OUTBREAK!
THE ENCYCLOPEDIA OF
EXTRAORDINARY SOCIAL BEHAVIOR

Hilary Evans, M.A.
Robert E. Bartholomew, Ph.D.

ANOMALIST BOOKS
San Antonio • New York

An Original Publication of Anomalist Books

Outbreak! TheE ncyclopedia of Extraordinary Social Behavior

ISBN: 9781938398452

Cover art by Walter Molino from *La Domencia del Corriere*
All images provided courtesy of the Mary Evans Picture Library (www.maryevans.com)
Book design by Seale Studios

For information about Anomalist Books, go to anomalistbooks.com, or write to:

Anomalist Books
5150 Broadway #108
San Antonio, TX 78209

For Veronique Campion-Vincent,
who shares our fascination for why people behave as they do

For my brother Paul Bartholomew
and my parents Emerson and Mary Bartholomew

Table of Contents

Foreword by Benigno Aguirre, Ph.D. ix
Introduction .... *x*
Preface xvi

Abdera Outbreak of Prose and Poetry 1
Adamites (Nudity Sect) 1
Alien Abduction Beliefs 3
Altered States of Consciousness 7
American Invasion of Canada 8
American Revivalism 9
Amou Barking Mania 16
Amsterdam Outbreak 17
Anabaptists 18
Andree Balloon Mania 23
Animal Noises, Epidemics of 25
Anxiety Hysteria 26
Assassins, Order of 28
Assembly Line Hysteria 31
Asteroid Panic 31
Aurora End-of-the-World Panic 32
Auxonne Possession Outbreak 32

Band Bus Hysteria 40
Band Mystery Illness 40
Barking-Off Squirrels Fad 40
Batavia Shipwreck 41
Battered Wife Syndrome 45
BBC Ghostwatch Scare 45
BBC Radio Hoax 46
Bekhterev, Vladimir Mikhailovich 47
Bequette, Bill 48
Berserk School 48
Bezpopovtzy Sect 49
Bird Flu Pandemic Scare 51
Blackthorn Barking Mania 53
Boarding School Fire Pandemonium 54
Boxer Rising 54
Brandenburg Mass Possession 57
Brechin Running and Jumping Fits 57
Brigand Great Fear 58
British Military Fainting Epidemics 62
Brooklyn Bridge Panic 62
Buffalo Martian Scares 62
Bus Bedlam 64

California Choral Collapse 67
California Telephone Illness 67
Cambrai Convent Outbreak 68
Cargo "Cults" 69
Castration, Voluntary 71
Cat Girls of India 71
Cat Massacres, Great 72
Catholic Scare 73
Cattle Mutilations 74
Cevennes Prophets 77
Chemistry Lab Mystery Illness 82
Chemtrails 82
Child Abduction Panic 83
Child-Eating Scare 86
Children's Crusades 86
Chilean Martian Panic 90
Chinese Needle Scare 90
Chinon Demonic Possession Outbreak 91
Cholera Panic 92
Christian Conversion Syndrome 95
Chupacabra Scare 96
Clay Eating Epidemic 96
Coca-Cola Scare 97
Collective Anxiety Attacks 98
Congo Witch Massacre 99
Copycat Behavior 99
Conspiracy Theories 103
Convent Hysteria 104
Coughing Orphans 109
Crazes 109
Cyber Ghost Scare 111

Dance Frenzies 116
Dancing Mania 117
De Martino, Ernesto 121
Defense Industry Suicide Cluster 121
Demon Possession 127
Derby School Fits 133
Doughiteli Strangelers 133
Doukhobors 134
Drunk Driving Hysteria 141

Ecuador Martian Panic 143
Edison Star Sightings 144

Enthusiasm Episodes ... 145
Epidemic of LSD Hallucinations ... 147
Extraterrestrial Tsunami Panic ... 147
Evil Spirit School ... 147

Facilitated Communication Mania ... 150
Factory Fainting Fits ... 151
Factory Hysteria Sweeps USA ... 151
Fads ... 151
Fainting Factory Workers ... 154
Fainting Football Cheerleaders ... 154
Fainting French Factory Girls ... 154
Fainting Vietnamese Schoolgirls ... 155
False Memory Syndrome ... 155
Familiarity ... 159
Fantasy-Prone People ... 160
Fashions ... 163
Fatima Solar Phenomenon ... 165
Feather Tickling Fad ... 170
Females and Mass Hysteria ... 170
Fibromyalgia ... 174
Filo Cargo Cult ... 175
Florida Land Boom ... 176
Florida War Scare ... 176
Flying Saucer, Origin of ... 177
Forced Marriage Syndrome ... 180
Frankie Avalon Mania ... 182
Fraternity Orders ... 182
Friedeberg Outbreak ... 186
Fumigation Hysteria ... 187

Garrotting Scares ... 193
Genital Shrinking Scares ... 194
Genital Vanishing Scares ... 203
Genocide Hysteria ... 206
Ghost Attacks ... 207
Ghost Dance (Native American) ... 208
Ghost Rocket Scare ... 208
Glossolalia, Contagious ... 211
Goblin Attacks ... 212
Goldfish Swallowing Fad ... 213
Great American Airship Wave ... 214
Greek Telephone Panic Attacks ... 224
Gulf War Syndrome ... 224

Halifax Disaster ... 235
Halifax Perfume Scare ... 239
Halifax Slasher ... 239
Halley's Comet Scare ... 242
Hammersmith Ghost Scare ... 244
Handsome Lake Sect (Native American) ... 245
Headhunting Scares ... 246
Hindu Milk Miracle ... 247
Hoorn Orphanage Possession ... 248
Hula-Hoop Fad ... 249
Hurricane Katrina Social Chaos ... 250
Husband Poisoning Mania ... 254
Hysteria ... 254
Hysterical Anorexia ... 258
Hysterical Blackouts ... 259
Hysterical Boredom ... 260
Hysterical Schoolgirls at Qawa ... 260
Hysterical Schoolgirls in Nepal ... 262

Images that Move, Weep, and Bleed ... 266
Incense Hysteria ... 273
India ET Scare and Riot ... 273
India Witch Scare ... 273
Iraq National Guard Mutiny ... 274
Iraq Prison Abuse Affair ... 275
Irradiated Mail Scare ... 277
Irvingites ... 278
Islamic Ecstatic Sects ... 280
Islamic Symbols Over Malaysia ... 282
Italian Fatigue Outbreak ... 284
Itching and Rash Frenzies ... 284

Jaca Possession Festival ... 289
Jewish Conversion Syndrome ... 290
Jumpers ... 291
Jumping Frenchmen of Maine ... 294

Kentorff Outbreak ... 298
Kentucky Fainting Outbreak ... 299
Kissing Bug Scare ... 299
Klikuschestvo Shouting Mania ... 300
Kokomo Hum ... 302
Koln Outbreak of Erotic Convulsions ... 302

Landes Outbreak ... 306
Laughing Epidemics ... 309
Lille Outbreak ... 311
London Earthquake Panic ... 313
London End-of-the-World Scare ... 313
London Monster Social Panics ... 314
London Monster Scare, The ... 315
Loudun Outbreak of Possessed Nuns ... 317
Louisiana Twitching Epidemic ... 323
Lourdes Visionaries ... 324
Louviers Outbreak ... 328
Lunar Influence ... 332
Lycanthropy ... 333
Lyonesse Believers ("Holy John" Sect) ... 339
Lyon/Saint-Etienne Demonic Outbreak ... 340

Mackay, Charles ... 345
Mad Cow Scares ... 346
Mad Gasser of Botetourt ... 347
Mad Gasser of Mattoon ... 350
Madrid Outbreak ... 355
Maine Factory Malady ... 356
Maliovanny Affair ... 356
Mangzo Cargo "Cult" ... 359
Marching Band Hysteria ... 359
Mars Earthquake Panic ... 360
Mass Hysteria ... 360
Mass Hysteria in Work Settings ... 364
Mass Hysteria in Schools ... 375
Mass Hysteria Synonyms ... 386
Mass Suicide Cults ... 386
Massachusetts Choral Mayhem ... 390
Masturbation Delusion ... 391
Maynard Experiment ... 397
Melbourne Airport Mystery Illness ... 397
Melin, Arthur Spud ... 399
Mercury Bomb Doomsday Scare ... 399
Merphos Poisoning Scare ... 399
Methodist Revival ... 399
Milan Outbreak ... 404
Milan Poisoning Scare ... 405
Millerite End-of-the-World Scare ... 406
Millenarist Migrations of Brazil ... 407
Mind Control Delusion, The ... 409
Miniature Golf Fad ... 412
Minnesota Fainting Epidemic ... 412
Miracle Hen of Leeds ... 413
Monkey Man Scare ... 413
Montreal Slasher ... 416
Moon Hoax, The Great ... 416
Mora Witch Affair ... 418
Moral Panics and Symbolic Scares ... 420
Morzine Outbreak (Possessed Town) ... 423
Motor Hysteria ... 430
Multiple Personality Disorder Epidemic ... 430
Mummy's Curse Fainting Fits ... 439
Mushroom Madness ... 440

Naked Cargo "Cult" ... 459
Naval Recruit Smoke Scare ... 460
Neurological Epidemic ... 460
New York Zoo Scare ... 460
New Zealand Sick Building ... 461
Nijmegen Convent Outbreak ... 461
Nîmes Outbreak of Possessed Nuns ... 462
Nuclear Disaster Hoax ... 463

Oat Bran Craze ... 464
Ohio Chorus Fainting Fits ... 464
Oklahoma Chorus Collapse ... 464
Operation Rid Fox ... 465
Orson Welles Martian Panic ... 465

Paderborn Outbreak ... 471
Palestinian Poisoning Panic ... 471
Paranormal Phenomena ... 474
Parent Hysteria (Mass Hysteria by Proxy) ... 477
Phantom Aircraft Waves ... 477
Phantom Florida Gas Poisoning ... 499
Phantom Hat Pin Stabber ... 501
Phantom Pregnancy Attacks ... 501
Phantom Slasher ... 502
Philippine Devil Hysteria ... 503
Phillip Knightley's Hook Hoax ... 504
Photocopied Ghost Scare ... 505
Pigsty Hysteria ... 505
Pittsburgh Furnace Scare ... 506
Plédran Demon Attacks ... 506
Pokémon Illness ... 508
Popish Plot, The ... 509
Portuguese Martian Invasion Panics ... 515
Possession ... 515
President Johnson "Cult" ... 517
Profanity and Blasphemy ... 518
Psychosomatic Illness ... 519
Puritanism ... 520

Quakers ... 529

Railway Spine ... 532
Red Scares ... 532
Revivalism ... 534
Rhode Island Martian Panic ... 536
Riots ... 537
Riveter's Ovaries ... 540
Rolling Stones Mania ... 540
Rumors ... 541
Running, Jumping and Climbing ... 544
Russian Poland Balloon Scare ... 546
Russian Sectarianism ... 546

Sabbatai Zevi the Messiah ... 551
Saint-Médard Convulsionnaries ... 555
Salem Witch-Hunts ... 561
Santen Convent Outbreak ... 566
Sardine Packing Hysteria ... 567
SARS Scare ... 567
Satanic Cult and Ritual Abuse Scare ... 568
Satanism ... 570
Saudi Teacher Fits ... 576
School Fainting Flurry ... 577
School Vampire Scare ... 577

School Writing Tremors ... 577
Scottish and Welsh Religious Excitement ... 579
Scottish End-of-the-World Scare ... 581
Scowerers and Mohocks Scare ... 581
Self-Flagellation Manias ... 582
Sexual Mores ... 583
Shared Psychotic Disorder ... 584
Sheep Panic, The Great ... 585
Showalter, Elaine ... 585
Sick Primary Schools ... 586
Sick School Staff Syndrome ... 587
Singapore Factory Hysteria ... 588
Skoptsi Castration Sect ... 588
Skunked Workers ... 592
Small Group Scares ... 592
Snake Handler Sect ... 595
Social Movements ... 599
Sorority Mystery Illness ... 599
Souponievo Outbreak ... 600
South Carolina Martian Panic ... 601
Space Alien Scare ... 602
Spirit Infestation as Mass Psychogenic Illness ... 602
Spirit Possession in India ... 603
Spiritualist Mania ... 605
Spouse Dropping Revival ... 614
Spring Break Riot ... 614
Springheel Jack Scare ... 614
Starpoint High Mystery Illness ... 616
Stevenage Mystery Illness ... 618
Stigmatization ... 618
Strawberries with Sugar Virus ... 623
Streaking Fad ... 624
Street Fainting Scare ... 625
Suicide Clusters ... 625
Swedish Preaching Epidemic ... 627
Syracuse Fog Scare ... 630

Taiping Rebellion ... 637
Tarantism ... 639
Teacher Hysteria ... 642
Tennessee School Hysteria ... 642
Terrorism Scares ... 642
Texas Earthworm Hoax ... 648
Theories of Mass Hysteria ... 648
They Saw a Game Study ... 657
Thuggee ... 657
Tollitis ... 661
Tom and his Followers ... 661
Tonsil and Adenoid Riots ... 665
Toulouse Possessed Village ... 665
Toxic Bus Controversy ... 667
Toxic Courthouse ... 669
Toxic Mold Fears ... 672
Tsunami Rumors ... 672
Tulip Mania ... 672

Ugandan Running Sickness ... 680
Ulster Revival ... 680
Umhayizo Bewitchment Hysteria ... 683
Unterzell Outbreak ... 683
Urban Legends ... 685

Vaccination Hysterias ... 689
Vampirism ... 691
Verzegnis Outbreak ... 699
Virgin Mary, Apparitions of ... 699
Virginia Fainting Epidemic ... 707
Virtual Life ... 707

Wacky Wallwalker Fad ... 711
Washing Mania ... 711
Water Monster Panic ... 712
Weather and Human Behavior ... 712
Welsh Pedophile Panic ... 713
Welsh Revival ... 716
Wertet Outbreak ... 721
Wheezing Malady ... 722
Whitechapel Murders Scare ... 723
White Slavery Scare ... 725
Wife Abuse Hysteria ... 726
Windigo Psychosis ... 726
Windshield Pitting Scare ... 728
Witch Mania ... 731
Wonder Horse Manias ... 740

Xenoglossossy ... 745
Xhosa Cattle Killing Prophecy ... 746

Zeitoun Luminous Phenomena ... 752
Zimbabwe Zombie School ... 752
Zoot Suit Riots ... 753

Index ... 755

Foreword

Outbreak! The Encyclopedia of Extraordinary Social Behavior by Hilary Evans and Robert Bartholomew is an extraordinary compilation of approximately 340 incidents of collective behavior spread over many countries on all continents, encompassing a time span of centuries. It is, without any doubt, the most ambitious undertaking of its sort, with entries ranging from the Children's Crusades to the Chilean Martian Panic, from Cyber Ghost Scares to the Popish Plot. Some of these entries are relatively well-known to specialists; others will be new to most, such as the Riveter's Ovaries and Railway Spine.

The authors' introduction explains that they have included incidents in which large groups of people behaved in an extraordinary fashion under the influence of fear and hope. It also includes a brief review of some of the existing explanations for this sort of behavior, such as the one proffered in Charles Mackay's Madness of Crowds formulation. The entries are divided into four categories: general themes, behavior, case histories, and reference entries.

This monograph will be an excellent resource for library references as well as for college-level teachers of collective behavior. Its wealth of information could, if used with scientific rigor, provide the basis for systematic comparative research on the causes, characteristics, careers and consequences of collective behavior. This is the potential disciplinary value of this excellent encyclopedia.

Benigno E. Aguirre
Professor of Sociology
Disaster Research Center
Department of Sociology and Criminal Justice
University of Delaware

Introduction

Social behavior is what people do collectively, either in groups or as individuals conforming to cultural patterns. It becomes extraordinary when it is so far at variance with contemporary mainstream standards of what is normal, rational or real, that labels such as "irrational" and "abnormal" come to seem appropriate. While such judgments are ultimately subjective, there must be a consensus view that the behavior is exaggerated, either in its expectations, its fears, or its response to the given circumstances. So it is when a community panics at attacks by a "phantom slasher" or hopefully awaits a rich "cargo" from the skies which will be brought to them in flying machines; so it is when members of a religious group fall into convulsions and act as though possessed by demons; so it is when articulate citizens insist they are being visited by extraterrestrial aliens or that their penises are being stolen.

These incidents do not occur in isolation. The *historical context* is essential if we are to understand the event. From medieval witch-hunts, dance frenzies and millennarist manias, to more contemporary episodes involving invading Martians in New Jersey, laughing manias in Uganda, and rumors of worldwide Satanist conspiracies, there is a general awareness of such occurrences, yet a widespread ignorance as to their frequency and nature. Everyone knows of stigmata, yet most are unaware that there are many hundreds of verified cases on record. When religious images were reported to be moving their eyes in 20th century Ireland, few related these marvels to meticulously-documented incidents of just the same kind in Italy two centuries earlier. When an American housewife claims to have been taken on board an extraterrestrial spacecraft, she too is following generations of other-world abductees. Before we judge the murderer who insists that "God made me do it," it is useful to know that he is part of a long tradition which seeks divine authority for deeds and misdeeds that are all-too-human.

The *social context*, too, is vital. Many individual episodes – that of the "devils" of Loudun, for example – have been thoroughly documented and widely discussed, yet rarely in the light of their time and their place. Often they are treated as one-of-a-kind occurrences, when in fact similar outbreaks were taking place throughout Western Europe, and for reasons which relate to the overall *zeitgeist* as much as to local circumstances.

Many events have drawn a brief flurry of media interest, only to be largely forgotten: the remarkable career of "Sir William Courtenay," for example. Some categories have attracted wide popular attention – notably witchcraft and Satanism, both of which have generated a copious literature, much of it of questionable value if not downright fallacious. Others, such as convulsionaries or slasher panics, are little known except to specialist researchers. Valuable studies have been made of some categories such as suicide clusters or mass psychogenic disorders, but there has been no comprehensive survey of these extraordinary social behaviors, still less a comparative study that not only sets one outbreak alongside another, but also sets both in their historical and cultural context.

This Encyclopedia gathers together the most notable of such happenings, covering a wide range of events which apparently have only one thing in common – that a great many people were driven, whether by beliefs not shared with the majority or by forces to which they were for some reason suggestible, to behave in an extraordinary manner. Either way, those involved were impelled to do things they would not normally do – and in many cases, which they *could* not normally do. The self-mutilation feats performed by members of Islamic Ecstatic Sects, or the painful ordeals cheerfully endured by the Convulsionaries of Saint-Médard, for example, verge on the incredible, yet the testimony to their actuality is overwhelming. And the fact that they are paralleled by similar occurrences – often in far distant countries and widely differing cultures – testifies to the certainty that these are not one-of-a-kind events, but manifestations of enduring traits in human nature.

By bringing these narratives together in a single volume, we are not only providing a convenient source of information that is not always easily accessed – our bibliography gives some idea of the diversity and often obscurity of the source material on which we have drawn – but also making a significant contribution to our understanding of why people behave in these extraordinary ways. For though each of these events possesses its own individual interest, they acquire additional meaning by juxtaposition and comparison: patterns emerge, similarities are revealed, enabling the identification of common factors that make possible a more complete and more fully rounded understanding.

From Belief to Behavior

Most extraordinary behavior occurs as the consequence of a *belief*. The Thugs, who ruthlessly murdered millions of innocent victims, were driven by their belief that they were thereby pleasing the divinity they worshipped. Throughout America in the 1980s, many came to believe that their country was threatened by a conspiracy of Satanists, with the result that thousands of innocent people were convicted for crimes that never in fact took place.

Two sentiments in particular drive extraordinary behavior: hopes and fears. Hopes that things will get better, fears that they may get worse. On the one hand, millennarist aspirations, the quest for a golden age in the future that will restore the mythical *L'Age d'Or* of the past. On the other hand, the ever-menacing forces of the Evil One – demons who seek our spiritual destruction, aliens who threaten humankind, cabals and conspiracies who seek to deprive us of our rights if not our lives.

Of the hopeful who were inspired by promises – held out to them by leaders who offered to conduct them to a promised land – the Taiping rebels, the Doukhobors, the followers of the Reverend Jones were all deluded by the Pied Pipers of their dreams. No less blindly, they may follow their leaders to death, as did the adherents of Heaven's Gate or the Bezpopovtzy sectarians. Millions of fanatics have undergone lesser ordeals – the Skopsti who castrated themselves, the Islamic fanatics who slash and scourge themselves, the martyrs of all times and all places who have died, voluntarily and often cheerfully, for beliefs which to others were empty and meaningless.

From Individual to Group

When an individual behaves in an extraordinary way – when he claims he has been instructed by God to kill prostitutes, when he believes he has been taken by extraterrestrials on a spaceship trip to Mars – we generally ascribe it to psychological aberration of some kind or another. But when a considerable number of people behave in the same extraordinary way, the explanation does not come so readily. While it is easy to believe that an individual may entertain an extravagant belief, it is not easy to believe that a number of people have simultaneously been overcome by the same psychological aberration.

Consequently, a major debate on which these events throw some light is the relationship of individual psychology to group psychology. Gustave Lebon and other commentators on crowd behavior have suggested that individuals lose their personality when they become components of a crowd,[1] while others deny that any such Jekyll-and-Hyde transformation occurs.[2] There are examples in our Encyclopedia which support either view: while many show people behaving en masse in ways they would never do on their own, there are also many which suggest that understanding the individual can contribute largely to our understanding of group behavior. For example, in many of our entries the participants display an impulse to strip off their clothes; for another, the urge to climb trees or high buildings is so widespread as evidently to represent a universal trait. The roots of such behavior surely lie in individual psychology, yet their manifestation on a group level must also be accounted for.

Every entry in this Encyclopedia involves a tension between the individual and the group of which he or she is a part – the same tension which is at the base of all human institutions from African tribal systems to the constitution of the United States and which underlies all political theory from Plato to Marx. In the words of William McDougall: "Each man is an individual only in an incomplete sense … he is but a unit in a vast system of vital and spiritual forces which, expressing themselves in the form of human societies, are working towards ends which no man can foresee."[3]

In assessing the extraordinary behaviors documented in these pages, we see that it is generally taken for granted that, when participating in a social group, the individual will become less of an individual, more of a unit in the group. Well, yes and no. Loss of personal identity is a symptom of psychopathology, but this is depersonalization in a form which is confined to the individual: it is, quite simply, a loss. The switch from being an autonomous individual to being a member of a crowd, on the other hand, implies *transfer*, not loss: an abandonment of personal goals and interests in favor of those of a collective with which the individual, for the time being at least, identifies himself.

The individual who participates in a group behavior is playing a part, however small, in fashioning the behavior of the group to which he has attached himself. If he could be questioned, he would probably insist that he is behaving as an individual, as himself; asked why, then, he is behaving like the rest of the group, he would reply – reasonably enough – that this is because he shares the values and interests, and is pursuing the same goals, as his companions.

The issues raised by the individual-group tension were a subject of debate in 5th century Athens and are no less so in the 21st century, but the dilemmas which Socrates sought to disentangle are those which we have to face, confronted by suicide bombers and terrorist martyrs. So the issues raised by our examples of extraordinary behavior possess a practical and urgent relevance. If we are to understand the present, the lessons of the past can save us from making tragic mistakes. How these extraordinary behaviors came about, how they commenced and how they spread, how they developed and metamorphosed, and how they eventually diminished and ceased – all these have very practical applications. For what emerges from our survey is the continuance and the resurgence of the human traits which found expression in these behaviors and will continue to do so unless we learn from past experience. Most of these behaviors – even those most optimistically initiated – eventually proved to be injurious to the community. By studying and understanding their dynamics, we may be able to prevent or control their recurrence.

In Search of Explanations

A great many thoughtful men and women have proffered theories of collective behavior. We have drawn on many of these authorities, but without adopting any single standpoint. The proliferation of debate on the subject is an indication of its complexity. It is our hope that by providing these case histories, we can play a part in bringing about a balanced understanding of the matter.

Time and time again, as we read these extraordinary narratives, we ask: how is it possible for intelligent, rational beings to be so sadly misled? Were their reasoning powers and their common sense overpowered by overwhelming social forces? Were they charmed into a zombie-like state by an irresistible charismatic personality? Has some regressive trait deprived them of their everyday powers of judgment? The horror of the witchcraft mania was able to sweep through Western Europe only because hundreds of thousands abandoned their normal reality-testing principles and accepted that demonic forces were about to take over the world. For thousands in 20th century America, a belief that thousands of children were being sacrificed to Satan clouded their minds and resulted in tragic consequences. Can these extravagances be explained by natural process and discernible social dynamics?

We fall back on phrases such as "mass hysteria" when workers in a factory believe themselves poisoned by a non-existent gas, but the process that is entailed is by no means self-evident. In such cases, it is harder to believe in a collective delusion, easier to believe that there is a veridical cause. Hence the readiness to believe in the 16th century that witches were physically flying to mountaintop rendezvous, or 20th century citizens to hunt for a "phantom slasher"or a "mad gasser." Time and again, when everyday rationalization is abandoned, disillusion – and sometimes tragedy – are liable to follow.

For all that, in general we have tried to maintain a neutral position regarding the questions raised by these incidents. We have no wish to stigmatize unusual behavior, and our use of the term "extraordinary" is not intended to be pejorative. That many of the events narrated in these pages were socially disruptive, and ultimately catastrophic for those involved, can hardly be denied. But it would be unjust to set aside the motivations and aspirations that prevailed when they occurred. For this reason we have sought to follow the advice of Michael Barkun: "By attempting to view behavior from the inside, in a contextual fashion, it may be possible to suitably explain events which at present serve only to suggest anarchy, superstition or 'madness.'"[4] In addition, when appropriate we have included informed comment, whenever possible by contemporaries, which may reflect different perceptions, and by later authorities whose input seems helpful. As an example of the first, we have cited Bishop Lavington's contemporary (and very entertaining!) comments on the Methodist revival in England; of the second, Louis Florentin Calmeil's suggestion that certain categories of behavior, which at the time were considered to be the work of the Devil, could be interpreted along psychosocial lines.

While some of the behaviors presented here may represent chronic forms of psychological disturbance, we believe it essential to set each one in its own context, with regard to the unique events and circumstances of each one, which point to a particular interpretation of reality for the participants, as contrasted with that of the outside investigator. It is not enough to view the behavior per se; its context and its perceived meaning are essential to a proper understanding. By adopting this approach, we find that some behaviors which are usually described in terms of individual or group pathology may more properly be attributed to the ways in which members of that particular culture are accustomed to express themselves. Thus, unfamiliar conduct codes and perceptual orientations, covert political resistance, local idioms of adaptation or negotiation, culture- and history-specific forms of deviant social roles – any or all of these may form a cultural setting that differs substantially from that of the investigator who approaches it from his own perspective. To take a simple example, most histories of the Boxer Rising in late 19th century China see the event from the point of view of Western observers, with the emphasis on the siege of the European legations and the murder of missionaries. But to adopt this perspective, or even that of the Chinese government of the day, is to fail utterly to understand the significance of the rising, which was essentially a native event, comprehensible only from a native perspective.

American cultural anthropologist Clifford Geertz has noted that "Man is an animal suspended in webs of significance he himself has spun. I take culture to be those webs, and the analysis of it to be therefore not an experimental science in search of law but an interpretive one in search of meaning."[5] Anthropologist Miles Richardson puts it this way: "Interpretative anthropology directly addresses the world in which we humans are. Conventional social science, in its search for underlying causes, explains away that world and in doing so alienates us from it and destroys its magic. When we are possessed, we do not exist within the category of psychological defense mechanisms. Instead, we are in the company of gods, who are all the more real for being human creations." According to Richardson, when we "reduce this world of contextual webs, of ghostly presences, to cause-and-effect languages of conventional social science ... we risk seriously misunderstanding our mode of being."[6] Above all, we must be mindful that we are dealing with human beings living in unique, often highly complex circumstances that do not easily lend themselves to superficial analysis.

This is particularly true of behaviors we would categorize as irrational. We must not hastily demonize the unconventional as bizarre or the exotic as strange, for there is a fine line between creativity and eccentricity, devoutness and fanaticism, different and deviant. How these behaviors are interpreted often depends on our social conditioning and cultural experiences. In this Encyclopedia, we take the view that in most if not all instances the behaviors in question are not sick, not bizarre, not irrational, not abnormal by the standards of those who participated in them. They may seem extraordinary to us, but they surely did not seem so to them. Had we been born into that culture, subjected to the same influences, we too might have acted in just that way. In this regard, studying their actions may give us a greater appreciation of how many ways there are to be human.

At the same time, however much we set aside our own feelings and seek to empathize with the participants, the fact remains that all these behaviors were considered exceptional by others, and the reasons why they were considered to be exceptional is part of our understanding of them. These were manifestations of minority values and attitudes, and they provoke the question: what were the forces which cause this or that minority to swim against the consensus stream, defying the rest of us at considerable cost to themselves?

The "Madness" of Crowds?

Charles Mackay, our eminent predecessor in exploring these vagaries of human behavior, entitled his classic book *Memoirs of Extraordinary Delusions,* with later editions adding "and the madness of crowds" to his title, thereby forcing an interpretation on his work he might not have approved.[7] As we have already indicated, we would avoid any such judgment. Delusion, though, is another matter; there can be no question but that a great many of the participants in these behaviors were indeed deluded, either by themselves or by others. Most of the behaviors described in this Encyclopedia came about as the result of delusion, including those generated by hysteria. However, it is important we understand what is meant by these terms.

A delusion is a false belief that is held despite evidence to the contrary. There are two types – social and psychiatric. To a psychiatrist, the word "delusion" usually refers to a range of conditions in which the sufferer exhibits psychosis. A psychotic has difficulty telling the difference between daydreams, hallucinations, and reality. Psychotic delusions are serious business and include schizophrenia (hearing voices that aren't there), affective or mood disorders such as depression, and paranoid psychosis where people feel others are out to get them or are conspiring against them.

Sociologists and social psychologists use the term social delusion in a different sense. It describes the spontaneous, temporary spread of false beliefs within a given population. There is usually no sign of psychological disturbance. Unfortunately, the term is frequently the source of confusion since it is often used as a catch-all category to describe a variety of different behaviors under one convenient label.

Social delusions differ from religious myths and popular folk beliefs in that they occur in an unorganized, spontaneous fashion, although at some later time social delusions may become institutionalized. For example, some church groups have incorporated into their teachings claims that thousands of satanic cult child sacrifices take place every year. You could not say that the members of such groups are psychotic or delusional in the psychiatric sense. Rather, they are likely to be comprised of normal persons who have acquired a view of the world that differs from that of the mainstream.

Hysteria, too, has become a catch-all term whose use can be misleading. It is a psychological disorder in which a person reports physical symptoms such as numbness, blindness, paralysis, or headache, yet after a thorough examination, a doctor is unable to find any organic cause. Occasionally, sufferers exhibit wild emotions and engage in histrionics – melodramatic outbursts whose subconscious purpose is to attract attention. In 1994, the American Psychiatric Association officially discontinued the use of the term hysteria due to its continuing misuse to stigmatize a variety of undesirable behaviors as "hysterical," especially unfounded assertions that females are inherently emotionally unstable.[8] The new term is "conversion disorder" which more accurately describes the process whereby mental conflict is converted into illness or disorder symptoms.[9] However, despite this attempt at banishment, the term continues to be widely used by psychiatrists, psychologists, psychoanalysts, and physicians. In this Encyclopedia we have generally used the terminology employed by the news report or study that is being cited. So bear in mind that whether it is referred to as hysteria, conversion disorder, or mass psychogenic or sociogenic illness, depends on the context.

For, alas, human behavior rarely fits into neat descriptive categories. What is hysteria in one context may be a natural response in another. Thomas Morgan writes: "the arrangement ... into species, genera, families, etc. is only a scheme invented by man (sic) for purposes of classification. Thus there is no such thing in nature as a species, except as a concept of a group of forms more or less alike."[10] Furthermore, some episodes can fit under more than one heading. For instance, a panic may be fueled by rumors and spark a riot. So where should we place it? That decision can only be a subjective one.

So don't look to this Encyclopedia for definitive explanations. Classification schemes are convenient, but they are also fallible. The compilers of this Encyclopedia are chroniclers, describers, reporters. Where appropriate, we comment on the behaviors and indicate explanations that were made at the time by observers, or proffered subsequently by informed authorities who had the advantage of hindsight. But such evaluations are tentative, speculative at best, for this is largely unexplored territory – and often disputed territory. For example, the phenomenon of stigmata, considered by some to be of divine origin, is recognized even by many religious authorities as being, albeit physical, a phenomenon of mental origin. Yet there is by no means consensus agreement on the matter, and still less on other alleged miracles such as moving images or divine apparitions. We have tried to present the testimony impartially, leaving all possibilities open, though we have not hesitated to indicate cases where the evidence is overwhelming, such as the delusion that hundreds of thousands of American children were being stolen for the purposes of satanic rituals. Delusion it certainly was, but how that delusion came about, and how it exerted so strong and so long a hold on so many intelligent people, is another question.

In any case, some outbreaks of social behavior seem to defy categorization – or explanation – so while listing them, we do not claim to explain them. For instance, when a reliable scientific journal reports that in 1892, pupils at a Hungarian girls' school exhibited outbursts of bird and animal noises, including the sounds of parrots, horses, and hounds, without greater detail, it is difficult at this date to tell what was actually going on.[11] The same can be said for the young women who were out picking currants near Wellington, South Australia, in August 1870, when they were suddenly seized by "fits" of "delirium."[12] Was there a hallucinogenic fungus on the currants? Perhaps the girls were being subjected to some severe stress, which triggered the outburst, but there is no mention of this in the newspaper report of the incident, and we may never know. At the same time, by setting them side by side with events where we *can* make a reasonable diagnosis, we may at least make an educated guess.

Explaining extraordinary behavior

Over and over again, those who have studied extraordinary behavior have exclaimed how amazing it is – but have not asked the crucial question, why did it happen? While we offer many possible explanations for the behaviors in various entries, these should never be considered to be the final word. Some of the most difficult to explain are those outbreaks that occur in developed countries, where people could be expected to know better. The Satanism scare in late 20th century America, for example, flourished in an educated and well-informed society possessing unequalled information technology. It seems that these advantages, far from blocking the spread of the delusion, actually facilitated it, demonstrating that no community, however sophisticated, is safe from such a tragic misconception, whether imposed from without or arising from its own communal psyche.

The Satanism scare occurred in the most highly developed nation on the planet, with every advantage that education and communications have to offer. This terrible delusion reminds us that the events we describe in this Encyclopedia are not just amazing stories; they are things which actually happened to real people, often to people like you and us. They may not have realized that they were behaving in an extraordinary manner, but they surely realized that something extraordinary was happening to them. In many cases, their response took the form it did because they subscribed, consciously or unconsciously, to a particular set of beliefs, and if we find their behavior extraordinary, it is because we do not share those beliefs. But in evaluating their response, we must try to look at the events through their eyes. If a nun went into convulsions and this was considered to be the work of the Evil One, it was because in her milieu that was the most probable explanation – and perhaps the only possible explanation, for neither she nor those around her could conceive of any other. In this regard, we could view such acts as being outside the traditional dichotomy of rational or irrational, but falling into the realm of behavior that anthropologist Richard Shweder calls "non-rational."[13] Non-rational is a more appropriate term as people's perceptual outlooks and mental frames of mind may support beliefs that foster social realities that are at extreme variance with contemporary mainstream western views of reality, rationality, and normality. This is important because throughout most recent history, it has been western scientists who have determined what standards of behavior are acceptable for the rest of the world's cultures.

Shweder observes that the Yir-Yiront Aborigines believe animal and tree spirits are responsible for pregnancy, while on the Arabian Peninsula it is widely held that breast milk from pregnant women is poisonous. Well now, should we view these people as crazy, irrational, or simply adhering to local folk beliefs? Throughout this Encyclopedia, we shall encounter people we may judge to be foolish or deluded, but before we judge them, we would do well to consider Henry David Thoreau's words: "If a man does not keep pace with his companions, perhaps it is because he hears a different drummer."[14]

Sources

1. Lebon, Gustave (1915[1895)]. *Psychologie des Foules.* Twentieth edition. Paris: Alcan. Originally published in 1895.
2. Stevenson, Robert Louis. (1886). *The Strange Case of Dr Jekyll and Mr Hyde.* New York: C. Scribner's sons.
3. McDougall, William. *The Group Mind.* Cambridge: University Press, 1921, p. 6.
4. Barkun, Michael (1974). *Disaster and the Millennium.* New Haven: Yale University Press, p. 132.
5. Geertz, C. (1973). *The Interpretation of Cultures.* New York: Basic Books, p. 5.
6. Richardson, Miles (1984). "Comments," in Paul Shankman, "The Thick and the Thin: On the Interpretive Theoretical Program of Clifford Geertz." *Current Anthropology* 25:275.
7. Mackay, Charles. ([1841]1852). *Memoirs of Extraordinary Popular Delusions and the Madness of Crowds Volume 1,* second edition. London: Office of the National Illustrated Library.
8. Bartholomew, Robert E. (1998). "Dancing with Myths: The Misogynist Construction of Dancing Mania. *Feminism & Psychology* 8(2):173-183.
9. American Psychiatric Association (1994). *Diagnostic and Statistical Manual of Mental Disorders* (3rd edition). Washington, DC: APA.
10. Clark, Ronald William. (1984). *The Survival of Charles Darwin.* New York: Random House, p. 23.
11. Bokai, cited in Szego, K. (1896). "Uber die Imitationskrankheiten der Kinder" [About the Imitative Illnesses of Children]. *Jahrbuch fur Kinderheilkunde* (Leipzig) 41:133-145.
12. *The Sydney Morning Herald,* August 25, 1870.
13. Shweder, R. A. (1984). 'Anthropology's Romantic Rebellion Against the Enlightenment, or There's More to Thinking than Reason and Evidence.' pp. 27-66. In R. A. Shweder and R. A. Levine (eds.), *Culture Theory: Essays on Mind, Self and Emotion.* New York: Cambridge University Press.
14. Thoreau, Henry David. *Walden.* Conclusion.

Preface

About this Encyclopedia

This book provides convenient access to accounts of extraordinary social behavior past and present. These accounts can be found scattered throughout the scientific literature, including sociology and anthropology texts, medical and psychiatric treatises and journals, as well as nonscientific sources such as memoirs and history texts. Never before, however, have so many sources on this topic been brought together in a single volume. Many are derived from non-English language sources; for instance, the entry on MASS HYSTERIA IN SCHOOLS draws on journals in French, German, Spanish, Italian, Swiss, and Malay. Several texts have not been reprinted since their original publication, and many are from hard-to-find pamphlets or obscure periodicals. Furthermore, many of those published accounts, which are easily available, often draw on second or third-hand or otherwise unreliable sources, with the result that many of them are defective if not actually erroneous. In other cases, "inconvenient" facts are quietly ignored; the Quakers and the Doukhobors, certain American fraternities, and many established churches tend to be reticent concerning uncomfortable episodes in their early history.

The Scope of the Book

We have tried to make our Encyclopedia as comprehensive as possible, but clearly we could not include every outbreak of extraordinary behavior throughout history; in any case, a good many run to a pattern you would find tiresome to read. The chronology appendix gives some idea of the enormous number of recorded collective outbreaks. We have described all the important ones known to us, together with a representative selection of others, which for one reason or another display points of uncommon interest. For example, we have selected only a handful of the vast number of incidents in which crowds claim to have witnessed MOVING IMAGES.

In cases where behavior manifested along similar lines in many instances, we have selected case histories representative of the whole; you will find examples of this in our entries on WITCHCRAFT, VAMPIRISM, and MULTIPLE PERSONALITY.

Our Sources

Whenever possible we have gone back to the original sources, and our bibliography indicates the range and diversity of material we have consulted. Often, only a single source is available, which means that we have no choice but to take an individual reporter's word for what happened. Thus in the case of the hysterical outbreak at LYON in 1687, for which we have only the investigating doctor's report, we have no choice but to accept his account of the matter. On the whole, though, we prefer to draw on a variety of sources, even though the testimony of one may contradict that of another. Thus, in the case of the AMSTERDAM outbreak of 1566, the number of those afflicted is stated as 30 by one contemporary commentator, as 70 by another; and though they are described as homeless orphans, we also find a reference to their "relatives." Again, how large was the crowd that witnessed the solar phenomenon at FATIMA? Estimates range from fifty thousand to a hundred thousand. In MASS SUICIDE CULTS, we narrate the death of over 500 followers of a religious sect in Uganda, who perished in a church fire during March 2000. One press report suggests that the leader lured his members into the church under false pretences and set it ablaze; other accounts suggest that the congregants were voluntary participants in their own immolation. In such instances, we reference both accounts and let you form your own opinion.

Steering a cautious way between such rocks and hard places, we have done our best to create a text that is both as coherent and as reliable as we can make it, exercising our judgment as to what to accept, what to reject. In a very small number of cases we have been unable to find anything better than uncorroborated references, for example, our opening item, the extraordinary outbreak at ABDERA. Under our entry MIRACULOUS CHICKEN OF LEEDS, Charles Mackay offers a brief but fascinating account of an "end of the world" scare in 1806, when many people were tricked into believing that a hen was laying eggs with the inscription, "Christ is coming." Mackay provides no sources for this story. In this as in some other cases, we have included them because of their exceptional interest, but the uncertainty of the provenance is always acknowledged.

A further difficulty is that what concerns us – the extraordinary behavior – is generally not the aspect of the matter that concerned the historian, so the material we need may be hidden or even omitted. For example, Braithwaite's standard history of the origins of QUAKERISM, admirable as it is, glosses over the extravagant behavior of some of the founder members of the Society, and we had to look elsewhere to find accounts of it.

Legend and rumor tend to exaggerate; they may even fabricate entirely. The history of the CHILDREN'S CRUSADES, for example, is a quicksand of possible error. The entire event may never have happened, and if it did, it is far from certain that it happened as the chroniclers reported it. Our account is only as dependable or otherwise as the original accounts. Political expediency has surely skewed accounts of the BOXER OUTBREAK in one century, the SUICIDE BOMBERS in another. Interpretation is often dictated by presumptions, thus the DANCING MANIA of the Middle Ages is almost universally interpreted as a stress-induced episode of mass hysteria, mostly affecting mentally disturbed women. However, an examination of contemporary chronicles makes it clear that men were affected in equal numbers and that the "dancers" were engaging in rituals intended to evoke divine favor during times of crisis. Hence the episodes may not have been as spontaneous and stress-induced as is so often assumed by later scholars. In other cases, such as THUGGEE and the ASSASSINS, the subject has given rise to myth as to whose veridicality scholars disagree. Our accounts consequently come with provisos, which we indicate, leaving you free to decide whether to accept Meadows Taylor's account of the one, Marco Polo's description of the other.

Categories

The sociological or psychological nature of many of the behaviors recounted in these pages is sufficiently uncertain that it is often difficult to assign them to any category, even in those instances where categories exist. In any case we are not here to make diagnoses, let alone pass judgments. Some categories that are already employed by social scientists, such as MASS HYSTERIA IN JOB SETTINGS and MORAL PANICS, seem to us useful and we have retained them. Others, such as Marian Apparitions, have seemed inadequate (would a clinical psychiatrist working in Japan understand the phrase?) and we have substituted alternatives. This is especially the case with local or culture-specific behaviors. For instance, an outbreak of hysterical twitching, shaking, and trance states among females in the jungles of Papua New Guinea in 1973 would be categorized by most scientists under the heading "mass hysteria," "psychogenic illness" or "conversion disorder." Since it is such a rare episode clearly triggered by forced marriage against the women's wishes, we have preferred to create our own specific category: FORCED MARRIAGE HYSTERIA. By drawing attention to the unique character of such incidents, we indicate what may be lost by forcing events into inappropriate pigeon-holes, and what may be gained by recognizing the diversity of extraordinary behavior.

Because of the ground-breaking nature of this work, it is often the case that no existing category is available. For instance, there emerges from many of our accounts a propensity of humans to make animal-like noises in emotionally-charged group settings, as at AMOU, or to indulge in reckless climbing under the influence of some morbid affliction, as at MORZINE. We have included "umbrella" entries to draw attention to these similarities and enable useful comparisons. Where for the sake of convenience we have been forced to create labels such as CONVENT HYSTERIA, which may give the impression that we are committed to a particular diagnosis, we have indicated that alternative explanations exist, such as that the unfortunate victims may indeed have been the victims of possession by the Evil One.

The Entries

For convenience of reference, the entries are presented in alphabetical order. However, they comprise four categories:

*General THEMES such as Fads, Rumors, Hysteria, Panics, Riots, Delusions, etc.

*Categories of BEHAVIOR such as Demon possession, Satanic cult scares, Flagellation manias, etc.

*CASE HISTORIES of specific outbreaks and manifestations, such as the "Mad Gasser" of Mattoon, the "War of the Worlds" broadcast, Thuggee or the Children's Crusade.

*REFERENCE ENTRIES to individual people and places. Most of these will be cross-referenced – e.g., "Wesley, John" will refer the reader to "Methodism in Britain."

*Cross-references are inserted generously, and references are provided for every item. The resulting bibliography constitutes a valuable research tool in its own right.

ABDERA OUTBREAK OF PROSE AND POETRY

Northern Greece: circa 300 BCE

In one of his satirical dialogues, "How history is written," the Syrian-Greek writer Lucian of Samosata (AD circa 120-180) gives a brief account of an extraordinary outbreak in the city of Abdera, in Thrace. Since this is the only known reference to the incident, it is best read in his own words:

> I have been told, my dear Philo, in the reign of Lysimachus,[1] the good people of Abdera were seized with a violent fever, which continued without intermission till about the seventh day: when some of them were relieved by a copious discharge of blood from the nostrils, and others by as plentiful a flow of sweat. However, though the fever thus left them, some effects were produced by it, extraordinary and whimsical enough. Their minds on a sudden became so enchanted with tragedy, that they roared out Iambicks, and uttered all in recitative. The *Andromeda* of Euripides became a favourite monody, and the speech of Perseus was chanted out most melodiously. Then was the city replete with tragedians pale and lean, all made fit for their parts by the seven days sickness.
>
> "Love, cruel king of God and men" was one of the fine flourishes which these heroes sounded forth, without ceasing.
>
> The cause of all this, in my opinion, was no other than Archelaus. Archelaus was a favourite player, who had exhibited the story of Andromeda in the middle of a very hot summer: so hot, that many persons, before they were well out of the theatre, were directly taken ill with a fever: while the fancied forms of Andromeda, Perseus and Medusa fluttered before their senses, and recalled their delighted attention to the strains of tragedy.[2]

COMMENT: According to *Webster's Geographical Dictionary*, the people of Abdera had a reputation for "stupidity." Whether this incident is an example of it, or even gave rise to it, is matter for conjecture. Lucian's flippant summary no doubt exaggerates, but he would hardly have used the story as an illustration if it had not had some foundation in fact.

It is noteworthy that the affliction combined physical and mental features. Its course seems to have commenced with a physical ailment, brought on by the heat, which left the sufferer weakened and suggestible, at which point he was overtaken by this remarkable collective delusion.

ADAMITES (NUDITY SECT)

Europe: 2nd to 17th Centuries

Though several sects have chosen to strip off their clothes from time to time, for example the QUAKERS and the DOUKHOBORS, this was for them an occasional practice, usually performed for a specific purpose such as demonstrating passive resistance to authority. For the Adamites, by contrast, it was a central tenet of their faith, derived from the Bible, in which the first humans created by God, Adam and Eve, are described as not wearing clothes.

Picart describes the Adamites as the oldest heretical sect of the Christian church, dating from the second century. They were one of many varieties of Gnostics who favored a return to the Church's earliest teachings, but accounts of their origin vary. "Their first principle consisted in imitating the nudity of Adam. This indecency was founded on the belief that by returning to a state of innocence, they became as simple and as pure as Adam and Eve while they lived in their terrestrial paradise."[3] However, according to their belief, the attitude of mind which condemned nudity was not decency but false modesty.

Their mode of worship is described thus:

When Adamites went naked in the streets of Amsterdam, the authorities disapproved. (Picart's "Superstitions" 1722)

Their assemblies were held underground, whence Epiphanius compares them to moles and their chapels to burrows and lurking-places. On entering, all persons of both sexes stripped themselves completely naked, and in that state went through the various rites of religion, calling their church Paradise. At the conclusion of the service they resumed their clothes, and appear to have confined their literal imitation of the habits of Paradise to the time of their fanatical worship. Its avowed object appears to have been that of extirpating carnal desire by familiarising the senses to strict self-control under the extremest form of temptation. But such customs were, of course, open to a very different interpretation, and the Adamites have been accused of indulging in every form of gross immorality. Nor indeed is it easy to see how such customs, however ascetic may have been the intentions of their originators, can have failed to degenerate rapidly into licentiousness.[4]

Augustine of Hippo said of them that they abhorred marriage, based on the somewhat improbable supposition that Adam and Eve did not have sexual relations until after they had been expelled from Eden for eating the Forbidden Fruit. This belief did not, however, make the Adamites any more chaste; they allowed themselves the use of women in common. For this purpose they had a particular place to which they went on certain days. There, naked and in silence, they awaited the signal: the words from the book of Genesis, "Increase and multiply." At this command they put in practice their teaching, without respect even for the most sacred blood-ties.

By contrast with these private practices, their public image was one of chaste respectability. Their behavior was modest, their lifestyle blameless. If any of their members had sexual relations outside the assemblies of the sect, they would be expelled just as Adam and Eve were expelled from the Garden of Eden. A questionable source reports that "at the close of the 16th century, those who wished to be initiated into the Adamite sect were required to walk, nude, in the midst of the assembly. Those who did not betray the sensibility of their flesh by a certain characteristic sign were admitted with applause: but the others were rejected as being too inclined to voluptuousness."

Adamite beliefs and practices reappeared periodically throughout the Middle Ages, notably in the 12th century under the leadership of the Dutch heretic Tanchelin (variously spelt), who taught the harmlessness of fornication, and again in the Dauphiné and Savoy in the 14th century. During the 15th century similar teachings emerged among several of the more radical Protestant sects to which the Reformation gave birth.

Their last recorded manifestation was in the 17th century, in the Netherlands, Bohemia, and England. There are several references to the presence of Adamites in England in the 1640s, for example a tract by Samoth Yarb [anagram of Thomas Bray] entitled, *A New Sect of Religion Descryed, called Adamites, deriving their religion from our father Adam. Wherein they hold themselves to be blamelesse at the last day, though they sinne never so egregiously, for they challenge salvation as their due from the innocence of their second Adam.* Their critics attributed wanton and lewd behavior to them, but none provided any reliable documentation and the accusations may have been no more than malicious hearsay.

Wherever the Adamites appeared, the authorities did their best to stamp them out. Prints from the early 18th century depict the private reunions of the sect, and the authorities of Amsterdam attempting to prevent Adamites from promenading naked in the streets of the city. While such displays of nudity no doubt gave offence, the Adamites' threat to society may have been perceived as more widely subversive, for they were supposed to be Antinomians who reject all moral law of whatever kind, recognizing no higher authority than the individual him/herself. We are told that many of the members of the sect chose to die rather than abandon their principles, and several women saw themselves as martyrs for their beliefs.

COMMENT: The term "Adamite" is little more than a label applied loosely to several autonomous sects who held roughly similar beliefs. Consequently what is said about any one community may not be altogether true of another. Furthermore, outside comments are generally hostile and may well include exaggeration or outright invention; some of Picart's information comes from a source that he admits cannot be altogether trusted.

The practices of the Adamites were ostensibly similar to those observed by many radical religious sects. The 16th century adepts of the Free Spirit were just one of many who held that they were above common laws and were therefore divinely authorized to have sex with anyone or everyone, just as they were permitted to rob or even kill.[5] The teachings of the SOUPONIEVO sect incorporated a similar belief as regards sexual relations.

But there is a clear difference between such sects and the Adamites, for whom nudity and free sex were not side-issues but central tenets. To outsiders, their conduct was shocking: "They couple in the buildings which serve them as temples, and to the abominations of unrestricted lust they add the greatest extravagances."[6] But the assemblies which struck observers as "indecencies" were not lascivious orgies, but had as their object the propagation of the human race in innocent obedience to God's will.

ALIEN ABDUCTION BELIEFS

Worldwide: 1960s to present

The alien abduction mania has affected thousands of people who are convinced that they have been taken, generally against their wills, on board extraterrestrial spaceships hovering in Earth's airspace. Though the great majority of these incidents involve isolated individuals, the overall similarity of their experiences, and the recognition by the "abductees" themselves that they are part of a widespread phenomenon, justifies treating alien abductions as a collective behavior.

The evidence that these abductions have really taken place is circumstantial and dependent almost wholly on individual testimony devoid of independent confirmation. Nevertheless the evident sincerity of the witnesses, the degree of consistency in the narratives, and the bizarre features of their experiences have persuaded reputable researchers to take the claims seriously. Above all, as folklorist Thomas Bullard points out, "More than any other type of UFO report, abductions promise answers to questions everyone has asked since the first flying saucer sighting. In these accounts we steal a literal look inside the UFO, see the occupants close up, and glimpse some clues about why they are here."[7]

CONTEXT: The widespread belief, born about 1947, that Earth was being visited by FLYING SAUCERS of extraterrestrial origin, led naturally to interest in their occupants. It was not long before people were claiming, first, to have seen them, and then to have met them. The first such alien entities to be encountered were generally benign and ostensibly well-intentioned. The "contactees" were frequently selected as being specially qualified; they would be invited on board the alien spaceships, entertained as privileged guests, and even taken to visit their home planets.[8] Some were given in-depth information about extraterrestrial life,[9] while others were entrusted with missions on behalf of the Inter-Galactic parliament and the like.[10] Some had sexual relations with aliens, sometimes willingly,[11] others under compulsion,[12] and at least one contactee was taken by her lover to give birth to their child under the more favorable conditions of his home planet.[13]

However, subsequent encounters revealed that the aliens were pursuing a more sinister agenda. Commencing with the Betty and Barney Hill case, described below, witnesses – mainly though not exclusively North Americans of European descent – told of being taken aboard the spaceships against their will and subjected to physical examinations, some individually, others as part of a group. For many, this was seen as the prelude to an invasion of the planet by the extraterrestrials,[14] and some asserted that a number of aliens were already here, mingling with humankind and preparing for a take-over in which the people of Earth would be reduced to the status of second-class citizens.[15]

The first widely publicized UFO abduction case occurred in the United States in 1961. The event would become widely known around the world and create a global awareness of "UFO abductions" as a real phenomenon. Near midnight on September 19, Betty and Barney Hill of Portsmouth, New Hampshire, were returning from a trip to Canada. They were driving near Indian Head, New Hampshire, when Betty became aware of an illuminated object, gradually growing in size, that seemed to be pacing their car. Over the next 30 miles (about 50 kilometers) they continued to watch the object. Betty grew increasingly frightened and persuaded Barney to stop. He got out of the car with his binoculars and said he saw a "craft" roughly thirty meters off, with a row of lights and six occupants. Barney raced back to the car yelling that he thought they were about to be captured. He got in and they sped away, arriving home some time later.

Ten days later, Betty began to experience a series of dreams that, when she had rearranged the various incidents, seemed to constitute a coherent narrative of abduction and examination aboard a spaceship. Barney was skeptical, but there were other puzzling features about their experience, particularly the curious fact that their journey seemed to

Betty and Barney Hill in 1966, five years after their claimed abduction; they hold John Fuller's The Interrupted Journey.

have taken some two hours longer than it should. Such puzzles encouraged Betty to explore the possibility that her dreams reflected reality, and she and Barney not only contacted UFO groups but paid several visits to the location of their adventure. They successfully identified the scene of their sighting, the precise section of the road where their car was stopped by the alien entities, and the clearing in the woods where the spacecraft landed.

In January 1964, Barney, who had been seeking therapy in hopes of relieving stress, was referred to Boston area psychiatrist Dr. Benjamin Simon, who decided to perform hypnotic recall sessions on the couple. Under hypnosis Barney recounted a story of being stopped by a group of short beings with bald heads, slit-like nostrils, and metallic-like skin, who escorted them to a spaceship, parked in a clearing. After being subjected to medical-like exams, the couple was released and told they would have no recollection of the experience. Betty, unaware of the story Barney had told, recounted a similar narrative, telling how a needle-like instrument was inserted into her navel. She was told it was a pregnancy test, while Barney recalled having a cup-like device placed on his genitals.

The fact that both recalled substantially the same story, apparently independently, has been taken by some as evidence that they were recounting actual events. However, Dr. Simon's own verdict was that the stories recalled by the couple under hypnosis derived from Betty's dreams. These dreams, which did not come to Betty as a coherent narrative but on her own admission had to be "edited" to form one, could in his opinion have been fantasies, and indeed Barney had consciously dismissed them as such. However, Betty's dreams remained the only version of events available to explain their experience, with the consequence that under hypnosis they were recalled by the couple as seeming fact.[16]

In September 1966 an article on the Hill episode appeared in *Look* magazine, and later that fall a full-length account, John Fuller's *The Interrupted Journey: Two Lost Hours Aboard a Flying Saucer*.[17] Subsequently the case has been retold and discussed countless times in UFO books and periodicals, and it provided the model for scores of other claimed abduction experiences, in which elements from the Hills' story are combined with material relating to the individual witness. First dozens and then hundreds of people, reading the Hills' story, claimed that they too had been the victims of a similar abduction. Many underwent regressive hypnosis to recover what they had supposedly experienced during their "missing time."

Though the stories told by the "abductees" were not only inherently improbable but also incompatible with one another, and moreover lacked confirmation by any independent evidence, the evident good faith of most of the witnesses and the ostensible plausibility of their accounts convinced a number of investigators to take them seriously.[18] This in turn led to a further escalation: a spate of studies and autobiographical narratives were published, support groups and services were formed, and psychiatrists welcomed a new and profitable market by providing counsel to people who feared they might have been abducted. The creation of this infrastructure served, in its turn, to further reinforce the belief system, building up to a veritable mania that ultimately involved many thousands of alleged abductees. A further indication of the strength of the belief was provided by investigators whose researches convinced them that they themselves had been abducted by aliens earlier in their lives.[19]

The proliferation of claims, from sincere witnesses who were evidently deeply disturbed by their experience, attracted the attention of serious researchers and behavioral scientists. For many, the fact that so many people were independently reporting similar experiences was evidence that those experiences must be real. However, others took a contrary, psychosocial view, arguing that the similarity of reports was a good reason to attribute them to folklore. This view was espoused by Bartholomew and others,[20] who proposed that abductees, if not strictly fantasy-prone, were at least psychologically predisposed in some way – "encounter-prone" as Kenneth Ring described them after identifying certain characteristic behavioral traits that enabled experiencers to be distinguished from the general population.[21]

Further reason to question the abductions-are-real position was provided by Lawson and McCall's "imaginary abductee" experiments[22] which demonstrated that anyone could, under hypnosis, present an abduction story which was indistinguishable from accounts that were purportedly veridical. While they did not prove that the latter were not factual, they showed that abductees *could* be fantasizing, as was claimed by those researchers who favored a psychosocial interpretation. On this hypothesis, what characterized the abductees was that they mistook their fantasies for reality.

However, the proponents of such alternative explanations remained in the minority. Belief in the physical reality of UFOs, and consequently that abductions by their occupants were physically real events, was widespread. In 1975, NBC television broadcast a two hour movie, *The UFO Incident*, recreating the Hills' supposed abduction with the strong implication that it was factual. Skeptical researcher Philip Klass described the movie as a "bombshell that would impact on public consciousness."[23]

By 1981, when New York artist Budd Hopkins published *Missing Time: A Documented Study of UFO Abductions*, he was justified in referring to the flood of abduction claims as "the invisible epidemic."[24] During the 1980s, numerous casebooks appeared detailing specific abductions, and major UFO investigation organizations largely abandoned their investigation of UFOs as such in favor of abduction claims. Many employed regressive hypnosis in the mistaken belief that this provided "the royal road" to the truth, though this had been specifically refuted by the Hills' Dr. Simon. Abductees came to be star attractions at the many UFO conferences held, mainly in the USA but also in Europe, Australia, and elsewhere. Their stories were published in the many UFO journals, and there was a flow of autobiographical books recounting their experiences. In 1987 an episode of the popular television series, *The Colbys*, which featured an abduction scene, would testify to the degree to which the phenomenon had become part of general awareness. Abductee support groups were formed and psychiatrists offered their services in counseling those who suspected they might have been abducted. Such people were encouraged to examine their bodies for implants, inserted subcutaneously at an earlier age, whereby the aliens were able to monitor the development of selected subjects.[25]

Further encouragement came with the 1987 bestseller, *Communion* by horror writer Whitley Strieber, which told of his abduction while insisting on every second page that it was "a true story." His sensational account, though full of unanswered questions and questionable claims, was made into a motion picture,[26] and that same year, Hopkins published *Intruders*, a follow-up to his earlier book recounting his further investigations, which was not only a bestseller but provided the basis for a TV mini-series.[27]

The extent of the abduction mania was measured – after a fashion – in 1991 when Hopkins and Temple University historian David Jacobs were approached to devise a survey on the incidence of the UFO abduction phenomenon. Conducted by the Roper Organization, it was based on 5,947 respondents. "The results indicated that millions of Americans might be abductees … The final analysis indicates that 2 percent of the American people – five million Americans – have experienced events consistent with those that abductees experienced before they knew they were abductees,"[28] wrote Jacobs, whose 1992 *Secret Life: Firsthand Accounts of UFO Abductions* – was a book-length exposition of his belief that the aliens were engaging in a secret, systematic breeding program with humans.

More recently, in British Columbia, Canadian UFO researcher Michael Strainic has noted that some local investigators tout the belief that *everyone* is an abductee and that *every* UFO sighting is a "hidden abduction." Strainic states: "I personally gave up on nearly all local abduction cases when the number (within 60 kilometers of Vancouver alone) blasted through the 300 mark. And especially since the largest number of reports were nearly incoherent..."[29] However, while he remarks "there certainly is a mania at work here," he concludes that there is "a tiny residuum of truly baffling cases, many of which have a paranormal quality." This was certainly true of the remarkable claim made in Hopkins' third book *Witnessed*, which tells the story of Linda Napolitano, who during the night of November 30, 1989, was allegedly abducted from her Manhattan apartment and taken aboard a UFO, which then dived into the river – an event witnessed, Hopkins claimed, by the Secretary-General of the United Nations (who, however, denied it).[30] This and other widely-publicized cases, such as the one presented below in our Case History, not only present behavioral scientists with a wealth of rich material but confront them with a formidable challenge to distinguish fact from fantasy.

Irrespective of whether the abductions were what they seemed, there could be little doubt that the witnesses were experiencing *something*. This was evidenced not only by their reactions at the time, which often manifested strong emotional trauma, but also by long-term effects, including personality and lifestyle changes.[31] As with most other features of the experience, this was seized upon by both believers and skeptics to support their case: believers claimed that these responses validated the veridicality of the myriad claims, skeptics asserted that they confirmed that the experiences were rooted in the individual's psychological history.

Sociologists were also interested in another category of witnesses, one that might be categorized as would-be abductees. The most notable of these were the group that formed round Dorothy Martin, who in 1954 believed that the United States was faced with imminent catastrophe but that her group would be privileged to be rescued by the aliens in their spaceships. The group was infiltrated by undercover sociologists interested to learn how the group would react if the catastrophe and the rescue failed to take place (which indeed turned out to be the case). Their account, entitled *When Prophecy Fails*, has become a classic of sociological literature, providing insight into the subtle processes whereby the human race indulges its capacity for self-deception.[32] Similar expectations have been raised and dashed by other groups, such as the followers of Taiwanese guru Teacher Chen who experienced a similar disappointment in 1979.[33]

COMMENT: There is considerable support for the extraterrestrial explanation of UFOs, and consequently for the veridical nature of abductions. At the same time, many features of the phenomenon suggest that the subject may be more appropriately studied by those in the fields of psychology and sociology, rather than astronomy or exobiology. Indeed, there is hardly any research discipline that might not be relevant. The folklorist, for example, could fairly claim that the origins of the mania lie in legends and the tribal beliefs of exotic cultures. Reports of visits to Earth by otherworldly beings have been a staple of folklore from the earliest times.[34] Many accounts include reports of humans being temporarily abducted by otherworldly beings, and these have led to exceptional behavior, notably during the WITCHCRAFT MANIA. Parallels to abduction stories can also be found in demon possession, shamanic trance, and the folk beliefs of many cultures. [35] John Musgrave and James Houran compare lore about the witches' Sabbat and UFOs, suggesting that both "share the same basic structure, common symbolism, and serve the same psychological needs of providing a coherent explanation for anomalous (ambiguous) experiences... This pattern of similarities suggests the possibility that UFO abductions are a modern version of tales of flight to the Sabbat."[36]

Another contributory source, itself perhaps derived from folklore traditions, is science fiction. Many writers have pointed out parallels between the science fantasies of the early 20th century and the UFO/abduction claims of the later 20th century.[37] Fred C. Smale's "The abduction of Alexandra Seine," published in 1900, prefigured aerial though not alien abduction.[38] By 1936, when Dona Stuart's "The Invaders" was published in *Astounding Stories*,[39] the Hills' abduction scenario was anticipated to a remarkable degree. The tales told by the late 20th century abductees were more sophisticated, more deeply "spiritual," more ecologically-concerned and more politically correct than their predecessors, but their raw materials are all to be found in the pulp science fiction of the 1920s-1930s.

For the behavioral scientist, abductees present a rich diversity of claimed experience, which throws light on the springs of human behavior. The astonishing complexity of the abduction phenomenon has encouraged many thoughtful researchers to perceive a deeper significance that goes beyond the psychosocial dimension: Leo Sprinkle and John E Mack, both university professors, discern a spiritual depth to the experience which could be of lasting significance to the human race[40] – a view which is, of course, emphatically endorsed by the abductees themselves, many of whom have felt their lives transformed by their experience and credit their alien abductors accordingly. Sprinkle has declared: "There are two themes to the extraterrestrial purpose. 1. ETs are here to rejuvenate planet earth, and 2. ETs are here to assist humankind in another stage of evolution… through a metamorphosis of human consciousness."[41] The case of Betty Andreasson, for example, involves a succession of experiences in which the surface narrative – intrusion, abduction etc. – was merely the prelude to a mystical saga which has persisted over several years.[42] For such as her, the abduction experience is an episode of personal spiritual development comparable to the religious conversion experience described by James and Starbuck.[43] Whether it has any basis whatsoever in fact remains an open question.

CASE HISTORY: On the basis of his analysis of some 1,700 abduction reports, folklorist Thomas Bullard felt justified in stating: "The abduction story consists of eight possible episodes – capture, examination, conference, tour of the ship, journey or otherworldly journey, theophany [religious or spiritual experience], return, and aftermath." However, he adds that "few reports contain all these episodes, only capture and return are universal."[44] His massive case-file, while largely repetitive, contains a remarkable diversity of experience, far more varied than, say, the confessions elicited in the course of the WITCH MANIA. No single abduction case is both typical and representative. We have chosen one which, in its bizarre narrative, gives some idea of the rich complexity of the abduction experience and explains its fascination both for investigators who believe that the stories do truly tell of alien visitations, and for behavioral scientists who suspect that a more down-to-earth explanation for them can be found in the human psyche.

The Kentucky Abduction Encounter January 1976[45]

Three ladies from near Stanford, Kentucky – Ms. Louise Smith, Ms. Mona Stafford and Mrs. Elaine Thomas – are driving home after a late birthday dinner when all see a bright 30-meter diameter disc-shaped object in the sky, which they will later describe in classic flying saucer terms. Smith, driving a car she purchased just this morning, loses control of it, finding herself moving at 140 km/h (85 mph) though her foot is not on the accelerator. Her companions become extremely alarmed, screaming for Smith to stop, and experience physical burning and blinding sensations. When they regain control they find themselves further on in their journey than seems possible. Yet when they reach home, they find, as did the Hills, that their journey seems to have taken an hour and a half longer than would be expected.

Although they do not seek publicity, word gets around, and civilian UFO groups show interest; an unseemly squabble ensues as to who should conduct the investigation. Eventually, hypnosis sessions are conducted by Leo Sprinkle, a respected professor of psychology at the University of Wyoming, Laramie. During the sessions, each of the three tells how she was taken apart from her friends to undergo something like a physical examination, but it isn't the same kind of examination in each case, and other circumstances are different. There is no specific detail as to the abducting process, nor any indication that the examination took place on board a spacecraft at all. Only Thomas gives anything like a detailed description of the aliens, whom she describes as several small figures about 1.20m tall, with dark eyes and grey skin. Anxiety is displayed by the witnesses during the sessions, and there is some suggestion of mystical and out-of-the-body experiences. Subsequently, all three women are considerably disturbed; they experience sleeping difficulties, inexplicable compulsive behavior, together with some ostensibly paranormal incidents. There are long-term personality changes: one of the three subsequently becomes more outgoing in her social behavior and takes to dressing more colorfully.

The fact that this was, initially at least, a collective experience, yet in other respects distinctly individual, adds to the challenge presented by this strange history. Despite the divergence, the three ladies seem to have shared essentially the same experience. Sprinkle, who examined them, commented, "Although it is not possible to claim absolutely that a physical examination and abduction has taken place, I believe that the tentative hypothesis of abduction and examination is the best hypothesis to explain the apparent loss-of-time experience; the apparent physical and emotional reactions of the witnesses to the UFO sighting; the anxiety and the reactions of the witnesses to their experiences which have occurred after their UFO sighting."[46]

This conclusion by Sprinkle, the contrary of Dr. Simon's diagnosis of the Hill case, demonstrates the divergence of views generated by the abduction phenomenon. Whether fact or fantasy, it is a remarkable instance of exceptional social behavior.[47]

See also: FANTASY-PRONE PEOPLE.

ALTERED STATES OF CONSCIOUSNESS

When an individual exhibits exceptional behavior, this is often attributed to the fact that he is in an altered state of consciousness (ASC). If collective behavior is to be accounted for in the same way, we would have to suppose one of two scenarios: either that each individual making up the group has independently entered into an altered state, or that there is such a thing as a collective altered state. No such state is known, though it is not inconceivable, and there appear to be kindred phenomena.

Commentators on group behavior accept that an individual acts differently when he is part of a group as opposed to when he is on his own. Some even go so far as to suggest that he undergoes a change of personality – that he becomes, in effect, a substantially different person. Even if this is so – which is far from being established – it is by no means clear that this necessarily amounts to an altered state. The question is made more difficult because no consensus exists as to what precisely constitutes an ASC. Definitions range from the specific and precise to the wide-ranging and inclusive.[48]

Anthropologist Erika Bourguignon regards ASCs as comprising a wide range of behaviors, which appear throughout this Encyclopedia: "Words such as 'trance' or 'spirit possession' are used widely, inconsistently, and often interchangeably. We may also read of dissociation, fugue states, hysteria, hallucinations, catalepsy, epilepsy, hypnosis, somnambulism, and so on. For our purposes, all of these psychiatric terms may be subsumed under the broad heading of 'altered states of consciousness.'"[49]

Bourguignon's studies of trance and possession trance found that "of a sample of 488 societies, in all parts of the world... 437, or 90%, are reported to have one or more institutionalized, culturally patterned forms of altered states of consciousness... [This] suggests that we are dealing with a matter of major importance, not merely a bit of anthropological esoterica."[50] They are culturally learned behaviors, which acquire importance to the community by embodying social and cultural symbols that serve to give it a sense of identity and cohesion.

When such behavior is institutionalized, it can hardly be said to constitute exceptional behavior. Though such practices as voodoo or the peyote cult may seem extraordinary to outsiders, they do not seem so to those who practice them, consequently they do not as a rule qualify for discussion in this Encyclopedia. It could indeed be argued that some of the behaviors described in these pages should not be regarded as exceptional – for instance, the self-mutilation practices of the ISLAMIC ECSTATIC SECTS, which are performed annually and can therefore be perceived as institutionalized. However, they merit inclusion because, though the practices as such may not be exceptional to those involved in them, the physical manifestations that result from them are indeed exceptional in that they transcend what is commonly thought of as possible.

Other behaviors described in this Encyclopedia seem more clearly to qualify as ASCs. The ecstatic trances in which the victims of CONVENT HYSTERIA claimed to be possessed by demons and exhibited a wide range of phenomena surely qualify as ASCs by any definition. The account of the children in the LANDES case leaves no doubt that a radical change in their personality took place. On the purely physical level, the children in the MORZINE epidemic performed feats of which they would not have been capable in their normal state.

There are two ways in which a group of individuals could collectively enter an altered state. It could occur biologically, if all members of the group took a drug or shared some other hallucinogenic experience such as the Native American sweat lodge. Other facilitating processes could be dance or rhythmic chanting. Some ISLAMIC ECSTATIC SECTS, for example, precede their performances, which seem to be conducted in an altered state, by dancing to the point of exhaustion. In many religious sects, such as the Russian SOUPONIEVO, prolonged dancing and chanting is a central feature of their ceremonies, as in Voodoo and countless tribal rituals. (See also DANCING MANIA.)

Alternatively, it could come about psychologically, the spectacle of one of their number, already in such a state, inspiring his companions by suggestion or imitation. Episodes of mass psychogenic illness/mass hysteria are commonly triggered by an "index case" (the first person to exhibit symptoms). There are many reports, especially in non-Western cultures, where the index case is described as experiencing some form of altered consciousness (described variously by such vague terms as hallucinations, possession, visions, trance, and trance-like states). Sometimes the altered state spreads to no one else; sometimes to a few group members; sometimes to all. Something of the sort seems to have occurred in many instances of convent hysteria in which the pattern seems to have been set by one member of the community, only to be followed by her companions, either by imitation or suggestion. This is evident at LOUDUN, where Sister Jeanne des Anges, the 25 year-old prioress, was the first to be affected, followed by her companions one by one until the entire community was hallucinating, convulsing, and claiming demon possession. In the TAIPING OUTBREAK, one charismatic individual inspired his followers to perform remarkable military feats. Whether all or even many of them were in altered states is now impossible to say, but certainly something of the sort must have occurred.

ASCs are particularly relevant to those of our exceptional behaviors that involve extraordinary physical phenomena, such as the SAINT-MEDARD CONVULSIONARIES and the ISLAMIC ECSTATIC SECTS. Researcher Andrew Weil tells of a drug-facilitated discovery:

> I had my first experience of non-hurtful pain under the influence of LSD. I found myself walking barefoot over a stretch of sharp stones near my house that I had never been able to walk on before. I was very aware of the pressure of the stones on my feet, but the sensation was simply strong and neutral. The sensation was so novel that I explored it for some time, running back and forth on the stones and jumping up and down on them. Yet at the end of this experience I had not the slightest marks on the soles of my feet. A few days later, when feeling ordinary, I tried to walk over the stones again but could not repeat my performance. Even a few steps hurt and left marks.[51]

It seems certain that the convulsionaries of Saint-Médard, and the Islamic self-mutilators, were in just such an altered state while performing their extraordinary feats, and these exceptional experiences give a clear indication of interaction between ASCs and bodily responses. Weil proposes a plausible explanation for how the body is capable, under these special circumstances, of transcending its normal physical limits.

Clearly, ASCs can be a crucial factor in many kinds of exceptional behavior, enabling manifestations of human ability that otherwise would not have taken place. For example, an Eskimo woman afflicted with PIBLOKTOQ survives convulsing for an hour or so, naked on the ice; only the "protection" afforded by an ASC enables her to survive what would, in her normal state, be an intolerable ordeal. Acting as a springboard, the ASC enables the individual to behave in ways which he/she could not have done in their normal state, whether it is the role-playing performances of those who suppose themselves possessed by demons, or the extraordinary gifts of SNAKE HANDLING or GLOSSOLALIA (speaking in tongues).

AMERICAN INVASION OF CANADA

Eastern Canada: 1915-1917

While Canada entered World War I in 1914, the United States did not declare war until April 1917. During much of this period, rumors circulated across Canada that German-Americans, owing their allegiance to the Kaiser, were planning to launch surprise bombing raids or espionage missions on their unsuspecting northern neighbors. At the time there were nearly 10 million German-Americans living in the U.S. As accusations were made on the flimsiest evidence, there were scores of false claims about scheming Germans in both the U.S. and Canada. The British consul-general Sir Courtney Bennett, who was stationed in New York, was notorious for spreading unsubstantiated rumors. In early 1915, Bennett made several wild claims about a plot involving upwards of 80,000 armed, highly trained German-Americans who he said were secretly training in the Western New York. The group was supposedly intent on invading Canada from along the northwestern New York state border. Despite the incredible, unfounded nature of his assertions, it was a reflection of the deep tension and suspicion of the period, that Canadian Prime Minister Sir Robert Borden asked his Police Commissioner to issue a report on the stories, which were assessed to be without foundation.[52]

See also: PHANTOM AIRCRAFT WAVES.

AMERICAN REVIVALISM

United States: 1735-1858

"Revivalism was perhaps an inevitable out-growth of the peculiar conditions of the isolated frontier life; and it undoubtedly had its value as an agency of moral reform and social solidarity.... The history of American Protestantism during the first half of the last [19th] century is a history of almost incessant turmoil of revivals, often accompanied by extreme emotional excesses."[53] As Mecklin observes, religious life in America has been perceived as in constant need of being revived. Many episodes were characterized by exceptional behavior. Though the history of American revivalism is almost continuous, springing up in one place when it dies down in another, three episodes in particular attracted attention by the conduct of the revivalists and their congregations, and this entry focuses on them while reminding the reader that similar behavior was liable to manifest anywhere at any time as religious fervor erupted sporadically. The incidents are: the Great Awakening in Massachusetts, 1735-1750; the Kentucky Revival, 1795-1805; and the Businessmen's Revival of 1857-1858.

The Great Awakening: The Revival In Massachusetts 1735-1750

From the start, the Europeans who colonized North America found themselves experiencing religious difficulties. Although for most of those who crossed the ocean, freedom of conscience was an important motivation, if not the most important, they quickly found that they did not always share the values of their neighbors, and there were continuous disputes among people who, fleeing intolerance in the Old World, might have been expected to practice tolerance in the New World. Instead, bigotry became as characteristic of America's ecclesiastical establishment as it had been in Europe. Then, at a time when Europeans were shaking themselves free of the WITCH MANIA, New England was shaken by the horrific SALEM WITCH TRIALS that put the colonists' beliefs to the test and found them sadly wanting. By the second quarter of the 18th century, however, things seemed relatively stable. But their religion continued to be the morose and pessimistic religion of the Puritans, heavy with guilt and premonitions of doom. The original austerity of the first colonists had softened and mellowed, and to those brought up in that austere tradition it seemed as though the colonies had sunk into depths of dissolution and debauchery. They were probably not as wicked as they thought they were, but the important thing is that they thought so.

Around 1734 a preacher named Jonathan Edwards came to the fore, determined to redeem the community from its sinful ways. He was a Yale-educated man of considerable intellect and even greater strength of purpose. He preached to the Bostonians a Calvinist version of Christianity in which the God of Love was replaced by a vengeful deity who would consign all his creation to damnation for the slightest departure from absolute faith and entire subservience to his will, as interpreted by the priesthood. So effectively did he preach this message that, in his own words, "there was scarcely a single person in the town [Boston], old or young, left unconcerned about the great things of the eternal world."[54] The themes of his sermons tended to be such as "Sinners in the Hands of an angry God" or "Wrath upon the Wicked to the Uttermost" or "The Eternity of Hell Torments." Other ministers followed his example, and for a few years New England was wracked by a religious upheaval that was all the more impactful because, for these people, religion was virtually their entire life. "All other talk but about spiritual and eternal things was soon thrown by; all the conversation in all companies, and upon all occasions, was upon these things only, unless so much as was necessary for people carrying on their ordinary secular business. Religion was with all classes the great concern, and the world was a thing only by the by... The town seemed to be full of the presence of God."[55]

A Boston newspaper described the effect of this new style of preaching: "They frequently fright the Little Children, and set them a Screaming; and that frights their tender Mothers and sets them to Screaming, and by Degrees spreads to a great part of the Congregation: and 40, 50 or an 100 of them screaming together, makes such an awful and hideous Noise as will make a Man's Hair stand on End. Some will faint away, fall down on the Floor, wallow and foam. Some women will rend off their Caps, Handkerchiefs, and other Clothes, tear their Hair down about their Ears, and seem perfectly bereft of their reason."[56]

On July 9, 1741, Edwards delivered his famous Enfield sermon. "The audience of New England farmers had gathered carelessly without thought of the avalanche of woe that was to sweep down upon them from the pulpit. And when it came, many cried aloud for mercy till the preacher could not be heard, and convulsively grasped the benches to prevent themselves from slipping into the pit..."[57] His message was that damnation awaited all who did not repent, and warned:

> If we knew that there was one person and but one, in the whole congregation, that was to be the subject of this misery, what an awful thing it would be to think of! If we knew who it was, what an awful sight it would be to see such a person! How might all the rest of the congregation lift up a lamentable and bitter cry over him! But alas! instead of one, how many it is likely will remember this discourse in hell! And it would be a wonder if some that are now present should not be in hell in a very short time, before this year is out. And it would be no wonder if some persons that now sit here in some seats of this meeting-house, in health and quiet and secure, should be there before tomorrow morning.

There was no counter-balancing promise of heavenly bliss; the best his hearers could hope for was *not* to be damned. Edwards relished detailed descriptions of the physical torments which awaited them – "Imagine yourselves to be cast into a fiery oven for a quarter of an hour... what horror would you feel at the entrance of such a furnace... and after you had endured it for one minute, how overpowering would it be to you to think that you had to endure it the other fourteen.... What if you must lie there for twenty four hours... for a whole year... for a thousand years... Oh! then how would your heart sink if you knew that you must bear it for ever and ever – that there would be no end, that for millions and millions of ages, your torment would be no nearer an end..."[58]

Edwards and his fellow-preachers were not without their critics. Dr. Charles Chauncy, pastor of the First Church in Boston, argued that the revival must be the work of the Devil to exhibit such extravagance and excess. He particularly criticized James Davenport, who addressed his congregation, "You poor unconverted creatures in the seats, in the pews, in the galleries, I wonder you do not drop into hell. It would not surprise me if I should see you drop this minute..."[59] So extreme was his enthusiasm that the General Assembly of Connecticut banished him from the colony.

The crying, the falling, the swooning, and convulsing came to be seen as the normal response, and a preacher would feel he had failed if he did not evoke such behavior. Chauncy was present at a meeting when the congregation was too serious and attentive for the preacher's taste, so he worked them up into a frenzy until they "melted and dissolved, and so overpowered that they fell down as if struck dead."[60] The preachers learned to control their congregations like an orchestra. One observer saw "about half a score of young women" thrown into violent hysteric fits, from which they would recover when the preacher moderated his tone, only to renew their fits when he raised his voice again.

The revival continued until 1744, when it began to lose its momentum. Opinion as to whether the "Great Awakening" did more good than harm remains divided. Certainly New England was made to examine its conscience, but many suffered in their minds, and at least one of his hearers was driven to suicide. Even Edwards subsequently confessed that many who converted during the revival later slid back "desperately hardened," and he himself was exiled from his post. Few today agree with Conant's contemporary view of the Great Awakening as "doubtless the most important event in American history."[61]

The Great Revival In The West: The Kentucky Revival Of 1800

The Great Awakening took place in the relatively civilized states of New England. By contrast, Kentucky was at this time perhaps the most backward corner of the United States, with an unenviable reputation as the harbor for fugitives from justice and other ne'er-do-wells who took refuge in its remote and lawless hills. Life, even for the law-abiding, was little more than a struggle for existence by poor people, mostly of Scottish or northern Irish origin, who brought nothing to their place of settlement and had to win everything from the land. Unremitting work filled their days; the only diversions were market-days and family gatherings. The only culture was religious – religious books the only reading, itinerant missionaries often the only visitors in country districts where it was not economically feasible to maintain a widespread network of established churches, chapels, or meeting-houses.

The preoccupation with subsistence, the fact that many settlers were from criminal or ignorant backgrounds, and the rough conditions of life generally – these led to an indifference as regards religion which dismayed the church leaders (mainly Presbyterians, Baptists and Methodists). The determination of the Protestant sects to convert the entire population meant that the whole of western America was continually traversed by preachers who trod or rode the various "circuits," going from one community to another, spreading God's word as they perceived it. But this enabled them to make contact only with scattered handfuls of people at a time. On the other hand it was unrealistic to expect settlers to quit their homes and travel long distances to attend church services in distant towns. The revival movement was seen as a way of correcting the situation.[62]

The starting-point of this revival was the arrival in Kentucky of the Reverend James McGready, a Presbyterian minister from North Carolina, a rough character who could hold his own with his rough parishioners. He brought a message of imminent damnation, of fire and brimstone, to which his audience was unaccustomed. He soon had them "weeping and talking about their souls… they spoke only of the need of the soul's salvation."[63] Other preachers working in the same fashion appeared, and soon their efforts were producing responses similar to those of METHODISM in England. John McGee, one such, reported: "I rose up and exhorted them to let the Lord God Omnipotent reign in their hearts, and submit to Him, and their souls should live. Many broke silence. The woman in the east end of the house shouted tremendously. I left the pulpit and went through the audience shouting and exhorting with all possible ecstasy and energy, and the floor was soon covered with the slain."[64]

But churches were few and far between in this territory, and hard-pressed farmers could not spare the time to make the long journeys required to get to them. This practical problem was answered with a very practical solution, the "camp-meeting," held in the countryside closer to where the farmers lived. In the summer of 1800, at the Gasper River, the church was too small to hold all who gathered to hear McGready. A suitable site was chosen in the nearby forest, where trees were felled – they would double as platforms for the preachers and seating for their hearers. "When night came they were far from surfeited with religious zeal. The women pieced together the extra sheets and quilts which they had brought with them in the wagons, and the men cut poles over which these coverings were stretched for tents. Some brought straw from the nearest farms and others foraged for provisions. And when the darkness fell, fires were kindled through the new-made village among the trees. The meeting lasted from Friday until Tuesday. The preaching, praying and singing continued almost without cessation save for a few hours in the early morning."[65]

It was not before Saturday evening that the attendees began to behave in any extreme fashion. Then two women became greatly excited; their excitement spread, and soon the camp was loud with sobbing and crying. The ministers spent most of the night passing between groups of the "slain."

Those who attended the Gasper River meeting told their neighbors, and enthusiasm for the meetings spread rapidly. This became the pattern for future events. Given that they came from 50, 100, even 150 km distance, a one-day event was not practicable, but there were far too many to be accommodated by the local population, so people came with provision for sleeping, some in their wagons, others in tents, enabling substantial numbers to gather. Furthermore, as the excitement increased, the night meetings became a most important feature of the gatherings, and the people were loath to leave the place at all.[66] The settlers were accustomed to camping as they travelled, and in any case their primitive homes were hardly more luxurious than camps. They brought their own provisions, though it was reported that in the excitement of the meeting, many seemed unconscious of the need of food and sleep. Such meetings were periodically attacked by rowdy mobs from the neighborhood, but the campers were as robust as their attackers and proved quite capable of taking care of themselves. "It is interesting to observe how often individuals of the same stratum were the first to be laid low by the spiritual blows struck by [the preachers]."[67]

Through 1801 and 1802, camp meetings were a prominent feature of life not only in Kentucky but also in the neighboring states of Ohio, North Carolina, Virginia, and parts of Pennsylvania. The meetings usually began on Friday, or even Thursday, and continued until the following Tuesday. People came from far and wide; sometimes entire settlements were deserted, every inhabitant away at the meeting. Attendance was often in the hundreds, sometimes in the thousands. At the larger meetings two or more preachers (as many as six or seven at the largest) might be preaching simultaneously, as at a fair, from individual stands, so that the singing, praying, and exhortation was continuous all day and sometimes all night, when the grounds would be illuminated with fires and candles.

The tone of the preaching was enthusiastic. The preachers – who might be Baptists, Presbyterians, or Methodists even at the same meeting – were rarely highly educated people, any more than their hearers, and the theme was a simplistic opposition of heavenly bliss for the saved who repent and everlasting fire and damnation for the unrepentant sinner. This was received by a vociferous and fervent congregation, who were often wildly excited. Elder Stone said of the Logan County meeting, in the spring of 1801: "Many, very many fell, and continued for hours together in an apparently breathless and motionless state, sometimes for a few moments reviving and exhibiting symptoms of life by a deep groan or a piercing shriek or by a prayer for mercy fervently uttered. After lying there for hours, they would rise, shouting deliverance."[68]

It was taken-for-granted that these were the outward signs of an inward grace bestowed by God; they were known as "exercises" and soon became an accepted feature of the meetings. A writer to the *New York Missionary Magazine* in 1802 stated:

> They were struck down and exercised in many different ways, although they generally trembled exceedingly, and were remarkably cold in their bodily extremities. After they recovered, some said they felt a great load about their heart, a little before the severity of the stroke; others said they were rather in a slumbering and inattentive way, not at all affected at that moment, with what they were hearing or had heard, when they were struck down in an instant as with a thunderbolt. Some were totally insensible of everything that passed for a considerable time, others said they were perfectly sensible of every word spoken in their hearing, and everything done to them although to the spectator they appeared in a state of equal insensibility. Many cried out exceedingly when they were first struck down; their cries were like those of the greatest bodily distress imaginable. But this was generally succeeded, in a little time, by a state of apparent insensibility which generally lasted much longer; and which, in some, was succeeded by the strongest appearance of extreme agitation and distress exhibited by incessant cries for mercy, and acknowledgements of unworthiness and ingratitude to a blessed Savior.[69]

At the Cain Ridge meeting in August 1801, attended by between 10,000 and 15,000 people, an observer reported: "I suppose I saw as many as 800 that were struck down mostly in the following manner: they say they feel very weak in their knees and a want of breath, gaping to gain their breath as one in the agony of death, and instantly fall and lay insensible from 15 minutes to 6, 8 or 10 hours."[70]

The noise of the vast crowd was compared to the roar of Niagara. A strange supernatural power seemed to pervade the entire mass of mind there collected. At one time the Rev. James Finley saw "at least five hundred persons swept down in a moment as if a battery of 1,000 guns had been opened upon them, and then immediately followed shrieks and shouts that rent the very heavens."[71] James Crawford, an old and respected minister, "informed me that he kept as accurate an account as he could of the number that fell on the occasion and computed it to be about three thousand, one in every six."[72]

Spontaneous preaching by children is a feature which recurs in a variety of other contexts, notably the CEVENNES PROPHETS. At the Cain Ridge meeting, August 1801, this was reported:

> I noted a remarkable instance of a little girl, by the name of Barbara, about 7 years old, who was set upon a man's shoulder, agreeably to her desire to speak to the multitude, which she did until she appeared almost exhausted, and leaned back her head on her bearer. A tender hearted old man standing close behind her, observed, "Poor thing, she had better be laid down"; at which she quickly turned round her head and said, "Don't call me poor, for Christ is my brother, God my father, and I have a kingdom to inherit, therefore don't call me poor, for I am rich in the blood of the Lamb."[73]
>
> At Indian Creek, Kentucky, July 1801 a boy from his appearance about twelve years old retired from the stand in time of preaching under a very extraordinary impression and having mounted a log at some distance, and raising his voice, in a very affecting manner, he attracted the main body of the people in a few minutes. With tears streaming from his eyes he cried aloud to the wicked, warning them of their danger, denouncing their certain doom if they persisted in their sins &c. Supported by two men he spoke nearly an hour. At another meeting a girl of about 10 years old was struck, and when able to speak began to exhort, continued two hours in prayer.[74]

As so often, it is difficult to say when compulsive movements begin to merit the label "dancing," but it is notable that "voluntary dancing was encouraged as a means of warding off other disagreeable exercises."[75] The term "disagreeable exercises" is doubtless a reference to participants who began to whirl around like a top. She continued for an hour without stopping, whirling at the rate of fifty times in a minute, and complaining of pain or distress only when the singing stopped.[76]

Some time after the Great Revival got under way, the most notorious of the "exercises" appeared at a meeting in eastern Tennessee: "the jerks." This seems to have been a particularly contagious phenomenon, very violent, and wholly beyond the individual's control, afflicting skeptics as well as believers. An entire congregation might be afflicted simultaneously; one observer (Peter Cartwright) speaks of having seen more than five hundred jerking at one time.[77]

Another observer was Lorenzo Dow, himself a preacher, who reported in his journal:

> I had heard about a singularity called the *jerks* or *jerking exercise*, which appeared first near Knoxville [Tennessee] in August last [1803], to the great alarm of the people, which reports I considered at first, as vague and false; but at length like the Queen of Sheba, I set out to go and see for myself. When I arrived in sight of this town I saw hundreds of people collected in little bodies; and observing no place appointed for meeting, I got on a log and gave out a hymn, which caused them to assemble round, in solemn attentive silence. I observed several invol-

untary motions in the course of the meeting, which I considered as a specimen of the jerks.

[Next day] I began to speak to a vast audience: and I observed about thirty to have the jerks; though they strove to keep as still as they could; these emotions were involuntary and irresistible, as any unprejudiced mind might discern... Hence to Maryville, where I spoke to about one thousand five hundred, and many appeared to feel the word, but about fifty felt the jerks. At night I lodged with one of the Nicholites, a kind of Quakers, who do not feel free to wear colored clothes. Whilst at tea I observed his daughter, who sat opposite to me at table, to have the jerks, and dropped the tea cup from her hand in the violent agitation. I said to her, "Young woman, what is the matter?" She replied, "I have got the jerks." I asked her how long she had it. She observed, "A few days," and that it had been the means of the awakening and conversion of her soul, by stirring her up to serious consideration about her careless state.

Sunday, February 19th, I spoke in Knoxville to hundreds more than could get into the court house. About one hundred and fifty appeared to have the jerking exercise, among whom was a circuit preacher, (Johnson) who had opposed them a little before, but he now had them powerfully; and I believe he would have fallen over three times had not the auditory been so crowded that he could not, unless he fell perpendicularly.

After meeting I rode eighteen miles to hold meeting at night. The people of this settlement were mostly Quakers; and they had said, as I was informed, the Methodists and Presbyterians have the jerks because they sing and pray so much, but we are a still, peaceable people, wherefore we do not have them. However, about twenty of them came in meeting [and] about a dozen of them had the jerks as keen and as powerful as any I had seen, so as to have occasioned a kind of grunt or groan when they would jerk.

20th. I passed by a meeting house, where I observed the undergrowth had been cut down for a camp meeting, and from fifty to one hundred saplings left breast high, which to me appeared so slovenish that I could not but ask my guide the cause, who observed they were topped so high, and left for the people to jerk by. This so excited my attention that I went over the ground to view it; and found where the people had laid hold of them and jerked so powerfully that they had kicked up the earth as a horse stamping flies. A Presbyterian minister observed, "Yesterday whilst I was preaching, some had the jerks, and a young man from North Carolina mimicked them, out of derision, and soon was seized with them himself; which was the case with many others; he grew ashamed, and on attempting to mount his horse to go off, his foot jerked about so that he could not put it into the stirrup; some youngsters seeing this, assisted him on, but he jerked so that he could not sit alone, and one got up to hold him on, which was done with difficulty." I observing this, went to him and asked him what he thought of it. Said he, "I believe God sent it on me for my wickedness, and making so light of it in others;" and he requested me to pray for him.

I observed his wife had it; she said she was first attacked with it in bed. Dr Nelson said he had frequently strove to get it, in order to philosophise upon it [study it scientifically], but could not; and observed they could not account for it on natural principles...[78]

[Standing on a log in the woods] Several of them desired I should pray with them; soon nine were sprawling on the ground, and some were apparently lifeless. The Doctors supposed they had fainted, and desired water and fans to be used. I replied, "Hush!" then they to show the fallacy of my ideas, attempted to determine it with their skill, but to their surprise their pulse was regular; some said, it is fictitious, they make it. I answered, "the weather is warm, and we are in perspiration, whilst they are as cold as corpses, which cannot be done by human art."

Here some supposed they were dying, whilst others suggested "it is the work of the devil." I observed, "if it be the devil's work, they will use the dialect of hell, when they come to;" some watched my words, in great solemnity, and the first and second were soon brought through, happy, and all in the course of the night."[79]

Dow was curious about the state of mind of the jerkers:

Friday, 19th [Oct 1804]. Camp meeting commenced at Liberty [Tennessee]. Here I saw the jerks, and some danced a strange exercise indeed; however, it is involuntary, yet requires the consent of the will; i.e. the people are taking to jerking irresistibly; and if they strive to resist it, it worries them much, yet is attended with no bodily pain, and those who are exercised to dance, which in the pious seems an antidote to the jerks, if they resist, it brings deadness and barrenness over the mind, but when they yield to it they feel happy, although it is a great cross; there is a heavenly smile and solemnity on the countenance, which carries a great conviction to the minds of beholders. Their eyes, when dancing, seem to be fixed upwards as if upon an invisible object, and they [are] lost to all below.[80]

Less common, though even stranger, were the outbreaks of "barking." Groups of people would fall on all fours, like dogs, growling and snapping their teeth at the foot of a tree while the minister preached. This was known as "treeing the devil," whom they supposed they were driving away as guard-dogs drive away unwelcome strangers.[81] Outbreaks of barking also occurred in the AMOU OUTBREAK and in several instances of CONVENT HYSTERIA.

In 1803, a further development was observed, one which had puzzled Wesley during the METHODIST MEETINGS. This was the sudden bursting into laughter, first by one individual, then taken up by others (see LAUGHING MANIA). Known as "the holy laugh," it

A revival camp meeting in the American backwoods. (Leipzig Illustrirte Zeitung, 1852)

was in no sense mocking or derisive; the afflicted people remained solemn and devout even as they laughed in chorus.[82]

Not all observers took so favorable a view of the camp-meetings. Several travelers have left accounts of meetings they attended. One of Grégoire's correspondents attended a five-day event in Dutchess County, New York. He watched as hundreds of families pitched their tents and arranged their baggage, while already the preachers were in action and singing could be heard. Soon he saw a good number of those present begin to shudder, then fall into convulsions, rolling and frothing at the mouth, shouting, and yelling. As night fell, lanterns were lit, giving the forest setting a romantic impression.

"The enthusiasm grew with each day as further arrivals swelled the number to four thousand. They formed groups of forty or fifty, in the centre of which some, mostly women and even children of six or seven, fell fainting to the ground. Compared with this, the chaos of the Tower of Babel would be a model of order and harmony. It is impossible to conceive to what excesses they gave themselves. One young girl, in a pious ecstasy, stripped off her clothes and threw herself into the river, where she drowned. Another woman was so deeply penetrated with the joy of being re-born, that she aborted the child she was bearing…." The traveler comments that, not only could he see nothing beneficial in these meetings, but he saw much danger as re-born "sisters" passed the night with "brothers" in name only. Another kind of danger was perceived by doctors who, since seven out of ten epileptics become so through fear, were concerned that the fear of hell-fire preached at the camp-meetings could lead to epilepsy.[83]

COMMENT: The French traveler Michaud, another of Grégoire's informants, said that the camp-meetings gave him some idea of the dances of the Maenads in ancient Greece; compared with this, he said, the lunatic asylums of Paris were strongholds of good sense.[84] But Lorenzo Dow did not doubt that even the physical symptoms of the revival were divine in origin:

> It appears that many have undervalued the great revival, and attempted to account for it on natural principles; therefore it seems to me, from the best judgment I can form, that God hath seen proper to take this method to convince people that he will work in a way to show his power; and sent the jerks as a sign of the times, partly in judgment for the people's unbelief, and yet as a mercy to convict people of divine realities.
>
> I have seen Presbyterians, Methodists, Quakers, Baptists, Church of England, and Independents, exercised with the jerks; gentleman and lady, black and white, the aged and the youth, rich and poor, without exception; from which I infer, as it cannot be accounted for on natural principles, and carries such marks of involuntary motion, that it is no trifling matter. I believe that those who are most pious and given up to God, are rarely touched with it; and also those naturalists, who wish and try to get it to philosophize upon it are excepted; but the lukewarm, lazy, half-hearted, indolent professor is subject to it; and many of them I have seen, who, when it came upon them, would be alarmed and stirred up to redouble their diligence with God, and after they would get happy, were thankful it ever came upon them. Again, the wicked are frequently more afraid of it than the small pox or yellow fever; these are subject to it; but the persecutors are more subject to it than any, and they sometimes have cursed and swore, and damned it, whilst jerking. There is no pain attending the jerks except they resist it, which if they do, it will weary them more in an hour than a day's labor, which shows that it requires the consent of the will to avoid suffering.[85]

The Businessmen's Revival, 1857-58

Americans would never again observe anything so spectacular as the Kentucky revival, but the "Businessmen's Revival" of 1857-1858 was sufficiently remarkable for it to be designated "the event of the century" by theologian Perry Miller of Harvard.[86] While most historians have described it as a consequence of the financial panic of October 1857, historian J. Edwin Orr has convincingly shown that the movement was already underway before the financial failure exploded. For instance, in May of that year, a corporate appeal entitled "Longing for Revivals" was issued by the General Assembly of the Presbyterian Church. "Christians were praying early in 1857 that the popular addiction to money-making might be broken."[87] Rather than look to a cause-and-effect sequence, both the financial crisis and the revival are best seen as consequences of a period of extraordinary materialism, which caused a revulsion in businessmen's minds at the same time as it led to a colossal financial failure that left Wall Street in a state of collapse, with trade and commerce throughout the country ruined or in difficulties. What is clear, though, is that the financial failure added greater urgency to the revival and dictated its character.[88]

On October 14, 1857, the financial crisis reached its crisis. In a single hour, banks closed and thousands of families were ruined. A few days later, "concerned by looks of anxiety on the faces of businessmen who passed by on the street,"[89] Jeremiah Lamphier, a lay missionary of the Dutch Reformed Church in Fulton Street, New York City, had the idea of an hour of prayer, from noon till one, specifically for the financial community. "This meeting is intended to give merchants, mechanics, clerks, managers, and businessmen generally an opportunity to stop and call on God amid the perplexities incident to their respective avocations."[90] The first day, three men sat in a small room on the third floor; the following day there were six. The day after, the room proved too small to contain all who came, and it was not long before there were meetings on all three floors of the building. "All sects are here: the formal, stately Churchman and the impulsive Methodist who cannot suppress his groan and his 'amen,' the sober, substantial Dutchman and the ardent Congregationalist, with all Yankee restlessness on his face; the Baptist and the Presbyterian, joining in the same chorus and bowing at the same altar. Not one woman is in the meeting."[91]

When hundreds came seeking admission, other churches followed the example. Soon *The New York Times* could report: "In this city we have beheld a sight which not the most enthusiastic fanatic for church observance could ever have hoped to look upon. We have seen in the business quarters of the city, during their busiest hours, assemblies of merchants, clerks, and working men, to the number of 5,000, gathering day after day for a simple solemn worship. Similar assemblies we find in other portions of the city: a theater is turned into a chapel, churches of all sects are open and crowded by day and by night."[92]

Soon there were meetings throughout the city, from which it spread to other towns throughout the country from Pittsburgh to New Orleans. The press added its voice: James Gordon Bennett's *New York Herald* competed with Horace Greely's *New York Tribune* in the number of column inches they devoted to the noonday meetings.[93] The excitement was intense and filled not only the churches but other less probable venues. John Allen's dancehall "which ranked with the worst the city had ever known" opened at midday for prayers, bringing together "his bartenders, musicians and prostitutes at noon to expound a passage of Scripture."[94] Burton's Theater, on Chambers Street, was opened for noontide prayer meetings:

> Half an hour before the time appointed to beginning the exercises, the house was packed in every corner from the pit to the roof. By noon, the entrances to the hall were so densely thronged that it required great exertions to get within hearing distance, and no amount of elbowing could force an entrance so far as to be able to get a sight of the stage. People clung to every projection along the walls; they piled themselves up on seats, and crowded the whole stage beneath, and above, and behind the curtain. The street in front was lined with carriages. The audience was composed principally of business men: there were about two hundred ladies, and not less than fifty clergymen.[95]

Not only businessmen were attracted. There were special meetings for groups such as firemen, a notoriously belligerent community. "Many mechanics come into the meetings blackened with smoke and dust of the forge and anvil... Numerous coloured persons also are present every day, and take seats, without any seeming objection on the part of their white neighbours."[96] The most sensational convert was a prize-fighter, Orville Gardner, and his public testimony "had a great impact upon a certain class of citizens."[97] Altogether it was estimated that up to a million converts were made in the course of the revival.[98]

The meetings had none of the wild excitement of the camp meetings. The preachers were heard with strong emotion, but in quiet. A teenage prodigy, Crammond Kennedy, attracted great crowds with his preaching, but the worst that could be said of him was that "his style sounded rather vehement" – he attracted none of the hysterical weeping of Jonathan Edwards or the Kentucky preachers. "Neither in 1857 nor in 1858 was there outbreaking of trembling, jerking, screaming, groaning, fainting, prostration, or dancing for joy."[99] It is perhaps significant to note that this was predominantly a male affair. Even when women were present, they were very much in the minority, and often there were no women present at all. Businesswomen were few and far between in the 1850s.

COMMENT: The underlying motivation of this revival was guilt. The financial crisis was perceived, if not as an explicit punishment, at least as an indication that Mammon had been worshipped to excess. Now, in a collective act of penitence, people turned back to the God of their fathers.

> Some weeks ago a merchant came here from Albany, and called on one of our New York merchants to buy some goods. At 12 o'clock the New York merchant looked at his watch, and asked to be excused for an hour. The other objected, as he was in haste to get through with his business. He replied that he must go to the prayer-meeting: it was of more importance than to sell his whole stock of goods. The gentleman from Albany inquired if he could not pray enough at morning and night, without leaving his business at noon? the merchant said he could not; and by persuasion and gentle force he induced his friend to go to the prayer-meeting with him. That man went into that meeting, became interested, and came out a converted man...[100]

These three episodes of American Revivalism, occurring in three quite different contexts, are notable as specific and largely spontaneous responses to particular circumstances – the perceived decadence of back-sliding New England; the spiritual desert of the Midwest; the materialism of the business world. By contrast, the revivalism of subsequent times was to take a quite different form – the preaching of charismatic individuals, from Aimée Semple McPherson and Billy Sunday to Billy Graham and today's televangelists. Though the early revivals had their popular preachers, they were, for all their excesses, responding to perceived needs. Their 20th century successors would impose their message on their audiences regardless of circumstances, arrogantly confident that they know what is best for their fellow men and women.

AMOU BARKING MANIA

France: 1613

Eighty women of the village of Amou, near Dax in the flat Basque region of southern France, were afflicted with a remarkable malady, known locally as Laïra, which was characterized by convulsions and dog-like barking.[101] The outbreak compares with several other behaviors described in this Encyclopedia where individuals present an array of symptoms that spread by contagion within an enclosed community, either by physical contact, by suggestion or by unconscious imitation.

CONTEXT: The barking mania was not an isolated occurrence but a relatively minor incident in one of the most virulent witch-hunts in French history. In 1609, King Henri IV received information from persons in authority that the region of Labourd, in southwest France, was infested with witches. He appointed two commissioners to investigate the matter, with powers to deal with the situation as they saw fit. One of the two was assigned to more pressing duties, leaving Pierre, sieur de Lancre, Conseiller du Roi at the Parlement de Bordeaux, (1553-1631) in sole authority. De Lancre was a thorough-going believer in the reality of witchcraft, and he considered it a grievous error of an earlier generation that witches should not be condemned to death but sent back to their priests as though their beliefs were simple illusion and false imagination. He held that the only way to get rid of witchcraft was to get rid of the witches themselves, and to this effect he burned six hundred of them.[102]

De Lancre surmised that the Labourd was infested with demons who had been expelled from India and Japan by Christian missionaries, and who had chosen to resettle in the region. Evidence for this was obtained from English and Scottish wine-merchants, trading with Bordeaux, who with their own eyes had seen the demons in flight over their vessels, heading like them for France.[103]

Hence it was no wonder that the region with its population of 30,000 was infested. The demons were able to recruit numerous local women as witches and even constrain the priests to do their will. Every household was contaminated and the witches were everywhere, of every age and every condition. The customary procedure of imprisonment and torture led to confessions that led, in turn, to widespread executions. Consequently the entire countryside was sensitized, its inhabitants fearful either of the witches themselves or of the inquisitors who might accuse them of practicing witchcraft. Sons accused their parents, brothers their sisters, husbands their wives. The convulsions and barking that took place in Amou were seen as just one further manifestation by the demons, and De Lancre did not doubt that those affected were victims or collaborators with Satan.

The two principal symptoms of the affliction were convulsions and dog-like barking, but remarkably, the women who were subject to convulsions were spared the barking, and vice versa. Those who went into fits of barking were said to be suffering from the *mal de laïra* – that is to say, the barking malady; they did not fall to the ground. Those who went into convulsions were at first diagnosed as suffering from epilepsy. They would sprawl on the ground, beating it with their bodies and limbs like savage animals, banging their heads against the roughest object they met with in their fall; it was far more violent than any natural epileptic fit. They turned their forces against their own persons, unable to prevent self-inflicted injury despite their own wishes.

Because the convulsions differed from natural epilepsy, De Lancre did not hesitate to regard the victims as witches, and the agent responsible as the Evil One. So too with the barking mania:

> It was a monstrous thing to see forty people in the church in this small parish, barking like dogs all at the same time, making such a concert in the house of God that one could not continue one's devotions. They barked like dogs at the time of the full moon, and this barking was renewed every time a witch came into the church, who passed this malady on to others. And even if the witch was not there, they would bark, calling on her by name… for God gave them in their affliction this precaution, of naming those who had brought this curse on them, so that they might be noted and delivered to justice…. Happily, many confessed voluntarily and were subsequently brought to the court. If a victim started barking in her own home, her family or her servants would look out into the street, to see who was passing: if it was the person she named, they ran out and held her, and many who were stopped in this way confessed to their crime.[104]

Calmeil, writing in 1845, agrees with De Lancre that this was not epilepsy, but instead of witchcraft he diagnosed *"une violente hystérie convulsive,"* and he compares it with cases of CONVENT HYSTERIA. Similarly, he notes that the barking also manifested itself in the convents of KENTORFF, SAINT-BRIGITTE, and AMSTERDAM, with the difference that in these cases those who were afflicted with convulsions also participated in the barking, whereas the village women of Amou did either one or the other.

COMMENT: The 19th century physician Calmeil exclaims: "What a spectacle! On one hand village women who mutilate themselves in the access of convulsions and girls who bark even in church, and on the other the judges and executioners who exterminate them! We must not lose sight of the fact that the presence of persons suspected of witchcraft, or even simply their memory, were enough to trigger the paroxysms of the *mal de l'aire*, and that these women attributed to distant sensations the feelings which sprang from within themselves, and led people to believe that they were impressionable at a great distance."[105]

The convulsions and the barking were clearly a hysterical response to the stress of living under constant threat either from the demons or from the judges. That leaves unanswered the question, why their stress should express itself in this form, echoing that of nuns whose stresses were of a very different kind. A tentative suggestion is that these symptoms are a primitive response employed in varying conditions. For a discussion, see entry ANIMAL NOISES.

AMSTERDAM OUTBREAK

Netherlands: 1566

The inmates of a Catholic orphanage in Amsterdam were collectively afflicted by an outbreak of convulsions and other compulsive behavior. Interpreted as demonic possession, it was initially supposed that exorcism was the appropriate treatment, but this did not prove effective.

CONTEXT: At this time the Netherlands were under Spanish domination, thanks to shrewd marriages on the part of the Hapsburg dynasty. Since the Spanish were Catholic and the Dutch inclined towards Protestantism, religious differences were added to the political situation, resulting in an overall tense climate in the country. To what extent this would directly influence orphans in a hospice we cannot say, but even if stress communicated itself to them only indirectly, it may have been a contributing factor. Bekker, writing in 1694 and from a Protestant – even a rationalist – point of view, notes that the orphanage where the children lodged was run by Catholics, and all the children were of that faith.

In March 1566, Adrian Nicolai, chancellor of Gueldres, reported that two months earlier, in a hospice in Amsterdam, thirty (another account says 70)[106] homeless boys and girls were strangely afflicted. Every so often, one or more children would throw themselves onto the ground in convulsions, and this torment lasted from 30 minutes to an hour or even longer. When they eventually got to their feet they had no sensation of anything out of the ordinary and supposed they had slept.[107]

Apart from the convulsions, they climbed walls and rooftops as if they were cats, without coming to any harm. They had a particular habit of running towards a piece of water that was nearby as if intent on drowning themselves, then stopping abruptly at the brink, explaining, "The big man [meaning God] does not permit it."[108] When anything angered them, their faces assumed expressions so horrifying and hideous that even the bravest seemed afraid of them. While in their trance state, they spoke in strange tongues, which were unknown to them, and they seemed to have knowledge of events taking place elsewhere, such as in the Municipal Council.[109]

The doctors tried various treatments without success, believing the children to be afflicted with a natural ailment. Their relatives, convinced that the children were bewitched, consulted sorcerers, but their efforts were no more successful despite their supposedly magic powers.

Finally, supposing that the children must be possessed by demons, exorcists were called in. These exorcists, according to their custom, began with lectures, conjurations, and tried all their devices, but "they lost their time." Worse, while they were being exorcised, the children vomited a huge assortment of objects – hairs, pins and needles, scraps of sheeting, fragments of glass and crockery. Despite all the efforts of the exorcists, the children were not cured; they relapsed into their sickness, to the astonishment of all.

Weyer, a doctor who, though he believed in the existence of Satan, was skeptical as to accusations of witchcraft, suggested that it was the devil who caused the children to vomit these objects, to encourage the belief that sorcery was responsible. This diagnosis seemed confirmed by the children's habit of making an exhibition of themselves on the doorsteps of certain women, grimacing and posturing. This was done, he suggested, with the intention that these innocent females might be accused of witchcraft and punished. They accused a certain woman named Bametie of casting a spell on them, and many believed them when they said they had seen her going out at night to practice her magic. The children climbed onto the bell tower of the chapel of the Holy Spirit, playing with their fingers on the bells, and singing with rough voices: "We shall not leave until we have seen Bametie burnt at the stake." However, it does not seem that she was arrested, let alone condemned.

History does not record how the outbreak ended. We can only suppose it faded away as the excitement diminished.

COMMENT: Most of the so-called marvels, Bekker suggests, were nothing of the sort. The children's pranks on ladies' doorsteps were childish mischief and nothing more: their speaking foreign tongues was mere gabbling, their knowledge of what went on in the council chamber could have been picked up by overhearing adults, and the objects they vomited were all commonplace items readily available. This is not to say that there was nothing to the outbreak, but such as it was, it was natural rather than supernatural. A century and a half later, Bekker would probably have agreed with Calmeil that the true diagnosis was contagious hystero-demonopathy.[110]

This case, like so many others, poses the problem of recurring symptoms. It seems unlikely that these children could have known of other outbreaks, yet the convulsions and subsequent amnesia, the urge to climb and run, the casting of blame on an innocent person, and the vomiting of needles are features which occur time and time again in such outbreaks, as though the unwitting children were unconsciously conforming to some stereotype.

See also: ANIMAL NOISES; CONVENT HYSTERIA; DEMON POSSESSION; RUNNING AND JUMPING

ANABAPTISTS

Germany: 1531-1536

"They were the radical party of the Reformation period [who] sought to reform the work of the Reformers."[111] The Anabaptists came into being in the 1520s as one of many 16th century sects who rejected the established church of Rome and sought to return to the ideals of primitive Christianity. They differed considerably among themselves: "They were not of one accord on the baptism of children. Some thought they should hold all possessions in common, others that all men should be free and independent. They inspired hatred towards magistrates, powers, the nobility, and promised a happy empire, where they alone would rule, after exterminating all the impious. They held that mankind should conduct itself only in accord with revelations, of which they had a great number, which they followed scrupulously. Others, beyond these excesses, deprived Jesus-Christ of his human nature, and others of his divine nature."[112]

The exceptional behavior described in this entry should not be seen as typical of this Christian sect, who for the most part were distinguished by principles that are today respected if not always adopted. While they regarded government as a necessary evil, they were opposed to war and military service, to capital punishment, and to the swearing of oaths. They favored a communal way of life. Their theology, in principle, derived from the scriptures and rejected any obstacle between the individual and his god. The mediation of priests was disallowed; instead, they relied on God to make his will known by revelation. Anyone who claimed a direct communication from Heaven was heard with respectful attention, while allowing for the possibility that the message was a false one emanating from the Devil. Their name came from their view that baptism should not be imposed on children too young to know what it means, but should be a voluntary decision made when the individual is mature enough to understand it; infant baptism was "an abomination in the sight of God."

Unfortunately, these views conflicted not only with Roman Catholic teachings but also those of the mainstream Protestant churches. Luther, Calvin, Zwingli, and others all attacked the Anabaptists fiercely. Melancthon, more mildly, wrote to the Anabaptist leader Rottmann begging him not to rock the boat: "We have enemies enough, they will rejoice to see us tearing and destroying one another."[113]

For many Anabaptists, millennarist dreams came to play a central role. Social ideals were intertwined with theological ones, further alarming the established authorities, secular as well as ecclesiastical. In particular, the communal experiment at Münster caused widespread alarm; though it was not representative of Anabaptism as a whole, it led to attacks even on quiet and well-behaved communities elsewhere in Europe. The young Emperor Carl V imposed a total ban on the sect, ordaining that they should be executed without awaiting the judgment of the Inquisition. Even outside the Empire, they were almost universally persecuted and sought refuge in countries where attitudes were more tolerant. Such multilateral opposition led to the virtual disappearance of the sect. Only a few sub-sects, such as the Mennonites, survived in America.

The Anabaptists At Münster:[114]

The Anabaptist episode in which exceptional behavior was most clearly manifested can be said to have originated with a German preacher named Melchior Hoffmann, a convert to Lutheranism from Catholicism whose views gradually evolved beyond Luther's into a doctrine that was, in all essentials, Anabaptism. Considering himself a divinely authorized prophet, he traveled northern Europe, proclaiming the imminent return of Jesus; he went so far as to provide a date, predicting that in 1534, at Strasbourg, 140,000 of the saved would win a great victory over their enemies, ushering in a new Golden Age. The city fathers, unimpressed at the prospect of playing host to the Second Coming, chased his followers out of the city, executing only the leaders. Hoffmann, either because they considered him mad or were hedging their bets, was imprisoned in a cage in a tower where after ten years he died.

The surviving Anabaptists shifted the designated place

to the German city of Münster, a prosperous trading city near the Dutch border, which was largely Lutheran in its views though ruled by a Catholic prince-bishop. Bernhard Rottmann, a Catholic priest who had converted to Lutheranism, emerged as their leading spokesman, and he too soon went beyond the Lutherans in his preaching. As the word spread, Anabaptists swarmed into the city, winning many converts among the citizens with their promises of a better life. It is likely that social reasons outweighed theological principles in the minds of most of the converts, who resented paying taxes to Catholic rulers and were drawn by the prospect of a community where all would share the good things of life. At the same time, "the idle, rogues, spendthrifts, thieves, and ruined persons, swelled the crowd of Evangelists."[115]

The Anabaptists gradually tightened their hold by instigating genuine reforms which encouraged people to believe that the earthly paradise would soon be a reality. The poor were fed and sheltered, and work was found for the unemployed. But the shadow of things to come fell with the imposition of a new moral order whose strict rules, enforced by harsh punishments, were at odds with the paradise image. Public floggings, prison, and death sentences awaited those who indulged in whoring, drunkenness, lying, and blasphemy.

But such restrictions seemed a small price to pay for their entrance ticket to Zion-on-Earth. "The chiliastic phantasy which Hoffmann's followers brought with them into Münster rapidly turned into a mass obsession, dominating the whole life of the poorer classes of the town."[116] Catholics were harassed: an Anabaptist preacher broke into a Catholic mass, seized the Host, and crumbled it into fragments, screaming "Look at your good God flying away!" When an opponent of the Anabaptists protested against one of their preachers' sermons, he was set on by a number of howling women who would have strangled him if he had not made his escape from the church. In 1533 large-scale public baptisms began; by the end of the year about one-third of the population had converted, persuaded that the Second Coming and the Apocalypse were round the corner. The thousands of converts came from all classes, from farm girls to merchants' wives; many spontaneously donated their jewelry and other treasures to the communal treasury. The Catholic nuns of Uberwasser, after being harangued by Anabaptist preachers, broke into revolt; they refused to observe abstinence and practice self-mortification, and determined to re-enter the world and marry. They became some of the most outspoken of the Anabaptists, among whom the women were often the most aggressively active. It was a crowd of women who forced their way into the city hall and accused the burgomasters, with their moderate Lutheran views, of being no better than papists.

Sporadic manifestations of fanatical zeal were commonplace. A preacher named Roll

> ...was seized with prophetic inspiration. He ran through the town, foaming at the mouth, his eyes rolling, his hair and garments in disorder, his face haggard, uttering at one moment inarticulate howls, and at another, exhortations to the impenitent to turn and be saved, for that the day of the Lord was at hand... A young girl of eighteen was possessed with a sort of oratorical fury, and preached with fire and extraordinary volubility before an astonished crowd.... A blind Scottish beggar ran about exclaiming that he saw strange visions in the sky... The Anabaptist women ran about the streets making the most extraordinary contortions and prodigious leaps, crying out that they saw the Lord surrounded by a host of angels coming to exterminate the worshippers of Baal...'[117]

The Prince-Bishop, living on his estates a few kilometers from the town of which he was the titular ruler, though nominally Catholic, was sympathetic to the Lutherans. His first efforts to discourage the Anabaptists were unsuccessful, and reluctantly, facing the reality of the situation, he sought to make a deal with them. But the protracted

Jan Beuckelson, aka Jan Van Leiden, Dutch Anabaptist leader. (Engraving by R Cooper)

negotiations broke down when one of the Anabaptist leaders deliberately withheld the Bishop's final offer from the council, the last hope for a peaceful solution. The people of Münster knew they were now surrounded by hostile forces, but they were confident the Lord would preserve them.

With Hoffmann in his cage at Strasbourg, the leadership of the Anabaptists passed to one of his converts, Jan Matthisson, a baker from Haarlem in the Netherlands. Unlike his mentor, he believed that their ends could be achieved only by force. One of his disciples, another Dutchman, Jan Boekelsen, better known as Jan van Leyden, came to Münster in January 1534 to co-ordinate Anabaptist activity in the city. On February 8, he and a prominent merchant named Knipperdolling ran wildly through the streets, calling on the citizens to repent. This provoked a hysterical outbreak among the populace, particularly among the women (many of them former Catholic nuns), a number of whom had joined the Anabaptists. "These women now began to see apocalyptic visions in the streets, and of such intensity that they would throw themselves on the ground, screaming, writhing and foaming at the mouth."[118] An eye-witness reported:

> The madness of the pagan bacchantes cannot have surpassed that of these women. It is impossible to imagine a more terrible, crazy, indecent, and ridiculous exhibition than they made. Their conduct was so frenzied that one might have supposed them to be the furies of the poets. Some had their hair disordered, others ran about almost naked, without the least sense of shame; others again made prodigious gambols, others flung themselves on the ground with arms extended in the shape of a cross; then rose, clapped their hands, knelt down, and cried with all their might, invoking the Father, rolling their eyes, grinding their teeth, foaming at the mouth, beating their breasts, weeping, laughing, howling and uttering the most strange inarticulate sounds... their words were stranger than their gestures. Some implored grace and light for us, others besought that we might be struck with blindness and damnation. All pretended that they saw in heaven some strange sights... Kneeling on the ground, and turning their eyes in one direction, they all at once exclaimed together, with joined hands, O Father! O most excellent King of Zion, spare the people! Then they repeated these words for some while, raising the pitch of their voices, till they attained to such a shriek that a host of pigs could not have produced a louder noise when assembled on market-day.[119]

Matthisson himself arrived in Münster later in February 1534 and assumed the leadership. The city was now virtually under the control of the Anabaptists, and their teachings were implemented vigorously. One of these was that material things intervene between the individual and his God; this provided the justification for vandalizing the churches, destroying sculptured altars and magnificent organs, choir stalls, stained glass, and other masterpieces of workmanship. Books and manuscripts, paintings and other works of art were slashed or burnt. Tombs were broken open, and anything that could be carried away was looted. The same process was extended to private premises; every home in the city was searched for "impurities" – all finery and ornament was smashed or taken and books and pictures were destroyed. Since life was now communal, there was no longer any need for money. So the private possession of money was forbidden; the leaders took it all for external payments. This again was in line with Anabaptist teachings to the effect that in the ideal community, everything would be owned in common; there was to be no private property, and indeed no one would need to work, for the Lord would provide. (The same delusion inspired the DOUKHOBORS in Canada, inspiring them to migrate to more favorable climes where food grows on trees without the necessity for labor.)

Next, Matthisson turned to the citizens of the city, and on February 26, 1534, he proposed "the purification of the New Jerusalem." He advised "that we kill without further delay the Lutherans, the Papists, and all those who have not the right faith, that there may remain in Zion but one body, one society, which is truly Christian... There is but one way of preserving the faithful from the contagion of the impious, and that is to sweep them off the face of the earth."[120] However he was persuaded by his followers that though no doubt morally desirable, such a procedure would be politically unwise in that it would win them dangerous enemies outside. Instead, those who still resisted Anabaptism were encouraged to leave. Many Catholics had already left, and now in February many more followed, together with moderate Lutherans, until several quarters of the town were entirely depopulated. The earliest were able to take their possessions with them, but later they were deprived even of their clothing and food before leaving the city.

The numbers of those leaving were more than made up by those taking their place. Preachers were touring the Netherlands to attract fellow-Anabaptists to join them in what purported to be the Promised Land, and it is a measure of the appeal of the image projected by their propaganda that so many were willing to leave home on these vague promises. Thousands of peasants and tradesmen in the Netherlands, dissatisfied with their lot under Spanish oppression, willingly joined the sect, which promised a better life. The authorities took ruthless action against them: any Anabaptist who was caught was liable to be summarily tortured and executed. A party of 15,000 formed in Holland to migrate to Münster, but it was halted before they got very far, and sent home, without their weapons and any valuables they happened to have. Others made better progress, pillaging and burning churches and convents as they marched, but were finally routed by the imperial forces and killed in great numbers. Nevertheless a substantial number succeeding in evading their enemies and made their way to the New Zion.

For these new arrivals, and for the ten thousand or so residents who chose to remain in the city, a process of re-baptism was initiated, and by March 3 every resident of the city was a "baptized-again" Anabaptist. For chosen individuals, there was also an additional baptism, the "Baptism of Fire" reserved for chosen men and women who were initiated into an inner elite. Following their initiation, there took place "frantic orgies too horrible to be described," at any rate by a Victorian parson.[121]

But now the inhabitants could see the army of the prince-bishop commencing the siege, which began on February 28, 1534, and would continue so long as the Anabaptists held power in Münster. Preparations were made to defend the city: the walls were strengthened and all eligible citizens were formed into militia. Mercenaries were enticed from the bishop's army with promises of better food and pay. Boys were given lessons in the arquebus. The women prepared pitch and sulfur to pour on the heads of attackers and stripped lead from the roofs to make bullets. Sentries were posted round the walls.

Within those walls, private life was increasingly dominated by the new leaders. The burgomasters, who had been elected "according to the flesh," were replaced by loyal followers of Matthisson, "elected according to the Spirit." Those who dissented from the leader's absolute rule were executed or imprisoned. The 24-year-old Jan Boekelsen, known as Jan van Leyden, showed his future mettle by publicly assassinating a prominent dissident with a dagger thrust.

On Easter Day, April 5, 1534, an extraordinary event took place. The previous evening, leader Jan Matthisson woke from a trance, declaring with enthusiasm that God the Father commanded him to put the enemy to flight, just him and a handful of followers. The next morning, the old prophet, clad in armor and furnished with a lance and a sword, rode out of the city gates towards the besieging army, while his fellow-citizens watched from the ramparts to see the miracle. Instead, they saw him instantly surrounded by a troop of the bishop's men, who ran him through with countless sword thrusts. His severed head was paraded, then stuck on a pole in full view of the city; his private parts were nailed to the city gate.

It was a sad blow to the besieged Anabaptists, but Boekelsen was equal to the occasion, and proclaimed that Matthisson's death was God's will. Formerly a tailor's apprentice, he had already proved himself a charismatic leader, as fanatical as his predecessor. Now he proceeded to establish himself as sole authority and despot, revealing that Matthisson's death had been shown to him in a vision, which also confirmed that he should take over as leader

Further visions followed. Boekelsen was now regarded not only as a prophet but as the divinely appointed leader, a favorite of Heaven, and he received greater adulation than Matthisson had ever known. Everything he ordered was a command from God himself. One of God's first orders was that the church spires and steeples should be demolished, partly in the interests of the defense of the city but also as a symbol of the old religion. The magnificent spire of the Uberwasser church, an architectural masterpiece, was one of the victims.

Next, Boekelsen had to consolidate his personal authority. One night in early April, after the work was done, he appeared in the market square, entirely naked. Crying on the people to repent, he ran through the streets until he collapsed. When he signaled that he was unable to speak, he was given paper on which to write. On it, he wrote: "I have been struck dumb for three days, so that I may properly receive God's vision."

After three days he revealed heaven's instructions. The city council was dissolved and replaced by a Council of Elders chosen by him. New laws were pronounced, imposing the death penalty for thirteen crimes: "blasphemy, disobedience, adultery, impurity, avarice, theft, fraud, lying and slander, idle conversation, disputes, anger, envy, and discontent against the government."[122] In practice, an individual's private life, as well as public, was now subject to continual monitoring: a person had only to incur the spite of a neighbor to be informed against. Every door had to be left open so that anyone could walk in at any time. A reign of terror began in which scores, probably hundreds, lost their lives for transgressing against the absolute ruler. All meals were taken communally, the brothers and sisters sitting separately, in silence. Portions of the Old Testament were read aloud. Everyone had to eat what was set before them.

A further inroad on private life came when, in July 1534, God told Boekelsen that polygamy was henceforth the law and every man could have as many wives as he wished. There was a sound reason for this, in that the population comprised three women to every man, due to many husbands having left the city without their families and also to the number of lapsed nuns. However, it does not seem to have been this practical reason which determined the decision, so much as the Biblical command to "be fruitful and multiply." This was not merely permission, it was an injunction. Every woman over fifteen must be married whether she wished it or not, and wives had to submit when their husbands introduced additional spouses into the household. The ruling provoked a rebellion, hoping to rouse the people against the increasingly rigorous regime, but the rebels were themselves attacked by Boekelsen's followers. Ninety-one rebels were beheaded or shot.

Thereafter, anyone who opposed the ruling was executed. Young girls of ten or eleven were picked by men old enough to be their grandfathers. At least one woman who refused to have sex with her imposed husband was beheaded. It was a license for lust, and Boekelsen's male followers – and some at least of his females – welcomed it. Boekelsen himself set a good example of obedience to God's will: he not only took over Matthisson's young wife, a former nun, but added a further sixteen, none of them older than 20. An eyewitness commented: "It was impossible, a few days later, to discover in the capital of Westphalia the last and feeble traces of modesty, chastity, and self-restraint."[123]

In September 1534, a prominent follower told the council he'd had a vision of Boekelsen as the new David, who would take the sword of justice and bring the divine will to all the world. It just so happened that he had with him in a bag a sword, some oil, a crown and a gold chain, rings for fingers, and a scepter. All these were reverently bestowed on the young leader.

It was patently a put-up job, but Boekelsen anticipated opposition by protesting that he was unworthy. However, if this was Heaven's will, God would find him more than ready. "Even if you all joined to oppose me, I will still rule, not only over this city but over the whole world, for the Heavenly Father has said it should be so. My kingdom which begins today shall never fail."[124] The crowd, which at first murmured against the appointment, now acquiesced. King Jan proceeded to establish the equivalent of a court. With his own privileged retinue, bodyguard, and servants, he moved into the palatial home of a merchant who had quit the town. Two crowns of pure gold encrusted with jewels were made for him, and fine robes were made for the man who only a few years before had been a tailor's apprentice. On public occasions he wore gold chains and other regalia. His faithful followers were rewarded by being allotted sections of Germany, a shopkeeper taking the title of Prince of Saxony, and so on. When God had given them the victory, they would govern Germany between them. It was as though they were all sharing in Jan Boekelsen's dream.

If victory was a dream, defeat was by no means certain. Militarily, at least, the defense was well planned and was proving effective against the bishop's every attack. But as the siege tightened, it became increasingly difficult for supplies to get into the city. Finally the blockade was complete, and Münster had nothing but its own resources to live on. Initially these had been adequate, supplemented by food brought in from outside. But now, as winter set in, the privations increased. The remaining cattle and horses were slaughtered and eaten. Soon thousands were starving: leather, candles, tree-bark, grass, cow-dung, and chalk had become foodstuffs. A mother ate her still-born baby. Sickness followed and so many died that their corpses had to be thrown into communal graves, whence they were likely to be dug up during the night and eaten. Those who survived – except for the army of 800 men – were in pitiable condition. Houses and streets resounded with moans and sobbing cries. Some dared to complain, but this was a capital offense for it meant questioning the will of God, and were beheaded. While some of the victims were real plotters and conspirators, others were those who from desperation had taken more than their share of food; a ten-year-old boy was hanged for stealing turnips.

The dream which had brought so many to Münster was turning to nightmare, and eventually, Boekelsen decided to allow those who wished to leave the city to do so. Some nine hundred took their chance and left the town, only to find themselves in the no-man's-land between the town walls and the siege fortifications. The besiegers refused to let them pass through, so they had to wander in this terrain, without food or shelter or any provisions. By the time the besiegers relented, seven hundred had died of starvation or sickness. The remaining two hundred were reluctantly allowed to pass through the lines.

The nightmare ended when two defectors, faced with the madness of their leader, showed the besiegers how to enter the city through one of the gates. On June 22, 1535, the bishop's men entered the city. The Anabaptists fought bravely, but though they had the will, they had neither the numbers nor the weapons to make a real resistance. The city was quickly taken. Many died during the defense, but Boekelsen was recognized while trying to escape and taken into custody along with two other Anabaptist leaders.

They would have done better to give their lives more heroically. Now they knew that not only would they die, but that the law required that they should die only after hideous torture. During the questioning that preceded his execution, however, Boekelsen maintained his position with intelligence and even wit, insisting that he was willing to answer to God for everything he had done. Six months later, on January 22, 1536, he and two others were executed in the market square at Münster. It was a slow and painful business, as the law required that the victims be kept alive and conscious for at least one hour of torture with red-hot pincers before being dispatched with a dagger into the heart. Boekelsen gave one involuntary cry against the pain but otherwise withstood the horrific ordeal with fortitude. His enemies concluded that only Satan could have given him such strength and courage.

COMMENT: Boekelsen is not an easy character to interpret, and commentators have varied in their assessment. Cohn says: "Boekelsen seems to have been a megalomaniac, whose behaviour cannot be adequately interpreted either simply as sincere fanaticism or simply as calculating hypocrisy."[125] Both elements were certainly present.

Though assertive, Boekelsen was no more than the leader. Many of his followers spontaneously manifested extremes of behavior: not only the preachers but the common people of all social classes who enthusiastically enrolled as citizens of the New Zion. The nuns who forsook their vocation, the merchants' wives who voluntarily donated their rich possessions, the women who stormed the Town Hall to accuse the burgomasters or who rounded on a churchgoer who dared to criticize the preacher – all these, whether or not we see them as deluded victims, were willing and eager. The Münster venture was a communal enterprise, a partnership between leaders and led.

ANDREE BALLOON MANIA

British Columbia-Manitoba: Canada 1896-97

During the nineteenth century, an intense popular interest in balloons and ballooning captivated Europe and North America.[126] Of all the ballooning exploits of this period, the most spectacular and ambitious was the heroic attempt by Swedish scientist Salomon August Andree to reach the North Pole.[127] In the early 1890s, discussion of such a trip was met with considerable press skepticism, but as the scientific reputation of Andree was considerable, he was eventually able to obtain sufficient funds in 1893 to undertake the journey. Such a voyage to this vast, uncharted territory was viewed as one of the last great adventures left on earth. Meticulous planning went into the trip and building the balloon, the *Ornen* (meaning Eagle). Andree's plans made headlines around the world from 1893 until he and his two crewmen froze to death in 1897 without ever reaching the Pole.

But this is only part of the story. In 1896, the year before his death, Andree and his crew had traveled to Danes Island on the northwestern tip of Spitzbergen, where he had constructed a giant building, 95-feet long and 100-feet high, to shelter the balloon from the harsh elements, so that it would be in excellent condition prior to the attempt. Andree had originally intended to make his polar expedition in 1896. On June 30, 1896, he had the balloon installed inside the structure, and he and the crew waited for favorable weather conditions to ascend. The attention of the world was focused on Andree, and governments with territory in the polar regions were asked to inform its citizens of the event and render any assistance to the aeronauts should they land there. The Canadian government and Hudson's Bay Company publicized to Native Canadian peoples that "it was probable the aerial voyagers might be driven southerly" and stray onto Canadian terrain.[128] The balloonists waited until mid-August, at which time they abandoned their attempt due to poor weather. However, the isolated communities in northern Canada did not know that Andree's expedition was cancelled, and they remained on the lookout for his famous balloon.

The reports of phantom balloon sightings began on the afternoon of July 1, 1896, when numerous residents in the city of Winnipeg claimed to see a balloon flying rapidly in the distance.[129] Several residents expressed the view "that it was Andree's balloon," but they were subsequently informed that Andree had not even left. Once this was realized, there was some discussion that the sighting could have resulted from a "toy balloon sent up in honor of the Confederation holiday." The press report concluded by noting that, "Whether miniature or real, the passage of the mysterious balloon caused a good deal of talk among citizens last night." Toy balloons were also known as "fire balloons" during this period. These items were quite popular and commonly sold at shops which dispensed fireworks. They were comprised of paper with candles attached near the mouth and made buoyant through the generation of heat.

On August 12, a sensational story appeared in the press, discussing an apparent sighting of Andree's balloon, as a telegram was received on August 11 by the government office in Ottawa, from the Superintendent of Indian Affairs in British Columbia, A.W. Vowell, who stated: "Credible information received by Agent Lomas from two Indian parties, separated by long distance at time of observation, that the Andree balloon had been sighted in latitude 55.15, longitude 127.40, pursuing a northerly course."[130] The location described in Vowell's dispatch would have placed the sighting about 100 miles up the Skeena River, some 500 miles north of Victoria. At the time of the observation, local residents were unaware that Andree had not begun his voyage.[131]

On August 13, more details of the dispatch became public. It was revealed that a boy had reported seeing a semi-circular black object near the setting sun, which soon disappeared about 40-feet above the timberline. The dispatch, dated July 3 and sent to Superintendent Vowell by Indian Agent R.E. Loring in Hazleton, concluded by noting that "the boy's description of the balloon and its action leaves no doubt as to its reality, and is no doubt Andree's balloon expected to have left Spitzbergen for the north pole" on July 1.[132] The same press account told of a second dispatch sent by Indian Agent Loring to Superintendent Vowell and dated July 10 from Hazleton. He wrote that Ghali, chief of the Kitsploux, observed a balloon-like object while trapping with a group of Indians on Blackwater Lake, above the head waters of the Skeena on the evening of July 3. He stated that the object was brightly illuminated and was traveling almost due north. Agent Loring also noted that the Indians living along the Skeena "were made aware that they were liable to see during the beginning of this month, a balloon going north, and of the purpose of its occupants, etc., and to report to me anything noticed by them of that description."[133]

In late September, Englishman J. Melville Stoddard, who was hunting with two Indians between Cross Sound and Mackenzie Bay at about the same time the sightings occurred, told journalists that he and his Indian companions at first became convinced they were looking at a balloon, possibly Andree's. However, when he viewed the distant object through his binoculars, it became evident that the "balloon" was an unusually shaped cloud, and it eventually dissipated. Stoddard noted that the Indians did not use the binoculars and remained steadfast in their conviction that it was Andree's balloon.[134]

Depiction of Andree's balloon caught in a storm over the Arctic ice. (French collectors' card)

Andree's second and final attempt to reach the North Pole transpired on July 11, 1897, when he ascended from Danes Island. The exact details of his demise were not known until 1930, when sailors visiting White Island, discovered the expedition's remains, including undeveloped film and notes describing the tragedy that befell them. Sixty-five hours after taking off, Andree was forced to land just 300 miles from his departure point after Arctic drizzle formed an ice coating on the balloon. He and his crew died on the arduous trek back to civilization. However, the world did not learn of this until 33 years later. In the days and weeks after Andree and his crew sailed into oblivion, his whereabouts again became the subject of intense press discussion, and those living in northern countries were told to keep a watch for his balloon.

The first sighting in 1897 was reported in Northern British Columbia by Rivers Inlet fisherman W. S. Fitzgerald, who was salmon fishing with a companion on the morning of July 10. At about 2:45 am they spotted a "great balloon-shaped body" that was "powerfully illuminated" and floating about a mile above a mountain range, when "all at once the thought burst upon us that it was a balloon and none other than Andree's."[135] The light appeared to drift southwesterly for about two hours, when it faded out of sight.[136] On July 12, several residents of a nursing home at Kamlooms, British Columbia, reported a similar illuminated object "fluttering" for over two hours before disappearing to the southwest.[137] Over the course of several days between the last week of July and August 3, several sightings of a "mysterious balloon or pillar of fire" were recorded in Victoria, British Columbia, including one by three women camping at Sidney, who watched it drift northerly over Salt Spring Island.[138] On early Sunday morning, August 1, three young men camping near Goldstream also reported what appeared to be a brilliantly glowing balloon.

On August 5, at Douglas, Manitoba, several residents observed an illuminated object about 11 pm, swaying in the sky and "resembling the shape of a massive balloon." It was traveling northward, disappeared after 45 minutes, and was assumed to be Andree's balloon.[139] During the early morning hours of August 6, two firemen on the Victoria city brigade, observed a bright aerial light hovering above Discovery Island for over two hours, moving in a general westerly direction. At one point, the pair thought they could discern "a dark body outlined behind the circle of intense light."[140] When the observation was denounced as the likely misperception of a toy balloon,[141] several local residents wrote in to support their claims.[142] On August 8, at 12.30 am, a family residing on the outskirts of Winnipeg also thought they saw Andree's balloon shining a bright light as it disappeared to the northwest after 45-minutes.[143] On August 13, at about 9 pm, thousands of Vancouver residents observed, for about 15 minutes, "a very bright red star surrounded by a luminous halo," which swiftly traversed the southern sky. This followed a sighting by several prominent citizens of Rossland, who watched it hover for some time before it faded from sight to the south.[144]

In September, there were two final reports. The first occurred on the evening of the 17th at about 6 pm, as several farmers residing near Souris, Manitoba, "distinctly saw a balloon floating over them at considerable height," traveling southwesterly. It was in sight for 5 minutes and the farmers were certain that a flag was protruding from the top of the vessel, suggestive that Andree was making a triumphant return.[145] Coincidentally, at this time there was much press speculation that Andree may have already reached the North Pole and would be heading back, although he had planned to trek back. The last report was by William Graham of Honora, Manitoulin Island in Lake Huron, who stated that on September 11 at 10 pm, he and several neighbors observed an illuminated object change colors from red to white to blue, which was also seen at nearby Gore Bay. Mr. Graham suggested that the object was Andree's balloon.[146]

It should be emphasized that almost certainly no one could or would have been able to fly in a balloon above Canada at this time, particularly under the observed conditions. Firstly, most balloons that were in use were tethered to a rope and used for show purposes. A so-called "free-flying" balloon traveling in such northern regions, and at night, would have been almost certainly suicidal, and have required considerable investment of time and money. No such attempt was ever recorded.

See also: "EDISON STAR" SIGHTINGS; FLYING SAUCER (ORIGIN OF); GHOST ROCKET SCARE; GREAT AMERICAN AIRSHIP WAVE; PHANTOM AIRCRAFT WAVES; RUSSIAN POLAND BALLOON SCARE.

ANIMAL NOISES, EPIDEMICS OF

Barking like dogs, mewing like cats, or uttering vague animal sounds, is a curious feature of many exceptional social behaviors. It occurs in some LAUGHING MANIA episodes, in the outbreaks of AMOU (1613), BLACKTHORN (1700), HOORN (1673), MORZINE (1857), NIMES (circa 1638), and among the convulsionaries of SAINT-MEDARD (1730s). It occurs during the Kentucky Revival of 1900 (see AMERICAN REVIVALISM), and it is also a feature of some Russian episodes, notably among the KLIKOUSCHESTVO (1861) and MALIOVANNY (1880s) sects. At Amou and Blackthorn, it is the most distinctive feature.

Typically, it was reported of the nuns of CAMBRAI (1491), who believed themselves possessed by demons, that "one saw them run across the fields like dogs, fly through the air like birds, climb on the trees and hang from their branches like cats, imitate the voices of different animals."[147] This suggests that the animal sounds were part of a multi-faceted identification with animals. (See also: RUNNING AND CLIMBING.)

The fact that people in so many scattered communities, over four centuries, should take to barking and howling suggests that this is an archetypal behavior. There can be no question of contagion from one episode to another, for the Russian peasants of the 19th century or village girls in Oxfordshire could not have known of similar conduct in France centuries previously. In any given incident – among the village women of Amou, for example – we may suppose that it spreads by imitation, but that does not explain how it originates.

Most episodes of seemingly strange collective behaviors occur to groups that are experiencing extreme emotional stress. Under such circumstances, people become prone to what psychologists term hyper-suggestibility. In such a state, it is common for people to imitate the acts of those around them. A classic modern-day example is The Holy Laugh Movement. During extremely emotional revival meetings associated with the Toronto Blessing Church in Canada, uncontrollable fits of prolonged laughter and animal noises are common. The movement began in the early 1990s and has since spread to many congregations around the world.

During meetings people have been observed, often collectively, to bark like dogs and roar like lions. Other common animal sounds include cackling, hooting, chattering (like monkeys), and meowing. One observer described a meeting as follows: "One of the leaders then explained that he was going to call upon several people to share a testimony... The first person... was apparently a Baptist preacher from England. He went to the front, began to speak and after a few sentences fell to the floor roaring and screeching. The leader reassured us that everything was all right. This roaring, he explained, was caused by the Holy Spirit... it is the roaring of the lion of Judah. This was apparently a common occurrence in their meetings."[148]

In explaining the animal noises during emotionally charged meetings, many adherents consider it to be a prophetic sign, and such sounds are encouraged, noting that it is symbolic in that "a man roaring like a lion is God prophesying that He is coming soon as a roaring lion."[149] However, this is clearly a post hoc explanation; there is no suggestion that the congregation deliberately commenced roaring like lions in full awareness and intent.

Such behaviors have also been interpreted as being consistent with Biblical scripture by suggesting that there would be strange signs near the end time. An observer of the Toronto Blessing describes one meeting as follows: "That room sounded like it was a cross between a jungle and farmyard. There were many, many lions roaring, there were bulls bellowing, there were donkeys, there was a cockerel near me, there were all sorts of bird songs.... Everything you could possibly imagine. Every animal you could conceivably imagine you could hear."[150]

During the Kentucky Revivals, some congregation members would roll on the floor or ground, and others quickly imitated this behavior, hence the term "Holy Rollers." Consider the emotional setting of the following description in which some congregants began to bark:

> At one meeting not less than a thousand persons fell to the ground apparently without sense or motion....Towards the close of this commotion, viz. about the year 1803, convulsions became prevalent....The rolling exercise consisted in doubling the head and feet together, and rolling over and over like a hoop....The jerks consisted in violent twitches and contortions of the body in all its parts....When attacked by the jerks, the victim of enthusiasm sometimes leaped like frogs, and exhibited every grotesque and hideous contortion of the face and limbs. The barks consisted in getting down on all fours, growling, snapping the teeth, and barking like dogs. Sometimes numbers of the people squatted down, and looking in the face of the minister, continued demurely barking at him while he preached to them. These last were particularly gifted in prophecies, trances, dreams, rhapsodies, visions of angels, of heaven, and of the holy city.[151]

While these behaviors may seem strange to outsiders, they should be perceived as products of their broader historical and religious context. In the case of the Kentucky Revivals, they were evidently a form of religious expression that was accepted within the particular subculture as a way to perform penance and worship or obtain divine favor. Whether these noises began as an archetype and were subsequently imitated is an unresolved question. Historian George Rosen remarks that collective barking was "a means of chastisement for sins" as congregants sometimes surrounded a tree while on all fours, yelping and barking so as to "tree the devil." Such acts were often considered to be a sign of piety or divine favor.[152]

The problem we face in understanding epidemics of animal noises is the lack of a more complete social and cultural context of the participants. In such cases as The Kentucky Revivals and the more contemporary Toronto Laugh Movement, they would appear too imitative. In some of the more historical, isolated episodes, we are left to guess at the context. What is clear, however, is that gatherings of people in many different cultures, across many centuries, have independently and spontaneously manifested this exceptional behavior.

ANXIETY HYSTERIA

MASS HYSTERIA involves the rapid spread of "conversion hysteria," a term coined by psychoanalyst Sigmund Freud, where illness symptoms appear with no physical cause. Known today as conversion disorder, this well-documented condition involves the conversion of psychological conflict into involuntary physical symptoms without a corresponding organic basis. Psychiatrists have identified two common types of conversion disorder: anxiety hysteria and MOTOR HYSTERIA. Motor hysteria appears gradually over time and usually takes weeks or months to subside. It appears in settings where people are repressed and have no way to channel their emotions. Twitching, shaking, and trance states are common. Both anxiety and motor hysteria share distinct features, the presence of which are reliable indicators of an outbreak. In both forms, there is no plausible organic basis for the physical complaints. Symptoms are transient and benign – in other words they come and go rapidly – and are relatively harmless. Episodes most often occur in a segregated group which is undergoing extreme stress. Symptoms tend to spread by sight or sound, and commonly begin in older or higher status persons.

Anxiety hysteria is of shorter duration, usually lasting no more than a few days, and is triggered by the sudden perception of a threatening agent, most commonly a strange odor. Symptoms typically include headache, dizziness, nausea, breathlessness, and general weakness. Outbreaks were rarely reported prior to the 20th century, but have dramatically increased in Western or developed countries. Incidents occur with little prior warning so there is usually not much pre-existing group tension. Most reported episodes occur in schools or factories.

Outbreaks of anxiety hysteria usually begin with illness symptoms in a single student or factory worker and spread rapidly to others nearby who experience a variety of stress-related complaints. Symptoms of the first person to be affected (the index case) are often dramatic, giving rise to sudden fear among workers or classmates. Often the first person affected has a medical condition such as an epileptic fit, schizophrenia, tonsillitis, or heat stroke. Usually the rest of the group is not aware of this. Information as to the specific cause of the symptoms is typically unknown and is only learned later. Soon after the appearance of the index case, others begin to attribute the cause to a strange odor that is assumed to represent a toxic gas, or an agent such as a communicable illness, that is believed to pose an immediate personal threat to the other workers or students. Commonly, food poisoning from the school or factory cafeteria is indicted. Rumors often spread like wildfire. Television and newspaper reports, recent events, local traditions, and superstitious beliefs exacerbate the situation.

In non-Western countries such as Malaysia, odors or food poisoning are rarely suspected. Instead, suspicion falls on an array of diminutive supernatural entities. In such settings, the index case typically exhibits screaming, crying, and over-breathing after seeing what is believed to be such spirits. Fellow pupils assume that the index subject is hexed or charmed, or that a ghost is roaming the school, triggering sudden, extreme anxiety as it is assumed they may be the next victims. The search for potential explanations among pupils is limited only by plausibility, as the lack of educational and life experiences can foster hypotheses that are potentially fantastic to adults or individuals living outside of the culture or subcultural milieu. Students who are in the closest spatial, visual, or social contact with the index case, and others who are affected, are most susceptible to developing symptoms. In the majority of cases, investigators identify a downward spread of symptoms along the age-scale, with the oldest student(s) affected first, followed by younger classmates. In Kenya, anxiety hysteria outbreaks are common and usually blamed on ghosts who are believed to strangle students; in actuality, those affected are simply hyperventilating.

Most outbreaks of anxiety hysteria last a single day and rarely more than a week. Lengthier cases or episodes involving relapses appear related to the inability of medical, school, and community leaders to convince the affected workers, or students and their parents, of the psychogenic nature of the symptoms. In rare instances where the imaginary agent is believed to persist, or authorities are not perceived to have thoroughly examined the premises, cases can endure sporadically for several weeks or months. Episodes of mass anxiety hysteria cease rapidly once the students are reassured that the phantom threat, most typically a harmless odor, has been eliminated or never existed.

Since the early 20th century, anxiety hysteria episodes were dominated by environmental concerns over food, air and water quality, especially exaggerated or imaginary fears involving mysterious smells. Outbreaks have a rapid onset and recovery and involve anxiety hysteria. Unsubstantiated claims of strange odors and gassings are a common contemporary trigger of hysteria outbreaks in schools. A typical incident occurred at a secondary school in Singapore in 1985, when pupils were suddenly stricken with chills, headaches, nausea, and breathlessness. Tests of the school and the students all came back negative. The episode began when several pupils noticed a strange smell and occurred amid a pre-existing rumor that a gas had infiltrated the school from a nearby building site.[153] This incident is similar to a mystery gas at a Hong Kong school a few years earlier affecting over 355 students ages 6-to-14. Before the outbreak there were rumors of a recent toxic gas scare at a nearby school. Several teachers had even discussed the incident with their pupils – some to the point of advising them on what action to take if it should hit their school.[154]

On July 8, 1972, in Hazlerigg, England, stench from a pigsty may have triggered an outbreak of stomach pain, nausea, faintness, and headache at a schoolchildren's gala.[155] That same year, headache and over-breathing affecting 16 pupils at a school in Tokyo, Japan, was traced to smog. A 1994 episode of breathing problems among 23 students in a female dormitory at an Arab school in the United Arab Emirates was triggered by a "toxic fire" that turned out to be the harmless smell of incense.[156] The perceived threatening agent must be seen as credible to the affected group. On any given school day, a fainting student would not be expected to trigger anxiety hysteria. Yet, if this occurred during the 1991 Persian Gulf War, and it coincided with the detection of a strange odor in the building, many of the naive schoolchildren might exhibit sudden, extreme anxiety after assuming that it was an Iraqi poison gas attack. This is just what happened at a Rhode Island elementary school during the Gulf War, coinciding with intense publicity about chemical weapons attacks on Israel and the possibility of terrorist attacks on the U.S.[157]

Since the early 20th century, strange odors have been a common trigger of anxiety hysteria in job settings, with environmental pollutant fears leading to lost productivity time. In 1988, an outbreak of breathing problems in male military recruits at their California army barracks occurred when the air was laden with a heavy odor from brush fires and mistaken for toxic fumes. A chance event combined to worsen the situation. Some recruits were "resuscitated" in the early confusion, as medics had wrongly assessed their conditions to be grave. These factors created more anxiety and further breathing problems. A study of the incident showed that those seeing the "resuscitations" or witnessing others exhibit symptoms were three times more likely to report symptoms.

What is the best way to handle short-lived outbreaks of anxiety hysteria? School and factory administrators should seek the cooperation of staff leaders, medical authorities, and respected community members to reassure those affected and the community that the agent believed to pose a threat was either imaginary or no longer exists. In non-Western countries, the services of witchdoctors or native healers are often rendered and may provide reassurance, although on occasion, they may make things worse. See also: MASS HYSTERIA IN SCHOOLS; MASS MOTOR HYSTERIA.

ASSASSINS, ORDER OF

Iran: 11th century

The word "assassin" is derived from "ashishin," which refers to someone who uses hashish, a drug derived from hemp leaves. The term is used in French for a murderer of any kind, while in English it is generally reserved for one who kills with political motives; in particular, it is applied to an Islamic sect that flourished in the 11th century in Persia and Syria. Members of the order are also known as Talinites (receivers of instruction) and Hasanites (followers of Hasan), but it is as ashishin that they are most widely known.[158]

CONTEXT: Beginning with the death in 632 of the prophet Mohammed, its founder, Islam was torn by rival sects, each supporting the legitimacy of one or other of his descendants. The most serious threats to the Sunnite (*sunna* = custom) establishment were the Shiite sect, who believed that Ali, Mohammed's son-in-law, was his true successor, and the Ismaili sect, another Shiite breakaway who followed Ismail, the disinherited son of the sixth Imam after Ali, rather than Musa who was acknowledged by the Shiites.

At the same time, Islam was threatened by invaders from the west. Though the First Crusade did not take place until 1095, complaints were already being voiced in Christian countries that it was shameful that the sites where their Christian religion had its origins should be under Islamic control. Subsequently, the rival Islamic sects would make use of the Crusaders to gain their ends. This led to an unfathomable history of opportunist alliances and sudden attacks in which religion and politics were inextricably mingled. It is against this background that the Ashishin flourished.

Hasan ibn al-Sabbah, the creator of the order, was an educated Persian – he had been a fellow-student of Omar Khayyam at Nishapur, in Persia – the son of a pious Shiite in northeastern Persia. He distanced himself from mainstream Islam even more than his father by adopting the dissident Ismaili form of Islam, itself a breakaway from the Shiite breakaway, combined with leanings towards Zoroastrianism, the ancient religion of Persia. This placed him in opposition to conformist Moslems, and this sectarian standpoint dominated his life. From his student days on he was intent on achieving power at any price. It is impossible to say whether he sought power on his own behalf or on behalf of the Ismaili sect, probably the two were combined, but it is certain that he regarded himself as the destined leader of the Ismaili cause, and to this end he took part in power politics first in Persia and then in Egypt where the Caliphate formed the center of Islamic authority. Though he achieved high positions both at Ispahan and at Cairo, he was distrusted, and failed to achieve his aims, some say because he was inefficient, others because he was over-ambitious.

Finally Hasan decided to find a remote and secure powerbase of his own, from which to act at a distance. In 1091, by devious means, he obtained control of the fortress-town of Alamut, known as "the Eagle's Nest" from its well-nigh impregnable situation in the Elburz mountains about 100 km northwest of Tehran. Here, now known as the Sheikh al Jebal – the Seigneur or Old Man of the Mountain – he imposed a severely ascetic lifestyle, not least on himself. The old and infirm were sent away, unless they were scholars. Musicians and singers were likewise excluded. No women were permitted to enter the inner citadel; even his wife was required to live in the village, which surrounded the citadel within the outer ramparts. Within this enclave he lived in voluntary seclusion. He never again left Alamut and until the end of his days was only twice seen on the battlements of his fortress. In the course of time he acquired several other strongholds in Persia and Syria, some by voluntary submission, others by unscrupulous force. The killing of enemies – and any who opposed his will were enemies by definition – was not simply a regrettable necessity but a sacred duty.

Those who shared the citadel with him were blindly devoted chosen followers to whom Hasan was a semi-divine figure. Volunteers came in their thousands to offer their services, but only a few were accepted, though others might be permitted to settle in the village. Those recruited into Hasan's service were elite, not altogether unlike the Crusader knights from the west; they shared a mystical companionship, dedicated to assisting Hasan in his aim of preparing a new humanity. Most were youths, some as young as twelve years old. Their dedication was total: Hasan inculcated in them the idea that there was no better death than to give their life in his service. They were trained in languages and martial exercises, and in the art of disguise and assimilation into communities, for they might be required to reside for months or even years playing a part in an alien community before accomplishing their mission. All this, over and above their spiritual education as adherents of the Ismaili religion, for the Order was essentially a religious one and Hasan himself, for all his ruthlessness, was a devoted Moslem who left a body of spiritual writings. It is not surprising that in the 12th century the ashashin found that, despite the difference in their religion, they had much in common with the Christian Knights Templar.

Their immediate function, however, was more practical than spiritual. The faithful followers – the fidawin – were dispatched on missions throughout the Islamic world, carrying out Hasan's orders. Frequently, those orders involved murder, and Hasan's envoys soon became an object of terror as ruthless assassins from whom none was safe.

Hasan had observed the use of hashish during his stay in Cairo and realized how he could put it to use for his own ends. The drug was to play an indirect but vital role in his system, not so much in the execution of his orders, but in the initiation that ensured that those orders would be blindly obeyed.

The process was simple in outline, elaborate in execution. Adjoining the citadel, Hasan laid out an extensive garden, which was described by the Arab historian Hâkem: "The Seigneur of the Mountain took into his service men who would be his faithful servants, dedicated to him heart and body. With this in mind, he built extensive gardens in his citadel to which water was conveyed, filled with exotic plants and wild animals and birds. In the middle of them was a kiosk on four floors, superbly ornamented and furnished with herbs and spices. Here there were slaves, ten male and ten female, just past the age of puberty, dressed in beautiful clothes and adorned with jewelry. Alleys of trees led to a building where the initiates lay on sofas and were given to eat and drink throughout the day."[159]

This account is confirmed by Marco Polo, who visited Alamut in the course of his voyage to the East in 1271 and "heard it told by several men of these countries"[160] He adds that "by means of small conduits, streams of wine, milk, honey, and the purest water are made to flow everywhere." Fifty years later, around 1320, the traveler Odoric de Pordenone further confirmed the account. While the accounts vary in detail, they are generally in agreement even though centuries had elapsed.

"The old man thought moreover of an unheard-of wickedness, that he should make men into bold murderers or swordsmen, by whose courage he might kill whoever he wished and be feared by all." The historians describe how the initiate was given a soporific in the morning and was carried unconscious into the garden. Awakened with vinegar, he found himself in the kiosk, welcomed by beautiful youths and girls who told him he was in Paradise. Were he dead, he would stay here forever, but as he was still living, this was only a dream. As for them, they were the houris and children of Paradise, ready to attend to his every wish. "And the ladies and the damsels stayed with them all day playing and singing and causing great enjoyment, and they did with them as they pleased, so that these youths had all that they wished, and never will they go out from thence of their own will." For a few hours he enjoyed the maximum of pleasure, and in the evening the Seigneur appeared and told him that he had been given a preview of the place reserved for him in Paradise. He must tell no one what he had seen and must never swerve from his devotion to Hasan for fear of forfeiting this place. The day culminated in a banquet at which he was again given a soporific. This time, when he woke, he found himself back in the real world, convinced that he had visited Paradise not simply in a dream but as a privileged foretaste. Now he was ready to do anything to get there again as a fidawi in the service of Hasan.[161]

According to Odoric of Pordenone, who gives a slightly different account, Hasan would carry out the garden ploy only as and when he needed someone killed: "When the Old Man wished the death of a man, he gave to one of these young men a drink which would make him sleep, took him out of Paradise and when he was awake he called him before him and told him that he would never see Paradise again unless he killed such-and-such a man, but if he killed him he would return to Paradise where he would enjoy delights beyond comparison with those of his first stay."[162]

This version is believable in light of the fact that the citadel contained thousands of men; it is said that the fidawin numbered forty thousand at the time of the order's greatest power. Clearly it would have been impracticable to process all of them through the garden ritual, and it would make sense to select and indoctrinate an operative only as required. Marco Polo, however, notes that when an initiate was brought back from the garden and recounted his adventure, he was made to do so in the presence of other recruits, so that they too would be eager to enjoy such pleasures.

He whom the Old Man ordered to go to die for his name reckoned himself happy, with sure hope of deserving to go to Paradise, so that as many lords or others as were enemies of the said Old Man were killed, because none feared death, and they exposed themselves like madmen to every manifest danger, wishing to die.

And when the Old Man wishes to have a great lord killed, he makes proof among his assassins of those who were better in this way. He sends several of the young men who had been in Paradise no great distance round him through the country, and orders them to kill that man whom he described. They go immediately and do their lord's command. And if one was caught he wished to die, believing that he would come back to this Paradise. And when those who are escaped are come back to their lord, they tell him that they had performed the duty well.

The Old Man of the Mountain, legendary leader of the Assassins, shows his authority by ordering two followers to kill themselves. (from Taxil,Le Mystères de la Franc-Maçonnerie)

The Old Man makes great rejoicing and great feasting for them. And he well knew him who had shown greater courage, for he had sent some of his men after each one secretly, that they might be able to tell him which is the boldest and best to kill a man.

The assassinations hit at all ranks, the lowly and the important, that Hasan perceived as enemies. The first assassination seems to have been a relatively lowly one, that of a *muezzin* (caller to prayer) who refused to convert to the doctrines of the Order and was killed to prevent him betraying them to the authorities.[163] The first notable operation on a prominent figure was the assassination of the Grand Vizir Nizam al-Mulik (a former schoolfellow of Hasan), during a visit to Baghdad on October 16, 1092. He was passing in procession through a narrow street of the city when a man disguised as a Sufi (a member of a mystical sect) dashed out of the crowd and threw himself onto the litter carrying the vizir, striking him with several dagger-thrusts near the heart. The vizir died on the spot. When the killer was tortured to reveal his motive, he admitted his deed calmly and smiling. He had done it for the greater glory of the Ismailite cause, on the express orders of the Seigneur of the Mountain. He predicted that this killing was merely the first in a series that would not cease until the Ismailis had achieved their ends.

And indeed further murders followed. Arasch-Nizami, cousin and right-hand man of the new Sultan, was killed, so was the emir Borsak, former governor of Baghdad, who was planning an attack on Hasan's fortresses. The total number of killings can only be guessed, but it has been calculated that they numbered in the thousands, including some fifty prominent persons.[164] Such deeds spread terror among the Islamic establishment, and many secretly switched allegiance to the Ismaili cause.

To carry out these operations was regarded as a great privilege, and this story was told: "A young fidawi had a mother who lived in the little village at the foot of Alamut. One day he left for one of these missions from which none ever returned. The mother, happy in the knowledge that her son was sacrificing himself for the honour of Persia and the Ismaili cause, put on her best clothes, praising Allah. The death of her son was something to celebrate, for Paradise would now open to him. A month later the son returned from his mission, miraculously safe and sound, but distraught to be still alive: his mother cut her hair, and blackened her face as a sign of mourning, and abandoned herself to despair."[165]

Hasan died in June 1124, aged about 90, but the tradition he created was maintained after his death and the ashishin remained a source of terror for years to come, to rival sects and western invaders alike, until in the 13th century their power crumbled before the Mongol invasion. Hasan had seven successors before the Mongol chief Hulagu besieged Alamut in 1256, starving the occupants to surrender.

Around 1190 Henri, Comte de Champagne and titular king of Jerusalem, was invited into an Ismaili castle. His host asked him to accompany him to the tallest tower, where two fidawin were standing. "These men obey me better than your Christian soldiers obey their lords," said the chief, and at a signal, the two men flung themselves from the tower to their death.[166]

COMMENT: For some, "the story can only be regarded as a romance,"[167] and the accounts given above can be neither substantiated nor refuted. Moreover, though there is a general conformity as to Hasan's methods, there are some difficulties. As Frere points out, the region of Alamut is not suited to sustaining a tropical garden of the kind described; it is very cold eight months of the year and very dry the rest of the time. Marco Polo was evidently speaking from hearsay rather than observation when he described "a luxurious landscape of gardens full of every kind of delicious fruit and every fragrant shrub on earth."[168] Frere suggests that this may have been no more than an illusion brought about by the use of hashish; one of the drug's properties is to induce hallucinations, so perhaps a combination of hashish and suggestion caused the initiate to see a terrestrial Paradise where there was in reality only a mediocre garden.[169] However, the existence of the garden itself is certainly a fact, for it can be seen to this day, and the beautiful young men and houris, of course, could have been substantial enough.

What is beyond question is the existence of a sect of dedicated killers who were inspired by an unquestioning devotion to the Ismaili cause and in particular to the Old Man of the Mountain. To secure such dedication, Hasan must have used exceptional means, so perhaps the account given by the historians is not so far from the facts.

The disregard for life, and indifference to torture, is found in other Islamic sects, notably the ISLAMIC ECSTATIC SECTS whose specialty is self-mutilation, which is frequently fatal. It is also a feature of THUGGEE, though the Thugs were not all Muslims. To what degree drugs play a part in the process is difficult to assess, but they certainly played a crucial role in the training of the Assassins.

ASSEMBLY LINE HYSTERIA

Huntington, West Virginia: November 4-7, 1977

An investigation by the National Institute for Occupational Safety and Health (NIOSH) concluded that a spate of illnesses in 48 employees of a shoe factory was the result of "assembly line hysteria." The episode began on November 4, when four employees were taken ill, and continued over four consecutive workdays. While workers at the Perry-Norvell Company were convinced that their illnesses were triggered by "toxic fumes from a new batch of glue," health authorities concluded that the bouts of dizziness and fainting were from over-breathing as a result of fear. The 14-page report of the investigation into the illnesses also found that those workers most severely affected had higher levels of job dissatisfaction. Another finding: workers under the greatest levels of financial and job stress were the hardest hit. Union representatives disputed the report, labeling it "a lot of bunk" and contending that the illness was caused by unsafe conditions at the plant. NIOSH medical officer Dr. Mitchell Singal who coordinated the study, said that mass psychogenic illness was "the only logical explanation."[170]

Stress-inducing working conditions: the stitching room at the Fine Welt factory, Endicott, NY, where more than 4,000 people were engaged in leather working and shoe making.

ASTEROID PANIC

United States: October 30, 1994

The broadcast of a CBS television network Sunday night movie, *Without Warning*, triggered fears that an asteroid was about to crash into earth. The program featured realistic, "live" reports from fictional disaster sites in Asia, Europe, and the United States. The film was broadcast as a news program, confusing many viewers. The "Evening World News" was presented like a real news program and reported that asteroids had already struck in Wyoming, France, and China, and more were on the way. At the end of the program, other meteors strike the earth and TV screens go black. Adding to the realism, 16-year-veteran television journalist Sander Vanocur anchored as he switched to apparent live footage of the aftermath of the impacts. The word "live" also appeared as actors and real reporters continued their deception.

During the airing, telephone calls poured into stations that were broadcasting the movie. Prior to the film's broadcast, the network advised audiences that the film they were about to see was a "realistic depiction of fictional events. None of what you are seeing is actually happening." [171] The problem was, after the initial warning, there was no advisory for the first 15 minutes of the film, which established the tone and mood. The program began like an ordinary Sunday night movie but was interrupted by news bulletins from respected organizations such as The Associated Press and Reuters, showing scenes of death and destruction. The movie even recreated a White House press conference during which it was announced that F-16 fighter planes equipped with nuclear weapons had been scrambled in order to blow up the asteroids before reaching Earth. [172]

It may have been no coincidence that the program aired on October 30 and was likely inspired by the infamous 1938 MARTIAN INVASION SCARE, which also aired on the same date. During the TV broadcast, the switchboard at the CBS headquarters in New York was jammed with anxious callers.

When the movie was over, one New York affiliate led their local news with viewer complaints about the broadcast. After covering the incident as a news story, the show's anchorman then said: "Now, here's the real news."[173]

AURORA END-OF-THE-WORLD PANIC

Europe: January 25, 1938

A brilliant aurora borealis or "northern lights" display terrorized people in much of Europe, many of whom thought it was the end of the world. According to one journalist: "Many villagers in more remote sections of Europe knelt in prayer as the northern lights spread across the sky last night." The vivid beams of purple, green, orange, red, blue and white light danced in the sky which was continuously changing between 6:30 and 8:30 pm. In London, many residents rushed into the streets to see the sky a vivid red, only to think that portions of the city were on fire; others believed that Windsor Castle was burning down.[174]

AUXONNE POSSESSION OUTBREAK

France: 1662

When trouble broke out among the nuns at Auxonne, near Dijon, it seemed for the most part to follow the traditional pattern of convent disorder. The nuns presented with convulsions, blasphemy, and aversion for the sacraments; their spiritual directors countered with the inevitable diagnosis of diabolical possession, followed by exorcisms and the hunt for someone to bear the blame. But in three respects the outbreak is of particular interest.

First, it not only affected the cloistered nuns, but also girls and women of all conditions from the town – old and young, rich and poor, religious and secular, and very unusually, Protestants as well as Catholics.

Second, many of the manifestations were ostensibly of what are today considered to be paranormal powers: selective and controlled anesthesia, glossolalia, telepathy, and precognition.

Third, when the local authorities had failed to put an end to the disorder, a Royal Commission, made up of churchmen and doctors, was created for the purpose of establishing the facts. The findings of the investigators provide valuable insight into the dynamics of such outbreaks.

CONTEXT: Auxonne, in northeastern France, was not in an area especially prone to religious strife, and the town was relatively untroubled in that respect. The source of the affliction lay within the convent. However, in one particular respect external events did play a part: it is on record that the nuns had read of the outbreaks at LOUDUN and LOUVIERS and were well aware of what had taken place there. So the resemblance of their behavior to that of the nuns in those two convents may well have involved a degree of simulation, conscious or unconscious.[175]

When the troubles in the convent came to public notice, they were said to have been going on for many years, since about 1652. But to begin with, the convent kept its troubles to itself. This may well be connected with the loose moral state of the convent at this time. Many of the nuns were young – the commissioners' report regularly refers to them as "girls" – and their two confessors, appointed in 1656, were aged 27 and 28. "Crises of nymphomania seem to have been the start of the matter," one historian states.[176] Eight of the nuns subsequently confessed to "great temptations of the flesh" for one of the confessors, Claude Nouvelet, even though he was described as "one of the ugliest men you ever saw."[177]

In 1658, reports of undesirable intimacy between the nuns and their confessors led to the dismissal of Nouvelet and his colleague Pelletier. Soon afterwards, Marie Borthon, known as Sister Saint-Sacrament, began to manifest symptoms similar to those reported at Loudun and Louviers: convulsions, howlings, hallucinations demonic or erotic, blasphemy, and a marked antipathy to anything sacred or pious. Exorcism was the usual remedy in such cases, but the director of the convent, Pierre Borthon, Marie's brother, suspecting that his sister might be pregnant, was reluctant and took the advice of the leading churchmen of the district. All agreed there was no need for exorcism and urged that Nouvelet should be put in prison.

Nevertheless Marie's confessor, Father Terrestre, alarmed at her condition, persuaded Borthon to proceed with exorcisms. The first was performed a fortnight before Easter 1658, and at first it seemed to be successful. Shortly after, Borthon died of a hernia, and it was whispered that this was his punishment for dismissing Nouvelet. Within a month Marie was manifesting the same symptoms as before and demanding that the two dismissed priests be reinstated. Hoping that this would restore Marie's health, Father Devenet, Borthon's replacement, agreed.

But by now the disorder was spreading. Eight of the nuns, followed soon after by six more, began to display the same symptoms as Marie, and all became candidates for exorcism. However, their spiritual director, Terrestre, was not acceptable to them as exorcist. In their fits, they attacked him physically and tore his vestments, insisting that only Nouvelet and Pelletier should perform the exorcisms. These took place twice daily in the church and also in the chambers of the nuns. The convent doors were open to the two young men at all hours: "Priests and nuns, the one as young as the other, were ceaselessly in contact by day and night." The exorcisms might be performed even when they were in bed, *visage contre visage* – face against face – "so close that only the nun's veil separated her face from that of her exorcist."[178]

Under these circumstances, it is not surprising that the exorcised nuns complained of carnal thoughts and a desire to quit religion. They had a marked antipathy towards anything holy and several admitted to "temptations against purity." "During the holy mass and in the course of their exorcisms, they spat out fearful blasphemies against God and the Holy Virgin, blasphemies which could only come from the mouth of a demon."[179]

Inevitably the question was posed: who was responsible for the epidemic? – for it was generally supposed that the devil needed a human channel through whom to work his wicked devices. On October 28, 1660, in the course of a solemn procession, intended as a public demonstration against the demons, Sister Gabrielle de Malo cried out "Barbe Buvée, calling herself Sister of Sainte-Colombe, is the witch and the sorceress!" whereupon she threw herself at Barbe, striking her and tearing away her nun's veil. Sister Marguerite Jannin threw a lighted candle at her and pummeled her; Sister Lazare Arnier tore off her headdress.

Father Devenet, instead of interfering, exorcised the nuns and inquired of the demons whether this accusation was true? They confirmed that it was as the nuns said.

Buvée, known as Sister Sainte-Colombe (=Holy Dove), had entered the convent as a 13-year-old novice around 1645. Now age 28, she had openly quarreled with Father Borthon, the late spiritual director. Borthon had three sisters and several other relatives in the convent, and it was his sister Marie who had been the first nun to be afflicted, so this alone offered grounds for suspecting Buvée. Moreover, she had openly criticized the intimate manner of the exorcisms: "The scapegoat of the exorcising priests and the nuns who claimed to be possessed was therefore clearly marked out."[180]

The testimony against Buvée is conspicuous in that, apart from the usual charges of magic and spellcasting, it contains erotic charges of every kind. Marie traced her own possession to kisses Buvée had given her and impure touching. Charlotte Joly claimed to have seen Buvée and Gabrielle de Malo mutually caressing each other under their skirts and accused Buvée of seeking to do the same with her. Sister Marguerite was assailed by demons who tried to rape her with batons made of rolled linen, which she found in her bed and threw in the fire. Buvée had touched her impurely and urged her to accompany her to the witches' sabbat; when the priests came to visit her, they placed consecrated hosts in her private parts. Sister Françoise Borthon confessed that she had been raped by a demon under the gallery, who then laughingly said that now all would know she was no longer a virgin. Subsequently Buvée had come down the chimney with two apostate priests, saying that Françoise was now pregnant and they must abort the birth to save her honor. Buvée had plunged her arm into Françoise's shameful parts, forced them open and made her bleed copiously. On another occasion Buvée had her sit on her knees and put her fingers inside her as a man would do. Her sister Humberte, still a novice, was put into trance at a sign from Buvée, then taken to Hell where she witnessed the damned being tortured. Buvée had lain on her like a man on a woman.

The charges veered further into fantasy when many of the sisters insisted that Buvée had twice become pregnant as a result of her coupling with demons. In both instances she had killed the child – had they not seen her, at four in the morning, leaving her room with a vase full of blood?

Though Buvée denied all these charges, the nuns' word – or rather, the demons speaking through her – was sufficient for the priests. She was confined to her room while a hearing was called. Charged with crimes of sorcery, of casting spells, of an infinity of lewd acts, and of infanticide on November 13, 1660, she was placed in a dark prison, manacled at ankles and wrists.

In the past, many such innocent women, charged with such crimes, were hurried to the stake. Buvée escaped thanks to the intervention of her family, who petitioned the Parliament at Dijon and succeeded in getting her transferred to the somewhat less harsh secular gaol in that town. In January 1661, the court overruled the Auxonne charges. Two months later she was released and subsequently pronounced innocent of all the charges against her.

But the departure of Buvée did not end the matter. Though the exorcisms continued, they appeared to be having no beneficial effect on the nuns, who were the center of the exorcists' attention for several hours every day. The convulsions continued, and many of the sufferers presented physical symptoms such as stomach trouble and vomited hair, small pebbles, pieces of wax, bones, and even living reptiles. Denise Parisot, a servant-girl in the employ of the lieutenant general of the town, threw up a live toad so large, the investigators wondered how it could have squeezed through her throat. Nevertheless the sisters were full of praise for the exorcists, for they had successfully removed from their wombs the sticks covered with sorcerers' foreskins which had been magically inserted there by the demons, as well as candles and other objects used by the sorcerers to perform their impure acts. Moreover, with holy water they had healed the swelling of the belly caused by diabolic coupling – for three of the sisters admitted they had surrendered their virginity to demons, while five others admitted performing acts which shame prevented them naming.

While some of these lewd events were supposed to have taken place within the convent, many more occurred at the sabbats to which, the nuns insisted, they were taken by the demons. On one occasion, some of the sisters were due to attend a sabbat the next day. When the time came, prevented from going, "they all fell into a kind of lethargy, in which state they remained for five quarters of an hour." One of them was Anne l'Ecossaise, known as Sister of the Purification, who subsequently reported that she had in fact been to the sabbat: "All her senses being closed, she was without movement, without word, without feeling, her arms crossed on her chest so stiffly that it was impossible to separate them, her eyes closed at first, then open, but immobile and unseeing. When she came out of this ecstasy, she told how she had been in spirit at the sabbat, and recounted all that she had seen there."

Three hundred years later, persons who claimed to be abducted by extraterrestrial aliens would be similarly observed, safe on Earth, at the time of their adventure in space.[181]

The priests took to patrolling the streets of Auxonne at night, claiming to be watching for witches on their way to a sabbat. Such activities had the effect of sensitizing the whole community to the presence of demons and sorcerers. For now girls from the town, including some Protestants, began to be affected by the epidemic, and they too were subjected to exorcism. Innocent people were denounced; two were even banished from the town for their own safety, for fear the townsfolk might attack them. A girl named Coudry, while being exorcised in the church, was asked if she knew of any who were witches. At once she pointed to a girl fruit-seller who had wandered into the church out of curiosity. The innocent girl was seized, and while being taken to prison she was stoned to death by women and children of the town and her body burned on an improvised pyre.

Such a state of affairs attracted notice beyond the city limits. The Bishop of Châlons-sur-Saône came in person to see how matters were. This led to the creation of a Royal Commission, comprised of four bishops, assisted by five physicians from the Sorbonne. After 15 days inquiry at Auxonne, they reported unanimously that the manifestations exceeded the power of nature and consequently could be ascribed only to the workings of the devil. Only one of the doctors, Morel, reserved his opinion that the phenomena could all be natural. Following the report, the sisters were dispersed to other convents, and isolation achieved what exorcism had failed to do.

Many of the phenomena ostensibly observed during the exorcisms would be classified as paranormal today. For example, the Bishop of Châlons performed several experiments on Denise Parisot. Once he commanded the demons controlling her to render her insensible to pain; he then stuck a pin under her fingernail and she showed no sign of feeling it. On commands from him, he caused the wound to bleed or not bleed. On another occasion she lifted up, with just two fingers, a heavy marble vase filled with holy water, and turned it the opposite way round, though it was so heavy that two strong men would have had difficulty in moving it from its pedestal. Sister Arivey of the Resurrection held for a long time a burning coal in her hand without leaving any trace of burning.

Denise also manifested remote sensing. On several occasions, the bishop gave her a mental command to come to him. Though resident in a distant quarter of the town, she came to him at once, declaring that she felt she had been commanded to come to him. Many subjects of the animal magnetizers in the early 19th century would manifest this ability, prompting the suggestion that the state of these exorcised girls was similar to that of animal magnetism.

The commission confirmed the bishop's assertion that "all these girls, whether secular or regular, to the number of eighteen, had the gift of tongues, and replied in Latin to the exorcists, sometimes by whole sentences and often making entire discourses in this tongue." These were not recited parrot-fashion from the ritual, but appeared to be genuine replies to questions. Anne l'Ecossaise understood what one of the exorcists said in Gaelic and translated it into French.

"All, or almost all of them possessed the gift of knowing the inmost and secret thoughts of others when they were directed to them: this was particularly striking when it was unspoken commands which were made to them by the exorcists, on several occasions, which they obeyed without any indication being given either in words or gestures. One nun predicted correctly that her sister would give birth to a boy, but with much pain: another was able to describe the events at a ball in the town."[182] While Sister Humberte de Saint-François was in convulsions, the bishop gave her a mental command to prostrate herself before the holy sacrament, her arms stretched out like the arms of a cross. She carried out this command that very instant, with extraordinary promptitude and precipitation. This happened so often that the churchmen ceased giving spoken commands, realizing that it was enough simply to think them for the commands to be obeyed.

Several of the nuns seemed to be gifted with clairvoyance. More than once they told the bishop or his priests particular and secret details relating to their family and homes. One day one of them correctly indicated to the bishop when he would make a journey to Paris, before he knew of it himself. They also sensed the approach of holy relics: "Simply to bring relics near them gave them violent access of fury, and often they would name the saint to which they belonged before they even saw them."

COMMENT: The fact that the Royal Commission included doctors from the Sorbonne, as well as churchmen, might be seen as a sign that the authority of science was starting to be taken into account. On the other hand, the fact that all but one of them agreed with the churchmen that the cause of the trouble was possession by the devil shows that science had yet to formulate independent criteria for the evaluation of such cases.

Reading the report from today's perspective, it is hard to disagree with Rapin, a doctor who dared to disagree with the churchmen. "There's nothing diabolical, precious little of sickness, any amount of trickery," was his conclusion.[183] It is hard to resist the suspicion that some of the feats were feigned – Denise's living toad "as large as a fist," for example. On the other hand, other feats sound as though they may have been genuine. When Denise stated that she had felt summoned by the bishop from the far side of the town, this corresponds to experiments conducted by the animal magnetizers.[184] Writing in 1845, Calmeil, no friend to animal magnetism and its marvels, was skeptical concerning the alleged paranormal feats.[185] However, though such phenomena are occasionally reported in other instances of convent hysteria, nowhere else are they described in such detail and given so much weight. When we are told that "the churchmen, seeing that the same thing happened every day, had got into the habit of never addressing these nuns except mentally," this is an unambiguous statement which cannot be set aside.

Clearly, some of the phenomena – such as commanding Denise to feel no pain and sticking a pin under her nail, causing the blood to flow or not flow, etc, are similar to the kind of demonstration given by hypnotists; so it is reasonable to think that a similar process is operating.

Other phenomena are of considerable psychological interest. The fantasy visit to the sabbat, when it was evident the sisters were lying entranced in their convent, was a clear demonstration that all such reports can be accounted for in this way. At a time when the physical reality of the sabbat was still generally accepted, the Auxonne incident was a valuable indication that it could be interpreted otherwise.

When the epidemic seemed to be over, the questionable death of a young girl directed attention again on Auxonne, and a further commission was ordered to re-open the inquiry. The report submitted to his superior by Doctor Bachet concluded with these words: "After a very exact research and a very curious and faithful observation of all that happened to these girls during the exorcisms, I can assure Your Grandeur that in all their actions whether of the body or the spirit, they did not show a single legitimate and convincing sign of true possession, neither in their understanding of tongues, nor in their knowledge and revelation of secrets, nor in heightened discourse, nor in the raising of their bodies in the air, nor in transport from one place to another, nor in movements so extraordinary as to surpass the forces of nature. In short, nothing happened in them which was not entirely human and natural."[186]

See also: CONVENT HYSTERIA; DEMON POSSESSION.

Sources

1. Lysimachus, one of Alexander the Greats' bodyguards, first governed and then ruled Thrace from 323 to 281 BCE.
2. Lucian. *Dialogues* (1779). Translated from the Greek by John Carr. London: W. Harvey, Volume 2, p. 540.
3. Picart, Bernard (1783[1730)] *Cérémonies et Coutumes religieuses de tous les Peuples du Monde.* [nouvelle édition 1783] Amsterdam and Paris: Laporte [originally published circa 1730]. Volume 3, p. 154. Except where otherwise stated, information is drawn from this source.
4. Blunt, John Henry (1874). *Dictionary of Sects, Heresies, Ecclesiastical Parties and Schools of Religious Thought.* London, Oxford & Cambridge: Rivingtons. p. 5, drawing on Epiphanius.
5. Cohn, Norman (1957). *The Pursuit of the Millennium.* London: Secker & Warburg, p. 186 et seq.
6. Picart, op cit., volume 3, p. 155.
7. Thomas E. Bullard (1998). "Abduction phenomenon" in Clark, Jerome. *The UFO Encyclopedia, Volume 1,* second edition. Detroit: Omnigraphics.
8. For examples, see Adamski, George. *Inside the Space Ships.* New York: Abelard-Schuman 1955; Bethurum, Truman. *Aboard a Flying Saucer.* Los Angeles: DeVorss 1954.
9. Denaerde, Stefan (1979). *Buitenaardse Beschaving.* Deventer: Kluwer 1979 [translated as *UFO Contact from Planet Iarga.* Tucson AZ: UFO Photo Archives 1982.
10. King, George (1965). *The Day the Gods Came.* Los Angeles: Aetherius Society; Muro, Maria Antonietta de, and Valenti, Orazio (circa 1979). *I Giganti del cielo: Eugenio Siragusa. Roma*: NEDI. Vorilhon, Claude "Rael." (1974). *Le Livre qui dit la Verité.* Vaduz: L'edition du message.
11. For example the Anibal Quintero case: Bowen, Charles (1977). "Saucer Central International," in *UFO Report* 5(1) (November).
12. See, for example the Villas-Boas case: Creighton, Gordon (1965). 'The Most Amazing Case,' in *Flying Saucer Review* 11(1) (January 1965) and subsequent issues.
13. Klarer, Elizabeth. (1980). *Beyond the Light Barrier.* Cape Town: Timmins.
14. Curran, Douglas (1985). *In Advance of the Landing: Folk Concepts of Outer Space.* New York: Abbeville.
15. Mandelker, Scott (1995). *From Elsewhere: Being ET in America.* Secaucus NJ: Carol Publishing.
16. Evans, Hilary, in *Magonia Supplement* 2005.
17. Fuller, John G. (1966). *The Interrupted Journey: Two Lost Hours Aboard a Flying Saucer.* New York: Dell. For an excellent analysis of the Hill case, see: Pflock, Karl, and Brookesmith, Peter (2007). *Encounter at Indian Head.* Jefferson Valley, New York: Anomalist Books.
18. Hopkins, Budd (1996). *Witnessed: The True Story of the Brooklyn Bridge Abductions.* New York: Pocket Books; Mack, John E. (1994). *Abduction: Human Encounters with Aliens.* New York: Scribner; Jacobs, David M. *Secret Life* (1992). New York: Simon & Schuster.
19. For example, Fowler, Raymond E. (1990). *The Watchers: The Secret Design Behind UFO Abduction.* New York: Bantam.
20. Bartholomew, R.E., Basterfield, Keith, and Howard, George S. (1991). "UFO 'Abductees' and 'Contactees': Psychopathology or Fantasy Proneness?" *Professional Psychology: Research & Practice* 22(3):215-222.
21. Ring, Kenneth (1992). *The Omega Project: Near-Death Experiences, UFO Encounters, and Mind at Large.* New York: William Morrow.
22. Lawson, Alvin H. (1977). "What can we Learn from Hypnosis of Imaginary Abductees?" *Mutual UFO Network Journal* 120:7-9.
23. Klass, Phillip J. (1989). *UFO Abductions: A Dangerous Game.* Buffalo, New York: Prometheus Books, p. 23.
24. Hopkins, B. (1981). *Missing Time: A Documented Study of UFO Abductions. New York: Richard Marek.*
25. Leir, Roger. (2000) *Alien Implants.* New York: Dell.
26. Strieber, 1987, op cit.
27. Hopkins, Budd (1987). *Intrusions: The Incredible Visitations at Copley Woods.* New York: Random House.
28. Jacobs, David M. (1999). *The Threat: Revealing the Secret Alien Agenda.* New York: Fireside, p. 123.
29. Personal communication between Michael Strainic and Robert Bartholomew, 10 December 2003.
30. Hopkins, 1996, op cit.
31. Gansberg, Judith M. & Alan L. (1980). *Direct Encounters: The Personal Histories of UFO Abductees.* New York: Walker.
32. Festinger, L, Riecken, Schachter, S. (1956). *When Prophesy Fails.* New York: Harper and Row.
33. Stevens, Anthony, and Price, John (2000). *Prophets, Cults and Madness.* London: Duckworth, pp. 2-3.
34. Evans 1998 passim.
35. Evans-Wentz, Walter Y. (1909). *The Fairy-Faith in Celtic Countries, its Psychological Origin and Nature.* Oberthur, Rennes; Vallee, Jacques (1969). *Passport To Magonia: From Folklore to Flying Saucers.* Chicago: Henry Regnery; Bartholomew, Robert E. (1989). *UFOlore: A Social Psychological Study of a Modern Myth in the Making.* Stone Mountain, GA: Arcturus Books; Musgrave John B., and Houran, J. (2000). "Flight and Abduction in Witchcraft and UFO Lore." *Psychological Reports* 86(2):669-678.
36. Musgrave and Houran (2000). op cit., p. 669.
37. Notably Méheust, Bertrand (1978). *Science-fiction et Soucoupes Volantes.* Paris: Mercure de France; Méheust, Bertrand (1985). *Soucoupes Volantes et Folklore.* Paris: Mercure de France; Méheust, Bertrand (1992). *En Soucoupes Volantes: Vers une Ethnologie des Récits d'enlèvements.* Paris: Imago; Meurger, Michel (1995). *Alien Abduction.* Amiens: Encrage.
38. Smale, Fred C. (1900). "The Abduction of Alexandra Seine" in xx magazine 1900, reprinted in Evans, Hilary, and Evans, Dik (1976). *Beyond the Gaslight: Science in Popular Fiction 1895-1905.* London: Muller.
39. Stuart, Dona (1936). "The Invaders" in *Astounding Stories* (June).
40. Sprinkle, Leo (1999). *Soul Samples.* Columbia NC: Granite Publishing; Mack, John E. (1999). *Passport to the Cosmos: Human Transformation and Alien Encounters.* New York: Crown; Mack 1994, op cit.
41. Sprinkle quoted in Jacobs, David M. (1998). *The Threat.* New York: Simon & Schuster, p. 209.
42. Fowler, Raymond E. (1979). *The Andreasson Affair.* Englewood Cliffs NJ: Prentice-Hall, and several follow-up volumes.
43. James, William (1902). *The Varieties of Religious Experience.* London: Longmans, Green.
44. Bullard in Clark, Jerome (1998). *The UFO Encyclopedia, Volume 1,* second edition. Detroit: Omnigraphics, p. 6.
45. *The APRO Bulletin* 25:5 (November 1976); *International UFO Reporter* 4:3 (March 1977); *MUFON UFO Journal* 220 (January 1977).
46. Sprinkle, Leo (1976), in the *APRO Journal,* op cit., p. 5.

47. Others sources consulted in creating this entry include: Jacobs, David M. [editor] (2000). *UFOs & Abductions*. Lawrence, Kansas: University of Kansas; Story, Ronald (1980). *The Encyclopedia of UFOs*. New York: Doubleday.
48. From an abundant literature: Evans, Hilary (1989). *Alternate States of Consciousness*. Wellingborough: Aquarian; Tart, Charles T. (editor) (1969). *Altered States of Consciousness*. New York: John Wiley; Wolman, Benjamin N. and Ullman, Montague (1986). *Handbook of States of Consciousness*. New York: Van Nostrand Reinhold.
49. Bourguignon, E. (1973). *Culture and the Varieties of Consciousness*. An Addison-Wesley Module in Anthropology 47. Reading, Massachusetts: Addison-Wesley.
50. Bourguignon, op cit., pp. 10-11.
51. Weil, Andrew T. "The Marriage of Sun and Moon," in Zinberg, Norman E. (editor) (1977). *Alternate States of Consciousness*. New York: Free Press, p. 46.
52. MacDonnell, F. (1995). *Insidious Foes*. New York: Oxford University Press; Mount, G.S. (1993). *Canada's Enemies: Spies and Spying in the Peaceable Kingdom*. Toronto: Dundurn Press, p. 40; Kitchen, M. (1985). "The German Invasion of Canada in the First World War." *The International History Review* 7(2):245-260.
53. Mecklin, John Moffatt (1926). *The Survival Value of Christianity*. New York: Harcourt, Brace, p. 1926, p. 23.
54. Davenport, Frederick Morgan (1905). *Primitive Traits in Religious Revivals*. New York: Macmillan, p. 106, quoting from Edwards.
55. Edwards, reported by Conant, William C. (1858). *Narratives of Remarkable Conversions and Revival Incidents*. New York: Derby & Jackson, p. 21.
56. *The Boston Post Boy*, cited by Godwin 1951, p. 124.
57. Davenport, op cit., p. 110.
58. Davenport, op cit., pp. 110-113, quoting from Allen 'Jonathan Edwards.'
59. Davenport, op cit., p. 119.
60. Davenport, op cit., p. 123.
61. Conant, op cit., p. 21.
62. Cleveland, op cit., p. 1916, chapter 1.
63. Davenport, op cit., p. 69.
64. Godwin, George (1941). *The Great Revivalists*. London: Watts, p. 153; Davenport, op cit., p. 70.
65. Davenport, op cit., p. 72-73.
66. Cleveland, op cit., p. 54.
67. Davenport, op cit., p. 65.
68. Elder Stone, cited by Davenport, op cit., p. 74.
69. Cleveland, op cit., p. 58.
70. Cleveland, op cit., p. 78.
71. Cleveland, op cit., p. 81.
72. Cleveland, op cit., p. 80; Davenport, op cit., p. 77.
73. Cleveland, op cit., p. 77.
74. Cleveland, op cit., p. 90.
75. Cleveland, op cit., p. 101.
76. Cleveland, op cit., p. 100.
77. Cleveland, op cit., p. 100.
78. Dow, Lorenzo (1855). *History of Cosmopolite*. Philadelphia: Rulison, pp. 183-184.
79. Dow, op cit., p. 207.
80. Dow, op cit., p. 215.
81. Davenport, op cit., p. 80.
82. Davenport, op cit., p. 81.
83. Grégoire, M. (1828). *Histoire des Sectes Religieuses*. [nouvelle édition] Paris: Baudouin, volume 4, p. 493.
84. Grégoire, op cit., p. 495.
85. Dow, op cit., p. 183.
86. Quoted in Orr, Edwin J. (1989). *My All, His All*. Wheaton, IL: International Awakening Press, p. 338.
87. Orr, op cit., p. 48.
88. This account is drawn from Conant, op cit., p. 357 et seq; Davenport, op cit., pp. 6-7; Orr, op cit., 1989, passim.
89. Orr, op cit., p. 53.
90. Orr, op cit., p. 54.
91. Quoted by Orr, op cit., p. 70.
92. Quoted by Orr, op cit., p. 72.
93. Orr, op cit., p. 71.
94. Orr, op cit., p. 75.
95. Conant, op cit., p. 362.
96. Conant, op cit., p. 364.
97. Orr, op cit., p. 74.
98. Orr, op cit., p. 333.
99. Orr, op cit., p. 274.
100. Conant, op cit., p. 383.
101. Calmeil, L.F. (1845). *De la Folie, Consideree Sous le Point de vue Pathologique, Philosophique, Historique et Judiciaire* [On Insanity, From the Point of View of Pathology, Philosophy, History and Justice]. Paris: Baillere, Volume 1, p. 503.
102. Robbins, Rossell Hope (1959). *The Encyclopedia of Witchcraft and Demonology*. London: Spring Books, p. 298.
103. De Lancre, Pierre (1613). *Tableau de l'inconstance des Mauvais Anges et des Demons*. Paris: Buon, p. 37.
104. De Lancre, op cit., p. 357.
105. Calmeil, op cit., Volume 1, p. 508.
106. Réal, quoted in Bekker, Balthasar (1694). *Le Monde Enchanté*. Amsterdam: Pierre Rotterdam, volume 4, p. 517.
107. Wier, Jean. [Weyer, Johann] (1885). *Histoires, Disputes Et Discours Des Illusions Et Impostures Des Diables, Des Magiciens Infames, SorcièRes Et Empoisonneurs*. Translated from the Latin original, published 1563. Paris: Bureaux du Progrès Médical, volume 1, p. 521.
108. Hoost, quoted by Görres, Johann Joseph von (1845). *La Mystique Divine, Naturelle et Diabolique*. Paris: Poussielgue-Rusand, 1855, translated from the German *Christliche Mystik*, volume 5, p. 231.
109. Hoost, quoted by Bekker, op cit., volume 4, p. 517.
110. Calmeil, L.F. (1845). *De la Folie, Consideree Sous le Point de vue Pathologique, Philosophique, Historique et Judiciaire* [On the Crowd, Considerations on the Point of Pathology, Philosophy, History and Justice]. Paris: Baillere, volume 1, p. 265.
111. Hastings, James (1908). *Encyclopaedia of Religion and Ethics*. Edinburgh: T & T Clark [published by volumes]. Volume 1, p. 106, "Anabaptism."
112. Picart, Bernard (1783[1730]) *Cérémonies et Coutumes religieuses de tous les Peuples du Monde*. [nouvelle édition 1783] Amsterdam and Paris: Laporte [originally published circa 1730], Volume 3, p. 148, "Religion des Anabaptistes."
113. Baring Gould, Sabine (1891). *Historic Oddities and Strange Events*, second series. London: Methuen, p. 220.
114. This account draws on the following sources: Arthur, Anthony (1999). *The Tailor-King*. New York: St. Martin's Press; Baring-Gould 1891, op cit; Cohn, Norman (1957). *The Pursuit of the Millennium*. London: Secker & Warburg; Hastings 1908, op cit.; Picart, op cit.
115. Baring-Gould, op cit., p. 221.
116. Cohn, op cit., p. 279.
117. Baring-Gould, op cit., pp. 259-264.
118. Cohn, op cit., p. 283.

119. Baring-Gould, op cit., pp. 264-265, quoting Kerssenbroeck.
120. Baring-Gould, op cit., p. 273, quoting Kerssenbroeck.
121. Baring-Gould, op cit., p. 268.
122. Baring-Gould, op cit., p. 290.
123. Baring-Gould, op cit., p. 300, quoting Kerssenbroeck.
124. Arthur, op cit., p. 111.
125. Cohn, op cit., p. 291.
126. Portions of this section on the Andrea balloon mania are excerpted from: Bartholomew, Robert E. (1997). "A British Columbia-Manitoba Balloon Mystery of 1896-97." *British Columbia Historical News* 30(4)27-29.
127. Rolt, L.T.C. (1966). *The Aeronauts: A History of Ballooning 1783-1903*. London: Longmans. p. 152.
128. "Can it be Andree? British Columbia Indians saw a balloon...The explorers driven far out of their course..." *Manitoba Morning Free Press*, August 12, 1896, p. 1.
129. "A mysterious balloon. Where was it from and whither bound?" *Manitoba Morning Free Press*, July 2, 1896, p. 4.
130. "Can it be Andree..." *Manitoba Morning Free Press*, August 12, 1896, p. 1.
131. Ibid., p. 1.
132. "It was no dream. The ghostly balloon seen by Winnipeggers," *Manitoba Morning Free* Press, August 13, 1896, p. 2.
133. "It was no dream." op cit., p. 2.
134. "Was only a cloud. How a balloon story originated in the mountains," *Manitoba Morning Free Press*, September 28, 1896, p. 3.
135. "That pillar of fire," *Victoria Daily Colonist*, July 18, 1897, p. 5; "Aerial mystery. The wonderful sight witnessed by two fishermen," *Manitoba Free Press*, July 20, 1897, p. 1.
136. "Aerial mystery..." *Manitoba Free Press*, July 20, 1897, p. 1.
137. "What is it?" [editorial], *Daily Colonist*, July 20, 1897, p. 4.
138. "Victoria news," *Daily News-Advertiser*, August 3, 1897, p. 5.
139. "Again the airship. Can Andree's balloon be visiting these parts," *Manitoba Free Press*, August 9, 1897, p. 3.
140. "That light in the air," *Victoria Daily Colonist*, August 7, 1897, p. 7.
141. "The ruddy moon. Late hours prove too much..." *Victoria Daily Colonist*, August 8, 1897, p. 2.
142. "That morning mystery," *Victoria Daily Colonist*, August 12, 1897, p. 6.
143. "Another aerial visitor," *Manitoba Morning Free Press*, August 10, 1897, p. 5.
144. "News of the province (Rossland)," *Daily News-Advertiser*, August 15, 1897, p. 6.
145. "A balloon again. This time seen over Souris," *Manitoba Free Press*, September 20, 1897, p. 8.
146. "Another Andree mystery," *Manitoba Morning Free Press*, September 28, 1897, p. 4.
147. Görres, Johann Joseph von (1845). *La Mystique Divine, Naturelle et Diabolique*. Paris: Poussielgue-Rusand, 1855, translated from the German Christliche Mystik, volume 5, p. 267.
148. Geraci, Gino (1995). "Look Before You Laugh." Accessed April 5, 2004 at: http://www.banner.org.uk/tb/look.html; Anderson, Dirk. "Great Signs and Wonders II." Accessed December 31, 2003 at: http://www.intowww.org/articles/art9708.htm.
149. Tarkowski, Edward. "Laughing Phenomena: Its History & Possible Effects on the Church, Part III: The Abrahamic Covenant And Joyous Feast of Tabernacles." Accessed December 31, 2003 at: http://users.stargate.net/~ejt/apos3.htm.
150. Needham, Dr. Nick. "The Toronto Blessing – Part One." Accessed December 31, 2003 at: http://www.geocities.com/bob_hunter/needham1.htm. Dr. Needham is from the Highland Theological College, Dingwall, Scotland IV15 9HA, United Kingdom.
151. Knox, Ronald (1950). *Enthusiasm*. Oxford University Press, pp. 560-561.
152. Rosen, G. (1962). "Psychopathology In The Social Process: Dance Frenzies, Demonic Possession, Revival Movements and Similar So-Called Psychic Epidemics. An Interpretation." *Bulletin of the History of Medicine* 36:13-44. See p. 35.
153. Goh, K. T. (1987). "Epidemiological Enquiries into a School Outbreak of an Unusual Illness." *International Journal of Epidemiology* 16(2):265-270.
154. Tam, Y. K., Tsoi, M. M., Kwong, G. B., and Wong, S. W. (1982). "Psychological Epidemic in Hong Kong, Part 2, Psychological and Physiological Characteristics of Children who were Affected." *Acta Psychiatrica Scandinavica* 65:437-449; Wong, S. W., Kwong, B., Tam, Y. K., and Tsoi, M. M. (1982). "Psychological Epidemic in Hong Kong." *Acta Psychiatrica Scandinavica* 65:421-436.
155. Smith, H.C.T., and Eastham, E.J. (1973). "Outbreak of Abdominal Pain." *The Lancet* 2:956-958; *Daily Mirror*, 10 July 1972.
156. Amin, Y., Hamdi, E., and Eapen, V. (1997). "Mass Hysteria in an Arab Culture." *The International Journal of Social Psychology* 43(4):303-306.
157. Rockney, Randy M., and Lemke, Thomas. (1994). "Response." Letter. *Journal of Developmental and Behavioral Pediatrics* 15(1):64-65; Rockney, R. M., and Lemke, T. (1992). "Casualties from a Junior High School during the Persian Gulf War: Toxic Poisoning or Mass Hysteria?" *Journal of Developmental and Behavioral Pediatrics* 13:339-342.
158. Where not otherwise indicated, information is derived from Frere, Jean-Claude (1973). *L'ordre des Assassins*. Paris. Culture.Art.Loisirs; Hastings, James (1908). *Encyclopaedia of Religion and Ethics*. Edinburgh: T & T Clark [published by volumes]; Larsen, Egon (1971). *Strange Sects and Cults*. London: Arthur Barker.
159. Hâkem quoted Frere, op cit., p. 180.
160. Polo, Marco (1938). *Descriptio Mundi*. [The Description of the World]. Latin original, translated into English, edited A. C. Moule and P. Pelliot. London: Routledge, volume one, p. 41 et seq: quotations are from Polo's account unless otherwise indicated.
161. Adapted from Hâkem, in Frere, op cit., pp. 183-184.
162. Odoric, quoted by Frere, op cit., p. 186.
163. Hastings, op cit., p. 139.
164. Larsen, op cit., p. 13.
165. Djouéiny, quoted by Frere, op cit., p. 190.
166. Larsen, op cit., p. 19.
167. Hastings, op cit., volume 2, p. 128.
168. Polo, cited by Larsen, op cit., p. 7.
169. Frere, op cit., pp. 187-188.
170. "Mass Hysteria Cited as Cause of 48 Ill in a Factory." *Chillicothe Constitution-Tribune* (Missouri), August 31, 1978, p. 6.
171. "Worried TV Viewers Call During Drama." *Herald-Journal* (Syracuse, New York), October 31, 1994, p. C4.
172. "TV Movie on Asteroid Crash Causes Real Fear in Viewers." *Daily Herald* (Chicago, Illinois), October 31, 1994, pp. 1 and 6.
173. "TV Movie on Asteroid Crash Causes Real Fear in Viewers." Op cit., p. 6.
174. "Aurora Borealis Startles Europe; People Flee in Fear, Call Firemen." *The Gleaner* (Kingston, Jamaica), January 28, 1938, p. 20.
175. Cauzons, Th. de. (1901-1912). *La Magie et la Sorcellerie en France*. Paris: Dorbon-Ainé, volume 1, pp. 140 and subsequent.
176. Cauzons, op cit., volume 3, p. 230.

177. Garnier, Samuel (1893). *Barbe Buvée et la Prétendue Possession des Ursulines d'Auxonne.* Paris: Bureaux du Progrès Médical, pp. vi, 2: all details are from this source unless otherwise indicated.
178. Garnier, op cit., p. 14.
179. Görres, Johann Joseph von (1845). *La Mystique Divine, Naturelle et Diabolique.* Paris: Poussielgue-Rusand, 1855, translated from the German Christliche Mystik, volume 5, pp. 238-246.
180. Garnier, op cit., p. ix.
181. See for instance the cases of Maureen Puddy and Gail Sunderland (see respectively, Magee, Judith (1978). "Maureen Puddy's Third Encounter." *Flying Saucer Review* 24(3):14-15; Randles, Jenny, and Whetnall, Paul (1981). *Alien Contact.* Suffolk: Neville Spearman.
182. Garnier, op cit., p. 15.
183. Cauzons, op cit., volume 3, p. 232.
184. Méheust, Bertrand (1999). *Somnambulisme et Médiumnité.* Le Plessis-Robinson: Institut Synthélabo pour le Progrès de la Connaissance, volume 1, p. 198. See also: Gauld, Alan (1992). *A History of Hypnotism.* Cambridge: University Press, p. 169.
185. Calmeil, L.F. (1845). *De la Folie, Consideree Sous le Point de vue Pathologique, Philosophique, Historique et Judiciaire* [On the Crowd, Considerations on the Point of Pathology, Philosophy, History and Justice]. Paris: Baillere, volume 2, p. 132.
186. Garnier, op cit., p. 80.

BAND BUS HYSTERIA

Penns Grove, New Jersey: August 1976

New Jersey health authorities blamed mass hysteria for a "mystery illness" that swept through two buses filled with students who were returning home from a band camp in Maryland. The buses, loaded with 130 students and their chaperones from Woodrow Wilson High School, stopped at a rest area on I-295 in the vicinity of Penns Grove, New Jersey, when several students reported feeling ill. They were examined at Salem County Memorial Hospital, complaining of dizziness, headache, nausea, and stomach cramps. School principal Larry Bosley said that once the first few students became ill, other students apparently grew anxious. It was at this point that school bandleader Byron King decided that all of the students should be examined at the hospital, and the buses were escorted there. Doctors later blamed the incident on "crowded buses and nervous excitement." All but four of the fifty students who were treated were released within three hours. Four others remained overnight under observation and were released the next day. Dr. Laurence Devlin Jr. of the Salem County Public Health Department called the incident "a classic case of mass hysteria." Based on his discussions with hospital physicians, he concluded that: "The kids had worked hard all week. It was hot and muggy and crowded on the buses. Several kids were sick and that set the others off." Authorities were emphatic that the students were not suffering from food poisoning.[1]

BAND MYSTERY ILLNESS

Eastern United States: November 24, 1978

Mass hysteria was suspected as the cause of a "mystery illness" that struck down 45 members of a high school band as they were returning home after performing in a Thanksgiving Day parade in Philadelphia, Pennsylvania. The students who became ill were part of a 108-member contingent who were on one of three busses heading back to Glen Este High School in Cincinnati, Ohio on Friday night. The primary symptoms were dizziness and nausea. Food and carbon monoxide poisoning were discounted by investigators. According to a report from United Press International, "One of the Este girls who eventually became sick said the students had stopped for dinner when one girl got sick on another bus. That illness prompted a discussion of Legionnaire's Disease and afterwards more students became ill." While some students were hospitalized overnight, all made quick recoveries and were released the following morning.[2]

BARKING-OFF SQUIRRELS FAD

Eastern United States: 18th century

In the 1790s, Kentucky woodsman Daniel Boone began betting his fellow marksmen as to who could "bark off" the most squirrels. So abundant were squirrels at the time, many hunters welcomed the challenge rather than simply shooting the little critters. Also known as "squirrel barking," hunters would kill squirrels by aiming at a piece of nearby bark. The object of the game was to see who could "bark off" the most squirrels in an allotted time. Naturalist John Audubon was an eyewitness: "Judge to my surprise, when I perceived that the ball had hit the piece of the bark immediately beneath the squirrel, and shivered into splinters, the concussion produced by which had killed the animal, and sent it whirling through the air, as if it had been blown up by explosion of a powder magazine."[3]

Frontier life in colonial Kentucky necessitated that inhabitants be skillful marksmen. This in conjunction with a penchant for gambling and Boone's popularity, led to the temporary, widespread emulation of squirrel barking within the region. So rampant was the practice, Audubon wrote that gambling on squirrel barking was taking place "on every tree around us." The practice proved so popular that Kentucky newspapers published regular columns detailing the outcomes of contests. In 1796, the *Kentucky Gazette* reported that one hunting party alone killed thousands of squirrels in a single day.[4]

See also: FADS.

BATAVIA SHIPWRECK

Western Coast of Australia: 1629

On June 3, 1629, the newly-built Dutch East Indiaman *Batavia*,[5] with 270 crew and passengers aboard and a fortune in cargo, seven months into her journey from Amsterdam to Java, ran ashore on Houtman's Abrolhos, a group of barren and uninhabited coral islands off the west coast of Australia. Most survived the wreck and managed to get ashore onto the islands. Separated into two main groups, the survivors managed to make a provisional lifestyle while a small party set off in a longboat to fetch help from distant Dutch settlements.[6]

What qualifies the event for inclusion in this Encyclopedia is the remarkable contrast in the behavior of the two main parties of survivors. On one island, a well-regulated community was created; it was orderly and made the best of the situation. On the other, a charismatic psychopath set up a mini-tyranny, which slaughtered scores of innocent people and subjugated the rest to fearful afflictions including torture, rape, and enforced killing. These contrasting reactions to an extreme situation provide a classic instance of how exceptional behavior can arise when individuals find themselves freed from the restraints customarily imposed by society.

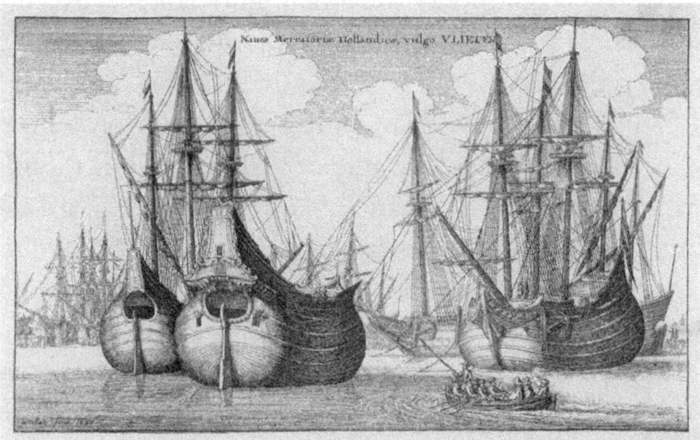

Engraving of Dutch trading vessels similar to the Batavia. (Wenzel Hollar engraving)

CONTEXT: This was a period of intense colonization, and the Dutch had overtaken the Portuguese in their near-monopoly of far eastern trade, chiefly in spices that played an important part in the diet of the time. Huge fortunes were made from this extremely lucrative trade by the Dutch merchants, but the wealth was dearly bought. Living conditions in the colonies were awful, added to the continual menace from the native population who might at any moment renege on the fragile trade agreements. Consequently, those who embarked on ships such as the *Batavia* were likely to be adventurers, greedy and even desperate; many had failed in their own country and were looking to recoup their fortunes. With them traveled soldiers sent to protect the settlements and officials to administer them. These, too, were not of the highest quality. The ship's complement of the *Batavia* was, consequently, a mixed bunch, many drawn from the least trustworthy strata of society. In a critical situation, anything might be expected from them. The situation was aggravated by the fact that the *Batavia* was known to be carrying a vast fortune in money and treasure, the wherewithal for the purchase of goods, bribery of natives, and so on.

Even while the journey was in progress, plans to seize the ship were being worked out by some of those on board, including the ship's captain, who was not the most senior person on board. Ultimate authority was held by Pelsaert, the official of the Dutch East India Company, which had commissioned the ship, planned the expedition, and provided the treasure. Whether this plotting would have come to anything can only be conjectured, because the ship was wrecked before any steps could be taken. Pelsaert was well aware, though, that some kind of conspiracy was afoot.

The wreck took place off the western coast of Australia, when the ship ran aground on some islands whose very existence was not known; indeed, Australia itself was known only as a great land mass to the east. Navigation at this period was a precarious art, particularly as regards longitude. Estimating currents and winds was so uncertain that it was quite usual for ships to find themselves off-course by many hundreds of kilometers.

The *Batavia* hit the coral reefs traveling at full speed, and it was immediately evident that even by jettisoning the valuable cargo there was no hope of saving the ship. Most of the crew and passengers got ashore, to find themselves on a barren coral island, uninhabited and devoid of fauna, with only minimal vegetation and no fresh water except from rain. The supplies salvaged from the wreck were quickly near-exhausted, and sea birds, fish, and sea lions were the only source of food.

There was no way the survivors could escape from the islands. Their only hope lay in rescue, and for this it was necessary to seek help from the Dutch settlements to the north, entailing a dangerous 3,500 km journey in an open longboat that had survived the wreck. So four days after the shipwreck, Pelsaert set off with the captain, a picked crew, and some favored passengers. As for those who remained – some two hundred – they could only wait and hope, surviving as best they could.

After the departure of Pelseart and the captain, the most senior among the survivors was Jeronimus Cornelisz, a recently appointed official of the East India Company. Apart from the authority due to his official rank, he was intelligent and persuasive, and was quickly accepted as leader. Some knew, and many others suspected, that he had been one of those plotting to mutiny and seize the ship, but that was forgotten now. To begin with, he managed affairs efficiently, but even as he did so, he marked out and gathered round him a group of men who were prepared to do as he told them without questioning. Several of them were men who had earlier shown the will to take part in the mutiny.

It was soon evident that the barren island, known as Batavia's Graveyard, could not support two hundred or so survivors, so Cornelisz set himself to reduce the population. First, parties were taken to explore the other islands, which could be seen close by. By this means, three separate settlements were created, which were hardly in contact or communication with one another, since the only boats were those at Batavia's Graveyard. In fact, Cornelisz knew that there was very little prospect for these other settlements; there was no reason to suppose that the other islands were any better furnished than his own, and he expected that, without even the meager resources retrieved from the wreck, which he had retained on his island, the exiles would soon die for lack of food and water.

In this he was fortunately mistaken. One group of twenty soldiers and sailors found themselves on a larger island, where after several days searching, located plentiful fresh water and indigenous fauna in the form of small wallabies to supplement the sea-birds and fish which otherwise were the only source of food. One of their number, a common soldier named Wiebbe Hayes, though having no official rank, soon emerged as a natural leader and organized the party efficiently. Forty-five others were marooned on an island named Seals' Island, and they too managed to achieve a precarious existence for a while.

This still left 130 on Batavia's Graveyard, and Cornelisz set himself to further reduce their number. It soon became clear that he was prepared to go to any lengths to achieve this. In the light of what was to come, his first step was a modest one: he found cause to execute three men for alleged crimes. Since they were plausibly guilty, the population accepted their deaths.

His next move was more secretive. Men whom Cornelisz suspected would not willingly submit to his rule were taken by boat, three or four at a time, ostensibly to explore other islands. Once out of sight, however, they were seized, bound hand and foot, and thrown into the water, where they were held under till they drowned. When the boats returned without them, it was presumed they had joined groups on other islands.

The survivors on Hayes' Island (as it became

known), when they found water, lit fires as arranged to signal the discovery. They expected that a party from the main group would come to join them. Cornelisz, however, did nothing, perhaps hoping that despite finding water they would not survive. But the signals had been seen by the party on Seals' Island, who set off on improvised rafts to Hayes' Island. They were seen by Cornelisz, who was unwilling to allow other groups to grow beyond his control. So he sent a boat to intercept them, brought them to Batavia's Graveyard, where all, children included, were promptly executed as traitors. The women were thrown into the sea where their heavy clothing caused them to drown.

Those on the island witnessed this horrific act, and though he justified his action by labeling them traitors, it was evident that this was nothing short of cold-blooded murder. However, enfeebled and confused by their situation, the others were powerless to intervene. Cornelisz's henchmen were not only the strongest men on the island – apart from anything else, they were better fed – but they possessed all the weapons. From this time on, any excuse – or none – would suffice for killing. Three more were executed on trumped-up accusations of theft, but often, no justification whatever was offered. To test the loyalty of one follower, Cornelisz, after inviting a married couple into his tent, ordered him to go and strangle their six-year-old child; willing or reluctant, the man did so, knowing that if he refused – or even hesitated – he himself would be killed.

Next, on the grounds that they were "useless mouths," he ordered that all those in the sick tent should be killed. Watched by his comrades, one of his followers went in and cut their throats one by one. Eleven were murdered on the first occasion, four more followed shortly. The remaining survivors realized that, from now on, to fall sick was to be summarily executed.

By such means, by July 14, less than six weeks after the wreck, nearly 50 of those on Batavia's Graveyard had been disposed of. This still left some 90, half of whom were either members of Cornelisz' gang of killers or men who, to save their own skins, had professed loyalty to him. His followers had *carte blanche* to do as they liked. They enjoyed better food – cask meat salvaged from the wreck rather than sea birds and sea lions; they drank wine and spirits instead of rainwater. They wore better clothes and helped themselves to anything they wanted. Possessing all the weapons, and the only serviceable boats, the others were powerless against them. Moreover, they were inspired with the hope of enjoying the spoils of the treasure salvaged from the wreck – enough to make every one of them wealthy for life. This gave them an additional reason for getting rid of the remaining survivors, who might prove dangerous witnesses in the future. They became ruthless killers; one, Jan Hendricxsz killed at least 17, Lenert van Os killed twelve.

Furthermore, while the earlier killings had been justified in some way, however speciously, they now became increasingly capricious. Some, indeed, bore all the appearance of killing for killing's sake. A particularly horrific killing comprised the family of the *predikant*, a priest traveling out to the colonies with his family. His wife and eight of his children were slaughtered before his eyes on no pretext whatever. He alone was spared, perhaps because some primitive fear led the killers to be chary of murdering a priest, and an adolescent daughter was taken by one of the men. Helpless, powerless, there was nothing the priest could do to save his family.

Cornelisz himself did not take part in the killing. His one personal attempt at murder was botched. A young mother had bravely kept her baby alive throughout the ordeals of the wreck, and its cries could be heard throughout the community. Cornelisz sent for the woman and offered her medicine to relieve its discomfort: it was in fact poison. The infant did not die, merely became sicker than ever. Cornelisz sent one of his followers to strangle the child, then another to kill the mother also.

By now, he had in one way or another brought about the deaths of more than a hundred persons. All the "useless mouths" had been eliminated. Those still spared were artisans whose services were useful to the community, but even their number was being reduced by further killings. One of the nastiest episodes occurred when Cornelisz decided that a boy net-mender could be dispensed with. A cabin boy, who was anxious to prove himself a man, begged to be allowed to do the killing but was refused because he was not strong enough. "When he was not allowed to cut off the head of the aforesaid youngster, Jan wept."

Unless they were pregnant, the females were spared. Some found protectors among the killers. Seven others were reserved for "common service" and subjected to periodic rape. The one woman of gentle rank resisted as long as she dared but eventually to save her life succumbed to share Cornelisz' bed, knowing that death was the alternative.

Cornelisz had not forgotten the survivors on the other islands. Though he could hope that they would eventually die of hunger, thirst, or some other cause, they were still a potential threat. He had already killed half the population of nearby Seals' Island; now he sent his men to deal with those remaining, most of them cabin boys and other youngsters. They were systematically hunted down. There were few hiding places, and all were caught in the course of time, and systematically killed. Those who were wounded were dragged to the shore and held under water till they drowned. Only a handful succeeded in escaping to Hayes' Island.

That island too presented a threat. Cornelisz realized that if he were to survive, the other community would have to be subjugated before a rescue ship arrived. So he ordered an expedition. Since his party had all the weapons, and controlled the most able of the men, he expected an easy victory.

By now, however, Hayes and his forty-odd companions had been well informed of the brutality and butchery on Batavia's Graveyard. One man who had been left for dead by Cornelisz' men had managed to steal a raft and make his way to Hayes' Island, and in all five groups had joined him, crossing the six or seven kilometers of water on home-made rafts or swimming behind wooden planks. They knew, too, that Cornelisz had slaughtered the entire population of Seals' Island, and knew that he could not afford to leave them in peace. Doubtless he would try to arrange a peaceful take-over, but Hayes knew better than to trust any offer of negotiation, sure that Cornelisz would kill them all if he possibly could. He prepared to defend his island with improvised defenses and homemade weapons.

When the first party of mutineers came, towards the end of July, Hayes was well prepared for them, even though the attackers possessed all the firearms and pikes. Rightly suspecting that treachery underlay their offers of peaceful co-operation, he refused to negotiate. Then, when twenty of Cornelisz' men tried to attack with force, they were beaten off. A second attack also failed. Desperate, Cornelisz came in person to make a third attempt; his supporters were killed and he himself was taken prisoner.

Spared for the time being on account of his position, Cornelisz was kept in isolation in a limestone pit where he was put to work plucking seabirds – an ignominious change of fortune for the self-appointed tyrant.

Meanwhile Pelaert and his companions had successfully completed their open-boat voyage to the Dutch Indies, reaching Java in less than a month. As soon as possible, a ship was dispatched to the Abrolhos, to rescue the people of the Batavia, if any survived, and if possible retrieve the treasure. As soon as the vessel was sighted, a boat from Hayes' Island went out to meet it. There, for the first time, Pelsaert learnt what had had happened during his absence.

Normally, Pelsaert would have taken Cornelisz back to the colony for justice. But he judged the danger to a small sailing ship of the prisoners, a band of desperate murderers who would stop at nothing, was too great a risk to take when it was a matter of safeguarding the other survivors. So he proceeded to carry out justice on the spot. Cornelisz and his leading henchmen were tried and found guilty; they were executed then and there. The lesser criminals were taken back to the colonies, where they too were tried and punished.

COMMENT: The survivors of the wreck, subjected to shortages of food and water, exposure to the elements, sickness, lack of familiar comforts, over and above the uncertainty of eventual rescue, were subjected to stresses that might excuse any exceptional behavior. Yet none, it seems, manifested among the survivors on Hayes' Island. The appalling contrast with the behavior of those on Batavia's Graveyard came about thanks to a number of interrelated circumstances, first and foremost being the fatal accident that among them was a psychopathic personality with the ability to impose his will on his companions.

There was a crucial difference between the parties on the two islands. Those that Cornelisz sent away to Hayes' Island were men he did not expect to be loyal to him, soldiers and sailors who, however rough by nature, were accustomed to discipline and to make the best of their circumstances. By contrast, those he kept with him included men he could rely on, chosen for their unscrupulous character, and consequently the most likely to behave as they did. Nevertheless, the willingness of his followers to abandon so completely the normal standards of social behavior is hard to explain without taking into account the fatal chance that among them was an individual whose anti-social tendencies had hitherto been held in check but were given free rein by the accidental circumstance of the shipwreck. What resulted was a reciprocal process of mutual self-advantage. By his position, Cornelisz was able to authorize his followers to indulge their greed and selfishness, justifying theft, rape, and murder. And the more they acted in obedience to his command, the more his right to command was reinforced. Had Cornelisz been drowned in the wreck, it is likely that the butchery of Batavia's Graveyard would not have taken place.

BATTERED WIFE SYNDROME

North America and Europe: 19th and 20th centuries

During the 20th century, psychiatrists identified a condition known as Battered Wife Syndrome whereby a husband periodically assaulted his wife, who would remain in the relationship due to low self-esteem and fear. While husbands are also battered, the word "wife" was used to identify the syndrome as the overwhelming majority of spousal assaults are on females. It is a testament to the power of social and cultural conditioning that until the early 1970s, Western social scientists, guided by popular opinion, contended that those being battered were at fault. From the time that psychoanalyst Sigmund Freud (1856-1939) began treating the problem of female assault by their partners, to the mid-1970s, victims were treated by health professionals as being to blame for "provoking" assaults and abuse.[7] During the mid-1970s, the focus finally shifted to the assailant. This fallacy was common at the time that Freud first highlighted the "disorder" in the latter 19th century. Consider the following excerpt from *The Physical Constitution of Battered Wives* (1886) by Furneaux Jordan, who was a respected instructor in physiology at Queens's College in Birmingham, England: "... I noticed that a very large proportion of the women who came into the hospital suffering from injuries inflicted by their husbands had ... peculiarities ... common to all of them. ...The friends and neighbours usually let it be known that these unfortunate women ... had sharp tongues ... and an unfailing – unfailing by repetition – supply of irritating topics on which to exercise them."[8]

BBC GHOSTWATCH SCARE

Great Britain: October 31, 1992

At 9:25 p.m. on Halloween, the British Broadcasting Corporation aired a 90-minute television program called *Ghostwatch*, billed as a live investigation of a "real" haunted house in England. The show discussed the supposed saga of Pam Early who, it was claimed, lived in a haunted house in Northolt, Middlesex, along with her two daughters. The family said they had been harassed by a variety of paranormal happenings.

An estimated 11 million people watched the program, which prompted 20,000 phone calls to BBC offices, most protesting the hoax. The program was successful in fooling many viewers because, not only was it realistic, but it featured prominent English TV presenters Michael Parkinson and Mike Smith who were shown "live" at the studio, while two "reporters" were said to be at the house. In reality, the show had been filmed several months earlier.

The show began with Michael Parkinson setting a serious tone: "The programme you are about to watch is a unique investigation of the supernatural. It contains materials which some viewers may find disturbing." The tension built gradually, and after a series of spooky sounds in the house, it appears that they have caught one of the girls – Susanne – creating the noises. Within a short time, it becomes evident that there really is a ghost as scratch marks suddenly and spontaneously appear on Susanne's face. Events quickly deteriorate as the girls start speaking a strange language, and Parkinson appears to be possessed by an evil spirit.

Scriptwriter Stephen Volk said the show was designed to fool the audience into thinking they were watching a "live" drama – but only for the first few minutes. "We thought that people might be puzzled for two, perhaps five minutes, but then they would surely 'get' it, and enjoy it for what it was – a drama. The curious thing about *Ghostwatch* is that while one part of the audience didn't buy it for a second, another part believed it was real from beginning to end."[9]

Ghostwatch triggered a firestorm of controversy, and was blamed for needlessly provoking traumatic reactions in youngsters across the country. *The British Medical Journal* published two separate reports of post-traumatic stress syndrome as a direct result of the program – both occurring in ten-year-old boys. Symptoms included sleeping difficulties, nightmares, anxiety attacks, depression, separation anxiety, memory problems, and intrusive thoughts and flashbacks about the show. One of the boys had to be hospitalized for eight weeks, though both eventually recovered.[10]

One young man's suicide was also linked to the show. Five days after airing, 18-year-old Martin Denham hung himself. Denham was intellectually impaired. The suicide note read: "Mother do not be upset. If there is [sic] ghosts I will now be one and I will always be with you as one. Love Martin."[11]

BBC RADIO HOAX

England and Ireland: January 1926

"London is in the grip of a terrible uprising of anarchists and unemployed ... Police and troops are powerless to hold the rioting mobs in check, and they have begun what promises to be a long reign of terror." Listeners across England and Ireland were stunned by the news that their government could topple at any moment in a bloody uprising by disgruntled workers. In truth, the streets were calm; people had been listening to a radio play. For the first time in history, thousands of listeners to the new medium of radio had been frightened by the use of realistic bulletins during what seemed to be a regular program. It would not be the last.

When most people think of infamous radio hoaxes, one event springs to mind: the Halloween Eve "Martian invasion" broadcast that frightened more than one million Americans in 1938. Surprisingly, the first major radio hoax took place twelve years earlier in England and Ireland. On January 16, 1926, Father Ronald Knox was conducting his regular Saturday evening radio show of comedy and entertainment. One of the segments was a twelve-minute skit on a fictitious riot in London. The drama broadcast reports of chaos and mob rule in central London resulting from a populist revolt. The idea for the skit hadn't come from thin air; at the time the British government was under great pressure from unions. In fact, one of the biggest strikes in the country's history was just months away—the British General Strike of May 3 to 12. This landmark event rocked the government to its foundations as more than one and a half million workers from various occupations took to the streets in protest in an unsuccessful bid to improve wages and working conditions for coal miners. In the lead-up to this standoff, there was great unease across the country as the Russian Revolution of 1917 was still fresh in people's minds. The stage was set for a mass delusion using the airwaves on a subject that seemed plausible: worker rebellion.

Knox was a famous Catholic priest and successful novelist who was respected and trusted by his audience. The episode began when he announced that he was about to present a skit on a London riot. Many listeners either missed the disclaimer, or weren't paying attention, and thought they were hearing actual reports of their government under siege.

The skit began with what appeared to be a typical discussion of eighteenth century literature, which was interrupted by reports that an unruly mob of unemployed workers was rampaging through London. Listeners heard that the Traffic Minister had been lynched from a pole, while trench mortars were used to destroy the famous clock, Big Ben. Announcer: "The Clock Tower, 320-feet in height, has just fallen to the ground, together with the famous clock, Big Ben...Fresh reports, which have just come to hand, announce that the crowd have secured the person of Mr. Wotherspoon, the Minister of Traffic, who was attempting to make his escape in disguise. He has now been hanged from a lamp-post in Vauxhall Bridge Road."[12]

Reaction was swift: jittery callers flooded newspaper and BBC offices to learn more details and try to ascertain if relatives living in the area were safe. Police and other government agencies were also deluged with calls. Some wanted to know if King George and Queen Mary had been safely evacuated. Several concerned citizens phoned the British Admiralty to inquire when the fleet was going to sail up the Thames and launch a counterattack by landing troops.[13] The BBC broadcast announcements throughout the evening, telling listeners that the show was just that, but at the time many people did not have radios and heard the news secondhand from neighbors who did. The countryside was rife with rumors about the "rioting in London." Suspicions turned to fear the next morning when newspaper deliveries were delayed owing to snowy weather. Many residents took this delay "as confirmation that the worst had happened."[14]

Parts of the Knox skit were highly realistic, including the sounds of shrieks from the crowd, explosions rumbling in the distance, and buildings crumbling. In fairness to Father Knox, anyone listening closely to the sarcastic content should have realized that the program was a skit, yet the BBC was such an authoritative and respected institution, and the drama's tone so serious, that it managed to fool many listeners. Another factor in creating the scare was the use of what sounded like regular programming, interspersed by "live" news reports. The following sequence is typical: "That concludes the news bulletin for the moment; you will now be connected with the band at the Savoy Hotel [gramophone dance music can be heard]... London calling..."[15]

Ironically, a few days after the broadcast, *The New York Times* published an editorial titled: "We Are Safe From Such Jesting," arguing that Americans were immune from similar scares. Later that year, in March 1926, a journalist for the *Syracuse Herald* in Western New York, interviewed the manager of one of America's top radio stations, asking if he thought a similar scare could happen in the United States. The executive, who was not identified, gave an arrogant response. "As for spreading a hoax of any kind, mischievous or otherwise, such a thing would never be thought of. It is beyond the bounds of possibility."[16] Authorities failed to anticipate what would happen in 1938, when Orson Welles would cause an even greater uproar with his broadcast of a Martian invasion that was heard across the entire continental United States, and history would repeat itself on a grander scale.

See also: ORSON WELLES MARTIAN PANIC

BEKHTEREV, VLADIMIR MIKHAILOVICH

A pioneering Russian psychiatrist and neurologist with a special interest in mass suggestion, Bekhterev was born January 20, 1857, in Sorali, Russia, and died in December 1927.[17] His book *Suggestion and its Role in Social Life* (1908) focuses on the destructive consequences of mass suggestion in Russia, Europe, and the United States.[18] A prominent neurological authority, his name is associated with several medical conditions

Russian neurologist Vladimir Mikhailovich Bekhterev, wearing uniform reflecting his status in the Soviet medical hierarchy. (Photo by K. Bulla in the Meledin collection)

including Bechterev's Nucleus, Bekhterev's Disease, and Bekhterev's Reflex. At age 70 in early December 1927, Bekhterev was summoned to the Kremlin by Joseph Stalin for advice, at which time he died suddenly and his body was quickly cremated. Rumors persist that the frank and outspoken Bekhterev was executed after diagnosing Stalin as exhibiting "grave paranoia."[19]
See also: RUSSIAN SECTS.

BEQUETTE, BILL

A former reporter for the *East Oregonian* newspaper, Bequette is credited with indirectly coining the term "flying saucer." On June 25, 1947, he interviewed pilot Kenneth Arnold who described seeing crescent-shaped objects moving "like a saucer would if you skipped it across the water." Bequette misunderstood Arnold's description, reporting to the Associated Press that the objects were "saucer-like." The term 'flying saucer' quickly entered the popular lexicon, the collective product of newspaper writers.[20]

Kenneth Arnold described the objects he saw as crescent-shaped.

CONTEXT: Bequette placed Arnold's story on the front page due to concerns that the sighting may have been of a foreign secret weapon. The incident coincided with the onset of the Cold War between the U.S. and Soviet Union.[21]

BERSERK SCHOOL

Miami, Florida: October 25, 1979

It has to be one of the most bizarre chapters in the history of American education: high school students and teachers suddenly going on a wild rampage through their school. Here is how Associated Press reporter Stephen C. Smith began his description of what happened: "Police say it was hysteria brought on by a hypnosis demonstration. Some students say it was demons. A school official calls it a political dirty trick...police say something sent students and teachers rampaging through a military school...smashing windows, ripping a door from its frame and screaming they were possessed by spirits."

The outbreak began after a 10th grade science project on hypnosis, during which several students passed out. Some students said there had been recent discussions on the supernatural at the school. The Academy's president and owner, Evaristo Marina, blamed the behaviors on the media swarm at the school, who arrived after several students passed out. "When you are a child and the fire, police, health and media people all come at once you can go crazy. It's like yelling fire in a crowded theater." Many of the school's 300 students were from Latin America. While no one was seriously injured, one student was treated for lacerations after shattering a window.

Fire and rescue personnel were first dispatched to Miami Aerospace Academy in Little Havana, after receiving a report that a child was unconscious. Fire official Dan LaMay said that several students collapsed from apparent hysteria, while others "flaked out all over the place." LaMay said: "I saw three girls. They had fainted ... There was some screaming about 'bloody Mary' and more screaming." LaMay believes that the students were induced to enter their frenzied state "by the sight of others who became hysterical – it was like a domino effect." When police were summoned to quell the chaos, they were shocked at what they saw. Officer Harry Cunnill said he found "people yelling and screaming they were possessed."[22]

BEZPOPOVTZY SECT

Russia: 1896

Bezpopovtzy means "without priests," and this group of sects was one of innumerable do-it-yourself breakaways from the Russian Orthodox Church, which believed in attaining a higher spiritual consciousness directly with God rather than via priestly middlemen. There were twenty or more sub-sects, including the DOUKHOBORS. The Bezpopovtzy sect was founded at Tiraspol, an industrial town on the Dniester estuary, 80 km from Odessa. Their history prefigures that of the HEAVEN'S GATE community in 20th century America, except that its 25 voluntary victims chose a more unpleasant way to go.[23 24]

CONTEXT: Tension between the *raskolniki* sects (see RUSSIAN SECTS) and the authorities was part of the Russian way of life, rising when the tsar or his ministers felt the need to take a stronger line or when a particular concern, such as anti-militarism in the case of the Doukhobors, became a topical issue. In the case of the Bezpopovtzy sect, the issue was the Russian government's census of 1896. This provoked a crisis in the Tiraspol community, for the counting of citizens was seen by them as an act of human presumption, since none but God can know the number of his creation.

The community had been founded by a man named Kovalev, whose grand-daughter, the widowed Kovaleva, now presided over the community. The leading spirit at this time, though, was an intelligent and energetic woman named Vitalia, and it was she who issued orders to the community; her devoted follower Fedor Kovalev, son of Kovaleva, saw that they were carried out.

When the census officials knocked at the door of the community farm, they were handed a note which stated that the inhabitants' beliefs would not permit them to cooperate with the census, and that they would sooner die. Why they chose to respond in quite so forthright a manner is not easy to understand without taking into account that they were in a state of constant stress due to the lifestyle their religion imposed on them. In farm buildings converted into hermitages, more or less isolated from the everyday world, they lived a life of constant prayer and fasting. In such an environment, halfway out of the world already, the notion of voluntary suicide may not have seemed so great a step. As with JONESTOWN and Heaven's Gate, it does not appear that any persuasion was required: suggestion sufficed.

That suggestion undoubtedly stemmed from Vitalia. "Impelled at first by an intense conviction, she confirmed herself in her role by auto-suggestion. The general atmosphere which prevailed in her hermitage while the censorship was being carried out; the continual discussion and debate about it; the fears and alarms which everyone felt as to the consequences; all this tended first to bring to their minds, and then to fix it there, the idea of burying themselves alive or to fast till death."[25]

As Advent approached, the disquiet of the solitary hermits and the villagers at Ternov increased. "Families spent entire nights keeping watch, uttering useless complaints, each one adding to the terror of the others. Women, children, Kovalev himself, when they asked Vitalia for guidance, returned with the assurance that the coming of the Antichrist was imminent, bringing with him war: each page of the census, bearing their name, was equivalent to branding them with a red-hot iron and condemning them to everlasting damnation." The only way to escape this fate, according to Vitalia, was for them all to starve themselves to death.

The ones who were most impressed by Vitalia's teachings were the adolescents, and in particular a 13-year-old girl named Praskovia, daughter of a certain Nazar Fomine. Admitted to Vitalia's intimate confidence, she seldom left her side and served as messenger between her and the villagers, playing a more important role than most of the adults. It was she who, indicating the prison, said, "That's where they will slit our throats, that's where they will make martyrs of us! We'll do better to bury ourselves in the ditch." To which her mother Domna agreed, saying,

"Well said, Paschenka, and I'll be with you!"

About halfway through December, after a sleepless night in Fomine's house, discussion raged as to what should be done with the children if, as they expected, the adults should all be imprisoned for failing to comply with the census. Since it was already decided that, in prison, the grown-ups would starve themselves to death, it was feared that the authorities would then proceed to baptize the children into the Orthodox faith, which was for them the worst of all possible fates. At this point Aniouschka, Kovalev's wife, clutching her youngest child in her arms, cried out that she would never allow her child to be condemned to eternal damnation, she would rather descend with her into the tomb! When Vitalia was told of this, she exclaimed, "Yes, she has the right idea! She is a prophet! She is lucky, she will be the first to be saved!" and she reproached Kovalev for his doubts, telling him that if he didn't support his wife in her intention, he would be responsible for sending three souls to damnation – his wife and their two children. Impressed by Vitalia, he was convinced when his mother backed her up; from this point on, he went along with the women's plan. Now the whole group was obsessed with the idea of the communal tomb, and all of them – most forcefully the women – repeated the vow:

> "To the ditch!" Vitalia urged them on as they made the final preparations, insisting that the Antichrist was already here, that the end of the world would take place not in a matter of years but in the course of two or three days. She insisted that anyone who hesitated would be trading the hope of eternal happiness for a few days of earthly existence. Everyone who heard her was thrown into utter despair. Moreover, she did not hide from them the fact that the death they were contemplating would be a terrible one – they would have to endure from one to three days of suffering in the tomb, before they entered into the celestial palace. But two or three days of torment, she exclaimed, they are nothing in comparison with eternal suffering! Can you count the raindrops as they fall? Well, as many drops of rain as there are, so many years of suffering there will be in hell. Better two or three days in the "ditch" and then the kingdom of heaven.

On the night of December 23, the designated first batch of victims congregated in the Fomine farmhouse. By eight o'clock that evening, the house was already full of people. In the cellar below, Fomine, Kovalev, and a laborer named Kravtzov pierced a hole in the cellar wall and dug into the soil beyond. After several hours, they had dug out a small room large enough that a person could lie sideways or lengthways – 3.60m wide and 1.40m high, but vaulted so that one could stand upright at the highest point. As the tomb neared completion, some of the women came down from upstairs to give a hand; all were in a state of great agitation.

Before the final moment, the victims put on their funeral clothes. A service of the dead was sung by all. Then Aniouschka and her two children were the first to enter.

> Such was the profound sadness, the continual praying, the preoccupations of mutual farewells, and finally the ecstasy which tonight had overtaken all who were resolved to bury themselves, such was the precipitation which had urged on all the operations, that not a moment's respite was left to the unfortunate victims; they were unable to arrest the course of events even for a minute to reflect on the horror of the hours which lay ahead of them.. After Aniouschka and her two daughters, one at the breast, the other three years old, it was the turn of Nazar Fomine with his wife and 13-year-old Praskovia; Kravtzov, the labourer; Elisabeth Denissov, sister of Vitalia; and Katchkov, the father of young Polia. Carrying torches, sacred books and icons, they entered the tomb. The children were laid on a sheepskin. The wall was closed behind them, and they sat down by candlelight. It is probable that they died before the last of the candles died, for when the tomb was opened the following April, deep burns were found on the table on which they had been placed.[26]

So clandestinely was it done, that residents in other nearby farms knew nothing of it, and the authorities had no suspicion when, on February 3, 1897, Vitalia and six others were arrested for non-compliance with the census and placed in preventive detention at Tiraspol. There, they refused all food and drink, stating that their religion would not permit them to eat food they had not earned by work. After several days of fasting, they were released by the Procurer but placed under house arrest in the Kovalev farm.

While in prison, they saw a meat-slicing device in the prison kitchen, and a cook jokingly told them this had been sent from St Petersburg to cut up the bodies of recalcitrant prisoners. This strengthened the Bezpopovtzy in their belief that the authorities planned to execute them, and they returned more determined than ever to avoid this fate.

No sooner were they back home than they began preparations for a second group of victims, and on February 12, four old women were buried alive. Two further groups followed: on February 27, Vitalia, after supervising the interment of the others, was a member of the last party, giving orders to the last. Even if she can be held largely responsible for the entire episode, one must admire her strength of mind that enabled her to watch others go to their deaths before following them herself.

In total, twenty-four people chose to die in this way. The only survivor was Kovalev himself, who had buried all the others and who alone knew what had happened. A simple-minded but not unintelligent man, he had sincerely carried out Vitalia's orders. He was sent to repent to a monastery where he is thought to have converted to the Orthodox Church.

COMMENT: While it is clear that Vitalia was the moving spirit behind this whole terrible episode, it could not have happened if the entire community had not shared her exalted state. They believed fervently in the teachings of their leaders and were genuinely alarmed by events which seemed to be forcing them into a situation where they had to choose between a voluntary death with the hope of salvation, or to wait for the authorities to do their worst and thus incur eternal damnation. Driven by their beliefs into this impasse, they chose to die.

BIRD FLU PANDEMIC SCARE

Worldwide: 2005

During 2005, a global fear ensued over the likelihood that an outbreak of Avian Influenza could create a global pandemic similar to or greater than the "Spanish Flu" of 1918-1919, which killed an estimated 50 million people after spreading from birds to humans. Avian Flu is nicknamed Bird Flu, as it occurs naturally in birds and to a lesser extent in other animals. Each year there are seasonal epidemics of influenza caused by sub-strains of flu viruses that are already in circulation among the population. Pandemics are rare occurrences that take place when a new flu subtype emerges – one that has never circulated among humans or has not circulated for a long period, resulting in illness and death rates much higher than seasonal influenza.[27]

The World Health Organization reports that between December 2003 and December 2005, at least 100 cases of Bird Flu were reported in humans, most after having contact with infected birds, usually poultry. While the transmission from birds to humans is rare, all flu viruses have the capacity to mutate into a new virus that spreads from person to person. Humans are particularly vulnerable to strains of Avian Flu as there is "little or no immune protection against them."[28] There were three flu pandemics during the 20th century: the "Spanish Flu" after World War I, the "Asian Flu" of 1957-58, and the "Hong Kong Flu" of 1968-69, the latter two outbreaks being mild. The global death toll from the Asian Flu was about one million, while the Hong Kong Flu killed between one and four million.

Several prominent scientists criticized the sudden fear of a Bird Flu pandemic in 2005 as alarmist, arguing that the likelihood of a pandemic was no greater than in previous years. Historian Paul Mickle cautioned that there have been similar past flu scares that failed to materialize, such as the 1976 Swine Flu panic. At the time, leading health officials in the United States warned of an impending pandemic that could kill one million Americans. The great Swine Flu scare began on February 6, 1976, when 19-year-old Army private David Lewis died at Fort Dix, New Jersey of what health officials would later identify as a highly communicable variation of the Swine Flu. Studies would later reveal that 500 other recruits at Fort Dix had contracted the same flu strain, but none died or were even seriously ill. Private Lewis was the only official American death from Swine Flu, but ironically, dozens died from side effects during the vaccination program. The inoculations began on March 1, with the goal of injecting all 220 million Americans. The government suspended the program on December 16, after 40 million Americans had received shots. At that point, Americans feared the vaccine more than contracting the Swine Flu.[29]

Science writer Michael Fumento says that while no one can accurately predict when the next flu pandemic will occur, "there is never such a thing as helpful hysteria. And the line between informing the public and starting a panic is being crossed every day now by politicians, public health officials, and journalists."[30] The 2005 fear of Bird Flu had reached such alarmist levels that during a question and answer session on the safety of Thanksgiving turkeys and bird feeders, one American woman suggested killing all domestic birds and poisoning food along bird migration routes.[31]

A classic example of media hype surrounding the fear of Bird Flu is a Reuters headline proclaiming: "Flu Pandemic Could Kill 150 Million, U.N. Warns." The health authority cited in the story had stated that the death toll from a Bird Flu pandemic was between 5 and 150 million. Just how these figures were arrived at is unclear. Fumento says that such wildly disparate figures are tantamount to wild guesses. He blames his media colleagues for focusing on the more alarmist "experts."[32]

Fumento lists several "experts" who have helped to exaggerate the Bird Flu threat. Topping his list of "Chicken Littles" is Dr. Irwin Redlener who heads the National Center for Disaster Preparedness at Columbia University. During a nationally televised interview on September 15, 2005, Redlener made the dramatic assertion that: "We could have a billion people dying worldwide." When questioned later by Fumento, he qualified this claim by saying: "one billion ill." The same TV program introduced the topic with the chilling words: "It could kill a billion people worldwide, make ghost towns out of parts of major cities, and there is not enough medicine to fight it ... It is called the avian flu."[33]

Fumento says that no one can predict the statistical probability of a Bird Flu outbreak in any given year. He dispels the notion that pandemics strike in predictable cycles, noting that humans and sick birds have been mixing for years without triggering a pandemic. "It's practically a state secret that the discovery of H5N1 (the Bird Flu virus) in poultry dates back not to 1997 but rather to 1959, when it was identified in Scottish chickens. ...So H5N1 has been flying around the globe for over four decades and hasn't done a number on us yet. That doesn't mean it won't ever; but there's absolutely no reason to think it will pick this year or next."[34]

In October 2005, Pittsburgh microbiologist Dr. Henry Niman issued the following warning about the 2005 Bird Flu strain: "We've known about the seriousness of H5N1 mutations and different forms of the virus for some time. We've had avian flu before, but this year the situation is extremely critical for a variety of reasons, including the many different strains detected and the unusually high mortality rate for some of those strains." Dr. Henry Niman's recommendation sounds like a script from a Hollywood film: "I would stock up on antiviral medication. Besides that, devise a plan to isolate yourself with enough food and water for an extended period of time."[35]

Dr. Niman and others have expressed concern over reports that thus far Avian Flu in humans kills just over half of those they infect. This scary figure is in stark contrast to the Spanish Flu that is estimated to have had a mortality rate of between 2.5 and 5 percent. Seasonal flu kills less than one percent. While these figures may seem chilling, they are misleading. The small number of Avian Flu deaths thus far has occurred in poor countries with substandard medical systems. Further, Fumento says the 50 percent mortality rate "comes from those ill enough to require medical attention – the sickest of the sick. Our experience with normal influenza is that many who become infected have no symptoms at all, nary a sniffle."[36] Wendy Orent, author of *Plague*, concurs: "We have no idea how many people in Asia contracted H5N1, came down with a mild infection, and became immune. Research from 1992 has shown that Asian chicken farmers have antibodies to many different forms of the H protein, including H5, in their blood."[37] University of Ottawa molecular virologist Earl Brown says that it is common for chicken farmers around the world to have antibodies to various Bird Flu strains.[38]

Orent states: "Evolutionary biology tells us that the worst-case scenario – a lethal, transmissible, world-destroying flu – cannot happen, any more than Ebola or Marburg can steal out of the jungle and destroy the human race. If we have an H5N1 flu pandemic, which is certainly possible, we have no logical reason to believe it will be deadlier than the pandemics of 1957 and 1968. We do not need 'a new Manhattan Project' ...to protect us from pandemic flu. We need an inoculation to protect us from disease hysterics."

British sociologist Frank Furedi, author of *The Politics of Fear*, notes the tendency for people to expect worst-case scenarios in a world where risk-free living is an impossibility. Furedi says that politicians are partly responsible for spreading the 2005 Bird Flu fear as a way to hedge their political bets so that in the unlikely event an outbreak were to occur, they cannot be accused of having not warned us. Furedi cites statements by Great Britain's Chief Medical Officer, Sir Liam Donaldson, as illustrating his point about creating needless fear of a Bird Flu pandemic. Donaldson has warned British citizens that a Bird Flu pandemic that will kill at least 50,000 citizens is inevitable, though he doesn't know exactly when. According to Furedi, "what we are faced with today is not so much a pandemic of a deathly virus but a pandemic of fear. Sir Liam knows that when he says that a flu pandemic is inevitable he will never be proved wrong. Such an unspecific warning about the risk of an avian flu that can mutate so it can spread easily between humans could have been made by chief medical officers in 1919 or 1920 or at any time since the 1918 influenza pandemic. Sir Liam's predecessors usually had the good sense not to issue such general warnings about a catastrophe that may or may not happen."[39]

Furedi says that even if 50,000 Britains were to die of Bird Flu, estimates by the British Department of Health are that about 12,500 citizens die from the flu during a typical year. "It is estimated that during the 1989-90 epidemic around 30,000 people died from the flu. Not quite 50,000 – but near enough. Every single death is a personal tragedy. Which is why we can do without additional doom mongering. The fact that we were spared of all the current morbid apocalyptic warning meant that in 1989-90 we could deal with our losses with dignity and then get on with our lives."[40]

Dr. Marc Siegel of the New York University School of Medicine says that while the fear of Bird Flu is real, the likelihood of an outbreak in 2005 was exaggerated. "If anything is contagious right now, it's judgment clouded by fear."[41] Dr. Gary Butcher of the University of Florida's College of Veterinary Medicine, concurs with Siegel's assessment of the threat. Butcher holds a doctorate in poultry virology and specializes is avian diseases. He calls the chances for an Avian Flu pandemic, a long shot. "For it to become dangerous to humans, it has to go through a pretty significant genetic change. If you put this in perspective, it's not going to happen. For a person to be infected now, it appears that the exposure level has to be astronomical."[42]

The internet has played a major role in accelerating the bird flu scare through the actions of bloggers – "techno-agitators and armchair epidemiologists who see each new flu report or update as a call to arms, and use their blogs as a medium to inform and scare the daylights out of each other."[43] Bird Flu bloggers typically contend that the mainstream media is doing an inadequate job of communicating the serious threat from the illness and vow to get the message out.

While there is a consensus among health authorities that Bird Flu cannot be transmitted to humans by eating poultry, executives from Kentucky Fried Chicken have made contingency plans to counteract the potential spread of such misinformation. Noting that chicken sales have dropped as much as 80 percent in parts of China in response to rumors that eating chicken can spread Bird Flu, the National Chicken Council has even set up a website to address consumer concerns (avianinfluenzainfo.com). Retail sales of chicken in the United States amount to 50 billion dollars annually, as the average American consumes 90 pounds of chicken per year.[44]

BLACKTHORN BARKING MANIA

England: 1700

Several inhabitants of the village of Blackthorn were afflicted with compulsive barking, similar to that in AMOU in France, a century earlier.

CONTEXT: Blackthorn is a village in Oxfordshire, 5 km southeast of Bicester. No particular reason is known why it should have been the scene of such an outbreak.

Dr. Thomas Willis had received reports of the outbreak, which attracted considerable attention as being the first time anyone had heard sick persons barking. Wishing to see this singular affliction for himself, he visited the village in person.

> In the family that I went to see there were five girls affected by the malady which caused such a stir in the region. On arriving in the village, I heard from a considerable distance their cries, and when I entered the house where they were, I saw that they shook their heads with much violence. Their faces exhibited no sign of convulsion, except that

> they yawned very frequently. Their pulses were steady, but at the end of their attacks it became somewhat feebler. Their cries resembled not so much the noise that dogs make when they bark, as the noise they make when they howl or complain. The sounds were also more frequent than those of dogs: the subjects uttered sobs with each breath they took.
>
> There were five sisters who were affected by this malady, although they were of very different ages, for the youngest was six and the eldest about fifteen. From time to time they had restful intervals during which they could talk among themselves, and at such times they had full use of their senses. Sometimes the ailment came back all of a sudden: they began to scream as before, until their strength gave out, whereupon they fell like epileptics onto beds which had been laid for them on the floor. For a time they would sleep in a profound silence: then their spirits returned and agitated them as before, they struck their chests and other parts of their body, and tormented those around them… I say nothing except what I witnessed for myself, and without the evidence of my eyes I would not have believed anything so extraordinary. The youth of these girls, the disinterestedness of their father and mother, and their state, did not permit me to suggest any artifice on their part.[45]

A further investigation, by Friend, seeking to discover the origins of the malady, established that it was mainly confined to two families who were linked one to the other by relationships. The attacks took place in a successive manner. His diagnosis was that when the first of the girls succumbed to the need to cry out, her cries took the form of blasphemies, roarings, and whistlings. Presumably, then, those of her companions who followed her example had contracted also this other form of delirium.

COMMENT: Though we have scanty information on this incident, it is interesting that it should take place at all. The behavior of the girls seems to have closely matched that of convent hysterics in 17th century France, yet the likelihood that English children aged from 6 to 15 would have heard of these others, and if they had heard of them, would be able to simulate their actions, is surely very slight, apart from the fact that Willis did not suspect "any artifice on their part."[46]

BOARDING SCHOOL FIRE PANDEMONIUM

New York City: January 1899

One evening in a cramped New York City boarding school, two roommates "took the globes off the gas fixtures for hair curling purposes" and forgot to put them back on. A few minutes later the curtains caught fire. Both girls screamed and fainted. Hearing the commotion, a group of dorm mates ran to their aid and quickly broke down upon seeing the fire: one fainted, several just stood there weeping, and a few ran away, while the rest shouted for the only male dorm worker to do something.

He arrived to see the three unconscious girls, the others screaming, and the curtains and adjacent woodwork ablaze. He stepped over the girls and ordered everyone else from the room. As they fled, "there was an enemy in the rear. A vigorous and practical woman from Texas had been inspired to go after some water. Returning in mad haste with a pitcherful of water borne triumphantly aloft, she collided with the retreating forces at the door. The pitcher struck the leader of the retreat squarely in the face and knocked out two of her front teeth, where upon the injured girl made the fainting trio a quartet and the water carrier dropped her pitcher and went into violent hysteria." By the time the teachers got there, the fire was out.

CONTEXT: In addition to being a fascinating study of group response to fear, the girls' reactions were remarkably conditioned by the zeitgeist. At the time of the incident, it was widely believed that girls were innately susceptible to stress, to the point where many had conditioned themselves to faint in response to stressful events.[47]

BOXER RISING

China: 1899-1900

The rising of the *Yi-ho-quan* – the Boxers United in Righteousness – was a popular movement directed against the incursion of Western powers into China as missionaries and traders. Apart from the political and religious aims of the movement, it was characterized by exceptional behavior in the form of spirit possession and the ritualistic performance of shaman-like magical practices intended to confer invulnerability on its followers.[48]

CONTEXT: The rising had its origin in the densely populated flat agricultural plain of northwest China, particularly the Shandong area, where life was predominantly a precarious peasant existence of chronic poverty and instability. This was due in part to the constant threat of natural disasters ranging from flooding of the Yellow River if rains were heavy, to drought if rains were insufficient. A contemporary observer estimated that a severe natural disaster could be expected every three years. Aggravating the natural forces were man-made menaces such as oppressive landlordism and widespread banditry.

Sectarian movements, promising a measure of security in these uncertain conditions, were a chronic feature of Chinese life. Far from seeing the Boxers as an exceptional response to an exceptional situation, it is more realistic to see them as one in a persistent series of groups that lay latent beneath the surface of society, making public appearances in response to political or economic circumstances. These groups were not necessarily subversive, and many – the Boxers included – were in principle loyal to the government even though their actions often ran counter to current government policy.

The precipitating factor that led to the Boxer rising was the conduct of foreign powers that, in the later part of the 19th century, increasingly imposed their missionary and trading ventures on China with arrogance and insensitivity for Chinese ways. The foreigners most involved were the Germans, the French, and the British. The German Catholic missionaries seem to have been the most extreme in their aggressive activities, and they received firm backing from their government that, in the pursuit of its own ends, disregarded the Chinese and treated their government with contempt.

An aggravating circumstance was that any Chinese who converted to Christianity obtained the favor and protection of the European nation that had converted him. A converted Chinese merchant could, for instance, count on European support if he went to the law, thanks to the pressure the missionaries were able to exert. Inevitably, a great many conversions were opportunist, and this led to a further degree of resentment, mixing social and political motives with religious ones, which did not count for so much and would not, of themselves, have occasioned anything worse than local disputes.

There had been sporadic attacks on Christian missionaries and converts throughout the 1890s. The war against Japan aggravated matters: the Japanese were foreigners, even if they were not Christians. In November 1897, the Juye incident occurred in which two prominent German Catholic missionaries were murdered though the principal target escaped. Two vagrants were executed for the crime, which no one believed they had actually committed, but this was not enough to satisfy the Germans who used the incident as a pretext to seize the port of Jiaozhou and to demand heavy reparations. The priests, especially the one who got away, seem to have been particularly obnoxious men, popularly accused of perverting justice on behalf of Christians, inflicting harsh punishments for alleged thefts, and even of raping local women.

In 1898, nature contributed to the climate of unrest with drought leading to famine. Families sold their children or gave them away to save them. Tree-bark and weeds were scavenged for food, snails and caterpillars were hunted. Later came widespread flooding when the Yellow River burst its banks and flooded hundreds of villages on the flat plain. Millions of peasants were forced to seek refuge on high ground or migrated to other districts; crops were destroyed and the famine worsened.

These were the conditions in which the Spirit Boxers made their appearance in early 1899 in the plain of the Yellow River.

Most accessible histories of the Boxer rising were written by western historians, for whom the outrages against missionaries and diplomats were the outstanding events. The Chinese documentation is entirely from the point of view of the authorities. Consequently, the inside story of the movement has

The execution of Boxer rebels by Chinese officials.

to be constructed from hints and fragments, with no first-hand account from within the sect. However, it is clear that the Boxers were building on a long tradition of sectarian group-forming going back over centuries, and their practices were derived from earlier movements.

Staging demonstrations from village to village attracted recruits. The appeal was to males only. The rituals were in the martial arts tradition, which was prevalent throughout China, combined with shaman-like practices involving spirit possession. A large element of magic was involved, almost entirely directed towards investing the initiate with invulnerability – to begin with against swords and suchlike weapons, but also against guns.

One observer declared that "the emissaries who went about to stir up the interest of people pretended to be possessed of a demon,"[49] but it is not evident that the claim was a deliberate pretence. The belief in spirits, and their ability to possess individuals, was endemic in China, and the claims may have been perfectly sincere. It is, in any case, important to realize that to a Chinese native and to a Western observer the word "demon" had quite different connotations. While to, say, a 17th century Christian nun possession by a demon was invariably a malevolent process, for a 19th century Chinese it was a voluntary act, performed as in voodoo for the purpose of acquiring magic abilities such as curing sickness and obtaining valuable attributes such as protection whether from the accidents of nature or from the animosity of ill-wishers. It is perhaps better to use the term "divinity," benevolent or malevolent as the case might be.

The possessing entity was invoked from a vast panoply of available divinities, each with its own attributes and history. They were well known to all through folklore, story-telling, and popular drama. The young men seeking initiation would gather in the center of a village where an altar had been erected. The individual seeking divine aid would make promises and, in return, would be given magic paper charms by the master. He would then recite a spell of *shang-fa* (receiving the magic), calling upon the divinity whose attributes he wished to share, then go into a trance, convulsing his body and panting until he felt himself possessed by the god, whose behavior he would unconsciously mimic. At first he would fall to the ground as though sleeping. Then he would rise, panting and frothing at the mouth. Picking up his weapons, he would start to dance wildly, fists flying and feet kicking, until the magic – and his strength – were exhausted. Even the most proficient could not maintain this for more than a few hours, yet he was supposed to practice this three times a day.

Such a process is typical of shamanism, of course, but with the Boxers what was otherwise an individual process was something available to all, not the privileged few but anyone who possessed the appropriate dedication. Each and everyone could invest himself with the powers of a divinity, but simple and easily suggestible minds took most easily to the process. In the absence of any first-hand account by one who went through the process, the state of mind of the initiate can only be guessed, but dedication and study were evidently requisite, driven by a sense of need and with a fervor directed at future well-being. A magistrate in 1899 reported a Boxer as claiming that his whole body had acquired *qi-gong* (literally, breath efficacy) with the result that it could resist spears and guns.[50] When, as inevitably happened, a supposedly invulnerable Boxer was injured or wounded, this must be because he hadn't performed the rituals correctly. Interestingly enough, the western forces found that the Boxers did indeed manifest something approaching invulnerability. A Naval officer on a British warship observed: "They work themselves into an extreme state of hypnotism and certainly do not for the moment feel body wounds. We have all learned that they take a tremendous lot of killing and I myself put four man-stopping revolver bullets into one man before he dropped."[51]

The Boxers were an all-male organization, vegetarian as regards diet, vowing not only never to steal but not even to covet wealth. They were strictly celibate, swearing to avoid "pollution by women." In 1900, a division of female adolescents was created, the *Hong-deng-shao* (Red Lantern Shining), and took part in the attacks on foreigners.

Conflict gradually escalated as the numbers increased. Individual Christians were attacked, then groups, then whole Christian villages, then the missionaries, then rich people irrespective of religion. Anything associated with the foreigners became an object of their violence: railway tracks were pulled up, telegraph wires were tugged down, and shops selling western goods were looted. They started fires in the belief that they would burn only Christian houses. Unfortunately the magic was not always successful, and in June 1900 several thousand buildings and 1,800 shops in Peking (Beijing) were destroyed when a deliberately-set fire spread from Christian to non-Christian homes. This may have been attributable to the presence of females, for the Boxers recognized that their magic would not work against women's "pollution." At this point the female division – the Red Lantern Shining – was deployed: "The Red Lanterns are all girls and young women, so they do not fear dirty things."[52]

Though often termed a "rebellion," the Boxer rising was nothing of the sort. It was not directed against the government, to which it was loyal. However, the government, powerless by comparison with the foreign powers installed in the cities, had no choice but to collaborate with the foreign powers in suppressing the movement. When the foreign legations had withstood the 55-day siege, the rising was effectively suppressed. The follow-up was conducted with appalling brutality, and exorbitant claims for reparations were made by the very powers whose initial arrogance and greed had brought about the uprising in the first place.

COMMENT: The Boxers were convinced that the gods were on their side, and would empower them to drive out the hated foreigners from their shore. The rituals they performed gave them the attributes of gods: the magic bestowed on them made them invulnerable. Without this belief in their own powers, they would never have banded together and embarked on their campaign. Thus it would be wrong to equate this with revolutions in France, Russia, or Latin American countries. The Boxer rising was an essentially Chinese affair and should not be judged out of context or by the criteria of other cultures.

BRANDENBURG MASS POSSESSION

Germany: 1594

In the Mark of Brandenburg, Germany, reports say that more than 160 persons were possessed by demons, enabling them to reveal marvelous things, including information about matters they could not possibly have known. Among these people, several were seen who had died shortly before. They went about urging people to repent, to give up their decadent clothes, announcing the judgment of god was at hand. They had demons who had taken up residence in their guts, and though they were demons, they were forced whether they liked it or not to exhort people to give up their evil ways and return to the true path. These demoniacs railed furiously against the pastors of the church wherever they went, and spoke of apparitions of good and evil angels. The devil showed himself in various guises when the sermon was preached in the temple. He flew in the air with a whistling noise.[53]

Unfortunately, information about this outbreak is meager. Evidently it was related to the prevalent witch-mania, but community outbreaks such as this were rare. The AMOU barking mania, for example, took quite a different form though the origin of both outbreaks was assuredly the general stress and unease of the witch-hunt, the fear of demon attack, and of accusations by the inquisitors or their collaborators. See also: CONVENT HYSTERIA, DEMON POSSESSION.

BRECHIN RUNNING & JUMPING FITS

Scotland: 1763-1764

In 1763 a number of children in a Scottish village were afflicted by a mysterious disorder, which matched, not only in its physical symptoms but also in the behaviors it induced, outbreaks occurring in other countries and at other periods, notably AMSTERDAM in the Netherlands and MORZINE in France.

CONTEXT: Although this outbreak occurred at a time when John Wesley was traveling the country conducting the Methodist revival, there does not seem to be any obvious link, and indeed there was no ostensible religious aspect to the Brechin outbreak.

Wesley gives a first-hand account of the disorder

in his Journal.[54]

Mr Ogilvie, the minister of the parish, informed us that a strange disorder had appeared in his parish between thirty and forty years ago; but that nothing of the kind had been known there since till some time in September last [1763]. A boy was then taken ill, and so continues still. In the end of January [1764], or beginning of February, many other children were taken, chiefly girls, and a few grown persons. They begin with an involuntary shaking of the hands and feet. Then their lips are convulsed; next their tongue, which seems to cleave to the roof of the mouth. Then the eyes are set, staring terribly, and the whole face variously distorted. Presently they start up, and jump ten, fifteen or twenty times together, straight upward two three or more feet [i.e. about 1 metre] from the ground. Then they start forward, and run with amazing swiftness two, three, or five hundred yards [200-500 metres]. Frequently they run up, like a cat, to the top of a house, and jump on the ridge of it as on the ground. But wherever they are, they never fall or miss their footing at all. After they have run and jumped for some time, they drop down as dead. When they come to themselves, they usually tell when and where they shall be taken again, frequently how often and where they shall jump, and to what places they shall run.

I asked, "Are any of them near?" He said, "Yes, at those houses." We walked thither without delay. One of them was four years and half old, the other about eighteen. The child, we found, had had three or four fits that day, running and jumping like the rest, and in particular leaping many times from a high table to the ground without the least hurt. The young woman was the only person of them all who used to keep her senses during the fit. In answer to many questions, she said, "I first feel a pain in my left foot, then in my head; then my hands and feet shake, and I cannot speak; and quickly I begin to jump and run." While we were talking, she cried out, "Oh, I have a pain in my foot; it is in my hand; it is here at the bending of my arm! Oh, my head! my head! my head!" Immediately her arms were stretched out, and were as an iron bar. I could not bend one of her fingers, and her body was bent backward, the lower part remaining quite erect, while her back formed exactly a half-circle, her head hanging even with her hips. I was going to catch her, but one said, "Sir, you may let her alone, for they never fall." But I defy all mankind to account for her not falling when the trunk of her body hung in that manner.

In many circumstances this case goes far beyond the famous one mentioned by Boerhaave; particularly in their telling before when and how they should be taken again. Whoever can account for this upon natural principles has my free leave: I cannot. I therefore believe, if this be in part a natural distemper, there is something preternatural too. Yet, supposing this, I can easily conceive Satan will so disguise his part therein that we cannot precisely determine which part of the disorder is natural and which preternatural.

COMMENT: We should not be tempted to read too much into the fact that Wesley reports this incident. He was always interested in curious happenings that he encountered in the course of his travels, not necessarily related to his own activities. Nevertheless he must have been particularly interested in the Brechin outbreak, insofar as it compared with the behavior of his more enthusiastic followers (see METHODISM IN BRITAIN).

What is remarkable about this otherwise relatively minor outbreak is that the children, who could hardly have known of other outbreaks of the kind, behaved in ways so similar to those observed elsewhere. The physical symptoms are not so surprising, as these could be the natural consequences of whatever disorder was afflicting them. But the similarity of the children's behavior – the running, jumping and climbing – seems to be more than a neurological response and perhaps demands a psychological explanation.

It would be interesting to know the nature of the disorder Mr. Ogilvie reports as having occurred some forty years earlier. He would hardly have mentioned it unless it had been of a similar character. On the other hand, a gap of forty years shows that this was not a chronic affliction in the neighborhood. See entry RUNNING AND CLIMBING for a broader discussion of this topic.

BRIGAND GREAT FEAR

France: 1789

In July, the month when the storming of the Bastille marked the outbreak of the French Revolution, a panic spread through most of provincial France that the common people were menaced by armies of brigands ravaging the country with the blessing of the anti-revolutionary nobility. Though closely connected to the events of the Revolution, it was based on unfounded rumors that reflected popular concerns and preconceptions. In the words of its leading historian, Georges Lefebvre, *"le peuple se faisait peur à lui-même"* [the people scared themselves].[55]

CONTEXT: The year 1789 was one in which the long-rumbling social and economic troubles of France finally erupted into revolution. The fact that these troubles had been building up for many years gave rise to a general feeling that "something" would have to happen to set things right. Political events, whether negative, such as the sacking of the popular minister Necker, or positive, such as the summoning of the *Etats-Genéraux* (an approximation to a representative government), heightened expectation, providing fuel for extravagant hopes on the one hand, profound fears on the other.

Throughout the early months of the year there had

been unrest in all parts of France, which sometimes amounted to something like a peasants' revolt. Politically, it was a period of great uncertainty. There were indications that reforms were on their way, but also signs that the authorities were determined to maintain the status quo. In such a situation, the populace did not know whom to trust or believe. The summoning of the *Etats-Genéraux*, the national parliament that incorporated the "Third Estate" – the working population – as well as the privileged aristocracy and the tax-free clergy, was hailed as a crucial first step, but the court and aristocracy seemed determined to prevent it from having a real say in the running of affairs. At the same time, the less enlightened aristocrats failed to appreciate the necessity for change and insisted on asserting their hereditary rights and privileges.

It is hardly an exaggeration to say that most of France was in a state of anarchy. Local authorities maintained order to a greater or lesser degree, but central authority was virtually non-existent. Widespread food shortages led to hoarding and black market activities. Riots and demonstrations, largely associated with the shortage and high price of food, had been sporadic hitherto, but through the spring and summer of 1789 they became widespread. Markets were disrupted, grain stores were pillaged, suspected hoarders attacked. These outbreaks reached panic level just before harvest time, when farmers feared that their crops might be stolen by gangs of strangers, perhaps directed by the aristocrats.

An important contributory factor was the difficulty of propagating information of any kind, let alone accurate information, outside the towns. Lefebvre speaks of "le grand silence provincial."[56] News from Paris could take three days to reach major provincial cities; remote towns and villages learnt of events with an even greater delay, and often in partial or imperfect form so that exaggeration and misinterpretation could easily occur. It wasn't easy to distinguish true information from false. A jeweler reported that at Charolles a brigand had been arrested with the great sum of 740 louis (gold coins) in his possession, and that at Bourbon-Lancy eighty strangers had come to pillage the town; the first of these statements was true, the second false, but the populace found both equally believable.[57]

The suspicions of the populace were directed primarily against the aristocracy, who had ignored their hardships for generations. The refusal of the governing class to relinquish their privileges and accept a more equitable tax system made them the natural enemy of the workingman. There were widespread fears of a conspiracy against the common people. So, one incident among hundreds, when on July 18/19 a soldier of the Garde Française, who had gone over to the side of the people, was taken ill in a Paris street, it was quickly rumored that the regiment had been poisoned by order of the aristocrats.[58] The populace believed the nobility capable of going to any lengths to retain their privileges and lands.

Consequently people were ready to believe stories that told them they had the right to attack châteaux throughout the country. Sometimes it was the *Etats-Genéraux* that authorized such attacks, sometimes even the King himself. Noblemen were forced to renounce the rights they had hitherto enjoyed – not just land ownership but feudal rights, and fishing and hunting rights. There was a widespread popular belief that henceforward they would not have to pay rents, tithes, and taxes. Whenever possible, aristocrats and their lawyers were forced to hand over documents concerning the ownership of land, taxes, and the like, generally to be destroyed. Also targeted were administrative buildings, lawyers' offices, abbeys, and monasteries (for the Church was a major landowner, not only exempt from taxation but receiving taxes in the form of compulsory tithes).

The fact that so many such incidents took place more or less simultaneously across the country led to the suspicion that there was some kind of conspiracy underlying them, expressed by one commentator on July 31, 1789: "The alarms which spread throughout the kingdom on almost the same day seem to be the consequence of a well-oiled plot, the result of disastrous projects intended to set all France alight. For one cannot imagine that, on the same day and almost at the same instant, almost everywhere the tocsin would peal out, unless agents who had been deliberately put in place had given the alarm."[59]

Yet in fact there was no evidence of conspiracy. Though the same kinds of incident were happening throughout the country, there was no concerted uprising. These were spontaneous incidents arising naturally from the rumors.

But the gentry in their châteaux were not the only danger perceived by the populace. An even more immediate menace threatened them: gangs of brigands roaming the countryside. This fear was not entirely without foundation. The catastrophic economic condition of the country meant that there were many people out of work and seeking it, leading to a large migrant population; these wanderers were easily perceived as a menace and interpreted as "brigands." No doubt some of them resorted to robbery, so the occasional existence of thieves was an undoubted fact. However, they were nowhere near so many or as organized as popular fears supposed.

Thus for either of the adversaries feared by the populace, aristocrats and brigands, there existed a rational basis in fact, however distorted. What was not rational was that the two fears came to be linked in the popular imagination. In principle the aims of brigands and those of aristocrats were diametrically opposed, but now the threatened peasant reasoned that the two might make common cause against him. Bands of brigands, paid or sponsored by the aristocracy, became the principal fear. Sometimes they were supposed to be simply vagrants, hired by the nobles to make trouble; other sources accused them of hiring mercenaries. Newspapers reported that 60,000 brigands were being imported from Italy, England, and Germany by the forces opposing the Revolution, in order to stir up trouble and put a spoke in the wheels of the *Etats-Genéraux*.[60]

A contrary rumor suggested that the fear of brigandage was encouraged – instigated, even – by the revolutionary leaders to encourage the peasant population to take up arms. But there was no evidence of this and in any case it was hardly necessary. When the peasants took up arms, they did so in simple self-defense of what they supposed to be their interests. Provincial towns and villages, feeling themselves threatened, and uneasily aware that they were not likely to get much in the way of protection from a government with other things to think about, began to form their own militias, until almost every community in France had provided itself with a defensive force of some kind. The effect was to increase the sense of emergency; people reasoned that if the municipality formed a militia to confront the danger, it was a sure sign that a real danger existed.

Such beliefs sprang up spontaneously and more or less simultaneously in many (though not all) parts of the country. Once generated, they spread and snowballed. Even those who did not believe in the conspiracy theory felt it best to be on their guard. One authority passed on a warning to another with these comments: "All in all, one can't trust a word these brigands say. But since, as the saying goes, there is no smoke without fire, and after what has been happening in Paris, it could be that such a confederacy has been formed. Consequently everyone is closing ranks and mounting guards by day and night. So you would do well to follow our example."[61]

As harvest-time approached, as militias were formed, as châteaux were burnt and nobles fled, the unease was transformed into panic. Warned to expect an enemy, it was not long before an enemy was sighted. A distant light, an unexpected sound were seen as signs; dust on a distant road suggested a column on the march. Now, any band of men would be seen as brigands to be repelled. Hundreds of incidents took place such as occurred at Maisières-la-Grande-Paroisse, near Troyes. On July 24, it was alleged that a group of brigands had been seen entering a wood: "The alarm bell was sounded and three thousand men gathered to give chase to these supposed brigands. But they turned out to be no more than a herd of cattle…"[62]

In almost every part of France such panic responses were taking place. At Sarlat, in the Dordogne, a curé ran to report that Limeuil had been burnt down during the night. At Luersac, the vicar of Saint-Cyr-le-Champagne hastened to announce that brigands were preying upon his village. Neither was true. A community that believed itself menaced would send a messenger to warn others, and on his way he would spread the news, giving the impression that the attack was actually in progress.

The pattern was much the same everywhere. On receiving a warning, the community would sound the tocsin: the bells would ring out across the countryside, often for hours on end, spreading the alarm. Women, imagining themselves already raped, then massacred with their children, amidst a village in flames, wept and wailed, fleeing into the woods or along the roads, with a provision of foodstuffs and a few necessities seized at hazard. The men might follow, after burying their most precious possessions and setting the livestock loose, but more likely they would join the other men, assembling at the call of the curé or some official. They would make their plans to defend the community, perhaps directed by the lord of the manor or an old soldier. All armed themselves as best they could; not all possessed firearms, but scythes and sickles would do. Sentinels were placed, the entrance to the village or a bridge would be barricaded, and parties were sent out to reconnoiter. After sunset there would be night patrols, and everyone remained on the qui vive. In larger communities, it was a real mobilization, with food, weapons, and ammunition being collected in a central place. Church services were held, imploring heaven's protection.[63]

When attack seemed imminent, there were dramatic scenes. A villager was overheard saying to his wife and children: "I will never see you again!" Another was just setting off with the militia, sounding fife and drum, when a messenger arrived, crying that the brigands were approaching. While women shrieked and children howled, the men prepared to defend their community. A mother spilt the soup she was serving, lamenting, "Oh, my poor children, you will all have your throats cut!"

> Anything could set off the alarm. A band went to protect a village, and saw lights burning on the other side of the village. They found it was another band of defenders come from another district. At Clermont-en-Beauvais, as happened elsewhere, a troop of peasants marching against the enemy was mistaken for the enemy themselves. The lights from chalk furnaces, bonfires of weeds, even the reflection of the setting sun in windows, gave alarm that brigands were setting fire to crops or grain stores. A monsieur de Tersac, hearing that the enemy was approaching with drums and trumpets, decided to look for himself: he found a group of harvesters, working by moonlight, singing at their work…[64]

Wilder rumors spread. The bandits were poisoning wells and springs. A well-dressed lady was mistaken for Marie Antoinette in person, and the Emperor of Austria (her father) was seen coming to her rescue. The English landed in force on the coast of Aquitaine: from the south came the Spanish, from the east the Piedmontese. Even Poles were seen, landing from the sea, for had not Louis XV married a Polish queen? It was thought the royal princes were leading bands of brigands: in Artois, the Prince de Condé was heading 40,000 men; the Comte d'Artois, brother to the king, led a similar number made up partly of Swedes and Norwegians, partly of convicts taken from prisons or from the galleys.

A few skeptical voices were raised. At Saint-Clair an officer on leave, on being told that four thousand brigands were at Lauzerte, commented: "I find it hard to believe anyone actually counted them." But even those who doubted the accounts felt obliged to act in case they might be true, rather than run the risk of ignoring a real threat. When an architect named Jacquet was reproached for reporting that forty thousand Spaniards were nearby, he was advised to keep quiet or he would be laughed at. But he didn't keep quiet, and he wasn't laughed at; people believed his story.

After the crops had been harvested, after so many false alarms, when not one village had had to defend itself against a band of brigands, the Great Fear died down of its own accord. But the embers were not wholly extinguished. At harvest time the following year, the same fears recurred, though on a much smaller scale, and even in later years they surged up here and there.

COMMENT: The most easily understood type of rumor is one that offers, first, a rational basis in reality; second, circumstances favorable to distortion of that reality; and third, conditions favorable to the propagation of that distortion. All three factors can be readily discerned in *la grande peur* of 1789. Lefebvre sums up the matter thus:

> The Great Fear had the same causes as earlier alarms, and the most effective of these were economic and social, causes which had always alarmed the countryfolk and which the crisis of 1789 merely intensified. So why did this fear, instead of remaining local, spread? Why was the parish, alerted to danger, in such a hurry to summon help? It was because, by the end of July, the sense of insecurity seemed more threatening than ever, and because on the eve of harvest people were more disturbed than they had ever been. The supposed aristocratic conspiracy, and the news that brigands were leaving Paris and the big towns, made the most harmless vagabond a figure of fear. Above all, the brigands had come to be perceived as instruments of the enemies of the Third Estate.[65]

The idea that two enemies should join forces, although their interests are ostensibly diametrically opposed, occurs in other contexts. There is an interesting comparison with the 20th century conspiracy theory, instanced for example in Williamson & McCoy, that "the force behind the 'International Bankers' who constitute the 'Hidden Empire' stems from Communist Russia" – that is to say, Western democracy is threatened by a coalition between the Jewish financial interests and the Soviet Union – again, two forces who one would normally suppose to be diametrically opposed.[66]

BRITISH MILITARY FAINTING EPIDEMICS

United Kingdom: 1951

A series of mass fainting incidents occurred among British military conscripts (Army, Navy, and Air Force) while standing in formation. The largest episode involved 100 female members of the Navy. Dr. Edward Sharpey-Schafer attributed the incidents to standing at rigid attention, which he said results in blood rushing to the feet and a sudden plunge in blood pressure. He said that as blood accumulates in the lower half of the body, it "diminishes the supply of blood to the brain."[67] Why should such outbreaks occur when lines of soldiers standing at attention happen all the time?

BROOKLYN BRIDGE PANIC

New York: May 30, 1883

Shortly after the Brooklyn Bridge was opened to the public for toll service (1 cent for people, 2 cents for sheep) on May 24, 1883, an unidentified pedestrian began to shout that the structure was collapsing. In the ensuing panic to get off, 12 people walking on the promenade were trampled to death by the fleeing crowd, and 40 others were hurt.[68] The bridge opened amid misgivings as to its safety, in the wake of several highly publicized bridge disasters earlier in the century. For instance, 25 years earlier, soldiers were marching across a bridge in Algers, France, when it collapsed, killing 200.[69]

The Brooklyn Bridge spans the East River. (Illustration by A. Tissandier in Les Voies Ferrees)

BUFFALO MARTIAN SCARES

Western New York: 1968 and 1971

Between 11 p.m. and 12:15 a.m. on Thursday, October 31, and Friday, November 1, 1968, popular Buffalo, New York, radio station WKBW, with a powerful 50,000 watt clear channel signal, aired a localized adaptation of the original script used in the 1938 *War of the Worlds* panic broadcast, triggering a regional scare. Despite heavy advance publicity, once the drama began, it was difficult to distinguish from regular programming. Buffalo radio historian Robert Koshinski describes it as remarkably realistic: "They played records, did commercials, played their jingles, and covered the story like they regularly covered stories."[70] The station's morning disc jockey, John Zach, said the quality was comparable to the Orson Welles drama.[71]

Program Director Jefferson Kaye wrote the script, which closely paralleled the 1938 version for the first few minutes, after which it became a local event set in modern-day Buffalo. Kaye and engineer Dan Kriegler intended to produce and direct the drama and had received permission to use the original 1938 script, but abandoned the idea when practice readings with staff announcers were lackluster and contrived as the language was dated and sounded phony.[72] Faced with the prospect of airing an incredulous broadcast bordering on the ridiculous, Kaye "spiced it up" by having the Martians land on the Buffalo island suburb of Grand Isle, a few miles south of Niagara Falls, letting staffers from WKBW radio and its television affiliate play themselves and report on the "Martian attack" as if it was a live event. The reporters (Jim Fagan, Don Lancer, Joe Downey, Sandy Beach and Irv Weinstein) were given basic details with which to ad-lib around and sent to mobile units in the parking lot, transmitting their reports back to the station, giving it an authentic, live quality.[73]

The pre-recorded production began at 11 o'clock when reporter Dan Neaverth signed off and aired a disclaimer. Joseph Downey then read the news, ending "with a seemingly innocent final story about mysterious explosions on Mars"[74] including an interview with an astronomer from local Niagara University.[75] Near the start of the program, disc jockey Sandy Beach did a typical show with occasional low-key news break-ins by Downey about reports of Martian explosions. Suddenly in the middle of the song *White Room* by Cream, a bulletin aired describing a major traffic jam on Grand Isle. During the recording, Kriegler and Kaye were at the station adding live sound effects.[76]

More music and commercials, then the Beatles' *Hey Jude* was interrupted by a bulletin about an explosion on Grand Isle. "It's been reported that a large meteor has smashed into the ground along the East River Road on Grand Island, setting off a series of fires. Several lives have been lost." Listeners were told that KB news director Don Lancer and other reporters were being immediately dispatched to the scene.[77] "To some this dramatic interruption was so real that they forgot they were listening to a Halloween program and thought an actual disaster had occurred," Koshinski said.[78]

Later, another reporter, said: "My God, Don, there's something crawling out of the top of this thing..."[79] "...The crowd's moving back... I'm moving back...I'm getting out of here...I tried to talk to the professor into moving out but he managed to talk some army lieutenant into approaching this thing... He and the professor are now approaching...Good God almighty Abraham, that was some sort of a red beam. They've burst into flames, the professor and the lieutenant. We're getting out of here. We've got to get out of here. The red beam, it's going off all over the place picking off people...one by one. There are bodies all over the place."[80]

Shortly after midnight, WKBW-TV reporter Irv Weinstein was zapped by a Martian heat ray, leaving Kaye alone to close the drama "by walking out onto Main Street and succumbing to the poison gas that had been wiping out the population of Buffalo all night. What followed was a somber close by Dan Neaverth that stuck to the original H.G Wells novel explaining that the Martians themselves were wiped out by the common germ despite their victory over humanity."[81]

Halfway into the program, the phone began ringing continuously with worried callers. Realizing the anxiety he was generating, Kaye asked his engineer to open his microphone to interrupt the broadcast to remind listeners of its imaginary nature. Kaye says that Kriegler steadfastly refused to do so, as the drama had been sold and he was worried over the possible loss of advertising revenue.[82] Kaye threatened to pull the reel off the wall and was finally given control of the microphone to make a 30-second disclaimer.[83] Buffalo police logged over 200 calls from concerned listeners, the majority from outside the immediate Buffalo area. People called from as far east as Bangor, Maine, and as far west as San Francisco, nearly 3,000 miles away. The station's signal can often be heard across much of the continental United States at night when its transmission carries farther.[84]

When the drama ended, and after taking savage verbal abuse from scores of irate callers, Kaye slid his resignation letter under the General Manager's door, certain that he would be fired in the morning. However, public and station officials were supportive, given their ample notification of the event, and the FCC offered no criticism of the episode.[85] Kaye recalls that after realizing they had been listening to a play, several people went to the station to complain. "One man came to the back door with a baseball bat and was threatening to bash my brains out." He thought the broadcast was real and headed toward Grand Isle to see the devastation, and in his haste, crashed his car into a utility pole.[86] Upon hearing reports of the "attack" in Canada, Canadian National Guard units were deployed along the major border crossings including the Queenstown Bridge, Rainbow Bridge, and Peace Bridge.[87]

While professionally done, the play was not without flaws that went unnoticed by many. "Several times reporters react to aircraft and explosions before the audience actually hears them because director Dan Kriegler had to add sound affects [sic] live to save tape generations. TV newsman John Irving describes Grand Island Bridge explosion and has survivors being swept away by rapids some half-mile away just seconds later."[88]

COMMENTS: The episode is enlightening in that station personnel took extreme measures to ensure that listeners would *not* be frightened, although Kaye admits anticipating that a few people might be fooled.[89] Fearing a possible FCC backlash if the play backfired, WKBW undertook an unprecedented advertising campaign for 21 days before the broadcast, airing frequent, daily promotions for the play, and mailing out hundreds of press releases to every police, fire, and emergency service agency within their eight-county area of primary listenership in Western New York and adjacent southwestern Ontario, Canada.[90] On the day of the broadcast, the *Buffalo Evening News* even published a regular radio and TV news column by J. Don Schlaerth, telling readers of the airing of the program at 11pm, complete with photos of WKBW's Dan Neaverth and DJ Don Wade.[91] The failure of many listeners to discern the fictitious nature of the drama highlights the dangers of airing radio dramas that include live bulletins, and realistic, localized scenarios with familiar personalities. Kaye says he learned a lesson from the event: "You should never over estimate the sophistication of your audience."[92] A modified version of the Kaye production aired in 1971, and despite repeated promotions as to the time and date, a few concerned listeners called the station and emergency services.[93]

See also: ORSON WELLES MARTIAN PANIC (1938), MARTIAN INVASION SCARE (1939), CHILEAN MARTIAN INVASION PANIC (1944), ECUADOR MARTIAN INVASION PANIC (1949), RHODE ISLAND MARTIAN INVASION PANIC (1974), PORTUGUESE MARTIAN INVASION PANICS (1988 and 1998).

BUS BEDLAM

Near Peoria, Illinois: May 2000

A bus load of fourth graders were returning home from a field trip when the driver was suddenly forced to pull over and evacuate the vehicle after eight of about a dozen occupants began gasping for breath. The incident began when two of the children, both asthmatics, became preoccupied with their breathing after leaving their inhalers home. Shortly after, six more were gulping for breath. The children quickly recovered in the hospital.[94]

Sources

1. Newill, Bill (1976). "Sickness Delays Return of Band." *Bucks County Courier Times*, (Pennsylvania), August 31, p. 1.

2. "Hysteria is Suggested for Students' Illness." *Daily Intelligencer* (Doylestown, Pennsylvania), November 28, 1978, p. 19.

3. Hoffmann, Frank W., and Bailey, William G. (1991). *Sports and Recreation Fads*. New York: Harrington Park Press, p. 33.

4. Hoffmann and Bailey, op cit., p. 33.

5. "Indiaman" refers to a ship trading with India, especially large vessels belonging to the East India Company.

6. All the details in this entry are taken from Dash, Mike (2002). *Batavia's Graveyard: The Story of the Mad Heretic Who Led History's Bloodiest Mutiny*. New York: Crown.

7. Caplan, P. (1985). *The Myth of Women's Masochism*. New York: Dutton; Davis, L. (1987). "Battered Women: The Transformation of a Social Problem." *Social Work* 32:306-311, see p. 306; Kutchins, H., and Kirk, S. A. (1989). "DSM-III-R: The Conflict Over New Psychiatric Diagnoses." *Health and Social Work* 14(2):91-101. See p. 91.

8. Skultans, V. (1975). *Madness and Morals: Ideas on Insanity in the Nineteenth Century*. London: Routledge & Kegan Paul.

9. Volk, Stephen (2003). "Faking It: Ghostwatch." *Fortean Times* 166 (January).

10. Simons, D., and Silveira, W.R. (1994). "Post-Traumatic Stress Disorder in Children after Television Programmes." *British Medical Journal* 308(6925):389-390.

11. Rickard, Robert (1992). "Whatever Possessed Parkinson?" *The Fortean Times* 67:38-41.

12. Knox, Ronald A. (1930). *Essays in Satire*. New York: E.P. Dutton, p. 285.

13. "The Radio Joke that England Took Seriously." *Syracuse Herald*, March 23, 1926.

14. "Britain is Alarmed by Burlesque Radio 'News' of Revolt in London and Bombing of Commons." *New York Times*, January 18, 1926, p. 3.

15. Knox (1930). op cit., p. 281.

16. "The Radio Joke that England Took Seriously." op cit.

17. "Vladimir Mikhailovich Bekhterev." http://www.whonamedit.com/doctor.cfm/905.html. Accessed February 22, 2003.

18. Bekhterev, Vladimir Mikhailovich. (1998)[1908] *Suggestion and its Role in Social Life*, third edition (translated from Russian by Tzvetanka Dobreva-Martinova). New Brunswick, New Jersey: Transaction Publishers.

19. "Vladimir Mikhailovich Bekhterev." op cit.

20. Bartholomew, Robert E. (2000). "From Airships to Flying Saucers: Oregon's Place in the Evolution of UFO Lore." *Oregon Historical Quarterly* 101(2):192-213. See pages 202-204.
21. Bartholomew, op cit., p. 206-207.
22. Smith, Stephen C. (1979). "Students Go Berserk at Miami School." *Austin Herald* (Minnesota), October 27, 1979, p. 3.
23. Blunt, John Henry (1874). *Dictionary of Sects, Heresies, Ecclesiastical Parties and Schools of Religious Thought*. London: Oxford & Cambridge, p. 73.
24. Bechterew, W.M. [Now spelled Bekhterev, V M] (1910). *La Suggestion*. [Translated from Russian by D. P. Keraval]. Paris: Boulangé, p. 99; Stchoukine, Ivan (1903). *Le Suicide Collectif dans le Raskol Russe*. Paris: Floury, p. 120. Except where otherwise indicated, all details are from these accounts.
25. Bechterew, op cit., p. 100.
26. Bechterew, op cit., p. 101, citing the account by Professor Sikorski in the Russian journal *Questions de médecine neuropsychique,* 1897.
27. "Key Facts About Pandemic Influenza," October 17, 2005, accessed December 4, 2005 at http://www.cdc.gov/flu/pandemic/keyfacts.htm. This site is operated by the Centers for Disease Control and Prevention, 1600 Clifton Road, Atlanta, GA.
28. "Key Facts About Avian Influenza (Bird Flu) and Avian Influenza A (H5N1) Virus," November 25, 2005, op cit.
29. Fumento, Michael (2005). "Fuss and Feathers Pandemic Panic over the Avian Flu." *The Weekly Standard*, November 21, accessed December 3, 2005 at: http://www.fumento.com/ disease/flu2005. html; Mickle, Paul (no date). "1976: Fear of a Great Plague." *The Trentonian*, accessed December 12, 2005 at: http://www.capitalcentury.com/1976.html.
30. Fumento, op cit.
31. Fumento, op cit.
32. Fumento, op cit.
33. Fumento, op cit.
34. Fumento, op cit.
35. Szymanski, Greg (2005). "Avian Flu May Come to America." Issue #41, October 10 issue of *The American Free Press*, 645 Pennsylvania Avenue SE, Suite 100 Washington, D.C. 20003, accessed December 12, 2005 at: http://www.americanfreepress.net/html/avian_flu.html.
36. Fumento, Michael (2005). op cit.
37. Orent, Wendy (2005). "We'll Survive the Bird Flu. Chicken Little." (September 12), accessed December 12, 2005 at: http://www.tnr.com/docprint.mhtml?i=20050912&s=orent0 91205.
38. Orent, op cit.
39. Furedi, Frank (2005). "Bird Flu Prophets of Doom Spread Nothing but Needless Alarm." *Daily Express* (18 October). Accessed December 12, 2005 at: http://www.frankfuredi.com/articles/ birdflu-20051018.shtml.
40. Furedi, Frank, op cit.
41. Chun, Diane (2005). "Experts Dismiss Scare Over Bird Flu." *The Gainesville Sun* (Florida), November 1, 2005, accessed December 12, 2005 at: http://www.gainesville.com/ apps/pbcs.dll/article?AID=/20051101/LOCAL/51101021/1078/news.
42. Chun, op cit.
43. Lianne, George, Karin, Marley, Danylo, Hawaleshka (2005). "Forget Sars, West Nile, Ebola and Avian Flu The Real Epidemic is Fear." *Maclean's*, October 3, volume 118, issue 40: 46-52.
44. MacArthur, Kate, and Thompson, Stephanie (2005). "KFC Preps Bird-Flu Fear Plan." *Advertising Age* (November 7), Vol. 76, Issue 45.
45. Calmeil, L.F. (1845). *De la Folie, Consideree Sous le Point de vue Pathologique, Philosophique, Historique et Judiciaire* [On the Crowd, Considerations on the Point of Pathology, Philosophy, History and Justice]. Paris: Baillere, volume 2, p. 310 citing Thomas Willis.
46. Note that Dupouy says they were in a convent, but Calmeil although seemingly drawing on the same source does not mention this, and Dr. Willis could hardly fail to mention it if this was the case.
47. "Just a Curtain Fire." *The North Adams Evening Transcript*, February 2, 1899, citing *The New York Sun*.
48. Esherick, Joseph W. (1987). *The Origins of the Boxer Uprising*. Berkeley: University of California Press. This is the major source for this entry.
49. Henry Porter quoted by Esherick, op cit., p. 217.
50. Esherick, op cit., p. 225.
51. Sublieutenant M. E. Cochrane of *HMS Centurion*, cited in Elliott, Paul (1995). *Warrior Cults*. London: Blandford, p. 173.
52. Esherick, Joseph W. (1987). *The Origins of the Boxer Uprising*. Berkeley: University of California Press, p. 297.
53. Calmeil, L.F. (1845). *De la Folie, Consideree Sous le Point de vue Pathologique, Philosophique, Historique et Judiciaire* [On the Crowd, Considerations on the Point of Pathology, Philosophy, History and Justice]. Paris: Baillere, Volume 1, p. 296, citing Goulard, *Histoires Admirables*, Volume 1, p. 60.
54. Wesley, John (1909). *The Journal of the Rev. John Wesley*. Edited by Nehemiah Curnock. London: Culley 1909 [Originally published at various dates from 1739 onwards], Volume 5, p. 73.
55. Lefebvre, Georges (1988). *La Grande Peur de 1789*. Paris: Armand Colin, p. 146.
56. Lefebvre, op cit., p. 96.
57. Lefebvre, op cit., p. 95.
58. Lefebvre, op cit., p. 84.
59. Maupetit, cited by Lefebvre, op cit., p. 160.
60. Lefebvre, op cit., p. 85.
61. Lefebvre, op cit., p. 176.
62. *Journal de Troyes*, cited by Lefebvre, op cit., p. 167.
63. Lefebvre, op cit., p. 179.
64. Lefebvre, op cit., p. 189.
65. Lefebvre, op cit., p. 169.
66. Williamson, George Hunt, and McCoy, John (1958). *UFOs Confidential!* Corpus Christi, Texas: Essene Press, p. 43.
67. "Medical Expert Solves Case of Swooning King's Army." *The Hopewell Herald* (Hopewell, New Jersey), August 22, 1951, p. 4.
68. See *Life Magazine*, May 24, 1954, accessed January 5, 2005 at: http://www.endex.com/gf/buildings/bbridge/bbridgenews/bblife1954/bblife1954.htm.
69. Corbett, Scott (1978). *Bridges*. New York: Four Winds Press, p. 100.
70. Personal communication from Robert Koshinski to Robert Bartholomew dated December 29, 2002, containing a description of the 1968 WKBW broadcast based on interviews with station personnel and having heard the original airing in 1968. Mr. Koshinski's information was originally published in the newsletter of the Buffalo Radio Pioneers. It is entitled: "WKBW and the 'War of the Worlds.'"
71. Telephone interview between John Zach and Robert Bartholomew on December 31, 2002. Mr. Zach was a disc jockey at WKBW at the time of the broadcast.
72. Telephone interview between Jefferson Kaye and Robert Bartholomew on December 31, 2002.
73. Telephone interview with Jefferson Kaye, op cit.
74. Koshinski, op cit.
75. Telephone interview with Jefferson Kaye, op cit.
76. Koshinski, op cit.; Telephone interview with John Zach, op cit.
77. Recording of the original 1968 'War of the Worlds' broadcast on

WKBW, first aired on October 30, 1968.
78. Koshinski, op cit.
79. Recording of the original 1968 'War of the Worlds' broadcast on WKBW, op cit.
80. Recording of the original 1968 'War of the Worlds' broadcast on WKBW, op. cit.
81. Koshinski, op cit.
82. Telephone interview with Jefferson Kaye, op cit.
83. Telephone interview with Jefferson Kaye, op cit.
84. Untitled. *Buffalo Evening News*, Friday November 1, 1968, p. 34.
85. Telephone interview with Jefferson Kaye, op cit.
86. Telephone interview with Jefferson Kaye, op cit.
87. Holmsten, Brian, and Lubertozzi, Alex (editors) (2001). *The Complete War of the Worlds: Mars' Invasion of Earth from Orson Wells to H.G. Welles*. Naperville, Illinois: Sourcebooks Inc., p. 77.
88. Koshinski, op cit.
89. Telephone interview with Jefferson Kaye, op cit.
90. Telephone interview with Jefferson Kaye, op cit.; Telephone interview with John Zach, op cit.
91. Schlaerth, J. Don. (1968). "Airwaves go Spooky in Halloween Spirit." *Buffalo Evening News*, October 31, 1968, p. 50.
92. Telephone interview with Jefferson Kaye, op cit.
93. Koshinski, op cit.
94. Smothers, M. (2000). "Mysterious Malady Strikes Kids on Bus." *Journal Star* (Peoria, Illinois) May 19.

CALIFORNIA CHORAL COLLAPSE

Santa Monica: April 13, 1989

On the evening of April 13, about 600 students from several area high schools were warming up in preparation for the 40th anniversary "Stairway of the Stars" concert. Suddenly, a single student fell ill. Before long, 247 students were experiencing headaches, dizziness, stomach pain, weakness, and nausea. Rescue personnel quickly converged on the building. Curiously, not one member of the audience reported feeling unwell. Psychiatrist Gary Small investigated the incident and concluded that the symptoms were caused by mass hysteria that was the result of "performance anxiety."[1]

CALIFORNIA TELEPHONE ILLNESS

1984

At 8:10 a.m. on March 27, 1984, a male worker in the western sector of a telephone operator's building at an unidentified facility in California, noted a strange smell resembling cleaning fluid or pesticide, and he began exhibiting nausea, headache, and irritation of the throat, nose, and eyes. At 9:40 a.m. he was granted permission to leave the building and see a doctor. Curiously, no other employees reported any odor or ill effects. At this point, other workers were given the chance to move to the eastern sector of the building. Meanwhile, at the doctor's office, the physician could find no clear indication of exposure to toxic fumes, but when pressed by the worker as to a possible chemical cause, he gave the patient a note saying that the symptoms were "compatible with irritant gas/fume exposure."[2]

CONTEXT: Overreaction by the first employee to report illness symptoms, and his diligence to convince fellow workers of their exposure to harmful fumes was a key factor in the outbreak. Other influences included the inability of the company's physician to recognize the psychological nature of the symptoms at an early stage and agreeing to write a note suggesting the possibility of exposure to a gaseous irritant. Overreaction by supervisors and responding emergency personnel further contributed to the episode.

By late morning he returned to the office and began telling everyone that he was suffering from petroleum distillate poisoning and had the doctor's note to prove it. Shortly after lunch he was reassigned to the eastern sector. Meanwhile, in the western sector four employees began complaining of strange odors and headaches, nausea and throat irritation. At 2 p.m. supervisors began querying workers in the west sector for any indications of illness or odors. Within 25 minutes there were numerous complaints of symptoms identical to what was reported earlier.

By 3:10 p.m. the west sector was evacuated, and 30 minutes later, after illness complaints in the east sector, the entire building was evacuated of 153 workers. A massive emergency response ensued including ambulances, fire trucks, and a rescue helicopter. Paramedics at the scene sent 58 workers in ambulances to area emergency rooms. Nine employees were assessed as having breathing difficulties so severe that it necessitated immediate injections of intravenous fluids. However, upon being assessed by area physicians, all of the employees were quickly released without receiving any therapy.[3]

It was later reported that a note found in the eastern sector had generated alarm among workers just before the illness outbreak. It read: "Whatever they used to clean the air-conditioning yesterday poisoned a bunch of us on the other side this morning. I just got back from Company Medical. That's why I'm over here."[4]

For the remainder of that day, and part of the next day, the building was evaluated by the California Occupational Safety and Health Administration. "No evidence of toxic fumes, gases, or chemical leaks or spills was found." Despite the negative results, erring on the side of caution, the building was closed until a comprehensive assessment could be undertaken. The building was searched meticulously, including "room equipment, insulation, walls, ceilings, drains, sewers, outside street, and surrounding businesses."[5]

On March 28, the building was re-opened at 6:45 pm, and the evening shift worked without incident. The next day at about 11:30 am, several workers reported a strange smell and feeling sick. The building was quickly closed and evacuated, with 28 employees being rushed to local emergency rooms (five of whom had reported symptoms during the initial March 27 episode). A thorough environmental assessment "failed to show evidence of significant toxins" and the facility was monitored 24 hours a day until April 11.[6]

On April 25, nine workers in the west sector reported a strange odor, and they were moved at their request to the east sector. Soon two employees in the east sector noted an odor and felt ill – one of them collapsing on the floor. This time a doctor was brought to the site and determined that those affected were suffering from anxiety and hyperventilation. Upon being reassured, the symptoms subsided and did not recur. In all, 81 workers were affected – 78 female.

At one point in early April, the initial worker to claim symptoms back on March 27, complained to co-workers that the continuous monitoring equipment was ineffective as it could not detect the presence of gasoline vapors. Why? He said he had soaked his shoes in gas to see if the fumes would register and it hadn't. When supervisors were told of his remarks, he was sent for another medical exam, at which point the employee denied soaking his shoes but said he had accidentally stepped in a gasoline puddle. The employee was ordered back to work.

Based on physician reports, of those workers sent to the emergency rooms for evaluation and treatment, "All symptoms were nonspecific and were compatible with effects frequently seen with anxiety and associated hyperventilation."[7]

COMMENT: The episode highlights the potential impact of psychosomatic symptoms in a single person, and how illness beliefs and symptoms can quickly spread throughout an entire business operation.

CAMBRAI CONVENT OUTBREAK

France: 1491

The outbreak in the convent of Cambrai, northern France, in 1491, is the first instance recorded in any detail of the cases of CONVENT HYSTERIA, which for two hundred years were to trouble the religious communities of Western Europe.[8]

CONTEXT: No particular incident seems to have triggered the outbreak, which we may suppose arose from the internal stresses frequent in cloistered communities. However, this was the period when the Church itself was starting to come under threat; in less than thirty years, Luther would launch the Protestant Reformation, and humanist ideas were already threatening the established church, notably in England and the Low Countries. Although nuns in their cloister would not be directly concerned with theological disputes, such threats may have contributed to an overall tension which communicated itself to them.

About the time of the festival of the Chaire de Saint-Pierre, demons began to trouble the sisters of the convent at Quercy and continued to torment them for four years and four months. The first of their number to be affected was Jeanne Pothière, but the affliction swiftly spread to her companions. Like her, they took to running across the countryside, throwing themselves into the air, climbing trees as though they were cats, and hanging from the branches, howling like animals, prophesying. The historian Görres reports: "One saw them run across the fields like dogs, fly through the air like birds, climb on the trees and hang from their branches like cats, imitate the voices of different animals. Apart from these physical manifestations, they were also reputed to reveal hidden matters and foretell the future. Whenever Henri, Bishop of Cambrai, or Gilles Nettelet, the dean of the church, made preparations to perform an exorcism, they knew about it in advance and exclaimed, 'Do you see the man with the horns who comes to threaten us?'"[9]

When all attempts to cure the women had failed, their names were sent to Pope Alexander VI in Rome, who read them out during mass in Saint Peter's on Holy Thursday, but this failed to produce the hoped-for results. It was taken for granted that the Evil One was responsible, and this was confirmed when the nuns were exorcised. Satan, speaking through the mouth of one of their number, declared that it was indeed Jeanne who had admitted him into the convent. He had been having sex with her since she was nine years old, on a total of 434 occasions, not including the "unnatural" acts they had performed together since her entry into religion.

Despite the fact that the Devil was regarded as the Father of Lies, his word was accepted on this occasion because Satan was supposedly incapable of lying during exorcism, and Jeanne was condemned to life imprisonment. Probably only her nun's vows saved her from the stake.

Despite the removal of Jeanne, the troubles persisted. Neither the exorcisms, nor medicines prescribed by the doctors, nor even the solemn mass held at Rome by the Pope, had any effect, and four years passed before the Cambrai nuns saw an end to their troubles, which gradually ceased of their own accord.

COMMENT: At the time, such outbreaks were invariably attributed to the Evil One, and no attempt was made to look for natural or psychosocial causes. This is as true of the victims themselves as of those whose duty it was to evaluate the occurrence; none of them questioned that they were possessed by demons who caused them to behave as they did.

Though little information is available concerning this outbreak, there is sufficient evidence to show that the behavior of the nuns was very similar to that displayed in such later outbreaks as KENTORFF, raising the question whether the nuns were on some level aware of the conduct of other nuns in other convents, or whether the symptoms such as running, jumping, and emitting animal noises were archetypal behaviors for persons in their situation, or whether a degree of simulation or psychic contagion was involved.
See also: CONVENT HYSTERIA, DEMON POSSESSION, RUNNING AND JUMPING.

CARGO "CULTS"

Melanesia: circa 1857 and ongoing

Beginning in 1857, Western observers in parts of Melanesia and the Pacific Islands first began to describe religious movements in which natives believed that their ancestors would return to life and usher in a golden age.[10] Cargo "cults" typically form around a charismatic prophet claiming to have visions of a dawning utopian age of native civilization and resurgence. It is widely held among adherents that the dead will dispense cargo goods to be shared with believers. Dubbed "cargo cults" by Western anthropologists, these movements are thought to have started when islanders observed cargo vessels and airplanes unloading modern goods. Cargo "cults" appear to be a response to European colonialism. The natives were exposed to industrial society, including an array of goods. Yet, despite their desire for Western wealth and technology, the lack of education and cultural differences made it extremely difficult for them to access or even understand the process through which outside factories produce goods that are shipped as cargo. Many "cultists" use misguided logic in assuming that because Europeans use these cargo objects and are far wealthier than the natives, that they know the cargo "secret." As a result, anthropologist Conrad Kottak notes that "cult" members often attempt to gain access to Western cargo through magical means by mimicking Western ways. According to Kottak, "having observed Europeans' reverent treatment of flags and flagpoles, cult members began to worship flagpoles, believing them to be sacred towers capable of transmitting messages between living and dead. Natives constructed airstrips in order to entice planes bearing canned goods, portable radios, clothing, wristwatches, and motorcycles. Near the airstrip they built effigies of towers, airplanes, and tin-can radios. They talked into these cans in a magical attempt to establish radio contact with the gods."[11]

In many of these movements, certain European goods are worshipped as sacred objects. The number of cargo movements proliferated in response to World War II when Allied forces used islands throughout the region as bases. Cargo cults are typically classified as nativistic, as members believe that the social order will become inverted with the natives on top and the Europeans at the bottom or are forced to leave the islands. They are also considered to be revitalistic, as members anticipate the re-emergence of a golden age during which their ancestors will return from the spirit realm.

Cargo "Cults" As Disturbance Or Adaptation

Collective displays of twitching, crying, spirit possession, trance states and fantasies associated with various "cargo cults" have sometimes been interpreted as forms of psychological disturbance. In the case of Melanesian cargo "cults," several writers describe these behaviors as types of collective hysteria,[12] although acknowledging semantic difficulties in their use of the term "hysteria" as most participants were clearly not hysterical in the clinical sense. Some authors interpret cargo movements as irrational fantasy reactions.[13] Sir Bruton G. Burton-Bradley postulated that many "cultists" are comprised of those with mental disorders and the socially marginal.[14] Religious philosopher and historian Mircea Eliade (1960) takes a psychotherapeutic perspective in which certain societies in Melanesia were suffering from a collective neurosis, with cargo movements representing the native's attempt at psychoanalysis.[15] In *The Religions of the Oppressed: A Study of Modern Messianic Cults*, Vittorio Lanternari describes functional aspects of such movements but also describes them as forms of "escapism" and "collective psychoses."[16] Australian missionary John Barr notes that many social interpretations of Melanesian cargo cults are based on the belief "that the society involved is somehow maladjusted,....and forms of 'social pathology' are considered to be integral aspects."[17] The former president of the British Sociological Association, Peter Worsley provides a well-known example in his classic study of cargo movements.[18] Other researchers view cargo movements as reflecting a dysfunctional social order in the face of strains brought on by rapid social and cultural change resulting from Western cultural contact.[19]

It should be acknowledged that many investigators also view cargo cults as "rational" or "logical" reactions to Western colonialism.[20] However, until relatively recently, negative descriptions were commonplace. Michel Stephen discusses the tendency of early authors to describe the phenomena with reference to mental disorder:

> In the now voluminous literature on Melanesian cargo cults one aspect which receives scant attention from serious scholars is the mass "hysteria" – the trances, shaking, speaking in tongues, wild dancing and emotionalism – which usually accompanies such movements. The omission is not surprising. For early observers, the government anthropologist like F.E. Williams, the "hysteria" was a symptom of social dislocation, the "anomie" caused by western civilization, while latter writers interpreted the cults as the protest of desperate, impotent peoples. More recently, scholars have stressed the positive elements of cargoism, in particular the elaboration of new moral codes and the creation of new and larger political units.[21]

Australian Historian P. Hempenstall takes a relativistic view, noting how from the Melanesian standpoint cargo myths and movements are rational attempts at problem solving on Melanesian terms.[22] "What western man has often seen as bizarre, irrational parodying of western civilisation has been in fact a creative response to a succession of modernisation crises, part of a continuum of experiments by Melanesians to bring the changes to their lives within their own frame of reference."[23]

See also: PRESIDENT JOHNSON CARGO CULT, NAKED CARGO CULT, MANGZO CARGO CULT, THE FILO CARGO CULT.

CASTRATION, VOLUNTARY

The vital biological role played by the male genitalia has given them a symbolic role that has in turn led to many exceptional practices. Emasculation of captive enemies is widespread among primitive people; aside from its symbolic significance, it serves the practical end of preventing an enemy from reproducing himself. Voluntary castration, on the other hand, is in this respect counter-productive, and serves no ostensible practical purpose. Nevertheless it has considerable appeal to the ascetics and penitents of many cultures.

Most frequently, the act is associated with chastity and sacrifice. Taught that any sexual act is inherently sinful, the individual may feel guilt for having performed such acts, or wishes to prevent himself from performing them, or is driven as an ascetic gesture to sacrifice the instrument of pleasure. However the motivation is interpreted, it evidently exerts considerable appeal, for throughout history there have been individuals and groups who have castrated themselves or chosen to be emasculated. Matthew reported that Jesus praised "eunuchs, which have made themselves eunuchs for the kingdom of heaven's sake."[24] While many have argued that his words were not intended to be taken literally, others offer cogent arguments to the contrary.

His words have inspired his followers through the centuries. Among prominent early Christians, one who probably castrated himself was the 2nd century heretic Montanus from Phrygia in present-day Turkey. "Phrygia was known in the ancient world as the home of strange religious practices featuring ecstatic dances, orgies, and self-mutilation, all of which believers participated in to become possessed by the deity of the cult. The worship of Cybele, a goddess who required her priests to be castrated, was strong in this area."[25] While there is no direct evidence linking Montanus with such pagan practices, some scholars consider it probable that he followed this example. Other prominent early Christians who underwent voluntary castration were Origen of Alexandria (2nd century) and Leontius, the patriarch of Antioch in the 4th century. At this period the practice became so prevalent that in 395 Pope Siricius had to intervene and prohibit it at the Council of Nicaea.

For voluntary castration to be singled out for papal prohibition suggests that it was widespread, but if there was anything approaching an epidemic is not known. Most acts of castration were individual acts; collective castration is virtually unknown. However, it was the outstanding feature of the Russian SKOPTSI sect, for whom castration for males and mutilation for females were central tenets of their beliefs from the 17th century onwards. More recently, it was part of the teachings of Marshall Applewhite's HEAVEN'S GATE suicide cult; when the bodies of the members of the group were examined after their collective suicide, it was found that eight of them had submitted to castration.

See also: GENITAL SHRINKING SCARES, GENITAL VANISHING SCARES.

CAT GIRLS OF INDIA

Dolagobind Hamlet, Orissa, India: July-August 2004

Between July and August 2004, at least a dozen schoolgirls began to exhibit fainting spells. Upon regaining consciousness they would behave like cats, meowing, walking on all fours, and clawing at their faces. The school, in the remote hamlet of Dolagobind in Orissa, India, was temporarily closed. The first sign that something was amiss was on July 26, when Sasmita Mohapatra, a Class 10 student, fainted during prayers. Later that day two more students fainted in a similar manner, only to regain their senses and start acting like cats. On other occasions they would act like cats then faint. School headmistress Manjubala Pande told journalists that the following day "some six-seven girls started crying, fell down on the floor making sounds like that of a cat. We immediately informed others in the village but after the faintings and behaviour repeated, we were forced to shut the school."[26] The girls were between the ages of 6 and 12. Each of the school's 75 students, including the affected girls, were then taken to a nearby hermitage where they were told to recite Vedic mantras in hopes of ridding them of the evil spirits. Other cleansing rituals were also being organized. Similar outbreaks were reported at other area schools.[27] Pande told the Indian News Agency: "They get normal after a few hours."[28]

CONTEXT: Possession states are a form of psychological defense mechanism against pent-up stress and reflect cultural beliefs. In modern India, cats are symbols of bad luck. In some places they are believed to be the incarnation of a witch. For similar outbreaks of collective meowing or cat-like behavior, see CAMBRAI OUTBREAK (1491), AMSTERDAM OUTBREAK (1566), SAINT-MEDARD CONVULSIONARIES (1730s and onward), HYSTERICAL SCHOOLGIRLS AT QAWA (1968).

Soon after the strange outbreaks at Dolagobind Girls' School, other schools within the region reported mass outbreaks of fainting, though there were no specific descriptions of meowing or other cat-like behavior. Other outbreaks were reported at the "Baulagadia UG, ME schools" in the Oupada section. Over a two-day period, no less than 20 students from a variety of classes lost consciousness. Some were taken to the Iswarpur Primary Health Center after complaining of nausea and vomiting but were examined and soon released. Panic swept through the school – and the region – amid rumors that the same evil ghost or ghosts responsible for the closing of Dolagobind Girls' School the previous month, were at work again.[29]

See also: ANIMAL NOISES, EPIDEMICS OF MASS HYSTERIA IN SCHOOLS.

A young Lancashire witch urges her familiar, a cat, to attack her victim. (John Gilbert in Harrison Ainsworth, The Lancashire Witches)

CAT MASSACRES, GREAT

Europe: Late Middle Ages

In parts of Europe during the latter Middle Ages, the pastime of killing and torturing cats was fashionable, especially at public events and carnivals. Princeton University historian Robert Darnton documents such events in his book *The Great Cat Massacre and Other Episodes in French Cultural History.* During a carnival in Burgundy, it was reported that youths would engage in *faire le chat,* in which a cat would be passed around to music as each person would tear out a chunk of fur and relish in its howling in agony.[30] During the festival of St. John the Baptist, crowds often lit bonfires, tossing into them objects that were believed to have magical power and bring good luck. A popular item was cats, "cats tied up in bags, cats suspended from ropes, or cats burned at the stake. Parisians liked to incinerate cats by the sackful ... [others] preferred to chase a flaming cat through the streets ... In the Metz region they burned a dozen cats at a time in a basket on top of a bonfire. The ceremony took place with great pomp in Metz itself, until it was abolished in 1765."[31] Darnton observes that the French took great pleasure in these activities. "Although the practice varied from place to place, the ingredients were everywhere the same: *a feu de joie* (bonfire), cats, and an aura of [the] hilarious..."[32]

A similar low regard for cats was held in Germany during the Middle Ages. In Nurnberg, a popular carnival sport involved the "cat knight" who "fought with a cat hung around his own neck, which he must bite to death in order to be knighted."[33]

CONTEXT: The mistreatment of cats in medieval Europe reflects the widely held belief that cats were considered familiars with the devil, and that certain animals such as cats could possess humans.

Such disdain for cats in medieval Europe may be responsible for shaping reports of hysterical nuns imitating animals noises, including cats, with the content of their possession and histrionics shaped by prevailing social-cultural beliefs. "I have read in a good medical work that a nun, in a very large convent in France, began to meow like a cat; shortly afterwards other nuns also meowed. At last all the nuns meowed together every day at a certain time for several hours together. The whole surrounding Christian neighborhood heard, with equal chagrin and astonishment, this daily cat-concert, which did not cease until all the nuns were informed that a company of soldiers were placed by the police before the entrance of the convent, and that they were provided with rods, and would continue whipping them until they promised not to meow any more."[34]

COMMENTS: This entry underscores the importance of interpreting seemingly bizarre behaviors from the perspective of their social and cultural milieu. In doing so, we can better understand the medieval treatment of cats in Europe and meowing nun episodes. In doing so, behaviors that may seem pathological on the surface can be seen to have had a plausible rationale at the time.

See also: MEOWING NUNS, CONVENT HYSTERIA.

CATHOLIC SCARE

United States: 1830-1860

During the American Catholic Scare of the mid-1800s, Catholics were portrayed as belonging to a dangerous, immoral cult that would engage in bizarre practices. Catholics were greatly feared, especially among conservative Protestants. Many people refused to hire Catholics and there were even moves afoot in state legislatures to block hiring them for employment. In some cities, anti-Catholic feelings were so high that fatal riots broke out and Catholic churches were burned down.[35] Many rumors circulated around the claim that Catholics were in cahoots with Native Americans in a scheme to violently overthrow the government.[36]

CONTEXT: The Catholic Scare flourished in an atmosphere of xenophobia, economic competition, and racial and religious discrimination of new immigrants, particularly those of German and Irish descent, who were viewed as a threat to the "American" way of life.

A feature of the American social landscape since colonial times, anti-Catholic sentiments rose dramatically in the 1830s, coinciding with the influx of Irish and German immigrants of Catholic persuasion.[37] The anti-Catholic scare was a natural outgrowth of the American nativism movement, which rose to prominence in the decades immediately prior to the Civil War. Nativism refers to the popular notion that established or native-born citizens felt superior to new or recent immigrants. Nativists opposed immigration and were especially fierce in their opposition to Catholics. It was widely rumored that German and Irish immigrants owed their ultimate allegiance to the Pope and not the President of the United States, and thus were part of a conspiracy to either undermine or overthrow the government.[38] They also posed an economic threat and brought with them strange customs. In 1849, the Order of the Star Spangled Banner was formed, quickly becoming a potent political force. Members of the Order were known as Know-Nothings, and they formed the Know-Nothing party, which lobbied national and state politicians to either halt or restrict immigration, especially involving Catholics. The party was named on account that if asked about their organization, their standard reply was: "I know nothing."[39]

It is estimated that between 1830 and 1860, anti-Catholic publications included at least 25 newspapers, 13 magazines, and 270 books, in addition to numerous pamphlets and almanacs.[40] This period was marked by several incidents of major violence. In 1834, a mob in Charlestown, Massachusetts, enraged by rumors of nunnery abuse, destroyed that city's Ursuline convent by setting it on fire. In 1839, Baltimore, Maryland, was rocked by three days of riots protesting the treatment of nuns at a Carmelite convent. In 1844, 13 people died in Philadelphia in riots that resulted in the burning of many Catholic homes and two churches. Anti-Catholic violence peaked in the mid-1850s when riots claimed the lives of ten people in St. Louis in 1854, while at least 20 died in August of the following year from rioting in the streets of Louisville, Kentucky.[41]

Rumors and misinformation abounded during this period, including claims that nuns were essentially sex slaves. Nunneries were portrayed as a threat to motherhood and family values,[42] and nuns were hardly viewed as celibate, making easy targets for the perverted desires of Catholic priests. Former priest William Hogan described how priests would wear down their "prey" by sympathetically listening to their most intimate secrets at close physical proximity in confessionals until these cloistered nuns would give up their virginity.[43] In 1836, Theodore Dwight claimed that behind closed doors and away from the watchful eye of friends and relatives, young nuns had their morals perverted by "the savage and brutal lusts of men professing to be ministers of religion."[44]

Scores of novels appeared describing how nuns, having managed to escape the clutches of the convent concubinage, fell in love, raised a family, and lived happily ever after in wedded bliss.[45] However, not every "escaped" nun was so lucky. *The American Nun* was a cautionary tale, telling the story of Anna, a heroine who decided against marrying her fiancé in favor of the convent, lured by the selfish, naive expectation of independence and adventure. She quickly realized her mistake but by the time she managed to escape and find her way home, her mother had died and a close friend had married her fiancé. The couple had produced a little girl named Anna. Overcome with guilt, conflict, and lament, the former nun soon died a mentally tortured and barren woman.[46]

The anti-Catholic fervor subsided in the 1860s as public attention was diverted to the more pending issue of the Civil War.

CATTLE MUTILATIONS

Midwestern United States: 1969 and ongoing

Between 1969 and 1980, widespread reports of mutilated cattle were recorded in the mid-Western United States. While mutilated animals have been reported in various countries and time periods prior to and after these events, the episode was particularly intense and was widely publicized.[47] During this period, farmers reported finding hundreds of dead cattle with missing body parts, especially the sex organs, mouth, and ears. The "mutilations" took place amid widespread speculation that either Devil worshippers or extraterrestrials were the culprits. Hundreds of press reports appeared during this time in the mainstream media, reinforcing these speculations and suggesting a UFO or satanic cult link.[48] Occasionally, it was claimed that the mutilations were part of a top secret United States government experiment using cattle. As mutilation stories began to attract media attention in the affected areas, the number of mutilation claims increased dramatically.

The modern wave of animal mutilation reports can be traced to the autumn of 1967 and media reports about the death of a three-year-old Appaloosa horse in the San Luis Valley of southern Colorado. The animal was supposedly found "mutilated" with surgical precision. Strange marks on the ground were found nearby and neighbors reported seeing a UFO in the area just prior to the incident. The carcass was reported to have been drained of blood and excessive levels of radiation were present at the site. The first scientist to examine the body was medical hematologist John Altshuler who suspected possible extraterrestrial foul play and noted the various anomalies. Yet, a closer scrutiny of media reports yields numerous inaccuracies. The horse was named "Lady" but was typically and erroneously identified as "Snippy." The case made worldwide headlines on October 5, 1968, when the Associated Press distributed the story. By mid-February 1968, nine other scientists had investigated the case and all were in agreement that the death was by natural causes. The University of Colorado sent three investigators to the site, while a separate, independent probe was conducted by six other researchers from the University of Nevada. They concluded that the absence of blood was common for a carcass in such a badly decomposed condition. It was surmised that small animals had eaten away the exposed fleshy parts of the body such as sex organs. As for the report of high radiation at the scene, based on an analysis of soil and autopsy samples, only incidental levels of background radiation were detected. Further, as for the cause of death, veterinarian Dr. Wallace Leary revealed that the horse had been shot twice by a .22 caliber weapon.[49]

Several scientific studies have been conducted in an effort to determine the nature of the animal mutilation phenomena. In each instance, a variety of mundane causes have been implicated.

The Stewart Study

Sociologist James R. Stewart of the University of South Dakota examined reports of animal mutilations in Nebraska and South Dakota during 1974. He concluded that the episode was part of a wider social delusion fueled by media publicity, noting that the organs of dead cattle are often cannibalized by an array of natural predators. Ranchers do not ordinarily scrutinize their animal carcasses, but with the flurry of mutilation publicity during this period, they suddenly began to pay special attention to the bodies of their dead animals for evidence of "surgical removal." Stewart believed that small nocturnal predators were the primary culprit as they have a difficult time penetrating cattle hides, eating the softest, most exposed parts. Further, sharp side teeth can give the impression of precise, surgical incisions. As for the "mysterious" absence of blood, it is well known that within a few days of death, blood coagulates, leaving an impression that the bodies were drained by some outside force, such as a cultist or alien.[50]

The Colorado Bureau Of Investigation Report

Following a flurry of cattle mutilation reports in Colorado, in 1975 the Colorado Bureau of Investigation (CIB) analyzed 203 mutilation reports in the state occurring between April and December. Nineteen cases were deemed suitable for testing by specialists at Colorado State University. In the 11 instances where the cause of death could be determined, all 11 expired from natural causes. While a tiny fraction of cases were determined to have involved the use of a sharp instrument, in every instance it was found that the incision had been made *after* the animal's death.[51]

In July 1978, CBI officials described the exhaustive nature of their probe and its findings. "During our investigation of the cattle mutilation problem in Colorado, the CBI laboratory examined approximately 40 hide samples. Of these, two were found to have been cut with a sharp instrument. In a six-month period, our agents spent 1,557 man-hours on this investigation, which included undercover operations. We were never able to identify any person or persons as being responsible for these, so-called, mutilations. The scientifically based evidence obtained points to cattle which died of natural causes being attacked by predators."[52]

The Owen Report

In 1979, University of Arkansas anthropologist Nancy Owen was awarded a $500 grant to study mutilations in the state, deciding to focus her investigation on a single, hard-hit area – Benton County in the northwestern part of the state. Owen's study was based on an analysis of 22 mutilation reports investigated by police and Sheriff's officers within the county. Her findings were released in January 1980. She found no concrete evidence to support more exotic explanations of cultists or extraterrestrials.[53] In the case of extraterrestrials, Owen points to a mysterious photograph that appears to depict a beam of light emanating from a mutilated animal. The photographer, a police officer, attributed the strange effect to a leakage of light or "static spark" when the picture was developing.[54]

While some "witchcraft altars" were, according to media reports, found in the vicinity of "mutilations," Owens remarked that "not every pile of rocks is a witchcraft altar. I'll be the first to admit I didn't get to check out the crime scenes firsthand, but the papers reported 'crude stone altars.' I think that could also be interpreted as 'piles of rocks.' Get off campus once in a while. Take a drive in the country and look for a field that DOESN'T have a pile of rocks in it."[55]

A mysterious white powder was found on some animal carcasses. A leading police investigator of the "mutilations" was certain it was plaster of paris, used to make castings. Analysis of the powder from one site was analyzed at the Oklahoma State University Animal Diagnostic University. The substance was identified as calcium sulphate, a common ingredient in plaster of paris.[56]

A survey of Benton County law enforcement officers identified a single over-riding concern about the "mutilations" – not of extraterrestrials or cultists, but of accidental deaths due to fear "that some innocent person might accidentally be shot and killed by a nervous rancher just trying to protect his property."[57] This was a real concern as several ranchers were conducting armed vigilante patrols at night in their vehicles. In summarizing police views, Owens writes that "although law officers do recognize the possibility that a human death might occur as the result of the mutilation phenomenon, the real threat, they believe, is not from those 'mysterious mutilators' but from the trigger-happy ranchers out to get them."[58]

The Rommel Report

In April 1979, the United States government approved a grant of $44,170 from the Law Enforcement Assistance Administration to investigate animal mutilation reports in the southwestern state of New Mexico. Former FBI special agent Kenneth Rommel was authorized to conduct the probe which ended May 27, 1980. None of the cases were linked to human slashers, with only relatively mundane, prosaic explanations found: predators, scavengers, and natural decomposition.

One of the first things Rommel did was to evaluate the 90 previously reported mutilation cases in New Mexico, observing that "I found nothing in the official reports to indicate that the animal was mutilated by any agents other than predators and scavengers. Available evidence strongly suggests that those animals died from natural causes or common injuries and were subsequently ravished by scavengers."[59] Rommel also soon discovered that many residents, including state officials and law enforcement personnel, supported the notion that a secret government operation was involved. "In short, the government conspiracy theory, though one of the most highly publicized theories in New Mexico has not one shred of evidence to support it."[60] Indeed, how could such a huge, complex operation be kept secret? Keeping such a secret would be even more implausible if the U.S. government were involved. Rommel states that it would be extremely difficult for "an organization as large and complicated as the government – with its complex system of checks and balances – to keep such a project secret. For judging from descriptions in the media, this conspiracy would have to involve personnel from numerous governmental agencies, including the CIA, the military, and animal diagnostic laboratories across the country. The ability of people from so many different agencies to maintain, for over five years, the secrecy required to conduct their grisly experiments would be a phenomenon rivaling that of livestock mutilations themselves."[61]

In all, Rommel examined 117 mutilation reports – several first hand. He also found no evidence to support other theories: cultists, extraterrestrials, or rumors that some ranchers themselves were killing cattle in order to collect insurance money. In his concluding remarks, Rommel offered advice to law enforcement officials who may be called to investigate future animal mutilation claims. "Don't use terms such as 'surgical precision,' which are conclusions. Stay with the facts, let the laboratory experts make conclusions. Also, don't be mislead by statements made by non-authoritative sources..."[62]

The Washington County Experiment

A separate investigation/experiment conducted by the Sheriff's Department of Washington County, Arkansas, in September 1979, also concluded that natural processes were involved. The Department took a diseased cow donated by local rancher Jack Perry who had previously reported two mutilated animals on his property, and induced death through an injection of tranquilizers. The cow died at 8:02 p.m. on September 4, after which the carcass was monitored for over 30 hours by a Sheriff's Department surveillance team that was watching about 300 feet away. Within only 18 hours, most of its organs were missing, the result of buzzards, blowflies, skunks, and other predators.[63] By the following day, the carcass resembled other "mutilations" in the county, as "the animal's tongue was gone, its eye removed to the bony orbit, anus 'cored,' internal organs (intestines, bladder, etc.) expelled, and little blood was evident at the scene. Who were the mutilators? Blowflies, skunks, and buzzards, who were still feeding on the carcass when the last photographs were taken September 6 at 11:00 a.m."[64]

Investigations In Oklahoma, Nebraska, North Dakota

In 1974, State authorities in South Dakota examined 12 reported mutilations. According to the Animal Diagnostic Laboratory at South Dakota State University, "each incident bore evidence of predatory animals."[65] Between 1974 and approximately 1980, about 140 "mutilations" were investigated by the Nebraska Highway Patrol, of which 20 necropsies were conducted. Human involvement was found in one case. The perpetrator was later arrested and prosecuted. He seems to have been greatly influenced by mutilation stories in the media.[66] During the late 1970s, a report from a special task force on cattle mutilation claims was sent to the governor of Oklahoma. Their conclusions: "All investigations that have been completed have indicated death due to natural causes and death due to disease. In no case has the observation and opinion of task force indicated man has been a primary factor in death or mutilation."[67]

CONTEXT: Conspiracy theories of government involvement and cover-up of the "mutilation mystery" may have been fostered by *zeitgeist*. Anti-government feelings and suspicions began to bloom soon after the "Snippy the horse" case, during the latter 1960s in response to the growing unpopularity of the Vietnam War.

CEVENNES PROPHETS

France: 1685-1703

In the closing years of the 17th century, an outbreak of extraordinary manifestations took place among the persecuted Protestants of the Cevennes region of southern France. Regarded as divinely inspired by those who favored them, as fanatical by those who opposed them, their behavior included ecstasies and convulsions, precognition and precocious preaching notably by young children, along with many related phenomena.

CONTEXT: In 1598 Henri IV, though he had converted from Protestantism to Catholicism for political reasons, issued the Edict of Nantes, granting religious freedom to French Protestants. In 1685, Louis XIV revoked the Edict, insisting that all his subjects adhere to Catholic teachings. But even prior to this, the authorities were cruelly oppressing the Protestant minority. Their temples were destroyed and their schools closed, their civil rights taken away and justice made a mockery. Many fled to more tolerant countries – Switzerland, the Netherlands, and Britain. Others submitted to a nominal conversion as the only means of survival.

When Protestantism continued to flourish in the Cevennes and Languedoc, Louis dispatched his military to enforce its abolition. A small but bitter civil war broke out, marked by appalling cruelty first on the Catholic side, then in retaliation by the Protestants. The "Camisards" (as the militant Protestants came to be known), though outnumbered and outgunned, had the advantage of local knowledge; they put up a heroic resistance and at one point could claim to control the region. In the end, the fighting was terminated by a kind of pragmatic tolerance, which was formally ratified at the time of the Revolution.

During the persecution, life was extremely hard for the Protestants: arrests, torture, and executions were commonplace. Among those nominally converted, schoolchildren were taught Catholic doctrine by day, then in the evening their mothers sabotaged their schooling, replacing it with Protestant teachings. The climate in thousands of Protestant homes was one of great stress combined with intense piety. Theirs was in every sense a lived religion, and the children would hear, for hours on end, the bible readings and prayers. With their temples destroyed and their priests in exile, each household became its own chapel, each householder his own priest. In the words of one commentator "the inspirés lived in a continual dream outside ordinary laws, in a state of mind which can be explained only by the times in which they lived and the inflamed milieu in which they breathed."[68]

The First Wave

Even before the revocation of the Edict, signs and wonders began to occur. In 1686 a man of Codognan had a celestial vision, and other apparitions quickly followed. Many experienced a remarkable phenomenon, the hearing of divine music in the air. A gentleman of Peyrolles reported: "At night, we heard the singing of psalms in the air, as though we were in a temple. Last Wednesday I was lying in my bedroom when, around midnight, I heard beneath the roof a strong and brilliant voice which woke me, followed by five or six voices which accompanied it and sang verses of Psalm V. Everyone in the house has heard it on several occasions, and indeed it has been heard by the whole district."[69]

A ten-year-old girl of Capelle d'Escroux was visited by an angel while guarding her cows. This aroused fervent interest, and the authorities felt obliged to put her in prison, where she predicted – correctly, as it turned out – that her judge would be hanged before the year was out. Isabeau Vincent, a 15-year-old shepherdess, began to preach in her sleep from which she could not be wakened, quoting from the scriptures, exhorting repentance, and predicting the future. Later she would go into ecstasies; a hostile critic described her lying on her back in the kitchen, her legs and stomach bare, while the admiring throng "listened to her pious nudities and contemplated the body in which the Holy Spirit resided." Many thronged to hear her, but her fame was fatal. She was arrested and thrown into prison, where she continued to preach, though exorcised in case she was possessed by Satan, and searched for the devil's marks in case she was a witch.[70]

Persecuted French Protestants of the Cevennes manifest remarkable gifts of prophecy and other phenomena. (Figuier, Merveilles de la Science)

The effect on observers was often contagious; many who met Isabeau, young or old, began to prophesy in the same way. An observer noted that "all these persons have the most beautiful appearance, the girls are like angels in beauty and gentleness when the charming and celestial state seizes them."[71] Typically, two young "angels" (as they came to be known), aged 11 and 12, claimed to be inspired by a (real) angel while guarding their flocks. They presided over numerous assemblies, preaching and prophesying. By 1688 there were up to six hundred "inspires" in the Dauphiné and the Vivarais, and the movement spread until the "little prophets" could be counted in the thousands.[72]

At this stage, some of the "prophecies" were to some degree millenarist, in that the more extravagant described apocalyptic visions in which Protestantism overcame the papacy. But the majority looked no further than for freedom to worship in their own way.

Several commentators have described the inspirés' ecstasies, which might take place in public (though secret) assemblies or in private homes. Typically, they would start by trembling, then stretch out their limbs, yawning, before falling to the ground. They clapped their hands, they threw themselves backwards, they closed their eyes, their stomachs swelled; they remained drowsily/passively in this state for several moments, then they would suddenly awake and utter whatever that came to their mouth. All insisted that the words came, not from themselves, but from the Holy Spirit. Subsequently they would have no recollection of what they spoke.[73]

The listeners were hardly less affected. Sometimes the entire congregation went into a kind of ecstasy: "The preacher spake with such force, that his audience were so affected that some of them cried out, others wept, others groaned, which made a kind of sabbat, no one listening to anyone else, except for the preacher… At Uzès, following the preaching of Daniel Raoul, the inhabitants embraced one another in the street or in their own homes, sobbing and sighing as if overcome with grief."[74]

Moved by such sights, Claude Brousson, a fervent supporter of the Protestants, reported to a friend in Holland that what he saw in the Cevennes were "such great marvels, that they will be the subject of amazement and admiration of the whole world."[75]

The Second Wave

The fearful punishment inflicted on the prophets if they were caught – many were tortured and executed, many more imprisoned or condemned to the galleys – proved a terrible deterrent and for a while, during the 1690s, prophesying died down for a while. The Catholics hoped that the older generation would die out and the young people of the region would settle down in the Catholic faith, but they were deceiving themselves. The Protestant faith might seem to have been extinguished, but it was smoldering beneath the ashes and in 1701 the flames burst out more fiercely than ever. By this time, many had fled the persecutions to take refuge in the "desert" of the mountainous Cevennes, and it was here that, in secret assemblies which on occasion attracted congregations of upwards of two thousand,[76] they gathered to share their faith. The religious excitement, combined with the continual danger of discovery and death, rekindled the prophetic raptures. A contemporary observer, David Flottard, estimated the number of inspirés as at least 8,000; he himself had witnessed "an infinite number."[77]

Jacques Bresson, who was abducted by the Catholic forces and forced to serve in their army but escaped and made his way to England, declared: "I saw in the Cevennes a great number of people – four or five hundred, I'm sure – of both sexes who received the Inspirations. All, when they were seized by the spirit, underwent agitations of one sort or another: but movements of the head, chest and stomach were the most common. When they began to speak, the spirit which animated them would almost always pronounce these words 'I tell you my child' and they spoke French throughout their ecstasy…"[78] [i.e., not in their everyday local patois].

Elie Marion gives a first-person account: "I felt as though a fire occupied my chest and caused me a kind of oppression which was not uncomfortable, but which made me utter deep sighs. My body was thrown back, and I stayed about 15 minutes in this state, slightly trembling… a few minutes later, an irresistible power took entire hold of me and compelled me to utter loud cries, interspersed with deep sighs, and my eyes filled with tears."[79]

Often, what impressed the listeners was the contrast between the inspirés in their normal and their inspired state. When two young women of Vigan, aged about 24, were arrested for preaching, their neighbor Mlle Sybille de Brozet secured their freedom by assuring the officials that in their normal state they were *pauvres idiotes* and it was only in the ecstatic state that they spoke coherently and in French.[80] Similarly, a M. Caladon reports: "Of the many people I saw fall into seizures, none impressed me as much as Jeanne, a poor idiot peasant, surely the most simple and ignorant creature our mountains have ever produced. When I was told that her preaching was wonderful, I refused to believe it. I couldn't imagine she could put four words of French together, nor that she would dare to speak in public. But subsequently I was present on several occasions when she spoke marvelously well. This Balaam's Ass had a mouth of gold, when the celestial intelligence made her speak. Never did an orator so command her audience: never were listeners more attentive and more moved than those who heard her. It was a torrent of eloquence…"[81]

The most notable feature of the outbreak was the preaching by small children, to which there is profuse testimony. Pierre Chaman of Uzès in 1701 saw a little boy of five years who fell to the ground, with agitations of his head and his whole body. Then he began preaching, predicting misfortunes to Babylon (= the papacy), blessings on the [Protestant] church, and exhortations to repentance. All was in French, which he could not speak in his normal state.[82] Isabeau Charras tells of a girl who preached not only in public assemblies but even at home while asleep.[83] Jacques Dubois of Montpellier reported seeing many hundreds of inspirés: "At Quissac I saw a boy of 15 months, in his mother's arms, whose whole body was shaking, particularly his chest. He spoke with sobs, in good French, distinctly and with raised voice, but with interruptions, so that you had to lean close to hear certain words. I have seen more than sixty children, of either sex, between 3 and 12 years, in a similar state. The preachings of these children tended always to exhort powerfully to change one's life, etc. They also predicted many things."[84]

Guillaume Bruguier reported: "When I was at the home of a certain Jacques Boussige, one of his children, aged 3, was seized by the spirit and fell to the ground: he was very agitated and gave himself great blows on the chest, saying at the same time that it was the sins of his mother which made him suffer. He added that we were in the End Times."[85]

Jean Cabanel observes that those who are touched with the inspiration become "the persons who have received the Graces, quit at once all kinds of libertinage and vanity. Some who were debauched become good and pious: and those who consort with them become more honest and lead exemplary lives."[86]

Paranormal Phenomena

The utterances of the prophets were not marginal phenomena, but were crucial to the rising. There are innumerable instances of foreseeing events, often with the very practical consequence of enabling them to avoid capture; or, if arrest was foreseen, predicting their eventual release to the day.[87] So far was this the case that Cavalier and other Camisard leaders were guided by prophecies continually; no action was taken without consulting the divine power.[88] Moreover, these were not general predictions but precise ones, stating for instance that a courier would shortly be traveling from Alès to Nîmes carrying certain letters; intercepted, such was found to be the case.[89]

The prophets were not privileged persons, but were of all classes – peasants, tradespeople, soldiers, and housewives. Some seemed to display psychic talents; Mathieu Boissier "at Geneva several times saw a girl from Languedoc, who had the inspirations. In her ecstasies she spoke many things which concerned me, of which it is impossible she could have been informed naturally. She had a wonderful communication with the divine spirit."[90]

Other paranormal incidents were claimed. Claude Arnassan and some forty companions, lost in the mountains while heading for a clandestine assembly, were in despair when a light like a huge star appeared in the sky and guided them to the place. Moreover, he asserts that this happened on many other occasions.[91]

An inspiré named Clary caused a big wood fire to be built, and stepped into the middle of it and preached while the flames rose higher than his body, raising his joined hands above his head and preaching to the kneeling crowd for at least a quarter of an hour, while his wife and others shrieked. Jean Cavalier, brother of the Camisard leader, who recounts the incident, was one of the first to embrace Clary when he emerged, sobbing, from the flames, and testified that his clothes showed no trace of the fire.[92]

Marion recounts that in 1702 he saw his own brother caught up by inspiration, and received a divine message that, by way of demonstrating that these prophecies were of divine origin, he should strike at his chest with a knife. "Have no fear, for I shall not permit you to be injured." A large pointed knife was brought: "he took it in his right hand and struck himself several times in the belly, with very great force: but his body resisted as if it were made of iron, and even his clothing was not pierced. Everyone was frightened and melted in tears."[93] (Compare ISLAMIC ECSTATIC SECTS.)

Another seemingly paranormal manifestation was the "heavenly music" attested to by many witnesses. Isabeau Charras insists:

> Although many have jeered at the singing of psalms which have been heard in several places as though coming from the skies, I can assure you that I have heard this divine melody with my own ears more than twenty times, in full daylight, and in the company of diverse persons, in places

far from any house, where there were no woods, or crevices in the rocks, or anywhere else where someone might be hidden. We considered every possibility: but these heavenly voices were so beautiful, that our peasant voices were surely not capable of producing such a concert. Part of the marvel was that not everyone who ran to hear the sounds could hear them. At any rate, several protested that they could hear nothing, while the others were charmed by this angelic melody. I remember distinctly hearing the words of the psalm "Lift up your hearts."[94]

COMMENT: For those outside the fervent Protestant milieu, the extravagances of the prophets were perceived as a kind of madness. The Catholics saw them as the work of the Evil One, and many Protestants disapproved or even condemned the goings-on as fanaticism. One of them, Brueys, defined it thus:

Fanaticism is properly speaking a malady of the spirit or a kind of melancholy and mania, which leads those who are affected by it to persuade themselves that they have the power to perform miracles and to prophesy. Melancholic and bad-tempered people can easily fall into this malady: if their temperament is destabilised by fasting, keeping vigils or over-fatigue, they begin to have vivid dreams of miracles and prophecies… until they are carried by their own self-importance to the point where they believe that they themselves are capable of performing miracles and prophesying… Though the Evil One is sometimes responsible for seducing the fanatics, for the most part this is a true illness that we cure as we do others, by using the appropriate remedies, and whose symptoms, surprising though they appear, are perfectly natural and whose cause is perfectly understood.[95]

Doctors were summoned from the Faculty of Medicine at Montpellier to examine some of the children. A contemporary, David Flotard, comments:

While they were unwilling to apply the term "prophets" to the children, neither would they agree that this was the devil's doing, nor that the children were mad. They would have treated them as impostors if they could, but they couldn't. Nor would they admit that the zeal of their religion had altered their brains and that prolonged meditation on the Apocalypse had turned them into visionaries. So what could they say? To rest silent would be an admission of failure, not good for their reputation. So they looked for a term which sounds as though it means something, but in fact is very vague: and they came up with the term "fanatics."[96]

The ability of the children to preach in French, a tongue they did not speak, is explained by the fact that in Languedoc the Bible was translated into French, even though as a rule the people spoke their own patois. Consequently the children were accustomed to hearing the French version, even if they could not understand it. This lends support to the idea that much of the preaching was accomplished by cryptomnesia – that is, the children were repeating parrot fashion what they had heard over and over again in their homes. While this certainly diminishes the extraordinary nature of the manifestation, it is still remarkable first, that small children were able to deliver a coherent discourse which often greatly affected those who heard it, and second, that hundreds if not thousands of children, some aged three or even less, were impelled to start behaving in this fashion. (For another instance see SWEDISH PREACHING MANIA.)[97]

A valuable comment is provided by John Wesley, who had the opportunity to meet one of the Cevennes prophets who had taken refuge in London:

I went about five in the evening to a house where was one of those commonly called French prophets. She [probably Mary Plewit] seemed about four or five and twenty, of an agreeable speech and behaviour… Presently she leaned back in her chair, and seemed to have strong workings in her breast, with deep sighings intermixed. Her head and hands, and, by turns, every part of her body seemed also to be in a kind of convulsive motion. This continued about ten minutes, till she began to speak (though the workings, sighings, and contortions of her body were so intermixed with her words, that she seldom spoke half a sentence together) with a clear, strong voice, "Father, thy will, Thy will be done. Thus saith the Lord, If of any of you that is a father, his child ask bread, will he give him a stone? If he ask a fish, will he give him a scorpion? Ask bread of me, my children, and I will give you bread. I will not, will not give you a scorpion…" She spoke much of the fulfilling of the prophecies [and more to the same effect].

Two or three of our company were much affected, and believed she spoke by the Spirit of God. But this was in no wise clear to me. The motion might be either hysterical or artificial. And the same words any person of a good understanding and well versed in the Scriptures, might have spoken.[98]

Though there is a danger in supposing Mary Plewit's performance to be typical of the Cevennes "preachings," there are sufficient indications in other reports to think it may be so. This first-person observation by a perceptive witness who might have been expected to be sympathetic to the persecuted Protestant reduces divine inspiration to human creativity, in which material obtained by cryptomnesia is reworked by the subconscious mind and regurgitated as a seeming revelation from on high. Wesley, with his customary acumen, anticipates what would surely be the verdict of any open-minded behavioral scientist.

Case History

Durand Fage describes what it felt like to prophesy. In February 1703, he is visiting relatives when Marguerite Bolle, a relative aged 23, falls into ecstasy and starts to prophesy. Later that day…

After noon, I was asked to read from a devotional text: and as I uttered the words "Increase our faith" I felt all of a sudden a weight on my chest, which stopped my breathing for a moment. At the same time floods of tears poured from my eyes, and I found it impossible to speak. No one was surprised, for all realised what state I was in. I remained in this state for an hour and a half; and the young girl having received a new inspiration, said that I was crying for my sins; which was true.

At six o'clock that evening, when I was in another house, I was suddenly seized with trembling, which spread till every part of my body was agitated. The weight on my stomach was less than it had been the first time. In this state, I felt an agreeable breath which was born inside me, which surprised me, though I was scarcely capable of thought. At the same time, my tongue and my lips were suddenly forced to utter vehemently words which I was totally surprised to hear, not having thought about anything and having no intention of speaking. The things which I said were principally exhortations to repentance: and this lasted three or four minutes. I fell instantly into a kind of faint, but this passed rapidly and was followed by a new trembling, which passed in its turn: after which I found myself completely free and in my normal state. But during the fortnight which followed, I had frequent sighings and shudderings that I could neither foresee nor prevent. My soul rose continually towards God. The ordinary diversions of my youth seemed not only contemptible, but insupportable. The thought of my sins occupied my mind all the time, and it was this which caused me to sob and shudder, so much so, that my mouth uttered unceasingly, "Mercy! Mercy!"[99]

CHEMISTRY LAB MYSTERY ILLNESS

Lawrence, Kansas: October 15, 2003

It began as a routine laboratory for an introduction to chemistry class in room 2028 at Malott Hall at the University of Kansas. On Wednesday morning at 8:30, students were going about their studies. Two students were at the front of the room taking notes, juniors Adam Yarnell and Megan Weatherly. A third student, Andrea Miller, also a junior, said that Yarnell stood up and appeared sick, then as he was trying to leave the room, he "fell face forward on the floor." As Miller tried to help Yarnell, she felt nauseated and walked out of the room. Shortly after, Weatherly fainted into the lap of her lab partner. Weatherly said that when Yarnell fainted, she stopped writing and looked up. "I don't know if I was scared for him or if I brought my head up too fast, but I started to feel really dizzy." When her dizziness persisted, she said: "I started feeling really hot and took off my sweatshirt. Then I just passed out."

Emergency personnel responded to the scene including Douglas County Fire and rescue. Members of the university's department of environmental health and safety also examined the site. The department's director, Mike Russell said there was nothing out of the ordinary in the lab. "There is nothing in this room that would be out of what would be expected in a lab. We didn't find any airborne chemicals at all." None of the students said they saw or smelled anything unusual during the incident, which Russell said could have been a coincidence caused by the warmth and people suddenly moving their heads and feeling dizzy. The students said they felt better after leaving the room. The trio refused medical treatment. At the time, the students were using three chemicals: potassium permanganate, phosphoric acid, and iron (II) chloride, which were very safe. Russell remarked: "It's all very benign chemistry. The biggest thing we would have to worry about is skin contact that could possibly lead to irritation." After the room was examined, the chemistry lab was reopened later in the day without any further illness incidents.[100]

CONTEXT: The key context here seems to be the setting, a chemistry lab, exacerbated by a series of freak coincidences. Any time someone suddenly becomes ill in a chemistry lab, there is a concern that it may be something harmful in the environment.

CHEMTRAILS

Worldwide: late 1990s and ongoing

Since the late 1990s, intense public interest has developed in the conviction that the United States military is engaged in a series of systematic, secret experiments involving the dispensing of chemical trails from high altitude jet aircraft. Scores of websites have appeared discussing the phenomena, usually accompanied by a myriad of conspiracy theories. It is also commonly believed that chemtrails are responsible for a variety of ailments experienced by people on the ground.

One conspiracy theory holds that chemtrails are created by the military as an inexpensive wireless communication system. Another theory insists that the chemicals are used to control the thinking of the masses. However, the most popular explanation centers around the view that these chemtrails are an attempt to modify weather on earth. Many websites claim that chemtrails are caused by secret United States military experiments being conducted with its allies, designed to produce a sky shield in order to protect earth from the ravages of global warming. Some point to a 1994 patent taken out by the Hughes aerospace company, which entails mixing jet fuel with a variety of reflective materials, including tiny aluminum oxide particles, that would provide the earth with a chemical sunscreen.[101]

In 1998, the issue of chemtrails became a prominent concern in parts of Canada, in particular the tiny town of Espanola in northern Ontario, where United States KC-135 aircraft were said to be making routine passes over the community and dispensing harmful chemicals. The concerns became so great that on November 18, a representative of Canada's New Democratic Party, Gordon Earle, presented a petition to parliament, calling for the covert spraying program to stop. At the time, many residents were claiming to be suffering from ill health as a result of the chemtrails, including dizziness, sudden fatigue, headaches, asthma, joint pains, and flu-like symptoms. The petition stated: "Over 500 residents of the Espanola area have signed a petition raising concern over possible government involvement in what appears to be aircraft emitting visible aerosols. They have found high traces of aluminum and quartz in particulate and rainwater samples. These concerns combined with associated respiratory ailments have led these Canadians... to seek clear answers from this government."[102] The petition went on to ask politicians to repeal any legislation that permits dispensing substances by Canadian or foreign aircraft "without the informed consent of the citizens of Canada thus affected."[103]

Based on an analysis of the chemtrail phenomenon, a meteorologist with the National Oceanic and Atmospheric Administration (NOAA) contends that the chemtrail scare is unfounded. Thomas Schlatter says that in understanding the so-called mystery, it is imperative to first define "contrail." The word is short for condensation trail, which form when high altitude jets disperse water vapor into the lower levels of the stratosphere (or high troposphere) resulting in saturated air. As for chemtrails (plumes of chemicals emitted from aircraft), Schlatter believes that they don't exist as such. That is, he believes that chemtrails are actually contrails.[104]

Schlatter states that normally contrails dissipate quickly, but this depends on the conditions. For instance, where very cold air temperature combines with high humidity, contrails have been known to stretch 100 miles in length. Whenever the temperature is -40F or lower, and the relative humidity is at least 70 to 80 percent, contrails will develop.[105]

CHILD ABDUCTION PANIC

Paris, France: 1750

"La Grande Peur de 1750" – the "Great Fear" – was that the authorities were abducting children from the streets of Paris. This fear led to a number of incidents, breaking out spontaneously in different parts of the city. Wild rumors were in circulation, and suspected abductors ran for their lives, pursued by crowds of citizens which swelled to hundreds or even thousands, culminating in violent rioting and even lynching. Ironically, while the rumors exaggerated the situation, they were founded in fact; children were indeed, in a manner of speaking, being abducted.[106]

CONTEXT: The Parisian mob, always volatile, was under particular stress in the mid-18th century as the result of a series of food shortages. In the 1740s they brought a great many vagabonds and vagrants from the country into the city, where they survived as best they could on the fringes of the community. The authorities sought to clear the streets of this riffraff by a series of ordinances; some of them were constructive, such as finding employment and housing for the vagrants, but they also proposed such alternatives as deporting the more undesirable to overseas colonies such as Louisiana.

Towards the end of 1749, these measures were put into effect with increasing stringency, leading to a sense of unease among the populace. At this period, the traditional loyalty of the people to the aristocracy and court was already fraying in a way that, forty years later, would lead to open revolution, and the police were seen less as guardians of order than as agents of the ruling classes, objects of fear and anger. On November 12, 1749, the authorities issued an ordinance which stated: "His Majesty commands that all the beggars and vagabonds who shall be found either in the streets of Paris, or in churches or church doorways, or in the countryside around Paris, of whatever age or sex, shall be arrested and conducted into prisons, to stay there as long as shall be necessary."[107]

To start with, the citizens welcomed these measures, for the streets were filled with undesirables. It was calculated that there were 15,000 beggars in Paris at the time, and respectable folk were glad to see the back of them. Gradually, however, the suspicion grew that the police were exceeding their authority; not simply clearing the children from off the streets, but arresting any children they found in the streets without discrimination, not stopping to inquire whether they had homes and families, and taking them away to imprisonment or forced labor. The fact that an agent received a reward for every arrest he conducted made it easy to believe that he would not be too scrupulous. Records show that many agents arrested the children of tradesmen, knowing them to have families and homes, but claiming to be acting under orders. It was even said that some agents held the children to ransom, forcing the parents to pay to prevent their offspring being taken. Several hundred children were arrested in this way. Agents, usually not in uniform, would accost children in the street and take them, without any form of inquiry, in a closed carriage directly to the Châtelet prison, without passing through the magistrate's court. Even young children might spend several days there before their families reclaimed them.

Remarkable rumors were in circulation as to why the children were being stolen. Some said they were being sent to the French overseas colonies in Mississippi, which may in truth have been the intention in some cases. But other suggestions were more bizarre; a widespread story was that one of the royal princes – or maybe it was a princess, or even the king himself – was sick, and required to bathe in human blood to be healed. The abducted children were to be slaughtered and drained of blood for this purpose.

The matter came to a head in May 1750, after a series of incidents throughout the preceding weeks. On May 1, police arrested six ("to make an example") out of some twenty youths, aged from 13 and 15, who were found gambling in the streets in the Faubourg Saint-Laurent. The quarter was alarmed. Some soldiers, who witnessed the incident, tried to obstruct the police and swords were drawn. The agents succeeded in forcing the boys into a carriage, which took them to the Châtelet prison. Fighting continued between soldiers and police.

During the ensuing weeks, a contemporary noted in his journal for May 16 that "rumour has it that Exempts (a kind of plain-clothes police auxiliary) are scouring the streets in disguise, in different quarters of Paris, and taking up children, girls and boys, aged from five or six to ten or more, and packing them into carriages or cabs which they have waiting at hand. These are the children of artisans, permitted to go as they will in the neighbourhood, or who have been sent to the church or to fetch something."[108] That same day, in the Marais quarter, a mother, holding her child's hand, saw a coach full of police, and cried out that the bastards were coming to steal their children. Almost at once a crowd gathered and the police were roughly handled, forcing them to take refuge in the nearest commisariat (police station). One person was killed and several injured.

Posters appeared on the walls urging everyone to be on the alert. Teachers advised parents to accompany their children to school and fetch them afterwards. In fact, many parents kept their children at home for fear they might be kidnapped. At one school for children of the poor, only 12 of its 85 pupils attended.

On May 22 incidents broke out independently in six places in the city: at Saint-Jean de Latran, in the Faubourg Saint-Denis, the rue du Gros-Chêne in the Marais, by the Porte Saint-Martin, at the Croix-Rouge crossroads on the rive gauche, and at the Pont-Neuf – all of them locations in the densely populated inner city where Parisians lived close to their place of work. Anything might spark off an incident – a child who thought he was being followed, a police spy recognized, anyone acting suspiciously in any way. Two peaceable pedestrians, strolling in the Marais, were seized by the crowd and assailed with blows for no other reason than that they were strangers in the neighborhood. Outside the College des Nations a drunken soldier tried to get a music student to play his instrument; immediately the cry went up that he was an agent in disguise, planning to abduct the boy.

Though each was unrelated to the others, the incidents followed much the same scenario. Someone would give the alarm and a group would gather, tradesmen would rush from their shops, craftsmen from their ateliers, servants from their homes, and the suspect – whether innocent or not – would take to his heels to escape the mob which he knew was disposed to strike first and listen afterwards. He would head for the nearest commissariat and hope to get there before the crowd caught up with him. If they did, he would be assailed with sticks, stones. Even if he reached the commissariat, the fugitive was not always safe; the building might be besieged by the crowd outside – sometimes numbering thousands – battering on the doors and demanding that he be released to them. If the authorities resisted, the crowd might disperse in time, or a force of police might have to be summoned. Dispersing the mob was not an easy matter; in one incident, twenty squads of troops, some on horseback, could get a mob to disperse only by firing on them, killing one and injuring 12 others.

Along with such goings-on, there was liable to be looting. When there was rioting at the Pont-Neuf, several dozen men rushed to the gunsmiths of the Pont-Saint-Michel quarter, demanding weapons – though without success. A whole district would be caught up in the panic, the mob filling the streets while the respectable closed their shutters and stayed home.

On May 23, at the Pont-Marie, an agent named Labbé was spotted with a child of 11. According to some, he was trying to arrest her; others said he was giving her money to buy cherries. Whatever the truth, some *gardes françaises* gave the alarm, and a crowd rapidly formed and rescued the child. The other agents faded away, but Labbé, seeing himself threatened by the mob, took to his heels. Twice he succeeded in giving them the slip, but he was found hiding in an apartment building, under a bed. He managed to get to the commissariat, but by now the crowd had become a lynch mob. The commissaire announced that Labbé would be sent to prison to await a judicial hearing, but the impatient mob broke into the commissariat and seized hold of Labbé. Though he managed to break away from them, they got hold of him and battered him to death with staves and stones.

A remarkable feature of the outbreak was that it seemed to break out spontaneously in different quarters of the city; there was at no time any concerted effort, nor a major riot involving the populace as a whole. Each incident was a local one, with its own dynamic, and yet each resembled the others. Perhaps for this reason, the authorities suspected that there was some kind of concerted effort of "a company of brigands whose purpose was to rouse the people." However, no evidence was produced for the existence of any kind of organization.

Following the riots, many arrests were made, but only three persons, who had played a prominent part in rousing the mob, were executed; one of them was only 16 years old, though with a history of delinquency. It was acknowledged that the police had exceeded their authority by removing from the streets children who had every right to be there, and the arrests ceased. However, it is evident from the official reports that the authorities were concerned not so much with the abuse of their powers by the police, as with the disturbance of public order, for which they blamed the rabble and the rabble-rousers.

COMMENT: The rumor that the children were being abducted for the sake of their blood, which would be used in the healing of a sick aristocrat, is almost a metaphor for the social division between the court and aristocracy on the one hand and the populace on the other, which clearly inspired The Great Fear. So alienated from his people was Louis XV by this time, that when he traveled from one of his chateaux, south of Paris, to another to the north, he made a detour through the Bois de Boulogne on a specially constructed road, rather than pass directly through the streets of his own capital.

When she heard the rumors being circulated, Madame de Pompadour, the king's mistress, wrote to her brother, "Speaking of stupidity, you are well aware of that of the people of Paris. I don't believe there is anything so stupid as to think that one wants to bleed their children in order to bathe a sick prince. I have to confess, I didn't think they were as imbecile as that."[109] Yet stupid as the rumor was, it expressed a social reality that La Pompadour would have done well to take to heart.

CHILD-EATING SCARE

Germany: Middle Ages

A widespread delusion appeared that Satan and his followers lived on human flesh. A story circulated that some men living near Berne and Lausanne had sold their souls to the devil and were eating their own children. Authorities stretched hundreds of men on the rack to gain confessions. In some instances, suspects were apparently burned to death. A number of mentally disturbed people voluntarily confessed to killing and eating children.[110]

CONTEXT: Medieval Europe was a hotbed of superstition, rumor, and fear surrounding the widespread belief in witchcraft. Witches were thought to be especially fond of eating children, and those who were missing, found murdered, or attacked by animals were sometimes thought to have been targeted by demonic agents.

CHILDREN'S CRUSADES

France and Germany: 1212

The story of the Children's Crusades embodies fact and fable, but historians are puzzled how much to accept as the one, how much to set aside as the other. Some go so far as to deny that they took place at all, noting that several contemporary chroniclers do not mention the episode; others offer alternative interpretations of such meager documentation as is offered.

Nonetheless, a fairly coherent and consistent narrative has come down to us from the period, and if the obviously fabulous elements are taken with a pinch of salt, it is a reasonably credible story. The account given here summarizes the events as recorded by contemporary or near-contemporary chroniclers. Their accounts are substantially in agreement, but while this may be taken as an indication that the event really did take place, it could simply be that they were all drinking from the same fountain.[111]

CONTEXT: Military expeditions, aiming at recovering the sacred sites of Christianity from the Islamic conquerors, had been mounted periodically since 1095 by the Christian powers of Western Europe. After initial chaos, they succeeded in winning Jerusalem, only to lose virtually all that they had won. A Third Crusade failed to reach Jerusalem, and in 1208 the Fourth had collapsed due to conflicting priorities among the Crusaders. But in 1212 there was still great enthusiasm for the cause, and the reigning pope, Innocent III, was actively promoting a renewed initiative. Throughout France and Germany the crusading ideal continued to be a source of inspiration, and it would be natural for young people to regard the Crusaders as heroes and dream of emulating their prowess.

The French Children's Crusade

The instigator and leader of the French Children's Crusade was Etienne (Stephen), a twelve-year-old shepherd boy from the small town of Cloyes, near Chartres. On April 25, 1212, he had witnessed the annual St Mark's Day procession, which that year was the occasion for propaganda for the Crusading cause; he was fired with enthusiasm. Shortly after this, he encountered a beggar who claimed to be a returned pilgrim from the Holy Land. After telling the boy about the dismal situation of the Holy Places, he revealed himself to be Jesus in person, and commissioned Etienne to preach a crusade to the children

Believing they had been appointed by God to recover the Holy Sepulcher, children set out for the Holy Land. (The Leisure Hour, 1852)

of France, promising that they would conquer where previous Crusaders had failed. He gave the boy a letter to Philippe-Auguste, King of France, commanding him to give Etienne any help he might need. It has been suggested that the stranger was not Jesus at all, but "undoubtedly a disguised priest, who had heard of Stephen's enthusiasm, and thought him a suitable instrument for the purpose of arousing the people."[112]

Eager to carry out this mission, Etienne headed for Saint-Denis, on the outskirts of Paris, where Philippe-Auguste was at the time. On the way he told of his adventure, and by the time he reached Saint-Denis he had attracted a crowd of followers eager to join his project. He is said to have presented the letter to the king, supporting his claim with miraculous stories. In one, when the sheep he was guarding had strayed into a field of grain one day, they went on their knees to him to beg forgiveness. Whether or not the king actually met the boy, he was not greatly impressed and asked the University of Paris for their opinion. They advised that the movement should be firmly discouraged; consequently, a royal edict ordered the children to return to their homes.

But though Etienne and the other children obediently returned to their towns and villages, they carried their enthusiasm with them, and gradually the idea of a Crusade by children took hold. Whether it was as spontaneous as it appeared to be, or whether it was secretly being manipulated by the clergy, is another matter. The great majority of those who were enthused were peasant children who had little to lose by leaving home, and to whom the idea of travel and adventure was exciting in itself, apart from the noble cause. But there were also some young nobles, perhaps eager to follow in the footsteps of crusading predecessors, or younger sons seeing a chance to make their own way in the world. They were mostly boys, but some girls also joined, some of whom wore male dress for protection.

A considerable number of adults joined with the children. Some were priests who perhaps felt that the children needed a few wiser heads among them, but every chronicle agrees that in addition there were vagabonds and riffraff of every kind.

> Many other men and women joined the armies from motives of a baser nature. All that were depraved in every sense found this a rare chance for profit. Abandoned women flocked in numbers in the expectation of fulfilling their infamous plans and of robbing as well as of ruining the youths. Thieves and sharpers never had such easy prey, and they did not neglect it. Every one whose disposition would lead them to consider this an occasion for gain or plunder, hurried to the rendezvous.[113]

Those who favored the project saw it as a divine inspiration, but others held that it was the devil's work – the explanation given by the medieval mind for anything out of the ordinary and not otherwise explicable. Hardly less far-fetched was the rumor that it was a plot of the Old Man of the Mountains, head of the Moslem sect of the ASSASSINS, who planned to make these Christian children his prey. The place chosen for the gathering of the Crusade was at Vendôme, near Blois. In June contingents arrived in the city from all over France. Some 15,000 are said to have come from Paris alone, half the total estimated at 30,000 by all the chroniclers.

They set off in August towards the Mediterranean at Marseille, via the Rhone valley. From being a humble shepherd boy, Etienne, their 12-year-old leader, was now regarded as a saint; he traveled in a splendid horse-drawn chariot, served by mounted attendants. Power had gone to his head, and the Chronicler Roger de Wendover said of him, "He was a child in years but accomplished in vice."[114]

The logistics of their journey can only be imagined. They carried no provision, so somehow food to sustain 30,000 hungry children had to be found. Even when the country folk were welcoming, living off the land was a severe problem. Populations who may have been sympathetic to the children were alarmed by the unscrupulous camp-followers who accompanied them. They traveled nearly 500 kilometers in about a month. Needless to say, these simple uneducated children had no notion of geography, and as each town came in sight the more innocent hoped it was their destination, asking, "Is that Jerusalem?"[115] The arduous walk through the summer's heat discouraged some, who abandoned the pilgrimage, while others died or were abducted. But these deductions were partially made up by new recruits, and it is reckoned that at least 20,000 reached Marseille.

Etienne had assured them that when they reached the sea, God would lay on a miracle. "Between waters, which are to be to us as a wall on the right hand and on the left, are we to cross the untrodden bed of the sea, and with dry feet will we stand on the distant beach by the walls of Acre or of Tripoli."[116] Unfortunately, no miracle was laid on for them. Whether this disillusion caused his followers to lose faith in their leader, we do not know, but nothing more was ever heard of Etienne de Cloyes.

However, two seemingly well-disposed merchants, Hugues Lefer and Guillaume Leporc, came to the aid of the crusaders, offering to convey them to Palestine. Some 5,000 – about one-sixth of those who had left Vendôme – took advantage of this offer, and with them were a number of adults, including 80 priests. They left France in August in seven vessels.

But they never reached the Holy Land. There were no reports of them from Egypt or Palestine, and nothing was known for 18 years. Then a priest, returning from North Africa, revealed that he had been one of the pilgrims, and told what had happened. Two days after leaving Marseille, two of the ships were wrecked in a storm on the uninhabited island of San Pietro, off the coast of Sardinia, where more than a thousand lost their lives. The five surviving vessels continued their voyage and reached the African coast. Most were taken to Beajïa on the Algerian coast, some 160 km eastward of Alger. There, the kindly merchants revealed that their true business was slave-running, and the children were sold as slaves or prostitutes. Others were taken to Alexandria where they suffered the same fate.

Not all came to a bad end. Some are said to have grown up and prospered in their new home. But most of the five thousand crusaders ended their lives as slaves, scattered throughout the Arab world. Later, exemplary tales would be told, such as how the Moslems in Baghdad sought to convert the children to Islam, but the children preferred to die as martyrs rather than renounce their faith. This is the closest they got to re-establishing Christendom in the land of the infidel.

The German Children's Crusade

The German crusade came into being at about the same time as that in France and is thought by some to have been inspired by the French initiative. Alternatively, it may have derived from a common inspiration, especially if a priestly conspiracy was at work. The story is essentially parallel to the French narrative, perhaps even suspiciously so. In the German case, it was a youth from a village near Köln, named Nikolaus, who was the prophet and leader. One chronicler refers to him as "a boy less than ten years old." A difference is that he was encouraged by his father, probably from motives of interest. He preached the crusade in the streets of Köln, where his message caught the popular imagination in the same way as Etienne's on the far side of the Rhine.

One aspect of the Crusade that must have seemed particularly impracticable was the idea that these unarmed children would take on the Saracens in battle. However, Nikolaus explained that the object of their crusade was not to fight the Saracens, but to convert them to the Christian faith. Baptizing the infidels was hardly a more realistic aim than battling them, but no doubt they hoped for miraculous aid when the time came.

The followers were drawn chiefly from the Rhineland and from neighboring Burgundy. The German crusade included a greater number of noble children than in France; some of these traveled with attendants. The city of Köln itself lost so many children that the effects were felt long after the event. Here as in France adults joined the children, and the chroniclers make frequent reference to the number of depraved women in the company. Consequently here as in the French Crusade it was not simply a company of innocent children who processed through the country, but also a following of less high-minded stragglers who would steal and otherwise misbehave at any opportunity.

The German crusaders left Köln in June or July, while the French were still gathering at Vendôme. The pilgrims divided into two parties, one which went directly over the Alps, the other taking a more roundabout route. The Alpine party was estimated by a contemporary chronicler as numbering 20,000.

The journey was tough enough on the plains, for no city could accommodate so many travelers, and the children were dependent on charity as they went. It is estimated that about half the number had fallen away by the time they reached the Alps: some had simply given up, others died from one cause or another, and still others were kidnapped or enslaved in the towns they passed through. The passage of the Alps via the Mont Cenis pass proved a more formidable obstacle than the children can have expected and reduced the number of pilgrims even further. Although it was mid-summer, travel conditions were harsh and there was little food to be had in these unpopulated regions. Many died, and many turned back. When the survivors descended into Italy, only about 7,000 of the original 20,000 were still plodding.

By the time they reached the Mediterranean coast at Genova on August 25, 1212, the children had walked more than 1,000 kilometers. They asked permission from the citizens to stay for one night, for the next day they would be on their way. For Nikolaus, like Etienne, had been promised that the sea would open up before them as it had for Moses leading the Jews from Egypt, and they would walk dry-shod to the Holy Land.

But the miracle did not take place for Nikolaus either, and the children found themselves helpless. One chronicle asserts that two shiploads of crusaders sailed from Pisa to Ptolemais, on the Nile, then the only port held by the Christians in the Holy Land. Some remained in Genova, where these attractive northern children were welcomed; the rest made their way to Rome, where they were received by the Pope. He convinced them of the impracticability of their project, and ordered them to return home and to set out again when they were older. Nikolaus, like Etienne, dropped out of history; none of the chroniclers records his fate.

Even less is known of the second German party, though it is said that their route ran through Switzerland, crossing the Alps through the St Gothard pass. They received a much more hostile reception when they reached Italy. "Many were murdered: others were stolen to be carried away to misery, dishonour, and slavery."[117] As if that were not enough, a severe drought was affecting Italy that summer, and many turned back or simply died from want of food. No more than two or three thousand can have survived by the time they reached Brindisi on the Adriatic coast. Here they were treated harshly; the girls were seized and enslaved. The boys were advised by the bishop to return home, and some took this wise advice. But others were said to have been taken in ships, promising to take them to the Holy Land. They were never heard of again, either in Italy or in the East, and it may be supposed that they met a fate similar to that of the French pilgrims. For those who took the bishop's advice and turned home, the return journey was miserable and humiliating. One chronicler commented: "They who used to pass through countries in parties and troops, and never without the song of encouragement, now returned singly and in silence, barefooted and famished. They were a scoffing to all men."[118]

One account records that, when the full extent of the disaster became known to the people of Köln, they hanged the father of Nikolaus, blaming him for the loss of their children.

COMMENT: The similarities between these narratives must raise suspicions that duplication has occurred; yet they also support the likelihood that some such events took place. The responses of historians have varied from total dismissal to attempts to reconstruct the events according to various theories. Several commentators have suggested that the children were not as young as has been supposed. Both Etienne and Nikolaus are said to have been twelve and nine years old respectively, but Collin de Plancy describes their followers as being between 12 and 15.[119] The Latin word *puer* does not necessarily imply a young boy, and psychohistorian Raffael Scheck has shown that the word could be applied to poor farm laborers of any age, raising the hypothesis that many of the crusaders were poor landless men rather than children.[120] But against any such theorizing is the fact that the whole point of the episode, whether fact or fantasy, lies in the tender age of the Crusaders, and any such reductionism makes nonsense of the story.

An alternative reductionist hypothesis is that the entire episode was a plot by the Roman Catholic

Church, with the intention of shaming adults into taking a more active part in rescuing the Holy Places. Thus the stranger who appeared to Etienne would be a priest in disguise, playing on the credulity of the boy. This theory, though, is invalidated by the failure of the Church to assist the children along the route or to welcome them when they reached the Mediterranean. They were helped by the monks as they crossed the Alpine passes, but so were all travelers. The young Germans who reached Rome were counseled to return home, and the bishop of Brindisi advised the other party to do the same. So it does not seem plausible that the Church of Rome bears any responsibility.

Unless further verification turns up, there are grounds for skepticism not only as to the details of the stories, but also as to whether they took place at all. At the same time the fact that so many chroniclers have recorded the event supports belief that something of the sort did in fact occur.

CHILEAN MARTIAN PANIC

Chile: 1944

Shortly after 9:30 p.m. on November 12, 1944, panic erupted in several Chilean towns and cities after the broadcast of a realistic 1938 radio drama loosely based on the H.G. Wells novel, *The War of the Worlds.* The play originated at a station in Santiago and was broadcast throughout the country on the Cooperative Vitalicia Network, causing thousands of terrified citizens to flee into the streets or barricade themselves in homes.[121] Hundreds were affected in Santiago; in Valparaiso, electrician Jose Villarroel became panic-stricken and died of a heart attack. The script was the brainchild of an American named William Steele, former writer for the popular United States radio drama, *The Shadow*. Ironically, and perhaps it is no coincidence, actor Orson Welles was the original voice of "The Shadow," and Steele was undoubtedly familiar with Welles who was involved in a similar radio panic in North America six years earlier.

Working with assistant Paul Zenteno, the duo set the invasion epicenter 15 miles south of Santiago in Puente Alto.[122] One provincial governor mobilized artillery units in preparation to repel the invading Martians. The broadcast was highly believable, including references to such organizations as the Red Cross and using an actor to impersonate the interior minister.[123] Accounts of the invading Martians appeared as a series of "news flashes." The drama described in vivid, gloomy detail the defeat of the military and the destruction of the Santiago Civic Center, along with air bases and artillery barracks. The broadcast described roads as jammed with desperate refugees fleeing the devastation.[124] Both the radio station and local press had announced the upcoming broadcast a week in advance, and once the play was underway, listeners were warned twice. After the broadcast, angry citizens pressured the government to close the station and suspend its creators but no official action was taken.[125]

See also: ORSON WELLES MARTIAN PANIC (1938), MARTIAN INVASION SCARE (1939), ECUADOR MARTIAN INVASION PANIC (1949), BUFFALO MARTIAN INVASION SCARE (1968), RHODE ISLAND MARTIAN INVASION PANIC (1974), PORTUGUESE MARTIAN INVASION PANICS (1988 and 1998).

CHINESE NEEDLE SCARE

China: December 2001-February 2002

Fear of being deliberately stuck with an AIDS-tainted needle swept through parts of China. The scare began shortly after Christmas in the city of Tianjin when several residents turned up at local hospitals seeking blood tests after claiming they had been secretly pricked by an AIDS-infected needle. The outbreak eventually spread to Beijing. The episode may have been triggered by several crimes in Tianjin involving threats of pricking victims with a needle. None of the needles were found to have been contaminated. In one high profile case, on January 12, police arrested a man for reportedly pricking a schoolgirl with a needle.

CONTEXT: China has strong media controls and as such, its people may be more vulnerable to such scares as people are forced to rely more on rumors and less on official media statements. Another contributing factor may have been concern over the spread of AIDS. At the time of the scare, there were conservative estimates of 600,000 HIV-positive cases in China, and predictions of an epidemic in the coming years.[126]

CHINON DEMONIC POSSESSION OUTBREAK

France: 1634-1640

The outbreak at Chinon was in a sense a sequel to the outbreak at LOUDUN, involving one of the principal figures from the earlier affair.[127]

CONTEXT: Chinon is a town in the Loire valley noted for its château. Though all France was troubled with claims of witchcraft and demon possession at this time, over and above the on-going conflict between the Catholic and Protestant communities, unquestionably the determining factor at Chinon was the presence of Father Barré as spiritual director.

One of the most fervent exorcists at Loudun had been Father Barré, who had persistently maintained that the sisters were truly possessed by Satan. When that outbreak came to an end, Barré was posted as parish priest to Chinon. He proceeded to apply the same methods here as he had at Loudun; the moment he heard anything in the confessions of his new parishioners that so much as hinted at the work of the Evil One, he interpreted it as demonic possession and proceeded forthwith to exorcism. As was always the consequence, this resulted in behavior that seemed to justify his diagnosis.

However, Barré's superiors were by no means convinced that the pious father was correct in diagnosing possession. The cardinal-archbishop of Lyon, the bishops of Angers, Chartres, and Nîmes, meeting at Bourgeuil, declared, after interviewing the supposedly possessed sisters, that they were simply suffering from depression (melancholia) and Satan was in no way involved. Barré swore on the Holy Sacrament that he was personally convinced that the devil was residing in the entrails of his parishioners, but the archbishop reproached him, saying, "Don't you see that, even though the sisters might not in fact be possessed, they would believe themselves to be so, as much because of their depressed state, as because they hold you in such respect."[128] However, Barré refused to submit to the ban which his superiors imposed and persisted in subjecting the nuns to exorcism. He was aided by the fact that two doctors called in as consultants had reached contrary opinions; Duclos inclining to believe the devil was responsible, Quillet denying it.

The sisters, who during the lifetime of Grandier at Loudun had known whom to blame for their condition, now needed to find another scapegoat. They focused on Father Santerre, the priest of Saint-Même, and denounced him to the authorities as a sorcerer. Appalled at the thought that he might suffer the same fate as Grandier, he appealed to the Parliament. From Paris came an order that Barré and the supposedly possessed nuns should all be put in prison, but the Intendant of the district, Laubardemont, who had played a major role at Loudun and who supported Barré in his belief that the possession was genuine, succeeded in delaying the carrying out of this order. A legal row erupted, Barré took his possessed nuns to the château where the exorcisms continued, and the sisters continued to behave as though they were possessed.

What finally brought the episode to an end was the attempt by one of the supposedly possessed women, La Beloquin, to incriminate the Giloire, a pious and popular priest. One morning Barré, the priest of the church of Saint-Jacques, arrived to find the altar streaming with fresh blood. When he inquired who was responsible, he received no reply, so he proceeded to exorcize La Beloquin and commanded the devil possessing her to reveal the truth. Satan duly obliged; when she had come to church early that morning, when no one else was around, Giloire had raped her on the altar itself

This accusation shook all good Catholics, since Giloire was the last person one could suspect of such a crime. The Magistrate conducted a thorough investigation, and a neighbor recalled that she had sold a fowl to La Beloquin the day before the alleged rape. The truth emerged – La Beloquin had taken the blood of the fowl with her to the church of Saint-Jacques, and when no one was looking, poured it on the altarcloth. Exposed, she was terrified, and purchased a ball of lead and inserted it in her womb, then began complaining of the pain she felt from a suppression of her urine that had been imposed by Giloire, whom she now accused of sorcery as well as rape. She demanded to be heard by the Archbishop of Tours. The archbishop, who favored the possession theory, happened not to be there, and his co-adjuror, of a more skeptical nature, agreed to help La Beloquin; he got two strong men to hold her, and two midwives to examine her. The lead was discovered, the ridiculous conspiracy was revealed, and La Beloquin was imprisoned.

That was the end of the affair. No doubt those responsible would have been severely punished, but neither the authorities, nor the parents of the supposedly possessed girls, many of whom came from the leading families of the town, including one of the judges, wanted publicity. Consequently the authorities contented themselves with exiling Barré to Le Mans, where he remained hidden for the rest of his days. As for the possessed girls, they were condemned to spend the rest of their life between four walls, where they were whipped every day in penance for their foolish behavior.[129]

This denouement brought to an end the infestation at Chinon, and also quieted things back at Loudun. By this time everyone had had enough of the business, and Aubin suggests that the revelation of conspiracy at Chinon may have made the sisters at Loudun wonder what would have been the outcome if they had been examined as minutely as the possessed females of Chinon. Thereupon calm returned to the minds of the sisters, and nothing more was heard about pacts of sorcerers and the harassments of the evil angels.

COMMENT: Though a minor affair compared with Loudun, the Chinon incident is interesting as a demonstration of how a single individual, sufficiently confident that he was in the right, could impose his views on a community at that time. Uneducated people of necessity looked to their priest for guidance in matters spiritual; they were in no position to question his insistence that, whether they knew it or not, they had been possessed by the devil. All over France and beyond, other men and women were being burned alive for supposed dealings with the Devil. The afflicted women of Chinon were fortunate not to suffer the same fate. As it was, for a period of several years, the populace of Chinon suffered as a consequence of the obstinate beliefs of their parish priest.

See also: CONVENT HYSTERIA, DEMON POSSESSION.

CHOLERA PANIC

Paris, France: 1832

The French Cholera Panic of 1832 provides a striking instance of a simple fear – the natural response to a very real menace – which, thanks to its social context, took on a political dimension, which in turn generated conspiracy rumors, which in turn escalated to rioting and a number of deaths, all caused only indirectly by the epidemic itself.

CONTEXT: France in 1832 was in a very unsettled state. The government of Louis Philippe, the "Citizen King" of the French, had been uneasily installed on the ruins of the Bourbon dynasty, restored after the defeat of Napoleon. The new regime displeased both the "legitimist" royalists on the right and the Republicans on the left. Sedition was seething below the surface, ready to erupt at any opportunity. The cholera epidemic provided just such an opportunity.

The plague had begun at Jessore, near Calcutta, India, on August 19, 1817, when an English doctor, Robert Tytler, was summoned to examine a patient suffering from a mysterious ailment. He diagnosed poisoning, but when, in a matter of days, the sickness

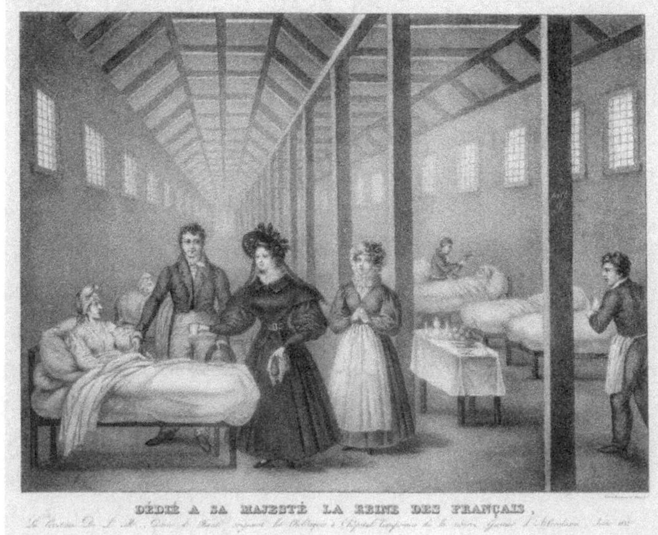

A cholera victim in a Paris hospital is cheered by a visit from a courageous countess. (Lithograph by Benard, Paris)

spread with fearsome rapidity, it was recognized that something more serious was involved. Identified as cholera, it spread from India to Ceylon and Indonesia, swept across China to Persia and in 1824 reached the Caucasus. By 1830 it was on the borders of Europe, and when Poland succumbed, Western Europeans began to feel menaced.

Cholera is now known to be an intestinal disease resulting from infection by the bacterium *Vibrio cholerae*, transmitted chiefly by contaminated water, but at this time the nature of the affliction was unknown, and medical authorities indulged in wild speculation both as to the ailment itself and how it spread. Some thought it was an airborne pestilence, others that it was contagious from person to person; ignorance in this matter led to ignorance as to how it might be checked, or at least avoided. All kinds of remedies were proposed ranging from friction or steam baths to burying up to the neck in straw from the stable. Various substances were recommended, such as purifying the room with sodium chloride in spring water. Others said that the *cholera morbus* was naturally endemic in the east, and took hold only when favorable moral conditions were found, as when a population panicked; stay calm, and it would pass over, for it was all in the mind.

If so, then France would surely be spared, for the righteous citizenry who had brought the Citizen King to the throne surely had the right to think that their virtues, domestic or political, would shelter them from an affliction that preferred to attack Indian peasants and Polish Jews, anarchists and dissidents who brought it on themselves by their degenerate lifestyles. For many, cholera was a punishment sent from on high, smiting those who offended against morality. The majority of Parisians felt that the danger was remote, and the doctors encouraged their optimism, pointing to the temperate French climate, the salubrious location of Paris, and the general prosperity of the country.

On February 1, 41-year-old Henri Veillot, a porter by trade, robust and in good health, suddenly fell ill of an ailment his doctor could not identify; two weeks later he was dead. Was it cholera? The doctors could not decide. In any case, it seemed an isolated case. Nevertheless, the authorities were taking no chances and precautions were stepped up, with provision made for first-aid stations and for isolation wards in hospitals. Some 40,000 leaflets were distributed, which warned the public against quacks and charlatans who might take advantage of the scare.

On March 26, the cholera struck for certain: four cases were reported. By April 1, there were 565. Only a hundred of the victims had died, but that sufficed to put the city into a state of panic. The price of medicines – or rather, substances popularly supposed to be remedial – rocketed. A packet of camphor, the most popular specific, shot from 5 francs to 24, and so with chloride and other medicines, all equally useless.

As the initial optimism proved false, Parisians looked for someone to blame, and now a political dimension became apparent. The right wing royalists blamed the 1830 revolution that overthrew the Bourbons and let undesirable fugitive émigrés into the country from Poland and elsewhere, bringing the *cholera morbus* along with their dissident tendencies. As if the cholera itself was not a sufficient affliction, each party saw how it might be exploited. For the republicans it was their opportunity to bring down the monarchy, for the royalists, a chance to restore the "legitimate" Bourbon dynasty. Though the queen and the princesses were helping with the epidemic, and rooms of the Tuileries palace were turned into workshops, the regime was attacked by both sides for its perceived mishandling of the crisis.

In fact the authorities had taken excellent measures to handle the situation, but the severity of the epidemic showed that more was needed. They recognized that one of the factors aiding the spread of the sickness was the appallingly insalubrious state of the narrow streets of central Paris, where filth and refuse lay in the streets, much to the delight of rats and other vermin. One of the measures introduced was a nightly removal of refuse, but this provoked fierce opposition from the two thousand rag-pickers and others who made a precarious living by scouring the streets of Paris every night for useable rubbish. The first night of the innovation, March 21, *la guerre des chiffonniers* – the war of the ragpickers – exploded. The dissidents saw their living destroyed. Rather than a social benefit, the street-clearing was seen as a government plot to suppress them. Bands of agitators set fire to the refuse wagons, and when the police intervened, fighting broke out. Next morning, rioting was widespread across the city. A gang of 150 ragpickers, armed with hammers, came to smash up the wagons. Troops put them to flight, but the police were attacked in several parts of the city. The newspapers of the left accused the government of depriving 10,000 people of the right to live – though in fact there were 1,800 ragpickers at the most.

The rioting was inflamed by a revolt in the prisons, where it was claimed the prisoners were being held in conditions favoring cholera. A prisoner was said to have died of the disease. Two hundred republicans brandishing the red flag attacked the Sainte-Pélagie prison in the name of liberty, smashing doors and windows, and might have broken into the prison if the municipal guard had not arrived in time. On April 1, the police, the municipal guard, and even the army were kept busy quashing local outbreaks and patrolling the streets, where most of the streetlamps had been smashed and the populace improvised barricades in the time-honored Paris manner. Street traders joined the rioters, as well as vagabonds and other riffraff. The city was home to some 1,600 fugitives from justice and 6,000 thieves and vagabonds for whom the police were a natural enemy.

From perceiving the street-cleaning operation as a government plot against the poor, it was a short step to a broader conspiracy theory, which was that there was no cholera at all, that the epidemic was itself a government plot introduced to suppress the workers and impose the regime on the populace. "The rich, the nobility and the bourgeois were accused, not only of not dying as others did from the cholera, but actually of conspiring with the doctors and priests to poison the people."[130]

The rumor spread from café to cabaret that it was arsenic-poisoning, not cholera, which was causing all the deaths. (In fact, the effects of arsenic are not dissimilar to those of cholera, so far as appearance is concerned, and similar accusations had been made during cholera outbreaks in Russia and Poland.) To make the rumor believable, left-wing enthusiasts acted out fake scenarios. For example, an individual would pretend to sprinkle poison into a shop or onto goods, and a crowd would surround him and drag him to the police. Naturally the supposed poisoner would make his getaway, but the effect had been produced, the public alarmed. On the Pont-Neuf, a child was given a flask of liquid and offered 20 cents to empty it into a public fountain. The child ran to tell its mother, who took the liquid to the prefecture where analysis revealed it to be a harmless herbal medicine. Poisoned food and wine were "found" in many places; sometimes, in the middle of the street, a man would fall, rolling on the ground in fearful convulsions, yelling that he had been poisoned. How much was genuine suggestion, how much false propaganda, none can say, but it had the same affect either way by stirring up popular uncertainty and suspicion. The evening of April 3, the police broke up a crowd who had seized hold of a man accused of poisoning a wine-merchant's stock; the crowd mutilated him so severely that he died before the police could get him to the commissariat. That same evening, fourteen foot guards were called to arrest six individuals accused of throwing arsenic into the jugs of a cabaretier and giving poisoned sweets to children; two companies of soldiers were barely able to protect them from being lynched by the workmen of the quarter.

Such incidents convinced many that the poisonings were real, and newspapers whether of the right or the left were happy to print the wildest stories against the government. According to the paper's viewpoint, the poisonings would be attributed to miserable revolutionary troublemakers on the one hand, on the other to the authorities, even the police themselves! Vigilante patrols searched any likely suspect. Confrontations took place here and there throughout the city.

Official denials followed, but inevitably they served only to inflame the populace by the very fact that the authorities recognized the existence of such stories. What had hitherto been suspicion became a certainty now that it was officially discussed, even though it was denied. Encouraged, the populace looked for victims – and found them. A Jewish fishmonger paused suspiciously in front of a bar. He was seized and searched; a packet of white powder was found. No doubt it was arsenic. The crowd threw themselves on him, and by the time the police arrived, they tore from the mob's hands nothing but a mass of bloody flesh. Near the Hotel de Ville, in the heart of Paris, a suspect was dragged out and his bowels ripped open; a coal merchant threw his entrails to his dogs.

Such rumors are not easily countered, but the authorities did what they could. When a man was accused of giving a poisoned cake to a small girl, Commissar Jacquemin divided the cake in two and ate half of it: "the crowd's fury gave place to hilarity." One of his colleagues drank from a supposedly poisoned bottle of vinegar, but such local debunking was insufficient to kill the rumor. The extremists continued to believe that the white powder was a poison chosen by the ministers to exterminate the poor, even though the official paper, *Le Moniteur*, announced that "no trace of poison has been found.... The bottles, the bread, the sweets, the meat, seized and supposed to be poisoned, have all been subject to analysis; they have been found absolutely pure. The white powder carried by the unfortunate fish merchant was camphor, which he carried as a preservative against the cholera."[131] Yet a large section of the populace continued to believe that the doctors and pharmacists were in league with the government to eliminate the poor.

Rumors ran rife as to how many were killed as a result of these excesses. The wildest guesses ran to fifty, but Lucas-Dubreton suggests that the number of actual deaths may have been only five, though many more were injured or roughly handled. But, as he adds, what is important is not the number of victims, but the effect on the morale of the population. La Duchesse de Dino, in a letter, observed, "Everything vanished in the face of the state of health and morale of Paris. How horrible that party politics should go so far as to exploit such an affliction in order to stir up the most bloody disorder!"[132] France, which considered itself the most civilized of nations, found itself on an equal level with the peasants of Poland or Hungary. Commentators sought to explain it by attributing it to a law of nature from which none could escape, or to bad elements in society which are found everywhere. Or, as the *Gazette d'Auvergne* proposed, it was a punishment from heaven "which swooped like a vulture on a city in disorder, surprised it in the midst of its pleasures and in the most perfect security, and proceeded to harvest for preference those who give themselves to excess of passion and brutal pleasures."[133]

While these distractions occurred, the cholera continued, with huge numbers being struck down daily. The rioting, which had initially drawn its impetus from the cholera epidemic, now became openly political, ultimately amounting virtually to a civil war. By the time the government succeeded in getting the upper hand over the mob, at least 70 police or soldiers had been killed, 326 wounded. Of the insurgents, 233 were killed, more than 600 wounded.

The cholera epidemic continued, carrying off 15 to 20 a day. In July the numbers started to rise again, but finally began to fall again in August, when the infection moved to Bordeaux. The official total of cholera deaths in Paris was 18,402, more if the suburbs were included; Lucas-Dubreton reckons the unofficial total must have been substantially higher. But by now the rumors of poisoning had faded, and the epidemic was seen for what it was, an act of nature, indifferent to the politics of left and right.

COMMENT: The process of blaming an unpopular establishment for a natural disaster has a long history. There is a clear parallel between the 1832 Paris panic and the late 20th century conspiracy theory which blames the AIDS virus on the machinations of the Pentagon.[134] The 1832 incident is unusual, however, in that those who sought to convince the public were not content with circulating rumors to that effect, but went to the trouble of faking the evidence.

Such rumors found ready ears, for the people were happy to believe that what menaced them was not an act of God, from which there was no escape, but an act of man, which could be combated.

CHRISTIAN CONVERSION SYNDROME

Uttarakhand, India: 1997

Strange psychological reactions were reported in the Uttarakhand region of Uttar Pradesh in northern India in response to a campaign by three missionary schools to convert Hindus to Christianity. According to reports, three Roman Catholic priests conducted a Christian "self awareness programme" on August 5, as children between the ages of 10 and 16 were taken to a church and made to recite prayers. Journalist Amita Verma said that, as the program reached an emotional climax, some students "started throwing up and reacting violently. Some children fainted while a few others went into convulsions. Five students were hospitalized while others reported signs of trauma." Similar responses were recorded during other self-awareness programs between July 28 to August 4. During each program, teachers were not allowed to enter the church as the priests gave their presentation.

One teacher told the press that several students who participated in the program were still not psychologically fit enough to attend school. "Their parents has [sic] told us that the children are behaving in an erratic manner. Some of them get up at night and call out to Yesu [Jesus] while others have not yet overcome the trauma."[135]

CHUPACABRA SCARE

The Americas and the Caribbean: 1975 to 1996

Between February and March 1975, reports circulated in Puerto Rico of a mysterious creature attacking domestic and farm animals, draining their blood, and scooping out chunks of their flesh. Residents claimed that they heard loud screeches and/or flapping wings coinciding with the attacks. Academics and police examined the carcasses, blaming everything from humans to snakes and vampire bats. Locals referred to the attacker as "The Vampire of Moca." This incident may have been spurred by the better known "cattle mutilation mystery."[136] In November 1995, similar attacks were reported on the island. Called "chupacabras,"[137] or goat sucker, named after a bird of the Caprimulgidae family that purportedly steals goat's milk,[138] the bizarre being was described as a "bristly, bulge-eyed rat with the hind legs of a kangaroo, capable of escaping after its crimes in high speed sprints."[139] It also exuded a sulfur-like stench. Stories had it that the bodies of animals were discovered disemboweled and drained of blood. One member of a Civil Defense team in a small city in the affected area said he was spending half his time responding to chupacabras calls. Some people, he reported, have been so distraught that they have been treated at hospitals.[140] Interest in the creature ran so high in May 1996 that a chupacabras home page received enough hits to be ranked in the top 5 percent of all web sites.[141] By March 1996, goat sucker stories had spread to the Hispanic community in Florida; by May, accounts of chupacabras attacks began to circulate in Mexico and soon after, to the Mexican-American community in Arizona. The chupacabras flap ended abruptly in mid-1996,[142] though sporadic reports continue.

CLAY EATING EPIDEMIC

Australia: 1974-1978

Between 1974 and 1978, an outbreak of clay eating was reported among a group of Aboriginal women in several North Australian coastal towns in the Northern Territory. Of 19 cases analyzed by psychiatrist Harry Eastwell, all were near or past childbearing age. The episode coincided with a period of turbulent social change as nomadic Aborigines were adjusting to Western ex-hunter-gatherer lifestyles. The arrival of imported foods rendered traditional good gathering patterns obsolete. Important social roles associated with hunting, foraging, and food distribution disintegrated. The role of post-menopausal females was especially ambiguous and ill defined. By 1974, many young mothers became unemployed, displacing the valued role of child-minding by middle-aged women who had been caring for the working mothers' children. Unable to gain employment or be productive members of society, these women suddenly found themselves poor, dependent, neglected, and depressed. The Aboriginal women studied reacted to their plight by eating clay.[143]

CONTEXT: The episode occurred during a period of rapid social change among Aborigines transitioning from a nomadic hunter-gatherer society to a modern Western lifestyle. Those affected may have been experiencing a period of social maladjustment as social roles involving foraging, hunting, and distribution of food were abruptly extinguished with the introduction of Western culture.

A basic ethos of Aboriginal hunter-gatherer society are sharing and reciprocation, which were weakened by the cash economy and sedentarianism. According to Eastwell, "Those who had once been the most efficient food suppliers have been reduced to the status of dependent consumers. They have nothing to reciprocate with, but they feel the obligation to do so, and dysphoria is the result."[144]

The handling and consumption of clay is psychologically comforting, often being rubbed on breasts to promote lactation. Clay is one of the first tastes of a newborn, and young females often play with clay babies and breasts.[145] Eastwell states that "pre-pubertal girls were given practice for their future role by playing 'mother' with two breasts of dried clay suspended by bark-string around their shoulders. A clay 'baby' was carried in a bark container in their hands. Clay thus has symbolism..."[146]

COMMENT: Eastwell considered the possibility that the clay eating was prompted by malnutrition. However, this hypothesis neither explains the sudden upsurge in clay eating in 1974, nor why food was in evidence in many of the homes of clay eaters.[147] Could clay eaters have been satisfying a craving for iron? Eastwell found "no difference in the hemoglobin levels of ingesters as compared with controls."[148] The consumption of clay did not appear to contribute to the health of the eaters, as most were constipated and two suffered near fatal intestinal obstructions requiring emergency colostomies.[149]

COCA-COLA SCARE

Belgium and France: 1999

On June 8, 1999, 33 pupils at a secondary school in the small town of Bornem, Belgium, near Antwerp, were rushed to a nearby hospital after they felt ill shortly after drinking containers of Coca-Cola. When the first 10 students reported feeling sick, the school nurse made inquiries, finding that the only common denominator the students shared was their having drank Coke. At this point, staff members reportedly went from room to room, asking students if they had consumed Coke and if they felt sick. Shortly thereafter, another 23 students reported feeling ill and were admitted to hospital. Symptoms included nausea, stomach pain, breathing difficulty, dizziness, and lightheadedness. However, examining doctors could find no indication of any abnormality as urine and blood samples were normal. None of the students were treated with medication, though some were given oxygen. Fifteen remained hospitalized overnight for observation as a precaution. On June 9, four more students were examined at the hospital complaining of similar symptoms, but their exams were also unremarkable. In all, 28 girls (out of 179) and 9 boys (of 101), ranging in age from 10 to 17, were admitted.[150]

The Bornem incident made headlines across Europe. In the following days, 75 Belgian schoolchildren claimed similar ill effects from drinking Coke at four other schools. These include students in Brugge (June 10, 11 affected), Harelbeke (June 11, 17 involved), Lochristi (June 14, 35 "sickened"), and also June 14 at Kortrijk, with 12 reporting illness.[151] The main symptoms in these subsequent school cases were abdominal pain, nausea, headache, trembling, and lightheadedness. Twenty-five percent of those affected were boys and 75 percent were female.[152] Coca-Cola announced a recall of certain barricaded Coke and Fanta containers on June 11, and by June 14, all Coca-Cola products were barred from sale in Belgium.

CONTEXT: The episode coincided with a major Belgian food scare commonly referred to as the "dioxin crisis." In early 1999, a tank filled with recycled fats used in the production of animal feed was inadvertently contaminated with PCBs, dioxins, and other pollutants. The incident led to a massive poisoning incident among chicken farmers when the feed was dispensed to the chickens. The delay in announcing the contamination to the public (the incident was leaked to the Belgian media in May) fomented a political confidence crisis that led to the resignations of the Ministers for Agriculture and Health.[153] In May 1999, it was widely reported in the media that animal feed in Belgium had been contaminated with several highly toxic agents, including dioxins, dibenzofurans, and polychlorinated biphenyls. The reports triggered widespread anxiety across Belgium, starting with a massive recall of chicken and eggs, and soon, of most dairy and meat products. By early June, at the time of the first Coke incident, the "dioxin crisis" was dominating Belgian news and all aspects of Belgian life.[154] "The issue of the safety of modern foods had become pervasive, with one of the main messages aired by scientists being that even minimal amounts of chemicals could seriously affect health."[155]

In the wake of media saturation of the "poisoning," symptoms quickly spread across Belgium. Between June 8 and 20, the Belgian Poison Control Center received 1,418 phone calls, of which 943 were from anxious callers concerning "one or more symptomatic subjects" who felt unwell after drinking Coke, and to a far lesser extent, other drinks: Fanta, Sprite, Minute Maid, Pepsi Cola, Lipton Ice Tea, Nestea, and Aquarius. There was no obvious geographical pattern to the reports and calls came from across the entire country.[156]

On June 15, Coca-Cola officials issued a statement claiming that they had pinpointed two causes of the outbreak. First, it was stated that transport pallets treated with fungicide were responsible for contaminating "the outside of some cans." Second, it was said that some bottles had been dispensed with "bad carbon dioxide."[157] These findings were then sent to prominent Belgian toxicologist D. Lison at the Catholic University de Louvain in Brussels, Belgium. After studying the results, Lison concluded that the chemical traces were unlikely to have caused illness, and the probable cause of the symptoms was mass hysteria.[158] "The analyses revealed the presence in some bottles of very low, but odorous amounts of hydrogen sulphide (about 5-15 ppb), possibly originating from the hydrolysis of carbonyl sulphide. Small amounts of 4-chloro-3-methylphenol were found on the outside of some cans (about 0·4 µg/can). In both cases, it is unlikely that such concentrations caused any toxicity beyond an abnormal odour. No other notable chemicals had been found."[159] A similar conclusion was reached by an Ad Hoc Working Group advising the Belgian Health Ministry.[160]

By the end of June, the episode had subsided. The recall is estimated to have cost Coca-Cola between US$103 and 250 million dollars. The ban on Coke products in Belgium was lifted June 23, 1999.[161] It wasn't until March 31, 2000, that a Belgian government report officially issued its conclusion that mass hysteria was the cause.[162] Reports of similar illness symptoms were reported from adjacent France during June, and it is thought that mass hysteria in the wake of the Belgian media publicity was also to blame.[163]

COMMENTS: Toxicologists have suggested that Coca-Cola officials contributed to the scare by underestimating the seriousness of the illness reports and its potential impact on sales of Coke products. Further, perhaps due to concerns over its secret Coke recipe, "they were very casual in providing data from the chemical analyses of their products. The documents that were received were often no more than faxed messages and loose notes, with insufficient details..."[164]

COLLECTIVE ANXIETY ATTACKS

American sociologist Jeffrey S. Victor has devised the concept of collective anxiety or panic attacks. Whereas anxiety or panic attacks are known to strike individuals, Victor believes that a similar process occurs in group settings. Working with fellow sociologist Robert Bartholomew, they have presented their work in *The Sociological Quarterly* as a way to explain some reports of imaginary illnesses that befall groups of people in schools, factories, and even whole communities.[165] These episodes have traditionally been diagnosed as hysterical conversion disorder (HCD) but the authors suggest that this blanket label is not invariably appropriate, and that some episodes, customarily so diagnosed, may not involve HCD at all. Victor states: "The explanation suggests that shared anxiety provoked by a belief in a threatening rumor can result in symptoms of sickness, when a location or situation is believed to be dangerous. If the rumor spreads widely enough, it can create a group 'definition of the situation' that can intensify fear and distort perception. A person's belief in the threat itself can cause psychological stress that distorts a person's somatic reactions, and expectations of feeling sick that result in symptoms of sickness. Any of a person's senses may be affected; sight, hearing, smell, taste, touch, and a person may feel nauseous, vomit or faint from the stress. These reactions are usually temporary and change when a person no longer believes that they are in danger."[166]

By viewing such episodes as collective anxiety attacks as opposed to HCD, they can be seen as distinct from those behaviors which have been traditionally diagnosed as mass psychogenic illness or that convenient but often misleading and confusing catch-all term, "mass hysteria," both of which carry the implication of a transient mental disorder. On the contrary, collective anxiety attacks are not symptoms of mental illness or disorder, nor are they even irrational actions, nor are they spread by emotional contagion. Instead, they have their origin in shared convictions, which often reflect aspects of deeply ingrained culture-specific beliefs. Victor and Bartholomew argue, for instance, that the famous case of the MAD GASSER OF MATTOON was the expression of a collective anxiety attack.

Seen in this perspective, though the response itself may be viewed by others as irrational, it is nothing of the kind from the perspective of the participants. As psychiatrist Julian Leff expresses it: "When a large group of people share a set of beliefs, however unusual they may seem to outsiders, they form a subculture which legitimises their convictions and invalidates their being labeled as delusions."[167]

A great many of the episodes narrated in this Encyclopedia, which seem to us to be based on social delusions, were considered rational not only by those involved but also by many observers at the time. For instance, to Roman Catholic believers in the 17th century, it was entirely rational to suppose that inmates of convents were being possessed by demons, since it was a tenet of their belief system, authorized by Rome and not to be questioned, that religious persons are at risk from demons who will possess them given half a chance.

CONGO WITCH MASSACRE

Democratic Republic of Congo: June 2001

Between June 15 and July 6, 2001, an estimated 200 inhabitants of the northeastern Congo were "hacked to death" as suspected witches who were blamed for causing various diseases that had ravaged the area.

A "Ju-Ju Man" (native healer) of the Ashanti people on the Gold Coast, West Africa.

The area in question is a disputed border territory with Uganda. According to Ugandan Army Brigadier Henry Tumukunde, "Villagers were saying that some people had bewitched others, and they started lynching them. By the time we discovered this, 60 people had already been killed...."[168]

CONTEXT: The belief in witchcraft in a traditional African society as causing an outbreak of various diseases appears to have been a major factor in the episode.

COPYCAT BEHAVIOR

Similarities between occurrences of extraordinary behavior are a feature of this Encyclopedia. Panic outbreaks, convent hysteria, and cult practices tend to follow patterns that are often predictable. These similarities can be ascribed to three main causes: fundamental human traits, contagion, and copycat behavior. It is seldom easy to say which of these processes is at work behind the similarity, and there is considerable controversy on the matter, leading, for example, to debates as to the effect of media reportage is encouraging or discouraging suicide clusters. Loren Coleman, in his study *The Copycat Effect*,[169] has been criticized for blaming the media as the single most influential factor in triggering the Copycat Effect in modern times. But Coleman denies such linkages. "[While] I talk about the media as a factor, I make the point several times...that I am not 'blaming' the media. Furthermore, my book deals in copycat behavior that greatly preceded the narrow use of the word 'media' (as in 'modern mass media'). I discuss behavior contagion, spread by word-of-mouth, for example, among the Greek suicide victims of 4th century B.C. That is one of scores of historical instances I give of the copycat effect that are neither modern nor media-driven."[170]

Many of the episodes cited in this Encyclopedia display unmistakable copycat behavior, some of which have common features. In religious outbreaks, a tendency to run, jump, laugh hysterically, or utter animal noises recur repeatedly. Shrieking, frenzied dancing, and dropping senseless to the ground are standard behavior at revivals, whether at a Methodist meeting in 18th century England or an American revival meeting. More subtle is the tendency towards familiarity displayed by people in altered states; in cultures which possess distinct modes of address for close relatives or for strangers, affected people tend to lapse into familiar modes – this manifested at Morzine, where victims would use the familiar "tu" rather than the formal "vous," and the children in the Swedish outbreak addressed their bishop with similar informality. Stripping off one's clothes is another stereotypical behavior-pattern; we find it among the ADAMITES, but also the DOUKHOBORS, the LOUDUN OUTBREAK OF POSSESSED NUNS, and the victims of pibloktoq.

Certain recurrent circumstances also tend to evoke similar behaviors. Conspiracy theories lead to the same kind of panics, and populations react to perceived threats such as mad gassers and phantom slashers in much the same way whether they occur in Malaysia or the United States. Possession generates much the same kind of behavior – blasphemy and obscenity were symptoms of diabolic possession in 17th century France and the hysterical *ikota* afflicted the Klikouschestvo sect in Russia two centuries later.

Many of these behaviors can be attributed to shared human characteristics: similar circumstances lead to similar responses. But the similarities often run deeper than surface behavior. When in 1858 Bernadette Soubirous claimed to meet the mother of Jesus in the grotto at Lourdes, she soon found herself one of some 50 other alleged visionaries. While it is possible that Mary was appearing to one and all, it seems more probable that the later claimants were imitating Bernadette. A pattern of behavior emerged, which came to be seen as a template whereby such encounters could be validated or rejected. Similarly, claims to be abducted by extraterrestrials have become formalized to the point where there is a virtual ritual to which abductees are expected to conform.[171]

There is no reason to think that such imitation is conscious. A person doesn't say to herself, I think I will become an abductee or a visionary. The experience is surely subconscious, and the motivation doubtless a psychological one which might be revealed by analysis. Rather, what seems to be happening is that the pattern is perceived as appropriate by the person's subconscious, perhaps as a coping strategy to resolve some personal crisis, and this need finds expression in following a recognized role model. The human need to feel part of the tribe – a "member of the wedding," in Carson McCullers' eloquent phrase – dictates the form the expression takes, involving conformity to group values and acquiescence in peer pressure.

This would seem to be the agenda followed by participants in suicide clusters, in which a spate of self-killing occurs within a limited group of people, generally in the same cultural circumstances. In such cases, as in panic outbreaks in schools and workplaces, it seems unquestionable that the effect spreads by contagion. Sociologists have traced the path by which, say, a fear of imagined sickness can spread from one person to another in a confined location.[172] No doubt, as with contagion of any kind, there has to be a predisposition on a person's part if he or she is to be affected. But whereas in the case of an illness, this would be physical, in the case of the extraordinary behaviors covered by this Encyclopedia, the predisposing factors would be initially psychological but escalating to psychosocial.

However, while this may be a valid description of the process, it falls short of explaining the problems raised by the phenomenon. For example, in the case of the Saint-Médard outbreak, not only did the participants copy one another's behavior, but they also acquired the same remarkable abilities to undergo extraordinary physical pain. This takes copycat behavior onto a deeper level, implying something more profound than superficial imitation. This is recognized by Coleman, who suggests that the trigger event speaks a "twilight language" that "generates an internal dialogue between the human consciousness and subconscious."[173] Some element in the individual's hidden self responds to this message and is driven to behavior that the rational self would likely reject.

Social And Cultural Influences: Suicide And Violence

The contention that direct or indirect exposure to acts of suicide can trigger clusters of similar acts was well established within mainstream science during the 19th century. Indeed, in 1841, eminent epidemiologist William Farr observed that "no fact is better established in science than that suicide is often committed from imitation."[174] The father of sociology, Emile Durkheim, was also convinced of this association, writing that "no fact is more readily transmissible by contagion than suicide."[175] Using a social learning theory of deviance, sociologist David Phillips began, in 1974, to develop his now influential theorem of suicidal copycat behavior which holds that highly publicized accounts of suicides in newspapers trigger similar acts. It is thought that these stories serve as role models for those seriously contemplating socially negative acts such as suicide.[176] In 1982, a similar link was made between watching television news programs that detail suicides and suicide waves.[177]

In his seminal study, Phillips labeled the association between press coverage of suicides and copycat behavior as the Werther Effect, based on a 1774 novel by German poet Johann Wolfgang von Goethe, *The Sorrows of Young Werther*. In the book, Werther dons boots, a blue coat, and yellow vest and sits at a desk before an open book, then shoots himself after being rejected by a female lover. Soon after publication, the book was banned in parts of Europe after a spate of similar reports of suicides with the bodies found dressed in similar attire and von Goethe's novel nearby.[178] A similar suicide epidemic was reported in 1903 following the publication of Otto Weininger's book *Sex and Character*, involving suicide in young, educated Jewish females.[179] There is now evidence from over sixty studies that media suicide reports trigger higher than expected rates of both attempted and completed suicides by people using the suicide method explicitly described by journalists.[180]

American criminologist Steven Stack has analyzed 42 studies involving 293 findings on the influence of the media and suicide. Stack found that studies of suicides involving political or entertainment celebrities were more than fourteen times more likely to trigger an imitation effect. Studies of real-life suicide accounts (versus fictional stories) were four times more likely to produce a copycat effect. Of these studies, newspaper-based stories were 82 percent more likely to affect suicide than television-based accounts.[181]

Critics contend that any links between media reports and suicide epidemics is a moral panic, as the research is not conclusive and an array of other variables could have been involved. They also contend that if the media were regulated to censor suicide stories, it would open a Pandora's Box to "cleanse" other undesirable influences in society.[182] On the other hand, even Jan Thorson and Per-Arne Oberg, who argue that the evidence for a suicide epidemic following the publication of the Werther book has been exaggerated, admit that the novel appears to have prompted some imitators.[183]

The Case Of Micronesia

One compelling example of an apparent copycat effect for suicides is the case of Micronesia. Between 1955 and 1965, not a single known suicide had been recorded on the island of Ebeye (population 6,000). Then in 1967, a young man from a prominent family hung himself after he was caught in a love triangle and was unable to make up his mind as to which lover he should commit to. Within three days, another young man on the island who was in a similar situation killed himself. Over the next decade, at least twenty more suicides were recorded on Ebeye that "bore an uncanny resemblance to the first initial suicide story, including the case of [a] young man who committed suicide after scrawling graffiti on a wall that bade farewell to his two girlfriends in a very public manner."[184] Suicides soon became a prominent feature of island life throughout Micronesia, which went from having one of the lowest suicide rates to having the world's highest rate per capita. On some islands the rate was thirty times more than of Great Britain.

Researcher Paul Marsden observed that the Micronesian pattern was reminiscent of the European "Werther" affair, as a significant number of deaths followed a roughly similar script involving teenagers. "After going out drinking with friends on a weekend night, often following an apparently trivial disagreement with parents, adolescents would find a rope, tie the end to a door knob or low branch, form a noose, place it around their neck and then lean forward," cutting off their air supply.[185] This social patterning of suicide in Micronesia prompted Marsden to remark: "It was as if exposure to suicide stories not only somehow influenced decisions to commit suicide, but also how to do it."[186]

Of course, suicide clusters or epidemics do not appear in a void but have unique contexts. Francis X. Hezel, an expert on Micronesian suicide, reported that several pre-existing cultural factors coupled with rapid social changes, appear to render Trukese males vulnerable to copycat suicides. First is their machismo attitude towards personal danger and death. As Hezel noted: "This sense of bravado underlies the readiness of youth to undertake exploits that others would regard as foolhardy. Some years ago, for instance, it became something of a fad in Truk to jump off a boat while drunk and swim to a distant island."[187]

A second cultural influence involves suffering as a show of love. According to Hezel: "The tendency of the young Trukese male to advertise his sufferings is most clearly exhibited in the graffiti that cover public walls and T-shirts: there the woes of the individual are set forth in fanciful language for the whole world to see. Especially prominent are the tales of unrequited love that have stung young hearts, complaints that are phrased with a strong tone of self-abasement. A common theme among youth, one that appears again and again in the graffiti and is echoed in Trukese love songs, is that a person's love is proved by his readiness to suffer. In former years a young man inflicted cigarette burns or knife scars on himself to prove the depth of his love to a sweetheart."[188] A third factor is the trait of Turkese males to repress their feelings in other aspects of living outside of love, depriving them of the ability to vent their emotions. Hence, a pattern of drunken behavior that results in suicide may be a way of expressing anger and shame.

A fourth contributing cultural factor in helping to explain the Turkese suicide epidemic appears to be the need for social recognition among young males amid rapid social changes. Turkese society has always placed a strong emphasis on the importance of contributing to their family's wellbeing by doing chores. In modern times, with the breakup of the traditional family and the dwindling of traditional demands on young males to assist in such family tasks as food preparation, there is a growing sense of diminishment of importance to their families. Hezel underscored this point, noting that suicide affords Turkese males a means of attaining recognition and social standing, albeit posthumously. "Some have alluded with a note of triumph to the funeral feast that would be held in their honor as if they expected to achieve in death the recognition that they had been denied in life." Hezel observed that at least three suicides, all involving adopted sons, were carefully timed to coincide with the anniversary of a death in their adoptive family "as a way of expressing their desire for full assimilation into the family and ensuring that the anniversary of their own death would be a major family event in years to come. One young man even left his footprint and signature in wet cement on the floor of the family meeting house to memorialize himself and his deed. The attraction that such a dramatic form of recognition holds for young Trukese is attested by one 13-year-old boy who exclaimed, while witnessing the funeral of a suicide victim not much older than himself, 'How nice it would be to have all those people crying and making a fuss over me!'"[189]

A person is driven to copycat behavior by a variety of motives that may ultimately relate to their individual psychology: a craving for social approval, a need for self-assertion, a personal identity crisis. By doing as others do, the individual shares the responsibility for their actions; the behavior of others legitimizes their own. Coleman focuses on violent behaviors, particularly suicides and murders, where statistics indicate the part played by factors such as location (the Golden Gate Bridge at San Francisco, the Eiffel Tower), the celebrity of the role model (actor James Dean, musician Kurt Cobain), and the timing of trigger events (anniversaries such as Hitler's birthday, religious feast-days). Heredity may play a part – suicides often "run in families" – but environmental factors provide the setting. Yet while these all play a contributory part, none can be said to *cause* the copycat behavior. For that, we must look to the personality whose interaction with his/her circumstances brings the behavior about.

A criticism of Coleman is that he advocates self-censorship and is unrealistic in calling for greater media balance and restraint in the way it reports on suicide and violence. Coleman rejects this notion in arguing that the mass media have created a fantasy world wherein the exaggerated perception of violence in American society as portrayed on TV shows and the news programs serve to create a sort of self-fulfilling prophesy that fuels copycat behavior. As Coleman puts it: "...the media should reflect more on their role in creating our increasingly perceived violent society. Honest reporting on the positive nature of being alive in the twenty-first century may actually decrease the negative outcomes of the copycat effect, and create a wave of self-awareness that this life is rather good after all. Most of our lives are mundane, safe, and uneventful. This is something that an alien watching television news from outer space, as they say, would never know. The media should 'get real,' and try to use their influence and the copycat effect to spread a little peace rather than mayhem."[190]

Copycat behavior is most evident and alarming in suicides and murders, but it is not confined to any narrow segment of human behavior. It is displayed in harmless fashions, fads, and crazes, as well as in harmful behaviors. Rather, imitation would appear to be a fundamental human trait. While the greater number of copycat behaviors relate to shared fears, as witness the number of panics and scares chronicled in this Encyclopedia, they may also be inspired by shared hopes, as exemplified by the Taeping and Boxer outbreaks in 19th century China or the 16th-to-19th century migrations of the peoples of Brazil and Peru.

CONSPIRACY THEORIES

A large proportion of the extraordinary behaviors described in this Encyclopedia spring from mankind's hopes or fears. The hopes are expressed in millennarist agendas, cargo cults, and migrations in search of utopian promised lands. The fears are likely to take the form of conspiracy theories. Just as millennarism represents an unjustified expression of people's hopes, so conspiracy theories are an exaggerated formulation of their fears.

A typical conspiracy theory purports to account for a controversial or enigmatic situation by attributing responsibility to the secret activities of a powerful group or institution. Most often, there will be a basis of fact, or at any rate circumstantial evidence to support the suggestion. As an example of the first, the POPISH PLOT of the 1670s developed as a consequence of real attempts by the Roman Catholic Church to reassert papal ascendancy over England; the 1605 Gunpowder Plot had been a clear indication of Catholic conspiratorial intentions. As an example of the second, the circumstances of the 1963 assassination of U.S. president John F. Kennedy were accompanied by sufficient conflicting evidence and unexplained incidents to justify suspicions that the official account was flawed.[191]

Not all conspiracy theories result in exceptional behavior. The Popish Plot did so, in that exaggerated suspicions led to extravagant rumors which in turn led to arrests and executions of innocent people. The Kennedy killing, on the other hand, while it generated an enormous and persistent controversy, never escalated into exceptional behavior.

For conspiracy theory to express itself in actions,

as against mere written or spoken arguments, there must be a perception that "something can be done about it." This in turn requires an appropriate formulation of the problem on the one hand, and its solution on the other. It also requires initiative, in the form of individual or group leadership.

Conspiracy theory writer Peter Knight has written, "As many commentators agree, conspiracy theories have long been identified as a peculiarly American obsession."[192] While this is largely true, however, they are certainly not exclusive to the New World, as several entries in this Encyclopedia show. Notably, conspiracy theories flourished among the Russian *Raskolniki* sects. (See RUSSIAN SECTS.) Thus the members of the Bezpopovtzy sect believed that their government was acting presumptuously in conducting a census of the population in 1896 – for, according to their beliefs, only God could know the number of humans he had created. When the authorities sought to enforce the census on the sect, its members perceived this as a government conspiracy specifically targeting them. Powerless to fight the government, they resorted to collective suicide. (See BEZPOPOVTZY.)

The Bezpopovtzy episode also illustrates a characteristic feature of conspiracy theory: the need to shift responsibility to some one else. Frequently, this involves demonizing some powerful group or organization. That someone else will usually be in a position of power – or ostensibly so. Jews, international bankers, communists, global companies, Freemasons, the United Nations – these are favorite targets. Sometimes they work in harness, thus by a remarkable juxtaposition, communists have been supposed to be in cahoots with international bankers, who themselves are of course supposed to be, or to be manipulated by, Jews.[193] These forces are often supposed to be seeking to "rule the world" – a vague and ultimately meaningless concept.

Such demonization is not necessarily harmful; it can on occasion be salutary open-minded speculation drawing attention to legitimate grievances or causes for concern. But it can also be very sinister and the potential dangers are many, as Richard Webster, investigator of the alleged North Wales pedophile ring, has expressed it: "Whenever we allow demonological fantasies to develop in our midst... there is always a danger that a process of self-delusion may take place... For, when small, zealous groups become seized by this kind of fantasy, they may well, as has happened repeatedly throughout history, construct a narrative so powerful that they cannot escape from its grip. There is then a very greater danger that they – or the agents of the church or state they succeed in mobilising – may begin unwittingly to 'create' the very evidence they need to intensify this fantasy..." He adds: "This danger is particularly acute when a delusion is based upon a palpable reality. For when fantasy is mixed with fact in unequal proportions, the fantasy can sometimes become even more dangerous and even more destructive."[194]

Apart from those who think that UFOs are being sent by extraterrestrials to take over Planet Earth, the only non-human menaces to figure widely in conspiracy lore are Satan and his demons, who play a leading role in many entries in this Encyclopedia. The huge amount of speculation that has been associated with this folklore figure is evidence of the need to find someone to blame. From hysterical nuns to criminals of all kinds, "the devil made me do it" has been a popular plea throughout the centuries. (See entries DEMON POSSESSION, EXORCISM, etc.)

But there is no lack of human scapegoats. As the authors of *Weapons of Mass Deception* demonstrate, misguided perceptions of other cultures can lead to demonization of entire communities or even nations. Two days after the 9/11/2001 terrorist attack on New York, columnist Ann Coulter told readers of the *National Review*, "This is no time to be precious about locating the exact individuals directly involved in this particular terrorist attack. We should invade their countries, kill their leaders and convert them to Christianity."[195] No doubt the perpetrators of the attacks were motivated by a similar demonization of the United States, seen as "Satanic" by the very cultures demonized by Coulter and like-minded Americans.

CONVENT HYSTERIA

From the late 15th century to the 18th century, outbreaks, generally involving supposed DEMON POS-

SESSION, periodically occurred in convents and orphanages maintained by the Roman Catholic church in western Europe. While all enclosed communities are vulnerable to stresses, which can erupt into outbreaks if some untoward event sets them off, this category stands apart not only by their religious setting, but also because the patterns of behavior remained remarkably consistent over a period of two hundred years. Moreover, these patterns presented many similarities to those observed in non-religious contexts, as well as in primitive cultures throughout the world.

While each outbreak of convent hysteria manifested individual features, all presented symptoms in common with others. In most cases the victims were nuns; in some they were children who for one reason or another had been taken into care by a religious community.

These outbreaks occurred at the time when the WITCH MANIA IN EUROPE was at its height, yet, though many of the manifestations were similar, there seems to have been a tacit consensus that witchcraft was not involved in them. It was presumed that these afflicted nuns, being by definition under divine protection, would not have voluntarily chosen to consort with demons, as witches were supposed to do; rather, they had been specially targeted by Satan in his on-going mission to suborn God's creatures. Consequently they received a quite different treatment from the authorities. If occasionally an individual was accused of practicing witchcraft, this was more with the intention of directing blame to a scapegoat, and the individual was generally someone on the fringes of the community, such as the midwife at Wertet or Else Kamense, the cook at Kentorff. The nuns themselves were rarely accused of witchcraft and consequently were hardly ever tortured to obtain full details of their story, nor executed for the crime of consorting with the devil.

The documentation for these outbreaks is sparse and uneven, and in most cases comes from Church records. The nearest we have to objective accounts come from medical reports. There can be little doubt that there were many more outbreaks than those for which records have survived. Weyer, for example, refers chiefly to those cases in which he was personally involved. No doubt other doctors were consulted for cases of which no records survive.

Inevitably, the records are frustratingly incomplete. Nevertheless, the degree of conformity between those that we have leaves no doubt that they ran to a pattern, with characteristic features occurring time and time again. These were:

Seemingly spontaneous commencement: Though underlying factors provided the enabling context, the outbreaks did not generally seem to be occasioned by any specific happening or circumstance. The commencement is probably best seen as analogous to the eruption of a volcano. For example, at Louviers the extremely severe austerities imposed on the nuns undoubtedly contributed; at Wertet, Weyer established that strict fasting during Lent triggered the outbreak.

Rapid spread: Frequently, a particular individual was identified as the first to manifest the trouble, but this very soon spread to others, sometimes to the entire community, as at Loudun. Facilitating this rapid spread was the isolation of the community, and the fact that all within it were subject to the same influences.

Physical manifestations: A wide range of these was reported, and an individual might switch rapidly from frenetic activity, such as convulsive seizures on the floor, to catalepsy. Manifestations included fainting; howling and shrieking; rapid movements of the head; rapid running; climbing on walls, trees and rooftops; and facial grimaces which were frequently reported by spectators as unbelievably horrible.

Verbal manifestations: The individual might switch from complaints about her plight to assertive imprecation. Blasphemy was frequent, as at Auxonne, the individual abandoning her normal piety to express antagonism to the priests, to church teachings, even to God himself. The Devil was honored. And language was often familiar, for example, employing the casual *tu* instead of the polite *vous* even when addressing a superior; it was frequently extremely obscene.

Animal-like noises: In convent after convent, the afflicted sisters would meow like cats, yelp like dogs, and so on. At Santen, they baaed like sheep. This particular symptom was also observed in some non-convent cases, such as AMOU and BLACKTHORN.

The afflicted persons claimed to be possessed by demons: Generally this claim was made spontaneously by the afflicted sisters; in other cases it was diagnosed by the authorities, including medical experts called in to evaluate. In many instances the sufferers would name the particular demons they had inside them, or the demons would identify themselves during exorcism.

Hallucinations: These occurred in many cases and might take all kinds of form – sometimes known persons, sometimes strangers; religious figures such as comforting angels; demonic figures either handsome and seductive or hideous and terrifying. Frequently, demons would manifest in the guise of benevolent beings, adding to the overall confusion. At Louviers monks and nuns appeared, who subsequently revealed themselves to be demons in disguise, and handsome young men appeared who tried to seduce the sisters. At Milan demons appeared not only in the form of monks but even of Jesus himself.

Obscenity and erotomania: Many aspects of the possessed sisters' behavior, physical or verbal, were lascivious in their nature. The temptations offered by the demons were generally erotic, and the sisters had frequently to resist demonic seduction – to which, at Louviers for instance, they were accused of submitting. Obscene language was commonplace when the victims were possessed, and their convulsions often simulated copulation or masturbation, shocking the spectators with their orgasmic character. The nuns of Aix, Auxonne, Köln, Loudun, and Louviers were particularly affected. [See PROFANITY]

A tendency to fantasy and an absence of everyday reality testing: The isolation of the nuns, and the lack of anyone dependable to turn to for help, detracted from the sisters' ability to use common-sense yardsticks to measure what was going on. In extreme cases, such as Madeleine Bavent at Louviers, the fantasy was so extreme as to be ludicrous – her description of eating roast infant at a sabbat, for example. It is a measure of the credulity of the times that these absurdities could even for a moment have been accepted as real.

Pointing the blame: In most cases, the afflicted persons, or their directors, sought to identify an individual responsible for the disorder. This might be one of themselves, as at Lille or Louviers, or someone marginally associated with the community, as at Wertet, or someone outside the community, as at Loudun. The person might be regarded as an innocent victim, but was more likely to be cast in the role of scapegoat, accused of practicing sorcery and punished accordingly.

The incompleteness of the record means that we cannot be sure how many of these recurrent features manifested in each case, but even from what we know, their conformity is remarkable. As with many other extreme behaviors discussed in this Encyclopedia, such as extraterrestrial abduction, the question to what extent these common features arose spontaneously, or by imitation conscious or unconscious, remains unresolved. While some features were no doubt modeled on known behaviors – the seizures, for example, took the form of pseudo-epileptic fits – others, such as the tendency to climb trees or walk on roofs, have no obvious model and challenge interpretation.

Nuns of the convent of Saint-Ursule develop "convent hysteria," claiming to be possessed by demons. (Taxil, Le Diable au XIXe siecle)

Shorter uses "symptom pool" as a convenient term for the models available for psychosomatic patients to draw on for the purpose of fabricating their supposed malady, and this seems very appropriate for the victims of convent hysteria who drew on the common stock of behavior patterns described above.[196] A nun who believed herself possessed by a demon would unconsciously "know" that she should not only go into a convulsive seizure but also utter blasphemies and obscenities.

How Convent Hysteria Was Diagnosed

In interpreting this behavior, three main options were available: that the victims were faking, that they were possessed by supernatural forces, or that they were suffering from some unidentified illness. In the great majority of cases, faking could be largely ruled out because of the apparent sincerity of the patients, the very real nature of their sufferings, and their ability to do things they would normally be incapable. Though no doubt some faking did occasionally occur, especially where children were involved as at Amsterdam and Hoorn, both church and medical authorities explicitly ruled it out as an explanation.

As for sickness, though some doctors suspected that some kind of natural malady might be responsible, they were unable to name it, and in any case this did not rule out the possibility that the devil was responsible for the sickness.

Consequently the explanation of choice was that the nuns were afflicted and possessed by some supernatural being. In principle, this could be either divine or diabolical, but since it was out of the question that such horrible afflictions could be God's work, they were attributed to the machinations of the Evil One. In virtually every case, demonic possession was diagnosed, with the doctors agreeing with the churchmen.

The nuns themselves were generally regarded – and regarded themselves – as innocent victims, but a search was usually made for one or more individuals who, consciously or otherwise, were acting as the devil's agent and were responsible for importing the demon into the community, usually by means of magical practices. It rarely happened that the nuns were unable to find someone who, on their say-so alone, could be cast in the role of scapegoat. This might be one of their number; at Santen, for example, a young novice who had entered the convent after an unhappy love affair was identified as having brought the demon into the community. In other cases, it might be someone among the spiritual advisers to the community, as notably at Aix. In yet other cases it might be someone outside the community altogether, such as Grandier at Loudun, whom none of the accusing sisters had so much as set eyes on when they accused him. In most cases the nuns' accusations were believed, especially when they came from the possessing demons, for the devil would surely know his own. The accused persons were liable to be tortured to extract a confession, then executed as heretics, as befell Grandier, Gaufridi at Aix, Boullé at Louviers, and other unfortunates.

A few protesting voices were raised against this procedure. The Flemish-born doctor Johan Weyer, who personally investigated some convent hysteria outbreaks, rejected the accusation of magic and believed that the accused individuals were innocent of the charges. What was afflicting the nuns was a kind of sickness, with natural causes. Nonetheless, he adhered to the prevailing belief that Satan was ultimately responsible.

Just why the devil should seek to win friends by subjecting them to these horrific sufferings was never made clear; to encourage a nun to climb trees might seem a strange way to win her soul. But the absence of plausibility and consistency did not discourage the churchmen from seeing the devil's hand in all these outbreaks. It was not until the 19th century that people seriously began to look elsewhere for an explanation.

How Convent Hysteria Has Been Subsequently Diagnosed

There are still those who continue to attribute behavior such as Convent Hysteria to the Devil: see DEMON POSSESSION. Generally, though, the consensus is that the afflicted nuns were suffering from a psychosomatic disorder, induced by the stresses of living in an enclosed same-sex community where fasting, penance, and other austerities were everyday conditions. Their disorder took the form it did to conform to prevalent beliefs that provided them with widely accepted models for their role-playing. Like Charcot's hysteric patients at La Salpetrière in Paris, consciously or unconsciously they knew what was expected of them and they put on an appropriate performance.[197]

Calmeil, writing in 1845, diagnosed the afflicted sisters as suffering from hystero-demonopathy. Doctors in his day and since have been hard put to find a term that adequately describes the condition, and the patients may be described as suffering from convulsive monomania, demonomania, demonopathy, or demoniac madness; religious madness or religious melancholy; or simple hysteria. The terminology has varied, but the diagnosis is one with which most medical opinion would concur. However, the labeling options reflect a basic question: should the focus be on the physical symptoms of the malady, or on its ostensible nature, or on its social context?

Shorter, in his valuable history of psychogenic illness, recognizes the difficulties of distinguishing between genuine organic illness and the pseudo-illnesses of the psychogenic kind.[198] One of his crucial criteria is motivation. By and large, patients do not consciously choose to be ill; so when they do, as in much of psychogenic illness, it is because they have a reason to do so, of which they are not consciously aware. In the case of Convent Hysteria, the motivations are not hard to discern. The conditions of convent life, the circumstances under which the young nuns entered it, the sexual frustration and dissatisfaction, and the jealousies and rivalries that inevitably arise in a closed community – all these provided ample incentive for the nuns to unconsciously initiate this type of behavior.

It is important to recognize that these communities were often made up of young women, sometimes adolescents. At Loudun few were over 30 and some under 20, while the prioress herself was only 26. The official reports at Auxonne refer to the nuns consistently as "girls." These were females physically in the prime of life, who would under different circumstances be socializing with the opposite sex, marrying, and bearing children. While some became nuns because they had a true religious vocation, there were also many who had not volunteered for convent life but were driven into it by family circumstances, by being, for one reason or another, not marriageable. It would be natural for them to feel frustration and resentment, whether open or repressed. This is reflected in the erotic character of so many of the outbreaks, whether in the sisters' physical actions, or in their language, or in the accusations they made against their colleagues or their spiritual advisers.

This motivation found expression in a selective borrowing from the symptom pool available. First and foremost was the fit. Taking the epileptic seizure as model, a highly stereotyped seizure became standard, to which all patients more or less conformed; this is particularly well described in our LOUVIERS entry. In several cases, contemporary observers guardedly mention the erotic nature of the convulsions. Today the orgasmic character of the seizures would be more readily recognized.

Several other kinds of psychosomatic behavior can be identified – the hysterical conversion leading to paralysis, anesthesia, and hyperesthesia. The rapid spread of the behavior throughout the community may have been accelerated by a kind of *folie à deux*. Hallucinations were a characteristic symptom that took many forms.

Other characteristic behaviors were drawn from the symptom pool to construct the syndrome, though it is not always obvious why. The uttering of animal-like sounds perhaps reflects the perception that demons are not human; the nuns would be aware that they are often depicted as monsters with animal features. The tendency to blasphemy and obscenity is a clear defiance of the Church and of propriety, such as the devil might be expected to indulge in. Similarly the familiarity – the *tu* instead of *vous* – can be seen as a defiance of authority. All these behaviors have also been noted in community outbreaks such as MORZINE.

Less easily accounted for is the tendency to run at great speed, or to climb trees, or to walk on high walls or the roofs of buildings. However, this is a notable feature of many Convent Hysteria outbreaks, and also occurred at Morzine. Why the nuns of Loudun or the children of Amsterdam should have manifested such a fondness for roofs is not self-evident. [See CLIMBING AND RUNNING.] These manifestations have not hitherto been taken into account by commentators, yet they are a conspicuous feature of the outbreaks and their recurrence requires explanation. While there is no obvious relevance to demons, neither are they predictable symptoms of hysteria as generally perceived, and it could be more profitable to consider them in conjunction with other physical phenomena such as those displayed by the CONVULSIONARIES OF SAINT MEDARD.

While psychology has gone a long way towards establishing Convent Hysteria as a psychosomatic affliction created by the victims' circumstances, there remain puzzling features of the outbreaks that show that we have by no means arrived at a complete understanding.

For individual outbreaks, see: AMSTERDAM, AUXONNE, BRANDENBURG, CAMBRAI, CHINON, FRIEDEBERG, HOORN, KENTORFF, KOLN, LILLE, LOUDUN, LOUVIERS, MADRID, MILANO, NIJMEGEN, NIMES, PADERBORN, ROME, SANTEN, TOULOUSE, UNTERZELL, WERTET.

COUGHING ORPHANS

Hungary: 1895

An episode of imitative coughing affected 5 of 45 children at a girls' orphanage in Budapest, in what seems to have been a typical instance of contagious behavior. Simple bodily actions such as yawning, sneezing, blinking, and so on frequently seem to spread in this way.[199]

CRAZES

The Concise Oxford Dictionary defines a craze as "a widespread but short-lived enthusiasm for something."[200] In popular usage the word craze denotes a temporary obsession or preoccupation with some object or activity. Crazes are similar to fads in that they are engaged in by large numbers of people, but are more intense, last longer, and are more serious. In general, crazes tend to involve fewer people than do fads. Sociologist Erich Goode defines crazes as "short-lived activities" that affect "fairly superficial areas of life." Unlike fads, however, Goode says that some people become obsessive or fanatical about these activities.[201] Crazes are often related to political bandwagons or money, such as financial booms, bubbles, and get-rich-quick schemes. During the DUTCH TULIP MANIA of 1634-37, the price of some tulip bulbs reportedly exceeded their weight in gold. Many crazes are related to quack health products or services such as "primal scream therapy" or "revolutionary" diet plans. Over the years there have been hundreds, perhaps thousands of diet books whose authors claimed to be "the" answer to being overweight; examples include "The Drinking Man's Diet" to the "Eat Anything You Want Diet."

What is the root cause of a craze? The craze involves a rush toward an object or idea that seems to provide a solution to a problem. When discussing crazes, it would be wise to remember the saying, "If it sounds too good to be true, it probably is!" Much of the literature on crazes falls under the heading of financial bubbles. The term "bubble" came into popular use in the early eighteenth century to describe property and share market booms.[202] During the KLONDIKE GOLD RUSH of 1897-98, as many as 100,000 Americans from all walks of life were enticed by sensational newspaper and magazine accounts of the vast riches to be found in the far north. They boarded trains for Seattle where they bought steamship tickets and headed for the Canadian Yukon Territory to seek their fortunes. Most were quickly disillusioned by the harsh, virtually unlivable conditions they encountered. In some places like Puget Sound in Washington State, entire factories and mills were deserted as workers left in droves – smitten by the lust of quick riches.[203]

Bursting Bubbles

In 1711, the South Sea Stock Company formed with the promise of reducing huge government debts built up between 1702 and 1713 during the War of Spanish Succession. An investment frenzy was soon underway as many people expecting to get-rich-quick rushed to buy real estate in several South Sea Islands. When the speculative bubble suddenly burst in October 1720, many people had lost vast sums of money, and England was plunged into a recession that lasted for several years.[204] In France a similar episode took place in 1720, thanks to the machinations of Scottish financier William Law. Frenchmen invested heavily in "the Mississippi Bubble," which promised them lucrative gains in Louisiana (a French possession at the time) – until after three years, like the South Sea Bubble, it burst.

During the FLORIDA LAND BOOM of the 1920s, it was predominantly Americans, who, entranced by the lure of quick riches, invested their life savings into inflated Florida real estate – land in some cases they had never laid eyes on and turned out to be almost worthless swampland. Many properties had deceptive names such as "Highlands" even though the land was just barely above sea level. Melbourne Gardens was advertised as suited for a house and garden, but in reality was 15 miles outside the city limits and without even an access road![205] In the face of wild, unrealistic expectations about immediate profits from quick re-selling, the boom was destined to go bust. The only question was when. An example of the speculation fervor is the case of D. P. Davis, who proposed building a small community using land dredged from the bottom of Tampa Bay. Investors bought three million dollars in lots on the first day alone that his scheme was open to the public – before dredging had even begun.[206] At the height of the boom, lots that sold for $1,500 in 1915, were selling for over two million dollars between 1925 and early 1926.

The Wall Street Crash of October 1929. (Illustration by Alfredo Ortelli in Illustrazione del Popolo)

In 1929 during the GREAT STOCK MARKET CRASH, many Americans threw caution to the wind and bought stocks on credit with the expectation of reaping huge profits. Why not, everyone seemed to be doing it and many experts were predicting no end in sight to the price boom. During the "Roaring 20s" the stock market rose to unprecedented heights as newspapers and magazines published account after account of people accumulating fortunes virtually overnight. Yielding to the share rush, ordinary Americans without much knowledge of the stock market and with only modest sums to invest, joined in the bull market. It didn't matter that they owed the other 90 percent because they were sure they would soon make double or triple that amount when the price continued to climb.

The mass media was instrumental in driving prices upward. Sociologist Richard LaPiere writes that between 1927 and 1929, newspapers and business magazines "were filled with hosannas for the New Era, in which prices – particularly stock market prices – were to continue indefinitely upward at an accelerative rate. The few writers who ventured to express doubt were quickly shouldered out of print by those who had caught the spirit of the new age."[207] Yet, the American stock market had reached unsustainable levels and was spiraling ever higher. Many investors were able to buy large numbers of shares at a fraction of the cost by buying on margin. Ten percent of the full price was a common down payment. Prices quickly rose faster than the stocks were worth. After a downward sell off that began slowly in August, the market crashed on "Black Tuesday" October 29, 1929. By early November 1929, some people had gone from being millionaires to standing in bread and soup lines in a matter of weeks.

The collapse of the American stock market triggered a depression across the industrialized world. Between 1929 and 1932, over 5,000 banks closed. In one school a frail-looking little girl was told by her teacher to go home and eat. She replied that she couldn't: "This is my sister's day to eat."[208] With the help of restored confidence in banks and massive public works programs, the Depression did not end until World War II. Unlike fads, crazes are far more likely to have disastrous outcomes.

CYBER GHOST SCARE

Southern India: September 2003

Two weeks of rumors and panic swept through the Indian city of Tiruchirappalli in the southern state of Tamil Nadu after reports that an internet ghost was terrorizing residents. School attendance had dropped considerably during the scare, which subsided after a police campaign to label the ghost as a hoax.

The episode can be traced to a Tamil-language newspaper that published a story accompanied by a photograph of a young boy posing by a tree. Behind him was what appeared to be the figure of a ghost with empty eye sockets, long hair, and no legs. According to the story, the boy had been at a picnic in the nearby Pulanjolai Hills, when a classmate took his photo by the tree. The student purportedly began vomiting blood before collapsing and dying. The boy in the photo supposedly went into a coma.

The report in the mass circulation paper led to fast-spreading rumors. The picnic spot where the ghost was allegedly spotted was deserted and many parents decided to keep children at home because of rumors about the ghost stalking young children.

The scare began to wane after police announced that they had determined that the picture was of a Malaysian girl, that it had been taken from the internet, and that the ghost had been added through the use of computer graphics. The photo had originally appeared in the Tamil newspaper *Thanthi* during October 2003. A senior Indian police official said: "Some prankster has downloaded the stuff from the internet and created a new scare out of an old photo." According to *The Asian Age*, at least one local psychiatrist said that he was still treating patients obsessed with the "ghost."

Sources

1. "Mass Hysteria Mars The Music." *Science News* (September 21, 1991) 140(12):187.
2. Alexander, R.W., and Fedoruk, M.J. (1986). "Epidemic Psychogenic Illness in a Telephone Operator's Building." *Journal of Occupational Medicine* 28:42-45. See p. 42.
3. Alexander and Fedoruk, op cit., p. 43.
4. Alexander and Fedoruk, op cit., p. 43.
5. Alexander and Fedoruk, op cit., p. 44.
6. Alexander and Fedoruk, op cit., p. 42.
7. Alexander and Fedoruk, op cit., p. 43.
8. Dupouy, E. (1907). *Psychologie Morbide*. Paris: Librairie des Sciences Psychiques, p. 106, drawing on Del Rio, Martin, *Disquis Magicae*.
9. Görres, Johann Joseph von (1845). *La Mystique Divine, Naturelle et Diabolique*. Paris: Poussielgue-Rusand, 1855, translated from the German *Christliche Mystik*, volume 5, p. 267, citing Massée's *Chronique*.
10. Steinbauer, Friedrich (1979). Melanesian Cargo Cults (translated by Max Wohlwill). London: George Prior Publishers, p. 5.
11. Kottak, Conrad P. (1987). *Cultural Anthropology*, fourth edition. New York: Random House, p. 278.
12. Williams, F.E. (1923). "The Vailala Madness and the Destruction of Native Ceremonies in the Gulf Division." *Papuan Anthropology Reports No. 4*. Port Moresby, New Guinea: Government Printer; Berndt, R.M. (1952). "A Cargo Cult Movement in the East Central Highlands of New Guinea." *Oceania* 23 (1-3):40-65, 137-158; Worsley, P. (1957). *The Trumpet Shall Sound: A Study of 'Cargo' Cults in Melanesia*. London: MacGibbon and Kee; Burton-Bradley, B.G. (1973). *Long Long–Transcultural Psychiatry in Papua and New Guinea*. Port Moresby: Public Health Department; Merskey, H. (1979). *The Analysis of Hysteria*. London: Bailliere Tindall; Robin, R. (1981). "Revival Movement Hysteria in the Southern Highlands of Papua New Guinea." *Journal for the Scientific Study of Religion* 20(2)150-163; Barr, J. (1983a) Forward. In G.W. Bays and W. Flannery (eds.). Religious Movements in Melanesia Today Volume 2. Goroka, and Socio-Economic Service.
13. Linton, R. (1943). "Nativistic Movements." *American Anthropologist* 45:230-240; Mair, L.P. (1948). *Australia in New Guinea*. London; Firth, R. (1951). Elements of Social Organization. Boston: Beacon Press.
14. Burton-Bradley, B.G. (1973). *Long Long–Transcultural Psychiatry in Papua and New Guinea*. Port Moresby: Public Health Department.
15. Eliade, M. (1960). *Myths, Dreams and Mysteries*. London. See also, Christiansen, P. (1969) *The Melanesian Cargo Cult: Millenarianism as a Factor in Cultural Change*. Copenhagen: Akademisk Forlag, p. 100.
16. Lanternari, Vittorio (1963). *The Religions of the Oppressed: A Study of Modern Messianic Cults*. New York: Alfred A. Knopf, p. 315.
17. Barr (1983a). op cit., p. vi.
18. Worsley, P. (1957). *The Trumpet Shall Sound: A Study of 'Cargo' Cults*

in Melanesia. London: MacGibbon and Kee.
19. Berndt, R.M. (1952). "A Cargo Cult Movement in the East Central Highlands of New Guinea." *Oceania* 23 (1-3):40-65, 137-158.
20. Hogbin, H.I. (1958). *Social Change*. London: Watts; Belshaw, C. (1954). *Changing Melanesia*. Melbourne.
21. Stephen, M. (1977). *Cargo Cult Hysteria: Symptoms of Despair or Technique of Ecstasy?* Occasional paper No. 1. Research Centre for Southwest Pacific Studies, La Trobe University, p. 1.
22. Hempenstall, P. (1981). *Protest or Experiment? Theories of 'Cargo Cults.'* Occasional Paper No. 2. Research Centre for Southwest Pacific Studies, La Trobe University, p. 2.
23. Hempenstall (1981). op cit., p. 7.
24. Matthew, chapter 9, verse 12.
25. George, Leonard (1995). *The Encyclopedia of Heresies and Heretics*. London: Robson Books, p. 218.
26. "Feline Spirits Force Orissa School to Close." August 5, 2004. Report from India's IANI news service accessed August 21, 2004 at: http://www.webindia123.com/news/show details.asp?id =44859&cat=India.
27. "School Shut Amid Fears That Some Girls Possessed." IANS News Service report of August 9, 2004. Accessed September 12, 2004 at: http://news.newkerala.com/india-news/index.php?action=fullnews&id=6702.
28. "School Shut Amid Fears That Some Girls Possessed." op cit.
29. "Mishra, Bibhuti (2004). "'Ghosts' continue to Stalk Schools in Orissa." Published by SAFY News on September 4 and accessed October 30, 2004 at: http://sify.com/news/offbeat/fullstory. php?id=13559208.
30. Darnton, Robert. (1984). *The Great Cat Massacre and Other Episodes in French Cultural History*. New York: Basic Books, p. 83.
31. Darnton, op cit., pp. 83-84.
32. Darnton, op cit., p. 83.
33. Sumner, William Graham. (1906). *Folkways: A Study of the Sociological Importance of Usages, Manners, Customs, Mores, and Morals*. New York: Ginn and Company, p. 599.
34. Hecker, Justus Friedrich. (1844). *Epidemics of the Middle Ages* (translated from German by B. Babington). London: The Sydenham Society, p. 127.
35. Pagliarini, Marie Anne (1999). "The Pure American Woman and the Wicked Catholic Priest: An Analysis of Anti-Catholic Literature in Antebellum America." *Religion and American Culture* 9(1): 97-128.
36. Rickard, Robert, and Michell, John. (2001). *Unexplained Phenomena: A Rough Guide Special*. London: Rough Guides Limited, p. 111; Bromley, David G., and Shupe, Anson. (1989). "Public Reaction Against New Religious Movements." Pp. 305-334. In Marc Galanter (ed.), *Cults and New Religious Movements: A Report of the American Psychiatric Association from the Committee on Psychiatry and Religion*. Washington, DC: American Psychiatric Association.
37. Lehtinen, Vilja (2002). *America Would Lose Its Soul: The Immigration Restriction Debate, 1920-1924*. Master's thesis, Department of History, Faculty of Arts, University of Helsinki, May, p. 16.
38. Ver Steeg, Clarence, and Hofstadter, Richard (1981). *A People and a Nation*. New York: Harper & Row, p. 287.
39. Ver Steeg and Hofstadter, op cit., pp. 287.
40. Billington, Ray Allen (1933). "Tentative Bibliography of Anti-Catholic Propaganda in the United States (1800-1860)," *Catholic Historical Review* 18(4):492-513.
41. Pagliarini, Marie Anne (1999). op cit.
42. Lewis Hippolytus Joseph Tonna (1852). *Nuns and Nunneries; Sketches Compiled Entirely from Romish Authorities*. London: Seeleys.
43. Hogan, William (1853). *Popery! As It Was and As It Is; Also, Auricular Confession; and Popish Nunneries*. Hartford, Connecticut: Silas Andrus and Son.
44. Dwight, Theodore (1836). *Open Convents; or Nunneries and Popish Seminaries Dangerous to the Morals, and Degrading to the Character of a Republican Community*. New York: Van Nostrand and Dwight, p. 114.
45. See for example: Harry Hazel (1845). *The Nun of St. Ursula, or the Burning of the Convent: A Romance of Mount Benedict*. Boston: F. Gleason; Anonymous (1855). *The Escaped Nun; or, Disclosures of Convent Life; and the Confessions of a Sister of Charity*. New York: De Witt and Davenport.
46. Lamed, Mrs. L. (1836). *The American Nun; or the Effects of Romance*. Boston: Otis, Broaders.
47. Stewart, James R. (1977). "Cattle Mutilations: An Episode of Collective Delusion." *The Zetetic* (presently *The Skeptical Inquirer*) 1(2):55-66; Hines, T. (1988). *Pseudoscience and the Paranormal: A Critical Examination of the Evidence*. Buffalo, New York: Prometheus, pp. 278-280.
48. See for examples: "Cattle Mutilations Remain a Mystery." *Eagle River News Review* (Wisconsin), January 26, 1978; "Mystery Still Surrounds Animal Mutilations." *Springdale News* (Arizona), November 26, 1978; "Tracking the Cattle Mutilators: Satanic Groups Suspected." *Newsweek* 95, p. 16 (January 21, 1980); "Did Horse Mutilator Come From Outer Space." *Gastonia Gazette* (North Carolina), May 24, 1980.
49. Saunders, David R., and Harkins, Roger R. (1969). *UFOs! Yes! Where the Condon Committee Went Wrong*. New York: World publishing, pp. 155-169; Condon, Edward Uhler (project director, and Gillmor, Daniel S., ed.), 1969. *Scientific Study of Unidentified Flying Objects*. New York: Bantam, pp. 344-347; Bartholomew, Robert E. (1991). "Mutilation Mania–The Witch Craze Revisited: An Essay Review of *An Alien Harvest* by Linda Howe." *Anthropology of Consciousness* 3(1-2):23-25 (March-June).
50. Stewart (1977). op cit., pp. 64-65.
51. Rommel, Kenneth M. (1980). *Operation Animal Mutilation Report of the District Attorney First Judicial District State of New Mexico*. Prepared for the Criminal Justice Department under Grant # 79-D-5-2-S, p. 175.
52. Rommel (1980). op cit., p. 176.
53. Owen, Nancy H. (1980). *Preliminary Analysis of the Impact of Livestock Mutilations on Rural Arkansas Communities, Final Report*. Prepared by Nancy Owen, project director, Department of Anthropology, University of Arkansas, Fayetteville, Arkansas 72701, for the Arkansas Endowment for the Humanities, University Tower Building, Suite 1019, Little Rock, Arkansas 72204, under grant number 001-102-79M, published in January.
54. Owen (1980). op cit., p. 16.
55. "Cattle-Mutilating Satanic Communist Space Aliens." In *The Arkansas Roadside Travelogue*, accessed July 26, 2003 at: http://www.aristotle.net/ ~russjohn/index.html.
56. Owen (1980). op cit., p. 16.
57. Owen (1980). op cit., p. 16.
58. Owen (1980). op cit., pp. 20-21.
59. Rommel (1980). op cit., p. 87.
60. Rommel (1980). op cit., p. 87.
61. Rommel (1980). op cit., p. 85.
62. Rommel (1980). op cit., p. 225.
63. Owen (1980). op cit., p. 17; (1979). "Birds, Flies Caused Cattle Mutilations, Sheriff Concludes." *Arkansas Gazette*, October 19, 1979.
64. Owen (1980). op cit., p. 17.
65. Rommel (1980). op cit., p. 204.
66. Rommel (1980). op cit., p. 204.
67. Rommel (1980). op cit., p. 210.

68. Rabaud, Camille (1896). *Les Petits Prophètes Huguenots*. Dole: 1896 [reprinted from an article in *La revue Chretienne]*, p. 8.
69. Ch. Bost (1912). *Les Prédicants Protestants des Cevennes*. Paris [cited in Joutard, Philippe (1976). Les Camisards. Paris: Gallimard/Julliard, p. 59].
70. Joutard, op cit., p. 61, quoting from a contemporary brochure, *Abrégé de l'histoire de la bergère de Saou Amsterdam, 1688.*
71. *Quoted by Crété,* Liliane (1992). *Les Camisards*. Paris: Perrin, p. 56.
72. Misson, Maximilien (1707). *Le Théâtre Sacré des Cevennes*. London, p. 5.
73. Misson, op cit., p. 6.
74. Joutard, op cit., p. 69, citing Bost.
75. Crété, op cit., p. 58, citing Bost.
76. Crété, op cit., p. 40.
77. Misson, op cit., p. 63.
78. Misson, op cit., p. 22.
79. Misson, op cit., pp. 73, 75.
80. Misson, op cit., p. 66.
81. Misson, op cit., p. 68.
82. Misson, op cit., p. 19.
83. Misson, op cit., p. 106.
84. Misson, op cit., p. 32.
85. Misson, op cit., p. 36.
86. Misson, op cit., p. 20.
87. Misson, op cit., p. 105.
88. Chabrol, Jean-Paul (1999). *Elie Marion, le Vagabond de Dieu*. Aix-en-Provence: Edisud, p. 57.
89. Misson, op cit., p. 117.
90. Misson, op cit., p. 12.
91. Misson, op cit., p. 28.
92. Misson, op cit., p. 53.
93. Misson, op cit., p. 82.
94. Misson, op cit., p. 110.
95. Joutard, op cit., p. 70, citing Brueys, A A. (1708). *Histoire du Fanatisme de Notre Temps*. Montpellier.
96. Misson, op cit., p. 62.
97. Richardot, Jean-Pierre. Note to a reprint edition of Misson, op cit., p. 122.
98. Wesley, John (1909). *The Journal of the Rev. John Wesley*. Edited by Nehemiah Curnock. London: Culley 1909 [Originally published at various dates from 1739 onwards], volume 2, p. 136.
99. Misson, op cit., p. 112.
100. Mills, Abby (2003). *University Daily Kansan* (student newspaper of the University of Kansas), accessed April 12, 2005 at: http://www.dailyillini.com/oct03/oct16/news/stories/ campus01.shtml.
101. Thomas, William (2002). "Stolen Skies: The Chemtrail Mystery." *Earth Island Journal* 34-35 (Summer).
102. Thomas, William, op cit., p. 35.
103. Thomas, William, op cit., p. 35.
104. Schlatter, Thomas (2000). "Weather Queries." *Weatherwise* (November-December):36-39.
105. Schlatter, Thomas (2002). "Weather Queries." *Weatherwise* (September-October):52-54. See p. 53.
106. All information in this entry is drawn from Farge, Arlette, and Revel, Jacques (1988). *Logiques de la Foule*. Paris: Hachette.
107. Farge and Revel, op cit., p. 40.
108. Barbier, a lawyer, quoted in Farge and Revel, op cit., p. 15.
109. Quoted in Farge and Revel, op cit., p. 112.
110. Hirsch, William. (1896). "Epidemics of Hysteria." *Popular Science Monthly* 49:544-549.
111. Most of the material is from Gray 1871, who cites references to six contemporary chronicles and twenty-four that were compiled shortly after. See: Gray, George Zabriskie (1871). *The Children's Crusade*. London: Sampson Low, Son, and Marston.
112. Gray, op cit., p. 30, citing Sporschild and others.
113. Gray, op cit., p. 47.
114. Roger de Wendover, cited by Gray, op cit., p. 139.
115. Choiseul d'Allecourt, cited by Gray, op cit., p. 144.
116. Gray, op cit., p. 132.
117. Gray, op cit., p. 116.
118. *Chronicon Argenteum*, cited by Gray, p. 125.
119. Collin de Plancy circa 1860: 269.
120. Raffael Scheck in *Journal of Psychohistory* 16 (2) Fall 1988.
121. "Those Men from Mars." *Newsweek* (November 27, 1944), p. 89.
122. "Those Men from Mars." op cit.
123. Bulgatz, Joseph. (1992). *Ponzi Schemes, Invaders from Mars & More Extraordinary Popular Delusions and the Madness of Crowds*. New York: Harmony Books, p. 137.
124. "Those Men from Mars." op cit.
125. "Those Men from Mars." op cit.
126. "AIDS Needle Attack Scare Spreads to Beijing." *Asia Economic News*, February 4, 2002, citing the Kyodo News Agency.
127. Aubin, Nicolas (1752[1693]). *Histoire des Diables de Loudun*. Amsterdam: 1752, re-issue of a publication in 1693, though it was in print earlier than this date, p. 367
128. Baissac, Jules (1890). *Les Grands Jours de la Sorcellerie*. Paris: Klincksieck, p. 537.
129. Baissac, op cit., p. 540.
130. Lucas-Dubreton, J. (1932). *La Grande Peur de 1832*. Paris: Gallimard. Unless otherwise noted, all material for this entry comes from this source.
131. *Le Moniteur*, 5 April 1832, cited by Lucas-Dubreton, op cit., p. 80.
132. Cited by Lucas-Dubreton, op cit., p. 82.
133. Cited by Lucas-Dubreton, op cit., p. 83.
134. Vankin, Jonathan, and Whalen, John (1992). *The Sixty Greatest Conspiracies of All Time*. Secaucus, NJ: Citadel Press, p. 295.
135. Verma, Amita (1997). "VHP Angry at Convent Conversion of Students." *The Asian Age* (August 27). Accessed April 17, 2006 at: http://www.hvk.org/articles/0997/0014.html.
136. Ellis, Bill. (1996). "Chupacabras Mania Spreads." *Foaftale News* 39:2-3.
137. Pronounced CHUP-ah-ca-bra.
138. Sylvia R. Gallagher of Huntington Beach, California, pointed out helpful information on the origin of the term goatsuceker.
139. Preston, J. (1996). "In the Tradition of Bigfoot and Elvis, the Goatsucker." *The New York Times*, June 2, p. 2E.
140. Navarro, M. (1996). "A Monster On Loose? Or Is It Fantasy?" *The New York Times*, January 26, p. A10.
141. Ellis, B. (1996). op cit., p. 2.
142. Erich Goode kindly provided sources for the chupacabras outbreaks.
143. Eastwell, Harry D. (1979). "A Pica Epidemic: A Price for Sedentarism Among Australian Ex-Hunter-Gatherers." *Psychiatry* 42:264-273.
144. Eastwell, op cit., p. 271.
145. Eastwell, op cit., p. 272.
146. Eastwell, op cit., p. 272.
147. Eastwell, op cit., p. 269.
148. Eastwell, op cit., p. 267.

149. Eastwell, op cit., p. 267.
150. Nemery, B., Fischler, B., Boogaerts, M., Lison, D., and Willems, J. (2002). "The Coca-Cola Incident in Belgium, June 1999." *Food and Chemical Toxicology* 40:1657-1667, see pages 1657-1658; Gallay, A., and Demarest, S. (1999). *Case Control Study Among Schoolchildren on the Incident Related to Complaints Following the Consumption of Coca-Cola Company Products, Belgium, 1999.* Scientific Institute of Public Health, Epidemiology Unit (November). http://www.iph.fgov.be/epidemio/epien/cocacola.htm, accessed April 10, 2002.
151. Nemery et al., p. 1658.
152. Nemery et al., p. 1659.
153. Bernard, A., and Fierens, S. (2002). "The Belgian PCB/Dioxin Incident: A Critical Review of Health Risks Evaluations." *International Journal of Toxicology* 21(5):333-340.
154. Schepens, P.J., Covaci, A., Jorens, P.G., Hens, L., Scharpe, S., and van Larebeke, N. (2001). "Surprising Findings Following a Belgian food Contamination with Polychlorobiphenyls and Dioxins." *Environmental Health Perspectives* 109(2):101-103; van Larebeke, N., Hens, L., Schepens, P., Covaci, A., Baeyens, J., Everaert, K., Bernheim, J.L., Vlietinck, R., De Poorter, G. (2001). "The Belgian PCB and Dioxin Incident of January-June 1999: Exposure Data and Potential Impact on Health." *Environmental Health Perspectives* 109(3):265-73; Bester, K., de Vos, P., Le Guern, L., Harbeck, S., Hendrickx, F., Kramer, G.N., Linsinger, T., Mertens, I., Schimmel, H., Sejeroe-Olsen, B., Pauwels, J., De Poorter, G., Rimkus. G.G., and Schlabach, M. (2001). "Preparation and Certification of a Reference Material on PCBs in Pig Fat and its Application in Quality Control in Monitoring Laboratories during the Belgian 'PCB-Crisis.'" *Chemosphere* 44(4):529-537.
155. Nemery et al., p. 1659.
156. Nemery et al., p. 1659-1660.
157. Nemery, B., Fischler, B., Boogaerts, M., and Lison, D. (1999). "Dioxins, Coca-Cola, and Mass Sociogenic Illness in Belgium." *Lancet* 354(9172):77(July 3).
158. Nemery, et al. (1999). op cit.
159. Nemery, et al. (1999). op cit.
160. Het Coca-Cola incident juni 1999 in België. Evaluatie van de gebeurtenissen, discussie, besluit en aanbevelingen." Ad hoc Werkgroep van de Hoge Gezondheidsraad. Ministerie van Volksgezondheid, Brussels, March, 2000. http://www.health.fgov.be/CSH_HGR/Nederlands/Advies/Coca-colaNl.htm, accessed April 10, 2003.
161. Anonymous (1999). "Coke adds life, but cannot always explain it" (Editorial). *Lancet* 354(9174):173 (July 17); Leith, Scott (2002). "3 Years After Recall, Coke Sales in Belgium at Their Best." *The Atlanta Journal-Constitution*, August 26, 2002.
162. Het Coca-Cola incident juni 1999 in België, op cit.
163. Nemery et al., p. 1662.
164. Nemery et al., p. 1665.
165. Bartholomew, Robert E., and Victor, Jeffrey S. (2004). "A Social Psychological Theory of Collective Anxiety Attacks: The 'Mad Gasser' Re-Examined." *The Sociological Quarterly* 45 (2):229-248.
166. Personal communication from Jeffrey Victor to Robert Bartholomew, February 1, 2005.
167. Leff, Julian (2001). *The Unbalanced Mind.* London: Weidenfeld & Nicholson, p. 29.
168. "Suspected Witches Killed in Congo." *Rutland Daily Herald*, July 6, 2001, p. A2.
169. Coleman, Loren (2004). *The Copycat Effect.* New York: Paraview Pocket Books, see especially chapter 17.
170. Loren Coleman, Personal Communication, July 31, 2008.
171. Bullard, Thomas E. (1989). "UFO Abduction Reports: The Supernatural Kidnap Narrative Returns in Technological Guise." *Journal of American Folklore* 102: 147-170.
172. Colligan, Michael J., Pennebaker, James W., Murphy, Lawrence R. (1982). *Mass Psychogenic Illness.* Hillsdale NJ: Erlbaum.
173. Coleman (2004). op cit., p. 237.
174. Marsden, Paul (2000). *The Werther Effect: Fact or Fantasy? Media Contagion and Suicide in the Internet Age: Critical Evaluation, Theoretical Reconceptualisation and Empirical Investigation.* Doctor of Philosophy research thesis, University of Sussex, Graduate Research Centre in the Social Sciences, p. 38.
175. Durkhein, Emile (1970[1951]). *Suicide: A Study in Sociology.* Translation by J.A. Spaulding and G. Simpson. London: Routledge & Kegan. Originally publish in French in 1897, pp. 141-142.
176. Phillips, David P. (1974). "The Influence of Suggestion on Suicide: Substantive and Theoretical Implications of the Werther Effect." *American Sociological Review* 39:340-354.
177. Bollen, K.A. and Phillips, D.P. (1982). "Imitative Studies in a National Study of the Effects of Television News Stories." *American Sociological Review* 47:802-809.
178. Phillips, David P. (1974). op cit.
179. Lester, David (2004). "A Possible Suicide Epidemic after Weiningers 'Sex and Character': A Comment on Thorson and Oberg." *Archives of Suicide Research* 8(3):293-294.
180. Blood, R. Warwick; Pirkis, Jane; Holland, Kate (2007). "Media Reporting of Suicide Methods: An Australian Perspective." *Crisis: The Journal of Crisis Intervention and Suicide Prevention* 28 (Suppl 1):64-69.
181. Stack, Steven (2000). "Media Impacts on Suicide: A Quantitative Review of 293 Findings." *Social Science Quarterly* 81(4):957-971.
182. Marsden, Paul (2000). op cit, p. 223.
183. Thorson, Jan, and Oberg, Per-Arne (2003). "Was there a Suicide Epidemic after Goethes Werther?" *Archives of Suicide Research* 7(1):69-72.
184. Marsden (2000). *The Werther Effect*, op cit., p. 13.
185. Marsden (2000). *The Werther Effect*, op cit., p. 14.
186. Marsden (2000). *The Werther Effect*, op cit., p. 14.
187. Hezel, Francis X. (1987). "Turk Suicide Epidemic and Social Change." *Human Organization* 48 (Winter):283-296. Article accessed online July 7, 2008 at: http://www.micsem.org/pubs/articles/suicide/frames/suiepidfr.htm.
188. Hezel, Francis X. (1987). op cit.
189. Hezel, Francis X. (1987). op cit.
190. Coleman (2004). op cit., p. 260.
191. There is a vast literature. A good overview of the problems can be found in Weisberg, Harold (1994). *Selections from Whitewash.* New York: Carroll & Graf.
192. Knight, Peter [editor] (2003). *Conspiracy Theories in American History.* Santa Barbara CA: ABC Clio, p. xi.
193. For an overview of perceived global menace, see 'New World Order' and related entries in Knight 2003.
194. Webster, Richard (2005). *The Secret of Bryn Estyn.* Oxford: Orwell, p. 10.
195. Coulter, Ann. (2001). "This is War." *National Review*, 13 September, in Rampton, Sheldon, and Stauber, John. (2003). *Weapons of Mass Deception.* London: Constable & Robinson, p. 145.
Rampton et al., p. 145.
196. Shorter, Edward (1992). *From Paralysis to Fatigue.* New York: The Free Press, p. 5.
197. Didi-Huberman, Georges (1982). *Invention de L'Hysterie.* Paris: Macula; Hart, Ernest (1896). *Hypnotism, Mesmerism and the New*

Witchcraft. London: Smith, Elder.
198. Shorter (1992), op cit., p. 97.
199. Szego, K. (1896). "Uber die Imitationskrankheiten der Kinder" [On the Imitative Illness of Children]. *Jahrbuch fur Kinderheilkunde* (Leipzig) 41:133-145; Schoedel, Johannes. (1906). "Uber Induzierte Krankheiten" [On Induced Illness]. *Jahrbuch fur Kinderheilkunde* 14:521-528.
200. Pearsall, Judy. (editor) (1999). *The Concise Oxford Dictionary*, tenth edition. Oxford: Oxford University Press, p. 334.
201. Goode, Erich (1992). *Sociology* (second edition). New York: Harcourt Brace Jovanovich, p. 516.
202. LaPiere, Richard T. (1938). *Collective Behavior*. New York: MacGraw-Hill, p. 512.
203. Park, Robert E., and Burgess, Ernest W. (1969). *Introduction to the Science of Sociology*. Chicago: University of Chicago Press, pp. 895-898.
204. Neal, Larry D. (editor) (1990). "How the South Sea Bubble was Blown Up and Burst: A New Look at Old Data." Pp. 33-56. In *Crashes and Panics: The Lessons from History* edited by Eugene N. White. Homewood, Illinois: Business One Irwin.
205. Bulgatz, Joseph. (1992). *Ponzi Schemes, Invaders from Mars & More Extraordinary Popular Delusions and the Madness of Crowds*. New York: Harmony Books, p. 68.
206. Turner, Ralph H., and Killian, Lewis M. (1972). *Collective Behavior*. Englewood Cliffs, New Jersey: Prentice-Hall, p. 134.
207. LaPiere (1938). op cit., p. 512.
208. Davidson, James W., Castillo, Pedro, and Stoff, Michael B. (2000). *The American Nation*. Upper Saddle River, New Jersey: Prentice-Hall, p. 705.

DANCE FRENZIES

Japan: 1705, 1771, 1830, 1867

Periodic episodes of collective emotional frenzy and chaotic dance have been recorded in Japan at times in the 18th and 19th centuries.

CONTEXT: Historian E. Herbert Norman labels these events as "mass hysteria" and notes that "outbreaks" conspicuously coincide with oppressive feudal regimes and during periods of social crises. Norman speculates that they may function as a social catharsis to long-standing repression, enabling the populace to release pent-up anxieties and frustrations. According to Norman, these events may represent a combination of hysteria and ritual through which a mass public catharsis is achieved under the guise of *okage-mairi*, a custom involving a pilgrimage to give thanks to the Sun Goddess by visiting the Ise Shrine.[1] Outbreaks were characterized by collective frenetic dancing, crying, singing, and obscene and bizarre behavior, including cross-dressing, amnesia, trance states, and other transient ailments.

During the "mass madness" episode of 1771, Shinto philosopher Motoori Norinaga was an eyewitness. He said that people clogged roads to make the pilgrimage, many of whom were carrying paper pictures which depicted obscene or absurd figures or events. "There is much roistering and noisy talk going on and some of it of a nature similar to the pictures. The people go along clapping their hands, shouting, singing 'okage de sa! nuketa to sa!' and becoming more and more excited. Both young men and old women forget their natural modesty and indulge in this frenzy so that it is quite a disturbing sight to see. They seem to have abandoned themselves to utter madness, as well as ribaldry and horse-play."[2]

During the autumn of 1867, another "hysterical dance frenzy" swept across Japan and paralyzed the ruling Tokugawa government during a tense political crisis. Amid great fear, fanatical nationalism, and wild rumors confusion and chaos reigned – brought about by the appearance of large crowds singing, dancing, weeping, shouting obscenities, and claiming amnesia. The dance frenzies allowed representatives of the Satsuma and Choshu clans to journey undetected past rival clan agents and government secret police in order to negotiate an agreement that gained the Emperor's support against the Tokugawa. The timing of the irregular pilgrimage was remarkable considering that such treks are organized about once a generation. Norman concludes that the stoic Japanese temperament, combined with unbearable economic hardships and repressive policies under feudal authority, induced a state of collective neuroses that unwittingly brought the government's fall. He describes the period immediately prior to the "outbreak" as characterized by peasant uprisings that had the effect to further intensify economic hardships. As government confidence was rapidly eroding, "alarming rumors and handbills warned the people of the evil intentions of the foreign powers. The superstitious were shaken by such portents as a comet in 1866, following which there was a serious failure of crops threatening famine. Class feeling was at a breaking point with commoners becoming restive under the humiliations which for generations had been visited on them by a feudal bureaucracy now losing its nerve..."[3]

Norman notes the relationship between Japanese dance frenzies and the more famous medieval danc-

ing manias involving masses of Europeans who, some argue, were engaging in a ritualistic mass catharsis by partaking in pilgrimages to St. Vitus shrines and chapels during periods of social, political, or environmental crises, including floods, famine, pestilence, and disease in order to obtain divine favor. Medical historians George Mora[4] and George Rosen[5] hold this position. Mora considers European dance manias as a socially appropriate means of "expression, through ritual, of deeply rooted emotional conflicts" that were at least partially resolved by engaging in what amounts to a psychotherapeutic coping strategy.[6] Norman views Japanese dance frenzies as a "safety valve," noting that it was no coincidence that it affected the population "after they had suffered some prolonged misery and affliction such as followed in the wake of the Black Death."[7]
See also: DANCING MANIA.

DANCING MANIA

Europe: 12th-17th centuries

A variation of TARANTISM spread through Europe between the twelfth and seventeenth centuries, where it was known as the dancing mania or St. Vitus dance, on account that participants often ended their processions in the vicinity of chapels and shrines dedicated to this saint. "Epidemics" seized groups who engaged in frenzied dancing, often naked, intermittently for days or weeks. Symptoms included screaming, hallucinations, convulsive body movements, chest pains, hyperventilation, sexually suggestive gestures, and even sexual intercourse as some outbreaks turned into mass orgies. Participants usually claimed that they were possessed by demons who had induced an uncontrollable urge to dance. Like tarantism, music was typically played during these "outbreaks," and was considered to be a potent remedy. It continues to be widely believed within the medical and psychiatric communities that the dancing mania grew out of widespread feelings of pessimism and despair from the effects of the Black Death, which had wiped out over half the population of Europe. This epic epidemic subsided about 1350, just two decades before what most scholars identify as the onset of the dancing mania – 1374.

Medical historian Benjamin Gordon provides the following description: "From Italy it spread to Aachen (Aix-la Chapelle), Prussia, and one morning, without warning, the streets were filled with men and women who joined hands, formed circles and seemingly lost all control over their actions. They danced together, ceaselessly, for hours or days, and in wild delirium, the dancers collapsed and fell to the ground exhausted, groaning and sighing as if in the agonies of death. When recuperated, they swathed themselves tightly with cloth around their waists and resumed their convulsive movements. They contorted their bodies, writhing, screaming and jumping in a mad frenzy. One by one they fell from exhaustion, but as they fell, others of the town took their places. These wild dancers seemed insensible to external impressions." Gordon says that the dancers would often exhibit epileptic-like convulsions as victims sometimes collapsed or fainted, gasping for breath. Some could be seen foaming at the mouth, only to spring "back to life" and continue dancing. During these events, some later said they saw Jesus and Mary in Heaven.[8]

Perhaps the most vivid, detailed account of these events is provided by German physician Justus Friedrich Hecker, who writes that about two decades after the Black Death had ravaged Europe, in 1374, "a strange delusion arose in Germany, which took possession of the minds of men" and quickly spread across the continent. Basing his descriptions on a number of eyewitness accounts, Hecker says

St. Vitus' Dancers on a pilgrimage to the Church of St. Willibrod, near Luxembourg. (After a drawing by P. Breughel)

that "assemblages of men and women were seen at Aix-la-Chapelle, who had come out of Germany, and who, united by one common delusion, exhibited to the public both in the streets and in the churches the following strange spectacle. They formed circles hand in hand, and appearing to have lost all control over their senses, continued dancing, regardless of the bystanders, for hours together, in wild delirium, until at length they fell to the ground in a state of exhaustion. They then complained of extreme oppression, and groaned as if in the agonies of death, until they were swathed in cloths bound tightly round their waists, upon which they again recovered, and remained free from complaint until the next attack."[9] Hecker states that the swathing practice "was resorted to on account of the tympany which followed these spasmodic ravings, but the bystanders frequently relieved patients in a less artificial manner, by thumping and trampling upon the parts affected. While dancing they neither saw nor heard, being insensible to external impressions through the senses, but were haunted by visions, their fancies conjuring up spirits whose names they shrieked out; and some of them afterwards asserted that they felt as if they had been immersed in a stream of blood, which obliged them to leap so high. Others, during the paroxysm, saw the heavens open and the Saviour enthroned with the Virgin Mary, according as the religious notions of the age were strangely and variously reflected in their imaginations."[10]

The events of 1374, which were first described in Aachen, continued for about four months. Between August 8 and early September they were observed in Koln, then in Maastricht, Harstal, Tongeren, Liege, and Trier between September 11 to the 14th, in Ghent during October 22 and 23, then on to Metz, France, Gelderland and Julich (northern Germany). They spread in a east to west, then north to south fashion, and were likely comprised of Hungarian pilgrims following a route that had been used as early as 1221.[11] After 1374, there are scattered references to phenomena in the region that closely resembles the dance mania. For instance, in 1428, a mini dance frenzy occurred among a group of women at a Zurich church. In Zabern in 1518, as many as 400 people danced at a St. Vitus chapel during a four-week period, coinciding with famine and disease.[12]

CONTEXT: Dancing manias coincided with catastrophic events: floods, famine, plagues, and epidemics. The most conspicuous coincidence is their appearance near the time of The Black Death. They also broke out during a period of European demon mania. In trying to understand these dance frenzies, a fundamental question focuses the debate as to their origins. Were participants engaging in religious rituals designed to appease a higher force in order to receive divine favor and protection from these devastating events and evil forces, inadvertently functioning as cathartic reactions to pent-up stress? Did these rituals involving prolonged prayer, deep emotional expressions, and wine consumption trigger twitching, shaking, and hallucinations? Were the disordered and hysteria-prone more likely to participate?

One of the best and earliest descriptions occurred in 1188 in Wales when Gerald de Barri described a curious ritual at a Brecknockshire church. It contains ritualistic parallels to the later dance manias. He writes about an annual August feast that was "attended by many people from a considerable distance, when those who labor under various diseases, received the health they desire through the merits of the blessed Virgin."[13] De Barri states that both men and women would dance at the church shrine of St. Almedha, beginning in the church, then continuing in the churchyard. Soon they were dancing "round the churchyard with song, suddenly falling to the ground as in a trance, then jumping up as in a frenzy, and representing with their hands and feet, before the people, whatever work they have unlawfully done on feast days; you may see one man put his hand to the plough, and another, as it were, goad on the oxen, mitigating the animal's sense of labour by the usual rude song; one man imitating the occupation of a shoemaker, another that of a tanner."[14] They would eventually be led back into the church, brought to the altar where they would be "suddenly awakened, and coming to themselves."[15] Perhaps festivals like this one, which includes the element of dancing at a religious site in expectation of divine favor, would eventually evolve into the dance mania.

The term "dancing mania" is Greek in origin,

from the word *choros* (dance), and *mania* (madness). In Germany it was referred to as *Tanzwut* (dancing frenzy or madness), *tanzplage* (dancing plague), and *chorea Germanorum*. Other medieval terms to describe the phenomena included choreomania, epidemic chorea, the lascivious dance, St. Vitus' dance, Chorea Sancti viti, Viti Saltus, St Guy's dance, St. John's dance, St. Anthony's dance, and the dance of St. Modestir.[16] The Swiss physician Paracelsus (1493-1541) identified three types of dancing frenzy: chorea imaginativa, chorea lasciva, and chorea naturalis. He was among the first to suggest that such acts were medical conditions and not caused by demonic possession.[17]

Theories: Fungus Poisoning

Some writers, most notably Swedish historian E. Louis Backman, contend that ergot poisoning was responsible for hallucinations and convulsions accompanying the dance mania. Nicknamed St. Anthony's Fire, after a Egyptian ascetic of the third century, ergotism typically coincided with floods and wet growing seasons, fostering growth of *claviceps purpura,* a fungus which forms on cultivated grains – rye in particular. Australian physician and ergot historian Caroline De Costa states: "The fungal spores are carried by the wind to the ovaries of young rye, where they germinate into hyphal filaments. These grow deeply into the rye, forming a dense tissue that gradually takes over the grain and hardens into a purple curved spur or sclerotium."[18] Hence, "ergot" is derived from the Old French word "argot," meaning cock's spur.

De Costa describes two main types of ergotism: gangrene (sometimes called chronic ergotism) and convulsive (also referred to as acute ergotism). Both seem fairly easy to differentiate as severe cases of the former "affected tissues became dry and black, and mummified limbs dropped off without loss of blood. Spontaneous abortion frequently occurred. Convulsive ergotism was often accompanied by manic episodes and hallucinations, especially a sense that the subject was flying; these symptoms were due to serotonin antagonism by various components of ergot related to lysergic acid diethylamide (LSD). The gangrenous and convulsive forms of ergotism could occur concurrently."[19] Clearly, if any dancing mania participants were suffering from ergot poisoning, it would be of the convulsive variety. While some dance manias coincided with floods and wet periods, many outbreaks did not. Convulsive ergotism could cause bizarre behavior and hallucinations, but gangrene ergotism more common and typically resulted in the loss of fingers and toes from gangrene, a feature that is distinctly not associated with dance manias.

Mental Disturbance

One common view by historians is that many "dancers" were mentally disturbed, as evidenced by the "bizarre" behaviors that often deteriorated into wild orgies or wild dances lasting for days and sometimes weeks. No wonder medical and psychiatric historians typify such episodes as a type of culture and history-specfic mass mental disorder affecting those overwhelmed by the stresses of the period. During outbreaks many immodestly tore off their clothing, walking about naked. Some screamed and asked to be tossed into the air; others danced feverishly in strange, colorful attire that was described as such by period observers. A few reportedly laughed or wept to the point of death. Women occasionally made howling noises and outrageous sexual gestures; others squealed like animals. Some rolled around in the dirt; others seemed to relish being struck on the soles of their feet and begged bystanders to do so. Justus Hecker attributed the cause to the stressful effects of the Black Death or bubonic plague that ravaged Europe and the world between 1347 and 1351. It is estimated that 75 million people died. In some European countries such as Italy, it is believed that half the population died. The dance manias began in 1374, at a time of widespread pessimism and despair.

Ritual

Surely some participants were hysterics, epileptics, mentally disturbed, or even delusional from ergot, but the question remains: What percentage? The large portion of the populations affected and the circumstances and timing of outbreaks suggests that a ritual is the best explanation, especially considering that episodes were pandemic, meaning that they occurred across a wide area and affected a high proportion of the population. While dance "maniacs" are typified as exhibiting spontaneous, stress-induced outbreaks of mental disturbance, primarily among females, sociologist Robert Bartholomew contends that they were most likely rituals of distress, and that history and culture has blinded researchers from understanding the conduct codes underlying the dancers' symbolic universe.[20]

In his study of the dancing mania, Bartholomew found, based on a representative sample of medieval chronicles translated into English by Backman,[21] that most participants did not reside in the municipalities where they danced but hailed from other regions, traveling through communities as they sought out shrines and churchyards to perform in. As a result, they would naturally have had unfamiliar customs and appeared to have acted strange. The largest and best documented dance plague, that of 1374, involved throngs of "dancers" in Germany and Holland who were "pilgrims" traveling from Bohemia, Poland, Hungary, Germany, and Austria. The behavior of these dancers was described as strange because – while exhibiting actions that were part of the Christian tradition and paying homage to Jesus, Mary, and various saints at chapels and shrines – other elements were foreign. Radulphus de Rivo's chronicle *Decani Tongrensis* states that "in their songs they uttered the names of devils never before heard of ... this strange sect." Petrus de Herenthal writes in *Vita Gregorii XI*: "There came to Aachen ... a curious sect." The *Chronicon Belgicum Magnum* describes the participants as "a sect of dancers." The actions of dancers were often depicted as immoral in their sex acts. Indeed, many dance manias turned into mass orgies. The chronicle of C. Browerus (*Abtiquitatum et Annalium Trevirensium*) states: "They indulged in disgraceful immodesty, for many women, during this shameless dance and mock-bridal singing, bared their bosoms, while others of their own accord offered their virtue." In *A Chronicle of Early Roman Kings and Emperors*, it states that a number of participants engaged in "loose living with the women and young girls who shamelessly wandered about in remote places under the cover of night." If most of the participants were pilgrims of Bohemian and Czech origin, as Backman asserts, during this period Czechs and Bohemians were noted for a high incidence of then sexual immorality, including annual festivals involving the free partaking of sex.

Bartholomew contends that episodes are best explained as due to deviant religious sects who gained adherents as they made pilgrimages through Europe during years of turmoil in order to receive divine favor. Their symptoms (visions, fainting, tremor) are predictable for any large population engaging in prolonged dancing, emotional worship, and fasting. Their actions have been "mistranslated" by contemporary scholars evaluating the participants' behaviors *per se*, removed from their regional context and meaning. Using this same line of reasoning, he considers tarantism as a regional variant of dancing mania that developed into a local tradition primarily confined to southern Italy.

Historians typically claim that the dance maniacs were hysterical and the proof is that they could not control their actions – that the urge to dance was spontaneous and uncontrollable. Again, a survey of period chronicles reveals another story. According to Bartholomew, dance manias were mainly comprised of pilgrims engaging in emotionally charged, highly structured displays of worship, which occasionally attracted locals. This social patterning is evident in a first-hand account on September 11, 1374, by Jean d'Outremeuse in his chronicle *La Geste de Liege*, which states: "there came from the north to Liege ... a company of persons who all danced continually. They were linked with clothes, and they jumped and leaped ... They called loudly on St John the Baptist and fiercely clapped their hands." Slichtenhorst, in describing the dance frenzy of 1375 and 1376 in France, Germany, and Gelderland (now southwestern Holland), notes that participants "went in couples, and with every couple was another single person... they danced, leaped and sang, and embraced each other in friendly fashion."

Many scholars assert that most dancers were hysterical females. Yet, revisiting of the descriptions of dancing manias based on early chronicles shows that both men and women were equally affected. Where the gender of the participants was noted, the following comments are representative: Petrus de Herenthal's chronicle *Vita Gregorii XI* remarks that "Persons of both sexes ... danced;" Radulpho de Rivo's *Decani Tongrensis* states that "persons of both sexes, possessed by devils and half naked, set wreathes on their heads, and began their dances;" Johannes de Beka's *Canonicus Ultrajectinus et Heda, Wilhelmus, Praepositus Arnhemensis: De Episcopis Ultraiectinis, Recogniti*, states that in 1385, "there spread along the Rhine ... a strange plague ... whereby persons of both sexes, in great crowds .... danced and sang, both inside and outside of churches, till they were so weary that they fell to the ground;" according to *Koelhoff's Chronicle* published in 1499, "Many people, men and women, old and young, had the disease [of dancing mania];" Casper Hedion in *Ein Ausserlessne Chronik von Anfang der Welt bis auff das iar nach Christi unsers Eynigen Heylands Gepurt M.D.* writes that in 1374 "a terrible disease, called St John's dance ... attacked many women and girls, men and boys;" and A. Slichtenhorst's *Gelsersee Geschiedenissen* states that "men and women were smitten by the fantastic frenzy."

For ST. VITUS DANCE, see DANCING MANIA.

DE MARTINO, ERNESTO

De Martino (1908-1965) was an Italian religious historian, philosopher, and anthropologist who documented contemporary TARANTISM episodes in Southern Italy in his acclaimed book, *La Terra del Rimorso* (*The Land of Remorse*).[22]

DEFENSE INDUSTRY SUICIDE CLUSTER

Britain: 1970s-80s

During the 1970s and 1980s, a number of people working on high-security military research in Britain, or in companies or institutions associated with such research, suffered accidents, frequently fatal, or killed themselves in circumstances that were often puzzling. Although individually each case received a mundane explanation, these often failed to satisfy colleagues and relatives of the victims; inquests tended to result in open verdicts (where no cause of death could be definitely identified). The police often seemed to be less than diligent in their investigation, and the authorities often seemed to be trying to conceal details.

The fact that so many incidents occurred in a narrow segment of the population, within a relatively brief time span, caught the media's attention and resulted in conspiracy theories, which may or may not be justified. Though officially each incident was regarded as an individual occurrence, and though there seemed nothing to directly link any victim with any other, it seemed to many to be more than coincidence that so many people, working in the same or related organizations on projects within the same general area, should fall victim at all, let alone in circumstances that were, in some cases, bizarrely improbable.[23]

CONTEXT: At the time of these happenings, the Cold War was still simmering, and Britain and the Soviet Union regarded each other as potential enemies. A great deal of research and development, largely concerned with electronic warfare, was being conducted in conditions of extreme secrecy. Those involved in this research were, by definition, security risks, and the possibility that they might pass their information to the other side, either voluntarily, or for cash, or consequent upon blackmail, was ever-present. Consequently, any unusual incident involving such people inevitably aroused suspicion. None of those listed here was seen to have been dishonest in any way, but the possibility may account for the evasive behavior of the authorities.

Note: Many of these scientists worked for companies in the General Electric group (GEC), including Marconi, Easams, and Plessey. The following abbreviations are used: BT is British Telecom; GCHQ is the Government Communications Headquarters at Cheltenham; MOD is the Ministry of Defence; ICL is International Computers Ltd.; RARDE is the Royal Armament Research and Development Establishment; and RMCS is the Royal Military College of Science at Shrivenham, Wiltshire. The incidents are listed in chronological order.

1972-3: Robert Wilson (43)

A former technical author for Marconi at Chelmsford, Essex. Wilson was clearing out his attic when he came across some confidential Marconi documents. When he took them to Marconi, he was interviewed at length. The next day he was cleaning his .45 revolver when he accidentally shot himself in the chest, though as a member of the local gun club he knew better than to clean a loaded gun with the muzzle pointed at himself. He himself described the accident as "grotesque." Around May the following year he had another accident. While servicing his car in his garage, he was overcome by fumes. This time the accident was fatal.

May 1973: Gerard Jack Darlow (22)

Employed by Marconi at Chelmsford. Found dead on his bed in his flat with a knife in his chest. He had previously made an unsuccessful suicide attempt.

March 1982: Keith Bowden (46)

Computer programmer and mathematics professor at Essex University engaged in computer work for Marconi. Killed in car accident after dinner with friends, when his well-maintained car went out of control on a divided highway, crossed the central median and plunged onto a disused railway line. Verdict: accident. Unusual circumstances: Police said he had been drinking, but family and friends denied this. Accident investigation revealed that the new tires on his car had been replaced with worn-out retreads, a likely cause of the accident.

July 1982: Jack Wolfenden (56)

Radio operator at GCHQ at Cheltenham. Though an experienced glider pilot, he had a fatal crash when his powered glider crashed into a Cotswold hillside in perfect flying weather. His girlfriend said he had been acting oddly, lethargic, and indecisive after returning from abroad. No indication of suicide. Verdict: accidental death. Unusual circumstances: The accident occurred within a few days of the appearance in court of Geoffrey Prime, a fellow worker at GCHQ, who was subsequently jailed as a spy; his files named several colleagues who might be blackmailed or bribed to pass information to the Soviets. However, the authorities specifically denied any connection between Wolfenden's death and Prime's conviction.

1982: Ernest Brockway (43)

Employed at Irton Moor, one of GCHQ's largest ground stations. He was found hanged in his home. Though he left no suicide note, suicide was presumed. His widow told reporters that her husband had been a sick man, and that she had been told by the authorities to say nothing. As with Wolfenden, the authorities denied any link with spying.

1983: Stephen Drinkwater (25)

Employed at GCHQ, Cheltenham, in the only department where it is permitted to make copies of classified documents. Found by his parents in his room asphyxiated with a plastic bag over his head. It was supposed he had been involved in a sexual experiment. Verdict: death by misadventure.

April 1983: Anthony Godley (49)

A Lieutenant Colonel and defense expert at RMCS. Disappeared one Saturday morning, seemingly with no word to anyone. He spent the night at a hotel in Dover, leaving without paying his bill. His car was found at Folkestone, where his yacht was missing and has never been found. He was presumed dead, particularly as he did not claim a substantial bequest left him by his father. Unusual circumstances: His widow left their married quarters at RMCS within 24 hours, without making any comment on her husband's disappearance.

1984: Dennis Skinner

He had worked for ICL, a defense contractor, in Moscow between 1968 and 1974. In 1984 he was working in Moscow for the Midland Bank. In June 1983 he had told the British Embassy in Moscow that he knew of a spy in the British security services and pleaded to return home. He was found on the ground at the foot of his apartment building, hundreds of feet below, a tracksuit top over his head. Although the apartment door was locked from the inside, the coroner (in England) directed the jury not to return a suicide verdict. Verdict: unlawful killing.

April 6, 1984: George Franks (58)

Radio specialist at GCHQ engaged in highly classified defense work. Originally said to have been found hanged in his Sussex home, leaving a suicide note. However, it was subsequently stated that he had died of a heart attack, and the verdict was natural causes. Unusual circumstances: The original statement seems to have been totally false, but how this error originated only adds to the mystery. The name of the victim was not at first disclosed, and a news blackout followed his death. The authorities explained this was out of concern for his family, yet no family member appeared except a sister who had not seen him for four months. A neighbor stated that Franks received only about two phone calls a week, mostly from a man who identified himself in code. Apparently anticipating his heart attack, Franks had bundled together a number of papers with directions that they were to be given to his sister only. However, they were given to the police and only some of them were passed on to his sister. A partially concealed half-empty malt whisky bottle and a bottle of tablets were found near the body, but they were said to have no relevance to his death. A friend revealed that he had been in serious dispute with his employers, GCHQ, but could not elaborate. Possibly this related to his taste for pornography, which had caused him difficulties at work, though "how the magazines were discovered and exactly why the matter was taken so seriously is not clear."[24]

1985: Stephen Oke (35)

Worked at GCHQ's listening post at Morwenstow, Cornwall. His work apparently had no security aspect, though he had access to sensitive material. Found hanging from a beam in the loft of his home while his wife and children were away for a few days. No apparent reason for suicide; open verdict. Unusual circumstances: A piece of string was tied round his hands, though the police said he could have tied it himself. Cigarettes were found nearby, though Oke did not smoke. An empty brandy bottle was found in the dustbin, though he disliked spirits.

March 1985: Roger Hill (49)

Radar designer with Marconi. Killed himself with shotgun at his family home. Verdict: suicide.

November 19, 1985: Jonathan Wash (29)

Digital communications expert who had worked for GEC and at BT. Fell from a hotel room in Abidjan while working in the Ivory Coast for BT. Verdict: open. Unusual circumstances: He had previously expressed fear that his life was in danger. Conflicting evidence left the exact circumstances of his death unclear and raised the possibility of a struggle before his fall. He had secretly booked a flight to Britain for the following day.

August 4, 1986: Vimal Bhagvani Dajibhai (24)

Pakistan-born computer programmer working for Marconi at Croxley Green on underwater defense. He was happily married and enjoyed life. He was in his last week of employment at Marconi and looking forward to a new job starting the following week. Apparently killed himself by jumping off the Clifton Suspension Bridge at Bristol, a location much favored by suicides. All who knew him insisted that suicide was highly improbable and out of character. Verdict: open. Unusual circumstances: He had driven some 150 km from his home at Ruislip to Bristol, a city he had never previously visited. Bottles of wine were found in his car, though he reportedly rarely drank, never when driving, and did not like wine. His trousers were found drawn down below his buttocks, and a possible puncture mark was on his left buttock. The authorities unexpectedly interrupted his cremation and called for a second postmortem but did not reveal the findings.

October 27-28, 1986: Arshad Sharif (26)

Pakistan-born computer expert with Marconi, Stanmore. He had previously worked for British Aerospace. He was due to get married that same month and was also expecting promotion at work. Killed himself at Siston Common, near Bristol, by tying one end of a rope to a tree, the other round his neck, then driving off in his car with the accelerator jammed down with a spanner. A tape recording left in the car was described by the authorities as tantamount to a suicide note, but its contents were never made public. Verdict: suicide. Unusual circumstances: He had driven some 200 km from his Walthamstow home to Bristol to do what he could have done anywhere. He spent the previous night at a guesthouse in Bristol used largely by employees of British Aerospace, where he had himself lived while working for them. There he displayed a wad of high-denomination banknotes. Four lengths of rope were used for the suicide, but a receipt for only one length was found in the car. On the day of his death he had an appointment with his Member of Parliament, presumably to discuss delays in the entry permit for his Pakistani bride.

January 14, 1987: Richard Pugh (26)

Defense telecommunications expert with MOD, engaged in defense projects. Found dead in his home at Loughton, Essex, with feet tied together and a plastic bag over his head, his body almost completely covered with rope. It was supposed this was a sexual experiment. Verdict: accident.

8 January 1987: Aviar Singh-Gida (27)

Signal-processing scientist from Pakistan, previously at RCMS, currently at Loughborough University on a grant from the MOD where he was employed in the Admiralty Research Establishment and involved in a signal processing project for them. He disappeared while working at a reservoir near Loughborough, Leicestershire, while his colleagues had gone off to buy lunch. The police carried out an intensive search on a scale that made it clear the authorities were very concerned to find him. Four months later, acting on a tip from the police, a Derby journalist traced him to a boutique in the porn district of Paris. Back in England, he had no explanation for his fugue beyond that he had been "in a state of confusion," which he attributed to work pressure. Unusual circumstances: his wife reported that he had been very disturbed by the death the previous August of Dajibhai, a former acquaintance. He was just a few weeks away from completing his four-year PhD.

January 12, 1987: John Brittan (52)

Senior scientist, formerly working at the RCMS, later for the RARDE at Chertsey. In December 1986 he had a car accident in which he lost control and drove into a ditch; he told colleagues he could not understand how it happened. In January he paid a working visit to the U.S., returning with a throat infection that kept him off work. January 12 was to have been his first day back at work, but he was found dead sitting in his car in the garage of his Camberley home, due to carbon monoxide poisoning. It was supposed that he had been warming up his car and had thoughtlessly failed to open the garage door. He had no reason to kill himself. Verdict: accidental death. Unusual circumstances: Most who choose this form of suicide connect a hose from the exhaust to the interior of the car. The fact that Brittan did not do this supports the accident explanation.

February 1987: Victor Moore (46)

Design engineer with Marconi Space Systems. It was alleged that he did not agree with some of the things he had to do. Said to have died in Portsmouth from an overdose of drugs. Verdict: suicide.

February 21/22, 1987: Peter Peapell (46)

Scientist at RCMS where he had been employed for 25 years, currently working for a MOD research department. Found dead in the garage of his home in Shrivenham, of carbon monoxide poisoning, after returning from a party with his wife about 3 a.m. She had gone straight to bed, but when she woke at about 9:30, she realized he was not there and went to look for him. She found him lying on the ground beneath the car in the garage, dead, with his head close to the exhaust and the engine running. She thought that he might have been checking for a knocking noise they had noticed on the drive home, but the garage light was broken and he had no flashlight. Suicide was improbable. He enjoyed his work and had just had a big pay raise, and their marriage was happy. Verdict: open. Unusual circumstances: It would have been virtually impossible to get his body into this position without opening the garage doors, yet they were closed. Deposits showed that the engine had been running for only a short time, certainly not the 6 hours between their return and the discovery of his body.

February 1987: Edwin Skeels (43)

Engineer with Marconi, Leicester. Found dead in his car with hose leading from the exhaust. Verdict: open.

March 30, 1987: David Sands (37)

Senior communications scientist working on defense projects for Easams, Camberley. Driving to work, he performed a sudden U-turn on the divided highway, A33, and drove at high speed down a slip road and crashed into an abandoned café. His car burst into flame and he was burnt beyond recognition. There was no sign of intent to kill himself and the verdict was open. Unusual circumstances: His car was carrying extra petrol cans, though this was said to be normal. Two days earlier, he had left the house telling his wife he wanted to buy some petrol. When he failed to return after six hours, she called the police. When he returned, he told her he had been "driving and thinking;" he was confused.

April 10, 1987: Stuart Gooding (23)

Variously described as research student, undergraduate, or scientific officer at RMCS. While on a diving expedition in Cyprus, he was killed in a car crash when a truck on a mountain road hit his hired car. Verdict: accident. Unusual circumstances: By coincidence, personnel from RMCS were involved in military exercises on the island at the time.

April 10, 1987: David Greenhalgh (46)

Though at first described as a "salesman," he was a NATO Defense Contracts Manager working for International Computers, which is not quite the same thing. Though the authorities insisted he was not currently engaged in sensitive work, he had recently been working on high-security matters. He was critically injured after a 13-meter fall from a railway bridge onto an embankment at Maidenhead, a few miles from his home, which he had left nearly four hours earlier en route for work. After several weeks in hospital, he recovered, but was unable to remember what happened before his fall.

April 14, 1987: Mark Wisner (24)

Software engineer at the Aeroplane & Armament Experimental Establishment at Boscombe Down. Found dead in his home at Durrington, wearing women's boots and suspenders, with a plastic sack over his head and cling-film over his face. He was said to be a transvestite in his leisure hours, and his death was perceived as an unsuccessful sexual experiment. Verdict: accident.

April 17, 1987: George Kountis

Experienced systems analyst at Bristol Polytechnic. His drowned body was found in his upturned car in the river Mersey at Liverpool. Verdict: misadventure.

April 17-18, 1987: Shani Warren (26)

Personal assistant at MicroScope, which became a GEC subsidiary less than a month later; the company was already collaborating with GEC on communications technology. Found drowned in half a meter of water on the edge of a lake. Police and medical experts thought suicide at least half-likely, despite the circumstances and the lack of motive, and the fact that she had made plans for the next few days. Verdict: open. Unusual circumstances: She was gagged, with a noose round her neck, her hands tied behind her back, and her feet tied together. A reconstruction showed that it was almost impossible she could have reached the water on her own. Suicide seemed supported by the fact that the only footprints were her stiletto heels, but the same reconstruction showed that someone wearing flat shoes would have left no marks. Her car, parked nearby, had a defective gearbox, and the contents were strewn around the grass nearby as though it had been searched. The police investigation was puzzlingly unenthusiastic.

May 3, 1987: Michael Baker (23)

Digital communications expert engaged on a defense project for Plessey at Poole, Dorset. On a fishing trip with two friends, his car crossed the highway and crashed through a barrier. His two companions were uninjured, but he was killed. Verdict: accidental death. Unusual circumstances: His mother reported that he had not wanted to go, but someone came to the door for him and he went. He was a part-time member of an SAS (Special Air Services) squadron with MOD connections.

June 1987: Frank Jennings (60)

Electronic weapons engineer at Plessey. Found dead of heart attack. No inquest.

January 1988: Russell Smith (23)

Laboratory technician at Atomic Energy Research Establishment, Harwell. Found dead halfway down a cliff at Boscastle, Cornwall. Verdict: suicide.

March 25, 1988: Trevor Knight (52)

Computer services manager at Marconi, Stanmore. He had previously worked for Marconi at Croxley Green, where Dajibhai worked, and at Stanmore, where Sharif worked, though it is not known whether he knew either of them. Found dead at the wheel of his car, with a hose connected to the exhaust, in his garage at Harpenden, Hertfordshire. He was known to have disliked his work and to be depressed by a number of traffic accidents, but his estranged wife and his current partner both found his suicide unexpected and surprising. Notes were found whose content was not disclosed; those who had seen them refused to comment. Verdict: suicide. Unusual circumstances: The previous day he had phoned his mother, sounding quite happy and discussing plans for the weekend.

August 1988: Alistair Beckham (50)

Computer engineer with Plessey Defense Systems at Addlestone, Surrey. Found dead in his garden shed at his home in Woking, with electric wire to mains. Verdict: open. Unusual circumstances: Earlier in the day he had discussed a forthcoming family holiday with his wife, and had arranged to pick her up that afternoon. He returned home, took the dog for a walk, bought the Sunday papers, and was preparing to do some DIY work.

August 22 or 23, 1988: Peter Ferry (60)

Retired army officer (Brigadier), working for Marconi on business development and involved with NATO. He was planning soon to retire from full-time work and work for Marconi part-time. He had been severely shaken by a car accident on August 2; though no one was seriously injured, he had been trapped in his car after being struck by a truck on the wrong side of a lane near his house. He was found in a cottage in the grounds of the Marconi factory at Frimley, Surrey. He had been electrocuted, having stuck two electric leads onto his teeth. No sign of foul play. Verdict: open.

September 1988: Andrew Hall (33)

Engineering manager with British Aerospace. Found dead in car with hose connected to exhaust. Verdict: suicide.

Unknown Date of Death: John Whiteman (31)

Computer software manager for British Aerospace at Warton, Lancashire. Found dead in his bath with an empty bottle of sleeping tablets and two empty whisky bottles. But no motive or sign of intention to kill himself. Stress at work was a possible factor. Verdict: open. Unusual circumstances: It is said that an autopsy revealed no trace of drugs and very little alcohol in his body.

COMMENT: Ostensibly, each of these deaths was either an accident or a deliberate suicide. Certain features, however, deserve a comment.

First, all the victims were working for companies or organizations involved in high-security work. Such people may well be under exceptional stress, but over and over again friends and colleagues testified to the physical and psychological health of the victim; only in a few cases was stress or depression signaled. Besides, as the *Independent* pointed out, "the pressure of work is also fierce in the money markets of the City, where equally large sums are at stake. Yet the suicide rate remains unremarkable."[25] Professor Colin Pritchard, of the Department of Mental Health at Southampton University, noted that four of the victims had "complained officially to their line-managers about the 'unscientific' nature of the projects they were working on – i.e. the tasks set were not feasible. They were thanked for their concern but were told it was imperative to continue for 'commercial' reasons.... All four had resigned and secured new jobs and were scheduled to join their new companies within days of their deaths. All four deaths were either extremely violent and/or bizarre. Such types of deaths are usually associated with the most extreme form of mental disorder, which is so disruptive that it is highly unlikely that such people could hold down a job, or that their extreme perturbation would go unnoticed. Yet all four men worked up to the day or within days of their deaths, and no one had noticed anything untoward."[26]

Second, the circumstances were frequently improbable and never adequately explained. Even though foul play was rarely a serious alternative explanation, in some cases there was a suggestion of third party interference. Police found the "suicide" of Peter Peapell to be well nigh physically impossible for a man on his own. Shani Warren's death presented many features that argue against suicide. If Keith Bowden's tires had indeed been replaced with defective ones, this could point to a murder attempt.

Third, as Collins points out, "The vast majority of the deaths were tinged with the suspicion that there were those in a position of authority who knew far more about them than was divulged at their inquests."[27] Perhaps this can be attributed to security considerations, but in many cases relatives declared themselves dissatisfied with the verdict and complained about the investigation. In some cases they insisted on pursuing the investigation themselves, though to no avail.

Inquiries by the authorities and by GEC reached the conclusion that the number of accidents and suicidal deaths was statistically unremarkable, and that the apparent cluster is simply a matter of coincidence. They deny that there was any link between the incidents; each should be seen as an individual occurrence. Individually, some of these cases may indeed have been quite mundane. There may have been nothing more to the disappearance of Singh-Gida, for example, than a momentary personal crisis. Nevertheless, certain features recur surprisingly often, such as the fact that three of the deaths occurred at Bristol, far from the victims' homes, whereas George Kountis from Bristol had his fatal accident far away in Lancashire. Again, that six should die, deliberately or by accident, in their garages is also noteworthy.

Conspiracy or coincidence? Even the most cynical conspiracy theorists do not propose a common modus operandi for all these incidents, and no one seriously suggests that the victims were linked in any way other than that they were working for companies associated with defense projects. The most plausible of the conspiracy theories is the speculation that some kind of "mind control" may have been applied to the victims, causing them to behave out of character, often bizarrely. This would explain why more than one victim referred to feelings of "confusion." It could account for Singh-Gida's mysterious fugue, Brittan's unexplained car accident and curious death, Wilson's improbable gun accident, and many more. The motive would be that these people, several of whom were planning to change jobs, constituted security risks. Such a fantasy explanation seems far-fetched, but then so were many of the circumstances.
See also: SUICIDE CLUSTERS.

DEMON POSSESSION

Popular beliefs in evil forces exist in every culture, though the offending entity is not necessarily perceived as a divinity incarnating evil; it may be a spirit of nature, or of the dead, who for some reason acts malevolently. The term "demon" originally had a neutral, even favorable connotation. This was true of the ancient Greeks, for example, and of countless non-Christian cultures throughout the world.[28]

"This connotation was changed into an evil one when Christianity condemned the deities and spirits of paganism."[29] Judeo-Christian dualistic theology elaborated a complex system of evil forces in opposition to God. The myth of Satan, whose arrogance inspired him to challenge the authority of God, leading to his banishment from Heaven together with his followers, is accepted as fact by those for whom the Bible is literally true; consequently the existence of the Devil and his demons is for many a simple truth. The literature on demons is voluminous, and the various attempts to catalog them and their attributes only highlight the fascination that evil entities exert, whether at the theological, the occultist, or popular level.[30]

The concept of the demon as enshrined in popular culture is a hybrid, mingling elements of the folklore "Evil One" with the more formalized figure devised by Church theology. Confusion between official and unofficial perceptions of the Evil One contributed to the WITCHCRAFT MANIA IN EUROPE and continues to cause misunderstandings of SATANISM, modern witchcraft, and other cult activities and beliefs.

In primitive cultures, it is widely believed that any unfortunate or unlucky event – the burning of one's haystacks, the sickness of an eldest son – is due to evil practices by magicians or witches working under the guidance and encouragement of the powers of evil.[31]

A shaman tries to heal a sick man by driving out evil spirits, at Mavaca, Venezuela. (Photograph by Hubertus Kanus)

Such beliefs, so far as external material events are concerned, tend to gradually die out as explanations in favor of natural forces. This is not true, however, of internal misfortunes in the personal sphere, where no such natural cause can be discerned. The individual who loses control and seems to be driven by forces outside himself remains liable to be considered a victim of malevolent entities, simply because no better explanation is available.

While the possibility of possession by benign entities was never excluded, it is conspicuously less frequent than possession by malign entities. A rare 19th century exception is cited of a Bavarian peasant woman observed by Baader, who noted: "If two states had up to that time been distinguished in her, the ordinary waking state and the magnetic (somnambulistic) waking state, it was now necessary to distinguish three: the ordinary waking state, the good magnetic waking state, and the bad magnetic waking state. The voice, gestures, physiognomy, sentiments, etc., were in the last two states exactly like heaven and hell. In particular the features changed so rapidly that one could hardly trust one's eyes, nor recognize her in the satanic fit as the same person who was in the good magnetic state."[32]

However, either this is an extremely rare occurrence or it has been rarely noted; the overwhelming majority of possessing entities are single-mindedly malevolent.

The idea of demonic possession is by no means confined to Christian teachings. It is the explanation of choice, in virtually every culture, for various otherwise inexplicable forms of pathological behavior. When an individual behaves as though he is not himself, this is taken literally: he has been possessed by something not himself. Anthropologist Edward Tylor eloquently describes the spectacle of possession:

> The possessed man, tossed and shaken in fever, pained and wrenched as though some live creature were tearing or twisting from within, pining as though it were devouring his vitals day by day, rationally finds a personal spiritual cause for his sufferings. In hideous dreams he may even sometimes see the very ghost or nightmare fiend that plagues him. Especially when the mysterious unseen power throws him helpless on the ground, jerks and writhes him in convulsions, makes him leap upon the bystanders with a giant's strength and wild beast's ferocity, impels him, with distorted face and frantic gesture, and voice not his own nor seemingly even human, to pour forth wild incoherent raving, or with thought and eloquence beyond his sober faculties to command, to foretell – such a one seems to those who watch him, and even to himself, to have become the mere instrument of a spirit which has seized him or entered into him, a possessing demon in whose personality the patient believes so implicitly that he often imagines a personal name for it, which it can declare when it speaks in its own voice and character through his organ of speech; at last, quitting the medium's spent and jaded body, the intruding spirit departs as it came.[33]

Such behavior manifests in countless contexts, including many described in this Encyclopedia. (See the many entries grouped under CONVENT HYSTERIA, for example.)

Nevius has pointed out the overall similarity of demon possession in China to that experienced in Western Europe in the Middle Ages. His findings about alleged possession cases could be applied without changing a word to the nuns of LOUVIERS or AUXONNE:

> The supposed demoniac at the time of "possession" passes into an abnormal state, the character of which varies indefinitely, being marked by depression and melancholy; or vacancy and stupidity amounting sometimes almost to idiocy, or it may be that he becomes ecstatic, or ferocious and malignant.
>
> During transition from the normal to the abnormal state, the subject is often thrown into paroxysms, more or less violent, during which he sometimes falls on the ground senseless, or foams at the mouth presenting symptoms similar to those of epilepsy or hysteria…
>
> The duration of the abnormal state varies from a few minutes to several days. During the transition period the subject often retains more or less of his normal consciousness… When normal consciousness is restored after one of these attacks the subject is entirely ignorant of everything which has passed during that state…
>
> Many persons while "demon-possessed" give evidence of knowledge which cannot be accounted for in ordinary ways… They sometimes converse in foreign languages of which in their normal states they are entirely ignorant…
>
> There are often heard rappings and noises in places where no physical cause for them can be found; and tables, chair, crockery and the like are moved about without, so far as can be discovered, any application of physical force…

Nevius says of his Chinese subjects: "The most striking characteristic of these cases is that the subject evidences another personality, and the normal personality for the time being is partially or wholly dormant. The new personality presents traits of character utterly different from those which really belong to the subject in his normal state, and this change of character is with rare exceptions in the direction of moral obliquity or impurity."[34] This predilection for PROFANITY is also characteristic of CONVENT HYSTERIA.

While the possessing "personality" generally ousts

the normal personality entirely, this is not always the case: Achille, one of Janet's patients, was either incompletely possessed, or alternated between the two personalities: "He murmured blasphemies with a dull, serious voice – Cursed be God, cursed be the Trinity, cursed be the Virgin. Then with a sharper voice, his eyes full of tears, 'It isn't my fault if my mouth utters these horrors, it isn't me…' I close my lips to prevent the words escaping, but it's no good, the devil makes my tongue move despite me."[35] What with entities benign and malign, and the ever-present possibility that seemingly benign entities may be the Evil One playing tricks, it is not surprising that the priests required manuals of instruction such as the *Malleus Maleficarum* to help them ascertain whom they were dealing with.[36]

Christian teaching distinguishes between obsession and possession. Obsession is when the demons remain outside the victim, making her life miserable in every way including poltergeist-type manifestations ("infestation") but leaving her essentially in command of herself. More serious is possession, when the demon enters the victim, controlling her actions and directing her thoughts. The process whereby this is effected, precisely what is located where when the act of possession takes place, is not evident, but clearly if demonic possession is a fact, it implies the factual existence not only of demons but also of some component in the individual into which, when circumstances permit, demons can intrude and settle like squatters.

A wide range of behaviors have come to be seen as symptomatic of demon possession, such as blasphemy and obscenity, glossolalia, nymphomania, disrobing, vomiting objects, and abnormal strength. So long as no better explanation was available, it was understandable that such behaviors should be attributed to a malevolent force, and the authors of such manuals as the *Malleus Maleficarum* can be in part excused, for a century would pass before Weyer and other doctors began to suggest a medical rather than a demonic explanation for such baffling conduct. Even then, Weyer did not dispute the existence of the Devil, only his ubiquitous responsibility.

The blanket of demonization was easily applied. "The Church has always considered the leapings, somersaults, falls and convulsions as signs of diabolic intervention. The Holy Spirit leaves the inspired individual in peace, whereas the demon drives his [people] out of themselves."[37] As a result, the nuns of Loudun, Louviers, Auxonne, and Wertet were presumed to be obsessed, infested, or possessed by demons, for they displayed the same symptoms that were recognized worldwide. It is important to recognize that demon possession is not necessarily a diagnosis made by doctors or churchmen; it is very often how the afflicted person himself defines his affliction. The nuns of Loudun and elsewhere not only believed themselves possessed, but they could name which demons were occupying them.

In Tylor's description quoted above, the possessing entity departs of its own accord, but Church authorities found that this did not generally happen; the possessing demon had to be expelled. The exorcist or his equivalent is an essential member of the social services, whether in 17th century Loudun or a Polynesian tribal settlement. Just as the symptoms described by Tylor could be those of afflicted nuns in 17th century France, the extravagant counter-measures, described in our entries on Loudun, Louviers, and elsewhere, are not substantially different from those adopted by any society at any period. Basically, they involve confronting the demonic forces with the more powerful forces supposedly made available by God to his priests. The demons are cajoled, threatened, or even negotiated with, until they agree to withdraw. (Interestingly, Japanese exorcists are more ready than their Christian counterparts to accept a negotiated surrender. Bälz observed a case in which the occupying fox-demon agreed to leave his victim provided certain favorite dishes of food, prepared in a particular way, were left at a certain place at a certain time, like ransom money. This was done, and the patient was punctually freed.)[38]

In Western Europe, the sustaining beliefs in demonism began to weaken in the later 17th century, when all but the most fervent believers came to realize that many of the people they had been exorcising as demon-possessed were simply ill. Thereafter, for a century or so, demonism was out of fashion. Then in the 19th and 20th centuries it arose again, inspired by spiritualism, mesmerism, and a renewed interest in the occult, which found expression in the writings of Bulwer-Lytton, Baudelaire, Poe, and many others. Magic was taken seriously by occultists such as Levi and Papus in France, the Golden Dawn and Crowley in Britain, and countless other marginal individuals and groups. This type of Satanism, however, is not properly demonism; it is a revolt, more or less serious, against establishment norms, a defiance of the powers that be (see entry on SATANISM). There is a large element of role-playing, and it is doubtful if many of those involved had any profound belief in the existence of the devil. Such practices are contingent on Christian belief; they have no meaning except as a counter or pastiche of the Church's position, and as such can be seen to share that position. As therapists, Baudelaire or Crowley would have been worse than useless.

It is otherwise with science, which from the 17th century gradually assumed authority in such matters, with the serious study of insanity and the growth of psychology. Parallel with the growing penchant for occultism came an increasing trust in the scientific method, so that by the 20th century the debate had polarized to a demonic explanation on the one hand, a psychological one on the other. The Catholic Church maintained its position with an authoritative publication in 1900 that stated: "The possibility of maladies caused by demoniacal influences must be accepted by every Catholic believer as a fact beyond doubt.... These maladies are due, under God's will, to supernatural forces and the might of evil spirits."[39]

Even those outside the Church were often uncertain what view to adopt. Behavioral scientists found it difficult to come to terms with individuals presenting acute anti-social or self-harming behaviors, or with anthropologists' reports in which superhuman powers appeared to be exerted. In 1983 a journalist claimed that "There is a growing conviction in the medical profession that many problems, which might seem to stem from some mental affliction, can be caused by invisible forces of evil." He added that this feeling was shared by large elements of the public at large: "Despite the sophisticated advances in science, vast numbers of intelligent and highly educated people accept the possibility of psychic invasion."[40]

This lack of confidence among behavioral scientists came at an unfortunate time, when interest in Satanism and the occult, in alien abductions and supernatural powers, was on the increase. Writing in 1921, Oesterreich had perceptively observed that, alongside the Catholic Church, "the second spiritual territory where belief in possession is cherished is the right wing of Protestantism."[41] His words became alarmingly true in the latter half of the 20th century, when there was a dramatic increase in demonism, notably among members of protestant churches of the charismatic and fundamentalist kind. Thousands of booklets and tracts were issued by the Churches, drawing attention to the dangers of dabbling in the occult, an umbrella that spread to include homeopathy, hypnosis, spiritualism, astrology, flying saucers, acupuncture, and the "New Age" generally. All these practices, perceived as dangerously anti-social, were considered to be the work of the Devil.[42]

The most widely debated phenomenon was demon possession, which spectacularly embodied the conflict between two opposed systems. Nor were the battle lines clearly drawn; many churchmen, even if they did not dispute the existence of the devil, questioned his power to possess a human being. In the other camp were scientists who were not confident that they had the requisite knowledge to cope with such situations, or indeed that science itself was the appropriate resource. Professor Sir William Trethowan, head of the department of psychiatry at Birmingham University, was probably expressing the view of most scientists when he wrote in 1976:

> From time to time doctors encounter patients who suffer from delusions of possession which are symptomatic of an ongoing psychotic illness... the fact that the subjects are mentally ill is usually fairly readily discernible, so that they are given appropriate treatment. More problematic, possibly, are other not necessarily psychotic but severely neurotic patients who exhibit hysterical and other symptoms and behaviours which resembles that occurring in so-called possession states... if such symptoms and behaviour are not recognised for what they really are, due to mental abnormality, the sufferers may not only fall into the wrong hands but be subjected to inappropriate treatment, including exorcism.[43]

Yet there were health practitioners who were not confident that their science could account for the behavior. Psychiatrist Richard Mackarness is quoted as saying: "I am certain that there are unseen good and evil forces, that people can become possessed, and that sometimes the only effective treatment is exorcism." At that time in 1983, he had had six patients whom he diagnosed as being possessed by demons and all were helped to recovery by Christian exorcism.[44]

Professional exorcists, some within the churches, others outside them, endorsed his views, needless to say. Most, if not all, were sincere people whose word must be taken seriously. Often their accounts of their activities describe the overwhelming impression they received of a force of evil emanating from the patient, and this convinced them that they were in truth up against some demonic power. Skeptics would say that this, too, was illusory, that the patient was indeed malevolent but that the malevolence was an aspect of his own personality, not that of some possessing entity.

Cases periodically occurred of exorcisms that not only failed to benefit the patient but ended tragically. The most notorious was that of Anneliese Michel, a 23-year-old, German university student whom priests assumed to be possessed by Lucifer, Cain, Judas, and Hitler, among others, and who died in 1976 from their ministrations.[45] In Britain, alarming cases occurred within the charismatic movement. In 1983, a researcher concluded, regarding the Charismatics: "They are contemptuous of attitudes and disciplines associated with what they call 'Churchianity.' They tend to be religious mavericks and there is often a danger that their unsupervised exorcisms may end in tragedy."[46] The Methodist church advised: "There should be a thorough pastoral investigation of the case including, save in totally exceptional circumstances, close and continuing collaboration with suitable persons qualified in medicine, psychology and the social services… The form of any service for healing for those believed or believing themselves to be possessed should be considered in consultation with the ministerial staff… Such a service should not be carried out when a person is in a highly excited state. It should not be unnecessarily prolonged. Publicity must be kept to a minimum."[47]

Those who hold that possession is illusion would regard exorcism too as illusion. In their view, exorcists are simply employing one fantasy to counter another, using a perceived authority to enforce the procedure. Just such a pragmatic approach was adopted in a late 20th-century case on the superstition-ridden island of Mauritius. Farida, a newly married woman brought up as a Muslim, became convinced (as the result of domestic conflicts) that she was possessed by demons. Her first recourse was to a magician. When his costly services failed to dislodge the demons, she was "cured" by a hypnotist/healer who staged a dramatic "exorcism" in which he performed Christian rituals (in which he did not believe for a moment) and treated her demons as if they were real entities – as indeed they gave every sign of being. The supposed demons were duly driven out by the supposed exorcism, and all was well.[48] If the patient was indulging in role-playing, the exorcist could play the same game. Another case, which had defied every method of treatment including exorcism and hypnotism, was resolved ingeniously by tricking the demon. "The doctors prescribed pills containing methylene blue, the sole effect of which is to colour the urine. This coloration produced a great effect on Alexandra and her devil; he no longer dared approach that part of the body which he believed to be poisoned."[49]

Within Islam there are similar differences of opinion. At one extreme are exorcists who believe that by punishing the patient they are punishing the possessing *djinn* (malevolent spirits) and who subject the afflicted person to fearful and often fatal torments. At the other extreme, the *iman* (priest) pronounces certain prayers, and if those are not effective, medical help is sought.[50]

A Statement on Exorcism adopted by the Methodist Conference in 1976 included this statement: "A belief in demons is explicable sociologically and psychologically. It is undeniable that there are people who claim to believe in demons, but – since demons do not exist – it is their belief with which we should deal, not demons."[51] Not many authorities are prepared to make so forthright a statement. Yet even belief in demons does not necessarily entail belief in the possibility of demon possession. American psychiatrist Paul Meier, a self-described "Biblicist," accepts the Bible as true and says, "I believe demons really do exist because the Bible says they do." Nevertheless he has written:

> I can honestly say that I have never yet seen a single case of demon possession. I have had hundreds of patients who came to see me because they thought they were demon possessed. Scores of them heard "demon voices" telling them evil things to do. It was at first surprising to me that all of these had dopamine deficiencies in their brains,[52] which were readily correctable with Thorazine or any other major tranquillizer. I discovered that all of the "demons" I was seeing were allergic to Thorazine and that, in nearly every case, a week or two on Thorazine made the "demons" go away and brought the patient closer to his real conflicts. These demons were merely auditory hallucinations. To have self-esteem, these patients were unconsciously amplifying their own unwanted thoughts so loud that they seemed like real voices. They felt less guilty when they could convince themselves that these thoughts were coming from an external source ("demons") rather than from within themselves.[53]

Case Study

It would be easy to find hundreds of sensational and dramatic cases of alleged demon possession, as the literature is only too readily available. Instead we have chosen a case from the 1960/70s that vividly presents the dilemma facing the authorities when confronted with an ostensible case. Father Trabold coped with the situation with admirable open-mindedness, adopting an attitude of reservation as to what was happening but of pragmatism with regard to the immediate requirement.

Father Alphonsus Trabold, a professor of comparative religion at St. Bonaventure University, New York State, like most priests, had rarely been called upon to deal with a case of ostensible possession. "I am not absolutely sure, even to this present day, whether or not these were cases of true possession, or whether there was some other explanation. However, at the time, I felt there was an emergency situation. Since I did not have time to try to use other means of helping this girl, I felt there was sufficient reason for acting and using my power as a priest to perform an exorcism."

The girl involved had experienced a period of infestation in her apartment, which was witnessed by herself and her roommate. She had reached the stage of obsession where she believed Satan was appearing to her and talking to her, threatening to take her over completely, and emphasizing that she could not escape him. When Trabold met her, she felt she was about to be possessed very soon.

She told him that she had sold herself to the devil some time ago, due to the fact that her father had been cruel both to her and to her mother, and she wanted revenge. Since she felt she could not ask God to do this, she invoked the Devil to do it. For some time she had been worshipping and serving him. This – or the conflict it caused – brought about an infestation, in the form of poltergeist phenomena. Then she began to have hallucinations of the Devil or demons that menaced her and threatened to take her over completely. She was in such a state that she was considering suicide. He tried to talk to the girl, using psychological methods such as suggestion, counseling, to help her. This went on for quite some time but he could not make any headway. She became more and more restless and more and more irritated by his efforts. "I was trying to use natural means and trying to help her in this way, through counseling and the like. All of a sudden she stared at me and said, 'He is laughing at you.' Of course, she meant the evil spirit. At this stage, I felt I had to take some drastic action – some form of prayer and exorcism. Let me stress that I considered this to be an emergency situation. I felt if the girl did not receive help immediately, she could very likely have tried suicide. Or, even if it were a case of purely psychological ailment, she could have become psychologically unbalanced if I did not act immediately."

During this stage, there were no paranormal manifestations, but Trabold did have "a feeling of an evil presence," notably when the girl said that he was laughing at her. Her eyes no longer resembled those of a human being: "It seemed as if I were looking into the depths of hell, itself; my soul froze with fear." It was at this moment that he felt he must begin saying prayers of a simple exorcism. He had to say them by heart because he did not have the ritual with him. But he remembered the main elements, and particularly that the exorcist must never plead with an evil spirit, he must *command*.

As he spoke, the girl lost consciousness. She crawled backwards over the big chair she was sitting in and fell to the floor. Commanded to leave, the apparent evil spirit said that he would not go. He then called on St. Michael, the warrior angel who defeated the rebel angels in the bible story, and Mary, mother of Jesus, conceived without sin and thus outside the power of Satan. The invocation of these names had a devastating effect on the girl, causing her great pain. But the opposition continued very strong, and the battle continued for quite some time. "How long, actually, I do not know. I persisted in the attack, always in a very authoritative way. Gradually, I felt the opposition was lessening. All the while, I was following the girl across the floor, saying different prayers, but keeping out of the way of the thrashing girl."

Gradually, as the opposition lessened, he lowered the tone of his voice. Finally, the girl calmed down. "I said to her, 'The spirit is gone, the devil is gone, he cannot harm you any longer.' Gradually, the girl opened her eyes and a beautiful smile came on her face. She said to me, 'Is he gone? Is he really gone?' I assured her he was. The beautiful expression that came on her face – I just cannot find words to describe it – the feeling of peace that came from her was so very, very strong. She did say, 'I feel so wonderful. I feel so good.'"

The following night she experienced the first perfect night's sleep she had had in many months. "While I have no absolute proof the exorcism was successful, the indication is that it was." Trabold's final verdict on the episode is balanced and perceptive:

> We are dealing here, of course, with a case of a person in great need. Whether or not we are dealing with a true diabolical being or whether we are dealing with a demon created by the mind of the person, it is extremely real for the person. So if an exorcism helps in any way, either in a supernatural way of actually driving out a real demon, or psychologically, simply by removing this demon of their mind, it is for me an act of healing. In such an instance, I believe some form of exorcism is warranted.
>
> I must, in all honesty, call your attention to a possible alternate explanation from the point of view of psychology. If she were suffering from merely a psychological delusion, and there was a deep suggestion within her that she was possessed by the devil, you would overcome this with a counter suggestion. If the person is so convinced the Devil is real and his influence is real, the only way you can help her, even on a purely psychological level, is to come down to her level of belief. You can show her you do have the power of dealing with such an entity and you can chase him out. Even if we are dealing with a case purely of a psychological state, the exorcism becomes a form of healing. To that extent, I think it is still fulfilling the healing ministry of Christ, even though it may not be the actual casting out of a demon.[54]

COMMENT: In this instance, as in the case of Farida cited above, the healer had considerable doubts as to the reality of what he was doing but recognized that the pragmatic approach was, under the circumstances, the only realistic one. By providing an authority-figure to impress the patient, countering the sensational forces of evil with even stronger forces of good, the conflict within the patient is satisfactorily resolved, the original autosuggestion being countered by an even stronger suggestion from the practitioner. Short of an emergency flying squad of trained psychotherapists able to deal with such situations, it would seem as though Trabold and the Mauritius hypnotist did pretty well by their patients.

DERBY SCHOOL FITS

Derby, England: 1905

Over five days during May of 1905, 45 pupils at a girl's school in Derby, England, exhibited fits of screaming and falling unconscious. They were described as weak and had to be carried home to rest. Suspecting a noxious gas or vapor was responsible, authorities placed mice in the classrooms, but they were unaffected.[55] No further details could be ascertained.

DOUGHITELI STRANGLERS

Russia: circa 1894

This peasant sect, conducting its activities inconspicuously in the Tzarevokokschaïsk district, came into prominence in 1894 following the discovery of numerous corpses showing signs of strangulation together with signs that the dead persons had been suffering from a serious disease.[56]

CONTEXT: The Doughiteli were a local sect whose activities, author Jean Finot suggests, had their origin in the traditional pessimism of the Russian peasant. What motivated them was no particular event, but their fatalistic attitude was that nothing good could be expected of continued existence, whereas death was not only a welcome release but a meritorious sacrifice.

Investigation after a missing person led police to a forest location, where it was found that this was not a single incident. A great many bodies were disinterred, each of them showing signs of death by strangulation.

Collective suicide was ruled out by the fact that the victims had evidently been killed, but the authorities considered the possibility that this was a criminal conspiracy. Further investigation led them to the persons responsible, but the question of their guilt remained.

Taken to court, the peasants admitted their responsibility, but not their blame. All the victims had been incurably ill or infirm; their life without purpose or hope of recovery, their prospect increasing infirmity and suffering. When an individual reached this stage, a *znacher* – the local sorcerer – was consulted (there were no doctors in this isolated region). If the sorcerer confirmed that the sufferer had no hope of cure, neighbors or relatives would convey him to an isolated spot, where the "Angels of Death" would put him to death, covering his head in a pillow and strangling him. The victim was then buried in the forest, covered with plants; no cross or stone marked his grave. Often even the closest relatives had no idea where he had been interred, and the police had great difficulty finding the bodies.

There was more to the practice than simple euthanasia; the custom contained a religious element. The victims were designated as martyrs and perceived as human sacrifices. In the eyes of these primitive people, someone who dies by harsh necessity has no merit in his death, whereas one who voluntarily foregoes a part of his existence, be it but the tail-end, is making an act of sublime piety. The authorities had no alternative but to take the perpetrators to court, but in every instance they were acquitted and no further action was taken.

COMMENT: While these activities can be likened to the practices of primitive tribes where it is customary to kill off the old and infirm when they cease to be useful members of the community, the similarity is only superficial. While in such usages it is the question of practical utility that predominates, in the case of the *doughiteli* there was a spiritual dimension that evidently persuaded the authorities that they were acting from what they perceived as the highest motives. Finot comments: "Their belief is simply the logical application of the pessimist theory. They may lack the terminology, but they have espoused its terrible consequences. What is the life of a simple moujik worth? Nothing or almost nothing. Is it not better to accelerate the coming of his deliverance? Let us then snap his lifeline, let us break the chains which tie us mortals to earth, let us bear him as an offering to the skies!"

Other behaviors treated in this Encyclopedia, such as THUGGEE and the ASSASSINS, sought to justify killing by claiming a divine dispensation from guilt, and many others involve a degree of indifference to death. In the case of the *doughiteli*, however, death was perceived as providing both a welcome and a fitting ending to life.

DOUKHOBORS

Russia and Canada: 18th Century to Present

The Doukhobors were one of numerous *raskolni* religious sects that sprang up in Russia in opposition to mid-17th century reforms in the Orthodox Church. Their idealistic beliefs and practices brought them into continual conflict with the authorities, and eventually the greater part of the sect migrated to Canada where they once again found themselves at odds with the secular government. Both in Russia and in Canada they frequently manifested exceptional behavior, which in Canada amounted at times to acts of terrorism.[57]

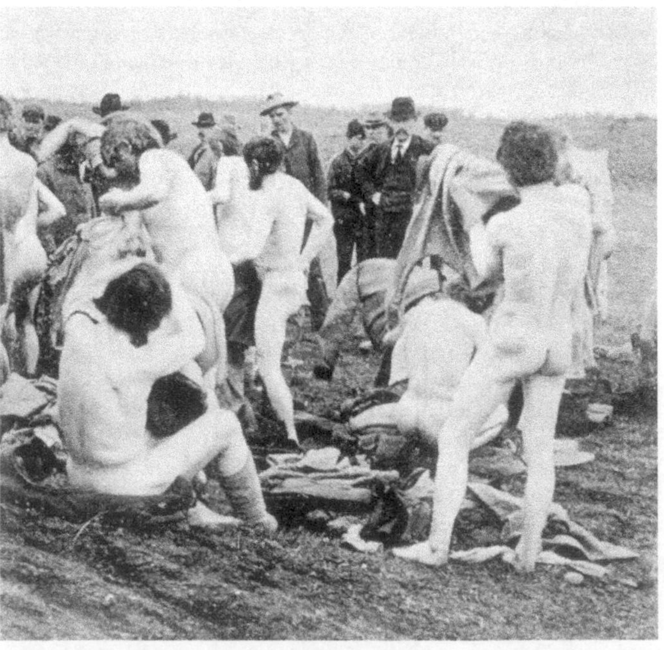

Canadian Police arrest Doukhobors at Yorkton and order them to dress. (Photo by W. Simpson)

CONTEXT: In their native Russia, the Doukhobors had been one of many intransigent sects the authorities contained as best they could, depending on the attitude of the reigning tsar, which varied from severe harassment to a conditional tolerance; it frequently meant exile to distant parts of the country. By migrating to Canada they hoped to find a place where they could behave as they wished, but they found themselves challenging authorities who, though initially well disposed, could not tolerate the sect's refusal to conform with the nation's fundamental laws.

The Doukhobors were essentially peasants, illiterate and uncultured. Even those who became their leaders, by force of personality or by their teachings, were only slightly more educated than their followers, but this was sufficient for them to impose their will on the rest and to be worshipped as reincarnations of Christ.

The Doukhobors In Russia

"Through long years of persecution they learnt to conceal their beliefs; and it is impossible to say with certainty and exactitude what, as a community, they have believed at any given moment, though the main trend of their thought, and the matters of practice on which they differed from their neighbors, are plainly discernible."[58] Starting from obscure origins, by mid-18th century the Doukhobors had formed a more or less coherent group whose leading principles were that all men and women are equal, that governments are unnecessary, and that the Church and its ceremonies are man-made superfluities since each individual – the peasant along with the tsar –contains within him/herself the Holy Spirit. Their first known leader, Sylvan Kolesnikov, added further teachings, such as rejecting icon-worship, but as a pragmatic survival technique he taught his followers that they should conform to the rites and ceremonies of the community they lived among; since they were meaningless, it did no harm to pay lip-service to them and thus avoid giving offence. Unlike the great majority of his followers, Kolesnikov could read, but he taught them to disregard the Bible as no more than an aid, preferring the "Living Book," their own orally transmitted gospel, which embodied the teachings of their leaders.

Crucially for the well being of the sect, Kolesnikov's successor Illarion Pobirokhin, a wool dealer from Tambov province, broke with the egalitarian principle by introducing the concept of divine leadership and proclaiming himself as Christ. He appointed a body of twelve "Death-bearing Angels" to punish anyone who relapsed from the faith or opposed his teachings. Few were disposed to do so, so even though he was arrested and sent to the salt mines, he was able to form a community in exile and exercise authority from afar. In view of the Doukhobors' traditional secretiveness, and the total absence of documentation, even those who knew the sect well confessed their puzzlement: "No one outside the sect (and probably no one in it either) is able clearly to define the component elements of divine incarnation, hereditary right, tribal expediency, and personal pushfulness, that go towards securing Leadership to one particular man."[59]

In the 1780s the sect became known as Dukhoborets (literally, "spirit-wrestlers") a term of derision which originally implied that they were wrestling against the Holy Spirit, but which they interpreted as meaning they were wrestling with the aid of the Spirit.

It followed from their beliefs that the taking of human life, no matter what the circumstances, was never permissible. During the wars against Napoleon, their anti-militarist beliefs brought them into conflict with the authorities when they not merely refused to fight but agitated to prevent others fighting. In 1799 ninety were exiled to Finland and a government order warned that anyone professing their beliefs would be liable to labor for life.

In 1802 the more tolerant tsar Alexander I invited the Doukhobors, along with other dissident sects such as the Mennonites, to settle in the Milky Waters, on the southern frontier of the country where they would be less of a nuisance. The settlers were mainly free peasants, who came from all parts of Russia. Their new leader, Savely Kapustin, rejected the survival technique of Kolesnikov, insisting on a stricter conformity to Doukhobor teachings and a more formal rejection of practices he considered unacceptable. A report on the sect published in 1832 stated that "the distinguishing trait in their character is obstinacy in their doctrine, insubordination to the Authorities, insults and slanders towards those who differ from them."[60]

In fact the situation was more serious than a mere attitude problem. When in the 1830s the authorities themselves conducted an investigation, they found wholesale evidence of torture, mutilation, decapitation, and burial alive. Within a few years, four hundred people had disappeared mysteriously and the assumption had to be that, despite their belief in the sanctity of human life, the Leaders had eliminated those who opposed them. The government presented the community with a choice: either they would be assimilated into general society, accepting liability for military conscription and converting to Orthodox Christianity, or they would be exiled to a penal colony in the Caucasus. Between 1841 and 1843 four thousand, including the new leader Ilarion Kalmikov, chose exile.

Kalmikov was not married, so in order that there should be an heir, his followers provided him, at the age of sixteen, with six virgins. One of them produced a son who became the next leader, Peter Kalmikov, who did the sect a favor by choosing as a bride a girl named Lukeria who revealed herself to be a forceful personality. After Peter's death in 1864 – which some thought due to poison – she controlled the community during its most peaceful and prosperous period. Thanks to hard work the settlements became wealthy, and the Doukhobor population increased to some 20,000 under her leadership. One of the original teachings crumbled when the settlers found they needed to carry guns to keep out brigands and hostile tribes. A further compromise came during the war with Turkey in 1877, when they furnished and transported military supplies for the Russian army.

The death of Lukeria in 1886 signaled internal squabbles, not least because towards the end of her life she had bestowed her favors on a young man named Peter Verigin, forcing him to divorce his wife and live with her. The sect was split when some refused to accept him as their leader, though a majority did accept him. The far from spiritual dispute over the sect's property resulted in Verigin being exiled in 1887. By calling himself Prophet, Christ, and Tsar, he was considered a disturber of the peace. He was banished to the Arctic province of Archangel, where he would remain for the next sixteen years.

In the same year, compulsory military service, which had existed in Russia since 1874, was introduced into the Caucasus. This led to further dissension among the Doukhobors, some of whom submitted, others resisted. Then in 1894 Nicolas II required all citizens to take the oath of allegiance. Verigin, though still in exile, advised his followers to refuse, and to oppose militarism in any form. They were already vegetarians; now he advised them also to reject alcohol and tobacco. Moreover, "sexual intercourse must stop during your time of tribulation. If we are to understand the truth we must not succumb to lusts of the flesh."[61] Such willful orders discouraged many of the more enlightened members of the sect, but some 7,000 – about a third of the community – conformed to his wishes.

At this time Verigin became much influenced by Tolstoy's teachings, some of whose writings he published in 1896, claiming them as his own. When Tolstoy met some leading Doukhobors, he was delighted to come across a group who shared his views, unaware that they had borrowed them from him. Tolstoy's translator comments: "Verigin's immature assimilation of Tolstoy's not infallible opinions has, I fear, not tended much to enlighten or clarify the mental perceptions of the sect."[62] Verigin's next order was very congenial to Tolstoy; he ordered that not only should his followers refuse military service, but they must destroy all offensive weapons. On Easter Day 1895, a Doukhobor conscript refused to go on parade, along with ten others. A series of anti-militarist demonstrations followed, culminating on the day of St. Peter and St. Paul, July 1895, when some 7,000 Doukhobors burned their weapons while others handed in their military reserve papers. The result was floggings and exile for many thousands. Tolstoy drew the world's attention to the plight of the sect and there was considerable sympathy in England. Donations poured in, and Tolstoy even wrote to Stockholm suggesting that the Doukhobors be nominated for the Nobel peace prize.

By now it was evident both to the Douhkobors

and to the authorities that no rapprochement was possible with those who held such extreme views and refused any compromise. So when in 1898 suggestions were made that they might emigrate, the government made no objection; one of the conditions was that, once gone, they should never return.

Various sites were suggested, ranging from Hawaii to Texas. A preliminary party of 1126 actually went to Cyprus, then under British mandate, but found the country unsuitable. The choice narrowed to Canada.

THE DOUKHOBORS IN CANADA

Canada welcomed hard-working immigrants who would help develop the country. When the first shipload of Doukhobors docked in January 1899 they were warmly welcomed, though on specified conditions. Their pacificism was respected; like the Quakers, they would be exempt from military service. But while the government was prepared to make this concession and to give them land, money, jobs, cheap transportation, and grants to settle the land, it required in return compliance with the nation's laws. The Doukhobor leaders signed their acceptance of these requirements.

Special trains carried the 7,354 Russians westwards to the lands that had been allotted them in Saskatchewan. At first everything looked promising. The new immigrants were hard-working and well-behaved and immediately set about creating well-organized self-supporting communities in the undeveloped country. It was not long, however, before they began to renege on their undertakings. In June 1900 they signified that because "the laws of your country are irreconcilable with what we consider the Divine Truth, and which we cannot break, we once more petition the Government of Canada to grant us exceptions concerning the use of lands, legality of marriage unions, and registration in order that we may be able to live in Canada without breaking the Divine Truth as we know it."[63]

From that time on, the history of the Doukhobors in Canada became, as it had been in Russia, a prolonged tussle between the sect and the authorities. From 1899 to the recent past there was scarcely a year without some protest or demonstration against anything that conflicted with their religious principles, many of which were religious only in the sense that they emanated from the leader they identified as Christ.

Almost from the start, about one third of the Doukhobors broke away from the main community, becoming "independents" who for the most part accepted Canadian laws and conditions, forming stable communities of individual homesteaders. This caused a split with those Doukhobors who continued to live communally. Much of the subsequent aggression perpetrated by the militant Doukhobors was directed against those who had in their view become traitors to the community.

As this dissension and truculence became manifest, many outsiders who had formerly espoused their cause became disillusioned. The British philanthropist Aylmer Maude, who had worked hard to bring them to Canada, wrote his book *A Peculiar People*[64] as "public penance" for having unwittingly misled the Canadian government as to the sort of people they were admitting into their midst.

The word of their leader, Peter Verigin, still in exile in Russia, was absolute as far as his more devoted followers were concerned, though some refused to accept his wishes. These became known as the "Butchers," while the more obedient were the "Fasters." Verigin's word was divine law for the Fasters. In new surroundings where they did not speak the language, where they were dependent on their leaders for physical sustenance and moral guidance alike, it is understandable that these illiterate peasants trusted their old leader. So when he commanded them to become vegetarians, they did not demur. "The bulk of the Russian peasants eat meat rarely, having some two hundred Church fast-days in the year, and being prompted by poverty to fast on most of the other days as well."[65] When he declared, "It is wrong to use money which bears the image of Caesar," they handed over their money to the immigration authorities. When he directed that "It is wrong to train horses or cattle to do our work," they set their livestock free on the prairies; most of the animals died or became the victims of predators, though the Mounted Police rounded up some 500 of the animals. As for the Doukhobors, they would pull their agricultural implements by human power, and much of the country was broken by plows tugged by teams of women.

But should they cultivate the ground at all? Verigin wrote, “It is wrong to till the soil, for being God’s earth it is wrong to spoil it when there are warm countries in which men live without working by eating fruit.” This could only be a directive that they should give up working the land altogether, and instead move to warmer climes where food in the form of fruit literally grew on the trees. (Fruit, their leader taught them, contains “compressed solar ether, that is to say, warmth-energy,” sufficient to sustain life.[66]) In October 1902, the first group of 2,000 set off towards the south – they had no more precise destination in mind – in a vague intention of finding a warmer homeland. “Winter was approaching, but the pilgrims were convinced that the Lord would, in consideration of them, send two summers that year and hold the winter off until they had reached the glory land.”[67] The Lord did no such thing and on October 25 the Canadian winter set in. They carried no clothes except those they wore. Many walked barefoot because boots were doubly prohibited, first because the use of leather contravenes God’s law, and second because “to make boots one requires needles, and needles, as is well known, are made in factories, and consequently it will not be possible to close the mines, where people are tortured to obtain ore.”[68] Some went bareheaded. They carried no provisions, either deliberately fasting or begging food as they went, for they believed that rich people would feed them en route. Indeed, they were housed and helped by the authorities or by people along the way who looked upon them as “a lot of harmless religious fanatics.” Nevertheless, they were hopeful, singing their traditional chants, and expecting any moment to reach the promised land.

Eventually, on October 28, a thousand women and children, sick, starving, and exhausted, abandoned the pilgrimage. Of those who continued, many became insane and one had to be restrained from attacking his companions. Finally on November 8, at a point where the road and the railway crossed, the remaining 450 men were forced, much against their will, into boxcars and railroaded back to their land, treatment which they later described as “cruelty and persecution” by police who were “no better than Cossacks.” To read the original reports by the Canadian Police is to realize the frustration the authorities felt as these ignorant, deluded peasants unthinkingly carried out the fantastic orders of their no less deluded leaders.[69]

In 1903 their leader Verigin – known as “Lordly” – was allowed to join them from Russia, after spending sixteen years in exile. After a fervent welcome by his followers who believed in him as Christ, he set about organizing resistance to the authorities, traveling about the Doukhobor settlements in a carriage pulled by six fine horses (evidently the reincarnated Christ was exempt from the principle of not using animal labor) and in the company of a harem of young girls (not for him, either, the sexual abstinence he recommended to his followers). They, for their part, accepted this as only right.

In May 1903 another pilgrimage took place, this time with many of the marchers making what was henceforward to be a characteristic gesture, stripping off their clothes, insisting that they did so to symbolize that they shared the freedom of Adam and Eve. Other Canadians did not appreciate the purity of their intentions, however, and one of the pilgrims reported: “We went in the manner of the first man, Adam and Eve, to show nature to humanity, how man should return into his fatherland and return the ripened fruit and its seed… We began to go naked… we went through sixteen villages in all… we were much beaten with twigs, all in blood, so that it was terrible to see us.”[70]

But the irony was that these villages were Doukhobor settlements, and those who attacked them were also Doukhobors – “Independents” who preferred to come to terms with the Canadian government and disapproved of such antisocial behavior. From this time on, divisions between different sections of the sect hardened, and the hostility of the hard-liners was directed as fiercely against the Independents as much as the government. The police stopped another march in the fall.

Their refusal to register their land as individual homesteads was founded on their belief that as true

Christians there should be no individual ownership of property. Though many Doukhobors secretly wished to settle in an acceptable way, they were too afraid of their leader. In the end their refusal to register the land led to a loss of their property rights, so that they found themselves with less than one-third of the land originally granted them. They refused to register births, deaths, and marriages. They opposed military training in schools, and this led to opposing state education of any kind on the ground that the principles taught in the schools conflicted with their own. From then on, demonstrations and disputes continued intermittently: displays of nudism, sometimes actually burning their clothes; hunger strikes; burning of money; and abstaining from work.[71]

In 1923 Doukhobor resistance entered a new phase when the first school on Doukhobor territory was burnt down; later in the year four more were destroyed. The burning of buildings, often their own homes and institutions, became the symbol of Doukhobor intransigence, and within the same year it had escalated to the bombing of government property or that of public companies such as power services.

Aggression also increased among their own kind. The homes and properties of the Independents were targeted. In 1924 the leader Verigin was killed in a train explosion. Though the perpetrator was never discovered, this act was evidently an assassination, though inevitably the new leaders spread the report that the Canadian government had carried out the murder. Not all believed this, and there were more breakaways, but among the humble rank-and-file membership of the community the effect was to increase their fear and uncertainty, their sense of persecution by the authorities, and consequently their dependence on their new leaders. So they willingly co-operated in the mounting campaign of resistance on behalf of what they had become convinced were their rights, which the authorities were withholding.

In 1927 a new leader, Peter Petrovich Verigin, son of the assassinated Peter Vasilivich Verigin, came from Russia to take over. Though he loathed his father, as leader he followed the same practices, pretending to co-operate with the government while secretly encouraging resistance. He told his followers: "I stand before you as perfect as man can be, but right after this meeting I will be entirely different to what you expect of me. For the benefit of our enemies I will smoke, drink, eat meat, and carry on as an ordinary man, an ordinary hoodlum. You alone will know why I act in this way." He was true to his word, collecting hundreds of thousands of dollars from the community, which he spent on gambling, girls, and liquor.[72] "He was notoriously bad at cards and usually too fogged by liquor to spot a cheat… he also demanded sexual gratification … the women considered it an honour and a duty. And if the men resented their daughters and wives being used in this way, few dared to speak."[73]

While outwardly he was friendly to Doukhobors of all kinds, whether independent or strict adherents, it was to these last – the "Sons of Freedom" as they styled themselves – that he was most attached. And it was they who carried out the exploits of practical resistance. To make it impossible for their children to attend government schools, 28 schools were burned in 1929. They had not abandoned the dream of migrating to a more favorable place, and one object of their terrorism was – by bombing, burning, filling the jails, and stripping off their clothes on the slightest provocation – to make the government so anxious to get rid of them that it would provide transportation to wherever they chose. In a typical incident, on July 13, 1929, after two school burnings, a hundred naked Sons of Freedom marched through the streets of Kamsack, Saskatchewan, with banners proclaiming their determination. The fire brigade was called to disperse them with their hoses. One young fireman was appalled to see that one of the naked victims he was hosing was his Doukhobor girlfriend.[74]

Young people were encouraged in hostility to the authorities, participating in outright terrorist activities. Teenagers grew up in the belief that setting fire to a building was an everyday activity. The Canadian flag was seen as that of the devil, government property a legitimate target for bomb attacks. Each new generation was taught that the authorities were to blame for this state of affairs. A recurrent complaint, when Doukhobors were brought to trial, was that the government had failed to attend to their "problem," though it was never formulated as to what their problem was.[75]

Fearful as terrorism is, it is hardly classifiable as "exceptional." Countless self-anointed cult leaders have matched the conduct of Peter Petrovich Verigin, and countless other followers have worshipped their leaders and carried out their orders with similar blind obedience. What set the Doukhobors apart was their readiness to carry out orders that were so patently to their disadvantage, such as destroying their own schools, community buildings, and even their own homes.

The younger Verigin's death in 1939 resolved nothing. When war broke out, though most Doukhobors were willing to serve the country in alternative service, the extremist Sons of Freedom refused to register even for that. From this point on, there was a definitive split between those who would and those who would not collaborate with the government. The Orthodox and the Independents rejected the new leader, Michael Orekov Verigin. Naming himself "Archangel," he was a blatant impostor who, nonetheless was accepted by the hardcore of the sect. For his part, he formed a sect within a sect, people who were willing to leave their families and live with him in wife-sharing freedom. "Man and woman must mingle all together without shame or fear, must break boundaries of devil."[76]

There followed a period of seemingly mindless terrorism, in which buildings were set afire for spurious reasons or no reason at all. "In a single night – February 6, 1944 – fire burned down the Canadian Pacific Railway station at Appledale, Gilpin School at Grand Forks, and Krestova No 5 Village. Four days later, a band of fire-marchers took possession of Kostova School, destroying it and the teacher's quarters."[77] In 1964, it was estimated that in the previous forty years a total of more than a thousand depredations by the Sons of Freedom had cost Canada's taxpayers more than $20 million, not to mention the cost of policing, sheltering, and feeding those involved in hundreds of demonstrations, nude parades, and hunger strikes.[78]

COMMENT: It could be argued that this money could have been saved if the Doukhobors had been left to themselves, but this raises the question whether a democratic state can contain a community that withholds taxes and forces its perceived problems on the rest of the country by its anti-social demonstrations. Today, in a period of greater tolerance, some kind of mutual accommodation has been achieved and the Doukhobor community is flourishing with minimal harassment from, or of, others. The sect has its own website, there are museums and audio-visual projects, a heritage village, and an international Doukhobor intergroup symposium. In 1995 the 100th anniversary of the burning of firearms was celebrated with choirs, dramas, and craft displays.[79]

As early as 1905 Aylmer Maude, who had assured the Canadian government that the Doukhobors would be valuable citizens, found that he had been misled. "Subsequent events showed that, though the Doukhobors are a worthy folk: industrious, cleanly, temperate, hospitable, thrifty, honest, and careful of their children, many of them are also ignorant, suspicious, fanatical, intensely clannish, and superstitious to the point of attributing divinity to their Leader."[80] This dangerous mix provided the means whereby the sect moved from being a set of people who held different *beliefs* from others to being a set of people whose *behavior* was different from others, bringing it into conflict with other parts of society. And it demonstrates how such a process reinforces group solidarity, the sense of persecution, the need to externalize responsibility, and the resorting to aggression in the name of self-defense.

But did the actions of the Doukhobors ever truly represent their own will, or were they simply following blindly leaders whose behavior frequently verged on insanity? Reporter Simma Holt has indicated a crucial contradiction between Doukhobor creed and practice: "From its known beginnings the history of the group has been the history of its leaders. Through the years these leaders have been notably shrewd and skilful men, many of them Christ-like in appearance. Most have posed as Christ and all have been accepted eagerly by this group which claims as a strict tenet of faith and life that each member listens only to the 'voice within' and each is of equal worth to the community. A society that professes to be communal and egalitarian became a despotism of the narrowest sort."[81]

While the self-appointed leaders of the Doukhobors have over the years provided instances of far-sighted leadership to the benefit of the community, the overall balance is heavily in their disfavor. They exploited their followers in every way – robbing them financially, abusing them sexually, and controlling their minds to accept their own, often arbitrary, ideas. To their greedy and selfish despotism on the one hand, and the unthinking submission of their followers on the other, must be attributed all the misfortunes of this unhappy people.

DRUNK DRIVING HYSTERIA

Elk Grove, Illinois: May 20, 1992

Eight students at Elk Grove High School collapsed while watching a mock drunk driving accident held at the school to deter teen drinking during the upcoming prom. The reenactment had been long planned, but took an emotional twist shortly before the event was scheduled when two students from the school were killed in a drunk driving accident following a night of heavy drinking. The planned assembly went ahead as scheduled despite the tragedy. In order to make the assembly more dramatic and memorable, school officials had the students' mangled sports car towed onto the football field as 1,700 students let out a collective gasp as they looked on in distress.

Seven of the eight students who became ill during the assembly were taken to a nearby hospital for "a combination of heat exhaustion and stress" after witnessing the crash reenactment. The program began with a 20-minute drama of a fictitious head-on collision between a family of four going fishing and a car of intoxicated prom-goers. During the reenactment, reporter Dave McKinney said, "a young boy died after being thrown from his parents' car, as did a girl dressed in a blood-stained, white prom gown. The drunk girl, played by junior and drama club member Pam Riley, was placed by paramedics in a black body bag in plain view of the student body."[82]

Sources

1. Norman, E. H. (1945). "Mass Hysteria in Japan." *Far Eastern Survey* 14(6):65-70.
2. Norinaga cited in Norman, 1945, p. 68.
3. Norman (1945). op cit., p. 66.
4. Mora, G. (1963). "A Historical and Socio-Psychiatric Appraisal of Tarantism." *Bulletin of the History of Medicine* 37:417-439.
5. Rosen, G. (1968). *Madness in Society*. London: Routledge and Kegan Paul; Rosen, G. (1962). "Psychopathology in the Social Process: Dance Frenzies, Demonic Possession, Revival Movements and Similar so-called Psychic Epidemics. An Interpretation." *Bulletin of the History of Medicine* 36:13-44 (paper delivered as the Fielding H. Garrison Lecture at the 34th annual meeting of the American Association for the History of Medicine, Chicago, Illinois, May 18 1961).
6. Mora, G. (1963). op cit., pp. 436-438.
7. Norman (1945). op cit., p. 68.
8. Gordon, Benjamin L. (1959). *Medieval and Renaissance Medicine*. New York: Philosophical Library, p. 562.
9. Hecker, J.F.C. (1970[1837]). *The Dancing Mania of the Middle Ages* (translated by B. Babington). New York: B. Franklin, p. 2.
10. Hecker (1837). op cit., pp. 2-3.
11. Rosen, G. (1968). *Madness in Society*. London: Routledge and Kegan Paul, p. 198.
12. Rosen (1968). op cit., pp. 201-202.
13. Rosen (1968). op cit., p. 200.
14. Rosen (1968). op cit., p. 200.
15. Rosen (1968). op cit., p. 200.
16. Bartholomew, Robert E. (December 2000). *Exotic Deviance: Medicalizing Cultural Idioms–From Strangeness to Illness*. Boulder, Colorado: University Press of Colorado, pp. 149-150.
17. Markush, R. E. (1973). "Mental Epidemics: A Review of the Old to Prepare for the New." *Public Health Reviews* 4(2): 353-442. See p. 406.
18. De Costa, Caroline (2002). "St Anthony's Fire and Living Ligatures: A Short History of Ergometrine." *The Lancet* (May 18) 359:1768.
19. De Costa, Caroline (2002). op cit.
20. Bartholomew, Robert E. (1998a). *Psychiatric Imperialism: Medicalizing Cultural Idioms–From Strangeness to Illness*. Doctoral thesis, James Cook University (Queensland, Australia); Bartholomew, Robert E. (2000a). op cit., pp. 127-152; Bartholomew, Robert E. (1998b). "Dancing with Myths: The Misogynist Construction of Dancing Mania." *Feminism & Psychology* 8(2):173-183 (May); Bartholomew, Robert E. (1994). "Tarantism, Dancing Mania and Demonopathy: The Anthro-Political Aspects of Mass Psychogenic Illness." *Psychological Medicine* 24:281-306; Bartholomew, Robert E. (2000b). "Rethinking the Dance Mania." *The Skeptical Inquirer* 24(4):42-47 (July-August).
21. Backman, E. L. (1952). *Religious Dances in the Christian Church and in Popular Medicine* (Translated by E. Classer). London: Allen and Unwin.
22. de Martino, Ernesto. (1961). *La Terra del Rimorso; Contributo a una Storia Religiosa del Sud*. Milano: Il Saggiatore; Anonymous. (1967). "Tarantism, St. Paul and the Spider." *Times Literary Supplement* (London), April 27:345-347.
23. The primary source for this entry is Collins 1990, supplemented by material on the Internet. See Collins, Tony (1990). *Open Verdict*. London: Sphere.
24. Collins, op cit., p. 139.
25. Editorial in *The Independent* (London), 26 August 1988.
26. Pritchard, Professor Colin (2000). "The Strange Case of the Dog that Failed to Bark." Southampton University *Viewpoint Online*, issue 409, 20 October.

27. Collins, op cit., p. 217.
28. Oesterreich, T.K. (1930[1921]) *Possession.* [Originally published in German 1921] London: Kegan Paul, Trench, Trubner. Oesterreich 1930 provides representative examples from many cultures.
29. Hastings, James (1908). *Encyclopaedia of Religion and Ethics.* Edinburgh: T & T Clark [published by volumes], volume 2, p. 565.
30. See, for example, Collin de Plancy (1844). *Dictionnaire Infernale.* Paris: P. Mellier; Gettings, Fred (1988). *Dictionary of Demons: A Guide to Demons and Demonologists in Occult Lore.* North Pompret, Vermont: Trafalgar Square Publishing.
31. See, for example, Evans-Pritchard, E.E. (1937). *Witchcraft, Oracles and Magic among the Azande.* Oxford: University Press.
32. F. von Baader (1858) cited by Oesterreich, op cit., pp. 20-21.
33. Tylor, Edward B. (1871). *Primitive Culture.* London: Murray, volume 2, p. 124.
34. Nevius, John L. (1892). *Demon Possession and Allied Themes.* Revell, Chicago, p. 143.
35. Janet, Pierre (1935[1897]). *Névroses et Idées Fixes.* Paris: Alcan 1897 (4th edition 1935), p. 384.
36. Sprenger, Jakob and Kramer, Heinrich (1928[1486]). *Malleus Maleficarum.* Translated into English by Montague Summers. London: Rodker.
37. Bizouard, Joseph (1863). *Des Rapports de L'homme avec le Démon.* Paris: Gamme et Duprey, volume 3, p. 34.
38. Bälz, cited by Oesterreich, op cit., p. 107.
39. August Stöhr, *Handbuch der Pastoralmedizin*, cited by Oesterreich, op cit., p. 200.
40. Watkins 1983, p. 7
41. Oesterreich, op cit., p. 208.
42. Countless books and pamphlets, too many to cite, were issued in the late 20th century condemning these and other practices.
43. Sir William Trethowan in *Journal of Medical Ethics* 1976, quoted in Watkins, op cit., p. 106.
44. Watkins, op cit., p. 113.
45. Goodman, Felicitas D. (1981). *The Exorcism of Anneliese Michel.* Garden City NY: Doubleday.
46. Watkins, op cit., p. 151.
47. Quoted in Watkins, op cit., p. 166.
48. Masson, Hervé (1975). *Le Diable et las Possession Démoniaque.* Paris: Belfond, p. 231.
49. Dupray, cited by Oesterreich, op cit., p. 108.
50. Watkins, op cit., p. 161.
51. Cited by Watkins, op cit., p. 166.
52. Dopamine is a neurotransmitter, a deficiency of which can cause Parkinson's disease, an excess of which may cause schizophrenia.
53. Korem and Meir 1980: 160.
54. Pelton, Robert W. (1979). *Confrontations with the Devil.* South Brunswick: A S Barnes, p. 34.
55. *The Complete Books of Charles Fort.* New York: Dover Publications, p. 851, citing the *Derby Mercury*, May 15, 1905.
56. *Volgar* (Russian periodical) March 1895, quoted by Finot, Jean (1918). *Saints, initiés et Possédés Modernes.* Paris: Charpentier, pp. 18-20.
57. Holt, Simma (1964). *Terror in the Name of God.* Toronto/Montreal, passim.
58. Maude, Aylmer (1905). *A Peculiar People.* London: Constable, p. 5.
59. Maude, op cit., p. 154.
60. Maude, op cit., p. 19, citing Orést Novitsky.
61. Holt, op cit., p. 17.
62. Maude, op cit., p. 160.
63. Quoted by Holt, op cit., pp. 29-30.
64. Maude, op cit.
65. Maude, op cit., p. 168.
66. Maude, op cit., p. 225.
67. Ferguson, Charles W. (1929). *The Confusion of Tongues.* London: Heinemann, p. 132; Maude, op cit., p. 217.
68. Maude, op cit., p. 226.
69. Holt, op cit., pp. 31-37: Ferguson, op cit., pp. 122-125.
70. Holt, op cit., p. 42.
71. Holt, op cit., p. 46.
72. Holt, op cit., p. 65.
73. Verigin quoted by Holt, op cit., p. 63.
74. Holt, op cit., p. 66.
75. Holt, op cit., pp. 7-8.
76. Holt, op cit., p. 95.
77. Holt, op cit., pp. 96-97.
78. Holt, op cit., p. 8.
79. www.doukhobor-homepage.com/history 2003.
80. Maude, op cit., p. 63.
81. Holt, op cit., p. 10.
82. McKinney, Dave (1992). "'Operation Prom Night' Crash Reenactment Hits Home. Heat, Stress Take Toll on 8 Students." *Chicago Daily Herald*, May 21, p. 4.

ECUADOR MARTIAN PANIC

February 1949

On the night of February 12, a radio play based on the novel *The War of the Worlds* by H.G. Wells sparked pandemonium in Ecuador. An Associated Press reporter on the scene said the broadcast "drove most of the population of Quito into the streets" as panic-stricken residents sought to escape Martian "gas raids."[1] The drama described strange creatures heading toward Quito after landing and destroying the neighboring community of Latacunga, twenty miles to the south. Broadcast in Spanish on Radio Quito, the realistic program included impersonations of well-known local politicians, journalists, vivid eyewitness descriptions, and the name of the local town of Cotocallao. In Quito, rioting broke out and an enraged mob marched on the building housing the radio station and Ecuador's oldest and leading newspaper, *El Comercio*. Rampaging mob members blocked the entrance to the building, hurling stones and smashing windows. Some occupants escaped out a rear door; others ran to the third floor.[2] Groups poured gasoline onto the building and hurled flaming wads of paper, setting fires in several locations, trapping dozens inside and forcing them to the third story. As the flames reached them, the occupants began leaping from windows and forming human chains in a desperate bid to reach safety. Some of the "chains" broke, plunging terrified occupants to their deaths.[3] Twenty people were killed and 15 injured.[4] Army soldiers were mobilized to restore order, rolling through the streets in tanks and firing tear gas canisters to break up the demonstrators and allow fire engines through.[5] Damage to the newspaper building was estimated at $350,000.[6] Help was slow to arrive as most mobile police units had been dispatched to Cotocallao to repel the "Martians," leaving Quito with a skeleton police and military presence.

The tragic events began with the sudden interruption of a regular music program with a special bulletin – "Here is urgent news" – followed by reports of the invading Martians in the form of a cloud, wreaking havoc and destruction while closing in on the city.[7] "The air base of Marisal Sucre has been taken by the enemy and it is being destroyed. There are many dead and wounded," the announcer said.[8] A voice resembling that of a government minister appealed for calm so the city's defenses could be organized and citizens evacuated in time. Next the "Mayor" arrived and made a dramatic announcement: "People of Quito, let us defend our city. Our women and children must go out into the surrounding heights to leave the men free for action and combat."[9] At this point, a priest's voice could be heard asking for divine forgiveness, followed by a recording of church bells sounding alarms throughout Quito. Positioned atop the city's tallest building, the *La Previsora* tower, an announcer said he could discern a monster engulfed in plumes of fire and smoke, advancing on Quito from the north.[10] It was at this point, according to a *New York Times* reporter, that citizens "began fleeing from their homes and running through the streets. Many were clad only in night clothing."[11] The panic was not limited to Quito. In some parts of the country hundreds of terrified Ecuadorians fled into the mountains to avoid capture, believing, according to the radio, that the Martians had already taken over much of the country.[12]

On February 14 and 15, Ecuadorian officials arrested at least 16 people, including the station's drama director Eduardo Alcaraz, for their role in either rioting or being responsible for allowing the radio play to air. Indictments were ordered against art director Leonardo Paez and station manager Alfredo Vergara, a Chilean scriptwriter, and his spouse, Maya Wong.[13] The station's operators claimed that Alcaraz and Paez were the broadcast's masterminds, having written and directed the play in secret.[14] Also arrested and charged with partial responsibility was *El Comercio*'s editor, Jose Alfredo Lierena.[15]

COMMENTS: The rioting, murder and public unrest is the most extreme reaction to a *War of the Worlds* radio recreation, exceeding even the original 1938 episode.

See also: ORSON WELLES MARTIAN PANIC (1938), MARTIAN INVASION SCARE OF 1939, CHILEAN MARTIAN INVASION PANIC (1944), BUFFALO MARTIAN INVASION SCARE (1968), RHODE ISLAND MARTIAN INVASION PANIC (1974), PORTUGUESE MARTIAN INVASION PANICS (1988 and 1998).

EDISON STAR SIGHTINGS

North America: 1885-early 1900s

In 1885, American inventor Thomas Alva Edison was conducting a series of experiments on wireless telegraphy between balloons near his Menlo Park laboratory in New Jersey. Achieving his best results at night, he began to send the balloons aloft at night. In order to illuminate and spot them, he attached lights. Newspapers afforded Edison's experiment considerable publicity. His telegraphic balloon trials were soon the subject of widespread rumors that gave rise to a popular folk belief surrounding the existence of the "Edison Star" or "electric balloon." Soon people began claiming to see this object in the sky. Decades after his experiments began, there were claims that Edison was experimenting with what was essentially a gigantic light bulb, intent on leaving a legacy by illuminating the entire continental United States at night.[16] One particular flurry of sightings occurred between March and April of 1897, when thousands of citizens reported seeing an imaginary arc lamp suspended in the sky. In 1897, rumors began to circulate that Edison was conducting "electric balloon" experiments with lamps capable of producing extraordinary candle power and cutting edge reflectors in an effort to project the light from one side of the country to the other. It is within this backdrop that the 1897 "Edison Star" sightings occurred.

The Electric Balloon Wave Begins[17]

On Tuesday evening March 29, a large crowd gathered in the city of Iron Mountain, Michigan, as rumors spread rapidly that a conspicuous object in the evening sky "was an electric light hoisted two miles high over St. Paul" in the adjacent state of Minnesota. One man claimed that it consisted of a storage battery attached to a tethered balloon.[18] A story circulated that the light was sent up at about 5 pm, was visible across the entire U.S., and was taken down mid-evening. Correspondingly, many residents claimed that they could see the balloon being slowly reeled in toward the earth at about 9 pm.[19] The following night in Portland, Maine, a large number of people gathered at various street corners and stared at Venus under the delusion that it was a "mammoth electric searchlight suspended by a block and tackle."[20] The "electric balloon" was seen in the vicinity Portland for several days in early April, and one newspaper noted that "Nine out of ten men and women who parade the streets nowadays are excited over it."[21] It was widely believed that they had observed an electric light suspended atop New Hampshire's Mount Washington, and residents in Dover and Foxcroft, Maine refused to accept that it was Venus.[22] In Bangor, Maine, one man was emphatic that he could see "by the light of the balloon, a faint outline of the frame which sustained the machinery." Meanwhile, a sensation was created in Waterville and throughout the Kennebec valley in Maine as the light was seen to suddenly move "as if it had been pulled down with a rope."[23]

Also during early April, rumors of the electric balloon swept across America, and it was even sighted for a week over Montreal, Canada.[24] One newspaper editor remarked that "No blizzard...ever swept over the country with greater rapidity or more thoroughly."[25] The *Augusta Chronicle* editors commented on the extent of the delusion: "...just think of the people of New England, the cultured east, in the state of Massachusetts where Boston is, taking the planet Venus for an electric light swung in the sky by Mr. Edison."[26] In Boston, a local astronomer remarked that he was unable to work as he was inundated with queries about "Edison's experimental star."[27] In Bearrien Springs, Michigan, the "electric star" was rumored to have been a monumental advertising ploy to promote a popular brand of soap manufactured at Michigan City. In supporting this story, one press account stated that "we all now know that many things are possible to electrical engineers."[28]

CONTEXT: To understand the sightings, we need to examine their context in relation to the events in America during the latter nineteenth century. The period between 1850 and 1897 was marked by unprecedented technological changes that permanently altered lifestyles. There was a widespread buoyant mood that almost any invention was possible. This sentiment was precipitated by a rapid series of technological innovations, including the invention of the gas mantle (1875), telephone (1876), gramophone (1877), filament lamp (1879), blow lamp (1880), motor car and steam turbine (1884), motorcycle (1885), diesel engine (1893) cinematograph and X-rays (1895), and radio (1896) to name a few.[29] In the final two decades of the century, Americans were preoccupied with popular literature on science and inventions. The string of rapid inventions and discoveries, in conjunction with a huge volume of both fiction and non-fiction stories on science and inventions, helped to foster an exaggerated optimism that almost any invention was conceivable. This period in American history has been aptly described as an age that was infatuated with science and its possibilities: "... the Frank Reade Library [was]...designed to meet the insatiable demand for tales of mechanical novelty by concentrating on a nonstop run of invention stories. The series opened on 24 September 1892 and continued for 19 issues. It was the first serial publication of any size ever to be devoted exclusively to science fiction stories; and every issue throbbed with the dynamism of coming things – robots, submarines, flying machines...and the rest of the imaginative bric-a-brac of an age that was in love with the great wonders of science."[30]

In his biography of Edison, Francis Jones commented that the inventor "often had a quiet chuckle" over the stories of his experimental light. He noted that Edison "received many letters on the subject, but he never replied to them, hoping that the absurd story would die a natural death," which it eventually did.[31] It is interesting to note that a quasi-religious mythos surrounded Edison, who was appropriately dubbed "the Wizard." According to Edison biographer Matthew Josephson, "the rustic neighbors of Menlo Park and nearby Metuchen gossiped about his having machines that could overhear farmers talking or even cows munching the grass in the fields a mile away. It was said that he had another machine which was supposed to measure the heat of the stars; and that illuminations of meteoric brilliance were seen blazing up through the windows of his laboratory and were extinguished as suddenly and mysteriously as they had appeared. Catching glimpses of figures gliding about the fields near his laboratory at midnight with lights and equipment, bent on missions none of them could understand..."[32]

Observations of the "Edison Star" appear to have been a symbolic projection of the prevailing technological mania and seemingly limitless faith in science and inventions that swept America at that time.

See also: FLYING SAUCER(ORIGIN OF), GREAT AMERICAN AIRSHIP WAVE, GHOST ROCKET SCARE, RUSSIAN POLAND BALLOON SCARE, ANDREE BALLOON MANIA.

ENTHUSIASM EPISODES

The Greek word *enthousiasmos* signifies inspiration or possession by a god, a form of behavior that plays a part in countless religious cultures or belief-systems past and present and in all parts of the world, many of which are covered in this Encyclopedia. If conduct were sufficient to qualify for the label, sects like the Russian SKOPTSI and the German ANABAPTISTS would be categorized as enthusiasts. Whitley, in an authoritative article, uses the term as a catch-all for all religious groups whose members seemed to be carried away by their beliefs and to have lost control of their behavior; by his criteria, Moslems (see ISLAMIC ECSTATIC SECTS) and Mormons would qualify.[33]

However, the term is more usually, and more usefully, applied particularly to the English sectarians of the 17th and 18th century and to those who carried their beliefs to the New World. The early QUAKERS who walked naked through the streets as a sign, the JUMPERS who jumped up and down in their chapels till exhausted, and the crowds jerking and falling at AMERICAN REVIVAL MEETINGS – these were usually labeled Enthusiasts, and the term was generally employed in a pejorative sense. "Almost always the enthusiastic movement is denounced as an innovation, yet claims to be preserving, or to be restoring, the primitive discipline of the Church."[34]

As perceived by its critics, enthusiasm implied exaggeration not so much in the beliefs held, as in the way those beliefs were expressed. The views of the Ranters, the Muggletonians, or the Swedenborgians might be extreme, but in 17th century England extreme views on spiritual matters were current coinage. It was in the way it manifested its beliefs that a sect left itself open to the charge of enthusiasm.

Enthusiasts were widely considered to be subversive, but if this was sometimes so, it was almost always secondary to their primary objective, the quest for a simpler and more direct relationship with the divine. They were intensely religious, and in their pursuit of their religious ideals they might show lack of consideration for the feelings of others, and they might despise public matters to a degree where they could be seen as dangerous radicals. But they were rarely political themselves and even such social changes as they recommended were for religious rather than humanitarian reasons. In 1653 the Fifth Monarchy Men, who believed that the overthrow of the monarchy was the prelude to the Second Coming of Christ, planned to destroy the cathedrals, dissolve the universities, and replace all laws by those of Moses.[35]

"Theirs was a desperate cry, a plea for riddance of all encumbrances between the individual soul and the naked Spirit."[36] Most, if not all, had come to believe they were in personal contact with God, who gave them instructions and counsel without any priestly go-between. If that included flouting man-made laws, so be it; God's authority was surely greater than man's. They believed they had the right to liberty of conscience, and this often led to liberty of behavior also. Even though nakedness might be offensive to others, if the Spirit moved them to strip, as it did the Quakers, they stripped.

Enthusiasts were an embarrassment to others who, having taken a few steps towards freedom by leaving the Church of Rome, were reluctant to take too many. Enthusiasm was always relative: there were no hard and fast lines as to where freedom tipped over into excess. Religious controversy raged over niceties of doctrine that to an outsider might seem mere hair-splitting. The Puritan sectarians "devised a vocabulary for their theology whose meaning was limited to the comprehension of the elect."[37] In 1635 Anne Hutchinson was banished from Massachusetts and excommunicated by the church fathers of Boston because they found her beliefs too offensive to be tolerated, yet the theology of this patently devout woman differed from theirs only in emphasis and interpretation.

The enthusiastic sects shared their general principles and differed from one another chiefly in nuances of doctrine and niceties of conduct. Writing in 1656, church historian Thomas Fuller colorfully expressed his views: "As in the small-pox (pardon my plain and homely but true comparison), when at first they come forth, every one of them may severally and distinctly be discerned, but when once they run and matter they break into one another, and can no longer be dividedly discerned. So though at first there was a real difference betwixt Familists, Enthusiasts, Antinomians (not to add high-flown Anabaptists) in their opinions, yet afterwards they did so interfuse amongst themselves, that it is almost impossible to bank and bound their several absurdities."[38]

In retrospect, it has becomes possible to take a more balanced view of enthusiasm, recognizing its positive contributions while deploring its excesses. Benjamin Warfield, lecturing in 1918, said:

> Protestantism, to be sure, has happily been no stranger to enthusiasm; and enthusiasm with a lower-case "e" unfortunately easily runs into that Enthusiasm with a capital "E" which is the fertile seed-bed of fanaticism. Individuals have constantly arisen so filled with the sense of God in their own souls, and so overwhelmed by the wonders of grace which

they have witnessed, that they see the immediate hand of God in every occurrence which strikes them as remarkable, and walk through the world clothed in a nimbus of miracle. To them it seems a small thing that the God who has so marvelously healed their sick souls should equally marvelously heal their sick bodies; that the God who speaks so unmistakably in their spirits should speak equally unmistakably through their lips.[39]

EPIDEMIC OF LSD HALLUCINATIONS

California: 1998

On September 23, three fourth-graders at a California middle school inadvertently ingested the powerful hallucinogenic drug LSD and were hospitalized. Eleven other students, who had sampled a white powder from a vial during the day, believed that they too had ingested LSD and were hospitalized. Despite exhibiting symptoms ranging from violence to hallucinations, tests were negative and the pupils were released within a few hours.[40]

EXTRATERRESTRIAL TSUNAMI PANIC

Morocco: May 25, 2006

In mid-May, the Ufological Research Centre posted information on its website, of extraterrestrials warning Earthlings of an impending tsunami disaster, resulting in anxiety and panic across Morocco. The Centre said that a tsunami could hit the Atlantic after a comet passes close to earth on Thursday May 25. The website said that Eric Julien, author of a book on extraterrestrials called *La Science Des Extraterrestres* (*The Science of Extraterrestrials*), claimed that on May 25 a fragment from a comet passing near the Earth would trigger a monster tsunami that would cause extensive damage to the Atlantic coast and the coast of Morocco. Julien said he was made aware of the disaster after receiving a psychic message from ETs. He claimed that the wave would reach 200 meters in height.

Despite assurances from scientists at NASA and the Moroccan meteorological agency, many residents living along the Moroccan coast left their homes and rushed to higher ground to wait out the expected carnage on May 25.[41] Part of Julien's website message read: "a series of giant waves, including one méga tsunami almost two hundred meters in height, will be born from a succession of underwater eruptions. These watery giants, decreasing with distance, will touch the majority of the Atlantic coasts; in particular, those most at risk lie between the equator and the tropic of Cancer. The victims of May 25, 2006, will be tens of millions. The devastated survivors will be more numerous still. The economic losses will be enormous, well beyond the scales of destruction hitherto tested by our civilization. North America and Europe will not be saved, but will be affected in less dramatic proportions. By extension, other remote countries will be also affected."[42]

EVIL SPIRIT SCHOOL

Northeastern Nepal: circa May 2003

The principal of a remote Nepalese school urgently contacted a group of psychiatrists from the public health department in Dharan to help prevent his school from being forced to close after parents, fearing attacks by evil spirits, refused to let their children attend school. A team of psychiatrists headed by Rabi Shakya visited the Nepal Rashtriya Secondary School in the Sunsari district and made the following report.[43]

The outbreak began with the 16-year-old daughter of the principal ("Miss A") who was described as very influential and "the centre of attention."[44] Miss A had met a psychotic woman two weeks earlier, when the elderly woman visited her village. Upon learning of the death of the "mad old woman," she feared that the woman's spirit might attack her and she grew anxious. That same afternoon, during the school lunch break, Miss A walked out to the tube well where students get their water. Suddenly she began to laugh for no apparent reason. Friends tried asking what was wrong. When some friends tried caressing her, she clinched them tightly and wouldn't let go. Dr. Shakya describes what happened next: "She clinched her teeth repeatedly, tightened her fists, shook her arms and body, went around the well and made funny noises."[45] By the look on her face, she was angry and appeared ready to fend off anyone who tried to stop her. A while later, she began weeping and threw away various possessions such as her glasses and pens.

Classmates grabbed her and forcibly brought her to a room inside the school, where, upon calming down, she told onlookers that she could recall nothing from the incident.

Soon other girls at the school experienced similar bouts of disorganized behavior whenever they walked near the well. The first few cases affected only Miss A's close friends at the school, but later it spread to other younger students who had witnessed the attacks. Of the school's 300 students, only 35 percent were female, yet the episode only affected females. In all, 70 were afflicted, all between the ages of 10 and 16. As more and more were stricken, bouts of strange behaviors occurred away from the well, such as in the bathroom or classrooms.

An investigation revealed that many of the affected students were poor, illiterate, had low social status, and were from agricultural backgrounds. With the exception of a single teacher, everyone else interviewed was convinced that the old woman's "evil spirit" was responsible for the strange behaviors.

Dr. Shakya decided to attack the problem through education. He gave a series of lectures during which he explained that the troubles were the result of a psychological phenomena known as mass hysteria. A trigger may have been tension created by having an all-male teaching staff. Curiously, while all of the boys interviewed believed that evil spirits were the cause of the trouble, they were also convinced that they were immune to the effects of evil spirits. Not a single girl under the age of 10 was affected. Another curiosity: it was widely believed that young children were immune from the effects of evil spirits. The bouts of strange behaviors slowly died down, and six months after the initial investigation, there had been only four new incidents. During this period, attempts to appease the "spirits" by sacrificing a goat and prayers, failed.

Sources

1. "Mars Raiders Caused Quito Panic; Mob Burns Radio Plant, Kills 15." *New York Times*, February 14, 1949 pp. 1, 7. Quote appears on p. 1.
2. "Mars Raiders Caused Quito Panic..." op cit.
3. "Mars Raiders Caused Quito Panic..." op cit.
4. "Wolf, Wolf." *Newsweek* 33(8) (February 21, 1949), p. 44.
5. "Martians and Wild Animals." *Time* (February 21, 1949), p. 46.
6. "'Invasion From Mars.'" *Times of London*, February 14, 1949, p. 4; Anonymous "When You Say That, Smile." *The Commonweal* XLIX, Number 20, pp. 483-484.
7. "Two Officials Indicted." *Times of London*, February 15, 1949, p. 4. Associated Press report.
8. "Two Officials Indicted." op cit.
9. "Two Officials Indicted." op cit.
10. "Mars Raiders Caused Quito Panic..." op cit.
11. "Mars Raiders Caused Quito Panic..." op cit.
12. Tovar, Enrique (1996). "The Martians Cause Panic." *La Nación* (The Nation), March 3, 1996.
13. "20 Dead in Quito Riot." *New York Times*, February 15, 1949, p. 5; Anonymous. (1949). "Quito Holds 3 for 'Mars' Script." *New York Times*, February 16, p. 15.
14. "Two Officials Indicted." op cit.
15. "Quito Holds 3 for 'Mars' Script." op cit.
16. Conot, R. (1979). *A Streak of Luck*. New York: Seaview.
17. The remainder of this entry is excerpted from: Bartholomew, Robert E. (1998). "Technology and Mass Delusion: Remembering Edison's 'Electric Star' Hysteria." *Technology: Journal of the Franklin Institute* 335A(1):65-67.
18. "There is no string to it. Venus, the evening star..." *Daily Tribune* [Iron, Mountain, MI], March 30, 1897, p. 3.
19. "There is no string to it." op cit.
20. "Venus was bright," *Daily Eastern Argus*, March 31, 1897, p. 3.
21. "See that balloon? Everybody is staring at Venus and Venus is fooling everybody..." *Bangor Daily Commercial* [Bangor, ME], April 3, 1897, p. 3.
22. "Dover and Foxcroft locals," *Bangor Daily Commercial* [Bangor, ME], April 2, 1897, p. 7.
23. "Dover and Foxcroft locals." op cit.
24. "Puzzled over a light. Citizens of Montreal see a strange star and wonder increases," *Piedmont Herald* [WV], April 16, 1897.
25. "Venus maligned" [editorial], *Milwaukee Journal*, April 6, 1897, p. 4.
26. "A light in the east," *Times and Democrat* [Orangeburg, SC], April 7, 1897, p. 4, citing verbatium from the *Augusta Chronicle* [ME].
27. "That experimental star," *Boston Evening Transcript*, April 15, 1897, p. 4.
28. "It is no fake," *Berrien Springs Era* [MI], April 7, 1897, p. 3.
29. de Bono, E. (1979). *Eureka! An Illustrated History of Inventions From the Wheel to the Computer*. London: Thames and Hudson.
30. Clarke, I.F. (1986). "American Anticipations: The First of the Futurists." *Futures* 18(4):584-596.
31. Jones, F.A. (1931). *The Life Story of Thomas Alva Edison*. New York: Grosset & Dunlap, pp. 174-175.
32. Josephson, M. (1961). *Edison: A Biography*. London: Eyre & Spottiswoode, p. 170.
33. W. T. Whitley in Hastings, James (1908). *Encyclopaedia of Religion and Ethics*. Edinburgh: T & T Clark [published by volumes], volume 5, p. 317.
34. Knox, Ronald A. (1950). *Enthusiasm*. Oxford University Press, p. 1.
35. Blunt, John Henry (1874). *Dictionary of Sects, Heresies, Ecclesiastical Parties and Schools of Religious Thought*. London, Oxford & Cambridge: Rivingtons, p. 160.
36. Lovejoy, David S. (1985). *Religious Enthusiasm in the New World*. Cambridge, MA: Harvard University Press, p. 71.
37. Godwin, George (1941). *The Great Revivalists*. London:

Watts. Godwin, p. 103.

38. Fuller's *Church History* volume ix, p. 3, quoted by Blunt, op cit., p. 147.

39. Warfield, Benjamin B. (1918). *Counterfeit Miracles*. New York: Charles Scribner's Sons, p. 127.

40. Telephone interview between Robert Bartholomew and Solomon Moore, reporter for the *Los Angeles Times*, March 14, 2000; Moore, Solomon, and Ramirez, M. (1998). "3 Sickened Pacoima Students Ingested LSD; 11 Other Hospitalized 4th Graders had no Drugs in System..." *Los Angeles Times*, September 25, 1998.

41. http://english.aljazeera.net/NR/exeres/F4396687-6C85-4C8C-B47A-3B8F785FE95C. htm.

42. http://exodus2006.com/cometfrags/Eric-Julien-25-MAY.htm.

43. Shakya, Rabi (2005). "Epidemic of Hysteria in a School of Rural Eastern Nepal: A Case Report." *Journal of the Indian Association for Child and Adolescent Mental Health* 1(4): 1-5 (the article appears in five pages, but the pages are unnumbered). While the report by Rabi Shakya fails to mention the date of the incident or the school involved, this was gleaned from the following press report, which is obviously a description of the same incident: "Mass Hysteria Hits Girls in Nepal school." Web site accessed on July 30, 2004 at: http://www.tribuneindia.com/2003/20030909/world.htm#5, citing the PTI news agency.

44. Shakya, op cit., p. 4.

45. Shakya, op cit., p. 2.

FACILITATED COMMUNICATION MANIA

Worldwide: 1990s

During the 1990s, a technique known as "Facilitated Communication" (FC) became popular in many schools. FC involved assisting intellectually challenged children to literally spell out their thoughts, while an aid guided their hand or hands and helped them to supposedly type out what the child was thinking. The technique was blamed for numerous unfounded sexual abuse allegations and claims that the assistants were unconsciously writing much, and in some cases, all of the child's thoughts.

FC was developed by Australian educator Rosemary Crossley and hailed as a breakthrough. The facilitator's job is to provide "continuous physical assistance to the handicapped person, helping him or her in pointing to pictures or letters on a communication board or in typing out messages on a computer keyboard."[1] FC was pioneered in the early 1970s when Crossley made a seemingly remarkable discovery in working with 12 children with communication impairments. With the aid of FC, she concluded that these children actually possessed intellectual abilities that were either in the normal or superior range. The technique was soon adopted in other parts of the world, and *The Facilitated Communication Digest* was founded.[2]

While some qualitative studies have supported FC, the more rigid, neutral, controlled studies have been consistently negative. Strictly controlled studies typically involve the elimination of "message passing" – that is, "conveying information in FC interactions that reflects what was previously said or done with a research participant in the absence of the facilitator, thus, conveying information and communication."[3] Hence, in their critique of FC, the leading opponents of the technique, researchers John Jacobson, James Mulick, and Allen Schwartz conclude that in reviewing the literature: "Relevant controlled, peer-reviewed, published studies repeatedly show that, under circumstances when access to information by facilitators is systematically and tightly manipulated, the ability to produce communication through FC varies predictably and in a manner that demonstrates that the content of the communication is being determined by the facilitator."[4] They argue that FC was a passing fad that represented the triumph of wishful thinking over sound scientific principles, as those most aggressively embracing this technique appeared to be human services advocates and social theorists who were aggressive advocates of equality and educational inclusion for the disabled. From this vantage point, as Jacobson, Mulick and Schwartz observe, it does not seem to be much of a leap to believe "that people with disabilities should have a full range of opportunities to the position that people labeled as disabled are, in fact, not disabled at all."[5]

FC has resulted in at least 60 allegations of abuse witch-hunts. In a review of such cases in the United States, in all but two instances, the legal proceedings were eventually terminated and the charges dropped.[6]

Harvard psychologist Dodge Fernald views FC as an example of "unintended cuing" that is akin to the case of Clever Hans, the so-called mathematical horse in the early 20th century (see WONDER HORSE MANIAS); later research on the impact of experimenters on their subjects; and the controversy over apes learning language.[7] The process involved in FC is also viewed as being akin to the unconscious production of automatic writing, channeling, and Ouija board use.[8]

Jacobson, Mulick and Schwartz view the rise of FC during the 1990s as the outcome of a social and political process that was part of an historical backlash against biomedicine and the behavioral sciences. They view the FC craze as a witch-hunt by some in the disabilities field. They state: "Similarities to historic witch-hunts are apparent in the actions of support groups led by personally dedicated pro-FC advocates who gain materially from promoting FC; the compatibility of FC and its rationales with current popular ideology (e.g., the goal of total inclusion for everyone now); strong appeals to emotional values; the disregard for disconfirming evidence; and the active suppression of heretics, or rather, critics. These are not the hallmarks of a scientific approach…"[9]

FACTORY FAINTING FITS

Syracuse, New York: circa June 1905

"An epidemic of fainting spells among girls in Pass & Seymour plant [sic] explained by neurologists as due to hysteria, on the same basis as 'the giggles' in girls' boarding schools. The expert explained that young women in an assembly are likely to become hysterical."[10]

FACTORY HYSTERIA SWEEPS USA

United States: August-October 1976

A series of mysterious illness outbreaks swept across the United States during the second half of the year, causing widespread concern. Health officials suggested that the cause was psychological in origin.

At least 300 workers of Essex International in Kittanning, Pennsylvania were sent home without pay as the facility temporarily shut down twice in early October while federal and state health authorities searched in vain for the cause. Similar outbreaks were reported at electronics plants in the nearby county of Jefferson, in Columbus, Ohio, and at Grants Pass, Oregon. The symptoms were the same in each case: nausea, headache, stomachache, breathing trouble, and "a sensation of being intoxicated."

In Jefferson County, the Rola-Jensen plant remained open while health officials continued to search for clues as to why 70 of 700 employees fell ill in September. According to Charles Straw of the Pennsylvania Occupational Safety and Health Administration, "We've been up there six times and we're no further ahead now than we were a month ago." Meanwhile in Columbus, state officials say that 80 of 600 workers at the Robertshaw Controls Company complained of feeling weak and nauseated after a new type of glue was used in early September. However, when use of the glue was discontinued in the production process, the complaints continued. Dr. George Shadler of the Ohio Department of Health said: "I feel we've gone as far as we can go." Between August 25 and September 8, the plant had to be shut down four times due to illness. Then when a propane leak was uncovered, officials were confident that they had solved the mystery, but workers continued to get ill. Finally, during the first week of October, an Oregon company that makes electronic components for the space industry reported that 50 workers had experienced similar symptoms. One possible explanation is that media coverage of these electronics plant ailments heightened safety and environmental concerns and awareness at other plants across the country.[11]

FADS

The word fad originated during the 1800s and is derived from "faddle" from the sixteenth century term "fiddle-faddle," meaning one who focuses on trivial matters or nonsense.[12] Fads occur when large numbers of people exhibit short-lived interest in trivial objects or activities. Fads can involve words, ideas, people, and habits. While interest in fads may be intense, those involved do not become obsessive and it doesn't become the central feature of everyday life. Fads may originate as symbols of high prestige and status, only to quickly die out as the novelty wears off and "everyone" is doing it. Sometimes youngsters will take up a fad as a way to rebel against authority. In other instances it's a way of saying, "Hey, I'm different and worth noticing – look at me." Some experts believe that fads tend to be more popular among young people because their identities are less stable or developed than those of older persons.[13] Other writers suggest that fads become more numerous during times of crisis, perhaps diverting attention from the more serious issues of the day.[14]

Arguably the biggest fad of the twentieth century was the Hula Hoop. A remarkable 30 million were sold in the United States over a four-month span in 1958.[15] Other classic fads include Cabbage Patch Dolls, streaking, gold fish swallowing, phone booth stuffing, Russian boots, pogo sticks, Davy Crocket coonskin hats, women's pocketbooks shaped like dogs, mini-skirts, and the words "groovy" and "no-brainer." Fads are, to use a fad cliché, "a flash in the pan," and often appear ridiculous after losing favor, but seemed like the hottest thing going in their heyday. Pet rocks and the coughing ashtray immediately spring to mind as classic examples. It's difficult to predict or control a fad. There isn't much you can do other than "ride it out."

A study of 735 fads by psychologist Emory Bogardus found that every fad could fit into one of several broad categories. These were: female dress and decoration (73%), male dress and decoration (11%), recreation and amusements (6%), and language (4%) with the remaining 6% involving cars, education, architecture, and culture.[16] Bogardus concluded that the typical fad maintains popularity for three months or less, while few fads can captivate the public's interest for more than six months.[17] There are notable exceptions however. Due to their spontaneous nature, it's difficult to tell what will be the next fad, only that there *will* be one.

Some sociologists discuss the *four phases of a fad.*[18] First is the *latent period,* where the fad exists but lies relatively dormant. Some writers contend that most or all fads are recycled from existing cultural themes that are later rediscovered and only give the appearance of being "the latest thing." For instance, the tree and flagpole sitting fads of the late 1920s and early 30s may seem unique, but can be traced to the "Pillar Hermits" of early Christian Europe.[19] The yo-yo enjoyed huge popularity in the early 1930s and again in the early 1960s, but was far from novel. A string attached to a spool has been used as either a toy or a weapon in various cultures dating back to ancient Greece. Something as seemingly original as bungee jumping has long been practiced in the jungles of Papua New Guinea where natives continue to leap off tall towers with only a vine tied to one ankle. The objective is to come within a few feet of touching the ground without dying. Occasionally, jumpers miscalculate – with fatal results. Before the Hula Hoop became one of the most popular fads in modern history, it experienced an obscure existence as a bamboo hoop in Australian gym classes, an idea that, in turn, had come from Pacific islanders. Yet, in 1958 when the Wham-O Company in the U.S. marketed it, 30 million polyethylene tubes were sold in one year before fading back into obscurity.

The next phase of a fad is the *breakout period,* where the item or activity is adopted by people other than those who used it in the latent phase, spreading mainly by word-of-mouth and the mass media. The spread is boosted when those who used it during the quiet, latent period, actively promote it. Until the early 1970s, Citizen Band radios were used mostly by truckers and sold at a few specialty locations such as select truck stops, truck garages, and obscure mail order catalogs. Once CB's started to "catch on" outside the trucker community, they soon found their way onto department store shelves and a wider audience. The plastic disk-shaped Frisbee was marketed in 1955 under the name "Pluto Platter," and renamed the following year as the Frisbee. As a similar game had long been popular at Yale University where students had a tradition of tossing pie plates, Frisbee tossing gained initial popularity on several Eastern U.S. college campuses where Wham-O recruited students to sell Frisbees. Wham-O officials claim that it was a coincidence that the pie tins that the elite Yale students had been tossing for years were from the Frisbie Pie Company of Bridgeport, Connecticut. Either way, the association certainly boosted the popularity of Frisbee tossing within the region.

The third stage is the *peaking period,* which is characterized by a rapid, dramatic increase in appearance, coinciding with frequent media coverage. During this phase, if a fad doesn't already have a readily identifiable name, the media coins one, such as the slicked-back "D.A." (duck ass) hair style of the 1950s. During the roaring 20s, a relatively small number of sassy young women defied the conservative mores of the period. They drank alcohol during the government Prohibition that forbade its manufacture or social use, smoked cigarettes in public when it was considered unlady-like, and wore bright red lipstick and bold, revealing dresses that flaunted their sexuality. They quickly gained the label of "flappers." Soon, older, traditional women began adopting some but not all of their habits such as short skirts, haircuts, and makeup. Some fads come ready-made, such as the Hula-Hoop; others, like the flappers, are soon given a label. During the peak period, it seems as though everyone's doing it, is talking about it, or has to have one. This saturation effect seems to portend their inevitable decline, as once fads peak, the excitement and novelty wear off.

The *decline period* begins when the excitement and interest quickly wane. Miller notes that in this stage the once "hot" item is thrown away or stored in closets or garages. If traces remain, it is because the fad has remained only with the few original users from the dormant or latent phase.[20] In the case of activities, the gold fish swallowing rage that swept across college campuses in the spring of 1939 lasted only two months before the novelty wore off and came to a screeching halt. Not only did goldfish swallowing become unpopular, it was viewed negatively. Soon what was initially viewed as a hilarious fad was being condemned as cruelty to fish, public health authorities were warning of the dangers of getting tapeworms, and communities were passing ordinances making it illegal. Many colleges even threatened to expel swallowers. Sometimes a fad will die out, only to be revived in a different form years later. This was the case for phone booth stuffing, which began when 25 students at a South African college set a world record by cramming into a single booth. While this 1959 fad lasted less than a year, public interest was rekindled as Volkswagen stuffing years later. Occasionally fads don't disappear but become part of the establishment, though their popularity and the fever-pitch of desire for them has faded. These include Frisbees, skateboards, yo-yos, and miniature golf. There was an explosive interest in miniature or Tom Thumb golf during the early 1930s, but soon people grew disinterested and most outlets went bankrupt.[21]

Fad words gain rapid acceptance for a short period. Language expert Jack Hart says they are identifiable by their vagueness. He gives the example of the word "no-brainer" which became vogue in 1994,[22] replacing such words as "apparent," "simple," "straightforward," "logical," "evident," and "clear." British journalist Charles Mackay describes a variety of fad words and phrases that spread through London during the 19th century. Words and phrases such as "flare up," "quoz," and "Does your mother know you're out!" were evoked to describe almost any act or situation, only to suddenly lose vogue. In America between 1900 and 1910, the word "go-getter" was seemingly on everyone's lips, followed by "doughboy" – a U.S. soldier (1917-1920). "Lounge lizard" was used to describe a womanizer in the 1920s; a "hepcat" was 1930s lingo for someone who was hip, while a "drugstore cowboy" was a 1940s teen who hung out at the local soda fountain. Our personal favorite is the 1960s phrase "See you later, alligator," which as children we thought was the epitome of cool, but now seems lame.

The Importance Of Fads

While fads, by definition, involve trivial things, understanding them can be important if you are in business. Being able to tell the difference between a fad and a long-term fashion or trend can translate into big money. Astute business executives can grow rich overnight by marketing fad products, as they initially sell like hotcakes, but they must then bail out just before interest plummets. However, be forewarned: marketing fads is not for the faint-hearted. One mistake and you can lose your shirt. Businesses hoping for stability by selling more enduring products may wish to steer clear of marketing fad items because of their unpredictable nature. For instance, near the end of 1958, some companies who had jumped on the hula-hoop bandwagon were left with warehouses filled with millions of unsold hoops and couldn't give them away.

Martin Letscher identifies several ways to tell a fad from a trend.[23] First, does it fit with changes in lifestyles? For instance, since most people today lead busier lives, a sudden interest in gourmet foods that take a great deal of preparation time would not be expected to last. Second, what are the benefits? Increasing chicken and fish sales coincide with the trend toward healthier living and are also a way of showing that you care for your family. It's hard to imagine the yo-yo offering comparable health or monetary benefits. Yes, during their fleeting periods of vogue, yo-yo contests were popular, but the prize money was a pittance even by today's standards, and certainly few people have ever managed to eke out a living as yo-yo professionals. Third, is it a trend or a side effect? This category is less straightforward than the others. Letscher again uses the example of the exercise trend, which he says is rock solid and here to stay. Yet certain new types of exercises may fade quickly, such as line dancing and exercise gadgets that target your buttocks or abdominal muscles. Category four is what other changes have occurred? Are there related trends? For instance, an interest in marketing vitamins would seem to be consistent with the long-term interest in exercise, healthy eating, and busy lifestyles. Another thing to look for in this category is whether there are carryover effects. He uses the example of the mini-skirt, which soared to popularity in the 1960s, resulting in interest in such items as pantyhose and causing tights to skyrocket.

FAINTING FACTORY WORKERS

Brooklyn, New York: March 1931

On the second floor of a building occupied by the Howard Clothes Company factory, about 30 workers suddenly smelled a foul odor, triggering a mass panic to get out. As they reached to street some fainted, others wandered about in a stupor. Other parts of the building were occupied but none was affected. No cause was ever found.[24]

FAINTING FOOTBALL CHEERLEADERS

Mississippi: September 12, 1952

On September 12, 1952, one-hundred-and-sixty-five teenage cheerleaders "fainted like flies" between the first and second quarters of a football game between the Monroe, Louisiana Tigers and a squad from Natchez, Mississippi. The girls, members of the Tigerettes Pep Squad, had paraded along Main Street prior to the game. When the first quarter ended, they mistakenly marched onto the field for their half-time performance, only to be embarrassingly called back over the loudspeakers. The girls ranged in age from 14 to 18.[25]

FAINTING FRENCH FACTORY GIRLS

Lille, France: June 1937

On approximately June 4, 200 girls, ages 16 to 20, "fell to the floor, while older workers stared in amazement." The incident happened at the Thumeries sugar refinery. Then, on June 15, a physician came to the plant to give advice on how to avoid future episodes of "mass swooning." During his presentation, another 30 girls fainted, and after several hours had passed, 40 more.[26]

More fainting attacks were reported in other French sugar refineries at about the same time – all involving female workers. While gas poisoning was the initial suspect, sophisticated tests of the premises "failed to find any traces of gas" and led to the conclusion among scientists that the cause was "psychopathological phenomenon induced by auto-suggestion."[27] One journalist suggested that nutrition may have been a factor, observing that most of the girls were age 17 and under and their salaries were paltry: earning $6.12 per week in the equivalent United States currency. It was suggested that the girls might have been suffering from malnutrition, as their salaries were insufficient to provide a balanced diet for developing bodies that were working 40 hours per week.[28]

FAINTING VIETNAMESE SCHOOLGIRLS

Phu Tho Province, Vietnam: Oct. and Dec. 2004

On October 18, 57 schoolgirls mysteriously fainted at Xuan Ang High School in Danang City in an incident that authorities attributed to "psychological disorders." Some of the girls were rushed to a nearby hospital but quickly recovered. The next day, 143 girls fell ill with similar symptoms: fainting, rapid pulse, and general anxiety. Twenty were kept in the hospital for varying periods as a precaution. Public health officials ruled out tainted food or environmental contamination.[29]

On Monday December 6, another school in the same city was stricken by what school authorities termed "mass hysteria." About 30 girls at Nguyen Hien High exhibited dizziness and seizures. Some of the girls suffered relapses after being examined and released by doctors. School Principal Pham Uc said the school was shut down on Monday morning after the episode. Another 15 students suffered similar symptoms at the school on December 4. At about the same time, several girls attending Phuong Dong Economics and Technology School in Danang suffered fainting spells over a 10-day period.

Ton That Thanh, Vietnam's Deputy Director of the Preventive Public Medical Service, said the outbreaks were the result of hysteria. Doctors examining the girls said that contributing factors might have included the current cold snap and some girls skipping breakfast. Officials at the city's Department of Education and Training were warning local students about the need to "dress warmly and eat breakfast before going to school."[30]

CONTEXT: Without more information, it is impossible to ascertain the cause of these incidents. It is unlikely that any of the episodes were triggered by cold weather or skipping breakfast. It is more probable that some type of unidentified stress, perhaps from exams or student conflict (common triggers in other school outbreaks), was responsible.

FALSE MEMORY SYNDROME

"False memory syndrome" is a loosely defined term referring to the "recovery" of false memories, typically during psychotherapy sessions, involving adults who claim that parents or relatives sexually abused them during childhood, and those memories were repressed due to the traumatic nature of the offense. It is known by a variety of synonyms: "repressed memories," "false memories," "hidden memories," "recovered memories," and "pseudo-memories."

Psychologist John F. Kihlstrom has proposed a more comprehensive definition of False Memory Syndrome: "A condition in which a person's identity and interpersonal relationships are centered around a memory of traumatic experience which is objectively false but in which the person strongly believes. Note that the syndrome is not characterized by false memories as such. We all have memories that are inaccurate. Rather, the syndrome may be diagnosed when the memory is so deeply ingrained that it orients the individual's entire personality and lifestyle, in turn disrupting all sorts of other adaptive behaviors. The analogy to personality disorder is intentional." In his definition, Kihlstrom further notes instances of avoidance and obsession. "False Memory Syndrome is especially destructive because the person assiduously avoids confrontation with any evidence that might challenge the memory. Thus it takes on a life of its own, encapsulated, and resistant to correction. The person may become so focused on the memory that he or she may be effectively distracted from coping with the real problems in his or her life."[31]

The term 'False Memory Syndrome' (FMS) was devised in the early 1980s by the False Memory Syndrome Foundation. The organization was formed in response to the dramatic escalation of child sex abuse claims that began to sweep across the United States during the early 1980s.

Several important books have been published, arguing for the reality of FMS. These include the emotional *Victims of Memory: Incest Accusations and Shattered Lives* by Mark Pendergrast, a Harvard-educated investigative journalist. Pendergrast's expose of the repressed memory movement recounts the sudden estrangement of his two daughters, Stacey and Christina, who he says were the victims of overzealous psychotherapists, and who at the time of the book's publication, were still alienated. Pendergrast chronicles the genesis of the movement. Prior to about 1970, incest and sexual abuse were widely viewed as rare occurrences, and through the mid-70s, most abuse claims involved conscious recall.[32] The organized search for repressed child abuse memories can be traced back to psychiatrist Judith Herman, affiliated with prestigious Harvard University. In her 1981 book, *Father-Daughter Incest*, Herman made reference to the existence of an informal network of private practice psychotherapists in the vicinity of Boston, Massachusetts, who were searching for patients with repressed memories of child sexual abuse. Herman's psychotherapy reportedly involved such techniques as dream analysis and the use of hypnosis to induce age regression.[33] By the mid-80s, the issue was being widely reported as an epidemic.

American Incest And Sex Scare – 1980s And Ongoing

In 1988, a landmark best-selling book further crystallized the movement: *The Courage to Heal: A Guide for Women Survivors of Child Sexual Abuse* by California creative writing instructor Ellen Bass and her pupil, Laura Davis.[34] The book sold nearly 800,000 copies.[35] The book seems to be based on a self-fulfilling prophecy. Pendergrast is a staunch critic of the book because the target audience is females who vaguely suspect they were abused but have no recall. He states: "Bass and Davis write, 'Often the knowledge that you were abused starts with a tiny feeling, an intuition. It's important to trust that inner voice and work from there. Assume your feelings are valid. ...So far, no one we've talked to thought she might have been abused, and then later discovered that she hadn't been. The progression always goes the other way, from suspicion to confirmation. If you think you were abused and your life shows the symptoms, then you were.'"[36] The vague nature of abuse signs and symptoms discussed by Bass and Davis are chillingly reminiscent of the SALEM WITCH-HUNTS, during which innocent people were accused and incarcerated for witchcraft based on the flimsiest of evidence and subjective impressions.

In *The Myth of Repressed Memory: False Memories and Allegations of Sexual Abuse*, University of Washington psychologist Elizabeth Loftus and writer Katherine Ketcham describe four tenets that fueled the sexual abuse incest scare. Loftus is a prominent psychologist and former president of the American Psychological Association.

The first factor was the view that *incest was occurring in epidemic proportions*. During the late 70s and early 80s, slowly gathering storm clouds were forming with claims that sex abuse occurred on a far greater scale that most people had ever imagined, and with books detailing case histories of female abuse. By the mid-80s, several so-called experts claimed statistical backing for the claims of Dr. Herman and others. According to a 1985 survey by the *Los Angeles Times*, about 38 million Americans were sexually molested during childhood.[37] The next year, Diana Russell published her startling book, *The Secret Trauma: Incest in the Life of Girls and Women*, claiming that of 930 California women randomly contacted and interviewed, over half reported sexual abuse before age 18 (factoring in claims of genital exposure without physical acts).[38] While Russell's study was flawed on several grounds, it helped to ignite the sex abuse "epidemic," such as interviewers being exposed to "ten hours of pre-interview indoctrination on the horrors of rape and incest."[39] One reason for the epidemic numbers of persons being labeled as having been abused during their childhoods was the new definition of incest and abuse. For instance, in *The Courage to Heal,* Bass and Davis offer examples that can be interpreted as either "violations of trust" or "nonphysical incestuous" behavior, including a father "leering when you entered to use the toilet" or if as a child you felt that "your stepfather was aware of your physical presence every minute of the day, no matter how quiet or unobtrusive you were. Your neighbor watched your changing body with an intrusive interest."[40]

A second factor in triggering the American sex abuse epidemic centers around the unsubstantiated assumption that *repression is commonplace*. As a result, many people who suspect they were the victims of childhood sexual abuse but cannot consciously recall it have allowed their therapists to hypnotically regress them so they can find out what happened.

The experience is also widely thought to serve a positive function for the victim – as cathartic release for memories that have purportedly been "bottled-up" for years. However, most child sex abuse victims *can* vividly recall their molestation. For them, the problem is, "they can't forget what happened to them, not that they don't remember it."[41] The evidence for repressed memories is not supported by any known theory of memory, which involves a rather straightforward process of encoding, storing, and retrieving. Forensic psychologist Terence W. Campbell states: "Do traumatic experiences interfere with the encoding state of memory, and if so, how does this interference occur?" The same questions can be asked for the storage and retrieval stages of memory. According to Campbell: "Current theories of trauma and memory loss neglect to answer these important questions. These theories suggest *why* people might engage in repression, but they fail to specify *how* repression supposedly occurs."[42]

A third factor in the sex abuse upsurge is predicated upon the belief that *recovery is possible once the repressed memories have been unveiled.* The final piece in the epidemic is the specific techniques used to reveal "hidden memories." Loftus and Ketcham state that when many patients first seek help from psychotherapists for various problems – from eating disorders to sexual difficulties and addictions – there is an assumption that the underlying cause is childhood sexual abuse. The so-called diagnostic criteria are highly ambiguous as to be present in almost anyone at some time. Psychotherapist E. Susan Blume offers 34 signs suggestive of incest including "Wearing a lot of clothing, even in summer; baggy clothes; failure to remove clothing even when appropriate to do so (while swimming, bathing, sleeping); extreme requirement for privacy when using bathroom."[43] Renee Fredrickson lists indicators of having been sexually abused, such as being terrified of the basement and sexual promiscuity.[44]

There are several different subjective methods used by psychotherapists to uncover "hidden memories." *Imagistic work* involves focusing on an image believed to be from childhood, then "describing in great detail every sight and sensation relating to the image and adding, whenever appropriate, subjective interpretations."[45] *Dream work* involves interpreting dreams related to possible sexual abuse. *Journal writing* is another method, as is *bodywork* where body massage and manipulation techniques can supposedly uncover hidden memories of abuse. Some therapists believe that such memories can be accessed by stimulating any one of the five senses.[46]

Another important consideration in the False Memory Syndrome debate is the number of studies suggesting that recollections of traumatic events are typically altered. A dramatic example of this process occurred when Loftus and her colleague Jacquie Pickrell reported that they were able to get a significant number of people to believe they had met and shook hands with the cartoon character Bugs Bunny at Disneyland when they couldn't have. About 1-in-3 subjects exposed to a bogus print ad picturing Bugs Bunny at Disneyland said they had met the character. However, the scenario was impossible as the Bugs Bunny trademark is property of Warner Brothers. Pickrell said she found the study "frightening" because "it suggests how easily a false memory can be created." Pickrell views the findings as potentially important for several areas of research. "It's not only people who go to a therapist who might implant a false memory or those who witness an accident and whose memory can be distorted who can have a false memory. Memory is very vulnerable and malleable. People are not always aware of the choices they make. This study shows the power of subtle association changes on memory."[47]

Critics Of False Memory Syndrome

A leading proponent of the widespread existence of repressed childhood sexual abuse memories is clinical psychologist James Hopper of Boston University who contends that many memory researchers – who argue that false repressed memories of abuse are more commonly creations and fantasies – lack first-hand psychotherapeutic experience.[48] Hopper argues that amnesia related to child sexual abuse in indisputable, that explanations other than repression can account for such experiences, and that based on conservative estimates, a minimum of 10% of adults experienced childhood sexual abuse.[49]

Psychologist Diana Elliott of the University of California at Los Angeles School of Medicine has conducted research to support the existence of dissociative or psychogenic amnesia, and refutes claims that psychotherapists commonly assist patients into inventing false memories of child sex abuse. Based on a random sample of 505 or 70% of Americans who answered a questionnaire on trauma and memory, 72% said they had experienced some type of trauma. Of these, 32% reported a delay in remembering the event. "This phenomenon was most common among individuals who observed the murder or suicide of a family member, sexual abuse survivors, and combat veterans ... The most commonly reported trigger for recall of the trauma was some form of media presentation (i.e., television show, movie), whereas psychotherapy was the least commonly reported trigger."[50]

Elliott offers an explanation for her findings, noting that as opposed to the process of normal forgetting, "theoretical writers in the area of trauma have suggested that some memory loss in trauma survivors may reflect dissociative avoidance strategies developed by the victim to reduce trauma-related distress."[51] Elliott continues: "From this perspective, traumatic memory loss may be understood as a form of avoidance conditioning, whereby access to memory is punished by the negative affect that accompanies the recall, thereby motivating the development of memory-inhibiting mechanisms. Such avoidance strategies might interfere with memory at any point during rehearsal, storage, or retrieval of material ... the more severe and chronic the trauma, the more painful the resultant affect should be, and thus, the more likely the victim's avoidance behavior would be reinforced ..."[52]

The American Psychiatric Association's *Diagnostic and Statistical Manual of Mental Disorders* (commonly referred to as the "Bible" of the mental health community) lists dissociative amnesia as a distinct diagnostic category. It is defined in part as the inability to remember key personal details, "usually of a traumatic or stressful nature, that is too extensive to be explained by normal forgetfulness ... This disorder involves a reversible memory impairment in which memories of personal experience cannot be retrieved in a verbal form (or, if temporarily retrieved, cannot be wholly retained in consciousness) ... and is not due to the direct physiological effects of a substance or a neurological or other general medical condition ..." The condition is described as appearing most often "as a retrospectively reported gap or series of gaps in recall for aspects of the individual's life history" that correspond to extraordinarily stressful or traumatic events.[53]

As for the prevalence of dissociative amnesia resulting from childhood sexual abuse, the DSM acknowledges the continuing controversy over the sudden "epidemic" during the 1980s and 90s but refrains from taking a definitive side. "In recent years in the United States, there has been an increase in reported cases of Dissociative Amnesia that involves previously forgotten early childhood traumas. This increase has been subject to very different interpretations. Some believe that the greater awareness of the diagnosis among mental health professionals has resulted in the identification of cases that were previously undiagnosed. In contrast, others believe that the syndrome has been overdiagnosed in individuals who are highly suggestible."[54]

Psychologist and trauma expert John Briere analyzed a sample of 450 people who were receiving therapy from mental health professionals for childhood sexual abuse. Nearly 60% said there was a period before their 18th birthday, "when they had no memory of their abuse."[55]

In a study examining adult recall of childhood trauma, headed by Judith Herman, 77 patients with childhood trauma memories were examined. Two sub-groups reported "a mixture of continuous and delayed recall (17%) or a period of complete amnesia followed by delayed recall (16%). Patients with and without delayed recall did not differ significantly in the proportions reporting corroboration of their memories from other sources."[56] According to Herman, "Twelve patients described a period of complete amnesia followed by delayed recall."[57]

Herman's research challenges claims made by Loftus and her colleagues on the subject of confirming evidence. Herman states: "Although patients were not asked whether they had any information which might confirm their memories of childhood abuse, 33 patients (43%) spontaneously described some type of corroboration. Only seven patients described having undertaken an active search for evidence that might confirm their memories; the majority of the patients who had such evidence had not actively sought it. Among the 25 patients who reported some degree of amnesia and delayed recall, nine (36%) reported having obtained confirming evidence for their memories, while among the patients who did not report any memory deficits, a slightly larger proportion (24 of 52, or 46%) reported obtaining corroboration. The difference between the two groups was not statistically significant."[58] Most commonly, abuse confirmation was reportedly made by family members who said they were either first-hand witnesses or heard of the molestation indirectly. A caveat of the study is that they did not try to independently verify the information from the patients.[59]

Oregon psychologist Jennifer Freyd argues that the theory of "betrayal trauma" can help to explain childhood sexual abuse amnesia. Freyd believes that amnesia is commonly used by sexually abused children as a means of adapting to their dilemma. On the one hand, they are being abused; on the other hand, they need to survive. Freyd says: "Betrayal trauma theory suggests that psychogenic amnesia is an adaptive response to childhood abuse. When a parent or other powerful figure violates a fundamental ethic of human relationships, victims may need to remain unaware of the trauma not to reduce suffering but rather to promote survival. Amnesia enables the child to maintain an attachment with a figure vital to survival, development, and thriving."[60]

According to Freyd:

> there is evidence that the most devastating psychological effects of child abuse occur when the victims are abused by a trusted person who was known to them ... If a child processed the betrayal in the normal way, he or she would be motivated to stop interacting with the betrayer. Instead, he or she essentially needs to ignore the betrayal. If the betrayer is a primary caregiver, it is especially essential that the child does not stop behaving in such a way that will inspire attachment. For the child to withdraw from a caregiver on which he or she is dependent would further threaten the child's life, both physically and mentally. Thus the trauma of child abuse by its very nature requires that information about the abuse be blocked from mental mechanisms that control attachment and attachment behavior. The information that gets blocked may be partial (for instance, blocking emotional responses only), but in many cases partial blocking will lead to a more profound amnesia.[61]

The Status Of False Memory Syndrome

There seems little doubt that False Memory Syndrome exists as some patients have invented "hidden memories" of childhood sexual abuse with the unwitting aid of their psychotherapist. The key question is: How prevalent is the creation of childhood sexual abuse? What percentage of patients who had no recollection of child sexual abuse prior to seeing their therapist for an unrelated issue invented such memories with the encouragement of their therapists using a variety of subjective techniques such as hypnosis and dream analysis? If, as many opponents of False Memory Syndrome believe, childhood sexual abuse is a hidden epidemic and molestation memories can be reliably uncovered, then we are dealing with a human tragedy. If, on the other hand, as researchers such as Loftus assert, False Memory Syndrome involving previous forgotten recall is common and comprised of subjective fantasies that are "teased out" by the therapist, then we are dealing with an equally devastating human tragedy. Childhood sexual molestation is a sinister crime perpetrated on innocent victims and can lead to a variety of psychological problems throughout one's life; false accusations are as equally catastrophic and far-reaching.

See also: SATANIC CULT AND RITUAL ABUSE SCARE, WELSH PEDOPHILE RING.

FAMILIARITY

A curious trait that recurs in many types of extraordinary behavior is that the affected individual lapses into an unwonted and often excessive familiarity. This is most easily seen in those countries where there is a distinction between the polite, formal form of address, and the familiar style used with close relatives, friends or inferiors, as in the *vous* and *tu* used in French, *du* and *Sie* in German, etc.

Many victims of supposed DEMON POSSESSION manifested this familiarity. Antoine Gay, who for more than thirty years was ostensibly possessed by Isacaron, prince of impurity, and two other demons of slander and avarice, was in his normal state well-spoken and respectful. "But what a contrast when he spoke as a demon, given full rein! Then he showed his anger and despair, and *tutoyait tout le monde sans exception*, even the highest dignitaries of the Church." That is to say, when possessed, he addressed everyone in the second person singular, normally reserved for close family or social inferiors.[62]

Behavior of a similar kind was observed in the case of the German stigmatic Theresa Neumann (see STIGMATIZATION): "On another occasion Therese Neumann is reported to have replied to parish priest Father Naber with the words, 'You can't speak to Therese now, she is asleep.' In this instance she not only used the third person, but also, in the original German, the familiar form 'du' for 'you' – a lack of respect quite untypical of the normal Therese, and again indicative of a shift in personality."[63]

Dr. Arthaud, one of the medical professionals who studied the hysterical epidemic of MORZINE (1857), noted that "during their crises, children who were in their normal state quiet and timid displayed an unheard-of insolence, surpassing all expression."[64] The archbishop of Skara, during the SWEDISH PREACHING EPIDEMIC (1841), said of the afflicted children that they "address everyone, regardless of their status, by the word 'thou.'"[65]

This trait occurs also in contexts where no exceptional behavior is involved. Bramwell, writing in 1903, provides a good example from his own experience. Sarah was a former servant girl in his employment, who subsequently came under his care as a patient:

> In her normal state Sarah was quiet, respectful, and somewhat shy and retained this character when I hypnotised her. Before coming under my care, she had been hypnotised and exhibited by a stage performer, and some time after, her mother told me that Sarah occasionally hypnotised herself, and that the condition then differed markedly from the one I induced. After some coaxing, the girl consented to hypnotise herself, and went through the following performance: - First, she closed her eyes and appeared to pass into a lethargic state; then a few minutes later awoke with a changed expression: instead of having a shy and modest air, her eyes sparkled and she looked full of mischief. In place of addressing me as "Sir" she put her hand on my arm and said in a familiar way, "I say." She then began to ask me impertinent questions about the persons she had seen at my house, and to criticse them in a particularly free and sarcastic fashion. The performance was so interesting and amusing that I got her to hypnotise herself on a good many occasions. The same phenomenon always appeared: she became familiar, inquisitive, and sarcastic.[66]

In all these instances, the lapse into disrespectful familiarity is evidently the spontaneous expression of a change in attitude – Wilson, speaking of Theresa Neumann, speaks of "a shift in personality" – resulting from the individual being in a special state. There is, however, a parallel with the practice of the QUAKERS, who in the 17th century purposely adopted the use of "thee" instead of "you" to indicate that they did not recognize social distinctions. Conscious or unconscious, it seems to betoken a refusal to accept authority, though not necessarily an outright hostility.

What is remarkable is that this same trait should manifest in such a variety of contexts. Clearly there is not the slightest likelihood that the children of Morzine would know how those of Sweden behaved: yet we find them innocently behaving in just the same way. This suggests that the adoption of the familiar style is the manifestation of some kind of archetypal process.

FANTASY-PRONE PEOPLE

During the early 1980s, psychologists stumbled upon a remarkable discovery: a small percentage of otherwise normal, healthy people are prone to extraordinarily vivid and involved fantasies. Even more remarkable, most of these people lead secret lives, and in many instances, not even their siblings or closest friends are aware of their rich fantasy world. Persons living within this self-absorbed world have trouble differentiating between imagination and reality, but typically outsiders have not the slightest clue that they were so heavily fantasizing. Based on early research by J. Hilgard in the 1970s,[67] Cheryl Wilson and Theodore Barber[68] found that up to 4% of the population might qualify as having fantasy-prone personalities ranging from mild to intense. It is also apparent that this condition fluctuates over time. At one point, a person may not even fit the definition of fantasy-prone, while at another time, they may merit classification as an intense fantasizer.

The breakthrough came when the two hypnosis researchers were administering a number of tests and interviews to excellent and poor hypnotic subjects.[69]

They observed that 92% who would be labeled as fantasy-prone estimated that they spent at least half their working day engaged in rich fantasizing. In comparison, no one in a control group reported doing the same. In terms of the intense, vivid quality of their experiences, Wilson and Barber[70] found that the fantasizers said they could typically see, hear, feel, and smell what people were describing, either in everyday conversations or on TV. An astounding 65% of fantasizers said that their daydreams were "as real as real," and that the fantasies occurred in an involuntary or automatic fashion. Once again, no one in the control group reported such experiences. "They see sights equally well with their eyes opened or closed. Also, imagined aromas are sensed, imagined sounds are heard, and imagined tactile sensations are felt as convincingly as those produced by actual stimuli... almost all of the fantasy-prone subjects have vivid sexual fantasies that they experience 'as real as real' with all the sights, sounds, smells, emotions, feelings, and physical sensations...(and they) are so realistic that 75% of the fantasizers report that they have had orgasms produced solely by sexual fantasies."[71]

An obvious question comes to mind: if this phenomenon is so common, how had it managed to elude some of the best researchers in the world throughout history? The explanation was that the findings didn't show up on standard tests but emerged only in detailed interviews.

The interviews also uncovered that 58% of fantasizers (versus 8% from the control group) said that a "large part" of their childhood play/interaction involved fantasies about people or animals ("imaginary companions"), reporting to have "clearly seen, heard and felt them in the same way that they perceived living people and animals."[72]

All but one fantasizer said that during childhood they lived for much or most of the time in an imaginary world. Further, 80% said that when playing with toy animals or dolls, they thought that they were alive, with feelings and distinct personalities. This behavior should not be confused with imaginary playmates, which are common in childhood and widely viewed as an indication of psychological well-being and creativity.[73] There were clear differences between the fantasizers and the controls: "Many of the 25 subjects in the comparison group also pretended their dolls or stuffed animals were alive; however, with three exceptions, they did so only when they were playing with them. Although they made-believe that the dolls and toy animals had personalities and said and did specific things, the make-believe play was always confined to a specific period and the toys did not seem to have an independent life."[74]

While playing make-believe games is an integral part of childhood around the world, it is not considered common for children to continue interacting with imaginary companions into adulthood – a feature that is common for fantasizers. Based on these findings, Wilson and Barber[75] hypothesize that many historical figures who claimed to experience paranormal happenings were actually fantasy-prone.

Barber and Wilson's findings may have implications for understanding many of the entries in this encyclopedia, including aspects of social delusions involving witchcraft, werewolves, child molestation scares, Satanic Ritual Abuse claims, Multiple Personalities, and "hidden memories." For instance, many episodes of mass hysteria are triggered by an index case – the first person to report symptoms or claim to see something extraordinary such as a ghost, spirit, or creature. Without the index subject, many outbreaks might never have developed. The UFO Abduction Phenomena is a classic example.

Fantasy-Prone Personalities And Alien "Abductions"

Sociologist Robert Bartholomew, psychologist George S. Howard, and UFO researcher Keith Basterfield have culled the UFO literature for accounts of persons claiming to have been abducted by extraterrestrials or who claim to be in contact with aliens to see how closely these people compare with Barber and Wilson's subjects.[76] They were able to find detailed biographical information on 154 UFO "abductees" and "contactees" dating as far back as the 16th century. The results were compelling. In 132 out of 154 biographies (86%), one or more of the key symptoms of fantasizers appeared among the subjects.

Ufos And "Psychic" Phenomena

Wilson and Barber[77] found a major link between persons reporting frequent "psychic" phenomena and fantasizers. Ninety-two percent of fantasizers in their study considered themselves to be psychic, reporting many instances of telepathy or precognition; this compares to just 16% of the controls.[78] In the sample of biographies, 75% of "abductees" and "contactees" reported psychic and/or telepathic or poltergeist experiences. It's likely that many of the remainder may have had such experiences, but did not appear in their biographies, which were primarily focused on their UFO, and not "psychic," experiences.

Out-Of-Body Experiences

Eight-eight percent of fantasizers in Wilson and Barber's study (compared to 8% of controls) reported "realistic out-of-the-body experiences."[79] In the UFO group, 21% reported "astral projection," "astral travel," "bi-location," "out-of-body experiences," or body floating. One early historical example involves the case of Massachusetts resident William Denton in the United States, who during the 1860s was a popular spirit medium who claimed to project his body astrally, enabling him to visit "Venusians," and describe to onlookers his "encounters."[80] [81]

Automatic Writing, Healing, Apparitions, Religious Visions

Automatic writing is a rare phenomenon that was found in just 8% of Wilson and Barber's comparison group, while 50% of their fantasizers reported such abilities that were guided by a spirit or intelligence. As for the UFO biographies, automatic writing was comparable to the control group. However, 24% of the sample were described as channels for regular written messages. Technically, this does not qualify, as there was not specific reference to automatic writing taking place, though if we combine the two categories, it would comprise 32% of the UFO sample.

Wilson and Barber found that two-thirds of fantasizers claimed the ability to heal (none in the controls), 73% said they had seen an apparition (16% in controls), and about a quarter of fantasizers had experienced religious visions (none in the controls). Among the UFO biographies, 14% reported apparitions, about 6% claimed the ability to heal, and 11% had religious visions. However, these figures are deceptive. For instance, the category of "religious visions" included only religious or spiritual experiences that were interpreted by the percipient as being separate from their UFO experience. To have included claims of UFO encounters with aliens who were claiming to be acting on behalf of a deity (most commonly Jesus), half of the biographies could be viewed as religious visionaries.[82] About 30% of the UFO sample reported a quasi-religious tone to their alien messages. A classic example is the case of Buck Nelson, a famous 1950s contactee, who during a flying saucer voyage was instructed to write the "Twelve Laws of God on Venus," paralleling the ten commandments.

Hypnotic Susceptibility

Hypnotic susceptibility is a difficult category to evaluate, as most UFO subjects never were hypnotized. Yet, there is compelling anecdotal evidence supporting the link between ease and degree of entering hypnotic states, and the UFO sample. UFO researcher Ann Druffel[83] writes about "a peculiar pattern" in abduction reports. "Time and time again in various cases, a primary witness will be easily regressed, giving a vivid and full account of the experience; any corroborating witness to the same case will either resist hypnosis altogether or prove a very poor trance subject."[84] Florida psychiatrist Berthold Schwarz concurs with this curious finding: "In my experience UFO contactees, unlike most across-the-board psychiatric patients, or so-called healthy people, have been usually easy to hypnotize or almost always go rapidly into deep somnambulistic trances."[85] Numerous other UFO researchers have made similar observations based on first-hand interviews with "abductees" and "contactees."[86] These findings correspond with results by Wilson & Barber[87] and Lynn and Rhue[88] who found a very strong relationship between hypnotic susceptibility and fantasizers.

Physiological Effects

Wilson and Barber[89] found that 19 fantasizers versus two among the controls, reported symptoms corresponding with the content of their fantasy.

> They state that "most said they had experienced quite frequently throughout their lives something such as the following: becoming physically ill when they thought (incorrectly) that they had eaten spoiled food or developing an uncomfortable and continuous itch when they (incorrectly) believed that they had been contaminated with lice. ...[One subject]...told us about the time she recaptured a neighboring child's pet frog that had escaped, remembered that she had been told that frogs cause warts, and then developed a wart on her hand that was highly resistant to treatment."[90]

Most fantasizers would become sick while watching violence on TV, or would experience sensations of hot or cold as if it were happening to them. One fantasizer recounted "how she was freezing as she sat bundled in a warm living room while she was watching Dr. Zhivago in Siberia on television."[91]

Physiological reactions were common in the UFO group, as the aftereffects reflected their contact scenarios. Perhaps the most famous example is that of Barney Hill who developed warts in a ring-like formation around his genital region, which corresponded to the placement of a cup-like device by his alien abductors.[92] The warts became inflamed during later regressive hypnosis sessions.[93] The most commonly mentioned symptoms in the UFO sample involved facial and body rashes, itching, burning eyes, dizziness, and headache, typically corresponding with alien examinations where the person is often stuck with a needle-like instrument and blood extracted, or exposed to intense light or X-ray-like machines. Similarly, psychogenic symptoms during mass hysteria episodes correspond with popular social norms. Curiously, similar symptoms were found in association with supposed victims of witchcraft during the Salem witch trials of 1692.[94]

Spiritual Themes

As well as frequent interactions with imaginary companions, many fantasizers developed a worldview that included the matter-of-fact existence of spiritual guardians and beings. "When they were children, almost all of the fantasizers believed in fairies, leprechauns, elves, guardian angels, and other such beings.... for some, encounters...were vivid and 'as real as real'; for instance, one told us how as a child she would spend hours watching in fascination the little people who lived in her grandmother's cactus garden that adults kept insisting were not there. With few exceptions, their belief in elves, fairies, guardian angels, tree spirits, and other such creatures did not terminate during childhood; as adults they either still believe in them or are not absolutely sure that they really do not exist."[95] Within the UFO sample, many subjects expressed a belief in seen or unseen guardians or spirits. Most interpreted these experiences within a religious context (Jesus of Nazareth, guardian angels), or having one or a combination of extraterrestrial guardian contacts and/or ongoing encounters with mythical beings like fairies.

Although the UFO sample contained only 20 cases where UFO encounter claimants discussed their interactions with guardians or other spiritual beings (and their continuing belief in their reality into adulthood), veteran UFO researcher Tim Beckley, who has interviewed scores of "contactees," makes the following observation:

> About eight years ago, as he traveled around the country while lecturing, well-known parapsychologist Brad Steiger noticed that many men and women he met, actually claimed memories of having come to this planet from "somewhere else," or to have experienced an interaction with paranormal entities since their earliest childhood. Steiger came to call these individuals "Star People" and noticed that they had many... physiological anomalies which obviously placed them apart from the rest of society.
>
> ...the pattern profile of the "Star People" contains the following elements: ...Had unseen companions as a child. Natural abilities with art, music, healing, or acting. Experienced ...psychic events. Had an unusual experience ...[at an early age] which often took the form of...a visitation by human-type beings who gave information and comfort. Have since maintained a continuing series of episodes with "angels," "elves," "masters," or openly declared UFO intelligences. ...despite a seemingly bizarre belief that they are not from here,...all appear normal and rational otherwise.[96]

See also: ALIEN ABDUCTION BELIEFS.

FASHIONS

Fashion can be defined as a prevailing custom or style conveying status and prestige. Part of an ongoing process in which each new style follows an existing one, fashions typically last from one to several years and often reemerge in a cyclical manner. Occasionally, they are discussed in terms of historical periods. Compared to fads, they are typically of longer duration, are viewed with greater importance, involve more participants, and are more predictable and less emotionally intense than fads. Fashions are most commonly applied to personal appearance, such as dress, grooming, or adornment, and are more likely to define a particular historical period, with elements surviving that era and having a more enduring impact on society. Hence, sociologist John Macionis remarks that "Because fashions show more historical continuity and ties to convention than do fads, the word *fashionable* is generally a compliment, while the word *faddish* is a mild insult."[97]

Fashions are believed to be similar in origin to FADS as they denote status, convey difference and independence, while simultaneously promoting a feeling of unity and security within the "in" group. Some scholars believe that fashions function "more to reinforce status distinctions than to allow people to express higher status," with people conforming to a particular style "because of normative constraint rather than contagion and mindless imitation."[98] In describing fashion, sociologist Thorstein Veblen used the term "conspicuous consumption" to describe those who purchase items with the explicit intention of flaunting wealth.[99]

Like fads, many sociologists and social psychologists consider fashions to pass through four distinct phases of interest. Sociologist David L. Miller summarizes these periods. First is the *latent phase* where the fashion exists in relative obscurity within a limited, typically small group. The *breakout phase* follows whereby the new style starts to gain a significant following after either discovering the fashion or being introduced to it by the small group of existing adherents. This is followed by the peak phase where the fashion is enthusiastically adopted and competing items are virtually ignored. The final decline phase is characterized by a rapid, widespread loss of interest.[100] However, as more people try to emulate the behavior of the wealthy by buying either the original or inexpensive copies, the once desired item experiences a loss of prestige and becomes "out of fashion" within the higher echelons of society. On rare occasions, the opposite effect can occur. In some societies with more egalitarian attitudes such as the United States, fashions may originate among the lower classes and be copied by the wealthy. For example, dungarees or blue jeans were initially worn by poor laborers but soon became popular among the wealthy, "especially those who identified with the socially disadvantaged. Jeans became the uniform of political activists in the civil rights and antiwar movements in the 1960s and, gradually, of college students across the country."[101]

Flappermania: A Classic Example Of A Fashion

On January 16, 1920, bowing to a wave of conservatism, the U.S. government officially banned the manufacture, sale, or transporting of alcohol anywhere in the country. The Prohibition era would last until 1933. Yet, at a time when traditional values were lauded, a new breed of young woman emerged who would soon epitomize the spirit of the "Roaring 20's." A relatively small number of rebellious, sassy women relished in breaking the conservative mores of the era and attracting attention to themselves. They puffed on cigarettes, discarded their bras and restrictive corsets, and wore high skirts that often concealed hip flasks, plunging necklines, and rolled-down stockings to just above or below the knee. The

A flapper on a bicycle. (Armand Vallee, La Vie Parisienne,)

press labeled them "flappers," a derogatory name for French street prostitutes who dressed and acted in a similar fashion, and who were a familiar sight to American soldiers in World War I.[102] Flappers reveled in accentuating their sexuality, caroused with men till the early morning hours in speakeasies (illegal Prohibition bars), often engaged in sex or sexual petting in the backseats of cars, and sipped on gin and kicked up their heels by dancing the Charleston to the jazz beat.

In order to achieve a boyish look dubbed *garconne* (French for "little boy"), women wound strips of cloth tightly around their breasts to flatten their chests.[103] Artist John Held Jr. helped to create the flapper image with his popular sketches that often appeared on the covers of well-known magazines. As one writer observed: "Held portrayed the flapper as he saw her, and she, in turn, became the flapper he portrayed."[104]

By the early 1920s, using their own lingo, flappers had become "the cat's meow" or "bees-knees" – something wonderful. Soon women of all ages around the nation aspired to look, and to a certain extent act, like a "jazz baby." Fueled by press coverage in newspapers and magazines, the few young flappers had set the trend for the rest of the country and the word flapper took on a new, more positive meaning – any assertive, fun-loving woman, especially those who bucked the system and liked to make bold fashion statements. Flappers came to symbolize a bold new spirit and sense of freedom that was the antithesis of what Prohibition represented.[105]

Despite the more positive connotation that soon came to be associated with the word, there were two types of flappers – the bold, radical trendsetters and the less extreme who dabbled in flapperhood. Writing in 1922, Ellen Welles described the difference between herself and the "hard-core" flapper, remarking: "I suppose I am a flapper. I am within the age limit. I wear bobbed hair, the badge of flapperhood...I powder my nose ... wear fringed skirts and bright-colored sweaters, and scarfs, and waists with Peter Pan collars, and low-heeled 'finale hopper' shoes. I adore to dance. I spend a large amount of time in automobiles. I attend hops, and proms, and ball-games, and crew races, and other affairs at men's colleges. But none the less some of the most thoroughbred superflappers might blush to claim sistership or even remote relationship with such as I. I don't use rouge, or lipstick, or pluck my eyebrows. I don't smoke...or drink, or...pet."[106]

"Flappermania" gripped the U.S. until the Great Depression when the radical flappers were forced, both socially and economically, to curtail their carefree behaviors, which were widely viewed as frivolous and undisciplined. However, in the true nature of a fashion, many of the changes that flappers helped to usher in were incorporated into American society, including greater independence and assertiveness in both dress and politics.

See also: FASHION.

FATIMA SOLAR PHENOMENON

Portugal: October 13, 1917

On this day, a crowd of between 50 and 100 thousand people gathered to observe an apparition of Mary, mother of Jesus, to some Portuguese children. They were said to have witnessed a remarkable atmospheric phenomenon in which the sun appeared to dance. This phenomenon was assumed to be a miracle that had previously been promised by Mary for this day.

There exists an enormous literature on Fatima, and versions of the story contain many contradictions and inconsistencies. Though witnesses were questioned on the day of the event, and newspaper accounts gave summary coverage, the full details were not published until much later; the first history that can be considered at all reliable was not written until 24 years after the event. Some features of the incident remain controversial, not least, whether it should be considered – as the Roman Catholic Church considers it – miraculous. In this entry, we are not concerned with the authenticity or otherwise of the alleged apparitions; we are concerned with the veridicality of the alleged miracle only insofar as it is reflected in the behavior of the observing crowd.

CONTEXT: The political and social circumstances within which this event took place were relevant to the way it was interpreted by the authorities, if not to the immediate response by the participants. Following the 1910 revolution in which a republic replaced the monarchy, Portugal was bitterly divided between the authoritarian right-wing, supporting and supported by the Roman Catholic Church, and the would-be progressive but inefficient and corrupt republic. Portugal had entered World War I in March 1916 on the side of the Allies and 40,000 troops (including visionary Lucia's 22-year-old brother Manuel) had been fighting in France since the spring of 1917. This would have contributed to an apprehensive climate in which any event such as the Fatima affair, manifestly supporting the Church's position, was certain to have a strong effect on public opinion. It was, therefore, very much in the Church's interests that the Fatima event should be received as an authentic miracle, and some commentators went so far as to accuse the Church of manipulating the entire affair.[107]

The Apparitions

Three young Portuguese children, Lucia Santos (10), and her cousins Francisco Marto (9) and Jacinta Marto (7), experienced a series of six encounters in which they claimed to see and speak with an entity subsequently identified as Mary, the mother of Jesus, though not resembling her as generally perceived. The first appearance was on May 13, 1917, when the children were minding sheep on land belonging to Lucia's family. Suddenly a "girl" appeared, declaring that she had come from Heaven, and asking the three children to come to this place at the same time on the 13th day of each month. She told them that on her final visit in October she would reveal her identity and declare her wishes.

The crowd at the Cova da Iria, during the final vision at Fatima. (Marchi, Fatima From the Beginning)

The incident, though at first received with skepticism, rapidly became public knowledge and when the children met the apparition for the second time on June 13, some sixty people were present. The apparition site was then fenced off. On July 13, some five thousand were present when the apparition told the children that in October she would work a great miracle so that everyone would believe them. On August 13, twenty thousand gathered, but the children had been taken to a nearby town by the prefect of the area; they did, however, have a vision elsewhere on August 19.

On September 13, a crowd of 20 to 30 thousand gathered. The apparition had nothing of importance to add, but many witnessed a mysterious luminous phenomenon. As Father Joan Quaresma, later a prominent churchman, testified: "I raised my eyes... and to my great astonishment saw, clearly and distinctly, a luminous globe moving from east to west, gliding slowly and majestically through space. Suddenly this globe, giving off an extraordinary light, disappeared from our sight, but near us a little girl continued to cry joyously, 'I can still see it... still... now it's dropping down!'"[108]

The narrative of the apparitions, including the solar phenomenon, is frequently contradictory. Both the visionaries and the investigators altered and embellished their accounts, making it virtually impossible to say precisely what occurred. As at LOURDES, there were others who claimed visionary experiences, though they were not officially recognized. The detailed study by Fernandes and D'Armada discusses these and other problematic issues.[109]

The Event Of October 13

Between the 5th and 6th apparitions, the three visionaries were taken from their homes to escape the crowds and lodged with a friend in a nearby village. They were pursued even here, and their protector, Donna Marques de Cruz, seeing the fanatical crowd, told them "My children, if the miracle you announce doesn't take place, these people are capable of burning you alive!" to which the children replied that they weren't afraid because the Lady would not deceive them.[110]

The crowd that gathered on the appointed day was certainly hoping for something marvelous to happen. The local republican authorities did their best to discourage attendance, and rumors circulated that a bomb would be detonated at the apparition site. Nonetheless vast numbers gathered at the site on the previous day, prepared to spend the night in the open air. Some came in vehicles of all kinds, but many traveled on foot, often barefoot, carrying their footwear on their heads. Many recited their rosaries or sang hymns.

The next morning was cold and rain was falling heavily, but the crowd was not discouraged. By now the attendance was estimated at 50 to 70 thousand; a professor from Coimbra thought it was 100 thousand. Towards midday (because of the war, Portugal had altered clocks to conform with other time zones, so in some reports one o'clock is cited), the children made their way with difficulty through the dense crowd, accompanied by Lucia's parents. Jacinta was crying and afraid. Lucia ordered that everyone should close their umbrellas, despite the pouring rain. Everyone did so. The ground was now a sea of mud.

At midday precisely Lucia exclaimed, "Here she is!" and fell into ecstasy. The two other children saw her also. Lucia spoke with the invisible apparition, who now revealed her identity: she was Nossa Senhora do Rosario. (According to Church teaching, Mary appears in a variety of forms reflecting attributes of her personality: "Our Lady of the Rosary" is one.). She wished for a chapel to be built in her honor. Mounted on a man's shoulders, Lucia was carried from group to group, announcing with theatrical gestures that Mary had just informed her that the war would end that day and the soldiers would return home.[111] (Lucia confirmed this unambiguous statement when interviewed by Canon Formigao that same evening.) To the embarrassment of believers, the war did not end till 13 months later, and Catholic commentators have been hard put to it to explain, or explain away, the apparition's mistake.[112] Their best effort has been to imply that the ending of the war was conditional on the people repenting of their sins, which they had failed to do. Mary also warned people not to continue to offend God, who was already more than sufficiently offended as it was.

Only Lucia saw, heard, and spoke to "Mary." Jacinta heard "Mary's" words. Francesco didn't hear them, but saw the apparition. When the apparition left, Lucia cried out, "Look at the sun!" Lucia's cry, however, was not so much to draw the attention of the crowd to the aerial display, as in exclamation at the vision which was being revealed to herself and her companions: the three of them now saw the Holy Family (Mary, Joseph and baby Jesus). But this was for the visionaries' eyes only; what the crowd saw was quite different. Barthas describes what happened next:

> Suddenly, the rain stopped, and the clouds, which had been opaque all the morning, cleared. The sun appeared at its zenith, like a silver disc, but which could be looked at with the naked eye without being blinded, and, at once, it began to spin on its own axis like a wheel of fire, projecting in all directions beams of light which changed their colour several times. The firmament, the ground, the trees, the rocks, the group of visionaries and the immense multitude seemed successively tinted with yellow, green, red, blue, violet. The sun stopped its dance for a few instants, then began again even more strikingly than before. It stopped, then began again a third time, more colourful and more brilliant than ever, a firework so fantastic that no inventor could create its like. Suddenly, all those who made up this multitude, all without exception, had the sensation that the sun was detaching from the firmament and, by zigzag leaps, was precipitating on them. A formidable cry arose from every breast, or rather, various exclamations which expressed individual feelings, but for all, a unanimous terror. Miracle, miracle! cried some. "I believe in God!... I hail you, Mary! ...My God, have mercy..." And now all these people were fallen on their knees in the mud and reciting the act of contrition.[113]

There were many eyewitness accounts, as well as newspaper reports, and all generally agreed with this description, though there were certain exceptions. Dr. Jose Proenca de Almeida Garret, a professor of natural sciences at the University of Coimbra, confirms this, with some added observations:

> Near the spot where the children were, there rose a column of light, bluish smoke. It rose to a height of about two metres above people's heads, then dissipated. It lasted several seconds. It vanished abruptly, then the same thing happened a second and a third time. I thought it must come from an altar where incense was being burnt, but

subsequently people told me no fire had been lit and nothing burnt....

About two o'clock the sun pierced the thick cloud cover which had hidden it until now, and began to shine clearly and intensely... I heard people compare the sun to a disc of matt silver, but this doesn't seem to me exact. It was a clearer colour, more brilliant and richer... not spherical like the moon. It seemed like a flat, polished disc, as if cut from the shell of a pearl... the clouds, travelling from east to west, did not mask the sun, so that one had the impression that they were passing behind, not before the sun... It's astonishing that for so long a time the crowd could stare at the sun, so bright and so hot, without being blinded... There were two interruptions when the sun shot out rays even more brilliant and striking, which obliged one to turn one's eyes away: this lasted about ten minutes... I have been present at a total solar eclipse, and this did not give at all the same impression.[114]

This phenomenon lasted ten minutes.

When the people recovered from the effect of this spectacle, they found that a further remarkable thing had occurred: their clothing, which shortly before had been drenched by the heavy rain and stained with mud, was now absolutely dry: "The rain continues to pour, and so strongly that despite our umbrellas, no one has a dry stitch of clothing. Suddenly the rain stops, the clouds melt away, letting the sun be seen in all its splendour. Our clothes are soaked, our bodies are cold: I remember still the delicious sensation that this warm caress of the sun gave me... [Then, after the dance of the sun:] If it is true that the brightness of the sun is enfeebled, its heat has lost none of its force. I feel my clothes now almost dry, when only a few moments ago they were soaking."[115]

COMMENT: There are a number of puzzling circumstances relating to the Fatima affair as a whole that have a bearing on the solar phenomenon:

1. The sheer improbability that Mary would choose these witnesses as recipients of her favor, and that she would proceed in this way – scheduling six visions during which little of substance was communicated; concealing her identity till the sixth; and finally accompanying her last ambiguous visit with a vision equally ambiguous. As subsequent controversy shows, it was very far from being the unarguable miracle that, Mary promised, would make everyone believe.

2. It is noteworthy, though understandable, that Lucia, the oldest, usually took the lead throughout the events. To all intents and purposes Mary was appearing to her alone. Her two cousins both died of illness soon after, and Lucia entered the religious life. Her memoirs, written in 1935 though not published till 1942, elaborate on the storytelling, telling of several apparitions previous to the 1917 apparitions, in 1915 and 1916, of a mysterious figure like "a statue of snow made transparent by the sun... like a person wrapped in a sheet."[116] Critics have thought it curious that she made no reference to this at the time when she was being closely questioned about the 1917 apparitions.[117]

With regard to the phenomenon itself, while there can be no doubt that a real event occurred causing so many people to react in so exceptional a way, some points should be noted:

1. No observatory noticed any unusual behavior on the part of the sun. Had the sun indeed acted as reported, the perturbation of the solar system would have led to the destruction of Earth and the other planets, to say the least. The phenomenon as reported, whatever it was, could have possessed no astronomical reality but was atmospheric only and restricted to a relatively small area.

2. The change of colors passed through the colors of the rainbow, and since it had only just stopped raining heavily, and the sun had only just broken through the clouds, conditions favoring a rainbow were very likely. Yet, though many use the word to describe the colors, none seemed to have considered the likelihood that the crowd was in fact enveloped within a rainbow. Martindale (a Catholic) points to many discrepancies in the accounts, especially on the potentially crucial question as to whether or not the sky became clear when the rain stopped. Several witnesses, for whom the solar phenomenon was perceived as taking place in a clear sky, asserted this.[118] To the contrary, the account by Professor Almeida Garret, quoted above, makes it clear that there was a continual passage of clouds. Martindale, after comparing the many testimonies, concludes firmly that "we have to discard all suggestions that the sky was perfectly clear." He quotes a non-Catholic spectator: "The heavy clouds did not 'roll away,' but through a hole in them you saw the sun. It was the colour of stainless steel. I then saw the sun spin round, and stop, and spin round again." Martindale suggested to a [Catholic] astronomer friend: "The air was satu-

rated with moisture: might it not, then, have acted as a lens, making the sun seem now larger, now smaller?" The astronomer replied: "Given layers of air at different temperatures and densities, I do not see why they should not produce the same effect as a series of lenses, and thus account for the observed result."[119]

3. It was subsequently established that the phenomena were observed by people five or more kilometers away, ruling out any possibility that the phenomena were the symptoms of a collective hallucination since these witnesses were not sharing in the expectancies and emotions of those present at the apparition site. One witness, nine years old at the time, saw the phenomena from his village of Alburitel, on a hill facing Fatima at a distance of about 10 kilometers. He was in school at the time when cries were heard from the street; schoolmistress and pupils rushed outdoors to where people were crying and pointing to the sky:

> The sun seemed to me pale and deprived of its usual sharpness; it seemed a globe of snow turning on its own axis. Then suddenly it seemed to descend in zig-zag, threatening to fall on the Earth. Fearful, I ran into the crowd. Everyone was crying, expecting from one moment to the next the end of the world. Near me was an unbeliever who had spent the morning jeering at those who made their way to Fatima... now he raised his hands to heaven, fell to his knees in the muddy street, saying over and over "Holy Virgin! Holy Virgin!" unable to say anything else. Meanwhile people continued to cry and to repent their sins. Then from all sides people rushed into the two chapels of the village, which were soon overflowing with people.
>
> During the long minutes of the solar phenomenon, objects located near us reflected all the colours of the rainbow: our faces were successively red, blue, yellow etc. These phenomena increased our terror. After ten minutes, the sun resumed its former place, pale and without brilliance. When the crowd were persuaded that the danger had passed, they became jubilant, crying out. 'Miracle! Miracle! Praise God!'[120]

The fact that people were affected at such a distance, while it rules out anything like a collective hallucination, nonetheless attests to the fact that the whole population was sensitized to reading a religious/miraculous explanation into what otherwise might have been supposed to be a natural phenomenon. Even though the people of this village had not seen fit to go to Fatima, they seem to have responded in much the same way to the phenomenon, implying a cultural response rather than a spontaneous reaction.

4. Many reporters were present, yet no authentic photographs of the phenomena exist; those that have been published claiming to be so are, if not proved fakes, dubious. There exist photographs of the crowd, but those which show them all gazing in the same direction do not show them staring up at the sky; their sight-line is almost horizontal, suggesting they are looking at something almost at ground-level, probably the visionaries themselves, rather than at the sun, which even in October would at midday be closer to the vertical than the horizontal.[121] Considering the popular appeal of the event and the massive media coverage, the lack of photographic evidence is an extraordinary omission.

5. Spinning or dancing suns are not exclusive to Fatima. They have been reported at other sites, notably another Portuguese site La Ladeira where, commencing in 1962, Maria del Concelçao attracted large crowds to her alleged meetings with Mary.[122] (Her visions have not received Church approval.) A film crew from the BBC *Everyman* program was present on one occasion, and when people started shouting that the sun was spinning, they turned their cameras upwards. Viewers saw rapidly moving clouds but nothing exceptional, though they might be sufficient to provide the basis for an illusion in the mind of someone in a suitable mental state of expectation.

6. The question, how many of the crowd actually saw the phenomenon, is not as simple as suggested by most writers, who cheerfully assume that all saw it. Barthas, quoted above, does not hesitate to describe the vision as unanimous, and no doubt a great many did see something they considered to be extraordinary. Yet even this is far from clear. While those who thought they had seen a marvel would be eager to testify, those who saw nothing might well be reluctant – or simply feel no need – to say so. Even as it was, some witnesses reported their negative experiences. Michel names six who saw nothing, even though all around them the enthusiastic crowd was describing what they saw.[123]

The Fatima phenomenon, thanks to its great impact on believers, has attracted a variety of alternative explanations. Some writers on UFOs have offered the hypothesis that some kind of extraterrestrial spacecraft was involved, and that the apparition was not of Mary, but some otherworldly being. Fernandes and D'Armada, in particular, have found parallels for most of the enigmatic incidents at Fatima, many of them in the UFO literature.[124] Whatever the value of such speculations, however, they do not affect the aspect that concerns us: the way the crowd reacted to what they saw.

It is reasonable to agree with Barthas when he writes: "It is manifest that the vision of this sign was not a purely subjective perception. It isn't possible that the sensations of this crowd of seventy thousand persons could be the fruit of their imagination. They were – and they could not be anything else – the result of luminous and atmospheric phenomena external to their eyes and brains." So far, so good, but he is perhaps going too far when he goes on to say, "The Queen of Heaven was playing, so to speak, with the rays of the sun to produce before them this magnificent firework display which so struck them."[125]

Cutting to the central features of what the Fatima pilgrims saw, it seems possible to perceive it as a remarkable atmospheric effect caused by the abrupt transition from a torrential downpour to intense sunshine (which at this latitude can be very strong even at this time of year); the clouds dispersing, though not completely, and perhaps providing some kind of lens effect; and a rainbow effect changing colors through the spectrum. Given the expectations of the crowd, it is not surprising that this striking phenomenon should be perceived as the promised miracle, a perception that could spread rapidly through a crowd already sensitized to such a possibility.

However, if some such reductionist explanation as this accounts for the physical aspects of the phenomenon, it fails to account for its timing and location. The synchronicity of the atmospheric effect at precisely the end of the sixth vision, when a miracle had been promised, and in the precise location where it had been predicted, is not easily ascribed to coincidence. At most, it can be argued that the crowd was ready to accept any exceptional occurrence as miraculous, and that it was Nature, rather than Mary, that provided a suitable candidate at the appropriate moment.

FEATHER TICKLING FAD

Massachusetts: early 1900s

As a testament to the common historical practice of interpreting a variety of behaviors deviating from the norm as a form of psychological disturbance, prominent Clark University Professor of School Health, William Burnham, made a curious remark in his book on school hygiene, *The Normal Mind.* A respected member of the American Medical Association, he described a "tickling epidemic" in Worcester, Massachusetts, during the early 1900s. Street vendors calling out "a tickle for a nickel" introduced a new toy – a long-handled feather duster – designed solely for the purpose of tickling people. Burnham states that the tickling craze captivated the city for several days as respectable citizens were not only tickling friends but also strangers on the street. "The demoralization of the manners of Worcester people in two or three days was astonishing. If Satan had come to the city in person, he could hardly have devised a surer method for perverting the minor morals of the community."[126]

CONTEXT: The episode transpired during a period when many types of collective behavior were widely viewed as forms of psychopathological "herd" suggestibility. As recently as the early 1950s, L.S. Penrose viewed such fads as the yo-yo and playing crossword puzzles as mild forms of mental disturbance.[127]

FEMALES AND MASS HYSTERIA[128]

Without question, females are over represented in epidemic hysteria episodes, but the reason for this situation is contentious. Some researchers consider biological factors as the primary determinant, while others argue in favor of a social conditioning hypothesis.

CONTEXT: Clearly, human behavior is a complex interaction between biology and genetics on the one hand, and society and culture on the other. While this Encyclopedia reviews both positions, the evidence is compelling that familiarity with the transcultural, transhistorical patterning of human behavior is vital in understanding the common unsubstantiated Western biomedical folk theory of innate female susceptibility to epidemic hysteria, by providing an ethnographically informed global and contextual viewpoint.

The Case For Biology

Psychiatrist Francois Sirois observes that in Western school outbreaks (where the vast majority of participants are also female), social conditions are fairly uniform for both boys and girls. He also notes that these episodes do not appear political or related to any obvious female repression, which so conspicuously typify occupational outbreaks.[129] Sirois analyzed 45 recent school outbreaks, noting that girls near puberty and menarche are the most frequently affected, and a large majority occur at the end of the school year and are associated with galas, graduation shows, and similar gatherings.[130] Sirois believes that as yet unspecified mechanisms associated with sexual arousal may trigger conversion reactions of a benign and age-specific nature.[131]

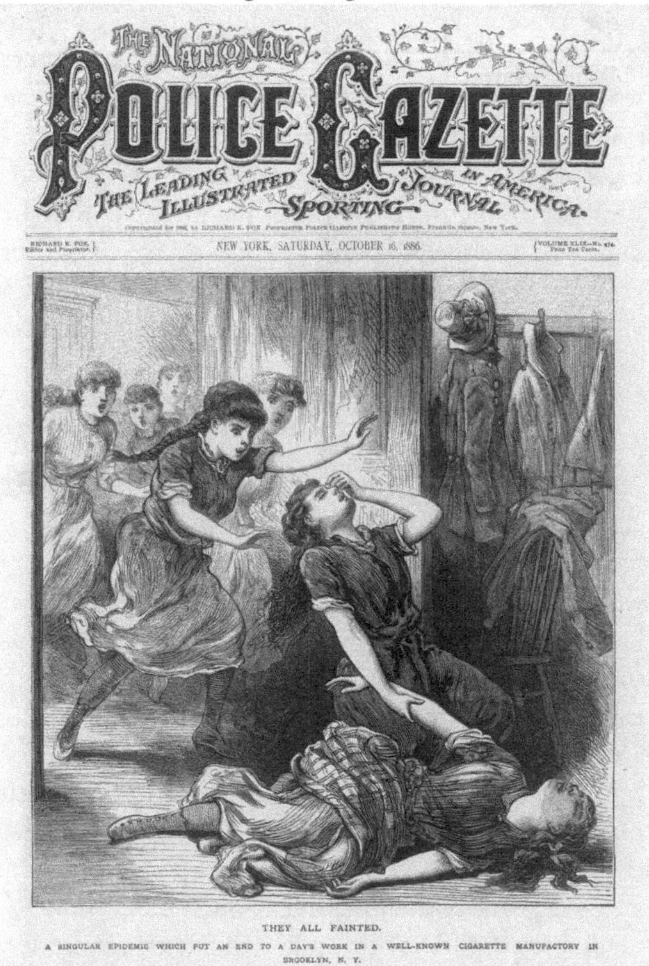
THE NATIONAL POLICE GAZETTE

THE LEADING ILLUSTRATED SPORTING JOURNAL IN AMERICA.

NEW YORK, SATURDAY, OCTOBER 16, 1886.

THEY ALL FAINTED.

A SINGULAR EPIDEMIC WHICH PUT AN END TO A DAY'S WORK IN A WELL-KNOWN CIGARETTE MANUFACTORY IN BROOKLYN, N. Y.

A hysterical employee affects the entire work force of a cigarette factory in Brooklyn, New York. (October 16, 1886)

Klein suggests that the susceptibility of menstruating females to panic disorder and hyperventilation syndrome renders them vulnerable to epidemic hysteria.[132] This is consistent with the presentation of symptoms in anxiety and motor cases, where the vast majority of participants exhibit anxiety-related symptoms and over-breathing. Hysterical disturbances such as psychogenic pain disorder and somatization disorder are more frequently diagnosed in females, with the latter occurring at a rate of about ten-fold of that in men.[133] Individual conversion disorders also appear to be more common in females than males, with reported ratios varying from between 2:1 to 10:1.[134] Any explanation of occupational mass psychogenic illness must also explain its occurrence in males. The only majority male episode appears in our survey (as mass anxiety hysteria) among a population of all-male military recruits at their California army barracks amid brush fires, an elevated pollution index, and pungent odors. The situation was exacerbated when some recruits unnecessarily received resuscitation as medics had prematurely assessed their conditions as warranting such measures. This unusual set of circumstances generated extreme anxiety among the remaining soldiers. Those observing the resuscitation, or witnessing others exhibit symptoms, were three times more likely to report symptoms.[135] [136]

The Case For Society And Culture

Sociocultural factors appear to be able to fully account for the over-representation of female participants in episodes. Females near puberty and menarche are exposed to psychosocial stresses that reflect these new life stages, including common perceptions of themselves as weak and biologically inferior.[137] Furthermore, workplace mass hysteria reports are virtually never characterized by a preponderance of females near puberty and menarche. Western females are typically socialized to cope with stress differently than males, with the former often acquiring emotionally expressive, sympathetic, submissive character traits.[138] Such female character traits are also evident in most non-Western countries, while males are typified transculturally by such characteristics as courage, self-reliance, and independence.[139] This socialization pattern may not only render females more vulnerable to mass psychogenic illness but more likely to seek treatment during an episode, as it is well-known that women are more likely to seek medical advice than men.

While there is a general psychiatric consensus that women somatize more than men, the actual role of gender is unclear as social factors including observer bias and methodological flaws can account for some of the discrepancies.[140] Social roles have also been shown to be the main determinant of gender differences in the incidence of depression.[141] While there is an aggregate over-representation of females who are diagnosed with psychiatric disturbances, Busfield concludes that "once the data are disaggregated what emerges is a gendered landscape...in which gender also intersects with other social characteristics such as age, marital status, social class and ethnicity. Moreover...the aggregate female predominance in admissions is relatively new."[142]

Females are also over represented in the types of jobs that tend to produce dissatisfaction. Sociologist Alan Kerckhoff observes that an entrenched part of industrial folklore holds that females perform better than males at tedious, boring, repetitious tasks. Hence, women are usually used for such positions: "When we review the work situations in which the best-documented cases of mass psychogenic illness have occurred, we find them to be strikingly similar. A room filled with rows of sewing machines operated by women, a series of long benches at which women assemble TV sets, a large room in which many women punch and verify computer data cards, and so on." Kerckhoff continues: "These are highly regimented work situations in which the workers are all carrying out very boring, repetitive tasks. Hour after hour, they do the same thing over and over again. In most of the cases reported, the degree of regimentation seems to be very high and the workers are permitted only infrequent breaks between which they are restricted in both physical space and their ability to vary their activities. It would be difficult to find situations that would be more conducive to a sense of tension and frustration."[143] As females are more likely to externalize emotive responses, if one views epidemic hysteria as the outward "manifestation of psychological stress or anxiety, one might expect those individuals who have been taught to subscribe to the traditional emotionally expressive female role to be most susceptible."[144]

Further, while men also work in tedious, repetitive jobs such as an auto assembly line, Michael Colligan and Lawrence Murphy of the National Institute for Occupational Health and Safety suspect "that the organizational climate and parity between labor and management are much 'healthier' in these setting than is usually evident in the more traditional female-intensive industries."[145] Another social explanation to account for the abundance of females as victims of mass psychogenic illness in the workplace may have to do with "off the job" stress which may render them more susceptible to psychological illness. Colligan and Murphy state: "An important consideration here would be the extent to which the affected women evidence role strain arising from the continuing conflicts of job demands and perceived domestic responsibilities. Mandatory overtime, for example, may be perceived as a mere irritant by the working male, but is likely to be catastrophic to the working woman who feels pressured to simultaneously assume full responsibility for such domestic activities as shopping, laundering and meal production."[146]

If one were to survey cultural anthropologists specializing in the study of trance and possession states, and ask them to explain the preponderance of females in epidemic hysteria reports, their responses would likely be affected by a curious observation that has been noted by ethnographers in various transcultural settings. In many cultures, people exhibit group trance and possession states that are occasionally accompanied by psychomotor dysfunction and/or transient somatic complaints. In most documented instances they involve females experiencing repressive or oppressive conditions or perceptions of themselves as weak and vulnerable.[147] Such cases show remarkable parallels with epidemic hysteria episodes. At least three anthropological perspectives use social and cultural factors to account for the preponderance of females in these group episodes of trance and possession, and transient somatic complaints. Yet in rare instances it occurs almost exclusively among males in situations of perceived weakness and/or extreme psychosocial stress, such as being socially manipulated and forced to live among strangers in a society based on matrilocal residence.[148] Any theory that attempts to explain the appearance of mass conversion symptoms in terms of innate female susceptibility must account for its manifestation in males.

Influential British anthropologist Ioan Myrddin Lewis has observed that there exists a global preponderance of females in spirit possession cults and charismatic religious movements within various cross-cultural settings. Lewis attributes this situation to their low social status and oppression in male-dominated societies where they are low on the power hierarchy.[149] Women in many of these societies often experience, sometimes collectively, trance and possession states, psychomotor agitation, and anxiety-related transient somatic complaints. Concordantly, epidemic hysteria is common among Malay females in conspicuously repressive, intolerable occupational settings in Malaysia.[150]

Sociologist Robert Bartholomew examined the appearance of epidemic hysteria in Malaysia, where episodes are numerous and almost exclusively affect Malay females in school and factory settings, and set out to find out why not a single case of epidemic hysteria has been recorded until about 1960.[151] He began with the work of Lewis, who views spirit "attacks" as functional and cathartic, allowing the oppressed to temporarily circumvent their position by inverting the normal social order. Concordantly, beginning in about 1960, the conservative Islamic *dakwah* movement spread across Malaysia, resulting in the implementation of strict Muslim rules and regulations, particularly in the educational system. Ethnic Indian and Chinese Malaysian students, of whom only a tiny portion are Islamic, were not required to adhere to these restrictions. In contemporary Malaysia, intolerable social situations are characteristic features of female Malay school and factory settings. Female redress is culturally unacceptable. Malaysian episodes of mass hysteria are typified by frank criticisms of authorities and administration policies, with the hysteria label deflecting the attribution of blame. Male headmasters who enforce strict academic and religious discipline typify female Malay educational settings.

Australian anthropologist Bruce Kapferer has an alternative anthropological explanation. He assumes that social factors can explain the preponderance of females in possession cults in cross-cultural settings but believes it is related to the global symbolic identity of females. Kapferer states that any explanation must consider "the shared constructions and typifications which men and women have of themselves and of each other."[152] A cornerstone of this position is the widespread transcultural reality, among both men and women, that women as a category are subordinate to men and are thus seen to be more susceptible to spirit possession.[153] If this approach is applicable, we should be able to identify cultural constructs that render female Malays vulnerable to collective spirit possession and conversion symptoms in schools and factories.

Ackerman reports that submissiveness to males is a female Malay cultural trait. Malays also hold a folk belief that they are inherently suggestible, especially females – a position even espoused by a former Malaysian Prime Minister.[154] Further, Malay females are believed to possess a weaker life force (*semangat*), making them susceptible to possession. This is the precise group that is affected by occasional episodes of mass spirit possession in educational and factory settings. So, in addition to repression and submissiveness, which typify episodes of workplace mass hysteria in Malaysia, cultural constructs of Malay female vulnerability to supernatural entities is another contributing factor to epidemic hysteria outbreaks. For example, in explaining an outbreak of mass spirit possession at a college hostel for female Malays, Raymond Lee and Susan Ackerman observed that events surrounding the episode were generally interpreted as spirit possession. "The ideas by which they made this interpretation were based on a world-view which places heavy emphasis on the supernatural and female vulnerability."[155]

Kapferer's perspective may also account for the

over-representation of females in global reports of general mass conversion reactions in schools and factories outside of Malaysia. While factors like male dominance in repressive settings and status ambiguity can engender episodes, a major overlooked element may involve conceptions about female perceptions of innate vulnerability in countries where epidemic hysteria cases occur.

Any discussion of social factors that are correlated with the preponderance of women in spirit possession religions and behaviors must include the meticulous research of anthropologist Erika Bourguignon who, like Kapferer, is critical of Lewis. Bourguignon believes that Lewis's thesis is only a partial explanation for a culturally-patterned model of altered states of consciousness (ASC) which results from a combination of economic and social structural factors. Using ethnographic data collected on 488 societies, she found that trance is predominantly a male phenomenon associated with less complex, low accumulation subsistence economies (i.e., hunting, gathering, fishing) that typically socialize for traits such as self-reliance, assertion, and independence. However, possession trance typically involves women in complex, high accumulation societies (i.e., pastoralism and/or agriculture), who in their ecological adaptations, socialize for obedience, compliance, and dependence.[156] In this latter instance, females entering possession trance deal with the spirits through impersonations and by dramatizing the importance of compliance made by these powerful spirits. Yet, since "humans play the roles of these impersonated entities, the ASC allow those in possession trance to act out their own needs for assertion, and they present them with an opportunity to manipulate others and their own real life situations as well."[157] This finding is entirely consistent with Malay society where females are socialized to be obedient and dependent. It is precisely in such societies that female Malays "will not seek spirit help to augment their own powers to be able to deal with a hostile group. Instead, the [sic] call on powerful, authoritative spirits to *act in their place*."[158]

To summarize, Bourguignon's findings indicate that trance is typically male and involves interaction with another to increase individual power in subsistence societies, while possession trance is common among females and entails becoming another, which allows subservient women to act out their needs for them.

See also: DANCING MANIA.

FIBROMYALGIA

The condition known as fibromyalgia, or FM, has long been steeped in controversy, and many medical practitioners question its very existence. According to the National Fibromyalgia Association, FM is a condition involving "chronic pain illness which is characterized by widespread musculoskeletal aches, pain and stiffness, soft tissue tenderness, general fatigue and sleep disturbances. The most common sites of pain include the neck, back, shoulders, pelvic girdle and hands, but any body part can be involved."[159] The Association claims that symptoms wax and wane with time, and that 3 to 6% of the United States population is afflicted.

Fibromyalgia is a subjective condition diagnosed in the absence of normal tests and examination findings. As D.L. Goldenberg observes, it is "not an entity that can be described and explained; it is rather a subjective experience comprising pain and fatigue."[160] Hence, P.A. Reilly notes: "In fibromyalgia, we may have created a monster. Is it now clinically, socially and financially appropriate to slay that monster?"[161]

Dutch scientists I. Hazemeijer and J.J. Rasker are two leading authorities on fibromyalgia, which they consider to be an imaginary condition. They outline the typical scenario through which the condition is "confirmed" and reinforced.[162] The typical patient is a middle-aged female who seeks help from her physician after experiencing a variety of ambiguous aches and pains over a period of several months. Symptoms include lethargy, unrefreshing sleep, constipation, and stomach pain. Examinations and tests are not able to identify any obvious medical problem. Further blood tests are performed: all unremarkable, as are radiographs. At this point, analgesics may be prescribed, but with little effect.

The patient is next referred to a specialist in rheumatology who repeats many of the earlier investigations and who suggests a diagnosis in part by counting the number of tender points – which can be a highly subjective process. The rheumatologist then explains the condition and gives the patient a booklet on the subject. Unsatisfied, the patient will often seek more information on the condition from a variety of popular sources, including internet websites, magazines, and the sympathetic views of relatives and friends, all of which tends to confirm their belief that they are suffering from fibromyalgia.

Next the patient may join a self-help group that reinforces his or her perception as a fibromyalgia patient. At the same time, "an organizing, reality-forming power of that domain has structured the observation of family doctors and rheumatologists" and a "looping effect" has occurred whereby "the individual patient and the concept have influenced each other."[163] In this regard, fibromyalgia is similar to mass psychogenic illness as it spreads through social networks.

The symptoms of fibromyalgia are so vague that if the sufferers had been referred to a different specialist, they may have been diagnosed with a different condition. For instance, a psychiatrist could have easily diagnosed them with chronic pain disorder. A gastroenterologist could have diagnosed irritable bowel syndrome. A neurologist could have diagnosed chronic fatigue syndrome.[164]

CONTEXT: Fibromyalgia appears to be a physician-created condition that is maintained within parts of the medical community and self-help groups, magazines, and internet web sites. Hazemeijer and Rasker believe that the therapeutic domain that gives rise to the reality of fibromyalgia – that is, the experts diagnosing it as a real condition – is the key to the future of fibromyalgia. Once this domain comes to accept the socially constructed nature of the "condition," they believe that "fibromyalgia syndrome can no longer exist."[165]

FILO CARGO CULT

Central Papua New Guinea: 1940-1947

In February 1940, a 17-year-old schoolgirl named Filo of the village of Inawaia was doing her morning gardening chores – work that she had long detested – when she had a vision. Filo said that A'aia, the creator spirit, appeared and instructed her to be prepared for changes that were about to occur to society. At the time of her vision, Filo, who would soon become known as "the prophetess of Inawaia," was unhappy because she had dreamed of marrying her uncle, Keama Gnu'u, a practice forbidden by local law, making Filo displeased with the existing social system. The social movement that was about to be founded upon her vision may have been a subconscious way for her to achieve her aspiration of becoming the wife of Gnu'u. After her vision, Filo told her parents what had happened, and that the creator spirit told her to tell the people that the missionaries were telling lies and that her people should immediately cease working, build altars, and pray more. All the pigs should be killed and eaten. Nonbelievers would perish.[166]

Upon hearing the story, Filo's parents reacted angrily, beating her, and ordering her back to the garden to finish working. Shortly thereafter, a flu outbreak in the area killed 60 people, at which point many villagers made a connection between the vision and the deaths, which were now widely seen as a divine sign. People stopped working, built altars, and every evening at 9 o'clock they gathered at the altars to pray for gifts. For those not following the new rules, the penalties would be harsh. For example, those who refused to abandon their garden work would be transformed into weeds; those continuing to hunt would turn into a cassowary (a large bird) or pig; and the bodies of those continuing to canoe would turn into the shape of a fish. Old rules of morality and marriage no longer applied and Filo took her uncle, Keama Gnu'u, as her lover.[167]

Among Filo's predictions, planes would soon fly in with canned foods, clothes, tools, books, cars, guns, and ammunition. She was adamant that the Europeans must be forcibly removed from their lands, and an attack was planned on the local Christian mission. Authorities were informed and soon armed police and government officers drove up in cars. Remarkably, the mob embraced the arrival of the vehicles, believing that they were the fulfillment of Filo's vision as the authorities brought with them weapons and ammunition. They were quickly disappointed upon realizing that the weapons were not going to be given to them but used against them. Filo was arrested and jailed for three months.[168]

In her absence, the movement remained popular. By the end of 1940, Filo would be pronounced a Queen, and her lover's brother, Konio Gnu'u, proclaimed that he was god, and his body was untouchable. Anyone accidentally touching him would have to pay money or risk being turned into a dog or losing their place in heaven. His cousin, Kavo Ipame, claimed to be Jesus Christ. Both claimed powers to heal the sick.

Upon her release, Konio Gnu'u said that Filo would return to the village on a majestic horse where there would be a big feast. In reality, the horse to be used had been neglected. The pathetic animal was so malnourished that it could not even walk. As for the planned feast, when Filo returned home to Inawaia, there was little food and people were hungry. Despite these obstacles and the disappointment of Filo's planned grand return, when she did arrive home (transported by the police), she was soon able to rally the populace around her. When hostilities again flared, Filo was arrested a second time, at which point the movement went on in secret. The movement persisted for several more years, underground, with clandestine prayer gatherings at which adherents prayed for cargo. Filo, for her part, threatened to turn anyone who opposed her into pieces of wood or snakes.

See also: THE NAKED "CARGO CULT," MANGZO "CARGO CULTS," PRESIDENT JOHNSON "CULT."

FLORIDA LAND BOOM

During the Florida real estate boom of 1924 to 1926, the state of Florida captivated the imagination of the nation. Americans engaged in a frenzied rush to buy land so that they could sell it at a higher price and make a quick "kill" or profit. As prices spiraled upward and more and more people got in on the "sure thing," many invested in Florida property without ever having seen the land – including swampland – they had purchased.[169] At the height of the boom in 1925, the *Miami Daily Herald* printed an edition totaling 504 pages of mostly real estate advertising, while other papers commonly printed editions of over 100 pages.[170] Many national magazines and newspapers contributed to the boom, publishing stories of people who became fabulously wealthy virtually overnight.

CONTEXT: The Florida property boom occurred during a period of exaggerated optimism and financial recklessness that typified the decade leading up to the great depression, an attitude that is widely regarded as being largely responsible for the economic disaster of the 1930s.

By March 1926, the real estate market began to crumble, banks were going bankrupt from the boom, and any hope of a recovery was buried on September 18 as a powerful, unpredicted hurricane slammed into the Miami area leveling 5,000 homes.[171] One writer noted that by 1928, Miami was the cheapest place to live in the country![172] Economist John Kenneth Galbraith observed that the Florida real estate boom was built on wishful thinking involving a make-believe world: "This is a world inhabited not by people who have to be persuaded to believe but by people who want an excuse to believe. In the case of Florida, they wanted to believe that the whole peninsula would soon be populated by the holiday-makers and sun-worshippers of a new and remarkably indolent era."[173] In his classic book on the STOCK MARKET CRASH OF 1929, Galbraith identified the Florida land boom and the desire to "get rich quick" with minimal effort as indicative of the attitude that led to the subsequent stock market collapse.[174]

See also: CRAZE.

FLORIDA WAR SCARE

Region, Florida: early October 1939

A balloon triggered a war scare among the Native American Seminoles in a remote part of the Everglades. After word of the outbreak of World War II filtered through the wilderness, they became excited upon spotting "a strange balloon high in the sky."

They followed it for 30 miles (some 50 kilometers) before alighting. The device was later identified as a weather balloon from the Miami weather bureau, used to monitor the stratosphere.[175]

FLYING SAUCER, ORIGIN OF

United States and worldwide: 1947

The first known use of the word "saucer" to describe an Unidentified Flying Object (UFO) occurred on January 25, 1878, when farmer John Martin told a reporter for the *Denison Daily News* that he observed an orange object "about the size of a large saucer" three days earlier near Denison, Texas. Contrary to the claims by many UFO writers, Martin's use of the word referred only to the size, not the shape, as saucer-like. While there are scattered historical references to disc-shaped objects, no consistent pattern emerges until after the Kenneth Arnold sighting of 1947, when witnesses began to use the word "saucer" to describe the shape of a UFO. The origin of the term "flying saucer" can be traced to a single press dispatch sent by a journalist at a Pendleton, Oregon, newspaper office, which was quickly disseminated worldwide by news wires.

CONTEXT: The flying saucer era began in the summer of 1947 during a period of Western fear over the rapid, global spread of communism and the potential threat of atomic warfare. It is within this RED SCARE context that waves of claims and public discourse about the existence of flying saucers as domestic or Soviet secret weapons flourished.

On Tuesday, June 24, 1947, Boise, Idaho resident Kenneth Arnold (1915-1984), owner of Great Western Fire Control Supply of Boise, installed fire-fighting equipment at the Central Air Service complex in Chehalis, Washington. There he learned of a missing C-46 Marine transport plane, believed lost in the vicinity of Mount Rainier, Washington. Relatives of the occupants were offering $5,000 to anyone who could locate the crash site. Though his next planned flight was to Yakima, Washington, Arnold decided to re-route over the search area in hopes of spotting the wreckage. Shortly before 3 p.m. on June 24, Arnold was flying his private plane near the Cascade Mountains when he saw what appeared to be nine glittering objects flying in an echelon formation from north to south near Mount Rainier. He kept the rapidly moving objects in sight for about three minutes before they passed southward over Mount Adams and were lost to view.[176]

Worried that he may have observed remote-controlled Soviet guided missiles, Arnold flew to Pendleton, Oregon, and went to the Federal Bureau of Investigation (FBI) office there. Finding it closed, he visited the offices of Pendleton's newspaper, the *East Oregonian*. Two reporters, Nolan Skiff and Bill Bequette, listened to Arnold's story for about five minutes as their deadline was fast approaching. Skiff hastily wrote a story that Bequette managed to squeeze onto the front page of the June 25 edition under the headline, "Impossible! Maybe, But Seein' is Believin', Says Flier."[177]

> Kenneth Arnold, with the fire control at Boise and who was flying in southern Washington yesterday afternoon in search of a missing marine plane, stopped here en route to Boise today with an unusual

From a hospital on Vancouver Island, Canada, nurse Doreen Kendall sees a hovering UFO with occupants. (Brian James, in Canadian UFO Report, July 2, 1970)

story – which he doesn't expect people to believe but which he declared is true.

He said he sighted nine saucer-like air craft flying in formation at 3 p.m. yesterday, extremely bright – as if they were nickel plated – and flying at an immense rate of speed. He estimated they were at an altitude between 9,500 and 10,000 feet and clocked them from Mt. Rainier to Mt. Adams, arriving at the amazing speed of about 1200 miles an hour. "It seemed impossible," he said, "but there it is – I must believe my eyes."

He landed at Yakima somewhat later and inquired there, but learned nothing. Talking about it to a man from Ukiah in Pendleton this morning whose name he did not get, he was amazed to learn that the man had sighted the same aerial objects yesterday afternoon from the mountains in the Ukiah section!

He said that in flight they appeared to weave in an [sic] out of formation.[178]

Bequette recalls that he then hurriedly keyed in a second similar report to the Associated Press (AP). "We were only minutes from 'putting the paper to bed' so we didn't have much time to give him [referring to Arnold]."[179] Both stories were misleading as Arnold had described the objects as crescent-shaped, referring only to their movement as "like a saucer would if you skipped it across the water."[180] However, Bequette's Associated Press account describing Arnold's "saucers" appeared in scores of newspapers across the country.

Bequette was obligated to file an AP story as member papers were required to provide the wire service with local teletype transmissions of reports that editors deemed to be of wider interest. Bequette later recalled that, at the time, Oregon papers belonging to the AP cooperative were linked by the "C wire." Bequette said that "Other papers were free to use stories from the C wire and the AP bureau took whatever stories the Portland editors thought had ... [broader] interest and transmitted them on the AP's main, or trunk, wire." Bequette filed his story onto the C wire, but he said it was picked up on the main wire, and by the following morning, "almost every newspaper in the country published the story on page 1."[181] Bequette's story appeared on teletype machines as follows:

PENDLETON, Ore., June 25 (AP) – Nine bright saucer-like objects flying at "incredible speed" at 10,000 feet altitude were reported here today by Kenneth Arnold, Boise, Idaho, pilot who said he could not hazard a guess as to what they were.

Arnold, a United States Forest Service employee engaged in searching for a missing plane, said he sighted the mysterious objects yesterday at three p.m. They were flying between Mount Rainier and Mount Adams, in Washington State, he said, and appeared to weave in and out of formation. Arnold said that he clocked and estimated their speed at 1,200 miles an hour.

Enquires at Yakima last night brought only blank stares, he said, but he added he talked today with an unidentified man from Utah, south of here, who said he had seen similar objects over the mountains near Ukiah yesterday.

"It seems impossible," Arnold said, "but there it is."[182]

This report was not technically responsible for the first use of the term "flying saucer." After examining press clippings between June 25 and 26, 1947, Herbert Strentz of the journalism department at Northwestern University found that the use of the term "flying saucer" is the collective product of American headline writers, and cannot be traced to any one person.[183] However, Bequette's AP report was the proto-article from which the term "flying saucer" was created. Of key importance was his use of the term "saucer-like" in describing Arnold's sighting. The term "flying saucer" allowed citizens to put "inexplicable observations in a new category."[184] Bequette's use of the word "saucer" provided a motif for the worldwide wave of flying saucer sightings during the summer of 1947,[185] and other waves since.[186] It also encouraged others who had observed mysterious aerial phenomena to report their sightings and heightened fears of a Soviet attack.[187]

In the June 26 edition of the *East Oregonian,* Bequette described Arnold as having seen "nine mysterious objects" that were "somewhat bat-shaped," and it was not until near the end of this account that he added that Arnold had "also described the objects as 'saucer-like.'" Many years later, Bequette remarked that he could not recall "whether or not Arnold used the words 'saucer-shaped craft,' but I am inclined to credit his version (that he only spoke of objects moving like a saucer if you skipped it across the water)."[188] This recollection of events is consistent with a description furnished by Arnold on June 26, 1947, when he appeared as a live guest on Pendleton, Oregon, radio station KWRC where he was interviewed by announcer Ted Smith. During the interview, Arnold never referred to the objects that he reported seeing two days earlier, as "saucer-like" or "flying saucers," but stated that they looked "like a pie plate that was cut in half with a sort of convex triangle in the rear."[189] The other notable feature of this interview is the atmosphere of excitement and Cold War urgency that is evident throughout. In his closing remarks, for instance, Ted Smith states:

"I know that the press associations ... [have] been right after you every minute .... It has been on every newscast over the air and in every newspaper I know of. ... I understand United Press is checking on it out of New York now, with the Army and also with the Navy, and we hope to have some concrete answer before nightfall. .... And we urge our listeners to keep tuned to this station because any time this afternoon or this evening, that we get something ... we'll have it on the air."[190]

The Oregon Journal of June 27 referred to Arnold as having seen "nine shiny crescent-shaped planes" and quoted him as saying they "were half-moon shaped, oval in front and convex in the rear." But many other newspapers, including the *East Oregonian*, continued to use descriptions that reinforced the "flying saucer" motif. The *Portland Oregon Daily Journal* of June 26 used such terms as "flying disk" and "shiny, 'piepan' shaped objects." The front page of the Boise, *Idaho Statesman* of June 27 used the term "flying saucers."

Domestic Or Foreign Secret Weapons

Why was Bill Bequette willing to believe Arnold's story and place it on the front page? Arnold was an articulate man, and in 1962 he even stood as a candidate for Idaho lieutenant governor. Another important factor was the recent memory of World War II, which had ended just two years before. Between 1944 and 1945, 93,000 Japanese Fugo balloon-carrying incendiary bombs were launched into the "jet stream" and sent in the direction of the Pacific Northwest in hopes of setting fire to forests and farmland. Only 297 were known to have reached the United States and Canada, causing relatively minor damage, although psychologically the threat struck widespread fear into coastal residents.[191] Memories of these secret Japanese weapons were still vivid in 1947, prompting speculations as to whether the flying saucers were "an indication of a similar activity on the part of the Soviet Union?"[192]

In the year immediately prior to the saucer wave, there were mass sightings of mysterious aerial objects, especially in Scandinavia and occasionally in other parts of Europe, and observers almost exclusively described them as resembling guided missiles or German V-rockets, with the most common descriptive term being "ghost rocket." This motif is a reflection of the immediate post-World War II political landscape and widely held view in Northern Europe at the time that remote-controlled German V-rockets confiscated by the Soviets at the war's end were being test-fired as political intimidation. Russian forces had occupied Peenemunde, the former center of German rocket science, and controlled much of northern Europe during this time, and it was unclear as to how much Scandinavian territory they might claim in the political uncertainty following the war.[193, 194] The 1947 saucer wave reflects a transition stage with "ghost rocket" sightings of the previous year.

From the time of Arnold's sighting until 1950, many observations of missile-like aerial objects were recorded, reflecting the popular notion that the mysterious sightings represented a domestic or foreign secret weapon. However, from the very beginning of the 1947 wave, most sightings were saucer-shaped, and by 1950, the missile motif had virtually disappeared, leaving most people to report disk or saucer-like objects. For instance, Bloecher's 1967 *Report on the UFO Wave of 1947* catalogs a minimum of 800 sightings during this wave alone. Of these, approximately two-thirds were saucer-shaped.[195]

During the 1947 "saucer" wave, almost no one believed the objects were of extraterrestrial origin. The American obsession with the Cold War and possible atomic conflict was reflected in the sighting explanations. Less than two months after Arnold's sighting, on August 15, 1947, a Gallup Poll revealed that 16% of respondents believed they were American or Russian secret weapons.[196] "Nothing [in the poll] was said about 'alien visitors,' not even a measurable 1% toyed with the concept."[197] Shortly after the publicity surrounding Arnold's sighting, the FBI investigated the likelihood that many reports were disinformation spread by Soviet agents trying to promote fear and panic, and through the end of July local Bureau offices conducted background checks on saucer witnesses.[198] These concerns reflect the American preoccupation with the spread of communism during this period. Two typical incidents reflect the social paranoia over the communist threat. After someone soaked a 28-inch "saucer" with turpentine and set it alight on top of a Seattle, Washington, house on July 15, 1947, someone erroneously thought they could see a hammer and sickle on the disc, causing FBI and military bomb experts to rush to the site.[199] Eight days later, when Oregon's wooden Salmon River Bridge was destroyed by a fire, the FBI investigated the possibility of communist sabotage. The ambiguous nature of the fire, and its appearance near the peak of a UFO wave, led to speculation that flying saucers were responsible.[200] During this period, the U.S. Air Force was concerned that the stimulus for some sightings may have been unconventional Soviet aircraft intended either to "negate U.S. confidence in the atom bomb as the most advanced and decisive weapon in warfare," "perform photographic reconnaissance missions," "test air defenses," or "conduct familiarization flights over U.S. territory."[201]

Unidentified Flying Meteors?

During the early 1990s, science writer Keay Davidson began researching the possibility that Kenneth Arnold saw a disintegrating meteor. Davidson says that Arnold's observation resembled previous fireballs. While Arnold said the objects were in view for up to three minutes, Davidson notes that time estimates under stress are commonly overestimated, such as a 1989 California earthquake that many San Francisco Bay Area residents estimated to have lasted over a minute; in reality, it lasted fifteen seconds.[202] There have been historical reports of individual meteors lasting up to fifty seconds (times that were also likely overestimated). Internal evidence from Arnold's account suggests that he overestimated the duration of the sighting by confusing the meteor fragments with the resulting contrail, which could have persisted for a number of minutes. Some large meteors break into smaller pieces as they burn. Davidson points out that Arnold described the objects as glowing tadpoles that would pulsate and flutter. "That sounds like chunks of a disintegrating meteor that glow, then dim as they cool," said Davidson.[203] Later, UFO researcher Brad Sparks of Irvine, California, found indirect evidence for the meteor hypothesis.[204] At almost exactly the same time as Arnold's sighting, Idaho Lt. Governor Donald Whitehead and Boise Justice J. M Lampert described "an object that bears a strong resemblance to a meteor contrail."[205] Whitehead said the object resembled a comet, was in view for about twenty minutes, and "had a brilliant head and a filmy smoke for a tail."[206] Why wasn't the meteor widely observed? Davidson reviewed weather maps and found that on June 24, 1947, "a huge system of bad weather covered much of Canada and the United States east of the Cascades."[207]

COMMENTS: What Arnold reported remains the subject of vigorous debate among UFO researchers. While we will likely never know exactly what he saw, the meteor explanation postulated by Brad Sparks and Keay Davidson seems to be the most plausible. Arnold's report is also important for the way that it highlights the notoriously unreliable nature of human perception and the role of the mass media in generating sighting waves. The media inadvertently misrepresented Arnold's description as "saucer-shaped," which appears to have structured subsequent UFO descriptions during that summer and since 1947 as disc or saucer-shaped.[208]

FORCED MARRIAGE SYNDROME

Papua New Guinea: October 1973

Between October 1973 and June 1974, an ongoing episode of illness diagnosed by local medical authorities as epidemic hysteria occurred at an Australian nursing school at Telefomin in the highlands of western Papua New Guinea. The "outbreak" began on February 22, 1973, when "A," a 20-year-old graduate of the local mission school of nursing was working at the clinic when she reported a headache, nausea, and her arms and legs began shaking. After a brief hospital stay and negative test results for various ailments, she was released but continued to experience a series of "fits," during which she would exhibit confusion, shaking, and a loss of consciousness. Later she would be unable to recall any of the events during the "seizures."[209] These "made a deep impression upon those closest to her, the nurses, for she was the most senior girl in the school, and greatly liked."[210]

On October 21, a 15-year-old primary school

girl ("B"), who had previously observed A's fits, was walking to the village when she developed similar symptoms, including striking out at others, and had to be subdued. After a failed exorcism she was taken to the Health Centre, where "C," a 12-year-old girl who had sprained her knee, was receiving treatment and witnessed "B" being admitted. As "C" left to go home, she began to complain of headache and confusion, and started hitting bystanders with a stick.

On October 24, a fourth case was reported, and by November 10, 15 females were afflicted. Sixteen girls exhibited a highly similar pattern starting with *ai raum* (feeling faint), *tingting faul* (mental confusion) and *hed i pen* (headache). Some reported feeling drowsiness (*hed i hevi*). Many said they felt a sudden cold chill and became deaf. In addition to partial amnesia, some became unsteady on their feet and others actually fell. Anthropologist Stephen Frankel, who interviewed subjects and observed many "fits" firsthand, noted that at this point the girls typically became violent. "Running was common, and attacks were made using any handy objects as weapons; they chose sticks and stones or just fists and feet, but never knives or arrows."[211] Curiously, Frankel observed that the violent behavior "was never indiscriminate despite their apparent loss of conscious control; they attacked close relatives, contemporaries and children most frequently, and avoided authority figures. They inflicted no serious injuries."[212] While some shouted verbal abuse, most were silent. After being restrained, most of the females seemed to return to normal within several hours, though two were "disturbed" for up to two weeks. Weeping and emotional liability was a prominent feature in four other cases.[213] There was no evidence that any of those affected had consumed any type of intoxicant, including alcohol, mushrooms, cannabis, pandanus, or areca nut.[214]

In all, 23 females between the ages 12 and 30 were afflicted. Those nurses the worst affected were the most enculturated to Western values, experiencing symptoms over an average of 12 days versus just over four days for those who were not nurses and had not been exposed to Western ways. In the region where the outbreak occurred tribesmen are renowned for dominating women. Females are restricted to pastoral duties: gardening, animal husbandry, childcare, and food preparation. They must also adhere to rigid female-only taboos, and their sexual lives are strictly controlled. Marriages are prearranged, with little means of redress for abusive or demanding husbands. Females are also prohibited from quarreling with elders and must internalize grievances. These conflicts were clearly evident in the case studies. For instance, "A" had married despite the protests of both her and her husband's parents. In January, she felt it necessary to leave her home village after continuous quarrels with her parents, opting to live with her husband in his village. Unfortunately for her, her husband left Telefomin in February to attend a college at Wewak, and shortly after his departure she had her first of a series of fits. She was taken to the Wewak Hospital near her husband and rapidly recovered, but when she left for Telefomin again, her fits returned. She eventually made arrangements to live with her husband at Wewak and her symptoms disappeared. Frankel remarks that without the husband's support, "the conflicts of her life at Telefomin became intolerable to her" and "was translated into physical symptoms."[215]

While the majority of marriages were arranged, some of the women, especially the more liberal, educated ones, such as those attending the nurses school, were able to chose their own partners but with a cost. According to Frankel, "It does seem that more women are succeeding in getting their way, but among the women affected here, marriage problems, particularly censure for marrying or attempting to marry against the wishes of the families involved, are a recurrent theme. 'A' succeeded, but has been criticized bitterly ever since. 'T' and 'V' are attempting to avoid marrying the men chosen for them, and both are having affairs with preferred partners, but they are under very strong pressure to conform."[216] One of the women to experience the "fits," "J," refused to marry the partner picked out by her elders and eloped. While the parents eventually succeeded in destroying the relationship, she still refused to marry the man chosen for her and she was involved in numerous quarrels. During one quarrel in particular, "a stick was thrust into her vagina. She is now married to a man chosen for her by her parents."[217]

The episode occurred during a period of intergenerational conflict. Elders were exerting strong pressure to conform with traditional values, while the younger generation was becoming used to Western ways, mostly through contact with the European school system.[218] As Frankel notes, "The most acculturated girls, who were affected here, might be expected to be the most sensitive to this."[219]

FRANKIE AVALON MANIA

Milwaukee, Wisconsin: July 1959

During a singing appearance by 18-year-old teen heart throb Frankie Avalon at a large ballroom, "Girls fainted at the rate of one a minute. They screeched for five minutes straight, trampled spectators, and mauled a police officer."[220] Such incidents didn't begin with popular music, as Rudolph Valentino was similarly "adored" in the 1920s.

FRATERNITY ORDERS

United States: 19th century

During the latter half of the nineteenth century, millions of American men, mainly middle-class, white-collar whites, flocked to join fraternal organizations which, even if in principle they proclaimed an ostensible purpose, in practice were little more than initiatory orders. The initial ritual of joining, and the subsequent rituals of rising through the successive grades of the hierarchy, were virtually the only function of these organizations. The cost of membership was high, yet the material benefits were few. The profusion of the orders, which numbered upwards of 300, and the number of eager candidates, which numbered more than 5 million in an adult male population of 19 million, amounted to a collective mania, and pose the question why so many men devoted so much of their time, energy, and money to this seemingly futile pursuit.[221]

The best known of these orders was American Freemasonry, and it provided the model for most of the others. In post-Civil War America the prospective joiner had hundreds to choose from, housed in some 70,000 lodges and temples throughout the country. Even in church-going America, lodges outnumbered churches in most cities by the close of the century. One could apply for membership of the Benevolent & Protective Order of Elks, the Grand Army of the Republic (if he were a veteran of the War between the States), the Grange – Patrons of Husbandry (farming), the Hibernians (if he was Irish), the Knights of the Golden Circle, of Labor and of Pythias, the Ku Klux Klan, the Loyal Order of the Moose, the Improved Order of Red Men (emulating Native Americans), and scores of others. A few sought to attract more forward-looking candidates with titles such as the Modern Woodmen of America, but most presented themselves as long-established: the Ancient Order of Foresters, or of Gleaners, for example.

Their ceremonies, though as freshly minted as their names, were replete with venerable language and trappings designed to reinforce the legendary origins of the order. But, in fact, not one of the orders was as ancient as it pretended. The Freemasons were one of the few who could genuinely claim more than a few decades of existence, but their boasted lineage to the time of Solomon was as dubious as the imagined ancestry of the later orders. The Odd Fellows claimed descent from Adam, nominated as the first Odd Fellow, and the Royal Antediluvian Order of Buffalo, purporting to date from before the Flood, was founded in 1822. Yet the truth was that masonry was an 18th century creation and most of the others did not exist till the 19th century; the Knights of Pythias, who traced their origins to the sixth century BCE, claiming Pythagoras as their founder, were created in 1864. Many of the rituals involved dressing up (or down) in costumes appropriate to their supposed origins, but little respect was paid to historical accuracy. The Knights of Pythias cheerfully superimposed the trappings of medieval knighthood on their supposed origins in classical Greece. The Shriners, who claimed they were founded by the son-in-law of the prophet Mohammed, indulged in a politically very incorrect travesty of Islamic practices. Some orders confessedly traced fictional origins: the Ben Hur Life Association was founded by Lew Wallace, author of the biblical epic *Ben Hur*, and the Brotherhood of American Yeomen drew its rituals from Sir Walter

Scott's romance *Ivanhoe*.

Orders that had existed in the early decades of the century had changed almost out of all recognition by mid-century. Formerly, they had been social clubs, like their forerunners in England, and convivial drinking was their chief activity. By the 1850s, however, they had become sober, abstemious, and serious to the point of being pompous. Even where temperance was not obligatory – though it often was – alcoholic beverages were likely to be proscribed at their gatherings. Typically, the lodge room of the Grange reassured visitors by displaying an open Christian Bible and the American flag, as well as the tools and implements of the farmer's profession.

Their purported aims were varied. Many, such as the Odd Fellows, appealed to a broad spectrum of members. Others, such as the Brotherhood of Locomotive Engineers or the Machinists & Blacksmiths Union, were directed towards a particular section of society. But despite their names, these were not mere trades unions; they too had their solemn rituals and venerated traditions. Most laid claim not only to mutual support and brotherhood between members, but also to philanthropic works in the wider community. In practice, however, charitable activities played a small part, if any, in their programs. A good many orders included mutual insurance benefits.

Instead, their practices were inward looking, and consisted overwhelmingly of ritual: the ritual of joining in the first place and then of initiation into the successive steps of the hierarchy. Each of these occasions was the subject of an elaborate ceremony, working to a scenario that was often custom-tailored in conscious imitation of real or supposed esoteric mysteries of ancient Egypt or Greece or the imagined chivalry of Medieval Europe. The Ancient Mystic Order of Bagmen of Bagdad, patronized by salesmen, paraded in pseudo-Arab costumes complete with fez. Although the rituals fulfilled much the same function as coming-of-age rites in tribal cultures, these were not regarded as appropriate models for Westernized Americans. The closest any approached to such rituals were those of the Red Men, supposedly modeled on the ceremonies of the Iroquois and other Native American peoples. Many of the rituals employed by other organizations were blatant imitations of Masonic ritual, and all shared the religio-mystical linguistic tone and the repetitive invocations characteristic of occultist ceremonial, and, above all, the solemnity with which they were performed.

Despite their often ludicrous character, the crucial importance of these ceremonial performances in attracting and retaining members can hardly be overestimated. It was the re-casting of their rituals in the direction of greater elaboration and greater solemnity that enabled the rapid growth of the Freemasons and Odd Fellows, who in turn provided the model for many of the others. "The revisions of ritual in the 1840s and 1850s were the culmination of a 'glorious reformation' that had transformed the lodges into temples and had conferred upon lodge masters the title 'Most Worshipful.' The lodge historians com-

President Washington at the altar of his Masonic Lodge, while planning the Capitol Building, Washington, D.C.

monly attributed the success of their order to the new ritualism of the mid-nineteenth century."[222]

Along with the rituals went all kinds of observances – secret signals of recognition or of distress, solemn oaths, passwords, and grips that differed according to the member's status within the order. Initiates were blindfolded, confronted with skeletons, and passed through simulations of Hades designed to test the candidate's fortitude. A symbolic significance was attached to every item and every gesture. Dress was an important element: officials wore costly uniforms, usually consisting of elaborately ornamented robes. Fantasies were enacted in carefully scripted dramas in which businessmen and shopkeepers exchanged their everyday garb for the vestments of High Priests, Roman Senators, Medieval Knights, or Native American chiefs. Candidates for the Mystic Shrine were represented as "poor sons of the desert, who are weary of the hot sands and the burning sun on the plain and humbly crave shelter and the protecting dome of the Temple." The candidate was often threatened with death, from which he was spared only by the plea of a kindly elder. The Homesteaders suggested that the candidate be tied to the back of a horse with burning brands tied to its heels, while the Ancient Order of Foresters simply proposed hanging him from the nearest forest tree.[223] The ritual generally represented symbolically a form of pilgrimage or quest, perhaps representing the American West or the journey to Jerusalem – all within the confines of the Temple. Just to what extent the candidate believed in this mumbo-jumbo was a matter for the individual, but the ceremony was designed to be genuinely frightening and doubtless often was. Skulls, skeletons, and coffins featured prominently among the props.

Significantly, the more profusely these quasi-religious trappings were introduced, the more the orders throve. Fraternity leaders recognized and acknowledged that their appeal lay in the "sacred" character of their ceremonies and went to great lengths to offer the right mix of esoteric verbiage and high-flown spirituality. Albert Pike, the most eminent Freemason of his day, declared that "every Masonic Lodge is a temple of religion, and its teachings are instruction in religion."[224] Paradoxically, even at a time when most American men were members of a church congregation, the lodges presented a challenge to the established churches. While many were specifically Christian, many others tended towards a form of deism or pantheism, acknowledging a rather undefined Supreme Being. This evidently appealed to those who were disillusioned by the established churches, while satisfying their need for some kind of god-figure. One clergyman calculated that of the young men in his town, some 5,000 were members of lodges, while fewer than 2,000 were church members

To this challenge, churchmen responded in one of two ways. Some denounced the orders: the Catholic Church vehemently opposed them; priests would often forbid members of their congregation to join the fraternities on pain of excommunication. (In 1881, however, Father Michael McGivney formed a Catholic order, the Knights of Columbus, which, while it eschewed the ritual performances of other fraternities, was clearly created to offer a Catholic alternative.) Other clergymen responded by joining the orders themselves; in 1891, it was estimated that about one in five New York church ministers were also members of fraternal orders.[225]

Clearly, though doubtless the majority of fraternity members were also churchgoers, the orders fulfilled a function that the churches were unable to provide. "If middle-class men built new temples, it was because existing ones had proved deficient; if they created strange new gods, it was because the ones with which they were familiar had failed them."[226] The secret of this appeal was clearly to be found in the ceremonies in which members were required to participate.

Typically, an initiation ritual comprised four elements. Fraternal officials insisted that members undergo the entire sequence of initiations provided by their order. In every major order at least one ritual developed each of the following themes: (1) an initiate at the outset of his task was portrayed as immature or unmasculine; (2) he overcame obstacles as he embarked on a difficult journey through the stages of childhood and adolescence; (3) this journey or ordeal reached a climax when he was killed (or nearly killed) by angry father figures; and (4) he was reborn as a man into a new family of approving brethren and patriarchs.[227]

This archetypal pattern – opera-goers will note that it is virtually a plot-summary of Mozart's Masonic opera *The Magic Flute* – evidently satisfied a psychological need comparable to the coming-of-age ceremonies of tribal cultures. The father-son, elder-younger dichotomy was a central theme: the candidate who presented himself for admission to an order was taking a step towards adulthood, and as he ascended in the order's hierarchy, ritual by ritual, he perceived himself as increasing in maturity. "Fraternal ritual succeeded when the participant allowed his imagination to transform the figure of a patriarch into a representation of his own father."[228]

For this, American men were prepared to pay substantial sums of money, as well as devote much of their leisure time. Thc cost of being a member was very great. "In 1897, a time when factory workers earned four to five hundred dollars a year, the *North American Review* estimated that the average lodge member spent fifty dollars annually on dues and insurance, and two hundred dollars on initiation fees, ritualistic paraphernalia, uniforms, gifts for retiring officers, banquets, and travel."[229] Since dues were paid into the order's coffers, they became extremely wealthy, enabling them to construct impressive temples that further enhanced their prestige. The effect of these high fees and expenses was to limit membership to the more affluent strata of society, and this in turn enhanced their elitist appeal.

Towards women, the orders adopted a hypocritical stance. Carnes suggests that because the churches were seen largely as the woman's domain – it is a fact that congregations contained a majority of women – a major appeal of the fraternal orders was their exclusive masculinity; the lodges were seen as more macho compared with the effeminate churches. It is interesting in this respect to compare the popularity of the fraternities with the Businessmen's Revival of 1857-8, (see AMERICAN REVIVALS) which was substantially a male-only affair, and which was significantly free from the "hysterical" manifestations that characterized most of the religious revivals described in this Encyclopedia.

In the face of growing feminism, a number of orders introduced women's auxiliaries, allowing them a certain degree of access to the lodges and instituting a kind of parallel order of their own. But it was generally recognized that this was whitewash; there was no question of admitting women to the inner sanctums of the orders, which remained an exclusively male preserve.

After 1900 a decline set in, and by 1920 the age of the lodges was well nigh over, with the depression of the 1930s giving the finishing stroke to all but a few. Those orders that survived had to change their image and their activities. The rituals played a diminishing role and community service and philanthropic enterprises became their *raison d'être*. For instance, the Knights of Pythias have outgrown their 19th century image and today focus on Service to Mankind, fostering peace and international understanding.

COMMENT: Though it has been widely supposed that men joined these organizations for the perceived social benefits, these have been shown to be generally marginal. Joining such an organization did not necessarily put a man on the fast track to commercial or social success. Rather, psychological gratification seems to have been the overriding motivation; this would involve bonding with peers or social superiors on the one hand, while excluding categories of people perceived as outsiders.

A crucial aspect of the fraternities, and one that surely contributed greatly to their appeal, was their secrecy. An essential element in the initiation was the candidate's solemn oath not to reveal the arcana of the order to anyone – not even his wife. Fearsome penalties were prescribed for any who should break this oath. In the 1820s, William Morgan, a former Mason, was abducted and presumably murdered when he threatened to go public with details of Masonic practices. But few were tempted to do so, for the sense of sharing a secret from the rest of the world added to the satisfaction of membership.

Secret societies have existed in all communities, and in some tribal cultures they are an essential dimension of life, intimately bound up with religious beliefs on the one hand, and such matters as kinship and interpersonal relationships on the other. Other societies have a political objective, which is often revolutionary in character, for whom secrecy is essential to survival. But no such constraints operated in the case of the American merchant or tradesman of the late 19th century, and the explanation must be sought elsewhere.

The fact that the fraternal orders were exclusively male is clearly significant. Yet in an era when male dominance was universal, a man had no need to join an organization to assert his manhood, or even to escape from females – wife or mother – who were in some way a threat or a constraint. Psychoanalytical explanations have been suggested but do not convince. Diminished self-esteem, often cited as a motive for joining cults or societies, does not apply in regard to the fraternal orders, which attracted social, political, and financial leaders, as well as their aspiring subordinates. However, it could be said that, for their members, the orders acted as a guarantor of the right to self-esteem.

A possible parallel is with today's "born-again" Christians. Joining a fraternal order resembled religious conversion in many respects and perhaps filled the same role in the individual's life. The young man who became an Odd Fellow or a Knight of Pythias was exchanging one way of life for another; by this rite of passage he was being admitted into the fellowship of wiser, more experienced men who had already penetrated more deeply into the realities of life. In accepting him among their number, they recognized his merits – or at any rate, his potential merits.

Paradoxically, though, this quasi-religious solemnity co-existed with a more frivolous motivation. Escapism also played its part. The orders were private worlds, where the humdrum demands of business, family, and daily activities could be temporarily forgotten, and where the individual could identify, for a while, with a medieval knight or a native warrior. The bogus claims to ancient origins, which surely deceived no one, demonstrate the play-acting that was clearly an element in the orders' appeal.

Though the American fraternal orders can be compared with organizations elsewhere – for example, German students' clubs with their dueling traditions – no other society has seen a movement on so massive a scale. So a further question is: Why were these fraternal orders specific to American males, of a certain social class, and at this period of time? Historian Arthur M. Schlesinger has memorably described his fellow-Americans as a "Nation of Joiners,"[230] so perhaps a part of the answer may be that American men are temperamentally nurtured to become Odd Fellows or Knights of Pythias. As to why the mania should have occurred at this epoch, the explanation must be found in social dynamics embodying a number of factors – the declining appeal of the established churches and the "threat" of feminism among them. Or perhaps the fraternal orders should be seen as a collective rite of passage whereby the American nation – or a substantial part of it – could come of age.

FRIEDEBERG OUTBREAK

Germany: 1593

In Friedeberg, in the Neumark region of Germany, some 150 persons were overcome by a hysterical affliction, which seems to be related to the fact that there had recently been fiery preaching against the devil for the first time in that region. When people began to be affected, public prayers were initiated, but publicizing the malady, which gave it official recognition, served to increase rather than diminish the contagion. And contagion certainly seemed to be operating, for observers noted that as soon as one person was overtaken, others in the vicinity followed.[231]

Unfortunately, this brief reference appears to be all that is known of the episode. Nonetheless it is of interest as being one of the earliest indications that a collective disorder could result directly from preaching. Later, similar manifestations would occur in response to revival preaching.

See also: METHODISM, REVIVALS, CONVENT HYSTERIA, DEMON POSSESSION.

FUMIGATION HYSTERIA

East Texas: June 15, 1983

On this day two college students were conducting a routine fumigation of a greenhouse belonging to the biology department on the campus of a university in Eastern Texas. The evening calm quickly turned chaotic when passersby noticed smoke pouring out of the greenhouse vents, and they summoned help. Emergency personnel rushed to the site and began evacuating the area around the greenhouse, dispersing the smoke, and urging people in the area to be treated at the hospital. Between 9 p.m. and 1 a.m., 119 people were examined at two local hospitals for organophosphate poisoning. About 30 patients were 11-to-14 year olds from a summer camp, who had been attending a dance in a building adjacent to the greenhouse during the fumigation – some of whom were aware of the nearby "smoke cloud" as the dance was going. While standing on the dance floor, one girl subsequently felt faint, at which point rumors circulated that "the cloud got her." Soon other students began to report feeling ill and worried chaperones took the affected students to the hospital.[232]

Investigators noted that physical symptoms indicating parathion poisoning, such as restricted pupils and respiratory distress, "were absent in the vast majority of victims who felt sick; fully 99 of the 119 persons evaluated at the two local hospitals showed no clinical evidence of organophosphate poisoning."[233] Further, many patients were clearly hyperventilating. Other complaints included stomach pain, headache, and a burning sensation of the skin or eyes.

CONTEXT: The episode was a confluence of a variety of different factors: the timing of the fumigation, the presence of the summer camp students and dance in the adjacent building, and the swooning schoolgirl, in combination with an exaggerated response by rescue personnel and doctors.

The actions of emergency personnel both at the scene and in the local hospitals appear to have made the situation worse. For instance, as emergency workers arrived on the scene, they were "exposed to a variety of suggestions for illness, including environmental cues (for example, the presence of ambulances and medical personnel and the sounds of sirens), the illness behavior of the index cases, and direct suggestion, when civil defense personnel told bystanders that the smoke was harmful." Furthermore, staff members at one hospital appear to have inadvertently worsened the situation "by giving patients a list of symptoms or by classifying patients with triage tags more appropriate for trauma situations."[234]

A similar exacerbation of the crisis occurred in the way that emergency personnel at the site and hospital talked to and treated patients. "The language used by emergency and hospital personnel while assessing and treating patients during episodes of mass psychogenic illness can be a powerful source of counter-suggestion. If staff use statements such as 'The effects of this chemical are temporary, not serious,' or 'You should be feeling better soon,' rather than continuing to question patients about headaches or breathing problems, they will promote calm. Reassurance and positive suggestion build an expectation of wellness and recovery and help promote symptom remission."[235]

Sources

1. Halasz, George (2003). "Can Psychiatry Reclaim its Soul? Psychiatry's Struggle Against a Dispirited Future." *Australasian Psychiatry* 11(1):9-11. Quote on p. 10.
2. Jacobson, John W., Mulick, James A., and Schwartz, Allen A. (1995). "A History of Facilitated Communication: Science, Pseudoscience, and Antiscience." *American Psychologist* 50(9):750-765. See p. 753.
3. Jacobson, Mulick and Schwartz, op cit., p. 754.
4. Jacobson, Mulick and Schwartz, op cit., p. 754.
5. Jacobson, Mulick and Schwartz, op cit., p. 761.
6. Margolin, K.N. (1994). "How Shall Facilitated Communication be Judged? Facilitated Communication in the Legal System." In Shane, H.C. (editor). *Facilitated Communication: The Clinical and Social Phenomenon*. Pp. 227-258. Sandiego, CA: Singular Press.
7. Fernald, Dodge (1996). "Tapping Too Softly." *American Psychologist* 51(9):988.
8. Hall, G.A. (1993). "Facilitator Control as Automatic Behavior: A Verbal Behavior Analysis." *The Analysis of Verbal Behavior* 11:89-97.
9. Jacobson, John W., Mulick, James A., and Schwartz, Allen A. (1995). "If a Tree Falls in the Woods..." *American Psychologist* 51(9):988-989. Quote on p. 989
10. "25 Years Ago From the Files of the Herald, June 5, 1906." *Syracuse Herald*, June 5, 1931, p. 10.
11. "Test Plants Where Workers Stricken." *Stevens Point Daily Journal* (Wisconsin), October 13, 1976, p. 5.
12. Pearsall, Judy (editor) (1999). *The Concise Oxford Dictionary*, tenth edition. Oxford: Oxford University Press, pp. 509 and 526.
13. Robertson, Ian (1987). *Sociology* (third edition). New York: Worth,

p. 549.
14. Turner, Ralph, and Killian, Lewis. (1972). *Collective Behavior* (second edition). Englewood Cliffs, New Jersey: Prentice-Hall, pp. 129-130.
15. Anonymous. (1986). "Fads: Did We Really Do Those Silly Things." *Life* 9:65-69.
16. Bogardus, Emory Stephen (1973). *Fundamentals of Social Psychology*. New York: Arno Press.
17. LaPiere, Richard T. (1938). *Collective Behavior*. New York: McGraw-Hill, p. 160.
18. Miller, David L. (1985). *Introduction to Collective Behavior*. Belmont, California: Wadsworth; Miller, David L. (2000). *Introduction to Collective Behavior and Collective Action* (second edition). Prospect Heights, Illinois: Waveland Press; Meyersohn, Rolf, and Katz, Elihiu. (1957). "Notes on a Natural History of Fads." *American Journal of Sociology* 62:594-601; Penrose, L. S. (1952). *On the Objective Study of Crowd Behavior*. London: H.K. Lewis.
19. LaPiere, Richard T. (1938). *Collective Behavior*. New York: McGraw-Hill, p. 203.
20. Miller (2000). *Introduction to Collective Behavior and Collective Action* (second edition). Prospect Heights, Illinois: Waveland Press p. 185.
21. Turner, Ralph, and Killian, Lewis (1987). *Collective Behavior*. Prentice-Hall: Englewood Cliffs, NJ, p. 146.
22. Hart, Jack (1996). *Editor and Publisher* 129(19):5 (May 11).
23. Letscher, Martin G. (1994). "How to Tell Fads from Trends." *American Demographics* 16(12) (December).
24. *The Complete Books of Charles Fort*. New York: Dover Publications, p. 854, citing the *New York World Telegram*, March 9, 1931.
25. Anonymous. (1952). "165 Girls Faint at Football Game; Mass Hysteria Grips 'Pep Squad,'" *The New York Times*, September 14, p. 1.
26. "Fainting Girls Close Refinery," *The News-Journal* (Mansfield, Ohio), June 16, 1937, p. 1.
27. "Mystery Story." *The Helena Daily Independent* (Montana), July 11, 1937, p. 14, citing *The New York Post*.
28. "Mystery Story." op cit.
29. Hanhnien News.com. Reported by Lien Chau and translated by Quynh Nhu, accessed June 1, 2005 at: http://thanhniennews. com/ society/?catid=3& newsid=2769.
30. Tra, Huu, and Hien, Dieu (2005). "30 High School Girls Faint in Danang City." Hanhnien News.com, Monday, December 6, 2004, accessed June 1, 2005 at: http://www.thanhniennews.com/ healthy/?catid =8&newsid=3690 (Translated by Quynh Nhu).
31. False Memory Syndrome Foundation (1997). *Frequently Asked Questions*. Brochure published by the False Memory Syndrome Foundation, 3401 Market Street, Suite 130, Philadelphia, Pennsylvania.
32. Pendergrast (1995), op cit., pp. 43-45.
33. Pendergrast, Mark (1995). *Victims of Memory: Incest Accusations and Shattered Lives*. Hinesburg, Vermont: Upper Access, Inc., pp. 46-47.
34. Bass, Ellen, and Davis, Laura (1988). *Courage to Heal: A Guide for Women Survivors of Child Sexual Abuse*. New York Harper/Perennial.
35. Butler, Katy (1994). "Self-Help Authors Freed From Liability; Suit Involving Incest Claims Continues." *San Francisco Chronicle*, September 6, p. A16.
36. Pendergrast (1995), op cit., p. 51.
37. Loftus, Elizabeth, and Ketcham, Katherine (1994). *The Myth of Repressed Memory: False Memories and Allegations of Sexual Abuse*. New York: St. Martin's Press, p. 142.
38. Loftus and Ketcham (1994). op cit., p. 49; Pendergrast (1995). op cit., p. 49.
39. Pendergrast (1995), op cit., p. 49.
40. Loftus and Ketcham, op cit., p. 143.
41. Coon, Dennis. (2000). *Introduction to Psychology: Exploration and Application* (eighth edition). Pacific Grove, California: Brooks/Cole Publishing, p. 343.
42. Campbell, Terence W. (1998). *Smoke and Mirrors: The Devastating Effect of False Sexual Abuse Claims*. New York: Plenum Press.
43. Loftus and Ketcham, op cit., p. 153.
44. Loftus and Ketcham, op cit., pp. 153-154.
45. Loftus and Ketcham, op cit., p. 156.
46. Loftus and Ketcham, op cit., pp. 158-164.
47. "'I Tawt I Taw' A Bunny Wabbit At Disneyland: New Evidence Shows False Memories Can Be Created." Science Daily News Release, University Of Washington, Juyne 12, 2001. Accessed at: http://www. sciencedaily.com/ releases/2001/06/010612065657.htm.
48. Hopper, James (2003). "Recovered Memories of Sexual Abuse: Scientific Research & Scholarly Resources." http://www.jimhopper. com/memory/#de.
49. Hopper, James (2003). op cit.
50. Elliott, Diana M. (1997). "Traumatic Events: Prevalence and Delayed Recall in the General Population." *Journal of Consulting and Clinical Psychology* 65:811-820. See p. 811.
51. Elliott, op cit., p. 812.
52. Elliott, op cit., p. 812.
53. American Psychiatric Association (APA) (1994). *Diagnostic and Statistical Manual of Mental Disorders* (4th edition). Washington DC: American Psychiatric Association, p. 478.
54. American Psychiatric Association (APA) (1994). op cit., p. 479.
55. Briere, J., and Conte, J. (1993). "Self-reported amnesia for abuse in adults molested as children." *Journal of Traumatic Stress*, 6, 21-31. See p. 21.
56. Herman, J. L., and Harvey, M. R. (1997). "Adult Memories of Childhood Trauma: A Naturalistic Clinical Study." *Journal of Traumatic Stress* 10:557-571. See p. 557.
57. Herman and Harvey, op cit., p. 563.
58. Herman and Harvey, op cit., p. 565.
59. Herman and Harvey, op cit., pp.565-566.
60. Freyd, J. (1994). "Betrayal Trauma: Traumatic Amnesia as an Adaptive Response to Childhood Abuse." *Ethics and Behavior* 4:307-329. See p. 307.
61. Freyd, op cit., p. 312.
62. Collin de Herté, writing as Victor de Stenay (1894). *Le Diable Apôtre par la Possession d'Antoine Gay*. Paris: Delhomme et Briguet, p. 3.
63. Wilson, Ian (1989). *Stigmata*. New York: Harper & Row, p. 87.
64. Blanc, Hippolyte (1865). *Le Merveilleux dans le Jansenisme &c*. Paris: Plon, p. 289.
65. Butsch 279: appendix to Wingård, C F af. (1846). *Review of the Latest Evils and Present state of the Church of Christ*. Translated from the Swedish. London: Rivington.
66. Bramwell, J. Milne (1930). *Hypnotism*. Third edition. London: Rider. Originally published in 1903. See p. 392.
67. Hilgard, J. R. (1970). *Personality and Hypnosis: A Study of Imaginative Involvement*. Chicago: University of Chicago Press. Hilgard, J. R. (1979). *Personality and Hypnosis: A Study of Imaginative Involvement* (2nd ed.). Chicago: University of Chicago Press.
68. Wilson, S. C., and Barber, T. X. (1981). Wilson, S. C., and Barber, T. X. (1981). "Vivid Fantasy and Hallucinatory Abilities in

The Life Histories of Excellent Hypnotic Subjects ("Somnambules"): Preliminary Report With Female Subjects." In E. Klinger (ed.), *Imagery, Volume 2, Concepts, Results, and Applications*. New York: Plenum Press; Wilson, S. C., and Barber, T. X. (1983). "The Fantasy-prone Personality: For Understanding Imagery, Hypnosis, and Parapsychological Phenomena." In A.A. Sheikh (ed.), *Imagery: Current Theory, Research, and Application*. New York: Wiley.
69. Wilson and Barber, 1983, op. cit.
70. Wilson and Barber, 1983, op. cit.
71. Wilson and Barber, 1983, op. cit., p. 351.
72. Wilson and Barber, 1983, op. cit., p. 346.
73. Pines, M. (1978). Invisible playmates. *Psychology Today* 12:38-42.
74. Wilson and Barber, 1983, op. cit, p. 346.
75. Wilson and Barber, 1983, op. cit.
76. Wilson and Barber, 1983, op. cit.
77. Wilson and Barber, 1983, op. cit.
78. Wilson and Barber, 1983, op. cit.
79. Wilson and Barber, 1983, op. cit.
80. Denton, W. (1873). *The Soul of Things*. Boston: privately published. Hudson, J. (1967). *Those Sexy Saucer People*. San Diego: Greenleaf Classics. Keel, J. A. (1975). op cit., pp. 871-896.
81. Of lone percipients reporting astral experiences, a quiet setting, such as meditation or resting in bed prior to sleep appears to induce the experience. Contactee William Ferguson always began his numerous encounters during meditation. His experiences were consciousness-raising, providing keen insights into his life.
"Upon my return to Earth....I thought I would go into the living room where an old gentleman...was staying at my house...to see if he would recognize me. As I went into the living room I spoke to him, but there was no response. He couldn't see nor hear me.... There were a lot of things I could do and think about and understand, that I never could have understood before. So I went back to the room where I had been relaxing,...and I looked for my body, but my body isn't there,... I again placed myself upon the lounge and remained quiet until my being was transformed back into this three-dimensional dense matter projection, and thereupon went into the dining room and told my wife about my experience." Ferguson, W. (1954). *My Trip to Mars*. Potomac, Maryland: Cosmic Study Center.
82. Brownell, W.S. (1980). *UFOs: Key to the Earth's Destiny*. Little Creek, CA: Legion of Light Publications, pp. 68-72.
83. Druffel, A. (1977). "Encounter on Dapple Gray Lane: Part 2." *Flying Saucer Review* 23:2.
84. Druffel, A., op cit., p. 21.
85. Schwarz, B. (1979). op cit.
86. Rimmer, J. (1984). *The Evidence for Alien Abductions*. Wellingborough: Aquarian. Lawson, A. (1977). What can we learn from hypnosis of imaginary abductees?" *The Mutual UFO Network Journal* 120:7-9; Moravec, M. (1985). Psychological influences on UFO "abductee" testimonies, M. Moravec and J. Prytz (eds.), *UFOs over Australia: A Selection of Australian centre for UFO Studies Research Findings and Debate*. Published by the Australian Centre for UFO Studies.
87. Wilson and Barber, 1981, op. cit; Wilson and Barber, 1983, op. cit.
88. Lynn, S., and Rhue, J. (1987a). Fantasy-proneness and Psychopathology. *Personality and Social Psychology* 53:327-336. Lynn, S., and Rhue, S. (1987b). Fantasy Proneness: Developmental Antecedents. *Journal of Personality* 55:1.
89. Wilson and Barber, 1983, op. cit.
90. Wilson and Barber, 1983, op. cit. p. 358.
91. Wilson and Barber, 1983, op. cit.
92. Rimmer, J. (1984). op cit.
93. Fuller. J. (1966). *The Interrupted Journey*. New York: Dial.
94. Hansen, C. (1969). *Witchcraft at Salem*. New York: George Braziller.
95. Wilson, S. C., and Barber, T. X., 1983, op. cit., p. 346.
96. Beckley, T. (1980). T.G. Beckley (1980). *Psychic and UFO Revelations in the Last Days*. New York: Global Communications, pp. 33-34.
97. Macionis, John. (1991). *Sociology*, third edition. Englewood Cliffs, New Jersey: Prentice Hall, p. 600.
98. Miller, David L. (2000). *Introduction to Collective Behavior and Collective Action*. Prospect Heights, Illinois: Waveland Press, p. 198.
99. Veblen, Thorstein (1889). *The Theory of the Leisure Class*. New York: New American Library.
100. Miller, op cit., pp. 181-182.
101. Macionis, op cit., pp. 598-599.
102. Panati, Charles. (1991). *Panati's Parade of Fads, Follies, and Manias*. New York: HarperCollins, p. 116.
103. Rosenberg, Jennifer (2003). "Flappers in the Roaring Twenties Part 2: Flapper Image and Attitude." The History Net, http://historyhttp:// history 1900s.about. com/library/ weekly/ aa022201b.htm.
104. Andrist, Ralph K. (1970). *The American Heritage History of the 20s & 30s*. New York: American Heritage Publishing, p. 130.
105. Panati, Charles. (1991). *Panati's Parade of Fads, Follies, and Manias*. New York: HarperCollins, pp. 116-117; Skolnik, Peter L. (1978). *Fads: America's Crazes, Fevers & Fancies From the 1890s to the 1970s*. New York: Thomas Y. Crowell, pp. 38-39.
106. Page, Ellen Welles. (1922). "A Flapper's Appeal to Parents." *Outlook* 132: 607.
107. De Sède, Gérard (1977). *Fatima, Enquête sue une Imposture*. Paris: Alain Moreau.
108. Michel de la Sainte Trinité, Frère (1983). *Toute la Vérité sur Fatima*. Saint-Parres-lès-Vaudes: Renaissance Catholique, volume 1, p. 272.
109. Fernandes, Joaquim, and D'Armada, Fina (1981). *Intervençâo Extraterrestre em Fatima*. Lisbon: Libraria Bertrand, p. 107.
110. Barthas, Casimir, and Fonseca, G da (1943). *Fatima, Merveille Inoui*. Toulouse: Fatima Editions. Revised and enlarged edition of the 1941 original), p. 80.
111. Avelino de Almeida and Canon Formigao, quoted by De Séde 115 and Michel 306.
112. Michel 306-309 offers ingenious but ultimately unconvincing explanations.
113. Barthas, op cit., pp. 85-86.
114. Dr. José Proënça de Almeida Garrett, cited in Agnellet 1958: 74.
115. Dr. Pereira Gens, cited in Michel 1983: 329-330.
116. Lucia 1980: 62.
117. Michel, op cit., I.11 et seq.
118. Michel, op cit., volume 1, p. 333.
119. Martindale C. (1950). *The Message of Fatima*. London, p. 81 et seq.
120. Ignacio Lourenço Pereira, missionary, cited by Barthas 243-4.
121. For example, the photo reproduced in Michel, op cit., p. 328.
122. Bouflet and Boutry 1997: 402.
123. Michel, op cit., p. 337.
124. Notably Fernandes and D'Armada 1981/2005.
125. Barthas, op cit., p. 241.
126. Burnham, William H. (1924). *The Normal Mind*. New York: D. Appleton-Century, p. 338.

127. Bartholomew, Robert E. (2000). *Exotic Deviance: Medicalizing Cultural Idioms–From Strangeness to Illness*. Boulder, Colorado: University Press of Colorado, p. 47.
128. The following section on why females are susceptible to mass hysteria episodes, is excerpted from Bartholomew, Robert E., and Sirois, Francois (2000). "Occupational Mass Psychogenic Illness: A Transcultural Perspective." *Transcultural Psychiatry* 37(4):495-524. See pp. 506-512.
129. Sirois, F. (1997). "Epidemic Hysteria: A Dialogue with Robert E. Bartholomew." *Medical Principles and Practice* 6:45-50.
130. Sirois, F. (1994). "Epidemic Hysteria: School Outbreaks 1973-1993." Unpublished manuscript, 25 pages.
131. Sirois (1997). op cit.; Sirois (1994). op cit.
132. Klein, D.F. (1993). "False Suffocation Alarms, Spontaneous Panics, and Related Conditions: An Integrative Hypothesis." *Archives of General Psychiatry* 50:306-317.
133. Golding, J., Smith, R., and Kashner, M. (1991). "Does Somatization Disorder exist in Men? *Archives of General Psychiatry* 48:231-235; American Psychiatric Association (1994). *Diagnostic and Statistical Manual of Mental Disorders*. Fourth edition. Washington, DC,: American Psychiatric Association.
134. American Psychiatric Association (1994). op cit.; Guggenheim, F.G. (1995). "Somatoform Disorders." Pp. 1251-1270. In Harold I. Kaplan and Benjamin J. Sadock (eds.). *Comprehensive Textbook of Psychiatry VI*, Volume 1 (sixth edition). Baltimore, MD: Williams and Wilkins, p. 1253.
135. Struewing J.P., and Gray, G.C. (1990). "Epidemic of Respiratory Complaints Exacerbated by Mass Psychogenic Illness in a Military Recruit Population." *American Journal of Epidemiology* 132:1120-29.
136. Here we exclude as epidemic hysteria, an episode of perceived genital shrinking among 50 male workers at a Thailand tapioca plantation that was recorded by Harrington (See Harrington, J.A. (1982). "Epidemic psychosis." Letter. *British Journal of Psychiatry* 141:98-99). This episode is more appropriately described as a collective delusion. See: Bartholomew, R.E. (1994). "The Social Psychology of 'Epidemic' Koro." *The International Journal of Social Psychiatry* 40:44-60; Bartholomew, R.E. (1998). "The Medicalization of Exotic Deviance: A Sociological Perspective on Epidemic Koro." *Transcultural Psychiatry* 35:5-38.
137. Martin, K.A. (1996). *Puberty, Sexuality, and the Self: Boys and Girls at Adolescence*. New York: Routledge.
138. Parsons T. (1955). "Family Structures and the Socialization of the Child." In T. Parsons and R. Bales (eds.), *Family, Socialization, and the Interaction Process* (35-131). New York: The Free Press; Colligan and Murphy (1979). op cit.
139. Bourguignon, E. (1979). *Psychological Anthropology: An Introduction to Human Nature and Cultural Differences*. New York: Holt, Rinehart and Wilson, pp. 149-150.
140. Wool, C.A., Barsky, A.J. (1994). "Do Women Somatize more than Men? Gender Differences in Somatization." *Psychosomatics* 35(5):445-452.
141. Jenkins, R. (1985). "Sex Differences in Minor Psychiatric Morbidity." *Psychological Medicine Monograph Supplement* 7:1-53.
142. Busfield, J. (1996). *Men Women and Madness: Understanding Gender and Mental Disorder*. London: Macmillan Press Ltd. See p. 30.
143. Kerckhoff, A.C. (1982). "A Social Psychological View of Mass Psychogenic Illness." In M. Colligan, J. Pennebaker and L. Murphy (eds.), *Mass Psychogenic Illness: A Social Psychological Analysis* (199-215). Hillsdale, New Jersey: Lawrence Erlbaum. See p. 211.
144. Colligan and Murphy (1982). op cit., p. 42.
145. Colligan and Murphy (1980). op cit., p. 41.
146. Colligan and Murphy (1980). op cit., p. 41.
147. Kapferer, B. (1983). *A Celebration of Demons: Exorcism and the Aesthetics of Healing in Sri Lanka*. Indiana University Press: Bloomington, Indiana; Bourguignon, E. (1979). *Psychological Anthropology: An Introduction to Human Nature and Cultural Differences*. New York: Holt, Rinehart and Wilson, pp. 149-150; Lewis, I.M. (1971). *Ecstatic Religion*. Harmondsworth, England: Penguin.
148. Siskind, J. (1973). *To Hunt in the Morning*. New York: Oxford.
149. Lewis, I.M. (1971). op cit.
150. Ong, A. (1988). "The Production of Possession: Spirits and the Multinational Corporation in Malaysia." *American Ethnologist 15*:28-42; Ong, A. (1987). *Spirits of Resistance and Capitalist Discipline: Factory Women in Malaysia*. Albany, New York: State University of New York Press.
151. Bartholomew, R.E. (1997). "Epidemic Hysteria: A Dialogue with Francois Sirois." *Medical Principles and Practice* 6:38-44.
152. Kapferer, B. (1983). op cit., p. 96.
153. Of course, it could also be argued that the young are subordinate to the old, and among youth, female participation in MPI episodes is overwhelmingly high.
154. Abdul Rahman, T. (1987). "As I See It... Will the Hysteria Return?" *The New Straits Times* (Malaysia), 6 July.
155. Lee, R.L., and Ackerman, S.E. (1980). "The Sociocultural Dynamics of Mass Hysteria: A Case Study of Social Conflict in West Malaysia." *Psychiatry* 43:78-88. See p. 85.
156. Bourguignon, E. (1978). "Spirit Possession and Altered States of Consciousness: The Evolution of an Inquiry." Pp. 477-515. In G.D. Spindler (ed.), *The Making of Psychological Anthropology*. Berkeley: University of California Press; Bourguignon (1979). op cit., pp. 258-261.
157. Bourguignon, E. (1974). *Culture and the Varieties of Consciousness*. An Addison-Wesley Module in Anthropology 47. Reading, Massachusetts: Addison-Wesley, p. 24.
158. Bourguignon, 1979, op cit., p. 261. Italics in original.
159. Http://www.fmaware.org/fminfo/brochure.htm.
160. Goldenberg, D.L. (1998). "Fibromyalgia and Related Syndromes." In J.H. Klippel and P.A. Dieppe (eds.). *Rheumatology*. Boston: Mosby.
161. Reilly, P.A. (1999). "How Should We Manage Fibromyalgia? *Ann Rheum Dis* 58:325-326.
162. Hazemeijer, I, and Raskerpp, J.J. (2003). "Fibromyalgia and the Therapeutic Domain. A Philosophical Study on the Origins of Fibromyalgia in a Specific Social Setting." *Rheumatology* 42: 507-515. See pp. 508-509.
163. Hazemeijer and Raskerpp, op cit., p. 509.
164. Hazemeijer and Raskerpp, op cit., p. 509.
165. Hazemeijer and Raskerpp, op cit., p. 512.
166. Steinbauer, Friedrich (1979). *Melanesian Cargo Cults* (translated by Max Wohlwill). London: George Prior Publishers, pages 26-29.
167. Steinbauer, op cit., pp. 27-28.
168. Steinbauer, op cit., pp. 27-28.
169. Bulgatz, Joseph. (1992). *Ponzi Schemes, Invaders from Mars & More Extraordinary Popular Delusions and the Madness of Crowds*. New York: Harmony Books, pp. 46-75.
170. Bulgatz, op cit., p. 51.
171. Schwarz, Frederic (2001). "Time Machine September." *American Heritage* 52(6):72.
172. Bulgatz, op cit.
173. Galbraith, John Kenneth (1961). *The Great Crash, 1929*. Boston:

Houghton Mifflin Company, pp. 8-9.
174. Galbraith, op cit., pp. 8-12.
175. "Wary of Weather Balloon." *The Frederick Post,* October 10, 1939.
176. Lagrange, Pierre (1989). "'It Seems Impossible, But There It Is.'" Pp. 26-45. In John Spencer and Hilary Evans (eds.). *Phenomenon: Forty Years of Flying Saucers.* New York: Avon; Arnold, Kenneth (1950). *The Flying Saucer As I Saw It.* Boise, Idaho: The author (pamphlet); Arnold, Kenneth, and Palmer, Ray A. (1952). *The Coming of the Saucers: A Documentary Report on Sky Objects that Have Mystified the World.* Amherst, Wisconsin: The authors; "Idaho 'Flying saucer' sighter dies," *Boise Idaho Statesman,* January 22, 1984; Clark, Jerome (1998). *The UFO Encyclopedia: The Phenomenon from the Beginning, Volume One: A-K* (second edition). Omnigraphics, Incorporated: Detroit, Michigan, pp. 139-143; Gardner, Martin (1988). *The New Age: Notes of a Fringe Watcher.* Buffalo, New York: Prometheus Books. Personal communication from Brad Sparks dated 1 February 2000. Sparks notes that Arnold's total time estimate kept varying from under two minutes to as many as four minutes.
177. "An Interview with Bill Bequette." Comprised of undated personal correspondence between French Sociologist Pierre Lagrange with Bill Bequette, made available to the public by Lagrange in 1998, p. 1. A small portion of Bequette's replies were in the form of face-to-face conversations in July 1988 with Lagrange and Bequette, the latter of whom was living at the time in Tri-Cities, Washington state, where the conversations took place.
178. Press report reprinted courtesy of Hal McCune, News Editor of the *East Oregonian.*
179. Ibid., p. 1.
180. Gardner, Martin (1957). *Fads and Fallacies in the Name of Science.* New York: Dover, p. 56; Story, Ronald Dean (1980). *The Encyclopedia of UFOs.* New York: Doubleday, p. 25; Sachs, Margaret (1980). *The UFO Encyclopedia.* New York: Perigee, pp. 207-208.
181. Ibid., p. 1.
182. This initial description of Arnold as "a United States Forest Service employee," is incorrect. See: "Boise flier maintains he saw 'em," *East Oregonian,* June 26, 1947, p. 1.
183. Strentz, Herbert J. (1970). *A Survey of Press Coverage of Unidentified Flying Objects, 1947-1966.* Doctoral Dissertation. Northwestern University, department of journalism. Brad Sparks (2000). op cit., is skeptical with this statement by Strentz as he provides no supporting details. These suspicions may be well founded. After searching hundreds of newspapers for UFO reports during the time of Arnold's sighting, to date Jan Aldrich has located but a single press report dated June 26, 1947 using the term "flying saucer."
184. Jacobs, David Michael (1975). *The UFO Controversy in America.* Bloomington, Indiana: Indiana University Press, p. 37; Blake, Joseph A. (1979). "UFOlogy: The Intellectual Development and Social Context of the Study of Unidentified Flying Objects." In R. Wallis (Ed.), "On the Margins of Science: The Social Construction of Rejected Knowledge," pp. 315-337. *Sociological Review Monographs 27.*
185. Hackett, Herbert (1948). "The Flying Saucer: A Manufactured Concept." *Sociology and Social Research* 32:869-873; Johnson, DeWayne B. (1950). *Flying Saucers – Fact or Fiction?* Master's thesis, University of California Journalism Department; Bloecher, Ted (1967). *Report on the UFO Wave of 1947.* Washington D.C.: The author.
186. Bullard, Thomas Edward. (1982). *Mysteries in the Eye of the Beholder: UFOs and Their Correlates as a Folkloric Theme Past and Present.* Doctoral dissertation, Indiana University Folklore Department.
187. Bloecher, op cit.
188. "An Interview with Bill Bequette," op. cit., p. 1.
189. "Transcript of KWRC Radio's Interview with Kenneth Arnold at Pendleton, Oregon on June 26, 1947 at 12:00 P.M," p. 2. Located, transcribed and made available to the public by French Sociologist Pierre Lagrange who found the tape while examining the papers of Ray Palmer, who co-authored *The Coming of the Saucers* (Amherst, WI and Boise, ID, The Authors) with Palmer in 1952. Brad Sparks op. cit., 2000 notes that Arnold himself added to the confusion surrounding the term "flying saucer" as on several occasions he used "saucer" shapes in his retellings.
190. "Transcript of KWRC Radio's Interview," op. cit., p. 2.
191. Stevenson, Henry (1995). "Balloon Bombs: Japan to North America." *British Columbia Historical News* 28(3):22-23. Stevenson also recounts the only recorded deaths from a Fugo balloon, which occurred in a tragic incident in Oregon on May 5, 1945, when the Reverend Archie Mitchell of the Christian and Missionary Alliance Church in Bly went for a picnic on Gearhart Mountain with his wife Elyse and five Sunday school students. Elyse and the children suffered horrific injuries and died shortly after approaching an object buried in the snow. The Reverend Mitchell was the only survivor (p. 23).
192. Menzel, Donald Howard, and Taves, Ernest Henry (1977). *The UFO Enigma: The Definitive Explanation of the UFO Phenomenon.* Garden City, New York: Doubleday & Company, p. 7.
193. Sundelius, B. (ed.) (1982). *Foreign Policies of Northern Europe.* Boulder, CO: Westview.
194. It is within this context of long-held Russian invasion fears and post-war political ambiguity involving possible Russian claims on Swedish territory, that plausible rumors began circulating as to potentially hostile Russian intentions. See: "Russians cry 'slander' to rocket-firing charge," *New York Times,* September 4, 1946, p. 10; "The Russians talk about lies and panic," *Svenska Dagbladet,* September 4, 1946, p. 3; "Sic transit," *Ny Dag,* August 6, 1946; "Sweden used as a shooting range," *Halsingborgs Dagblad,* July 26, 1946; "Rocket, meteor or phantom?" *Aftonbladet,* August 7, 1946; *Smalands Folkblad,* July 27, 1946; "The ghost bomb a serious threat. 'Monster in miniature for the next war,'" *Svenska Dagbladet,* August 7, 1946, p. 7; Bartholomew, Robert Emerson (1993). "Redefining Epidemic Hysteria: An Example from Sweden." *Acta Psychiatrica Scandinavia* 88:178-182; Liljegren, Anders, and Svahn, Clas (1989). "Ghost Rockets and Phantom Aircraft." Pp. 53-60. In John Spencer and Hilary Evans (eds.). *Phenomenon: Forty Years of Flying Saucers.* New York: Avon.
195. Bullard (1982). *op. cit.,* p. 259.
196. Gallup, George (1947). "Nine out of Ten Heard of Flying Saucers." Public Opinion News Service, Princeton, N.J., August 15, 1947.
197. Gross, Loren Eugene (1982). *UFOs: A History Volume 1 July 1947-December 1948.* Scotia, NY: Arcturus Books, p. 30.
198. Maccabee, Bruce Sargent (1977). "UFO Related Information from FBI file: Part 1." *The UFO Investigator* (November), official publication of the now defunct National Investigations Committee on Aerial Phenomena, p. 3; Gross, L. (1982). op. cit., p. 16.
199. Gross, L. (1982). op. cit., p. 37.
200. Arnold, K., and Palmer, R. (1952). op. cit., pp. 188-189; Gross, L. (1982). op. cit., p. 29.
201. Declassified formerly top secret United States Air Force Air Intelligence Report produced for the Directorate of Intelligence in Washington, D.C. on April 28, 1949, entitled, "Analysis of Flying Object Incidents in the U.S., Summary and Conclusions," NO. 100-203-79, CY. NO. 102 OF 103, p. 2. This document was made available to the public by Jan Aldrich.

202. Davidson, Keay. (1997). "Flying Saucer Saga," *San Francisco Examiner Magazine*, June 1, 1997, pp. 12-13.
203. Ibid., p. 13.
204. Letter from Keay Davidson to Robert Bartholomew dated 24 January, 2000; Davidson, Keay. (1999). *Carl Sagan: A Life*. New York: John Wiley & Sons, p. 440.
205. Letter from Keay Davidson to Robert Bartholomew dated 24 January, 2000.
206. Whitehead, Lampert Join 'Disc List,'" *Idaho Daily Statesman*, July 3, 1947, p. 1.
207. Davidson, Keay (1997). op cit., p. 13.
208. For a more detailed description of the origin of the term "flying saucer," see, Bartholomew, Robert E. (2000). "From Airships to Flying Saucers: Oregon's Place in the Evolution of UFO Lore." *Oregon Historical Quarterly* 101(2):192-213.
209. Frankel, Stephen. (1976). "Mass Hysteria in the New Guinea Highlands: A Telefomin Outbreak and its Relationship to other New Guinea Hysterical Reactions." *Oceania* 47:105-133. See pp. 107-108.
210. Frankel, op cit., p. 117.
211. Frankel, op cit., pp. 111-112.
212. Frankel, op cit., p. 112.
213. Frankel, op cit., p. 112.
214. Frankel, op cit., p. 113.
215. Frankel, op cit., p. 115.
216. Frankel, op cit., p. 120.
217. Frankel, op cit., p. 121.
218. Frankel, op cit.
219. Frankel, op cit., p. 112.
220. Prime, Mary (1959). "Frankie Avalon's Telephone Call Throws Camp into Panic." *The Zainesville Signal* (Ohio), August 19, 1959, p. 6A.
221. The primary sources for this entry are: Axelrod, Alan (1997). *The International Encyclopedia of Secret Societies and Fraternal Orders*. New York: Facts on File 1997; Carnes, Mark C. (1989). *Secret Ritual and Manhood in Victorian America*. New Haven, CT: Yale University Press.
222. Carnes, op cit., p. 29.
223. Quoted in Axelrod (1997). op cit., p. 210.
224. Pike quoted in Carnes, op cit., p. 75.
225. Carnes, op cit., p. 61.
226. Carnes, op cit., p. 65.
227. Carnes, op cit., p. 125.
228. Carnes, op cit., p. 124.
229. Carnes, op cit., p. 4.
230. Schlesinger, Arthur M. "Biography of a Nation of Joiners." *American Historical Review* 50 (October 1844).
231. Lea, Henry Charles (1957). *Materials Toward a History of Witchcraft*. New York: Yoseloff, volume 3, p. 1045, drawing on Horst Zauberbibliothek.
232. Elkins, G. E., Gamino, L. A., and Rynearson, R. R. (1988). "Mass Psychogenic Illness, Trance States and Suggestion." *American Journal of Clinical Hypnosis* 30:267-275.
233. Elkins et al., op cit., p. 447.
234. Elkins et al., op cit., p. 448.
235. Elkins et al., op cit., p. 448.

GARROTTING SCARES

London: 1856 and 1862

Garrotting came into practice in the early fifties, and was essentially a winter crime, favoured by the secrecy and the isolation of a London fog. The method is well known, and needs no detailed description. The thief approaches his victim from behind, and suddenly throws his arm round his neck, tightening the pressure even to suffocating point, when, strangulation being near, outcry is impossible. Other thieves – one or more – then turn out the pockets of the helpless prisoner.[1]

Street robbery was nothing new, of course, but garrotting was street robbery with a scary difference. Magazines of the day described the method as an attack from behind, bringing the arm under the victim's throat across the adam's apple, cutting off the air till the victim was unconscious, rendering him powerless to resist and leaving him on the ground writhing in agony, "with tongue protruding and eyes starting from their sockets."[2]

Crime statistics are notoriously difficult to establish, partly because of uncertain definition, partly because crimes reported are not necessarily equivalent to crimes committed. However, after studying the statistics, social historian R. Sindall concluded not only that the streets of Victorian London were substantially safer than those of neo-Elizabethan London, but also that they did not become significantly more dangerous during the period of the garrotting scares. In other words, it was the perception of danger, not the danger itself, which caused the panic. In November 1856 the London *Times* editorialized that there existed parts of London "inhabited by a numerous and respectable population" where a man cannot walk "without imminent danger of being throttled, robbed, and if not actually murdered, at least kicked and pommelled within an inch of his life."[3] That winter that newspaper published no less than seven editorials and 31 letters on the subject, many calling for extreme legal action such as the reinstatement of hanging for the offence. The judges responded to the popular feeling, and sentences became heavier: in November 1856 two garrotters were sentenced to life.

The garrotting panics first escalated in 1856, then subsided in the following spring and during 1857 only to burst out anew in July 1862. This second wave of panic was triggered by an attack on a Member of Parliament, Mr. Pilkington, who was returning along Pall Mall, one of the most respectable streets of

A man frightened by his own shadow during a garrotting (mugging) scare. (Punch, January 1863)

London, at 1 a.m. after a late sitting of that famously hard-working body. (The attack achieved literary fame when Trollope borrowed it for his political novel Phineas Finn.) Seemingly, the number of garrotting assaults rapidly increased, but this may simply have been due to press coverage and/or an increase in police activity in response to public demand.

Unlike the exploits of the Hammersmith Ghost and Springheel Jack, the garrotters were never thought to be anything but real flesh-and-blood criminals. In 1862, 27 offenders of this class were arraigned at the same time at the Central Criminal Court. Very heavy sentences were imposed on all, and the crime was scotched for a time, though not entirely eliminated. Judges had the power to impose flogging, and this acted as a powerful deterrent, but not so powerful as to stop garrotting altogether. In 1895-6, a gang led by a man named Smith, known as "the countryman," carried out some fifty attacks in two months in the Borough of Southwark. He eventually shot himself when cornered by the police after a robbery.

Although crime historian Major Arthur Griffiths describes garrotting as "a winter crime" performed under cover of darkness or fog, many attacks took place in broad daylight. "One gentleman was garrotted in the afternoon near Paternoster Row, another in Holborn, a third in Cockspur Street," three busy streets with plenty of passers-by. "A young lady of 15 was attacked in Westbourne Crescent about 4 pm. While she was half-throttled the thieves tore off her necklace and dragged the pendants from her ears. They had meant to cut off her hair, which was long and fine, and worth a considerable sum, but just then the ruffians were frightened from their prey." Though the garrotters were a genuine menace, the alarm they aroused in the minds of Londoners was out of all proportion to the real danger. Anti-garrotting devices were on sale to protect the victim and injure the attacker, including spiked collars such as are worn by some dogs.

One feature of the scares was that they were perceived as essentially an attack on the middle class. It is not surprising that the satirical journal *Punch*, quintessentially a middle-class publication, dedicated much of its coverage to the garrotting menace during this period, for example making absurd suggestions for protective devices. Another noteworthy aspect is that though the garrotting scare was felt to be peculiar to London, in fact the pedestrian in either Liverpool or Manchester was in relatively much greater danger. But the *Daily News* was referring to London when it spoke of "a lair of footpads and assassins by night."

By the 1860s, the popular press was greatly more accessible to the general public than it had been in the time of the London Monster or Springheel Jack, and the garrotting scare not only spread by word of mouth but also was fueled by the newspaper coverage. Significantly, though the image of the garrotter became a symbol of popular terror, no one individual or group was singled out, with the consequence that the menace remained shadowy and undefined. This was because, though a number of attacks undoubtedly took place, the panic was disproportionate to the reality, inflated by exaggerated press reports.

GENITAL SHRINKING SCARES[4]

Asia: 1865 and ongoing

Koro is the term used by the medical and psychiatric communities to describe a rare condition whereby a subject is suffering from a delusion that his or her genitals are shrinking. Such cases typically persist for years or decades and are almost universally described as an abnormality. Less than one hundred cases have been recorded in the scientific literature, though with increasing frequency in recent years. This entry will focus on even rarer episodes of "epidemic" *koro*, whereby symptoms and perceptions quickly spread through a particular region, and attempt to answer the question: Should these collective episodes be viewed a mass psychosis or social delusion?

Koro: A Brief History

Koro is a Malay word that has gained acceptance as standard psychiatric nomenclature to describe cases of perceived genitalia shrinkage or retraction and accompanying panic. Of uncertain derivation, it may have arisen from the Malay word *keruk*, "to shrink,"[5] or the Malayo-Indonesian words for "tortoise," *kura*, *kura-kura*, *kuro*. In Malaysia and Indonesia, the penis, especially the glans, is commonly referred to as a tortoise head. "The fact that a tortoise can withdraw its head with its wrinkled neck under its shell literally into its body, suggested...the mechanism...in '*Koro*' ('kura') and gave it its name."[6] While the condition of genital retraction is described in ancient Chinese medical texts, *koro* first entered the Western scientific literature with a report by Dutch physician J.C. Blonk in 1895, involving a native healer among the non-Chinese Macassaran peoples of southern Celebes in the Netherlands Indies (now Sulawesi, Indonesia).[7]

While the origin and nature of *koro* continues to be debated within transcultural psychiatry, there is a consensus that both individual and epidemic forms of this condition represent a mental disorder. *Koro* is typically defined as a culture-specific syndrome involving delusions of genitalia shrinkage, acute anxiety, psychosomatic complaints, and a conviction in some subjects that death will occur once the genitalia fully retract. The condition is primarily confined to parts of Asia where it has extensive cultural traditions and related beliefs (southern China, Malaysia, Indonesia, Thailand, India), and is most commonly reported among Chinese descendants in Southeast Asia and southern China. There are references to *koro* in Mandarin (*suoyang*), Cantonese (*sookyong*), parts of Mainland China (*shook yang, shook yong, suk-yong, so in tchen*), and among the Buginese (*lasa koro*) in southern Sulawesi. All of these words translate into "shrinking penis." Among the Tagabawa Bagobo peoples of south-central Mindanao, the Philippines, it is termed *lannuk e laso* (approximate translation being "retracting penis"). In sections of northeast India, it is referred to as *jinjinia* ("tingling") or *jhinjhini* ("tingling disease"), *disco* near Calcutta (a generic word for any type of novelty), and *kattao* ("cut off") among the Northern Bengalese. In Thailand the term is *Rok Joo*.[8]

During the past four decades, sporadic individual cases have been reported in the psychiatric literature with increasing frequency across a disperse cultural and geographical spectrum, among subjects of diverse ethnic backgrounds: an Israeli Jew[9] and Israeli Jewish immigrants from Yemen and Soviet Georgia;[10] Americans;[11] and an American of Greek heritage;[12] Canadians of Anglo-Saxon[13] and French descent;[14] subjects from the Sudan,[15] South Africa;[16] France,[17] Nigeria,[18] Italy,[19] Great Britain,[20] a British-born citizen of West Indian parentage,[21] and a Greek Cypriot British immigrant.[22]

The earliest known reference to a condition involving the shrinking or retraction of human genitalia appeared in the Chinese medical book *Huangdi Neiching*, meaning *Yellow Emperor's Classic of Internal Medicine* (circa 200 to 300 B.P.), describing *suo-yang*, a fatal condition of male genital retraction into the abdomen.[23] Many subsequent Chinese medical texts referred to this condition as *shook yin*, a disease affecting male *and* female genitalia. As recently as 1967, some Chinese medical practitioners considered it to be an actual disease.[24]

The contemporary psychiatric consensus typifies *koro* as an hysterical variant of universal categories of human sexual dysfunction, precipitated by culture-specific *koro*-related folk beliefs and/or Freudian concepts of castration anxiety. It has been variously classified as an obsessive-compulsive disorder,[25] pathological castration fear,[26] psychosexual disorder,[27] and acute hysterical panic syndrome.[28] Hong Kong psychiatrist Pow Meng Yap[29] typified his patients as young, poorly educated men with immature dependent personalities lacking in sexual confidence. Berrois and Morley suggested the presence of a unitary psychiatric disorder which varies according to social and cultural context, basing their argument on the presence of *koro*-like symptoms in 15 non-Chinese subjects who hailed from disperse geographical locations and claimed no prior knowledge of *koro*-related folk beliefs.[30] Ronald Simons also argues for a universal biological etiology ("genital retraction taxon").[31]

Canadian psychiatrist Raymond Prince contends that a pan-human fear of castration and impotence in males are the root stimulus for both individual and "epidemic" *koro*, citing as supporting evidence, numerous examples of castration themes across history and cultures, especially involving female castigators.[32] While this does not explain why females also experience *koro*, Prince notes that male episodes are more serious and common, and he is unable to locate a single female case description.[33] However, the neglect of female cases may be an artifact of the historically male-dominated medical profession. For instance, of the cases investigated by Sachdev and Shukla in India, nearly as many females as males were affected.[34] A supporting factor may involve prohibitions in some societies with *koro* traditions, such as parts of Indonesia, where males are not allowed to prevent the shrinking by holding the vulva or nipples.[35] Further, the male genitals appear to be more physiologically plastic than female breasts, nipples, or vulva. The male testicles and penis are vital for reproduction (the penis may not be essential in the case of *in vitro* fertilization), while the female breast and nipples are not. Of the female breasts, nipples, or vulva, the latter, more vital organ, shows the least physiological plasticity.

"Epidemic" *Koro*: China

Koro "epidemics" have been reported in India, Thailand, China, and Singapore. More than 2,000 inhabitants in a remote area of Guangdong, China, were affected by *koro* between November 1984, and May 1985. University of Hawaii psychiatrist Wen Shing Tseng and his fellow researchers note the prevalence of a popular folk belief within the region which was related to "evil-induced genital retraction."[36] Men within the region are socialized to practice restraint in matters of sexual desire and activity, as excessive semen discharge is believed to weaken physical and mental health, even inducing death. Further, many residents believe that certain spirits of the dead, especially female fox maidens, wander in search of penises that will give them powers. In fact, each of the 232 "victims" surveyed by Tseng were convinced that an evil female fox spirit could cause *suoyang*, and 76 percent had witnessed "victims" being "rescued."[37] Most of these cases occurred at night following a chilly sensation, which would precipitate a feeling of penile shrinkage. "Thinking this to be a fatal sign and believing that they were affected by an evil ghost, they became panic stricken and tried to pull at their penises, while, at the same time, shouting for help."[38]

The following description was given by an 18-year-old agriculture student on Leizhou Peninsula, and happened near the end of a major penis-shrinking scare in 1984-85.[39] "I woke up at midnight and felt sore and numb in my genitals. I felt ... [my penis] was shrinking, disappearing. I yelled for help, my family and neighbours came and held my penis. They covered me with a fish net and beat me with branches of a peach tree ... The peach tree branches are the best to drive out ghosts or devils. They said they'd catch the ghost in the net. They were also beating drums and setting off firecrackers. ...They had to repeat the procedure until I was well again, until the ghost was killed by the beating." It is noteworthy that during this episode, several children reported shrinkage of their tongue, nose, and ears, reflecting the prevalent ancient Chinese belief that any male (*yang*) organs can shrink or retract.[40]

A separate "epidemic" in 1987 affected at least 300 residents in the vicinity of Haikang Town on the Leizhou Peninsula of Guangdong Province.[41] *Koro* is endemic in parts of southern China, with sporadic annual reports, occasional case clusters, and confirmed epidemics in 1865, 1948, 1955, 1966, and 1974, all of which involved at least several hundred residents.[42] While recognizing the importance of rumors and traditional beliefs in precipitating episodes, Tseng and his colleagues consider epidemics in southern China to be a psychiatric disorder ("genital retraction panic disorder") that primarily affects susceptible individuals such as the poorly educated and those possessing below normal intellectual endowment who are experiencing social crisis or tension.[43]

J. Legendre reports on a *koro* episode affecting about twenty males in a school at Szechwan, China. The "outbreak" occurred in 1908, persisted for several days, and is the earliest known *koro* episode for which descriptions of events are available.[44] Legendre described the incident while he was in Se-tchouan (Szechwan) province. The events began during "the 10th moon of the 32nd year of Quang-Sou" (circa 1908), when he heard rumors that numerous pupils attending the schools of la Ville Jaune (Yellow City) were reported to have been simultaneously afflicted with *so in tchen*. This "illness" involved perceptions that the penis was shrivelling, followed by a sudden shrinkage and disappearance into the abdominal cavity. It was reported that death would ensue if immediate treatment could not induce a re-emergence of the organ. Intrigued by these stories, Legendre visited the affected schools, talked with several administrators, and managed to ascertain that the episode began one evening and affected a single pupil who noticed "that his penis was no longer as developed as he had known it to be." The student "immediately diagnosed 'so in tchen,' so well known and dreaded in his country, and without hesitation" he applied "methodical tractions" to his penis. In the course of the same evening and the following day, approximately 20 more cases appeared in male students attending the schools. They were all treated with tractions placed on the penis, and all recovered within a few days.[45]

Legendre was able to locate and interview the final student stricken, "at that time out of danger but not completely restored and still staying indoors." The "affliction" began four days earlier when he apparently felt "light pains" in his genital area, persisting for several hours. The pupil stated that his penis had shrunk to between 3 and 4 centimetres. Legendre examined the subject, noting that his physical condition was unremarkable, having a healthy tongue, normal temperature, and a soft and painless stomach. His genitals appeared to be entirely normal in terms of size and health. Legendre speculated that his subject most likely experienced "light alimentary intoxication expressed in insignificant abdominal symptoms," and it was possible that "fairly notable shrinkage" may have occurred. He attributes the cause of the "imaginary illness" to Chinese superstition. "The scared imagination of Celestial youths, inheritors of twenty centuries of superstition, and legatees from long ancestry to an exclusively literary culture, had not hesitated to attribute this syndrome to the rank of a feared, morbid entity."[46]

In a concluding commentary, Legendre states his conviction that *so in tchen* and *koro* are the same "imaginary illness." He also describes it as an "exotic pathology" and "Asian psychosis," which occurs both individually and in collectives. As for its cause, he speculates that it is related to the Chinese fear of impotence and not being able to produce a male descendant to continue their family heritage and to be able to conduct family religious rituals that are believed to ensure the happiness of their deceased ancestors' souls in the afterlife. Legendre observed that "If I did not see before my very eyes the notes that I took then, I would think I had dreamt it, the adventure of these young people was so entertaining and improbable."

Based on traditional Chinese humoral medical theories, it is widely believed that *koro*- related conditions result from an imbalance of the *yin* (female) and *yang* (male) forces. *Koro* occurs when the *yin* dominates the *yang*, whereby any protruding male or female body parts are considered to be *yang* (i.e., penis, breasts, nipples, tongue, nose, hands, feet, ears), and can potentially shrink or retract.[47] Hence, curative or prophylatic measures include the application or consumption of *yang* elements, such as ginger, powdered black pepper, liquor, or red pepper jam, or tying the penis with a yam stem.[48] There also appears to be a second, separate belief system that engenders *koro* epidemics in Hainan Island, China, involving ghosts and fox spirits who steal penises.[49]

Thailand

Another *koro* episode transpired in northeast Thailand between November and December 1976, affecting an estimated two thousand, primarily rural Thai residents in the border provinces of Maha Sarakhan, Nakhon, Nong Khai, Thani, and Udon. Besides bisexual genitalia shrinkage, symptoms included panic, anxiety, dizziness, diarrhoea, discomfort during urination, nausea, headaches, facial numbness, and abdominal pain. Some patients temporarily lost consciousness, and men were fearful of imminent death.[50] Most sufferers "recovered within one day and all within one week."[51]

The episode apparently began at a technical college in Udon Thani Province with rumors that Vietnamese immigrants had deliberately contaminated food and cigarettes with a *koro*-inducing powder. It is significant that during this period, the minority population of as many as sixty-thousand Vietnamese immigrants living in northeastern Thailand were ostracized for their economic power and clannish behavior. In the month prior to the episode, anti-Vietnamese sentiments in the region were strong with allegations by Thailand's Interior Minister that there was "solid evidence" of a plot whereby "Vietnamese refugees would incite rioting in northeast Thailand, providing Vietnam with an excuse to invade" on February 15. As the episode continued, the poisoning rumors became self-fulfilling as numerous Thai citizens recalled that previously consumed food and cigarettes recently purchased from Vietnamese establishments had an unusual smell and taste. However, an analysis of suspected sources by the Government Medical Science Department "detected no foreign substance that could possibly cause sexual impotence or contraction of the male sex organ."[52]

The episode appears clearly related to the worldview of the Thai population that was almost exclusively affected. Thailand is situated in the vicinity of several Southeast Asian countries with *koro* traditions. It appears that *koro* rumors, combined with pre-existing awareness of the "disease," served to foster and legitimize its plausible existence. For instance, 94 percent of "victims" studied "were convinced that they had been poisoned."[53] Further, contradictory statements issued by authority figures in the press undermined the negative Government analysis of alleged tainted substances. Jilek and Jilek-Aall note that Thai newspapers cited security officials as attributing the tainting substances believed responsible for precipitating the *koro* in food to a mixture of vegetable sources undetectable by medical devices.[54]

India

Another epidemic of *koro* occurred in the Assam, Meghalya, and Bengal regions of India during the summer and fall of 1982. Cases apparently numbered in the thousands, as males claimed penile shrinkage while females perceived their breasts were getting smaller. The panic reached such proportions that medical personnel toured the region, reassuring those affected with loud speakers.[55] Parents typically tied string to their sons' penises to reduce or stop retraction, a practice that occasionally produced penile ulcers. While there was evidence of pre-existing *koro*-related beliefs among some residents, the episode spread across various religious and ethnic groups, social castes and geographical areas via rumors. Based on psychiatric interviews with 30 "victims" (17 male, 13 female), while Sachdev and Shukla were unable to identify obvious signs of psychological disturbance, they support Rin's psychoanalytical interpretation involving castration anxiety, oral deprivation, and cultural conditioning.[56]

Singapore

Between October and November 1967, a major genital-shrinking scare swept across the tiny Southeast Asian island nation of Singapore as clinics and hospitals were inundated by nervous citizens who were convinced that their penises were growing smaller and would eventually disappear, at which time, many believed that they would die. Frantic "victims" used string, rubber bands, clamps, and even clothespins in a desperate effort to prevent further perceived retraction. Occasionally such actions resulted in serious damage to the penis. Friends and relatives often held the penis in relays until help was obtained from medical doctors or native healers. At the height of the "epidemic," Singapore Hospital's outdoor clinic treated nearly 75 cases each day. The episode coincided with rumors in the Singaporean press that eating pork vaccinated for swine fever before slaughter could cause genitalia shrinkage. One sensational report even claimed that a pig had died after receiving an inoculation and experiencing penile retraction.[57] After several weeks, the scare subsided when authorities from the Singapore Medical Association and Health Ministry conducted press conferences to reassure the public that the threat was baseless and imaginary.

C.L. Mun describes two characteristic cases. The first involved a 16-year-old boy who burst into the clinic with his parents, shouting for a doctor to help him quickly as "he had 'Shook Yong.' The boy looked frightened and pale and he was pulling hard on his penis to prevent the organ from disappearing into his abdomen. The doctor explained and reassured both parents and patient. A tablet of 10 mg. of chlordiazepoxide was given at once and he was sent home with two days' supply of chlordiazepoxide. There was no recurrence. The boy had heard about *Koro* in school. That morning he took 'Pow,' which contained pork, for breakfast. Then he went to pass urine and noticed his penis shrunk at the end of micturition. Frightened, he quickly grasped the organ and rushed to his parents shouting for help."[58] In a separate episode, a mother hurried into the clinic clutching the penis of her four-month-old baby and asking the physician "to treat her child quickly because he had *Koro*. The child had not been well for two days with cold and a little diarrhoea. The mother was changing his napkin and washing his perineum when the child had colic and screamed. The mother saw the penis getting smaller and the child screamed and [she] thought he had *Koro*. She had previously heard the rumors. The mother was first reassured, and the baby's cold and diarrhea treated. The child was all right after that."[59]

It is noteworthy that the Republic of Singapore and surrounding nations have lengthy traditions of *koro* folk beliefs. Several tropical disease textbooks mention previous episodes in nearby West Borneo and Celebes. Chinese medical books from the nineteenth century describe *koro* as a "disease." Pao Sian-Ow's treatise, *New Collection of Remedies of Value*, which was published in 1834, states authoritatively that *koro* is a physiological condition that occurs when "the penis retracts into the abdomen. If treatment is not instituted at once and effective, the case [patient] will die. The disease is due to the invasion of cold vapors and the treatment is to employ the 'heaty' drugs."[60] At the time of the initial rumors and inaccurate press reports that contaminated pork was causing *koro*, its reality was institutionalized and legitimated within the Singaporean society to the extent that some Chinese Singaporean physicians believed that a physical disease called *koro* actually existed and could cause shrinkage of one's genitalia.[61]

"Epidemic" *Koro* As Psychological Disturbance

Due to the large number of people affected and abrupt onset, biological explanations have been excluded in favor of psychological models that seek to identify unresolved conflicts and abnormal personality traits. Gwee and colleagues consider epidemic *koro* to be a culture-bound panic syndrome.[62] Harrington interprets them as a form of "epidemic psychosis" paralleling the European DANCING MANIAS, TARANTISM, and contemporary episodes of mass psychogenic illness.[63] Ronald Simons argues that, as in individual cases, mass episodes also reflect the existence of a universal genital retraction syndrome.[64]

Indian Psychiatrist Arabinda N. Chowdhury is the most prominent, vigorous advocate for *koro* epidemics representing a psychological abnormality. Chowdhury[65] studied the penile length perceptions of 40 single male *koro* subjects who were affected during the 1982 episode involving thousands in North Bengal, India. Since two years after the episode, most "victims" perceived themselves to possess shorter penises than control subjects, it was concluded that they were vulnerable to "outbreaks" as they suffered from "dysmorphic penis image perception." Chowdhury views this as an abnormal psychiatric condition akin to other body image disorders such as anorexia and bulimia, where victims who are undernourished perceive themselves as obese.[66] However, these drawings were made retrospective to the epidemics and may have reflected greater genital anxiety and concern (vis-à-vis controls) as a result of their previous traumatic *koro* experiences. Further, "body dysmorphic disorder" typically begins in adolescence, does not occur abruptly in epidemic form, and persists for years with diagnoses marked by denial and resistance. Collective *koro* involves different accompanying features (extreme anxiety, fear of dying), desire for immediate treatment, and complete recovery within a few minutes, hours, or days following reassurance.[67] For example, in an Indian epidemic, the majority of cases lasted between 15 and 60 minutes,[68] while in China, 60 percent of the subjects surveyed experienced symptoms from 20 to 60 minutes.[69] In all collective episodes, subjects may experience occasional relapses, but symptoms always dissipate within a few days, although genital-related anxiety may endure.

Individual *koro* reports are rare even in countries with *koro*-related folk beliefs, with Yap locating 19 cases in Hong Kong during 15 years;[70] Gwee encountering three Singaporian subjects;[71] and Rin treating two Taiwanese patients.[72] (There have also been sporadic cases from Guangdong, China.)[73] Individual cases are associated with physiological and psychiatric origins that, in rare instances, may be exacerbated by folk beliefs. Of less than 100 individual case reports in the scientific literature, most unambiguously exhibited major psychiatric pathologies (e.g., schizophrenia, affective disorder) associated with sexual inadequacies or conflicts, occasionally coinciding with organic disease[11] or drug ingestion. For instance, while *koro* has been associated with phimosis,[74] urogenital system pathology,[75] prostate removal,[76] brain tumors,[77] and stroke,[78] these patients typically have identifiable affective disorders accompanying their organic disturbances. Wen Shing Tseng notes that most of Berrois and Morley's subjects "manifested incomplete symptoms (as a *koro* case is defined). Such *koro*-like states, as secondary symptoms, are usually observed as a part of the primary psychiatric condition, such as affective disorder or psychosis."[79] For instance, in most individual cases in settings with no prior knowledge of the phenomenon, a belief that the penis will fully retract with fatal consequences is not reported.

In 1992, Tseng conducted detailed psychometric testing of 214 epidemic *koro* victims in southern China (41 female), with a control group, and third group of 56 patients presenting with minor psychiatric conditions.[80] Surprisingly, the controls tested highest for levels of problems associated with work, school, and their interpersonal lives. The only aberrant findings were elevated phobic and anxiety levels, but no difference with controls on sub-scales related to neurasthenia, hypochondriasis, and dissociation, suggesting that *koro* should not be classified as a depersonalization condition or dissociative disorder, while the similarity with controls for symptoms of neurasthenia or hypochondriasis argue against its placement as a somatoform disorder.[81] While on the basis of these findings, Kirmayer concludes that *koro* appears as a condition evoked by severe anxiety that is exacerbated by folk beliefs and social stresses, he also describes *koro* as a pathogenic syndrome related to castration anxiety.[82]

"Epidemic" *Koro* As A Normal Response

American Sociologist Robert Bartholomew and Canadian husband and wife psychiatric team Wolfgang Jilek and Louise Jilek-Aall of the University of British Columbia, argue that while isolated, individual cases reflect mental disturbance, "epidemics" involve normal populations who are conforming to social and cultural norms. They point out that all subjects experiencing collective episodes involve populations with extensive *koro*-related traditions or beliefs, and that episodes are best explained as collective social delusions precipitated by group dynamics and cultural, physiological, and cognitive factors.

It is crucial to emphasize that during each incident of mass *koro*, there was unambiguous evidence of *koro*-related cultural traditions exacerbated by folk beliefs related to sexual potency, semen loss, etc., that facilitated the episode and made the rumors of genitalia shrinkage (or other *yang* organs) plausible. The 1967 Singapore outbreak occurred amid widespread rumors that the consumption of pork, vaccinated for swine fever prior to slaughter, could precipitate genitalia shrinkage. The panic ended abruptly after authority figures from the Singapore Medical Association and Health Ministry held public news conferences to dispel fears. At the time of the initial *koro* rumors, its existence was legitimated within Singaporean society to the extent that some Chinese Singaporean physicians believed that a physical disease called *koro* actually existed and could cause genital shrinkage.[83] In arguing for the existence of a pan-human castration anxiety among males, Prince notes that only 25% of the Singaporean victims (95% male) had previous knowledge of *koro*-like conditions.[84] However, as the literature on social delusions demonstrates, rumors need only be plausible to be cogent and initiate reality-testing to confirm or deny their existence. Many social delusions begin with false social beliefs that are held by a relatively small portion of the population and an absence of any cultural traditions related to these convictions, such as episodes of phantom gassers,[85] slashers,[86] Martians,[87] windscreen pitting,[88] and monsters.[89] Other episodes begin with cultural traditions held by a few individuals and become increasingly plausible to the remaining population in the wake of rumors, misperceptions, and media reports. Examples include waves of claims and public discourse surrounding widespread sightings of legendary creatures such as Sasquatch,[90] extinct animals like the Tasmanian "tiger,"[91] or supernatural beings such as fairies.[92]

By considering the social and cultural context of "epidemic" *koro* participants *and* those diagnosing the "disorder," Bartholomew argues that the psychiatric designation of participants as psychologically aberrant is pejorative and Eurocentric, imposing Western standards of normality, reality, and rationality. Such pathological interpretations reflect the medicalization of sexual variance, and unlike rare, sporadic individual *koro* cases without related social or cultural beliefs, no consistent pattern of psychological disturbance has been identified. While Dr. Chowdhury typically utilizes Western-based personality inventories and profiles to demonstrate that subjects are sexually maladjusted, the results of these findings are ambiguous. For instance, in examining the behavioral profiles of 162 *koro* subjects with 160 controls (all Indian males), it was found that those experiencing epidemic *koro* had a greater incidence of aberrant sexual behavior, conflicts, and guilt. However, "aberrant" can also be viewed as creative, inventive, expressive, intense, or different. These subjects may have been more sexually conscious. Further, sexual "difficulties" per se do not necessarily validate the existence of a psychosexual disturbance, as historically such arbitrary labels have been couched in "neutral" medical terminology, when in fact, they were unsubstantiated assumptions reflecting prevailing social and cultural mores (e.g., masturbation, homosexuality, premarital intercourse). As psychiatrist Thomas Szasz remarks, the acceptance of terms such as "sexual disorder," "pathology" or "dysfunction," assists in their mythological conceptualization. "Our language informs and even defines our perceptions. When we talk about sexual dysfunctions the implication is that the labels for such alleged disorders name abnormal sexual conditions that exist – in the same sense in which, say, [colon cancer]...exists. This is simply not true."[93]

The characteristic features of epidemic *koro* unambiguously meet the standard social science criteria for the constitution of a collective social delusion, with participants experiencing the cognitive consequences of deviant perceptual sets and the psychosomatic consequences of sexual social realities that become self-fulfilling and real in their consequences. While some contemporary behavior models of social delusions attribute episodes to irrationality and/or societal "strains" (social disorganizational theories), pathological explanations of collective behavior are thoroughly discredited.[94] Yet, because *koro*-related folk beliefs are not plausible social realities among mainstream Western-biased psychiatric evaluators, images of psychological disturbance continue to be the predominant explanatory models.

It is important to make a clear distinction between the medical/psychiatric use of the word delusion as a persistent pathological belief associated with a psychotic condition, as opposed to its loose usage to denote the collective sharing of a temporary false belief. Throughout this entry, the term "social delusion" refers to the nonpathological mass adherence to a false belief. This terminology is consistent with their common sociological usage. The issue is often confusing and requires clarification as many social scientists continue to loosely use such terms as epidemic hysteria, mass psychopathology, and collective mental disorder interchangeably with social delusions.

Genital-Shrinking Scares As A Social Delusion

Virtually all known "victims" of collective *koro* return to a normal state of health within hours or days after being convinced the "illness" is over or never existed. Cases share a similar range of symptoms, including anxiety, sweating, nausea, headache, transient pain, pale skin, palpitations, blurred vision, faintness, paraesthesia, insomnia, and the *koro*-related "delusionary" conviction. The appearance of these symptoms per se, is not necessarily indicative of psychopathology, as they reflect the spectrum of normal physiological responses to extreme anxiety. The inclusion of the "delusionary" conviction and perception within the collective *koro* symptom pattern is consistent with perceptual psychology research that supports the predisposition of observers to interpret information patterns in a particular manner that is significantly influenced by their mental set at the time. Studies on the fallibility of human perception and conformity dynamics are apposite.[95] The accuracy of eyewitness testimony is notoriously unreliable, remarkably subject to error, and preconditioned by mental outlook.[96] The selective and organizational nature of perception is based more on inference than reality, allowing for interpretations that often differ substantially from reality. Hence, "inference can perform the work of perception by filling in missing information in instances where perception is either inefficient or inadequate."[97] The variance of interpretations from objective reality is especially pronounced involving the perception of ambiguous stimuli or conflicting information patterns within a group setting, which will result in members developing an increased need to define the situation, depending less on their own judgment for reality validation and more on the judgment of others. Since individuals are more dependent upon others and less on themselves in their construction of social reality, an opinion, attitude, or conviction "is 'correct,' 'valid,' and 'proper' to the extent that it is anchored in a group of people with similar beliefs, opinions and attitudes."[98] Individuals continually engage in reality testing by comparing their perceptions with those of others around them.

What constitutes reality for any individual or group is socially constructed,[99] a process that assists in maintaining social continuity and meaning.[20] Since an integral part of ordering reality is the forming of perceptual sets that we view the world through, culture is a constellation of perceptual sets through which order and meaning are maintained.[100] Similarly, the possibility that certain peoples could erroneously believe their genitalia to be shrinking, or disappearing altogether, has typically received deviant, abnormal, or psychopathological evaluations by Western-trained scientists who, through cultural conditioning, find such realities to be implausible.

Enhancing Physiological Factors

Social and cultural folk beliefs related to *koro*, are exacerbated by physiological factors. Edwards cites physician-investigated cases of genital retraction due to both physical trauma and unknown reasons, in addition to the common experience of genital shrinkage in response to cold, excessive physical exertion, and aging.[101] One case reported in 1886, describes a physician-investigated incident involving penile hyperinvolution:

> A. B--. a healthy, steady, single man, aged twenty-seven years, shortly after he had gone to bed one night, felt a sensation of cold in the region of the penis. He was agitated to find that the organ, a fairly developed one, was rapidly shrinking, and was, he thought, finally retiring. He at once gave the alarm, and I was hastily summoned from my bed to attend him. I found him highly nervous and alarmed. The penis had almost disappeared, the glans being just perceptible under the pubic arch. The skin of the penis alone was visible, and looking as it does when the organ is buried in a hydrocele, or, in an extreme degree, as it does after death by drowning. I reassured him, and gave him some ammonia, and found next day that the natural state of things had returned. But he remained weak and nervous for some days. He could give no explanation of the occurrence, and the un-natural condition has never returned.[102]

The penis, scrotum, breasts, and vulva are the most physiologically plastic external body parts, regularly changing size and shape in response to a variety of stimuli. Mun states that diminution of penis size typically occurs in conjunction with illness and following micturition.[103] Patrick suggests that the appearance of penile retraction may result from abdominal gas or a vigorous cremasteric reflex.[104] Anxiety can also induce discernible penile circumference reduction,[105] while Thase and colleagues found a significant relationship between diminished penis tumescence and depression.[106] This may explain the appearance of perceived penile reduction or retraction as a secondary condition to affective disorders, as in virtually all cases the "delusion" of penis diminution ceased once the primary psychiatric condition was effectively treated with drugs and/or psychotherapy.[107]

Since a reduction in penile size can occur in response to normal anxiety and mood disorders, the exhibition of individual *koro* occurring in persons with no knowledge of related folk beliefs cannot necessarily be considered a delusion per se, and cannot, by definition, be classified as delusional in societies with *koro*-related traditions. The common psychiatric definition of "delusion" involves an erroneous belief that is not ordinarily held by other members within the subject's culture or subculture, while a "bizarre delusion" is one the individual's culture would consider as entirely implausible.[108] In societies experiencing epidemic *koro*, it is normal practice for relatives to support the belief, which often involves relatives and friends holding the penis until assistance, typically from a native healer or physician, can be obtained.[109]

Defining The Consequences Of Beliefs As Psychiatric Entities

While "epidemic" *koro* may reflect a state of temporary psychological disturbance, a sociological explanation seems more likely. Social realities need only be plausible to the affected group, no matter how seemingly implausible to those outside of the particular affected social dynamic. Such beliefs alter perceptual sets and are formed within a complex mosaic of social, cultural, physiological, and cognitive influences. By focusing on the "exotic" nature of *koro*-related folk realities per se, and underemphasizing their social and cultural context in engendering extreme anxiety, Western-trained scientists place their own social realities (including the speculative art of psychoanalysis), as superior, with their implicit assumption that no rational or psychologically healthy individual in their "right mind" could possibly believe that their genitalia (or nose, ears, or tongue in the case of some pre-adolescents) were shrinking and that death may ensue. As a result, unfamiliar social reality is viewed as an "exotic" syndrome; fear appropriate to the perceived circumstance becomes "sexual neurosis" and "panic reaction;" the consequences of anxiety are viewed as "hysterical conversion;" and concern over sexual potency is interpreted as "obsession," "phobia," and "castration anxiety;" while cultural tradition is mistranslated as "delusionary belief."

Participants in charismatic religious movements commonly experience a variety of transient signs and symptoms that are the consequences of beliefs and emotional zeal: psychomotor agitation, ecstatic states, fainting, tingling, uncontrollable crying, laughing, visions, etc. Mainstream psychiatry no longer typifies these meaning-oriented expressions of emotions and beliefs as disorders or syndromes, as in recent years various minority religious movements have gained popularity and familiarity in Western countries.[30]

Bartholomew views the continuing designation of epidemic *koro* as an example of the inappropriate placement of medical labels onto unpopular or unfamiliar non-Western behaviors. He states: "To devalue foreign social realities, that is to say those beliefs defined as such by Western-trained scientists, because of the fantastic nature of the beliefs, or to classify them as exemplifying irrationality or psychopathology, is to obscure their symbolic meaning whereby diversity is transformed into eccentricity, and variance becomes abnormality. To medicalize the perceptual consequences of deviant worldviews and resultant psychosomatic reactions is to deprive the non-Western world of its own cultural heritage, and to ignore and censor the enormously rich and diverse ethnographic record."[110]

GENITAL VANISHING SCARES

Africa: Mid-1970s and ongoing

Sporadic episodes of what locals describe as "magical genitalia loss" have been recorded in parts of Africa with major "outbreaks" recorded in the mid-1970s, 1990, and again in 2001. Nigerian-born psychiatrist Sunny Ilechukwu offered a firsthand report in 1975 when he was working in a hospital in the northern Nigerian city of Kaduna.[111] One day a police officer approached him with an unusual request. The officer was accompanied by two men engaged in a dispute. One man was adamant that the other had stolen his penis by making it vanish. The officer explained that his superiors wanted him to settle the claim by obtaining a medical report to either support or refute the claim. The man claimed that he was walking down a street when the other man passed by him dressed in robes that brushed against him. At that point he said he "felt his penis go." Dr. Ilechukwu listened to the story with incredulity, refusing to handle the case, but eventually agreed to perform a physical exam in full view of the parties. "The patient stood and stared straight ahead until it was announced that his genitals were normal. Reacting in disbelief, the patient glanced down at his genitals and suggested that they had just reappeared! The policeman then indicated that charges would be filed against the man for falsely reporting an incident."[112]

CONTEXT: The role of sociocultural traditions in triggering episodes is evident as many Nigerian ethnic groups "ascribe high potency to the external genitalia as ritual and magical objects to promote fecundity or material prosperity to the unscrupulous. Ritually murdered persons are often said to have these parts missing."[113] The reality of vanishing genitalia is institutionalized to such an extent that during a 1990 episode, several influential Nigerians, including a court judge, protested vehemently when police released suspected genital thieves, and many knowledgeable citizens "claimed that there was a real – even if magical –basis for the incidents."[114] One Christian priest supported cultural beliefs in genital theft by citing a biblical passage where Christ asked "Who touched me?" because the "power had gone out of him," claiming that it was a reference to genital stealing.[115]

The "Epidemic" Of 1990

Dr. Ilechukwu also investigated a major Nigerian episode of "vanishing genitalia" in 1990. He found that episodes usually involved men, but sometimes women, walking in public places. Accusations were typically triggered by incidental body contact with a stranger, which was interpreted as intentionally contrived, followed by unusual sensations within the scrotum. The affected person would then grab their external genitals to confirm that all or parts were missing, after which he would shout a phrase such as "Thief! my genitals are gone!" and accuse the passerby.[116] The "victim" would then completely disrobe to convince quickly gathering crowds of bystanders that all, or part, of his genitals were actually missing. The accused was threatened and usually beaten (sometimes fatally) until the genitals were "returned." While some "victims" soon realized that their genitalia were intact, "many then claimed that they were 'returned' at the time they raised the alarm or that, although the penis had been 'returned,' it was shrunken and so probably a 'wrong' one or just the ghost of a penis."[117] In such instances, the assault or lynching would usually continue until the "original, real" penis reappeared. During this period, Ilechukwu described the scene in Nigeria as tense as genital theft claims and beatings spread quickly across the country. "Men could be seen in the streets of Lagos holding on to their genitalia either openly or discreetly with their hands in their pockets. Women were also seen holding on to their breasts directly or discreetly by crossing the hands across the chest. It was thought that inattention and a weak will facilitated the "taking" of the penis or breasts. Vigilance and anticipatory aggression were thought to be good prophylactics.[118]

Penis "Theft" Attacks Of 2001: Nigeria And Benin

During the first two weeks in April 2001, at least 12 people were lynched by enraged mobs in the southwestern Nigerian state of Osun. Each of those murdered were accused of engaging in magically stealing someone's genitals. The most dramatic incident occurred on Friday, April 6, when several hundred members of the Christian sect "Brotherhood of the Cross" attended an annual convention in the town of Ilesa. Sect members reportedly went house-to-house to gain new converts, when someone claimed their penis had been stolen.[119] Osu resident Kunle Eniola reportedly accused one member of the religious group of using witchcraft to steal his penis. After the accusation was made, a crowd soon gathered around the bus to show their support of Eniola. As the bus began to pull away, "members of the crowd gave chase in other vehicles. They eventually stopped the bus and set it alight. The eight were unable to escape."[120] In one instance, a woman was saved by police at the last minute "after a mob put a tyre around her neck and was about to set her ablaze. A similar outbreak of violence during the previous month in the state of Oyo resulted in six people being burned to death after being captured by angry mobs. In an effort to counter the violence, government officials issued television and radio appeals for calm and ordered plainclothes detectives to patrol the streets in several major cities.[121]

During November 2001, a similar outbreak of violence took place in the small neighboring country of Benin; police were patrolling the capital after vigilantes murdered five people – four of whom were burned alive while another was "hacked to death." According to BBC reporter Karim Okanla in Cotonou, the attacks had a pattern and would start after someone began shouting out that their penis had been robbed. "An angry mob would then descend on any passerby deemed to look suspicious, strip them naked and then douse them in petrol before setting them alight. No one in the crowd would stop to question their actions or ask whether the accused might possess magical powers..."[122]

Ilechukwu believes that sociocultural beliefs related to magical genitalia loss in Nigeria, render sexually maladjusted individuals susceptible to "attacks." Sociologist Robert Bartholomew takes issue with Ilechukwu's pathological interpretation of those experiencing "magical genitalia loss," noting that this position is based on Ilechukwu's clinical assessment of just two cases. Bartholomew states: "This generalization is not warranted especially as the widespread reports of magical genitalia loss in Nigeria can be explained in social psychological terms and without reference to individual or group pathology."[123] He notes the importance of examining the worldview and perceptual outlook of "victims" who live in a mental world that accepts the reality of such beliefs as taken-for-granted.

Anthropologist Richard Shweder emphasizes the importance of explicating the meaning of "foreign" conduct codes and suggests that many "exotic" beliefs are not amenable to evaluation through the traditional dichotomy of rational or irrational, but are *non*rational.[124] In the case of magical genitalia loss, Bartholomew remarks that "perceptual outlooks may support beliefs that foster social realities that are at extreme variance with Western constructions of reality, rationality, and normality. Similarly, the possibility that certain peoples could erroneously believe their genitalia to be shrinking, or disappearing altogether, has typically received deviant, abnormal, or psychopathological evaluations by Western-trained scientists who through cultural conditioning, find such realities to be implausible. In fact, 'rationality' appears to be a social construct that varies transculturally."[125]

American sociologist Neil J. Smelser's widely used paradigm to explain collective behavior typifies Ilechukwu's position. Many "mass hysteria" studies implicitly or explicitly utilize Smelser's contention that grandiose structural elements in society facilitate irrational, abnormal "hysterical" episodes. However, while Smelser's perspective is used to argue that such elements as extraordinary "ambiguity," "anxiety" and "structural strains" are present in all episodes, these categories are only identified after "outbreaks," and are so vaguely defined as to be present in all societies during all periods.[126] Ilechukwu relates the "epidemic" of magical penis "loss" claims in Nigeria during 1990 to political and economic upheavals.[127]

The Sudan Episode Of 2003

In September 2003, a penis vanishing scare swept through the Sudanese capital of Khartoum in northeast Africa. The episode began amid rumors that certain sinister sorcerers were strolling through the city and shaking the hands of various males, after which their penises were said to have vanished. A contributing factor in the rapid spread of the rumors was the use of cellphones with text messages.[128] Initial reports indicated that the sorcerers were members of a Sudanese tribe. Another account held that a West African was the culprit, while later there were stories that several West Africans were responsible. According to journalist Kamal Hassan Bakhit of the Arabic daily newspaper *Al-Quds Al-Arabi* based in London, "the source of the horror is a foreign citizen from a West African country who is roaming through the city marketplace and draining men's virility via a handshake..." As a result, many people were refusing to shake the hands of any stranger.[129] While most victims claimed the temporary genital theft involved a handshake, one man said that while shopping at a market, he was approached by another man who handed him a comb, requesting that he comb his hair. Upon doing so, after a few seconds, he claimed to feel an unusual sensation and his penis vanished. "It was also claimed that once 'Satan's Friend' drains a man's virility, he demands that his victim pay him over four million Sudanese pounds (about $3,000) to get it back."[130]

Police and government officials in the Sudan responded to the claims and counterclaims by arresting 40 people after they filed complaints of genital theft, while 50 others were also incarcerated on "suspicion of sorcery and fraud. Many West Africans were brought into police stations for questioning, amid attempts by groups of people to assault them. The police were forced to devote a great deal of effort to dispersing rioters." The country's attorney general, Salah Abu Zayed, said that the first person to make a complaint of genital theft was charged with disturbing the peace as an examination by a physician revealed his genitals were in tact.[131]

According to Dr. Nour Al-Huda, a senior police officer, it was determined, after interviewing the suspects, that they were in reality the victims. "They were accused of something they knew nothing about... One of the accused had been informed by his wife that his daughter was suffering from sharp pains and that she was going to be operated on. He rushed to the hospital, but on the way stopped to ask a man where the operating room was – and was surprised to discover that this man was accusing him of being one of those who were causing impotence via handshakes. He found himself under suspicion at a time when he was hurrying to reach his daughter in the operating room…" Al-Huda believes that many of the men affected "were under the influence of suggestion. Since they were prepared [mentally] for this to happen, they honestly felt that they were ill."[132] Sudanese psychiatrist Taha Ba'asher compared the episode to that of pseudo-pregnancy where women who think they are pregnant actually develop bloated stomachs and symptoms similar to those of pregnant women.[133]

The head criminal attorney general, Yasser Ahmad Muhammad, said the wave of genital theft rumors and accusations "broke out when one merchant went to another merchant to buy some Karkady [a Sudanese beverage]. Suddenly, the seller felt his penis shriveling as a result of sorcery. It was the first complaint regarding the matter. Afterwards, the matter reached the media and this caused sensitivity among many."[134] He said that every person who filed a genital theft complaint was taken to the hospital for an examination. In each case, "their penises were normal." While many withdrew their charges in court claiming they had recovered their "missing" penis, others continued with the charges. The Sudan's Health Minister, Ahmad Bilal Othman, said that the claims of genital theft were without any scientific grounds.[135]

A Sudanese newspaper columnist, Ja'far Abbas, addressed the episode in the Saudi Arabian daily *Al-Watan*: "Even though what I write today will harm 'tourism' in Sudan, I consider it my duty to warn anyone who wants to come to Sudan to refrain from shaking hands with a dark-skinned man. Since most Sudanese are dark-skinned, he had better avoid shaking hands with anyone he doesn't know…" In another column in *Al-Rai Al-A'am*, he discussed the report in which a man said his penis vanished after being given a comb from a stranger. "No doubt, this comb was a laser-controlled surgical robot that penetrates the skull [and passes] to the lower body and emasculates a man ... I wanted to tell that man who fell victim to the electronic comb: 'You jackass, how can you put a comb from a man you don't know to your head, while even relatives avoid using the same comb?!'"[136]

While magical genital theft at the hands of witches or sorcerers may seem to be strange by Western standards, there is actually a Western tradition of such acts in medieval Europe. Witches were credited with the power of hexing their clients' victims in this way, even having the ability to tie a faithless lover's penis in knots.

COMMENTS: Episodes of "magical" genitalia "theft" highlight the point that plausibility is a key factor in the development of mass hysterias and social delusions. There is a discussion of such phenomena as vanishing genitalia in one of the most influential and notorious books in human history. In 1486, Dominican monks Jakob Sprenger (1436-1495) and Heinrich Kramer (circa 1430-1505) published the *Malleus Maleficarum* (*The Hammer of Witches*), which served as the blueprint for the identification and execution of tens of thousands "witches" throughout Europe.[137] On page 119 there is a description of two separate reports in which men claimed that their penises had been stolen or made to vanish as a result of a witches' spell. In both instances the spell was removed and the "member" was said to have reappeared.

GENOCIDE HYSTERIA

Rwanda, Africa: 1994

During the 1994 Civil War in Rwanda and sporadic clusters of flighting that have occurred since, it is estimated that at least half a million inhabitants were massacred along ethnic lines. During April of 1997, more than 30 teenaged students from the Nyanza Secondary School were attending a solomn ceremony for the remains of their murdered relatives from 1994. Rwanda psychiatrist Athanase Hagengimana and his American counterpart Lawson Wulsin report that during the ceremony, "They developed acute emotional reactions such as agitation, seeing vivid images of genocide and weeping for over two days after the ceremony ended. The children fled the scene; the government ordered the school to close." A similar outcome took place during another reburial servive. These episodes have been diagnosed as "mass hysteria" by a consulting psychiatrist.[138] Wulsin and Hagengimana report that in the wake of the killings, an epidemic of mental disorder occurred, estimating that in the wake of the genocide, as much as 20 percent of adults may be suffering from Post Truamatic Stress Disorder (PTSD). "The sudden, overwhelming trauma afflicting most civilians and the persistence of unpredictable threats four years after the 'end' of the war (a period now commonly known as 'the insecurity' in Rwanda) have caused an epidemic of PTSD and related psychiatric disorders," they state. In addition, they report a dramatic increase in the number of individuals with relatively minor physical complaints, experiencing conversion disorder. "One soldier, referred from the front line, presented with aphonia, pseudoparalysis of the right side of the body and contractions of the right hand, particularly the index finger (his trigger finger)." Another soldier lost his parents and siblings in the genocide. "In January 1998 he lost his auditory acuity and developed la belle indifference. Audiometry done in the Ear, Nose and Throat (ENT) service was normal."[139]

GHOST ATTACKS

Kenya: 2000

In 2000, a series of "ghost attacks" were reported across Kenya at primary and secondary schools, especially in rural areas. At the Kathuma Primary School in the Kitui district, evil spirits reportedly invaded the school and tried to strangle students as the pupils experienced breathing difficulties. Other incidents occurred in the Kirinyaga district at the Wang'uru Girls Secondary School; at the Gathigi Primary School about 30 miles (50 kilometers) north of the capital, Nairobi; and at the Kambaa Girls High School not far from Nairobi. At the Kambaa school it was claimed that ghosts had thrown stones onto the hostel roof during the night. Many girls blamed the events on a staff member who was said to have been responsible for conjuring them up. The episode forced school officials to temporarily close their doors and send the students home. The Gitogo co-educational secondary school was temporarily closed during mid-July after several boys claimed to have been attacked by a ghost in their hostel, with the fear climaxing into a stampede. Some students required hospital treatment. The belief in ghosts and demons is common in rural areas, and so-called ghostbusters are widely used to rid the premises of the evil spirits. Some schools even held fundraisers to collect money to hire witch doctors. In early June, after a series of ghost attacks at the Itokela Girls Secondary School, a Kenyan businessman reportedly confessed to triggering the episode by sending the ghosts to the school. The man agreed to pay for the grounds to be exorcised from the spirits. The arrest occurred after many of the girls showed up at the district commissioner's office asking that something be done. The "ghosts" reportedly relished pushing the girls down. The motive was said to have been revenge after his daughter was unhappy with her treatment at the school and left.[140]

A similar scare was reported during 2001. Concerned by the ongoing presence of a "mysterious illness" striking down students, the Loreto Day Secondary School in Kenya, was closed in early October amid a devil-worship scare. The mood at the Catholic school was reportedly tense. The closure caused tension in the neighboring Loreto-Matunda Secondary School. The Uasin Gishu District Education Officer, Julius Bissem, said it was imperative to close the school in an effort to reduce the level of stress among students "following claims that some students were engaged in devil worship."[141] When interviewed by journalists in Eldoret town, students said that the problems began to surface shortly after the school reopened for the new term. Many students were upset that school officials had decided to re-admit several Form Three students who had been suspended for allegedly practicing "devil worship." "Since we came back, ghosts have been visiting our school." One of the disgruntled students claimed that a few Satan-worshipping classmates were responsible for the mysterious affliction, noting that over 100 students had been admitted to hospitals.[142]

Not long before officials decided to temporarily close the facility, there were reports that a local prophet was predicting that the building would be destroyed by a fire. At this point, tension at the school reached a climax. There were also rumors that the school was "being protected against the Holy Spirit by an angel Rael."[143] The school is sponsored by the Eldoret Catholic Diocese. The episode occurred amid a backdrop of widespread fears within the region that devil worship was a major problem in many schools.

GHOST DANCE (NATIVE AMERICAN)

Mid- and Western United States: 1889-1891

The "Ghost Dance" of the Plains Indians of the United States was essentially a type of utopian movement. It was a reenactment of a vision received by an Indian prophet. It foretold of a time when Native Americans across the United States would be unified and their political control of the land would be restored. Word of the Ghost Dance spread across the Western U.S. Anthropologists view the ghost dance as a deliberate attempt to recreate a utopian world. Such activities arise among oppressed people whose culture has been suddenly and radically changed. The dance provided hope as it swept across the plains just as Native American culture had been devastated by European Americans who forced them onto reservations and exterminated their buffalo. The Native Americans were a beaten, demoralized people with no means to fight back against European weapons. The Native American world was in shambles and the Ghost Dance promised a new vision of what they longed for.[144]

It wasn't long before the "Indians" were in emotional disarray. A medicine man from a Nevada tribe claimed to have a vision from God instructing him to instruct his people on how to perform the "ghost dance." If they did, a new harmonious era in Indian-White relations would dawn. It involved frenzied all-night dancing for five successive nights and was to be repeated every six weeks. The dance spread quickly to many tribes west of the Mississippi River. Sociologist David Miller remarks that: "In some tribes, dancers often trembled violently and fainted ... some dancers would stand rigidly for hours in a trance-like state. During their faints or trances, dancers said they were transported to the Happy Hunting Ground, where they visited with their dead ancestors."[145] During the dances, some had visions of the perfect world to come. Ironically, the movement faded rapidly after some American Army soldiers became frightened and began firing at a gathering of Indians. The incident occurred after they wrongly thought that the dancing was a preparation for war. On December 29, 1890, about 300 Native Americans were massacred at Wounded Knee Creek in what is now South Dakota. The ghost dance religion soon died out, along with their dreams of a dawning utopia, though some remnants continue today.

Ghost Dance of the Sioux Indians. (Amedee Forestier in Illustrated London News, 1891)

GHOST ROCKET SCARE

Scandinavia: 1946

During May and September of 1946, widespread fear was in evidence across Scandinavia and especially Sweden as thousands of inhabitants reported seeing rocket-like projectiles in the sky.[146] At the time, Soviet military forces were occupying Peenemunde, Germany's former center of rocket science. This situation gave rise to a widespread folk belief that the observations were of German V-rockets being test-fired in an effort to intimidate the Swedish public. In October, Swedish defense officials released the results of their four-month investigation of nearly 1,000 sighting and "crash" reports. With no concrete evidence that a single rocket over-flew Sweden during this period, most sightings were attributed to either meteorological or astronomical causes.

Astronomer Louis Winkler correlated the sightings to the appearance of geomagnetic comets and the periodic disbursement of their orbital streams in conjunction with intense solar activity.[147] The result was a spectacular series of auroras, meteors, and cometary spray streaking into the atmosphere. Winkler remarked: "The uniqueness of the ghost rocket activity is emphasized by additional and accompanying phenomena. Scandinavian newspapers gave accounts of spectacular auroras occurring over Helsinki on Feb 26 and Stockholm on July 26. The preliminary aurora correlates well with the spray date of Encke on February 25, whereas the July 26 aurora corresponds to the onset of the main ghost rocket activity."[148]

CONTEXT: The historical and political contexts were of pivotal importance in the shifting interpretation of the objects from meteorological and astronomical origins to Soviet-made rockets. There is a long history of Soviet-Swedish mistrust including espionage accusations, heated political rhetoric, disputed land boundaries, and wars.[149] Further, prior to and encompassing the episode, numerous public officials issued statements affirming the rockets' existence, including high ranking Swedish military officers, politicians, police, journalists, and scientists. Near the close of the Second World War, German V-rockets pounded parts of England, causing horrific damage. Fears existed that V-rockets would rain down on Sweden from its longtime Soviet nemesis. The Soviets were in control of much of northern Europe at this time, and there was great uncertainty as to their intentions with Scandinavia and how much territory they might attempt to claim in the chaotic aftermath of the war.[150] It is within this context of centuries-old Russian invasion fears and post-war political ambiguity involving possible Russian claims on Swedish territory that plausible rumors began circulating as to potentially hostile Russian intentions.

An alleged "ghost rocket" over Scandinavia in 1946.

As early as mid-March, there was speculation in the Swedish press that the Soviets might test-fire rocket bombs over Sweden. It was at this time that the Swedish News Agency Tidningarnas Telegrambyra published a report warning of the possibility of such test-firings. By late April when several earth tremors shook the regions of Skane, Blekinge, Kalmar, and near the Danish island of Bornholm in the southern Baltic, a newspaper suggested that they may have been Russian atomic weapons tests.[151]

Starting in early January, numerous reports began to appear describing unusual meteors and glowing clouds. For instance, on January 4, many people in the southern part of Sweden reported seeing luminous clouds casting red, purple, and green hues on the snow-covered landscape. In one incident at a military training post in Revingehed, during one spectacular auroral display, a horse "lowered his head towards his legs" and "army watch-dogs crawled into their kennels."[152] Remarkable observations of meteors were recorded northwest of Stockholm at Fransborg, on January 9,[153] in Jamtland on the same day,[154] and across the Dalarna region on the 17th.[155] These and other sporadic reports of intense auroral and astronomical activity continued through early May, and were defined as natural in origin.[156] Other strange celestial activity was reported between January and May of 1946, including a mirage at Gagnef,[157] an eerie light in Dalarna,[158] a rainbow-halo at Helsingfors,[159] and a mock sun ("like two suns had risen") above Fagerhult.[160] In May there were reports of ball lightning at Vaderobod[161] and Svaneke,[162] a "mysterious light" above Stockholm[163] and on the 21st, a yellow fireball passed near Halsingborg.[164] But starting on May 24th, citizens began to redefine what had been previously described as celestial phenomena, as potentially hostile missiles. This major shift began with the sighting of an object over Landskrona when a security officer reported a "fireball with a tail" while another witness reported seeing a "wingless cigar-shaped body" that was expelling exhaust sparks.[165] It wasn't long before press reports began describing these sightings as Soviet weapons with such terms as a "V-bomb,"[166] "V-1-bomb,"[167] "remote-directed bombs,"[168] "rocket bomb,"[169] and "projectile."[170]

On May 27, in the wake of reports of wingless planes and fireballs at many locations including Hagalund, Karlskrona, Halsingborg, and Huddinge, it was suggested that these observations were foreign experiments using "remotely controlled bombs."[171] From this time through early June, there was a transition period where aerial objects were labeled as either meteors or missiles.[172] A massive wave of "rocket projectile" sightings occurred in June across the entire country. On the 8th, a former pilot reported seeing "a rocket with intermittent exhausts" at Eskilstuna.[173] The next day a "ghost rocket" was observed streaking across Southern Finland, further elevating fears in Sweden.[174]

In the grips of a nationwide panic, on June 12th Swedish defense officials distributed a memo to their military units across the country requesting them to get observers to fill out questionnaires on the mysterious sightings. The memo read in part: "It cannot be ruled out that these [recent sightings] could be connected to tests, by a foreign power, of types of remotely-piloted weapons."[175] From mid-June to early July, reports of fireballs and missiles were common, including several spectacular reports.[176] By July 10, military officials were appealing to the public for help in reporting mysterious aerial objects or sounds.[177] At about the same time, the military was also involved in highly public inspections of many "crash" sites. These events appear to have only further heightened anxieties and crystallized the belief that sightings were of Soviet-fired V-rockets. While military officials investigated at least 28 crash reports firsthand,[178] and while 30 "ghost bomb" fragments were recovered and analyzed, not a single piece of evidence was ever found to confirm their foreign-power origin.[179]

Once the widespread belief in the rockets' existence solidified, many ordinarily mundane events and circumstances were redefined as rocket-related. Two fires of unknown origin were attributed to ghost bombs.[180] When a barn in a mid-Norrland village fell down on August 11, for no apparent reason,[181] the collapse was "connected to the appearance of the ghost rockets," which were spotted in the area on the same day. Police later determined the cause as a tornado.[182] As the wave continued, the explanations for various happenings grew increasingly speculative. When three cows on a Jamtland farm were found dead with no obvious cause, farmer Andera Edsasen believed that a ghost rocket had dispensed poison.[183] In some instances the explanations were outlandish. Following an infestation of metal fly caterpillars in several southern provinces during mid-July, one citizen told military officials that he thought some of the mystery rockets contained caterpillars. Meanwhile, rumors circulated that the projectiles were stuffed with political leaflets.[184] Ghost rockets were even blamed for the crash of a B-18 bomber on August 12,[185] until an investigation rejected the theory.[186] Perhaps the most improbable sighting occurred on that same day when no less than eight people reported seeing luminous "ghost bombs" flying just above the ground and traveling north over Karlstad. A more mundane cause was soon found: "the ghost projectiles were soap bubbles made by a little boy who sat on a sofa...with a newly bought bubble apparatus and a can of soap-water."[187]

During the period, many people thought they had found parts of ghost rockets or evidence of their existence. In central Sweden, military personnel examined a report of a "pit in the ground" as a possible "ghost bomb mark."[188] One "projectile find" near a "crash" site was identified as a steam valve spindle.[189]

When a farmer said he had discovered a "missile" embedded in the ground near Blekinge[190] it seemed as though the authorities might finally get the proof they were looking for. Further scrutiny revealed the object as an airplane antenna.[191] On the evening of August 20, many citizens of Nyhem were certain that a rocket projectile had passed by, ending with a display of sparks spraying into the air. The next day the carcass of a magpie was found "which had met its fate in the high voltage lines."[192] Colonel Sven Ramstrom termed the tendency of some citizens to misperceive meteors as ghost rockets as suffering from "the bomb psychosis."[193] As the sightings were waning in late July, other reporters used such terms as "rocket psychosis"[194] and "war psychosis."[195]

Many Swedish authorities publicly expressed their fear that the Soviets were testing rockets that would soon be carrying atomic warheads that could result in the demise of their country. Per Persson, New York editor of the *Svenska Dagbladet*, remarked: "If these projectiles carried explosive charges of atomic bomb character and if they were directed against industrial centers...Sweden would be destroyed and the war would be over."[196] Other writers concurred, describing the situation as "a premonition of 'push-button war.'"[197] One editor dramatically asserted: "Now we know what it's all about – trial shootings. And Sweden is the target, or a part of it."[198] Some used poetry to express their fears of a looming nuclear disaster.[199] For instance, one person wrote: "Trembling people walk about wondering what will happen... Limitless is our wonder, no one knows what it will bring, just now upon the sky, here the horned beast was seen... Terrible is a summer's night, listen to the laughter of the ghosts, when on the wheels of the atom bombs, they play tag in the heavens."[200]

While phantom rockets were occasionally spotted in other Scandinavian countries during the episode,[201] and also Europe,[202] none compared to the intensity and volume of the Swedish reports.

The Final Report

When the Swedish Defense Staff released the findings of its four-month investigation on October 10, 80 percent of the nearly 1,000 reports were categorized as having been of celestial origin. While the remainder could not be conclusively identified, there was no unequivocal evidence that they were foreign rockets.[203] The report read in part:

> The majority of sightings with certainty result from celestial phenomena... [which] often occur but usually do not attract any special attention. Since the interest of the general public was awoken...[they] started to take a closer note of them...therefore the large number of reports.
>
> Some sightings cannot, however, be explained but this should not be attributed to some sort of object of a different kind. Not enough information is in hand...to be able to draw firm conclusions with any certainty concerning their nature, origin and appearance...Through a collaboration with astronomers it was clear that the two "peaks" in July and August probably were caused by meteors or meteorites.
>
> Even at an early date measures were taken through which the military authorities tried to maintain a certain watch over the aerial territory, seeking to clarify the origin of the phenomena. ...[Radar tracking] proved impossible to establish...what kind of object it was...[Of the many alleged crashes]...remains mainly consist of coke or slag-like formations... In no case has anything come forth that can be considered as if the material came from any kind of space projectile. In certain lakes very thorough investigations have been made because of supposed crashes. So far, however, no find has turned up which can be presumed to originate from a V-type weapon.

The following year, there were a small number of sporadic sightings of rocket projectiles over Sweden.[204] Most sightings of unusual aerial phenomena were interpreted as either meteors[205] or "flying saucers,"[206] the latter reflecting Swedish press reporting of the flurry of flying disk observations in the United States during the summer of 1947.

See also: PHANTOM AIRCRAFT WAVES, FLYING SAUCERS, GREAT AMERICAN AIRSHIP WAVE, "EDISON STAR" SIGHTINGS, RUSSIAN POLAND BALLOON SCARE, ANDREE BALLOON MANIA, BRITISH COLUMBIA-MANITOBA in CANADA.

GLOSSOLALIA, CONTAGIOUS

Theologist Anthony Hoekema defines glossolalia as "a spontaneous utterance of sounds in a language the speaker has never learned and does not even understand. This tongue-speaking is usually done only in certain types of religious groups."[207] Within the Christian tradition, some followers, especially in certain denominations such as Pentocostalists, view such actions as indicating a type of prayer, prophesy, or possession by a Holy Spirit.[208] Glossolalia comes from the

Greek, *glossa* (tongue) and *lalia* (speaking). The literal translation is "tongue speaking."[209]

The seemingly spontaneous, collective exhibition of glossolalia or "speaking in tongues" is a common feature reported among participants of emotionally charged services of ecstatic religious groups. A survey of Christian writings from 100 AD to 1900 indicates that the prevalence of glossolalia has waxed and waned over the years, but overall it was rarely reported, and when it was, it occurred mostly in persecuted minorities.[210] For instance, in the fourth century, Father Chrysostom seemed mystified by Paul's mention of speaking in tongues in Corinthians 12 and 14: "This whole place is very obscure; but the obscurity is produced by our ignorance of the facts referred to and by their cessation, being such as then used to occur but now no longer take place."[211]

During the first half of the nineteenth century, the scientific community typically viewed glossolalia as an abnormality. An early study by Emile Lombard in 1910, views it as a form of crowd psychology in impressionable people, representing a form of infantile regression.[212] In 1912, Oskar Pfister used concepts developed by Sigmund Freud to view speaking in tongues as a type of hysterical neuroses involving regression to an infantile stage.[213] In 1927, George Barton Cutten reinforced the association between tongue-speaking and hysteria, which involves control of one's mind by the subconscious among the poor and uneducated. He also interprets it as an infantile response, "showing itself not only by its appearance among the most primitive and untrained in a community, by its similarity to the reactions of children.[214] During the 1960s, pathological interpretations of glossolaliacs began to shift to that of more normal individuals. During this period, South African psychiatrist L.M. Vivier found that half of the tongue-speakers profiled had psychiatric or psychological problems, though he noted that there may be therapeutic benefits.[215]

In recent decades, less ethnocentric, more contextual studies view glossolalia as learned behavior that anyone can be engaged in and is communicated via religious ritual. The late prominent psychologist Nicholas Spanos wanted to determine whether tongue speaking is an altered state of consciousness or learned behavior and examined these possibilities in an experimental setting. "The present findings are consistent with the social learning hypothesis that glossolalia can be acquired with relative ease by almost anyone with the requisite motivations. All of our subjects were unfamiliar with glossolalia prior to their participation in this study. Nevertheless, after only two brief training sessions, that included practice at glossolalia, encouragement, and modeling, 70% of them spoke fluent glossolalia throughout the entire post-test trial and all of the remainder spoke recognizable glossolalia throughout most of the post-trial interval."[216] Theologian Killian McDonald, in his study of the history of tongue-speaking, remarks that "Though some glossolalics may be suffering from some neurotic or psychotic form of pathology, there is not sufficient evidence to show that glossolalia should be interpreted as per se deviant or pathological."[217]

GOBLIN ATTACKS

Mhondoro, Zimbabwe: June and July 2002

In July 2002, a phantom goblin scare swept through the St. Mark's Secondary School in Mhondoro, Zimbabwe. The headmaster of the school, which is operated by the Anglican Church, reportedly fled the school and was hiding out amid claims by parents that he was in control of tiny creatures who were sexually harassing both female pupils and teachers.[218] Commotion surrounding the hysteria forced the school's temporarily closure. The community was in an uproar over the accusations and angry parents were turning up at the school, demanding to see the Headmaster.

Several students and teachers told journalists that they had also been beaten by "invisible objects." In all, at least 30 students said they had been attacked. One teacher who did not want to be identified for fear of being victimized, said that some of the students were possessed by evil spirits: "I witnessed one incident when a student went into a trance...He was demanding meat, threatening that after finishing with the students, the spirits would attack the teachers next. We are living in fear here." The outbreak coincided with mid-term exams.

The strange turn of events left the school's assistant headmaster in the "hot seat," having to deal with the community. Somewhat "shell-shocked," he was reportedly referring inquiries to the Ministry of Education, Sports and Culture. He also insisted that his name not be published in the newspapers citing Public Services regulations. In trying to put on a "brave face," he was quoted as saying: "Everything is now back to normal and I understand lessons have resumed." Despite the reassurance, his words did not seem to be taken seriously and the situation seemed to be far from normal.

The first signs of trouble began six weeks earlier when some students claimed that "mysterious beings" were harassing them in their hostels at night. The creatures were known as *zvikwambo* and *mubobobo* in Shona, and *tokoloshe* in Zulu. According to one student: "About 30 students have been victims of the attacks and we can't bear spending another night at this haunted place ... A friend of mine was bitten on the arm after she wrestled with a ghost which wanted to sleep with her."

Several of the school's female teachers were said to be thinking about quitting their jobs. Just like their students, the teachers said they were being sexually assaulted at night by strange creatures. A statement issued by some of the teachers read in part: "Sometimes we get up in the morning to find the bedding mysteriously wet and we suspect foul play."

GOLDFISH SWALLOWING FAD

United States: March-May 1939

In 1939, a goldfish swallowing fad swept across the United States. The episode began on March 3, at Harvard University in Boston, Massachusetts. While showing off his aquarium, Harvard freshman Lothrop Withington Jr. boasted to a classmate that he could eat live fish. Acting on a $10 bet, Withington agreed to eat a live goldfish in the freshman dining room on March 3rd. When the time came, and with a crowd gathered around, Withington dipped his hand into a small bowl, grabbed a 3-inch goldfish, tipped his head back and let go of the fish. He began chewing the fish, followed by a hard gulp. The flamboyant Withington next proceeded to brush his teeth before sitting down to dine on a meal of – fish.[219] The mass media were instrumental in spreading news of the incident as word of the dare had circulated across the campus and throughout the Boston community. As a result, several major Boston newspapers sent reporters to cover the event and take photographs.[220]

CONTEXT: The origin of goldfish swallowing seems to have begun with a well-publicized chance event and followed a classic fad pattern, beginning with a person of high class and status (a Harvard University student), who spread an innovative act to other college campuses as students emulated these behaviors and set new records for the number of goldfish swallowed, thereby raising the status and prestige of those engaging in such acts. But the fad soon lost its novelty, as there was little prestige in swallowing goldfish or other objects, and the fad quickly died out.

A student at Franklin and Marshall College quickly outdid Withington by swallowing three goldfish whole. In a series of one-upmanship, students at colleges across the country were going one better. Each day brought press reports of new records. A Michigan University student downed 28 fish. Not long after, someone at MIT swallowed 42. The record was eventually set at 210 fish, although some unconfirmed claims totaled just over 300. At the height of the fad, students were not limiting their quarry to fish but were publicly swallowing earthworms, live mice, magazines, and phonograph records.[221] One student even bit the head off a live snake.[222]

As the fad spread and variations on the goldfish theme grew more outrageous, it began to be seen by some schools in a more negative light. When a student at Klutztown State Teachers College in Pennsylvania swallowed 43 goldfish, he was suspended for "conduct unbecoming a student."[223] An anatomy professor at UCLA cautioned against the eating of more than 150 goldfish, while physicians cautioned against the possibility of choking to death or falling ill from worms that could be carried by raw fish.[224]

The fad ended abruptly in the spring as classes came to an end and students left for home.

COMMENTS: While goldfish swallowing revivals occurred in the U.S. during the late 1960s, the extent of the episode is minor in comparison to 1939.

See also: FADS.

GREAT AMERICAN AIRSHIP WAVE

United States: 1896-1897

Between November 17, 1896 and mid-May 1897, "airship fever" spread across the United States as thousands of Americans became convinced that one of their citizens had perfected the world's first practical heavier-than-air flying machine. At the height of the rumors, it is estimated that tens of thousands of people reported seeing the craft. On many occasions, the sightings occurred simultaneously in different regions, prompting some to remark that there must have been an entire fleet. The vessel was typically described as oval or cigar-shaped with an attached undercarriage, and sporting a powerful headlight. Huge fans or wings were protruding from both sides. Occasionally observers said that the wings slowly flapped up and down in a motion similar to that of a bird.

Witness descriptions of the craft's maneuvers far exceeded the technology of the period. The airship was almost exclusively seen at night, and the Wright Brothers fragile attempt at piloted powered flight at Kitty Hawk, North Carolona, would not occur until December 17, 1903, during which the longest period of sustained flight was less than one minute.[225] While many crude prototypes were in development at this time, they were impractical. For instance, Albert and Gaston Tissandier's motor-powered electric dirigible of 1883 and 1884 in France was hailed as a success, yet the vessel could not even maintain its position against the wind.[226] We can also rule out the possibility that citizens were misperceiving a balloon as night flight was treacherous, and a sudden wind gust could have disastrous consequences. Aviation historian Charles H. Gibbs-Smith states emphatically that airships reported during the 1896-97 wave were technologically impossible: "I can say with certainty that the only airborne vehicles, carrying passengers, which could possibly have been seen anywhere in North America...were free-flying spherical balloons, and it is highly unlikely for these to be mistaken for anything else. No form of dirigible...or heavier-than-air flying machine was flying – or indeed could fly – at this time..."[227]

CONTEXT: The episode occurred at a time when America was experiencing a technology mania and its citizens were enchanted with stories in science fiction serials and articles in popular journals devoted to the subject of science and invention. This literature provided the public with "a steady diet of aeronautical speculation and news to prime people for the day when the riddle of aerial navigation finally would receive a solution."[228] The topic was nothing short of a national obsession.[229] In the words of one writer, it was "an age that was in love with the great wonders of science."[230]

During this period of rapid technological change there was a widespread feeling that nearly any invention was possible. The second half of the nineteenth century was marked by a series of revolutionary inventions that would affect all aspects of life. Between 1876 and 1896, there were such inventions as the telephone, gramophone, filament lamp, motor car, steam turbine, diesel engine, and X-rays, to name a few. In the 20 years preceding the airship mania, the American public was preoccupied with popular literature on science and inventions. A special interest was the age-old dream of humans soaring in a heavier-than-air flying machine as "magazines devoted to science and engineering vied with Jules Verne's *Robur the Conquerer* and other fictional publications to describe the flier which would soon succeed."[231] This social climate fostered an exaggerated optimism in the belief that the perfection of the world's first heavier-than-air flying machine was imminent.

Between 1880 and 1900, the exploits of backyard tinkerers in America and Europe were closely followed by journalists who typically portrayed them in their newspaper and magazine articles as heroes or adventurers. Science fiction writers glorified them. Historian David Jacobs writes that during this time, the U.S. patent office in Washington, D.C., received hundreds of submissions that were often shrouded in secrecy as suspicious, distrusting inventors withheld key information on their experimental craft.[232]

In the late 1890s many people in the United States obtained patents for proposed airships. Most people believed someone would soon invent a flying machine, and many wanted to capitalize on the fame and fortune that would certainly come to the first person to launch an American

> into the skies. As soon as someone had a glimmer of an airship design, he immediately applied for a patent. These would-be inventors constantly worried over possible theft or plagiarism...[and] most people kept their patents secret. Given this atmosphere and the numerous European and American experiments with flight, it is not surprising that secret inventor stories so captured the public imagination and seemed such a logical explanation for the airship mystery.[233]

It was within this backdrop that the *Sacramento Evening Bee* published a telegram on Tuesday, November 17, 1896. It said that a New York-based entrepreneur was vowing to pilot his recently perfected airship to California, which he expected to reach within 48 hours. That evening, hundreds of people in Sacramento reported seeing an airship.[234] The incident created a statewide sensation. It began between 6 and 7 p.m. when a bobbing light was seen to the east, drifting southwest. News of the sighting quickly spread and citizens came out of their homes and establishments to gaze skyward. At one point the light appeared to descend near distant housetops along the skyline when a witness steadfastly claimed that they could hear barely audible voices warning: "Lift her up quick! You are making directly for that steeple!"[235] Some electric railway car employees supported this account, claiming that while passing near East Park, they could hear music and human voices in the sky.[236] Railcar worker R. L. Lowry even said he could discern people in the distant vessel, which appeared "as an oblong mass, propelled by fanlike wheels operated by four men, who worked as if on bicycles."[237] Many California newspapers described the Sacramento sightings as plausible or in factual terms, supporting the growing belief that a California man had invented the world's first practical heavier-than-air flying machine and was secretly testing it at night.

Airships And Yellow Journalism[238]

Mass sightings across California began on November 19, as a mysterious light was seen near Eureka.[239] The next afternoon the airship was spotted near Tulare.[240] That evening numerous Sacramento residents again observed what appeared to be a light "attached to some aircraft;"[241] in Oakland, witnesses claimed to discern huge fan-like propellers; while others said they saw giant wings attached to each side of an airship.[242] On November 22, between 5 and 6 p.m., hundreds of Sacramento residents watched what they thought was an airship with a brilliant arc lamp pass to the southwest.[243]

During the last week of November and first week of December, airship sightings were reported in such California communities as Red Bluff,[244] Riverside,[245] Antioch,[246] Chico,[247] Visalia,[248] Hanford,[249] Ferndale,[250] Box Springs,[251] Salinas,[252] Maxwell,[253] Tulare,[254] Merced,[255] Fresno,[256] and Pennington.[257] There were scattered sightings in the adjacent states of Oregon,[258] Washington,[259] Nevada[260] and Arizona[261] during the episode, which received minor press coverage. The wave was primarily confined to California, where widespread sightings continued until dramatically declining by mid-December, with the exception of a few intermittent cases from around the state.

An interesting feature of the California episode were several reports of close encounters with terrestrial airship pilots or crew who typically offered to give the witness a ride in the vessel,[262] although one involved an encounter with what appeared to have been Martians. Two men had contact with three beautiful beings standing about seven feet tall. The "strange beings" had slender builds and hairless faces and heads. Wearing no clothing, their bodies were covered with a silky smooth growth. "Each of them had swung under the left arm a bag to which was attached a nozzle, and every little while one or the other would place the nozzle on his mouth, at which time I heard a sound of escaping gas. It was much the same sound as is produced by a person blowing up a football." Upon returning to their airship and flying off, it was noticed that the vessel "expanded and contracted with a mus-

Sketch of an "airship" seen over San Francisco with "wings" or "fins," a birdlike tail, and a searchlight. (Nov. 23, 1896)

cular motion."[263]

Starting with a trickle of reports in mid-January 1897, and climaxing during April before petering out in May, speculative stories about the possible existence of an airship and inventors, and reports of other sightings, appeared in almost every state, but virtually spared the west coast states where the episode began in November 1896.

Press sensationalism played a major role in creating and perpetuating the sightings, first in California, and later across the United States. Amid intense public interest in airship development, newspaper editors published a barrage of articles speculating as to whether someone had invented the world's first practical airship. Publisher William Randolph Hearst remarked in the *San Francisco Examiner* that he could not recall a clearer example of "Fake journalism ... than the persistent attempt to make the public believe that the air in this vicinity is populated with airships. It has been manifest for weeks that the whole airship story is pure myth."[264] Hearst was notorious for exaggerating or fabricating news stories in order to sell his papers, and his position on the existence of the airship was charactistically hypocritical in order to exploit the situation and increase sales. During November and December 1896, his *San Francisco Examiner* adhered to a strict editorial policy of deriding the airship's existence. Meanwhile, Hearst's flagship newspaper in the eastern United States, the *New York Journal*, was publishing sensational accounts proclaiming the California airship's reality. A bitter rival of Hearst at the time, the *San Francisco Call*, took great relish in pointing out this conspicuous discrepancy, which it said proved the "Jekyll and Hyde features of 'Little Willie's' journalistic character."[265] The Examiner's skeptical position on the California airship was almost certainly in response to claims made at the very beginning of the wave in *The Call*, suggesting the airship's reality.

"Yellow journalism" typified the period prior to and encompassing the sightings, and refers to the reporting of sensational, exaggerated, and often falsified stories in order to boost circulation. This strategy was common among many American newspapers between 1880 and 1900.[266] Other editors attacked the sensationalism of the airship rumors and sightings by portions of the California press.[267] However, while yellow journalism in California was instrumental in propagating the episode, witnesses were usually seeing something, typically stars and planets. Within this context of newspaper saturation and public enchantment with aeronautics, a new definition of plausible reality was created, where past and concurrent events, objects and circumstances, were redefined to reflect this new meaning.

The California airship wave had been building up for about a week and dominated the California press amid sensational, near saturation-level press coverage, when sightings spread to nearby states, and eventually across the country. One of the first sightings in the Pacific Northwest was at McMinnville, Oregon, on the night of November 24, when a report in that city's *Telephone-Register* referred to the incident with a brief two-sentence story: "Tuesday night several of the boys about town saw the Sacramento air ship sail over this city, at least they saw lights in the heavens. This they swear to."[268] A deluge of airship sightings ensued across the Pacific Northwest, except in Oregon. This prompted the Portland *Evening Telegram* to remark that "It is news to say that the ship has not been seen in Portland" and had nearly missed the state altogether.[269]

1897: The Sightings Rekindle Nationwide

Airship sightings spread across the rest of the country. The following is a survey from several states and represents but a fraction of the reports.

Illinois

The state of Illinois was inundated with airship reports during April 1897. The first known sighting took place in Nashville during the first week of that month, as many residents spotted a balloon-like airship with a large red light at 8 pm.[270] On April 8th, a Rock Island police officer claimed that while on his east end beat, he was startled by an illuminated vessel a half mile overhead. He described it as having "a glittering steel hull, with dim wing-like fans on either side, and it swayed gently in its flight."[271] On April 9th hundreds of people observed it over Chicago, Evanston, Niles Center, and Schermerville.[272] On the night of April 10th, scores of Jacksonville residents watched the airship pass over the city. "It was seen by all the police officers on duty, the firemen and hundreds of citizens."[273] By the evening of the 11th, the sightings reached Springfield as Richard Schriver, foreman of the county jail, watched it for 30 minutes with another man. It was described as "a radiating light not unlike a locomotive headlight."[274] At 8 p.m. in Lincoln on April 12th, "More than fifty people stood on Pulaski Street and whenever the lightening flashed and the clouds separated" they thought they could discern the airship's light in the distance.[275]

On April 13th, over 200 people saw its white and green lights as it passed near Lincoln at 8 pm, while 30 minutes later it was seen over Moline by several farmers, including Benjamin Carr who said it was "a cigar-shaped body or hull, apparently about 15 feet long, with large wing-like projections on each side."[276]

These are just a handful of hundreds of Illinois sightings that occurred during April. Not only are there striking parallels between the airship wave and present-day UFO reports, but there were also reports of close encounters. We will briefly mention here just three Illinois close encounter cases out of the many that occurred across the nation during 1897.

Artist's enhancement of an "airship" photographed by newsstand dealer Walter McCann in 1897 over Chicago.

According to the front page of the *Decatur Daily Republican* of April 16, 1897, the airship landed near Springfield the previous night. Farmhand John Halley and local vineyard owner Adolf Wenke said that it landed three miles west of the city along the Jefferson street road. They said a long-bearded man emerged and inquired where he was. "Inside the car was seated another man and also the scientist's wife." He said they usually rested during the daytime in remote parts of the country in order to conceal the vessel's huge wings. When they asked the scientist his name, "he smiled and pointed to the letter M., which was painted on the side car." After bidding the farmers farewell, he pressed a button and the ship flew off.[277]

The *Springfield News* also reported on an airship touching down near Carlinville on April 12th. It was reportedly spotted between the town of Nilwood and Girard about 6:15. William Street, Frank Metcalf, and Ed Temples and the telegraph operator all saw it at Girard. "These men saw it alight, and a man get out and fix some part of the machinery. They started for the place where it had alighted, but within a quarter of a mile it rose and disappeared from view" to the north.[278]

A fourth-hand encounter report came from Elburn, in Kane County, on April 10th. According to a report on the front page of the Rockford *Daily Republic* of April 12th, "Trainmen running through there say that the operator says that some stockmen say that some farmers say that the ship had a breakdown near there and came down for repairs."[279]

Near the height of the wave, the following is a modest sample of Illinois sightings that appeared in the *Chicago Tribune*:

> Mount Vernon, Illinois, April 15.--(Special.)--What is thought to have been the mysterious airship was seen here by more than 100 persons last night. ...
>
> Carlyle, Ill., April 15.--(Special.)--The airship was seen this evening travelling rapidly in a northwesterly course...
>
> Quincy, Ill., April 15.--(Special.)--The Wabash passenger train which arrived here at 10 o'clock tonight raced for 15 minutes with the alleged airship. They first sighted the thing near Perry Springs, 52 miles east of Quincy... All of the passengers saw it, but all they could see was two lights, one white, the other red.
>
> Hillsboro, Ill., April 15.--(Special.)--...the airship was seen in the western heavens by a number of reputable citizens last evening.[280]

Toward the end of the month, the press grew increasingly skeptical in their discussion of the airship, and several mass sightings were being attributed to pranksters after the remains of tissue balloons or fire balloons were found in the vicinity of the sightings. There were also instances where illuminated kites were sent skyward and accounted for some sightings. Among the skeptical was a journalist for the *Monmouth Daily Review* who noted that "The 'airship neck' will have to be counted a modern malady as much as the 'bicycle face' and other kindred ills."[281] At the *Chicago Record* it was observed that the airship had been sighted at several places at once.[282]

MICHIGAN[283]

In Michigan too, the most intense period of phantom airship sightings occurred between April and May of 1897, coinciding with a flurry of similar reports in nearby Iowa and Missouri.[284] During the last week of March, there were several reports of mysterious aerial lights in Michigan, but these were interpreted as either a strange "meteor" that was observed for an hour at Holland,[285] or "ghost lights" on Boughner and Mills Lakes near the village of Shearer, which resulted in several inhabitants leaving the vicinity due to this "ghost scare."[286] A similar episode was reported in the bay off Caseville, where a fluttering light was thought to have been ghosts from the steamer Oconte, which sank near Big Charity Island several years earlier.[287] Also, a mysterious nocturnal light seen by Rodney Heddon near his farm in Byron was attributed to the ghost of his deceased father.[288]

The first Michigan airship sighting occurred in the village of Alma on Saturday evening, April 10th in the western sky.[289] At Benton Harbor at 7:45 p.m. on the following night, it was observed for 15 minutes flying high above Lake Michigan by a group of residents on Morton Hill before it faded off to the northwest.[290] The vessel was described as having red, green, and blue flickering lights, and was also seen at St. Joseph, Michigan, at about the same time.[291] An hour later, several hundred people saw the aerial "machine" floating above Black Lake near Holland, including prominent citizens Dr. J.D. Wetmore, and Mr. C.L. King, manager of the large King Basket Factory.[292] Near Niles, Michigan, two men saw bright aerial lights during the evening, of what may have been the airship,[293] while at 10 p.m. it was seen by three Mendon residents.[294] On April 12th, some 20 "reputable citizens" in Battle Creek, claimed to observe the vessel pass two miles west of the city at 8:55 pm. "Sparks flew forth and the ship began to slowly settle to within about half a mile from the earth."[295] It was 25-to-30 feet long and remained near the ground a few moments, when a buzzing noise was heard. "Again the sparks flew out as if from an emery wheel and the machine began to rise slowly...[and] the lights went out."[296] Some witnesses even claimed they could discern faint voices coming from the "craft."[297] The object disappeared to the southwest.[298] When the brilliantly illuminated airship was spotted by several residents in Kalamazoo on the same evening, it was said to be moving about 50 miles per hour as it passed northwesterly. The editor of the *Kalamazoo Gazette*, Andrew J. Shakespeare, also observed the object.[299] The most sensational report of the evening was from the town of Pavillion, where residents George W. Somers and William Chadburn saw an illuminated object explode in the air, leading them to assume that the airship had exploded. Several other residents heard the noise but saw nothing. When part of an electric appliance was found lying on the ground the next morning, it was thought to have come from the airship, as were mysterious tiny fragments of an unknown material found scattered near a barn in the town of Comstock.[300]

On Tuesday night, April 13th, the airship mania continued. When a mysterious glow was noticed in the southern sky over Kalamazoo, the cry of airship immediately when up. It was subsequently realized that the illumination was a reflection from Thomas Moore's barn burning down on South Burdick Street.[301] Meanwhile, George Parks and his wife reported that an airship swooped to within 100 feet of a field on their Pennfield farm, 5 miles north of Battle Creek, claiming that a wheel fell off, embedding itself into to ground. The wheel was three feet in diameter and on display at their farm.[302]

As the sightings continued, press editors grew increasingly incredulous as numerous hoaxes came to light and the stories grew more outlandish. A carrier boy for the *Battle Creek Daily Moon* claimed to have found a letter dropped from the vessel.[303] A sensation was caused in Pontiac on the evening of the 15th as hundreds of persons were certain that the airship had passed about 250 feet above Saginaw Street, but were disgusted to hear that enterprising students had hauled lanterns up on the flag staff of the Grove school.[304] On the same evening, hundreds of Lansing residents reported seeing the airship, which was later identified as a toy balloon.[305] Also referred to as "fire" or "paper" balloons, such items were popular during the period and typically sold at stores selling pyrotechnics. They consisted of paper balloons with candles attached near the mouth that made the object buoyant through the generation of heat.

By mid-April, the airship episode peaked. The following excerpt from the *Saginaw Courier-Herald* gives a flavor of the widespread nature of the sightings:

> Corroboration of the visit of the flying air-ship to this city [Saginaw] yesterday morning has been received from many sources....
>
> Charlotte, Mich., April 16.--The mysterious air ship was seen by many people last night...
>
> Hudson, April 16.--This morning's Hudson Gazette contained an account of the passage of the Airship over this city...last night. It...was also seen at Pittsford, Clayton and Cadmus...
>
> Hart, April 16.--A large crowd witnessed a strange sight Wednesday night. Something floated over Shelby...
>
> Olivet, April 16.--The airship was observed here Wednesday night by a large crowd...
>
> Battle Creek, April 16.--The aerial phenomenon, construed by some to be an airship, was seen by many persons here Wednesday evening...
>
> Middleville, April 16.--This village takes the cake in regard to airships. Several responsible residents claim to have seen two of them Wednesday evening... A car attachment had colored lights and scattered sparks, and what was supposed to be smoke.
>
> Lansing, April 16.--Many citizens of Lansing are willing to swear that they saw the airship last evening.[306]

From this point on, witnesses were mercilessly ridiculed in most press accounts, although sightings continued until early May when they tapered out, with reports in Manistee,[307] Saginaw,[308] Davison,[309] Three Rivers,[310] Saline,[311] Grant,[312] Marquette,[313] Marshall,[314] Geneseeville,[315] Sidnaw,[316] Dayton,[317] and Flint.[318] After a report by several people in Wyandotte, it was noted that beer season was open.[319] One journalist quipped that an American had "the same right to see airships that he has to see pink-winged elephants and man-eating cockroaches."[320] Another reporter warned that if the sightings did not abate soon, large numbers of citizens were in danger of getting cricks in their necks. One newspaper reported that the sea serpent was "green with envy over the notoriety being enjoyed just now by its rival the airship."[321] Meanwhile the *Saginaw Globe* commented that future historians should note "the fact that the airship is always seen on Saturday night, when a large portion of the population is in a proper mood to see such things."[322] One writer told of being pleased by three consecutive days of rain, since during this time "nobody claims to have seen the airship."[323] A press editor sarcastically urged sinners to repent, noting that the Bible predicts the appearance of strange signs and wonders during the Last Days, and that the airship may portend that "the day of judgment draws near."[324]

A humorous incident was recounted near Galesburg, when a hunter came upon a hole that appeared to contain a metal instrument. "Visions of airships and grappling hooks arose before him and he made all speed to town" to relay his finding to the local newspaper office. While the paper reported that an anchor dropped from the airship had made a deep hole, a subsequent investigation revealed "a steel trap in the entrance of a skunk's dwelling place."[325]

Ohio

The state of Ohio also experienced a series of airship reports during April 1897. One of the earliest sightings occurred at Kenton, where many residents reported seeing an airship at about 7pm on April 14th.[326] An hour later, a Casstown farmer, James McKensie said that while feeding his hogs, a huge bird-like airship passed by just 150 feet off the ground.[327] At 10:30 pm, several people in Hillsboro saw an airship with red lights.[328] It was observed by several prominent Dunkirk residents at about 4 a.m. on April 15th, as several witnesses including the marshall, William Mahon, claimed to hear voices coming from the vessel "but could not distinguish what they were seeing." Resembling a wagon bed, it had "large wings extending on either side."[329] That very evening it was sighted over Akron.[330]

After widespread sightings over Cincinnati that occurred between late Saturday night and early Sunday morning on April 17-18, one newspaper made fun of the reports.[331] At about the same time, it was also spotted over Columbus.[332] When Toledo residents Howard Wern and his father M.B. Wern saw the airship on Saturday night April 24th, they were willing to sign an affadavit.[333] In Cleveland, Jed Wickham, cashier at the county clerks office, saw it while walking in the city at about 10:30 pm. After staring at the aerial light for a while, he could discern that it "was shaped like a cigar and right about it was a balloon-shaped affair. It seemed to be stationary for quite a while, and then it moved slowly off to the southeast."[334] On the 28th, Cincinnati police officer John Ringer and half a dozen citizens spotted the light of what he believed was the airship while standing at the corner of 8th and Walnut streets at 10 pm.[335] Other people in the city claimed to see it independently.[336] One of the last Ohio sightings was over Norwalk on the evening of May 9th where some people out of a group of a dozen or so who saw it thought they could hear music coming from the vessel.[337]

There were several Ohio reports of close encounters with airship pilots and their earthly crew. For instance, in Bradford, Ohio, three men (David Brant, Michael Roach, Oscar Richards) said that the airship landed and they conversed with those on board.[338] A Lancaster man who refused to give his name, described in great detail his meeting with the crew and being given a tour of the contraption.[339] On the 26th, an airship 40 feet long with bat-like wings reportedly startled a farmer while he was milking near Pigeon Roost in Perry County. The crew told him that a California hermit had unraveled the secret of flight and their experimental airship was being supported by a group of capitalists.[340]

Kentucky

The Kentucky sightings were primarily confined to mid-April to mid-May. Just prior to this time, at least one Morganfield resident was holding nightly parties on the roof of his house in expectation of seeing the airship that had been reported in other parts of the country.[341] The first known sighting occurred on Monday evening, April 12th, near Adairsville. The airship caused a sensation among the inhabitants when it was spotted at 8:30 pm. nearly a mile high. It had a bright headlight attached to a steel body 25-to-30 feet long that sported wings or propellers and a red lantern at the tail.[342] The local African-Americans panicked at the sight and many "shouted and prayed as if they thought the millennium was at hand."[343] Early the next morning, two miles south of Louisville, farmer Augustus Rodgers claimed to observe an illuminated oblong-shaped airship traveling about 100 miles per hour just 400 feet above the ground. After calling to his wife, they "saw a form, like that of a man, standing at the front of the ship and directing its course," and the vessel soon disappeared to the southeast.[344] At about the same time, John S. McCollough, who resided near Churchill Downs, reported that a brilliantly lighted airship passed overhead while he was traveling by horse near the city; he claimed that a piece of half-burned coal fell from the vessel.[345]

On the evening of April 15th, several Russellville residents observed the airship "plainly and distinctly," including Mayor Andrews and prominent dry goods merchant Colonel James McCutchens. The illuminated object sailed out of sight westward.[346] It was also spotted that night by many people in the communities of Todd,[347] Clarksville,[348] and Hopkinsville.[349] The following day, the managers of the Nashville Centennial Exposition used the growing public interest in the airship to their advantage to gain free publicity by claiming that the vessel was real and the owners were under contract to place it on display.[350] On the 16th at 8:30 pm, hundreds of people in Cairo saw the airship pass slowly just above the western horizon.[351] At about this time, Samuel Bunnel of Mercer County made perhaps the most incredulous report when he seriously claimed to view the airship through his telescope; he said the airship contained winged angels with exquisite garb.[352]

On April 18, scores of people in Bowling Green saw in the western sky for about an hour a large moving light that was widely assumed to have been the airship.[353] There was "great excitement" in Madisonville on the night of April 20th as "the streets were crowded with people watching the aerial wonder," among them Mayor Holeman A. Worley.[354] On the same evening, it was seen passing over Rich Pond, where well-known merchant H.F. Jordan proclaimed:

"I saw the airship and it was a beautiful sight."[355] By April 20th, the craze had reached such proportions that newspapers were carrying airship-related advertisements. For instance, one ad read: "The Airship a Certainty.--Make this doubly sure by buying one of our choice carpets, and your 'HEIRSHIP' will not be questioned."[356] Another proclaimed that the airship had been seen with two men on board, one of whom dropped a message which urged people to attend a local sale.[357]

On the 21st, several policemen and citizens in Louisville spotted a brilliant aerial light, which many assumed to be a flying machine. Captain John Tully of the No. 6 Engine house and the entire company also witnessed the light upon returning from a fire call. "One of the men called attention to the peculiar sight, and the men at once concluded that it was the air ship," which subsequently disappeared to the northwest.[358] At about this time, three men in Berea claimed the airship passed overhead at about 10 pm.[359] On April 23rd, numerous residents in Lewisburg were convinced that they saw the craft pass to the southwest. "Its outlines were plainly observed and many good citizens will swear that it was the aerial flyer."[360] One newspaper reported the incident as follows: "Lewisburg, April 24.--A profound sensation was created here last night by the discovery of the lights of an airship moving in a south of west course and at a great height. It was witnessed by a great number of our most reputable citizens. There can be no doubt whatever that it was the airship that is said to have been seen in so many places."[361]

Also on the night of the 24th, a Louisville man employed as a clerk for the Louisville and Nashville railroad gave a particularly vivid description of the airship. Thomas J. Casey stated that he was behind his home when he heard a buzzing sound and saw the cigar-shaped ship about 200 feet up.[362] He claimed to discern the outline of a man standing in the lower rear section. "He looked at me and I waved my hat. Two other men were sitting in the helm."[363] The object rapidly disappeared to the south. Station keeper Thomas O'Neil of the central police station also reported seeing the airship at about the same time.[364] The ship, which "carried a very bright light," was again sighted by Clarksville residents on Sunday evening the 25th, flying half a mile high to the southwest.[365]

Many newspaper editors were skeptical, attributing the observations to either irrationality precipitated by emotional excitement, or to alcohol or opium intake. The editors of the Paducah *Daily News* ridiculed witnesses, referring to them as "rubbernecks," and the airship as the "queer aerial voyager" and "strange lightening bug."[366] When hometown lawyers Tom Wallace and Jess Scott said they watched the airship fly over Mayfield on April 14th, the *Mayfield Mirror* quipped that they must have been viewing the vessel "through a bottle."[367] In the *Louisville Courier-Journal*, it was sarcastically suggested that there must be an "aerial flotilla" due to the volume of sightings.[368]

During late April, as the episode peaked, the claims grew more outlandish, and the belief in the flying machine's existence began to erode rapidly. Some Kentucky residents even maintained that they had found letters dropped from the airship.[369] In Corbin, a businessman who also served as church deacon claimed to be in possession of a piece of metal that he said had fallen from the airship.[370] By April 30th, the sightings had declined dramatically. One of the last sightings was recorded on the 30th when Gillis Hendricks, a section foreman with the Louisville and Nashville railroad, reported seeing a cone-shaped airship with blue and white signals. The account states that "Hendricks' story is laughed at."[371] [372]

Pennsylvania

On the evening of April 17, 1897, a heavier-than-air flying machine was seen by many residents of Derry. They described it as cigar-shaped with red, green, and white lights; they said that a car could be seen "hanging about ten feet from the ship entirely enclosed."[373] Four nights later, numerous citizens of Erie said that a mysterious vessel passed over that city at an estimated height of 2,000 feet and was plainly visible. One of the witnesses was Mr. J.S. Scheer, who said it carried bright lights and was "quite long and shaped like a cigar. It had two wing-like fans on each side and a huge propeller on the stern."[374] On the same evening, the airship was reported from Sharon, Pennsylvania: Jay Latimere, C.S. Wallace, and Attorney E.E. Andrews claimed that the airship passed over "at a high rate of speed. They say three men were on board, and the ship was plainly visible. They are reliable citizens and their story is generally believed. The ship was cigar shaped and seemed to have wings and a propeller.[375]

One of the last Pennsylvania reports came from four persons at Fairplain on the evening of April 27. One observer was a correspondent for the *Erie Daily Times* who noticed a brilliant light in the sky at about 8:45. The vessel had red and green lights that were discernible, "would tossle up and down a ways and then it seemed to fall quite a ways down, but would rise as soon as it fell to its old line of travel." Nearly an hour after first spotting it, the airship sank in the western sky. The correspondent stated emphatically that "no one can convince me that it was 'only a star' I saw. I firmly believe it was the 'airship.'"[376]

On the night of April 12th, an Allegheny man said the airship landed near his home on Troy Hill and he was taken for a ride in the craft. In conversing with the crew, they "Simply told me to go home, and if I met people who told me they did not believe that machines were made that could fly to tell them that I saw one and had a ride in it."[377]

Colorado

In the state of Colorado, one of the first known sightings was in the city of Denver on Thursday evening April 8th, when an assistant weather observer saw "two bright yellow lights" moving rapidly west from the dome of the Federal Building at 7:45 pm. The *Denver Times* speculated that it was an airship.[378] The next report occurred on the night of April 11th at Boulder when an immense airship, 100 feet long and sporting two wings, was seen hovering above the city.[379] On April 17, a man in Cripple Creek made an incredible claim. James H. Graham said that on Saturday evening he was in his barn when something crashed onto the roof. He got a stepladder, climbed onto the roof, and claimed to have found a battered sardine can that contained a message from the airship occupants who purportedly said they were from Boston and Paris, France.[380] Graham said that after reading the note, he scanned the sky intensely and saw an object sinking over Mt. Pisgah. This was the first of many incidents involving citizens claiming to have received notes dropped from the craft.[381] The next day, the *Denver Times* reported that about three thousand people saw a cigar-shaped airship near Cripple Creek for two hours before disappearing from sight.[382] When the Glenwood Springs *Avalanche* reported on this sighting three days later, the number of witnesses had inflated to ten thousand.[383] The *Rocky Mountain Daily News* reported that there were only several hundred observers.[384]

On Sunday night April 18th, prominent Florence businessman Charles Bates, reported seeing an apparent airship passing slowly southward.[385] At about 1 a.m. on the 21st, a nightwatchman at the Silver Lake mine, Mr. T.K. Holden, saw the airship within 2,000 feet of the ground. In supporting the story, a local newspaper described him as "a man of good standing in the community, noted for his truth and veracity, and at all times strictly temperate in his habits, never drinking anything stronger than Hood's Sarsaparilla."[386] In the early morning of April 22nd at about 1 am, the airship was seen by 20 miners of the Aspen and Durant mines, passing westerly over Smuggler Mountain. The *Aspen Daily Times* used the misleading headlines: "Mysterious Airship, It passed over Aspen Yesterday Morning;" it also admitted in the same issue: "The only thing visible was a bright light resembling the headlight of a locomotive."[387] A typical sighting occurred on the night of April 24th near Grand Junction.[388]

> GRAND JUNCTION, Colo., April 25.--The air ship was seen here last night by Orson Adams, Jr., cashier of the Mesa County State Bank. The aerial voyager was pursuing a northwest by north course at an elevation of about 2,500 feet, seemingly moving at a terrific speed and finally vanishing behind a low hanging bank of black clouds. Mr. Adams is somewhat averse to discussing the matter, realizing the skepticism of most people as the to actual existence of the ship, but he stated...this morning that he was never surer of anything in his life... [He saw] a cylinder-like craft with outriggers and fan-shaped sails. A steely light beamed from the stern of the sky-scraper as she receded from view. The story has been circulated quite extensively here today and there is considerable excitement, as Mr. Adams is known as a practical and conservative citizen, who is not likely either to invent or misstate facts.

During the episode, there were at least two reported close encounters with airship occupants, but unlike their modern extraterrestrial counterparts in flying saucers, they contained airship inventors and crew. In one case, four men claimed to have come across the vessel at a remote location behind a hill near Loveland. They were introduced to the inventor, Professor E.K. Afatisi of Worcester, Ohio, and Mr. R. E. Jones, a Chicago businessman "who furnished the money for the experiment and the trial trip."[389] Two Montrose residents claimed that the cigar-shaped vessel passed so near that they could discern voices.[390] Not to be out done by contemporary UFO crash claims like those at Roswell, New Mexico, a prospector claimed that he had seen the remains of the airship after crashing near Fulford, Colorado.[391]

On May 6th, airship interest was briefly rekindled when the Mayor of Florence, Colorado, had a sighting:

> An airship was seen by Prof. George Kellar, Principal of the Schools, and Mayor Lewis, while on their way home from a church meeting last night about 10:30.
>
> Professor Kellar describes it when first seen as cigar shaped with bow and stern curved upwards. It was so brilliantly lighted that it illuminated a cloud through which it passed. It was visible for ten or twelve minutes and tacked about, changing the appearance of its outline to something resembling a big wedge. It disappeared below the horizon to the northwest. [392]

Near the end of the wave, as reports died down, the Colorado press grew increasingly skeptical and published shorter and shorter stories on the subject, such as the two-sentence accounts in the *Silver Plume Silver Standard* on May 8th and 15th, and the Gilpin County Observer of May 7th.

The Northwest

Many airship reports were recorded in Montana during April 1897. One of the earliest known sightings occurred at Havre at about 5:30 a.m. on Saturday morning April 17th.[393] At about this time, several people in Minot also claimed to have seen it.[394] At 7 p.m. on April 22nd, a mysterious airship was reported traveling westward over Miles City.[395] It was again seen above Miles City, this time by many residents, on the evening of April 27th. The editor of the *Yellowstone Journal*, Samuel Gordon was one witness who became convinced that it was a heavier-than-air flying machine:

> It being deep dusk and the air full of a gray mist of driving rain, it was impossible to make out the ship itself; the point of brilliance made by the headlight appeared to obscure all in its immediate vicinity, nevertheless there were some sharp-eyed observers who claimed to trace the familiar cigar-shaped cylinder...and at one time shouts were plainly heard, clear and shrill though greatly mellowed by distance. For over three-quarters of an hour the queer craft was closely watched by many of our best citizens... Suddenly at about 7:40...the light went out, and in the gathering darkness all was lost to view.[396]

According to the editor of the *Helena Daily Herald*, it was later learned that at the same time as this sighting, several mischevious boys had sent aloft a kite with a lantern attached to the bottom, and occasionally "gave vent to their pleasure in wild, shrill shrieks."[397] Later that night at about 10:15 pm, several Fort Benton residents saw an illuminated object that some thought was the airship.[398]

There were also sightings in adjacent states. For instance, in Wyoming, around May 1, 1897, a party of railroad workers claims to have spotted the airship about 20 miles east of Cheyenne. They said it was visible for seven minutes and was just 200 feet off the ground.[399]

To the west in Washington State, the airship was spotted on Thursday evening April 15, 1897. Several residents observed the mysterious flying object passing over Spokane between 8 and 8:30 pm. According to the Spokane *Spokesman-Review*, one witness was Miss T. Kiesling, a nurse who saw it for half an hour: "While I watched it the light changed from a dazzling whiteness to a bright green. It was like nothing I ever saw before in the sky." Another witness was Jack L. Ford, who estimated the illuminated object to have been two miles high. He said it was larger than a star and appeared to move around in the sky. Based on witness descriptions, the newspaper reported that those who saw it were "certain that it was a machine for navigating the air, the work of humans, and bearing evidence of containing people who were directing its progress."[400]

About three weeks later in early May, an even more spectacular sighting report occurred at the small town of Marble Siding, about seven miles from Northport along the Spokane Falls & Northern railroad.

> Marble, Wash., May 5.--The town of Marble was greatly excited today over the appearance of an airship. Some men working at the mill discovered it as it appeared over the mountains at the southern part of town, and watched it disappear in a northeasterly direction. It was in full view, and the fans could easily be recognized. It had an apparatus in front resembling a rotary snowplow...that seemed to be revolving rapidly. The whole thing moved very rapidly, and was only a few minutes passing from view. It was seen by nearly all the mill crew and myself passing away in a northerly direction. The citizens were quite worked up over its appearance, having read of the existence of such a machine as an airship. If anyone doubts the authenticity of this, every man in town can vouch for it. E.E. Horton...[401]

The Wave Wanes

Press skepticism and ridicule increased from

about mid-April onward. In Minnesota, the *St. Paul Pioneer-Press* described local airship observations with the disingenuious headline: "Of course they saw it."[402] The *St. Paul Dispatch* attribed another mass sighting to Venus "slowly sinking to the horizon."[403] The editor of the *Minneapolis Tribune* scoffed at the claims, attributing them to "the star 'Alpha Orionis,' which has been wandering about the heavens for ten million years" and was currently prominent.[404] To the east, the *Wisconsin State Journal* quipped: "Every bird that essays the zenith these days incurs the imputation of being an airship."[405] *The Evening Wisconsin* offered two explanations: "One is that all the air is full of airships. The other is that a good many people are lying." It suggested that the evidence favored the latter.[406] When the vessel was spotted near Lancaster on Saturday night April 10th, a report in the *Racine Daily Journal* bluntly proclaimed: "Fake airship at Lancaster," offering the view that it was yet another tissue balloon.[407] As the wave was abruptly ending in Indiana, sighting reports were afforded brief space, and witnesses were mercilessly teased. The editor of the *Ligonier Banner* wrote: "If you want to know anything about the airship that passed over here Saturday night ask Operator Schwab and he will tell you all about it."[408] Another headline proclaimed embarassingly: "The airship fake."[409] When it was spotted at Rensselaer, the reporter began his account: "Of course somebody in Rensselaer had to see the airship."[410] When several residents of Lake Station reported seeing the flying machine in late April, a local paper devoted one sentence to the incident: "Some of the Lake people have sighted the airship, or claim they have."[411] Following a sighting near Seymour, Indiana on May 7, one headline read: "Sure it was the air ship."[412]

The 1896-97 wave can be interpreted as a form of mass wishfulfillment, as in the wake of rumors of a secret airship, Americans of the late 1800s projected their hopes and expectations onto the ambiguous night-time sky, creating a Rorscach Ink Blot that was a social barometer of the times. Octave Chanute captures the seemingly limitless enthusiasm and optimism of the period when he remarked: "...let us hope that the advent of a successful flying machine...will bring nothing but good into the world; that it shall abridge distance, make all parts of the globe accessible, bring men into closer relation with each other, advance civilisation, and hasten the promised era in which there shall be nothing but peace and good-will among all men."[413]

See also: PHANTOM AIRCRAFT WAVES, FLYING SAUCERS, GHOST ROCKET SCARE, "EDISON STAR" SIGHTINGS, RUSSIAN POLAND BALLOON SCARE, ANDREE BALLOON MANIA.

GREEK TELEPHONE PANIC ATTACKS

Athens, Greece: October 1975

During a two-week period in 1975, a fainting "epidemic" swept through the Athens Telephone Center, affecting an estimated 250 of the center's 990 work force. Major symptoms included the sensation of choking accompanied by hyperventilation, nausea, dizziness, excessive sweating, and dry mouth. At least 154 of the 250 who reported fainting actually fell to the ground but did not lose consciousness.[414]

A team from the psychiatry department at the Athens University Medical School conducted a battery of tests, comparing a sample of 16 "normal" workers with those who were affected. It was concluded that the fainting episodes were not related to conversion disorder or epidemic hysteria, but transient "anxiety attacks" as a result of various environmental stresses in the facility. Potential stressors were identified as excessive noise, temperature, having too many people in one area, and high humidity. Episodes were labeled as "panic attacks" as "there was no loss of consciousness and most subjects expressed an excessive fear of impending threat against their health."[415]

GULF WAR SYNDROME

Middle East: 1991 and ongoing

Many British and American veterans of the Persian Gulf War have reported a variety of illness symptoms that they attribute to their exposure to an array of potential hazards: biological and chemical weapons, depleted uranium munitions, pesticides, oil fumes, vaccinations against such potentially fatal exposures to the plague and anthrax, and taking pyridostigmine bromide as a prophylactic for contact with organophosphate nerve agents. However, despite widespread media publicity and medical discussion about the existence of "Gulf War Syndrome," (GWS) the most common symptoms, according to one study examining the medical records of 18,495 Gulf War veterans, were identified as fatigue, joint aches and pains, rash, sleep disturbances, headache, and memory/concentration problems. They found no evidence of toxic exposure. In fact, two-thirds of victims reported that their symptoms did not appear until after the war was over. In 40 percent of cases, it took a year or more for symptoms to materialize. The researchers noted that the classic symptoms of "Gulf War Syndrome" are typical of the general population.[416] Science writer Michael Fumento observes that because many hundreds of thousands of veterans are involved, "In such a pool you're going to have every illness in the book. Because modern medicine is not an exact science, you're also going to have a certain number of illnesses for which no firm cause is identified."[417] Indeed, Fumento has counted over 100 symptoms of Gulf War Syndrome, and says it's "no exaggeration to say that every ailment any Persian Gulf vet has ever gotten – has been labeled a symptom of GWS."[418]

In an investigation into the political aspects of the condition, Fumento made a compelling case for the socially constructed nature of "Gulf War Syndrome," which he argues was founded on rumors, exaggerations, human nature, and both shoddy and sensationalistic reporting. After interviewing numerous experts, including Gulf War veterans, and reviewing studies on the subject, Fumento concluded that the hoop-la surrounding what he calls "Gulf Lore Syndrome" constitutes an episode of mass hysteria. He poignantly writes:

> Welcome to the world of Gulf Lore Syndrome. It is a world in which science is replaced by rumor, in which vets are presented as medical experts while real medical experts are ignored. It is a dimension in which authoritative review studies by eminent scientists are scorned and disdainfully labeled "Pentagon studies" because they reach the "wrong" conclusions – even if done by civilian organizations. Yet incredible accounts of such symptoms as skin-blistering semen and glowing vomit are taken as gospel. It is a "reality" constructed by crusading reporters, activists, demagogic congressmen, and, sadly, by Persian Gulf vets who have become convinced they are the victims of a conspiracy deeper and broader than anything on the X-Files.[419]

Fumento says the misinformation and myths about "Gulf War Syndrome" can be traced to the first supposed victim, an Army Reservist named Michael Adcock, who died from a spreading lymphoma in 1992, at the age of 22. His mother testified before Congress that her son developed his cancer from something he was exposed to in the Persian Gulf, and the media publicized these claims widely. Yet a review of his case reveals that this was impossible as Adcock's first lymphoma symptoms were discovered after he had been in the Gulf for just six days. In reality, it takes on average, about 10 years for a lymphoma to develop.[420]

Researchers have been unable to identify a new symptom or illness cluster that is unique to military participants in the Gulf War. The popular, widespread use of GWS is in reality a misnomer that serves to confuse the issue.[421] Two of the leading experts on GWS, British psychiatrist Simon Wessely and historian Lawrence Freedman, suggest substituting such terms as "Gulf War Illness" and "Gulf War health effect" as more accurately describing the situation, though they acknowledge that this is unlikely to be adopted given the political and medical entrenchment of the term.[422]

In summarizing the vast medical literature on GWS, Wessely and Freedman emphasize the difference between the terms disease and illness. Disease refers to incidents where there is evidence of pathological dysfunction, whereas illness involves persons reporting symptoms of distress and suffering, yet there is no evidence that physicians are dealing with a pathological condition. Wessely and Freedman note

U.S. Infantry patrol in the Saudi desert. (Photo by Jack Novak)

that except for deaths from injuries, Gulf veterans from both the United Kingdom and United States do not have higher mortality rates. Gulf War veterans from the United States are no more likely to be hospitalized (relative to controls), with three exceptions: mental health diagnoses, musculoskeletal disorders (which have been linked to mental health issues), and unexplained symptoms without evidence of organic disease (which have also been linked to psychological factors). Indeed, just one disease has been claimed to be elevated among Gulf veterans – motor neuron disease – the supporting evidence for which remains inconclusive and fails to explain ill health claims in all but a fraction of Gulf veterans.[423]

Wessely and Freedman observe that clusters of medically unexplained symptoms (that is, symptoms for which there is no identifiable underlying pathology) are commonplace in the medical literature following terror attacks and in military service veterans. After World War I, physicians observed a variety of unusual symptoms in returning soldiers, including physical and psychological fatigue, and numerous aches and pains, nightmares, and insomnia. Yet for all of their efforts, no one could pinpoint a definitive physical cause. In these and other wars, these symptoms became known by such names as "Effort Syndrome," "Soldier's Heart," and "Shell Shock." Each of these illnesses was never found to have a pathological basis and slowly faded away and eventually became discarded diagnoses. According to Wessely and Freedman: "Now, few talk about Soldier's Heart or Effort Syndrome, but these were the Gulf War Syndromes of their day."[424]

Despite a century of research into medically unexplained symptoms on returning veterans, and despite hundreds of studies, the most plausible explanation to account for these illness clusters – given the lack of an underlying pathology in these men and women, and until a medical breakthrough occurs that can definitively explain these symptoms – is that they are of a psychological origin triggered by extraordinary stress.

Sources

1. Griffiths, Major Arthur (1898). *Mysteries of Police and Crime.* London: Cassell and Company, Volume 3, p. 230.
2. Sindall, R. (1987). "The London Garotting [sic] Panics of 1856 and 1862." *Social History* 12(3): 351.
3. Sindall, op cit., p. 352.
4. Portions of this entry have been excerpted from Bartholomew, Robert E. (1998). "The Medicalization of Exotic Deviance: A Sociological Perspective on Epidemic *Koro.*" *Transcultural Psychiatry* 35(1):5-38.
5. Gwee, A.L. (1968). "*Koro*–It's Origin and Nature as a Disease Entity." *Singapore Medical Journal* 4: 119-122.
6. Van Wulfften Palthe, P.M. (1936). "Psychiatry and Neurology in the Tropics." In C. de Langen and A. Lichtenstein (Eds.) *Clinical Textbook of Tropical Medicine.* Batavia: G. Kolff and Company, p. 536.
7. Blonk, J.C. (1895). "*Koro.*" *Geneeskundig Tijdschrift voor Nederlandsch-Indie* 35: 562-563.
8. Bartholomew (1998). op cit., p. 24.
9. Modai, I., Munitz, H., and Aizenber, D. (1986). "*Koro* in an Israeli Male." *British Journal of Psychiatry* 149:503-505.
10. Hes, J.P., and Nassi, G. (1977). "*Koro* in a Yemenite and a Georgian Jewish Immigrant." *Confinia Psychiatrica* 20: 180-184.
11. Malinick, C., Filaherty, J.A., Jobe, T. (1985). "*Koro*: How Culturally Specific?" *International Journal of Social Psychiatry* 31(1):67-73; Kendall, E.M., and Jenkins, P.L. (1987). "*Koro* in an American Man." *American Journal of Psychiatry* 144(12):1621; Scher, M. (1987). "*Koro* in a Native Born Citizen of the U.S." *International Journal of Social Psychiatry* 33(1):42-45.
12. Edwards, J.G. (1970). "The *Koro* Pattern of Depersonalization in an American Schizophrenic Patient." *American Journal of Psychiatry* 126(8):1171-1173.
13. Arbitman, R. (1975). "*Koro* in a Caucasian." *Modern Medicine of Canada* 30(11):970-971; Ede, A. (1976). "*Koro* in an Anglo-Saxon Canadian." *Canadian Psychiatric Association Journal* 21:389-392; Waldenberg, S. (1981). "*Koro.*" *Canadian Journal of Psychiatry* 26: 140-141.
14. Lapierre, Y.D. (1972). "*Koro* in a French Canadian." *Journal of the Canadian Psychiatric Association* 17: 333-334.
15. Baasher, T.A. (1963). "The Influence of Culture on Psychiatric Manifestations." *Transcultural Psychiatric Research Review* 15:51-52.
16. Menezes, S.B. (1992). "A Case of *Koro* and Folie a Deux in a Shona Family." Letter. *South African Medical Journal* 82(6):483.
17. Turnier, L., and Chouinard, G. (1990). "Effet Anti-*Koro* d'un Antidepresseur Tricyclique" (Anti-*Koro* Effect of a Tricyclic Depressant). *Canadian Journal of Psychiatry* 35(4):331-333; Bourgeois, M. (1968). "Un *Koro* Charentais" (Transposition Ethnopsychiatrique). *Annales Medico-Psychologiques* 126: 749-751.
18. Ifabumuyi, O.I., Rwegellera, G.G. (1979). "*Koro* in a Nigerian Male Patient: A Case Report." *African Journal of Psychiatry* 5:103-105.
19. De Leo, D., Mauro, P., and Pellegrini, C. (1989). "An Organic Triggering Factor in *Koro* Syndrome? A Case Report." *European Journal of Psychiatry* 3(2):77-81.
20. Barrett, K. (1978). "*Koro* in a Londoner." Letter. *The Lancet* ii: 1319; Constable, P.J. (1979). *Koro* in Hertfordshire. *The Lancet* i:163; Cremona, A. (1981). "Another Case of *Koro* in a Briton." Letter. *British Journal of Psychiatry* 138:180; Adeniran, R.A., and Jones, J.R. (1994). *Koro*: Culture-Bound Disorder or Universal Symptom?" *British Journal of Psychiatry* 164: 559-561; Hawley, R.M., Owen, J.H. (1988). "*Koro*: It's Presentation in an Elderly Male." *International Journal of Geriatric Psychiatry* 3(1):69-72.
21. Smyth, M.G., and Dean, C. (1992). "Capgras and *Koro.*" *British*

Journal of Psychiatry 161:121-123.
22. Ang, P.C., and Weller, M.P. (1984). "*Koro* and Psychosis." *British Journal of Psychiatry* 145:335.
23. Tseng, W.S., Mo, K.M., Hsu, J., Li, L.S., Ou, L.W., Chen, G.Q., and Jiang. D.W. (1988). "A Sociocultural Study of *Koro* Epidemics in Guangdong, China." *American Journal of Psychiatry* 145 (12): 1538-1543. See p. 1538.
24. Gwee, 1968, op cit.
25. Van Brero, P.C.Z. (1897). "*Koro*, eine Eigenthumlich Zwangsvorstellung." *Allgemeine Zeitschaft fur Psychiatrie* 53: 569-573.
26. Kobler, F. (1948). "Description of an Acute Castration Fear, Based on Superstition." *Psychoanalytical Review* 35: 285-289.
27. Rack, P. (1982). *Race, Culture, and Mental Disorder*. London: Tavistock Publications, p. 148.
28. Gwee, A.L. (1963). "*Koro*–A Cultural Disease." *Singapore Medical Journal* 4: 119; Prince, R. (1992a). "*Koro* and the Fox Spirit on Hainan Island (China)." *Transcultural Psychiatric Research Review* 29:119-132. See p. 120.
29. Yap, P.M. (1965). "*Koro*–A Culture-Bound Depersonalization Syndrome." *British Journal of Psychiatry* 111: 43-50. See p. 49.
30. Berrois, G.E., and Morley, S.J. (1984). "*Koro*-like Symptoms in a Non-Chinese Subject." *British Journal of Psychiatry* 145: 331-334.
31. Simons, R.C. (1985). "Introduction: The Genital Retraction Taxon." In R.C. Simons and C.C. Hughes (Eds.) *The Culture-Bound Syndromes*. Boston, Reidel.
32. Prince (1992a). op cit.; Prince, Raymond (1992b). "A Symposium on the Vulnerable Male: Cultural Variations on the Castration Theme." *Transcultural Psychiatric Research Review* 29: 87-90.
33. Prince, 1992a, op cit., p. 119.
34. Sachdev, P.S., and Shukla, A. (1982). "Epidemic *Koro* Syndrome in India." *The Lancet* ii:1161.
35. Slot, J.A. (1935). "*Koro* in Zuid-Celebes." *Geneeskundig Tijdschrift voor Nederlandsch-Indie* 75:811-820.
36. Tseng, 1988, op cit., p. 1538.
37. Tseng, 1988, op cit., p. 1539.
38. Tseng, 1988, op cit., p. 1540.
39. Jilek, W. G. (1986). "Epidemics of 'Genital Shrinking' (*koro*): Historical Review and Report of a Recent Outbreak in Southern China." *Curare* [The German Journal of Ethnomedicine] 9:269-282. See p. 276.
40. Tseng, W.S., Mo, K.M., Hsu, J., Li, L.S., Ou, L.W., Chen, G.Q., and Jiang, D.W. (1987). *A Socio-Cultural and Clinical Study of a Koro (Genital Retraction Panic Disorder) Epidemic in Guangdong, China.* Paper presented at the Conference of the Society for the Study of Psychiatry and Culture, Quebec City, Quebec, Canada, September 16 to 19; Tseng (1988). op cit., p. 1538.
41. Tseng, W.S., Mo, K.M, Li. L.S., Chen, G.Q., OU, L.W., and Zheng, H.B. (1992). "*Koro* Epidemics in Guangdong, China: A Questionnaire Survey." *The Journal of Nervous and Mental Disease* 180 (2): 117-123.
42. Tseng, 1992, op cit., p. 117; Jilek, W.G. (1986). "Epidemics of 'Genital Shrinking' (*koro*): Historical Review and Report of a Recent Outbreak in Southern China." *Curare* 9:269-282, see p. 274; Murphy, H.B.M. (1986). *The Koro Epidemic in Hainan Island.* Paper presented to the Regional Conference of the World Psychiatric Association's Transcultural Psychiatry Section, Beijing, China, August 17-31.
43. Tseng et al. (1988). op cit., p. 1542; Tseng et al. (1992). op cit., p. 117.
44. Legendre, J. (1936). "Une Curicuse Epidemie (*Koro*)." *Presse Medicale* (Paris): 1534, translated from French and published in: Bartholomew, Robert E., and Gregory, Jane (1996). "'A Strange Epidemic:' Notes on the First Detailed Documented Case of Epidemic *Koro*." *Transcultural Psychiatric Research Review* 33:365-366.
45. Legendre, op cit.
46. Legendre, op cit.
47. Gwee, 1963, op cit.
48. Tseng et al., 1988, op cit.
49. Prince, 1992a, op cit., p. 128.
50. Jilek and Jilek-Aall, 1977a, op cit., p. 58.
51. Suwanlert, S., and Coates, D. (1979). "Epidemic *Koro* in Thailand–Clinical and Social Aspects." Abstract of the report by F.R. Fenton appearing in *Transcultural Psychiatric Research Review* 16: 64-66. See p. 65.
52. Jilek and Jilek-Aall, 1977a, op cit., p. 58.
53. Suwanlert and Coats, op cit., p. 65.
54. Jilek and Jilek-Aall, 1977a, op cit., p. 58.
55. Chakraborty, A., Das, S., and Mukherji, A. (1983). "*Koro* Epidemic in India." *Transcultural Psychiatric Research Review* 20: 150-151.
56. Sachdev and Shukla (1982). op cit.
57. Ng, B. (1997). "History of *Koro* in Singapore." *Singapore Medical Journal* 38(8):356-357.
58. Mun, op cit.
59. Mun, op cit.
60. Gwee, 1963, op cit, p. 120.
61. Gwee, 1968, op cit., p. 4.
62. Gwee, A.H., Lee, Y.K., Tham, N.B., Chee, K.H., Chew, W., Ngui, P., Wong, Y.C., Lau, C.W., and Tsee, C.K. [Commonly referred to as "The *Koro* Study Team"] (1969). "The *Koro* 'Epidemic' in Singapore." *Singapore Medical Journal* 10(4): 234-242.
63. Harrington, J.A. (1982). "Epidemic Psychosis." Letter. *British Journal of Psychiatry* 141:98-99.
64. Simmons (1985). op cit., p. 152.
65. Chowdhury, A.N. (1989a). "Penile Perception of *Koro* Patients." *Acta Psychiatrica Scandinavica* 80: 183-186; Chowdhury, A.N. (1989b). "Dysmorphic Penis Image Perception: The Root of *Koro* Vulnerability." *Acta Psychiatrica Scandinavica* 80: 518-520.
66. Chowdhury, 1989a, op cit., p. 183.
67. American Psychiatric Association (1994). *Diagnostic and Statistical Manual of Mental Disorders*, fourth edition. Washington, DC: American Psychiatric Association, pp. 467-468.
68. Sachdev and Shukla (1982). op cit.
69. Tseng et al., op cit, p. 1540.
70. Yap, 1965, op cit.
71. Gwee, 1963, op cit.
72. Rin, H. (1965). "A Study of the Aetiology of *Koro* in Respect to the Chinese Concept of Illness." *International Journal of Social Psychiatry* 11:7-13.
73. Cai, J.B. (1982). ("Five Case Reports of Suo-Yang Zhen"). *Chinese Journal of Neuropsychiatry* 4:206; Mo, G.M. (1991). *Sociocultural Aspects of a Koro Epidemic in Southern China.* Paper Presented at the International Symposium on Cultural Psychiatry in Budapest, Hungry (August 26-28).
74. De Leo et al., op cit.
75. Cohen, S., Tennenbaum, S.Y., Teitelbaum, A., and Durst, R. (1995). "The *Koro* (Genital Retraction) Syndrome and its Association with Infertility: A Case Report." *Journal of Urology* 153(2): 427-428.
76. Puranik, A., and Dunn, J. (1995). "*Koro* Presenting After Prostatectomy in an Elderly Man." *British Journal of Urology* 75(1):108-109.
77. Durst, R., and Rosea-Rebaudengo (1988). "*Koro* Secondary to a Tumour of the Corpus Callosum." *British Journal of Psychiatry* 153:

251-254; Lapierre (1972). op cit.
78. Anderson, D.N. (1990). "*Koro*: The Genital Retraction Symptom after Stroke." *British Journal of Psychiatry* 157: 142-144.
79. Tseng et al., 1988, op cit., p. 1538.
80. Tseng et al., 1992.
81. Kirmayer, L.J. (1992). "From the Witches' Hammer to the Oedipus Complex: Castration Anxiety in Western Society." *Transcultural Psychiatric Research Review* 29: 133-158. See pp. 137-139.
82. Kirmayer (1992). op cit., p. 139.
83. Gwee, 1968, op cit.
84. Prince, 1992a, op cit., p. 121.
85. Johnson, D.M. (1945). "The 'Phantom Anesthetist' of Matoon: A Field study of Mass Hysteria." *Journal of Abnormal Psychology* 40: 175-186.
86. Jacobs, N. (1965). "The Phantom Slasher of Taipei: Mass Hysteria in a Non-western Society." *Social Problems* 12: 318-328.
87. Cantril, H. (1940). *The Invasion From Mars: A Study in the Psychology of Panic*. Princeton: Princeton University Press.
88. Medalia, N.Z., and Larsen, O. (1958). "Diffusion and Belief in a Collective Delusion." *Sociological Review* 23: 180-186.
89. McCloy, J.F., and Miller, R. (1976). *The Jersey Devil.* Wallingford, Pennsylvania: Middle Atlantic Press.
90. Stewart, J.R. (1989). "Sasquatch Sightings in South Dakota: An Analysis of an Episode of Collective Delusion." In G. Zollschan, J. Schumaker and Greg Walsh (Eds.) *Exploring the Paranormal.* Bridport, England: Prism Press.
91. Park, A. (1986). "Tasmanian Tiger: Extinct or Merely Elusive." *Australian Geographic* 1: 66-83.
92. Kirk, R. (1812). *The Secret Commonwealth of Elves, Fauns and Fairies*. London: Longman; Evans, H. (1984). *Visions, Apparitions, Alien Visitors*. Wellingborough: Aquarian; Evans-Wentz, W.Y. (1909). *The Fairy Faith in Celtic Countries, Its Psychological Origin and Nature.* Rennes, France: Oberthur.
93. Szasz, T.S. (1990). *Sex by Prescription*. Syracuse, New York: Syracuse University Press, p. 4.
94. Goode, E. (1992). *Collective Behavior*. New York: Harcourt Brace Jovanovich; Goode, E., and Ben-Yehuda, N. (1994). *Moral Panics: The Social Construction of Deviance*. Oxford: Blackwell; Turner, R.H., and Killian, L.M. (1987). *Collective Behavior*, third edition. Englewood Cliffs, New Jersey: Prentice-Hall.
95. Asch, S.E. (1955). "Opinions and Social Pressure." *Scientific American* 193: 31-35. Zimbardo, P. G. (1972). "Pathology of Imprisonment." *Society* 9: 4-8.
96. Buckhout, R. (1980). Nearly 200 Witnesses can be Wrong. *Bulletin of the Psychonomic Society* 16: 307-310. Buckhout, R. (1974). Eyewitness Testimony. *Scientific American* 231(6): 23-31. Ross, D.F., Read, J.D., and Toglia, M.P. (1994). *Adult Eyewitness Testimony: Current Trends and Developments*. Cambridge: Cambridge University Press.
97. Massad, C. M., Hubbard, M., and Newston, D. (1979). "Selective Perception of Events." *Journal of Experimental Social Psychology* 15: 513-532. See p. 531.
98. Festinger, L. (1950). "Informal Social Communications." *Psychological Review* 57: 271-280, p. 272.
99. Beerger, P., and Luckmann, T. (1967). *The Social Construction of Reality*. New York: Anchor Books.
100. Conner, J.W. (1975). "Social and Psychological Reality of European Witchcraft Beliefs." *Psychiatry* 38: 366-380. See p. 367.
101. Edwards, J.E. (1984). "Indigenous *Koro*, a Genital Retraction Syndrome of Insular Southeast Asia: A Critical Review." *Culture, Medicine and Psychiatry* 8:1-24.
102. Edwards (1984). op cit., pp. 15-16.
103. Mun, C.I. (1968). op cit., p. 641.
104. Patrick, E. (1971). "Emotional Stresses in University Students." In N.N. Wagner and E.S. Tan (Eds.) *Psychological Problems and Treatment in Malaysia*. Kuala Lumpur: University of Malaya Press, p. 85.
105. Oyebode, F., Jamieson, M.J., and Davison, K. (1986). "*Koro* - A Psychophysiological Dysfunction." *British Journal of Psychiatry* 148: 212-214.
106. Thase, M.E., Reynolds, C.F., Jennings, J.R. (1988). "Nocturnal Penile Tumescence is Diminished in Depressed Men." *Biological Psychiatry* 24:33-46.
107. Ang (1984). op cit.; Kendall and Jenkins (1987); Turnier and Chouinard, (1990). op cit.
108. American Psychiatric Association (1994). op cit., p. 765.
109. Vorstman, A.H. (1897). "*Koro* in Westerafdeeling van Borneo." *Geneeskundig Tijdschrift voor Nederlandsch-Indie* 37: 499-505; Arieti, S., and Meth, J.M. (1959). "Rare, Unclassifiable, Collective, and Exotic Psychotic Syndromes." In S. Arieti (Ed.) *American Handbook of Psychiatry*. New York: Basic Books; Gwee, 1963, op cit.; Mun, op cit.
110. Bartholomew (1998). op cit., pp. 23-24.
111. Ilechukwu, Sunny T.C. (1988). "Letter from S.T.C. Ilechukwu, M.D. (Lagos, Nigeria) which Describes Interesting Koro-like Syndromes in Nigeria." *Transcultural Psychiatric Research Review* 25: 310-314.
112. Bartholomew, R.E. (1994). "The Social Psychology of 'Epidemic' Koro." *The International Journal of Social Psychiatry* 40(1): 46-60.
113. Ilechukwu, 1988, op cit., p. 313.
114. Illechukwu, 1992, op cit., pp. 96-97.
115. Ilechukwu, 1992, op cit., pp. 101-102.
116. Ilechukwu, Sunny T.C. (1992). "Magical Penis Loss in Nigeria: Report of a Recent Epidemic of a Koro-Like Syndrome." *Transcultural Psychiatric Research Review* 29: 91-108. See p. 95.
117. Ilechukwu, 1992, op cit., p. 95.
118. Illechukwu, 1992, op cit., p. 96.
119. Dan-Ali, Mannir (2001). "'Missing Penis Sparks Mob Lynching." British Broadcasting Corporation, April 12, accessed June 26, 2003 at: http://news.bbc.co.uk/1/hi/world/africa/ 1274235.stm.
120. Smith, Alex Duval (2001). "Eight Die in Arson Over 'Theft' of Penis." *The Independent*, April 12.
121. Dan-Ali, Mannir, op cit.
122. "Benin Alert over 'Penis Theft' Panic." British Broadcasting Corporation, Tuesday, 27 November, 2001, 15:51 GMT.
123. Bartholomew, Robert E. (2000). *Exotic Deviance: Medicalizing Cultural Idioms–From Strangeness to Illness*. Boulder, Colorado: University Press of Colorado, p. 104.
124. Shweder, R. A. (1984). "Anthropology's Romantic Rebellion Against the Enlightenment, or There's More to Thinking Than Reason and Evidence." Pp. 27-66. In R. A. Shweder and R. A. LeVine (eds.), *Culture Theory: Essays on Mind, Self and Emotion*. New York: Cambridge University Press.
125. Bartholomew, 2000, op cit., p. 106.
126. Bartholomew, R.E. (1989). "The South African Monoplane Hysteria: An Evaluation of the Usefulness of Smelser's Theory of Hysterical Beliefs." *Sociological Inquiry* 59:287-300.
127. Ilechukwa, 1992, op cit.
128. "Panic in Khartoum: Foreigners Shake Hands, Make Penises Disappear." The Middle East Media Research Institute, Special Dispatch Series No. 593 (October 22, 2003), accessed December 8, 2003 at: http://memri.org/bin/articles.cgi?Page=archives&Area=sd&ID=SP593 03 citing a report in *Al-Quds Al-Arabi* (London), September 24, 2003.
129. "Panic in Khartoum: Foreigners Shake Hands, Make Penises

Disappear." op cit., citing a report in *Al-Quds Al-Arabi* (London), September 22, 2003.
130. "Panic in Khartoum: Foreigners Shake Hands, Make Penises Disappear." op cit., citing a report in *Al-Quds Al-Arabi* (London), September 22, 2003.
131. *Al-Rai Al-A'am* (Sudan), September 23, 2003, cited in "Panic in Khartoum: Foreigners Shake Hands, Make Penises Disappear." op cit.
132. *Al-Sharq Al-Awsat* (London), October 9, 2003, cited in "Panic in Khartoum: Foreigners Shake Hands, Make Penises Disappear." op cit.
133. *Al-Sharq Al-Awsat* (London), October 9, 2003, op cit.
134. *Al-Rai Al-A'am* (Sudan), September 24, 2003. cited in "Panic in Khartoum: Foreigners Shake Hands, Make Penises Disappear." op cit.
135. *Al-Rai Al-A'am* (Sudan), September 24, 2003. cited in "Panic in Khartoum: Foreigners Shake Hands, Make Penises Disappear." op cit.
136. "Panic in Khartoum: Foreigners Shake Hands, Make Penises Disappear." op cit.
137. Sprenger, Jakob and Kramer, Heinrich (1928[1486]). *Malleus Maleficarum*. Translated into English by Montague Summers. London: Rodker, p. 119.
138. Wulsin, Lawson R., and Hagengimana, Athanase (1998). "PTSD in Survivors of Rwanda's 1994 War." *Psychiatric Times* 15(4) (April), accessed December 31, 2003 at: http://www.psychiatrictimes.com/p980412.html.
139. Wulsin and Hagengimana (1998). op cit.
140. Okoko, Tervil. (2000). "Ghosts Invade Kenyan Schools." Pan Africa News Agency, July 19; "Ghosts Beat Up Pupils At Kenyan School AFP news agency, July 20 2000, citing local newspapers; "I hired ghosts to torment schoolgirls." *The Star* (South Africa), June 5, 2000 (Reuters report).
141. Barasa, Lucas (2001). "School Closed Over Devil Worship Fears." *The Nation* (Nairobi) October 5.
142. Barasa, Lucas, op cit.
143. Barasa, Lucas, op cit.
144. Schultz. Emily A., and Lavenda, Robert H. (1995). *Anthropology: A Perspective on Human Culture.* Mountain View, California: Mayfield Publishing, p. 545. Davidson, James, Castillo, Pedro, and Stoff, Michael. (2000). *The American Nation.* Upper Saddle River, New Jersey: Prentice-Hall, pp. 519-520.
145. Miller, David L. (2000). *Introduction to Collective Behavior and Collective Action* (second edition). Prospect Heights, Illinois: Waveland Press, p. 423.
146. While a small percentage of 'rocket' reports transpired over the remainder of Scandinavia, the vast majority of reports were in Swedish territory.
147. "A new aurora - the most beautiful for ages," *Sydostra Sveriges Dagblad,* March 29, 1946; "The magnetic storm the most powerful ever," *Sydostra Sveriges Dagblad,* March 30, 1946.
148. Winkler, L. (1984). *Catalogue of UFO-like data before 1947.* Mt. Ranier, MD: Fund for UFO Research, p. 4.
149. Vayrynen, R. (1972). *Conflicts in Finnish-Soviet Relations: Three Comparative Case Studies.* Tampere: Tampere University; Orvik, N. (1973). *Europe's Northern Cap and the Soviet Union.* New York: AMS.
150. Sundelius, B. (ed.) (1982). *Foreign Policies of Northern Europe.* Boulder, CO: Westview.
151. "Nuclear tests or settling on the bottom of the Baltic?" *Helsingborgs Dagblad,* April 27, 1946.
152. "Luminous morning clouds frightened horses and dogs," newswire report from the Swedish Newspaper Agency Tidningarnas Telegrambyra appearing in various domestic newspapers on January 8. The atypical nature of the phenomena was noted by weather observers in Horby and Uppsala according to the 1946 edition of *The Swedish Weather Bureau Yearbook.*
153. Letter from Defense Staff Archives from Alice Ahlsen, Fransborg, Barkarby, July 11, 1946.
154. *The Swedish Weather Bureau Yearbook* (1946), *op. cit.*
155. *Borlange Tidning,* January 18, 19, 24, 26, and February 2, 1946; *Dala-Demokraten,* January 19, 1946; *Saters Tidning,* January 19, 1946.
156. There were also numerous reports of meteoric and auroral activity between February and early May, 1946. Among the most prominent was a fireball in Vasterbotten county, parts of Vasternorrland and Norrbotten, and in Western Finland on February 17, and a possible train of meteors on February 21 in the counties of Vasterbotten, Vasternorrland, Kopparberg, Gavleborg, Uppsala, Ostergotland and Skaraborg, while an unprecedented aurora borealis was reported for several days in late March. For descriptions of these and other reports, see: *Norra Vasterbotten,* February 19-21; *Vasterbottens-Kuriren,* February 21-23; *Ornskoldsviks-Posten,* February 18; *Hufvudstadsbladet,* Helsinki, Finland, February 22, 24, 26, 28, and March 3, 7, 10; *Borlange Tidning,* February 22; *Sundsvalls Tidning,* February 23; *Falu-Kuriren,* February 22; *Smalands Dagblad,* February 22; *Mora Tidning,* February 25; "Northern lights continue," *Norra Vasterbotten,* March 26; "Fireball flew over the town yesterday," Sundsvalls Tidning, April 25.
157. *Mora Tidning,* January 14, 1946.
158. *Saters Tidning,* January 15, 1946; *Mora Tidning,* January 18, 1946.
159. *Hufvudstadsbladet,* February 22, 1946.
160. *The Swedish Weather Bureau Yearbook* (1946).
161. *Smalands Dagblad,* April 6, 1946.
162. "Ball lightning knocked down pedestrians in the streets," *Sydostra Sveriges Dagblad,* May 4, 1946.
163. "Does a mysterious light betoken clearer May weather?" *Morgon-Tidningen,* May 4, 1946, p. 1.
164. "Mysterious fireball also observed in Halsingborg," *Helsingborgs Dagblad,* May 29, 1946.
165. "Mystery in the sky in Skane: 'Wingless, cigar-shaped body' amazes Landskrona inhabitants," *Morgon-Tidningen,* May 28, 1946, p. 12. A sighting at about the same time by a Danish border guard near the parish of Rudbbl described a rapidly moving "bright light, followed by a tail." See "The Danes see a mysterious fireball too," *Morgon-Tidningen,* May 29, 1946, p. 7.
166. "The V-bomb over Landskrona a piece of fireworks?" *Goteborgs-Tidningen,* May 25, 1946.
167. "The wingless airplane could be a V-bomb," *Dagens Nyheter,* May 26, 1946.
168. "Remote-directed bombs haunt both here and there," *Morgon-Tidningen,* May 27, 1946; "Ghost flier or remote-controlled bombs?" *Aftontidningen,* May 27, 1946.
169. "Night workers took shelter from the rocket bomb in Landskrona" *Aftonbladet,* May 25, 1946; "Rocket bomb or what?" Strange aerial body over Landskrona," *Landskrona-Posten,* May 25, 1946.
170. "Fire-spewing 'log'–meteor or projectile?" *Expressen,* May 25, 1946.
171. "The meteor over Karlskrona–remote directed experiment bomb," May 27, 1946, *Sydostra Sveriges Dagblad,* May 27, 1946; "New mysterious 'fireball' over naval yard. Experiment with secret weapon?" *Expressen,* May 27, 1946; "Mysterious sky appearance also in Stockholm," *Morgan-Tidningen,* May 28, 1946, p. 12.
172. "Sky phenomenon in Eskilstuna," *Morgon-Tidningen,* June 13, 1946, p. 5; "Flaming red meteor in southern Finland," *Morgon-Tidningen,* June 22, 1946, p. 6; "Mysterious plane over Gavle.

Long grey object disappears in smoke cloud," *Svenska Dagbladet*, July 2, 1946, p. 3; "Mysterious object crossed through the sky over Flurkmark," *Vasterbottens-Kuriren*, June 5, 1946 and police reports from investigation in Trehorningen, September 20 in Defense Staff files; Kroksjo information taken from Defense Staff files, War Archives, Stockholm.

173. "V-bomb seen over Hugelsta on Whitsun Eve," *Eskilstuna-Kuriren*, June 11, 1946; *Dagens Nyheter*, June 11, 1946; *Svenska Dagbladet*, June 12, 1946; Notes in Defense Staff files.

174. "Ghost rocket also over our country. Sightings in several places," *Hufvudstadsbladet*, June 11, 1946; *Helsingin Sanomat*, June 11, 1946; "Ghost rocket an ordinary meteor," *Dagens Nyheter*, June 12, 1946; "Flying bomb or meteor, one asks in Finland," *Helsingborgs Dagblad*, June 12, 1946; Tidningarnas Telegrambyra newswire reports on June 10-11, 1946; reports number 68/3:43/1946, 69/3:43/1946 and 82/3:55/1946 from the military attache from the Defense Staff files.

175. Memo entitled "Headquarters, Defence Staff Department L (Air Defence) nr 7:49. June 12, 1946. Reports concerning light phenomena." The memo was issued "On order of the Supreme Commander," and signed by T. Bonde (acting chief of the Defence Staff) and co-signed by Nils Ahlgren (head of the Air Defense department of the Defense Staff).

176. Letter in Defence Staff files, from S.H. Liljhage, Chief of Staff of the Western Airbase, Gothenburg, describing a telephone report to the local base by engineer Berglund; Report filled in on July 5, 1946 at 6 p.m. to the research officer on duty at the Defence Staff from the duty officer at the 117 infantry regiment at Uddevalla filed in the Defence Staff archives; "Meteor or radio bomb," *Svenska Dagbladet*, July 10, 1946, p. 3; "A radio-controlled projectile over Medepad yesterday," *Sundsvalls Tidning*, July 10, 1946; "Rocket projectiles have taken over the ghost flier's role. Vaxholm and Sundsvall saw mysterious space rockets," *Morgon-Tidningen*, July 10, 1946, p. 1; "The rocket-projectile crashed on Bjorkon," *Sundsvalls Tidning*, July 11, 1946; "The light phenomena continue. No solution yet to the findings at Nolvikssand," *Sundsvalls Tidning*, July 12, 1946

177. "Enigmatical paper find from 'ghost bomb.' Dalarma-Varmland also has had visits," *Morgon-Tidningen*, July 11, 1946, p. 1; "The military has a bomb fragment," *Svenska Dagbladet*, July 11, 1946, p. 9.

178. Based on a large number of former secret documents from defense staff archives examined by Anders Liljegren and Clas Svahn. In numerous other cases, local police were ordered to conduct investigations.

179. Liljegren, A., & Svahn, C. "Ghost rockets and phantom aircraft." In J. Spencer & H. Evans (eds.), *Phenomenon: Forty Years of Flying Saucers*. New York: Avon, 1989, pp. 53-60.

180. "Ghost rocket caused the Svartvik fire?" *Sundsvalls Tidning*, July 31, 1946; "Ghost bomb was not the cause of the Svartvik fire." *Svenska Dagbladet*, August 1, 1946, p. 1; Tidningarnas Telegrambyra newswire of July 27, 1946; "Ghost rocket in the hen house?" *Stockholms-Tidningen*, July 28, 1946; "Space projectile causes a fire?" *Svenska Dagbladet*, July 28, 1946, p. 5; "MT continues to say there have been many fires... in the dry weather, some probably started by arson. Sparks not ghost bomb, the true cause...a blasting cap," *Morgon-Tidningen*, August 1, 1946, p. 3.

181. "Ghost rocket crashed a barn in a Norrland village," *Goteborgs-Tidningen*, August 12, 1946.

182. "A tornado demolished the barn," *Stockholms-Tidningen*, August 13, 1946.

183. "Poisonous material from rocket bombs?" *Morgon-Tidningen*, August 13, 1946, p. 7.

184. Letter from Jan Flinta, Stockholm, August 9, 1946 to the Defence Staff; *Varmlands Folkblad*, July 19, 1946; *Sundsvalls Tidning*, July 20, 1946; *Nya Wermlands-Tidningen*, August 1, 1946.

185. "Did the accident plane collide with a returning ghost rocket?" *Expressen*, August 13, 1946.

186. Space rocket not the cause for the Valdshult accident," *Jonkopings-Posten*, July 15, 1946; "Investigation of the B18 accident: The pilot lost control," *Expressen*, August 16, 1946; "Fatal accident: The...crash not because of space rocket," *Morgon Tidningen*, August 16, 1946, p. 11.

187. "Ghost bomb theory fell apart like a soap-bubble," *Varmlands Folkblad*, August 13, 1946; *Expressen*, August 13, 1946.

188. "Pit in the ground a ghost bomb mark?" *Svenska Dagbladet*, August 3, 1946, p. 3.

189. "The 'projectile' is a steam valve part. Experts agree," *Svenska Dagbladet*, August 16, 1946, p. 3; "Ghost bomb screw a steam valve," *Morgon-Tidningen*, August 16, 1946, p. 7.

190. "Ghost phenomenon hidden in a moss in a Blekinge wood," *Dagens Nyheter*, August 4, 1946.

191. "Airplane antenna taken for a ghost bomb," *Morgon-Tidningen*, August 6, 1946, p. 7; "The mysterious find was an airplane antenna," *Sydostra Sveriges Dagblad*, August 6, 1946.

192. "Steep-diving magpie in Nyhem causes ghost rocket fever," *Ostersunds-Posten*, August 22, 1946.

193. "Bomb crash at Sigtuna exposed as meteorite," *Stockholms-Tidningen*, July 24, 1946.

194. "The reality behind the 'ghost bombs,'" *Stockholms Tidningen*, July 26, 1946.

195. "The ghost bombing," *Halsingborgs Dagblad*, July 27, 1946.

196. "The ghost bombing." op cit.

197. Advertizement for *Se* magazine appearing in *Svenska Dagbladet*, August 16, 1946, p. 9.

198. "The ghost bombs," *Vasternorrlands Folkblad*, July 26, 1946.

199. A poem in Copenhagen's *Berlingske Tidende*, July 31, 1946: last page, made reference to a recent sensational ghost rocket sighting over Byen, expressing relief that the "rocket" was actually a meteor. "People breathed a little scared in Hong ....It was like a great meteor in and arc over the region below. People thought at once of this rocket which travels so mysteriously... ....But surely people can be at ease on Hong. It was not a great power on an expedition of war." On July 12, a poem titled "Anxiety on the air" appeared in the *Vasterbottens Folkblad*, stating in part: "What is it that's flying here and there...That man can never rest in peace, of atoms and other troublesome things, in a calmer world some may believe–but I, I believe in nothing." Other poems on the ghost rockets include: "The great riddle," *Stockholms-Tidningen*, August 18, 1946; "The ghost rocket in Denmark," *Dagens Nyheter*, August 19, 1946.

200. *Morgon-Tidningen* of July 12, 1946, p. 8.

201. "Ghost rocket explodes in Denmark," *Svenska Dagbladet*, August 14, 1946: last page; "Space projectile over Helsinki," *Svenska Dagbladet*, August 15, 1946: last page; "Another Danish sighting," *Svenska Dagbladet*, August 15, 1946, p. 3; "Many ghost rockets over Denmark," *Svenska Dagbladet*, August 17, 1946, p. 13; "Danes find metal piece of a ghost bomb," *Morgon-Tidningen*, August 22, 1946. p. 1; "12 'ghost bombs' up till now over Denmark," *Svenska Dagbladet*, August 22, 1946, p. 13; "Ghost rockets over Norway," *Svenska Dagbladet*, July 19, 1946, last page.

202. "Ghost rockets over France too," *Svenska Dagbladet*, August 21, 1946, last page; "Carrier cancels Athens air show," *New York Times*, September 6, 1946, pp. 1, 11; "Ghost bomb over Austria," *Svenska Dagbladet*, September 13, 1946: last page. Edoardo Russo of Torino, Italy (personal communication, 16 January 1997) summarizes press reports from 14 Italian daily newspapers surveyed between July and

October 1946, yielding 70 articles on these mysterious aerial objects over Italy. He states: "'strange bolides' at Imola and 'rocket projectiles' in Bologna of September 17, 'flying bombs' over Vercelli and a 'fire bolide' again at Imola on the 18th, 'luminous bolides' at Turin on the 19th, at Florence on the 21st and on the 22nd, 'bright signals' over Rome on the 20th, more 'rocket projectiles' at Livorno on September 20 and in Bari on October 5, 'flying bolides' in Trieste on October 12 and even a 'fire disc' at Varazze on October 4." Most of these reports described rapidly moving luminous objects with trails. While initially connected to the 'ghost rockets' by journalists, they were later explained as meteorological events by astronomers. These reports include: "Bombe volanti anche a Vercelli?" *Il Giornale Di Torino*, September 20, 1946; "Il bolide luminoso. Chi l'ha visto?" *Gazzetta d'Italia*, September 21, 1946; "Un bolide luminoso nel cielo di Firenze, *Nazione Del Popolo*, September 22, 1946; "I bolidi misteriosi. L'opinione di un astronomo sull natura..." *Nazione Del Popolo*, September 24, 1946; "I proiettili razzo sull'Italia sono fenomeni cosmici," *Corriere Di Sicilia*, September 25, 1946; "Proiettile razzo nel cielo di Livorno," *Corriere Tridentino*, October 1, 1946; "Un corpo luminoso nel cielo di Bari," *Giornale Alleato*, October 6, 1946; "Un bolide volante avvistato a Bari," *La Prealpina*, October 6, 1946; "Anche nel cielo di Trieste i misteriosi razzi," *Voce Libera*, October 10, 1946; "I razzi luminosi di Trieste sono frammenti di una cometa," *La Prealpina*, October 13, 1946.

203. Defense Staff press release published by the *Tidningaras Telegrambyra* news agency, October 10, 1946.

204. "Ghost rockets over Hudiksvall," *Aftonbladet*, October 7, 1947; "'Space projectile' over Appelviken," Dagens Nyheter, October 23, 1947, and Ministry of Foreign Affairs Archive.

205. "Fireball with tail appeared before Lulea inhabitants," *Norrlandska Social-Demokraten*, August 5, 1947; "Fireball over Stockholm," *Ostergotlands Dagblad*, December 22, 1947; Letter in the Defence Staff Archives from G. Pettersson, warrant officer with Gota Artilleriregemente, Gothenburg, submitted to the Stockholm Defence Department on 20 November, 1947, describing a luminous ball over Gothenburg, November 17, 1947 at 1740 hours.

206. "Flying saucer over Stockholm," *Stockholms-Tidningen*, July 12, 1947; "'Flying saucer' over Ostersund," *Stockholms-Tidningen*, July 25, 1947; "Flying saucer over Haparanda," *Norrlandska Social-Demokraten*, August 6, 1947; "Flying saucer over Finspang," *Ostergotlands Dagblad*, August 18, 1947; "Flying saucer or meteor over Helsingborg," *Helsingborgs Dagblad*, October 19, 1947.

207. Hoekema, Anthony A. (1966). *What About Tongue-Speaking?* Grand Rapids, Michigan: William B. Eerdmans Publishing Company, p. 9.

208. Samarin, W.J. (1972). *Tongues of Men and Angels: The Religious Language of Pentecostalism*. New York: MacMillan.

209. Hoekema, op cit., p. 11.

210. Hoekema, op cit., pp. 10-11.

211. Hoekema, op cit., p. 16.

212. McDonnell, Kilian (1976). *Charismatic Renewal and the Churches*. New York: The Seabury Press, p. 232.

213. Pfister, Oskar (1912). *Die psychologische Enträtselung der Religiösen Glossolalie und Automatischen Kryptographie*. Leipzig: Franz Deuticke.

214. Cutten, George Barton (1927). *Speaking with Tongues: Historically and Psychologically Considered*. New Haven, Connecticut: Yale University Press, p. 162.

215. Vivier, L.M. (1968). "The Glossolaliac and His Personality." *Beitrage zur Ekstase*. T. Spoerri (editor). Basel: S. Karger, p. 169.

216. Nicholas P. Spanos, Wendy P. Cross, Mark Lepage, and Marjorie Coristine, "Glossolalia as Learned Behavior: An Experimental Demonstration," *Journal of Abnormal Psychology* 95:1 (1987), 21-23. See p. 23.

217. McDonnell, op cit., p. 152.

218. "Headmaster Flees as Hysteria Grips School." *The Daily News* (Zimbabwe), July 30, 2002.

219. Panati, Charles. (1991). *Panati's Parade of Fads, Follies, and Manias*. New York: HarperCollins, pp. 156-157; Skolnik, Peter L. (1978). *Fads: America's Crazes, Fevers & Fancies From the 1890s to the 1970s*. New York: Thomas Y. Crowell, pp. 73-75.

220. Marum, Andrew, and Parise, Frank. (1984). *Follies and Foibles: A View of 20th Century Fads*. New York: Facts on File, p. 67; Panati, op cit., p. 156.

221. Marum and Praise, op cit., p. 68; Skolnik, op cit, pp. 73-75.

222. Panati, op cit., p. 157.

223. Marum and Parise, op cit., p. 68.

224. Panati, op cit, 156; Marum and Praise, op cit., p. 68.

225. Sanarov, V. (1981). "On the nature and origin of flying saucers and little green men." *Current Anthropology* 22:163-167; Gibbs-Smith, C.H. (1960). *The Aeroplane: An Historical Survey of its Origins and Development*. London: Her Majesty's Stationary Office; Gibbs-Smith, C., (1985). op. cit.

226. Jacobs, D.M. (1975). *The UFO Controversy in America*. New York: Signet, pp. 27-28.

227. Clark, J., & Coleman, L. (1975). *The Unidentified: Notes Toward Solving the UFO Mystery*. New York: Warner, p. 133.

228. Clark and Coleman, op cit., p. 133.

229. Clarke, I.F. (1986). "American anticipations: the first of the futurists." *Futures* 18(4):584-596.

230. Clarke, op cit., p. 589.

231. Bullard, T.E. (1982). *Mysteries in the Eye of the Beholder: UFOs and their Correlates as a Folkloric Theme Past and Present*. Doctoral dissertation, Indiana University Folklore Department.

232. For actual reproductions of some of the original patents, see Lore, G., & Deneault, H. (1968). *Mysteries of the Skies: UFOs in Perspective*. Englewood Cliffs, New Jersey: Prentice-Hall, pp. 16-17, 38-39.

233. Jacobs, D. (1975). *op. cit.*, pp. 27-28.

234. "Voices in the sky...people declare they heard them and saw a light," *Sacramento Evening Bee*, November 18, 1896, p. 1.

235. "Voices in the sky..." op cit., p. 1.

236. "Voices in the sky..." op cit., p. 1.

237. "A lawyer's word for that airship," *San Francisco Chronicle*, November 22, 1896, p. 16.

238. This section on 'Airships and Yellow Journalism' is excerpted from: Bartholomew, Robert E. (2000). "From Airships to Flying Saucers: Oregon's Place in the Evolution of UFO Lore." *Oregon Historical Quarterly* 101(2):192-213 (Summer).

239. "Singular phenomenon," *Western Watchman* [Eureka, CA], November 21, 1896, p. 3; "That mysterious march," *Western Watchman*, November 28, 1896, p. 3.

240. "Sailed high overhead," *The Call* [San Francisco], November 22, 1896, p. 13.

241. "That airship again," *The Call* [San Francisco], November 21, 1896, p. 3.

242. "Saw the mystic flying light," *The Call* [San Francisco], November 22, 1896, p. 13.

243. "Have we got 'em again," *Sacramento Evening Bee*, November 23, 1896, p. 1.

244. "A singular phenomenon. Was it an airship..." *Red Bluff Daily People's Cause*, November 24, 1896.

245. "The airship again," *Riverside Daily Press*, December 10, 1896, p.

5.
246. "A strange phantom," *Weekly Antioch Ledger*, November 28, 1896, p. 3.
247. "Seen again. Many people of Chico gaze at the supposed airship," *Morning Chronicle-Record* (Chico, CA], November 25, 1896, p. 3.
248. "The air ship," *Weekly Visalia Delta*, November 26, 1896, p. 2.
249. "Seen at Hanford," *Weekly Visalia Delta*, November 26, 1896, p. 2; "The air ship. The vessel seen again..." *Weekly Visalia Delta*, December 3, 1896, p. 1.
250. "Was it an air-ship?" *Ferndale Semi-Weekly Enterprise*, December 1, 1896, p. 5.
251. "The air ship," *Riverside Daily Press*, December 2, 1896, p. 5.
252. "Observations," *Daily Colusa*, December 1, 1896, p. 2.
253. "County news," *Daily Colusa*, December 3, 1896, p. 3.
254. "Our neighbors," *Weekly Visalia Delta*, December 3, 1896, p. 3; "The air ship at Tulare," *Tulare County Times* [Visalia, CA], December 3, 1896, p. 4.
255. *Merced Express*, December 4, 1896, p. 3.
256. *Fresno County Enterprise* [Selma, CA], November 27, 1896, p. 4.
257. "Pennington points," *Sutter County Farmer* [Yuba City, CA], December 4, 1896, p. 6.
258. McMinnville *Telephone-Register* [OR], November 26, 1896, p. 3.
259. "The tourist of the air" [editorial], *Tacoma News* [WA], November 28, 1896, p. 4; "Beats the airship," *Tacoma News* [WA], November 30, 1896, p. 2.
260. "The airship of Winnemucca," *Carson City Morning Appeal*, November 26, 1896, p. 3; "The airship," *Reno Evening Gazette*, December 3, 1896, p. 1; "The airship again," *Reno Evening Gazette*, December 5, 1896, p. 3; "That airship," *Carson City Morning Appeal*, December 6, 1896, p. 2; "Airship burned," *Carson City Morning Appeal*, December 9, 1896, p. 3; "Airship yarns," *Territorial Enterprise* (Virginia, NV), December 12, 1896, p. 2; "What could it have been?," *Central Nevadan*, December 10, 1896, p. 3; "The air ship. It reached Carson Saturday night," *Carson Weekly*, December 7, 1896, p. 6.
261. "Local briefs," *Arizona Gazette* [Phoenix, AZ], December 4, 1896, p. 8.
262. "Others who saw it" [letter], *San Francisco Call* [San Francisco], November 23, 1896; "Piercing the void, or on to Honolulu," *San Francisco Examiner*, December 2, 1896; "How about this. A San Josean declares that he traveled on the ship," *Oakland Tribune*, December 1, 1896, p. 1; "We are in it," *San Luis Obispo Tribune*, December 11, 1896, p. 1; *San Jose Daily Mercury*, December 1, 1896, p. 8; Marysville Daily Appeal, December 2, 1896, p. 3; "The airship described by fishermen," *The Call* [San Francisco], December 3, 1896, p. 1; "...Strange and circumstantial story of a sailor passenger," *The Call* [San Francisco], December 5, 1896, p. 2.
263. "Three strange visitors. Who possibly came from the planet Mars," *Evening Mail* [Stockton, CA], November 27, 1896, p. 1.
264. "The airship nuisance," *San Francisco Examiner*, December 5, 1896, p. 6.
265. "Hearst and his two faces. Editor Hearst has one opinion in the east and another here," *The Call* (San Francisco), December 5, 1896, pp. 1-2.
266. Hiebert, Ray Eldon, Bohn, Thomas W., and Ungurait, Donald F. (1974). *Mass Media: An Introduction to Modern Communication Media*. New York: David McKay Company, pp. 209-210; Tebbel, John (1952). *The Life and Good Times of William Randolph Hearst*. New York: E.P. Dutton.
267. "A necessity," *San Luis Obispo Tribune*, December 18, 1896, p. 3; "A journalistic failure," San *Francisco Examiner*, December 6, 1896, p. 6; "Coincidents," *Merced Express* [Merced, CA], December 4, 1896, p. 3; "Credit where it is due," *San Francisco Chronicle*, December 5, 1896, p. 6.
268. *McMinnville Telephone-Register*, November 26, 1896, p. 3.
269. "That California Airship...It Slid over Portland in the Fog," *Evening Telegram* (Portland), December 1, 1896, p. 3.
270. "Airship gets into Illinois. Nashville Man sees a Strange Sight..." *Chicago Record*, April 6, 1897, p. 1.
271. "Saw the Airship," *Argus* [Rock Island, IL), April 9, 1897, p. 5.
272. "See Airship or Star," *Chicago Tribune*, April 10, 1897, pp. 1, 2.
273. "Seen at Jacksonville. The Airship Creates Great Excitement in that City," *Quincy Morning Whig*, April 11, 1897, p. 8; *Jacksonville Daily Journal*, April 11, 1897, p. 4.
274. "Saw a Light. High Above the State House Last Night," *Springfield News*, April 12, 1897, p. 1.
275. "Seen by Lincolnians," *Lincoln Weekly Courier*, April 13, 1897, p. 8.
276. "Air-Ship..." *Daily Republican* [Decatur], April 13, 1897, p. 1.
277. "A Springfield Story," *Decatur Daily Republican*, April 16, 1897, p. 1.
278. "Airship Repaired in llinois," *Springfield News*, April 14, 1897, p. 7.
279. "...Seen in Rockford Again Saturday Night," *Daily Republic*, April 12, 1897, p. 1.
280. "Sees Man Fishing from Air Ship," *Chicago Tribune*, April 16, 1897, p. 4.
281. "The Air Ship," *Monmouth Daily Review*, April 12, 1897, p. 1.
282. *Chicago Record*, April 15, 1897, p. 5.
283. This section on airship reports in Michigan is excerpted from: Bartholomew, Robert E. (1998). "Michigan and the Great Mass Hysteria Episode of 1897." *Michigan Historical Review* 24(1):133-141.
284. "Strange aerial craft," *Saginaw Courier-Herald*, April 11, 1897, p. 4.
285. "Wolverine tidbits," *Detroit Free Press*, March 24, 1897, p. 4.
286. "Weird lights. Seen in two little lakes in Ogemaw County," *Detroit Evening News*, March 29, 1897, p. 4.
287. "Caseville has a mystery. Strange light moves at night in the bay..." *Saginaw Globe*, March 30, 1897, p. 1.
288. "State notes," *Detroit Free Press*, April 9, 1897, p. 3.
289. Mysterious airship," *Saginaw Courier-Mail*, April 14, 1897, p. 3.
290. "Airship seen here. It was moving in a northwesterly direction..." *Benton Harbor Evening News*, April 12, 1897, p. 1.
291. "It bore colored lights. Benton Harbor people claim they saw the airship," *Detroit Free Press*, April 14, 1897, p. 3.
292. "Is seen at Holland," *Benton Harbor Evening News*, April 12, 1897, p. 1; *Grand Haven Daily Tribune*, April 12, 1897, p. 1.
293. "Queer object. Seen in the skies last evening–might have been airship," *Niles Daily Star*, April 12, 1897, p. 2.
294. "All sorts," *Evening News* [Detroit], April 15, 1897, p. 4.
295. "The air ship. It was seen to pass over Battle Creek last night," *Battle Creek Daily Moon*, April 13, 1897, p. 4; "The airship with us. It was seen by responsible citizens in a number of cites...," *Saginaw Evening News*, April 13, 1897, p. 2.
296. Ibid., p. 4.
297. "High in the air. Airship taking spin over Michigan. If the testimony of sober men is accepted," *Evening News* [Detroit], April 13, 1897, p. 4.
298. "Shower of sparks. Marks the air ship's path in Michigan...," *Grand Rapids Evening Press*, April 13, 1897, p. 3.
299. "Air ship or not," *Kalamazoo Gazette*, April 14, 1897, p. 4; "Shakespheare saw it. The Kalamazoo editor gives his version of the air ship," *Saginaw Evening News*, April 16, 1897, p. 1.
300. "Went to smash. Airship said to be scattered over Kalamazoo County," *Evening News* [Detroit], April 13, 1897, p. 4.

301. "Not an air ship. Just a reflection in the sky of the light from a burning barn," *Kalamazoo Gazette*, April 14, 1897, p. 1.
302. "Airship again. Broken wheel dug up near Battle Creek," *Evening News* [Detroit], April 15, 1897, p. 4; "That airship. Well-to-do Battle Creek farmer claims to have found a wheel from the mysterious craft," *Saginaw Courier-Herald*, April 16, 1897, p. 1.
303. "Dropped from the clouds. A message from the airship picked up on Maple Street," *Battle Creek Daily Moon*, April 16, 1897, p. 5; "Letter from airship. Received by a paper in Battle Creek," *Evening News* [Detroit], April 16, 1897, p. 4.
304. "Trip of the airship..." *Saginaw Courier-Herald*, April 17, 1897, p. 5.
305. "Seems to be catching. Stories told about an airship in Michigan," *Detroit Free Press*, April 17, 1897, p. 3.
306. "Trip of the airship...Seen at different points throughout the state as well as in other parts of the country," *Saginaw Courier-Herald*, April 17, 1897, p. 5.
307. "That air ship. The cigar-shaped body gives us a call," *Manistee Daily News*, April 17, 1897, p. 5; "Was it an air ship?" *Manistee Daily Advocate*, April 20, 1897, p. 1.
308. "People who saw it. Three citizens of Saginaw claim to have been favored," *Saginaw Evening News*, April 17, 1897, p. 7; "That airship again..," *Saginaw Courier-Herald*, April 21, 1897, p. 5.
309. "Are adrift in the air...," *Flint Daily News*, April 19, 1897, p. 3.
310. "Michigan news. Some citizens of Three Rivers are positive the airship passed over that place Saturday night," *Saginaw Globe*, April 19, 1897, p. 2.
311. "Beats any fish story...," *Detroit Free Press*, April 20, 1897, p. 3.
312. "That rapid airship. Now the citizens of Grant, Newaygo County, claim to have spied it," *Muskegon Daily Chronicle*, April 20, 1897, p. 2.
313. "Air ship passed over...," *Daily Mining Journal* [Marquette], April 23, 1897, p. 8; "Out in broad daylight...," *Flint Daily News*, April 24, 1897, p. 3.
314. *Daily Chronicle* [Marshall], April 27, 1897, p. 3.
315. "The airship at Geneseeville," *Flint Daily News*, April 28, 1897, p. 2.
316. "Airship seen at Sidnaw," *Daily Mining Journal* [Marquette], April 28, 1897, p. 8.
317. "Fragments of Flint," *Flint Daily News*, May 1, 1897, p. 3.
318. "The airship in Flint," *Flint Daily News*, May 11, 1897, p. 3.
319. "Saw the airship. Bock beer season has opened...," *Evening News* [Detroit], April 18, 1897, p. 9.
320. *Evening News* [Detroit], April 18, 1897, p. 2.
321. "Around the state," *Muskegon Daily Chronicle*, April 14, 1897.
322. *Saginaw Globe*, April 26, 1897, p. 2.
323. *Detroit Free Press*, May 3, 1897, p. 4.
324. *Kalamazoo Gazette*, April 23, 1897, p. 4.
325. "Stories of the state," *Evening Press* [Grand Rapids, Michigan], April 23, 1897, p. 3.
326. "The Air Ship...Seen by Kenton People Last Evening," *Kenton News-Republican*, April 15, 1897, p. 3.
327. "Farmer Scared," *Cincinnati Enquirer*, April 16, 1897, p. 1.
328. "Airship Travels..." *Cincinnati Commercial Tribune*, April 16, 1897, p. 1.
329. "Talking Heard by the Citizens as the Airship Passed Over Dunkirk..." *Cincinnati Enquirer*, April 16, 1897, p. 1.
330. "The...Air Ship. It has been seen by Akronians..." *Akron Daily Beacon and Republican*, April 16, 1897, p. 1.
331. "Was Plainly Seen..." *Cincinnati Commercial Tribune*, April 18, 1897, p. 20.
332. "Soared over Columbus," *Cincinnati Commercial Tribune*, April 18, 1897, p. 20.
333. "Will Swear to It," *Cincinnati Enquirer*, April 28, 1897, p. 1.
334. "Saw the Airship," *Cleveland Plain Dealer*, April 29, 1897, p. 3.
335. "The Airship Seen," *Cincinnati Commercial Tribune*, April 29, 1897, p. 8.
336. "He Saw the Airship," *Cincinnati Commercial Tribune*, April 30, 1897, p. 8.
337. "That Airship Again..." *Cleveland Plain Dealer*, May 11, 1897, p. 3.
338. "Saw the Aeribarque," *Cincinnati Enquirer*, April 27, 1897, p. 8.
339. "Aeribarque..." *Cincinnati Enquirer*, April 25, 1897, p. 9.
340. *Perry Country Tribune*, April 29, 1897, p. 8.
341. "Party of Morganfield people anxious to see the airship," *Louisville Evening Post*, April 13, 1897, p. 3.
342. "The air-ship in Kentucky," *Louisville Courier-Journal*, April 15, 1897, p. 5.
343. Ibid., p. 5.
344. "Airship passed in the night," *Louisville Evening Post*, April 13, 1897, p. 6.
345. Ibid., p. 6.
346. "Airship. Mayor and reputable citizens of Russellville saw it last night," *Louisville Evening Post*, April 16, 1897, p. 5. Also see: *Owensboro Daily Inquirer*, April 16, 1897, p. 1.
347. "Todd people saw it," *Louisville Evening Post*, April 16, 1897, p. 5.
348. "Seen in Clarksville," *Louisville Evening Post*, April 16, 1897, p. 5.
349. "Seen in Christian County," *Louisville Evening Post*, April 16, 1897, p. 5.
350. "...Nashville's Centennial managers say it will be exhibited there," *Louisville Evening Post*, April 16, 1897, p. 2.
351. *The Cairo Bulletin*, April 17, 1897.
352. "Must have been hitting the pipe," *Louisville Times*, April 19, 1897, p. 2.
353. "...The airship seen by Bowling Green people last night," *Louisville Evening Post*, April 19, 1897, p. 3.
354. "Flitted by," *Louisville Evening Post*, April 21, 1897, p. 2; "Madisonville's got 'em now," *Louisville Courier-Journal*, April 22, 1897, p. 4.
355. "Omnipresent. That airship is everywhere...," *Louisville Evening Post*, April 23, 1897, p. 3.
356. *Louisville Evening Post*, April 20, 1897, p. 8.
357. *Owensville Messenger*, April 27, 1897, p. 5.
358. "Pillar of fire. Strange light seen in the northern heavens," *Louisville Courier-Journal*, April 22, 1897, p. 9.
359. "Seeing the airship," *Owensville Messenger*, April 24, 1897, p. 4.
360. "Aerial flyer. Seen by reputable citizens of Lewisburg last night," *Louisville Evening Post*, April 24, 1897, p. 2.
361. "Saw the airship," *Owensboro Daily Inquirer*, April 25, 1897, p. 1.
362. Another press account gives his address as 1227 13th street.
363. "Saw the air ship," *Louisville Courier-Journal*, April 25, 1897, section II, p. 6.
364. Ibid.
365. "They saw it," *Louisville Evening Post*, April 26, 1897, p. 2.
366. "Made of thin air," *Daily News*, April 19, 1897, p. 2. For similar descriptions, see: "News via airship. A heavenly lightening bug...," *Paducah Daily News*, April 23, 1897, p. 3.
367. *Mayfield Mirror*, April 16, 1897.
368. "Madisonville's got 'em now," *Louisville Courier–Journal*, April 22, 1897, p. 4.

369. "That air ship," *Louisville Courier Journal*, April 30, 1897, p. 5.
370. "...Dropped from the airship as it passes over Corbin," *Louisville Evening Post*, April 27, 1897, p. 5; "Letter. From the navigator in the air ship," *Louisville Courier-Journal*, May 1, 1897, p. 9.
371. "Saw the airship. A Middlesborough man willing to make an affadavit," *Louisville Courier-Journal*, May 2, 1897, section I, p. 10.
372. The section on the Kentucky sightings is excerpted from: Bartholomew, Robert E. (1997). "Mass Hysteria in Kentucky 100 Years Ago." *Kentucky Association of Science Educators and Skeptics* 10(2):1, 3, 6-7.
373. "Airship Going East. Many Prominent Citizens of Derry Say They Sighted It," *Pittsburgh Dispatch*, April 19, 1897, p. 7.
374. "Passed Over Erie. The Mysterious Ship was Plainly Seen Last Night..." *Erie Daily Times*, April 22, 1897, p. 8.
375. "Flew Past Sharon. Mysterious Flying Machine Said to Have Been Seen There," *Erie Daily Times*, April 22, 1897, p. 8.
376. "Save the Airship. Correspondent's Statement is Verified..." *Erie Daily Times*, May 4, 1897, p. 2.
377. "Rode in a Flying Machine. An Allegheny Man...Grave Yard Cocktails Blamed," *Pittsburgh Dispatch*, April 12, 1897, p. 2.
378. "Was It An Airship? Strange Spectacle seen over the City Last Night," *Denver Times*, April 9, 1897, p. 6.
379. *Boulder Daily Camera*, April 12, 1897, p. 1.
380. "Now at Cripple...the Airship. Message from the Clouds." *Denver Times*, April 19, 1897, p. 1; "An Airship Hovered Near Us," *Florence Daily Herald*, April 19, 1897, p. 1.
381. See, for examples: "Runaway Airship. Paper Parachute Brings Word From a Mysterious Aerial Visitor," *Rocky Mountain Daily News*, April 16, 1897, p. 5; "Air Ship Visits Here," Colorado Springs Gazette, April 22, 1897, p. 5; "Again the Air-Ship. This Time Colorado Springs Is the Victim of a Hoax," *Rocky Mountain News*, April 22, 1897, 3; "That Air Ship...A Message Dropped From the Sky," *Silida Mail*, April 27, 1897, p. 3; "That Famous Air Ship..." *Silver Cliff Rustler*, April 28, 1897, p. 1; "Airship Again..." *Denver Times*, April 30, 1897, p. 1; (no title), *Silida Mail*, May 11, 1897, p. 3a.
382. "Now at Cripple...the Airship. Message from the Clouds." *Denver Times*, April 19, 1897, p. 1.
383. "It Hung Over Cripple Creek," *Avalanche* (Glenwood Springs), April 21, 1897, p. 1.
384. "Mysterious Airship. Cripple Creek Residents View a Very Strange Rover over the Gold Camp," *Rocky Mountain Daily News*, April 20, 1897, p. 1.
385. "Saw the Airship," *Florence Daily Herald*, April 20, 1897, p. 1.
386. "A Strange Phenomena..." *Silverton Standard*, April 24, 1897, p. 9.
387. "Mysterious..." *Aspen Daily Times*, April 22, 1897, p. 7.
388. "Saw the Airship..." Rocky Mountain News, April 26, 1897, p. 2.
389. "Loveland is 'Way Ahead," *Loveland Reporter*, April 29, 1897, p. 4.
390. "Airship Again. Two Men at Montrose Were Evidently Out Too Late," *Denver Times*, April 30, 1897, p. 1.
391. "That Airship Again," *Avalanche* (Glenwood Springs), May 3, 1897, p. 3.
392. "Airship Again Over Us..." *Florence Daily Herald*, May 6, 1897, p. 1.
393. "City and State," *Daily River Press* (Fort Benton, MT), April 19, 1897, p. 3.
394. *Chinook Opinion*, April 22, 1897, p. 1.
395. *Yellowstone Journal* (Miles City, MT), April 24, 1897, p. 2; "No Longer A Mystery. The Much Talked of Air Ship Pays Miles City a Visit," *Helena Herald*, April 26, 1897, p. 3.
396. "Air Ship at Miles," *Helena Daily Herald*, April 28, 1897, p. 3.
397. Ibid., *Helena Daily Herald*, April 28, 1897, p. 3.
398. "From Friday's Daily," *River Press* (Fort Benton, MT), April 28, 1897, p. 6.
399. "Throughout Wyoming," *Daily Boomerang* (Laramie), May 6, 1897, p. 3.
400. "Saw an Air Ship. Peculiar Aerial Visitor seen over Spokane last night..." Spokane *Spokesman-Review*, April 16, 1897, p. 6. Also see "Spokane Saw the Airship," *Walla Walla Union*, April 17, 1897, p. 4.
401. "Saw an airship in Broad Daylight..." *Spokesman-Review* (Spokane), May 7, 1897, p. 1. For other accounts of this sighting, see: "A Washington Airship," *Ellensburg Localizer*, May 15, 1897, p. 2; "State News," *Chelan Leader*, May 14, 1897, p. 1.
402. *St. Paul Pioneer-Press*, April 14, 1897, p. 2.
403. *Ibid.*
404. *Minneapolis Tribune*, April 12, 1897, p. 4.
405. *Wisconsin State Journal*, April 13, 1897, p. 2.
406. "The airship mystery," *Evening Wisconsin* [Milwaukee], April 12, 1897, p. 4.
407. *Racine Daily Journal*, April 12, 1897, p. 2.
408. "Wawaka news nuggets," *Ligonier Banner*, April 22, 1897, p. 1.
409. *Indianapolis Sentinel*, April 19, 1897, p. 6.
410. *Rensselaer Republican*, April 22, 1897, p. 1.
411. "Lake Station," *Hobart Gazette*, April 30, 1897, p. 8.
412. *Indianapolis Journal*, May 9, 1897, p. 2.
413. Quoted in 1893, from Gibbs-Smith, C.H. (1985). *Aviation: An Historical Survey from its Origins to the End of World War II.* London: Her Majesty's Stationary Office, p. 221.
414. Boulougouris, J.C., Rabavilas, A.D., Stefanis, C.N., Vaidakis, N., and Tabouratzis, D.G. (1981). "Epidemic Faintness: A Psychophysiological Investigation." *Psychiatria Clinica* 14:215-225.
415. Boulougouris et al. (1981). op cit., p. 216.
416. Kroenke, K., Koslowe, P., and Roy, M. (1998). "Symptoms in 18,495 Persian Gulf War Veterans. Latency of Onset and Lack of Association with Self-Reported Exposures." *Journal of Occupational Medicine* 40(6):520-528 (June).
417. Fumento, Michael (1997). "Gulf Lore Syndrome." *Reason* 28(10) (March), accessed May 2, 2006 at: http://www.fumento.com/biggulf.html.
418. Fumento, op cit.
419. Fumento, op cit.
420. Fumento, op cit.
421. Wessely, Simon, and Freedman, Lawrence (2006). "Reflections on Gulf War Illness." *Philosophical Transactions of the Royal Society* 361:721-730; Gray, G.C., and Klang, H.K. (2006). "Healthcare Utilization and Mortality Among Veterans of the Gulf War." *Philosophical Transactions of the Royal Society* 361:553-569.
422. Wessely and Freedman, op cit., pp. 721-722.
423. Wessely and Freedman, op cit., pp. 721-722.
424. Wessely and Freedman, op cit., p. 722.

HALIFAX DISASTER

Canada: December 6, 1917

The explosion of a ship laden with explosives in the harbor of Halifax, Nova Scotia, was one of the greatest man-made disasters in history. The response of the populace, and the behavior which resulted, were the subject of a landmark study by Samuel Henry Prince of Columbia University, which the author claimed to be "the first attempt to present a purely scientific and sociological treatment of any great disaster."[1] While only occasionally could the behaviors involved be described as extraordinary, we include the event in this Encyclopedia because the detailed record of the event provides a unique yardstick by which to measure the popular response to catastrophe.

CONTEXT: At about 8:45am the French vessel *Mont Blanc*, laden with more than 2500 tons of explosives destined for the war in France, was sailing to join a convoy before crossing the Atlantic. At the entrance to the Narrows, she collided with an empty Norwegian vessel, the *Imo*. The impact was not severe, but fire immediately broke out on the French ship. The captain, pilot, and crew, expecting the ship to blow up at any moment, lowered the boats and headed for the nearest shore, away from the city, where they made for the woods. (They were subsequently blamed for neglect of public safety, but neither captain was held responsible for the disaster.)

The unmanned ship drifted, burning fiercely, for twenty minutes, and ended up against Pier 6 in the heart of the harbor. The dramatic sight attracted crowds of spectators, unaware of the imminent danger. "It was the best fire I ever saw in my life," one eyewitness reported.[2] But then at 9:05, the ship blew up. She was totally destroyed, her entire fabric and contents hurled into the air, to rain down in the form of red-hot debris over a wide area of the town. The violence of the explosion shook the entire city, causing damage similar to that of an earthquake, and was heard more than 30 kilometers away. The entire dockyard area was leveled at once by the immense gas-blast, which "wrought instant havoc everywhere. Trees were torn from the ground. Poles were snapped like toothpicks. Trains were stopped dead. Cars were left in twisted masses. Pedestrians were thrown violently into the air, houses collapsed on all sides. Steamers were slammed against the docks. The sky rained iron fragments, piercing a thousand roofs..." The exploding ship set up a wave two meters high in the harbor waters, causing further destruction and drowning some 200. On shore, as 3,000 tons of red-hot metal showered down, the wooden pier was instantly set ablaze, the fire spreading rapidly throughout the harbor area. In the residential streets, countless individual fires were started when the stoves, burning in every home dur-

Vessels make their way through the ice in Halifax harbor.

ing the Canadian winter, were overturned.

Had there been a wind, probably the entire city would have been caught up in a single almighty conflagration. Even as it was, there were so many individual fires, together with the burning fragments showering down from the sky, that it created an impression of a city on fire. "For some time after the Mont Blanc blew up the city was unnaturally quiet. Then it was bedlam. Everything that was ordered, familiar and tranquil was gone and horror, fear and chaos reigned in their place. The elements of civilized society were broken down and for many all that remained was the jungle law of self-preservation."[3] At first all was confusion. Some ran to the cellars. Some ran to the streets. Some ran to their shops. Those in the shops ran home. The streets were filled with the dead and dying, the hideously injured, and the distraught.

One hour after the explosion, the spreading flames reached the powder magazine in the Navy Yard, setting off fears that a second explosion was imminent. Panic resulted, made the more urgent by the exhortation of the military to leave the endangered northern quarter and flee south. The actions of the fire services produced a sudden cloud of mingled steam and smoke, which onlookers perceived as an indication that the powder magazine had taken fire.

> It is said that some civilian in the crowd pointed with his cane to the cloud of smoke. He may also have shouted, or spoken his thought to his nearest neighbor. But the mere hint, the mere wind of the word would be enough. The crowd turned at once and surged back from the apparent danger, heading south and spreading alarm. Panic ran through the city. With incredible swiftness, the rumor went round that there was great danger of a second explosion from a powder magazine, that all people were to leave their houses and take refuge in the parks and open spaces. There was nothing vague about the rumor. Soldiers everywhere conveyed this definite statement. They were on foot, knocking at house-doors, or in vehicles such as motor-lorries, telling the people to "go south" and even throw themselves on the ground in the open spaces. It is hardly likely that these men should have done so without proper authorization, but it seems impossible to discover whether any orders were definitely given to this effect. The hardship, suffering, and death caused by this panic can hardly be estimated.
>
> The "second alarm," overtaking the populace before they had time to adjust to the initial catastrophe, must be regarded as a second disaster. Its results were calamitous as the panicking crowds raced to safety. Harbor operator William Fowlie, lying injured and unable to move, watched "the struggling terrified mob streaming past him until, in a matter of seconds the street was empty, there was not a living creature to be seen: everyone had fled and he was alone."[4]
>
> The well and strong, infants, the old, and the bed-ridden, some of whom had not left their homes for years, found themselves in this mob expecting they knew not what... Some people undoubtedly lost their heads for the time being... men were seen running with their eyes staring as if German bayonets were behind them. Motors sped southward through the streets with refugees clinging to the footboards, and the screeching horns helped to spread alarm... The currents of population swirled and eddied according to impulse. There was the impulse, first, to reach a place of safety. The instinct of those injured was to reach some spot – hospital, doctor's office, drug shop – where they could find relief for their hurt. Those who were unhurt wanted to escape from danger... or to assist their helpless friends.[5]
>
> Then came the orders of the soldiers, for the people to fly southward, to the open spaces – anywhere. Another explosion was imminent. Then came further outbreaks of the flight impulse... The crowd needed no second warning. They turned and fled. Hammers, shovels and bandages were thrown aside. Stores were left wide open, with piles of currency on their counters. Homes were vacated in a twinkling. Little tots couldn't understand why they were being dragged along so fast. Some folks never looked back. Others did, either to catch a last glimpse of the home they never expected to see again or to tell if they could from the sky how far behind them the Dreaded Thing was... Many were scantily clad. Women fled in their night dresses. A few were stark naked, their bodies blackened with soot and grime... With blanched faces, bleeding bodies and broken hearts, they fled from the Spectral Death they thought was coming hard after, fled to the open spaces where possibly its shadow might not fall.[6]

Between them, the explosion and the resulting fire and flood brought about the deaths of 1963 people, according to the official figures, though this is widely considered to be a serious underestimate. Some 9,000 more were injured: 25 limbs had to be amputated, 199 were blinded, and upwards of 250 eyes had to be removed, destroyed by shattered glass. Hospitals treated the more than 4,000 injured, private doctors many hundreds more. About 6,000 lost their homes, and 25,000 were left without adequate shelter. A total of 1630 homes were completely destroyed, and 12,000 more were damaged; the destruction of property was estimated at 35 million dollars. The population of Halifax had been 50,000; now, nearly one person in five was dead, injured, or homeless.

The immediate effect of this combination of disasters – the explosion, the flood, and the fire – was total social disintegration. All services – telephone, lighting, public transport – were out of action. Communication was non-existent, so no one knew either the extent of the disaster or the risk that there might be more to come. Many hundreds of families had lost one or more members, or were in need of medical care. Many more had lost their homes. Dwight Johnstone, an observer, commented that "Halifax had become in a trice a city of dead bodies, ruined homes and blasted hopes."[7]

Though immediate steps were taken to control the fires, locate and assist the injured, and house the homeless, the authorities were in no position to provide immediate relief on the necessary scale. Until the fire services could be organized, coping was limited to individual efforts. One man was helping to control a fire when he learned that the house next door was on fire, and that there were four children in it. "The parents went on like maniacs, but it was not possible to get the children out."[8] Those who survived the destruction of their homes poured out into streets which "were filled with the strangest apparitions: men, women and children with their faces streaming with blood from head wounds dealt by flying glass, faces chalk-white with terror and streaked with red, faces black with the 'black rain' and smeared with blood. The dead, the dying and the severely injured lay about the streets..."[9]

Analyzing the reaction of the populace, Canadian sociologist Samuel Henry Prince noted that in the first instance most were simply stunned. One commentator compared it "to being suddenly stricken with blindness and paralysis." Many felt utter helplessness, resulting in an inability to act or to think rationally. Individuals lost their sense of proportion: a motorist, fleeing the stricken area in his car, was stopped by soldiers who wanted to requisition it as an ambulance. His answer was, "Oh! I'd like to help, believe me, but this is a new car and the last thing I want is to get blood all over the seats." They took it anyway.

"The nervous shock and terror were as hard to bear as were the wounds." It was early afternoon, perhaps five hours after the explosions, before a semblance of co-operative rescue work began. People accustomed to concerted action were the quickest to respond; the actors and actresses of the Academy Stock Company organized the first relief station for the injured about midday on the morning of the disaster.

Many hallucinated shapes corresponded to their fears. Naturally enough, since Canada was at war, an attack by the Germans was thought by many to be the cause. "The first thought in many minds was 'the Germans, at last!' They were shelling the city from the harbour or dropping bombs from the air..."[10] Cadet Brooke was one of many who assumed the German fleet was bombarding the port. Before he grasped the extent of the disaster, the reaction of Colonel Thompson, Assistant Adjutant-General, was "At last, the war has come to us. I'm glad. People will know that we are in it."[11] Individual experiences seemed to confirm those fears. "It is no wonder eyes looked upward when there came the crash, and when seeing the strange unusual cloud beheld the Zeppelin of fancy." Mrs. Dickinson, a doctor's wife, shouted to a neighbor, "You mustn't stay out in the open, my dear. It's not safe. It's the German Zeppelins, you know – they're dropping bombs." A man standing on the heights overlooking the harbor clearly saw a German fleet maneuvering in the distance. Evidently the city was being bombarded by their guns and a resident had heard a German shell shrieking as it passed overhead. One rumor claimed that "the Germans have landed in Purcell's Cove and the Militia's calling for volunteers." One man had seen fifty U-boats with his own eyes. German residents – or even folk with Germanic names – were instantly suspect: "they had the dynamite on them! Going to hang them, they are..." Some were stoned in the street or chased by angry crowds. A certain Herr Hobrecker was said to have a concrete gun emplacement under his lawn for the use of an invading army. On the morning of the disaster his maid was reported opening all the windows of the house, long before the explosion. Evidently she had advance warning of the blast. A mob attacking the house found that it had been damaged by the explosion and that the family had left, but they ransacked the place anyway.[12] Many aliens were placed under arrest, though all were soon released when it was recognized that they could have played no part in the disaster.

An alternative supposition was that this was the end of the world. Many fell to their knees in prayer. One woman was found in the open yard of her ruined home repeating the Christian general confession. "There were instances, not a few, of those who 'saw' in the death-cloud the clear outlines of a face."

Delusion was another feature. "This was especially noticeable in the hospital identification, particularly of children. A distracted father looked into a little girl's face four different times but did not recognize her as his own, which in fact she was. The opposite occurrence was also noted: a fond parent time and time again 'discovered' his lost child, 'seeing' to complete satisfaction special marks and features on its little body. This phenomenon was repeated in numberless instances at the morgue."

Individual response varied widely. Amnesia afflicted one soldier who had been working continuously for two days in relief work. Without knowing what he was doing, he took a train to Montreal, where, later in the day he was found wandering and taken to hospital where he recovered. Dr. Shacknove, one of the first medical men to respond to the emergency, after working for hours on end with the wounded, was thrown off his mental balance by emotion and exhaustion and hanged himself in his office. A married man who had lost his wife and children attempted to take his own life. The hospitals housed many mothers who had given premature birth.

One dramatic incident could scarcely be duplicated in its tragic and pathetic features. An old man who a few hours before had left his wife and two beautiful daughters in their comfortable cottage in the destroyed area and had gone into the south end of the city on business, returned to find only the smoking ruins of his happy home, and after long effort recovered all that was left of his wife and daughters, the charred remnants of those he had parted from a few hours before in the full enjoyment of life, happiness and home. Seeking in vain in the destroyed region for any receptacle for the remains, he finally found an old oat sack. He nearly filled it with all that was left and staggering under the weight of his burden and his sorrow, with his back bent and his head bowed, he marched off, like Atlas of old, doomed to carry the load the fates had imposed.[13]

In contrast to these individual responses, collectively there came about a tremendous sense of community. Countless unpaid volunteers worked twelve or fourteen hours a day, often disregarding their own bereavement or their own injuries. One man was found working in the ruins although half his face had been blown off. A chauffeur carried the wounded to the hospital trip after trip despite a broken rib and stopped only when he collapsed. "I have never seen such kindly feeling. I have never seen such tender sympathy," one observer noted. Hundreds threw themselves voluntarily into relief activities, even though they themselves were injured or had lost relatives, friends, or their homes.

According to MacMechan, "there was no plundering or robbery," but this is not borne out by others. Witnesses testified to a certain amount of casual looting:

Few folk thought that Halifax harbored any would-be ghouls or vultures. The disaster showed how many. Men clambered over the bodies of the dead to get beer in the shattered breweries. Men taking advantage of the flight from the city because of the possibility of another explosion went into houses and shops, and took whatever their thieving fingers could lay hold of. Then there were the nightly prowlers among the ruins, who rifled the pockets of the dead and dying, and snatched rings from icy fingers. A woman lying unconscious on the street had her fur coat snatched from her back...

Although Chief of Police Hanrahan was later to deny vehemently, at least in public, that orders to shoot looters had been carried out, the fact is that six men were killed resisting arrest by service patrols. Profiteers proliferated. Landlords raised their rents as the demand for accommodation rose. Plumbers demanded overtime money, bricklayers insisted that plasterers should not poach on their trade. Truckmen charged exorbitant prices for carting goods and baggage. Merchants boosted prices: one shopkeeper was attacked by a customer when he asked a little starving child thirty cents for a loaf of bread. Many of the port's prostitutes had fled the town, but those who remained found that business was brisk with the sailors and the workers brought into Halifax to help with reconstruction.[14]

A witness who had experience of the fighting in France made a comparison. "There is a difference in the expression of those instantly killed [in Halifax] compared to those in France. In France, the faces of dead soldiers wear a look of determination, teeth clenched, brows drawn. These wore a look of surprise, surprise not fear. The mouths were open and the eyes staring as if they were looking at they knew not what."[15]

COMMENT: Research consistently shows that, contrary to popular belief, people behave with mutual support and restrained purposefulness during disasters.[16] The citizens of Halifax responded to catastrophe with classic behaviors, collective and individual. The initial explosion took them all by surprise and stunned them with the rapidity and intensity of its destructive force. In an instant they saw their homes destroyed, their relatives killed, their city, its services, and infrastructure massively destroyed. Though at this stage there was no collective panic, there were many individual acts by terror-stricken people driven out of their minds by their situation.

Those who could bring their minds to reflect, tried to account for what was happening to them in terms of their beliefs, fears, and expectations. For many the first option had to be an attack by the Germans; for a few it seemed the end of the world.

Panic came with the rumor of a second explosion. This time the danger was explicit, and people had a general idea what to expect. And this time there was something they could do about it – get away to a place of safety, as far from the powder stores as possible. Even subsequently, rumors of further danger sparked terror: "For a long time after the disaster all of those who had experienced it lived subconsciously on the knife-edge of panic and twice, at least, thousands fled into the open country again on rumors of new dangers."[17]

On the whole, the people of Halifax responded with discretion and self-control. Within a remarkably short time they were coming to terms with the catastrophe and organizing help. Exceptional behavior was limited to individuals, or to the crowds who were for a while driven by panic.

HALIFAX PERFUME SCARE

Canada: circa 1990 to present

In February 2000, an anti-scent ban took effect across Halifax, Nova Scotia, including all municipal buildings, schools, courts, libraries, and many work settings. The city council vote in favor of the ban was 15 to 8. Science writer Michael Fumento says that what began innocently enough in Halifax in about 1990 soon spread across the region and by about 2000 "about 80% of Halifax's 146 schools have some form of scent-free policy. Anti-fragrance policies also appear to be the norm at most of the city's workplaces: Most of the city's public institutions, and a number of private businesses, now request or demand that workers be scent-free." Fumento observes: "…there's nothing that qualifies as science that indicates that –while a few persons among hundreds of millions may have allergic reactions to this perfume or that deodorant – there is anybody with a true health reaction to artificial smells as a whole anymore than there is anybody who reacts to any product beginning with the letter 'f.'"[18]

In one incident during March 2000, the Royal Canadian Mounted Police arrested a schoolboy for assault. His crime: wearing cologne and Dippity Doo hair jel. The episode began when 17-year-old Gary Falkenham was attending a school at Sheet Harbour when his teacher complained that he repeatedly disregarded the anti-scent policy. In other incidents, an elderly woman was forced to leave City Hall for wearing perfume; another was kicked off a bus.[19]

Local journalist Stephanie Domet defended the policy: "The rest of the country may think we're a bunch of crackpots, but I believe some people are canaries in a coal mine. We've created a world where some people are overly sensitive to chemicals. So is it really that much of a hardship for you to not be able to pour on the Charlie?"[20]

CONTEXT: Michael Fumento described the milieu in which the anti-perfume scare took place. He said, "it is spread by antichemical activists, Internet innuendo, newspaper and magazine reporters who treat alleged victims as experts while ignoring the real experts, and by a handful of doctors who rake in the big bucks by treating the fragrance phobes."[21]

HALIFAX SLASHER

Northern England: November-December 1938

Between Monday November 21 and Friday December 2, fear and terror paralyzed daily life in several communities in the vicinity of Halifax (estimated population 98,000) as many believed that a crazed, razor-wielding maniac dubbed "the Halifax Slasher" was roaming the streets in search of his next victim.[22] Authorities later concluded that there never was a slasher and peoples' imaginations were playing tricks on them. There were so many reports in so many locations, often several in a single night, that at one point, bewildered police thought there may have been three slashers. Slasher historian Michael Goss recounts the reporting of three "attacks" within about an hour on a single night. "On reaching work ... a man discovered two slight cuts in his raincoat; he couldn't remember having been approached nor attacked, but thought he'd better notify the police anyhow. Half an hour later a volunteer watcher (who said that, as husband and father, he was going to do all he could) chased a suspicious character over a wall... 30 minutes or so onwards after a nervous boy claimed that he'd been clutched on the shoulder, a Hume Street patrol similarly failed to make anything of 'a man up to no good ... lurking the shadows.'"[23]

In a series of events remarkably similar to the PHANTOM SLASHER OF TAIPEI, by the time Scotland Yard got involved on Tuesday November 30th, the affair had peaked but the slasher seemed to be everywhere and jittery residents were in the throngs of a collective anxiety attack. In all there were estimated to have been between 200 and 400 slasher reports. At the height of the scare, hundreds of vigilantes patrolled the streets and police had deputized 80 citizens to join in the hunt. As news of the sensational events in Halifax spread, "slashings" were reported as far away as Manchester and London.

One unfortunate man was nearly lynched by a mob of 200 after being mistakenly fingered as the slasher. Police arrived just in time to whisk him to safety – he had been cornered and pinned against a wall.[24] It seemed only a matter of time before the irate citizens ripped him to shreds. Another near disaster involved Hilda Lodge, who told police that she was slashed on November 25th. She soon recanted, admitting that she had scratched her own face and arms with a broken vinegar bottle. Between her report to police and her confession that she'd made up the story, Clifford Edwards, in the wrong place at the wrong time, was nearly "dismembered by a frenzied mob" intent on finding her "attacker."[25] In London, an elderly woman ran into a pharmacy for treatment after being "slashed" by a man she said had brushed against her, after which she noticed a scratch on her hand. As it turned out, the mark was simply a run-of-the-mill scratch!

Events involving Mrs. Constance Wood were typical of the scare. In the early morning of November 28, Mrs. Wood was standing near the front gate of her home. Suddenly, as a man in a raincoat dashed by, she was knocked down and felt a stinging pain in her left arm. The slasher had apparently lacerated her arm twice and ripped her sweater. She began sounding the alarm, crying out for help. Her screams echoed through the neighborhood, sparking several separate chases involving tall men who had the misfortune of being in the area and wearing raincoats. An interview with Mrs. Wood in *The Yorkshire Evening Post* was revealing, as it was evident that she and neighbors had been living in fear and semi-paranoia in the week before the incident and were actually anticipating an attack. And what of her "slash" marks? A closer examination revealed two minor cuts – not from any slasher – but from where she apparently hit the ground and tore her sweater.[26]

By the first week of December, reports were declining rapidly as the press grew critical of the episode, which was being increasingly attributed to "hysteria" and imagination. This new wave of press skepticism appeared after several "victims" confessed to having slashed themselves for attention. In two separate incidents, young women said that they had fabricated attacks in order to get the attention of their boyfriends, whose affections were waning.

Chronology Of Events

The first "victim" was 21-year-old Miss Mary Sutcliffe, who told police that she was slashed on the wrist by a man standing near a street lamp. It was Monday night November 21st. Mary had worked the late shift at a toffee factory. At about 10:10 pm, she was nearing Lister Lane and said that a man suddenly stepped from under a street lamp two yards away, his arm raised as if about to strike her.[27] Mary said she instinctively raised her hand to deflect the anticipated blow and felt a strange but not painful feeling in her wrist. She turned and ran for home. It was only upon arriving that she noticed blood dripping from her wrist from a deep cut that took four stitches to close. There were a couple of oddities about the "attack." It happened in a densely populated neighborhood and the area was well lit.

Three days later, on the evening of the 24th, the "slasher" was born. Mr. Clayton Aspinall, a caretaker of the St. Andrew's Methodist Sunday School, was standing by a side door of the Church, just 300 yards from where Miss Sutcliffe had reported her encounter. As his eyes searched for latecomers to the various meetings scheduled at the church that evening, he heard the patter of rapid footsteps and saw a young man running through a narrow lane and heading directly for him. Mr. Aspinall had to take a step back to give him room to pass by, and as the figure passed, his hand struck Mr. Aspinall in the head. Mr. Aspinall suffering cuts to his head and on two fingers of his right hand that he had thrown up at the last minute top protect himself. While the blow may have been intentional, in hindsight it is not possible to be certain, and it may have been accidental. After the incident, the *Halifax Courier & Guardian* carried the headline: "£10 Police Reward for Arrest of Halifax 'Slasher.'" Police and community reaction to the Aspinall incident was swift, as public warnings and special security arrangements were quickly made. It was as if residents were anticipating that more attacks by slasher maniac were inevitable.

CONTEXT: A series of actual slashings that occurred 11 years earlier in Halifax may have set the stage for the 1938 wave of fear. On Wednesday February 16, 1927, a handsome 26-year-old, named James Leonard, was given a six month prison term after being convicted of stalking and slashing the clothes of six different girls in the city. Leonard used a razor in his misdeeds. In 1938, he was crossed off the suspect list, as he was instantly recognizable for his prominent nose – a feature that was not once described by the 1938 victims. Yet in 1927, most of those he attacked noted his nose and he was easily identified and arrested. It was within this context – a city with a relatively recent outbreak of real slashings – that the incident involving Sutcliffe took place.

After the Aspinall incident, the following evening, there were four new slashing reports and the scare exploded. At about 6:20 on the 25th, Mrs. Annie Cannon, 39, was leaving work and overheard saying that she hoped "the slasher" didn't "get" her. Shortly after, while walking down an alley, she said that a man appeared, striking her left shoulder and causing her to fall and hit her head. The man ran off. Mrs. Cannon was only slightly hurt but had a three-an-a-half-inch gash in her sweater, which went through to the blouse underneath, as if slashed by a sharp instrument.

It wasn't long before the slasher stories unraveled and the bubble of fear burst for good. On Tuesday November 29, grocery store manager Percy Waddington admitted to authorities that he had made up his account of having been slashed. The next day a 15-year-old Carlton boy confessed to making a false slasher report. Then the floodgates of confession opened wide. On December 1, Hilda Lodge broke down under police questioning, admitting to having broken a vinegar bottle by smashing it against a wall, then scratching her face and arms with the jagged glass. "I don't know what made me do it," she said. That same day 19-year-old Beatrice Sorrell admitted that she had a fight with her boyfriend, then bought a razor blade and went out and slashed her sweater in hopes of getting him to pay more attention to her. Around this time, another victim with boyfriend problems was Lily Woodhead. They had a lover's spat on November 27. Her boyfriend refused to walk her to the bus, said he didn't want to see her again, and gave her the distinct impression that he didn't care if she lived or died by saying: "I should not be surprised if there was a slasher in the road tonight." She said the slasher appeared, knocked her down and gave her several cuts and scratches. In reality, the insecure Miss Woodhead had been carrying a razor, apparently in the event of just such a break-up.[28]

More confessions poured in during early December. In Manchester, Marjorie Murphy broke down and confessed that her slashing injuries, which she suffered while on her way to the laundry, were an accident. A Huddersfield boy made a similar confession. Meanwhile, in Doncaster, a 15-year-old girl said she had made her slasher story up after having read about it in the newspaper.[29]

The price tag of the scare was high, as the episode involved 112 police officers working 2,069 hours at a public expense of £180.7.6d.[30] In Manchester, Michael McKeiven, 46, a man well known for his fragile mental constitution, committed suicide by ingesting aspirin tablets after his workmates accused him of being the slasher.[31] Perhaps the *Halifax Courier & Guardian* of December 2nd summed up the episode best: "The theory that a half-crazed, wild-eyed man has been wandering around, attacking helpless women in dark streets, is...[erroneous]. There is no doubt that following certain happenings public feeling has grown, and that many small incidents have been magnified in the public mind until a real state of alarm was caused."[32] In fact, by some accounts, Scotland Yard considered the only legitimate attack to be that of the first victim, Mary Sutcliffe, who suspiciously claimed a second attack on November 29th. Her mother had walked Mary to the front door of her house and had just turned away. Mary fell to the ground on her doorstep with a slash on her clothing and a small cut to her chest. The time was 4:45 pm. Several neighbors were at home along Allerton Lane. Police were nearby and got to the scene within five minutes. Despite all of these factors, no one got a good look at the "slasher," who had seemingly vanished into thin air.

See also: PHANTOM SLASHER OF TAIPEI; PHANTOM HATPIN STABBER.

HALLEY'S COMET SCARE

Worldwide: 1910

In 1881, astronomer Sir William Huggins was analyzing light spectra from comets when he discovered the presence of the lethal gas cyanogen. When it was later determined that the Earth would pass through the tail of Halley's Comet during its next fly-by, there was global anxiety and panic.[33] Concern began to mount on February 7, when the *New York Times* uncharacteristically published a speculative and rather sensational front-page story that astronomers at the Yerkes Observatory had identified bands of poison gas in the comet.[34] The article's tone was chilling, stating that cyanogen was deadly, noting that if "a grain of its potassium salt touched to the tongue ...[it was] sufficient to cause instant death." The article went on to portray an image of growing alarm by astronomers around the world. "The fact that cyanogen is present in the comet has been communicated to Camille Flammarion [a highly respected French astronomer] and many other astronomers, and is causing much discussion as to the probable effect on the Earth should it pass through the comet's tail. Prof. Flammarion is of the opinion that the cyanogen gas would impregnate the atmosphere and possibly snuff out all life on the planet."[35] The article was misleading in that Flammarion was the only astronomer at Yerkes to express grave concerns, though it clearly pointed out that his viewpoint was not in agreement with most scientists.[36] Indeed, soon after, Flammarion recanted his position, though this act received less fanfare in the press. Meanwhile the *New York Times* quickly followed the account with an editorial in an attempt to reduce anxiety caused by their earlier story. But while it was stated that the Earth could pass through a dozen comet tails without any effect, the initial damage was done.[37]

Like many newspapers during the episode, the *Washington Post* gave mixed messages. While Flammarion's doom and gloom scenario was criticized by several of his colleagues, in the very same article a journalist reported: "On the other hand, it is pointed out that the spectroscope has shown that there is a large quantity of cyanogen gas in the atmosphere surrounding Halley's Comet, and some chemists, such as M. Dastre, say that being practically without odor, the presence of the gas would not easily be perceived. A mixture of this gas with air would lead to certain poisoning."[38] As if this wasn't pessimistic enough, the article ends with a warning of the comet's danger by scientist M. Armand Gautier who said "that in the presence of fire or a small electric spark, a mixture of cyanogen gas and air will explode."[39]

Less than a week before the comet was to pass closest to earth, the *Washington Post* was still generating anxiety by referring to the inexact nature of astronomy when it comes to the understanding of comets: "COMET QUITS ITS PATH. Wanders From Predicted Orbit; Surprises May Follow." The sub-heading was even more alarming: "POISON IN ITS TAIL AGAIN. Cyanogen, Which Disappeared in March, Is Now Revealed by Spectroscope. Prof. Deslandres Says Hypothesis That Gas Is Liable to Affect the Earth's Atmosphere Is Not at All Absurd." The article cites French astronomer Maurice Hamy of the Paris Observatory, reporting "that the length of the tail has increased from five to ten degrees in three days." The implication was clear: with a bigger tail, the Earth could expect to be exposed to more poison gas.

On May 14, *Harper's Weekly* magazine published different views on the projected impact of Earth's rendezvous with Halley's Comet. American astronomer D. J. McAdam of Washington and Jefferson College discussed some possible disaster scenarios, including comet gases penetrating the atmosphere and causing widespread illness. "When we pass through its tail in

May we will be in a stream of hydrogen, probably mixed with marsh gas and other cometary gases. Disease and death have frequently been ascribed to the admixture of cometary gases with the air. Enough of such gases as are in the comet's tail would be deleterious." This assertion was without scientific merit. But this scenario was rosy in comparison to a second possibility, a theory once proposed by British astronomer Richard Proctor who speculated that if a comet with a hydrogen dense tail were to pass through Earth's oxygen-rich atmosphere, it could spark a cataclysmic explosion "leaving the burnt and drenched Earth no other atmosphere than the nitrogen now present in the air, together with a relatively small quantity of deleterious vapors."[40] In discussing Proctor's theory, McAdam failed to tell readers that it had been thoroughly discredited.

CONTEXT: The episode was preceded by waves of claims and public discourse by many astronomers and journalists, speculating on the possibility that deadly gas in the comet's tail could poison earth.

Reaction In The United States

On the night of Wednesday, May 18th, New York time, the comet was projected to pass through the tail, though most scientists agreed that any poisonous substances would be so rarefied that the atmosphere would not be affected.[41] Some alarmed citizens went so far as to stuff rags in doorways, while opportunists sold gas masks and "comet pills" to counter the effects of the gas. Others made light of the concern and held comet parties.[42]

Across America there was great concern. One of the areas particularly affected was Chicago. On May 17th, much of Chicago was in a state of great anxiety as most residents were preoccupied with the comet, fearing that "the tail will wipe out all life."[43] One report described the talk of the city: "All else is forgotten. Comets and their ways and habits have been the principal topic discussed in the streets, cars, and elevated trains to-day..."[44] New York City residents were also on edge as one man reportedly leaped from an Eighth Avenue street car onto the pavement, fearing the comet had struck the car after he heard a loud thud.[45] In Lexington, Kentucky, it was reported that "excited people are tonight holding all-night services, praying and singing to prepare ... [to] meet their doom."[46]

In parts of Kentucky and North Carolina, African American farm laborers held all-night prayer services, fearing the world was about to end.[47] In numerous communities in western Georgia, the reaction was similar.[48] Meanwhile, thousands of mostly foreign miners in Wilkes-Barrie, Pennsylvania, refused to go underground, instead demanding to spend what they thought were their last hours alive, in prayer. Miners near Denver, Colorado, took the opposite strategy, going back into the mines in hopes of avoiding or limiting their exposure to the comet's tail.[49]

In the rural town of Towaco, New Jersey, two gentlemen convinced the local populace that they were scientists intent on studying the comet. They asked residents to write descriptions of the event and said they could get the best view at 3 a.m. on the 19th on Walkman Mountain. They even offered prizes ($10, $5 and $2.5) for the top three descriptions. The night turned disastrous. First, heavy fog rolled in, making viewing impossible. Then, by the time the weary residents had reached their homes in the early morning, they found several empty chicken coops and hundreds of missing chickens.[50]

The Global Reaction

A similar drama unfolded in other parts of the globe. While major panics were recorded in Russia and Japan, in Rome Pope Pius X denounced the hoarding of oxygen cylinders.[51] In Bermuda, a former

Halley's Comet also caused a panic in 1456 when Constantinople residents were terrified by its appearance.

British colony, upon the report of the death of King Edward VII, some citizens said the comet's head flared and the tail turned red. Many dock workers then "fell on their knees and began to pray. They thought that the end of the world was surely coming" and refused to work.[52] The workers were adamant that the observation was a portent that war would occur during the reign of the new King, George. They were also convinced that a great disaster would strike earth: "They were speechless with fear and worked themselves up in their paroxysms of religious zeal to a ... frenzy."[53] The men only returned to work after the comet had faded from view in the morning sunlight. There were even several reported suicides in different countries due to the comet's appearance.[54] In San Juan, Puerto Rico, hundreds marched in a candlelight parade through the streets and sang religious songs.[55]

In Italy, so many people were hoarding oxygen cylinders,[56] that not a single pharmacist in Rome had an oxygen tank on hand as they "had all been taken by persons in splendid health who had been frightened lest the fumes of the gases from the comet should choke them."[57] France also saw the hoarding of oxygen as many private residents placed the cylinders in the cellars, which were then sealed off in hopes of keeping the poisonous cyanogen at bay.[58] Those living in the rural areas seemed to be more anxious, though much of the country celebrated with "comet suppers" and "comet balls." The mood in Madrid, Spain, was festive, though the skies were cloudy.[59] While some in London used oxygen cylinders, most residents were in a mood to celebrate the occasion. The party atmosphere was true in many British cities. Festive comet gatherings were the order of the day in Germany as well with people sporting everything from comet hats to comet umbrellas and even brands of alcohol.[60] In Switzerland, parties were held through the night.[61]

In sections of South Africa, the comet fostered "an extraordinary amount of nervousness," as one man placed a newspaper ad which read: "Gentleman having secured several cylinders of oxygen and having bricked up a capacious room wishes to meet others who would share the expense for Wednesday night. Numbers strictly limited."[62] In Russia, many St. Petersburg residents spent the night of May 18 praying somberly in churches.[63] Crucifixes could be seen on the hilltops around Mexico City as prayer vigils were held in some cases, 10 days prior to the 18th in an effort "to avert the impending disaster with music, incantations, and weird ceremonies." When the morning broke over the horizon the next day, the masses celebrated with feasts and dancing, as if their actions had saved earth from the comet's harm.[64]

HAMMERSMITH GHOST SCARE
London: 1830

There is no folly more predominant... than a ridiculous and superstitious fear of ghosts and apparitions...The inhabitants of the London suburb of Hammersmith were much alarmed by a nocturnal appearance which for a considerable time eluded detection or discovery. In the course of this unfortunate affair, two innocent persons met with an untimely death; and as the transaction engaged the attention of the public in a high degree, we shall fully relate the particulars of it.

Joseph Taylor's book on apparitions is a skeptical work, and the story of the Hammersmith Ghost confirmed his finding that "servants, nurses, old women, and others of the same standard of wisdom, to pass away the tediousness of a winter's evening, please and terrify themselves with strange relations, till they are even afraid of removing their eyes from one another, for fearing of seeing a *pale spectre* entering the room."[65]

In December 1803 rumors began to circulate in the London suburb of Hammersmith, that a mysterious figure, resembling a ghost, had been seen in the lanes at night. Ghosts were commonly supposed to be revenants, spirits of the dead rising from the grave and returning to revisit the living, wearing the shrouds in which they had been buried. On December 29th, the neighborhood watchman, William Girdle, saw the apparition. He chased after it; it fled, throwing off a sheet in the process, and got away.

The discarding of the sheet ought to have made it evident that this was no ghost, but a human impostor. But not every account could be so easily explained. Thomas Groom, a brewer's servant, told how he was walking through Hammersmith churchyard with a fellow servant when he was assaulted by something that clutched at his throat; yet he saw nothing. When others added such scary details as horns and glassy eyes, the notion spread that the figure was truly supernatural. A rumor spread that it was the reappearance of a man who had cut his throat in the neighborhood about a year before. From this point, the notion of a ghost from the grave was the prevailing belief.

Neither man, woman, nor child would pass that way for some time, particularly after an event in January 1804, when a poor woman, far advanced in her pregnancy of a second child, was passing near the church yard at about two o'clock in the morning and beheld a figure rise from the tombstones. It was tall and very white. She attempted to run, but the entity soon overtook her and pressed her in its arms. She fainted. Neighbors eventually discovered her unconscious body, roused her, and kindly led her home. She was so shocked that she took to her bed and died two days later as a consequence of her terror.

Several self-appointed vigilantes lay in wait on different nights, hoping to catch the ghost, but there were so many bye-lanes and paths leading to Hammersmith that it always managed to be in an unguarded area and continued to "play his tricks" every night, to the terror of pedestrians. Nor were all the victims on foot: a wagoner was driving a team of eight horses when he was confronted by the figure. Though he was carrying sixteen passengers, he jumped to the ground and fled, leaving his wagon, horses, and passengers to the mercies of the ghost.

Francis Smith shoots bricklayer Thomas Milwood, believing him to be the "Hammersmith Ghost." (Engraving by Phiz in Benson's Remarkable Trials)

On January 3rd, Francis Smith, an excise officer, determined to lie in wait for the apparition, armed with a gun, in Black Lion Lane. He must have thought luck had favored him when the supposed entity came in sight. He challenged him twice but received no reply, so he fired at the figure, which fell. He told John Locke, a wine merchant, that he had shot the ghost – but it was found to be Thomas Milwood, a bricklayer, who wore white clothing as was customary in his occupation. Milwood had already alarmed people on more than one occasion and had been warned to cover up his white working clothes with a greatcoat. This he had neglected to do – with fatal consequences. At the coroner's inquest, this rash act was judged willful murder, and Smith was accordingly committed to jail. At the ensuing sessions at the Old Bailey, on January 13th, the jury at first found him guilty of manslaughter, but since the crime being deemed murder in the eye of the law, the judge could only receive a verdict of guilty or acquittal. He was consequently found guilty, and was sentenced to be hanged in a few days' time, but was pardoned on condition of being imprisoned one year.[66]

There are no reports of the ghost being seen from that time on, and we may suppose that Milwood's tragic end discouraged the "ghost," who was never identified.

HANDSOME LAKE SECT (NATIVE AMERICAN)

Western New York State: circa 1800

Handsome Lake (1735-1815) was the founder of a Native American religious movement at the turn of the 19th century on land that is now New York State. A tribal chief, he started a revitalization movement at a time when Iroquois society and culture were disintegrating. The Iroquois suffered the consequences of having supported the British during the Revolutionary War and were eventually sent to live on small reservations, which prevented them from continuing their once vibrant, traditional practices of hunting and horticulture. Displaced from their homeland and under the control of the U.S. government, Iroquois life deteriorated and was marked by the heavy consumption of alcohol and frequent arguments among tribal members. It was within this context that Handsome Lake, an alcoholic himself, began to experience visions that he believed were from otherworldly spirits. He said that the spirits had issued a warning to be passed on to the tribe – the Iroquois must either change their way of life or they would perish.[67] Handsome Lake's visions contained a plan for surviving the present crisis. The Code of Handsome Lake spelled out what the natives needed to do in order to adjust to the new social order. The Code called for an end to self-bickering, witchcraft, and drinking alcohol.

In the late 1700s, Handsome Lake was seriously ill for several years, apparently from his drinking habit. During this time he became very spiritual and meditated. Soon he reported receiving revelations from "the Creator" and "four beings" who appeared to him. Following this first vision, he was physically revitalized and quickly began to spread the news of his revelations. Anthropologist Arthur Parker, who studied the movement firsthand, observes that the great appeal of The Code was "that it presents in their own language a system of moral precepts and exhortations that they can readily understand. The prophet, who is called 'our great teacher' ... was a man of their own blood, and the ground that he traversed was their ancestral domain. Patriotism and religious emotion mingle, and, when the story of the 'great wrongs' is remembered, spur on a ready acceptance."[68]

The Code served a practical function, helping the "Indians," who hated Europeans and rejected Christianity, to adjust to their situation on their own terms. Anthropologist Conrad Kottak remarked: "This revitalization movement helped the Iroquois survive in a drastically modified environment. They eventually gained a reputation among their non-Indian neighbors as sober family farmers."[69] More than 200 years after its founding, the Handsome Lake religion still has members in Western New York State and adjacent Ontario province in Canada. A typical text from The Code is as follows: "Now the Creator of mankind ordained that people should live to an old age. He appointed that when a woman becomes old she should be without strength and unable to work. Now the Creator says that it is a great wrong to be unkind to our grandmothers. The Creator forbids unkindness to the old. We, the messengers, say it. The Creator appointed this way: he designed that an old woman should be as a child again and when she becomes so the Creator wishes the grandchildren to help her, for only because she is, they are. Whosoever does right to the aged does right in the sight of the Creator."[70]

HEADHUNTING SCARES

Southeast Asia: 20th century

Periodic headhunter, ritual sacrifice, and kidnapping scares have been recorded in parts of Indonesia and Malaysian Borneo since the seventeenth century.

CONTEXT: Episodes coincide with real or rumored government construction projects and a local belief that such developments require a head or body to be laid in the foundation or on a special pillar nearby to ensure an enduring structure.[71]

During March 1937, the first Indonesian Prime Minister, Soetan Sjahrir, was living on the Moluccan island of Banda in Dutch Indonesia, where he described a headhunting rumor-panic that swept through his village.[72] The episode coincided with rumors that a *tjoelik* (someone who engages in headhunting for the government) was operating in the area and searching for a head to be placed near a local jetty that was being rebuilt. According to tradition, government construction projects would crumble without such an offering. Sjahrir said that "people have been living in fear" and were "talking and whispering about it everywhere," and after 7 p.m. the streets were nearly deserted.[73] There were many reports of strange noises and sightings. Sjahrir stated: "Every morning there are new stories, generally about footsteps or voices, or a house that was bombarded with stones, or an attack on somebody by a tjoelik with a noose, or a cowboy lasso. Naturally, the person who was attacked got away from the tjoelik in a nick of time!" Sjahrir described the scare as an example of "mass psychosis."[74]

For several weeks in late 1979, a headhunter kidnapping rumor-panic suddenly broke out on the island of Borneo. Anthropologist Richard Drake was studying the Mualang peoples living on the Belitang Hulu River in Kalimantan Barat (Indonesia) when the episode occurred. Soon guards were posted around the village, rubber tapping ceased, and a local school closed for insufficient attendance. A variety of ordinarily mundane events and circumstances were defined as kidnapper-related, such as noises and rustling in the jungle. The scare was triggered by rumors that the government was constructing a bridge in the region and needed a body to place in the foundation to strengthen it. Drake agued that these episodes reflected antagonistic tribal-state relations that were characterized by distrust and suspicion of a distant, central government.[75] A similar headhunting scare swept through parts of Indonesian Borneo in Kalimantan in 1997.[76]

COMMENTS: Headhunting scares highlight the importance of plausibility in spreading social delusions. Episodes only occur in regions where there exist cultural traditions of such headhunters, in conjunction with a belief in their continuing reality.

HINDU MILK MIRACLE

Worldwide: September-October 1995

On September 21st, many Hindus around the world became excited, believing that idols of Lord Ganesh (the elephant deity) was drinking milk offered by followers. As news of the "miracle" spread, other idols were reportedly drinking milk, including statues of Nandi (the bull) and Lord Shiva (usually depicted as a human with snakes straddling his neck). The "miracle" reportedly began when an unnamed worshipper in India had a dream that Ganesh was thirsty for a drink of milk. Believing the dream, the worshipper is said to have gone to a nearby temple and offered a spoonful of milk to a statute of Ganesh, which promptly drank it. News of the "miracle" spread quickly. Within 24 hours, millions of Hindus around the world were flooding into temples in order to see the miracle for themselves or offer spoonfuls of milk to Ganesh.[77]

Based on media reports, most milk drinking "miracles" occurred between September 21 and the end of the month. Reports endured into October, when they continued to taper off.

Skeptics noted that many of the milk-drinking idols were composed of baked clay – a highly porous material that readily absorbs liquids through its capillary system. Polymer chemist Julia Higgins from Imperial College in London described what she believed was occurring: "Break a flowerpot, dip it in water, and the water disappears like mad."[78] American paranormal research fellow Joe Nickell observed that in the case where the statue is glazed, "only a bit of the glaze need be absent, say from a tooth (as indeed seemed the case in one statue), for capillary attraction to work."[79]

The former Indian secretary for science, Yash Pal, dismissed the "miracle" as an illusion. He said the excitement was created by the capillary effect and surface tension. Scientists from the National Council for Science and Technology Communication (NCSTC) uncovered evidence of this process by mixing red dye with a spoon of milk and observing that it was "sucked in by capillary action dripping from the idol's body."[80] This helped to explain why milk was pooling at the bottom of many of the statues. Through the process of surface tension, the milk need not directly spill out, but milk molecules are "pulled from the spoon by the texture of the statues."[81] Indian Rationalist Society secretary Sanal Edamaruku noted that when a spoon of milk is placed over a wet idol that has been ritually washed, the spoon, which is usually slightly tilted at an angle, transfers the milk onto the idol. "The basic principle behind it is that when two drops of a liquid are brought together it leads to the formation of one drop."[82]

During the mania, the price of all types of milk across India skyrocketed to as much as twenty times their normal price.[83] Police had to be summoned to guard temples and maintain order, and government officials ordered additional milk supplies to placate the throngs of would-be worshippers.[84] One journalist estimated that in New Delhi alone an average of 300 people attended its 5,000 roadside temples that dot the landscape.[85]

HOORN ORPHANAGE POSSESSION

Netherlands: 1673

The orphanage at Hoorn, in the Netherlands, was the scene of an outbreak in 1673, which ostensibly was entirely physical in its nature.[86] The adolescent boys and girls, all age twelve or more, were abandoned children, described as libertine and debauched.

CONTEXT: Religious matters do not seem to have been an issue here, nor indeed was any external factor. The disorder seems to have arisen among the children, spreading among them by contagion. Orphanages are, by their nature, unstable communities where unrest is easily brought about, and where contagion readily occurs.

There is no record of how the outbreak began. By the time the authorities became aware of the situation, it was already under way. The children were usually taken by surprise by the fits, which as a rule afflicted them when they saw others affected or heard them shouting and barking. Some of them, to avoid the contagion, ran away when they saw another affected, but this did not protect them unless they had sufficient time to reach the door of the house and get outdoors. Soon, so many of them had been affected that there were scarcely sufficient staff to care for the patients.

The contemporary account by the Amsterdam theologian Bekker, one of the most level-headed observers of such phenomena, provides so detailed a record that it merits quotation in full:

> This evil consisted in that these children fell suddenly into a faint, and at the same moment they were as though out of themselves. They tugged and tore at themselves, striking at the ground with their legs and arms and even with their heads, crying, yelling and barking like dogs so that it was a terrifying thing to see. The bellies of some of them pounded so fearfully, that one would have said there was a living creature moving about inside them or even that a barrel was being rolled within their bodies. So strong were these movements that it took three, four, five or even six persons to hold them: one would take the head, two others the hands, one sat on the legs and sometimes another to sit on the belly to prevent them moving. When they were motionless at last, they were stiff as a bar of iron, so that with one person holding the head and another the feet, they could be carried anywhere, without making any movement. Sometimes this happened for several hours on end, and even at night, until 11pm, midnight, one, two or three o'clock: this happened to a girl named Catherine, daughter of Lucas, who was one of the oldest girls in the house, who was attacked at 8 am, just as the bell called them to breakfast, and she was in this state without interruption until four hours after midday, when the bell called the children to their evening collation. When this patient came to herself again, she believed she had been in that state only for a moment, because she could hear the bell still ringing, and when she heard grace being said for the evening meal she thought it was for breakfast.[87]

The other occasion for the onset of the fits occurred while the children were at their devotions, in the church during preaching or catechism, for instance. The fits happened almost every day, and after a while the preaching had to be suspended. The directors of the orphanage assigned certain hours for prayer, but the more fervently they prayed and the more earnestly they begged God to take away this affliction, the more the children suffered and the longer their fits lasted. However during the Carnival, which lasted for nearly a week, the children who were the most tormented by this malady were the most libertine and the most debauched in their behavior. It was as though their ailment had been replaced by a kind of internal fire that drove them to activity.

Doctors were called in but were baffled by the phenomena. Consequently it was supposed that this was the work of the devil, regarded by the Protestants as the ultimate source of evil, but they did not personalize him as did the Catholics, and did not consider exorcism to be a practicable solution. It was found that the most effective remedy was public prayer, and services were held in all the churches except in those of the papists (Catholics). After that, the children were lodged singly in houses of the townspeople. No sooner was this done, than the children began to recover. Little by little the sickness diminished, and sooner or later all who were removed were cured, except for two young girls who continued to have fits for some time after.

COMMENT: The fact that the outbreak took place in a community of streetwise adolescents at once suggests imposture, but the authorities seem to have recognized from the start that the physical symptoms could not have been simulated.

Was it, then, the work of the Devil? Bekker, a minister and a theologian, considered the possibility, and concluded that the weight of the evidence argued against this explanation. He pointed out that the children already had a reputation for bad behavior: "they would surely be happier running in the streets than confined in church."[88] The malady affected them most when they were together, and least when they were away from the hospice. Without putting it into so many words, he seems to have regarded the outbreak as a rebellion, conscious or unconscious, against the discipline of the orphanage, and though he does not deny the reality of the malady, he speculates that the children may have exaggerated the severity of their affliction so as to escape confinement.

Be that as it may, a problem remains, one that is true of many other outbreaks featured in this encyclopedia: how was it that the behavior of these children, who could hardly be aware of similar happenings far removed in time and place, should resemble them not simply in general outline but in detail – in the nature of the seizures, and the animal-like utterances, for example?

See also: CONVENT HYSTERIA, DEMON POSSESSION.

HULA-HOOP FAD

Worldwide: 1958

Often dubbed the greatest fad of the 20th century, the Hula-Hoop took the United States by storm in early 1958. A bamboo or rattan hoop had long been in use by Australian grade-schoolers as a fun exercise tool in gym classes and by some Pacific islanders who gyrated it with their hips.[89] After noticing an interest in Australian hoop sales, ARTHUR SPUD MELIN, co-founder of the Wham-O Manufacturing Company, made several prototypes using polyethylene plastic. During this time, Melin's wife Suzy discouraged him from proceeding: "He said it would be huge. But I said, 'You can't put that on television. They just banned Elvis Presley's hips from the Ed Sullivan Show.'"[90] Melin listened to his instincts and in the spring, he began traveling around Southern California, giving demonstrations in schools and other venues in hopes of drumming up interest. The mass media quickly picked up on the local interest in the colorful hoops that spanned three-feet in diameter, and it spread like wildfire to the east coast. Soon amateur competitions (usually endurance contests) or "hoop-ins" were being held across the country.

CONTEXT: The popularity of the hula-hoop coincided with criticism, in conservative circles, of Elvis Presley's hip gyrations and may have reflected a shift in public attitudes regarding the body and sexuality at the dawn of the liberal 1960s.

Once hula-hoop mania set in, it seemed as though every psychologist had a theory for its phenomenal growth. Explanations ranged from a subconscious

Japanese hula-hooper Isaki Fukishima (center) fatally injures his back at Scizuka, Tokyo. (Walter Molino in La Domenica del Corriere, December 1958)

eroticism evoked by gyrating the hips, to the hoop representing a symbolic vagina, to encirclement offering a sense of security. A few even claimed that it symbolized God as it had no beginning or end. It may have simply been fun and novel.[91]

Scores of companies quickly jumped on the bandwagon, offering a variety of spin-offs – everything from the Spin-a-Hoop to the Hoop-D-Doo and the Hooper-Dooper, selling for one to two dollars. By some estimates, between 100 and 120 million hoops were sold in the U.S. and abroad in 1958, and at one point, at least 47 varieties of hoops were on the market.[92] As the hoop-la peaked, practitioners became more creative and outlandish in their uses of the hoop, including getting it to climb stairs, diving into one floating in a swimming pool, and using it in animal stunts.[93]

As hoop interest quickly waned in the fall of 1958, manufacturers tried to rekindle interest, but to no avail. Attempts at revival included hoops with bells, hoops that made musical sounds – even a hoop that could be used as an umbrella.[94] By November, hoop sales plunged and the fad was over as quick as it began. Surprisingly, when the hula-hoop fad came to a sudden, unexpected, abrupt end in the fall, Wham-O was left with millions of unsold hoops and posted a $10,000 loss for 1958.[95] Despite well-planned attempts to rekindle the Hula-Hoop hoop-la, all have failed. In 1967 Wham-O introduced the Shoop-Shoop Hula Hoop (the ball bearings inside made a swoosh sound), and in 1982 it was the Peppermint Hula Hoop (complete with a peppermint aroma). Despite promotional campaigns, including attempts to market hula-hoop exercise classes,[96] and brief spurts of interest in 1988 and 1992,[97] none has been able to captivate the public's interest anywhere near the extent of the 1958 Hula-Hoop fad. More recently, Maui Toys has tried marketing the Wave Hoop (filled with water), the non-edible Scented Hoop (fruit or bubble gum), and the Razzle Dazzle Hoop, without great success.

When the hoop fad began to quickly wane in the U.S., there was a sudden, brief surge of international interest in parts of the Middle East, Europe, Japan, and Asia. In Japan, the Prime Minister even demonstrated his hoop skills, and there was fascination for the hoops across much of the Soviet block.[98] Hula-Hoops were introduced at $1.98 and sold for $2.79 at their peak, but by the time the fad went bust, stores couldn't even sell them for 50 cents.

COMMENTS: Social scientists still cannot explain the hula-hoop's sudden, intense popularity and subsequent disinterest during 1958.
See also: FADS.

HURRICANE KATRINA SOCIAL CHAOS

New Orleans, Louisiana: August-September 2005

On August 29, 2005, Hurricane Katrina made landfall near Buras-Triumph, Louisiana, as a Category 4 storm, causing extensive damage along coastal Louisiana, Mississippi, and Alabama. The city of New Orleans, about 10 feet (3 meters) below sea level, was especially hard hit from flooding after the antiquated levee system surrounding the city was breached by the storm surge. Katrina resulted in at least 1,320 deaths, the displacement of over a million residents, and an estimated 100 billion dollars in damages.[99] This entry will focus on the social, psychological, and folkloric response to Katrina, including evidence that the reports of widespread social chaos in New Orleans following the hurricane were exaggerated.

Shortly after Katrina struck the Gulf coastal region of the southeastern United States, there were sensational media reports of mayhem and mob rule across New Orleans, including claims of children with their throats slit, gangs roaming the Superdome raping and murdering terrified evacuees, gunfire aimed at rescue personnel, a surge in murders, and serious looting. Attempts to confirm these initial reports by interviewing witnesses at the scene and checking police records portray a very different picture, however.

On September 1, CNN reported that the Superdome evacuations had been suspended after a ferrying helicopter was fired upon. Officials from the Louisiana National Guard subsequently denied the report.[100] Later that day during a live, nationally televised news briefing, Louisiana Democratic Senator Mary Landrieu said, "We have gotten reports, but unconfirmed, of some of our deputies and sheriffs that have either been injured or killed." This also proved unfounded. As of September 1, just one law officer out of thousands in the region, had been reported shot – a self-inflected leg wound that occurred during a struggle.[101] According to a spokesperson for the Louisiana National Guard, Major Edward Bush, who was deployed to the Superdome: "It just morphed into this mythical place where the most unthinkable deeds were being done."[102] Bush continued: "Rumor control was a beast for us... People would hear something on the radio and come and say that people were getting raped in the bathroom or someone had been murdered. I would say, 'Ma'am, where?' I would tell them if there were bodies, my guys would find it. Everybody heard, nobody saw. Logic was out the window because the situation was illogical."[103]

The impression of chaos at the Superdome was widely broadcast in the media and promoted by city officials. On September 6, New Orleans police superintendent Eddie Compass told TV interviewer Oprah Winfrey chilling accounts of babies being raped there. Mayor C. Ray Nagin also contributed hype when he said on the same broadcast that the Superdome was a major crime scene: "They have people standing out there, have been in that frickin' Superdome for five days watching dead bodies ... watching hooligans killing people, raping people."[104]

As of September 27, New Orleans District Attorney Eddie Jordan stated that he had received just one report of attempted sexual assault and not a single official report of rape. As for confirmed homicides, there had been four.[105]

Washington Post reporters Robert Pierre and Anne Gerhart suggest that a major reason for the rumors was the lack of communication with Louisiana residents as most communication systems were disabled in the aftermath of the storm. Pierre and Gerhart quote Denise Bottcher, press secretary to Louisiana Governor Kathleen Babineaux Blanco, who said: "The television stations were reporting that people were literally stepping over bodies and violence was out of control [in the Superdome]... But the National Guardsmen were saying that what we were seeing on CNN was contradictory to what they were seeing. It didn't match up."[106]

Sociologist Robert Granfield says that the flurry of false reports of criminal mayhem in New Orleans in the wake of Katrina reflect popular American beliefs about minorities and the poor. In several instances, Granfield said that rumors were reported as reality. "Reporters had neither the time nor the ability to investigate these claims, and so repeated them as facts. One gunshot or drowning or stolen television became 10, and 10 became 100. Hungry people taking bread off shelves were generalized into 'massive looting' and then typified as the rule, not the exception."[107] Granfield contends that the accounts of widespread murder and mayhem were readily believed because for years the media has been hyper-inflating the news in order to sell their product to the public and keep them watching. In reality, Granfield says that in the United States, "crimes against person and property are the lowest since 1973. The public, constantly exposed to lurid news stories of child murder, bombings, rapes, and other kinds of violence is not aware of the declining crime rate. Many apparently believe that we're just one police department or one National Guard unit away from anarchy."[108] Another reason why the gloom and doom reports out of New Orleans were believed, Granfield says, is that "the alleged perpetrators were those to whom they attribute moral lassitude, lack of self-control and criminal nature – the urban minority poor." The result, Granfield says, was a mass delusion involving journalists and the public. "Official hysteria reigned, the facts were misrepresented, the press could not investigate and reported the worst, which in turn supported public assumptions about that population. We were left with an 'idea' of the New Orleans disaster that, now, as the facts continue to come out, is as shocking and shameful as the behavior we assumed to be true."[109]

Urban Myths And Katrina

Scores of urban legends circulated in the aftermath of Katrina, many involving crimes or bad behavior supposedly committed by displaced New Orleans residents. One classic example was the story of the "Utah evacuees." According to the claim, many evacuees, upon arriving in Utah, immediately tried to sell drugs, re-form gangs, and commit rapes. The following account was obtained in a mid-September email by Snoops.com, an organization that gathers and analyzes rumors. This account was purportedly from a relief worker on the scene: "Let me tell you a few things about the wonderful group of evacuees we received here in Utah. The first plane arrived with 152 passengers. Of the 152; 10 were children. 3 of these children had been abandoned by their parents. As these passengers attempted to board the plane, the National Guard removed from their person; 43 handguns... 20 knives, one man had 100,000 dollars in cash, 20 pounds of Marijuana, 10 pounds of Crack, 15 pounds of Methanphetamines, 10 pounds of various other controlled substances including Heroin."[110]

It was then claimed that upon reaching Salt Lake City, two passengers immediately began smoking marijuana. During their medical exams, several parents were supposedly found to be using their children to conceal looted goods – the price tag still on the items. About a third of passengers who disembarked there were said to have been angry that they weren't going to San Antonio or Houston, and most of the evacuees processed on the planes had lengthy criminal records.[111]

The email continued: "By the second night in the shelter, there was one attempted rape of a relief worker, sales of drugs on-going and a gang had begun to rebuild. When the people arrived at the shelter, they were given the opportunity to dig through piles of donated clothes from local church groups. Many complained that they were second hand clothes... This past Saturday, workforce services held a job fair. 85 of the 582 evacuees attended. 44 were hired on the spot. 24 were asked back for a second interview. Guess the others had no desire to work."[112]

A check of the facts found the account to be without substance. The first Katrina evacuees to arrive in Utah reached there on September 3, and as would happen to later arrivals, they were temporarily housed at a Utah National Guard training center, Camp Williams, where they remained until September 27th when they found more permanent housing. Governor Jon Huntsman said that the background of each evacuee was checked and that "None of the guests at Camp Williams have criminal records that would justify booking them into jail."[113]

Rumor expert Barbara Mikkelson said that of 582 evacuees sent to Utah, just 42 had criminal records. "Yet stories about drug sales, gangs re-forming, and an attempted rape are unsupported by the Utah news media. Though we looked and looked, we couldn't find reportage of any such incidents."[114]

Utah Department of Public Safety spokesman Derek Jensen said the wild tales of unruly evacuees "are just not true. The evacuees have been cooperative and behaved themselves pretty well while they were here." In fact, during their three-week stay, police did not issued a single citation. His sentiments were echoed in a statement issued by the Utah Governor: "Guests on the base have displayed exemplary behavior and been cooperative with volunteers and law enforcement. No major crimes or incidents have been reported at Camp Williams since the arrival of our guests."[115]

Mikkelson found similar unfounded accounts of outrageous behavior by transplanted evacuees in other parts of the country. "In Tennessee, similar whispers about rapes, robberies, and murders resulted in hundreds of alarmed local residents rushing to purchase guns for their protection. Police in that region assert the crime rate has not jumped since the arrival of the evacuees…Oklahoma, which has also opened its arms to thousands of those displaced by the hurricane, has also experienced the rumors of rapes and violence. While a spokesperson for the Oklahoma Highway Patrol did admit there had been a few fistfights at Camp Gruber (an evacuation center in that state), he also said life at the camp had been relatively quiet."[116]

Mikkelson believes that the rumors of Katrina evacuees behaving badly resonate with common fears about outsiders changing communities. "By presenting the evacuees as rude or ungrateful or as the crime-riddled worst dregs of society, garden variety xenophobia is cloaked in the more respectable mantle of entirely defensible fear for one's safety and/or distaste for objectionable behavior. In such fashion, the internal tug of war between the selfless ('My heart goes out to these people; what can I do to help?') and the self-centered ('I like my town just the way it is; I hope the refugees don't come here') is quelled."[117]

Water Quality

News agencies commonly described the New Orleans floodwaters as "witch's brew" and "toxic soup" of pollutants that could easily prove fatal if swallowed, and would pose a long-term health threat to those inhabiting the area. Yet tests of water during the first week of September, indicated otherwise. Most of the pollution was from feces, trace amounts of pesticides and petroleum-based chemicals, and slightly higher than normal amounts of metals.

Chris Piehler of the Louisiana Department of Environmental Quality said that based on the water quality tests taken shortly after the storm hit, there were no "specific toxic pollutants at any levels of concern." When asked if water pollutants could pose a hazard for returning residents, he said bluntly: "No. The limiting factor is going to be what structures are going to be salvageable and which ones are not."[118] Jerry Fenner, the head of the environmental health assessment team dispatched to New Orleans from the nearby Centers for Disease Control and Prevention in Atlanta, Georgia, echoed Piehler's sentiments: "all the test results show there shouldn't be any long-term problems of health and habitability."[119] Based on the results from daily water samples taken by the Environmental Protection Agency, floodwaters around New Orleans yielded levels of hexavalent chromium, arsenic, and lead above agency drinking water standards. Yet, in a statement issued by the EPA, agency officials were not too worried about the results: "These compounds would pose a risk to children only if a child were to drink a liter of flood water a day. Long-term exposure [a year or longer] to arsenic would be required before health effects would be a concern." A prime ingredient in the floodwater was fecal matter that came from the city's underground sewage system after the city's sewage treatment plant stopped operating. As disgusting and unhealthful as this may sound, by September 7th, the presence of fecal bacteria was declining and health officials said it would not have a lasting effect on the water quality. Fenner said: "The stuff will desiccate and you can clean it up. You fertilize your lawn? It's the same thing."[120] Further, and contrary to popular belief, the city's drinking water does not come from Lake Pontchartrain, where officials were pumping the floodwater, but the Mississippi River.[121]

Many media analysts expressed views that due to the chaotic conditions in the days after Katrina, many journalists on the scene based their reports on fragmentary accounts from unverifiable sources. In the words of Matthew Felling of the Center for Media and Public Affairs: "The fog of war and the gusts of a hurricane both cloud and obscure vital truths...What we're seeing here is no different than the reports of museum looting right after U.S. troops entered Baghdad. It's not that different from election night 2000 when some journalists prematurely declared a winner. In all three cases, the public would have been served by a bit more patience and less feigned certainty."[122]

Global Warming?

As for widespread media claims that Katrina was a superstorm created by global warming, scientists from the National Oceanic and Atmospheric Administration attribute the record number of hurricanes in the United States during 2005, to "natural occurring cycles in tropical climate patterns near the equator. These cycles, called 'the tropical multi-decadal signal' typically last several decades (20 to 30 years or even longer). As a result, the North Atlantic experiences alternating decades long (20 to 30 year periods or even longer) of above normal or below normal hurricane seasons. NOAA research shows that the tropical multi-decadal signal has caused the increased Atlantic hurricane activity since 1995, and is not related to greenhouse warming."[123]

How does Katrina compare to other hurricanes in the region? It was much weaker. Katrina made landfall as a Category 4 with gusts in excess of 140 mph (225 kph). In 1969, Hurricane Camille, roared onto the Mississippi coast as a Category 5, while in 1980, Hurricane Allen, another Category 5 storm, came ashore near Brownsville, Texas. Both hurricanes had sustained winds of approximately 190 mph (306 kph).[124] Meteorologists report that social and political factors are responsible for ever-increasing damage amounts in the aftermath of hurricanes. According to Brian Handwerk of National Geographic: "The global risk of hurricane disaster is increasing due to human activity. Populations are concentrating along the world's coastlines – particularly in large urban areas. Improved forecasting and emergency response have lowered hurricane casualty rates, but as more people and infrastructure move into harm's way, storms are likely to become more destructive."[125]

HUSBAND POISONING MANIA

Italy and France: 1600s

British writer and poet CHARLES MACKAY documents how a poisoning mania was popular in Italy during the 1600s. Slow poisoning became a common, albeit illegal, means of avenging wrongful acts or marital infidelities, especially by a husband. "Italians of the sixteenth and seventeenth centuries poisoned their opponents with as little compunction as an Englishman of the present day brings an action at law against any one who has done him injury."[126] A profitable network of black market poison vendors even emerged to meet the spiraling demand. By 1659, Pope Alexander VII was informed that "great numbers" of women had admitted in confessionals to poisoning their husbands. One group of wives who met regularly to plot their deeds was arrested and punished: "La Spara, Gratiosa, and three young women, who had poisoned their husbands, were hanged together at Rome. Upwards of thirty women were whipped publicly through the streets; and several, whose high rank screened them from more degrading punishment, were banished from the country and mulcted in heavy fines. In a few months afterwards, nine women were hanged for poisoning; and another bevy, including many young and beautiful girls, were whipped half naked through the streets of Rome."[127]

A suspicious guest hesitates before accepting a glass that may prove fatal. (J. R. Herbert, The Gemof the Season, 1849)

CONTEXT: Mackay attributes the popularity of slow poisoning to a few high profile cases that were widely reported among the upper class, which spread by "insane imitation" from a herd mentality.[128] The spread from higher to lower status people resembles the proliferation of fads.

Despite these actions, authorities of the period had a difficult time trying to extinguish the practice. Mackay writes: "This severity did not put a stop to the practice, and jealous women and avaricious men, anxious to step into the inheritance of fathers, uncles or brothers, resorted to poison. As it was quite free from taste, colour, and smell, it was administered without exciting suspicion. The skillful vendors compounded it of different degrees of strength, so that the poisoners had only to say whether they wanted their victims to die in a week, a month, or six months... The vendors were chiefly women, of whom the most celebrated...was in this way accessory to the death of upwards of six hundred persons."[129]

A similar spate of husband poisonings occurred in France between 1670 and 1682. During this period, slow poisoning became such a common form of murder that King Louis VIV attempted to deter such acts by punishing those convicted with torture and live burning.

HYSTERIA

This innocuous-looking eight-letter word is arguably the most ambiguous, confusing, misunderstood, and controversial term in the history of science. It is the objective of this entry to clarify the concept. In the field of psychiatry alone, hysteria has been used to describe no less than ten different individual behavioral manifestations, including the histrionic personality, forms of psychosis, and psychogenic pain disorder.[130] Its general usage by physicians and psychiatrists is to describe a disturbance of the nervous system whereby patients exhibit an alteration or loss of function resulting in illness symptoms that are unconsciously exhibited and have no corresponding organic basis.

Hysteria generally manifests as some form of conversion disorder – that is, a mental problem is "converted" into a physical symptom. Primary and secondary gain are two mechanisms that have been hypothesized to explain conversion disorder. In the former, a psychological need or conflict becomes internalized, and in doing so the symptoms offer a partial solution to the internal conflict. Such cases are typified by "a temporal relationship between an environmental stimulus that is apparently related to a psychological conflict or need and initiation or exacerbation of the symptom," which often manifests as a symbolic projection "and partial solution of the underlying psychological conflict."[131] Secondary gain is attained through the avoidance of undesirable activities, as in the case of leg paralysis that engenders sympathy and prevents a spouse from deserting his or her mate.

The concept of hysterical conversion, like so many other psychiatric disorders, suffers from the problem of ambiguity, that is, the diagnostic criteria are highly ambiguous and open to interpretation and misdiagnosis. This is especially true of the notion of hysteria – perhaps hysteria more than any other condition as it is said to be able to mimic virtually any organic illness.[132] The problems associated with hysteria are formidable. For instance, how does one tell the difference between someone who is unconsciously exhibiting a conversion reaction, and a malingerer who is deliberately producing symptoms? As if this wasn't complicated enough, some studies indicate that a majority of subjects who have been diagnosed with conversion actually have undiagnosed neurological disorders that are difficult to detect during the early stages.[133]

Malingering is a contentious term that is typically defined as the conscious feigning or exaggeration of physical or psychological symptoms with the intent to achieve some goal. Malingering is notoriously hard to verify. For example, how does one determine whether a patient is faking symptoms in order to avoid work, school, criminal prosecution, or military service? Others have been known to feign symptoms so as to receive financial settlements through lawsuits, state assistance, romantic attention, or sympathy.[134] Psychiatrists use the term "secondary gains" when referring to subjects with symptoms that are not intentionally produced. The problem is, there is a fine, ambiguous line between such terms as malingering, conversion, and dissociative disorders, the latter category referring to patients entering trance-like states. As one research team noted, "some patients with dissociative (or conversion) disorder appear to add deliberate exaggeration to basic unconscious mechanisms."[135] Diagnostic challenges, such as differentiating between these three conditions, render psychiatry, psychology, and psychoanalysis especially problematic and prone to diagnostic fads and fashions. A classic example is the once popular treatment of a surgical lobotomy in order to treat certain psychiatric conditions.

HYSTERIA AS MYTH

Controversial American psychiatrist Thomas Szasz views hysteria as an atypical form of communication triggered by "problems in living." Szasz contends that hysteria is a neither an illness nor a disorder.[136] In fact, Szasz believes that there is no such thing as mental illnesses, only persons experiencing "problems in living" who have been erroneously labeled as sick. Other writers argue that hysteria does not exist. For instance, the past editor of the prestigious *British Journal of Psychiatry*, Eliot Slater (1965), has made such a claim. Slater followed the progress of 112 people who were diagnosed with hysterical symptoms. About ten years later he checked on their conditions. Surprisingly, he found that 60% were suffering from organic illness, 8% were experiencing either depression or schizophrenia. Slater reported that the rest of the patients were exhibiting Briquet's Syndrome or vague signs and symptoms that were labeled as hysteria. Based on these findings, Slater remarks: "The diagnosis of 'hysteria' is a disguise for ignorance and a fertile source of clinical error." He concludes that: "No evidence has yet been offered that patients suffering from 'hysteria' are in medically significant terms anything more than a random selection.... The only thing that 'hysterical' patients can be shown to have in common is that they are all patients."[137] Despite his views, the existence of hysteria as a clinical entity as widely accepted today.

Hysteria has been conceptualized and interpreted in myriad ways depending on the academic tradition and time period. Historian Mark Micale surveyed these approaches and noted the different levels of analysis. He stated that its disease history has been viewed

> ...as a scientific, clinical, social, economic, political, sexual, cultural, and aesthetic construction. It has been interpreted as a chapter in the history of medical thought, an episode in the discovery of the unconscious, a study in mind/body relations, and an example of the misdiagnosis of organic disease. It has been written about as a repressed cry for sexual release, an exhibitionistic erotic performance, and a passive, pathological escape from social oppression; as a caricature of femininity, an exploration of masculinity, and a codification of misogynistic male science; as an exercise in scientific pornography and a program for gender normalization. It has been studied as a social metaphor, a literary typos, a visual icon, and a surrogate form of religious experience; as a morbid manifestation of Victorian civilization, a secret strategy for professional expansion ... (and) discussed as an actual psychiatric disorder.[138]

Hysteria As Disorder

The study of conversion symptoms has a checkered history of abuse and misuse, due in large part to ambiguous diagnostic criteria and uncertainty surrounding the exact processes involved. However, while Harvard anthropologist Arthur Kleinman considers conversion symptoms to be "a great mystery at the heart of psychosomatic medicine," he believes that "enough is known about conversion symptoms to describe them as the literal embodiment of conflicted meanings, somatic symbols that have psychological and social uses."[139] This continues to be the mainstream position and virtually all textbooks on psychiatry and abnormal psychology support this view of conversion as a clinical entity. In defending the concept and its use, Miller concedes that while models of hysteria have major weaknesses, health professionals have long noted a consistent pattern whereby patients describe symptoms that upon more thorough examination clearly have no discernible pathology.[140] "If 'hysteria' refers to this and nothing more then the term does carry useful meaning."[141]

Epidemic hysteria involves the rapid spread of individual conversion reactions. In comparison to singular hysteria, the topic of mass hysteria has received little in-depth study, with most reports being comprised of brief descriptions of apparent incidents. As with hysteria, while the exact processes involved in the manifestation of conversion reactions are unclear, physicians have noted a constellation of signs and symptoms across history and cultures signifying psychological distress or disorder for which there is no identifiable toxicological, viral, or bacteriological cause. As in individual conversion disorder, episodes are typified by an anxiety-generating agent within the victims' environment, and symptoms appear within close temporal proximity of exposure to the stimulus.

Misuse Of The Term "Mass Hysteria"

Scientists, especially those trained in the Western tradition, have long marginalized an array of deviant or unfamiliar behaviors and beliefs under the stigmatizing label of "mass or epidemic hysteria." The list is lengthy and includes such heterogeneous collective behaviors as mass suicide,[142] riots,[143] Nazism,[144] lycanthropy,[145] and excessive masturbation (masturbatory "insanity").[146] Pyromania clusters have also been labeled as epidemic hysteria,[147] as have fads, fashions, booms, and crazes.[148]

Further exacerbating confusion over the ambiguous definition of what constitutes "epidemic hysteria," is the interdisciplinary nature of the subject matter and the use of a variety of methods and assumptions that are used to interpret social delusions. For instance, medical practitioners typically write on singular episodes of mass psychogenic illness, which they have been encountered in the geographical vicinity of their practice.[149] Sociologists often describe community-wide incidents involving the spread of false beliefs or perceptions, such as sightings of strange or legendary creatures[150] or phantom windshield pit marks.[151] Psychologists often focus on the psychometric characteristics of participants;[152] social psychologists have examined the impact of rumor and gossip;[153] while psychoanalytical frameworks have been used to identify deeply rooted psychic conflicts within the subconscious.[154] Political scientists are known for using the vernacular meaning to characterize the overzealous or unfounded adherence to a particular view.[155] Historians typically limit their discussion of such behaviors to medieval dancing frenzies,[156] while anthropologists focus on the cultural circumstances of episodes and the position of repressed subordinate females in patriarchal societies.[157] Folklorists study the influence of urban legends in triggering social delusions that may foster hysterical symptoms, while journalists have probed the newspaper impact in perpetuating the widespread contemporary belief in flying saucers.[158]

Overambitious Classification Schemes

The rapid spread of conversion symptoms in small, close-knit groups at schools and work settings is thoroughly documented and appears indisputable. It is a universal syndrome that varies in accordance with the social and cultural context. It is unfortunate that those professionals who most often encounter episodes and write about them in science journals – psychiatrists and physicians – are not specialists in the social sciences such as sociology or social psychology. As a result, they have superimposed a universalist model of collective conversion reactions onto a variety of human behaviors involving the rapid spread of false beliefs and emotional expressions in community or regional settings. In this sense, "mass hysteria" has evolved into a convenient, grand diagnostic rubric under which distinctly separate behaviors have been erroneously categorized. Such diverse social phenomena as witch-hunts, stock market selling panics, kissing bug scares, and communitywide headhunting fears have all been placed under this singular heading. Yet, rarely do any of these people exhibit conversion disorders. Remarkably, many researchers evaluate the behavior per se, without regard to the broader social, cultural, historical, religious, and political circumstances. While conversion reactions can spread throughout a town or region, such events are not commonly documented, and there are only a relatively small number of reports in a literature spanning centuries.[159]

Some behaviors that have been stigmatized with the label of "mass hysteria," date back centuries, such as descriptions of the "tulip mania" in Holland between 1634 and 1637, whereby exorbitant prices were paid for tulip bulbs. Some sociologists and social psychologists continue to describe this event with such terms as "craze," "irrationality," and "mass hysteria." However, in examining the episode within its wider context, Peter Garber argues that the seemingly irrational aspects of the "tulip mania" were exaggerated. He disputes Charles Mackay's claims that many citizens neglected their jobs, becoming overwhelmed by crowd psychology with the obsessive desire to obtain tulip bulbs, as sensational (see DUTCH TULIP MANIA).[160]

Too often, the bizarre nature of the participants' social realities is used to justify the existence of abnormal group behaviors. Simply because participants hold beliefs that appear obviously false to those outside of their social and cultural dynamic does not make those convictions irrational or illogical. The human variation in norms, values, beliefs, and practices is remarkable, and the array of social realities that lie outside the narrow Eurocentric tradition is enormous. Examples include such culturally accepted behaviors as cannibalism, sorcery, animism, headhunting, polyandry, homosexuality, and bestiality. Psychiatrists Arieti and Meth write that "In the West, suicide is considered a sign of emotional disorder, in Japan, it is normal for a samurai in certain circumstances. Among the islanders of Dobu (Melanesia), no sane woman leaves her cooking pots unguarded for fear of being poisoned. To us this behavior would indicate paranoia."[161] A tolerance of social realities that deviate from those held by a particular evaluator is crucial because it often appears that no normal or reasonable person would engage in what appears to be obviously sick, immoral, irrational, or disordered behavior. A key point is that social realities alter perceptual outlooks. Because human perception is notoriously poor and people are prone to interpreting information patterns that reflect their worldviews, the rapid spread of false beliefs in community settings are not typically precipitated by mental disturbance and rarely result in psychogenic symptoms.[162]

Clearly, the often loose and inappropriate usage of the such words as "mass" or "epidemic hysteria" to describe various social phenomena that are separate from the condition of conversion reactions within individuals or groups has created, and continues to create, considerable confusion among scientists and the lay public.

A Modern Plague?

More recently, Princeton University English professor Elaine Showalter has created a firestorm of controversy after arguing that several contemporary maladies are actually forms of hysteria. In *Hystories: Hysterical Epidemics and Modern Media*, Showalter claims that such conditions as Chronic Fatigue Syndrome, Gulf War Syndrome, and the subject of "recovered memory" are each hysterical in nature, without an organic basis. Other conditions that she places under this label include alien abductions, satanic ritual abuse, and multiple personality disorder. Based on studying these subjects, Showalter contends that a characteristic pattern emerges in these psychosomatic disorders that reflect societal distress.

> They usually begin in a fairly small, isolated community. With chronic fatigue syndrome, it was Incline Village, Nevada. With Gulf War Syndrome, it was a single battalion. You get a lot of vague symptoms and complaints. Then you need a charismatic doctor or scientist who begins to [define] it. That gets picked up by the media, and more and more doctors hear about it and they pick up more and more patients. When it reaches some sort of critical mass, patient groups start to organize and it politicizes. At that point, sufferers begin to ask for things: They want more money, they want insurance, they want disability, they want recognition, whatever.[163]

Reaction to Showalter's book was so heated that she actually hired a bodyguard for certain public events.[164] She believes that these various subjects reflect the present-day social obsession with paranoia and government conspiracies. She says that such obsessions have always been with us but not at the current level. "Something like alien abduction, which is a form of recovered memory, is similar to apocalyptic beliefs historians describe around the year 1000," she says.[165] Showalter believes that many people in modern Western society tend to externalize their problems and blame various possible causes except for their own unconscious. "We have this image of our society as a therapeutic culture. It's true – there's been an incredible proliferation of therapy: You know, the 12-step programs, the Recovery Channel, the friendly neighborhood hypnotherapist, and so on. But there's a much stronger hostility to the idea that the unconscious [mind] might be responsible for problems: If I'm unhappy as an adult, then my father must have molested me. If I don't fit my ideal of how I should behave, then obviously I'm a victim of a satanic cult," she said.[166]

See also: MASS HYSTERIA; MASS ANXIETY HYSTERIA; MASS MOTOR HYSTERIA; THEORIES OF MASS HYSTERIA; INTRODUCTION; MASS HYSTERIA IN SCHOOLS; MASS HYSTERIA IN JOB SETTINGS; SATANIC CULT AND RITUAL ABUSE SCARE.

HYSTERICAL ANOREXIA

Tennessee: January 2000 and ongoing

In October 2001, a visiting nurse uncovered a mysterious neurological condition in a community of Old Order Amish girls – one of whom was said to have been "near death." While the specific location of the cluster was kept confidential, it was in the southern U.S., and based on the affiliation of medical personnel involved, most likely in the state of Tennessee. A subsequent investigation revealed that beginning in January 2000, the mysterious illness began to affect five girls ages 9-to-13, living in a traditional Amish community. The girls suffered serious weakness and anorexia. Four of the victims were so adversely affected that they could not even hold their heads upright and required help with eating, dressing, bathing, and going to the toilet.

The term Old Order Amish refers to approximately 200,000 members of an extremely conservative Christian religious community that is found in various parts of the United States and Canada. The community is typified by their farming lifestyle, a refusal to use technology, and maintaining social separation from non-Amish, which is often achieved by conversing in a German dialect. In contrast, New Order Amish are more liberal. All of the affected girls lived within 2.5 miles of one other.

A description of the case of "Cassandra" is typical and shows the exhaustive nature of the medical investigation, which included ruling out chemical or pesticide exposures, and drinking from a common water supply. Cassandra was friends with two other affected girls. In May 2001, she began to have bouts of headache and stomach pain. Her parents allowed her to be examined at a hospital after she became unresponsive to tactile or verbal stimuli. Tests of her brainwave function and a magnetic resonance image of her brain were normal. After a dramatic improvement, she again began developing symptoms soon after returning home. In August she became unresponsive while lying down at night. By September, she was unable to get out of bed and was suffering from arm, leg, and neck weakness. Three months earlier, her neighbor and friend developed similar complaints. In December of 2001, after having been bedridden for three months, unable to even hold her head, and unresponsive to family members for four days, her relatives allowed her to be examined at a teaching hospital.

An interdisciplinary team of doctors gave Cassandra a battery of tests for everything from proper liver function to illicit drug use. A pediatric neurologist diagnosed "psychogenic unresponsiveness" after noting that Cassandra's symptoms were not consistent with her medical exam and the results of an EEG. A psychiatrist concurred with this assessment, and concluded that she was suffering from conversion disorder. Cassandra was observed to roll over and move her limbs while sleeping, yet could not do so while awake. Cassandra's condition gradually improved and she was eventually discharged.

The other girls exhibited similar inconsistencies. For instance, Debra would not speak during a normal waking state, yet spoke fluently when injected with an anesthesia during a medical procedure. Betty could not so much as lift her head while being examined, yet was seen to raise her head off a pillow in order to adjust her head bonnet.

The episode occurred during a local church crisis. Members of the Old Order Amish were unhappy with recent changes to church standards, which resulted in a rift over the fees that Amish men could bill for work done outside the community. Consequently, 20 percent of the community relocated to other regions, and about 10 percent of the families who remained were actively "shunned" – a culturally appropriate form of discipline whereby the remaining families deliberately avoided socially interacting with the other family members. While none of the afflicted girls were members of the shunned families, the community was rife with tension and divisiveness.

CONTEXT: The outbreak occurred amid serious conflict in the community that would undoubtedly have caused tension among the girls, with friends either leaving the region or being "shunned." Further, the episode targeted a group of girls – four of whom were the oldest female siblings in the family – an added social responsibility. Four were also either 12 or 13 years old, another added source of stress as most girls in the community left school at age 14, at which point they were expected to accept significant responsibilities for homemaking activities, including cooking, sewing, and general domestic duties, all supervised under the watchful eye of elders.

The investigative team noted that the symptoms resulted in behaviors (stoicism and silence) valued by the Amish during periods of stress and crises, and as such appear to be a culture-specific manifestation of conversion disorder.[167] [168]

HYSTERICAL BLACKOUTS

Great Britain: September 1978 to June 1980

The episode, which spread throughout an unidentified British co-educational school, started with a single female pupil who began blacking out and overbreathing after her father's death. By the month's end, nine girls were affected. Over 21 months, 60 girls and three boys ages 12-to-15 experienced 447 "blackouts." In addition to fainting, other symptoms included over breathing, twitching of the arms and legs, and occasionally frothing at the mouth.[169]

Investigators noted that those affected fell into three groups. The first group was comprised of a small core of eight girls who had most frequent and severe attacks. Each had serious emotional disturbances, came from dysfunctional families, or had significant others with enduring medical conditions. "The first girl affected started to have attacks after the death of her father. Two others, whose mothers were nurses, had been treated for epilepsy; one of these girls also had a subnormal sister and the other a sister who fainted with migraine attacks. A fourth girl lived with her father, who had attacks of vertigo, and a grandmother who was demented and had blackouts."[170]

A second group of eight girls had less severe attacks and frequently associated with the first group.

Their attacks tended to cluster around a single term. While having more stable family backgrounds relative to the first group, they were experiencing a host of medical problems including two cases of goiter, a drug overdose, and anorexia nervosa.[171]

A third group, comprising 44 girls and three boys, had only one or two attacks each, usually after seeing one of the more severely affected students "black-out."[172]

Ninety percent of the time the symptoms involved fainting, with the other ten percent consisting of hyperventilation. Less common complaints included limb twitching, headache, stomach pain, and dizziness.[173]

Also see: MASS MOTOR HYSTERIA.

HYSTERICAL BOREDOM

Canada: 1972

In 1972, a poor, remote village of Native Americans of Cree and Ojibway descent was the scene of hysterical fits. Psychiatrists who went to the village interviewed 13 of those affected, between the ages 11 and 18. Upon arriving, they were struck by the dreary quality of life and how miserable the afflicted children seemed. They complained of fatigue, irritability, headaches, and nightmares prior to having hysterical fits, during which they would often run into the woods. Episodes coincided with their intense feelings of anger and depression over social and cultural isolation in the dull village. Strict Christian rules were enforced: there was little privacy, prearranged marriages were typical, and parentsí decisions were absolute. Histrionics and the use of the sick role as attention-seeking devices were prominent. On a number of occasions, several females intentionally held their breath so as to attract attention by receiving artificial respiration. The antics of the afflicted children, desperate to "spice up" their dreary existence, developed a soap opera-like quality. Episodes often drew scores of neighbors and turned into huge social events complete with refreshments and snacks even being served. The "fits" eventually subsided after the psychiatrists stopped the social functions surrounding the incidents, improved family communication, and increased recreational and educational activities.[174]

CONTEXT: Within a backdrop of poverty, and both physical isolation and both social and cultural transition, Native Canadian Cree and Ojibway found themselves trapped between two worlds. Their hysterical symptoms drew attention to their plight and eventually brought help in the form of Canadian psychiatrists.

COMMENT: Repression of the human mind and spirit are as equally remarkable as the ways in which the oppressed use their imagination and creativity to cope.

HYSTERICAL SCHOOLGIRLS AT QAWA

Fiji: October 1968

On November 13, 1968, a medical officer from Labasa Hospital on the Fijian island of Vanau Levu was urgently summoned to the nearby Qawa Primary School in response to a medical emergency. Upon arriving, he found 13 Fijian girls of Indian descent afflicted with a mysterious ailment. Conspicuously, all of the girls were acting "in almost exactly the same manner. They were all over-breathing, taking deep inspirations and exhaling with a musical wheeze, at a rate of about 50 respirations per minute. Some were standing, some sitting, some tended to faint and quickly recover."[175] Eight of the girls were sent home, while the remaining five were hospitalized for observation and more careful examination. The exams proved uneventful, revealing no abnormalities except for slightly elevated body temperatures of about 99F. After several hours they were released to their parents.

After further investigation by a government physician named R. G. Randall, it was determined that the "mysterious illness" was mass hysteria that began in a single pupil during early October. On November 8, two classmates exhibited similar symptoms of twitching and over-breathing. The next day, several more girls were affected. In all, 17 girls between the ages of 12 and 14 exhibited symptoms, while an 18th subject was an eight-year-old girl. Indian boys also attended the school but none were affected.[176]

CONTEXT: The episode occurred to a group of Hindu schoolgirls whose parents were convinced were possessed by angry Fijian spirits from a nearby desecrated pool. The hysterical symptoms were eventually resolved with the cooperation of Hindu, Islamic, and Fijian native healers, and reassurance from psychiatrists who had the foresight to allow the traditional ethnic healing ceremonies to take place.

Dr. Randall was able to trace the episode back to a 12-year-old "trigger girl" with a long history of emotional disturbance, including hysterical blackouts and over-breathing. The girl had made numerous visits to doctors and native healers in the area prior to the Qawa incident.[177]

On November 14, the parents of most of the afflicted girls, including all of those who had been hospitalized, were taken to an Indian healer by their parents. Dr. Randall then requested that all of the affected girls meet with a psychiatrist named D.N. Sell at the hospital on November 15, but only one pupil showed up. During the meeting she reported feeling "dizzy and strange" and soon "began to overbreathe and twitch her hands and arms." After reassurance by Dr. Sell, she began to calm down and recover.[178] The next day, authorities were able to convince five of the afflicted girl's parents to bring them to the hospital. Dr. Sell saw the group "sitting on a bench on the hospital verandah. Each was hyperventilating with hands and arms twitching and "moueing" sounds coming from their throats in perfect chorus and identical pitch. Each was sent off singly, their symptoms subsiding as they left."[179]

By November 25, five more pupils were affected, bringing the total to 18. After Dr. Snell's visit to the hospital, and following his advice, the school was closed for one week, and those affected were sent home to rest and kept separated from each other. The symptoms gradually subsided and the school soon reopened.[180] While the parents followed Dr. Snell's advice, most remained convinced that the cause of the trouble was a bulldozing accident that damaged part of a sacred pool near the school playground. The parents believed that a supernatural force possessed the girls and it was up to them "to determine which power or spirit *(shaitan)* had been roused and how it should be exorcised."[181]

The parents of the girls turned to various members of the community for help. Although all the affected girls were Hindu, a Muslim woman, who had reputedly acquired healing powers from the Fijian island of Taveuni, was approached to help. Amina, who lived in the nearby village of Bulileka, met with seven of the pupils, placed her hand behind their heads, and rubbed coconut oil on their throats while telling them to calm down and not worry. "Immediately the hysteria left the girls and they calmed down," only to relapse after leaving the woman's compound with their parents.[182] The girls then returned to the compound, as they felt protected there. Amina then recommended that school officials approach the Fijian owners of the pool who should appease the disturbed spirits by presenting them with a *yaqona* – the Fijian national drink. Fiji has a long tradition of offering *yaqona* to appease the spirit world.[183] A Fijian chief conducted the ceremony, which included the yaqona to the pool spirits, noting that the damage was an accident and that those involved should be excused. After the ceremony the girls left Amina's compound but were again stricken with symptoms.[184] With Muslim and Fijian healers being ineffective, the parents turned to a Hindu priest *(pandit)* who asked the Hindu elephant god for help in appeasing the disturbed spirits of the pool during a public Om Shanti ceremony. The following Monday school re-opened, during which five of the original 18 began hyperventilating. The girls were reassured, with the appeasement ceremonies being noted. Two were sent home but returned the next day – which was free of any "attacks." From that day on, no more incidents were recorded.

The so-called "trigger girl" was asked not to return to school and was treated with a sedative (Largactil). She eventually recovered and was able to cope without medication when last evaluated in February 1969.[185]

COMMENT: Due to the multi-ethnic community in which it occurred, this was a particularly complex episode of mass hysteria to resolve. It illustrates how people of diverse backgrounds, living as neighbors, can cooperate to resolve problems. Indian and Fijian residents "combined their beliefs and rituals to appease the spirits and as far as they were concerned, to cause the girls to recover and to remove the troubles from the school and to prevent further troubles from occurring."[186] The episode appears to be a case of mass motor hysteria triggered by the buildup of anxiety from the index case and rumors surrounding the desecration of the adjacent pool, whose disturbed spirits possessed the girls as revenge. Once the girls were convinced that the spirits were appeased, and with some reassurance from school and medical authorities, their anxiety diminished and the symptoms subsided.

See also: MASS HYSTERIA IN SCHOOLS.

HYSTERICAL SCHOOLGIRLS IN NEPAL

Sunsari District, Nepal: 2003

Nearly two-dozen schoolgirls in Nepal began to exhibit outbursts of involuntary laughing or crying over several months during the summer of 2003. The emotional "fits" affected girls between the ages of 13 and 16 from the Nepal Rashtriya Secondary School. According to the school's headmaster, Daya Shanker Chaudhari, doctors had diagnosed the students as having contagious hysteria. Nepalese health experts from the BP Koirala Institute of Health Science attributed the outbreak to the exclusively male teaching staff at the school. Psychiatrist Binod Dev stated: "There were only male teachers in the school and the disease had occurred due to suppressed feelings which the girls could not express in front of the male teachers." Local folk theories, which many of the affected girl's parents believed, held that "the girls were under the influence of supernatural powers and they had even sacrificed a black goat, besides offering special prayers to Gods." Eventually, the health authorities were summoned when the episodes did not subside.[187]

Sources

1. Prince, Samuel Henry (1920). *Catastrophe and Social Change.* New York: Columbia University Press. Quotations and details are taken from this source unless otherwise noted.
2. Archibald MacMechan, "The Halifax Disaster," reprinted in Metson, Graham (editor) (1978). *The Halifax Explosion.* Toronto: McGraw Hill Ryerson, p. 29.
3. Bird, Michael J. (1962). *The Town That Died.* Toronto: McGraw-Hill Ryerson, p. 88.
4. Bird (1962), p. 111.
5. Metson, op cit., pp. 36-41.
6. Dwight Johnstone cited by Prince, op cit., pp. 42-43.
7. Prince, op cit., p. 32.
8. Metson, op cit, p. 43.
9. Metson, op cit., p. 18.
10. Metson, op cit., p. 14.
11. Metson, op cit., p. 33.
12. Bird, op cit., p. 160.
13. Metson, op cit., p. 108.
14. Bird, op cit., p. 152.
15. Metson, op cit., p. 43.
16. Shalev, Arieh Y., professor of psychiatry at Hebrew University, Jerusalem, in *New Scientist,* July 16, 2005, p. 20.
17. Bird, op cit., p. 151.
18. Fumento, Michael (2000). "Canadians Smell a Rat: Aqua Velva Cologne." *Human Events* (June 9).
19. McLaren, Leah (2000). "Non-Scents in Nova Scotia: Halifax Hysteria." *The Globe and Mail,* April 29.
20. McLaren, op cit. "Charlie" is regional North American slang for perfume.
21. Fumento, Michael (2000). "Canadians Smell a Rat: Aqua Velva Cologne." *Human Events* (June 9).
22. Goss, M. (1987). *The Halifax Slasher: An Urban Terror in the North of England.* London: Fortean Times.
23. Goss, op cit., p, 27.
24. Goss, op cit., p. 44.
25. Goss, op cit., p, 27.
26. Goss, op cit., pp. 16-19.
27. Goss, op cit., p. 6.
28. Goss, op cit., pp. 15-16, 28-29.
29. Goss, op cit., p. 30.
30. Goss, op cit., p. 12.
31. Goss, op cit., p. 30.
32. Goss, op cit., p. 30.
33. Sagan, Carl. (1985). *Cosmos.* New York: Ballantine Books, p. 66.
34. "Comet's Poisonous Tail. Yerkes Observatory Finds Cyanogen in Spectrum of Halley's Comet." *New York Times,* February 7, 1910, p. 1.
35. "Comet's Poisonous Tail." op cit.
36. Flaste, Richard, Noble, Holcomb, Sullivan, Walter, and Wilford, John Noble. (1985). *The New York Times Guide to the Return of Halley's Comet.* New York: Times Books, p. 68.
37. Flaste et al., op cit., pp. 68-69.
38. "Discuss Halley's Comet." *The Washington Post,* February 6, 1910, p. 15.
39. "Discuss Halley's Comet." op cit.
40. McAdam, D.J. (1910). "The Menace in the Skies: I. The Case for the Comet." *Harper's Weekly* 54:11-12 (May 14), see p. 12.
41. Moore, Patrick, and Mason, John. (1984). *The Return of Halley's Comet.* New York: W.W. Norton, p. 71; Flaste, Richard, Noble, Holcomb, Sullivan, Walter, and Wilford, John Noble. (1985). *The New York Times Guide to the Return of Halley's Comet.* New York: Times Books, p. 61.
42. Moore and Mason, op cit., p. 71; Sagan, op cit., p. 66.
43. Flaste et al., op cit., p. 63.
44. Flaste et al., op cit., p. 63.
45. Flaste et al., op cit., pp. 63-64.
46. Sagan, Carl, and Druyan, Ann (1985). *Comet.* New York: Random House, p. 140.
47. "Southern Negroes in a Comet Frenzy." *The New York Times,*

February 19, 1910, p. 1.
48. "Comet Jerusalem's Omen." *The Washington Post*, May 11, 1910, p. 1.
49. "Miners Refuse to Work." op cit., p. 1.
50. Littmann, Mark, and Yeomans, Donald K. (1985). *Comet Halley: Once in a Lifetime*. Washington DC: American Chemical Society, p. 43; Flaste et al., op cit., p. 58.
51. Sagan and Druyan (1985). op cit., p. 140.
52. Flaste et al., op cit., p. 75.
53. Flaste et al., op cit., p. 75.
54. Sagan and Druyan. op cit., 140.
55. Flaste et al., op cit., p. 80.
56. Sagan and Druyan. op cit., 140.
57. "Pope Not Impressed by Halley's Comet." *The New York Times*, May 29, 1910, p. 2.
58. "Parisians Feared Comet Would Kill." *The New York Times*, May 22, 1910, p. 3.
59. Harpur, Brian (1985). *The Official Halley's Comet Book*. London: Hodder and Stoughton, pp. 48-49.
60. "Berlin Comet Picnics." *The New York Times*, February 19, 1910, p. 1.
61. "Rush to Alpine Heights." *The New York Times*, February 19, 1910, p. 1.
62. "Alarm on the Rand." *The New York Times*, February 19, 1910, p. 1.
63. "Night Services in Russia." *The New York Times*, February 19, 1910, p. 1.
64. "Mexicans Pray, Then Dance." *The New York Times*, February 19, 1910, p. 1.
65. Taylor, Joseph (1815). *Apparitions, or the Mystery of Ghosts*. London: Lackington, Allen, p. 156.
66. Newgate Calendar.
67. Kottak, Conrad P. (1987). *Cultural Anthropology*, fourth edition. New York: Random House, p. 276.
68. Parker, Arthur C. (1913). *The Code of Handsome Lake, the Seneca Prophet*. Albany, New York: The State University of New York at Albany, p. 7.
69. Kottak, op cit., p. 276.
70. Parker, op cit., p. 35.
71. Barnes, R.H. (1993). "Construction Sacrifice, Kidnapping and Headhunting Rumours on Flores and Elsewhere in Indonesia." *Oceania* 64:146-158; Forth, G. (1991). "Construction Sacrifice and Head-Hunting Rumours in Central Flores (Eastern Indonesia): A Comparative Note." *Oceania* 61:257-266; Drake, Richard Allen (1989a). "Construction Sacrifice and Kidnapping: Rumor Panics in Borneo." *Oceania* 59:269-278; Drake, R.A. Letter to Robert Bartholomew dated August 19, 1989.
72. Sjahrir, Soetan. (1949). *Out of Exile* (translated from Dutch by Charles Wolf). New York: Greenwood Press, p. 164.
73. Sjahrir, Soetan. (1949). op cit., p. 164.
74. Sjahrir, Soetan. (1949). op cit., p. 164.
75. Drake, op cit., 1989b.
76. Stephen, Ignatius (2003). "No More Headhunters so Borneo Travel Chiefs go for more Tourists." Bruni Direct (March 2). Http://www.brudirect.com/DailyInfo/News/Archive /Mar02/250302/nite01.htm, accessed April 14, 2003.
77. Srivastava, Vinita (1995). "Milking a Miracle." *The Village Voice* (October 17):12, 16.
78. Nickell, Joe (1996). "Milk-Drinking Idols." *The Skeptical Inquirer* 20(2):7.
79. Nickell, Joe (1996). Op cit.
80. Jayaraman, K.S. (1995). "India's 'Milk Miracle' is Hard to Swallow." *Nature* 377(6547):280 (September 28).
81. "Milk-Drinking Idols Draw Millions in India." *Syracuse Post-Standard*, September 22, 1995, p. D1.
82. Nickell, Joe (1996). op cit.
83. Nickell, Joe (1996). op cit; Srivastava, Vinita (1995). op cit., p. 12.
84. Anonymous (1995). "Milk Miracle Makes Masses Mental." *The Skeptic* 3(4):13.
85. "Milk-Drinking Idols Draw Millions in India." op cit.
86. Bekker, Balthasar (1694). *Le Monde Enchanté*. Amsterdam: Pierre Rotterdam. Volume 4 p.523. All other authorities, explicitly or otherwise, use him as their source.
87. Bekker (1694).
88. Bekker (1694). Volume 4, p. 528.
89. Oliver, Myrna (2002). "Obituaries: A Melin, 77; Introduced Frisbee and Hula Hoop." *Los Angeles Times*, June 30, 2002, p. B-15.
90. Hansell, Saul (2002). "Arthur Melin, 77, Promoter of the Hula-Hoop, Is Dead." *New York Times*, July 1, 2002, p. B-6.
91. Hoffmann, Frank W., and Bailey, William G. (1991). *Sports and Recreation Fads*. New York: Harrington Park Press, pp. 185-187; Skolnik, Peter L. (1978). *Fads: America's Crazes, Fevers & Fancies From the 1890s to the 1970s*. New York: Thomas Y. Crowell, pp. 112-115; Panati, Charles. (1991). *Panati's Parade of Fads, Follies, and Manias*. New York: HarperCollins, pp. 264-265.
92. Panati, op cit., p. 264; Hoffmann and Bailey, op cit., p. 185.
93. Hoffmann and Bailey, op cit., pp. 186-187.
94. Marum, Andrew, and Parise, Frank. (1984). *Follies and Foibles: A View of 20th Century Fads*. New York: Facts on File, p. 105.
95. Hansell, op cit., p. B-6.
96. Jones, Noa (2001). "Come On, Get Hoopy! The Hula-Hoop is more than just a Retro Toy; it's an Energizing Art Form." *Los Angeles Times*, April 8, 2001, p. E-2.
97. Stevenson, Richard W. (1998). "The Hula Hoop is Coming Around Again." *New York Times*, March 5, p. 35; Lili, Cui (1992). "Hula Hoop Craze in Beijing." *Beijing Review* 35(13):40-41 (March 30).
98. Marum and Parise, op cit., p. 105.
99. http://en.wikipedia.org/wiki/Hurricane_Katrina, accessed NovePierre, Robert, and Gerhart, Anne (2005). op cit.mber 27, 2005.
100. Pierre, Robert, and Gerhart, Anne (2005). "News of Pandemonium May Have Slowed Aid." *The Washington Post*, October 5, 2005, p. A8.
101. Pierre, Robert, and Gerhart, Anne (2005). op cit.
102. Rosenblatt, Susannah, and Rainey, Jamers (2005). "Katrina Takes a Toll on Truth, News Accuracy." *The Los Angeles Times*, September 27, 2005.
103. Harper, Jennifer (2005). op cit.
104. Harper, Jennifer (2005). "Media, Blushing, Takes a Second Look at Katrina." *The Washington Times* (Washington, DC), September 29, 2005, p. A1.
105. Harper, Jennifer (2005). op cit.
106. Pierre and Gerhart, op cit.
107. Donovan, Patricia (2005). "New Orleans – What Urban Myths Say About U.S." Press release issued by the Sate University of New York at Buffalo, accessed November 28, 2005 at: http://www.buffalo.edu/news/fast-execute.cgi/article-page.html?article=75960009.
108. Donovan, Patricia (2005).
109. Donovan, Patricia (2005).
110. Mikkelson, Barbara (8 October 2005), http://www.snopes.com/katrina/personal/utah.asp, accessed November 29, 2005.

111. Mikkelson, op cit.
112. Mikkelson, op cit.
113. Mikkelson, op cit.
114. Mikkelson, op cit.
115. Mikkelson, op cit.
116. Mikkelson, op cit.
117. Mikkelson, op cit.
118. Brown, David (2005). "Floods' Pollutants Within the Norm. Oil Spills Seen as the Only Exception." *The Washington Post*, September 15, 2005, p. A15.
119. Brown, op cit.
120. Brown, op cit.
121. Brown, op cit.
122. Harper, op cit.
123. NOAA Attributes Recent Increase in Hurricane Activity to Naturally Occurring Multi-Decadal Climate Variability." Accessed December 12, 2005 at: http://www.magazine. noaa.gov/stories/mag184.htm.
124. Handwerk, Brian (2005). "Eye on the Storm: Hurricane Katrina Fast Facts." National Geographic News (September 6), accessed December 12, 2005 at: http://news.national geographic.com/news/2005/09/0906_050906_katrina_facts.html.
125. Handwerkk (2005). op cit.
126. Mackay, Charles. (1852). *Memoirs of Extraordinary Popular Delusions and the Madness of Crowds Volume 2*. London: Office of the National Illustrated Library, p. 576.
127. Mackay, op cit., p. 579.
128. Mackay, op cit., p. 574.
129. Mackay, op cit., p. 579.
130. Kendell, R.E., and Zealley, A.K. (eds.). (1993). *Companion to Psychiatric Studies*. Fifth edition. Churchill Livingstone: London; Weintraub, M.I. (1983). *Hysterical Conversion Reactions: A Clinical Guide to Diagnosis and Treatment*. Lancaster, UK: MTP Press.
131. American Psychiatric Association. (1987). *Diagnostic and Statistical Manual of Mental Disorders*, third edition, revised. Washington, DC, American Psychiatric Association, p., 257.
132. Rack, P. (1982). *Race, Culture, and Mental Disorder*. London: Tavistock Publications, p. 141.
133. Alloy, L., Acocella, J., and Bootzin, R. R. (1996). *Abnormal Psychology: Current Perspectives* (seventh edition). New York: McGraw-Hill, p. 197.
134. Carson, R. C., Butcher, J. N., and Mineka, S. (1996). *Abnormal Psychology and Modern Life* (tenth edition). New York: Harper Collins, p. 254; Meyerson, A. T. (1989). "Conditions not Attributable to a Mental Disorder." Pp. 1396-1399. In H. Kaplan and B. Sadock (eds.), *Comprehensive Textbook of Psychiatry*. Baltimore, MD: Williams and Wilkins. See p. 1396.
135. Gelder, M., Gath, D., and Mayou, R. (1994). *Concise Oxford Textbook of Psychiatry*. Oxford: Oxford University Press, p. 123.
136. Szasz, T. S. (1974b). *The Myth of Mental Illness*. New York: Harper and Row.
137. Slater, E. (1965). "Diagnosis of 'Hysteria.'" *British Medical Journal* 1:1395-1399. See p. 1399.
138. Micale, M. S. (1995). *Approaching Hysteria: Disease and its Interpretations*. Princeton, New Jersey: Princeton University Press.
139. Kleinman, A. (1988). *Rethinking Psychiatry: From Cultural Category to Personal Experience*. New York: The Free Press, p. 41.
140. Miller, E. (1988). Hysteria. Pp. 245-267. In E. Miller and P. J. Cooper (eds.), *Adult Abnormal Psychology*. London: Churchill Livingstone; Miller, E. (1987). "Hysteria: Its Nature and Explanation." *British Journal of Clinical Psychology* 26:163-173.
141. Miller (1987). op cit., p. 171.
142. Faguet, R. A., and Faguet, K. F. (1982). "La Folie a Deux." pp. 1-14. In C.T.H. Friedmann and R. A. Faguet (eds.), *Extraordinary Disorders of Human Behavior*. New York: Plenum Press.
143. Smelser, N.J. (1962). *Theory of Collective Behavior*. New Jersey: Prentice-Hall.
144. Cartwright, F. F., and Biddiss, M. D. (1972). *Disease and History*. New York: Thomas Y. Crowell, p. 210; Brown, R. W. (1954). Mass Phenomena. Pp. 833-873. In G. Lindzey (ed.), *Handbook of Social Psychology Volume 2*. Cambridge, Massachusetts: Addison-Wesley, p. 59.
145. Goshen, C. E. (1967). *Documentary History of Psychiatry*. London: Vision.
146. Gilbert, A. N. (1975). "Doctor, Patient, and Onanist Diseases in the Nineteenth Century." *Journal of the History of Medicine and Allied Science* 30(3):217-234.
147. Boling, L., and Brotman, C. (1975). "A Fire Setting Epidemic in a State Mental Health Center." *American Journal of Psychiatry* 132:946-950.
148. For a comprehensive list and discussion of over forty behaviors inappropriately identified as "epidemic hysteria," refer to Bartholomew, R. E. (1990). "Ethnocentricity and the Social Construction of 'Mass Hysteria.'" *Culture, Medicine and Psychiatry* 14(4):455-494.
149. Tan, E. S. (1963). "Epidemic Hysteria." *Medical Journal of Malaya* 18:72-76.
150. Stewart, J. R. (1989). "Sasquatch Sightings in South Dakota: An Analysis of an Episode of Collective Delusion," pp. 287-304. In G. Zollschan, J. Schumaker and G. Walsh (eds.), *Exploring the Paranormal*. Bridport, England: Prism Press.
151. Medalia, N. Z., and Larsen, O. (1958). "Diffusion and Belief in a Collective Delusion." *Sociological Review* 23:180-186.
152. Kerckhoff, A. C., Back, K. W., and Miller, N. (1965). "Sociometric Patterns in Hysterical Contagion." *Sociometry* 28:2-15.
153. Shibutani, T. (1966). *Improvised News*. Indianapolis, IN: Bobbs-Merrill.
154. Benaim, S., Horder, J., and Anderson, J. (1973). "Hysterical Epidemic in a Classroom." *Psychological Medicine* 3:366-373.
155. Selvin, D. F. (1989). "An Exercise in Hysteria: San Francisco's Red Raids of 1934." *Pacific Historical Review* 58(3):361-374.
156. Sigerist, H. E. (1943). *Civilization and Disease*. Ithaca, New York: Cornell University Press.
157. Ong, A. (1988). "The Production of Possession: Spirits and the Multinational Corporation in Malaysia." *American Ethnologist* 15(1):28-42; Ong, A. (1987). *Spirits of Resistance and Capitalist Discipline: Factory Women in Malaysia*. Albany, New York: State University of New York Press.
158. Strentz, H. J. (1970). *A Survey of Press Coverage of Unidentified Flying Objects, 1947-1966*. Doctoral dissertation, Northwestern University, Department of Journalism; Johnson, D. B. (1950). *Flying Saucers – Fact or Fiction?* Master's thesis, University of California Journalism Department, Los Angeles.
159. Bartholomew, R. E. (1997b). "Epidemic Hysteria: A Dialogue with Francois Sirois." *Medical Principles and Practice* 6:38-44.
160. Garber, Peter M. (2000). *Famous First Bubbles: The Fundamentals of Early Manias*. Cambridge, Massachusetts: MIT Press; Garber, Peter M. (1989). "Tulipmania." *Journal of Political Economy* 97:535-560; Garber, Peter M (1990). "Who put the Mania in the Tulip Mania?" Pp. 3-32. In Eugene N. White (editor). *Crashes and Panics: Lessons from History*. Homewood, Illinois: Business One Irwin.

161. Arieti, S., and Meth, J. M. (1959). "Rare, Unclassifiable, Collective, and Exotic Psychotic Syndromes." Pp. 546-563. In S. Arieti (ed.), *American Handbook of Psychiatry*. New York: Basic Books, p. 560.
162. Bartholomew, R. E. (1993). "Redefining Epidemic Hysteria: An Example from Sweden." *Acta Psychiatrica Scandinavica* 88:178-182; Bartholomew, R. E. (1994b). "The Social Psychology of 'Epidemic' Koro." *The International Journal of Social Psychiatry* 40:44-60.
163. Brown, Pryde (1997). "Syndrome Syndrome (Gulf War Syndrome and Belief in Alien Abduction as Psychosomatic Disorders)." *Reason* 29(3):21 (July).
164. Personal communication between British psychiatrist Simom Wessely and Robert Bartholomew dated October 2001.
165. Brown, op cit.
166. Brown, op cit.
167. Cassady, Joslyn, Kirschke, David, Jones, Timothy, Craig, Allen, Bermudez, Ovidio, and Schaffner, William (2005). *Journal of the American Academy of Child and Adolescent Psychiatry* 44(3):291-297.
168. All of the victims names are pseudonyms.
169. Mohr, P.D., and Bond, M.J. (1982). "A Chronic Epidemic of Hysterical Blackouts in a Comprehensive School." *British Medical Journal* 284 (27 March):961-962.
170. Mohr and Bond, op cit., p. 961.
171. Mohr and Bond, op cit., pp. 961-962.
172. Mohr and Bond, op cit., p. 962.
173. Mohr and Bond, op cit., p. 962.
174. Armstrong, H., and Patterson, P. (1975). "Seizures in Canadian Indian Children." *Canadian Psychiatric Association Journal* 20:247-255.
175. Parke, Aubrey L. (1995). "The Qawa Incident in 1968 and Other Cases of 'Spirit Possession.'" *The Journal of Pacific History* 30:210-226, citing the *Fiji School of Medicine Journal* 4(12):4 (December 1969).
176. Parke, op cit., p. 217.
177. Parke, op cit., p. 218.
178. Parke, op cit., p. 218.
179. Parke, op cit., p. 218.
180. Parke, op cit., p. 219.
181. Parke, op cit., pp. 218-219.
182. Parke, op cit., p. 220.
183. "Yaqona (Kava)." Islands Travel, Lot 7, Qanville Estate, Box 10146, Nadi Airport, Fiji, South Pacific. Http://www.fiji-island.com.
184. Parke, op cit., p. 220.
185. Parke, op cit., p. 223.
186. Parke, op cit., p. 226.
187. "Mass hysteria hits girls in Nepal school." *The Tribune* (Chandigarh, India), September 9, 2003, accessed December 4, 2003 at: http://www.tribuneindia.com /2003/ 20030909/world.htm#5.

IMAGES THAT MOVE, WEEP, AND BLEED

Worldwide: various periods 1524 to present

Images of gods, saints, and heroes have been venerated by mankind since ancient times and have often been endowed with some of the attributes of the beings they represent. Simply by touching them, for instance, it was supposed that one could acquire some of their virtue to heal or protect, to promote fertility or good fortune. From this it is a simple step to supposing that the images themselves could be animated by the entity, and this is evidenced when they seem to move, weep, and bleed. Animated images have been recorded since the earliest times. In Ancient Egypt, the celebrated statue of Memnon was supposed to utter a cry at sunrise – and indeed it did, though in this instance it was not the deity who spoke but the stone struck by the sun's heat.

Chroniclers have periodically reported collective experiences of such phenomena, which continue to occur in all cultures. As a measure of their frequency, the French Catholic expert Bouflet, in a list he admits is far from complete, catalogued 101 cases between 1953 and 1990. Of these, the Church has favorably recognized 15, though they are not necessarily regarded as miracles.[1] Most of the recorded instances have taken place within the Roman Catholic community and are of religious figures – Jesus, various saints, but predominantly Mary, the mother of Jesus. To the Church, these events are miraculous; to non-believers, they are illusions aided by suggestion. However, even if this latter view is correct, the psychological processes involved are by no means simple and straightforward.

Not all these cases constitute collective experiences in the sense that large numbers see them simultaneously. The greater number are one-off cases, yet even when the manifestation takes place in a domestic setting, friends, neighbors, and ecclesiastical authorities are called in to testify to the event, and it is usually not long before swarms of people throng to the site. Consequently almost every case can be legitimately classified as a collective experience. The most revealing, however, are those cases that occur in clusters, and our entry presents and considers a few of these.

CONTEXT: Moving images have been reported in many places at many times, and often there is no ostensible reason to relate them directly to any particular social context. However, many take place at times of crisis, as exampled by the Italian 1850s cluster, which occurred at a time when Pope Pius IX had been forced to retire from Rome due to the nationalist *Risorgimento*, triggering a traumatic conflict of interest among the Italian population. In the cases mentioned below, the Rome outbreak is clearly related to political events, whereas the Irish cluster has no obvious trigger and seems to relate to a state of mind rather than a specific event.

Brescia and Pistoia, Italy, 1524: One of the earliest instances of which we have a firm description took place at a time when both the French and Imperial armies were active in Italy, each striving to seize as much territory as possible. The major cities were besieged, taken and re-taken, and the country between them was ravaged and looted by the soldiers. The chief sufferers, as always, were the common people, not only directly from the fighting but also from food shortages frequently amounting to famine, to which acts of man were added acts of god in the form of flooding and pestilence.

On the seventh Sunday after Easter, Pentecost, when worshippers were gathered in the church of Our Lady of Grace in Brescia before a painting representing the holy family, the figure of Mary was seen to open and close her eyes, with an air of solemnity yet of kindliness; she then joined and separated her hands; the child Jesus that she held in her arms raised his eyes and hands towards his mother; and rays of light shot from the eyes of Saint Joseph. A thousand people, including the bishop and many priests and laypersons of quality, witnessed this event.[2]

At about the same time, the image of Mary in the old porch of San Giovanni of the Temple at Pistoia began moving her eyes "like a living being." Though hostile invaders threatened both these towns, other towns equally under threat did not share the alleged miracle.

Rome And Elsewhere In Northern Italy 1796-1797: From June 1796 to January 1797, a veritable epidemic of moving images occurred in Rome and other towns in the Papal States. Most of the hundred or more reported were statues or paintings of Mary, but images of Jesus also took part. The phenomena included movements of the eyes, the flowing of tears, and sweating. Some were taken as warnings of misfortune, others as tokens of hope. A commission appointed by Pope Pius VI took depositions from nearly a thousand witnesses, testifying on behalf of thousands more. (Marchetti estimates there were more than 60,000 witnesses in all.[3]) Eighty-five of the strongest witnesses were questioned rigorously and at length, so that there exists a wealth of detailed eyewitness testimony. For each manifestation, statements were taken from at least four witnesses. Marchetti lists them by name, age, and profession in his account. This is not only the most prolific of moving-image incidents, but also the most thoroughly investigated and documented.

The first manifestation took place in the church of San Nicolo di Lorenesi, where at sunset one evening in June 1796 Nicolo Rinaldi saw the Madonna open and close her eyes several times. He did not speak of it until news came of a similar event, on June 25, from the city of Ancona, where the Virgin of San Ciriaco behaved in the same way.[4] Crowds came to see it with their own eyes and an account was printed and published; the news created a profound sensation. On July 9, the Madonna of the Archetto did the same (see Case History below). Before the end of that day, the prodigy was repeated throughout Rome. Work stopped, workshops closed, and the streets and churches were crowded until late at night. The next day, July 10, the streets were thronged from daybreak. The same phenomenon was reported at six major churches, and from private or public chapels and oratories. Eventually, more than a hundred images, in churches, chapels, and private premises were reported as moving. This continued throughout the latter part of 1796 and into 1797, then gradually ceased.

The manifestations took place either indoors or in narrow streets. The images were mostly oil paintings or frescoes, but there were several sculptures, and one chalk drawing on paper. The two-dimensional images were usually behind protective glass, though in at least one case this was removed to give a clearer sight. In one remarkable case, the painting was so dark that its subject could barely be made out, but witnesses affirmed that it grew brighter, enabling the movements to be clearly seen. In virtually every instance, what was seen was a vertical movement of the eyes of Mary or Jesus.

The effect on the spectators varied from one to another: "One saw, at the same moment, some prostrate themselves, others weep, others strike their breasts, or in some other manner give signs of what they saw, and what they felt in their hearts… There was a general commotion, a spirit of penitence and sudden change which followed immediately in this great metropolis the series of affecting prodigies it had witnessed… someone who had been away and returned among us after a brief absence might have doubted that we were the same people, and recognised the city only by its great buildings. Dress, manners, language, changed in an instant. The streets, the squares, the shops, the homes, the churches presented changes which could seem unbelievable even to us who witnessed them. At every step one came across a chapel continuously surrounded by a pious crowd, prostrating themselves, begging for grace, or applauding with grateful joy the miracle being performed in their presence. Some seemed struck with remorse, others struck their breasts, others had their eyes full of tears."[5] Spontaneous processions passed through the streets, moving from one miraculous image to another, chanting canticles as they went and bursting into cries of Viva Maria and other such words. The boys led the cortege, followed by the men, then the women and children; many were barefoot, many others carried scourges with which they belabored themselves. The churches stayed open late into the night or even throughout the night. Rather than stir up religious fervor, the priests found themselves having to dampen the enthusiasm so that the nights should not be too disturbed. "During these great days of Rome, one heard no profane songs, the names of God and Jesus were not used with disrespect, no indecent word was uttered, there was no quarreling, no drunkenness. One could believe oneself in Paradise."[6]

The attitude of the authorities was guarded, but a good many of the clergy, at first skeptical, were convinced by the evidence of their own eyes. Far from being blinded by their credulity, they went to considerable lengths to objectively verify what they saw. They shifted their sight lines, they made repeated visits under different light conditions, they climbed ladders to examine the images at close quarters with magnifying glasses, or employed telescopes for those they could not approach. Marchetti comments:

> Everyone knows that Rome, the capital of the Christian World, contains a populace drawn from many states and nations; and that the knowledge of the Holy Scriptures, and the culture of the fine arts are, one can say it without exciting jealousy, here carried further than anywhere else. The natural sciences themselves are not neglected, nor the rules of criticism, and the most up-to-date principles are applied in their study. Consequently those people deserve our pity who, strong in theory, tell us in grave and scientific tones that the impression which so many people said they had experienced was due to refraction of the sun's rays, the position and vibrations of light, the fatigue and shifting of eyes fixed for too long on an object, the reflection of windows, the diversity of angles of perspective, and above all an imagination formed and excited by devotion. No doubt there was a degree of justice and sense in these suggestions, but in a city like Rome they were as inappropriate as if an academician had presumed to warn the shepherds on the hills not to be confused by a meteor. Foreigners who found themselves in our city at this time can bear witness that there was no one who didn't take these possibilities into account: even for the man in the street, working men and even a good many of the women, they were the subject of every conversation. By exchanging with one another their observations and difficulties, the common people became so instructed in the effects of light and sight, that when they discussed them they sounded like a group of scientists warning themselves against illusions. When witnesses were questioned, they were specifically asked to give their reasons for rejecting a natural cause rather than a supernatural operation.[7]

There were skeptics a-plenty, but time and time again they came to scoff and went away persuaded – "burning with eagerness to put a stop to what they conceived to be popular fanaticism, who when they arrived on the spot were constrained by the evidence to cry and weep like the others."[8]

Rome Was Not Alone: Frascati, Todi, and at least eight other towns in the papal domains were similarly blessed. The epidemic reached its height in August and continued until January, when Napoleon entered Ancona and ordered that the miraculous image should be covered with drapery. This was done, and "the order of the future emperor was doubtless heard by all the madonnas of Italy, for about this time all the miracles diminished."[9]

Despite the profusion of witnesses, not everyone who was present on these occasions saw the miracles, and of those who saw them, many had to wait many hours and even make several visits before they could see any movement. This lends strength to an explanation in terms of subjective experience, for as French folklorist P. Saintyves comments, if the movements were a physical fact, then the fact that some didn't see them was also a kind of miracle.

He is inclined to think that the priests – and in particular the Jesuits – encouraged the claims. The first episode in Rome was at a Jesuit church. He even speculates that they may have touched up the images, but only a few lent themselves to this possibility. Naturally, the Church favored a miraculous explanation in principle, but in practice they went to commendable lengths to examine natural possibilities, and consequently the Rome cluster constitutes one of the most closely documented instances of exceptional behavior.

Limpias, Spain, 1919: Huge crowds were attracted to a figure of Jesus on his cross in the parish church at Limpias, near Santander, after the figure was seen to move its eyes and to become covered with a moisture-like perspiration. Throughout the summer and autumn visitors streamed to see it – three to four thousand a day. Countless pilgrims claimed to have seen the phenomenon, and statements, often on oath, were taken from some 2,500, though they did not all concur as to what they saw:

> Many said that the Savior looked at them; at some in a kindly manner, at others gravely, and at yet others with a penetrating and stern glance. Many of them saw tears in His eyes; others noticed that drops of blood ran down from the temples pierced by the crown of thorns; some saw froth on His lips and sweat on His body; others again saw how He turned His head from side to side and let His gaze pass over the whole assembly of people; or how at the Benediction He made a movement of his eyes as if giving the blessing; how at the same time He moved the thorn-crowned head from one side to the other. Others had the impression that a deep, submissive sigh was wrested from His breast; some believed they saw him whisper…[10]

Thurston notes, with regard to these sightings, that most of those present did not see the phenomenon, and that the sightings were not always spontaneous and simultaneous as at Rome. Often, they were not seen until the witness had been present for several hours. There were, however, some manifestations that resembled those of Rome:

> On Saturday, April 10, 1930, at half-past twelve in the afternoon, nearly all who were in the church were so surprised by the manifestations that they simultaneously gave expression to their interior excitement through loud prayers and cries. The folk who were conversing outside in the church square hastened out of natural curiosity into the church, where they at once became witnesses of the changes. They, too, began forthwith to shout aloud, so that the sound penetrated farther and farther. Workmen occupied in the vicinity left their work and went into the house of God. The same thing happened to them. They did not need first to ask the cause of the general tumult, for the greater number of them saw the same apparitions.[11]

Some of the sightings appear to have been much more complex than elsewhere; several persons claimed to have seen the successive phases of the death of Jesus enacted by the crucified figure, including a change of appearance of the dying victim. Electric lighting was installed to give visitors a better view, but this did not affect the number of sightings. Close inspection was permitted, and attempts were made to photograph the changes, but none was successful.[12]

Ireland 1985:[13] Nearly two centuries later an outbreak of moving images occurred in southern Ireland, like Italy a predominantly Roman Catholic country. By contrast with the Rome cluster, the Irish sightings took place in some forty mainly rural locations. The first incident occurred near Ballinspittle, 30 km south of Cork. A grotto housing a life-size, plaster-covered concrete image of Mary had been set up in 1954, the "Marian Year" commemorating the 100th anniversary of the Papal pronouncement of the Immaculate Conception of Mary. It was illuminated after dark by eleven star-like lights encircling the head.

Passing the grotto at dusk, about 10 p.m. on July 22,1985, 17-year-old village girl Clare O'Mahony received the impression that the statue, which she saw at a distance of some 30 meters, was rocking to and fro. She went home and told her mother and other villagers, who came to see for themselves; they received the same impression. One recalled, "I thought I'd better go and see what these nutcases were up to. I joined about forty other people saying the rosary. Then I saw the statue move. I got a terrible fright. I thought it was going to fall on some youngsters below."[14]

The news spread rapidly. The following evening a few score local people gathered at the site, and from the fourth day on, crowds numbering thousands, some coming from considerable distances, gathered every evening from 10 pm. By the third week some 100,000 pilgrims had visited the site, many coming by the daily coach service that had been started. Loudspeakers broadcast prayers at 20-minute intervals. Tradesmen provided food and police controlled the huge crowds.

Soon, reports were coming in from other Irish locations. At Dunmanway, 30 km west of Ballinspittle, Mary was seen moving in a similar grotto. Beer lists 47 sites in all, though none attracted as many visitors as Ballinspittle. Generally the phenomena were similar, but some were more unusual. At Asdee, in an incident that actually pre-dated Ballinspittle but was not widely reported till later, a 7-year-old girl saw both Jesus and Mary. At Mount Melleray, three local children told how the image of Mary had left its pedestal and walked toward them, telling them "God is very angry with the world."

Though the pattern was similar overall, there were many individual variations. Spectators saw rocking movements not only forwards and back but also sideways, as well as twisting of the body, gestures of the arms, and eyes that glittered. At one roadside shrine, Mary moved her hands and was seen breathing. At Cratloe in County Clare spectators saw the face of

Christ superimposed on that of his mother, while others saw the likeness of Padre Pio and the face of a pope. Elsewhere, demons were reported.

An unusual incident occurred on October 31, the night of Halloween, when three men vandalized the image at Ballinspittle, climbing the barrier and smashing the face with hammers and axes, while shouting to the crowd "You stupid fools, worshipping a plaster statue!" The men were arrested but were acquitted of any offence on the technicality that the image was not located in a place of divine worship. The statue was repaired by its creator and replaced, but by this time the crowds were diminishing.

The Catholic clergy generally stayed away from the sites, no official pronouncement was made, and visitors were generally, though ineffectually, discouraged. Many nuns, however, were among the visitors. Significantly, it was not only doubters who felt that all these apparent movements were illusory optical effects caused by the way the statue was lit. A good many of the spectators, including those who saw the movement, accepted that this was the explanation. A team of psychologists from Cork University confirmed this view.[15] "None of those who believed they had possibly seen a miracle appeared to be awestruck as a result. They talked of what they had 'seen' in matter-of-fact tones. 'She sort of smiled and looked round to her left.' 'Her eyes opened and closed and then she nodded.' 'She made as if to raise her hands up and then she stopped.' I gathered no reports of people falling to their knees in wonderment or being transfigured or experiencing any sort of ecstasy."[16]

Colm Tobin, introducing a collection of contemporary articles about the moving statues, lists possible triggers ranging from unemployment and hunger strikes to boring summer television. But what emerged from the collection is a sense that the Catholic Church in Ireland was on the defensive, its teachings on matters such as divorce and abortion questioned and often attacked. The alleged miracles are perhaps most easily seen as an expression of these tensions.[17]

Weeping And Bleeding Images: Apart from moving their eyes, religious images are often alleged to weep or bleed, as was occasionally the case at Limpias. In 988, in the abbey of Pucelles at Orléans, France, the figure of Jesus on a crucifix began to weep, as Jesus himself had wept for the destruction of Jerusalem. Other uncanny events followed, and no one was surprised when, soon afterwards, a catastrophic fire devastated the center of the city. The weeping crucifix was taken by all to have been a forewarning of the disaster.

Though weeping and bleeding images are ostensibly a phenomenon similar to moving images, there is a crucial difference. In the case of moving images, there is no objective evidence that anything has taken place. The phenomenon consists of spectators seeing the movement, which, since not everyone sees it, is a subjective process. In the case of weeping and bleeding images, the evidence in most cases is objective; the tears and blood, whether or not they are genuine, are there for all to see. Thus, moving images provoke exceptional behavior, in the form of a collective hallucination of some kind (whether divinely inspired or otherwise); weeping and bleeding images do not. Consequently they are only marginal to the subject matter of this Encyclopedia and our mention is intended only to put the moving images into a wider context.

Like moving images, weeping and bleeding images are frequently reported and generally taken to be a sign from Heaven. So, when in June 1796, the eyes of the statue of the Madonna in the cathedral of Ancona, Italy, were found to be filled with tears, this was seen as an indication that Mary was distressed at the harsh treatment of the Roman Church by Napoleon.

When weeping and bleeding images are found in private homes, their message seems to be a more personal one. Typically, on August 29, 1953, in a humble home in Siragusa, Sicily, there stood a crude popular image of the Virgin, which had been given to Angel and Antonia Gusto as a wedding present. Pregnant, epileptic, and sick, Antonia was kneeling before the statue in prayer when she saw tears trickling down its face. At the same moment she felt marvelously recovered from her sufferings. The weeping continued so long as the image was in the house, but stopped when the police took it away for testing. When it was returned to its owners, the statue began to weep again and continued to do so for three days. Seventeen bishops affirmed the miracle, which was recognized by the Church. Today a chapel houses Our Lady of the Tears.[18]

The phenomenon seems to be confined to Catholic believers, but it is by no means limited to traditionally Catholic countries. At Akita, Japan, a statue of the Virgin began to bleed in June 1973. It also perspired, giving off a scent of lilies and roses, and later it began to weep as well. This happened 101 times until it finally stopped in 1981.[19] A few years later, in 1985, an image began to weep at Naju, in Korea. In both these cases, as at Siragusa, the owner of the statue was a sick lady, and it would seem that the phenomenon was an expression of sympathy on the Virgin Mary's part.

The phenomenon invariably attracts large crowds who flock to see a miracle with their own eyes. Unfortunately, this encourages some individuals to fabricate miraculous images of their own. In July 1967, London faith healer Alfred Bolton admitted that the blood in the miraculously bleeding crucifix, which had so impressed his patients, came from pieces of butcher's meat he had placed there himself.[20]

In 1986, California physicist Shawn Carlson was intrigued by reports that a weeping statue had drawn more than 300,000 visitors to the church of Saint Nicolas in Chicago. Church officials would not allow him to make a scientific study of the statue, so he set out to replicate the phenomenon. In 1987, at a meeting of the American Committee for the Scientific Study of Religion, he created a sensation by producing a copy of the Mona Lisa – which wept tears.

Carlson did not claim that the Chicago statue was a fake. All he set out to do was to show that there could be a natural explanation. The technique he used was very simple, using ingredients that would have been available to hoaxers throughout the centuries. However, he would not reveal them in case he decided to go into the business of selling weeping images![21]

COMMENT: It seems to us that it takes a deal of courage, and critical faculties of some new-fangled kind, to persuade oneself that all these witnesses were mistaken, and that they went on being mistaken over and over again, and in the same way, about something that was visible to all, and that the entire multitude of those present fell along with them in illusion and error, in the same way and at the same moment. Of course, some physical circumstance might deceive such and such an individual, and his senses might report something that had no objective reality. But how can one imagine so many witnesses, on their guard against any surprise, all falling into so gross an error? How can we conceive that such an illusion should be born in the eyes or the imagination of so many people at the same instant, neither earlier or later? And this, several times in a day over a period of months?[22]

After hearing such a wealth of testimony, much of it from professional men and citizens of position, Marchetti can hardly be blamed for subscribing to the miracle explanation: if the testimony can be accepted, nothing short of a miracle can account for it. The only alternative he considered – collective illusion fueled by suggestion – would have to be on a scale so massive that he found it unacceptable, for not only would it affect hundreds and even thousands in the same place and at the same instant, but over and over again through a period of months. To the skeptic, for whom subjective illusion is the preferred explanation for all moving-image manifestations, the scale, spontaneity, and simultaneous nature of the Rome outbreak constitutes a powerful challenge.

The Limpias case, where so many people saw so many different things, argues strongly in favor of the subjective nature of the experience. If, as Christians believe, to God all things are possible, it could be that each individual saw something different because Jesus was operating a different miracle for each member of the congregation. Behavioral scientists would prefer to think that each witness created his own illusion.

Many witnesses of the Irish phenomena, even while they affirmed what they perceived, accepted that some kind of optical illusion was involved. This ambiguous response introduces a psychological element into the moving-image process that adds to the complexity of this type of extraordinary behavior.

Case History

Father Juvenal Goani, a 46-year-old Franciscan priest who had served the Church as a missionary and in other capacities, was one of the 86 witnesses questioned in depth by the Roman Church's investigative body. On October 29, 1796, he described his personal experience three months earlier, relative to the image known as the "dell'Archetto," publicly displayed in a small street on the wall linking the palazzo Casali to the house of the brotherhood of San Antonio. The oil painting, behind glass, shows Mary in a humble attitude, joining her hands over her breast. The figure is in half-profile. The open eyes, with visible pupils, are directed downwards towards the observer. The painting, about three and a half palms in height, is surrounded by silverwork, hence it is protected by a metal grille. The image is very popular and well known to the people of the area.

On the 9th of July last, in the morning, the prodigy had barely commenced before I was informed of it by Piero, a lay brother, who came out of breath and full of joy to tell me that the eyes of the Virgin of the Archetto were moving. I didn't give any credence to this news, thinking that it was an enthusiasm of the people, in whom an excess of piety had created the illusion, and who wished to see the same kind of prodigies as had been reported from the town of Ancona. Brother Piero sought in vain to persuade me, adding that the spectators were unanimous as to what they were seeing, but I didn't change my opinion.

Some time later, leaving my room, I saw from the balcony a great number of people coming and going in the street below. I considered this tumultuous concourse as fanaticism. Despite this, however, I was driven by curiosity to go and see this image for myself, though I was still convinced that the reports were false. When I met three of my colleagues in the doorway, who all attested the reality of the thing, I made no reply. In the street I met monsignor Catali, and having passed through the door facing the tennis-court, and finding ourselves immediately under the wall which holds the image, we positioned ourselves before it at a distance of about a metre. I knelt to pray, then retired a short distance to where I could clearly see the entire effigy. An enormous number of people filled the narrow street facing the image. The faithful prayed continuously at the tops of their voices, and over and over again I heard them cry, Viva Maria, there she is, moving her eyes! Although I was watching attentively, I saw no movement, confirming my earlier opinion that this was an effect of heightened imagination due to excessive devotion to the Virgin.

For about three quarters of an hour I watched with a critical eye. Mgr Casali tired and left; but I stayed there, willing to remain three or four hours so that I should be able to say I had stayed that long without seeing the prodigy. Then suddenly, at a moment when I was thinking the least about it, standing still, my eyes fixed on those of the Virgin, I saw a movement in her eyes, clearly visible; I saw her eyeballs move, her pupils rise by degrees until they were almost entirely hidden by her eyelids, so that only the whites of her eyes could be seen. Then after a short space of time I saw the pupils drop back to their former position. After a very brief interval, I saw them rise again, then lower once more. This perpendicular movement was repeated twice more. It is easier to imagine than to describe the state that I was put into by a sight so marvellous and for which I was so little prepared. I can only say that I could not contain my feelings, and that tears ran from my eyes.

I must record some remarkable circumstances which accompanied this prodigy. First, at the moment when the Virgin's eyeballs began to move, I saw a certain very light cloud which somewhat obscured the white of her eyes. But this cloud dissipated very promptly, and when she raised her pupils, I saw the eyeballs white as before. The second circumstance was that this perpendicular moment was performed with such grace and majesty, that it aroused not only devotion but feelings of respect and veneration. Third, at the same moment that I observed the supernatural movement, it was confirmed by the cries, the tears and the extraordinary acclamations of the entire gathering, expressive of the joy they felt at the sight.

For me the fact was now a certainty, for I had seen it with my own eyes: but I still had to reassure myself that no artifice was involved. The wax dripping from one of the candles burning in front of the image gave me the opportunity. I took a ladder which was close at hand, and, on the pretext of attending to the candle, climbed till I was on a level with the Virgin's eyes. As I adjusted the candle, I was looking closely at the image, to see if there was any lineament, slit, or other sign however small which might indicate that behind the canvas there was some artificial device to make the eyes move. I was quickly assured that the canvas was perfectly smooth, without the slightest sign of fraud, artifice or alteration. Satisfied at having entirely cleared all doubts, I retired praising God and glorifying the Virgin. The least I could do was to manifest, to everyone I met, my feelings as to the reality of this miracle.

I did not return to the image that day, but the crowds remained and were back the next and the following days. Then on Monday 11th I had an idea for another test, which would enable me to counter objections. I provided myself with a compass, and went to the image at 10 in the evening, when there were relatively few people about, partly because of the hour but also because by now other such prodigies were taking place in other parts of the city. For about a quarter of an hour I waited, saying prayers but never taking my eyes off the image. Then I saw the movement as before, and at the same moment the crowd burst into cries. I then took the ladder, asking those present to forgive me if I made an experiment which would serve to authenticate the prodigy. I then mounted the ladder and was able to measure the amount of white which was visible when she raised and lowered her pupils, and found it to be about five lineas [a linea is the 12th part of a thumb]. When she lowered her eyes, no white was visible as her pupil met the lower eyelid. After such an experiment, what more could I ask? I shared my findings with the spectators, convincing them all there was no illusion.

He pointed out that the street was so narrow that the sun could not reach the image, and that the glass that covered it was kept perfectly clean by the guardian. He possessed excellent sight and didn't wear spectacles. "Having studied physics, I am well aware of the effects of the imagination and optical illusions, which occur when one is taken by surprise, and when the sensory input is not clear-cut, constant or uniform. But clearly I was not in such circumstances, consequently my imagination was neither affected nor heightened, nor were my eyes deceiving me."[23]

This remarkable account, given in response to rigorous questioning, shows that no simplistic explanation can be imposed on the eyewitness testimony, which was forthcoming in such quantities. Goani was well aware of possible alternatives, and took proper care not to be deceived. It is pertinent to point out that his most crucial test was carried out at 10 o'clock at night, consequently by artificial light, and that candles were burning – and doubtless flickering – in front of the image. Nevertheless, it is hard to affirm that what he was measuring with his careful compass measurements, performed up against the glass covering of the painting, was nothing but an optical illusion.

INCENSE HYSTERIA

United Arab Emirates: 1994

On November 13, a fire was reported to have broken out at the female student dormitories of the United Arab Emirates University. As emergency personnel arrived it was believed that toxic materials were involved, as 23 teenage students had become ill and were rushed to two nearby hospitals. Their symptoms included chest pressure, difficulty breathing, dizziness, shaking, screaming, and crying. Some were coughing and complained of sore throats. Blood tests and physical exams revealed nothing unusual and symptoms quickly resolved. Upon further investigation of the premises, it was realized that the suspected "toxic fire" was actually the harmless smell of burning incense.[24]

INDIA ET SCARE AND RIOT

India: August 2002

One man was killed and 12 injured after rioting erupted in northern India during a scare involving a purported extraterrestrial spaceship terrorizing residents. Violence broke out in the state of Uttar Pradesh when hundreds of frightened villagers stormed the Barabank police station, angry with police for not providing sufficient protection against the "aliens." The attack on the police station followed seven mysterious deaths in the region that were attributed to a mysterious aerial object, which villagers claimed struck during the night by burning and/or scratching its victim. Some locals had dubbed the phantom assailant *muhnochwa*, which means "face scratcher."[25]

CONTEXT: Uttar Pradesh is one of the poorest, underdeveloped Indian states and is infamous for inhabitants making incredible claims.[26] In 1996, residents were terror-stricken by accounts of a man-like creature reportedly stealing babies. A pack of wolves was later identified as the culprit.[27]

In addition to space aliens, one folk theory advanced by Police Deputy Inspector General K.N.D. Dwivedi held that "anti-national elements" (Pakistani spies) had used genetic engineering to produce a super insect. Pakistani spies are a common scapegoat for numerous problems in India.[28] The scare prompted the formation of vigilante squads in some villages. Local physicians, who treated those claiming to have been injured by the spacecraft beam, dismissed the claims as psychological in origin, with most of the injuries being inadvertently "self-inflicted by panicked villagers."[29]

COMMENT: An editorial in the *Indian Express* attributes the scare to poverty, disease, and lack of education, noting that life expectancy for a female child born in Uttar Pradesh is "20 years less than her sister in Kerala."[30] As one travels the area they will encounter a mood of despair that is rare "even by Indian standards."[31] Given these circumstances, it is not surprising that "a mind bereft of education and overwhelmed by the iniquities and burdens of daily life is prone to fear, superstition and wild imagination. ...The official government explanation, based on a report submitted to the home department by IIT, Kanpur, for the *muhnochwa* is likely to be the rare phenomenon of ball lightning. When the rains die down, says the report, so too will the sightings. ... But until eastern UP gets down to improving the lives of its people, it will only be a matter of time until the next strange thing comes along."[32]

INDIA WITCH SCARE

New Delhi, India: March 2005

Waves of fear rippled through the city of New Delhi amid rumors that a witch was wandering the city and visiting homes, only to strike some occupants dead. The witch supposedly appeared as a hungry old woman who showed up at homes and asked for an onion. Upon receiving the onion, reports said that she took out a knife and cut the onion in two, whereupon blood squirted out from the vegetable. The person giving the onion then supposedly dropped dead on the spot from her black magic. Authorities reported that many natural deaths were being blamed on the witch. Especially hard hit was the outer suburb of Sagarpur where hundreds of houses were sporting freshly painted maroon and yellow palm pictures, which were believed to ward off witches. In recent years there have been several incidents of suspected female witches being lynched in parts of eastern India, including the states of Jharkhand and Orissa.[33]

COMMENT: Certain parts of India have rich traditions about witches with black magical powers accosting residents as they open their doors.

IRAQ NATIONAL GUARD MUTINY

Tallil, Iraq: October 13, 2004

At least 18 part-time U.S. National Guard reservists who were called up to serve in the Iraq War of 2003 reportedly led a temporary "mutiny" by refusing orders to travel as part of a supply mission. The incident happened near the southeastern Iraqi city of Tallil after the reservists were asked to transport fuel along a route that was the subject of frequent attacks by Iraqi insurgents. One of the reservists, Amber McClenny, phoned her mother and said that she and her comrades refused to go as it was a "suicide mission" and pleaded with her to raise the alarm. "Mom, I need you to raise pure hell," was part of a message left on the answering machine. Other reservists made similar calls to relatives and the issue made headlines across the U.S. Complaints included being ordered to use old vehicles that frequently broke down and had not been fitted with protective armor. U.S. military officials, afraid that similar incidents could spread and concerned over the impact on morale, would not use the word "mutiny," but instead described it as "a temporary breakdown in discipline."[34] The reservists were initially placed in detention but later released and the unit temporarily broken up. Insubordination in time of war is viewed as serious, and punishment is often swift and harsh. The soldiers hailed from the same South Carolina Reserve, which likely fostered a strong sense of cohesion.[35] Reservists have long been referred to in America as "weekend warriors" and until the Iraq War were almost exclusively confined to domestic duties such as border patrol and airport security. Many may not have been psychologically ready to serve overseas in a war zone. At the time of the incident, about 169 members of the Army National Guard and Reserve had died while serving in Iraq.

U.S. military expert Phillip Carter noted that insubordination was very common among U.S. troops in World War II – troops whose training was similar to today's reservists. But nowadays, Carter said, there is a big gap between the level of readiness of regular versus reserve soldiers, as the latter train just two weeks during the summer and one weekend per month. He says that reservists in the "mutiny" unit had to "learn how to drive their big rigs and maintain them, but they hardly have time to practice convoy defense or route reconnaissance. The lack of training time is compounded by other resource problems in the reserves. Many reserve leaders don't have significant active-duty experience, so they lack the expertise necessary to train their units on these important missions. Reserve equipment – particularly in the National Guard – suffers from decades of neglect. It is not uncommon for reservists and National Guardsmen to drive vehicles that are older than they are."[36]

Carter said that reservists are mobilized and trained in the very basics of warfare, then are on their way to Iraq in few weeks "with the hope that they survive and gel as a team in the ultimate Darwinian environment. The reservists in Iraq lack the training, equipment, leadership, and resources to do their job."[37] Surveys support his contention that reserve morale is much lower than Marines and active duty troops.[38] Writing in the journal *Armed Forces & Society*, military mutiny expert Joel E. Hamby reported that there are eight major factors that typically contribute to the formation of mutiny, among the most valuable being leadership. Other factors include training, alienation, environment, primary groups, values and hope, combat experience, and discipline.[39]

IRAQ PRISON ABUSE AFFAIR

Iraq: 2003-2004

On April 28, 2004, the popular U.S. television newsmagazine *Sixty Minutes* broadcast disturbing photos of Iraqi inmates being abused by U.S. soldiers at Abu Ghraib prison near Baghdad. The report and those that followed created outrage around the world, especially in Arab countries. The outlandish antics that were reported at the prison sounded like horror fiction, except that they were caught on video by some of those taking part in the mistreatment. Photos depicted both male and female soldiers laughing and giving thumbs-up signs, while posing beside naked Iraqi inmates who were coerced into performing a variety of humiliating sexual acts. One picture depicts an Iraqi prisoner standing on a box with a sack covering his head and wires leading from his hands. In an apparent bid to "break" the prisoner and get him to talk, he was allegedly told that if he fell from the box, he would be electrocuted. Other allegations included soldiers urinating on prisoners, beatings, and even homicide. Some prisoners were deliberately exposed to dogs in order to upset them; in Islam, The Holy Koran forbids touching the nose of a dog or you must wash the affected body part seven times.

The episode came to light on January 13, 2004, when a U.S. soldier stationed at Abu Ghraib prison reported the prisoner abuse to his superiors. The next day a criminal investigation of the claims was begun. On January 16, Brigadier General Mark Kimmitt, the U.S. military's chief Iraqi spokesman, informed the media of the abuse allegations and that an investigation was underway. How could American soldiers engage in such perverse acts? Two classic sociological studies on group behavior help shed light on such crimes.

CONTEXT: The Iraq abuse scandal underscores the power of the situation on conformity and group dynamics. In the case of Abu Ghraib prison, it was lack of a powerful central authority figure and inadequate accountability. The episode is surprising in showing the extent to which seemingly normal, healthy, "good" people can rapidly turn into brutal, unfeeling abusers under suitable conditions.

Zimbardo Prison Experiment: Slow Descent Into Hell

"Male College Students Needed for Psychological Study of Prison Life..." Thus began an ad placed in a local newspaper in 1971. During that summer, three psychologists at Stanford University in California, Craig Haney, Curtis Banks, and Philip Zimbardo, headed an experiment to test the power of circumstances on human behavior – in this case, the effect of arrest and incarceration on healthy people. They oversaw the construction of a mock prison in the basement of the psychology building, and then recruited mock guards and "prisoners." This was no haphazard experiment, but was conducted in consultation with ex-convicts. The guards would come and leave after eight-hour shifts; the prisoners remained incarcerated 24-hours a day. And how was it decided who got to be a guard and who a prisoner? By the flip of a coin. Each participant was paid $15 per day. The experiment was videotaped. The field of more than 70 initial applicants was pared down to 24. All of the students were screened ahead of time for psychological disturbances, medical problems, or a history of drug abuse or crime. So the experiment began with a group of young, healthy, intelligent university students.

The experimenters wanted to simulate a real prison environment. For the "prisoners," the experiment began with a surprise. On a quiet Sunday morning, local police were enlisted to drive up and perform mock arrests of the soon to be "prisoners" at their residences. They were handcuffed, read their legal rights, and then whisked off to the Psychology Department with sirens blaring. There they were strip-searched, sprayed for lice, issued standard prison uniforms, fingerprinted, blindfolded, and chains were placed around their ankles. In an effort to make them feel anonymous, each prisoner was given an identification number and could only be referred to by that number. A stocking cap was placed over their heads to simulate having their hair shaved. Head shaving is common in prison and military settings, and is intended "to minimize each person's individuality, since some people express their individuality through hair style or length. It is also a way of getting people to begin complying with the arbitrary, coercive rules."[40]

Though the experiment was scheduled to last two weeks, within six days the "guards" had become so abusive to their "prisoners" that the experiment was abruptly called off. In noting the similarities between his study and the events at Abu Ghraib prison, Zimbardo states: "I have exact, parallel pictures of naked prisoners with bags over their heads who are being sexually humiliated by the prison guards from the 1971 study."[41]

Parallels With Iraq Abuse

A former president of the American Psychological Association, Zimbardo says that given the poor climate and lack of authority at the prison, as detailed in Major General Antonio Taguba's report on the abuses, the outcome was predictable. In the report, the person in charge of the prison, Brigadier General Janis Karpinski, was criticized for being a weak leader who rarely visited the site of the abuses. Personnel overseeing the prisoners were improperly trained for their duties, did not have standard procedures to follow, were not well disciplined, and suffered from poor morale. The prison was short-staffed and the basic necessities of everyday life were lacking for the soldiers, who were living in constant fear of attacks by insurgents outside the prison walls. Discipline was so lax that various breaches of protocol, from following proper documentation procedures to prisoner escapes, went unpunished by superiors. "This was over a two-month period. This was not one day. I bet it was like my study, where each day it escalated, it got worse and worse and worse. Here's where hell becomes the ordinary situation."[42] How ordinary? So much so that the abusers even photographed themselves and their colleagues engaging in hideous acts. While the main task of the soldiers was guarding prisoners, their duties grew unclear when intelligence officers gave vague orders to "soften up" the inmates. The chain of command, and who was accountable for what, was ambiguous at best.[43]

Zimbardo says that the Stanford Prison Study is so well known and understood that military officials should have foreseen the potential for abuse even given the poor environment at the prison.

How Far Would You Go To Obey Authority?

Between 1961 and 1962, a Ph.D. student named Stanley Milgram was interested in reports of atrocities by German soldiers during World War II. Were these people mentally aberrant and blindly obedient as a result of the dysfunctional Nazi social structure, or were they normal and conforming to group norms? His dramatic study strongly suggested the latter was true. In fact, it could be argued that under the circumstances, if the Nazis had not committed atrocities, it would have been aberrant.[44]

Here is how the experiment was set up. Milgram places an ad in a local newspaper recruiting subjects for an experiment at Yale University "on learning and memory." People of various ages, incomes, and occupations are chosen. When they arrive for their appointments, an official-looking experimenter wearing a white lab coat meets them. A second subject (in fact, an actor) is strapped into a chair in an adjacent room, and an electrode is attached his arm. It is explained that each time the learner gets a wrong answer, the learner will receive an electric shock. The first subject is brought back to the first room and is seated in front of a metal box with a series of switches that start from "slight shock" (15 volts) at one end, up to "danger: severe shock" (450 volts) at the other end. In reality, the box does not give shocks but the operator does not know this. He must begin by asking the learner questions and with each incorrect answer, he begins to gradually increase the shock level by 15 volts.

At the 75-volt level, the learner lets out a grunt. At 90 volts there are more grunts. At 120 volts, the he complains that the shocks are painful and owwwes and ahhhs. At 150 volts, he cries out: "Let me out of here! I refuse to go on!" As the voltage level continues ever higher, the learner pleads for the shocker to stop, making statements such as "You have no right to hold me here!" and "My heart's bothering me! Let me out of here." The shocker hesitates, then consults with the man in the lab coat who orders him to continue or he will not be paid. The shocker hesitates, looks confused and frustrated, but continues with higher and higher levels of shocks after each wrong answer until reaching the "severe shock" level. At 300 volts, the learner starts pounding on the walls, demanding to be let out. By the 330-volt mark, there is dead silence from the next room. The lab coat man now enters and says that any failure to respond should be viewed as a wrong answer and a higher level of shock should be given.

If you were in this person's shoes, what would you do next? Before the experiment, Milgram surveyed a number of scientists and asked them how many subjects they thought would actually continue giving what they thought were shocks all the way to the end (450 volts). The experts estimated that just one in a thousand might do so. When Milgram conducted this very experiment he found that nearly two-thirds of seemingly normal men and women thought they were giving the learner a potentially lethal 450 volts! As for those who refused to go to the very end, the vast majority delivered what they thought to be high shock levels. Milgram's experiment has been replicated with similar results in many European countries, South Africa, and Australia. His experiment underscores the power of authority and peer pressure on conformity.

As hard as it may be to believe, the Zimbardo and Milgram experiments suggest that under the right circumstances, the majority of people are likely to have engaged in similar behavior as was reported in Iraq. It is conjectured that the situation at Abu Ghraib prison was a real-life occurrence of these experimental conditions. This was an impressive vindication of experimental work in social science in throwing light on real-life human behavior.

IRRADIATED MAIL SCARE

United States: 2002

In the wake of the anthrax mail attacks attributed to possible terrorists during the fall of 2001, the U.S. Postal Service began to irradiate mail in an effort to thwart a potential attack by killing biological agents. But an investigation was launched after Congressional and postal employees handling the treated mail complained of various symptoms: headaches, nausea, eye irritation, rashes, and a strange metallic taste.

A spokesman for one of the two firms hired to conduct the irradiation, Titan Scan Technologies of Lima, Ohio, Will Williams, said, "It just doesn't make sense ... Either they're getting sick from something else or it's mass hysteria." Williams said that the irradiation process, while new to postal workers, had been used for years without complaint in the medical profession. "When medical people open up cartons of supplies that have been irradiated, they don't get sick. After a decade of using this process worldwide, all of a sudden somebody [in Washington] is saying there are health consequences."[45]

Writing in the respected *Bulletin of the Atomic Scientists*, Bret Lortie was critical of Congressional probes into an issue that he said was already thoroughly researched. "As any reader of the *Bulletin* knows, irradiating mail is akin to microwaving it: There's no residual radiation. Too bad Sen. Charles Grassley didn't know that before requesting a full investigation," Lortie said.[46] The U.S. Office of Compliance distributed 14,000 surveys (presumably by mail!) to House and Senate workers, asking if they had any health reactions linked to handling mail. A mere 215 workers replied, reporting such common symptoms as headaches (51%) and itching (31%). Other symptoms reported included nausea, rashes, burning eyes, and bloody noses. Still not satisfied, Congress ordered the National Institute for Occupational Safety and Health (NIOSH) to analyze the Capitol air for a host of "contaminants that could be on the irradiated mail – such as carbon monoxide, volatile organic compounds, formaldehyde, ozone, polynuclear aromatic hydrocarbons, toluene, and particulate matter..." They found that the levels were either zero or below those that could impair health.[47]

In January 2002, 11 employees of the United States Commerce Department in the Herbert Hoover Building in Washington, D.C., developed breathing difficulties, nausea, and throat irritation after handling irradiated mail. A hazardous-material inspection team found the building to be safe, leading federal law officers to conclude that the symptoms were prompted by "mass hysteria." A possible trigger for the incident was a harmless package of paper. According to a Washington, D.C., Fire Department official, a ream of photocopier paper packaged in plastic gave off a strong odor when opened. One theory held that a large number of letters with plastic wrapping or plastic address windows were irradiated, emitting hazardous fumes. Federal law officers flatly rejected the idea, saying that irradiated mail does not emit toxic fumes. One government official speculated that the incident might have been fueled by urban legends about irradiation.[48]

CONTEXT: The irradiated mail scare occurred in the context of a decades-old concern over the safety of the irradiation process. In their investigation, NIOSH concluded that the irradiated mail complaints were psychological, stemming from 911-related stress and "heightened awareness."[49]

IRVINGITES

Britain: 1830-1834

Irving, a popular Presbyterian preacher in London, inspired his followers with enthusiasm for the principles of the first Christians, which he believed had been authenticated by divine "gifts," notably of healing, prophecy, and speaking in tongues. When these gifts manifested among his followers, he saw this as confirmation of his belief that the second coming of Jesus was imminent. His church became a nine days' wonder, attracting not only popular excitement but respectful attention from distinguished people.

CONTEXT: By this date the excesses of METHODISM had calmed, and dissent from the Anglican establishment had become respectable. Nevertheless many considered that the priest-ridden established churches of the day lacked the simple directness of the primitive Church, and to this they attributed the absence of the wonders that marked early Christianity. Henry Drummond, a wealthy London banker, was the moving spirit in a society established for the purpose of studying biblical prophecies that led to a belief in the restoration of "gifts," which characterized the early Church and which were supposed to have ceased with the death of the Apostles. The career of Joanna Southcott and the proliferation of small sects, such as the Jezreelites, showed that many in Britain were looking for such marvels, and it was in this context of expectation that Irving flourished.[50]

In 1822 Edward Irving (1792-1834), a young Scottish Presbyterian minister, was appointed to the Caledonian Chapel in London, a little known backstreet church with only about 50 members. In a short time, his eloquent and enthusiastic preaching attracted wider attention. He was brought to the notice of Lord Macaulay, was friendly with Thomas Carlyle, and a distinguished Member of Parliament referred in a debate to Irving's sermon as "the most eloquent sermon that I ever listened to." Soon huge crowds were thronging the chapel, which became too small to hold his would-be audience, and larger premises were found.

Irving himself seems to have been modest and likeable, by no means seeking power or position for himself. However, he was much impressed by Henry Drummond and others who looked back to the early Christians and their simple, direct relationship with God, which was expressed in the gifts of healing, prophecy, and speaking in tongues. "Irving was deeply moved, and made it a constant matter of earnest prayer that such might come to pass in his day and time. This and the expected near advent of the Lord was the chief burden of his work."[51]

In 1830, at Port Glasgow in Scotland, a young woman named Margaret Macdonald manifested the "gift of tongues," and shortly afterwards another Scottish girl, Mary Campbell, did the same. These manifestations accompanied seemingly miraculous cures, for both women were suffering from consumption and expected to die of it. Campbell declared her voices to be those of Pacific Islanders; typical phrases were *Oorin hoopo tanto noostin* or *O fastos sungor*. However, since no one was familiar with the language of the Pelew Island people, their authenticity could not be verified.[52]

Irving, hearing of these incidents, at once took them as evidence that God was about to restore the old miraculous gifts to mankind, and the utterances in foreign tongues signified to him that God's purpose was a worldwide one. "These facts fired his warm heart, and with a strong belief that he was soon to see the descent of his Lord and Master, he prayed and waited for the promised 'gifts' which were to herald the visible descent of the Lord, who was to come and sit upon his millennium throne."[53]

His prayers were answered. In July 1831, two of Irving's congregation manifested the gift of tongues and prophecy, and the epidemic spread rapidly. To begin with they manifested only in private meetings, but on October 16, Irving introduced them into the public service of the church. Eyewitnesses "dwell upon the startling effect of the outcry, and the rush of the young woman [Miss Hall, a respectable governess], either unable to restrain herself or alarmed at what she had done, into the vestry, whence proceeded a succession of doleful and unintelligible cries, while the audience of fifteen hundred or two thousand people, standing up and straining to hear and see what was toward, fell into utter confusion."[54]

London was stirred to the depths by this unusual display, which to the press was a nine-days' wonder. The church trustees, however, found this intrusion on their sedate Presbyterian form of worship intolerable. In May 1832, Irving was ejected from the church, convicted of heresy, and was no longer recognized as a minister. His followers set him up in a church of his own.

Edward Irving. (Engraving by J. Rogers)

The prophecies in a known language consisted of more or less random phrases; insofar as they could be understood, they were either meaningless rhapsodies, contradictory, or incorrect. Those which purported to be in other languages could not be translated, so could not be evaluated, though many saw wisps of known languages in such phrases as *Gthis dil emma sumo* and *Casa serahastha caro, yeo cogo nomo.*[55] Notwithstanding the apparently meaningless character of the utterances, the speakers were remarkably fluent. Individuals who were normally reticent and shy would, when the "power" seized them, speak more gracefully and more rapidly than in their normal state.

Though many of the prophecies were dubious, Irving continued to believe that all was the work of God, and a committee was created to evaluate them. Those manifestly not of divine origin were attributed to evil spirits. Two young children of an Anglican clergyman, a friend of Irving's, spoke with tongues, but so outrageous were their utterances that they had to be exorcized. One zealous follower, Richard Baxter, received a divine instruction to go to the Court of Chancery where a message would be given him, after which he would be cast into prison. He went, but no message came, and he was not cast into prison. He concluded that the Evil One had deluded him.[56]

Irving's friend, the writer Thomas Carlyle, deplored the scenes in his church. In a letter to his mother, he wrote "Last Sabbath it burst out publicly in the open church, for one of the 'Prophetesses,' a woman on the verge of derangement, started up in the time of worship, and began to speak with tongues, and, as the thing was encouraged by Irving, there were some three or four fresh hands who started up in the evening sermon and began their ragings; whereupon the whole congregation got into foul uproar, some groaning, some laughing, some shrieking, not a few falling into swoons: more like a Bedlam than a Christian church."[57] *The Times* was even more outspoken: "Are we to listen to the screaming of hysterical women and the ravings of frantic men? Is bawling to be added to absurdity, and the disturber of a congregation to escape the police and tread-mill because the person who occupies the pulpit vouches for his inspiration?"[58]

Discouraged by criticism, rejected by the church, broken in health, and perhaps burnt out by his enthusiasm, Irving died in 1834 at the age of just 42. The church he founded continued after him but never again attracted wide popular attention.

COMMENT: "My persuasion concerning the unknown tongue, as it is called ... is that it is no language whatever, but a mere collection of words and sentences... The whole work is a mimicry of the gifts of the Spirit – the utterance, in tongues, a mimicry of the gift of tongues – and so of the prophesyings, and all the other works of the power. It is Satan, as an angel of light, imitating, as far as permitted, the Holy Spirit of God."[59] To Robert Baxter, who had felt it himself, there was no doubt that the power that drove the tongue-speakers was real: what was less certain was that it was divine, and he concluded that it was not.

Nevertheless, the manifestations were impressive to those who heard them. The fluency of the speakers, overtaken by the "force," was quite remarkable. Oxley, writing in 1889, regarded them as "common psychic phenomena," seeing them as precursors of spiritualism.[60] On the other hand, Warfield, commenting in 1918, had no hesitation in saying, "Of course, we are in the presence here of hysteria."[61]

See also: GLOSSOLALIA.

ISLAMIC ECSTATIC SECTS

From Morocco in the west to Malaysia in the east, Islam has given birth throughout its history to groups, sects, or brotherhoods that seek salvation through ecstatic practices. Each of the major religions contains elements that hope to reach paradise through mortification and penance. But whereas for the most part these practices are conducted on an individual basis – Christian ascetics, Hindu fakirs – in Islam they tend to be public and collective.

Ecstatic practices were established within Islam from a very early date after the Prophet Muhammad received his revelations. They probably derived in part from indigenous practices of the nomads, in part from the practices of mystical groups encountered by the Muslims as they spread throughout western Asia. Processional ceremonies took place round sacred stones, prefiguring the ceremonies of the Mecca pilgrimage, and it has been suggested that the procession of Joshua round Jericho, narrated in the Bible, was such an event.[62]

Mysticism in Islam was inspired, as with many movements within Christianity, by the perception that the religious establishment had become too worldly. As a consequence of their conquests, Muslims had acquired great wealth. Just as so many Christian sects revolted against the power and riches of the Roman Catholic Church, seeking the simplicity of the early church, so there was a nostalgia among Muslims for the pastoral simplicity of Islam's desert origins. This led to a more rigorous adherence to fundamental values, and found its expression not only in intellectual spiritual attitudes and teachings but also in practical physical forms. Ecstasy, which led to annihilation of self, was honored, and the physical processes whereby ecstasy was achieved became the practice of some of the sects. Rhythmic chanting of repeated phrases, accompanied by the beating of tambourines, drums, and cymbals, typified the ceremonies of the Rafa'ia, followers of Ahmed-el-Kebir-er-Rafa'i. The members would form a chain, each with his hands on the shoulders of the one before, and all together would throw their bodies forward and back, while shouting and chanting. "Some fell to the ground, totally unconscious: others rushed to the snakes, braziers and red-hot swords already prepared for them, which they grabbed, licked, gnawed with transports of eagerness until the moment when, dripping with sweat, their eyes out of their head, frothing at the mouth, they too fell to the ground, a horrible spectacle."[63]

In Algeria, Tunisia, and Morocco countless groups of this kind were formed. While claiming local origins, they followed much the same pattern as the Rafa'ia. Not all indulged in extreme behavior. In the upper classes of society, meditation and charitable works were more usual. But several sects, notably the Aïssâoua, the Hamadcha, and the Degougiyyîn, went in for violent performances. In 1931 a French traveler provided an eyewitness account of the members of the Derkâoua of Fez, Morocco:

The fakirs arrive one by one, greet one another and kneel. When a sufficient number have arrived, the *muqâddam* begins to read from one of the sacred books, reading gently and commenting on the passage, with discussion among the gathering. Then all form a circle and the *dikr* begins to improvise on a beautiful song, with a slow rhythm, to which those present respond with a forward and backward movement of their bodies, accompanying the song with the repeated phrase *La ilaha illa Allah*, their cheeks inflame, their eyes close or open wide-eyed and staring. The rhythm becomes more accentuated; suddenly, simultaneously, all spring to their feet and the chanted phrase is reduced to simply *Llah*. The fakirs grow more excited and begin to dance, cries uttered on all sides. The excitement grows, all are sweating, turbans unroll, heads are thrown back and haggard eyes are turned upwards, blinded by an ineffable light, drunken with the verses of the chant. Breathing becomes heavier and more urgent, yet all is perfectly ordered and rhythmic. The singer cries 'Houwa! houwa! (he is in me) and all tremble while a smile embellishes all faces. Legs tremble. Finally all collapse in a state of total annihilation.[64]

In 1858 a correspondent to a French weekly described an event that took place each Friday, at three in the afternoon, at the tomb of the marabout Sidi-

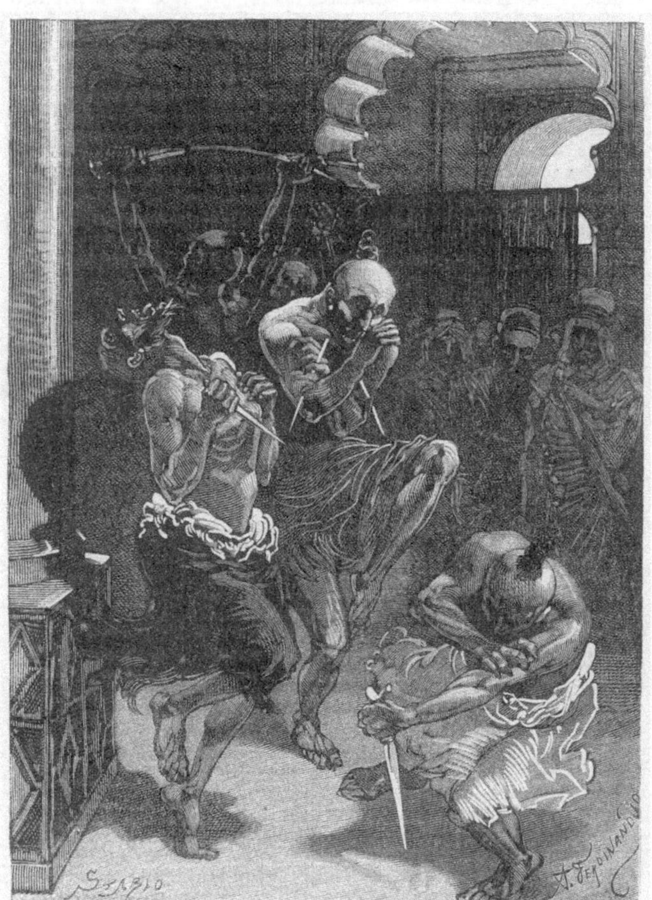

Fanatics at Kairouan, Tunisia, feel no pain as they mutilate their bodies. (Ferdinand, Remedes de la Bonne Femme)

Bou-Annâba, in a cemetery in the rue des Zouaves at Constantine, Algeria. A group of the Aïssoua sect arrived and commenced a sacred dance to the sound of a tambourine, accompanied with a religious chant. At first it was no more than a rhythmic step; gradually the pace quickened, to culminate in leaping and convulsive contortions:

This is when the overexcitement of the sectarians explodes in unexplained, if not inexplicable feats. Some pierce their cheeks with little iron skewers, others swallow the most abrasive objects, the most dangerous substances, nails, tessera of pots, powdered glass; some, turning their mouths into furnaces, fill them with glowing coals; the least carried away chew on Barbary fig leaves with their thousands of prickles.

These feats are nevertheless the most commonplace, the simplest. On solemn feast days, you will see these fanatics pierce themselves with yataghan and dagger, strike themselves with spades and bars of iron made red-hot in braziers, eat scorpions and play with the most dreaded serpents, provoking them to bite. Yet it is rare that any of them succumbs to these murderous practices. All emerge safe and sound from these terrible ordeals, during which death in its most implacable form menaces them.[65]

French anthropologist Philippe de Félice witnessed a demonstration by the Aïssoua in Algeria:

After partaking kif [cannabis] they begin chanting. They make movements of their body which become more and more precipitated. Their heads are thrown back and forward, forward and back so violently that you would think them separated from their bodies, joined only by skin and soft flesh. This is the ischdeb, their "dance" particular to them, if such contortions merit the word. Their eyes become haggard, their mouths froth, they seem completely mad.

Then begins the unbelievable feats for which they and some other sects are famous. These demented creatures are presented with knives and daggers, with which they pierce their arms and cheeks, without a drop of blood flowing from the wounds. Then they are offered dishes on which are scorpions and grey vipers. They throw themselves on these creatures and devour them. They eat cactus leaves, and glass lamps. This singular repast is followed by the fire ordeal. They walk barefoot on burning coals, and the smell of burnt flesh rises.

Then one, after taking off some of his clothes, leans against a sword with two handles held by two of his comrades. He lies down in such a way that his head hangs to one side, his legs to another, so that his whole body is pressing down on the sword blade. To increase the pressure, one companion climbs onto his back. Yet when the man stands up again, there is only a long red line on his skin. Another kneels, takes a huge nail and hammers it into the back of his own skull. One of us, asked to pull it out again with pincers, has to make a great effort to withdraw it, which he does while the man gives an unforgettable grimace of pain.

It will be objected that I and my companions were the victims of trickery. While it is possible, I have to say that our hosts invited us at every moment to test for ourselves. We examined the live scorpions and snakes. We felt the sharpness of the blades. We saw inside the mouth of the glass-swallower, where there was no sign of bleeding, suggesting that the flow of blood had been temporarily stopped. And the same may apply to the wounds they inflicted on themselves, none of which resulted in bleeding.

> Could we have been the victims of hallucination? None of us at any time lost full awareness, and I observed everything that happened with lucidity as if observing a scientific experiment. Therefore I accept the testimony of my eyes, even though I admit my inability to explain what I saw.[66]

Similar practices take place in Iran, where Sufi mysticism accompanies the practices of the Shi'ite schismatics. In the month of Moharram is celebrated the "Day of Blood" at Tehran, where half a million men dressed in white robes process through the streets, their heads covered with ashes, abandoning themselves to an ecstasy of mourning for Imam Husain, murdered in 680, regarded by Shi'ites as the true successor of the Prophet. For several days they torture and mutilate their bodies and even indulge in group suicide. An early 20th century account:

> With the encouragement of their companions, and excited by the contagion of the crowd, they seize the swords handed to them. Then their excitement becomes deadly, they whirl round and round waving the weapons over their heads. Their cries dominate those of the crowd. To enable them to withstand what they are about to suffer, they must have arrived at a state of catalepsy. They step forwards and back, from side to side, like automata, without any apparent command. At each step, rhythmically, they strike their heads with their sabres. Blood flows. Their white robes turn scarlet. The sight of this blood completes the disarray of their brains. Some of these voluntary martyrs collapse, hacking with their sabres this way and that: red froth flows from their clenched jaws. In their frenzy they sever veins and arteries, and die on the spot, before the police have time to carry them to the first-aid station installed behind the closed front of a shop.
>
> The crowd, regardless of the blows of the police, close round these men and drag them to another part of town where they continue their massacre. There's not a person in the crowd who is conscious of what he is doing. Those who are not taking part offer sustaining drinks and drugs to those who are. The martyrs strip off their shirts, now sacred relics, and give them to others. Many who hadn't intended to participate, in the general agitation become thirsty for blood. They demand weapons, tear off their clothes, wound themselves this way and that. If someone falls, the crowd closes over him, kicking or treading him with their feet. Is there a more beautiful death than to die on the day of Achourah, when the gates of eight paradises are wide open for the holy ones, to which each man yearns to go? The soldiers, commanded to keep order, are overtaken with the excitement, strip off their uniforms and join in the massacre. The hallucination overtakes even the children; near a well, a woman, drunken with pride, hugs her child who has just mutilated himself. Another comes running, who has gouged out one of his eyes; a moment later, he has deprived himself of the second; his parents look at him with joy.[67]

Similar practices are found in India. In 1985, a visitor to Ahmadabad during the Muharram festival found the streets filled with more than 150 thousand chanting spectators. Among them were groups of frenetic dancers, many with their cheeks and tongues transfixed with skewers, their bodies streaming with blood as they lashed their backs with whips and chains. Others would grab hot embers from a fire pit and hurl them among the crowd. Interestingly, many Hindus take part in these practices alongside the Muslims.[68]

COMMENT: There is a striking parallel with the CONVULSIONNAIRES DE SAINT-MEDARD, albeit occurring in a totally different cultural context. There too, individuals were able to inflict upon themselves the most fearsome injuries with little or no pain, and with no lasting ill effect. In both cases, moreover, the participants derived immense satisfaction from their ordeal. The author of the 1858 account compares the two, saying of both that they present "an ensemble of phenomena before which science is left silent, when it doesn't hide its inability to explain in an outright denial." While it is possible that a certain amount of legerdemain is involved in some instances, the greater part of the phenomena are unquestionably genuine and remain equally unexplained by conventional science. Philippe de Félice suggests that anesthesia may be induced in part by drugs, in part by excitement. There is a clear parallel with the "non-hurtful pain" such as that experienced in drug-induced states. (See ALTERED STATES OF CONSCIOUSNESS.)

A parallel can also be drawn with the SUICIDE BOMBERS of the late 20th/early 21st century who willingly give their lives in a political cause, having been instructed that this is Allah's will, and with the promise of Paradise before them.

See also: ASSASSINS.

ISLAMIC SYMBOLS OVER MALAYSIA

Klang: July 29, 1992

On the night of July 29, 1992, beginning at about 11 o'clock, some 200 students and a female instructor at the Hishamuddin Secondary Islamic School in Klang, State of Selangor, reported witnessing a variety of "miraculous" sights in the sky during a five-hour period. This included the word Allah (God) in Jawi script (Arabic writing, the original language of the Koran), followed by the appearance of a fetus in the womb, women with their aurat exposed (body parts which must be covered according to Islamic custom), and two dead bodies. A total of 26 images were reported. The following evening, July 30th at about 6:50 p.m., the words "Allah" and "Muhammad" reportedly appeared in Jawi script while all of the students were praying in a school field. Unlike the first episode, this time the script was said to be much larger. During both episodes, the images were reportedly formed in, on, or by clouds. There are no known photographs or video tape recordings of the reported events, but based on an investigation by Dr. Jariah Abdullah of the Chemistry Department at The University of Kebangsaan Malaysia, 26 drawings of the perceived images were made by students.[69]

In reviewing the Klang episode, we are left with eyewitness testimony, which is insufficient scientifically acceptable evidence that something miraculous occurred.[70] Known sociological and psychological processes can explain the Klang sightings. This is consistent with research on perceptual psychology, the branch of the behavioral sciences that deals with how people perceive and process information. There is a consensus among perceptual and social psychologists that observers tend to interpret information patterns in a particular manner – and these patterns are significantly influenced by their mental set at the time. In this regard, it is important to understand the context of the sightings.

The Islamic Crisis

The "miracle" coincided with a flurry of reports, beginning in about 1990 and involving mostly Muslims, of the appearance of Islamic symbols, most typically Arabic Jawi script, in a variety of countries and settings. For example, on June 12, 1990, in Algeria, the Islamic Salvation Front Party won an upset election victory. While the party leader was speaking to a crowd of supporters who were standing and shouting, "Allah Akhbar" ("God is great!"), in the direction of Mecca (the Muslim Holy Land), a cloud reportedly formed the shape of the word Allah in Jawi letters. There was great excitement and people fainted and wept.[71] In 1990, there were many reports of Arabic script appearing in eggplant (referred to in some countries as egg fruit or aubergine). For instance, in Nottingham, England, during March, Islamic accountant Hussain Bhatti cut open an eggplant and was convinced it contained Jawi script. In another case, Farida Kassam of Leicester, England, reported that the seeds had formed a pattern that was similar to "Yah-Allah" ("God is everywhere") or "Ya-Allah" ("God exists").[72]

CONTEXT: During times of extreme excitement, joy, crisis, anxiety, or uncertainty individuals and groups often see what they want to see in an unconscious attempt to seek psychological comfort and security, or to reconfirm expectant fears. During the 1980s, two Islamic countries, Iran and Iraq, fought an ongoing war that was divisive to the Islamic community. Further exacerbating this situation was the military coalition of Muslim and Western countries that was formed in 1991 in order to regain the sovereignty of Kuwait after its occupation by Iraq. Additionally, there have been great challenges and adversities faced by Muslims in Bosnia-Herzegovina and in parts of the former Soviet Union. Under such circumstances, Islamic individuals and groups may have been susceptible to misperceiving ordinarily mundane events and circumstances relative to their specific beliefs, and hence, Muslim-related. In regards to the Klang "miracle," it is significant that the students were all Islamic, were attending an Islamic school, and were returning from receiving Islamic instruction. Furthermore, the two episodes occurred in nocturnal settings involving ambiguous objects (clouds) at a distance. So it is not surprising, given the aforementioned circumstances, that clouds should be interpreted according to their view of the world.

At least 26 drawings of the pictographs were made by the students. These included a human body, a red-colored eye like a person who is very angry, and a long tongue that appeared to be cut into pieces. The observer said the tongue pieces then appeared to merge and form a whole tongue again. This happened three times. Another picture was described as follows: a woman was running and her hair was flowing or pulled, then the hair caught fire and burned. The face then changed into that of an ugly animal that was screaming from pain (the movement of the mouth appeared like it was in pain). The face then turned into a skeleton and the hair became stiff. Other students described what was interpreted as the flapping wing of a bird; a female with a pig face; a scorpion; a big snake with shiny eyes; a man with a dark dog's head; two people arguing, then shaking hands; a man wearing a turban and bowing towards the Ka'ba in Mecca, praying with his forehead touching the floor; a Malaysian map upside down with Singapore on the top, then focusing on the map of Singapore only; a liquor bottle; a cross which changed into a dome; a cooked chicken; a fish; a map of Saudi Arabia; a tombstone; a bird; and a hand trying to reach for something but unable to get it, with a round mark appearing on the palm.

COMMENT: This variety of eyewitness testimony testifies to the subjective nature of the sightings.

ITALIAN FATIGUE OUTBREAK

Italy: 1978

During October 1978, an epidemic of malaise and fatigue swept through an Italian electro-mechanical plant, affecting 427 of 5,000 workers. Most of those affected were female. Complaints included headache, dizziness, skin and eye irritation, dry mouth, bad mouth taste, stomach pain, itching, and general weakness. A few workers passed out. The outbreak was triggered when a female assembly worker suddenly felt faint. Within moments, "other female workers from areas scattered all over the plant also began to feel weak and slumped to the floor."[73] As a result, the plant was forced to close. After a preliminary investigation of the premises was negative, the plant was soon reopened. Within a few hours of resuming work, dozens of employees, almost all of them female, began to exhibit similar symptoms as in the first incident, and their plant was again shut down. After two more unsuccessful attempts to restart production, management decided to close the facility and thoroughly clean the workplace. Extensive environmental testing was negative and some medical personnel described the building air quality as "like mountain air."[74]

CONTEXT: The episode occurred amid an atmosphere of poor worker-management relations. After interviewing and examining each of the affected workers, most were unhappy with their level of job stress; they complained about the excessively repetitious nature of their work, mental fatigue and monotony, and production pressures.[75]

Treatment consisted of separating the most severely affected from the rest of the group by providing hospital treatment in a nearby town and reassuring workers of "the benign nature of the epidemic."[76] Within two weeks of the initial report of symptoms, the plant reopened after an agreement between the union and management. Despite occasional, isolated reports of mild malaise over the next few months, production remained on schedule.

ITCHING AND RASH FRENZIES

Princeton University historian Elaine Showalter notes that mysterious itching and rashes are well documented in the archives of history. "The skin is extremely vulnerable to emotion and stress, as seen in blushing, flushing, hives or eczema – and itching, like yawning, is a notoriously suggestible symptom."[77] Such episodes fall under the category of short-lived MASS ANXIETY HYSTERIA, triggered by the perception of exposure to a potentially threatening agent that can affect the skin.

Outbreaks of mass psychogenic itching and rash have been reported in school and occupational settings (see MASS HYSTERIA IN WORK SETTINGS). The symptoms exhibited typically mirror the perceived threat. For instance, skin rashes develop in work settings where it is believed employees come into contact with a potentially offending agent. Examples include reports of itching and rash among ceramic and textile workers in the United Kingdom during the 1970s and 80s that was attributed to mass hysteria.[78]

Typically the index case (the first subject affected) draws considerable attention to their symptoms, and soon fellow workers exhibit similar symptoms. Between May and June of 1978, an outbreak of psychogenic itching and rash near Leeds, England, was investigated by dermatologist W. J. Cunliffe, who was asked to examine eight male tool operators (ages 18-

53) at a nearby unidentified job setting. They were so concerned with a recent outbreak of skin problems that they considered quitting their jobs unless the trouble could be stopped. The workers were convinced that the different cutting oils, which commonly got on their skin, were the offending agent. After working with the same oil for several years, they noticed that their skin problems developed soon after changing to a new oil. The symptoms began with an employee who had a long-standing case of eczema, which coincidentally flared up at the time of the oil change. This initial high profile incident resulted in co-workers examining their skin for possible problems, whereupon they found itchy spots on their back and chest. A dermatological examination revealed that "all had acne, commensurate with their age and past history of acne." Dr. Cunliffe noted that the symptoms quickly subsided after "frank discussion with the management and with the men as individuals as well as a unit."[79]

CONTEXT: Outbreaks of itching and rash are triggered by anxiety and suggestion, incubated in an atmosphere of plausibility, and almost exclusively involve students or workers who believe they have been exposed to an agent that can cause such symptoms.

The most commonly reported episodes occur in schoolchildren (also see, MASS HYSTERIA IN SCHOOLS). A classic example occurred at 9:15 a.m. on February 22, 1982, when two 4th grade girls at a rural elementary school in West Virginia, complained of severe itching and rash.[80] By noon 32 students were affected, and by the time new cases stopped breaking out the next day, 57 of 159 total students were affected. Medical exams and tests of air, water, and food were negative, as was a thorough examination of school grounds. Investigators found that symptoms spread by word of mouth, with the highest attack rates occurring among the younger, more impressionable, children. After the initial two cases, subsequent symptoms usually began with an itching sensation after learning of a previous case, and only then did the rash appear – and only on parts of the body that were easily assessable to the hands (forearms, abdomen, neck, shoulders, middle and lower back). Investigating physicians noted that during exams, "children were actively scratching, and the rash distribution was noted to change. Several children who were surreptitiously observed a half hour after the interview exhibited no scratching, and their rash disappeared."[81] The rash disappeared when students left the school or during recess, and returned once they were back inside the building. The school's small size and high pupil interaction rate in the halls appear to have contributed to the outbreak. Girls were affected more by a ratio of almost 3 to 1. Symptoms gradually diminished over about 20 days.

Sometimes reports appear in the media but are not thoroughly investigated by medical authorities, and while the exact cause may never be known, the episodes are strongly suggestive of psychosomatic illness. One such example occurred in June of 1984, as an itching frenzy was reported in the Malaysian state of Kuala Terengganu. The episode swept through 15 members of a class of eight-year-old female students for half an hour.[82]

South Africa

Another typical case occurred in South Africa between February 14 and 25, 2000, when an outbreak of itching was reported among students at schools in Free State Province. A total of 1,430 mostly female pupils were affected at 13 schools located in the townships of Mangaung and Heidedal. It is likely that the itching occurred in other schools, but they were not studied.[83] Most of those involved were in grades 8, 9, and 10, though a small number of primary school students also reported itching. Students would report itching upon entering the school grounds; only a tiny fraction said that the itching continued when they returned home. A small number of instructors, mostly women, also reported itching. The itching never persisted for more than a few hours in any student, and the average length of a school outbreak was six days. Prominent folk theories blamed Satanism and claims that some boys had sprinkled itching powder in the girl's toilet.

Interviews and questionnaires determined that the spread of symptoms occurred primarily via line of sight after observing others scratching. The typical pupil reported that they felt a rush of hot air over their body just prior to the itch, often followed by hyperventilation, headache, tingling of the limbs, light-headedness, and chest tightness. Students were treated with antihistamines, given Calamine lotion, or bathed in Jeyes Fluid (an antiseptic).

Investigators could find no organic or toxicological cause, and while entomologists found book lice, it was concluded that they could not have been responsible for the symptoms. To reassure students and anxious parents, the school buildings were fumigated. The episode quickly ceased when the school reopened and the principals followed strict guidelines that called for any new cases to be sent home. They were not allowed back in school until their itching sensations subsided.

The "Bin Laden Itch"

Between October 2001 and June 3, 2002, a mysterious skin rash affecting thousands of mainly primary schoolchildren in dozen of schools was reported at widely separated locations in 27 states of the United States and parts of Canada.[84] The rashes persisted from a few hours to 14 days and were not accompanied by other symptoms. There was no evidence that the skin rash could be spread from person to person.[85] According to the Centers for Disease Control and Prevention (CDC), the rashes appeared to be different kinds with different causes. "With 53 million young people attending 117,000 schools each school day in the United States, it is expected that rashes from a wide range of causes will be observed. Environmental factors or infectious agents can cause rashes among groups of school-aged children. Rashes caused by infectious agents usually are preceded or accompanied by symptoms such as headache or fever. However, in these reports, none of the children showed signs of systemic illness, and the rash appeared to be self-limiting."[86] Health officials have ruled out the possibility of environmental causes, with the exception of one school that had high levels of skin and dust particles. CDC physicians stated that an infectious agent was improbable, as such agents are typically associated with fever or headache, but "in these reports, none of the children showed signs of systemic illness, and the rash appeared to be self-limiting."[87]

The rash of rashes began during the post-September 11th ANTHRAX SCARE. While it's likely that these skin conditions always existed within the school system, during the bio-terror scare students were paying more attention to their skin and school nurses were more likely to report such incidents. Dry skin and itching are notorious during the winter months in the U.S., as people spend more time indoors and the air is typically dry due to cold Canadian air masses and the use of heating systems.

CDC officials stated that among the various potential causes of rashes are those with environmental origins, such as bacteria and fungi, physical agents like fiberglass, chemical agents such as pesticides and cleaning products, allergens, and insect bites.[88] In a few cases, students faked the rash by rubbing themselves with sandpaper in an effort to close the school.[89]

Sources

1. Bouflet, Joachim (1991). *Encyclopédie des Phénomènes Extraordinaires dans la vie Mystique: Tome I: Phénomènes Objectifs*. Paris: F. X. de Guibert (L'Oeil), p. 290.
2. Don Felice Astolfi *Historia Universale*, 1624, quoted by Saintyves, P. (1912a). *Les Reliques et les Images. Volume 1.* Légendaires. Paris: Mercure de France, p. 85; also Marchetti, D. Jean [Giovanni] (1799). *Memoires Concernant les Prodiges Arrivés à Rome dans Plusieurs Images, Particulièrement de la T[rès] S[ainte] Vierge.* [French translation of the original Italian, 1707] Hildesheim: Schlegel, p. xl.
3. Marchetti, op cit., p. xiv.
4. Marchetti, op cit., p. 62.
5. Marchetti, op cit., pp. xvii, 48-49.
6. Marchetti, op cit., pp. 50-51.
7. Marchetti, op cit., pp. viii-ix.
8. Marchetti, op cit., p. xxv.
9. Saintyves, op cit., p. 91.
10. Kleist, Baron von (1922). *The Wonderful Crucifix of Limpias* [original German, translated by E F Reeve]. London: Burns Oates & Washbourne, p. 14.
11. Kleist, op cit., pp. 144-145.
12. Thurston, Herbert (1934). *Beauraing and Other Apparitions.* London: Burns Oates & Washbourne, pp. 50-52.
13. Toibin, Colm (1985). *Seeing Is Believing.* Mountrath, Eire: Pilgrim Press; Beer, Lionel (1986). *The Moving Statue of Ballinspittle and Related Phenomena.* London: Spacelink. Details are taken from these two sources unless otherwise indicated.
14. Beer, op cit., p. 15.
15. Peter Kellner in Tobin, op cit., p. 31.
16. Eamonn McCann in Tobin, op cit., p. 36.
17. Tobin, op cit., p. 7 and passim.
18. "Les Miracles," special issue of *Historia* (magazine) 394 bis: Paris 1979, p. 81.

19. Tatsuya, Shimura (1985). *La Vierge Marie Pleure au Japon.* Hauteville, Switzerland: Parvis.
20. *Sunday News* (New Zealand) 9 July 1967.
21. Carlson, Shawn, quoted in Broch Broch, Henri (1992). *Au Coeur de L'extraordinaire.* Bordeaux: L'horizon Chimérique, p. 296.
22. Marchetti, op cit., p. xvi.
23. Marchetti, op cit., pp. 13-28.
24. Amin, Y., Hamdi, E., and Eapen, V. (1997). "Mass Hysteria in an Arab Culture." *The International Journal of Social Psychology* 43(4):303-306.
25. Philip, Catherine (2002). "'Killer Alien' Sparks Panic Riots in India." *The Australian*, August 21, p. 10.
26. Waldman, Amy (2002). "Seeing and Believing." *New York Times*, August 25, p. 10.
27. Waldman, op cit.
28. Philip, op cit.
29. Philip, op cit.
30. Editorial. "The Next Strange Thing." *Indian Express*, August 21, 2002.
31. Editorial, op cit.
32. Editorial, op cit.
33. "'Witch' Causes Mass Hysteria." March 18, 2005. News 24.com, accessed May 1, 2005 at: http://www.news24.com/News24/World/News/0,,2-10-1462_1678524,00.html.
34. Rawe, Julie, Allbritton, Christopher, Baughn, Alice Jackson, and Richards, Constance E. (2004). "Mutiny on The Convoy?" *Time*, October 25, 2004, p. 24; Babbin, Jed (2004). "From Mare Island to Tallil. Will the Army Prosecute Mutineers?" National Review Online, accessed November 5, 2004 at: http://www.nationalreview.com/babbin/babbin 2004101908 35.asp.
35. Tyson, Ann Scott (2004). "Defiance in Iraq: Orders Refused." *The Christian Science Monitor*, October 18.
36. Carter, Phillip (2004). "The Reserve Mutiny. How the Iraq War is Crippling the Army Reserve." October 18, 2004, accessed November 5, 2004 at: http://slate.msn.com/id/2108357.
37. Carter (2004). op cit.
38. Carter (2004). op cit.
39. Hamby, Joel E. (2002). "The Mutiny Wagon Wheel: a Leadership Model for Mutiny in Combat." *Armed Forces & Society: An Interdisciplinary Journal* (Summer 2002) 28(4).
40. Zimbardo, Philip G. (2004). 'Slide Show.' Accessed July 27, 2004 at: http://www.zimbardo.com/zimbardo.html (Philip G. Zimbardo's Homepage). See also: Haney, Craig, Banks, Curtis, and Zimbardo, Philip (1973a). "A Study of Prisoners and Guards in a Simulated Prison." *Naval Research Reviews* 9, 1-17 (September). Washington, DC: Office of Naval Research; Haney, Craig, Banks, Curtis, and Zimbardo, Philip (1973b). "Interpersonal dynamics in a simulated prison." *International Journal of Criminology and Penology* (1):69-97.
41. "How Psychology Can Help Explain The Iraqi Prisoner Abuse." Special Fact Sheet on the Prison Abuse Scandal issued by the Office of Public Communications, American Psychological Association Washington, DC and published on the Association's website, accessed July 28, 2004 at: http://www.apa.org/pubinfo /prisonerabuse.html. Psychologists Philip Zimbardo, Brett Pelham and Steven J. Breckler contributed their expertise to the Fact Sheet.
42. Stannard, Matthew B. (2004). "Stanford Experiment Foretold Iraq Scandal 'Inmates' Got Abused in Psychology Study." *San Francisco Chronicle*, May 8, p. A15.
43. Stannard (2004). op cit.
44. Milgram, Stanley (1974). *Obedience to Authority.* New York: Harper and Row; Milgram, Stanley, Reinert, J. (1970). "Would you Obey a Hitler?" *Science Digest* 67:34-39 (May); Milgram, Stanley (1970). "If Hitler asked you to Electrocute a Stranger, Would You?" *Esquire* 73:72-73 (February).
45. Taylor, Guy (2002a). "Irradiated-mail Health Woes 'Mass Hysteria,' Officials Say." *Washington Times*, January 30, p. 1. Quotations taken from the January 30 article. See also: Taylor, Guy (2002b). "Rumors Spread Hysteria Epidemic." *The Washington Times*, January 12, 2002, p. 8.
46. Lortie, Bret (2002). "The Envelope, Please." *Bulletin of the Atomic Scientists*, 58(6):9-10 (November-December).
47. Lortie, op cit.
48. Taylor, op cit., 2002a, 2002b.
49. Lortie, op cit.
50. The principal sources for this entry are Blunt, John Henry (1874). *Dictionary of Sects, Heresies, Ecclesiastical Parties and Schools of Religious Thought.* London, Oxford & Cambridge: Rivingtons; Oxley, William (1889). *Modern Messiahs and Wonder Workers.* London: Trubner.
51. Oxley, op cit., p. 54.
52. M'Kerrell (1831). *Apology for the Gift of Tongues* quoted by Blunt, op cit., p. 229.
53. Oxley, op cit., p. 55.
54. Warfield, Benjamin B. (1918). *Counterfeit Miracles.* New York: Charles Scribner's Sons, p. 141.
55. Pilkington's *Unknown Tongues* quoted by Blunt, p. 230.
56. Baxter, op cit., p. 1833.
57. Thomas Carlyle, quoted in Cutten, George Barton (1927). *Speaking with Tongues: Historically and Psychologically Considered.* New Haven, Connecticut: Yale University Press, p. 98.
58. *The Times*, quoted in Cutten 100.
59. Baxter, op cit., pp. 134-135.
60. Oxley, op cit., p. 52.
61. Warfield, op cit., p. 153.
62. Félice, Philippe de (1947). *Foules en Délire.* Paris: Albin, p. 149.
63. Dupont and Coppelani, quoted by Félice, op cit., pp. 155-156.
64. Unnamed correspondent, Félice, op cit., p. 159.
65. Léo de Bernard, in *Le Monde Illustré*, 16 January 1858.
66. Félice, op cit., pp. 163-165.
67. Quoted in Félice, op cit., p. 170.
68. Cardoza, Rod, "The Ordeal of Muharram," in *Natural History* (September 1990).
69. Abdullah, J. (Undated). *A Report of the Interview with the Female Teacher and Students at the Hishamuddin Secondary Islamic School, Klang.* Confidential Report: The Author; Bartholomew, R. E. (1993). *Miracle or Mass Delusion: What Happened in Klang, Malaysia?* A study compiled for Pusat Islam, The Prime Minister's Department, Kuala Lumpur, Malaysia.
70. By miraculous, we mean the occurrence of an incident which is beyond the known natural laws of physics.
71. *The Daily Telegraph*, June 16, 1990.
72. See, *The Best of the Fortean Times* edited by Adam Sisman. New York: Avon Books, 1992, p. 63.
73. Magnavita, N. (2000). "Industrial Mass Psychogenic Illness: The Unfashionable Diagnosis." *The British Journal of Medical Psychology* 73(3):371-375 (September), p. 372.
74. Magnavita, op cit., p. 372.
75. Magnavita, op cit., p. 372.
76. Magnavita, op cit., p. 373.
77. Showalter, Elaine (2002). "Scratching the Bin Laden Itch." *New Statesman* (July 29) (131):12. Showalter, op cit.

78. Cunliffe, W.J. (1978). "Psychic Possession Among Industrial Workers." Letter. *Lancet* ii, 44; Maguire, A. (1978). "Psychic Possession Among Industrial Workers." Letter. *Lancet* i, 376-78; Ilchyshyn, A., and Smith, A.G. (1985). "Gum Arabic Sensitivity with Epidemic Hysteria Dermatologica." *Contact Dermatitis* 13:282-283.
79. Cunliffe, op cit.
80. Robinson, P., Szewczyk, M., Haddy, L., Jones, P., and Harvey, W. (1984). "Outbreak of Itching and Rash." *Archives of Internal Medicine* 144:1959-1962.
81. Robinson, op cit., p. 1960.
82. "15 Pupils Hit by Mystery Itch." *The New Straits Times* (Kuala Lumpur, Malaysia), June 6 1984.
83. Rataemane, S.T., Rataemane, L.U.Z., and Mohlahle, J. (2002). "Mass Hysteria Among Learners at Mangaung Schools in Bloemfontein, South Africa." *International Journal of Psychosocial Rehabilitation* 6:61-67.
84. No authors listed. (2002). "Update: Rashes Among Schoolchildren–27 States, October 4, 2001-June 3, 2002." *Morbidity and Mortality Weekly Report* (Center for Disease Control, Atlanta) (2002). 51(24):524-52) (June 21), posted on the CDC website without specific page numbers at: http://www.cdc.gov/mmwr/preview/mmwrhtml/mm5108a1.htm; No authors listed. (2002). "Rashes Among Schoolchildren–14 States, October 4, 2001-February 27, 2002." *Morbidity and Mortality Weekly Report* (Center for Disease Control, Atlanta) 51(8):161-4 (March 1), posted on the CDC website without specific page numbers at: http://www.cdc.gov/mmwr/preview/mmwrhtml/mm5108a1.htm
85. Ibid.
86. "Rashes Among Schoolchildren–14 States, October 4, 2001-February 27, 2002." op cit.
87. "Rashes Among Schoolchildren–14 States, October 4, 2001-February 27, 2002." op cit.
88. "Rashes Among Schoolchildren–14 States, October 4, 2001-February 27, 2002." op cit.
89. Bartholomew, Robert E., and Radford, Benjamin (2002). "Rash of Mysterious Rashes may be Linked to Mass Hysteria." *Skeptical Inquirer* 26(3):8.

JACA POSSESSION FESTIVAL

Spain: 1881

In the ancient town of Jaca in the Spanish Pyrenees, the annual feast of Orosia, its patron saint, on June 25, was traditionally the occasion for remarkable scenes in and around the cathedral. On this day in 1881, a Spanish doctor, José Reig y Gasco, was present at the festival and observed scenes resembling the demonic possession cases of the 17th century. This entry is based on his report.[1]

CONTEXT: The festival, held every year, was attended by Spanish and French peasants from the surrounding countryside, a mountainous region. They were ignorant, illiterate, extremely superstitious, and very attached to their religious practices (Roman Catholic). They were brought up to attribute misfortunes of every kind to the devices of the Devil or the spells of sorcerers. This was matched by the strength of their devotion to the Church, which to them represented the only power that could withstand the forces of evil.

On this day peasants from the surrounding countryside crowded into the town and thronged into the chapel of the cathedral to pay their respects to the image of the saint. Most of them were in search of a remedy for their ailments. Processions accompanied by dancers and musicians took place throughout the day, culminating in a "sacred festival" in the cathedral. Then those who wished would spend the night in the cathedral, where dancers performed before the image of the saint. The tumult was tremendous and order difficult to maintain. An old book prescribed that "to avoid indecent rites in so sacred a place, the vicar-general and the priests must make periodic rounds of the church." Many groups formed in the chapel of Santa Orosia, which was splendidly decorated and bright with light. It is here that exorcisms took place and miraculous healings were alleged to occur.

Among those who came hoping for a cure, the convulsionaries and those who believed themselves possessed by demons formed the greatest number. Unusually, the men outnumbered the women. Any number of conditions could bring on this state: the onset of puberty, genital disorders, excessive impressionability, worry, overwork, fear, jealousy, unrequited love, or lack of affection. Any of these, reinforced by intense piety that often amounted to excessive devotion, could result in periodic seizures, which were invariably blamed on the actions of malevolent demons. Among associated symptoms that presented were hyperesthesia of the skin, in which the gentlest touch or the slightest pressure of any kind of object irritated the afflicted person. But in some cases this hypersensitivity alternated with the reverse, analgesia, where the patient lost all feeling. Sometimes this was accompanied by other forms of sensory loss. The individual would lose his sense of taste, of smell, of hearing, or his eyesight would become "tired" and his eyes took on a fixed look.

The onset of seizures was announced by a general feeling of malaise, pain in the legs, waves of heat with the face going red, a sense of oppression, palpitations, cramps, and strange internal sensations. This led to jerking in the arms and legs, which in turn led on to full convulsions, cramps, and contractions that seemed to affect every muscle in the body, the facial muscles in particular, twitching and giving them a very strange appearance. Bloody froth even appeared at the mouth. Afflicted persons would utter spasmodic laughing, crying, and howling, together with groans of despair. They moved their arms and legs incessantly, clenching and unclenching the fists, and striking the ground fiercely with their feet. Then some would sink into an ecstatic or cataleptic state where they lost all feeling, lying motionless, oblivious to the tumult around them, for a considerable time.

To cope with those who claimed to be possessed by demons, the priests would customarily perform exorcisms or conjurations of the demon, reciting prayers and sprinkling the afflicted person's entire body with holy water. Additional succor was provided by members of religious fraternities, who sought to help the afflicted person by holding out sticks at the end of which was an iron crucifix to be kissed. Women, usually elderly, applied chaplets (strings of prayer beads) to the body of the patient, striking them so vigorously that they almost amounted to flagellations. Before the conjuration, the patient would attach slippers, sandals, or cords to his hands, as a kind of defensive magic. At the height of his seizure, the patient was asked how many demons he had within him, and by what part of his body he wanted them to be expelled. Usually he answered, by the hands or feet. Then he would cry out louder than ever, his convulsions growing more violent, until the shoes on his feet or on his hands were shaken off. This was taken as the sign that a demon had been expelled, to the great wonder of the spectators who would often go into contortions themselves, crying out loud. Their howls, joined with the sound of music and dancing and the songs of the pilgrims, made an infernal bacchanal, which in Dr. Gasco's opinion contributed to the spread of the malady among the spectators.

Eventually, after these rites, the afflicted persons were left exhausted and drained, their bodies covered with perspiration. They would fall into a prostration that was generally the precursor of stupor or sleep.

COMMENT: It is clear from Dr. Gasco's account that a considerable role-playing was involved in these seizures. The afflicted people knew, at some level of awareness, what was expected of them, and gave an appropriate performance. The attaching of footwear or cords to the hands was in itself a manifestly conscious act. Since the rites were conducted publicly, every one who witnessed them would be aware of the protocol if they should ever be afflicted in their turn.

The resemblance of the Santa Osoria seizures to those reported from many locations in the 17th century is striking. The same symptoms were manifesting in a quite different context, among people who could have no notion of what had taken place in French convents two hundred years previously. (See CONVENT HYSTERIA and cases such as LOUDUN.)

Dr. Gasco himself, and Paul Richer, a colleague of the French neurologist, Jean-Martin Charcot, who cites him in his classic work on La Grande Hystérie, believed these people to be truly sick. Whatever other ailments might be afflicting them, they were unquestionably victims of collective HYSTERIA.

JEWISH CONVERSION SYNDROME

Italy: 1554

An outbreak of hysteria afflicted eighty-two young girls of Jewish origin in an orphanage in Rome. Soon after their baptism, they suddenly suffered an attack that was at once diagnosed as possession by demons.[2]

CONTEXT: Most of the children were of Jewish birth and upbringing but had been converted to Christianity. Presumably they were constrained to do so as a condition of being taken into care, though this is not stated. If so, this would understandably have led to emotional stress with sentiments of guilt at renouncing their faith. The ceremony of baptism, formalizing their conversion, could have triggered the outbreak. The scenario is borne out by the statements made during their exorcism.

The Bishop of Paris, Cardinal de Gondy, was in Rome at this time, and on hearing of the outbreak, he sent a Benedictine monk from his entourage to exorcise the supposed demons. Unfortunately, according to Jean Bodin, a prominent French political philosopher turned witch hunter, Cardinal de Gondy met with no success despite six months of strenuous wrestling with the powers of darkness. This may be an indication of the violence of the children's sentiments, though it equally lends itself to the possibility that the exorcisms themselves perpetuated the outbreak by conferring on it the recognition of authority and by proposing an external cause – the Devil – who could be blamed for whatever was afflicting the children.

However, the exorcisms were successful in one respect. The Benedictine did manage to establish communication with the Evil One. When asked why he had possessed these girls, the Evil One replied that he had done so on behalf of the Jews who resented that these children, born in the Jewish faith, should have accepted Christian baptism.[3] It was surmised that Satan made this accusation in the hope that Pope Paul IV would have the Jews of Rome killed, and indeed the Pope was so vexed by the affair that he proposed to banish all the Jews from the city. But he was dissuaded from this course by a Jesuit advisor who argued that they could not be to blame, for no human being can send a devil into another person's body; this is something that only demons could do.[4]

Though Johann Weyer, an influential Dutch physician (also known as Jean Wier, Johannes Wier) and others mention the case, no description of the children's behavior is offered.[5] We are simply told that the attacks persisted over a period of two years.

COMMENT: It is understandable that among so many children, compelled to renounce their faith and adopt another, one or more might suffer an attack of self-reproach that might manifest in the form of a hysteric attack. In such an enclosed community, in which all shared the same trauma, the symptoms might well spread to the others.

See also: CONVENT HYSTERIA, DEMON POSSESSION.

JUMPERS

England, Wales, America: 18th to 20th Centuries

For a period of some two hundred years, jumping, as a form of worship, was practiced by Protestant Christians in the British Isles and the United States. To outside observers it seemed an extravagant display, an indecorous defiance of conventional reverence. To the jumpers themselves, however, this was not only an acceptable way in which to express adoration – they pointed to precedents in the Old Testament – but also a form of spiritual exaltation to its participants. To what extent the jumpers considered themselves a sect or movement is not easily discerned, but contemporary commentators did not hesitate to speak of the "Welsh Jumpers" as a coherent sect, and America's "Holy Jumpers" applied the term to themselves consciously.

CONTEXT: In its most specific form, jumping was associated with METHODISM and may have derived directly from the spontaneous manifestations occasioned by John Wesley's immensely effective preaching. In this context, it can be seen as a secession from the passivity of traditional religion, imposed by authoritarian establishment, and an active affirmation of the individual's unmediated relations with his god. The practice seems to have been confined to those classes of society to whom religion was virtually the only cultural activity, providing a basis of community life far stronger than political affairs or other group activities. It seems to have been fairly localized.

The Cornish Jumpers

The practice of jumping seems to have originated in Cornwall in the 1760s. One commentator traced the origin to an incident in a Methodist chapel at Redruth, when a member of the congregation, in the middle of the service, "cried out 'What shall I do to be saved?', manifesting the greatest uneasiness respecting the condition of his soul. Others cried out in the same form of words, and shortly after behaved as if afflicted with pain."

Word of these goings-on spread rapidly, and hun-

Welsh "Jumpers." (Nightingale's Religious Ceremonies)

dreds were attracted out of curiosity to see these afflicted persons, only to fall into the same state themselves. The chapel remained open for several days and nights, and almost at once similar behavior was reported not only in other neighboring towns in Cornwall, but also in small villages. However, it was confined to Methodist chapels, and "it seized none but people of the lowest education."

The outbreaks were invariably triggered by the original words "What must I do to be saved?" Those who succumbed seemed overcome by anguish and fell into convulsions; others cried out, like persons possessed, insisting that they saw Hell open to receive them. The clergy responded to their congregations by exhorting them to confess their sins and warned that those who resisted would be liable to eternal torment. This inflamed the over-excited congregation still further. Then, when he felt that his discourse had produced its full effect, the preacher held out the hope of salvation to those who repented, and then a remarkable reaction took place: now, those who were in convulsions felt they could hope to enjoy the wonderful freedom of the children of God. However, their convulsions continued, and "they remained, during this condition, so abstracted from every earthly thought, that they stayed two and sometimes three days and nights together in the chapels, agitated all the time by spasmodic movements, and taking neither repose nor nourishment."

According to contemporary estimates, some four thousand people were afflicted with "the convulsive malady," which was meticulously described by a contemporary observer:

> There came on at first a feeling of faintness, with rigour and a sense of weight at the pit of the stomach, soon after which, the patient cried out, as if in the agonies of death or the pains of labour. The convulsions then began, first showing themselves in the muscles of the eyelids, though the eyes themselves were fixed and staring. The most frightful contortions of the countenance followed, and the convulsions now took their course downwards, so that the muscles of the neck and trunk were affected, causing a sobbing respiration, which was performed with great effort. Tremors and agitation ensued, and the patients screamed out violently, and tossed their heads about from side to side. As the complaint increased, it seized the arms, and its victims beat their breasts, clasped their hands, and made all sorts of strange gestures. The observer who gives this account remarked that the lower extremities were in no instance affected. In some cases, exhaustion came on in a very few minutes, but the attack usually lasted much longer, and there were even cases in which it was known to continue for sixty or seventy hours. Many of those who happened to be seated when the attack commenced, bent their bodies rapidly backwards and forwards during its continuance, making a corresponding motion with their arms, like persons sawing wood. Others shouted aloud, leaped about, and threw their bodies into every possible posture, until they had exhausted their strength. Yawning took place at the commencement in all cases, but as the violence of the disorder increased, the circulation, and respiration became accelerated, so that the countenance assumed a swollen and puffed appearance. When exhaustion came on, patients usually fainted, and remained in a stiff and motionless state until their recovery. The disorder completely resembled the St. Vitus's dance, but the fits sometimes went on to an extraordinarily violent extent, so that the author of the account once saw a woman, who was seized with these convulsions, resist the endeavours of four or five strong men to restrain her. Those patients who did not lose their consciousness were in general made more furious by every attempt to quiet them by force, on which account they were in general suffered to continue unmolested until nature herself brought on exhaustion. Those affected complained, more or less, of debility, after the attacks, and cases sometimes occurred in which they passed into other disorders: thus some fell into a state of melancholy, which, however, in consequence of their religious ecstacy, was distinguished by the absence of fear and despair; and in one patient inflammation of the brain is said to have taken place. No sex or age was exempt from this epidemic malady. Children five years old and octogenarians were alike affected by it, and even men of the most powerful frame were subject to its influence. Girls and young women, however, were its most frequent victims.[6]

The Welsh Jumpers

Selena Lady Huntingdon was patron to a kind of Methodist sect that came to be known as the Countess of Huntingdon's Persuasion. Some of these went in for jumping. John Wesley, in 1774, heard an account of the Jumpers at Hay-on-Wye: "Some of them leaped up many times, men and women, several feet from the ground; they clapped their hands with the utmost violence; they shook their heads; they distorted all their features; they threw their arms and legs to and fro in all variety of postures; they sung, roared, shouted, screamed with all their might, to the no small terror of those that were near them. One gentlewoman told me she had not been herself since, and did not know when she should."[7]

Dr. Evans, about the year 1785, witnessed one of their meetings held in the open air, on a Sunday evening, near Newport in Monmouthshire on the Welsh border:

> The preacher concluded his sermon with the recommendation of jumping; and to allow him the praise of consistency, he got down from the chair on which he stood, and jumped along with them. The somewhat flimsy arguments produced to support this practice were citations from the scriptures in which leaping occurs, which were twisted into providing a reason for jumping. He expatiated on these topics with uncom-

mon fervency, then gave an impassioned sketch of the sufferings of the Saviour, and rousing the passions of a few around him into a state of violent agitation. About nine men and seven women, for some little time, rocked to and fro, groaned aloud, and then jumped with a kind of frantic fury. Some of the audience flew in all directions; others gazed on in silent amazement! They continued their exertions from eight in the evening to near eleven at night.[8]

The practice was still operating in the early 19th century. The Reverend Bingley reports that at a chapel in Caernarvon he more than once attended the chapel of "a singular branch of Calvinistical Methodists, who, from certain enthusiastical extravagancies which they exhibit in their religious meetings, are denominated *Jumpers*." The concluding hymn of their gatherings "consists only of a single strain, having but one verse which is repeated over and over, sometimes if their spirit of enthusiasm is much excited, for half an hour or even upwards of an hour."

It is sung once or twice over without any apparent effect. The first motion to be observed is that of the upper parts of their body from right to left. They then raise their hands, and often strike one hand violently against the other. Such is the effect produced even on strangers, that I confess whenever I have been among them at these times, my intellects became greatly confused: the noise of their groaning and singing, or oftentimes rather bellowing, the clapping of their hands, the beating of their feet against the ground, the excessive heat of the place, and the various motions on all sides of me, almost stupified my senses. The less enthusiastic move off soon after the hymn is begun, among these, every time I attended them, I observed the preacher to make one; he always threw a silk handkerchief over his head, and, descending from the pulpit, left his congregation to jump by themselves. At intervals the word "*gogoniant*" (praise or glory!) is frequently to be heard. The conclusion of this extravagance... has been described by one of their own countrymen with more justice than I am able to give to it. "The phrensy [sic] (he says) so far spreads, that to any observation made to them, they seem altogether insensible. Men and women indiscriminately cry and laugh, jump and sing, with the wildest extravagance imaginable. That their dress becomes deranged, or the hair dishevelled, is no longer an object of attention. And their raptures continue, till, spent with fatigue of mind and body, the women are frequently carried out in a state of apparent insensibility. In these scenes, indeed, the youthful part of the congregation are principally concerned, the more elderly generally contenting themselves in admiring, with devout gratitude, what they deem the operations of the spirit. Their exertions on these occasions are so violent, that were they often repeated in the week, the health of the people must be materially affected. When they leave the place, they often seem so much exhausted, as scarcely to be able to support the weight of their bodies, and the hardest labour they could be employed in would not so much waste the animal spirits, or weary their limbs, as an hour spent in this religious frenzy.

Besides these common meetings, they have their general assemblies, which are held twice or thrice in the year at Caernarvon, Pwllheli, and Bala, in rotation. At the latter meetings they sometimes assemble so many as five or six thousand people, who come from all parts of the adjacent country to hear the popular preachers. The general meeting at Caernarvon is holden [sic] in the open air, upon the green near the castle. Here, not contented with their enthusiastic extravagances on the spot, many of the country people have been known to continue them for three or four miles [5 or 6 km] of their road home.[9]

THE AMERICAN JUMPERS

As late as 1907, New York City received the missionary visit of the "Holy Jumpers," a Christian dancing sect moved to compassion by the wickedness of the great city. Leuba quotes a newspaper report:

The "Holy Jumpers" are now preparing to move from their idyllic country home in western New Jersey to the wickedest quarters here. Between their dances, which include every manner of step, from the Dervish's whirl to the sailor's hornpipe, they will warn New Yorkers of the destruction that is bound to come in a pillar of fire. The Jumpers will make extraordinary efforts to interest the city in the weird gyrations which give them their name, and if they are successful they will establish a colony and missionary school such as they have in Denver, their parent city. At any stage of the 'Holy Jumpers' meetings the inspiration to dance is likely to seize on members. With a shout of joy one begins. Perhaps he starts by waltzing alone around the ring. Another joins him. They grasp shoulders and the waltz livens into a movement like a very rapid two-step. Then they stop, face each other, and whirl like Dervishes, ending their performance by jumping high in the air, and sometimes half turning before reaching the ground. Excited by the dance and singing and the shouts, others join, women skip about like school-girls, and seize and drag one another into the circle. By and by the whole assemblage is whirling and jumping and shouting, but the women never dance with the men.[10]

COMMENT: Jumping is a very simple action, and it would be easy to find similar actions as part of religious practices in various parts of the world, the dances of New Zealand Maoris, for example. In July 1903, a group of Russian Orthodox worshippers at Irkutsk, Siberia, were reported as "exalted peasants manifesting their piety by uttering ferocious cries and dancing frenetically, jumping in the Russian style, turning on themselves, until the moment when, worn out, they fall as if dead to the floor, where they lie in ecstatic trance." The neighbors complained about the noise, but they persisted.[11]

The Christians of Western Europe, however, have tended not to employ physical movements in their ceremonies, so that it was something of a surprise to find such innovations appearing after 17 centuries, less of a surprise that those who behaved in this way were thought at first to be afflicted. The terms used by contemporary observers – "malady," "complaint," "disorder," "frenzy" – testify to the prevailing view that the Jumpers were suffering from some kind of ailment the patient (as the individual was perceived) caught as s/he might catch any other infection.

Such a view was the more understandable because the symptoms were the same in every case. This uniformity seemed to point to a malady the individual might catch, rather than a mode of behavior arising from the individual. Nevertheless, it is a strange malady that has this as its only symptom, and it seems more promising to look towards some nervous compulsion triggered by psychological factors.

John Wesley was not favorably impressed by what he heard of the Jumpers. "They are honest, upright men who really feel the love of God in their hearts. But they have little experience, either of the ways of God or the devices of Satan. So he serves himself of their simplicity, in order to wear them out and to bring a discredit on the work of God."[12]

Jumpers raise the recurring question, how should we assign values to spontaneous individual behavior on the one hand, to conformity to a collective pattern on the other? The fact that certain words triggered the jumping response is surely significant, but by what process does a form of words develop into an instantly recognized command? And if we assume contagion, how does this arise from cultural conditioning?

JUMPING FRENCHMEN OF MAINE

Maine: 18th and 19th centuries

The phrase "Jumping Frenchmen of Maine" refers to a famous condition in the annals of neurology and cross-cultural psychiatry, the origin of which remains contentious. In the northeastern United States along the northern fringe of Maine and New Hampshire, and in the adjacent Canadian province of Quebec, small pockets of people, especially in isolated communities and lumberjack camps, exhibit dramatic responses when suddenly startled. These include a combination of jumping, screaming, swearing, flailing out and striking bystanders, and throwing objects that may be in their hands. The most extraordinary feature of these displays is "automatic obedience" – briefly doing whatever they are told. "Jumping" is (or was) especially prominent among residents of French-Canadian heritage, and in Maine, hence their nickname the "Jumping Frenchmen" of Maine. The condition is commonly referred to in the standard medical and psychiatric nomenclature as the "Jumping Frenchmen of Maine" disorder or syndrome. There are two main theories to account for "jumping." Some consider it a nervous disorder of probable genetic origin; others interpret the condition as a social phenomenon grounded in operant conditioning. Because the last scientific study of jumping dates to 1986,[13] and this study examined subjects aged 55-77, it is questionable as to whether the syndrome still exists, so jumping will be described in the past tense.

CONTEXT: The "Jumping Frenchmen" phenomenon was unique in the context of the environment of isolated logging communities in the northeastern United States and Canada during the 18th and 19th centuries, and may have originated as a formalized response to "the kicking horse game."

"Jumping" has long been part of the heritage in this region. In 1902, Holman Day published a book on Maine folklore, *Pine Tree Ballads*. He included a poem, "The Jumper," describing in a heavy rural Maine dialect, a man who jumped at the slightest stimulus, and who unintentionally struck his wife in bed on numerous occasions after being startled by the whistle of a passing train. He wrote in part:

An' wan tra'n she go pas' on night,
Long 'bout de tam' I sle'p mos' tight.
An' w'en she whees-el, "Whoot-too-too!"
I jomp lak' wil' cat, I tal you.
I heet ma wife gre't beeg hard slams
An' black her eye mos' seexteen tam's.
Till las' she go off sle'p down stair,
–She say I worse as greezly bear,
Bot w'at yo' t'ink? I sore dis true,
I nevaire know w'at t'ing I do.[14]

The "Jumping Frenchmen" first gained public attention in 1878, when prominent New York neurologist George Beard told a meeting of doctors that he had heard stories of a group of lumberjacks in northern Maine who suffered from a strange nervous condition. When startled, they struck out at nearby people or objects. In 1880, Beard boarded a train to the Moosehead Lake region of Maine to see the phenomenon first-hand. He was not disappointed and wrote his observations in an 1880 edition of *The Jour-*

nal of Nervous and Mental Disease.[15] He encountered numerous "jumpers." One 27-year-old man sat in a chair while holding a knife that he was about to use to cut tobacco. Suddenly he was struck hard on the shoulder and ordered to "throw it." The knife flew from his hand and struck a beam. He again forcefully commanded the man to "throw it." Beard wrote, "He threw the tobacco and the pipe on the grass at least a rod away with the same cry and the same suddenness and explosiveness of movement." Beard noted that the condition appeared to run in the family. He found that jumping began in childhood, lasted a lifetime, and was rare in women. Beard described the jumpers as physically and mentally strong. He speculated that jumping was caused by temporary degeneration from exposure to their rustic environment, but made no conclusions about racial heredity, or a diminished capacity to make rational judgments.

Modern Investigations Of "Jumping"

Interest in "jumping" was rekindled in the 1960s and led to a debate as to whether it was a disorder or habit. In 1963, neurologist Harold Stevens examined a 59-year-old man of French-Canadian descent, whose father was a northern Maine lumberjack. Stevens noted that the man was easily startled, and when struck by a reflex hammer, "he jumped about ten inches off the bed." He said the man exhibited similar reactions to the sound of a telephone ring or an instrument dropping on the floor.[16]

Reuben Rabinovitch, a Canadian neurologist, wrote in 1965 about his childhood experience with "jumping." He said that while growing up in Quebec, Canada, the exaggerated reflex was common to all of the children in his village. Each spring, lumberjacks came out of the woods and set up camp nearby, sharing their food, music, and entertainment. In this way, Rabinovitch was exposed to "the horse kicking game," in which children snuck up on their victim and suddenly poked them while making the neighing sound of a horse. The "victim" then jumped up in the air and flailed out while blurting out a horse cry. A vital part of logging camps, horses were used to haul logs to the riverbank where they could be floated to their destination. The horses were often temperamental and the lumberjacks could be badly hurt from being kicked when entering a stall. Typically one lumberjack would sneak into the stall next to his intended victim's horse and wait. When the victim arrived, the prankster would "reach over and suddenly and violently poke his victim and give vent to the loud neighing cry of an enraged horse. This would most often frighten the victim into jumping away from what he thought was his own horse about to kick him."[17] Dr. Rabinovich's anecdote suggests that social and cultural factors were important in the development of "jumping."

Dr. E. Charles Kunkle, a Maine neurologist, also emphasized the influence of learned roles in analyzing the game reported by Dr. Rabinovitch. Kunkle noted that this game involved subjects who, when startled, were "expected to produce a formalized response of jumping violently, flailing out, and shouting angrily, often imitating the cry of a kicking horse." Adults, especially those in isolated communities and lumberjack camps, sometimes practiced this "horse play." Kunkle felt that this represented a "socially conditioned reflex, reinforced by example and by repeated stimulation..." Kunkle described jumping as a "part of regional folklore." As a physician he was able to talk to and examine fifteen jumpers. Dr. Kunkle said that jumping seemed to develop and flourish in "relatively closed and unsophisticated communities and in entirely masculine work groups."[18]

In 1986, two Canadian neurologists, Marie-Helene Saint-Hilaire and Jean-Marc Sainte-Hilaire, and psychologist Luc Granger, published their study of eight jumpers in the region of Beauce, Quebec, where men traditionally worked as lumberjacks in Maine. In six of those examined, the symptoms began with their work as lumberjacks. One man, when startled "would run, swear, throw an object he was holding, strike at bystanders, or obey commands." He said that one time he "jumped from a height of 10 feet (3 meters) after a sudden command." The researchers noted that all eight subjects would scream, most would throw an object in their hand or strike out, and half briefly obeyed commands shouted at them immediately after being startled, such as "jump," "run," or "dance."

Is "jumping" nature or nurture? Roughly similar behaviors have been recorded in various parts of the world. Soon after the publication of Beard's reports, "jumping" gained international prominence, and the search began to locate global variants. Within a few years, various exotic behaviors – rituals, idioms, and conduct codes – remotely resembling "jumping" were lumped under the same rubric and miscategorized as identical. These included *latah* in Malaysia, *imu* among the Japanese Ainu, *miryachit* in Russia, and *ramenajana* in Madagascar. It is unlikely that the few similar reports in widely separated geographical and cultural locations refer to kindred behaviors, as most supporting documentation is anecdotal, incomplete, and unconvincing.[19] Some scientists believe these symptoms occur in rare individuals suffering from a dysfunction of the human startle response known as hyperstartle, with local culture shaping the response.[20] Others think it is more common and akin to a regional habit.[21] It appears that "jumping" resulted from a set of social conditions that may be related to other examples of hyperstartle. There is probably a genetic predisposition to excessive startle in the general population, but this does not explain the prevalence of "jumping" in isolated Maine communities. While certain medical conditions can cause excessive startle (magnesium deficiency, tetanus, degenerative brain disorders), jumpers have no known medical condition.[22] This suggests a social and cultural linkage.

Rabinovitch suggested that as lumberjacks were confined to the northern woods from autumn to spring, they invented distractions in their isolation and boredom involving the only people available, men and horses. The jumping syndrome then grew out of the lumber camps and moved to surrounding towns and villages. "Jumping" appeared to die out with the passing of the traditional logging camp. Tractors replaced horses, lumberjacks became less isolated, and the incidence of "jumping" declined. The experts have noted that even severe "jumpers" lost their exaggerated responses as they were removed from the continual stimuli,[23] which suggests an origin in operant conditioning in a closed community – learning based on the consequences of the response. According to the principles of operant conditioning, acts that are reinforced tend to be repeated, while those that are not, tend to diminish in frequency.

COMMENTS: A plausible explanation for "jumping" is that it began as a local idiom that became institutionalized among a select group of people. If logging camp inhabitants lived with the knowledge that they may be surprised by a sudden "poke," and exaggerated startle was the expected response, then this conditioned social reflex became a normal part of social intercourse. Kunkle suggested this when he wrote that "jumping may represent a special variety of socially conditioned reflex, reinforced by example and by repeated stimulation from attentive colleagues."[24]

The JUMPERS in England, Wales, and North America take a different form (not in reaction to startle) and occurs in a religious context. Are the same forces operating here, exploiting a common basic physical trait; or is the similarity purely coincidental?

Sources

1. Richer, Paul (1885). *Etudes Cliniques de la Grande Hystérie.* Paris: Delahaye et Lecrossnier, p. 863 et seq. Much of the account is drawn from an eye-witness account by José Reig y Gasco in *El Siglo Medico* 11 September 1881, p. 584, translated and printed in *Journal de Médécine de Paris*, pp. 23-24, 1881.
2. Bodin, Jean (1604[1598]). *La Démonomanie des Sorciers.* Rouen: imp. Raphael 1604 [identical to 1598 edition but with additions], p. 398.
3. Calmeil, L.F. (1845). *De la Folie, Consideree Sous le Point de vue Pathologique, Philosophique, Historique et Judiciaire* [On the Crowd, Considerations on the Point of Pathology, Philosophy, History and Justice]. Paris: Baillere, volume 1, p. 262.
4. Lea, Henry Charles (1957). *Materials Toward a History of Witchcraft.* New York: Yoseloff, volume 3, p. 1051.
5. Wier, Jean. [Weyer, Johann] (1885). *Histoires, Disputes Et Discours Des Illusions Et Impostures Des Diables, Des Magiciens Infames, Sorcières Et Empoisonneurs.* Translated from the Latin original, published 1563. Paris: Bureaux du Progrès Médical, volume 1, p. 522.
6. Cornish, J. (1814). "On a Convulsive Epidemic in Cornwall, Caused by a Religious Excitement." *Medical and Physical Journal* 31:373-379. Reprinted in Hecker, J.F.C. (1854). *The Epidemics of the Middle Ages* translated by B G Babington London: The Sydenham Society.
7. Wesley, John (1909). *The Journal of the Rev. John Wesley.* Edited by Nehemiah Curnock. London: Culley 1909 [Originally published at various dates from 1739 onwards], Volume 6, p. 37.
8. Nightingale, the Rev J. (1835). *The Religions and Religious Ceremonies of All Nations.* London: Sherwood, Gilbert and Piper, p. 247.
9. Bingley, the Rev W. (1814). *North Wales, Delineated in Two Excursions, etc.* London: Longman, Hurst, Rees, Orme and Brown.
10. Leuba, James H. (1929). *The Psychology of Religious Mysticism.* London: Kegan Paul, p. 15.
11. *Le Petit Journal* 19 July 1903.
12. Wesley, op cit., Volume 5, p. 28.
13. Saint-Hilaire, Marie-Helene, Saint-Hilaire, Jean-Marc, and

Granger, Luc (1986). "Jumping Frenchmen of Maine." *Neurology* 36:1269-1271.

14. Day, Holman F. (1902). *Pine Tree Ballads*. Boston: Small, Maynard & Company, p. 252.

15. Beard, George M. (1880). "Experiments with the 'Jumpers' or 'Jumping Frenchmen' of Maine." *Journal of Nervous and Mental Disease* 7:487-490.

16. Stevens, Herald (1965). "Jumping Frenchmen of Maine" (Myriachit). *Archives of Neurology* 12:311-314. See p. 313.

17. Rabinovitch, R. (1965). "An Exaggerated Startle Reflex Resembling a Kicking Horse." Letter. *Canadian Medical Association Journal* 93:130.

18. Kunkle, E. Charles (1967). "The 'Jumpers' of Maine: A Reappraisal." *Archives of Internal Medicine* 119:355-357.

19. Bartholomew, Robert Emerson (2000). *Exotic Deviance: Medicalizing Cultural Idioms–From Strangeness to Illness*. Boulder, CO: University Press of Colorado.

20. Simons, Ronald C. (1996). *Boo! – Culture, Experience, and the Startle Reflex*. New York: Oxford University Press.

21. Bartholomew, Robert E. (1999). "The Conspicuous Absence of a Single Case of *Latah*-Related Death or Serious Injury." *Transcultural Psychiatry* 36(3):369-376.

22. Kunkle (1967). op. cit., p. 358.

23. Saint-Hilaire et al. (1986), op cit., p. 1271.

24. Kunkle (1967). op. cit., p. 357.

KENTORFF OUTBREAK

Germany: 1552

One year after the outbreak at SAINTE BRIGITTE, the nuns at Kentorff (variously spelled: Kintorp, etc.) near Strasbourg, were afflicted in a similar manner. The monastery was known as "the noble convent" because many of the nuns were from aristocratic families, but their birth did not spare them from convulsions and contortions of the body that made the authorities suspect an outbreak of epilepsy. Little by little the contagion spread until every one of the inmates was afflicted. However, some of the symptoms were interestingly different from those observed at WERTET and other earlier outbreaks.

Dutch physician Johann Weyer[1] spoke with one of the nuns, Anne Lengon, who was among the first to be afflicted. She told him how, when the hysterical access overtook one of them, it would set off the others, even if they were not actually present. They would howl like animals. In this state, they no longer recognized their companions and would throw themselves, one against another, hurling them to the ground, biting them and scratching them with teeth and fingernails – yet they seemed to feel no pain. When separated, they attacked their own bodies, since they had got it into their head that it was necessary to mortify themselves. Those who suffered the convulsions were also seized with spasms of the throat. Before the attacks began, they would announce themselves by fetid breath – taken to be an indication of the presence of a demon – and a burning sensation on the soles of the feet.

Anne said that if she spoke during an attack, it seemed to her that it was someone else speaking, and afterwards she had no memory of what she had said. But when someone told her what she had said, she was ashamed that such words should pass her lips. She said also that she found it difficult to pray, and even felt an aversion to her customary devotional exercises, which she blamed on the demon.

The devil would show himself to them in the form of a black cat, or in the false likeness of Else Kamense, the cook, or of her mother or her brother. This led them to suspect that Else was in league with the Evil One, and when some of the sisters denounced her as a witch, their word was readily accepted even though she had been afflicted along with the others. She would talk nonsense, and this seemed added proof that she was bewitched. It was alleged that she mixed poisonous substances with their food, which brought on the malady. Though tortured to confess, she denied this accusation. But the sisters' word was enough for the judges, and the unfortunate cook was condemned to be burnt alive, along with her mother for good measure.

Anne was taken away from the convent by her family and resolved not to return. Now that she had left the community, she was no longer afflicted, though when she received letters from the Mother Superior, she was overtaken with trembling in all her body, as though she was about to suffer the convulsions again. Soon after this she married and never again had any trouble.

However, the execution of the cook and her mother did nothing to stop the malady, rather the reverse. For now that the matter had become publicly notorious, the affliction spread beyond the walls of the convent, and women and children who had heard of the nuns' experience began to manifest it also. Moreover, five men seemed possessed by maniac delirium and behaved as if possessed, making wild accusations against certain women of the neighborhood, claiming to be transported to their homes though in fact they never left the house of the priest who was examining them.

In the nearby village of Houel, many men were possessed by demons. As a consequence, many women were accused and thrown into prison.

COMMENT: Here, as at WERTET, Weyer recognized the work of Satan, but he insisted that the cook was wrongly accused.

Writing in 1907, Dr. Edmond Dupouy, from his own observations, confirms that bad breath often announces a maniac or convulsive attack, and at the same time sweat and urine give off a nauseous stench.[2]

See also: CONVENT HYSTERIA, DEMON POSSESSION.

KENTUCKY FAINTING OUTBREAK

Louisville: April 1878

An epidemic of fainting among girls at the Louisville High School was being attributed to tight lacing.[3] The chances that the girls *all* simultaneously felt themselves to be too tightly laced are slim. This must have been suggestion at work.

KISSING BUG SCARE

United States: 1899

The "kissing-bug" is a generic term for numerous insect species that suck blood from mammals, so-called for their tendency to pierce the exposed skin of sleeping victims, most often on the face and especially the lips. Other common names include the "assassin bug," "cone-nose" and "big bed bug." Its romantic nickname became popular during the summer of 1899, when scores of Americans claimed to have been bitten on the lips while sleeping.

After biting its victim, the kissing bug would ungraciously defecate on the host, a practice that can transmit potentially fatal Chagas disease. In the fecal matter is a parasite that can severely damage the heart, nervous system, brain, colon, and esophagus. The bug is rampant in parts of Central and South America where a quarter of the population is at risk, an estimated 17 million are infected, and 50,000 deaths occur annually.[4] Risk factors include living in open-air houses and residing near forest habitats where the bugs are more likely to thrive. However, the species of kissing bug on the United States mainland rarely bites humans, and when they do the chance of contracting Chagas is extremely low, as their more polite American cousins do not defecate while feeding, greatly reducing the transmission risk.[5] The bug's notorious reputation outside the U.S. may have sparked what became known as "the great kissing bug scare" of 1899.

The scare can be traced to *Washington Post* police reporter James F. McElhone, who, in the course of making his journalistic rounds in mid-June, began to note an influx of patients seeking treatment for "bug bites" at the Washington City Emergency Hospital. Upon interviewing hospital physicians on June 19, he learned that several people had indeed been treated for redness and swelling, typically on the lips, "apparently the result of an insect bite."[6] Curiously, no one ever saw their attackers in the act. On June 20, McElhone published a sensational, speculative account of the "bug bites," describing victims as having been "badly poisoned" and warning that it "threatens to become something like a plague."[7] Other Washington papers quickly reported the story, followed by papers along the east coast and then nationwide.[8]

Soon any insect bite or swelling or pain of any kind on or near the face was attributed to the evil "kissing bug." Leland Howard, the entomology chief for the U.S. Department of Agriculture in Washington, D.C., described the ensuing scare as a "*newspaper* epidemic, for every insect bite where the biter was not at once recognized was attributed to the popular and somewhat mysterious creature."[9] At the Philadelphia Academy of Natural Sciences, entomologists analyzed the remains of "kissing bugs" collected by purported victims. Among the insects identified were houseflies, beetles, bees, and a butterfly.[10] Newspaper accounts of kissing bug "attacks" grew increasingly sensational.[11]

One report from a Chicago woman more closely resembled a vampire attack than a bug bite.[12] At the height of the scare, beggars in the city of Washington, D.C., bandaged themselves and went about soliciting donations, claiming to have been out of work and requiring donations to subsist until their full recovery from kissing bug bites.[13] Due to the apparent psychogenic nature of the episode, Dr. Howard compared the scare to medieval European reports of TARANTISM.[14]

KLIKUSCHESTVO SHOUTING MANIA

Russia: 1861

An outbreak of ostensible collective possession occurred in Russia in the spring of 1861. However, this was not a unique event, but a kind of manifestation that had been reported throughout Russia since the 16th century, and which in 1910 was described as still presenting in the same form as in the earliest accounts.[15]

CONTEXT: Vladimir Bekhterev, the neurophysiologist and psychiatrist, stated: "The Russian possession is quite simply a variant of the hysterical possession due to popular beliefs which attribute to so-called sorcerers the power to deteriorate people by various means, bewitching them or casting a spell on them: this is known as *portcha*. It leads to hysterical attacks characterised by convulsions and contortions, during which the sufferers accuse by name those who have bewitched them. This takes place most frequently during religious services and at the moment of great church solemnities."[16]

Though widespread throughout Russia, *portcha* is particularly prevalent in northern Russia, while in the south it is almost non-existent. In Siberia, on the other hand, it is of almost daily occurrence, and different forms of it are found among the Lapp and Khirgiz peoples.

In the spring of 1861, people on the farm of Boukreiewski, in the administrative district of Ekaterinoslav, were overcome with seizures. Those afflicted were thrown to the ground, where some lay inanimate while others were convulsed by violent outbursts of laughing, weeping, barking, or uttering the sounds of birds. They cried out, claiming to have been bewitched by sorcery, and named those who, in a few days' time, would in their turn be afflicted with the same malady. Some of these predictions were fulfilled, and altogether seven people were afflicted.

This was a particular instance of a widespread form of hysteria, which is basically the same wherever it occurs, though it will take particular forms according to the particular circumstances. The most notable characteristic is shouting: the sufferer starts by crying aloud at the top of his/her voice. This is what gives the behavior its name, *klikuschestvo*, which comes from the verb *klikatj*, to shout. Sometimes what is uttered are meaningless sounds of varying intensity and intonation. These cries may resemble sobbing, or animal sounds, the barking of dogs or the "coucou" of birds. They may be interrupted by a loud hiccup or by retching sounds. In other instances, the sufferer will enunciate clearly articulated words. These vary greatly, but the most common are along the lines of "Oh! I feel terrible, oh, I'm really sick, oh, how I su-u-u-ffer!" and so on. The victim may proclaim from the start that someone has introduced devils into his body as the cause of his suffering, and then he will proceed to name the person responsible.

Though the shouting was the most common element, it was rare for it not to be accompanied by other symptoms. As a general rule, the sufferer would fall to the floor, and without ceasing to cry out, would struggle, agitating his body in all kinds of movements. He rolled on the ground, his body jerking in an uncontrolled manner, striking the floor with his arms and legs, twisting this way and that. These movements were subject to alternating spasms and calm periods. The fits could be as brief as ten minutes, or as long as two or three hours. Bekhterev noted: "In the cases I have observed, the phenomena I have described are accompanied by grimacing. Truly, when one observes a possessed person during his attack, one is stupefied by the repulsive facial distortions which he performs." He noted that, after the attack, sufferers had no memory of it, provided it was allowed to progress through all its phases.

Once it has started with one individual, it easily spread to others, and this could be very rapid, almost immediate. On one occasion, around 1890, it occurred during a wedding ceremony in a village in the Moscow district, where the bride herself was the first to be afflicted. In a matter of moments the malady spread among the wedding party until fifteen of the guests were affected in the same way.

The outbreak on the Boukréiewski farm was exceptional in that it occurred at home. These attacks occur most frequently during church services, and particularly at the moment when the priest performs certain ritual acts, such as the laudes or reading from the gospels. This is precisely what was reported from the Middle Ages, and is not necessarily of religious significance. Church services were one of the few occasions during which the community assembled, so that a manifestation during the service can be seen as a kind of public testimony that the sufferer is possessed by demons. During these attacks, he would speak, as it were, in the name of the demon currently resident in his body.

Though most often these attacks, once they have run their course, have no further consequences, there are exceptions. In 1879, in the village of Vratchévo in the Novgorod district, a peasant woman named Ignatieva was suspected of being a sorceress who had bewitched the community. The dates of various calamities seemed to correspond with her activities. At the approach of Twelfth Night in January 1879, Ignatieva asked a farmer named Kouzmine for some curdled milk. He refused to give her any. Soon after, Kouzmine's daughter was afflicted with *klilouschestvo* and, in the course of her attacks, claimed to have been bewitched by Ignatieva. In a neighboring village a peasant woman Maria Ivanova was afflicted in the same way. And then, towards the end of January, in the village of Vratchevo, Caterina Ivanova, a farmer's daughter married to a retired soldier, was also struck down. She recounted that her sister, who had recently died from the same malady, had insisted on her deathbed that Ignatieva had bewitched her. Thereupon her husband made a formal complaint to the local police who came to the village and opened inquiries. However, before the authorities could determine the facts, a peasant named Nikiforov had roused his neighbors, claiming that Caterina, speaking with the demon's voice, foresaw that Ignatieva was planning to cast a spell on Nikiforov's wife. Thereupon the villagers enclosed the unfortunate woman in a cottage, closing all the doors and windows, and set fire to it. Subsequently, three of those involved in the murder were ordered to do penance in the church, while the rest were pronounced innocent.

COMMENT: Another account of this affliction is given by T. K. Oesterreich, writing of a malady by the name of *ikota*, which is another name for *klikuschestvo*:

> It generally consists in a peculiar prolonged and obviously obsessive hiccupping (ikota means nothing more than hiccupping), but may, in more serious cases, come to neighings, bleatings or other animal cries. The victims are also constrained to shout insults and use filthy words, and are subject to twitchings and contractions, wild writhings upon the ground, etc. in short, the picture is exactly the same as that offered by the possessed of western Europe. The malady affects only or almost exclusively women and is very common. It is considered as a form of possession. Naturally it only attacks the uneducated lower classes and is even characteristic of the particularly ignorant peasantry; it is a peasantwoman's and not a townswoman's complaint...The autosuggestive character of the ikota is clearly attested by the manner in which this state is cured: by holy pictures, the exercises of the Church, the putting on of harness, or finally by immersion in holy-water on the day of the Epiphany.[17]

Bekhterev affirms that the basic requirements for this affliction are the popular beliefs in the existence and power of the Evil One and in sorcery. He blames the Orthodox Church for encouraging the peasant population to hold these old beliefs in order to strengthen its hold over the community. With such beliefs as a starting point, suggestion and auto-suggestion will play their part as soon as circumstances provide an occasion, and the predisposed mind, once alerted, can read malevolence into the simplest action by the suspected person – offering food or drink, or even simply passing them on the road. He writes:

> There can be no doubt that the psychic characteristics of sorcery and possession in Russia derive, like that of ordinary demon possession, from the superstitions and religious beliefs of the common people. The lower classes are deeply infected with the idea that the evil spirit can seize hold of a person and cause morbid phenomena to manifest. Just as belief in God leads to the conviction that heavenly wrath can lead to sickness, so the impure spirit can induce pathological afflictions, not only operating himself, but also through the agency of sorcerers devoted to him. The morbid state, in the eyes of the common people, is the result of portscha [sorcery] and will frequently take the form of possession of the klikouschestvo kind.
>
> ...This accounts for the characteristics of the affliction: the convulsive attacks in church at particular moments of the ritual; their shouting

and their animosity against those they consider to be responsible for bewitching them; their frequently observed tendency to utter insults, obscenities, and blasphemies; their sacrilegious attitude to sacred icons; and sometimes a tendency to prophesy.

It follows, in the folklore of popular belief, that the doctors can do nothing for those afflicted; only the sorcerer who imposed the affliction can remove it, unless a more powerful sorcerer intervenes, or divine grace brings about a miraculous recovery.[18]

Though he is writing with particular reference to these Russian afflictions, it is evident that Bekhterev's conclusions apply to a great many of the behaviors in this Encyclopedia. The villagers of his country behave in almost precisely the same way as, for example, the villagers of PLEDRAN in Normandy or BLACKTHORN in England.

KOKOMO HUM

Kokomo, Indiana: 1999 and ongoing

A small city in north central Indiana, Kokomo (population 50,000) is the center of a controversy over the reported presence of a mysterious humming noise. Since 1999, city officials have been besieged by complaints from at least 90 residents who claim that the hum is not only irritating but in some cases is ruining their health.[19] Claims about the presence of a low-frequency hum, popularly known as the "Kokomo hum," have been the subject of national media attention. Symptoms associated with the hum include diarrhea, insomnia, nausea, dizziness, headaches, memory loss, and tremors.[20]

CONTEXT: Concerns over various humming sounds and their possible negative effects on health occurred during a litigious period in Western society characterized by a preoccupation in the popular media with elaborate theories of conspiracies and government cover-ups. Such noise fears may also reflect an increasing emphasis on, and discussion of, concern over environmental pollutants.

A preliminary study of one Kokomo neighborhood by an acoustics engineer detected a low frequency sound at about 55 decibels and 15 hertz, too low to be heard by the human ear.[21] Bennett Brooks of the Acoustical Society of America notes that the origin of the sound is unclear. "Those levels of sound could be coming from road traffic on even distant highways, air or rail activity or possibly just some industrial plants or even commercial buildings in the area. And, in fact, those levels could be caused just by the wind in the trees."[22] Brooks cautions that the range of ill-effects attributed to the low frequency hum could be entirely imaginary, noting: "The levels that will rattle dishes on a wall...haven't been shown to cause health problems, other than perhaps people waking up at night worrying."[23]

Most city residents say that they cannot hear the noise, beyond the mundane sounds of city life. But one resident, Diane Anton, said a barely audible, throbbing vibration caused her house to vibrate and made her ill including short-term memory loss, nausea, and hand tremors. She said the constant humming noise wore her down over time and forced her to move away from Kokomo.[24]

Similar claims of ill-health associated with the presence of low-frequency sound have been recorded in Taos, New Mexico, since 1991, but the source has neither been determined nor has any conclusive link been established to ill-health, including sleep problems, earaches, irritability, and general discomfort.[25] In the early 1990s, the "Taos Hum" gained national media recognition, and ever since, people from across the United States have reported mysterious humming noises and similar accompanying health problems as in Kokomo.[26] Investigative journalist Oliver Libaw noted that various investigations of the Taos Hum "failed to measure any low-frequency vibration that experts believed could cause either the noise or the infirmities reported by those who heard it."[27]

In parts of London and South Hampton, scores of English residents have complained of irritating low frequency sounds since the 1940s, which they claim affects their well-being. An organization has been formed to investigate the reports (The Low Frequency Noise Sufferers Association), nicknamed "the Hummers."[28]

KOLN OUTBREAK OF EROTIC CONVULSIONS

Germany: 1564

The nuns of the Nazareth convent at Köln were afflicted over a number of years with erotic convulsions.

In 1564, these increased to such an extent that Dutch physician Johann Weyer, who examined the convulsing nuns, believed they had been infected with "the demon of lubricity."[29] The entire community seemed taken up with unrestrained debauchery.

CONTEXT: The WITCH MANIA was at its height at this time, particularly in Germany, and this may have affected the nuns, but the nature of the affliction suggests that it stemmed from the youthfulness and frustrated instincts of the sisters.

A 14-year-old nun named Gertrud, who had been enclosed in the convent since the age of 12, was the first of the sisters to be affected. Sounds of laughter coming from her cell revealed that she was visited at night by an incubus who entered her bed. Although she tried every night to chase her demon lover away by protecting herself with a consecrated stole, this proved insufficient. One night when one of her companions was lying on a couch in the same room, for the purpose of defending her against this apparition, the poor girl became terrified when she heard the sounds of the struggle in Gertrud's bed, and she in her turn was overtaken by convulsions and became delirious. She became very nervous, uttering strange and inconsistent words, which greatly distressed her.

A demon, in the form of a frog, seduces a married noblewoman. (Martin van Maele)

Other sisters had the same experience, and the malady became more intense when the poor nuns had recourse to illegitimate remedies. (Weyer does not specify what he means by this, but perhaps he was referring to some kind of magic.) In their convulsions, the afflicted sisters seemed endowed with a degree of physical strength that was almost unbelievable and that could not be controlled by the will. They would be thrown down on their backs, then, holding their arms as though to embrace a man, they would go through the movements of intercourse. During this time they kept their eyes closed. When they opened their eyes again, it was with an expression of shame and embarrassment, as if they had been greatly troubled.

In May 1565, Weyer himself visited the convent to investigate the happenings, along with a number of observers, including two other doctors, one of them his own son. They read the horrible letters this young girl had written to her lover, though none of them doubted that Gertrud had written them while she was possessed.

A curious circumstance was that while they were being afflicted, the nuns didn't suffer from the plague; and if they suffered from the plague, they were not harassed by the demons. Weyer gave God the credit for preventing Satan from afflicting the nuns with two evils at the same time.

He traced the origin of the outbreak to some dissolute young men, who made the acquaintance of one or two nuns while playing tennis, and afterwards clambered over the walls and made love with the nuns. When the authorities put a stop to this, the devil seized the opportunity and sent demons into the convent in the likeness of these young gallants, who "manifested to each in turn the shameful villainy of these sexual movements."

Subsequently Weyer wrote letters of advice to the nuns, suggesting how they might bring the affliction to an end in a suitably Christian way. He does not explain his suggestions, but presumably they were effective since nothing more was heard.

According to French political philosopher Jean Bodin, there was a dog in the convent the nuns declared to be a demon, though Bodin believed it was a real dog. This dog would get beneath the skirts of the nuns "in order to abuse them." He mentions a woman of Toulouse who had similar relations with a dog; when she confessed, she was burnt. Something of the same sort happened at Hensberg, Germany, where the nuns were afflicted and committed the sin they called "the silent sin." In their ecstasies, their convulsions were very violent and interspersed with "cynical movements of the pelvis." After these crises, the nuns were in a state of prostration, and breathed with difficulty.[30]

COMMENT: Weyer seems to have been well aware that frustrated sex instincts were the basis for the sisters' condition, and Dr. Edmond Dupouy does not hesitate to call it nymphomania.[31] This is borne out by the description of the convulsions. In other instances of CONVENT HYSTERIA where their "shameful" character is noted, nowhere else is it specifically indicated that they mimicked the sexual act, though the nuns at LOUDUN certainly shocked spectators with the orgasmic character of their convulsions.

Ironically, it is Bodin, the ruthless witch-hunter, who makes the thoroughly sensible suggestion that might have prevented this and other such outbreaks: "In view of these happenings, I counsel the reader, that one should not force the will of young girls who have no vocation for a celibate life."[32]

See also: CONVENT HYSTERIA, DEMON POSSESSION.

Sources

1. Wier, Jean. [Weyer, Johann] (1885). *Histoires, Disputes Et Discours Des Illusions Et Impostures Des Diables, Des Magiciens Infames, Sorcières Et Empoisonneurs.* Translated from the Latin original, published 1563. Paris: Bureaux du Progrès Médical, Volume 1, p. 532. This is the source on which all other commentators draw.
2. Dupouy, E. (1907). *Psychologie Morbide.* Paris: Librairie des Sciences Psychiques, p. 110.
3. *Oshkosh Daily Northwestern,* May 1, 1878.
4. Figures were for 2002, obtained from the Seattle Biomedical Research Institute, 4 Nickerson Street, Suite 200, Seattle, Washington. Refer to: http://www.sbri.org/Mission/ disease/ Chagas.asp.
5. Ibid.
6. Howard, Leland O. (1899). "Spider Bites and 'Kissing Bugs.'" *Popular Science Monthly* 56 (November):31-42. See p. 34.
7. McElhone, James F. (1899). "Bite of a Strange Bug." *Washington Post,* June 20.
8. Howard (1899), op cit., p. 34.
9. Howard (1899), op cit., p. 34. Italics in original.
10. W.J.F. (1899). "Editorial." *Entomological News* 10 (September): 205-206.
11. Murray-Aaron, Eugene (1899). "The Kissing Bug Scare." *Scientific American* (new series) 81 (July 22):54.
12. "Weird Tales of Kissing Bug." *Chicago Daily Tribune,* July 11, 1899, p. 2.
13. Howard (1899), op cit., p. 34.
14. Howard (1899), op cit., pp. 35-36.
15. Bechterew, W.M. [Now spelled Bekhterev, V M] (1910). *La Suggestion.* [Translated from Russian by D P Keraval]. Paris: Boulangé. Bechterev, p. 137, citing Schteinberg, writing in *Archives Russes de Médécine Légale,* 1870. All information in this entry is from Bechterev unless otherwise indicated.
16. Bechterev, op cit., p. 138.
17. Oesterreich, T.K. (1930[1921]). *Possession.* London: Kegan Paul, Trench, Trubner [Originally published in German 1921], p. 205.
18. Bechterev, op cit., pp. 143-144.
19. Huppke, Rex W. (2002). "Strange Doings Abuzz in Kokomo–Many Claim Illness from Mystery Noise." *Bergen County Record* (Bergen County, New Jersey), June 13, 2002; Martinez, Matt (2002). "Profile: City Council in Kokomo, Indiana, Authorizes a Study to Investigate the Source of a Sound that has Caused many Residents to Become ill." All Things Considered (National Public Radio program), May 22.
20. Huppke, Rex W. (2002). "Strange Doings Abuzz in Kokomo–Many Claim Illness from Mystery Noise." *Bergen County Record* (Bergen County, New Jersey), June 13, 2002.
21. Martinez, op cit.
22. Martinez, op cit.
23. Libaw, Oliver (2003). "The Kokomo Hum. Reports of Mysterious Noise and Illness in Indiana." ABC News report filed February 14, 2003 and archived at: http://abcnews.go.com/sections/us/DailyNews/kokomohum020213.html.
24. Huppke, op cit.
25. Lambert, Pam (1992). "Hmmmmmmmmmmmm...? (Ground Noise in Taos, New Mexico)." *People Weekly* 38 (12):61-62 (September 21); Begley, Sharon (1993). "Do You Hear What I Hear? A Hum in Taos is Driving Dozens of People Crazy." *Newsweek* 121 (18):54-55 (May 3); Huppke, op cit.
26. Donnelly, John (1993). "Mysterious, Annoying 'Taos Hum' a Baffling Detective Story." Knight Ridder/Tribune News Service, July 9, 1993.

27. Libaw, op cit.
28. Donnelly, op cit.
29. Wier, op cit., volume 1, p. 539.
30. Bodin, Jean (1604[1598]). *La Démonomanie des Sorciers*. Rouen: imp. Raphael 1604 [identical to 1598 edition but with additions], pp. 399, 401-402.
31. Dupouy, op cit., p. 113.
32. Bodin, op cit., p. 402.

LANDES OUTBREAK

France: 1732

The outbreak of supposed demon possession at Landes, near Bayeux in Normandie, though a relatively minor incident, is of unusual interest due to the fact that the father of some of the afflicted children provides us with a detailed first-person account of the girls' behavior.[1]

CONTEXT: No external influences seem to have exerted particular pressure on those afflicted, though it is worth bearing in mind that this was the Age of Enlightenment, when traditional religious beliefs were being widely challenged. Louis XIV's struggles with the Protestants were recent, and the convulsionaries of SAINT-MEDARD were commencing their activity. It is against this background that in 1723, Le Sieur de Laupartie, the local seigneur, appointed as the priest of his parish, the Abbé Heurtin. The excessive enthusiasm of this priest – "he saw miracles everywhere"[2] – had earlier obliged his superiors to prohibit him from performing ecclesiastical duties. Laupartie, however, had for some time had his eye on the abbé, who he hoped would bring up his four daughters in exemplary piety.

The following year, the 10-year-old eldest daughter, who was preparing for her First Communion, fell suddenly into a terrible delirium.

Until then, this girl had given her parents nothing but obedience and tenderness. Since the cradle, her moral and religious education had not been neglected for an instant, yet suddenly she was uttering obscenities, insulting everyone around her, and blaspheming against God. Whenever she was urged to return to her former pious habits, she became furious and made demonstrations which her family found difficult to repress. Her father, desolated at this change in his daughter, did not hesitate to suspect the work of the Evil One. Churchmen agreed, and she was taken to the convent of Bon-Sauveur, at Saint-Lô, to be exorcised. This succeeded admirably, and before the end of the autumn the young girl was returned home and took her first communion. It seemed that all was over.

Eight years later, a new access of anti-religious delirium assailed the family. This time it began with the youngest sister, Claudine, now aged nine, who in her turn had been afflicted with convulsions and demonopathy. She was possessed, she claimed, by a demon named Crêve-Coeur (Break-Heart). The abbé at once prescribed exorcisms, to which her father agreed, for he saw this as a sign that the devil had targeted his family and was plotting their ruin.

The first exorcisms, performed by the abbé himself, were not effective, but during one of her attacks Claudine revealed that she would be delivered from the affliction on the feast-day of Saint-Louis. The family rejoiced. The church was packed that day, when all witnessed her deliverance and there was a celebratory banquet at the château. But soon after, the attacks began again. Indeed, some of the servants asserted that they had never ceased. Now, besides Claudine, her eldest sister again and also a third sister were afflicted, together with a female in the service of the house. All, it seemed, were possessed by demons.

Moreover, the convulsions now spread beyond the Laupartie household. Two nuns of Bayeux in charge of the education of children of the people, the servant-girl of the priest de Landes, and a young peasant girl from this village, all succumbed to the same affliction, and thereafter it spread throughout the parish.

The Sieur de Landes himself wrote an extremely revealing first-hand account of the children's behavior, as expressed in their words and actions, which is worth presenting at length for the explicit detail of its observation:

The girls of Landes frequently and suddenly display an aversion and an inconceivable hatred towards God, and particularly against the holy sacrament. They heap on it a thousand blasphemies, a thousand execrations, which it would be horrific to report. In addition they have often spat upon the tabernacle [case containing the sacrament], they look at it with glaring eyes, saying they wish with all their heart that some enemy would take out the lie it contains and reduce it to cinders, or give it to them to stamp on with their feet to avenge them for the torments which it makes them suffer.

You would need to see it to credit the extent of their hatred and spite against their fathers and mothers. Often they can't bear to see them or speak to them: they refuse to use the terms "father" and "mother," for which they substitute the most injurious and spiteful terms. There is no insult they have not applied to their parents, no evil they have not wished on them. They go so far as to strike them, to tear their clothes, to bite them viciously, to break and damage things, and in short do everything in their power to cause them distress and irritation. They even urge the servants to behave in the same way.

If in their moments of freedom from their fits they happen to give any satisfaction, if they show any signs of goodness or gratitude, or utter the words "mon pere" or "ma mere," they fall on the ground in a syncope, or a moment later enter into the greatest rage against them, and are filled with remorse for having given this little contentment.

They seem to breathe nothing but evil; they seem to take a delight in seeing evil done. There is nothing of that kind that they do not wish for themselves and for others, now and forever, such as that a thunderbolt or the house should fall on them; that the whole world should perish and be damned along with them. They cherish the ill-behaved, they treat them as friends and comrades and heap praise on them.

By contrast, it makes them sad or very angry to see any good done, to see virtue practised, above all to see God worshipped and his praises sung, or to receive sacraments, particularly communion. They cry out to the communicants that they will be poisoned, that they will regret it. They detest virtuous people, and their aversion against the priests is greater, and particularly those known for their saintly character.

It is only with the greatest difficulty that one can get them to pray to God or perform any pious act. They enter into the matter with extreme fury, they fall at once into a faint, and every least word one tries to make them utter, they answer that they have forgotten what they have to say, and their tongue is tied so that, even with the greatest effort, they can utter no more than the first syllable. Whereas their tongue is perfectly free to pronounce a thousand curses…

They have great difficulty in hearing the divine office, the holy sacrament, but above all the mass… They say that they suffer terrible headaches and violent stomach pains; they have fearful agitations, they proffer a thousand execrable blasphemies against the sacrament; they bark, they whistle, they cry, they howl. They pass out at the blessing of the holy sacrament and the elevation of the host, and feel a pain at the heart when the priest takes communion, and at this time they utter a thousand curses.

They have equally great trouble when making their confession. As soon as they enter the confessional, they lose their reason and become violently agitated. They shout and vomit injuries against the confessor whom they often strike. They bite their own arms and hands, tear their clothes and everything they encounter; they complain that they have forgotten the sins they have committed, their tongues are tied against saying any word accusing themselves.

Nothing approaches the resistance and horror they show for the holy sacrament. They are seized with fear and trembling, they utter fearful cries, they strike themselves, they bite themselves cruelly; they grind their teeth, they bark, swear, blaspheme, they act like mad dogs… only with the greatest difficulty does one get them to receive the sacrament with reverence and piety; after which they are tranquil for a while…

Their exorcisms are also extremely terrible…they spare nothing to irritate Christ, and beg to be thrown into hell rather than serve to glorify him… and all their paroxysms are redoubled when the devil is reminded of his former happiness and commanded to leave the girls…

What they say about religion is horrible. They talk like heretics or atheists, and excite others to think likewise. All heresies and the most relaxed morals are to their taste. They add sometimes that all religion is a lie, and that it is false to think that there are devils, or even a God.

They seem to take delight in telling lies or speaking ill of people, which they do with a great malice and facility. Some have even gone so far as to say it is they who should be worshipped and adored… In certain moods they become melancholy, and then the temptation to destroy themselves is so violent they often they do not dare to approach windows, nor water, nor to have knives or scissors and other such things near them.

They break all kinds of things, tear their clothes, even the possessions they love most. They strike their heads with their fists, tear their arms and hands with their teeth or cut them with scissors. They do the same to people who come near them, so that often they have to be tied up.

They say that the different impressions of hate, anger and despair which suddenly come into their heads are felt as though a very heavy burden, or extreme heat or cold. They often feel unbearable pain in their arms or their legs, which passes in an instant from one part of the head to another, from one arm to the other or one part of the arm to another part.

Sometimes their fits last for three quarters of an hour without stopping, and when they are in their convulsion four or five of the strongest are not enough to hold them. Yet at such times their pulse is normal and as level as if they were in perfect repose, and if there is any fluctuation, it is negligible.

I have said that it is sometimes necessary to tie them, and there is one in particular who needs to be restrained. Yet it is usually quite useless with this girl, for however carefully her body is tied, her arms and legs, in her bed or in a chair, with all the knots under the bedstead or behind the chair, and though they are tied so tight that she can't move any part of her body, one has hardly turned one's back before she is found in a moment untied…[3]

A symptom that manifests in several such cases, barking like dogs, was particularly pronounced in this case, as at AMOU and other outbreaks. Several of the afflicted girls were prone to it, but "one among them did it with such force and so exact a resemblance to the largest dogs that it was difficult to distinguish her barking from theirs, if one was not actually on the spot or warned in advance. Moreover, she was often in a syncope, her body bent backwards in a bow, to the astonishment of the doctors who witnessed it."[4]

Another phenomenon that manifested among the afflicted was the ability, during exorcism, to respond to unspoken commands on the part of the priests. (This occurred elsewhere, notably at AUXONNE.) However, the oldest girl was studying Latin, and might have responded subconsciously to commands given by the priests in that language.

Another manifestation that occurs in other such outbreaks was the tendency to climb, without any sense of danger. Laupartie records:

> They show an astonishing courage, or rather recklessness, in exposing themselves to the greatest dangers, where they would have been lost a hundred times if God had not protected them, or perhaps I should say, if the same force which drove them to the acts had not also sustained them by a special command from God. One of them on several occasions walked on a high wall, both forwards and backwards, with great rapidity, yet without making a single false step. She was also thrown with great violence into a well, with nothing to support her but by clinging to the edge by her hands. Another girl passed her whole body through the upstairs windows, stairs and attics, exposing herself to danger in a way which made those who saw her tremble... and in all these cases they were in a trance.[5]

One of the girls was subject to fits of hiccups that sometimes lasted two or three hours without stopping, and which were so violent that she complained her stomach was broken. Several had eating problems, no matter how hungry or thirsty they felt, either because they were in a fit of rage or in a faint, or because they could not get anything down their throats, which they said were blocked.[6]

A report that the afflicted girls had psychic abilities was not supported when one of them declared that a document, a contract between Satan and a local farmer named Froger, would be found in the latter's hay-loft. Armed with this information, Laupartie obtained a search warrant, but no contract was found. Nonetheless, the abbé felt justified in sending a report on the case to the Faculté de la Médécine of the Sorbonne, at Paris, for their opinion. After due consideration, on March 13, 1735, the doctors concluded, somewhat strangely, that the girls were indeed possessed by demons "even if one could explain these happenings by the forces of nature, because the devil, careful of his own interests, would not reveal his part without much difficulty, for fear of being driven from his dwelling."

However, the satisfaction of the abbé was short-lived. Monsigneur de Luynes, the Archbishop of Bayeux, decided to look more carefully at the evidence. At first he was inclined to agree that it was a case of possession. So two bishops, five grands-vicaires, and nine priests were assigned to perform exorcisms on the afflicted girls. However, disagreements broke out among them, and de Luynes intervened personally. Despite being attacked physically by one of the girls, he continued his inquiry, and formed the opinion that the best way to deal with the outbreak was to remove the girls from the influence of the abbé, who were packed off to the abbey of Belles-Toiles. The girls were then separated one from another, whereupon the manifestations ceased as though by magic.[7]

COMMENT: This is the most vivid and detailed account we have of any of these hysterical outbreaks, and it is all the more valuable because it is provided without the religious coloring that so often distorts the testimony. Consequently it throws considerable light on the nature of the behavior, its motivation – however unconscious – and the response of the girls to whatever was afflicting them. French medical historian Louis Florentin Calmeil drew our attention to the similarities with the hypnotic state, comparing the girls – regarding their ability to respond to unspoken commands, for example – with the somnambules, who were so much a subject for discussion in the early 19th century when he was writing.

Just as in a hypnotic trance, where the subject can control his/her senses on the orders of the hypnotist, so these girls seemed to be able to suspend their normal sensory responses in the belief that the devil wished it so: "The patients of Landes, convinced that the demon did not wish them to recite prayers, or read pious readings, or hear the words of the preacher, became sometimes dumb when asked to repeat prayers, blind when they opened a church book, deaf when the priest gave his sermon; and even when they retained the use of their sensory faculties, a sudden obliteration prevented them from using their mental faculties."[8]

His conclusion, like that of the archbishop, was to lay the primary blame on the over-enthusiastic abbé who inflamed first the daughters of the house, driving them through fear and guilt to the idea that they might be possessed by the Devil. Thereafter the same fears spread through the household and then to others in the parish, until it seemed as though the entire community was infected.

See also: ANIMAL NOISES.

LAUGHING EPIDEMICS

Episodes of uncontrollable, prolonged laughter, typically accompanied by bouts of RUNNING, crying, and disobedience have been recorded in parts of Africa since at least the 1960s. The overwhelming majority of those affected are students.

CONTEXT: Between 1962 and 1963, "laughing mania" erupted in several schools in Uganda and Tanganyika (now Tanzania). The first report was in January 1962, from the village of Bukoba on the western shore of Lake Victoria in Tanganyika, 25 miles southeast of the Ugandan border. Those afflicted exhibited fits of uncontrollable laughing, crying, and running. Over an 18 month period, more than 1,000 natives were affected, mostly schoolchildren, by what is known to locals as *endwara ya kucheka* ("the laughing trouble").[9] Authorities eliminated the possibility of a physical illness and attributed the symptoms to "mass psychology" from the highly superstitious population. Symptoms lasted from a few hours to 16 days. Other symptoms included talkativeness, general agitation, and attempted violence. Locals believed spirits of their dead ancestors triggered the episode.[10] In July 1963, episodes were reported in Uganda at Kigezi northwest of Bukoba, and at Mbale in northeastern Uganda near the border with Kenya. These latter two episodes had heavy elements of running and violence. Blood and cerebrospinal fluid studies on several patients were normal.[11] During this period, other outbreaks were reported in Tanganyika in the vicinity of Bukoba, to the south in Nshamba, Kanyangereka, and Ramashenye, and in Kashasha to the north.[12]

According to pediatrician G.J. Ebrahim of the Muhimbili Hospital in Tanganyika, a common folk belief held that those afflicted were responding to commands from ancestral spirits. He said, "The illness usually involved several individuals simultaneously in a home or a school. Patients ran about aimlessly, sleeping out of doors near ancestral graves. They frequently wore white chicken feathers on their heads or a twig from a specific tree."[13]

In May 1966, an outbreak of uncontrollable laughing and crying recurred in Musoma on Lake Victoria in northern Tanzania. The behavior affected 40 pupils and forced the closing of two schools for 14 days. Health Ministry spokesman Charles Mywali said that, based on previous episodes, "It spreads like wildfire among schoolchildren, particularly girls, one girl starts to laugh her head off and all the others follow. Nobody can control them and the only answer is to separate them for a couple of weeks."[14]

During July 1971, an episode of laughing and disobedience occurred in Ankole, Kajara County, Uganda. Classes were disrupted at the Rugarama Primary School when an ordinarily shy, 20-year-old male with a poor academic record, attending Primary 7, began to act strangely, exhibiting inappropriate, uncontrollable laughter, disobeying authority, making bizarre gestures, grimacing, and disregarding personal hygiene. Soon at least 50 other students began imitating and elaborating on the behavior of the first child. Behaviors included seemingly involuntary laughter, grimacing, headache, stomach pain, using foul language, refusing to obey teachers, threats of violence, tossing stones, and wandering about the school compound and nearby bush aimlessly. Unbeknownst to the other students and teachers at the time, the initial student affected was later diagnosed with acute schizophrenia and hospitalized.[15]

In May 1976, schoolchildren in Mwinilunga, Zambia, seemed to be in a mental "fog," in addition to exhibiting twitching, laughing, and running. It affected 126 students at a secondary school for at least three days. Pupils walked around as if in a daze and appeared anxious.[16] Investigators noted that "the recent strict disciplinary measures taken by the new administration, such as rigid separation of boys and girls, may have prepared the emotionally charged background."[17]

In mid-March, a secondary school in remote northern Botswana was closed for three weeks after an outbreak of illness symptoms and disruptive acts that were interpreted by the government's Health Services director as "mass hysteria." At least 93 pupils were afflicted at the Okavango Community Junior Secondary School. Some press reports described many students as appearing to be in a trance-like state.[18] Additional cases were reported at nearby primary schools in Gumare, and some residents were reportedly affected. Symptoms included uncontrollable, unprovoked laughing, weeping, screaming, talking, and sometimes acting in a violent manner. Journalist Wene Owino stated: "Afflicted students have caused injuries to their teachers and themselves besides destroying school property."[19] School officials initially suspected a malaria outbreak, but blood tests were free from the presence of any parasites. Some villagers attributed the episode to witchcraft, demanding that school officials bring in a traditional healer, but the administrators refused.[20] Violent acts were a major factor in closing the school, as students threw a variety of dangerous objects at their classmates and sometimes other teachers. During one meeting at the school between worried parents and education authorities, a student brandishing a rife disrupted the gathering, forcing them to take cover. Police managed to capture the student before anyone was harmed.[21] The "outbreak" began about February 20th.

Paterns

Episodes of Laughing Mania are most evident in Central and East Africa and typically occur to pupils in missionary schools.[22] British psychiatrist Simon Wessely classifies them as a culture-specific form of epidemic hysteria involving long-term repression that is incubated in repressive social settings. Typical symptoms include twitching, shaking, dissociation, screaming, crying, and histrionics. Laughing and running are occasionally reported, most commonly in Africa. Wessely refers to such episodes as MASS MOTOR HYSTERIA as they involve motor dysfunction.

Ebrahim has investigated several African incidents of Laughing Mania and believes they are rooted in social and cultural factors. Elders in African society are "all-powerful." Conflict arises when children attending missionary schools are exposed to radically different ideas that may conflict with and challenge traditional beliefs, resulting in CONVERSION REACTIONS that reflect the stress between young and old, convention versus innovation, East versus West. Ebrahim believes the episodes are triggered by "emotional conflict aroused in children who are being brought up at home amidst traditional tribal conservatism, while being exposed in schools to thoughts and ideas which challenge accepted beliefs."[23]

Contemporary Laughing Epidemics

Similar epidemics of uncontrollable, prolonged laughing, sometimes in conjunction with making animal noises, have been reported during the 1990s and early 21st century. These behaviors have been reported at religious meetings associated with a church in Toronto, Canada. The group known as the Toronto Blessing is credited with starting the Holy Laugh Movement or Laughing Revival in Canada, which then spread around the world. The movement has its beginnings in the Toronto Airport Church in 1992. The church pastor and catalyst for the movement is Rodney Howard-Browne, who came to Toronto after practicing in South Africa, where he had been involved in the World Faith Movement. During meetings, "Some weep uncontrollably. Some laugh hysterically. Some topple over or crumple silently to the floor, while others jerk, twitch, kneel drunkenly, karate-chop the air, scream, sway, double over with abdominal spasms, roar or bark."[24] In addition to barking like dogs and roaring like a lion, other congregates have been observed to begin cackling like a chicken, howling like a wolf, hooting like an owl, chattering like a monkey, or meowing in cat-like fashion.[25]

One pastor who attended a meeting described what he saw and experienced:

> One of the leaders then explained that he was going to call upon several people to share a testimony… The first person…was apparently a Baptist preacher from England. He went to the front, began to speak and after a few sentences fell to the floor roaring and screeching. The leader reassured us that everything was all right. This roaring, he explained, was caused by the Holy Spirit...it is the roaring of the lion of Judah. This was apparently a common occurrence in their meetings. The speaker concluded his message by telling us that the Holy Spirit was now mov-

ing in our midst and anyone who felt any shaking, trembling, or numbness was to understand that those feelings or manifestations were from the Holy Spirit and those who were experiencing those things should raise their hands and a member of their ministry would come and pray with them. Many people began experiencing this uncontrollable shaking of their bodies. Many fell on the floor roaring and screeching. Some were laughing hilariously.[26]

In explaining the animal noises during emotionally charged meetings, many adherents consider it to be of a prophetic nature, noting that it is symbolic in that "a man roaring like a lion is God prophesying that He is coming soon as a roaring lion."[27] Such behaviors have also been interpreted as being consistent with Biblical scripture suggesting that there would be strange signs near the end time. An adherent of the Toronto Blessing described one meeting as follows: "That room sounded like it was a cross between a jungle and farmyard. There were many, many lions roaring, there were bulls bellowing, there were donkeys, there was a cockerel near me, there were all sorts of bird songs.... Everything you could possibly imagine. Every animal you could conceivably imagine you could hear."[28]

Some members reported hearing a strange buzzing sound in their ears, others felt a sensation of being very heavy, while still others felt weightless or tingling throughout their body. One attendee, Greg Makeham, described his experience while attending a Toronto Blessing revival: "Soon, people were falling down like nine-pins, and there was much holy laughter, shaking, and other manifestations...One could hardly see the carpet for all of the bodies laying thereon…My pastor didn't even touch me...and I was on that ground in no time at all! And for the first time ever, holy laughter came over me, and I was laughing, and shaking, and laughing, and shaking, and laughing... for at least 30 minutes, maybe for an hour!"[29]

Often a spirit of uncontrollable laughter seizes those affected. This laughter can last literally for days. In his video, "The Coming Revival," Rodney Howard-Browne described an episode involving a man who became intoxicated with the Holy Spirit "and laughed uncontrollably for 3 days."[30] Austrian physician Franz Mesmer, the father of hypnosis (sometimes referred to as Mesmerism), is reported to have produced a variety of collective symptoms, including laughter, during the 1780s in France. "Mesmer marched about majestically in a pale lilac robe, passing his hands over the patients' bodies or touching them with a long iron wand. The results varied. Some patients felt nothing at all, some felt as if insects were crawling over them, others were seized with hysterical laughter, convulsions or fits of hiccups. Some went into raving delirium, which was called 'The Crisis' and was considered extremely healthful."[31]

See also: UGANDAN RUNNING SICKNESS, MOTOR HYSTERIA.

LILLE OUTBREAK

France: circa 1608-1618

This convent outbreak was characterized by the fact that blame for the hysterical behavior of the nuns was directed towards a single unlikely individual, whose extravagant confession was accepted by the authorities despite being not simply improbable but physically impossible.

CONTEXT: The Franciscan convent of Sainte Brigitte was located near Lille, in northern France. One of the sisters had earlier witnessed the exorcism of Father Gaufridi at AIX-EN-PROVENCE, in 1611, leading to his torture and death on little more than the say-so of a hysterical nun and the two exorcists, Michaelis and Domptius, who were fresh from their triumph at Aix and were now the spiritual advisers of the sisters at Lille. This traumatic experience, one of the most scandalous episodes in French religious history, surely played a part in bringing about the Lille outbreak three years later. The sisters must also have been aware of the trials and executions of the WITCH MANIA in various parts of France and other countries, and of the fighting in the CEVENNES between Catholics and Protestants, all of which may have contributed to a state of uneasiness and suggestibility.

A number of the sisters were afflicted, apparently without any prior precipitating event, with unusual anguish of mind and painful sensations. This sprang from one to another and with increasing violence. Some were troubled in their mind, others relapsed into a languishing condition, and some became choleric and impatient. They developed a horror of the confession, and being thus deprived of spiritual support, gave way to despair. Newcomers to the convent succumbed rapidly to this prevailing state of mind, yet the moment they set foot outside the convent walls they felt cured. At length they became convinced that they had been possessed by demons.[32]

The next step was to find who was responsible for bringing the demons into the convent, for the Church's teaching was that the Devil could not enter a religious community unless he had, as it were, an agent within the walls. The sisters convinced themselves that this could only be Sister Marie de Sains, though until then she had held a great reputation for piety and virtue. But it was now suspected that this had been a hypocritical cover for the practice of sorcery. In 1613, three of the nuns, under exorcism when it was supposed that the Devil, speaking through the nuns, was compelled to speak truth, accused Sister Marie of being responsible.

At first, amazed, she denied everything, but then she suddenly confessed to all and everything. She had cohabited with demons, and claimed to be pregnant with a child given her by the Prince of the Sabbat. She had had two previous children in this way and had also committed sodomy and bestiality with dogs, horses, and snakes. She had practiced sorcery on countless people, using a magic poison made to a recipe that Lucifer himself had given her, compounded of sacramental hosts and wine stolen from the mass, powder from a goat, human flesh and bones, the crushed skulls of infants, hair and fingernails, and the seminal fluids of a sorcerer. This concoction, Lucifer had assured her, was very effective, and indeed, she had proved its efficacy by the number of people she had killed with it.

When visited, separately, by Jesus and his mother Mary, both of whom were anxious to save her, she rejected their help with insults. She went so far as to strike Jesus in the face and injured Mary. But the worst of her atrocities were saved to the children of Lille:

> She confessed that she had disembowelled living children and caused a great many others to die in various ways, in order to offer them as a sacrifice to the demon. Often, after she had strangled them, she crushed their still-beating hearts with her teeth, especially when they were born to Christian parents. "I have cut the throats of a great many children in this town and in the neighbourhood, and when they were put in the ground, I dug them up and took them to our nocturnal assemblies. I killed a lot of them thus, or else I poisoned them with poison given me by the demons. Sometimes I pulled their hair out, or I pierced their hearts or temples with needles. I have thrown many into flaming furnaces; I have drowned others; I have roasted many on a spit; I have boiled others in pots or threw them into the latrines; some I burnt alive, others I gave to lions to eat, or wolves, serpents and other animals; I have hung some up by their legs, arms or necks, or by their shameful parts; I have smashed their heads against the wall, then I have flayed them and cut them into pieces as though to salt them. Others I threw to the dogs. There are some that I crucified, to insult the Saviour, and on each occasion this is the form of words I employed: This I do out of spite for the Creator, I offer to you, Lucifer and Beelzebub, and all you other demons, the body and the soul and all the members of this child."[33] [34]

The Archbishop of Malines, hearing this confession, observed that though he had seen and heard many things during his seventy years, he had never heard anything that approached the crimes and abominations of this nun, which were beyond all imagination. Indeed, comments Madden:

> They were indeed more than this, they were beyond the possibility of perpetration. She could not have committed them unless her whole life without intermission had been devoted to the crimes of murders without numbers, stranglings of innocent children, ravaging of graves, feeding on human flesh, revelling in orgies of superhuman turpitude, sacrileges unheard of, poisonings of all degrees of swiftness or slowness of operation, acting variously on the mind, the body, and the soul, and banquetting and junketting incessantly with demons at their Sabbath and in their synagogue of sorcery; and unless, indeed, that life had been extended to at least three times the ordinary term of human existence, and that the elements of all the perversity that was ever heard of in the most debased minds of the most degraded criminals were concentrated in her heart.[35]

Even the shocked archbishop may have had some inkling of the possibility that Marie was mad rather than possessed, for instead of consigning her to be burnt at the stake as a witch and heretic, he condemned her to be imprisoned for the rest of her life at Tournai, with austere penances, which was harsh enough if she was in fact innocent.

One of the notable features of the outbreak was the ability of the nuns, particularly Marie but also all the others, to improvise long discourses while in a state of delirium or ecstasy. These were equally fluent whether pro- or anti-religious, according to the state of the individual, and favorite themes were the Apocalypse and the Antichrist. No one seemed surprised that Marie was able to recite verbatim the lengthy discourses made by Beelzebub at the Sabbaths. Three of the possessed nuns, Sister Peronne, Sister Françoise, and Sister Catherine, supplied detailed accounts of the demonic lifestyle and Satan's plans for the coming of the Antichrist. Fluency, which manifests only in an ecstatic state, is found in other cases in this Encyclopedia, notably the Prophets of the Cevennes.

The incomplete records do not tell us whether the state of the convent was at once improved when Marie was sent away, but it seems unlikely, for we know that two other sisters from Lille were subjected to trials: one of them, Simone Dourlet, was accused of wickedness similar to Marie's, and indeed Marie was one of the witnesses who begged her to confess, as she had done. After five days of almost non-stop exorcism, she, like Marie, broke down and confessed to a wide spectrum of implausible wickedness. In 1617 a third nun, on trial in Germany, confessed to the same repertoire of demonic coupling and demon-assisted murders, only to retract everything, insisting she had lied from start to finish. She was kept in prison under the most severe conditions, confessing and retracting by turns, but in the end she was released.

Overall, the outbreak lasted nearly ten years. "Of those who declared themselves the victims of sorcery, several after languishing for a long time died; others fell into a state of miserable imbecility, neglected their attire, and became lost to all sense of propriety. And to crown their misfortunes, these unfortunate creatures were exposed to the vulgar curiosity of the ignorant and unfeeling, to their jeers and their scorn... no one treated them as if it was believed, or in the slightest degree suspected, that they were insane."[36]

COMMENT: No case of this kind demonstrates more clearly the astonishing credulity of the authorities, whether churchmen or secular officers, who were called upon to judge the behavior of these afflicted people. As Madden notes, Marie's confessions were quite literally impossible: she could not physically have performed so many crimes, to say nothing as to whether she could have summoned up the necessary will to commit them. As one commentator asked, where in Lille would she have found lions to feed the babies to?

At the same time, we can understand how the judges would be impressed by the remarkable fluency that enabled the sisters to give such copious accounts of the devil's doings. The creativity released by altered states of consciousness should not surprise us, given the vividness and complexity of our dreams, but the nuns' judges were not equipped to cope with it when displayed in the context of a trial for sorcery.

The treatment of the sisters, by subjecting them to repeated exorcism and interrogation until they made an "acceptable" confession, inevitably invites comparison with the kind of brainwashing imposed by Soviet officials to obtain "confessions" during their show trials. The question of enforced confessions is considered in WITCH MANIA.

See also: CONVENT HYSTERIA, DEMON POSSESSION.

LONDON EARTHQUAKE PANIC

London, England: 1761

On February 8, 1761, minor earth tremors shook London. While damage was minor, the impact was visible in the form of several damaged chimneys. By sheer coincidence, another tremor shook London exactly a month later (March 8), stimulating discussion about the possibility of more quakes. A "psychic" then predicted that London would be leveled in a third quake on April 5. "As the awful day approached, the excitement became intense, and great numbers of credulous people resorted to all the villages within a circuit of twenty miles, awaiting the doom of London." People paid exorbitant sums to find lodgings in such places as Highgate, Harrow, Hampstead, Blackheath, and Islington in hopes of being spared the quake's wrath. Many of the poor remained in London until two or three days before the predicted disaster, then left to camp in fields in the countryside. The quake never occurred.[37]

LONDON END-OF-THE-WORLD SCARE

England: Mid-January 1955

A strange cloud descended on London during the afternoon and plunged the city into darkness, "bringing the vast metropolis nearly to a state of mass panic." The blackout lasted about ten minutes. Meteorologists theorized that the freak incident was the result of smoke accumulating under an exceptionally thick cloud layer. Outside the Croydon Town Hall, a man shouted, "The end of the world has come!" In response, some residents "fell to their knees on the sidewalks and prayed." A Piccadilly Circus newspaper seller said, "It was pitch dark and then the place went silent." He continued: "It was lonely, frightening and awful. Then someone began to scream he'd gone blind. I was getting my wind up when it all of a sudden came clear." The cloud enveloped London without warning and left just as quickly.[38]

LONDON MONSTER SOCIAL PANICS

London, England: 18th and 19th centuries

London's monster scares are typical of incidents that occur from time to time in every community, causing the populace, or a section of it, to respond by riot, panic, or insurrection. The many examples of popular panic presented in this Encyclopedia show that such incidents may be triggered by religious differences (e.g. the POPISH PLOT), by concerns of public health (e.g., the JUNE BUG), through fear of an unknown predator (e.g. the MATTOON GASSER), or any other collectively perceived threat of uncertain origin.

All such events have periodically troubled British cities. In most cases, however confused the motivations of the populace, the instigating event was evident. The Porteous Riots of 1736 broke out when the Edinburgh Town Guard fired on a mob demonstrating at a smuggler's execution. The Gordon Riots of 1780 began as a "no popery" putsch against Catholics but escalated from a religious to a political affair culminating in full-scale attacks on the authorities. On Bastille Day 1791, the chemist Joseph Priestley had his house sacked by the Birmingham mob, his library and writings destroyed, because he expressed sympathy with the French Revolution. In the 1930s Communists and Fascists clashed in the streets of London for explicit ideological reasons.

But besides these identified or perceived enemies, there were unseen predators, in which elements of the unnatural or even the supernatural combined with physical fears to scare the populace. The monster scares, which have from time to time arisen among the citizens of London, did not cause them to respond by indulging in exceptional behavior as such; what makes the incidents exceptional is the way in which each was perceived *sui generis* and ascribed a local habitation, a name and attributes of its own. Diverse though these events were in many ways, they shared a common denominator: fear. Each of the "monsters" became some kind of bogeyman, reflecting and embodying the latent terrors of the Londoner.

They differed from traditional folklore bogies – witches, demons – by the fact that their exploits were flesh-and-blood crimes performed by flesh-and-blood perpetrators. Yet the popular imagination endowed them with larger-than-life features – Springheel Jack was widely believed to be a supernatural being, the Hammersmith Ghost was one by definition, the London Monster was thought by some to be an evil spirit. Even when the crimes were all too human – the Mohocks, the garrotters – the predators acquired a superhuman dimension by what they did and how they did it, while the horrific character of the Ripper's killings made him seem less than human.

Considered as a group and in retrospect, the most salient feature is that the predators were all male and the victims in most cases female, though the Mohocks and Garrotters also attacked males for the purpose of mutilation or robbery. Consequently it can reasonably be supposed that the primary motivation involved some degree of sexual perversion. This is confirmed by the nature of the attacks, targeting thighs and buttocks in the less serious cases, involving sadistic murder in the more serious ones.

Since none of the London monsters was ever convincingly caught, though some arrests were made, psychiatric evaluation of the motivation involved is a matter of speculation. However, some light is thrown by cases elsewhere that afforded greater opportunity for study. Dr. Jan Bondeson has pointed to a number of parallel occurrences in other countries.[39] The streets of Paris in 1819 were infested with *piqueurs* who attacked women in the buttocks or thighs with sharp instruments, customarily rapiers attached to canes or umbrellas. The attacks were very like those of the London Monster and may have been carried out in imitation of them. Here too there was widespread public alarm, vigilantes, offer of rewards, and a similar dying down of the scare after an individual had been arrested – though, as with Williams in London, with considerable doubts that he was really responsible. At Bozen, Germany, there was a similar outbreak by a so-called *Madchenstecher* (girl-stabber) in 1828-9, where a soldier confessed, then another at Leipzig in the 1860s, Strasbourg and Bremen in 1880, and Mainz 1890. In the United States in the 1890s, a serial attacker nicknamed "Jack the Cutter" was active in Brooklyn attacking women, and in 1906 "Jack the Stabber" in St Louis was similarly occupied until his capture.

In 1819, the same year as the Paris outbreak, a similar wave of assaults on women took place in Augsburg, Germany; here again some kind of copycat procedure can be supposed. Remarkably, 18 years later, a man named Carl Bartle was finally arrested and confessed to being the *madchenschneider* (girl-cutter). Since the man was clearly mentally disturbed, he was subjected to a medico-legal examination. He explained that the sight of blood had always obsessed him; his first attack, carried out when he was 19, had given him intense pleasure culminating in ejaculation.

It is fair to conclude that sexual perversion, amounting in some instances to sadism, underlay all the London monster attacks. What takes them out of the world of individual psychology – and qualifies them for inclusion in this Encyclopedia – is that each in turn triggered a public response that perceived the attackers, not as deranged individuals, but as larger-than-life creations.

The tendency of the populace was, wherever possible, to designate *a single monster*. In fact, it is certain that a single perpetrator could not have carried all the incidents attributed to the London Monster or Springheel Jack. Even if there was indeed an individual who initiated the series, he was soon followed by copycat individuals who deliberately sought, or were psychologically driven, to emulate his deeds. This tendency was most marked in the case of the Whitechapel murders where, though five of the killings were almost certainly the work of a single serial killer, popular alarm created a folklore figure that after a hundred years has not lost its appeal. Thus Peter Sutcliffe, a 20th century serial killer who confessed to 13 killings between 1975-1981, was named "the Yorkshire Ripper" in deliberate evocation of his 19th century predecessor; he, too, targeted prostitutes, claiming to have received a mandate from God to destroy them.

In contrast to many of the urban panics recorded in this Encyclopedia, such as the CHILD-ABDUCTION panic in 18th century Paris, or the POPISH PLOT in 17th century England, the issues were neither political, nor religious, nor related to public health or other community issues. Instead, they had their roots in human pathology and, perhaps for that reason, awoke an atavistic fear in the populace, endowing them with a monstrous significance.

See also: CHILD-ABDUCTION PANIC, CHOLERA SCARE, GARROTTING SCARES, THE HAMMERSMITH GHOST, THE LONDON MONSTER, POPISH PLOT, SCOWERERS AND MOHOCKS, WHITECHAPEL MURDERS.

LONDON MONSTER SCARE, THE

London, England: 1788-1790

Over a period of two years, ladies in central London – mostly young ladies – were subjected to attacks by male molesters. Such incidents occur in all cities, and street life in 18th century London was notoriously rough and violent. However, the assaults carried out during this period tended to be of a particular kind, leading to the supposition that they were the work of a single predator, who was unimaginatively nicknamed "The London Monster."[40]

The incident considered the first of its kind took place in May 1788, when a young wife, Maria Smith, was approached in Fleet Street by a thin, short, ugly man wearing a cocked hat. He began talking to her in an indecent, eager way, talking and walking beside her till she reached her destination. When she asked him to stop following her, he grinned and made no reply. As she knocked on the door of the house she was visiting, he jumped onto the step beside her and struck her violently below the left breast and on the leg. Inside the house, it was found that she had been stabbed in the thigh with a sharp instrument like a lancet or a penknife, and only her corset had protected her from a similar wound to the chest. She was exceedingly disturbed by the attack, and later claimed that the shock confined her to bed for many months, when her life was despaired of.

This attack set the pattern for the majority of the subsequent attacks, of which Dr. Jan Bondeson lists 55 in all, though he accepts that some of them may have been either imagined attacks or attention-seeking inventions. Most targeted single women walking in the streets, usually young, respectable and even elegant; occasionally groups of two or three were threatened. The attack was generally initiated by obscene talk and indecent suggestions. Then perpetrator would then suddenly slash the victim, usually on the buttocks or thighs. There was never any serious attempt at rape or killing, but some of the wounds were quite severe. The fact that the attacks were generally similar supported the popular suspicion that one person was responsible for all the attacks, and several of the descriptions seemed to bear this out.

By April 1789 there had been a sufficient number of these attacks for Londoners to feel seriously alarmed. The Bow Street Runners and others who formed the rudimentary police force of London at this date had no success in catching or even discouraging the monster. At a meeting in Lloyd's coffee house, a wealthy insurance broker, John Julius Angerstein, opened a subscription for a reward, and a group of gentlemen subscribed a total of £100 – a very considerable sum in those days, equivalent to nearly £10,000 in today's money. Posters announcing the reward were put up, and soon all London was looking for the Monster. In the St. Pancras district, 15 gentlemen set up a nightly patrol between half an hour before sunset and 11 pm, and numerous other self-appointed vigilantes set out to win the reward.

Though Angerstein's intention had been to put Londoners on the alert, the effect was to increase the alarm of the female inhabitants. Rumors proliferated. Some thought the Monster to be an evil spirit who could make himself invisible to escape detection, while others believed he was a master of disguise who could change his appearance at will. Another theory was that he was a mad nobleman who had vowed to maim every beauty in London – a theory discounted by the fact that some of the Monster's victims were less than beautiful. Any man was looked at with apprehension; the *Oracle* newspaper reported: "It is really distressing to walk our streets towards evening. Every woman we meet regards us with distrust, shrinks sideling from our touch, and expects a poignard to pierce what gallantry and manhood consider as sacred."

Inevitably, one result was to bring about a spate of false identifications and even false arrests. Angerstein admitted that his reward did no better than have several innocent people accused and sometimes beaten up by vigilantes before being dragged to the magistrates' office. He commented:

> It became dangerous for a man even to walk along the streets alone, as merely calling or pointing out some person as THE MONSTER, to the people passing, was sufficient to endanger his life; and many were robbed, and extremely abused, by this means. No man of gallantry dared to approach a lady in the streets after dark, for fear of alarming her susceptible nature. The whole order of things was changed. It was not safe for a gentleman to walk the streets, unless under the protection of a lady.

As always in such cases, anyone who behaved in any suspicious manner was liable to be pointed out and even attacked. "One Monster-hunter arrested his employer after beating and pummelling him: another took his brother-in-law into custody and brought him to Bow Street. One lunatic arrested a butcher at gun point, after finding a bloody knife in his pocket."[41] A drunken naval lieutenant, whose coat matched a victim's description, was committed to Clerkenwell prison but soon after was discharged when his supposed victim, who shrieked when first confronted with him, subsequently admitted she couldn't be sure he was the man. Numerous such incidents took place.

The best way to avoid the Monster was, of course, to stay at home. For those unwilling to do so, however, protective measures were sought. It was reported that several ladies ordered underwear made from sheet copper, to wear beneath their skirts. The less well off improvised more rudimentary armor with cardboard and the like.

Although most of the victims described their attacker in similar terms, many others did not. There can be little doubt that no one person was responsible for all the attacks, apart from the fact that in some cases more than one attacker was involved. Although most spoke of "the" monster, Angerstein's later poster declared that "there is great Reason to fear that more than ONE of these WRETCHES infest the streets." Criminals realized that the monster scare gave them unprecedented opportunities: a pickpocket had only to shout "The Monster!" to distract attention from his pilfering. And not all the supposed victims were what they seemed. A Miss Barrs, daughter of a fruit merchant on Marylebone Street, gave a vivid account of how she had been attacked, but investigation revealed that she had cut her own clothes and gave herself a cut in the calf to make herself a celebrity.

One variant of the attacks was for the attacker to thrust into the lady's face a nosegay of real or artificial flowers in which a sharp instrument was concealed, thereby cutting her features. When a young Welshman named Rhynwick Williams was arrested on June 13, 1790, the fact that he was employed in a manufactory of artificial flowers was seen as damning, though the actual circumstances of his arrest were very dubious. His principal accuser, Anne Porter, identified him as the man who had made obscene talk to her and slashed her clothing, and it was true that Williams, a weak and less than admirable character, was in the habit of chatting up women in the street. This was not an unusual practice at the time, but there were other circumstantial reasons to suspect him. He admitted to knowing Miss Porter, by sight if nothing else. But he denied the attack and produced a watertight alibi for the evening in question. Nevertheless he was arrested, tried, convicted, and committed to Newgate where he was imprisoned for several years.

It is possible that Williams was responsible for some of the alleged attacks, but not a scrap of evidence showed this beyond a reasonable doubt. Apart from his alibi, the identification made by Anne Porter was doubtful and there was plenty of counter-evidence. Even if there was a single "monster" who set the pattern, no one villain could have carried out all the attacks. The fact that the attacks ceased after Williams' arrest encouraged the public to think the Monster had been laid to rest, but it is equally likely that the arrest scared off those responsible for the attacks.

LOUDUN OUTBREAK OF POSSESSED NUNS

France: 1632-1638

The long drawn-out occurrence of supposed demonic possession among the Ursuline nuns of Loudun is the most lavishly documented instance of CONVENT HYSTERIA. As in so many such outbreaks during the 16th and 17th centuries, the victims were perceived as being possessed by the devil, except by those who suspected outright imposture. Political and social circumstances combined to make this a very public affair, attracting widespread interest. The case generated an enormous wealth of commentary both at the time and subsequently, offering widely divergent perspectives.

CONTEXT: The outbreak at Loudun, in central France, occurred at a time when there was widespread concern about the supposed activities of the Devil. The town had recently suffered an epidemic of plague, in which one-quarter of the population had died, and many were inclined to see all such disasters as the work of the Evil One. However, by mid-September 1632 the epidemic was over, and while it is tempting to read significance into the fact that the trouble in the convent began in the same month the epidemic ceased, this may have been no more than coincidence. More to the point is that at this time witchcraft trials were taking place sporadically in all parts of Western Europe, and the sisters must have been aware of them. Crucial to their affliction is the matter of the priest Urbain Grandier, who came to be accused by the nuns of bewitching them. That accusation might not have been made if the idea of witchcraft had not been prevalent. The trouble in the convent was clearly bound up with Grandier's career and downfall, and any interpretation of the sisters' behavior must be evaluated in this context.

The convent at Loudun: At this time more than half the population of Loudun was Protestant. While Henri IV's Edict of Nantes imposed religious toleration in principle, in practice those who were not Catholics were liable to discrimination if not outright hostility. Though they were in a majority in Loudun, Protestants were on the defensive, and the setting up of another Catholic community in 1626 was perceived, no doubt correctly, as a maneuver in the religious cold war. From the start the nuns were made aware that their presence was resented.

Also relevant to what was about to happen was the social status of the nuns: they were without exception ladies of rank. The prioress, Jeanne de Belcier, known as Sister Jeanne des Anges, was of noble birth; Sister Claire de Sazilli, who played a conspicuous part in the affair, was related to the highly influential cardinal Richelieu whose cynical hand was to play a crucial part in the affair; and their fifteen companions were also from good families, cultured, educated, and refined.[42]

Despite their fine connections, however, the convent was anything but wealthy. The nuns had no funding, and when they first arrived they slept on palliasses on the floor. The convent was a poor lodging-house with only three rooms in which they slept like schoolgirls in dormitories, and they were dependent on charity for food and linen. The Ursulines are a teaching order, and the nuns took in girl boarders to provide themselves with an income.

Finally, it is important to bear in mind that the nuns were all young women. The prioress herself was only 25 years old when she took office. The oldest of her companions was 36, the youngest 18, most were in their twenties.

The first outbreak: Sister Jeanne, the prioress, born in 1602 and difficult and unstable as a child, surprised her family by taking the veil, which she may have done to spite them. Her behavior as a nun continued to be perverse, as although her zeal for good works was admirable, she showed a macabre preference for nursing patients with horrific physical symptoms. At the same time she schemed with shrewd calculation to obtain promotion, and got her way when she was appointed prioress at Loudun in 1627. Granted it was a small pond, but at the age of 25 she was the biggest fish in it.

As prioress, her behavior continued to provoke comment, as she seemed to spend more time in intrigue than in prayer. Then, in September 1632 her health was mysteriously affected: her symptoms included nervous irritability, violent convulsions, catalepsy, and hallucinations. Almost immediately several of her companions were affected in the same way. Some of the sisters claimed they were disturbed at night by specters. This may have started as a practical joke by their boarders – the building was reputed to be haunted – but soon became more serious. The ghost of a recently dead confessor struck one of them, for no obvious reason. A black globe threw Sister Marthe to the ground. Nuns would leave their beds and wander round the convent, and even mount on the roofs, a curious trait echoed in other cases. (See RUNNING AND CLIMBING.) Such behavior suggested that they might be possessed by demons, and on October 5, an exorcism was performed on the prioress, ostensibly establishing that this was the case. It would prove to be the first of a countless number, and continued almost daily for seven years.

The demons possessing Jeanne were seven in number and her companions also suffered from multiple possession. How did the demons obtain access to these innocent women who would normally be protected by their piety? It was the common assumption in such cases to look for a human agent through whom the Evil One was able to do his will. Since the nuns were, by definition, innocent, someone from outside was sought. On October 11, 1632, one of the demons possessing Jeanne, under exorcism, named the one responsible: the priest Urbain Grandier.

Urbain Grandier: The story of Urbain Grandier, though crucial to the history of the outbreak, need not be recounted here beyond what is relevant to the nuns' attitude and actions.[43] Since he had a reputation as a womanizer and had once been taken to court for getting a pupil pregnant, any sexual accusation relating to him was likely to be readily believed. Handsome and charming, he inspired jealousy and hostility: "It was a question who would throw the first stone…jealous husbands, priests he had offended, women he had abandoned, matrons who had offered themselves to him in vain."[44] With an imprudence that would prove fatal, he had even contrived to make an enemy of the powerful politician, Cardinal Richelieu.

Jeanne never so much as set eyes on Grandier

until they were confronted at his trial. It was, however, characteristic of her that, when the confessor to the convent died and a replacement was needed, she picked Grandier about whom she had heard so much from town gossip. To her surprise and displeasure, he turned down the offer, pleading that he was too busy already, though this may have been an excuse to avoid getting involved in the affairs of the convent. This was the start of the nuns' obsession with him, in which lust and resentment were mixed. The image of Grandier seemed to haunt the sisters: "They had no thoughts but for him, even though they did not even know him by sight."[45]

Piqued by this refusal, Jeanne offered the post to a priest named Mignon who was an open enemy of Grandier, one of a group of Loudun citizens who were looking for any way to discredit the priest. The sisters' affliction gave him the opportunity he needed. It seems likely that it was he who put it into Jeanne's head that Grandier was responsible for sending the demons into the convent. Indeed, one possible hypothesis is that the naïve nuns were manipulated from start to finish by Grandier's enemies, and that their entire behavior was an imposture aimed at destroying him.[46] However, this simplistic explanation is not easily reconciled with an examination of the sisters' behavior, and the fact that their affliction continued after his death. Most commentators, then and now, take the view that they were genuinely afflicted, though not necessarily in the way they supposed.

Jeanne said she was visited by Grandier's apparition, "radiating a fascinating beauty," and made lewd suggestions to her and caressed her shamelessly. In her autobiography she wrote: "At this time, Our Lord permitted that there was thrown a curse on our community by a priest named Urbain Grandier…this wretch made a pact with the devil to destroy us and to turn us into women of bad life. To do this, he sent demons into the bodies of eight nuns, to possess them."[47]

This is a somewhat partial view of the matter, to put it mildly. The convent was now literally like a madhouse. The sisters were subject to temptations of impurity: "It was a sad sight to see these unfortunate females, like dogs on heat, run by night and day along the alleys of their garden, calling aloud on this man whose image fascinated them."[48] Jeanne wrote candidly in her autobiography: "At that time, the priest I have spoken of employed demons to excite in me a passion for himself. He made me yearn to see him and hear him speak. Many of my sisters shared these same feelings, but without telling one another. On the contrary, each of us kept her feelings from the others as much as we could…When I did not see him I burned with love for him, and when he presented himself to me and sought to seduce me, our good Lord gave me a strong aversion to him. Then all my feelings changed and I hated him worse than the devil himself."

We must bear in mind that at this time neither Jeanne nor any of the others had set eyes on Grandier. These passionate sentiments arose simply from what they heard of him from others.

The scandalous behavior in the convent was now public knowledge, and those parents who had entrusted their children to the sisters, and were delighted to have such well-connected teachers, now felt that things had gone too far and withdrew them. This deprived the Ursulines of their principal means of subsistence. The highborn ladies had no choice but to do menial sewing work, for which they were paid less than the going rate by employers who despised them. They became more and more beholden, economically as well as psychologically, to the handful of people who showed them any kindness – the exorcists, that is to say, the enemies of Grandier.

The exorcisms, which were intended to drive out the demons and which sometimes continued all day long, served only to heighten the tension in the convent, already sufficiently exacerbated by fasting, prolonged prayers, and discipline. The nuns had no chapel of their own, so the daily exorcisms were publicly performed in four churches of the town; anyone who chose could watch. As news of these happenings spread, sightseers came from all over France and even from beyond. For anyone traveling for curiosity, this was one of the sights to see. The hotels were filled. The future playwright Thomas Killigrew, who was touring France at the time, came to see the spectacle and recorded both his disgust and his skepticism.

Inevitably, the nuns were expected to put on a

show while being exorcised, and the transcripts reveal glimpses of reluctance and hesitation on their part, insistence on the part of the exorcists. The pressure on the women to comply with the exorcists' demands was very great. They had little choice but to say what the exorcists wanted them to say, and to back it up with convincing demonstrations of demon possession, which gave authority to their accusations.

Many who witnessed the spectacle described the nuns' behavior. They would strike their own bodies with incredible rapidity. They twisted their arms and legs, writhed in convulsions on the ground, their faces wore horrible grimaces; they threw themselves backwards until their heads touched their feet and would walk in this position with great speed and for a long time. They were insensitive to pain while in the ecstatic state. They uttered cries so horrible that those who heard them said they had never heard anything like it before. They would howl like dogs. They made use of expressions so indecent as to shame the most debauched of men, while their acts in exposing themselves and inviting lewd behavior from those present would have shocked the inmates of a brothel. The nobly born Sister Claire was particularly demonstrative: "She fell on the ground, blaspheming, in convulsions, lifting up her petticoats and chemise, displaying her private parts with no shame, and uttering obscenities. Her gestures became so indecent that the audience averted their eyes. She cried out again and again, abusing herself with her hands, 'Come on then, fuck me!'"[49]

There was continual friction between the law officers on the one hand, concerned that justice should be done to Grandier, and on the other, the exorcists who considered that possession was a matter for the Church. For example, the legal officers wanted to separate the nuns, lodging them apart, so that they would not influence one another. The exorcists, and through them the sisters themselves, refused. The convent was so poorly equipped that six or seven nuns were sleeping in each room, so that suggestion, if not outright confabulation, was a real possibility.

Except when she was being exorcised, Jeanne kept to her bed. Though the nuns failed the three formal tests of possession – the ability to speak strange languages, to reveal knowledge they did not possess, and to perform physical feats beyond natural capability – Grandier's enemies insisted that the possessions were genuine, that the demons were who they claimed to be, and that Grandier was responsible. At one point the nuns tried to retract their accusations, but Grandier's accusers merely saw this as a further subterfuge of the devil. Distorted reports were sent to Richelieu, already hostile, who considered the evidence sufficient. He gave orders to his unscrupulous agent, named Laubardemont, to arrest the priest. On November 30, 1633, Grandier was arrested and thrown into prison.

Yet again the nuns were exorcised. Confronted with the prisoner, Jeanne renewed the violence of her attacks, the obscenity of her language, and her cynical attitude. "Sixty witnesses deposed to adulteries, incests, sacrileges and other crimes committed by the accused, even in the most secret places of the church, as in the vestry where the holy host was kept."[50]

Further accusations came from women from outside the convent who were now being affected in the same way as the nuns. Aubin, who took a skeptical view of the whole matter, said of one of these: "Although the number of possessed women was very great, we see that nevertheless not many achieved fame during the exorcisms and were able to adopt postures and fall into convulsions. Just as the Superior [Jeanne] excelled among the nuns, so Elizabeth Blanchard carried away the prize among the secular ladies."[51]

Blanchard declared herself to be possessed by no less than six devils, and to have had sex with Grandier, who when confronted with her protested that he had never met her. Nevertheless her accusations were taken seriously and contributed to the list of counts against the priest. From then on the machinery of justice proceeded inexorably; the wretched man had no chance. Though he protested his innocence under the most appalling tortures, on August 18, 1634, he was condemned to death and publicly burnt the same day, under terrible circumstances, on a pyre which had been prepared in advance since the verdict was a foregone conclusion. Many were aware that this was a travesty of justice but were afraid to say so. Two of those who inflicted the sentence died insane shortly afterwards.

After the death of Grandier: Even though Grandier, the supposed agent of Satan, was no more, the nuns continued to be possessed by demons, and the exorcists felt it was their duty to continue their ministrations until they were cured. Their displays were as violent as ever.

In January 1635, Jeanne developed a false pregnancy – ostensibly from having relations with a demon – and had no periods for three months. She considered various ways to abort it, and even contemplated killing herself rather than bear a diabolic child. Fortunately it didn't come to that because the exorcists succeeded in persuading the demon to destroy its own handiwork, and suddenly the prioress was no longer pregnant.

Exorcism, intended to eject the demon, served only to excite the nuns. Father Surin, a Jesuit chosen as the principal exorcist, took up his duties on December 24, 1634. He was a fanatic whose behavior was hardly less extreme than that of his patient. In their private sessions, which took place daily and often lasted for hours on end, he made the prioress strip naked and, under pretext of punishing the demon inside her, had her whip herself. In her autobiography she said she remembered none of this, beyond a confused memory of taking her clothes off. Dr. Louis Calmeil commented:

The temporary delirium of the intellectual faculties and the moral sense, the insane actions, the muscular phenomena, were especially exhibited during the exorcisms, and during the most solemn religious rites. In the intervals of repose, the sufferers endeavoured to return to their usual exercises of prayer, to resume their customary duties and the demeanour and comportment befitting young women of their rank and profession. Almost always the arrival of an exorcist sufficed to throw into disorder the nervous system of these unfortunates. No sooner was Satan summoned, than blasphemies and imprecations were the only things heard.[52]

Erotomania was evidently an aspect of the nuns' illness. This is clear from the nuns' passionate lusting after Grandier, their lascivious contortions and uttered obscenities under exorcism, and the face-to-face confrontation of male exorcists and young nuns. On one occasion Sister Claire "was so tempted to lie with her great friend whom she said was the accused Grandier, that when about to receive the sacrament, she suddenly rose and hurried to her room where, having been followed by another of the sisters, she was observed with a crucifix in her hand with which she was preparing to assuage her wicked desire, having already slipped it under her skirt for this purpose." This sacrilegious masturbation was the closest she could get to the object of her passion.[53](Sister Claire was not the only nun to use the crucifix as a dildo; this also occurred during the infestation at LOUVIERS.)

Between May and September 1635, the demons were expelled one by one from their home inside Jeanne. In February 1637, she was afflicted with an illness that was miraculously cured thanks to a dream in which Saint Joseph and her guardian angel came to her with a magical ointment that put her right. (It should be noted that Jeanne herself was given to concocting medicines and salves.) A few drops fell on her chemise, and with these she pursued a second career as miracle-worker, taking the precious garment to the king himself, whose wife Anne of Austria was ill. Many women came to touch the garment, which was said to ensure a successful birth.[54]

A fact that supports the reality of the afflictions is that several of the exorcists were themselves affected. Father Surin, who had himself exorcised the prioress, was subject to horrendous demon attacks. Madden comments, "It is impossible to read Surin's account of his own mental and spiritual sufferings, his possession and obsession as he imagined by evil spirits, without coming to the conclusion that the frequent exorcisms he was engaged in, and their deplorable results, had drawn him into the same monomaniacal disease."[55] By all accounts, though, he already had a reputation for bizarre behavior before he came to Loudun.[56] Surin was harassed throughout the rest of his life and for twenty years was more or less mad with lucid intervals. Two other exorcists – Father Tranquille, Father Lucas – were harassed by demons, and two other officials involved in Grandier's death lost their reason.

With the expulsion of Jeanne's demons, the long affair came to an end. The priory was closed down, the nuns dispersed. Jeanne wrote her autobiography, though it would be two centuries before it was published. Loudun became an everyday provincial town again.

COMMENT: At the time of the affair, there were

really only two explanations for the nuns' conduct: either they were genuinely possessed by the devil, or they were faking. Only later was a third option proposed: that they were afflicted with a natural, though psychosomatic, disorder.

That genuine possession by the devil was a real option is something we must take seriously, as indeed it was accepted by all the commentators of the day. As a recent historian pointed out, "the typology of witchcraft was not born from some sick brains. It resulted from a mass of analyses accumulated over centuries thanks to the devoted work of many of the best minds of Europe, inquisitors, theologians, magistrates, men of rigorous mentality and of faith, driven by a sense of duty towards society divine and human."[57] Johan Weyer, a doctor distinguished by his open-minded attitude towards witchcraft, nevertheless believed firmly in the devil, and made a register of them – 72 princes of darkness, 7,405,926 "ordinary" devils, forming 111 legions each with 6666 fiends.[58]

Aldous Huxley commented: "Modern Catholic historians are unanimously agreed that Grandier was innocent of the crime for which he was tried and condemned, but some of them are still convinced that the nuns were the victims of a genuine possession. How such an opinion can be held by anyone who has read the relevant documents, and who has even the slightest knowledge of abnormal psychology, I confess myself unable to understand. There is nothing in the behavior of the nuns which cannot be paralleled in the many cases of hysteria recorded, and successfully treated, by modern psychiatrists."[59]

Writing in the mid-19th century, Madden proposed this diagnosis:

> In this case of the nuns of Loudun, we find a nervous hysteric disorder, connected with convulsive affections, trance, and catalepsy, not only allowed to run its course, but turned astray by injudicious treatment, and eventually converted into an epidemic madness, by the super-excitation of long-continued exorcisms, breaking out among a number of nuns in a convent, plunging a whole community into terror, causing several deaths, and the wreck of many understandings. The accounts can leave no doubt on any reasoning intelligent mind, that the nuns of Loudun were afflicted with hallucinations, which had all the known characters of monomania; that they had a full conviction on their minds of being possessed by evil spirits; that they feigned things which were incompatible with actual evidences of a sane mental condition; that they were capable of reasoning right on every subject, except the one on which their fixed ideas were disordered.[60]

This still leaves a choice of secondary options available. For instance, could it be that the nuns, even if genuinely victims of hystero-demonopathy or whatever label their affliction is given, were, during Grandier's lifetime, putting on a show for the benefit of his accusers, and after his execution, keeping up the show to justify their previous behavior?

Many were skeptical, even at the time. When the prioress was examined by a doctor named Duncan, he held her arm to prevent her falling and going into convulsions, saying that if she had a demon inside her, it would be able to free her from his grasp. The demon failed to release her. The Cardinal of Lyon, speaking to one of the exorcists, said: "Don't you see that, even if these women were not genuinely possessed, they believed themselves to be so because you told them they were."[61]

Imposture and delusion, autosuggestion, and suggestion from others, all these were undoubtedly present in the complex psychosocial malady that afflicted the nuns of Loudun. Figuier commented: "One primordial fact, indubitable and which rises with the most evident clarity from every contemporary account, is the real and not simulated existence of a nervous ailment among the Ursulines. This malady was a convulsive hysteria with various complications."[62] How could it be otherwise, when the nuns were exorcised, sometimes as many as six times in one day, over a period of seven years? The prioress herself was an unstable creature predisposed to abrupt changes of behavior, as witness the way in which her passionate feelings for Grandier changed abruptly to hate. She was a dominant personality and it is not surprising that her delusions transmitted themselves to her fellow nuns whose behavior was a carbon copy of hers. Living under wretched conditions, in a town generally hostile to them, and where almost the only people favorably disposed to them were the exorcists themselves, it is small wonder that these women who hardly knew their own minds responded to suggestions from this group of determined and ruthless men who certainly knew theirs.

See also: CONVENT HYSTERIA, DEMON POSSESSION.

LOUISIANA TWITCHING EPIDEMIC

Louisiana: January 28, 1939

In the spring of 1939, a progressive high school in Louisiana, in the southern U.S., was the scene of a twitching "outbreak" among anxious schoolgirls. The episode occurred in the village of Bellevue, affecting seven girls ages 16-to-18 who were described by their principal as "among the brighter members of their respective classes."[63] The twitching spread after the first student affected was able to avoid dance classes and rekindle her boyfriend's affection. Researchers surmise that after observing the success of the initial case, over the ensuing weeks, six classmates also obtained unconscious benefits from their newly acquired illness status.

CONTEXT: The prominence of dancing and festivals were an integral part of life in the Bellevue region of Louisiana in 1939, and throughout the year students were allowed to dance in parts of the school during their noontime break after lunch. Investigators suggest that the spread of the symptoms to other schoolgirls occurred because they may have been "rendered more suggestible by the strain and fatigue induced by the events [various dances and festivals] of the preceding days and nights."[64]

The episode began on Saturday January 28, when Helen, a 17-year-old student and a popular and prominent member of the senior class, was attending the annual Alumni Homecoming Dance. She went to the dance strictly as an observer, as she had an aversion to dance. After watching others dance for a while, her right leg began to briefly twitch and jerk. Over the next several weeks, she experienced several "attacks" of increasing intensity and duration. Some "fits" even occurred at home, though to a lesser extent. At times while playing basketball at school, Helen would be forced to stop as her leg began twitching. Soon, news of her twitching spread throughout the school, and several students, ignorant as to the nature of her symptoms, urged her to stay away from school, fearing that her problem was contagious and they could "catch it."[65]

On Tuesday February 21, during Mardi Gras celebrations, the second girl to develop "nervous twitchings" was 16-year-old Millie who came from a poor, troubled family and prior to her symptoms had been receiving treatment from a doctor for several weeks for "nervous difficulties."[66] That night Millie had attended a dance in nearby Ferryville, returning to a friend's house about 1 a.m. early Wednesday, and shortly thereafter "developed an involuntary convulsive jerking in the diaphragm, chest, and neck."[67] She attended school that morning, but her twitching continued. She left school at noon to be examined by a physician who prescribed several days of rest at home.

The next day at school, several students saw Helen experience what was now one of her commonplace twitching "attacks."[68] Shortly after 9:30 in French class, a third girl, 16-year-old Frances, exhibited "involuntary spasmodic movements." She was removed from the class and sent to the nurses' office. During this time, a fourth girl, Geraldine, who sat next to Frances, grew anxious and she began to twitch. She told investigators: "And then I started jumping. Then they carried me upstairs to the infirmary, and I started crying. They gave me ammonia but that didn't help. Plenty girls [sic] tried to hold me down, but they couldn't."[69]

While the afflicted girls were being taken to the infirmary, an angry mother upset with school administration, drove to the school and loudly demanded that her children be taken out of school. Between the shouting mother, the twitching girls being taken to the infirmary, and a series of public address announcements that were viewed as alarming by many pupils, rumors circulated of "strange goings-on." Concern even spread to the community and soon other parents were arriving at the school to withdraw their children, fearing that a contagious illness was spreading through the school. As more and more students walked through the halls and went to their lockers before departing, tension among students grew as it was assumed by the commotion that "something was up." The principal called an emergency assembly to calm and reassure students that everything was okay.

But the assembly was a failure, and as students left the meeting, the hallways were chaotic. "With the break-up of the assembly ... the children scurried around and pressed forward in an attempt to see and hear what they could of the hysterical subjects. Some were to be seen in the principal's office; others were being administered ammonia-water ... in the infirmary; still others, who had not developed the motor disturbances, but who contributed even more largely to the general confusion because of their uncontrolled fearful crying, had been taken to the nearby teacherage."[70] One observer quipped: "You've seen a stampede? That's how it was. The children were running up and down and all around trying to get a wiff here and a wiff there."[71] School closed early, but on one bus ride home, several students were making humorous remarks about the day's events, when the driver reportedly joked: "If you want to talk about the jerks, why don't you practice them." Shortly thereafter, Mildred, 17, began to exhibit involuntary twitching and jerking on the bus.[72]

When school opened the next Monday, a local public health authority reassured students that the episode was not contagious, though half of the school's 275 pupils were not in attendance. The symptoms slowly subsided. It would take a week before the school returned to normal.

Two Louisiana State University sociologists, Edgar Schuler and Vincent Parenton, investigated the episode and concluded that several factors combined to trigger the twitching. First, several days before the big dance where Helen first began to twitch, school physical education classes were turned into mandatory dance instruction classes. Helen's illness status allowed her to "beg off" taking the dance instruction while enabling her to rekindle her boyfriend Maurice's waning interest in her. Helen was being compelled to take part in an activity (dancing) that she neither liked nor was good at. "The jerking of her leg muscles obviously made it impossible for her to dance, so the painful conflict situation was resolved with no discredit to the subject."[73]

A good dancer, Maurice was showing a romantic interest in an attractive, spunky freshman newcomer to the school named Gretchen, who gained notoriety for her skillful tap-dancing abilities. "Her appeal to Maurice was apparently irresistible, and he did not trouble to conceal his admiration. In fact, he bestowed his senior class ring on her as a symbol of his esteem."[74] Schuler and Parenton concluded that Helen's twitching was an unconscious means for her to gain attention and affection from Maurice. "...Helen was both by temperament and training entirely incapable of consciously making a bid for the attention of her boyfriend, but that unconsciously and involuntarily she may have been achieving precisely this end through ...[hysteria]."[75] Helen was subsequently successful in winning over Maurice's affection.

In explaining the spread of the symptoms from Helen to her fellow students, Schuler and Parenton stated that the six other girls who exhibited symptoms were "apparently unconsciously influenced by the repeated suggestion of the initial case, but possibly rendered more suggestible by the strain and fatigue induced by the events of the preceding days and nights [celebrations going on at the time]..."[76] Since Helen, the first affected, had high social standing with in the school, and community, "there was...no ostracism or penalty to be attached to an unconscious imitation of her behavior...[and] served as a satisfactory device for gaining attention...in...a thoroughly unconscious or unintentional manner."[77]

LOURDES VISIONARIES

France: 1858

In the small French town of Lourdes, near the Pyrenees, a 13-year-old girl claimed to meet and speak with an otherworldly figure, subsequently identified as Mary, the mother of Jesus, on 18 separate occasions. Fifty or more others, mostly children, claimed similar visions. Though some of these other visionaries seemed pious and sincere, ultimately the Roman Catholic Church found that only the original visionary, Bernadette Soubirous, had experienced an authentic encounter. The others had been deluded, by either themselves or the Devil. However, many of the "false" visionaries were considered authentic at the time, and the episode raises the problem of establishing criteria of veridicality where no objective corroboration of subjective experiences is offered, particularly when the alleged experience is one that is generally considered impossible.[78]

Lourdes is not unique in attracting "false visionaries." At FATIMA, Portugal, where in 1917 three children claimed to have encountered the Virgin Mary, similar claims were made by a 12-year-old girl, Carolina da Capelhina, and an unnamed child from Espite.[79] As at Lourdes, the Catholic Church did not accept the testimony of these rival claimants, and they are not usually mentioned in accounts of the events.

CONTEXT: France at this time was divided between two ideologies: one royalist, religious, and largely reactionary, the other republican, anti-clerical, and generally progressive. While this did not necessarily involve ordinary people to any great extent, it did mean that every public event – and the Lourdes sightings rapidly became a public event – acquired political dimensions, which determined how it was received by authorities clerical or secular. On the whole, the Lourdes affair was handled with discretion and restraint. Nevertheless anti-authoritarian attitudes affected the course of events and influenced the response of the populace on the one hand, the authorities themselves on the other.

In 1851 France had become an Empire again, thanks to Napoléon III's coup d'état. In 1854 Pope Pius IX had pronounced the dogma of the Immaculate Conception, whereby the miraculous virgin birth of Mary became a tenet of Catholic belief. After Bernadette's sixteenth encounter, she told how she had asked the apparition who she was, obtaining the reply, *"Que soy era Immaculada Councepciou"* ("I am the Immaculate Conception" in the local patois, which Mary very considerately spoke because Bernadette was unfamiliar with French.) Catholics hailed this as divine confirmation of the papal announcement, while to skeptics the faulty syntax suggested that the words came from Bernadette's imperfect understanding.

The 1858 apparitions were by no means the first to occur in the region; there was a considerable prehistory of such events. There was also widespread belief in fairies and demons, sorcerers and popular magic. The visionaries grew up in a culture in which folklore and religion were intertwined, and in which Bernadette's apparition would be readily accepted and rapidly identified. The fact that it bore little resemblance to the traditional image of Mary became a problem only when a sculptor was asked to make a statue for the Grotto.[80]

The idea that Mary might return to Earth and reveal herself to one or more privileged people was not a new one. The Lourdes children would have been aware of many such events, particularly two quite recent instances in France, at Paris in 1830 and at La Salette in 1846. Consequently the people of Lourdes had little difficulty in identifying as an encounter with Mary the experience of Bernadette and the other visionaries, even if the authorities were more hesitant.

The question whether any of the visions, Bernadette's included, was veridical, was disputed at the time and remains so. In this account we are concerned only with the claims that were made and the behavior they inspired.

Commencing on February 11, 1858, a simple, sickly, pious 13-year-old girl of humble family, Bernadette Soubirous, claimed 18 encounters with a shining white being who was, after the sixteenth appearance, identified as Mary, the mother of Jesus. They took place in a cave known as the Grotto, beside the river on the outskirts of the town. Bernadette's claims had a tremendous impact on the town, dividing the population into those who believed she was indeed meeting Mary and those who considered her deluded. Few thought her an outright impostor. Though the authorities, religious or secular, were reluctant to commit themselves, her claims were widely and enthusiastically accepted by a great many of the townspeople, and it was not long before visitors were coming from farther afield.

Bernadette had 17 visions before anyone else claimed a similar experience. Then in early April there came a stream of claims, continuing through the ensuing weeks. Public opinion was as divided about them as about Bernadette's, but there was a general feeling that if Mary was visiting the town, it was only to be expected that others would see her. Henri Lasserre, the first historian of the happenings, expressed the prevailing uncertainty:

> In a different or indeed opposed sense there took place strange happenings of which it is important to take note. On three or four occasions, several children and women claimed to have visions like Bernadette. Were these visions authentic? Was the diabolical mystique seeking to confuse itself, in order to cause trouble, with the divine mystique? Or

> was there simply, at the bottom of these singular phenomena, a derangement of the mind, an exaltation of spirit, or mere trickery on the part of naughty children? Or should we look for hostile hands, concealed in the shadows of evil, who thrust these visionaries forward in order to discredit the happenings in the Grotto? We do not know.[81]

Lasserre was an inaccurate and tendentious writer, and a later commentator, the Jesuit Herbert Thurston, was more precise:

> We find that already even before 13 April there were at least two visionaries who claimed to have seen Our Lady as Bernadette had seen her. We find that new visionaries were continually declaring themselves – Père Cros speaks of as many as thirty or forty who were in evidence at the same date. We find that several of these were as devoutly believed in and encouraged by the clergy as Bernadette herself had been. We find that new claimants came forward as late as 18 September.[82]

Father Léonard Cros, to whom Thurston refers, was the Jesuit author of the first thoroughgoing examination of the Lourdes story; his book was so controversial that it was refused publication in his lifetime. He quoted a contemporary, Brother Léobard, as saying that "the devil caused an infinity of visionaries to surge up. We saw them indulging in the greatest extravagances. Did they see anything? Yes, there is every reason to suppose that many of them saw the Evil One, in this guise or that. Many of my pupils claimed to see visions. They stayed away from school. Their extravagances were produced not only at the Grotto and at the river, but also at home, where they improvised a little chapel…" Another, Brother Cérase, said: "A crowd of little boys and girls claimed to see the Holy Virgin. I thought it was nothing but play-acting, and I had serious doubts concerning the visions of Bernadette, which I never went to observe."[83]

More recently Father René Laurentin, in his comprehensive documentation of the Lourdes episode, has gone to some trouble to establish more accurate numbers, and proposes a fairly reliable figure of 48 individual visionaries, together with some groups and others anonymous or unidentified.[84] While not the "ifnity" or even the "crowd" of Cros's informants, the claims of 50 or so visionaries constitute a substantial phenomenon.

For those who were not individually interrogated, there is often insufficient documentation. Thus, little more is known of Claire-Marie Cazenave, a 22-year-old couturière, than that she was *une fille vertueuse* but inclined to be imaginative and *exaltée*; she claimed to see visions on two occasions. In regard to others, there are character problems. The police chief described the middle-aged Honorine Lacroix, who claimed to see the Virgin on April 10, as "a wretched and abject prostitute," though this should not have disqualified her as a recipient of divine favor. In principle, the same should apply to Catherine Laborde, whose sister Marie told Cros, "My sister, aged five or six, also had visions. One day at the Grotto she cried out 'There's the Devil!' and later 'Stop, the Holy Virgin says not to be afraid.'"[85]

When questioned, 18-year-old Julien Cazenave (evidently a common name in the town, for three of the visionaries bear it) told a coherent and not implausible story, but his conduct gave cause for suspicion. He led groups to the Grotto where he danced up and down, wearing a crown of olive leaves (this may relate to a folklore custom concerning the feast of Saint-Jean) and making faces at the devil, and required his companions to kiss the ground forty times. He advised them to tell their rosaries because God himself was doing so, though some thought it improbable that God would say prayers to Mary – as one cynic remarked, "it's the world turned upside down!" He was further accused of setting off in a run in pursuit of the apparition, conduct thought unbecoming a true visionary.

Also challenging credibility was Marie Bernard, whose vision failed to conform to accepted notions of how apparitions should be. She claimed to see a group of people – identified by the others as the Holy Family – including an old man holding keys (Saint Peter?) and a younger one who tugged at his moustache. On a second occasion, she saw the same people but they were making *gestes peu décents* [indecent gestures]! Her confessor admitted that he paid little attention to her story, believing it to be an attempt by the Evil One to cast a shadow on the true apparitions.[86]

But Cros, who personally spoke with most of the other visionaries, was impressed by 17-year-old Joséphine Albario, who was generally respected by the townspeople, and by Marie Courrech, the subject of our case history, which follows. Though the Church officially questioned no one, many voluntarily made statements that were included in the reports sent by the mayor and the police chief to the Préfet of the district. Witness Jean-Baptiste Estrade had this to say concerning Albario:

> We arrived [at the Grotto] at the moment when a young girl of the town seemed to have fallen into one of those pathological states which resemble catalepsy. A dozen women made a circle round her and watched her with amazement. We approached, and found the young girl on her knees in the attitude of a Mater Dolorosa. Her expression, though lacking the supernatural grace of Bernadette, was beautiful, transcending the ordinary. Her hands were joined, she prayed with sighs, and large tears fell down her cheeks. From time to time spasms interrupted her prayers. My companions were so struck by this tableau that they knelt… I have to confess, I had a strong impression in the presence of this young girl, and for a moment I thought I saw in her a new and genuine ecstatic. Nevertheless something undefined bothered my admiration and seemed to warn me that the truth did not reside here. I made a mental comparison with the ecstasies of Bernadette, and realised that whereas there I had been transported, here with Joséphine I was simply surprised. With the first, I felt a truly celestial action: with the second, I found only the agitations of an overexcited organism. I retired with my doubts and uncertainties.[87]

Most of the "false visionaries" emerged during April and May and then soon faded away as interest in them evaporated and the attention of all was focused on Bernadette. Nevertheless, some new claimants appeared as late as September, and Marie Courrech (see below) had her last vision on Christmas Day.

COMMENT: The swarm of "false visionaries" benefited from the fact that, as Bernadette's visions came to an end, the people were left unsatisfied. Their appetite for marvels had been whetted and they hoped for more and greater manifestations. While in many cases there seems little to support their claims, Cros was evidently troubled by the thought of the alternative diagnosis, that these other visionaries were one and all victims of diabolic manipulation. "Our opinion is that there was illusion of the imagination or the handiwork of Satan, and most likely the two together."[88]

A crowd throngs to Lourdes, led by Hope, who is blindfolded, and a feeble priest, while Death brings up the rear. (Steinlen)

Estrade's experience with Joséphine Albario indicates how the evaluation of an apparition experience is as subjective as the experience itself. Cros, who was the first to pay serious attention to the "false" visionaries, was clearly unhappy to dismiss them all so summarily, and the trouble he took to obtain their accounts at first hand suggests that he may have felt the Church had too prematurely dismissed them. For skeptics who doubt whether even Bernadette herself encountered Mary, the line that separates her experience from those of the "false visionaries" is by no means self-evident.

Case History[89]

Marie Courrech was an orphan, age about 30, and employed as a domestic servant in the household of the Mayor of Lourdes, Monsieur Lacadé. "She ran about the house all day, there was so much work; looking after the children, doing the bedrooms, shopping, cooking…" A contemporary described her as "very ignorant and very humble." She was, in fact, illiterate. Everyone, whether or not they believed in her visions, considered her to be honest and pious. "I loved the Holy Virgin since I was a child," she said. When Bernadette was asked if anyone else had seen Mary, Marie was the only one she acknowledged: "There is the servant of the mayor who has also seen her, on the last day that I saw her [16 July]." Cros took down her account in person:

> The first time I heard about Bernadette, they said she was bewitched, crazy. I came to the Grotto one morning only. It seemed to me that she saw something: I never had a bad opinion of her. The sight of her gave me pious feelings: I prayed (on my knees) like the others, I wanted very much to see her, that's all.
>
> The 17 April I went down to the Grotto to pray there, I didn't want to go, others asked me, Would you like to come to the Grotto? I don't care to go, I haven't got time. Someone asked M. Lacadé [her employer], he allowed me to go. There were three or four of us, it was two or three in the afternoon. We found other people there, praying. I placed myself facing the niche [where Bernadette had seen the apparition] about ten paces distant, and we began to pray. I had great devotion and recited the rosary. I hadn't finished the rosary, I was gazing at the niche, when I saw something like a person, but without any light either before, during, or after. That day, I was astonished, so much so that I didn't know where I was: I was happy, not knowing I was at the Grotto. The person I saw was 15 or 16 years old, dressed all in white, I

didn't pay attention to her face, nor her feet, or her hands. It vanished and I was astonished to find myself there, with these other women. I got up and walked away; I was crying. I spoke with the women; they had seen nothing. Back home, I felt the need to be alone and to cry; I wept as I went about my work. That evening I asked myself, My god, what can this be? I thought it might be an illusion created by the demon, I thought all kinds of things.

For two or three days I didn't think of going back, but then the following week one day I felt a strong urge to go there. I went down before daybreak before mass, which I heard on my way home. I went down alone to the Grotto, I wasn't afraid. I positioned myself in the same place, on my knees, with my rosary… a few minutes later, it appeared, I don't know how. I saw the Holy Virgin quite clearly, in a long white veil which reached to the ground; and a little of her blond hair, wide blue eyes, smiling except when she said to me, Pray for the sinners…. I didn't see her for long, two or three minutes, then she vanished… She said to me, Go and drink, take the water three times. Saying that she vanished.

Her friend Antoinette Garros testified:

In her ecstasies, she looked just as Bernadette did, but she had more joy than Bernadette… One day she was in ecstasy on the far side of the river from the Grotto, on her knees, and she seemed to want to throw herself into the river to reach the Grotto. Her eyes were focussed on the niche. I held her by the waist, I felt her struggles, I could feel her heart pounding like violent blows… People watching began to shout, Let her go: if she crosses the river, it will be a miracle. But I didn't listen to them, I was more intent on preventing her drowning herself, and I said to myself, if the Holy Virgin wants her to cross the river, she can snatch her out of my arms.[90]

Marie's apparitions continued until nearly the end of the year, the last known episode being on Christmas Day. Subsequently she tried to enter a religious house: "The sisters of the Immaculate-Conception at Lannemezan told me I needed a dowry of 5000 francs. Then at Saint-Vincent-de-Paul, they refused me because I had been a servant. It was the same thing at the Carmel of Bagnères."

Many accepted that Marie's apparitions were authentic. She made one or two predictions, such as that a supposedly dying child would recover, which proved correct. She seems to have been universally liked and respected. However, although she was questioned about her experiences, the Church never formally interrogated her and no formal evaluation of her claims was made. Instead they were informally rejected along with those of all the visionaries except Bernadette. To a cynic, it might appear that the Church felt that one visionary at a time was as much as they could handle.

LOUVIERS OUTBREAK

France: 1642-1647

The recently founded Franciscan convent of Saint-Elizabeth at Louviers, near Evreux in Normandy, became almost at once the scene of extraordinary behavior on the part of several of the sisters, who were rapidly diagnosed as being possessed by demons. One of the nuns was accused of importing the demons into the convent, and she in turned accused three priests, with fatal consequences.

CONTEXT: No particular external cause for the outbreak presents itself, though the prevailing religious conflicts and witch hunting may have added to the normal stresses of convent life. This convent had for its spiritual director Father Pierre David, an austere ascetic who encouraged the nuns towards an exceptionally high degree of spirituality. "They indulged in all kinds of mortifications, passing their nights in prayer, fasting with excessive strictness, torturing their flesh with flagellation, and to crown all these fine works, rolling half-naked in the snow."[91]

At the death of Father David in 1628, his place was taken by Father Mathurin Picard, who continued to follow the ambivalent regime of his predecessor, together with his assistant Thomas Boullé. When Picard in turn died in the autumn of 1642, the nuns, whose minds were already unsettled by these austere practices, became less stable than ever, especially when their new spiritual director gave them contrary instructions. One by one, over the course of a few months, eighteen of the fifty sisters were affected with convulsions and monomania, and those who had previously been the most pious were now the most inclined to blasphemy and worldliness.

The accounts of their behavior, as recorded by the bishop's investigators, run to hundreds of pages and cover a wide range of conduct. Running through them, however, is one constant thread: an antipathy to everything that until then the sisters had considered most sacred. These nuns, so pious previously, found it impossible to pray, or even to behave respectably. "A hundred times a day one hears them carried away, blaspheming against God, one comes across them spitting on the sacrament, shouting obscene oaths. From time to time they give way to transports of frenzy, and commit countless extravagances. In the night they are afflicted with visions, they mutter to themselves, and disturb the repose of the community, filling the air with their plaints and the sound of their howlings."

Their physical convulsions were extraordinary. A contemporary observer noted that "they bend themselves backward in the form of a bow without using their hands, in such a manner that the whole body is supported on the forehead more than on their feet, and all the rest is in the air, and they remain a long time in this posture, and repeat it seven or eight times. Yet after such feats and a thousand others, continued for as much as four hours at a stretch, and in the hottest weather, they emerge from these paroxysms as healthy, cool and calm, and the pulse as firm and as regular, as if nothing out of the way had happened to them."[92]

They were also subject to fainting fits: "They come out of this fainting fit without employing any remedy, yet in a manner even more wonderful than that in which they fell into it; first stirring the ankle, then the foot, then the leg, then the thigh, then the abdomen, then the chest, then the throat, and finally by a great movement dilating those parts, the face which until now has in no way reflected the mind within, suddenly regains its expression with hideous grimaces; then, howling anew, they fall back into their previous violent agitations and contortions."

Most saw apparitions, of all kinds. Sister Marie de Saint-Nicolas was visited by the apparition of Father Picard, who sat on her bed at four in the morning and boasted that one of the sisters was already "entirely one of us." Sister Marie du Saint-Sacrament was visited by a naked man who tried to drag her with him when he left via the chimney. Some saw attractive figures who sought to seduce them, others saw horrible monsters. Many saw monks and nuns who at first seemed benevolent but turned out to be demons in disguise. Some sought to entice them with lewd suggestions, others to terrify them. It's no wonder the nuns were confused.

Some of the nuns manifested the urge to climb, which has been encountered in other cases (see RUNNING AND CLIMBING). Sister de Saint-Esprit, despite being described as "a very large girl," was thrown down backwards onto the stone floor, landing on her head yet feeling no pain. She climbed onto a wall three meters high, walking along it to a place where there was no way down, where the demon threw her down onto stones and tiles, whence she was not injured, though "a little frightened and stunned." Sister of the Saint-Sacrament "under the influence of a demon, climbed a tree, where she was seen by the alarmed nuns in imminent peril of her life, proceeding from the trunk to the small branches, and supporting her whole weight on them, and moving with such apparent lightness and absence of all effort, that a bystander exclaimed, 'She is flying like a bird.'"[93]

Other seemingly paranormal manifestations were reported. Esprit de Bosroger, the provincial of the Capuchins who accompanied the Bishop of Evreux as an observer, recorded: "One morning Sister du Saint-Esprit was ravished and in a state of ecstasy. The bishop who was exorcising her ordered the demon to leave her free. Instantly she went into contortions and a fit of rage, and suddenly her demon took off like lightning and threw this girl into a fairly large fire, and thrust her face and her hand between the fire-dogs; people ran to pull her out, and saw that neither her hand nor her face were in the slightest degree burned."[94]

The convent as well seemed a particular source of fascination. On a hundred occasions the nuns, coming away from the exorcisms or on other occasions, were thrown into the well and were found clinging to the rim with their shoulders on the surrounding ledge, in such positions that observers wondered that they could support the weight of their bodies.

The sisters themselves were convinced that they were possessed by devils, and this was confirmed when François de Péricard, Bishop of Evreux, came in person on several occasions to visit the nuns, hoping that his presence would calm things. But the sisters persisted in their claims, and identified by name the particular demons that infested each of them.[95] In February 1643, after a sermon demonstrating that God was almighty and the power of the devil limited, one of the nuns, 36-year old Madeleine Bavent cried out, "We shall soon see if the power of Satan is so insignificant!"

It was a turning point in the affair, in which Madeleine played the leading role from then on. She was accused by her companions of practicing sorcery and of being responsible for bringing the demons into the convent.

On March 1, 1643, the possessed sisters charged Father Picard, the recently deceased spiritual director of the community, with being a sorcerer, and Anne de la Nativité led the accusation that he, in turn, had instructed Madeleine Bavent in the magic arts. She had been one of the first to be afflicted with convulsions and had from the start claimed to be possessed by a demon. At first she professed to be astonished by these accusations, but whether she was really guilty, or because the accusations acted on her by suggestion, she admitted her guilt – not only of practicing magic, but of a number of other crimes which became more and more extravagant the longer she confessed.

Among her claims were that Father David, and his successor Father Picard, preached in the nude and encouraged the sisters to strip naked in order to "achieve the perfect innocence of our first parents, who before the fall walked naked and unashamed…the most holy sisters were those who stripped themselves stark naked and danced before him in that state. Stark naked they appeared in choir; stark naked they walked in the garden-path. But this is far from being all. He delighted in bidding us stroke and handle one another with lustful caresses and embraces, so that – alas that I must needs avow it! – we not unseldom gave ourselves to the most impure and monstrous couplings, which Nature abhors…I have even seen the crucifix from the altar abused in this foul fashion of lust."[96] (The use of the crucifix as a dildo also occurred at LOUDUN.) There is much more to the same effect.

Accused, Sister Madeleine, in turn, became accuser. She insisted that she had seen the superior of the convent and other nuns, including Anne de la Nativité, at the sabbat.[97] But her judges chose to ignore these counter-accusations, while believing every word that she uttered against herself, without taking into account that this was a desperate attempt by a condemned prisoner, sick, suicidal, and surviving in isolated and severe conditions, to defend herself against accusations by her fellow nuns. She was tried and condemned to a lifetime of solitary confinement in austere conditions. She begged in vain not to be imprisoned alone, where the devil could do what he liked with her. In her dungeon she made several attempts to kill herself, including swallowing powdered glass, slashing her veins, and stabbing herself, but she survived all.

In this state of mind, she was brought out to serve as witness in a further trial, and gave evidence against the deceased former directors David and Picard, together with Thomas Boullé. She added to her previous confessions by describing the sabbats to which she was taken by these evil priests. On these occasions she had committed every conceivable crime of blasphemy and sexual perversion: dancing with a demon who was half-man half-goat, committing sodomy with Father Picard, watching Father Boullé fornicate with the Queen of the Sabbat, and coupling with him herself and many others as well. She had witnessed murders; when a witch gave birth to a child, she helped to kill it and cut it up to make charms and had eaten roasted infants. She had also signed a written document selling herself to the devil.

Despite the fact that she was ill, weakened, and driven out of her mind by the severity of her prison life, and despite the fact that none of her claims was substantiated, these ravings were accepted as legal evidence. Not entirely without question, but when the judge suggested to her that she had done these things only in her imagination, she insisted that she had really been physically present and done these things.

The sisters had accused Madeleine, and Madeleine had accused the priests. The word of these nuns, despite their deranged mental state, was sufficient for the Parliament of Rouen. Boullé vehemently denied all the charges against him, even under torture, throughout the four years during which his trial dragged cruelly on. But the exorcisms continued, the convulsions continued. The authorities were desperate to bring the affair to a close, and they could see no other course but the prosecution of Boullé, the only one of the three accused priests still alive. He was condemned to do penance, to be tortured, and then to be burnt alive. On August 21, 1647 he was drawn through the streets on a sledge and then, tied to the exhumed corpse of Mathurin Picard, he was burnt to death in the square at Rouen where Jeanne d'Arc had been burnt a century or so earlier.

Boullé was not the only victim. A certain man named Duval, suspected of practicing sorcery, was brought before Madeleine and recognized by her as having been present at the sabbat. On no other evidence than her say-so, he too was burnt alive. The Mother Superior, Simone, was summoned for interrogation, but she had already discreetly retired to Paris. The other sisters were dispersed to other nunneries, and the Louviers convent was demolished.

In that same year Madeleine wrote her autobiography. Montague Summers, who translated it into English for the first time, said "that her confession is substantially true cannot be questioned."[98] This is clearly not the case. Summers was a thoroughgoing believer in the reality of diabolical possession, and he was willing to accept as substantially true a narrative that is a blatant distortion of the facts when it is not outright invention. Yet it is not easy to believe that he accepted as fact Madeleine's account of the sabbat where "Blessed Lord Himself appeared and blasted the priest, of whom not a hair was left, with His Divine Wrath… Our Lord appeared a second time, and at his side was seen Our Lady, attended by two Saints. In great wrath He reduced the three miscreant priests to ashes, and never has man since set eyes on them…"[99]

The hysterical novices of Louviers are required to take the Holy Sacrament naked. (Martin van Maele)

COMMENT: One of the features of the Louviers outbreak was the physical contortions displayed by the supposedly possessed nuns. As in so many cases, notably the SAINT MEDARD CONVULSIONNAIRES, observers could not believe that young people, who were not professional acrobats or trained gymnasts, could perform these feats, not only without injury to themselves but without showing any sign of fatigue. "And yet, commented Bosroger, "we see that these young women are healthy, although they have suffered these convulsions night and day during four years, and for three or four hours daily have been subjected to exorcisms over a period of two years."

The erotic aspect of convent hysteria was particularly evident in the Louviers outbreak, and it seems that the spiritual directors of the convent, Father David and his successor Picard, may have been responsible for permitting it open expression. Having the sisters to strip naked to simulate the innocence of Eden has a ring of authenticity, compared with the obvious fantasies, and the hints at lesbian relationships and mutual masturbation may well have had their origin in fact.

The parallel between Madeleine's supposed experiences at the sabbat, and the allegations by alleged victims of satanic ritual abuse (i.e., 1980s/1990s in North America) [see FALSE MEMORY SYNDROME] are very striking. The fact that similar scenarios can be described after the lapse of 300 years, despite the advances in understanding which have taken place, and despite the fact that contemporary healthy American housewives are not subject to the same stresses as 17th century nuns given to extreme penitential practices and under the influence of obsessed priests, is a disquieting one.

See also: CONVENT HYSTERIA, DEMON POSSESSION.

LUNAR INFLUENCE

The belief that human behavior is affected by the phases of the Moon is not only deeply entrenched in popular belief but also supported by serious testimony and numerous studies. Other studies, however, fail to support the belief, and scientists remain generally skeptical.

The derivation of our word "lunacy" from the Latin word for the Moon shows that the idea has deep roots. The 17th century mystic Teresa of Avila suffered when the Moon was full.[100] Two centuries later, Swedish scientist Jöns Berzelius made a similar discovery after suffering periodic migraines for 14 years. When a journey took him to a part of the world where the lunar calendar was different, the timing of his migraines changed, and he realized they were linked to the Moon's phases.[101]

Doctors in ancient times took it for granted that their mental patients would be disturbed by the full moon. In the 2nd century, Italian doctor Galen asserted that the fits of his epileptic patients were governed by the lunar cycle. In London's Bethlehem Hospital during the 18th century, severe patients were chained, even flogged, at the full moon, to curb their violence. Studies show that during this time alcoholics are more likely to go on a spree, somnambulists are more likely to walk in their sleep, and pyromaniacs are more likely to start fires. Nor is it only the mentally afflicted who are affected; a German proverb warns, "When the moon shines into the window, the maid breaks many pots."

The notion that werewolves and vampires are especially active at the full Moon might be brushed aside as an old wives' tale,[102] but in 1972, psychiatrists in Florida found a correlation between homicides and lunar phase. In 1974, a similar study in Texas found no such correlation, but then, two years later, a further study found that almost all kinds of crime – rape, robbery, assault, drunkenness, and disorderly conduct – occur more often during the full moon phase. Curiously, homicide was the one exception.[103]

In the face of such conflicting testimony, it is perhaps not surprising that establishment medicine remains skeptical, dismissing the widespread popular belief as naïve. In 1985, a review of 37 studies concluded that "the moon was full and nothing happened."[104]

Yet in many parts of the world farmers, who more than anyone have to take nature into account, plan seedtime and harvest to match the lunar timetable. Silas Deane, an 18th century American minister, gathered in his apples at full Moon so they would keep better.[105] In 1923, an English biologist named Fox demonstrated that the reproductive cycle of certain marine animals coincides exactly with lunar phases.[106] And a 1936 study established that more women begin their menstrual periods at the full or the new moon than at other times.[107]

Though scientists are skeptical that the Moon can affect behavior, in 1978 Arnold Lieber argued that if the Moon can affect huge bodies of water to create Earth's tides, it might also affect the water contained in the infinitely smaller bodies of animals and people. He proposed the existence of "biological tides."[108] Alternatively, the moon's phases might affect terrestrial magnetism, to which humans are sensitive – some strongly so. In 1963, American doctor Edmund Jannino speculated that the lunar effect might be caused by fluctuations in body electricity caused by the Moon.[109]

"The Influence of the Moon on the Heads of Women." (17th century caricature by Lagniet)

The French folklorist Pierre Saintyves, commenting on a belief among the natives of Guinea that the new moon triggers convulsions in certain women suffering from the convulsive ailment known as the "glé," suggested that, contrariwise, it was the belief that it was so that brought on the seizures. But this fails to explain how the belief arose in the first place. Be that as it may, traveler Jean Perricault saw the glé affect an entire crowd of women, and this is only one among countless instances where popular practices reflect such a belief.[110]

Whether or not the lunar effect has any biological basis, the belief in it may be associated with popular practices. The Moon's phases could thus be a contributing or enabling factor in extraordinary social behavior, whether directly, by affecting people en masse, or indirectly, by affecting especially susceptible individuals who in turn set off others by suggestion or imitation.

LYCANTHROPY

Lycanthropy is derived from the Greek words *lukos* or wolf, and *anthropos* meaning man. The literal translation is wolfman.[111] Werewolf comes from the Anglo-Saxon word "wer" or man, and "wulf," wolf. Werewolf traditions can be found in a variety of cultures including Italy (*lupo manaro*), France (*loup-garou*), and Cyprus (*vrykolakas*).[112] Within the context of contemporary medicine, lycanthropy is a generic term used to describe "an unusual psychiatric syndrome involving the delusion of being an animal" and manifests "as a transient symptom of severe psychosis."[113]

Montague Summers' classic study of werewolf beliefs in ancient times offers a broad definition of the topic and its characteristic features. He states that "a werewolf is a human being, man, woman, or child (more often the first), who either voluntarily or involuntarily changes or is metamorphosed into the apparent shape of a wolf, and who is then possessed of all the characteristics, the foul appetites, ferocity, cunning, the brute strength, and swiftness of that animal." Summers notes that in the vast majority of accounts, the werewolf is perceived both by him or her self and others to have completely assumed the form of a wolf. This transformation is usually temporary but occasionally is said to be permanent. "The transformation ... can be effected by certain rites and ceremonies, which in the case of a constitutional werewolf are often of the black goetic kind. The resumption of the original form may also then be wrought at will. Werewolfery is hereditary or acquired..."[114]

The notion that a human could transform into a wolf is ancient. In the first century, Petronius wrote *Cena Trimalchionis*, a novel about a *versipella* or werewolf. As historian Rossell Robbins points out, this story was influential in shaping medieval conceptions of werewolfism. The story is commonly retold by medieval demonologists, helping to explain why "its four essential features appear in most later stories of lycanthropes; transformation in moonlight, removal of all clothes, urination or some other charm to permit regaining human shape, and sympathetic wounding."[115] This latter condition involves a report of someone wounding a werewolf, such as cutting off its paw, only to shortly thereafter come upon a human with an identical wound (the assumption being that the wounded person had actually transformed into the wolf).

Most Hollywood depictions of werewolves are very different from medieval European accounts. Hollywood films typically portray werewolves as two-legged creatures that are half man, half wolf. Medieval lycanthropes transformed into four-legged wolves, though sometimes witnesses claimed they could discern certain physical or facial features of the accused. Other Hollywood fictions include the notion that shooting a werewolf with a silver bullet can kill it.[116]

Werewolves And Witch-Hunts

Coinciding with the medieval European witch-hunts, fear and accusations of lycanthropy swept across the continent, especially between the 16th and 17th centuries, owing mainly to the notion that werewolves were demonic agents. During this period it was widely believed that witches could shape-shift into the form of various animals, especially wolves. Traditions of humans shape-shifting to and from an animal form are common around the world, with those purportedly achieving such feats commonly regarded as shamans, wizards, warlocks, and sorcerers. In Lapland, there are traditions of were-reindeer; in Malaysia it is were-leopards; in parts of Africa there are accounts of were-elephants and were-crocodiles; Native American stories tell of the were-buffalo, while South Americans have stories of were-eagles and were-serpents.[117]

CONTEXT: The prominent fear of wolves during the Middle Ages coincides with the depopulation of the countryside from the Black Death, the widespread abandoning of villages, and the rise of wolves in previously cultivated and deforested areas.[118] Anthropologist H. Sidky writes that chronicles of the 15th and 16th centuries "frequently reported the presence of roaming wolves in both urban and rural areas. Wolves preyed heavily on livestock and other domestic animals (due to the extermination of many of their natural prey by hunters), and on occasion they also attacked humans."[119] Psychotic delusions, hallucinations, fantasies, and rumors reflect the cultural context, and given the preoccupation with wolves during this time, and the widespread belief that persons, usually witches, could transform into wolves to do the Devil's bidding, it is not surprising to find numerous accounts of lycanthropy. Church of England vicar, folklorist, and historian Sabine Baring-Gould has stated:

> Whatever may have been the cause ... it is not surprising that the lycanthropist should have imagined himself transformed into a beast. The cases I have instanced are those of shepherds, who were by nature of their employment, brought into collision with wolves; and it is not surprising that these persons, in a condition liable to hallucinations, should imagine themselves to be transformed into wild beasts, and that their minds reverting to the injuries sustained from these animals, they should, in their state of temporary insanity, accuse themselves of the acts of rapacity committed by the beasts into which they believed themselves to be transformed. It is a well-known fact that men, whose minds are unhinged, will deliver themselves up to justice, accusing themselves of having committed crimes which have actually taken place, and it is only on investigation that their self-accusation proves to be false; and yet they will describe the circumstances with the greatest minuteness, and be thoroughly convinced of their own criminality.[120]

Werewolf Trials Of The 16th Century

As a result of the widespread fear of wolves and witchcraft, scores of accusations, trials, incarcerations, and executions for lycanthropy first began on a large scale during the 1500s. This century was marked by several prominent werewolf trials. As with witchcraft trials of the period, those suspected of lycanthropy were often social deviants. The scope of the lycanthropy "epidemic" in parts of Europe is remarkable. By some estimates, between 1520 and 1630, 30,000 people across France faced werewolf accusations.[121]

Peter Stubb (1589)

The most infamous of the 16th century lycanthropy trials, notorious for its cruelty, was the gruesome fate of Peter Stubb (sometimes spelled Stube, Stubbe, Stump, or Stumpf) who was tried near Köln (Cologne), Germany in 1589. Stubb was disliked in the community since childhood and was blamed for numerous accounts of missing children, murders, rapes, and livestock attacks. In short, without any unambiguous confirming evidence, Stubb was a convenient scapegoat for the various evils – both real and imagined – in the Cologne region during the latter 16th century.[122] During this much-publicized event, he confessed to shape-shifting from a man into a wolf and prowling the countryside at night, committing numerous murders. Eyewitnesses also testified to seeing him change to and from the lupine form. He claimed to accomplish this transformation with the aid of a belt. When he removed the belt, his human form returned. His testimony set off a search for the belt in a particular valley, though it could not be found. Some even speculated that the belt had been taken back by its original owner – the Devil.[123]

On October 31, a large crowd gathered in the nearby town of Bedburg to observe Stubb's execution. According to the court pronouncement, Stubb was sentenced "first to have his body laid on a wheel, and with red-hot burning pincers ... the flesh pulled off from the bones; after that, his legs and arms to be broken with a wooden axe or hatchet; afterward to have his head struck off from his body; then to have his carcass burned to ashes."[124] The court also sentenced Stubb's mistress Katherine Trompi and daughter Beel to die by incineration on the same day.

Gilles Garnier (1573)

Another high profile case was that of Gilles Garnier of Armanges who went on trial for his life in

1573. Following a series of reported attacks involving a werewolf that had supposedly carried away several children, the Parliament of Dole in Franche-Comte issued a proclamation urging local inhabitants to hunt down and kill the creature. Suspicion turned to Garnier, who along with his wife were described as poor, "sullen recluses."[125] On November 9, a small girl was attacked by a large wolf, only to be rescued by a group of peasants. As the creature was fleeing into the dusk, some thought that the animal's features resembled those of Garnier. Six days later, when a 10-year-old boy was reported missing, rumors spread that Garnier was responsible. He and his wife Appoline were taken into custody and put on trial for devouring several children while taking the form of werewolves.[126] Franche-Comte, a tiny country situated between France to the west and the Swiss Federation to the east, was the scene of numerous werewolf trials during this period.

Garnier was an excellent candidate for a werewolf as he was viewed as a social misfit with few friends, and he had the misfortune of having been born with eyebrows that bridged across his forehead. One writer remarked: "The man, Gilles Garnier, was a sombre, ill-looking fellow, who walked in a stooping attitude, and whose pale face, livid complexion, and deep-set eyes under a pair of coarse and bushy brows, which met across the forehead, were sufficient to repel any one from seeking his acquaintance. Gilles seldom spoke, and when he did it was in the broadest patois of his country. His long grey beard and retiring habits procured for him the name of the Hermit of St. Bonnot, though no one for a moment attributed to him any extraordinary amount of sanctity."[127]

Garnier was stretched on the rack and quickly confessed to killing various children from the region, including a vicious attack on a little girl just outside Dole on about October 6. Garnier provided vivid details, noting that he stripped the body of all clothes before eating her and telling authorities that the flesh was so tasty, he carried some of it home for his wife to feast on. Garnier and his wife were condemned by the Parliament of Dole to be burned alive, January 18, 1574.[128] To make matters worse, if such is possible, Garnier was charged for prosecution costs. The sentence read as follows: "Seeing that Gilles Garnier has, by the testimony of credible witnesses, and by his own spontaneous confession, been proved guilty of the abominable crimes of lycanthropy and witchcraft, this court condemns him, the said Gilles, to be this day taken in a cart from this spot to the place of execution, accompanied by the executioner (*maître executeur de la haute justice*), where he, by the said executioner, shall be tied to a stake and burned alive, and that his ashes be then scattered to the winds. The Court further condemns him, the said Gilles, to [pay] the costs of this prosecution."[129]

Jean Grenier

In the vicinity of Bordeaux, France, in 1603, a mildly retarded shepherd boy, Jean Grenier, was tried for lycanthropy. The episode began one beautiful spring day when several girls met Grenier while tending their sheep. He immediately struck them as odd: "His small pale-grey eyes twinkled with an expression of horrible ferocity and cunning, from deep sunken hollows. The complexion was of a dark olive colour; the teeth were strong and white, and the canine teeth protruded over the lower lip when the mouth was closed. The boy's hands were large and powerful, the nails black and pointed like bird's talons. He was ill clothed, and seemed to be in the most abject poverty. The few garments he had on him were in tatters, and through the rents the emaciation of his limbs was plainly visible."[130] Perhaps out of being mischievous or trying to impress the girls, he then told them that

French villagers hunt a werewolf.

he was a werewolf, then burst into a frightful fit of laughter. Terrified, the girls fled.

One girl who tended her sheep with Grenier, and whom he would frighten by telling stories of his so-called werewolf exploits, was Marguerite Poirier, 13. Her parents had not taken her seriously until one day she told them of being attacked by a wolf-like creature. She then repeated some of the things Garnier had reportedly told her about being a werewolf. "Jean had often told her that he had sold himself to the devil, and that he had acquired the power of ranging the country after dusk, and sometimes in broad day, in the form of a wolf. He had assured her that he had killed and devoured many dogs, but that he found their flesh less palatable than the flesh of little girls, which he regarded as a supreme delicacy. He had told her that this had been tasted by him not unfrequently, but he had specified only two instances: in one he had eaten as much as he could, and had thrown the rest to a wolf, which had come up during the repast. In the other instance he had bitten to death another little girl, had lapped her blood, and, being in a famished condition at the time, had devoured every portion of her, with the exception of the arms and shoulders."[131] The attack on the girl, coupled with a series of recent killings of area children, cast suspicion on Grenier as the likely culprit.

Authorities soon arrested Grenier and tried him for murder. He freely confessed to having murdered numerous children in the area after turning into a wolf and prowling the countryside under the cover of darkness. Furthermore, he implicated his father and a neighbor in helping him. They were arrested but later released.

Grenier's testimony seemed to grow more and more incredible, confessing to murdering over 50 children and several grown-ups, including an elderly woman whose flesh Jean described as "tough as leather" and inedible.[132] In summarizing Grenier's confessions, Justice De Lancre wrote that Grenier deposed the following: "When I was ten or eleven years old, my neighbour, Duthillaire, introduced me, in the depths of the forest, to a M. de la Forest, a black man, who signed me with his nail, and then gave to me and Duthillaire a salve and a wolf-skin. From that time have I run about the country as a wolf..."

Grenier also confessed to attacking Marguerite Poirier:

> My intention was to have killed and devoured her, but she kept me off with a stick. I have only killed one dog, a white one, and I did not drink its blood.
>
> When questioned touching the children, whom he said he had killed and eaten as a wolf, he allowed that he had once entered an empty house on the way between S. Coutras and S. Anlaye, in a small village, the name of which he did not remember, and had found a child asleep in its cradle; and as no one was within to hinder him, he dragged the baby out of its cradle, carried it into the garden, leaped the hedge, and devoured as much of it as satisfied his hunger... In the parish of S. Antoine do Pizon he had attacked a little girl, as she was keeping sheep. She was dressed in a black frock; he did not know her name. He tore her with his nails and teeth, and ate her. Six weeks before his capture he had fallen upon another child, near the stone-bridge, in the same parish. In Eparon he had assaulted the hound of a certain M. Millon, and would have killed the beast, had not the owner come out with his rapier in his hand...
>
> He accused his father of having assisted him, and of possessing a wolf-skin; he charged him also with having accompanied him on one occasion, when he attacked and ate a girl in the village of Grilland, whom he had found tending a flock of geese.[133]

The Parliament of Bordeaux reviewed the evidence, had the boy examined by two physicians, and eventually ruled that Grenier was suffering from a malady (though this illness was attributed to a demon) and that he was fabricating his werewolf exploits. He was sentenced on September 6, 1603, to spend the rest of his life in a monastery, where he died "a good Christian" in 1610.[134]

Medical And Psychiatric Interpretations

Lycanthropy and Mental Disturbance

There are several possible medical conditions that could potentially explain cases of werewolfism. Most obvious is the condition of lycanthropy whereby patients hold the delusion that they are animals. A survey of lycanthropy cases by psychiatrist Paul Keck found that most thought themselves to be wolves, four presented as dogs, two thought they were cats, while one each thought they were a rabbit, a tiger, and even a gerbil. These cases were noted to occur in conjunction with other serious psychiatric conditions, including schizophrenia, pseudoneurotic schizophrenia, schizoid personality disorder, organic brain syndrome, major depression, and bipolar disorder.[135] Other conditions associated with lycanthropy include hysterical neuroses involving dissociation and psychomotor epilepsy.[136] Hence, the condition where one thinks they have transformed into an animal, while not common by any means, has been frequently recorded in the contemporary scientific literature, and we have no reason to believe it was any less common during the Middle Ages. In fact, during this period it was widely believed that humans could shape-shift into a variety of animal forms.

Consider the following case from the *American Journal of Psychiatry*, involving a 56-year-old woman with a life history of schizoid personality. She became psychotic "immediately after an attempted reconciliation through sexual activity with her husband [as] she believed that she had become a wild dog. When seen in the emergency room, she was making barking sounds, crouched down, cowering in the corner, extending her hands in claw-like fashion."[137] As is typical of such cases, her symptoms were transient, and when she was not exhibiting canine behavior, appeared tense and expressed the notion that she was demonically possessed. Five months later, after discontinuing her anti-psychotic medication, she drove herself to the hospital in an apparent altered state of consciousness. "During the first night in the hospital she intermittently growled and clawed at the air while crouching on the floor, obviously in a panic."

Another case study of lycanthropy was reported in 1977 and involves a 49-year-old Texas woman who was obsessed with wolves and even had dreams about them. During her twenty years of marriage, she exhibited "compulsive urges" of adultery, lesbianism, and bestiality. A week prior to admission, while attending a family gathering, she acted on her feelings when, over a 20-minute period, she stripped naked, "assumed the female sexual posture of a wolf, and offered herself to her mother."[138] The next night, following sex with her husband, she suffered a two-hour psychotic episode – growling, gnawing, scratching at the bed, and claiming that Satan entered her body and transformed her into an animal. She also exhibited auditory hallucinations. During this episode, she was not under the influence of any drugs.[139] The woman was hospitalized for four weeks until her condition began to stabilize. Prior to this time, she had several relapses during which she would utter statements such as "I am a wolf of the night; I am a wolf woman of the day...I have claws, teeth, fangs, hair...and anguish is my prey at night...the gnashing and snarling of teeth..." At other times she would stare at herself in a mirror and remark that her eyes looked strange. At times, according to her psychiatrists, she felt "sexually aroused and tormented. She experienced strong homosexual urges, almost irresistible zoophilic drives, and masturbatory compulsions – culminating in the delusion of a wolflike metamorphosis. She would gaze into the mirror and see 'the head of a wolf in place of a face on my own body – just a long-nosed wolf with teeth, groaning, snarling, growling...with fangs and claws...'" While gazing into the mirror, she was observed by others to be making animal-like sounds.[140]

As previously discussed, while wolves and dogs are two of the more common forms that mentally disturbed subjects believe they can transform into, they are by no means the only ones. The following case study involves a man who thought be was a cat. In what has to be one of the most remarkable and bizarre psychiatric delusions ever recorded, in 1990, three Harvard psychiatrists described the case of a 26-year-old, male research scientist who was being treated for major depression. During his initial interview, he stunned the psychiatrist by telling him that during childhood he felt closer to his cat Tiffany than his parents, that he had long suspected that he was actually a cat, and that Tiffany confirmed this when he was 11, after teaching him to "speak cat." He claimed that as a child he was often tied to a tree near the family dog and "pretended to be a dog himself." While angry at his parents, during this period he looked at Tiffany with idealized thoughts and considered her his "surrogate parent." "When alone, he began to regularly hunt with cats, to eat small prey and raw meat, to have sexual activity with cats in serial monogamous relationships, and to converse with them by mewing and feline gestures. He reports that the activities have been continuous and are not confined to episodes of depression. He frequently visits tigers at zoos, talks with them in tiger language, pets them through the bars and collects their loose fur. While previously unsure what kind of cat he was, by age 17 he had concluded that he was a tiger-like cat due to his large size and affinity to tigers. For the past 7 years, his greatest but unrequited love has been a zoo tigress named Dolly, whom he had hoped eventually to release. When she was recently sold to a zoo in Asia, he was inconsolable and attempted to hang himself."[141]

A remarkable aspect to this case is that the patient was "gainfully employed," served as his high school class president, and had been involved in several relationships with women persisting from one three years, though he found female humans to be "far less attractive than cats."[142] In public, the man wore tiger-striped clothing and sported well-groomed facial hair and long nails, which gave him a distinct feline appearance. He maintained his secret cat identity until age 17, and received "almost continuous" drug and psychotherapeutic treatment since age 18.[143]

Porphyria

One illness that could have brought about lycanthropy accusations is porphyria, a generic term used to describe a family of related disorders affecting normal body metabolism involving an increased production and secretion of porphyrin. Severe cases can cause horrific facial scaring and ulceration, the disintegration of cartilage and bones, and facial deformities. Neurological and mental disturbances, including delirium and psychosis, have been reported. Sufferers tend to go out only at night due to extreme photosensitivity. Certain victims of porphyria suffering from mental disturbance and wandering the countryside at night, could, especially during the Middle Ages, have been mistaken for a werewolf.[144] Porohyria can also cause receding gums, giving the appearance of teeth that are long and fang-like, and produces a reddish-colored urine that could have been interpreted by medieval Europeans as supporting the notion that the werewolf had consumed people.[145]

Hypertrichosis

Congenital generalized hypertrichosis, also known as werewolf syndrome, has been suggested as a possible cause for some lycanthropy reports. This extremely rare condition is caused by a mutant gene that triggers the growth of thick, copious hair on the face and upper body. Hair typically sprouts on all parts of the face, even the eyelids.[146]

Rabies

Rabies is an acute viral infection affecting the nervous system. It is transmitted in the saliva of an infected animal and, if not promptly treated, is fatal. A common disease in medieval Europe, rabies may be associated with werewolfism for two reasons. First, rabid wolves, like other rabid animals of today, would likely have acted uncharacteristically, viciously attacking humans. There are numerous stories of wolves attacking and often killing people during the Middle Ages. While many accounts may sound exaggerated, it's possible that many wolf attacks involved rabid animals. This state of affairs may have promoted the belief in werewolves and innocent persons being accused of having perpetrated the attacks before changing back to human form. A second possibility is that people bitten by rabid animals, including wolves, would have developed rabies and gone insane. Rabies in humans typically develops within two months and results in a rapid deterioration of one's mental capacity, including hallucinations and strange behavior.

Feral Children

Some writers suggest that feral children in medieval Europe may have been mistaken for werewolves.[147] There are numerous accounts of feral children. An offshoot of the feral children theory is held by Christopher Baxter who believes that some lycanthropy cases may have involved autistic children who were abandoned by their parents.[148]

Hallucinogens

A number of people put on trial for lycanthropy described rubbing on magic ointments prior to shape-shifting into various animals, including wolves, lending credence to the role of certain drugs in the process. Writing in the early 1600s, the chief justice of Burgundy, Henry Boguet, supported this idea, noting that "The confessions of Jacques Bocquet, Francoise Secretain, Clauda Jamguillaume, Clauda Jamprost, Thievenne Paget, Pierre Gandillon and George Gandillon ... [all] said that in order to turn themselves into wolves, they first rubbed themselves with an ointment, and then Satan clothed them in a wolf's skin which completely covered them, and then they went on all-fours and ran about the country..."[149] During his confession, Pierre Bourgot told of stripping naked and smearing his body with a strange salve that could transform him into a wolf.[150] Montague Summers provided numerous examples of ointments reportedly being used in relation to werewolf accusations.[151] In medieval Europe, witches were notorious for rubbing their bodies with ointments that had different transformative powers, most prominent being the "flying ointment." However, it was also believed that witches used ointments for lycanthropy.[152]

In 1615, Jean de Nynauld, a physician, provided the most extensive and detailed description of ointments in relation to both witchcraft and lycanthropy. For transforming into a werewolf, Dr. de Nynauld concludes that Satan does not possess the power to transform humans into animals, and that lycanthropy can be explained as hallucinations potentially triggered by a variety of ointment ingredients, including such substances as henbane, opium, nightshade, parsley, and belladonna root.[153] These substances were supposedly boiled down in the fat of murdered children but were more likely "boiled down with oil."

Some werewolf reports may be attributable to ergot poisoning from eating *claviceps purpura*, a fungus that thrives in cold, damp conditions. Rye is particularly susceptible to the growth of the fungus, which eventually becomes part of the human food supply in the form of flour and rye bread – a common staple in many parts of medieval Europe. Ergot can elicit a host of abnormal psychological symptoms, including hallucinations and disorientation, and is closely related to the popular 1960s psychedelic drug lysergic acid diethylamide or LSD.[154]

Lycanthropy: An Overview

A variety of factors may have contributed to the influx of accusations, confessions, and trials for lycanthropy in later medieval Europe. While feral children, drug ingestion, certain psychiatric conditions, excessive hairiness, and porphyria may each have contributed to the werewolf scare during the 16th and 17th centuries, one overriding factor is paramount. Demonomania, or fear of the devil, which characterizes Europe during this period, appears to have been the dominant factor in the "epidemic," as werewolves were widely thought to have been witches. Suspicions of witchcraft and werewolfism were typically cast on social deviants, many of whom were tortured into confessions, often naming others, and in the self-fulfilling search for evil, condemned themselves and the others accused to be burned at the stake. It is important to realize that to most medieval Europeans, werewolves, like the belief in witches, were real. Their existence was an unquestioned fact of everyday life, and reflects the power of self-fulfilling prophecies. In the words of Walter Lippman, "under certain conditions men respond as powerfully to fictions as they do to realities, and...in many cases they help to create the very fictions to which they respond."[155] Werewolf and witchcraft beliefs had a powerful impact on medieval Europe, resulted in horrific injustices to fellow humans, and shaped the course of history.

LYONESSE BELIEVERS ("HOLY JOHN" SECT)

Cornwall, England: late 1980s

The belief that there is a submerged city between Land's End, the western tip of Cornwall, and the Scilly Isles, is an old one. Though belief in it persists, it is a false belief, as we will explain.

Historian Davies Gilbert, in his 1838 *Parochial History of Cornwall* writes: "The editor remembers a female relation of a former vicar of St. Erth who, instructed by a dream, prepared decoctions of various herbs, and repairing to Land's End, poured them into the sea, with certain incantations, expecting to see the Lionesse country rise immediately out of the water."[156]

The more recent Holy John episode shows that the legend still has the power to inspire. Trivial as it is, the incident is typical of countless minor events in which an inspired and charismatic figure succeeds, for a while at least, in attracting followers who share his vision.[157]

Holy John was a karate teacher of middle-class upbringing, prone to reading books of a vaguely mystical nature. He was in prison on a minor drug-possession charge when he had a vision that changed his life. "A great earth goddess named The Lady, and her consort Pan, were going to return to rule Britain and save us from impending ecological disaster. There would be floods and some of the land would be lost for ever. Cars would be washed away by the waves. The unjust would scatter, the old world would perish and a new Arthurian age would dawn." The vision directed him to go west, where the fabled city of Lyonesse, located off the Cornish coast, would rise from the waves.

Released from prison, in 1985 Holy John traveled in a van as far west as Britain allows, to Cornwall. Accompanying him were a group of followers whom he had already attracted to his prophecy. In a disused quarry near the town of Saint Just he set up a community. He continued to experience dreams and visions, which he recorded in a book illustrated with drawings depicting the gods and goddesses he saw in them.

Some of his followers lived in his cottage; others camped on the cliff. John would talk to them about his visions, and explain that the institution of marriage would disappear and all women would be shared. He taught his followers astral traveling and how to have visionary dreams of their own, which he would interpret. They, in turn, began to have strange experiences, seeing mysterious ships and submarines off the coast, or UFOs flying overhead. One of his followers would later recall that "It was like living in a legend." One of the attractions was Cornwall itself, a region that fascinates many. "A lot of people who had come to Cornwall already felt there was a mysterious purpose in why they had come here. John put this into focus. He crystallised their mystery, he gave it a mythology, and he made it seem right."

Sadly, after some two years, disillusion took the place of illusion. His followers resented the rules of Holy John and his second-in-command, Black Steve. Arguments led to expulsion. The final deception was the failure of Lyonesse to emerge on the day in spring predicted by their leader. For some of his followers this was the last straw, and they left soon after. Others remained, hoping that the promised event would occur, but after a year or so, the community, as such, finally dissolved.

COMMENT: The legend of Lyonesse was founded on a linguistic error. Folklore historian Jennifer Westwood writes: "There are many legends of lost lands off Western Europe, and they are probably not so much folk-memories of actual inundations as 'explanations' of visible remains such as those on Scilly." In the Breton legend of Tristan and Iseult, Tristan's native land is *Loenois,* the Old French name for Lothian in Scotland, and this was confused with Leonois in Brittany; and *Cornouaille*, a Breton district, was confused with Cornwall. When the Cornish antiquary, Richard Carew, failed to find Lyonesse in Cornwall, he assumed it to be the lost land of tradition – and so the legend was created.[158]

The body of King Arthur is borne to Lyonesse on a mysterious boat. (Stella Langdale)

LYON/SAINT-ETIENNE DEMONIC OUTBREAK

France: 1687-1690

Fifty pious persons of the parish of Cambon, near Saint-Etienne, were afflicted with convulsions, which they blamed on the devil, as was customary at the time. Fortunately, a local doctor took a different view and was able to put an end to the outbreak with very simple means.[159] Though a very minor outbreak compared with many in this Encyclopedia, the Lyon affair marks a significant step in the shift from unquestioning obedience to traditional Church teachings to a growing recognition that medical science might have better answers.

CONTEXT: The afflicted people were all from a local rural community, but the origins of the outbreak are not known. This was, however, a period of intense religious activity, with witch trials taking place throughout the country. Those involved in this outbreak seem to have carried piety to excess, and when one of their number succumbed to the strain of excessive devotion, others followed by contagion.

The women suffered from convulsions, cries, and other afflictions, including barking like a dog, or braying, bleating, whinnying, or making other animal noises. Typical was Marie Volet, a woman of excessive piety in whom devotion had gradually built up to something approaching paranoia. Superstition and scruples worked on her in such a way that her most innocent thoughts and actions became suspect to her conscience; almost anything was liable to throw her into the clutches of the Evil One. She lost sleep and her appetite, and she confused her spleen with her womb, which she fancied was sending black vapors to her brain, convincing her that she had indeed been possessed by the demon.

As this idea took hold of her imagination, an extraordinary reversal took place in her behavior. Abruptly, what had hitherto been the objects of her devotion and veneration – the blessed water, the sacred relics, the prayers, the Eucharist –now became objects of antipathy. She cried out, using savage words that some took to be Hebrew, others Arab, and yet others the language of demons. She would go for a week without eating, and claimed to have had no sleep for a fortnight. She went into convulsions and her face contorted with hideous grimaces. Her body was deformed into strange postures and shaken with fearful and terrible agitations.

For three years Marie was a victim of these afflictions. Several churchmen at the church of the Grands-Carmes in Lyon tried to exorcize her but without success. Yet Dr. de Rhodes, of the medical college of Lyon, set her right in the space of a fortnight, simply by using mineral water. At first, thinking he was trying to cure her with holy water from the church, Marie refused it. So de Rhodes ordered her nurse to walk with her to a mineral water spring. Having got her used to that, which she could see was natural, the nurse brought her artificial mineral water, saying that it came from the same source, which Marie believed, and drank it every morning for a fortnight. This caused her to vomit bilious elements of all colors, and she progressively recovered her reason. She then returned to her own parish without a trace of the possession that had afflicted her for so long, and she was now able to hear sacred things spoken of without going into convulsions. Back home, she continued to improve, resuming the weaving by which she had formerly made her living.

Dr. de Rhodes also took care of a woman from the village of Millery, 12 km south of Lyon: "I went to see a so-called possessed woman who, by her savage words and her contorsions, was considered as being possessed by a demon. I made her drink some emetic wine, which made her vomit countless 'yellow and green demons,' which were the cause of her supposed possession, and which now rendered her again her liberty."[160]

He goes on to say that if the same treatment were applied to the fifty ladies of Cambon, it would probably sort them out also. Evidently, the fact that he succeeded in curing patients who had failed to profit by their exorcisms impressed even the clergy, for after his success at Cambon they would ask him to examine sick people before they jumped to the conclusion that they were infected by the Evil One.

Sources

1. Calmeil, L.F. (1845). *De la Folie, Consideree Sous le Point de vue Pathologique, Philosophique, Historique et Judiciaire* [On the Crowd, Considerations on the Point of Pathology, Philosophy, History and Justice]. Paris: Baillere, volume 2, p. 400: all details are taken from this source unless otherwise indicated.
2. D'Hauterive, Ernest (1902). *Le Merveilleux au XVIIIe Siècle.* Paris: Juven, p. 48.
3. Calmeil, op cit., volume 2, p. 400, citing Le pour et le contre de la possession des filles de la paroisse de Landes.
4. Calmeil, op cit., volume 2, p. 410.
5. Calmeil, op cit., volume 2, p. 410.
6. Calmeil, op cit., volume 2, p. 414.
7. D'Hauterive, op cit., p. 54.
8. Calmeil, op cit., volume 2, p. 412.
9. Conley, Robert. (1963). "Laughing Malady a Puzzle in Africa. 1000 Along Lake Victoria Afflicted in 18 Months - Most are Youngsters. Schools Close Down." *New York Times*, August 8 1963, p. 29; Anonymous. (1963). *New York Times*, August 9 1963, p. 4.
10. Rankin, A. M., and Philip, P. J. (1963). "An Epidemic of Laughing

in the Buboka District of Tanganyika." *Central African Journal of Medicine* 9:167-170; Ebrahim, G.J. (1968). "Mass Hysteria in School Children, Notes on Three Outbreaks in East Africa." *Clinical Pediatrics* 7:437-438. See p. 437.

11. Ebrahim, G.J. (1968). op cit.

12. Ebrahim, G.J. (1968). op cit., p. 437.

13. Ebrahim, G.J. (1968). op cit, p. 437.

14. Anonymous. (1966). "Two Schools Close in Tanzania Till Siege of Hysteria Ends." *New York Times*, May 25, p. 36.

15. Muhangi, J. R. (1973). "Mass Hysteria in an Ankole School." *East African Medical Journal* 50:304-309.

16. Dhadphale, Manohar, and Shaikh, S.P. (1983). "Epidemic Hysteria in a Zambian School: 'The Mysterious Madness of Mwinilunga.'" *British Journal of Psychiatry* 142:85-88.

17. Dhadphale and Shaikh, op cit., p. 87.

18. Nkala, Gideon (2000). "Mass Hysteria Forces School Closure." Middle East Intelligence Wire, March 13.

19. Owino, Wene (2000). "Mass Hysteria Causes School's Temporary Closure." Pan African News Agency, March 8.

20. "Medics Call for School's Closure as Students Go Crazy." Pan African News Agency, March 3.

21. "Medics Call for School's Closure as Students Go Crazy." op cit.

22. Rankin and Philip, op cit., Kagwa, B. H. (1964). "The Problem of Mass Hysteria in East Africa." *East African Medical Journal* 41:560-566; Ebrahim, op cit.; Muhangi, op cit.

23. Ebrahim, op cit., p. 438.

24. Geraci, Gino (1995). "Look Before You Laugh." Gino Geraci is the Senior Pastor of the Calvary Chapel, South Denver, Colorado USA. Accessed December 31, 2003 at http://www.banner.org.uk/tb/ look.html; Anderson, op cit.; Needham, Dr. Nick. "The Toronto Blessing–Part One." Accessed December 31, 2003 at: http://www.geocities.com/bob_hunter/needham1.htm. Dr. Needham is from the Highland Theological College, Dingwall, Scotland IV15 9HA, United Kingdom.

25. Geraci (1995). op cit.; Anderson, Dirk. "Great Signs and Wonders II." Accessed December 31, 2003 at: http://www.intowww.org/articles/art9708.htm.

26. Anderson, op cit.

27. Tarkowski, Edward. "Laughing Phenomena: Its History & Possible Effects on the Church, Part III: The Abrahamic Covenant And Joyous Feast Of Tabernacles." Accessed December 321, 2003 at: http://users.stargate.net/~ejt/apos3.htm.

28. Needham, op cit.

29. Makeham, Greg (1995). "12 Months of the Toronto Blessing." Accessed December 31, 2003 at: http://members.iinet.net.au/~gregga/toronto/testimonies/12tb-1.html.

30. Needham, op cit.

31. Needham, op cit., Part 2, citing Richard Cavendish, *The Magical Arts*, p. 180.

32. Calmeil, L.F. (1845). *De la Folie, Consideree Sous le Point de vue Pathologique, Philosophique, Historique et Judiciaire* [On the Crowd, Considerations on the Point of Pathology, Philosophy, History and Justice]. Paris: Baillere, volume 1, p. 511, drawing on Lenormand, J. *Histoire de ce qui s'est passé sous l'exorcisme de trois filles possèdèes ès pays de Flandres*. Paris 1623: this is the primary source for this story.

33. Görres, Johann Joseph von (1845). *La Mystique Divine, Naturelle et Diabolique*. Paris: Poussielgue-Rusand, 1855, translated from the German Christliche Mystik, volume 5, p. 328.

34. Calmeil's version differs from Görres in some details.

35. Madden, R. R. (1857). *Phantasmata or Illusions and Fanaticisms of Protean Forms Productive of Great Evils*. London: T.C. Newby, volume 2, p. 265.

36. Madden, op cit., p. 269.

37. Mackay, Charles. (1852). *Memoirs of Extraordinary Popular Delusions and the Madness of Crowds Volume 2*. London: Office of the National Illustrated Library, p. 259.

38. "Smoke Cloud puts London in Total Darkness." *The Salisbury Times* (Salisbury, Maryland), January 17, 1955, p. 1.

39. Bondeson, Jan. (2000). *The London Monster*. London: Free Association, p. 176.

40. All details are from Bondeson, op cit.

41. Bondeson, op cit., p. 35.

42. Jeanne des Anges, Soeur (1886). *Autobiographie edited by Gabriel Legue and Gilles de la Tourette*. Paris: Bureaux du Progrès 1886 [originally written 1640s, but not published at that time], p. 7.

43. The best general source is Legué, Gabriel (1880). *Urbain Grandier*. Paris: Baschet.

44. Jeanne des Anges, op cit., p. 10.

45. Jeanne des Anges, op cit., p. 20.

46. Robbins, Rossell Hope (1959). *The Encyclopedia of Witchcraft and Demonology*. London: Spring Books, p. 312.

47. Jeanne des Anges, op cit., p. 64.

48. Jeanne des Anges, op cit., p. 20.

49. Jeanne des Anges, op cit., p. 20.

50. Des Niau, quoted in Robbins, op cit., p. 313.

51. Aubin, Nicolas (1752[1693]). *Histoire des Diables de Loudun*. Amsterdam: 1752, re-issue of a publication in 1693, though it was in print earlier than this date, p. 200.

52. Calmeil 1845, volume 2, p. 13.

53. Carmona, Michel (1988). *Les Diables de Loudun*. Paris; Fayard, p. 332, quoting one of the witnesses at Grandier's trial.

54. Jeanne des Anges, op cit., p. 36.

55. Calmeil, L.F. (1845). *De la Folie, Consideree Sous le Point de vue Pathologique, Philosophique, Historique et Judiciaire* [On the Crowd, Considerations on the Point of Pathology, Philosophy, History and Justice]. Paris: Baillere, volume 1, p. 307.

56. Jeanne des Anges, op cit., p. 36.

57. Carmona, Michel (1988). *Les Diables de Loudun*. Paris; Fayard, p. 17.

58. Carmona, op cit., p. 18.

59. Huxley, Aldous (1986[1952]). *The Devils of Loudun*. London; Chatto & Windus 1952 [Folio Society edition 1986], p. 168.

60. Madden, op cit., volume 1, pp. 323 and 344.

61. Figuier, Louis (1886). *Histoire du Merveilleux dans les Temps Modernes*. Paris: Hachette, p. 245.

62. Figuier, op cit., p. 245.

63. Schuler, Edgar A., and Parenton, Vernon J. (1943). "A Recent Epidemic of Hysteria in a Louisiana High School." *Journal of Social Psychology* 17:221-235. See p. 225.

64. Schuler and Parenton, op cit., p. 232.

65. Schuler and Parenton, op cit., p. 228.

66. Schuler and Parenton, op cit., p. 228.

67. Schuler and Parenton, op cit., p. 229.

68. Schuler and Parenton, op cit., p. 229.

69. Schuler and Parenton, op cit., p. 230.

70. Schuler and Parenton, op cit., p. 231.

71. Schuler and Parenton, op cit., p. 231.

72. Schuler and Parenton, op cit., p. 231.

73. Schuler and Parenton, op cit., p. 233.

74. Schuler and Parenton, op cit., p. 227.

75. Schuler and Parenton, op cit., p. 227.
76. Schuler and Parenton, op cit., p. 232.
77. Schuler and Parenton, op cit., p. 233.
78. There is a vast literature relating to Lourdes, though most writers make little or nothing of the visionaries other than Bernadette. Unless otherwise indicated, material for this entry is drawn from the histories of Cros and Laurentin.
79. Fernandes, Joaquim, and D'Armada, Fina (1981). *Intervenção Extraterrestre em Fatima*. Lisbon: Libraria Bertrand. Fernandes & D'Armada 1932/2005, p. 107.
80. Laurentin, René (1965). *Mary's Place in the Church*. London: Burns & Oates.
81. Lasserre, Henri (1877). *Notre Dame de Lourdes*. Paris: Société Générale de Librairie Catholique, p. 340.
82. Thurston, Herbert (1955). *Surprising Mystics*. London: Burns & Oates, p. 255.
83. Cros, L-J M. (1926). Histoire de Notre-Dame de Lourdes d'après les Documents et les Témoins. Paris: Beauchesne, volume 2, p. 319.
84. Laurentin, René (1957). *Lourdes, Documents Authentiques*. Paris: Lethielleux, volume 2, p. 88.
85. Laurentin, op cit., volume 2, p. 72.
86. Cros, 1926, op cit., volume 2, p. 66.
87. Estrade, Jean-Baptiste (1953). *Les Apparitions de Lourdes*. Lourdes: Imprimerie de la Grotte. Re-edition of 1899 original, p. 169.
88. Cros, 1926, op cit., volume 2, pp. 99-100.
89. Cros, 1957, p. 126: also less fully in Cros, 1926, op cit. and Laurentin, 1957. op cit.
90. Cros, 1926, op cit., volume 2, p. 96 et seq.
91. Calmeil, L.F. (1845). *De la Folie, Consideree Sous le Point de vue Pathologique, Philosophique, Historique et Judiciaire* [On the Crowd, Considerations on the Point of Pathology, Philosophy, History and Justice]. Paris: Baillere, Volume 2, p. 73. Except where otherwise indicated, the facts are taken from his account which is drawn from contemporary sources.
92. Lebreton, quoted by Calmeil (1845), op cit., p. 78.
93. Calmeil, op cit., p. 108.
94. Baissac, Jules (1890). *Les Grands Jours de la Sorcellerie*. Paris: Klincksieck, p. 547 citing Bosroger.
95. Baissac, op cit., pp. 545-546.
96. Bavent, Madeleine (1930). *The Confessions of Madeleine Bavent*. Original publication 1652: translated and edited by Montague Summers, London; Fortune Press, p. 7.
97. Baissac, op cit., p. 360.
98. Bavent, op cit., p. vii.
99. Bavent, op cit., p. 51.
100. Teresa of Avila, Letters, quoted in Sackville-West, Victoria. (1943). *The Eagle and the Dove*. London: Michael Joseph, p. 38.
101. Katzeff, Paul (1981). *Full Moons*. Secaucus NJ: Citadel, p. 206.
102. Alain, Chantal (1989). *L'effet Lunaire*. Montréak: L L'etincelle, p. 162.
103. Lieber, Arnold (1978). *The Lunar Effect*. Garden City NY: Anchor Press/Doubleday, p. 31 et seq.
104. Kelly, Rotton & Culver (1985-1986). "The Moon was Full and Nothing Happened." *The Skeptical Inquirer* 10(3), page 129 (Winter).
105. Alain, op cit., p. 103.
106. Oliven, John F. "Moonlight and Nervous Disorders: A Historical Study." *American Journal of Psychiatry* 99:579, reprinted in Corliss, William R. [compiler] (1982). *The Unfathomed Mind*. Glen Arm MD: Sourcebook Project, p. 717.
107. Lieber, op cit., p. 52.
108. Lieber, op cit., p. 109.
109. Katzeff, op cit., p. 265.
110. Saintyves, P. (1937). *L'Astrologie Populaire*. Paris: Emile Nourry, p. 183.
111. Thomas, Clayton L (editor) (1989). *Taber's Cyclopedic Medical Dictionary* (sixteenth edition). Philadelphia, Pennsylvania: F.A. Davis, p. 1057.
112. Sidky, H. (1997). *Witchcraft, Lycanthropy, Drugs, and Disease: An Anthropological Study of the European Witch-Hunts*. New York: Peter Lanf, p. 215; Summers, Montague (1973). *The Werewolf*. Secaucus, New Jersey: The Citadel Press, p. 17.
113. Kulick, Aaron, Pope, Harrison, and Keck, Paul (1990). "Lycanthropy and Self-Identification." *The Journal of Nervous and Mental Disease* 178(2):134-137.
114. Summers, 1973, op cit., p. 2.
115. Summers, 1973, op cit., p. 325.
116. Cohen, Daniel (1991). *The Encyclopedia of Monsters*. New York: Avon, p. 250.
117. Summers, 1973, op cit., p. 21.
118. Sidky, op cit., p. 220.
119. Sidky, op cit., p. 220.
120. Baring-Gould, Sabine (1865). *The Book of Werewolves: Being an Account of a Terrible Superstitution*. London: Smith, Elder and Company, p. 151.
121. Wellert, Robb, and Grossman, Gary H. (Producers) (1998). *History's Mysteries: Legends of the Werewolves*. Weller/Grossman Productions for the History Channel.
122. Foster, Joseph Arnold (editor) (1940[1590]). *A True Discourse, Declaring the Damnable Life and Death of One Stubbe Peter*. East Lansing, Michigan: Reprints of English Books.
123. Robbins, Rossell Hope (1966). *The Encyclopedia of Witchcraft and Demonology*. New York: Crown, pp. 489-490.
124. Robbins, op cit., p. 490.
125. Robbins, op cit., p. 212.
126. Robbins, op cit., p. 213.
127. Baring-Gould (1865). op cit., p. 76.
128. Robbins, op cit., p. 213.
129. Mackay, Charles (1852). *Extraordinary Popular Delusions and the Madness of Crowds. Volume 2*. London: Office of the National Illustrated Library.
130. Baring-Gould (1865). op cit., p. 88.
131. Baring-Gould, op cit., pp. 91-92.
132. Ashley (2001). op cit., p. 67.
133. Baring-Gould, op cit., pp. 93-95.
134. Robbins (1966). op cit., pp. 234-235.
135. Keck, Paul, Pope, H.G., Hudson, J.I., et al. (1988). "Lycanthropy: Alive and Well in the Twentieth Century." *Psychological Medicine* 18:113-120.
136. "Werewolves–A Medical Perspective." Complementary Medical Association, accessed July 23, 2003 at: http://www.the-cma.org.uk/HTML/werewolf.htm.
137. Jackson, Pauline M (1978). "Another Case of Lycanthropy" [Letters]. *American Journal of Psychiatry* 135(1):134-135. See p. 134.
138. Rosenstock, Harvey A, and Vincent, Kenneth R. (1977). "A Case of Lycanthropy." *American Journal of Psychiatry* 134(10):1147-1149.
139. Rosenstock and Vincent (1977). op cit., p. 1148.
140. Rosenstock and Vincent (1977). op cit., p. 1148.
141. Keck et al. (1988). op cit., p. 135.
142. Keck et al. (1988). op cit., p. 136.
143. Keck et al. (1988). op cit., p. 135.

144. Sidky (1997). op cit., p. 239.; Ashley, Leonard (2001). *The Complete Book of Werewolves*. New Jersey: Barricade Books, p. 87; Berkow, Robert (Editor-in-Chief). (1997). *The Merck Manual of Medical Information*. Whitehouse Station, New Jersey: Merck and Company, p. 690; Clayton (1989). op cit., p. 1451.
145. (1998). "The Science of Hallowe'en (Scientific Angle on Mythology)." *The Economist* (October 31):89.
146. Glausiusz, Josie (1996). "Strange Genes. (Genes for Hirsutism, Dwarfism and Bedwetting Traced in 1995." *Discover* 17(1):33.
147. Ashley (2001). op cit., pp. 92-93.
148. Baxter, Christopher. (1977). "Johann Weyer's De Praestigiis Saemonum: Unsystematic Psychopathology." Pp. 53-75. In (Sydney Anglo, editor) *The Damned Art: Essays in the Literature of Witchcraft*. London: Routledge and Kegan Paul.
149. Boguet, Henri (1929). *An examen of witches drawn from various trials of many of this sect in the district of Saint Oyan de Joux, commonly known as Saint Claude, in the county of Burgundy, including the procedure necessary to a judge in trials for witchcraft, by Henry Boguet, chief judge in the said county*. Translated by E. Allen Ashwin and edited by the Rev. Montague Summers. London: John Rodker, p. 154.
150. Summers, 1973, op cit., p. 104.
151. Summers, 1973. op cit., pp. 104-109.
152. Summers, 1973, op cit., p. 105.
153. Nynauld, Jean de (1615). De *la Lycanthropie, Transformation, et Extase des Sorciers*. Paris: J. Millot.
154. Wellert and Grossman (1998). op cit.
155. Lippmann, W. (1922). *Public Opinion*. New York: Harcourt, Brace, cited in MacDonnell, F. (1995). *Insidious Foes*. New York: Oxford University Press, p. 2.
156. Westwood, Jennifer (1985). *Albion*. London: Granada, p. 28.
157. All details for this entry are from Shaw, William (1994). *Spying in Guru Land*. London: Fourth Estate, unless otherwise indicated.
158. Westwood (1985). op cit., pp. 27-28.
159. Calmeil, L.F. (1845). *De la Folie, Consideree Sous le Point de vue Pathologique, Philosophique, Historique et Judiciaire* [On the Crowd, Considerations on the Point of Pathology, Philosophy, History and Justice]. Paris: Baillere, volume 2, p. 182, quoting de Rhodes' *Lettre sur les maladies auxquelles les eaux minérales artificielles sont propres*. All the facts are from this source.
160. Calmeil, op cit., volume 2, p.182.

MACKAY, CHARLES
1814-1889

He moved to London in 1832 where he worked as an assistant editor of the *Morning Chronicle* (1838-1844), and later became editor of the *Illustrated London News* (1852-1858).[1] Mackay's book, *Memoirs of Extraordinary Popular Delusions* was first published in 1841 when he was just 27. A revised second edition was published in two volumes a decade later under the title *Extraordinary Popular Delusions and the Madness of Crowds*. Some of the frequently written upon social delusions discussed in the book include financial speculations – the Mississippi Scheme, South-Sea Bubble, Tulipomania, in addition to broader topics: The Crusades, Witch Mania, Slow Poisoners, Popular Follies of Great Cities, and Popular Admiration of Great Thieves.

Charles Mackay, author of Extraordinary Popular Delusions and the Madness of Crowds.

While the book was not enthusiastically received when it first appeared and was criticized for being superficial, interest in the book was rekindled in 1932 by Wall Street stockbroker and millionaire Bernard Baruch who claimed that he owed much of his financial success to reading Mackay.[2] Joseph Bulgatz remarks that, with the help of writers such as Baruch, it soon became a rite of passage for new employees on Wall Street to be given the book as a primer on the potential of human folly.[3] Mackay believed that when placed in a crowd, ordinarily rational people will regress, submitting to the herd mood – a common view of the crowd at the time of his writing. While this theory of crowd contagion is no longer accepted in psychological and sociological circles, his book continues to be widely cited in newspapers, magazines, and even scientific journals as providing historical examples of the human propensity to follow the herd. For instance, after the share market "crash" of 1987, *The Economist* described the sudden, massive sell-off by noting: "The crash suffered by the world's stock markets has provided a beginning and middle for a new chapter updating Charles Mackay's 1841 book *Extraordinary Popular Delusions and the Madness of Crowds* which chronicled Dutch tulip bulbs, the South Sea bubble... It was the madness of crowds that sent the bull market ever upward ... (and it) ... is mob psychology that has now sent investors so rapidly for the exits."[4]

MAD COW SCARES

1985 to present

Just as possession is considered nine-tenths of the law, from a psychological standpoint, perception is nine-tenths of reality. During public scares and panics, the truth is often irrelevant. It's what people *believe* to be true that counts most, and since 1985, there has been a widespread perception in many parts of the world, including the United States and England, that eating beef products from cows places one at a significant risk for contracting 'mad cow' disease.

"Mad Cow" is a medical mystery that continues to baffle scientists. Unlike other diseases that are caused by bacteria, a virus, or microbes, the culprit is a prion or misfolded protein. Science writer Maggie Fox explained the problem this way: "Proteins are made by cells following instructions laid out in the genes. But like a cardboard box, a protein must be folded to function and they sometimes get folded into the wrong shape. Usually a cell will recognize this and cause it to be broken up."[5] In the case of Mad Cow, something goes wrong. The disease afflicts many animals including deer, sheep, and cats. Dogs and horses appear to be immune, but no one is sure why. Yet, for all of the mystery surrounding Mad Cow and kindred diseases, it is clear that these illnesses do not pose a credible health threat for the average human. While the death of a single person is one too many, the odds of getting "mad cow" are one in one million. But fear of the unknown makes people uneasy.

The main threat from Mad Cow is the psychological impact. Shortly after the U.S. Agricultural Department announced on December 23, 2003, that a single Holstein cow from a farm near Yakima, Washington was suspected as having Mad Cow, the reaction was staggering. Within 24-hours, eleven countries had announced total bans on the import of American beef. Fears over getting Mad Cow shook the foundations of the fast-food industry. The price of McDonald's and Wendy's stock plunged about 5%, and the U.S. dollar plummeted to record lows against the Euro and other currencies. When within weeks it was determined that the sick cow was from a herd in Canada that had eaten feed prior to the ban on ground-up animals in the feed supply, concern over the safety of U.S. beef began to subside.

Tracing The Scare

During the latter 1980s and early 1990s, at least 150,000 European cattle were diagnosed with Mad Cow Disease. Then there was a government announcement that ten residents of the United Kingdom had recently died from Creuzfeldt-Jakob Disease (CJD), a disease related to Mad Cow. The announcement sparked concerns across Europe that people could get Mad Cow from eating contaminated beef. In reaction, the European Commission banned imports of British beef and related products.

The European Mad Cow scare began on December 22, 1984, when cow number 133 on a farm in Sussex, England, started to shake uncontrollably. It also had trouble walking and became uncharacteristically aggressive. Within two months the animal was dead. When tests were conducted to determine the cause of death, scientists were stunned at the condition of the brain, which was pocked with tiny holes. They had seen this condition before in other animals but not cows. It was evident that the animal had the dreaded disease known as spongiform encephalopathy. The situation soon grew worse as more cows on the farm began to exhibit similar symptoms.

Mad Cow disease is the popular name for Bovine Spongiform Encephalytis or BSE for short. Bovine has to do with cattle; spongiform refers to sponge-like holes that dot the brain of afflicted animals; encephalytis is derived from the Greek words for brain and disease.[6] The epidemic among cattle has been traced to cattle feed from the ground-up remains of BSE-infected sheep that entered the food supply through cattle feed.

Rigid feeding restrictions were implemented, and the number of BSE cases peaked by 1993, affecting three-tenths of one per cent of British cattle herds.[7] Fear over a possible human epidemic of Mad Cow gained momentum in 1995 when it was widely reported that a British citizen named Stephen Churchill had died of a strange new affliction resembling BSE and Creutzfeldt-Jakob disease. Many people, including health authorities, were fearful that this new disease, termed new variant Creutzfeldt-Jakob disease, would soon sweep through the human population. Some scientists issued frightening scenarios. For instance, in 1997, scientists at London's Imperial College issued a prediction that as many as 10 million people could soon be struck down by new variant CJD. Such estimates turned out to be grossly exaggerated. For example, by 2002, the number of new variant JCD deaths was placed at just 17 and the predicted influx in cases never materialized.[8] Meanwhile, the number of regular CJD cases held steady at about one per million.

COMMENT: The risk of a human getting a BSE-related illness is extremely rare. BSE expert Dr. Jean Weese is confident that the beef supply is safe to eat: "We've simply not seen any evidence of this prion in red muscle mass. From everything researchers have been able to determine, it only turns up in brain and spinal tissue."[9]

MAD GASSER OF BOTETOURT

Botetourt and Roanoke Counties, Virginia: 1933-1934[10]

Between December 22, 1933 and early January 1934, residents in rural, mountainous Botetourt County, Virginia,[11] became the focus of national media attention after a series of alarming reports that a maniacal gasser was prowling the neighborhood at night and spraying citizens in their homes with a noxious chemical. Near the end of the episode, a flurry of cases was reported from adjacent Roanoke County.

CONTEXT: The episode is a reflection of what military historian Elvira K. Fradkin termed the "poison gas scare,"[12] as numerous writers of the decade warned of the dangers of gas warfare.[13] Residents of rural Virginia, preoccupied with the threat of chemical weapons, began to redefine various mundane events and circumstances as gasser-related.

The episode began in the tiny community of Fincastle, when a mysterious figure reportedly struck at the Cal Huffman farmhouse on three separate occasions between Friday evening December 22 and early Saturday morning of the 23rd. The first incident began at about 10 p.m. when Mrs. Huffman detected a gassy odor and became nauseous. Despite the incident, she retired to bed while her husband remained awake in hopes of catching the perpetrator if there was a repeat attack. About 30 minutes later the smell of gas permeated the house and Mr. Huffman telephoned police who arrived about midnight; their investigation was unrevealing. Immediately after county police officer O.D. Lemon left at about 1 a.m., a third attack reportedly transpired. This time, all of the seven or eight family members experienced choking fumes that made them temporarily ill. The Huffman's 20-year-old daughter Alice was most seriously affected, having fainted, and when nearby Troutville physician S.F. Driver arrived on the scene, thinking her gravely ill, he dramatically administered "artificial respiration" in order to "resuscitate" her. In just a few hours she appeared completely recovered. She later relapsed and was described as "seriously ill," but physicians attributed the symptoms to "nerves."[14] After this third attack, Mr. Huffman and another person inside the house thought they might have seen a man running away.[15] The only vague clue found at the scene was a woman's high heel shoe imprint near the window where the gas was believed to have entered the house, and a second print under a porch where it was thought the gasser may have hidden.[16]

The next press report appeared in the Wednesday edition of the *Roanoke Times* of December 27, treating the gasser attacks as factual ("Gas Attacks on Homes Continue"), and adding a new case involving Mr. and Mrs. Clarence Hall of Cloverdale. The couple returned home Sunday night at about 9 p.m. after a church service and within five minutes detected sickening fumes that left a sweet taste in their mouth. Symptoms included extreme nausea, smarting eyes, and weakness. The next evening a relative thought they saw a figure with a flashlight near a side window of the Hall residence.[17]

The "gasser" struck again on Wednesday the 27th

at Troutville, as acetylene welder A.L. Kelly reported that he was attacked about 10 p.m. while in an upstairs room. Curiously, no one else in the house was affected.[18] This was followed by a temporary cessation of press coverage and reported incidents, with the view expressed that the gasser "has concluded to call a halt to the series of mysterious attacks."[19]

The gas attacks resumed on Thursday night, January 11, at about 10 p.m. when a woman living at Howell's Mill, several miles west of Fincastle, reported hearing muffled voices in the yard followed by a rustling shade by a window that had been broken for some time. As the room immediately permeated with the smell of gas, "Mrs. Moore grabbed her baby and ran out to give the alarm, but not until experiencing a marked feeling of numbness." The couple living upstairs, who owned the house, were unaffected by the "gas" and were unaware of the incident until hearing Mrs. Moore's cries.[20] Once again the press had reported the gasser's existence as an absolute fact, beginning its account as follows: "Nocturnal dispensers of a nauseating and benumbing gas were abroad in Botetourt county again last night..."[21] The owner of the house, Homer Hylton, stood guard over the residence the remainder of the night fearing another attack. It was subsequently revealed that on about the same night, the home of G.D. Kinzie in Troutville was gassed by what one physician concluded was potentially lethal chlorine gas.[22]

On Tuesday night, January 16, Mr. F.B. Duval told police that upon arriving at his home near Bonsack about 11:30, he learned that his family had been gassed. On his way to meet police, he caught a fleeting glimpse of a man running to a nearby car, and assumed that he was the perpetrator.[23] Friday evening, January 19, at 7:30 p.m., a Mrs. Campbell was sitting near a window at her Carvin's Cove home when she noticed the curtains flutter, immediately followed by a strange odor which made her ill.[24] On Sunday night January 21, Mr. and Mrs. Howard Crawford retuned home in Colon at about 9 p.m. after visiting friends, when Mrs. Crawford, while trying to light a lamp, was staggered by fumes.[25]

By Tuesday January 23, the fear of being the gasser's next victim had reached such proportions that families in remote sections of the county were sleeping with neighbors, and vigilante farmers were "reported patrolling roads at late hours of the night or sitting on their doorsteps with guns in their hands."[26] One police officer expressed concern "that some innocent person passing a house or calling upon a neighbor may be wounded or killed through nervousness" by those fearing they were next on the gasser's list.[27] On the morning of the 24th, Mrs. R. H. Harteel of Pleasantdale returned home at about 4:30 a.m. after sleeping with a neighbor, only to find that the house had been gassed.[28] During the day of the 24th police needlessly heightened tensions after an internal misunderstanding resulted in their erroneously announcing three separate attacks on homes in the vicinity of Carvin's Cove two nights earlier.[29] In actuality, there had been one report, at the residence of a man named Reedy. Immediately upon detecting the odor, one of his sons grabbed a shotgun, ran outdoors, and fired at what appeared to be a man running across a field, but apparently missed.[30] The escalating number of reports prompted members of the Virginia State Assembly to introduce a bill calling for a prison term of up to 10 years or a fine of $500 or one year's jail for anyone convicted of releasing noxious gases in public or private places. In the event the incident caused injury, the gasser "would be deemed guilty of malicious wounding and punished with from between one and twenty years in the penitentiary in the discretion of the court."[31] The bill was passed after a vote of the House of Delegates at the Capitol on Tuesday, January 30.[32]

On the evening of Sunday, January 28, five people at the Ed Stanley residence near Colon Siding were overcome by noxious fumes while sitting in a room. Symptoms included a severe choking sensation and nausea. While none of the victims had lost consciousness, a Mrs. Weddle had to be carried from the house suffering extreme nausea. When one of the victims, Frank Guy, managed to reach fresh air, he saw what appeared to be four men running near the woods, so he grabbed a shotgun and fired.[33] The next day, the county Board of Supervisors voted to offer a $500 reward for apprehension and conviction of the culprit or culprits.[34]

Increasing Skepticism

With the lack of concrete evidence, an inkling of skepticism began to appear in press reports for the first time on the 24th, perhaps triggered by the first obvious false alarm. The first hint occurred in Fincastle on the night of the 24th, when a colored woman living near the jail, Mamie Brown, dashed from her residence screaming that she had been gassed. A crowd quickly formed and was led to her house by jailer C.E. Williamson, who determined that someone "had tossed a common fly killing fluid into the kitchen – apparently as a joke."[35] At about 9 p.m. on the 25th, a watchdog at the Chester Snyder Farm near Cloverdale began barking. Prepared for the gasser, Snyder immediately leaped out of bed, grabbed a shotgun, and fired at the outline of a man walking in a nearby field.[36] The incident may have been unrelated to the "gasser," and although it was reported as a potential attack, on January 28, a journalist jokingly interviewed Mr. Snyder's dog. "He [the dog] was friendly and apparently willing to 'make copy,' but when he was asked whether a man he detected prowling...was the 'gas' man, the pup merely pointed his ears...and barked a single bark."[37] By January 30, some citizens expressed the view that "the whole gassing case is a mere hoax, or figment of imagination of reported victims."[38] Further, while believing in the reality of the gasser, a Dr. Driver told a meeting of the county Board of Supervisors that not all cases appeared to be genuine gassings. It was also disclosed that at one of the homes "attacked," the offending fumes were traced to a coal stove.[39] The statement of sheriff L.T. Mundy typified the mood at this time, declaring himself a "doubting Thomas" until getting gassed himself. Meanwhile, his wife was busy stuffing keyholes on their farm in an effort to thwart the gasser.[40]

Shift To Roanoke County

In early February, the attacks shifted for the first time outside of Botetourt County. The first of these "attacks" was reported from near the Botetourt County line in adjacent Roanoke County. It occurred early on the evening of February 3, when three people were sickened by fumes at the Hamilton residence, as the family was entering their home after an absence of several hours.[41] Within three hours, the last case investigated as a possible attack in Botetourt County occurred on Saturday evening February 3, at the Troutville home of Mr. A.P. Scaggs, making seven people ill, as well as the dog.[42] As usual, the attack occurred between 8 and 9 p.m. and a doctor was summoned to treat the victims, all of whom soon recovered fully, including the pet.[43] While there were claims of subsequent gassings in Botetourt County, none involved actual symptoms or the detection of gas by residents. For instance, the next evening when John Shanks noticed a suspicious car not far from his home near Troutville, he fired three shots into the air as the vehicle disappeared. At about the same time, another Troutville man became fearful of a gas attack after hearing a vague noise on his porch. Police, however, noted that the incidents were vague and may have been unrelated to the gasser.[44]

The gasser next struck in a residential section of Roanoke at about 8 p.m. on Wednesday, February 7, as Mrs. A.H. Milan of Rorer Avenue was alone in her living room with her 12-year-old daughter, when a "funny" smell was noticed coming from the door. Several minutes later, Mrs. Milan suddenly felt very ill, while her daughter experienced temporary dizziness.[45] She spent the night in the hospital as a precaution, although her daughter suffered no after-effects.[46] The following night, Roanoke police received five additional reported attacks within two hours, only to be frustrated by a stark lack of clues. The first call was received at about 8:55 p.m., when an employee of the city health department and three family members detected a strange smell in their home and briefly felt faint. Most of the calls consisted of residents smelling fumes but not becoming sick. One of the reports was a clear false alarm when a maid over reacted upon hearing a car stop near her residence.[47]

The following night, February 9, seemed to usher in a major turning point as the Roanoke County "gassings" peaked with seven separate reports investigated by police, who curiously noted that "In no instance did the officers detect any nauseating fumes, and no occupants of any of the homes were affected."[48] In most instances, the police readily detected a mundane source of the odors. In one case, three detectives rushed to a home, only to implicate coal fumes from a stove. At another house, gasser fumes were believed to have emanated from a passing car.

> Residents at 316 Howbert Avenue, Wasena, detected strange fumes near a furnace register about 8:25 but no one suffered any ill effects and police said they believed the fumes had come from the furnace. No one was seen or heard about the house before the odor was detected...
>
> Three reports were received between 10 and 11 o'clock...at 551 Washington Avenue, S.W.–both occupants and police detected fumes, but they came from a thawing automobile radiator which contained alcohol. Several persons were playing bridge when the fumes were noticed. Police found that an automobile had been driven into a garage at the rear of the house and the smell of alcohol was decidedly noticeable.
>
> A resident at 311 Broadway, South Roanoke, entered a bedroom and detected a peculiar odor. Police said they failed to find any trace of a noxious gas.
>
> Residents at 811 and 813 Shenandoah Avenue, N.W., noted a peculiar odor about 11 o'clock. Police said they believed that the occupants had smelled sulphur in coal smoke from passing trains.[49]

On the morning of the 10th, when the seven pseudo-attacks of the previous night were reported, a further revelation eroded confidence in the gasser's existence. It was disclosed that Mrs. E.L. Langford, who became suddenly ill on Thursday evening February 8 after hearing a gas canister strike her door, was being released from the hospital after recovering, while the noise was believed to have been rice thrown at her door. Three other residents of the dwelling had been unaffected.[50]

On the following night, February 11, five more gassings were reported as police reported a potential break in the case, announcing that a bottle had been used to scoop up a sweet-smelling oily liquid found in the snow near the scene of a suspected attack at a home in Botetourt County, the first incident reported in that county in over a week.[51] On February 12, a local chemist told police that the mystery liquid was a mixture of substances that were harmless to humans and most likely an insecticide "similar to that of fly exterminators used in practically every household."[52] Reported gassings ceased entirely in both counties after the night of the 11th. In all, Roanoke police had received 19 calls, the last of which occurred when several officers responded to a "gassing" that was traced to burning rubber, and prompting them to suggest that the "gas man" was "a product of overwrought imaginations."[53] This conclusion was supported by an editorial in the *Roanoke Times,* which proclaimed: "Roanoke Has No Gasser."[54] In this article it was stated that "This newspaper has so believed from the first [in the gasser's nonexistence], but it seemed best to permit the police to go ahead and investigate without whatever handicap they might be under were cold water to be thrown on their search in advance." Despite this claim, in an earlier editorial in the same newspaper, it was clearly stated that the gasser was real, concluding that "the series of gas attacks is being engineered by irresponsible practical jokers, with more zest for adventure than brains."[55]

See also: MAD GASSER OF MATTOON, TERRORISM SCARES.

MAD GASSER OF MATTOON

Mattoon, Illinois: 1944

During September 1944, residents of Mattoon, Illinois, made national headlines after a series of reported gas attacks by someone dubbed the "phantom anesthetist." Mattoon police investigated over two dozen separate gassing claims and scores of other reports involving shadowy figures prowling after dark, later concluding that the events were figments of the imagination. Shortly after the publication of a study the following year by Donald Johnson in the *Journal of Abnormal and Social Psychology*, the episode became a classic within the social science annals.[56] It is arguably the most widely cited example of "mass hysteria" during the 20th century. Since the 1950s, most introductory textbooks on sociology and social psychology that discuss mass behavior cite Johnson's article, as does virtually every book on collective behavior. Physicist Wily Smith contends there was a real gasser.[57] His argument is based on eyewitness testimony and recollections of the event – both of which are notoriously unreliable, and both of which Smith takes at face value. The incident has appeared in popular books and articles on mysteries and the paranormal, where it is typically discussed as an unsolved crime or the work of a supernatural entity.[58]

CONTEXT: The episode was incubated in a hotbed of sensational press coverage, widely publicized fears of Nazi poison gas attacks, an escaped Nazi scare in Mattoon, and a local robbery/break-in wave. The Mattoon scare occurred when the United States was at war, indeed — shortly after D-day when a German retaliation would not have been surprising.

Based on an analysis of press reports and interviews by Robert Bartholomew,[59] the "mad gasser" saga began about 11 p.m. on Friday, September 1, when housewife Aline Kearney retired to her bedroom with her three-year-old daughter Dorothy. Her husband Bert was out driving taxi. Her sister Martha was awake in a front room, while Aline's other daughter and Martha's son slept in a back room. Suddenly Aline perceived a sickening, sweet odor that she attributed to a gardenia flower patch next to an open window, just inches from her bed. She summoned Martha to see if she could smell it. She could not and left the room. As the scent intensified, Aline noticed that her throat and lips felt dry and burning, and there was a paralyzing sensation in her legs. She screamed for Martha, who again rushed in but this time said she *could* detect a strange odor. After being told of the "paralysis," Martha alerted a next-door neighbor, Mrs. Earl Robertson, who phoned police about the "gassing." Meanwhile, Mr. Robertson searched the area without success. Police found no trace of an intruder.[60] After hearing of the "attack," Mr. Kearney reached home about 12:30 a.m. and claimed to glimpse a figure near the bedroom window. Police again searched fruitlessly. He said the man was tall and wore dark clothes and a skullcap.[61] [62]

The *Daily Journal-Gazette and Commercial Star*[63] (hereafter referred to as the *Gazette*) was Mattoon's only large-circulation newspaper and read by 97 percent of families.[64] It reported that unnamed authorities surmised that someone might have sprayed the bedroom with poison gas. Mrs. Kearney said that the paralyzing sensation in her legs abated after 30 minutes. Her daughter also felt temporarily ill. The others in the house were unaffected.[65]

Alarmist Press Coverage

From the start, the mass media sensationalized the initial gassing claims, encouraging a retrospective interpretation of events, shortly after the start of the episode. Accordingly, people in Mattoon began redefining recent ambiguous events and circumstances as gasser-related. On September 2, the *Gazette* published the first "gasser" report, claiming, "Anesthetic Prowler on Loose." His existence was treated as fact. The sub-headline read: "Mrs. Kearney and Daughter First Victims...Robber Fails to get into Home."

Later, other residents reported "gassings" but only *after* reading the *Gazette's* initial sensational account. These four additional "attacks" were reported to have occurred at homes before or near the time of the Kearney incident. At about the same time as the Kearney "attack," *The Chicago Herald-American* of September 21 reported that Mrs. George Rider later said she was alone with her two sleeping children, awaiting her husband's return from work. Having an upset stomach, she began drinking excessive amounts of coffee. She later told a doctor that she had consumed "several pots" and then took stomach medication before vomiting.[66] Until this point, there was no sign of the gasser. She next lay in bed near her children with the window shut. She then heard a peculiar noise – like a "plop" – followed by an odd smell accompanied by a feeling of lightheadedness.[67] And with this came finger and leg numbness. Just then her baby began coughing. She assumed that the gasser had forced the fumes through a bedroom window.[68]

On September 8, the *Gazette* reported that Mr. and Mrs. Orban Raef claimed the gasser struck at their residence the night before the Kearney "gassing." He and his wife were asleep at 3 a.m. when, he claimed, fumes came through the bedroom window. Both experienced "the same feeling of paralysis" and felt unwell for 90 minutes. Friends sleeping in another room were unaffected.[69] The same issue of the *Gazette* reported that Mrs. Olive Brown told police that months earlier, she too had been "gassed," but did not report it, fearing ridicule. She said that near midnight, "she had an experience similar to that related by persons during the past few days."[70]

Police did not lend credibility to the first few gassing claims. This was noted in a September 8 *Gazette* editorial criticizing authorities for neither believing Aline Kearney nor the four reports that quickly followed by residents claiming "gassings" only after learning of Mrs. Kearney's claim. The *Gazette* states that police attributed these early reports to "imagination."[71] Police did not publicly exhibit concern until about September 5, yet police skepticism is not reflected in the early press reports.

On Saturday, September 2, the *Gazette* published the first report on the incident in banner, six-column headlines: "Anesthetic Prowler on Loose." Not only was the gasser treated as fact, the sub-headline implied that more gassings may follow: "Mrs. Kearney and Daughter First Victims ... Robber Fails to get into Home." The four additional gassing claims are dubious, as no one reported them to police, fled their home, told friends or relatives, or bothered to consult a physician. As Robert Ladendorf and Robert Bartholomew remarked: "Just imagine – you suspect someone has sprayed poison gas into your home making you and your family ill: dizziness, burning lips, vomiting, partial limb paralysis. It was well-known that poison gas could cause permanent disabilities or prove lethal. And what do these early 'gas victims' do? They remain in the house and soon after the supposed attack, go back to sleep without telling a soul! This behavior makes no sense unless, after learning of the mad gasser, those involved in the three earlier 'attacks,' began redefining ambiguous events and reconstructing what had actually happened."[72]

Wily Smith states because there were gassing reports prior to Mrs. Kearney's on September 1, and they occurred late at night, it is "very unlikely that word of the incidents could have spread so quickly. As they were not reported in the newspaper until two days later, they simply had to be real events."[73] Smith's argument would seem to hold little merit as he bases his assumptions on Johnson's statement that there were four earlier gassings, for which all of the evidence is circumstantial and retrospective. This might have become evident if Smith had examined the original Mattoon press reports, which he did not. By his own admission, Smith said, "I am a physicist, not a psychologist," and he made no mention of studies on the fallibility of human memory and perception.[74]

In re-examining Mrs. Kearney's report in the *Gazette* on September 2, neither she nor her sister mentioned a prowler. Mrs. Kearney is quoted saying that her sister contacted a neighbor, Mrs. Earl Robertson, who called police. The newspaper then indicated that Mr. Robertson searched the yard and neighborhood, "but could find no trace of the prowler. Police also searched without success." Not until Mr. Kearney arrives is there mention of a prowler at the bedroom window. In the article's lead and a following reference to Mrs. Kearney's parched and burned lips from "whatever was used by the prowler," the unnamed reporter surmises that there is a prowler spraying gas through the window. The "mad gasser" was a *Gazette* creation that combined the first incident involving Aline Kearney's strange odor and "paralysis" with Bert Kearney's claim of a prowler in the second incident. No one reported seeing an "anesthetic prowler." A headline writer simply created the phrase. The term "anesthetic prowler" was a media construction of the *Gazette* and quickly became a self-fulfilling prophecy as evidenced in the next four prowler reports. The *Gazette* sensationalized the events further by suggesting that there would be more victims in the sub-head for the first headline: "Mrs. Kearney and Daughter First Victims."[75]

Escalating Fear

Between September 5 and 6, gasser reports spread beyond the *Gazette* to most Illinois newspapers. These reports quoted authorities, such as the Mattoon police commissioner and mayor and army experts, all of whom described the gasser as real. Additional gasser claims continued to be reported. Most of these reports were either alarmist or asserted the gasser's real existence. On September 5, Mrs. Beulah Cordes claimed to be "overcome" by fumes after finding a cloth on her porch and sniffing it. It was analyzed at a crime laboratory where a chemical expert could detect no trace of gas, saying it must have evaporated.[76] Mattoon Mayor E. Richardson suggested that mustard gas could account for the numbness, while army experts from the Chicago-based Chemical Warfare Service favored chloropicrin.[77] Richard Piper, superintendent of the Illinois Bureau of Criminal Identification and Investigation, confidently proclaimed: "The existence of the anesthetic, or whatever it is, is genuine."[78]

The major Chicago newspapers provided coverage on September 6. Most sent reporters to Mattoon and afforded the story considerable space. Johnson reports that these papers had a significant Mattoon readership, undoubtedly affecting public perceptions. The *Chicago Daily Tribune* was read by 24% of residents; the *Chicago Daily News* reached 20%.[79] Although the *Chicago Herald-American* covered only 5% of Mattoon,[80] its audience during the gassings was likely higher. Johnson said *The Herald-American*'s alarming headlines and photographs were often cited to him in the course of his investigation.[81]

By September 6, a nightly barrage of gassing reports was overwhelming Mattoon's modest police force of two officers and eight patrolmen.[82] On September 8, about 70 people poured onto Dewitt Avenue, after hearing that the gasser was spotted nearby. When someone in the crowd detected a strange odor, others in the group were convinced that they had been "gassed."[83] On September 10, the *Chicago Herald-American* described the incident with its typical sensationalism, beginning its front-page account this way: "Groggy as Londoners under protracted aerial blitzing, this town's bewildered citizens reeled today under repeated attacks of a mad anesthetist who has sprayed deadly nerve gas into 13 homes and has knocked out 27 known victims."[84]

On September 9 and 10, hundreds of citizens gathered near City Hall to hear the latest news. As a patrol car responded to a call, it was followed by a procession of vehicles with curious occupants. This prompted Police Commissioner Wright to order his officers to arrest "chasers."[85] Vigilante gangs of men and boys roamed the streets on foot and in vehicles, toting everything from clubs to rifles and shotguns. The Commissioner feared that a jittery resident with a gun would shoot innocent people.[86] One woman whose husband was away in the army loaded his gun for protection, only to blow a hole in the kitchen wall.[87] These kinds of events would seem absurdly humorous, if it were not for their potential to harm innocent suspects.

By September 9, several more "gassings" were reported, as the *Gazette* continued to describe the episode in its typical sensational fashion and banner page one headlines: "'Mad Gasser' Adds Six Victims! 5 Women and Boy Latest Overcome." The most vivid gassing claim was also reported on the 9th, as sisters Frances and Maxine Smith claimed a series of attacks on their home. Frances was a prominent community figure and local grade school principal. On Wednesday night the two said they were frightened by "noises outside their bedroom windows" and thought it may have been the gasser. The following night, they claimed three attacks. Like the previous "gassings," the *Gazette* of September 9 presented this incident as absolute fact.

> The first infiltration of gas caught them in their beds. Gasping and choking, they awoke and soon felt partial paralysis grip their legs and arms. Later, while awake, the other attacks came and they saw a thin, blue smoke-like vapor spreading throughout the room.
>
> Just before the gas with its "flower-like" odor came pouring into the room they heard a strange "buzzing" sound outside the house and expressed the belief that the sound probably was made by the "madman's spraying apparatus" in operations.[88]

Separate weekend incidents resulted in two women being hospitalized for "gassings" but they were later diagnosed as having "nervous tension."[89]

By Monday the 11th, ten Springfield police officers were mobilized to Mattoon. Each car had a local volunteer to assist with directions, and each officer carried a shotgun.[90] Three police officers from Urbana were also dispatched. It was also disclosed that two FBI agents had arrived to determine the type of gas the "madman" was using "to knock out his victims."[91] That night a woman was so scared of a possible attack that she was hospitalized for "extreme mental anguish."[92]

The Skeptical Stage

There was a sudden shift in claims by the press and institutions of social control (i.e., police and politicians) on September 11 that described *much* of the recent events as "mass hysteria." With a small army of police on patrol, Commissioner Wright joked that they were often able to answer a call "before the phone was back on the hook." [93] At 11:30 a.m. Mrs. Eaton Paradise told police, "I've just been gassed." Racing to the house, they found the culprit – a bottle of spilled nail-polish remover.[94] This and many other obvious false alarms prompted Police Chief Cole to announce on the 12th that it was *all* "mass hysteria" triggered by chemicals from local factories that drifted across the city by shifting winds.[95]

On Wednesday the 13th, reporters were now describing the gasser as the "phantom anesthetist" and "Mattoon Will-o'-the-Wisp." The *Gazette* reported on two more false reports overnight involving a cat on a porch and someone locked out of their car.[96] By September 14, under a barrage of ridicule by police and the press, gassing reports in Mattoon had stopped. The *Gazette* began its account of a prowler claim the previous night by saying: "One call! No paralyzing gas! No madman! No prowler!"[97] On the 15th, the *Gazette* reported that police in Cedar Rapids, Iowa, stated that a frantic woman telephoned, claiming that a man holding a spray gun outside her window had gassed her room. Police said "they found no madman and no gas, but did find a billy goat tied in the yard and an odor that seemed to come from the animal."[98]

Heretofore the gasser's strongest media advocate, the *Chicago-Herald American*, suddenly turned scathingly critical of gasser claims by publishing a series of interviews with a prominent Chicago psychiatrist about the "phantom prowler," "non-existent madman," "wave of hysteria," and "gasser myth," equating it to the Salem witch hysteria of 1692.[99] An editorial on the 19th in the *Decatur Herald* made fun of imaginative Mattoonites, noting that autumn was a season of odors: flowers, picnic fires, industrial wastes, and rotting Victory garden produce. "Our neighbors in Mattoon sniffed their town into newspaper headlines from coast to coast."[100] A reporter for *Time* joked that gasser symptoms in Mattoonites consisted of temporary paralysis, nausea, and "a desire to describe their experiences in minutest detail."[101] Other letters to the *Gazette* during late September ridiculed the episode. On the 26th, an army officer said Mattoon residents had more advanced poison gas training than his unit;[102] on the 29th another writer described the incidents as "hysteria."[103]

The Poison Gas Scare

Dozens of popular and scientific periodicals around this time also discussed the "poison gas peril" in publications such as *Newsweek*, *Popular Science*, and *The American Journal of Public Health*.[104] As the tide of World War II turned increasingly in favor of the Allies, so did concern that desperate German commanders might resort to gas warfare.[105] In fact, the Allies were so concerned that the Germans might use poison gas during their June 6, 1944, D-Day invasion of Normandy, that they had a plan to retaliate within 48 hours with two bombing raids of 400 planes each, all loaded with chemical weapons designed to hit selected targets. Gas warfare expert Frederic Brown states that D-Day was the "most dangerous period for German [gas] initiation" – a credible threat that was widely discussed in the press later that year.[106] The mad gasser appeared just two and a half months after D-Day.

About the time of the first gassing report in Mattoon by Aline Kearney, newspapers in Champaign, Chicago, and Springfield carried wire service articles about gas use. The August 30 *Champaign News-Gazette* included a page 1 article: "Believe Nazis Prepared To Use Gas." On August 31, the *Chicago Herald-American* had one on page 2 ("Report Nazis Plan Poison Gas Attack") and another report in the September 1 issue on page 2 ("Allies Ready If Nazis Use Gas"); and an Associated Press article in the (Springfield) *Illinois State Journal* on September 1 ("Unlikely Gas To Be Used In War") appeared on the day of Mrs. Kearney's alleged gassing. The AP article stated: "If Nazi extremists bent on ruling or ruining should employ gas against civilian populations in a bitter end resistance, the allies would be in a position through air strength to drench German cities...Recurrent rumors that the Germans are preparing to initiate gas warfare bring no official reaction here."

In the Mattoon event, the Mattoon *Daily-Journal Gazette* was responsible for initiating the scare, while a deluge of subsequently published gassing claims propagated the episode, and despite early reluctance, state officials and police, FBI officers and local opinion leaders soon embraced the hypothesis that a real gasser was prowling the community. Near the end of the episode, this process began to work in reverse, as both the press and police were soon embracing the mass hysteria hypothesis. This view was given final legitimization in a series of articles in the *Chicago Herald-American* by local psychiatrist Harold Hulbert, who proclaimed the gasser mythical and a case of "mass hysteria."

While certainly unusual, given the war scare context, the case of the mad gasser is not so bizarre. During the 20th century, strange odors were the most common trigger of epidemic hysteria in both job and school settings.[107] It is a sign of our present times, which are dominated by occupational safety legislation and environmental fears. Given the recent concern over chemical and biological weapons attacks by terrorists, episodes similar the phantom anesthetist may be set to recur.

MADRID OUTBREAK

Spain: 1628

The malady that struck a community of Benedictine nuns of the convent of San Placida in Madrid was a public scandal. The convent had been founded by the family of Donna Teresa de Sylva, who though only 26 years old was its abbess, and its spiritual director was Father Francisco Garcia, a learned and holy man. The thirty sisters were all virtuous ladies who had chosen to embrace the monastic life.[108] With such credentials, life at the convent should have been serene and untroubled. Instead, all but five of the sisters were overtaken by a terrifying affliction they could only attribute to the Evil One.

CONTEXT: At this time the witch mania was at its height, and this may have affected the state of mind of the Madrid sisters. However, there does not seem to have been any immediate cause for the outbreak.

In September 1628, one of the nuns, Sister Francisca, gave signs, by her words and gestures, of being in a "supernatural" state of mind and body. Their spiritual director and confessor Father Garcia was summoned. He exorcised her and diagnosed that she was possessed by a demon. During the following months three other nuns were afflicted in the same way, and on December 28, Sister Teresa, the abbess herself, succumbed. She said later that she began to feel interior movements so extraordinary and novel that she was persuaded they were not natural. She begged Garcia to exorcize her, but he refused, trying to convince her it was her imagination.

Finally, however, he agreed to perform the exorcism. She felt relieved but fell into "a kind of swoon, and delirium, doing and saying things of which she never had an idea in her life." She said that for three months she rarely found herself in her natural condition: "Nature gave me so tranquil a character that, even in my childhood, I had none of the characteristics of childhood, and had no fondness for the games and sports which children generally enjoy. In the light of that, one must see it as supernatural that, now that I have arrived at the age of 26, a nun and even an abbess, I should commit such follies of which I have never previously been capable."[109]

By the end of the year, 25 of her flock of 30 were afflicted in the same way. Expert theologians were called in, and the exorcisms were repeated daily. Father Garcia, a pious and learned man, spent days and nights at the convent to renew his efforts and established that 25 demons, led by one named Peregrino, had taken possession of the nuns.[110]

The sisters tried to cope with the situation by inflicting discipline – corporal penance – on one another, but this was no more effective than the exorcisms. The trouble persisted for three years, when finally the Inquisition of Toledo brought the situation to an end by arresting the confessor, the abbess, and some of the nuns. They were lodged in their secret prisons at Toledo. Garcia was denounced for corrupting the nuns, and they, in turn, were accused of only pretending to be possessed. In 1633, the trial closed with Garcia and the nuns being accused of falling into the heresy of the *Alumbrados* (meaning "the illuminated ones," fanatics). They were condemned to perform severe penances and were separated and dispersed to different convents. The abbess herself was sent away for eight years.

When she returned to her convent, her superiors commanded her to demand a revision of her trial. She agreed to do so and wrote an account of the matter, not out of self-love, but for the honor of her nuns and the reputation of the order of Saint Benedict. Fortunately she had influential friends who persuaded the Supreme Council of the Inquisition to review the case. In 1642, the Council accepted that the nuns were completely innocent but continued to blame

Father Garcia for his imprudence in holding conversations with the demons, to satisfy his own curiosity, before he drove them out of the sisters.

From beginning to end, no one questioned that the nuns had really been possessed by demons. Garcia himself, though condemned, was blamed only for being irregular in his mode of exorcism.

COMMENT: Irish physician Richard Madden observed: "The only evil Garcia appears to have done the community was by the long continuance of his exorcisms for a period of three years. This abused practice alone, with all the concomitant terrors of the belief in its necessity, with all its tendencies to fix ideas which had become hallucinations, and to confirm, day after day, the terrible belief of possession by devils, was sufficient to drive the timid into monomania, and the monomaniacs into incurable furibond madness."[111]

Suggestible females on the one hand, a sincere but narrow-minded spiritual adviser on the other, seem to have enabled the affliction to spread. But for its beginnings, we should probably look to whatever caused Sister Felicia to enter her "supernatural" state. Unfortunately, the account gives no hint of what that may have been.

See also: CONVENT HYSTERIA, DEMON POSSESSION.

MAINE FACTORY MALADY

Portland, Maine: May 1972

State and local authorities were left grasping at straws to explain why 36 women at a suburban children's clothing factory were suddenly stricken while on the job. All of the victims were taken to the Osteopathic Hospital of Maine. One theory held that a temperature inversion held down carbon monoxide from the parking lots to the point where it was sucked into the plant's intake system. According to another theory, the cleaning fluid dichloride was responsible, but officials doubted that there were sufficient quantities of the substance to cause the symptoms. The victims were not from any one part of the plant but scattered throughout the facility. A check of the plant's ventilation system found it to be in perfect working order.

An official from the State Department of Health and Welfare, Dr. Daniel C. Hoxie, discounted the carbon monoxide theory, noting: "I personally feel that the first few faintings may have triggered some psychological reaction among the workers." Dr. Hoxie also postulated that a few workers might have "had the flu and all the others reacted hysterically." All but three of the workers were examined and released while three others remained overnight under observation.[112]

MALIOVANNY AFFAIR

Russia: 1880s-1890s

On March 31, 1892, a 48-year-old wheelwright, Kondrath Maliovanny, was committed to the asylum at Saint Cyril, on the outskirts of Kiev, as being insane in his person and also for propagating a false religious doctrine, Maliovannism. The eminent neuropathologist V. M. BEKHTEREV (then generally spelt Bechterev in the West) found it appropriate to study not only the man himself but also the sect made up of followers of his teachings, whose extravagant behavior matched that of their megalomaniac leader.[113]

CONTEXT: This affair seems to have started from the inspiration of a single individual, who having aroused himself to a state of spiritual, mental, and physical excitement, proceeded to arouse a similar enthusiasm in others. Leader and followers alike were no doubt affected by the social climate currently prevailing. Professor Sikorski, who like Bekhterev studied the outbreak at first hand, refers to "a general effervescence" in the Russian people.[114] This was indeed a period of effervescence in Russia, with the emancipation of the serfs still a living memory for many, with the nihilists and their terrorist operations an on-going affair, and the social unrest which would explode in 1905 already fermenting. The tendency of Russians to flock to new sects (see RUSSIAN SECTS, BEZPOPOVSKY, DOUKHOBORS, KLIKOUSCHESTVO, SKOPTSI, SOUPONIEVO) did the rest.

To understand Maliovannism, it is necessary to know something of its originator, for he was the pattern on which his followers, consciously or unconsciously, modeled themselves. He was a wheelwright from the town of Taraschtschi, in the Kiev district. His parents were alcoholics, and he himself had been addicted to alcoholic beverages in his earlier years. He also suffered from insomnia and melancholic attacks and was periodically obsessed with the idea of killing himself. At age 48, he was married and the father of seven. Though illiterate, he spoke fluently and clearly, and once he started speaking, he was liable to be carried away by the flow of his words.

When Lutheran Protestantism made its appearance in Russia, he was attracted to this new form of Christianity and switched from his Orthodox affiliation in 1884. He became a fervent convert. He renounced alcohol but through intense prayer and singing arrived easily at a state of ecstasy that gave him the excitement he had formerly obtained from drinking. In 1889 he began to hallucinate, particularly odors. While praying he was often aware of scents that seemed to him not of any earthly origin. He perceived these as a kind of announcement of the presence of the Holy Spirit, who, he came to believe, paid him personal visits. He also saw bright stars that had never been seen before, but which he said were seen in 25 empires and reported in newspapers the world over.

Shortly after this he persuaded himself of his ability to fly 25 cm above the ground; not only that, but others claimed to see him do it. This, together with the visits of the Holy Spirit, the scents, and the stars, convinced him that he had been chosen by God the Father, with whom he believed himself to be in permanent and direct communion. Naturally enough, since he now realized that he was the new Christ – or rather, *the* Christ, as the Jesus of the Gospels had never existed. The Gospels were nothing more than prophecies relating to himself.

In 1890, he became subject to convulsions during prayer, which began in his arms and gradually took over his entire body. This, he explained, is what happens when one is penetrated by the Holy Spirit. His followers, a growing number of whom were attached themselves to him, were greatly impressed. Many of them, especially the women, began to experience similar shakings and tremblings that ended in convulsive seizures. These became a regular feature of their meetings, even if Maliovanny himself was not present. Professor Sikorsky notes, "In their reunions, they wait impatiently for a first attack to manifest in one of them: this spectacle delights them, animates and enthuses them. As soon as the convulsions begin, the entire assembly is as though uplifted and transported with joy…for they regard it as the revelation of divine action working inside mankind."[115]

The convulsions into which they fell were similar to their leader's. Three kinds were observed: the least frequent being cries, bursts of laughter, sobbing and weeping, hiccups, belching and the like (by contrast, among the KLIKOUSCHESTVO sufferers, these were the most prevalent symptoms). More common were rhythmic and miming movements such as are found in hysterical patients, particularly those that imitate domestic actions or movements relating to their work activities. Each individual would generally have his or her own mannerisms, which were the same every time. The variety of behavior was described by one witness: "It's a general racket, a tumult of cries and confusion. Some fall as though struck by lightning, others utter shouts of enthusiasm or complaint, cry, leap, clap their hands, strike their faces or their chests, tug out their hair, stamp their feet, dance, utter every possible cry or exclamation expressive of their emotion, be it joy or happiness, despair or fear, terror or surprise, prayer or expressions of physical pain, hallucinations of scent or taste or others which they feel. Finally there are those who bark like dogs, whinny like horses or imitate other animals. Frequently the convulsions persist until the subject is totally exhausted."[116]

Maliovanny also began to prophesy. As savior of the world, he was privy to God's intentions and confidently announced the imminence of the Last Judgment, over which he would preside as the supreme judge. Consequently he counseled his followers to repent their sins. He taught them that since the end of the world was nigh, there was no point in working or amassing material goods. God would provide, and because they were the first to support the true God, they would be the first to receive the heavenly rewards, while those who failed to recognize the true God would be damned. So the Maliovannites stopped working and abandoned their responsibilities. They sold their goods, using the proceeds to sustain themselves during these last days of earthly existence. Their fields were left uncultivated; many sold their last cow and had to buy from orthodox people the milk for their children. If they were asked why they were so inactive, they answered that it was God's will. However seemingly illogical their actions, they could justify them by saying they were impelled by God or his Holy Spirit.

Not surprisingly, such activities alarmed the authorities, and in 1890 they decided that Maliovanny should be subjected to mental tests. At the asylum of Saint Cyril, at Kiev, he was examined and found to be afflicted with a systematic delirium, which had already reached a chronic state. He was confined there for a year without his megalomania abating one jot. He would declaim the scriptures and preach sermons, but these were no more than a deluge of incoherent phrases, accompanied by movements, gestures, and intonations, all of them stereotyped and repeated over and over again. Though his followers dutifully took down his words in the belief that they were divine utterances, they followed no logical course or logic; they even lacked sound grammar or syntax, though Sikorski confessed that they exhibited a "lyrical verve."

From studying Maliovanny, Bekhterev and his colleagues turned to his followers and had to confront the question: how was it possible that people who were in other respects not noticeably stupid should believe Maliovanny's extraordinary claims?

Sikorski, who examined a number of them, found that many were subject to hallucinations, which they described in detail. They manifested one symptom in particular, which occurs in other extraordinary behaviors but rarely if ever to the same degree: hallucinations of smell, which Sikorski found predominated in 80 percent of those he examined.

The next most important were hallucinations of the other senses, especially a sense of lightness. Many reported feeling as though they had left the ground and were lifted in the air. Others had aural and visual hallucinations: they heard commands from God or the whispers of the Holy Spirit, or they saw the skies open and saw the blessed occupants of Heaven. They also saw multi-colored stars of a size and brilliance they had never before seen, moving about the skies in an extraordinary manner. These experiences were, of course, similar to those that Maliovanny experienced himself.

Above all, they replicated their leader's convulsions with the deepest satisfaction. It is self-evident that his example lay at the origin of all these symptoms, and that they were adopted unconsciously by force of suggestion. Bekhterev draws attention to the fact that it was not only the adults who were affected, but also small children from 3-to-8 years old, who certainly did not share their parents' religious exaltation and were incapable of realizing that they, like their elders, were possessed by the Holy Spirit. Yet they, too, succumbed to the force of suggestion.

COMMENT: Few of the extraordinary behaviors described in this Encyclopedia illustrate so vividly the process of suggestion, for there is nothing in the conduct of his followers that did not originate with Maliovanny himself, and yet, once implanted, it manifested in his absence. This was clear to Bekhterev, who had no doubt that suggestion was the explanation for the extraordinary spread both of Maliovanny's teachings and of the physical symptoms, which were their outward expression:

> However uninstructed the Russian common people may be, they are none the less informed as to the fundamental teachings of religion. Their common sense would always reject with indignation the idea that an unlettered bourgeois should claim to be the Christ, God the Father and the Holy Spirit, and that the Christ of the gospels is nothing but a myth.
>
> But suggestion intervenes. Into the more or less predisposed brains of those around him, it implants all that he tells them about himself and the world around him. Result: an epidemic develops, which gradually assumes such proportions as to alarm the authorities.[117]

As to the predisposition which made it possible for suggestion to impose on him, the cultural factors mentioned previously played a crucial enabling role. Given the prevailing socio-political climate, the excitement of Maliovanny's revelations overwhelmed his followers' sense of reality.

But, predisposed though his followers may have been, Bekhterev places the primary emphasis on suggestion and provides the example of one of Maliovanny's partisans:

> Ballotte, like Maliovanny himself, had converted from Orthodoxy

to Lutheran protestantism, and for five years had suffered agonies of conscience in consequence. In April 1892 he became a follower of Maliovanny, and in a few weeks received his first hallucination: he saw a huge book with large writing in the sky. Maliovanny came to him in dreams as the Saviour, and ordered him to burn down his cottage, so that all could see that his faith was the true faith. This order obsessed him to such a degree that in broad daylight he set fire to his cottage. Unfortunately the fire spread not only to his own outhouses but also to the house of his neighbor, who may not have been too impressed by this demonstration of Ballotte's faith.[118]

MANGZO CARGO "CULT"

Huon Peninsula, Eastern Papua New Guinea: 1946 and ongoing

Natives in this region have, on occasion, become so emotionally excited about the expected arrival of cargo goods from Europeans, that they have exhibited collective trembling, a burning sensation in the stomach, and visions. During visionary states, ancestor spirits reportedly communicated their concern about the neglect of graves. The missionaries were criticized for imparting only book knowledge, while the Mangzo followers were said to have been enlightened directly through God's voice. Young boys were especially susceptible to spirit possession.[119]

Between 1946 and 1948, missionaries were shunned, and instead the locals prayed for the arrival of heavenly manna and blessings for their new social order. This nearly led to disaster, when one of the leaders, Ginu, promised the arrival of cars and other goods, but only if they sacrificed an entire village. While this plan was scrapped, he had sex with a native girl, Mawawe, then stated: "If I kill her and her blood flows the goods will come." He then picked up an axe, chopped off her head, and buried her. Not only did the promised goods not come, but Ginu was arrested by an administration officer.[120]

At this point, one of the greatest sales in the history of New Guinea was about to take place. The owner of the Kalasa trade store cut prices drastically in order to give locals a taste of the cargo utopia to come. People could not understand why goods were ordinarily so costly and why the purchase of food involved such complex calculations. Thus, a system of "good prices" was introduced, whereby for example, if he bought a bag of coconuts for three shillings, he sold it for just one shilling. He also bought garden fruits at a high price and sold it cheaply. He did the same with coffee and other items. Naturally the store became very popular and it fed the belief that a better life was coming. As Friedrich Steinbauer remarked: "Here was evidence of how smoothly business activities could be run if only the New Guineans took over the management. Here was proof for the exploitation practiced by Europeans. The people were not mistaken after all in expecting cargo."[121] A European missionary put an end to the bonanza when he uncovered the store's debt during an annual stocktaking.

See also: NAKED CARGO-CULT, FILO CARGO-CULT, PRESIDENT JOHNSON CARGO-CULT, CARGO CULTS.

MARCHING BAND HYSTERIA

Alabama: September 21, 1973

On September 21, 1973, 57 of 120 members of an Alabama marching band either fainted or felt ill shortly after performing at a high school football game. The incident occurred on a hot, humid evening after band members had traveled 100 miles to reach the away game. The game was particularly exciting as the favored visiting team lost 7 to 6. The band successfully performed their seven-minute half-time routine, remaining on the field in a kneeling position while their counterparts from the rival school performed. When the rivals' drill was completed, the visiting band briefly stood at attention, marched to the grandstand, and were seated, when without warning, a girl fainted. Over the next ten minutes, five other girls suffered a similar fate. During the following twenty minutes, the girls rested on benches and several were sent to the hospital. During this period, many more band members reported feeling sick. Many of those affected seemed to be over-breathing, felt a tingling sensation in the limbs, and developing a choking sensation. Some also reported stomach pain or cramps, dizziness, nausea, and weakness.[122]

CONTEXT: During an exciting football game, a group of wind instrumentalists in a marching band were apparently dressed too heavily for the warm weather conditions. This appears to have triggered minor dizziness and fainting, which in turn, generated extreme anxiety in other band members who subsequently succumbed to mass hysteria.

A second wave of symptoms occurred as band members were boarding busses after the game. Over the next three days, ten more girls were stricken, with five overall experiencing relapses. Tests for food poisoning –the initial suspicion – were ruled out. Heat stroke was also eliminated as the cardinal symptom, and fever was absent. While heat may have played a minor role, according to Dr. Richard Levine of the United States Public Health Service who investigated the episode, mass psychogenic illness was the primary culprit. Levine states that "the discipline of a precision marching drill, the discomfort of wearing heavy clothes in a hot environment, the excitement and disappointment at losing a close game – suggests that the setting...was appropriately tense for mass hysteria to occur."[123]

A Remarkably Similar 1964 Episode

In the course of his investigation, Dr. Levine made an interesting discovery. A similar episode occurred in the U.S. under nearly identical circumstances in 1964. While the specific location is not given for purposes of anonymity, like the Alabama incident, the episode affected girls in a high school marching band at an exciting away football game. "The band had worn heavy woolen uniforms on a hot day, and the visitors, although their team was favored to win, had lost. Except for the prominence of symptoms of fainting and syncope, this reported epidemic shows a striking resemblance to the one described here."[124] Levine accounts for the greater incidence of fainting and syncope in Alabama as an initial "reaction to heat exacerbated and propagated by mass hysteria."[125] The first group of girls to be affected were all from the wind section and were dressed the heaviest with high-wasted 100% wool trousers "and an impermeable plastic jacket overlay." Levine believes that with an air temperature at the time of 73 F, it's likely that some of the girls experienced syncope, but mass hysteria soon took over. Levine concludes: "It seems reasonable to postulate a dual cause for the epidemic involving heat syncope and hysteria, with heat syncope figuring more prominently in the first wave of illness where it served to trigger a subsequent outbreak of mass hysteria."[126]

MARS EARTHQUAKE PANIC

Mendoza, Argentina: July 28, 1939

Minor earth tremors, which caused no damage, triggered a panic as scores of residents, "fearing the world was coming to an end, ran for their homes, prayed, screamed and fired guns into the air."

CONTEXT: The incident occurred amid media publicity that the planet Mars was exceptionally close to Earth, leading residents to conclude that the proximity to Mars was responsible for the quakes.[127]

MASS HYSTERIA

Mass hysteria refers to the rapid spread of illness signs, symptoms, and related beliefs within a cohesive group for which there is no plausible organic cause.[128] Common synonyms include mass psychogenic illness, mass sociogenic illness, epidemic hysteria, and hysterical contagion. Before the 20th century, it was often referred to with such pathological labels as "psychic disturbance"[129] and "epidemic insanity."[130] In the fourth edition of *The Diagnostic and Statistical Manual of Mental Disorders* (often referred to as the "Bible" of the mental health community), the term hysteria was officially discontinued by the American Psychiatric Association (APA), superseded by the term "conversion disorder."[131] This designation more accurately describes the process involved – converting psychological conflict into involuntary physical symptoms.[132] Another reason for its discontinuation was and continues to be misuse of the term to stigmatize a variety of undesirable behaviors as "hysterical," including unfounded assertions that females are innately emotionally unstable.[133] Despite its discontinuance by the APA, the term "mass hysteria" continues to be widely and commonly used across various disciplines including psychiatry and medicine.

The characteristic features of hysterical contagion include: (1) symptoms with no plausible organic basis, (2) that are transient and benign, (3) have rapid onset and recovery, (4) and occur in a segregated group

(5) in the presence of extraordinary anxiety. Furthermore (6) the symptoms are spread via sight, sound, or oral communication, (7) beginning in older or higher status students, (8) and affecting a preponderance of female victims. Treatment involves identifying and eliminating or reducing the perceived stress-related stimulus.[134]

CONTEXT: Episodes must be interpreted within their unique circumstances. Until recently, scientists lacking sociocultural sensitivity have erred in over-ambitiously superimposing a universal model of hysterical contagion onto various episodes involving the rapid spread of false beliefs and unpopular emotional displays. In this sense, "mass hysteria" has become a convenient, grandiose diagnostic rubric under which various heterogeneous behaviors have been erroneously categorized. Mass suicide, cargo "cults," witch-hunts, financial panics, communist infiltration scares, the Dutch tulip mania, head-hunting rumor-panics, and flying saucer sightings have all been labeled as "mass hysteria." Yet, rarely do any of the participants in these behaviors discussed in this Encyclopedia exhibit conversion symptoms; even rarer are attempts to provide thorough descriptions of the participants' social, cultural, historical, and political circumstances. Too often, the bizarre nature of the "victims" social realities is used to support the existence of abnormal group or "hysterical" behavior. Researchers must be mindful that the human variation in norms, values, beliefs, and practices is remarkable, and the array of social realities that lie outside the narrow Eurocentric tradition is enormous.[135]

Mass hysteria is both under-reported and often a significant financial burden to responding emergency services, public health offices, and environmental agencies.[136] Excluding the abundance of literature on medieval DANCE MANIAS and TARANTISM, there are few books and articles in English on historical aspects of mass hysteria.[137] British psychologist Simon Wessely identifies two types – anxiety and motor hysteria. The former is of shorter duration, typically a day, and involves sudden, extreme anxiety shortly after the perception of a bogus threat. The second type involves the slow build-up of stress, is confined to intolerable social settings, and features trance-like states, histrionics (melodramatic reactions), and psychomotor dysfunction (shaking, twitching, contractures), usually persisting for weeks or months.[138]

The Middle Ages

Pre-20th century mass hysteria reports are dominated by motor hysteria incubated by continuous exposure to excessive anxiety in work, school, or religious settings. From 1400 to 1800, strict Christian religious orders appeared in Europe. Coupled with a popular belief in WITCHCRAFT and DIABOLIC POSSESSION, dozens of epidemic motor hysteria outbreaks occurred in nunneries (see CONVENT HYSTERIA). Episodes typically lasted months and occasionally years. Histrionics were a notable feature of the syndrome. Many young girls were reluctant "inmates" of these orders, forced by relatives to join and take vows of chastity and poverty; subsisting on bland, meager diets; and engaging in repetitious prayer sessions and lengthy fasting rituals. Even minor infractions were met with flogging and incarceration. The hysterical fits appeared under the strictest administrators. Priests summoned to exorcize the demons often accused unpopular individuals of bewitching the nuns and were typically banished, imprisoned, or burned alive. Witchcraft accusations were also a way to settle old scores under the guise of religion and justice. These rebellious nuns would use foul, blasphemous language, and expose genitalia, rub private parts, and thrust their hips in mock intercourse.[139] Community members often flocked daily to witness these spectacles, while priests tried to exorcize the demons. An outbreak was recorded in a U.S. convent as recently as 1880.[140]

At Loudun, France, Father Urbain Grandier was burned at the stake in 1634 for bewitching a convent into hysterical fits.[141] Occasionally nuns were executed, as in 1749, when strange movements and trance states swept through the Unterzell convent near Wuzburg, Germany. Sister Maria von Mossau was convicted of casting spells and beheaded.[142] At Cambrai, France in 1491, nuns exhibited fits and yelped like dogs; in 1560 in Xante, Spain, they "bleated like sheep, tore off their veils, [and] had convulsions in church."[143] At a French convent, the sisters meowed daily for several hours.[144] During this period, certain animals were believed to be demonic familiars.[145] Convent outbreaks fomented in an atmosphere of long-term, pent-up anxiety, fostering dissociation and hyper-suggestibility, reflecting the *zeitgeist*.

Under similar conditions in modern-day Malaysia, outbreaks of motor hysteria affect adolescent Muslim females sent by their parents to isolated boarding schools. One episode affected 36 girls over five years, as native healers *(bomohs)*, intermittently summoned to exorcize demons, failed to alleviate the bouts of emotional tantrums, twitching, shaking, and demon possession. The battle with totalitarian administrators culminated in 1987 when the desperate girls took hostages, demanding change. The girls were not held legally accountable, claiming impunity through possession. Their symptoms subsided only after their transfer to a liberal school.[146]

18th To The Early 20th Century

Between the 18th and early 20th centuries, the industrial revolution fostered outbreaks of mass motor hysteria in oppressive Western job settings, especially factories. Reports from England, France, Germany, Italy, and Russia included convulsions,[147] strange movements,[148] and neurological symptoms.[149] The first reported outbreak occurred in February 1787, as English cotton mill workers exhibited violent convulsions and feelings of suffocation.[150] It may have been no coincidence that this episode was recorded one year after Edmund Cartwright's invention of the power-loom, which both revolutionized and dehumanized the textile industry.[151] The absence of motor hysteria reports in Western countries during the second half of the 20th century may reflect union gains and rigorous occupational health and safety regulations. The disappearance of reports in the former Soviet Union mirror the rise of anti-capitalist, Western-style political systems antagonistic to Western capitalist regimes.[152]

During the same period, extreme discipline in some European schools – German, Swiss, and French in particular – triggered motor hysteria including convulsions,[153] contractures,[154] twitching, shaking and trembling,[155] and laughing.[156] In 1893, fits of contagious shaking and convulsions swept through a girls' school in Basel, Switzerland, rendering pupils unable to complete in-school written assignments. Symptoms subsided after school was dismissed and then relapsed upon re-entering the school.[157] A decade later a similar outbreak hit the same school.[158] In 1892, hand tremors, followed by trance states and amnesia, affected students at a German school, persisting for about 100 days.[159] At a German school in Chemnitz, students began exhibiting arm and hand tremors during their grueling and monotonous writing exercise hour. Symptoms subsided after electric shocks were given and rigorous mental arithmetic drills were substituted during writing time.[160]

Twentieth century mass hysteria reports in school settings are dominated by contamination fears of food, air, and water. The overwhelming majority of cases involve imaginary or exaggerated concern about strange odors. Outbreaks had a rapid onset and recovery and involved anxiety hysteria.[161] A 1985 incident in Singapore affected 65 students and a teacher who suddenly exhibited chills, headaches, nausea, and breathlessness after noticing a strange smell. Prior to the outbreak there were rumors that a harmful gas was infiltrating the school from a nearby building site. Student interviews determined that those who believed the rumors succumbed while "those who were indifferent to it were immune."[162] In 1972, schoolchildren at a gala in Hazlerigg, England, were enveloped by a sickening stench and began complaining of headaches, stomach pain, nausea, and dizziness. The odor was later traced to a pigsty.[163] That same year, headache and over-breathing affecting 16 pupils at a school in Tokyo, Japan, was traced to a pungent smog.[164] In the United Arab Emirates in 1994, a "toxic fire" that filled an Arab dormitory with a mysterious odor and sent 23 students to the hospital with breathing difficulties was actually caused by harmless incense.[165]

Strange odors were also a common 20th century trigger of mass anxiety hysteria at work settings[166] with pollution fears reducing productivity at data processing facilities,[167] communications offices,[168] and assembly plants.[169] A 1988 outbreak of breathing difficulty among U.S. Army recruits in California coincided with a strong odor from brush fires that were mistaken for toxic fumes. Some recruits were "resuscitated" in the early confusion, as medics had wrongly assessed their conditions to be more serious. These factors heightened anxiety and increased breathing problems. A study showed that recruits seeing the "resuscitations," or others exhibiting symptoms, were three times more likely to report symptoms.[170]

Chemical And Biological Warfare

During the 20th century, strange odors and the presumed presence of toxic gases were also commonly blamed in episodes of mass hysteria that spread to communities,[171] occasionally involving the fear of chemical and biological weapons. During World War I, 90,000 people on both sides were killed by poison gases and over a million were injured.[172] The psychological specter of "the poison gas scare" haunted the American psyche for the next three decades, triggering several prominent hysteria episodes.[173] In rural Virginia between 1933-34, there were dozens of reported nocturnal gas attacks involving someone spraying victims inside homes. After expending significant time and resources, authorities concluded that all cases had mundane origins – from backed-up chimney flues to flatulence.[174] Another "mad gasser" scare occurred in Mattoon, Illinois, in 1944 and was attributed to fear, imagination, and press reports of the possible German use of poison gas.[175] The Martian invasion scare of 1938 reflected the preoccupation with poison gas, as in a survey of listeners who were frightened, 20 percent assumed that the Martian "gas raids" were in fact German gas raids on the United States.[176]

Since the early 1980s, fear of the use of chemical weapons on civilian targets in several in war-torn regions, in conjunction with the detection of strange odors, has triggered large-scale outbreaks of mass anxiety hysteria. Episodes involved rumors of poison gas against ethnic minorities, including the ethnic Albanian mistrust of Serbs in the former Yugoslavia,[177] Palestinian suspicion of the Israelis,[178] and Georgian distrust of Moscow.[179] Even when chemical weapons have been used, such as dispersing of Sarin nerve gas on the Japanese subway system in 1995 by the Aum Shinrikyo sect, real attacks have triggered several mass hysteria episodes involving benign odors.[180]

The September 11, 2001, attacks on the U.S. have fostered an exaggerated response to a genuine terrorist threat, prompting numerous episodes of hysterical contagion in response to heightened anxiety.[181] At a metropolitan subway station, a man sprayed an unknown substance into the air, sickening 35 people with nausea, headache, and sore throats. It was later identified as a common window cleaner.[182] Over 2,300 anthrax false alarms occurred during the first two weeks of October 2001, many involving psychogenic symptoms.[183]

Future Trends

Historical and transcultural manifestations of mass hysteria mirror social, cultural, and political preoccupations that define each era and reflect unique beliefs about the nature of the world. In the 21st century, mass hysteria is likely to reflect fears over terrorist threats and environmental concerns.

COMMENTS: A fundamental problem with the concept of conversion disorder is that, like so many other psychiatric conditions, the diagnostic criteria are vague and subject to misdiagnosis, especially hysteria, which is said to mimic any organic disease.[184] This poses many challenges, the least of which is: How does one differentiate between a unconscious conversion and someone feigning symptoms? Complicating matters, no one is certain of the exact mechanism whereby there is a conversion or channeling of psychosocial distress into physical symptoms. For instance, a woman who worries that she may have heart disease might experience chest pain. Some people undergo temporary blindness after witnessing unspeakable horrors. There are reports of soldiers who are opposed to killing, experiencing sudden arm paralysis when trying to fire their gun in battle. In each case, doctors can find nothing physically wrong. While Harvard psychiatrist Arthur Kleinman considers hysteria to be "a great mystery at the heart of psychosomatic medicine," he believes that "enough is known about conversion symptoms to describe them as the literal embodiment of conflicted meanings, somatic symbols that have psychological and social uses."[185]

MASS HYSTERIA IN WORK SETTINGS

Mass hysteria in job settings can be defined as any illness symptoms and related beliefs that are collectively reported at a worksite and have no identifiable pathogenic explanation. Episodes are assumed to be a variant of individual "conversion hysteria," a term devised by Sigmund Freud to explain the converting of psychic conflict and anxiety into involuntary symptoms for which there is no corresponding organic basis. Mass hysteria at worksites refers to the spread of conversion symptoms and anxiety states within a particular group of employees following exposure to a common stressor, either real or imagined. Reports are commonly referred to as occupational mass psychogenic illness. Episodes occasionally appear under the label of factory hysteria, assembly line hysteria, and hysterical contagion.

A variety of chemical sensitivity syndromes have been labeled as occupational mass hysteria, including Environmental Hypersensitivity, Multiple Chemical Sensitivity Syndrome, Sick Building Syndrome, and Total Allergy Syndrome. While many of these cases have characteristic features of mass hysteria, such as symptoms closely following social networks,[186] the psychogenic status of these "syndromes" remains contentious. For instance, some reports of Sick Building Syndrome may stem from a confluence of environmental circumstances and agents: indoor air pollution, poor ventilation, and the synergistic effect of a mixture of various low level toxic substances.[187]

CONTEXT: Western reports of hysteria episodes in job settings appear to line up almost exclusively under the social factor category, and non-Western ones are largely cultural. It appears that those experiencing hysterical contagion in the West are responding to external factors arising from powerlessness (i.e., low participation in decision-making, performing boring tasks, job insecurity, low pay, conflict with supervisors). In non-Western settings, a critical factor is the endemic belief structures harbored in the minds of sufferers. When discussing non-Western beliefs that appear to engender outbreaks, we must be careful to use the term "folk beliefs" and avoid words such as "superstitions," as most dictionaries define "superstitions" as involving a lack of logic and reasoning. Another culture's assumptions, and therefore the steps in reasoning, may differ from one's own. This suggests that to refer to another culture's beliefs as superstitions is ethnocentric. While many reports of mass hysteria at job sites tend to describe the illness associations made by the affected people and groups as false or erroneous, such descriptions are pejorative as there is no demonstrable alternative or agreed upon agent. Therefore, we have substituted such words as "unsubstantiated" and "perceived illness." There are two main types of "outbreaks."

Mass anxiety hysteria is common in modern Western societies and involves a group of workers who are suddenly exposed to what they perceive to be an imminent threat. Symptoms are usually transient, benign, and include over-breathing, headache, and nausea. Mass motor hysteria predominates in non-Western settings and builds slowly over weeks or months, being incubated in an atmosphere of pre-existing tension among dissatisfied workers who exhibit trance-like states, histrionics, falling, and occasionally psychomotor disruption such as shaking or twitching. A third pattern of reports involves the re-labeling of ever-present symptoms after attention is drawn to such symptoms by medical authorities and the media.

Reports of mass psychogenic illness at work drew scant attention in the scientific literature until the late 1970s when there was a sudden upsurge in published episodes, especially in the United States, attracting interest and concern from the public health community. In fact, during the 1970s "epidemic" of workplace

Women making packets of bacon in a British factory, circa 1960.

cases studied by Michael Colligan and L. Murphy, the researchers were surprised that their survey of the scientific literature unveiled just two previous cases during the twentieth century – both in the U.S.[188] The first was the 1962 "June Bug" outbreak at a textile factory in Spartanburg, South Carolina;[189] the second was a 1974 episode in a data center at a mid-western university.[190] The waxing and waning of reports may reflect the prevailing medical *zeitgeist* and philosophical approaches in the social sciences to defining and recognizing the problem.

Presentation Patterns

Based on a survey of the literature, three patterns are evident. The first two patterns correspond to Simon Wessely's classification scheme of mass hysteria, dividing episodes into two categories: MASS ANXIETY HYSTERIA and MASS MOTOR HYSTERIA.[191] In the former, a group of workers are suddenly exposed to extreme anxiety in the form of the presence of what they perceive to be an imminent personal threat. There is no extraordinary pre-existing stress within the group. Employees react by exhibiting a variety of ambiguous, transient symptoms that are benign in nature. Mass motor hysteria usually builds up slowly over weeks or months and develops in an atmosphere of pre-existing stress among employees who are dissatisfied with their jobs. Typical symptoms include trance-like states, histrionics, bouts of falling, and on occasion psychomotor agitation such as shaking or twitching muscles. A third pattern of reports involves the relabelling of ever-present symptoms.

(1) Mass Anxiety Hysteria

Mass anxiety hysteria is most prevalent in Western or developed countries. In the majority of reports, the onset of symptoms coincides with the perception of an unfamiliar smell that is assumed to be detrimental to worker health. Occasionally suspicion focuses on an infectious agent, as in the case of skin rash that is observed in a fellow worker. Investigators are often able to identify an "index case" (the first person to report illness symptoms) that often exhibits symptoms in a dramatic fashion. Sometimes, unbeknownst to co-workers, the index case is actually suffering from a medical condition such as skin problems, epilepsy, or a psychological disorder.

Upon observing the index case, colleagues within close visual or social contact rapidly redefine the situation, attributing the symptoms to a plausible toxic agent in their work environment. As a consequence, co-workers may exhibit sudden, extreme fear for their personal well-being. Social and cultural protocols inhibit workers from leaving the job setting as to do so may prompt peer ridicule, management sanctions, or even dismissal. This situation generates internal conflict which gives rise to anxiety and conversion symptoms within the close-knit group of employees. The presence of such health complaints unconsciously allows workers who are very concerned for their health to be excused from duty on permissible grounds. In other words, their illness status deflects the potential attribution of blame for their actions.

Workers typically exhibit a broad range of psychogenic symptoms that represent the physiological consequences of anxiety. Over-breathing (hyperventilation) is an especially common symptom. The symptoms experienced usually mirror the perceived threat. For example, employees of ceramics manufacturers often develop skin rashes, while headache, lightheadedness, and nausea are common complaints in settings where an unusual odor is detected. Once medical authorities or company management convincingly discredits the threatening agent, symptoms often dissipate quickly, although on many occasions, claims by such figures are not widely viewed as credible, especially when unions and the mass media are involved. Sometimes episodes continue intermittently for weeks or months, usually in situations where workers feel that management is more interested in making a profit than in employee well being. Whenever an episode is labeled as epidemic hysteria – even by medical authorities – such pronouncements may do more harm than good by generating worker hostility and resentment of the "hysterical" label or suggestions that their symptoms are "all in their head." This situation fosters an array of folk theories.

It is widely believed that epidemic hysteria in work settings involves cathartic reactions to built-up emotions that foment in an atmosphere of either labor-management conflicts and/or job dissatisfaction.[192] In the case of mass anxiety hysteria, such associations appear unfounded given the distinctive presentation pattern whereby the presence of psychogenic symptoms occur almost always after the sudden, unexpected perception of a strange odor or agent. Strained management-labor relations and employee dissatisfaction are common in many job settings without any reports of hysteria outbreaks. The role of accumulating anxiety in triggering hysterical reactions is clearly in evidence in repressive work environments that engender motor hysteria.

Example: Over-breathing in response to Diesel Fumes
On April 21, 1982, three employees of a manufacturing plant of electronic components in Pennsylvania exhibited headaches, nausea, and disorientation. Suspecting a defective air conditioner, the system was examined for leaks but none were identified. Five days later a car engine was being tested in a sealed off part of the plant, when diesel fumes escaped onto the production floor. Workers became alarmed when they smelled the odor fearing toxic fume exposure. Between April 21 and May 24, 98 of the plant's 220 workers reported becoming ill and 30 were taken to the local hospital emergency room. The work site was closed twice during this period.

In late May the plant was the subject of a thorough investigation from members of the National Institute for Occupational Health and Safety (NIOSH), a team of local physicians, and an environmental consulting company. Nothing out of the ordinary was found. Further, medical tests at the local hospital for toxic chemical exposure were all negative, though an analysis of blood gases in seven workers indicated "respiratory alkalosis consistent with hyperventilation."

According to a final report on the episode from the Centers for Disease Control: "The poorly defined nature of the employees' illness, the absence of exposures to environmental contaminants in concentrations exceeding current occupational standards and criteria, and the presence of symptoms similar to those of hyperventilation suggest that this incident was an outbreak of psychogenic illness. The release of diesel fumes into the plant from an automobile engine may have contributed to a heightened awareness of various odors in the plant. The air-conditioning system was restarted on June 14; no unusual employee illness at the plant has since been reported to NIOSH."[193]

Example: The June Bug Scare of 1962
While an unfamiliar or foul odor is the most common Western trigger of hysteria episodes, occasionally it is the plausibility of the existence of a perceived threatening agent such as a bug. Over a ten-day period during the summer of 1962, a dress-making factory in Spartanburg, South Carolina, was the subject of intense media interest after 62 employees began feeling ill with what appeared to be insect bites. Symptoms included nausea, fainting, headache, disorientation, rashes, and general weakness, but all the employees quickly recovered. An investigation was conducted by the Centers for Disease Control and an entomologist or bug expert visited the plant. No plausible explanation for the symptoms could be found. In all, 59 females and 3 males from a pool of 965 workers were affected.

A sociological study of the case was conducted by Alan Kerckhoff and Kurt Back of Duke University and Norman Miller of the University of Chicago who concluded that the symptoms and belief in the "bug" began in workers who were socially isolated, then spread quickly, especially through social networks. The acceleration in spread is "a function of the fact that, as more cases appear, the behavior becomes increasingly legitimized – increasingly accepted according to an evolving generalized belief in the group involved." While "outsiders" are slower to accept the reality of the "bug," as more and more workers exhibit symptoms, "the sheer size of the affected category makes the credibility of the phenomenon greater. We thus find that ultimately 'everyone' believes in 'the bug'... and cases begin to occur throughout the population. It thus becomes a 'crowd response.'"[194]

The episode began when a 22-year-old female worker fainted shortly after complaining that she thought an insect had bitten her. According to co-workers, the woman had a history of fainting, having done so "at least five times during the previous year." Three days later a second worker came forward to report that she too had been bitten five days earlier. She told doctors that her main symptom "was that she felt like a balloon ready to burst."[195] That same afternoon, physicians examined a third female worker after she fainted during her shift. The employee "had been under a physician's care for nervousness of several months duration."[196] Later that same day, a fourth woman from the plant sought medical attention after feeling a crawling sensation on her leg and shortly thereafter felt faint. Of 62 workers examined by physicians, 37 said they felt nauseated, 23 reportedly fainted, 19 reported "almost fainting," 22 had headaches, 14 felt dizzy, 8 said they just felt nervous, while 7 said they were bothered by cramps.[197] During the "outbreak," nine of the 62 workers described complaints that were not associated with bug bites. One worker felt "numb and couldn't breathe;" another said there was a burning pain in her leg calf; one worker was having trouble turning their head; and two said they just felt nervous. After a thorough search of the building for insects, the only biting insect found on the premises was a chicken mite, and it was not capable of generating the reported symptoms.[198]

Example: Mystery Gas And The Power Of The Mind

One morning in 1972 on the campus of a major university in the Midwestern United States, a mysterious ailment spread through workers at a data processing facility. The "outbreak" began one Wednesday morning when employees said they detected a "strange and burning odor" and the plant was closed. A similar series of events occurred the following day. Over a 48-hour period, 35 of the company's 60 female employees were affected. Ten workers were at the university's hospital. Symptoms included dizziness, fainting, burning or watery eyes, nausea and vomiting. Several workers were clearly hyperventilating. All of the affected employees were in a single large room on the first floor. The room housed about 60 machines, including 30 noisy keypunch devices.[199]

On both Wednesday and Thursday, environmental scientists combed the building for a possible cause and took air samples. All the tests were negative. At this point, something highly unusual occurred. One of the emergency room physicians and an environmental studies professor gathered the staff together and told them a concocted story. They said that their studies indicated that an "atmospheric conversion" had occurred causing smoke from a nearby power plant to build up over the data center. Most of the workers seemed to have believed the bogus explanation, and symptoms disappeared the next workday, with the exception of a single hyperventilating employee who was quickly isolated and told to go home.[200]

Social psychologist Sydney Stahl of Purdue University investigated the episode, noting that the incident coincided with worker stress from an adjacent construction site, which was very noisy and including occasional, unexpected dynamite blasts that shook their building and the constant use of heavy machinery, included pneumatic hammers. One event in particular appeared to trigger the illness – the placement of a diesel engine near an open window of the data center. While most of the employees commented on their concern over the fumes, tests for the presence of noxious fumes were negative.[201] It was also determined that workers reporting the most severe symptoms were the most unhappy with their jobs. Stahl states that "Those who fainted and vomited were invariably the persons who had attempted to look for other jobs or expressed the highest levels of dissatisfaction with the work conditions, the nature of the relationship between the supervisor and the workers, and the restrictive dress code."[202]

(2) Mass Motor Hysteria

Mass motor hysteria typically occurs in repressive job settings, and is incubated in an atmosphere of pre-existing employee dissatisfaction and poor labor-management relations. There are two distinct sub-types: some are primarily shaped by cultural influences, others by social influences. In making the distinction between cultural and social, "cultural" refers to traditional ways of thinking and feeling, while "social" concerns the conditions or circumstances prevailing at the time of the incident.

The Industrial Revolution And Social Forces

The first cluster of similar reports involve descriptions of psychomotor dysfunction and dissociation in Western and Asian settings prior to 1948. Most of these episodes conspicuously coincide with the onset of the Industrial Revolution, which was characterized by repressive, brutal management policies. Typical practices included excessive work hours, the employment of young children, low wages, unsanitary and unsafe working conditions, and few rights. It is, therefore, perhaps no coincidence that the first recorded episode of mass hysteria at the workplace occurred at a Lancashire, England, cotton factory in 1787:

> ...a girl, on the fifteenth of February, 1787, put a mouse into the bosom of another girl, who had a great dread of mice. The girl was immediately thrown into a fit, and continued in it with the most violent convulsions, for twenty-four hours. On the following day, three more girls were seized in the same manner; and on the 17th, six more. By this time the alarm was so great, that the whole work, in which 200 or 300 were employed, was totally stopped, and an idea prevailed that a particular disease had been introduced by a bag of cotton opened in the house. On Sunday the 18th, Dr. St. Clare was sent for from Preston; before he arrived three more were seized, and during that night and the morning of the 19th, eleven more, making in all twenty-four. Of these, twenty-one were young women, two were girls of about ten years of age, and one man, who had been much fatigued with holding the girls... The symptoms were anxiety, strangulation, and very strong convulsions; and these were so violent as to last without any intermission from a quarter of an hour to twenty-four hours, and to require four or five persons to prevent the patients from tearing their hair and dashing their heads against the floor or walls. Dr. St. Clare had taken with him a portable electrical machine, and by electric shocks the patients were universally relieved without exception. As soon as the patients and the country were assured that the complaint was merely nervous, easily cured, and not introduced by the cotton, no fresh person was affected.[203]

It is probably no coincidence that the year before this episode, Edmund Cartwright invented the power-loom, which helped to revolutionize the textile industry, superseding the handwork order and further dehumanizing the workplace. During this period many adult males lost their factory jobs to women and children who were considered better suited for such jobs. American sociologist Neil Smelser, in his study of the Lancashire cotton industry during the time of the outbreak, describes how the cotton industry displaced the family's traditional economic and educational function, placing a great deal of social and psychological stress on female cotton mill employees.[204]

Why are modern-day episodes of motor hysteria in Western work settings so rare? It may reflect a heightened emphasis on worker rights, improved worksite safety conditions, occupational legislation, and certainly the greater influence of unions as compared to some 200 years ago. Why has there been a dramatic reduction in the number of motor reports in Communist countries during the 20th century? The answer may be associated with the rise of anti-capitalist political systems.

Cultural Influences: Outbreaks In Southeast Asia

Southeast Asia is an excellent place to glean insights on the relationship between mass hysteria and culture. A second category of mass motor hysteria occurs among indigenous peoples of Malay ethnic descent employed at factories in Malaysia or adjacent Singapore, a former Malaysian state. Episodes are almost always confined to Malay females of Islamic faith and are situated in an atmosphere of worker unhappiness or management conflict. Channels of negotiation or protest are either non-existent or restricted, and there is an absence of unions through which grievances may be redressed. Cultural and religious traditions inhibit workers from directly confronting their almost exclusively male superiors with grievances. This is especially true of female Malays who are raised to respect authorities and elders.[205] Such situations present an intolerable dilemma for many workers who feel trapped. Many female workers are under financial and peer pressures to stay on the job, yet to remain employed leads to great psychic conflict. It is within this context that frustration and continuous psychosocial pressure building over weeks or months begin to affect a tiny fraction of workers who start exhibiting trance and possession states, histrionics, and occasional bouts of psychomotor agitation, such as shaking, tremor, or twitching. "Because of their supernatural world-view and lack of formal education, the observation of 'possessed' colleagues fosters extreme and immediate anxiety, and an array of folk theories pertaining to the presence of a demonic agent. For instance, among many workers of Malayan descent, a pervasive belief exists in the unquestioned reality of *Jinn* and *toyl* spirits, or the cogency of magic potions, spells, hexes and charms."[206]

In conjunction with the supernatural worldview of the typical Malay worker, it is common for employees who either see or learn of their fallen comrades to suddenly grow anxious and hyperventilate. Over-breathing often spreads quickly throughout the workforce. Those most affected are workers in closer proximity to the initial dramatic cases exhibiting dissociation/histrionics or having the closest social ties to them. Altered states of consciousness occasionally take the form of spirit possession, which can be dramatic, unnerving, and highly convincing to eyewitnesses who interpret them in accordance with Malay folk beliefs.

Most Malays live in a mental world inhabited by an array of tiny animistic beings known as *toyls,* who supposedly stand just a few inches high; wandering apparitions called *hantus*;[207] and *Jinn* creatures, which are referenced in the Muslim Koran (whence the belief of holding a Genie in a bottle is derived). These mass hysteria episodes in Malaysian and Singaporean factories typically persist from a few days to a month, eventually subsiding once certain worker demands have been met. Often management hires a male Malay native healer (*bomoh*) to perform ceremonies or exorcism or appeasement at the factory site. Often the *bomoh* will sacrifice a goat or chant incantations intended to ward off the "evil spirits." *Bomohs* perform an invaluable service as they act as a mediator between the disgruntled workforce and management. Bartholomew and Sirois have noted: "Often the affected employees convey to the *bomoh* their dissatisfaction with intolerable working conditions which are believed to have attracted the evil or mischievous spirits. Because of the *bomoh's* status and typical male gender, he serves as a mediator between the employees and management, in an attempt to improve working conditions. Episodes may persist if dissatisfaction remains, and the entire cycle is repeated."[208] Since the mid-20th century, reports of mass motor hysteria in Western job settings are virtually unheard of. Why? Presumably greater exposure to Western values, worker and human rights in more egalitarian political systems provide immunity by offering outlets into which they can channel frustrations – unions, non-government organizations, alternative political parties or systems, etc.

Example: Hysteria In Singaporean Factory Workers

During the 1970s, a series of mass hysteria episodes swept across factories in the tiny island city-state of Singapore in Southeast Asia. Singapore was a former state in Malaya (now Malaysia) until it gained independence in 1963. W.H. Phoon of the Singapore Labour Ministry documented several of the mass hysteria episodes.[209] We will describe the first two 'outbreaks.'

The first incident occurred at a television assembly plant during January 1973. On the evening of Saturday the 13th, a female employee began screaming and fainted. As her supervisor and several colleagues carried her to the medical clinic on a different floor, she screamed out and struggled against them. Before long, other female workers exhibited similar symptoms, and plant officials closed the factory later that night, reopening the following Tuesday. Of the plant's 899 workers, just 97 were male, and most of the workers were Malays. Curiously, of the 84 workers stricken with "spells," all were female Malays. During the two days the plant was shut down, management hired a *bomoh* to exorcize the evil spirits. The day the factory reopened, more women had spells.[210]

The episode soon spread to two nearby factories. On January 17, a nearby electrolytic capacitor factory reported that 16 female employees were having similar spells. Several days later, another nearby factory reported a single case. Most of those affected in these two additional factories were female Malays. Phoon and his colleagues identified three distinct types of cases. First were "hysterical seizures," which were typified by screaming, fierce struggling, and violence. Many of those affected exhibited extraordinary strength, often requiring several men to restrain them. Injections of tranquilizers such as Valium were ineffective. Those affected would ignore attempts to reassure them or not respond to any questions posed to them or would scream even more after inquiries were made. Between screams and shouts, some would break out in laughter, interspersed by more screaming. Some said they could see "a dark figure" who was about to strangle them.[211] A second category of affected worker seemed to exhibit trance states. "While being violent, or before becoming violent, a worker would suddenly speak as though she was someone else, and claim that a 'jin' or spirit was speaking through her. Such states persisted for no more than several minutes." A third presentation type were those exhibiting "frightened spells." These are workers who "expressed a feeling of unexplained fear, and might complain of feeling cold, numb, or dizzy."[212]

A second "outbreak" was reported in a dried cuttlefish factory on September 29, 1973, when a female employee began to suddenly scream and cry. When she became violent she exhibited exceptional strength and several men were needed to restrain her. Two more women soon followed with similar outbursts. The "attacks" resumed on Thursday morning, October 4, when ten workers were stricken, including three repeat cases from the 29th. The scene was one of chaos and confusion, and officials closed the plant that afternoon. In all, 28 females and two males were affected out of a total of 350 workers. The main symptoms were screaming, weeping, and violence. Some employees claimed to see visions of a dark-skinned man with hairy arms. Like the previous outbreak, all of those involved were Malays. While management brought in a *bomoh* to rid the premises of evil spirits, sporadic cases continued to be recorded even after the exorcism. Some workers reported as many as five separate "attacks."

Phoon notes that Malays have a strong belief in the existence of spirits, including some that can supposedly possess another person's body. He hypothesizes that "because of internal conflict generated by unhappiness and the inability to self-express or vocalize their unhappiness, for fear of social disapproval, the Malay women react by 'mass hysteria,' i.e., it is used as a 'safety valve.'" Due to the widespread popular belief in possessing spirits, the exhibition of mass hysteria, "far from being condemned, is accepted without any social disapproval. On the contrary, it generates concern and sympathy on the part of parents, colleagues and perhaps even management."[213]

Chan and Wong have also investigated episodes of "hysterical fits," including screaming and trance-like states, in Singaporean factories. Based on their analysis of four cases they note that 107 of the 108 workers affected were female and most of those were Malay, despite the majority of the Singaporean population being Chinese. A strong relationship was found between being afflicted and a worker's ethnicity and worldview. Of employees reporting "attacks," only three said they were not followers of Islam, Hinduism, or Buddhism. The outbreak form appears to reflect the female role in Malaysia and Singapore at the time of the incidents. The outbreak mirrors the intensity of animistic beliefs among the affected groups of workers. The intensity of animistic beliefs among Malays was greatest and seemed to reflect their socialization process. Malay children are typically exposed to "stories of the powers of evil spirits and taught to avoid certain dark places, such as cemeteries. Evil spirits are often used as threats when the child misbehaves. This could explain the deep-seated animistic beliefs of the Malays and their intense subconscious fear of evil spirits." On the other hand, most Singaporean Indians (who are typically Hindu but occasionally Christian or Buddhist) were raised "to believe in spirit possession and spirit mediums. In the social context of Singaporean Hinduism, there is nothing remarkable about...trance states, with many ordinary devotees entering into such states during certain ceremonies." The Chinese, however, socialize their children very differently, usually threatening them "with corporal punishment or the police. They seem to approach 'dealings' with spirits and deities [with business-like pragmatism]." Their relative lack of fear and control of evil spirits "may explain their relative 'immunity' to hysterical behavior."[214]

Relabelling Endemic Symptoms [215]

This category is more controversial. It involves subjects who redefine a variety of mundane, commonplace complaints that are prompted, maintained, and reinforced by an over-vigilant medical community and other exacerbating factors.

Example: Myalgic Encephalomyelitis or Mass Hysteria?

One example is characterized by epidemic malaise, emotional lability, depression, gastrointestinal upset, muscle aches, mild fever, and headache, which have been documented since 1934. Episodes primarily occur in closed, socially cohesive populations of general hospital staff, physicians, interns, and female nurses, the latter being most heavily affected. Symptoms are protean, often exhibiting considerable variation between outbreaks. Reports have appeared under a variety of descriptive labels: benign myalgic encephalomyelitis (ME),[216] epidemic neuro-myasthenia,[217] Iceland Disease,[218] and poliomyelitis-resembling.[219] While several researchers argue that an unidentified virus elicits the symptoms,[220] no causative agent has been conclusively identified. Many episodes appear concurrently with epidemics of poliomyelitis in fatigued hospital staff who are in unavoidable close contact with potential vectors.

The origin of these outbreaks has been the subject of medical debate since the publication of three *British Medical Journal* articles suggesting a psychosocial origin,[221] enforced by the re-labeling by a hypervigilant medical community of a variety of mundane complaints that are endemic within the general population. These articles elicited considerable consternation among many in the medical community who seemed defensive and determined to implicate an organic etiology in order to vindicate themselves from the stigmatic label of epidemic hysteria, convinced that their educated colleagues were somehow immune from such episodes. Even experienced scientists supporting the presence of an unknown viral agent have concluded that a significant number of participants in the benign myalgic encephalomyelitis and epidemic neuromyasthenia episodes were almost certainly exhibiting conversion symptoms,[222] or at the least, some of the patients were exhibiting psychogenic reactions.[223]

The most famous of these "outbreaks" occurred at the Royal Free Hospital in London, which began during mid-July of 1955, when a doctor and a sister in one of the ward's fell ill on the same day and became patients in their own hospital. Eventually nearly 300 people were affected with malaise, headache, nausea, depression, weepiness, and sore throat. The epidemic spread but thorough investigations failed to identify any definitive cause. The belief that it was an unknown virus reigned until 1970 when two British psychiatrists, Colin McEvedy and Alfred Beard, reexamined the episode and suggested that many of the symptoms were likely generated by the mass hysteria. Their diagnosis created a firestorm within the medical community. While the episode was initially diagnosed as hysteria, when internists were affected and it was perhaps common knowledge that internists were not vulnerable to hysteria, the symptoms were relabeled as a previously undescribed affliction.[224] As Geoff Watts remarks on the attitude of many staff at the Royal Free, "Hysteria may be a diagnosis fit for schoolchildren and other ordinary folk, but not for medical staff, especially those of 'various seniority.' And even if nurses might fall victim to the condition, consultants – men, especially – could not. So the unpleasantness at the Royal Free had, at all costs, to be organic not psychological."[225] McEvedy and Beard suggested that concerns over a polio epidemic had generated anxiety among hospital staff, producing ambiguous symptoms reflecting their anxiety.

The existence of ME continues to be shrouded in controversy. Consider the following description of the "illness" by an organization dedicated to ME research: "Myalgic encephalomyelitis (ME) is a disabling, often painful and little-understood disease of unknown origin and uncertain outcome. Its duration appears to be variable: some people seem to recover completely, or experience periods of remission and relapse; others develop a condition of unresolving physical and/or cognitive disability, while a further small but significant minority deteriorate to a housebound and ultimately immobilised state. Since case history research on ME is still in its infancy, and the disease is chronic, this last category may be considerably larger than has been supposed."[226]

Example: Repetition Strain

A second example within this category involves variations of WRITER'S AND TELEGRAPHIST'S CRAMP, appearing under the contemporary label of REPETITIVE STRAIN INJURY (RSI) since 1982. The "epidemic" of occupational over-use injuries in Australian keyboard users during the mid-1980s has been attributed to "hysterical" contagion by numerous researchers, including Australian psychiatrist Yolande Lucire.[227]

One view is that many of those exhibiting the

symptoms of repetitive strain were consciously feigning injury to receive worker compensation benefits or less strenuous work duties. Ireland argues that the Australian RSI epidemic of the 1980s was triggered by the lackadaisical social and political climate, including a weak "work ethic."[228] Another view is that the Australian RSI epidemic was a "compensation neurosis" whereby "victims" experience a "disproportionate disability and delayed recovery from a genuine injury. This is generally attributed to an unconscious desire for secondary gain, usually, but not necessarily, financial. Other gains can include invalid status, attention from others and freedom from unwelcome work."[229] This position is articulated by Australian researchers Gabriele Bammer and Brian Martin. "The financial gain is thought to arise because the workers' compensation system is seen as providing an opportunity for workers either to receive an income without working (through weekly payments) or to obtain large windfalls of money (through lump sum settlements, either in lieu of weekly payments or as a result of a successful common law damages suit against the employer). The explanation also maintains that, once the financial gain has been obtained, immediate recovery and usually return to work follows, whereas other treatments are ineffective."[230] Another view, championed by Lucire, was that of conversion disorder of mass hysteria, which differs from compensation neurosis in that there is no injury involved. The pain is seen as emanating "from unresolved psychological conflict or emotional disturbance. Put another way, the conflict is converted into imaginary pain, which in turn allows an escape from the conflict."[231]

Despite these explanations, which may account for a relatively small number of RSI injury claims, there is considerable evidence that "victims" were experiencing a constellation of mundane symptoms that became redefined by the Australian medical community, and subsequently in patients, to a new cause. Exacerbating the situation was the prominence of numerous RSI cases that became the focus of false compensation claims by malingerers.[232] A further factor inappropriately implicating mass hysteria were reports that most patients were female, which, as one research team noted, "is a characteristic of epidemic hysteria."[233] Such analyses were flawed in that they sought to understand the origins of the RSI influx independent of its local context and meaning. For instance, most Australian keyboard operators are female, and while RSI experiences were not uniquely Australian, the scale of the "ailment" was.[234] The social context is of key importance in this regard as work-related compensation injuries are viewed as a right among Australians, and a consensus emerged prior to the "epidemic" that the Workers' Compensation system was an easy target for exploitation by simply obtaining a doctor's certificate.[235]

Australian physician David Bell examined the epidemiology or spread of RSI, noting that it followed social networks and was clearly neither an illness nor an injury, but spread by the motivation (conscious or unconscious) for compensation.[236] Another complicating factor was intervention in the dispute and support of the strong Australian trade unions and the highly ambiguous diagnostic criteria for determining the presence of RSI.[237] As a result of these circumstances, the diagnosis became a nebulous catchall category for an array of endemic aches and pains, with its mysterious pervasiveness and persistence in Australia earning it the nickname "kangaroo paw."[238] A consensus has since emerged among researchers that the diagnosis of RSI was a broad, over-inclusive, vaguely defined rubric embodying "the causal theory that the symptoms were an injury caused by repetitive movement and overuse. Its creation gave legitimacy to complaints of arm pain as a reason for absence from work and a basis for claims under workers' compensation."[239] This helps to explain why the incidence of writer's cramp among Australian keyboard telegraphists in 1971 was 14 percent (Ferguson 1971), yet symptoms were virtually nonexistent "in countries where [workers'] compensation was not paid for it."[240]

Episodes of writer's cramp in the latter half of the nineteenth century,[241] and telegraphist's cramp during the first three decades of the twentieth century,[242] have a remarkable parallel to RSI "outbreaks" and occurred under similar circumstances. While telegraphist's cramp was covered in 1908 under the British Workman's Compensation Act and was initially attributed to a variety of organic causes such as muscle failure, the Postal Clerk's Association eventually concluded that it resulted from "nervous instability" in conjunction with fatigued muscles.[243] In fact, by 1912, up to 60% of British postal workers reported symptoms. Remarkably, simultaneous surveys conducted in continental Europe identified only sporadic incidents among telegraphists, while the incidence in the United States of "cramp symptoms" was between 4% and 10%.[244]

While the majority of these various RSI epidemics dating back to the nineteenth century are explainable as the re-labeling of endemic symptoms that were supported by the medical community, simple re-labeling cannot entirely explain the epidemiology. However, occupational stress was likely a major exacerbating factor. There is a relationship between workplace mass hysteria reports and the gradual accumulation of somatic symptoms, which can be linked to psychosocial factors in the workplace. This association is especially strong with regard to musculoskeletal complaints. For instance, a ten-year study by Leino and Hanninen found that psychosocial factors in work settings "were associated with, and predicted the change in the occurrence of musculoskeletal disorders when age, gender, social class, and physical work load were controlled for."[245] In summarizing the literature on this area, British psychiatrist Simon Wessely remarked: "It would be tedious to list all the studies that have considered the influence of psychosocial factors at work and the development of upper limb disorders." He notes a similar pattern in these studies: "A recent systematic review found 76 relevant references, and concluded that monotonous work and feeling under pressure were closely associated with musculo-skeletal symptoms. Certain themes reappear time and again. These are job content (unstimulating); control (low participation in decision making); interpersonal relationships (conflict with supervisors) and general career development (uncertainty, insecurity, poor pay)."[246] Wessely further remarked: "There is now a consensus that the psychological environment does affect the production of somatic musculo-skeletal symptoms, with a general relative risk of two."[247]

The Pattern Of Report Incidence[248]

Episodes of mass hysteria in work settings can be a confusing topic, often due to the array of terms used by authors to label such cases. Susan Ackerman and Raymond Lee's ethnographic description of mass hysteria at a Malaysian shoe factory was labeled "a spirit possession event."[249] When a group of female Australian textile workers exhibited dizziness over a 12-day period in 1956, and the cause was identified as psychogenic in origin, the report appeared incognito under the title: "Fumigation with Dichlorethyl ether and Chlordane: Hysterical Sequelae."[250] Other misleading or ambiguous episode descriptions include "acute illness,"[251] and "epidemic of 'shocks.'"[252] P.J. Sparks and colleagues entitled their report "An Outbreak of Illness Among Aerospace Workers."[253] A historical review of mass hysteria episodes in various settings, including the workplace, appeared in an article by Dr. Robert Markush under the title of: "Mental Epidemics: A Review of the Old to Prepare for the New."[254] Then there is the problem of assessing a variety of contentious medical syndromes and whether some, all, or any involve psychogenic symptoms: Sick Building Syndrome, Multiple Chemical Sensitivity Syndrome, Total Allergy Syndrome, and Environmental Hypersensitivity. The jury is still out as to what percentage of cases, if any, which are initially labeled under these headings, may involve mass psychogenic illness.

Since hysterical contagion is referred to by a variety of descriptive labels, reviews are prone to information bias as the literature is more diffuse than researchers may realize. Those reviewing the literature on mass hysteria in occupational settings face a formidable task in locating cases distributed across a variety of interdisciplinary journals in such domains as general, occupational and epidemiological medicine; psychology; sociology; anthropology; and psychiatry. Occupational mass psychogenic illness is subsumed within the epidemic hysteria literature – a literature fraught with similar labeling problems. The diversity of names used to label "epidemic hysteria" is a source of further confusion, often implying the presence of mental disorder (e.g., shared psychopathology, mass psychosis), sometimes denoting normalcy (group conformity, social contagion), and occasionally described in neutral terms (mass phenomena, collective behavior). Bartholomew identified 82 separate synonyms for the term.[255] A further exacerbation is the interdisciplinary nature of the topic, prompting the use of diverse methods and assumptions in interpreting social delusions. Physicians typically write on singular cases of mass psychogenic illness they have encountered, while sociologists often discuss community-wide episodes involving unsubstantiated beliefs or perceptions. Psychologists tend to focus on the psychometric characteristics of those affected, social psychologists usually explore the influence of rumor and gossip, and psychoanalysts often seek to identify deep-seated subconscious psychic conflicts. Historians usually limit discussion to medieval dancing "manias." Anthropologists emphasize the cultural context of outbreaks and the position of subordinate females within repressive social structures. Some folklorists study the influence of urban legends in precipitating collective delusions, in addition to similarities between recurring folkloric genres, while journalists examine the mass media's impact in perpetuating such mass phenomena. Finally, political scientists are known to employ the vernacular meaning to describe what they may view as overzealous or unsubstantiated adherence to a particular opinion that is unfounded.

The enigmatic temporal clustering of scientific reports on mass hysteria at work may reflect the prevailing medical *zeitgeist* and psychiatric ideology in terms of the recognition, prevalence, and seriousness of episodes.[256] A major factor affecting the seemingly sporadic report pattern is the scientist's awareness of cases. This was well illustrated from psychologist Michael Colligan's attendance at an American Footwear Manufacturers Association Conference, when nearly half of the audience acknowledged familiarity with episodes.[257] Robert Bartholomew has served as a consultant to several multinational corporations operating in Malaysia, and the Malaysian Ministry of Human Resources, and is aware of four episodes since 1992, one of which involved more than 300 workers. The managers in these factories are reluctant to disclose incidents fearing adverse publicity, a view reinforced by the media-sensitive government that is concerned with any portrayals of the country as backward, primitive, or underdeveloped. In fact, during a spate of at least 17 school episodes in 1971, the Malaysian government prohibited the press from reporting on mass hysteria cases.[258]

Another factor affecting the clustering of reports may be the heightened public and scientific awareness of occupational and environmental issues that can foster hypersensitivity and preoccupation with workplace health. For example, as Sick Building Syndrome (SBS) has risen in prevalence during the past two decades, environmental legislation has grown concurrently voluminous. As a result, various mundane symptoms that are prevalent in any general population may have become re-labeled and attributed to a new cause. This may account for the almost exclusive confinement of SBS to Western countries. Preoccupation with workplace contamination is a powerful theme that is thoroughly entrenched in the Western psyche. For instance, John Cornwell's *The Power to Harm* examines the circumstances leading up to a 1989 killing spree by a printing plant worker in Louisville, Kentucky. Cornwell remarked: "For years [Joseph] Wesbecker thought that he and his co-workers were being poisoned by toxic fumes in the printing plant, and toward the end he talked of himself being 'sodomized' by the company. Whatever the literal accuracy of these assertions, a powerfully metaphorical perception of a 'toxic' and 'abusive' workplace haunts the story of Wesbecker's last three years at the plant."[259]

Concluding Remarks

It may be less confusing and more accurate to refer to the three discernible mass hysteria presentation types as a syndrome since the symptom pattern is distinct and consistent over time. Investigators of outbreaks with psychogenic features have a responsibility to thoroughly examine the occupational environment for the presence of infectious or toxicological agents. Incomplete environmental investigations following outbreaks of illness symptoms among the predominantly female workforce at a garment industry in Mayaguez, Puetro Rico, resulted in management labeling the complaints as hysterical contagion. But a more thorough subsequent examination revealed the presence of toxic fumes that had precipitated degenerative diseases, respiratory tract damage, and even death.[260]

Most episodes of collective psychogenic illness in the workplace are readily identifiable, even before environmental testing is completed, by the presence of most or all of the following characteristic features, the presence of which should heighten suspicions of a psychogenic origin: extraordinary anxiety among a segregated group of workers; ambiguous, benign, transient symptomatology, featuring a rapid onset and recovery; transmission via sight, sound, and along social networks; and a disparity between affected workers and cohorts of equal or greater exposure who remained asymptomatic. Conspicuously absent from this list is female susceptibility. If one takes the position that sociocultural factors can account for the disproportionate number of female participants in episodes, the over representation of females may not be considered a risk factor by some researchers. However, if we do, a high female "attack" rate can be added to this list.

Since the 18th century, various authors have documented a fascinating array of occupational mass psychogenic illness forms, from writer's cramp to repetitive strain injury, and fainting factory workers to epidemic malaise. It remains to be seen what new forms future episodes will take and the corresponding medical label it will receive. A key factor in the prevalence of future episodes will hinge on how workers are treated. It is clear that an underlying factor in many outbreaks is related to the dehumanizing aspects of certain types of jobs and the way management treats employees. For decades, those studying occupational mass psychogenic illness episodes have sought the causes by scrutinizing the affected workers. It is now evident that building trust and open communication between workers and management can prevent many episodes. For instance, in episodes of mass anxiety hysteria involving the perception of strange odors (the most common type), such a climate can prevent outbreaks or reduce their extent as open communication channels and trust serve to dissolve suspicions, rumors, and cover-up and conspiracy theories that typify outbreaks. In episodes of mass motor hysteria, both listening and responding to worker concerns can reduce the long-term build-up of anxiety that eventually trigger outbreaks. The general incidence of mass hysteria can be further reduced by focusing on other areas such as resolving supervisory conflicts, providing stimulating positions that offer appropriate pay, future security and career development, and, above all, by treating workers with respect, equality, and sensitivity. It is also likely that the number of documented reports of mass anxiety hysteria, mass motor hysteria, and the re-labeling of existing symptoms is significant and likely represent but a tiny fraction of what has actually occurred.[261]

Episodes of both mass anxiety and motor hysteria continue to be reported in Malaysia and reflect the exposure of traditional Malay peoples to dehumanizing working conditions – typically in Western multinational factories. In the 1990s Robert Bartholomew worked as a management consultant in several Malaysian factories where mass motor hysteria was a common occurrence and where workers often wore t-shirts that read in broken English: "Human being is not machine." This led him to remark: "In an age of technology, assembly lines, deadlines and quotas, where profit margins are often placed ahead of people, and workers can feel like numbers, we could do well to listen to these voices."[262]

MASS HYSTERIA IN SCHOOLS

"Epidemic hysteria" refers to the rapid spread of conversion hysteria and/or anxiety states within a particular student cluster, shortly after exposure to a common threat, which is either real or imagined. This definition encompasses groups of students off school premises, participating in school-related activities such as a field trip, sporting event, dance, play, chorus, concert, or marching band. For reasons of manageability, excluded from this definition are episodes of a non-spontaneous nature, i.e., fainting, twitching, shaking, glossolalia, altered states of consciousness, and related phenomena originating in an organized, ritualized, or institutionalized manner, such as deliberately induced ecstatic states in school-related charismatic religious organizations. The rapid spread of illness signs, symptoms, and related beliefs for which there is no plausible organic basis, but occurring within a school-related context, was commonly reported in Europe during the second half of the 19th century. Episodes were rarely reported in the scientific literature between 1910 and 1950, but have risen steadily since.[263]

CONTEXT: There are two main types of mass hysteria in school settings. The first type, mass motor hysteria, predominates in non-Western traditional cultures among pupils exposed to pre-existing psychosocial stress and usually enduring repressive academic and religious discipline, thereby triggering trance states, psychomotor agitation (twitching and shaking), and histrionics. In non-Western countries, motor symptoms may reflect cultural change and conflict with elders. In Western settings they usually involve fainting or twitching in an unconscious effort to get out of schoolwork or a related intolerable situation. Anxiety hysteria episodes predominate in Western settings and are typified by the sudden appearance of extreme anxiety in the wake of a redefinition of a mundane event such as illness in a fellow student or an unfamiliar odor, which is perceived as an immediate threat in the form of contamination or illness.

What may have been the first known documented case of mass hysteria in a school setting was recorded in Lille, France in 1639, when fifty students at an all-girls' school became convinced that Satan was controlling their actions. Religious zealot and headmistress Antoinette Bourgignon had them believing that tiny black angels were flying about their heads, and that the Devil's imps were everywhere. Soon, each of the students confessed to witchcraft, flying on broomsticks, and even eating baby flesh. The students were nearly burned at the stake but were spared when blame shifted to the role of Bourgignon, who narrowly escaped herself.[264] While it is not known whether conversion or anxiety states were present, it is a likely supposition given the circumstances. The episode occurred near the end of the European WITCH MANIA of 1400 to 1650, when at least 500,000 people were executed following wrongful allegations of witchcraft.

German girls' school circa 1900. Such schools were hotbeds for mass twitching and shaking outbreaks in response to lengthy, tedious writing and memory exercises.

Most researchers assume that the stimulus for group episodes, collective or otherwise, is a variant of individual "conversion hysteria," a term devised by psychoanalyst Sigmund Freud to describe the converting of psychological trauma and conflict into involuntary physical complaints that have no organic basis. A classic example is the pacifist soldier conscripted into the military who experiences temporary arm paralysis when trying to fire a weapon. The link between conversion hysteria and mass hysteria is natural since the major symptoms of the latter are characteristic features of collective episodes. These are: symptoms with no plausible organic basis; that are transient and benign; with rapid onset and recovery; and occur in a segregated group; in the presence of extraordinary anxiety. The symptoms are spread via sight, sound, or oral communication; occur down the age-scale, beginning in older or higher status students; and exhibit a preponderance of female participants near puberty and early adolescence.[265] Symptoms are believed to enable victims to unconsciously avoid undesirable situations and activities while simultaneously receiving support and attention.

Some researchers suggest abandoning the terms "mass hysteria" or "epidemic hysteria," arguing that use of the word "hysteria" is prejudicial to females.[266] While the use of more neutral terminology in describing school episodes has become more common ("mass psychogenic illness" and "mass sociogenic illness" being the most widely used alternatives), "mass hysteria" and "epidemic hysteria" remain the most commonly used terms to describe reports. The occasional use of such phrases as "group mental disorder" has potentially stigmatizing connotations. Pathological labels also appear to be inaccurate, as attempts to identify abnormal personality traits in victims are inconclusive.[267] Further complicating the topic is the confusion over the ambiguous meaning of the word "hysteria," which has been used to describe no less than ten separate behavioral patterns, including the histrionic personality, psychogenic pain disorder, and different forms of psychosis.[268]

Presentation Patterns

Based on the descriptive features of episodes, two readily identifiable presentation patterns are notable. These patterns correspond closely with what British psychiatrist Simon Wessely terms "mass anxiety hysteria" and "mass motor hysteria."[269] The former is of shorter duration, usually one day, and involves sudden, extreme anxiety shortly after exposure to a perceived threat. The second type occurs in intolerable social settings and includes such characteristic features as dissociative states, histrionics, and alterations in psychomotor activity, typically enduring for weeks or months. Two additional, rarely reported episode types are also noted. The third is termed "mass hysteria by proxy," involving the re-labeling of mundane symptoms in students by hypervigilant authority figures. A fourth type involves echo or sympathy with the behavior of a particular student.

Type One: Mass Anxiety Hysteria

Mass anxiety hysteria is common in developed countries and occurs in a social setting where there is no pre-existing anxiety. Episodes typically begin in a single pupil who exhibits illness signs and symptoms that quickly spread to fellow schoolmates, and on occasion, to teachers and staff who report a broad range of ambiguous, anxiety-based somatic complaints. Sometimes the index case (the first to exhibit symptoms) is a school employee or visiting parent. The initial "victim" often behaves in a dramatic fashion, creating intense anxiety among those within visual proximity. Frequently the index case is suffering from a medical condition, such as epileptic seizure, schizophrenia, or heat stroke. Typically, classmates learn such information retrospectively, well after the episode has spread, and other pupils attribute the illness behavior to an unusual smell that is assumed to represent a toxic gas leak or a communicable agent such as an infectious disease, which is perceived as an immediate personal threat. Within the first 24-hours of an outbreak, food poisoning from the cafeteria is commonly suspected. Several factors may exacerbate the situation: the news media, rumors, recent events, superstitious beliefs, and local traditions.

Noxious odors or food poisoning are rarely suspected in non-Western countries, where the prime culprit is typically believed to be one of scores of tiny supernatural beings. The index case often begins screaming, weeping uncontrollably, and over-breathing after seeing what they believe is one of these spirit entities. Classmates may assume that the initial "victim" is "hexed" or "charmed," or that a ghost roams the school grounds. As a result of observing the index pupil, classmates experience sudden, extreme anxiety as they assume they may be the next targets. "The search for potential explanations among pupils is limited only by plausibility, as the lack of educational and life experiences can foster hypotheses that are potentially fantastic to adults or individuals living outside of the culture or subcultural milieu. Students who are in the closest spatial, visual or social contact with the index case, and subsequent victims, are most susceptible to developing symptoms."[270] In most cases, symptoms spread downward, with older students being affected first, followed by younger schoolmates; at the very least the index case is a prominent group member.[271]

The typical episode persists for less than a day and often just a few hours. Occasionally, a particular manifestation will recur in waves, lasting more than a week, and very rarely longer than a month. In such instances, when the threatening agent is believed to persist, or authorities are not perceived to have taken the students' claims seriously or thoroughly examined the premises, symptoms can endure sporadically for several months. These lengthier relapse reports are often exacerbated by mass media coverage and speculation about the event. Such cases also appear related to the inability of law enforcement, politicians, medical personnel, school officials, and community leaders to convince the affected students and their worried parents of the psychological origin of the symptoms. Episodes of mass anxiety hysteria cease rapidly once the students are convincingly reassured that the phantom threat, most typically a harmless odor, is likely to have been eliminated or never existed.[272]

Example: Hyperventilating Schoolgirls in Britain

A classic episode of mass anxiety hysteria involved over-breathing schoolgirls in Blackburn, England. The affair occurred at a girls' secondary school in 1965 and was investigated by physicians Peter Moss and Colin McEvedy,[273] whose study was published in *The British Medical Journal.* On October 6, a majority of the schoolgirls attended a church service under Royal patronage. Unfortunately, when the service was delayed, students had to wait for three hours. During this time 20 girls fainted. The next day, the fainting episode was the main topic of discussion. At the morning assembly, a girl fainted. While this was not especially uncommon (the assembly averaged two or three fainting pupils per week), soon after the assembly dispersed, four girls reported feeling dizzy and thought they might faint, so authorities and sat them on chairs in a corridor near the center of the building. During the first two class periods, six more girls reported feeling faint and were asked to sit in the hallway with the other four girls. School officials grew concerned that if one of the girls were to actually faint, they might injure themselves by striking the floor, so the 10 girls were asked to lie on the floor in the corridor. "By positioning the first group of symptomatic girls in the highly visible corridors, the situation appeared more dramatic and the epidemic spread by line of sight soon after the mid-morning break."[274] By the middle of the afternoon, 141 pupils were exhibiting a constellation of symptoms including feeling faint, lightheaded, dizzy, and shivering, along with reports of abdominal pain, nausea, breathlessness, backaches, facial numbness, and tetanic spasms.

Ambulances and emergency personnel converged on the scene and during the ensuing chaos transported 85 students to the hospital. Mass media reports exacerbated the situation, stoking the levels of anxiety in the community as newspapers described the episode as a "mysterious illness." Medical tests were negative, and over the next 15 days, several waves of cases occurred at the school in a declining fashion. In all, about 30 percent of the school's 550 pupils were affected. Drs. Moss and McEvedy concluded that placing the first few "faints" in such a highly visible, strategically positioned corridor near the middle of the building was counterproductive and seemed to have heightened anxieties. "What became epidemic was a piece of behaviour consequent on an emotional state: excitement or, in the latter stages, frank fear led to over-breathing, with its characteristic sequelae – faintness, dizziness, paraethesiae, and tetany. Once learned, this self-reinforcing piece of behaviour restarted spontaneously when the school was assembled. By day 12, however, the hysterical nature of the epidemic was generally accepted, and a firm line prevented the behaviour propagating as extensively as it had on the previous occasions."[275]

Example: Malathion Poisoning Scare

Another typical case of anxiety hysteria involved a pesticide-poisoning scare at a Tucson, Arizona, elementary school in 1987. On Friday morning, April 24, a man sprayed trees and scrubs with Malathion in his backyard, which was adjacent to the school. At about 9 a.m., two teachers separately reported to the office via the intercom that they detected a strong odor. An office worker then used the intercom to notify the other classes of the situation and to request that they keep their doors and windows shut until the odor subsided. Despite instructions to the contrary, a teacher took her class outdoors where they encountered an even stronger smell. They quickly reentered the building and went to the cafeteria, where some students exhibited headache, nausea, and dizziness. At this point, an office attendant who observed the student complaints grew worried and telephoned for outside help and summoned the principal, who was away from school.[276] When emergency personnel arrived, they "found a class of 12 children in the cafeteria complaining of headache and nausea. The fire chief arrived a short time later and ordered additional paramedic units, firefighters and the Hazardous Materials (HazMat) Team on the basis that an unknown and possibly toxic substance was causing illness."[277] As more emergency responders arrived, they went to each classroom to check on the condition of the students and teachers. Other responders fanned out to locate the source of the odor, which was soon located. At this point, more and more students began to report feeling ill, prompting authorities to make the decision to set up a triage station on the school grounds with local physicians summoned to the scene to treat the affected students on site. This plan was soon abandoned when the paramedic coordinator decided to evacuate the grounds and transport each of the 296 students to eight different medical facilities. At this point, the school grounds looked like a scene from a disaster movie with nearly a dozen fire departments on the scene along with numerous law enforcement officers, over 100 emergency responders, and county health and emergency services personnel, in addition to reporters and film crews and concerned parents trying to check on the welfare of their children.[278]

At the hospitals, the symptoms soon subsided and none of the patients was described as seriously ill. Symptoms reported at the hospitals mimicked those of anxiety – upset stomach, headache, runny eyes, headaches, weakness, sweating, difficulty breathing, dizziness, and blurred vision.[279] When physicians observed and examined each of the 296 students, "No clinical findings of anticholinergic poisoning were noted..."[280] The man who sprayed the pesticide told investigators that he diluted approximately 22 milliliters of Malathion into 15 liters of water. An inspection of the remaining fluid in the bottle used supported his claim that he had mixed the ingredients properly.[281] A sample of the Malathion used was analyzed both by the manufacturer and the state agriculture department; their findings were unremarkable.

Malathion is widely used in the United States and it gives off a strong odor. It has even been used in lotion form to control head and body lice.[282] How likely is Malathion exposure to cause breathing problems similar to those recorded during the school spraying incident? "Studies on respiratory exposure to malathion have shown that inhalation of an aerosol of 12g of 25% malathion (2.4g) in a room with no ventilation failed to produce any observable effects in humans exposed for 1 h [hour] periods, twice a day for 42 consecutive days."[283]

A number of observers at the school noted that the scene was very chaotic and tense, with some authorities openly disagreeing as to what course of action to take. In their report on the episode, Paul Baker and Donald Selvey noted that several physicians on the scene indicated in their notes the presence of anxiety reactions that might have been prompted by the "heat of the moment." The two researchers concluded that the episode was due to mass hysteria, not Malathion poisoning. "The severity of the psychological stress associated with this event may be best exemplified by a verbal exchange between the paramedic coordinator (triage nurse) and the school principal after the latter questioned the decision to alter the evacuation plan. The paramedic coordinator is alleged to have threatened to have the principal arrested for interference."[284] Baker and Selvey further observe that other observers at the scene suggest that "emergency responders did not consider the effects of their actions on the children; notably, that the constant shouting of orders to children teachers, the principal and parents frightened many people."[285] The episode is typical of mass hysteria reports: it occurred at a school, had a preponderance of female or young victims whose symptoms were spread by sight and sound, and displayed a rapid onset and recovery.

Example: Ghost Attacks in Thailand

On occasion, anxiety hysteria will be recorded in non-Western settings, though the trigger is rarely food contamination or poisoning, or a strange odor. The culprit is typically, but not always, evil spirits or ghosts. One incident occurred in mid-January 2001, in Thailand. About 100 students attending a school camp in Nakhon Ratchasima province suddenly fell ill for no apparent reason. An investigating physician said the students were exhausted after a long day of exercise and grew fearful that ghosts haunted the camp. Dr. Somchai Chakraphand said the exhaustion "built up on top of the general belief that spirits and ghosts haunted the area. The students' fear increased and this led to hyperventilation and eventually to breathing problems." The episode began when one girl, who was singing around a campfire, screamed after believing she saw a ghost. Most residents in the region have a strong belief in ghosts and malevolent spirits.[286]

Example: Poisoning Fears in Ethiopia

In rare instances, mass hysteria can occur exclusively to males. During the first week of February 2003, at Addis Ababa University in Ethiopia, more than 36 male students fainted in the wake of concern over the unexplained deaths of two fellow students the previous week. The episode occurred amid rumors that the pair had been poisoned. According to the hospital authorities where the group was taken, no evidence of this could be found. All tests were negative, including analyses of urine, blood, and stool, in addition to X-rays. Some of the students complained of weakness, but according to hospital physicians "all their vital signs were normal." Fearing the further spread of "mass hysteria," university officials canceled exams.[287]

Type Two: Mass Motor Hysteria – In Western Settings

The second episode-type occurs when students are exposed to prolonged, pre-existing tension. During the 20th century cases were mostly confined to technologically impoverished, non-Western schools in traditional societies, or European schools between 1800 and 1910. Based on an analysis of 53 cases from 1808 to 1994, sociologist Robert Bartholomew and psychiatrist Francois Sirois remark that in settings that gave rise to episodes, "both male and adult-dominated power structures often foster strict disciplinary routines among pupils, especially females. Students have little means of redress as negotiation or protest channels with authorities are inhibited or nonexistent."[288] Students are faced with a dilemma since school is mandatory, they cannot exit the anxiety-provoking situation. "By staying at home and feigning illness, homework is still required. Besides, such avoidance strategies will remove them from social contact with many schoolmates. The inescapable, intolerable situation engenders intense frustration which is internalized during the ensuing weeks or months."[289]

This pattern was most prominent in Europe during the latter 19th and early 20th centuries in response to strict educational practices in many schools in such countries as Switzerland, France, and especially Germany. While the degree of severity in rules often varied between districts, it is conspicuous that schools experiencing hysteria "outbreaks" had several characteristic features in common: extreme pressure to perform; the practicing of tedious, repetitive, wearisome, monotonous memorization drills in writing and arithmetic; and an absence of creativity and individuality. During this period, French primary schools had curriculums that were described as "too intense" and "far too much composed of memory work."[290] Exacerbating this situation was the fear of legal repercussions or being dismissed. Article 1384 of the French educational code discouraged physical activities and games as teachers were responsible for any mishaps occurring under their supervision.[291] In some of the more rigorous French schools, teachers and parents placed enormous performance pressures on pupils who knew that if their grades slipped, there was a lengthy waiting list of students to take their place. "With such dismissal constantly hanging over their head, pupils appear to be always at high pressure."[292] French secondary schools (*lycees*) were described by one outside educator as "a veritable prison-house for all pupils from the youngest equally to the oldest, with a system of continual espionage known as *surveillance* (every minute of the day being duly apportioned, even recreation policed), relieved...by scarcely a human feature." One British educator described the French teaching method as consisting of "monotonous and reiterated preaching" during which at the end of each lesson, "a tireless *resume*" must be committed to memory.[293] The situation in Germany was not much better. The discipline in some German school districts was so strict that an observer wrote that even "corporal punishment in the elementary schools is harsh and severe,"[294] while another writer noted that some schools were instilling discipline that resembled what one might find in the German military instead of school, including rigid obedience, order, and self-control.[295] During this period, the education system in

Switzerland was similar to the German system,[296] with discipline high, games infrequent, and free thought and creativity suppressed.[297]

Example: Trembling Schoolgirls

A typical case of this nature occurred at a girls' school in Basel, Switzerland during 1893, as contagious trembling and convulsions affected 20 students who were prevented from completing in-school written assignments. Symptoms virtually disappeared after school hours, returning only upon re-entering school grounds.[298] In 1904, the same school was swept by a similar outbreak affecting 14 classes of pupils ages 11-to-15. The main symptom was a vibrating tremor in the right hand and forearm, which began in two students on June 11. Over the ensuing weeks the symptoms gradually spread until 27 pupils were affected amid rumors that the school would be closed for six weeks if the tremors continued to spread. The administrators instead announced that the school session would continue and the affected pupils were instructed in a special classroom with the same teacher for a month. The students were well fed, given a reduced workload, and suffered no blame or punishment for their inability to complete written work resulting from their tremors. Despite some disruptions in their arithmetic and handwriting performances, the symptoms gradually diminished. There were six cases of relapse but the outbreak soon ended.[299] A similar episode took place at Gross-Tinz, Germany, between June 28 and mid-October 1892, but the initial hand tremors soon affected the entire body and 8 of the 20 victims exhibited altered states of consciousness and amnesia.[300]

Between 1905-1906, P. Schutte described a "trembling disease" that swept through several schools in Meissen, Germany. The symptoms reportedly affected otherwise healthy children who apparently had excessive writing assignments. Schutte states: "The unique aspect of the 'Trembling Disease,' is that it occurs in epidemic form, that is, is communicated from one person to the other. The patients are mainly children from the age of 9 to 13 years, and predominantly girls of the elementary and middle school 'Burgerschule,' who are placed together with 35 classes in the same building...The characteristic symptoms first make themselves noticeable by a mild shaking of the right hand, which is always shaken only in a radial-ulnar direction. The trembling often extends to the forearm and sometimes it also seizes the left side...The trembling phenomena occur with varying frequencies, sometimes also at night, and they last from a few minutes to half an hour. During the intervals the children usually feel entirely well, except for a certain nervous excitement, until the attack again sets in with more or less renewed vigor. This condition can last for weeks or months..." [301] At the time of his writing, the twitching episode was stubbornly persisting.

Example: Twitching Epidemic in Louisiana

In 1939, an episode of spasmodic twitching struck seven girls ages 16-to-18 at a Louisiana high school. Twitching spread after symptoms in the first pupil enabled her to avoid dance classes and rekindle a boyfriend's waning affection. Investigators surmised that after observing the success of the initial case, six others obtained benefits from their newly acquired illness status over the ensuing weeks.[302] See also, TWITCHING EPIDEMIC IN A SOUTHERN SCHOOL.

Example: Pregnancy Test Fears at a Louisiana School

Motor symptoms accompanied a pregnancy scare that occurred in an African-American school in Louisiana, a conservative state in the U.S. south, in 1962, where 21 girls and one boy experienced "blackout spells" over six months. Symptoms included dizziness, headaches, epileptic-like fits, tremors, and catatonic posturing. Most of these "spells" lasted a few minutes and occasionally up to an hour. Most of the affected students, who ranged in age from 10-to-17, were sexually active. Anxiety that fueled the outbreak coincided with rumors that all of the girls were going to be given pregnancy tests, and those testing positive would be sent to a correctional school. Treating those affected with sedatives was ineffective, and visits by outside authorities only exacerbated symptoms. Only with the gradual reduction of anxiety did the outbreak subside seven months later.[303]

Type Two: Mass Motor Hysteria – In Nonwestern Settings [304]

During the present century, mass motor hysteria is most evident in schools within Malaysia and Central and Eastern Africa. The African outbreaks usually affect missionary schools.[305] A typical African case was investigated by Dhadphale and Shaikh and involved an outbreak of twitching, mental confusion, uncontrollable laughing, running, and anxiety in 126 students at a secondary school in Zambia during May 1976.[306] The researchers noted that "the recent strict disciplinary measures taken by the new administration, such as rigid separation of boys and girls, may have prepared the emotionally charged background."[307] African physician G. J. Ebrahim noted that African children are dominated by their "all-powerful elders." Conflict arises from exposure to foreign ideas that challenge traditional beliefs, with escape being sought through conversion reactions. According to Ebrahim, the outbreaks are fueled by "emotional conflict aroused in children who are being brought up at home amidst traditional tribal conservatism, while being exposed in school to thoughts and ideas which challenge accepted beliefs.[308] Also see, LAUGHING EPIDEMICS IN AFRICA.

In Malaysia, the widespread appearance of mass motor hysteria in schools coincides with rapid social and cultural changes,[309] especially Islamic revivalism, which has rapidly gained influence since the early 1960s. Islamic by birth, Malays comprise just over half of the population. Yet, mass motor hysteria is almost exclusively confined to female Malays attending religious boarding schools. Episodes have become endemic in Malaysian schools since 1962.[310] Malaysian Islamic religious schools are notorious for their strict discipline and lack of privacy, where even basic choices such as which school to attend, courses to take, careers to pursue, and friendships to develop are decided upon by others.[311] In coeducational Islamic schools, boys and girls are strictly segregated, even within the same classroom. Students must account for their whereabouts at all times. Interaction with boys is strictly prohibited, courting is forbidden, and even visits by relatives are closely monitored in special public rooms. Hence, mass motor hysteria in Malay boarding schools typically occurs amid "a general feeling of unhappiness about some new condition of study or rule among the girls."[312] In conjunction with such oppressive practices, social, cultural, and religious protocols prohibit female Malays from direct confrontation with their superiors.[313]

With the continued presence of strict religious discipline, eventually a small number of students begin exhibiting conversion symptoms. Such events foster widespread anxiety as to the existence of demonic agents within the school that seem to present an immediate personal threat. Malaysian psychiatrist Jin-Inn Teoh and colleagues report a "monotonously similar" pattern in Malaysian schools whereby "girls would scream, shout, and run aimlessly all over in terror, with severe hyperventilation followed by muscular twitchings and tetanic spasms of the limbs." Some of these Malay schoolgirls "would fall on the floor in a trance-like state, as though in a stupor. Occasionally one or two of the subjects would speak up on behalf of the group, voicing their misdemeanors and frustrations. Very often they became abusive. They characteristically took hints and cues from one another. Most of the subjects...would swear amnesia. On questioning, the girls would complain of seeing fearsome objects... Some would see dark flying objects or an ugly woman eight feet tall. The occupants of one hostel complained that a hungry spirit was always stealing their food and raiding the refrigerator. Others complained of ghosts stealing their underwear and jamming their doors."[314]

It is vital to realize that while the interpretations of these events by the pupils may seem bizarre by Western standards, they are entirely consistent with popular Malay folk beliefs.[315] Animistic customs and superstitions are prevalent in Malay society, as there is a widespread belief in the existence of various supernatural forces such as the efficacy of magic potions, spells, amulets, charms, and curses, which are easily obtained by consulting a witchdoctor (*bomoh*) whose services remain popular. There is also a prevalent belief in the existence of supernatural beings known as the *Jinn* which are described in the Koran, in addition to diminutive fairy-like *toyl* creatures, and ghosts (*hantus*) from Malay culture. Extreme anxiety, hysterical conversion, and hyperventilation spread rapidly among pupils in close proximity, in visual contact, or with the strong social ties, when the initial cohort exhibits dissociative states. These trance-like states sometimes take the form of spirit possession, which can be dramatic and convincing to observers. In virtually every non-Western episode of this type, the services of one or more native healers are solicited to exorcize the evil spirit(s). Repression-induced conversion symptoms typically persist from one month to several years, depending on the changes implemented by authorities in response to the outbreak. If discipline is eased, and anxiety levels decline, episodes usually subside. However, if the intolerable situation persists, outbreaks can endure indefinitely.

Contemporary Western episodes are uncommon but occasionally occur. One outbreak of mass motor hysteria took the form of epidemic fainting, dissociation, and histrionics among several pupils at a girls' school near London, amid serious interpersonal and sexual conflicts following the death of a former schoolmate and lesbian advances by a school mistress.[316] In this instance, instead of the "drop attacks" being instigated by academic discipline, the school premises served as a stage where the girls' personal problems appeared in the form of hysterical conversion dramas over the better part of a year.

The presentation of mass motor episodes is remarkably similar to scores of hysterical fits, dissociation, and psychomotor agitation among nuns secluded primarily in European Christian convents between the 15th and 19th centuries.[317] Like their Malaysian counterparts, young females were typically coerced by elders into joining socially isolating religious orders practicing rigid discipline in confined, all-female living quarters. Male associations were forbidden. Mass motor hysteria conspicuously appeared under the strictest administrations. Instead of witch doctors, priests were summoned to exorcize the "demonic" spirits, and disliked individuals were often accused of casting spells. In both instances, the inmates released frustrations by uttering disrespectful, often blasphemous remarks, and engaging in aggressive sexual and threatening behavior, their possession status providing them with impunity.

While Malay schoolgirls often call for the dismissal or transfer of their restrictive headmaster, possessed nuns typically accused a despised colleague or restrictive convent priest of causing their condition via witchcraft. Malaysian episodes usually subside when school figures relax rules or the offending official is removed, while in convents, symptoms disappeared soon after the accused was either transferred, banished, imprisoned, or more commonly, burned at the stake. While Malaysian episodes typically persist for a few months, and occasionally years, convent outbreaks usually endured for several years, since lengthy church inquisitions were required and exorcisms were performed in order to remove the offending administrator and for punishment to be decided. During this waiting period, the nuns remained in their repressive situation, which continued to incubate symptoms.

Example: Contemporary Demon Possession

Between May and August 1999, hundreds of adolescent girls began exhibiting signs of 'demonic possession' at a church boarding school in Umtata, Grahamstown, South Africa. The symptoms were in response to apparent strict discipline and began during an examination period and included bouts of screaming, crying, writhing, foaming at the mouth and trance states. The 'fits' were especially intense during prayer time and at large gatherings.[318] According to the School rector, Reverend Ebenezer Ntlali: "Many girls began to scream or run wildly and most collapsed as their legs became wobbly. They were biting on their teeth, foaming at the mouth and experiencing stomach cramps that caused huge lumps just below their chests. There was also the twitching and jerking of their bodies as if they had suffered epileptic seizures, while their eyes rolled backwards until only the whites were visible."[319]

Many of those afflicted reported terrific headaches. A 19-year-old student named Bongeka Bulo said: "Many pupils also complained of excruciating headaches, blindness and memory loss. The pain was terrible and it felt as if something from inside my head was going to fall out. But it all stopped once the priest started praying for us." Another pupil, Makhosi Majozi, 16, said that she could only recall remembers being stricken with a headache followed by the sudden loss of sight. She said: "I have no recollection of what happened next and when I awoke I was in hospital."[320]

Type Three: Mass Hysteria By Proxy

One case surveyed involved the re-labeling of mundane symptoms in a closed, cohesive group, which was instigated and maintained by the erroneous beliefs of concerned parents. The case began in September 1988, at an elementary school near Atlanta, Georgia, when at a routine social gathering in the cafeteria, the mother of a pupil remarked that her child had experienced several health problems since the start of the term. Soon other mothers began examining their children for similar illness signs, including headache, fatigue, and vomiting. A folk theory soon emerged that the school building was making their kids sick. Their suspicions solidified further on October 11, when a natural gas leak at the school prompted an evacuation. A series of subsequent minor gas leaks fueled further parent fears, despite health assurances by experts to the contrary. While many parents picketed the school and spoke out about their children's safety to the mass media, tests of the school grounds by health specialists were negative. Investigators remarked that the children exhibited few public illness displays, did not seek attention, and maintained high attendance rates through the term, with health concerns "expressed almost exclusively by the mothers."[321] The minor health problems reported by the parents in their children were attributable to ever-present, mundane childhood illnesses.

Type Four: Mass Sympathetic Or Echo Hysteria

A fourth rarely reported category of mass hysteria in schools appears to involve extreme sympathy for and/or identification with a fellow student who is particularly esteemed. In London, England, during February 1907, a girl with infantile palsy of the left arm fractured her right arm. She returned to class several weeks later and "within a few days three children had lost the use of their left arms, and a fourth...had such severe pains in her left arm that she held it to the side and could not be persuaded to use it." The episode ended soon after a Dr. Hogarth used suggestion to move their arms freely again. While the details on this case are scant, it clearly does not fit any known pattern. It appears that the pupils affected were not particularly anxious but somehow identified with the injured girl with prolonged empathy to the point where they too began to exhibit symptoms.[322]

This category may correspond to what psychologists David Levy and Paul Nail term "echo contagion," which they define as "a case of social contagion in which an unconflicted recipient imitates or reflects spontaneously the affect or behavior of the imitator."[323] In such episodes, the person being imitated acts in a manner that is desirable or attractive to the imitator, yet such mirroring of the other other's behavior occurs "at a lower level of cognitive processing," and hence, the responses appear to be relatively involuntary and unconscious.[324] M.H. Small lists 958 cases records of school children engaging in imitative behaviors of classmates, other adults, or teachers. In 337 cases the behaviors were described as occurring unconsciously, including imitating the position of lips, the head, hands, frowns, squinting, drawls, and cross-eyes.[325]

Conclusions And Containment Strategies [326]

The characteristic features of epidemic hysteria in school settings are consistent across diverse geographical and historical periods. The classic school outbreak involves a socially cohesive group of female pupils near puberty and early adolescence who are exposed to a stressful stimulus. Transient symptoms spread and subside rapidly, and occasionally reoccur. School episodes manifest as variants of a unitary syndrome that is typified by collective anxiety states and hysterical conversion symptoms, with the medical and cultural *zeitgeist* accounting for the variance in descriptions and nomenclature. Symptoms within each presentation type are interpreted within the prevailing sociocultural milieu. Demonic possession predominates in non-Western traditional societies experiencing mass motor hysteria, while chemical and food contamination scares typically involve mass anxiety hysteria, reflecting contemporary Western preoccupations with environmental concerns. While major theories vary in explaining symptom presentation, each acknowledges the pivotal role of extreme psychosocial stress.

By its very nature, epidemic hysteria outbreaks have the potential to generate public controversy since most investigators view it as a diagnosis of exclusion that can never be confirmed with positive medical test results. A notable exception to this view is argued by Simon Wessely who does not consider it to be a diagnosis of exclusion since the syndrome is characterized by several distinct features, the collective appearance of which almost certainly indicates the presence of epidemic hysteria syndrome.[327] However, prior to the results of medical and environmental tests and detailed interviews with affected students, physicians can only note the transient, ambiguous, benign symptomatology, preponderance of female victims, and lack of a plausible pathogenic agent during the initial phase of the outbreak.

A diagnosis of epidemic hysteria syndrome can only be reasonably determined retrospectively, after eliminating the presence of organic or toxicological pathogens. During the early stages of any outbreak, investigators should be cautious in attributing a psychogenic origin to unidentified illness symptoms, prior to receiving laboratory findings. An outbreak of abdominal pain, nausea, and vomiting at a London elementary school in 1990, included such classic epidemic hysteria features as rapid onset and recovery, over-breathing, line of sight transmission, and a high female attack rate. Yet, subsequent investigation revealed cucumber pesticide contamination.[328] It may, therefore, be advisable to close the school until such negative results are returned. Closure should also assist in reducing the stress levels among the students and temporarily break up the group. This will allow time for investigators to determine, in detail, if most or all of the characteristic features of epidemic hysteria syndrome are present.

While mass anxiety hysteria reports dominate the 20th century scientific literature, and mass motor hysteria was more prevalent during the 19th century, it does not necessarily follow that mass anxiety hysteria was less common in the past century. It may be that during the 19th century, psychoanalytic-oriented observers took more notice of prolonged outbreaks affecting small numbers of students, while ignoring more short-lived, large-scale episodes by passing them off as the behavior of "immature" schoolgirls.

In managing episodes, school administrators must identify the underlying stressor(s) and take appropriate measures to reduce or eliminate their anxiety-generating effects. This is much easier said than done, as epidemic hysteria diagnoses often engender hostility from defensive parents who challenge claims that the outbreak was "psychological." For instance, physician Joel Nitzkin received a series of threatening telephone calls from belligerent parents,[329] while other investigators note considerable public resentment to the epidemic hysteria label,[330] including Cartter and colleagues who observed that "some parents insisted that we had accused their children of faking symptoms."[331]

In controlling short-lived mass anxiety hysteria, administrators should seek the co-operation of teachers, medical authorities, and high status community members to reassure students and parents that the agent believed to pose a threat was either imaginary or no longer exists. In non-Western countries, the services of native healers are often rendered and provide reassurance.

For more enduring mass motor hysteria, emphasis should be on identifying and resolving the precipitating conflict. Public confrontation, exhortation, and other coercive measures typically aggravate the situation. In controlling outbreaks or their recurrence, it would be useful to utilize counseling and open communication to counteract misinformation and rumor. In locations such as Malaysia and East and Central Africa, the presence of native healers typically exacerbates episodes, since motor symptoms usually take longer to subside than anxiety hysteria. Hence, while the native healer's assistance is viewed as confirming the presence of malevolent spirits, the persistence of cases reaffirms that the school grounds have not been completely exorcised. This supports Wessely's conclusion that in order to control mass motor hysteria measures must be implemented "to remove the advantages of the sick-role by the withdrawal of social validation."[332] This could take the form of advising teachers to handle any new cases by appearing confident while publicly labeling the incident as psychological in nature and removing the child from the sight and sound of any pupils, and sending them home if necessary, until their condition completely subsides. This is consistent with the most historically successful means of controlling epidemic hysteria in schools: disbanding and isolating the group affected, such as granting them leave from school until their symptoms subside. We should also be mindful that the number of documented reports involving mass anxiety hysteria is significant and likely represent but a tiny fraction of what has actually occurred.[333] The same can be said for episodes of mass motor hysteria.[334]

MASS HYSTERIA SYNONYMS

A confusing aspect to the study of mass hysteria, are the many synonyms that have been used to describe the rapid spread of conversion symptoms within a particular collective. In addition to mass hysteria, other common contemporary labels include mass psychogenic illness, mass sociogenic illness, and epidemic hysteria. Less common descriptions include: psychic epidemic,[335] moral epidemics,[336] *folie communiquée*,[337] epidemic insanity,[338] emotional contagion,[339] psychic disturbance,[340] acute psychic contagion,[341] morbid contagion,[342] psychic suggestion,[343] unconscious suggestion,[344] epidemic *folie a deux*,[345] social insanity,[346] automatic imitation,[347] hallucination by suggestion,[348] hysterical epidemic,[349] psychic mass infection,[350] collective hysteria,[351] mass psychosis,[352] contagious frenzies,[353] mass psychopathology,[354] mass hysterical attacks,[355] mass delusion,[356] anxiety hysterical reaction,[357] behavioral contagion,[358] socially shared collective madness,[359] shared group psychopathology,[360] mental epidemic,[361] mental contagion,[362] collective hypnosis,[363] shared psychopathology,[364] hysterical contagion,[365] hysterical psychosis,[366] behavior contagion,[367] collective mental illness,[368] mass psychology,[369] communicated hysteria,[370] collective psychosis,[371] group hysteria,[372] social contagion,[373] collective epidemics,[374] mass suggestibility,[375] crowd hysteria,[376] collective "hysteriform" manifestation,[377] psychic contagion,[378] group epidemic,[379] group mental disorder,[380] mass madness,[381] epidemic transient disturbance,[382] associative illness,[383] transient collective psychosis,[384] transient hysterical reactions,[385] psychogenic anxiety syndrome,[386] contagious psychogenic illness,[387] collective stress syndrome,[388] communicable hysteria,[389] epidemic psychological disturbance,[390] epidemic transient situational disturbance,[391] psychological epidemic,[392] psychotic epidemics,[393] collective mental disorders,[394] psychogenic epidemic,[395] group contagious hysteria,[396] group conversion reaction,[397] epidemic psychogenic illness,[398] mass systemic psychogenic illness,[399] mass anxiety hysteria,[400] mass motor hysteria,[401] collective stress reaction,[402] and mass anxiety epidemics.[403]

MASS SUICIDE CULTS

Groups that engage in mass suicide are often labeled by social scientists as *escapist* or *utopian* movements and are commonly identified as "cults." Such groups seek radical changes in society but do not challenge the existing system. Instead, members retreat or withdraw from what they view as "corrupt" or "unjust" systems of government, and thus typically limit contact with the outside world. The Jim Jones-led People's Temple movement fled to Africa and eventually committed suicide in 1978 in Jonestown, Guyana (see PEOPLE'S TEMPLE MASS SUICIDE). Suicide "cult" members often leave behind documents describing how they feel unable to remain in the existing "immoral" system, promising a new utopian life for true believers who keep the faith. HEAVEN'S GATE members expected that after committing suicide an alien spaceship with fantastic technology would whisk them off to a new realm of existence.

Psychologist Dennis Coon defines a cult as "a group in which the leader's personality is more important than the beliefs she or he preaches."[404] In summarizing findings from several cult studies, Coon takes the position that they often use powerful recruiting techniques, including isolating the initiate, making him or her feel guilty and fearful, and requiring displays of commitment that slowly increase over time. In terms of recruitment, Coon states that it would seem that most cult joiners are essentially normal but are often experiencing significant mental stress in their lives, either from indecision over which career path to pursue or feeling alienated from friends and relatives. Many are in despair following a busted romance. Others are having a tough time living on their own, away from the security of their families. The common link is that potential cult joiners are most vulnerable during times of personal crisis. As for the actual conversion process, Coon observes that it often starts with members expressing to potential recruits deep feelings of love and understanding. In addition to this bombardment of affection, soon the potential convert is isolated from outsiders and engaged in rituals such as chanting for long periods of time or activities that carry on throughout the night, depriving them of sleep. Such actions slowly drain a person's physical and mental strength. Soon it becomes hard to think with a critical eye. Coon says that during the early stages the recruit is asked to make modest commitments such as staying overnight. Soon the requests escalate, until the new member hands over their money and possessions. It is at this point that the victim is in trouble. "Once in the group, members are cut off from family and friends ... and the cult can control the flow and interpretation of information to them. Members are isolated from their former value systems and social structures. Conversion is complete when they come to think of themselves more as group members than as individuals. At this point obedience is nearly total."[405]

On November 18, 1978, about 900 followers of Jim Jones' PEOPLE'S TEMPLE were involved in a mass suicide in their remote jungle camp in Guyana. Most died willingly, some unwillingly, either by swallowing a lethal concoction of purple cyanide-laced Kool Aid or were shot. Above Jones' throne read the haunting words: "Those who do not remember the past are condemned to repeat it." Coon notes that cults like Jonestown use an array of tactics to wear down members to reach a state of dependency and commitment. The Jonestown members were isolated in and "intimidated by guards and lulled by sedatives. They were also cut off from friends and relatives and totally accustomed to obey rigid rules of conduct, which primed them for Jones' final 'loyalty test.'"[406]

In The Eye Of The Believer

Many suicide groups and unfamiliar or new religious movements have been labeled as "cults." Yet, "cult" can be a troublesome word. Members of most groups that are labeled "cults" do not commit mass suicide and obey the law. It is important to remember that there is a fine line between what many scientists label as an unacceptable fanatical "cult," and what is considered to be "devout" and acceptable. The difference is often based on the number of followers and their political influence. During the American CATHOLIC SCARE of 1830 to 1860, Catholics were labeled as cultists with bizarre practices. All kinds of rumors and misinformation were circulated, including claims that nuns were essentially sex slaves. Many people refused to hire Catholics, and rioting even broke out in some cities. How times change. Roman Catholicism is now a major American religion. The word "cult" carries with it negative images such as members who are mentally disturbed or the victims of "brainwashing." Jeremiah Gutman notes that when certain religious practices seem strange or unpopular, "A religion becomes a cult; proselytization becomes brainwashing; persuasion becomes propaganda; missionaries become subversive agents; retreats, monasteries, and convents become prisons; holy ritual becomes bizarre conduct; religious observance becomes aberrant behavior; devotion and meditation become psychopathic trances."[407]

It is also worth noting that while some acts or beliefs may appear strange or bizarre to outsiders, a cult's members are not necessarily sick. Take the 1978 group suicide at Jonestown, Guyana, for example. The mass media and some psychiatrists painted a picture of mentally disturbed members based solely on the acts *per se*. Yet, given the relative isolation with outside contact, autocratic social hierarchy, sense of persecution, and belief in the existence of a utopian life after death, the event can be viewed as exemplifying conformity to group norms like *hara-kiri* among Japanese pilots during World War II, or the Indian suttee throwing herself onto her husband's funeral pyre,[408] or contemporary SUICIDE BOMBERS in Sri Lanka and the Middle East.

In some mass suicides such as Jonestown, at least

a few group members who opted out at the last moment appear to have been murdered by other zealots. Then there is the issue of young adults and children who are not old enough to have formed a perspective on what mass suicide entails. They will never experience growing old and raising a family. Too young to know better, they have been conditioned by their parents or friends into participating in such events. To the outsider, there is a clear issue of immorality and psychological coercion with such group suicides, yet there is no compelling evidence to suggest that most, or even many, followers were psychologically disturbed. It may be that they are simply acting out the consequence of their worldview. Equally controversial are views such as those held by Jehovah's Witnesses who are convinced that if they receive a transfusion of someone else's blood, their souls will be contaminated. For this reason, based on Biblical interpretation, most Jehovah's Witnesses refuse blood transfusions even when to do so threatens their life. Yet, there are numerous examples of Jehovah's Witnesses refusing to do so for their young children who are not yet old enough to formulate opinions on their own. Does this constitute coercion? Is it an immoral act or an act of love?

A Brief Survey Of Mass Suicide Cults

In about 1868, a mass suicide was reported near Perm Province, Russia. A peasant came to believe that the end of the world was near and convinced his neighbors that the only solution was mass suicide. He led his family and a group of men, women, and children into the woods where they dug catacombs. After three days they all dressed in shrouds and renounced the Devil. The leader then ordered them not to eat or drink for 12 days and they would enter heaven. When some of the children, clearly in agony, began sucking grass and eating dirt, some members appealed for the children to be spared, but the leader refused. Two members then fled, which frightened those remaining and prompted the leader to announce that the time of death was at hand. He ordered the children massacred and continue their fast. The police then found them. Facing capture, members hacked the women to death with hatchets. Police managed only to save the leader and three others.[409]

About 28 years later, a mass suicide by live burial was recorded in Siberia, Russia. The incident involved at least 25 members of a Russian religious sect and occurred in a remote Siberian religious community. A charismatic leader had convinced his followers that the antichrist had come to Earth, the end of the world was imminent, and whoever took their life before the apocalypse would be rewarded in heaven.[410] (See also: BEZPOPOVZY SECT)

Thirty-three bodies belonging to a religious cult called "Benevolent Mother" were found in August 1987, by police in Tongin, South Korea. The corpses were found bound, gagged, and piled on a factory attic in a murder-suicide pact. Apparently "one person wearing rubber gloves strangled or poisoned the others then killed himself or herself." The victims had badly bruised necks and showed no signs of resistance and were apparently high on drugs.[411]

Heaven's Gate: Abnormality Or Religious Diversity?

At 3:30 p.m. on March 26, 1994, the San Diego County Sheriff's Office received an eerie emergency telephone call, which claimed that there had been a mass suicide. Upon investigating, authorities found the bodies of 39 members of the "Heaven's Gate" cult at the group's posh mansion at 18241 Colina Notre in Rancho Santa Fe, a wealthy suburb of San Diego, California. Cult members believed that their spirits would be taken aboard a spaceship that was hiding behind the Hale-Bopp comet. They ranged in age from 26-to-72, were celibate, and some members had even castrated themselves.[412] In the final hours they donned a uniform of long black pants and shirts, and black Nike sneakers emblazoned with the shoemakers' trademark comet-like "swoosh" insignia. A note left behind read: "Take the little package of pudding or applesauce and eat a couple of tablespoons. Pour the medicine in and stir it up. Eat it fairly quickly and then drink the vodka beverage. Then lay back and rest quietly."[413] Ironically, one victim was 59-year-old Thomas Nichols, brother of Nichelle Nichols, who played Lieutenant Uhara on the hit television action-adventure outer space program *Star Trek*.[414]

Social psychologist Frederick Pope views the incident as a form of *folie a deux* or psychosis of association. "The Heaven's Gate cult is a prime example of 'induced psychosis' in which someone who is psychologically stronger gets weaker members to change their belief system."[415] Science writer Martin Gardner viewed those who committed suicide as having been under some type of "brainwashing," which suggests that no one in their "right mind" could engage in such acts and be normal. "To me the saddest aspect of this insane event was the firm belief, expressed on the incredible videotapes, that cult members were killing themselves of their own free will. Nothing could have been more false."[416] While acknowledging that the group did not engage in physical coercion, he assumes that some form of psychological coercion was used. "Although Do [Marshall Applewhite] always told his robots they were free to go at any time – and hundreds had done just that – so powerful was his control over the minds of those who stayed that they believed anything he said, obeyed every order."[417]

Religious scholar Ronald Steel took a culturally and historically relativistic view of the group and their suicide. Steel observed that the groups' central views on such issues as pacificism, celibacy, and community are found in mainstream Christianity, noting that every religion seems strange or weird to those who reject its tenets. Steel argued that religions are intended to "offer solace, explain mysteries, provide standards of behavior and offer the promise of escape to a better world. The Heaven's Gate group would appear to be particularly benign, and even praiseworthy, in that its members were gentle, industrious, supportive and kind to one another. They did not try to coerce others into joining them. All they asked was to be left alone."[418] Steel said that the Shaker sect was similar to Heaven's Gate in many respects, including avoiding confrontation with political leaders by living in isolated enclaves, separated from the corruption of mainstream society. Other parallels include the professing celibacy, "communal ownership, pacificism...equality of the sexes and freedom to leave the collective."[419]

Solar Temple

In October 1994, the charred bodies of 53 members of the Swiss-based Order of the Solar Temple "cult" were found in clusters, as the buildings they were in were set ablaze. The sites were located in Switzerland and Canada. They may have committed suicide in a ritual intended to save the world from ecological disaster. Many had apparently taken drugs, then placed plastic bags over their heads and tightened them. They believed that death by ritual suicide brings rebirth.[420] On March 22, 1997, a mass suicide reportedly occurred near Casimir, Quebec Province, Canada. Five Order of the Solar Temple cult members died in a fiery event after rigging propane tanks and gasoline to a house and detonating them.[421]

Just after 10 o'clock on Friday morning, March 17, 2000, some 517 members of an apocalyptic cult (Movement for the Restoration of the Ten Commandments of God) – men, women, and children – may have committed mass suicide in Kanungu, Uganda, after getting rid of their possessions and crowding into a church that was set on fire. In the following days, the bodies of 394 more victims were found at three other sites in this West African country.[422]

American religious scholar J. Gordon Melton observed that based on examining reports of the event, two radically different interpretations were possible. One view suggests that the event was a mass murder by group leaders who may have lured members into the building with the expectation of some type of religious miracle. Melton stated: "This view is consistent with the lack of rumors that an act of suicide was planned, the lack of concern about the group by family members and government observers, the fact that no members appear to have left their children at home, or the fact that some group members did not themselves refuse to attend the final service."[423] On the other hand, there is information that could be interpreted as evidence of a voluntary mass suicide. "This view is consistent with the actions of the group during the last week of destroying worldly possessions and saying goodbye to friends and relatives, indulging themselves with meat and drink, and the obvious preparation of the church building."[424]

On about April 4, 2000, police in Peru took into custody 86 members of the Quillabamba Pentecostal Religious Sect after they tried committing mass suicide by starving to death. At the time, members were undergoing a 40-day fast in the remote Mesa Pelada jungle region of the Andes Mountains. Police located the group with the aid of concerned relatives. While some followers fought with authorities and tried resisting arrest, most were unable to muster sufficient energy to struggle, as they were too weak from fasting. One police officer was quoted as saying, "the fanatics were letting themselves die while praying and chanting."[425]

COMMENTS: The question as to whether mass suicide should be considered legal or is moral engenders strong emotions on both sides of the debate. Since the 1990s, considerable attention has been focused on the issue of physician-assisted suicide for terminally ill persons. There is growing acceptance of such acts. But what if a group of physically healthy people voluntarily considers it their religious duty to end their lives? Should this be allowed to happen? Are they brainwashed? Mentally disturbed? Religiously devout? Could anyone in their "right mind" commit such acts? Perhaps if a group desires to commit mass suicide, they should be allowed to if all of the members are above a certain age and are able to fully comprehend the permanent and radical nature of their actions. Yet, if younger group members have had little or no exposure to outside views, they would almost certainly go along with their peers. Would it be morally acceptable to allow such acts? The issue of allowing mass suicide creates thorny issues on both sides of the debate, issues that are not easily resolved.

There are numerous examples of voluntary, culturally condoned ritualistic suicides in such places as Europe, Russia, and ancient Greece.[426] Suicide clusters involving self-incineration do not *necessarily* indicate mental disturbance when viewed from the symbolic universe of the "victims." Such events were occasionally recorded among Buddhists during the 1960s and 1970s in protesting the Vietnam War.

> ...self-sacrifice by suicide brings secondary gains to the victim in the personal attainment of a "divine" state (e.g., Nirvana for the Buddhists), posthumous glorification which often immortalizes a martyr, or winning honor or glory for the individual's family or group. Religious or political figures, as exemplified by the Buddhists, may identify at times so completely with a cause that they perceive their lives solely as instruments for attaining the goals of the group, allowing total submission to control. Thus, a command or even a suggestion to commit a sacrificial suicide would provide sufficient motivation for a person with such extreme zeal or devotion.
>
> The Buddhist self-incinerations may thus be characterized as an epidemic which resulted from the confluence of several conditions: (1) a conducive atmosphere of open conflict and emotional tension; (2) a dramatic and powerful expression of a widely shared emotion–a passionate expression laden with complex symbolic meaning which served to intensify and focus the ubiquitous emotional tension; and (3) a population of individuals whose religious devotion, personal commitment, and unquestioning obedience perhaps made them particularly susceptible to suggestion from their leaders who may have encouraged the sacrifices for political purposes.[427]

MASSACHUSETTS CHORAL MAYHEM

Templeton, Massachusetts: May 20, 1981

In East Templeton, Massachusetts, 102 elementary students boarded buses to their central school building to join 300 other students from area schools in order to rehearse for a major evening concert. About 1,000 people, mostly parents, were expected for the event. Within 30 minutes of rehearsing, several students collapsed, clutching their throats and stomachs. Symptoms included itchy eyes, lightheadedness, fainting, hyperventilating, and weakness. Of the nine students who had fainted, six were examined at a hospital and were back in time for the performance.

That evening, 75 minutes into the concert, 29 students were stricken with similar symptoms, and 15 were rushed to the hospital. Physicians could find nothing unusual with their patients, except for a few cases of pink eye and nervousness. After they were given a battery of tests, doctors made a startling announcement: the 13 students who gave urine samples all tested positive for the presence of the chemical *n*-butylbenzene sulfonamide, which is a common component in plastics and insecticides. Stories that the students were somehow poisoned spread through the community. But soon more samples were taken, this time using glass rather than plastic containers, and no trace of the chemical was found. It was later determined that the chemical *n*-butylbenzene sulfonamide had come from the containers themselves.

The scare soon diminished, and investigators concluded that the incident was an episode of mass hysteria. Among their curious observations: not one adult in the audience fell ill, and despite students from four elementary schools taking part in the concert, all but one who fell sick was from East Templeton Elementary. Their conclusion: excitement and nerves had led to the incident.[428]

MASTURBATION DELUSION

Europe and America: 18-19th centuries

The masturbation delusion of the 19th century is exceptional in that it involved extraordinary behavior not on the part of panicking mobs or obsessed fanatics but of physicians and scientists of the highest repute, moral and religious leaders of unimpeachable standing. Weighted with their authority, the delusion infected countless lesser minds that accepted and repeated their dictates.

The delusion consisted of the belief that masturbation is uniquely harmful to those who practice it, leading inexorably to feebleness and debility, through a wide assortment of ailments, then to madness, and ultimately death. The delusion was subscribed to, and often vehemently promoted by, men and women in the highest scientific positions throughout Western Europe and North America, as well as churchmen and others with the moral clout to ensure that they would be listened to with respect. Yet in support of these affirmations there was not a scrap of scientific evidence. Instead, scientific and medical findings were distorted and manipulated to give a wholly erroneous impression. As a result, millions of children were subjected to a reign of terror in which horrific mental suffering was often accompanied by physical torture.

CONTEXT: Masturbation is practiced throughout the world, in almost every known culture. "It is found among the people of nearly every race of which we have an intimate knowledge, however natural the conditions under which men and woman may live," sexologist Havelock Ellis declared more than a century ago, and he provided examples showing that among Africans "no secret is made of it...it is treated as one of the most ordinary facts of life. Throughout the East masturbation is very prevalent, especially among young girls..." and so on.[429] Culturally, the area in which the delusion was promulgated was almost wholly Judeo-Christian, and the teachings of the Jewish and Christian religions formed its basis. In particular, they taught that any sexual activity outside marriage is sinful, particularly when – as with masturbation – it is non-procreative. The pleasure that accompanies sexual activity, being simply a biological device to provide an incentive, was not to be sought for its own sake. Consequently, masturbation always ranked high on the list of forbidden acts.

In practice, however, this was little more than a technicality. During the centuries previous to the 18th, the taboo on masturbation, insofar as any taboo existed, was wholly a theological one, stemming from what the Church believed were God's wishes on the matter. Doctors saw no reason to stigmatize masturbation on medical grounds; at most they would discourage excess, as with any other form of sexual activity.[430] Indeed, the eminent 16th century anatomist Falloppio encouraged parents to stimulate their son's penis on the grounds that repeated erections would

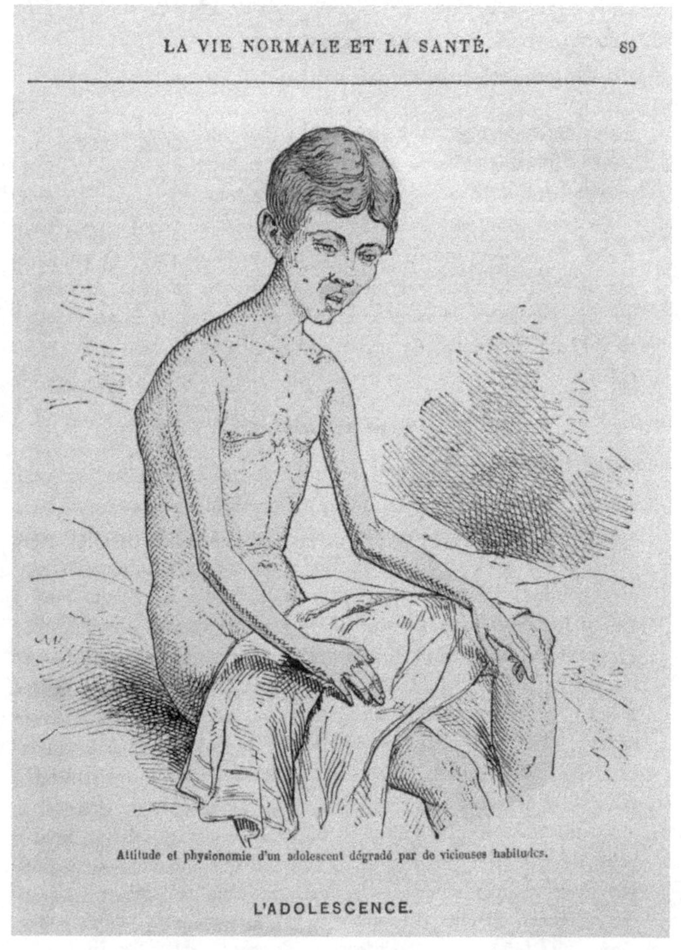

A "pathetic" masturbator displays the inevitable symptoms.

make it larger and thus capable of giving greater pleasure to a future wife.[431]

At the beginning of the 18th century, however, the taboo acquired a supposedly scientific dimension, with the publication of writings purporting to demonstrate the deleterious consequences of masturbation. The ball was set rolling by the 1710 publication, by an anonymous English author (plausibly identified by Laqueur as hack writer John Marten[432]), of *Onania or the Heinous Sin of Self-Pollution*. Though, as its title suggests, it was the moral aspects of the matter which were its focus, his book echoed the spirit of the Age of Enlightenment in finding a "scientific" dimension for the moral teaching: masturbation was identified and soundly denounced as a serious medical hazard.

Though Marten had no professional standing, his book was immensely popular and led to more serious discussion. However, it is doubtful whether the delusion would have taken firm root without the authority of a recognized professional. One of those who had been profoundly influenced by the English book – which was widely translated – was a Swiss physician of high repute, Samuel-August Tissot, who in 1758 published (at first in Latin, later in French) *LíOnanisme ou Dissertation Physique sur les Maladies Produites par la Masturbation*. (Incidentally, though both these authors employ the term "onanism" as though it were synonymous with masturbation, it is nothing of the sort. The crime of Onan, a biblical figure, was to spill his seed upon the ground rather than impregnate his sister-in-law. Not only is masturbation not condemned in the Bible, it is not so much as mentioned.)

Following these two very influential books, the dangers of masturbation were supposed to be built upon an ostensibly solid medical foundation. Masturbation was perceived as responsible for a wide range of ailments, ranging from digestive disorders to deteriorating eyesight and leading to insanity. For Tissot, the masturbator was a criminal, whose condition "more justly entitles him to the contempt than the pity of his fellow creatures."[433] Moreover – and this was to be a key factor in the creation of the delusion – Tissot purported to show that masturbation was more harmful to the individual than "normal" forms of sexual activity. His book sold in vast quantities and was widely translated; his great reputation ensured that his statements carried authority. Though his case histories were dubious and his reasoning faulty, he appeared to be providing abundant evidence that masturbation led to degeneration of the individual, culminating in madness and death.

From then on, the chorus of condemnation of masturbation increased in volume throughout the rest of the 18th century and reached a crescendo in the 19th. Attitudes were similar throughout Europe and North America. In 1780, the American physician Johann Frank insisted that onanism had become so widespread in American schools that the authorities could not take too much care to stamp out this plague.[434] The medical-scientific aspects of the subject were accepted without question, the only differences of opinion being as to how many maladies should be attributed to the practice.

By the early 19th century, virtually all authorities accepted the belief as fact. Benjamin Rush, the most respected physician in America, asserted in 1812 that masturbation led to a whole range of ailments, including pulmonary consumption, dimness of sight, vertigo, epilepsy, loss of memory, and ultimately death.[435] In France, the 1819 *Dictionnaire des sciences medicales* confidently claimed that "the continual excitement of the genital organs is liable to give rise to almost all the acute or chronic illnesses which can disturb the harmony of our functions."[436] Diagnosis became a self-fulfilling process. Since masturbation led to so many ailments, clearly anyone suffering from any of these ailments was probably guilty of masturbation, and since almost every patient admitted to masturbating at one time or another, the sequence of cause and effect was self-evident. The list of believers included many of the greatest names in medicine. In France, the eminent Jean-Etienne-Dominique Esquirol took it for granted that no respectable medical authority could doubt the harmfulness of the practice: "Masturbation is recognized in all countries as a common cause of insanity…by lowering the powers of resistance it reduces the patient to a state of stupidity, to phtisis, marasmus, and death."[437] The idea took root in England in the 1820s and in Germany in the 1830s.

Doctors everywhere echoed the view of French physician Reveille-Parise who in 1828 declared: "In my opinion, neither plague, nor war, nor smallpox, nor a crowd of similar evils, have resulted more disastrously for humanity than the habit of masturbation: it is the destroying element of civilized society."[438]

However, as Lesley Hall has shown,[439] the matter was not quite so simple. She demonstrates that the delusion presented significant changes of emphasis. At first, following *Onania* and Tissot, the emphasis was on the physical consequences of masturbation. This emphasis gradually shifted to what it did to the mind, driving the patient insane. As the 19th century progressed, the masturbatory hypothesis became more specifically applied to madness. Some doctors, among them the distinguished Henry Maudsley, identified specific types of insanity that could be linked to masturbation. To his credit, Maudsley subsequently withdrew his 1868 assertions, but for a while "masturbatory insanity" was an essential element of diagnosis, explaining a wide range of psychiatric conditions.

Male voices outweighed female voices here as elsewhere, but masturbation was no less vilified by women. The eminent American doctor Elizabeth Blackwell saw masturbation as the precursor of "all other forms of unnatural vice," and feminist writer Mary Wollstonecraft considered "private vices" (she clearly intended masturbation) to be "a public pest."[440] Towards the end of the 19th century masturbation came to be associated with "neurasthenia" rather than madness, and for those who continued to condemn it in the 20th century, it was regarded rather as a psychological defect. However, these were trends of emphasis rather than clear-cut distinctions; underlying them there persisted the almost unquestioned conviction that self-abuse (as it was now widely labeled) was one of humankind's most terrible scourges and must be eradicated by whatever means offered themselves.

Sanctioned by the authority of the medical authorities, popular authors felt it their duty to echo their judgment in terms accessible to the general public. Thus the American self-appointed "Professor" Fowler let loose in 1875 with a diatribe whose exaggerated terms bear witness to the well-nigh unbelievable extremes to which the masturbation delusion carried those who subscribed to it: "Neither Christendom nor heathendom suffers any evil at all to compare with this...Pile all other evils together – drunkenness upon all cheateries, swindlings, robberies and murders, and tobacco upon both, and all sickness, diseases and pestilence upon all, and war as the cap-sheaf of them all – and all combined cause not a tithe as much human deterioration and misery as does this secret sin."[441]

To stigmatize a schoolboy or girl enjoying a solitary orgasm as worse than the ravages of the Huns might seem extreme, but such expressions of horror were commonplace. The prolific Dr. Rengade, author of many excellent books of popular information, can be taken as representative of popular European authors. This is his take on masturbation – "the most shameful of all vices," in his 1881 book *La Vie Normale*:

> A frivolous conversation, the reading of a book, the sight of an attractive person, sometimes a single word, suffices to excite these burning souls, to inspire erotic dreams whose inevitable consequence can only be a spontaneous pollution or one brought on by masturbation. Defying all surveillance, the adolescents seek solitude: they hide, without waiting for nightfall which is most favourable to these vile manoeuvres, and may indeed succeed, simply by friction of the thighs, to satisfy their shameful passion even beneath the eyes of parents or teachers. Miserable beings, of whatever sex, who, deficient in willpower, abandon themselves to these superficial joys, who cannot live without these sorry pleasures! Soon it becomes a veritable mania which drives them to devote themselves to it. The brain exhausts itself in unhealthy overexcitement which the organs, overtaxed, refuse to obey. Haggard, panting, the wretched creature struggles to provoke the voluptuous spasms which lead only to fatigue. Soon, the eyes grow ringed and lifeless in their sockets, the lips hang flabby, the nostrils become pinched, the features grow to resemble a monkey's rather than a human's, the head droops in shame, the shoulders are bowed, the limbs become emaciated: and these first signs are swiftly followed by more serious symptoms–phthisis, epilepsy, hysteria, imbecility, madness and consumption.[442]

The remedies proposed by the good doctor were incessant surveillance, early rising, going to bed late when sleep will come swiftly, daily baths and cold showers, severe diet, gymnastic exercises, manual tasks, and exhausting country walks, all backed by remonstrances and reproaches from the parents.

As a physician, Rengade was concerned only with the physical consequences of the practice, but in Britain and America it was the interweaving of science with morals that gave the delusion a double force. The best-selling Sylvanus Stall can be taken as representative in this regard, His *What A Young Boy Ought To Know* sold in the hundreds of thousands and was widely translated: "If you were ever to fall a victim to this vice...you would begin to lose faith in all that is good, and as you persisted in your sin, you would grow less and less like Jesus, and more and more like Satan."[443]

But of course he also points out, at some length, the physical consequences. The masturbator, he wrote,

> ...gradually drops back towards the foot of his class...he no longer has his accustomed pleasure in the vigorous romp, the hearty laugh, the good fellowship which characterizes a boy with a vigorous mind and a strong body...the health gradually declines. The eyes lose their luster. The skin becomes sallow. The muscles become flabby. Every little effort is followed by weariness. Work becomes distasteful and irksome. He complains of pain in the back, of headache and dizziness. The hands become cold and clammy. The digestion becomes poor, the appetite fitful. He sits in a stooping position, becomes hollow-chested, and the entire body becomes wasted, and many signs give promise of early decline and death.[444]

How the public responded to this teaching and preaching can only be surmised from scraps of information that slip past the taboo that ensured the subject was rarely mentioned except in the form of warnings. Many masturbators carried on covertly, no doubt. The historian of the MORZINE OUTBREAK mentions, quite casually, that the country girls would meet for group masturbation. At more sophisticated social levels, diaries and autobiographical narratives bear witness to the torment of moral guilt and physical terror induced by the likes of Rengade and Stall.

Along with the identification of masturbation as the root cause of so many ailments came discussion as to how it could be eradicated. Moral condemnation could go only so far with an impetuous youth, so more practical means had to be found. In simple cases, prevention was tried before cure. Little girls should be discouraged from riding hobbyhorses, boys from sliding down stair banisters. The bicycle and the treadle sewing machine were recognized as dangerous. Vigorous activity just before bedtime, leaving the child too fatigued to indulge his/her vice, was advised. Cold baths were prescribed. François Raspail, in his manual of health, recommended that the child's genitals should be wrapped in a heavy layer of camphor powder, which should also be sprinkled on the bed sheets or between the mattress and the sheets before putting the child to bed. The child could even wear a bathing suit with a bag of camphor strategically placed.[445] The hands could be tied to the bedpost. Ingenious devices were designed, such as enclosing a spiked cage to enclose the penis, which became uncomfortable if erection occurred. "Chastity belts" of various types were available for boys and girls.

One rather surprising solution was proposed early in the 18th century. In *A Modest Defence of Publick Stews*, Bernard de Mandeville, a Dutch physician practicing in England, proposed the establishment of authorized brothels, providing a healthier outlet for young men than masturbation. Though moral objections prevented the idea from being accepted, other later opponents of masturbation would discreetly advocate this solution, though it failed to address the equally alarming propensity of females to the vice.[446]

Surgery was also advocated. About 1858, Dr. Isaac Baker Brown, a prominent London surgeon, proposed clitoridectomy – the surgical removal of the clitoris – for female masturbators who would then have less incentive to indulge in a practice that otherwise would lead them to hysteria, epilepsy, and convulsive attacks. This operation was still being advocated in the United States as late as 1894.[447] Back in 1786 S. G. Vogel had suggested that infibulation – preventing full erection by fastening the foreskin to the penis with silver wire – might be an effective preventive; comparable methods might be employed on girls. In 1864 the great French physician Broca told how he had performed an operation on a five-year old girl who had been masturbating repeatedly, despite surveillance and even the wearing of a chastity belt. By joining the labia, leaving only a small hole to pee through but covering the clitoris, he reduced the girl's access to her sensitive parts. He was, however, criticized – not for performing the operation, however, but rather as to whether this was the most effective method. A colleague wondered why he had not tried cauterization, which he himself had used effectively on a boy, making his genital area so painful as to effectively discourage masturbation.[448]

In 1891, London surgeon James Hutchinson proposed that male circumcision would effectively reduce the "shameful habit," while his colleague T. Spratling went further, recommending "the complete section of the dorsal nerves of the penis," while for females he advocated "nothing short of ovariotomy." Alas, even surgery was not certain of success. A Dr. Richet in 1864 told how he had performed a total amputation of the clitoris of a 27-year-old girl, but within a year she had learned to obtain relief by masturbating her vagina. A Dr. Guèrin concurred, describing his own attempt to cure a patient: "I totally destroyed the clitoris without managing to extinguish the desire to masturbate."[449] But in 1894 Dr. Eyer, of St John's Hospital in Ohio, reported greater success when his patient, a little girl whose clitoris he had hacked away, reported, "You know there is nothing there now, so I could do nothing."[450]

These surgeons describe their procedures in clinical terms, much as they would the removal of an appendix or any other operation. They make no reference to the psychological trauma involved, not only subjecting the young patients to terrifying surgery but involving them in a horrific experience of induced guilt. Dr. Yellowlees, in England, told in 1876 how he had been struck by "the conscious-stricken way in which they submitted to the operation on their penises."[451] The child was made to feel an outcast, a sinner, performing an unnatural act, which was vile in the eyes of God and of all decent men and women. The result was that children were terrorized, and in extreme cases this could lead to suicide. In uncounted instances, it led to feelings of guilt and self-recrimination that recur not only in case histories but also the literature of the period, ranging from Dean Farrar's story of school life, *Eric*, or little by little to Leo Tolstoy's *The Kreutzer Sonata*. Yet, while some doctors deplored the psychological effects of inculcating guilt and remorse, others welcomed it as a means whereby the patient would be driven to voluntarily abandon the practice. In 1844 a French doctor named Debreyne declared that masturbators "must be threatened with dishonour, with ignominy, with all the horrors of the most painful, the most degrading and the most shameful maladies and finally with an early death to be followed by eternal punishment."[452] A colleague, Dr. Devay, taught his young patients that their penis would become gangrenous as a result. Privately he admitted that there was no truth in this whatever, but insisted that the lie was justified if it served his purpose.

These examples illustrate the extraordinary circular arguments of the delusion. Doctors justified the threatening consequences they knew to be false, in order to discourage practices which they believed to be harmful in other ways. They demonstrate that, while it was unquestionably the ostensibly scientific aspect of the delusion that enabled it to take such universal hold, it would hardly have done so without a strong moral basis, explicit or concealed. At this time, when almost everyone in advanced societies still, if only nominally, subscribed to Judeo-Christian beliefs, medical authorities did not hesitate to interweave science and religion. Thus Mary R. Melendy, an American doctor and author of popular guides to sexual behavior, wrote to mothers: "Go teach your boy...about these organs that make him specially a boy. Teach him that they are not impure, but...made by God for a definite purpose. Impress upon him that if these organs are...put to any use besides that for which God made them – and He did not intend they should be used at all until man is fully grown – they will bring disease and ruin upon those who abuse and disobey those laws which God has made to govern them."[453] Needless to say, she does not indicate where God promulgated any such laws, which would – if they existed – hardly be compatible with medical reality.

Indeed, the strength of the moral aspect of the delusion is illustrated by the comment of one of the first medical men to declare that masturbation is no more harmful than sexual intercourse, Sir James Paget. Even while insisting that the practice is not the monster it had been made out to be, he concluded by saying, almost reluctantly, "I wish that I could say something worse of so nasty a practice: an uncleanliness, a filthiness forbidden by God, an unmanliness despised by man."[454]

Because masturbation is by definition generally a solitary act, and because given the climate of opinion most people kept quiet about their activities, there are no figures to show how prevalent the practice was or how many children were affected. When in 1949 Alfred Kinsey, professor of zoology, and his colleagues at Indiana University, presented their report on the sexual habits of the American male (followed in 1953 by a sequel on the female), they disclosed that 93% of American males, and 62% of females, indulged in masturbation, despite the fact that the taboo was still very widely imposed.[455] Since there is no reason to think that human nature had changed dramatically in the previous 100 years, we can suppose that even at the height of the delusion, and in the face of such a barrage of denunciation, almost every child felt the urge to masturbate, and that a very high percentage yielded to that urge. That the practice was widespread was generally admitted, but authorities with rare exceptions did not ask the obvious question: why, in that case, were the numbers of mad people relatively few?

Although throughout the duration of the delusion a few skeptical voices had been raised, this was only in medical circles and not in public. It was not until the very close of the 19th century that ideas began to change, and even then it was only slowly and reluctantly. A prominent influence was the English sociologist Havelock Ellis, whose writings were initially banned, but whose authority went a considerable way towards shaking the entrenched belief. Although he was able to report in 1900 that "recent authorities are almost unanimous in rejecting masturbation as a cause of insanity,"[456] the delusion was slow to die. Freud and his followers, even if they no longer held extreme views, did not question that masturbation was harmful. (The importance Freud attributed to the subject is indicated by the fact that there are more than 100 references to masturbation in his collected works, as well as some 50 to auto-eroticism.) Even though medical authorities generally came to concede that masturbation had few if any harmful effects, Kinsey, writing about male masturbation in 1949, noted that the consequences of the delusion were still much in evidence half a century later:

> It must be realized that masturbation is taboo and even strongly condemned among certain groups; and while college men more often admit their experience, there are males in some other groups who would admit almost any other kind of sexual activity before they would give a record of masturbatory experiences... Millions of boys have lived in continual mental conflict over this problem. For that matter, many a boy still does. Many boys pass through a periodic succession of attempts to stop the habit, inevitable failures in those attempts, consequent periods of remorse, the making of new resolutions and a new start on the whole cycle. It is difficult to imagine anything better calculated to do permanent damage to the personality of an individual.[457]

The situation was similar for the female. Four years later, Kinsey reported:

> In view of the more than two thousand years of religious condemnation of masturbation, fortified by the ostensibly scientific opinions of physicians and other professionally trained groups, it is not surprising that many individuals, both female and male, are considerably disturbed when they masturbate. Among the females in the sample who had ever masturbated, approximately half had experienced some psychologic disturbance over their experience... This means that some millions of the females in the United States, and a larger number of the males, have had their self-assurance, their social efficiency, and sometimes their sexual adjustments in marriage needlessly damaged–not by their masturbations, but by the conflict between their practice and the moral codes.[458]

COMMENT: "Masturbational insanity was real enough," declared Dr. Alex Comfort, but it was not the ignorant masses who were insane, rather "it was affecting the medical profession," whom he stigmatized as "anxiety makers."[459] Thomas Szasz commented: "We may wonder how learned men and the public alike could believe such nonsense, flagrantly contradicted by observation easily made among both men and animals," and attributed it to the fact that man "is more interested in preserving popular explanations, which tend to consolidate the group, than in making accurate observations which tend to divide it."[460]

Thomas Walter Laqueur's 2003 thesis analyzed the concept of masturbation as a cultural phenomenon rooted in time: the delusion was, paradoxically, a child of the Age of Enlightenment, when the status of the individual in relation to society was in the course of transformation. Masturbation, so essentially an individual practice, was felt to be anti-social, so when Marten and Tissot offered grounds, however dubious, for demonizing the practice, their views were enthusiastically embraced.[461]

Thus the masturbation delusion served a stabilizing purpose. It allowed people to continue to accept the Judeo-Christian moral code and perpetuate it into a scientific age. Fundamental to the delusion was the puritanical credo that any form of self-indulgence is inherently blameworthy, and non-procreative sexual activity especially so. Consequently, when ostensible scientific support for demonizing masturbation was offered, it was welcomed by moralists and scientists alike. They accepted the false reasoning that led to the belief in masturbatory insanity because it justified their subconscious conviction that masturbation was wrong. The moral judgment not only preceded, but continued to underlie any supposed scientific evaluation.

MAYNARD EXPERIMENT

Maynard, Iowa: April 1971

The Maynard Experiment illustrates the herd mentality and how people will reinterpret events to conform to their view of reality.[462] On April 14, Michael Potratz, a student at Maynard's West Central High School, asked student Russell Bantz if he had seen a UFO flying near the Mrs. James Bantz farm the previous night. Bantz replied that he hadn't but suggested going to the site on the edge of town and looking for evidence that a UFO might have been there. Once there the boys came upon what seemed to be a landing site – a scorched circle 10 feet (3 meters) in diameter, and four smaller circles. News of the "UFO landing" quickly spread around town as the boys called the local radio station, K-O-E-L, and the story was broadcast as a breaking news story. Soon nearly 500 people visited the site. Within 24-hours of the initial "discovery," numerous Iowa newspapers had published the story of the mysterious Maynard circles, and several people in eastern Iowa gave reporters detailed accounts of having seen a strange aerial object between 10 and 11 p.m. on the night of April 13. Among them was a man in Tripoli, Iowa who said that he had not only seen the UFO but was certain from watching its maneuvers "that it was going to land."[463]

In reality, the "landing" had been staged by students in John Forkenbrock's sociology class in response to their teacher's suggestion to conduct an experiment in mass media psychology and the influence of the media. Among the conclusions of the students partaking in the study: "The media are not always reliable and can be used. The media were responsible for exaggerating the UFO incident before all the facts had been taken into consideration. The media can be misled and can mislead."[464]

MELBOURNE AIRPORT MYSTERY ILLNESS

Victoria, Australia: February 21, 2005

On Monday morning February 21, the Australian media broadcast news of a mysterious "gas leak" blamed for breathing problems, dizziness, nausea, headaches, and vomiting among 57 people in the vicinity of the Virgin Blue terminal at Melbourne Airport. An investigation by Victorian emergency services personnel yielded no leak, and air quality tests were unremarkable. The incident disrupted a third of domestic passenger flights for two days and cost Virgin an estimated three million dollars,[465] not to mention the financial burden of responding emergency services and government agencies.

Victorian Premier Steve Bracks ordered Emergency Services Commissioner Bruce Esplin to "investigate and analyse any matters pertinent to a comprehensive understanding of the incident." The report was issued on 24 March concluding that the illness cluster was a mystery and "a cause for the incident may never be known."[466] Based on a review of the Esplin report, it is evident that the most obvious diagnosis was excluded: mass psychogenic illness (MPI). Inexplicably, this possibility was not even considered.

According to the Esplin report, at 7:12 a.m., the Airport Coordination Centre (ACC) was notified that a female W. H. Smith newsagent worker had collapsed at the base of the escalators in the southern domestic terminal, mezzanine level. The Aviation Rescue and Firefighting Service (ARFF) responded, and she was transported to hospital. The drama occurred in full view of those in her workplace. The report failed to cite a cause for her condition, but witnesses told a journalist that she "was under stress and hadn't eaten for hours."[467] The Esplin report concluded that the incident "was considered unrelated then and later to the incident that developed." No rationale for this conclusion was given.

At 8:48 a.m., the ACC learned that a second female employee at the same newsagent collapsed inside the store. ARFF responders found her conscious and breathing. At 9:02 a.m., a female American Express counter employee, who was just 15 meters from the second incident, collapsed and vomited. She was the only victim to vomit that day and the only one of three people working the counter to fall ill – points missing in the report.[468] At 9:05 a.m., the immediate vicinity of the incidents was cordoned off and air sampling undertaken. Tests revealed that the air was normal.

The next person to feel ill was a nearby Group 4 security guard who approached ambulance personnel treating the second woman. He then phoned his union, which alerted and advised that Group 4 staff should be checked out by the Melbourne Ambulance Service (MAS). Shortly thereafter, two security guards from Virgin's departure screening point, just 600 meters from the earlier collapses, reported ill. The next two Group 4 staff counted as ill were union members reporting to the MAS, as per union instructions. This was not made clear in the report.

Amid the hoopla, at 9:55 a.m., two Virgin Blue staff, whose counter overlooked the drama, arrived at the triage, saying that they too felt ill. The ARFF Commander immediately ordered the entire southern terminal evacuated and closed. Specialized air testing commenced for breathability, flammability, and foreign agents. The readings were unremarkable and the sector's air conditioning unit was found to be working properly in "full fresh" mode.

Another curious omission: there was no mention in the report of a scare among Group 4 staff and customs workers in the airport's international section. Upon noticing mysterious fumes and feeling sick, they made three separate emergency calls to the incident controller. Firefighters soon pinpointed the causes: a coat of fresh paint in one incident, new rubber bollards in a second, and dust in a third.

In its subsequent investigation, the Esplin report ruled out exposure to food and water, and said that the symptoms "were relatively nonspecific and did not correlate closely with any particular illness." Further tests of the air conditioning system determined that it was functioning properly during the incident. By 6 p.m., medical personnel had evaluated 57 people and taken 47 to the hospital. All were released the same day except one, a patient with an existing medical condition (asthma). In fact, by 2:10 p.m., some patients were already arriving back from hospital.

This episode shares many classic features of mass hysteria. The outbreak began with a dramatic singular incident (an index case) and was primarily spread by line-of-sight and sound, and later by telecommunications. Symptoms were transient and benign, with a rapid onset and recovery, and consistent with stress. There was an absence of clinical or laboratory evidence of organic etiology, and no identifiable causative agent was found despite air quality tests and an epidemiological study that ruled out common exposure to water or food. Media reports and witnesses suggest a preponderance of female victims, though the Esplin report does not provide a gender breakdown. The report neglects to note the selective nature of the malady – that of the 57 "victims," emergency personnel on the scene report that just two or three were passengers. In one instance, a passenger taken to hospital was a woman complaining of a headache – a headache she'd had ever since she boarded a plane at Coolangatta in Queensland.

The incident escalated once emergency services were advised to don protective clothing and masks at 10:05 a.m., serving to confirm suspicions that there was a serious health threat in the terminal. The report admitted that "loose language" by the media and agency personnel likely exacerbated the situation – including such words as "toxic," "noxious," "chemical," and remarks that subjects "were dropping like flies." In one news interview, an ambulance spokesman said that "a lot of people were actively vomiting."[469] Another said that many "became violently ill," including "severe vomiting."[470] Despite normal air quality checks and failure to locate a plausible source of a potential contaminant, in subsequent days many media outlets continued to describe the episode as an unidentified chemical or gas leak.[471] Journalist Patrick Carlyon suggested "that the sight of emergency crews in protective gear actually increased fears and amplified the outbreak." Meanwhile, a fire official said that "the only evidence of a contaminant were the symptoms themselves."[472]

Once state and commonwealth emergency services declared the area safe at 6:20 p.m., anxiety levels were reduced and there were no further illness reports. This treatment is consistent with other similar MPI incidents and involves identifying and eliminating or reducing the perceived stress-related stimulus.[473]

CONTEXT: The initial collapse of the woman at the base of the escalator appears to have caused anxiety in bystanders and led to a series of similar stress-related signs and symptoms based on a belief that a toxic agent was responsible. The escalating response by rescue personnel as more and more people felt ill fostered further anxiety, especially as the rescue personnel were wearing protective gear. It is clear from broadcast interviews with victims that concern over a chemical or biological attack was on the minds of many. Since September 11, 2001, there has been an escalation in the number of MPI reports involving the perceived use of chemical or biological agents, and particular concern over the targeting of mass transit. This may have been the lens through which many airport officials interpreted the initial events. The passengers are transients, but airport staff are "captives" of their work, and hence, may have viewed the events through a different perceptual prism, engendering greater anxiety. In this sense, the episode was a reflection of the times, preoccupied with environmental concerns and fear of chemical and biological attacks. Thus far, the fear of such incidents has proven more harmful than any real event.

It is conspicuous that mass hysteria was not even considered. It may be that the stigma and controversy often surrounding such diagnoses was a factor in excluding its consideration.[474] The report's conclusions may have been influenced by political and not medical considerations. Failure to render a MPI diagnosis in the face of compelling evidence may undermine perceptions of science and create unnecessary public unease.

MELIN, ARTHUR SPUD

A prominent designer and marketer of enormously popular fad products, Arthur Melin (pronounced Mah-LIN) was responsible for the appearance of the HULA-HOOP and Frisbee. He co-founded the California-based Wham-O Company in 1948, and died in June 2002 at age 77.[475]

See also: FADS.

MERCURY BOMB DOOMSDAY SCARE

Italy: July 14, 1960

In early July, a bearded Italian pediatrician from Milan lead a small group of followers to a mountainside refuge to survive a cataclysm that he predicted. Dr. Elio Bianca claimed that Earth would be devastated when someone was going to accidentally detonate a "mercury bomb" at 7:45 a.m. on July 14. Bianca claimed that when the "bomb" ignited, Earth would be tilted off its axis, triggering a deluge of Biblical proportions. About 100 followers set up a survival station at the 7,150-foot level (2,200 meters) on Mount Blanc in the Alps. But when the time came, nothing happened. It was just as well, as their plan to survive the disaster had hit a snag: the "10 boats they ordered to navigate after the deluge had not arrived from a sporting goods store in Genoa."[476]

MERPHOS POISONING SCARE

Auckland, New Zealand: February 1973

Fifty drums of the relatively harmless defoliant merphos were being unloaded at a wharf when it was noticed that several barrels were leaking, and a chemical smell permeated the air. Authorities were wrongly told that merphos was extremely toxic. An emergency was declared, an evacuation ensued, and some 400 dock workers and local residents were treated for a variety of psychosomatic complaints, such as headaches, breathing problems, and eye irritations.[477]

METHODIST REVIVAL

England: 1739 and later

The rise of Methodism prefigured the growth of REVIVALISM with its strategy of encouraging religious belief by means of large gatherings of people addressed by a preacher, generally in the open air. It prefigured them also in another way: the response to the preaching frequently took the form of manifestations of extraordinary behavior, including dropping to the ground, crying out, fainting, convulsions, and catalepsy, at first by individuals and subsequently by many. Those involved perceived these manifestations as signs of spiritual grace. Those not involved considered them pernicious and reproached the Methodists for appealing to the emotions via ENTHUSIASM EPISODES. The controversy continues to the present day, when many Christian sects choose a form of worship that appeals to the emotions rather than the intellect.

The creation of Methodism, in the 18th century, was, like the proliferation of sectarianism of the 17th century, a protest against the established church, which was accused of having abandoned the principles that had inspired the original Christian church. We are not here concerned with the doctrinal questions and the associated theological controversies, except insofar as they led to the manifestations of extraordinary behavior. In this new form of Protestantism, justification by faith took precedence over justification by works. This gave rise to forms of behavior that seemed to be sanctioned by the emphasis on personal salvation; they were perceived as expressions of a direct personal relationship with God without the mediation of priests. The men and women in the street were not concerned with the finer theological points, but they responded eagerly to John Wesley's impassioned evangelical preaching. Their response was "not the product of individual mental processes but of emotional reactions to instinctual needs – needs that probably are largely subconscious."[478]

At the same time, while the cries and convulsions were seen as the workings of divine grace on the guilt-torn penitent, these manifestations of individual behavior were expressed in a collective setting. They were a source both of gratification and of embarrassment to the preachers whose work brought on such dramatic – and initially unexpected – effects.

CONTEXT: Ostensibly, the Methodist revival was a purely religious affair, but the social milieu in which it took place dictated its form. Methodism addressed itself particularly to the lower classes in English society, both in the countryside and in the manufacturing towns. Social conditions at this period were harsh, and working people, apart from suffering widespread poverty, had virtually no access to cultural facilities and inadequate access to spiritual resources. "In the eighteenth century, the pulses of religion beat intolerably slow."[479] Ignorant and brutal, they had virtually no notion of what religion might mean for them until Wesley came to them with his insistence, first that they needed salvation, and second that he would show them the way to it.[480] For most of the converts, it was a conversion not from an alternative form of religion but from virtually no religion at all.

The principal instigator of Methodism was John Wesley (1703-1791), who as a student at Oxford joined his brother Charles's group, known derisively as "Methodists," of which he became leader. After visiting America as a missionary rather unsuccessfully, he returned to England and proceeded to institutionalize his church, which involved traveling the country and preaching either in halls or in the open air. He was a charismatic preacher, forceful and direct, and his meetings were immensely popular. In September 1773, at the age of 76, he preached to 32,000 at Gwennap Pit.[481] It was during such meetings that the manifestations occurred with which we are concerned, and first-hand documentation comes from Wesley's own *Journals*.

An early hint of things to come was given on January 21, 1739, in London:

> While I was expounding, a well-dressed, middle-aged woman suddenly cried out as in the agonies of death. She continued to do so for some time, with all the signs of the sharpest anguish of spirit. When she was a little recovered, I desired her to call upon me the next day. She then told me that about three years before she was under strong convictions of sin, and in such terror of mind that she had no comfort in anything, nor any rest day or night; that she sent for the minister of her parish, and told him the distress she was in; upon which he told her husband she was stark mad, and advised him to send for a physician immediately. A physician ordered her to be bleeded, blistered, and so on. But this did not heal her wounded spirit. So that she continued much as she was before: till the last night… gave her a faint hope…[482]

But it was at Bristol, two months later, that a more extreme response to his preaching began to manifest:

> 17 April: I expounded the fourth chapter of the Acts. We then called upon God to confirm His word. Immediately a young woman named Cornish (to our no small surprise) cried out aloud, with the utmost vehemence, even as in the agonies of death…Soon after, two other persons, Elizabeth Holder and James Worlock, were seized with strong pain, and constrained to "roar for the disquietness of their heart." But it was not long before they likewise burst forth into praise to God their

Saviour.[483]

On April 21, "A young man was suddenly seized with a violent trembling all over, and in a few minutes the sorrows of his heart being enlarged, sunk down to the ground…"[484] Many who attended his preaching came out of curiosity, or even hostility: often they found it difficult to believe the manifestations genuine:

30 April: Many were offended at the cries of those on whom the power of God came; among whom was a physician, who was much afraid there might be fraud or imposture in the case. Today one whom he had known many years was the first (while I was preaching) who broke out "into strong cries and tears." He could hardly believe his own eyes and ears. He went and stood close to her, and observed every symptom, till great drops of sweat ran down her face and all her bones shook. He then knew not what to think, being clearly convinced it was not fraud nor yet any natural disorder. But when both her soul and her body were healed in a moment, he acknowledged the finger of God.[485]

Many in his audience were offended by the disturbances caused by these people. On May 1, his voice could scarcely be heard amidst the groanings and cries. A Quaker, displeased at what he considered to be the dissimulation of those creatures, was biting his lips and knitting his brows, when he dropped down as if thunderstruck. After writhing in agony, he raised his head and cried aloud, "Now I know thou art a prophet of the Lord."[486]

20 May: Although they saw "signs and wonders" (for so I must term them) yet many would not believe. They could not indeed deny the facts; but they could explain them away. Some said, These were purely natural effects; the people fainted away only because of the heat and closeness of the rooms, and others were sure it was all a cheat; they might help it if they would? Else why were these things only in their private societies? Why were they not done in the face of the sun? Today, Monday the 21st, our Lord answered for Himself. For while I was preaching in the open air, and before more than two thousand witnesses, one, and another, and another was struck to the earth, exceedingly trembling…Others cried out with a loud and bitter cry, What must we do to be saved?

In the evening I was interrupted almost as soon as I had begun to speak, by the cries of one who was "pricked at the heart," and strongly groaned for pardon and peace…. Another person dropped down, close to one who was a strong asserter of the contrary doctrine. While he stood astonished at the sight, a little boy near him was seized in the same manner. A strong man, Thomas Maxfield, who stood up behind fixed his eyes on him, and sunk down himself as one dead; but soon began to roar and beat himself against the ground, so that six men could hardly hold him. I never saw one so torn of the Evil One. Meanwhile many others began to cry out, inasmuch that all the house (and indeed all the street for some space) was in an uproar.[487]

Both Wesley and his colleague George Whitefield found that field preaching in the open air was particularly effective. Whitefield declared, "I never was more acceptable to my Master, than when I was standing to teach in the open Fields. I always find I have most Power, when I speak in the open Air."[488] He gloried in the response of his hearers: "The Tide of Popularity began to run very high – I carried high sails. Thousands and ten thousands came to hear me – my Sermons were everywhere called for – when I preached, one might walk upon People's Heads –Trees and Hedges full, all hush'd when I began – God only can tell how the Hearers were melted down – I was crowded, admired, sainted, Hands kissed, hugged – they melt, weep, hang upon me – receive me as an Angel of God…" There was much more to the same effect.[489]

Later in 1739 Wesley returned to London, and the same effects now occurred here also. No doubt by this time word had spread of what might be expected to happen at his meetings, and we must allow for contagion by suggestion. He saw "many hysterical and many epileptic fits; but none of them were like these in many respects….one woman was offended greatly, being sure they might help it if they would – no one should persuade her to the contrary; and was got three or four yards [3-4 meters] when she also dropped down, in as violent an agony as the rest."[490]

One problem that puzzled Wesley was the rapid spread of symptoms from one person to another: "If one Member suffered, all the Members suffered… One, and another, and another sunk to the Earth." He saw no alternative explanation but that it was the spirit – whether divine or diabolic – infecting one after another. Bishop Lavington, Wesley's most eloquent critic, while confessing his ignorance as to precisely how this contagion occurs, had little doubt that it was a natural process. "It hath been observed of Superstition, and Enthusiasm in particular, that they are very catching and infectious, running like wild Fire from Breast to Breast." He goes so far as to suggest "that a corrupted and polluted Imagination is capable of corrupting and polluting the ambient Air, so that those who suck it in shall be thrown into the same Malady."[491]

The strength of Wesley's appeal was the personal interest he took in his followers. The meetings were the public face of his mission, but he continually made private visits where his human side was much in evidence. On October 12, "I was sent for to one of those who was so strangely torn by the devil that I almost wondered her relations did not say, 'Much religion hath made thee mad.'"[492] The behavior of some of the people he visited in this way is reminiscent of the victims of CONVENT HYSTERIA described elsewhere in this Encyclopedia. Sally Jones, in the following instance, could have been one of the afflicted sisters of LOUDUN:

> 23 October: I was exceedingly pressed to go back to a young woman, Sally Jones, in Kingswood. The fact I nakedly relate, and leave every man to his own judgment of it. I went. She was nineteen or twenty years old, but, it seems, could not write or read. I found her on the bed, two or three persons holding her. It was a terrible sight. Anguish, horror, and despair, above all description, appeared in her pale face. The thousand distortions of her whole body showed how the dogs of hell were gnawing at her heart. The shrieks intermitted were scarce to be endured. But her stony eyes could not weep. She screamed out, as soon as words could find their way, "I am damned, damned; lost for ever. Six days ago you might have helped me. But it is past. I am the devil's now. I have given myself to him. His I am. Him I must serve. With him I must go to hell. I will not be saved. I must, I will, I will be damned." She then began praying to the devil.... We interrupted her by calling upon God: on which she sank down as before, and another young woman [Betty Somers] began to roar out as loud as she had done... it being about nine o'clock. We continued in prayer till past eleven; when God in a moment spoke peace into their souls...[493]

Wesley was himself very puzzled by such behavior. While confident that it was the outward sign of his followers' process of salvation, he took a scientific interest in their conduct, as he had a lifelong interest in science and took part in experiments in electrotherapy. He interrogated his followers, hoping to understand what was happening to them:

> 30 December 1742 at Tanfield, near Newcastle: I carefully examined those who had lately cried out in the congregation. Some of these, I found, could give no account at all how or wherefore they had done so; only that of a sudden they dropped down, they knew not how; and what they afterwards said or did they knew not. Others could just remember they were in fear; but could not tell what they were in fear of. Several said they were afraid of the devil, and this was all they knew... One of them told me, "I was as if I was just falling down from the highest place I had ever seen. I thought the devil was pushing me off, and that God had forsaken me."[494]

On March 12, 1743, he conducted further questioning of followers who had been afflicted, and concluded: "These symptoms I can no more impute to any natural cause than to the Spirit of God. I can make no doubt but it was Satan tearing them..."[495] Bishop Lavington, on the other hand, observes that all these symptoms are present in "natural distempers," and sees to reason to look for a supernatural cause.[496]

For all his science, Wesley believed firmly in the existence of the Devil, but this did not prevent him from taking a pragmatic view of things, displaying common sense and quiet humor. On January 13, 1743, at Shottery, near Stratford-on-Avon, "Mrs. K, a middle-aged woman, had been for many weeks past in a way which nobody could understand; she had sent for a minister, but almost as soon as he came began roaring in so strange a manner (her tongue hanging out of her mouth and her face distorted into the most terrible form) that he cried out, 'It is the devil, doubtless!' and immediately went away. I suppose this was some unphilosophical [that is to say, unscientific] minister, else he would have said, Stark mad! send her to Bedlam! [an asylum for the insane]"[497] Indeed, Bishop Lavington might well have done so, for he quotes authorities – including Roman Catholic exorcists – to the effect that "the Exorcist must not easily believe any one to be possessed by the Devil, but must well know the Signs, whereby one possessed is distinguished from those who labout under the Black Bile, or any Distemper."[498]

Other Methodist preachers continued to have these effects on their followers. On May 20, 1769, John Berridge, Vicar of Everton, Bedfordshire, was preaching, and one in his audience left a vivid record of the scene:

> I heard many cry out, especially children, whose agonies were amazing. One of the eldest, a girl ten or twelve years old, was full in my view, in violent contortions of body, and weeping aloud, I think incessantly during the whole service. And several much younger children were agonizing...What sounds of distress did I hear! The greatest number of them who cried or fell were men; but some women and several children felt the power... and seemed just sinking into hell. This occasioned a mixture of various sounds, some shrieking, some roaring aloud. The most general was a loud breathing, like that of people half strangled and gasping for life. And indeed almost all the cries were like those of human creatures dying in bitter anguish. Great numbers wept without any noise; others fell down as dead; some sinking in silence, some with extreme noise and violent agitation. I stood on the pew-seat, as did a young man in the opposite pew, an able-bodied, fresh, healthy countryman. But in a moment, while he seemed to think of nothing less, down he dropped, with a violence inconceivable. The adjoining pews seemed shook with his fall. I heard afterwards the stamping of his feet, ready to break the boards, as he lay in strong convulsions at the bottom of

the pew...

The violent struggling has broke several pews and benches. Yet it is common for people to remain unaffected in church, and afterward drop down in their way home. Some have been found lying as dead in the road.

And now did I see such a sight as I do not expect again on this side of eternity. The faces of the three justified [i.e. converted] children, and I think of all the believers present, did really shine; and such a beauty, such a look of extreme happiness, and at the same time of divine love and simplicity, did I never see in human faces till now. The newly justified eagerly embraced one another, weeping on each other's necks for joy.[499]

A particular manifestation was outbursts of laughing, which puzzled both Wesley and his critics. At one of his meetings several broke out into "horrid Fits of Laughter," which they could not control; others rebuked them, but were suddenly seized in the same manner. "Thus they continued for two Days, a Spectacle to all." Wesley, needless to say, held the Devil responsible. Bishop Lavington took a different view: "Though I am not convinced that these Fits of Laughing are to be ascribed to Satan, I entirely agree with

John Wesley preaching in Cornwall.

Mr. Wesley, that they are involuntary and unavoidable; and don't in the least question the facts. Physical Writers tell us, that Laughing-Fits are one Species of a Delirium, attending on some Distempers." And he reminded us that similar laughing fits afflicted the CEVENNES PROPHETS and that Oliver Cromwell at the battle of Dunbar "did laugh so excessively as if he had been drunk" and was afflicted in the same way just before the battle of Naseby.[500]

As the years went by, the intensity of response to the field-meetings diminished, even while their popularity remained as great as ever. On July 14, 1759, Wesley reported from Cambridge: "One brought good tidings from Grantchester, that God had there broken down seventeen persons last week by the singing of hymns only; and that a child, seven years old, sees many visions and astonishes the neighbours with her innocent, awful manner of declaring them."[501] From this time on there are few mentions of extraordinary behavior in his *Journals*. This may have been simply that they had become a matter of course, and that they continued as ever though unrecorded, or, as seems more likely, now that the first shock of his mission was over, his followers responded less violently. However, extraordinary behavior of a similar kind continued to take place elsewhere in Britain. See also: JUMPERS, SCOTTISH AND WELSH RELIGIOUS EXCITEMENT, AMERICAN REVIVALISM.

COMMENT: Wesley's most eloquent critic was George Lavington, Bishop of Exeter, who compared the enthusiasm of the Methodists to that of the Papists, also citing several other outbreaks described in this Encyclopedia. Lavington did not claim to know all the answers, but recognized that what was happening at the Methodists' meetings was nothing new:

But to what Causes shall we ascribe these surprising and strange Appearances and Effects? I am persuaded that we know not enough of Nature, and the Ways and Works of Providence, - of the Powers, Extent and Boundaries of Natural Enthusiasm; of Disorders in Body or Mind; of superior Spirits, good and evil; of Ecstasies, Raptures, and Visions; of (supposed or real) Witchcrafts, and diabolical Possessions; of Magic and Sorcery; or even of Counterfeits, and juggling Impostures; and the like - We are not, I say, sufficiently acquainted with these Things, so as to determine precisely to what Cause we should ascribe, and how account for, every Particular of these strange and amazing Narratives of Mr. Wesley...Whether all be not mere Diabolical Operation, or Magical Imposture, or Juggling Artifice, or Natural Enthusiasm highly worked up by a cunning Operator, or the Effect of some unaccountable Distemper, - and how far all, or any of these may be concerned, and where to fix their Boundaries, I confess myself unable to determine. Though in general it is clear enough, that the Mystery of Iniquity is working.[502]

Wesley, though far from a typical man of his period (he strongly disapproved, for example, of Voltaire and Hume) was shaped both by beliefs left over from the past and by a critical approach characteristic of the Enlightenment. So we find him believing in the Devil but also in the curative properties of electricity, as well as regretting the disbelief in witchcraft but espousing vegetarianism. His *Journals* display an admirable good sense on every page: an open-minded attitude to ghosts, a skepticism as to the sea serpent, and an acceptance of precognition. "How hard it is to keep the middle way: not to believe too little or too much."[503] Moreover, though he was meeting scores of people every day of his life – and often hundreds – he never forgot that he was preaching to individuals, and his journal is full of personal anecdotes that show the crowds he addressed were not for him mere collections of humanity but made up of individuals each with their own faces, names and attributes.

Consequently, his own observations on the manifestations that occurred during his preaching are not cold records but intimate observations of the greatest interest for the psychologist and sociologist. On November 25, 1759, he found himself at Everton, and observed:

A remarkable difference since I was here before. None now were in trance, none cried out, none fell down or were convulsed...The danger was [i.e. when he started his ministry in 1739] to regard extraordinary circumstances too much, such as outcries, convulsions, visions, trances; as if these were essential to the inward work, so that it could not go on without them. Perhaps the danger is [twenty years later] to regard them too little, to condemn them altogether; to imagine they had nothing of God in them and were a hindrance to His work. Whereas the truth is: (1) God suddenly and strongly convinced many that they were lost sinners, the natural consequence whereof were sudden outcries and strong bodily convulsions: (2) to strengthen and encourage them that believed, and to make His work more apparent, He favoured several of them with divine dreams, others with trances and visions; (3) in some of these instances, after a time, nature mixed with grace; (4) Satan likewise mimicked this work of God, in order to discredit the whole work...Let us even suppose that, in some few cases, there was a mixture of dissimulation - that persons pretended to see or feel what they did not, and imitated the cries of convulsive motions of those who were really overpowered by the Spirit of God; yet even this should not make us either deny or undervalue the real work of the Spirit. The shadow is no disparagement of the substance, nor the counterfeit of the real diamond.[504]

Wesley had come to terms with the behavior of the more extreme members of his congregations, but he continued to deplore excess. Speaking of the over-enthusiastic preaching of one of his colleagues, George Bell, he said, "The reproach of Christ I am willing to bear, but not the reproach of enthusiasm, if I can help it."[505] He thought poorly of the Prophets of the Cevennes[506] [his verdict is given in the entry for that phenomenon], and deplored the antics of the Jumpers.[507] We can only guess what he would have thought of the occurrences during the American Revivals.

Ironically, just as he condemns others for their excesses, so he himself is condemned. Lavington, bemused by Wesley's attempts to assign to the Devil and to God their respective responsibilities in these matters, commented, "I must confess, I see little Difference, whether they are Bedevil'd, Bewitched, Bejesuited or Bewesleyed."[508]

MILAN OUTBREAK

Italy: 1590

Thirty nuns in a convent, described as virgins of lowly birth, in the neighborhood of Milan, were afflicted with hallucinations.[509] These were of the Evil One, whom they saw in different and very suggestive forms. But at other times, to frighten them, he would appear in the form of a lion, a serpent, a bear with an open jaw as though to devour them, or a soldier threatening them with a dagger and with a fierce dog, which he threatened to unleash unless they did as he told them. Most devious of all, he would appear to them in the form of a monk, and even as Jesus on the cross, who incited them with his discourse to impious thoughts and actions. Fortunately, the chronicler tells us, their simple nature and the support of God shielded them from these attacks.

The scanty accounts do not mention any behavior other than seeing visions, except in the case of one of the sisters who came from a good family. She felt such a great heat throughout her entire body that, despite the coldness of the weather, she was obliged to go into the garden and roll in the snow until she had extinguished the fire that Satan had lit inside her. (A similar behavior occurs in PIBLOKTOQ.) Another nun had a vision of Saint Ursula, behind whom appeared a long procession of demons disguised as nuns, with a banner at their head. They made impious suggestions; when she rejected them, they left, while uttering curses on the unfortunate sister.

This particular sisterhood seems to have got off very lightly compared with other instances of convent hysteria.

See also: CONVENT HYSTERIA, DEMON POSSESSION.

MILAN POISONING SCARE

Milan, Italy: 1630

In 1630, the "Great Poisoning Scare" swept across Milan, Italy.[510] Acclaimed Italian writer Count Alessandro Manzino describes the episode in detail in his book, *I Promessi Sposi* (*The Betrothed*). Across Europe at the time there were widespread fears that certain people were intent on spreading plague throughout the continent, either through witchcraft or "contagious poisons." The seeds of the scare of 1630 were sown the previous year when King Philip IV signed a dispatch that was sent to the governor of Milan, warning to be on the lookout for "four Frenchmen" who had escaped from a Spanish prison and who may be on their way to the city, intent on spreading plague by use of "poisonous and pestilential ointments." The episode was nearly forgotten but was resurrected when the plague broke out in Milan in May 1630, and some residents began to suspect a plot involving poison, as vague fears and suspicions crystallized into a specific incident.[511]

CONTEXT: The episode coincided with pestilence, plague, and a prediction that the Devil and evildoers would poison the city's water supply.

On the night of May 17, some residents claimed that they had observed some people placing what seemed to be poison on a partition in the city cathedral. The head of the city's health board and four health committee members went to the cathedral to deal with the crisis. At this point, various items had been removed from the building. Health officials could find no evidence of poison, though judging from the scene, the removal of the items lent credence to rumors the cathedral had been poisoned. Alessandro Manzino stated: "This mass of piled-up furniture produced a strong impression of consternation among the multitude, to whom any object so readily became an argument. It was said, and generally believed, that all the benches, walls, and even the bell-ropes in the cathedral, had been rubbed over with unctuous matter."[512]

When city-dwellers awoke the next day, they grew even more fearful upon finding a mysterious stain on various doors and walls across the city. "In every part of the city they saw the doors and walls of the houses stained and daubed with long streaks of I know not what filthiness, something yellow wish and whitish, spread over them as if with a sponge."[513] Disregarding the possibility of some mischievous act, there was alarm that the sign of the awaited poisoning was at hand. Members of the Health Board inspected the markings and conducted experiments with the substance on dogs without any harmful effect. Some people said they thought the markings were done in jest.[514] Despite these reassurances homeowners lit straw and burned the spots. Meanwhile, numerous people became the subject of great speculation as the possible culprit. "While the Board was thus making inquiries, many of the public, as is usually the case, had already found the answer. Among those who believed this to be a poisonous ointment, some were sure it was an act of revenge of Don Gonzalo Fernandez de Cordova, for the insults received at his departure; some, that it was an idea of Cardinal Richelieu's to desolate Milan, and make himself master of it without trouble; others, again – it is not known with what motives – would have that the Count Collalto was the author of the plot, or Wallenstein, or this or that Milanese nobleman."[515]

Soon, strange stains were again seen in various places across Milan: walls, doors, and public entrances. Fears intensified and "all eyes were on the lookout" for the "poisoners." In the scare that ensued, many people were killed, beaten, or imprisoned.

Josephi Ripamontii described two eyewitness accounts. In the first, an elderly man was spotted in church wiping a bench before sitting on it, when he was accused of smearing poison on the seat: "…an old man, more than eighty years of age, was observed, after kneeling in prayer, to sit down, first, however, dusting the bench with his cloak. 'That old man is anointing the benches!' exclaimed with one voice some women, who witnessed the act. The people who happened to be in church...fell upon the old man; they tore his gray locks, heaped upon him blows and kicks, and dragged him out half dead, to convey him to prison, to the judges, to torture. 'I beheld him dragged along in this way,' says Ripamontii, 'nor could I learn anything further about his end; but, indeed, I think he could not have survived many moments.'"[516]

In another incident, Ripamontii recounts that three young visiting Frenchmen were studying various antiquities, including the Milan cathedral. They were standing outside the building, apparently admiring the architecture. "One, two, or more passers-by, stopped, and formed a little group, to contemplate and keep their eye on these visitors, whom their costume, their headdress, and their wallets, proclaimed to be strangers, and, what was worse, Frenchmen. As if to assure themselves that it was marble, they stretched out their hands to touch it. This was enough. They were surrounded, seized, tormented, and urged by blows to prison. Fortunately, the hall of justice was not far from the cathedral, and by still greater good fortune, they were found innocent, and set at liberty."[517]

In another instance described by journalist CHARLES MACKAY, a pharmacist and barber named Mora, who was found with several preparations containing unknown potions, was accused of being in cahoots with the Devil to poison the city. Protesting his innocence, he eventually confessed after prolonged torture on the rack, admitting to cooperating with the Devil and foreigners to poisoning the city and anointing the doors. Under duress he named several accomplices who were eventually arrested and tortured. They were all pronounced guilty and executed. Mackay stated, "The number of persons who confessed that they were employed by the Devil to distribute poison is almost incredible," noting that "day after day persons came voluntarily forward to accuse themselves."[518]

COMMENT: As Alessandro Manzino shows us so vividly in his marvelous book, Italy at this time was suffering from invading foreigners, particularly Spanish and French, to say nothing of the intrigues of the Popes and the feuding families of Milan, Florence, and elsewhere, so the populace was kept in a state of chronic alarm, which surely kept everyone on edge to react to any kind of rumor or suspicion.

MILLERITE END-OF-THE-WORLD SCARE

New York and worldwide: circa 1830 to 1850

In the year 1816 farmer William Miller (1782-1849), previously a skeptic on religious matters, developed an interest in religion and began fervently studying the Bible. Within two years he became convinced that certain passages from the Book of Revelation pointed to the second coming of Christ. In his interpretation of the Bible, Miller placed great emphasis on Daniel, 18:14: "Unto two thousand and three hundred days; then shall the sanctuary be cleansed."[519] He was convinced that this was a reference to the Apocalypse, and despite his shyness he reluctantly became a preacher at a local Baptist church. In the 1830s he set up a small church of his own in the small town of Hampton, near the southern Adirondack Mountains of New York State. Here he began to preach that the world would soon end by the hand of God. His preaching attracted followers who became known as Millerites, and his teachings became known as Millerism.

By early January 1843, Miller felt able to be more precise, predicting that Christ would reappear "sometime between March 21st, 1843, and March 21st, 1844."[520]Adherents of Miller reportedly soon gave away their property and possessions, left their jobs and families, and held prayer gatherings until Ascension Day arrived in March 1843. By some accounts, followers climbed up trees to be the first to greet Jesus and be carried to heaven. But when the time came, nothing happened. It is claimed that Miller never predicted a specific date in March but that overzealous followers had. When March 21, 1844, passed without incident, ("The Great Disappointment"), Miller reviewed his calculations and soon announced that he had been mistaken: the new Ascension date was actually the following year — October 22, 1844. Many of his followers remained loyal to Miller. But when the time came, again nothing happened.[521]

How had Miller reached his conclusions for October 22? In the eighth chapter of the Prophet Daniel, there is a reference to 2,300 days. At the time, many Biblical scholars believed each day referred to a year. Miller calculated that "490 years" (the seventy "weeks" mentioned in Daniel 9:24) were "cut off" from the 2,300 years, leaving 1,810 years. It was assumed that Christ died early in 31 A.D. with 3.5 years of Daniel's 70th week still to run. Adding those 3.5 years to 31 A.D. brings us to late 34 A.D., at which time the 1,810 remaining years supposedly began. 1810 + 34 brings us to 1844. Technical considerations placed the date in October 1844."[522] The modern Adventist Church grew out of the Miller movement.

CONTEXT: According to historian Paul Boyer, it would be a mistake to view Miller and his followers as crackpots. He noted that "it's very hard to find how the Millerites were different from other Americans. They were ordinary Americans. Many of them were involved in other reform movements. Joshua Himes in Boston, for example, was also involved in the abolitionist movement. Sarah Grimke was involved in the women's rights movement and the anti-slavery movement. People were drawn to Miller out of a larger cultural climate of the moment. And they were not cranks. They were not fringe people. They were ordinary Americans who found his interpretation compelling."[523]

William Miller, who predicted the End of the World.

MILLENARIST MIGRATIONS OF BRAZIL

Brazil: 15th to 20th century

People of virtually every culture cherish the image of another land, far-off in place or time, where the shortcomings of their present habitat will be set right: "shires where the girls are fonder, towns where the pots hold more."[524] But whereas most people, like A.E. Housman's Shropshire lads, resign themselves to the sad fact that the longed-for land is only a dream, the Tupa-Guarani and other indigenous peoples of Brazil have periodically been persuaded that the Land Without Evil, of Immortality, of Perpetual Rest, of their legends was an attainable reality. Even before the arrival of the conquistadors from Europe, there had taken place a series of messianic migrations in which entire populations abandoned their homes and set out in quest of the promised land. Those dwelling inland headed either eastward to the Atlantic coastlands, or westward to Peru's Pacific shore. Conversely, those who dwelt on the coast sought it in the jungle interior. What we know of these events derives partly from oral traditions and partly from the observations of the European chroniclers. Ironically, when these newcomers learned of the natives' quests, they in turn perpetuated the tradition when they set out on equally fruitless expeditions of their own in search of El Dorado.[525]

In the early 16th century, there was considerable religious ferment among the indigenous Tupinamba peoples, who had themselves migrated from the interior to the Atlantic coast before the arrival of the Portuguese. Now, shamans persuaded their people that they could cease working in the fields, for the crops would harvest themselves of their own accord, ensuring abundance for all. Their enemies would yield to them. The elderly would become youthful again. So work was abandoned, and the populace devoted themselves to ritual dancing, by day and night, by way of working the requisite magic to ensure the generosity of their gods.

These signs, the shamans told them, preceded the imminent end of the world, a disaster presaged not only by their own tradition of an earlier civilization destroyed by catastrophe, but now reinforced by the European missionaries who preached terrifyingly of a fearsome Day of Judgment at which the undeserving would be condemned to perpetual torment. This horrific event might overtake them at any moment. So, in 1539, thousands abandoned their settlements in search of the promised land where dwelt the divine hero who had created their world; here, they would be safe. They believed that shamans and warriors went to this land when they died, and that even common people might be admitted if they give proof of courage and endurance during their lifetimes.

Courage and endurance were certainly called for during the nine-year westward journey, which took them across Brazil, traversing the continent at its widest point, to the Peruvian coast. They were encouraged by their shamans, who seemingly performed miracles to obtain food and water for them, and protected them from hostile tribes by making them invisible. But they reached the Pacific only to find that the promised land wasn't there. Disillusioned, some stayed on as settlers, others returned.

This was just one of many such hopeful journeys. Often the inspiration came from an individual prophet called a *pagé*, who attracted a cult or a crowd of followers and was credited with semi-divine status. Several such prophets arose during the 16th and 17th centuries. Frequently they owed much of their appeal to their opposition to the Europeans, who in the colonial tradition were increasingly enforcing their political rule, imposing their values and their religion on the native population. One such prophet attracted an enthusiastic following when he predicted the extermination of all Christians, whatever the color of their skins. Another took a contrasting approach, claiming that his mother was the Virgin Mary and that he was a new Christ sent to complete the work of the first.

Every Guarani prophet claimed some kind of divine authority. He might be the reincarnation of a heroic ancestor, or even be a god himself, possessing the power to destroy the world with a breath if he so chose. He could communicate with the heavens through his special messengers and proved his powers by performing seeming miracles, commanding demons and angels; he would claim healing powers which he said were bestowed on him by the gods. A French chronicle of 1614 tells of one such prophet, part native part Portuguese, who attracted a following of about 10,000 around Rio de Janeiro, urging them to embark on a migration northward. As the horde proceeded, their numbers increased at every village they passed through, until undeterred by the hardships of their journey, the mass of fanatical people approached Pernambuco, where they were halted by the inhabitants. The prophet died, while the number of his followers was reduced to a handful by hunger and disease.

Other such migrations continued to occur intermittently. At the end of the 19th century a native messiah, calling himself the Second Christ, arose among the natives of the Içana River in northwest Brazil. He won their confidence by healing the sick, then ordered them to stop tilling the land, for the era of wealth and happiness was about to arrive when the soil would yield its fruits without any need for work. When he was finally arrested, the movement collapsed. But the belief in the golden age persisted even into the 20th century. An observer in 1921 found that Paraguayan settlers on the Brazilian coast still retained the dream of crossing the ocean to the magical land their ancestors had hoped but failed to find. In a village of the Nandeva-Guarani, more than a hundred inhabitants succumbed to an ailment involving discouragement and tedium, sometimes taking the form of a suicidal mania in hope of attaining another life where death does not exist. Their remedy was to devote themselves intensively to rituals that they trusted would enable them to escape from life into a state of mystical beatitude and personal perfection. A more literal flight from reality was promised to another community of tribes people at Praia Grande, who were observed performing ritual dances and incantations with the aim of reducing their weight. Once they became light enough, their shamans assured them, they would be able to fly across the Atlantic to the Land Without Evil.

COMMENT: Although desire for material gain and freedom from hardship provided strong incentives for these mass displacements, their religious and messianic character is unmistakable. Those who instigated the migrations were shamans and prophets. As with CARGO CULTS and the Russian *raskoliniki* (see RUSSIAN SECTARIANISM), the religious, economic, and political motives are intertwined and inseparable, but it would seem that though such motifs as opposition to the Europeans and bettering their lifestyle play a part, they are only secondary to what can be seen as a more transcendental or spiritual aspiration. By contrast, when in the mid-16th century the Europeans, inspired by the natives' tales, set out under Pedro de Ursua in search of El Dorado, it was the prospect of material treasure alone that provided the lure.

MIND CONTROL DELUSION, THE

United States and elsewhere: 1940s-1970s

Scientists have long strived to enhance the quality of human life through the modification of behaviors deemed negative by the individual (e.g., obsessive compulsive disorder), society-at-large (e.g., Tourette's Syndrome), or the state (e.g., Communist dissidents advocating radical political change), in order to "correct" behavior, cure their ills, or enhance performances. A wide range of means has been proposed to modify behavior, ranging from drugs to surgery to the "talking cure" to hypnosis, with varying success. One of the greatest contemporary myths centers on what we term "the mind control delusion." The concept of "brainwashing" (commonly referred to as "coercive persuasion" by social scientists) has not yet been established within mainstream science, either involving an individual or en mass.

The Myth

Claims that certain governments have instigated programs to discover how people may be conditioned to change their views can be traced back to Soviet Russia, where Stalin set out to justify his purge of political rivals and opponents by a series of "show trials" in which political opponents "confessed," seemingly willingly, to crimes of which they were palpably innocent.

> The central element of Soviet brainwashing was total control over the prisoner and his environment, control so total that the prisoner's entire existence was manipulated according to the wishes of the brainwasher...In Soviet hands, the brainwashing process was a sophisticated means of interrogation designed to weaken the will of the prisoner to the point of no resistance. The prisoner was then required to memorize his role from the script of his trial and perform it well before the public. Prisoners were handled one by one and no attempt was made at indoctrination and conversion. Soviet interrogators worked quickly, applying psychological pressure through isolation, sensory deprivation and old-fashioned torture.[526]

Alan Scheflin and Edward Opton have charted an escalating scale of brainwashing based on the procedures of Communist states. The Soviets were not interested in indoctrination, they required merely compliance leading to pseudo-confession. The Chinese authorities sought to convert dissidents, but failed to achieve permanent results with foreigners; whether they were more successful with their own recalcitrant population is not known. American soldiers captured by the Communists during the Korean War were supposedly brainwashed to the extent that some of them expressed views favorable to their captors, even admitting – falsely – that the United States had engaged in germ warfare. The Koreans were looking for a show of change of heart, which they could exploit for propaganda purposes. Their efforts gave rise to a category of behavior epitomized by Richard Condon's classic novel, *The Manchurian Candidate*. However, they obtained no long-term conversions, so in retrospect it can be said that none of these techniques had any durable success. "Brainwashing" is simply not a very efficacious procedure, even if it obtains some short-term benefits for the perpetrators.

This, however, was unknown to U.S. authorities during the period of the Korean and Vietnam Wars, and U.S. fears led to a vast, extremely costly and ultimately fruitless program aimed at countering the methods used by potentially hostile countries, and if possible, out-doing them. "There can be little question that the CIA used Stalin's trials of the thirties, and that of Cardinal Mindszenty, as an excuse, a justification rather than a reason, to explore the possibilities of manipulating the mind."[527] The U.S. program was not only the most ambitious but the most methodical and scientific. Given the immense resources available, there was every expectation that they would achieve more than the Communists.

Full details of the research carried out by the CIA and the U.S. Army (working separately and competitively, not sharing their findings so that, for example, the Army was not aware that the CIA had discovered the dangerous effects of LSD) are not yet available, and much never will be as many records were not only concealed but destroyed. Those concerned have been understandably reluctant to divulge more than they were obliged to, and much of what has emerged has been censored or sanitized. Enough has emerged, however, to make it clear that "the objective of Operation Mind Control...has been to take human beings, both citizens of the United States and citizens of friendly and unfriendly nations, and transform them into unthinking, subconsciously programmed 'zombies,' motivated without their knowledge and against their wills to perform in a variety of ways in which they would not otherwise willingly perform. This is accomplished through the use of various techniques called by various names, including brainwashing, thought reform, behavior modification, hypnosis, and conditioned reflex therapy."[528] In pursuit of their aims, the specialists working for the U.S, government employed a staggering range of methods: "The Security office planned to use outside consultants to find out about such techniques as ultrasonics, vibrations, concussions, high and low pressures, the uses of various gases in airtight chambers, diet variations, caffeine, fatigue, radiation, heat and cold, and changing light."[529]

Research was carried to its extreme in the CIA's Project MKULTRA whose aims were "behavior control, behavior anomaly production and counter-measures for opposition application of similar substances. It was an 'umbrella project' which supervised research on radiation, electroshock, various fields of psychology, psychiatry, sociology, and anthropology, graphology, and paramilitary devices and materials."[530]

"One hundred and thirty-nine different drugs... were tested...The most promising drugs were given to unwitting subjects in normal social conditions."[531] They were inspired by the findings of the eminent behaviorist J. D. Watson, who asserted that not only moment-to-moment behavior, but the entire lifestyle of the individual could be manipulated by appropriate conditioning. "Give me the baby, and I'll make it a thief, a gunman or a dope fiend...The possibilities of shaping in any direction are almost endless...Men are built, not born."[532]

James V. McConnel, head of the Department of Mental Health Research at the University of Michigan, underlined this claim by saying, apparently in all seriousness, "We want to reshape our society drastically, so that all of us will be trained from birth to want to do what society wants us to do. Today's behavioral psychologists are the architects and engineers who are shaping the Brave New World of tomorrow."[533]

Sid Gottlieb, working for the CIA, outlined the needs he perceived, calling for "operationally pertinent materials along the following lines: a. Disturbance of Memory: b. Discrediting by Aberrant Behavior: c. Alteration of Sex Patterns: d. Eliciting of Information: e. Suggestibility: f. Creation of Dependence."[534] In pursuit of these aims, CIA researchers were prepared to go beyond laboratory testing, to

> ...covert testing of materials on unwitting U.S. citizens...in blatant disregards of the civil rights and civil liberties of Americans, and of their health and safety as well...For nearly ten years the minds of Americans had been surreptitiously infiltrated with powerful and dangerous chemicals such as LSD...The CIA records disclose that in numerous instances the subjects became quite ill, sometimes to the point of requiring hospitalization, and an occasional death occurred...Oblivious to the extreme dangers that could be produced, or not caring, since secret programs cannot be called to account, the CIA blithely continued invading the minds of unsuspecting citizens...Enough evidence now exists to demonstrate conclusively that the CIA violated the law with its domestic experimentation programs. It is not difficult to conclude that the CIA was aware of the illegal and unethical nature of its activities all along.[535]

Some subjects were volunteers, for instance prison inmates who were promised incentives – usually drugs – if they cooperated, but even they were not told what was being done to them. Prostitutes were employed to lure men into "safe houses" where they could be given spiked drinks. Meanwhile magicians were consulted as to how substances could be surreptitiously administered to unwitting subjects. An unidentified member of the TSS (Technical Services Staff) told John Marks: "We thought about the possibility of putting some LSD in a city water supply and having the citizens wander around in a more or less happy state, not terribly interested in defending themselves."[536] The possibilities offered by LSD seemed to foreshadow the kind of effect they were seeking:

> Only a speck of LSD could take a strong-willed man and turn his most basic perceptions into willowy shadows. Time, space, right, wrong, order, and the notion of what was possible all took on new faces. LSD was a frightening weapon, and it took a swashbuckling boldness for the leaders of MKULTRA to prepare for operational testing...They thought they could use it to find out what went on in the mind underneath all the outside acts and pretensions. If they could get at the inner self, they reasoned, they could better manipulate a person – or keep him from being manipulated.[537]

But what the CIA learned was pretty much what the Communists had already learned: that affecting the populace en masse, applying some kind of fits-all procedure – though it might achieve some useful negative results, though it would enable them to disorient and confuse people, though it might weaken many of their responses, in short, while it might *reduce them as people* – would not really enable the manipulators to exercise any useful degree of *positive* control over the individual. "The researchers learned...that the quality of a person's reaction was determined mainly by the person's base personality structure (set) and the environment (setting) in which he or she took the drug. The subject's expectation of what would happen also played a major part. More than anything else, LSD tended to intensify the subject's existing characteristics – often to extremes. A little suspicion could grow into major paranoia, particularly in the company of people perceived as threatening."[538] Another TSS member told Marks: "What we subsequently found was that when you came down, you remembered the experience, but you didn't switch identities...This wasn't the kind of thing that was going to make a guy into a turncoat to his own country."[539]

Nevertheless, a substantial number of people have claimed to be the victims of governmental mind control, not only in the U.S., Jim Keith, a noted conspiracy theorist, cited testimony from several such persons, of whom the best-known was Candy Jones, who told in her ghosted autobiography how she had been used as an unwitting courier by the U.S. government.[540] It has been suggested that these supposed victims were deluded, but if so, those delusions in themselves reflect a widespread anxiety that stems from well-established facts.

Investigators Marks, Bowart, Scheflin, and Opton have documented the persistence of the U.S. government in seeking to control the minds of populations and individuals. What they found was that it would be relatively simple to destroy people's normal behaviors, but that would be only the first and relatively easy step. The further step, of then getting people to do what the authorities wanted them to do, was far more difficult. "The magic mushroom never became a good spy weapon. It made people behave strangely but no one could predict where their trips would take them. Agency officials craved certainty."[541] So, though no doubt experimentation has continued, the original efforts at mass mind control have been abandoned as impracticable. The aim was to find foolproof, "scientific" methods of mind control that would not require individual treatment. But "for every experiment suggesting that a particular behavior change is due, say, to the effect of electricity applied to a center of the brain, there are others which suggest that the effect is a result of some psychological response to the initial stimulus."[542] Every brain is one-of-a-kind, and no standardized method of mind control emerged from the millions of dollars spent on searching for one.

As the U.S. government wound down its efforts, one of its leading protagonists, Dr. Sidney Gottlieb, commented:

> It has become increasingly obvious over the last several years that this general area had less and less relevance to current clandestine operations. The reasons for this are many and complex, but two of them are perhaps worth mentioning briefly. On the scientific side, it has become very clear that these materials and techniques are too unpredictable in their effect on individual human beings, under specific circumstances, to be operationally useful. Our operations officers, particularly the emerging group of new senior operations officers, have shown a discerning and perhaps commendable distaste for utilizing these materials and techniques. They seem to realize that, in addition to moral and ethical considerations, the extreme sensitivity and security constraints of such operations effectively rule them out.[543]

As Scheflin and Opton observe, "Law, religion, morality and conscience are all more or less ephemeral, but...as long as a man's thoughts remain his private possession, domination ends at the scalp."[544] The history of mind control is the story of attempts to get beneath the scalp, to tamper with people's thoughts. Without question, they succeeded in so far that they learned how to assault, disarrange, interfere, harass, even destroy. But to *control* thought, to re-direct it, has eluded the most devious would-be manipulators. In the end, Marks concluded, "the human psyche proved so complex that even the most skilled manipulator could not anticipate all the variables. He could use LSD and other drugs to chip away at free will. He could score temporary victories, and he could alter moods, perceptions – sometimes even beliefs. He had the power to cause great harm, but ultimately he could not conquer the human spirit."[545]

MINIATURE GOLF FAD

United States: 1920s

While diminutive golf courses using natural grass had long been used in Great Britain in front of some inns, a variation of this idea became very popular in the United States in the late 1920s. In 1927, Garnet Carter of Chattanooga, Tennessee, built "Fairyland," America's first known course.[546] The fad was so popular that soon hundreds of miniature golf courses appeared in Florida to boost the popularity of hotels there.[547] It quickly caught on, and the tiny courses began popping up like mushrooms across the country. So big was this fad that shortly after the onset of the depression, people commonly joked that miniature golf was the only industry hiring.[548] Miniature golf was an undeniable boost to the ailing economy. Near its peak in the Fall of 1930, an estimated four million people a day were playing on any one of as many as 40,000 courses, providing jobs for some 200,000 people and reaping profits of $225 million dollars.[549]

CONTEXT: The sudden, meteoric rise of miniature golf, affordable and accessible to most Americans, coincided with the sudden, precipitous decline of the American economy.

Known by such names as "midget golf,"[550] "half pint golf,"[551] Lilliput golf,[552] and "Tom Thumb golf,"[553] some neighborhoods protested their appearance due to the large rowdy crowds that were sometimes associated with them. A typical afternoon round of "mini-golf" cost 30 cents, 50 cents at night, and extra 75 cents if you desired a caddie to carry your clubs.[554] At a time when money was in short supply, the miniature golf boom seemed to have been a product of the Great Depression, being the right game at the right time. At a time when the national economy was in shambles and a cloud of psychological malaise of doom and gloom hung over the country, miniature golf was "fun, entertaining, cheap and a great place to bring a date."[555] The fad began to fade by the end of 1930, and most establishments soon went bankrupt, despite proprietors trying various innovations to keep or attract customers, such as outlandish hazards and driving ranges.[556] As a testament to its rapid decline, by the end of 1931, the publication *Miniature Golf Management,* which served mini-golf operators, had folded, but not before reporting that during the winter of 1931 not a single California mini-golf course had registered a profit.[557]

COMMENT: While miniature golf continues today, its popularity is but a shadow of its former self. During an upsurge in miniature golf in 1989, there were only an estimated 1,800 courses across the U.S.,[558] and during another resurgence in 2001, just 6,000 courses had popped up across the nation, far fewer than when the fad was in its heyday.[559]

See also, FADS

MINNESOTA FAINTING EPIDEMIC

Minnesota: November 10, 1927

Educational Psychologist Willard Olson of the University of Minnesota was called upon to investigate a fainting "epidemic" at an unnamed co-educational high school (presumably in the state of Minnesota) with an enrollment of 270 pupils, exactly half of each sex.[560] The episodes began on November 10, when three girls apparently fainted in an assembly hall after someone took a camera flash picture. This incident was followed by a series of fainting spells in subsequent weeks. By December 6, nine girls in all had fainted. The girls were between the ages of 14 and 17, and in all but one instance, they appeared to be temporarily unconscious. After each incident the affected girl was taken to a restroom to recover. It was noted that the first girl to faint was known to have fainted in the past. After the Christmas vacation, no further cases were recorded.

CONTEXT: Episodes of individual fainting are relatively common in large school assembly settings. The initial incident, involving three fainting girls after a camera flash, was a highly public event and may have made others anxious.

Professor Olson offered the following conjecture: "Apparently the excitement, the crowded condition of the room, and the sudden explosion of the flashlight powder were sufficient stimuli for the fainting response in a girl already somewhat predisposed. The added excitement and suggestion at this event was sufficient to overcome two others. In the days that followed, the incident was the subject of much discussion and many students were probably in a... unhealthful mental state. In this condition, others succumbed to what ordinarily would be inadequate stimuli."[561]

MIRACLE HEN OF LEEDS

Leeds, England: 1806

A panic spread through Leeds, England, and environs that the end of the world was at hand. The episode began when a hen from a nearby village began laying eggs inscribed with the words, "Christ is coming." Large numbers of people flocked to the site to examine the eggs and see the "miracle" firsthand. Many were convinced that their days on earth were numbered and suddenly became devoutly religious. Excitement quickly turned to disappointment when a man "caught the poor hen in the act of laying one of her miraculous eggs" and soon determined "that the egg had been inscribed with some corrosive ink, and cruelly forced up again into the bird's body."[562]

MONKEY MAN SCARE

New Delhi, India: May 2001

During May 2001, residents in the vicinity of New Delhi were terror-stricken by reports of sightings and attacks by a mysterious creature dubbed "the monkey man." Most reports came from east Delhi, and encounters were almost exclusively reported at night by persons sleeping atop their suburban homes in the open air while trying to remain cool during a heat wave that was accompanied by rolling electricity blackouts.[563] Most people reported the creature as half-human, half-monkey, and having razor-sharp fingernails, super-human strength, and a leaping ability. However, descriptions varied widely. Some said it had steel claws and could press an invisibility button on a belt around its waist. Many witnesses said the creature was between 3 and 6 feet tall (1 to 2 meters), but some said it was the size of a cat. In mid-May, at the height of the scare, vigilante groups roamed the city armed with sticks. Journalists described the tense scene: "Wandering bands of vigilantes guard neighborhoods with wooden cudgels, daggers, field-hockey sticks, ceremonial swords and pikes made from butchers' cleavers...In the early hours, police fire flares over cultivated ground to see if the Monkey Man is hiding in the darkness. The area's 500-strong police force has been tripled. Some legislators are demanding the central government send in elite commandos to deal with what they call 'the crisis.'"[564]

CONTEXT: Monkeys can often be spotted running wild through the streets of New Delhi, especially on the city outskirts, occasionally attacking bystanders or entering homes. During the heat wave, residents who were forced to sleep on their housetops may have felt vulnerable to such attacks, generating anxiety, rumors, and misperceptions of mundane occurrences.[565] Sanal Edamaruku of the India Rationalist Association observed that the Monkey Man sightings conspicuously coincided with an Indian television series on the popular Hindu monkey deity "Hanuman," which has super-human strength and the ability to leap incredible distances.[566]

At least two people died from the scare, and dozens more claimed attacks, typically suffering cuts and bruises. One man leapt off the roof of a one-story building in the suburb of Noida. A pregnant woman died after falling down a staircase. Both had awakened to cries that the creature was nearby.[567]

One witness described his encounter in broken English: "I open the curtain and I saw a hand...Then

I heard a noise, a noise like a monkey makes, and I started running towards the stairs and he chased me. Then I tripped over something in the hall and fell down the stairs...He didn't follow, but I could see he had a dark face and an iron hand."[568]

The evening of May 16 was typical – police received about 40 phone calls claiming attacks or sightings across the city, often simultaneously. In one instance, a rat had clearly bitten the "victim." Another caller said they were testing police response time in case the monkey man showed up.[569] Upon closer examination, several of the "fresh wounds" reportedly made by the Monkey Man were determined to have been two or three days old, as many people faked injuries to gain media publicity.[570] One man was arrested wearing a monkey mask while breaking into a house.[571] By the end of the third week, reports to police rapidly subsided. A police probe concluded that the danger was imaginary.[572]

The mythical King Ravana tries to punish the monkey god Hanuman by setting his tail alight.

Edamaruku viewed the reports as rumors exacerbated by circumstances, noting that most "attacks" occurred during power outages after midnight. "Somebody makes a sound that a monkey's coming and everybody's panic [sic] and running and you get some scratches somewhere while running...You're afraid that it's caused by a monkey."[573]

The Monkey Man Study

Dr. D. K. Srivastava of the University College of Medical Sciences in Dilshad Garden, Delhi, served as the Medical Superintendent of the Guru Teg Bahadur Teaching Hospital during the period of the episode. The hospital, located in East Delhi in the heart of the scare, treated a total of 51 alleged monkey man-related injuries between May 10 and 26. The majority of victims were males between the ages of 20 and 30, poorly educated, and of low social and economic status. In fact, 94 percent of cases involved residents from "the resettlement or Jhuggi-Jopri clusters, i.e. very low socioeconomic strata, mainly clustered in single belt (region wise) having poor environmental sanitation and a high level of pollution. This population is more vulnerable [to social delusions]...due to their low educational level as evident from the fact that only 2 victims were educated more than higher secondary level, i.e., class XI standard."

According to a study of the episode by Dr. Srivastava and Indian physician S.K. Verma, most reports occurred at night and coincided with power outages.[574] The two were part of a medical investigation team of five physicians including themselves, two senior forensic medical specialists, and a chief medical administrator. They randomly selected 18 of the 51 cases for a more thorough analysis. Of the 18 cases analyzed, 11 were allegedly caused by the monkey creature and seven were the result of injuries sustained in fleeing. All appeared to be accidental in nature. Two-thirds of the cases occurred between a relatively narrow span from between midnight and 6 a.m. Srivastava and Verma noted that this was the time when people are most likely to be in the deepest state of sleep and prone to falling as they get up to go to the bathroom in the night. The likelihood of accidental falls also increased given the common lack of proper lighting that is more common among the poor. "The fact that 67% of incident [sic] occurred during the power failure in the area can be a strong collaborating factor for such accidental fall/injuries."

Srivastava and Verma said that the evidence "points towards an accidental nature of injuries among the victims of this outbreak. Factually, none of the victims actually saw the alleged monkey man. Every one described an imaginary figure giving vague description [sic]. Further, the victims also did not refute the chances of being injured accidentally."

How did Srivastava and Verma account for the preponderance of male victims? The first reported victim was male. They suggested that subsequent media coverage of the case worried other males that they too might become victims as the monkeyman might be targeting males. Secondly, they believed local male/female sleeping patterns could account for the "targeting" of males as the "majority of cases were reported from outside the covered area of house [i.e. open] where mostly male members of family [sic] sleep during summer time due to lack of proper housing."

COMMENT: While strange creature encounter reports may seem ridiculous and incredible to those outside of the cultural milieu, social delusions only require plausibility to be deemed real. Early in their investigation, some police officials helped to foster the Monkey Man scare after theorizing that the creatures were "remote-controlled robots being maneuvered by Pakistan's Inter-Services Intelligence."[575]

Bear-Man Attacks In India During May 2001

As the monkey man scare was subsiding in late May, another phantom animal attack terror took place in northeastern India. In the Nalbari district of Lower Assam, a mysterious bear-like creature was reportedly wreaking havoc among locals. A few said it resembled a wolf-man. Vigilante groups were being formed to stay awake through the night to protect the sleeping. According to Prafulla Kalita, a government worker in Nalbari town, "People say it roams about, often becoming invisible before attacking them." Many sightings were reported in the Nathkuchi and Tihu region.[576]

Descriptions given by villagers in a local newspaper indicate that the creature "has a furry body, looks like a bear and disappears when rays of light are directed toward it. The villagers are spending sleepless nights and the situation has become even worse with erratic power supply, especially after sunset."[577] Nalbari's Deputy Commissioner, B. Kalyan Chakravarty, rejected the claims as "figments of people's imagination." Chakravarty believed that publicity surrounding the monkey man scare in New Delhi was responsible for the reports. "We sent out teams of officers, including the police, to these villages, and after careful examination found that it is just some kind of panic created following reports of the monkey-man in Delhi. Such stories always create sensation among the villagers, who easily give in to superstitions and ghost stories."[578]

Terrified villagers desperate to capture the creature sought help from the Army who were in the region carrying out a counter-insurgency operation. Colonel Sanjeev Sinha, of the 5 J-K Light Infantry unit based in Nalbari, said that their investigations had turned up empty. "We sent out men to verify the incidents, but till date not one person has been able to substantiate his claim that he had seen a mysterious creature."[579] In an effort to quell fears, the Assam Science Society issued a report dismissing claims about the creature's existence. Based on interviews with 16 "victims," in each instance the person was sleeping at the time the "attack" was reported. The report read in part: "The people said they first heard a noise on the tin roof of their houses, following which they felt that something was trying to clutch them with sharp nails. But every person admitted they were half-asleep when they experienced this."[580]

According to Ramani Nath, a schoolteacher from Tihu village, "We first heard a loud bang at night. Then we saw something black and furry resembling a bear, and before the beast could attack, we switched on the lights and the creature disappeared." She also noted: "I have seen many people with injury marks on their body, some with minor scratches and others with cut marks on their legs and hands."[581] Some accounts have the creature sporting metallic claws reminiscent of monkey man stories. A judge in the

Nalbari district, B. Kalyan Chakravorty, said authorities were doing everything they could to calm frayed nerves. "We have sent police patrols to instill confidence among the villagers although I think it is nothing but hallucination...There are some reports of people being scratched but there are no tell-tale signs of sighting the animal as such."[582]

The Indian Wolfman Scare Of 1996

During the summer of 1996, a phantom animal attack scare swept through Ahmedabad, terrorizing the inhabitants of the Jashodanar-Vatwa and Isanpur's industrial area. During the episode, 19 persons were reportedly injured, either by the creature or in trying to get away from its clutches. According to Dr. Dharmila Shah of the L.G. Hospital in Maninagar, many people showed up for treatment of a variety of injuries but weren't certain exactly how they had occurred. Some attributed the "attacks" to a wolf creature that could walk on two legs. One local resident, Mehrzaban Beramji, said that during the scare "we used to sleep the days and keep a watch in the night, with pick-axes, sickles, spears, lathis and mashals torches. That fortnight drove enough fear amongst small children who would not venture out after dark." Not surprisingly, the creature was never caught.[583]

MONTREAL SLASHER

Ontario, Canada: 1954

Police announced that many of the 22 reports of a mysterious slasher cutting women on their legs over a weeklong period in late January were determined to have been the result of "mass hysteria." In the wake of the news, police were imposing "a partial news blackout on further cases." Many of the women said that the "slasher," thought to be carrying a razor, smiled or laughed after slashing them. All of the "attacks" occurred at stops for either streetcars or buses during rush hour and near the heart of the city.[584]

MOON HOAX, THE GREAT

Worldwide: 1835

During the summer of 1835, a series of newspaper reports appearing in the *New York Sun* caused a worldwide sensation. Created by journalist Richard Adams Locke, a Cambridge-educated amateur astronomer and journalist, and *Sun* publisher Benjamin Day, the paper claimed that famed British astronomer Sir John Herschel had perfected the world's most powerful telescope in a South African observatory and could actually see living creatures on the moon.

CONTEXT: Princeton University comparative literature professor Eileen Reeves contends that many readers were willing to believe the spectacular claims about "bat men" on the Moon because of its South African link and discussion of "dark people," corresponding with the American slavery debate that was current at the time.[585]

On Friday, August 21, *The Sun* published a brief account under the heading, "Celestial Discovery." "The *Edinburgh Courant* says – 'We have just learnt from an eminent publisher in this city that Sir John Herschel at the Cape of Good Hope, has made some astronomical discoveries of the most wonderful description, by means of an immense telescope of an entirely new principle.'" There was no further mention of the "discoveries" until the first article in a series appeared on Tuesday, August 25, describing the telescope and the anticipated discoveries. It was apparently intended to establish credibility. The telescope was said to weigh 14,826 pounds (6,731 kg) and to

Life on the Moon, allegedly observed by Sir John Herschel through his telescope.

have the capacity to magnify objects 42,000 times.[586] The appearance of the series coincided with Herschel's well-publicized expedition to South Africa, which he undertook the previous year to use his powerful new telescope that was being set up at a Cape Town observatory. Written in highbrow, scientific language, the articles were purportedly excerpts from the "*Edinburgh Journal of Science*," which in fact had become defunct years earlier.

The second article described lush vegetation and rocks of great beauty before making an even more fantastic claim – the discovery of various life forms on the Moon, including a bluish-gray creature the size of a goat, a powerful looking bison-like mammal, and an array of colorful birds. "In the shade of the woods on the south-eastern side, we beheld continuous herds of brown quadrupeds, having all the external characteristics of the bison, but more diminutive than any species of the *bos genus* in our natural history. Its tail is like that of our *bos grunniens*; but in its semi-circular horns, the hump on its shoulders, and the depth of its dewlap, and the length of its shaggy hair, it closely resembled the species to which I first compared it."[587]

On the 27th, Herschel reportedly classified nine separate types of mammals, including a creature that looked like a two-legged beaver. "The last resembles the beaver of the earth in every other respect than in its destitution of a tail, and its invariable habit of walking upon only two feet. It carries its young in its arms like a human being, and moves with an easy gliding motion. Its huts are constructed better and higher than those of many tribes of human savages, and from the appearance of smoke in nearly all of them, there is no doubt of its being acquainted with the use of fire. Still its head and body differ only in the points stated from that of the beaver, and it was never seen except on the borders of lakes and rivers... [where it] has been seen to immerse for a period of several seconds."[588]

His most astonishing observation came on the fourth day when it was reported that flocks of human-like forms could be seen flying about with bat-like wings. The creatures were given the scientific name of "Vespertilio-homo" meaning bat-man. These beings were described as living in angelic innocence, peacefully co-existing with their fellow creatures in an environment apparently devoid of carnivores. The plausible scientific description of these strange creatures continued: "We could then perceive that they possessed wings of great expansion, and were similar in structure to this of the bat, being a semi-transparent membrane expanded in curvilineal divisions by means of straight radii, united at the back by the dorsal integuments."[589] He went on to describe great oceans and land masses,[590] providing his final installment on Monday, August 31.[591] In this article readers were told that the reflection chamber was damaged and further observations were not possible. By the time the series ended, the *Sun*'s circulation had soared to 19,360, making it the highest circulation of any paper of the day.[592]

During the affair, rival newspapers, frantically trying to confirm the claims, were faced with the dilemma of possibly missing out on one of the greatest stories in recorded history – or being part of a monumental embarrassment if it proved untrue. They could not wait the several weeks it would take to contact Herschel who was incommunicado in a remote part of South Africa, so many newspaper editors and publishers took the gamble and reprinted the story on their front pages.[593] Even the *New York Times* was hoodwinked, remarking that the writer "displays the most extensive and accurate knowledge of astronomy, and the description of Sir John's recently improved instruments...[and] the account of the wonderful discoveries on the moon, &c., are all probable and plausible, and have an air of intense verisimilitude."[594] Locke also published the articles in a pamphlet and sold sixty thousand copies within a month to meet the public's insatiable appetite for the story.[595]

The New York-based *Journal of Commerce* newspaper eventually unmasked the hoax after Locke admitted to fabricating the entire series of events,[596] though the *Sun* publisher steadfastly refused to acknowledge it. On September 16, 1835, the following editorial appeared in *The Sun*: "Certain correspondents have been urging us to come out and confess the whole to be a hoax; but this we can by no means do, until we have testimony of the Scottish or English papers to corroborate such a declaration. In the meantime, let every reader of the account examine it, and enjoy his own opinion." When word of the episode finally reached Herschel, he reportedly erupted with laughter.[597]

Brian Thornton undertook a more recent interpretation of the episode by examining a sample of editorials and letters to the editor of New York newspapers during the affair. His analysis suggests that the extent of the excitement was exaggerated and that *The Sun* claims were meant with considerable skepticism at the time, though many readers accepted the accounts as fact.[598] The episode is noteworthy in that it may mark the beginning of modern tabloid journalism.[599]

MORA WITCH AFFAIR

Sweden: 1664-1676

The Scandinavian countries suffered far less than more southerly regions from the European WITCH MANIA, which makes the sudden and vicious outbreak in late 17th century Sweden all the more difficult to understand.[600] When reports from the countryside alleged that witchcraft was taking place, the authorities were at first reluctant to take action. But as complaints continued to be made, despite the protests of doctors, they decided that rigorous measures were needed. The number of those executed has never been established, but it seems likely to approach 200, including some children, and many other children were severely punished.

CONTEXT: Local social conditions seem to have played the major part, for the origins of this affair came not from any external circumstances but sprang spontaneously from within the affected population, which was rustic and ignorant. No individuals are named as leading the movement, which seems to have derived its content from popular beliefs concerning magic and witchcraft. The stories told by the children are full of folklore details that must have had their origin in fireside storytelling. Thus the Evil One is a red-bearded fellow wearing a pointed cap, similar to figures in popular Swedish tales, rather than the conventional Evil One associated with witchcraft in southern Europe.

In December 1664, a five-year-old boy from Ävdalen, in central Sweden, was bribed with food by villagers to testify against his own family for practicing witchcraft. He asserted that he himself had been taken with them to sabbats on a mountain known as the Blakülla, where they dined on fine food and then beat one another with the furniture. It is remarkable that so unsubstantial a case was taken to court, but so it was, only to be dismissed as a childish fantasy or a dream.

However, it set a pattern for further such accusations. In July 1668, 15-year-old Eric Ericsen accused 18-year-old Gertrud Svensen of stealing several children for the Devil. A spate of such accusations followed, and a great many women were charged, on the basis of testimony by children, of attending the sabbats on the Blakülla. The children were agreed on what they had seen. They told how the witches would call on the devil, crying "Come, Antesser, carry us to the Blakülla!" whereupon he would shortly arrive in answer to their summons. He had a red beard and a pointed cap, and wore red shoes and blue stockings. Yes, he would take the witches to his feast, but only on condition they brought children with them, as many as possible. They might either bring their own children, or borrow them from other homes, leaving dummies that exactly resembled them in their place, so that their parents wouldn't notice. Then off they

The witches gather on the Blakülla in Mora, Sweden.

would fly, mounted on goats or other beasts, on sticks or even astride the bodies of sleeping men; often several children would ride a single mount. They would leave the house through the window; prudently, the devil had first removed the panes of glass, which explains why they weren't found broken next morning.

Their destination was the Blakülla, a place known only to the devil and his associates. It was a lovely meadow with a pretty gate. On arrival the witches had to sign their names in the devil's visitor book (cutting their fingers to use their own blood as ink) and swear obedience to him. Then they were baptized in the name of the devil. After that, the grown-ups enjoyed a delicious feast of cabbage soup and cheese, while the children had to stand leaning against the wall. Dancing and fighting then followed, while the devil, with uncharacteristic modesty, would take the women, one after the other, into a private room to have sex with them. As the skeptical Dutch commentator Balthasar Bekker observed, the devil was evidently partial to mature ladies, for most of the accused women were old hags. The children were reported as being in "strange fits" after being brought home from these excursions, perhaps because at the sabbat the Devil had shown them "a great, Frightful, Cruel Dragon" who would be let loose on them if they confessed to the judges. The children also told of "a White Angel, which did use to Forbid them, what the Devil had bid them to do, and Assure them that these doings would not last long; but that what had been done was permitted for the wickedness of the People. The White Angel would sometimes rescue the Children, from going in with the Witches."[601]

Despite these improbabilities, the courts found 18 women guilty – four of them children. Some had confessed under torture, others were convicted on the testimony of children or fellow villagers. A higher court confirmed the sentences on the seven who confessed, who were then beheaded on top of a funeral pyre and burned.

But the investigations seemed to show that the practice of witchcraft was far more prevalent in the region than had hitherto been supposed, notably in the parish of Mora, where the peasants had actually sent a delegation to Stockholm requesting that action be taken by the authorities to protect their children against perceived danger from the witches. "Such was the perilous Growth of this Witchcraft, that Persons of Quality began to send their Children into other Countries to avoid it."[602] The initial recommendation was that prayer, rather than torture and imprisonment, should be used. But the mass prayer sessions, instead of calming the populace, added fuel to the flames. Ordinary citizens turned themselves into vigilantes, eagerly helping the investigators. Normal standards of testimony were overridden; children had only to point at an individual, and she would be arrested.

In August 1669, a royal commission began its inquiries with a Day of Humiliation. Three thousand people gathered to hear the preaching. The commissioners listened as hundreds of children and their accomplices, the adults who supported them, told of being taken to the Blakülla. On the basis of their testimony alone, for there was no corroborating evidence, 23 more persons, most of them women, were sentenced to death; fifteen of them, who had confessed, were executed at once. The parish priest, who described it as "a horrible spectacle," reported that several thousand people came to witness the executions. The 47 who denied the charges were sent to the nearby town of Falun, where it wasn't long before they too were burned. Not all the victims were grown-ups. The children accused some of their own fellows: 15 children were burned as witches; 36 more, considered less guilty, had to run a gauntlet through lines of men wielding whips; and 20 aged under nine were lashed on their hands once a week for a whole year.

By drawing attention to the widespread nature of the evil, these harsh measures only caused the epidemic to spread more widely. In 1670, reports of more than 300 witches and literally thousands of possessed children were submitted to the authorities. For a while, in the summer of 1675, it became an upper-class entertainment to visit the hospitals where the possessed children were housed. Further commissions were dispatched to other parishes.

Legal experts attached to the commissions considered the trials to be irresponsible and strongly protested against the way in which the statements of small children, and the dubious adult accomplices who encouraged them, were taken as reliable evidence despite the absence of any factual confirmation. The courts replied that this was the only evidence they had, and together with the priests, they succeeded in getting many more death sentences passed. An unknown number of children were affected, and more than a thousand people were arrested and interrogated on the children's say-so. Some children were credited with the ability to identify witches, and were actually paid for their witch-finding services. Not only was this practice liable to abuse, but it naturally led to a protection racket, the shrewd children threatening to accuse people who did not reward them. These children were actually encouraged by priests and parish officers.

The exact number of executions is not known, but it has been suggested that there were at least a hundred additional executions in 1675, the final year of the outbreak. Finally, the governor of the district, who had all along been reluctant, forbade any further executions and received the backing of the king. The commission in the north was stopped. The children began to admit that their accusations were lies, and the last accused women were freed. By 1676 this tragic episode in Swedish history was over.

COMMENT: Generally speaking, the European witch mania was the result of a doctrine being imposed from above, by the ecclesiastical authorities. Although the readiness of villagers to accuse a suspected member of the community was helpful, in that informers identified potential victims, this was a secondary process and would not of itself have brought about the widespread network of accusation and counter-accusation whereby the victims played into the hands of the inquisitors.

In the Mora affair, the contrary seems to have been the case. Village vindictiveness unquestionably brought about the initial incident. Family feuds, neighborly differences, and intra-family quarrels all triggered accusations.

A dominant feature of this Swedish epidemic is the part played by children. The accusations came primarily from children, though it is clear that adults frequently put them up to it. Hundreds of children were said to be possessed, and it was their vivid, if infantile descriptions of the sabbat, with profuse detail, that convinced the authorities to take the matter seriously. The presence of children at the sabbats was insisted on forcibly: the witches were required to take children with them, either their own or children abducted from neighbors.

This accounts for the content of the accusations. The banquet at the sabbat consists of cabbage soup, because the peasant children knew of no finer fare. The "White Angel" who sometimes appears in a rescuer capacity is a folklore entity who plays no part in witchcraft accounts in other countries.

A hideous corollary to the role of the children is the ruthless way in which, when accused by their fellows, they were punished. Children were occasionally executed in other parts of Europe, but nowhere else as viciously as in the Swedish outbreak.

MORAL PANICS AND SYMBOLIC SCARES

Moral Scapegoats: An Overview[603]

The term "moral panic" was popularized by sociologist Stanley Cohen in 1972 and is now an established field of study within sociology. In his seminal book, *Folk Devils and Moral Panics: The Creation of the Mods and Rockers*, Cohen analyzes the exaggerated public reaction to a relatively minor disturbance involving two youth factions (the "Mods" and "Rockers") in Clacton, England, during Easter Sunday of 1964.[604] In formulating his now classic definition, Cohen utilizes a labeling or interactionist view of deviant behavior. Instead of categorizing those who deviate from the norm as a category existing in society and awaiting discovery by authorities, Cohen views deviance as relative, emphasizing the role of social controlling agents (police, politicians, and the media) in both creating and maintaining the deviant label. Cohen states: "A condition, episode, person or groups of persons emerges to become defined as a threat to societal values and interests; its nature is presented in a stylized and stereotypical fashion by the mass media; the moral barricades are manned by editors, bishops, politicians and other right-thinking people... Sometimes the panic passes over and is forgotten, except in folklore and collective memory; at other times it has more serious and long lasting repercussions and might produce such changes as those in legal and social policy or even in the way the society conceives itself."[605]

Sociologist Jeffrey Victor offers a more succinct definition, noting that contemporary moral panics are "characterized by widely circulating rumor stories disseminated by the mass media" and lead to increased fear and hostility among "a significant segment of a society, in reaction to their belief about a threat from a category of moral deviants. Careful, empirical examination at a later time, however, reveals that the perceived threat was either greatly exaggerated or nonexistent,"[606] as occurred with the Popish Plot in 17th century England or the anarchist threat in 19th century America.

CONTEXT: Moral panics are more common during periods of social crisis and serve as a convenient scapegoat mechanism. Jeffrey Victor states: "When, in times of turmoil, new forms of deviance are needed by a society in order to provide scapegoats for deep social tensions, they will usually be invented. Rapid change in a society results in widespread dislocation in people's lives, and the resulting frustration, fear, and anger cause a great many people to seek scapegoats. These scapegoats are, in turn, 'invented' by moral crusaders to bear the blame for threats to a society's past way of life and basic moral values."

The Five Indicators Of Moral Panics

More recently, sociologists Erich Goode and Nachman Ben-Yehuda identified five moral panic indicators: concern, hostility, consensus, disproportionality, and volatility.[607]

Firstly, there must be sufficient concern and even fear about the perceived threat to the community well-being. The concern should be measurable in some way through such means as opinion polls, public commentary via the media, or through organized social movements.

Secondly, the public concern must engender increased hostility towards the identifiable group or category that is perceived as threatening to the community. The advent of hostility towards those responsible for the threat produces a dichotomy of stereotypes consisting of "good" or respectable individuals who want to rid themselves of the undesirable threat posed by the "folk devils." H.D. Barlow draws a parallel between the good versus evil continuum by observing how police routinely round up suspects for crimes based on stereotyped characteristics such as age, race, or socio-economic background.[608] It is worth noting that it is not sufficient for a finger to be pointed at the threatening group: there must be ostensible grounds for hostility. A classic example is the Reichstag Fire in the Nazi demonization of Communists, when on February 27, 1933, Hitler used this event to marginalize Communists and Socialists as the fire was widely thought to have been a sign to begin a revolution.

Thirdly, for a moral panic to materialize, there must be agreement or consensus that a problem or threat exists among at least some section of the society. Goode and Ben-Yehuda contend that moral panics may, however, be limited to a region or section of society. However if the number of people affected is insubstantial, there would be little chance that a moral panic exists.[609]

Fourthly, there is the indicator of disproportionality. There is an assumption that the degree of public concern or numbers of people affected by a moral panic may be disproportionally high compared to the reality of the actual threat posed by the moral panic. Goode and Ben-Yehuda state: "In moral panics, the generation and dissemination of figures or numbers is extremely important – addicts, deaths, dollars, crimes, victims, injuries, illnesses – and most of the figures cited by moral panic 'claims-makers' are wildly exaggerated. Clearly, in locating the moral panic, some measure of the objective harm must be taken."[610] While the degree of objectivity is an important consideration when examining claims about the existence or size of a moral panic, the concept of the moral panic is contingent on disproportionality. For if the degree of disproportionality cannot be determined, it is impossible to conclude that a given episode of concern represents a case of moral panic, as the supposed threat could indeed be a real one. Media amplification and stereotyping are clearly relevant to the disproportionate way in which a threat is portrayed and raises the issue of social constructionism.

Fifthly, moral panics, by their characteristics, exhibit *volatility* in that they may erupt at any time and just as easily subside. Some moral panics leave a residue in terms of ongoing social movements after they have abated, while others dissipate without trace leaving the moral and social fabric of the society intact. However, while they may be short-lived experiences, moral panics may have historical antecedents that have lain dormant over time and re-occurred in the same or other locations. For example, the Renaissance witch craze "flared up at one time and place and subsided, burst forth later in another location and died down, and so on."[611] It should be emphasized that while volatile, moral panics are fundamentally related to structural conditions such as various demographic, political, and gender factors that contributed to the early modern witch-hunts.[612]

Actors In Moral Panics

Much of the moral panic literature examines the underlying motives of the various actors involved. Examples include the Renaissance witch crazes,[613] the Israeli drug abuse panic,[614] and the American drug abuse panic.[615] When analyzing moral panics, it is also important to consider which specific groups emerge as a threat to societal values and interests. Moral panics in themselves do not speak to a silent majority that is simply out there waiting to listen. Rather, they provide raw materials in the form of words and images where individuals are encouraged to identify their deepest interests in terms of initiating or sustaining a moral panic.

The contemporary mainstream sociological approach to studying moral deviation is social constructionism, and advocates of this perspective treat the dimension of claims-making as the primary focus of analysis. Goode and Ben-Yehuda identify five groups of actors who typically have pivotal roles in the creation and perpetuation of moral panics.[616] Firstly, *the media* may be a major vehicle for reporting moral panics and may be responsible for exaggerating the amount of attention given to a particular event. The press may also distort events, fueling mass hysteria over a perceived threat to society. There is also a dimension of *public* concern. There must be some raw material in the first place out of which a media campaign can be built. Without sufficient factual information, public hysteria is unlikely to eventuate, thus negating the possibility of a moral panic. Hence, the media's exaggerated reportage of an event must touch a responsive chord with the public before concern is sufficient to constitute a panic. *Law enforcement* comprise the third group of actors. In times of perceived or real danger to the community, citizens expect that the police and the law courts will act to protect individuals' personal safety. During these occasions ties between the police at local and national levels are strengthened in order to more effectively deal with the problems that Cohen calls diffusion.[617] The next category involves *politicians and legislators* who symbolically align themselves against the perceived forces of evil during periods of societal crisis. They often take immediate action by altering existing laws or by increasing sanctions for infringements against the common good of society. Finally, at some stage moral panics generate appeals or campaigns that may result in the formation of fully-fledged *action groups* who attempt to cope with the new threat. These consist of what Howard Becker termed "moral entrepreneurs" who believe that existing remedies to the problem are insufficient, thus necessitating the formation of a collective response to remedy the situation.[618]

Theories Of Moral Panics

There are three major models used to explain moral panics. According to the *grassroots model*, moral panics emanate from the general public's widespread concern over an event or issue. These expressions of concern also spread to other sections of society such as the law, politicians, and the media. The level of concern initially may not be overt but may build up until the level of strain is such that immediate action is called for to find a solution to the threat. For instance, vigilante patrols might be instituted. As a result, action groups are formed to address the issue. A central characteristic of the grassroots model is that large numbers of citizens perceive a real danger from the threat in terms of their values and personal safety.

The *elite model* follows the Marxist tradition by arguing that elite or the most powerful members of society consciously undertake a campaign to generate and sustain a moral panic across society as a whole. The motive for this course of action is to divert the public's attention from the real problems of society so that the elite can maintain its power base. This enables the elite society members to sustain their domination over the media and the direction of government policies over issues such as law enforcement and the control of resources. This analysis has been advanced by arguing that individuals are persuaded to "experience and respond to new contradictory developments in ways which make the operation of the state power legitimate, credible and consensual."[619]

The *interest group theory* contradicts the elite model by maintaining that the middle class/professional group is more likely to emanate and sustain a moral panic. Goode and Ben-Yehuda argue that professional associations such as church leaders may have a stake in highlighting an issue and be responsible for focusing media attention away from a particular position.[620] This may contradict the interests of elite groups and provide interest groups with their own source of power in terms of the direction or timing of moral panics. While members of interest groups may sincerely believe they are advancing a cause, they may also be advancing their status and power at the same time.

These three theories of moral panics are not mutually exclusive and may be combined. Thus, for example, the early modern witch-hunts derived both from popular beliefs in cures and misfortune but were also "informed" by elite theories of demonic conspiracies. See also: SALEM WITCHHUNTS, RED SCARES, WHITE SALVERY SCARE, CATHOLIC SCARE, WITCH MANIA (EUROPE), FALSE MEMORY SYNDROME.

MORZINE OUTBREAK (POSSESSED TOWN)

Italy-France: 1857-1864

The outbreak of hysterical behavior in the small, remote town of Morzine seemed an isolated event with no ostensible cause. In retrospect, however, it can be seen as a landmark case, bridging between old folk-beliefs and modern science. When it broke out, the symptoms were attributed to demon possession, as at LOUDUN or LOUVIERS two hundred years earlier. But by the time it subsided, the doctors had been able to demonstrate the viability of a natural, as opposed to a supernatural, explanation. Because of the significance of this remarkable event, which distressed the community for seven years, it is described here in some detail.

The symptoms presented at Morzine were strikingly similar to those previously displayed in CONVENT HYSTERIA and other outbreaks, yet here they presented among the townspeople as a whole rather than within an enclosed community such as a convent. Several hundred people were affected, mostly women, including a very high proportion of children. Occurring at a time when scientific medicine was broadening its scope, it provided a unique opportunity for study. Several competent medical men came to observe its phenomena, which sparked off a controversy among scientists and churchmen, and triggered widespread popular interest.

CONTEXT: Morzine is a small town in Haute-Savoie, occupying a very isolated mountain-girt position in the Alps of eastern France. This geographical isolation, which went along with a social and cultural isolation, was unquestioningly a crucial factor in determining the character of the outbreak – and perhaps for enabling it to occur at all. At the time of the incident the population numbered some 2000. The inhabitants, though peaceful and honest, were poorly educated and little developed by the limited culture of the area; fewer than one in ten could read or write. They were strongly pious (Catholic) but retained old beliefs in magic and the devil.[621] They were fond of tales of past times and fantastic legends. It is said that during the winter preceding the outbreak the population had been much taken with the new amusement of table-turning (see SPIRITUALISM), which may have contributed to make the populace more than commonly suggestible.[622]

Many of the men went out of the town to find work, leaving their womenfolk on their own to run the household and look after the livestock, as well as running the family. This also meant that there were an exceptional number of unmarried women. The women's normal evening activity was the "*veillée*," or gathering in one another's homes to drink coffee and exchange stories and gossip. News and rumors alike were swiftly propagated.

A further circumstance of possible relevance was that a somewhat similar incident, though affecting only a single individual, had taken place in the neighborhood shortly before. In 1852 or 1853, a ten-year-old girl named Sylvie had manifested similar behavior in a nearby village. Taken by the church authorities to Besançon, she was declared to be possessed by the devil, and was cured by exorcism. The people of Morzine would have been well aware of the matter.[623]

Yet another circumstance, which however seems to have played no significant part in the affair, is the fact that on April 23, 1860, during the course of the outbreak, Morzine changed from being an Italian town – or to be precise, Sardinian – to being French, thanks to the territorial deal that Napoleon III made after giving military assistance to the Risorgimento. The fact that no commentator has mentioned this except in passing suggests that it was of little or no consequence to the Morzine population and further evidence of their introverted outlook.

The first manifestation of the symptoms occurred on March 14, 1857.[624] A ten-year-old girl named Péronne Tavernier was coming out of church, where she had been preparing for her first communion. By chance, she saw a little girl, who had almost drowned, fished out of the river. A few hours later, at her school desk, Péronne suddenly fainted. She was carried home and was unconscious for several hours. This was the first of several such attacks.

Some weeks later Péronne and her friend Marie Plagnat were minding goats in the fields when Péronne had one of her attacks, and Marie had one too. They were found stretched on the ground, side by side, in an unconscious state. From then on, both girls would lapse into trance-like states five or six times a day. But now, instead of lying motionless, they experienced hallucinations, notably of serpents, and they mimed such actions as opening and reading a letter that sometimes pleased them, sometimes disgusted them. Later, in their normal state, they said they had received letters from the Virgin Mary in Paradise, who said nice things to them, or from the Devil in Hell, who wrote horrid things.

In May, Marie's nine-year-old sister was affected. She would cry out, her eyes turning this way and then rush out of the house and started climbing trees. But she was soon cured by the simple means of intimidation: her father threatened to kill her if she persisted. Then it was the turn of her 15-year-old sister Julienne, who suddenly noticed a scar on her thigh and went into crisis, claiming to be possessed by seven devils. Their brother Joseph, seeing his three sisters behaving in this way, ran into a stream carrying a stick with which he proceeded to batter the water and turn over the stones for a quarter of an hour.

One of the predictions made by Marie was that Péronne's father would himself be afflicted with the malady and would die. This he did, after refusing food for more than a month, clenching his teeth when anyone tried to feed him. His entire family was afflicted with the malady, and their animals died of a mysterious ailment.[625]

Slowly, from isolated cases, the epidemic spread, within families to begin with, or to next-door neighbors, but gradually it was diffused throughout the town. After eight months, 27 had been affected, mostly young girls. If one in a household was affected, it was rare for none of the others to follow. A few months later, more than a hundred men, women, and children of Morzine were experiencing trances and convulsions, seeing hallucinations, and performing acrobatic feats. They lost their appetite, particularly for their customary food. They had a strong repugnance for work and for attending church, both surprising for this pious and hard-working rural community. For the local population, addicted to folktales, there was no doubt that this was the work of magic, and a neighbor or an old maid would be accused of practicing sorcery.

Some claimed they were afflicted only after seeing a black dog they said was the shape taken by Champlanaz, a man suspected of practicing magic. All this was beyond human remedy; only magical or spiritual powers could cope with it. Consequently, the demand that the victims be exorcised came not from the Church and its inquisitors but from the people themselves. Ironically, the Church, which in the past had been the first to impose exorcisms, now refused to do so. Monsignor Rendu, Bishop of Annecy, rejected the priest's request, insisting that the malady was a natural affliction. Perhaps he was mindful of the utterance of the Cardinal of Lyon, at LOUDUN, who said to one of the exorcists, "Don't you see that even if these girls were not possessed, they would come to believe they were on your say-so?"[626]

Nonetheless, the people of Morzine were determined that exorcisms were the answer, and the priest, who shared their opinion, agreed to perform them. At first they took place privately, in the homes of the afflicted, but the populace demanded a visible sign that the Church was concerned with them. So in 1858 a public exorcism took place in the church. The result, said a medical commentator named Richer, was just what was to be expected. The church was packed: as soon as the ceremony commenced, an appalling transformation took place: "One saw nothing but convulsions on all sides, all one could hear was cries, cursing, blows against the seats, insults and threats directed at the exorcists." The experiment was not repeated. The priests and populace reverted to private performances in their own homes. Exorcisms were carried on clandestinely for the next 18 months until the authorities came to hear of them and the priests were forbidden by their superiors to perform the rituals.

When exorcised, the demons spoke through the mouths of the afflicted. But whereas in the 17th century those who spoke were well-known demons – Lucifer, Beelzebub, and the like – at Morzine it was the spirits of dead people, now damned and suffering in Hell, who possessed the victims in a process more akin to reincarnation, or recovering past lives, than to demon possession of the traditional kind. They spoke to warn the living not to follow their example: "I am plunged into eternal fire because I ate meat on a Friday… I've been dead for 31 years, I skipped mass, I disobeyed my parents, I played cards with dissolute people, I blasphemed, I spoke ill of the judge, I'm damned and that's how it should be…"[627] No one seems to have questioned the theological implications of these communications from Hell. Interestingly, the person who stated she was damned for eating meat on a Friday went, every Friday, to the town hall to request a slice of bacon, which she ate eagerly and sometimes raw.[628]

Instead of resolving the epidemic, the exorcisms served to spread it more widely and more rapidly than ever. Exasperation against the supposed sorcerers, thought to be the authors of the affliction, increased. One of them, chased by a crowd of 30 or 40 armed with sticks, forks, and axes, owed his life only to a rapid escape. Dr. Constans, who was investigating the situation on behalf of the authorities, was told by respectable citizens that they were sorry to see him wasting his time, for there wouldn't be an end to the trouble until the sorcerers had had their necks cut, or burned in the public square.[629]

The attacks of the later victims were not like those of Péronne and Marie. To begin with, phenomena of ecstasy, catalepsy, and somnambulism were the rule; now, victims started by having hallucinations. One was haunted by a black dog, another saw a man change into a bird and fly away.[630] Then followed convulsions, as had been the case, Richer notes, at Loudun and Louviers. Dr. Tavernier, the first doctor to investigate, described the progress of seizures:

> A person who is about to have a seizure begins with light tremblings in the arms. The face muscles have light spasms, the eyes flicker and bulge, she utters groans, then, suddenly, her arms bend and stretch, and this spreads to the whole body. Now, her body convulses in all directions as in a violent chorea (jerks), until the head nearly touches the feet; the eyes, sometimes open, sometimes closed, roll with an extraordinary rapidity. Then she starts to curse, in an earnest, raised voice. If she is spoken to, without irritating on contradicting her, she replies violently with all kinds of insult. The convulsions grow more violent during the seizure, the pulse increases, body heat remains normal, the face animated; then comes complete anesthesia, at least as regards the skin: you can pinch or prick her, she seems to feel nothing. If the fits are prolonged, the convulsions cease for a while and she will let herself slump against a wall or furniture, or fall as if exhausted: but after a minute or so she will suddenly leap up as though she has acquired a new secretion of nervous energy, and the convulsions begin again with the same intensity. After the seizure she wears a look of surprise, as if emerging from a dream, not knowing where she is, and ordinarily starts to laugh, having no memory of what has happened, and returns to normal.[631]

In September 1860, after Morzine had passed under French authority, Doctor Arthaud was sent to Morzine to investigate. He established that the children, when in their seizures,

• were in perfect health,

• spoke French fluently, though in their normal state they could speak only a few words, otherwise using the local patois,

• were cheeky and familiar to the point of insolence, though normally they were shy and timid,

• would blaspheme against anything sacred,

• had knowledge of events happening at a distance,

• would give appropriate replies to questions asked in other languages such as German or Latin (though apparently they did not reply in these tongues),

• would announce the time of the start and finish of their fits,

• possessed unwonted strength, so much that it required four men to hold a girl of ten,

• and though they manifested all kinds of convulsions, falls, and hitting, they did themselves no harm,

• and they performed feats which would seem impossible, such as climbing trees 40-50 meters tall with extraordinary rapidity, jumping from one tree to another, descending head down, and so on.[632]

So far as the authorities were concerned, the religious option was out. As the priests were trying to expel demons from the bodies of the afflicted, the doctors wanted to expel them from their minds.[633] On September 30, 1860, the priest, who had hitherto supported the people in their belief in demon possession and their faith in exorcism, publicly declared his belief that he had been mistaken. In view of the medical studies, he said, it was clear that the malady was natural. The effect was immediate and violent: the honest priest was well nigh lynched. The entire congregation rose, striking with anger against the benches and chairs, shouted insults at the preist, and menaced and cursed him, forcing him to interrupt his discourse. Twenty girls and young women who had previously been afflicted now underwent a seizure in the church, and one of them threw a book at the priest's head. The women wanted to climb the pulpit to tear out his eyes, and many went out of the church shouting insults as they left.[634]

The residents of the town were now in a dilemma. There was no one left whose authority they could accept. The church, which they had hitherto trusted, was now in cahoots with the state, and they were left on their own. It is perhaps not surprising that they were disoriented, not knowing where to turn. From this time on, those who still thought that exorcism was the answer had to go outside Morzine to be exorcised, and many did so.

At this point, it seemed to the authorities that the choice was between curing or punishing, and they inclined to the second. The epidemic became a matter for policemen rather than churchmen. The *sous-préfet* of the district issued an order that anyone who had a seizure in public would be arrested. The effect was that the townspeople directed their anger against the secular authorities, who were perceived as acting as agents of the Evil One. In April 1861, the *adjoint*, Berger, narrowly escaped being thrown into the river by a furious crowd, along with two others suspected of sorcery. When slanderous rumors were circulated concerning him, those responsible were imprisoned and fined. When Dr. Arthaud left the town, the fits burst out again: "it seems that the more one occupied oneself with the malady, the worse it got: each intervention by the authorities being followed by a redoubling of the convulsive crises."[635]

When it was seen that the malady was persisting and if anything escalating, the French authorities on April 26, 1861, sent in an even bigger gun, Dr. Constans. He was a very senior medical man, inspector general of the insane, and commanded considerably more clout than his predecessors. Troops were sent to enforce the state's decrees, but they were ordered to mix with the residents, not to appear to be a threat. The afflicted were dispersed to hospitals in the region – a massive operation, since often it meant separating mothers from their families, so that both had to be provided for. But the idea was firm: not one sick person was to be left in Morzine. The difficulty was that, since the authorities made it an offence to have a seizure in public, many made sure that they had them only in their own homes, so that their affliction was not generally known. Some tried to hide, but one by one they were winkled out. In the hospitals to which they were sent, the treatment was work and distraction. As far as possible they were separated, because as long as they remained in groups they tended to set one another off.

Dr. Constans' view was that the population had got this way because of their heredity: of the 120 afflicted he examined, 59 were imbeciles, epileptics, idiots, and the like. He noted the symptoms. Some looked sickly and acted feebly, while others displayed excessive and uncoordinated agitation. Others, in contrast, seemed to be in perfect health, but their character changed. All those things that were normally most important to them – their families, their friends, their religion, even their own children – became indifferent to them. All seemed to manifest an extreme impressionability: normally hard working, now they were unable to apply themselves to any occupation. If they took up some work, they soon changed it for something else, or gave it up altogether. They became capricious in their appetite and would often go for days without eating. They drank too much black coffee. Once they began to have seizures, these would recur at unpredictable intervals, and without any correlating cause. The sight of a stranger, or hearing a displeasing word, or the sight of anything suggesting religion, could bring on convulsions. (The wife of Dr. Tavernier spoke to one of the victims, saying that she had brought a very powerful relic from Rome that could cure her. When the victim agreed, Mme Tavernier touched her on the forehead with the supposed relic – which was of course nothing of the sort – and the patient immediately went into convulsions.) Many tried to conceal their condition, but the greater number "loved to make a spectacle of themselves." They took delight in telling strangers – speaking as though possessed by demons – of things they had done on Earth, and what they did in Hell.

When they spoke, their faces expressed the utmost fury, distorted and frothing at the mouth. In their paroxysms, they would overturn furniture and throw stools or anything that came to hand at anyone present, shouting all the while. They would hurl themselves at people to strike them, even friends and relatives. They stretched on the ground, supporting themselves on their head and their feet. Such seizures would normally last 10 or 20 minutes, or as much as half an hour, but if it was brought on by the presence of a stranger, especially if it was a priest, it was likely to go on until that person left the house. After a while the movements became less violent, and the victim would gradually come to herself and look around her with an astonished air, rearrange her hair, put her bonnet on again, drink a little water, and take up her work just as before the fit. What's more, she would seem in no way fatigued despite the physical violence of her movements. She would insist that she had no recollection of what she had said or done, but Dr. Constans suspected this was not always the case.

Richer observes that, by contrast with the nuns in CONVENT HYSTERIA cases, there seemed to be no erotic element in the fits. If a victim's clothing was ever so slightly immodestly disarranged during her seizure, it would be almost immediately adjusted even though she seemed to be unconscious. In the 17th century cases, the afflicted nuns mingled obscenities with their blasphemies, but though at Morzine a notable symptom was the shouting of blasphemies at relatives, doctors, priests – anyone who represented authority – lewd and obscene speech was almost unknown. A rare exception was the usually timid and well-behaved Jeanne P., who was reproached for unloosing a three-minute tirade of filthy obscenities: "Oh no, sirs," she answered, "you are mistaken, that wasn't me," with the implication that it was the Devil speaking.[636]

On the other hand, some of the Morzine victims manifested a feature noted in other cases, which was that of barking like a dog. While generally their senses were normal, during the seizure anesthesia was always present, but only those parts of the body which were being convulsed. If a victim were agitated only in the upper half of her body, her legs would retain their normal feeling. Their smell and taste were normal, ammonia and chloroform having their customary effect. Actually their sense of smell and hearing were apt to be hypersensitive during the seizures.

A further remarkable phenomenon was the agility of the victims, a symptom frequently observed (see RUNNING AND CLIMBING) though seldom so markedly as here. A dramatic instance occurred as the Plagnat family was returning from the father's funeral. Suddenly, twelve-year-old Joseph quit the procession, raced towards an enormous pine tree, and climbed rapidly to the topmost branch, where he hung head down, singing and waving. His elder brother called up to him, saying this was no time to be playing games. The reproach brought the boy to his senses, but now, realizing his dangerous position, he was petrified with fright. His brother, seeing how things were, cried out, "Devil, go back into this child so that he can climb down!" At once Joseph lost his fear, and skimmed down the tree, head downwards, with the speed of a squirrel.

Dr. Constans' view, rightly or wrongly, was that the men who seemed to be afflicted were not really so. In their case, he thought, one should look to alcoholism, epilepsy, or some mania, which they masked as hysterodemonopathy, following the example of the women and girls afflicted by the fashionable malady. Whether or not he was correct in this diagnosis, his methods seemed to be effective. In January 1862, the authorities believed they could be optimistic, as a decline in numbers was noted: only 13 were now afflicted at Morzine, and all but one of these was sent away. Some of those who had been sent away were now returned and believed cured. Throughout this and the following year, things seemed to be steadily improving.[637]

Then in January 1864, the Church, following a request from the people of the town, sent seven missionaries to the town. The sound of the church bell, announcing the start of the mission, sent several women into convulsions, writhing in contortions and crying out as in the first days of the epidemic. However, this time the priest, knowing what to expect, sent the afflicted at once to their own homes where they would receive personal visits from the missionaries. These priests were forbidden to carry out exorcisms. Instead, what they did was to perform ambiguous rites, not exorcisms exactly, but intensive prayers that troubled the women almost as much. Within a week of sermons and public meetings, eighty cases were recorded.

The secluded town of Morzine, Haute-Savoie, was the scene of an outbreak of collective hysteria.

In April 1864, the prefect of the department paid a visit to the town, and asked to meet and talk to some of the afflicted, hoping to see what plain speaking and common sense would do. Only 20 attended the meeting, held in a schoolroom. They soon went into seizures, rolling on the floor, breaking furniture, and shouting, "Fucking prefect, fucking doctors, there's nothing you can do, only the priests can help us." They attacked the prefect with abuse, oaths, and blasphemies; they kicked and struck him, as though they would tear him to pieces. They leapt with unnatural strength high in the air, foaming at the mouth, and overpowered the policemen present. One smashed a window with her arm, and a fight broke out when a doctor threw water on the face of a woman in seizure and her husband took offence.[638]

The following month, May 1864, the Church's authority, Bishop Monseigneur Magnin, paid the town a visit. This provoked the most violent scene of the entire epidemic. Even as the bishop made his way into the town, he was greeted with insults by the afflicted, fireworks from the disrespectful. People came in from neighboring villages, and the town square was packed. The *sous-prefêt*'s official report stated that, to begin with, seven or eight girls went into seizures. Soon 60 to 80 women had fallen to the ground with fearful cries, rolling between the graves of the cemetery that overlooked the square where the bishop dismounted from his carriage. "Wolf of a bishop! Tear his eyes out! He hasn't the power to cure a girl! He can't rid a girl of the Devil" – such cries continued as he went into the church where 30 or 40 women were already in fits. Only by lifting aside women on the floor-stones could a way be cleared for him to reach the altar. He knelt in prayer for nearly an hour while the tumult raged all around him. Their relatives tried to restrain the afflicted, but with prodigious strength they pulled themselves free and fought their way towards the altar. Only a squad of policemen prevented one woman from striking the bishop; others were stopped just in time from overturning a catafalque with lighted candles.

> So passed this terrible evening, which it is impossible to describe precisely. However, it gives some idea of the appalling disorder which reigned everywhere to say that at more or less the same moment, in the entire commune, in the cemetery, on the public square and the streets, and in the interior of the church, women could be seen in prey to atrocious convulsions, rolling on the ground, agitating their legs and their hands, striking the ground and uttering the same words as before and furious cries.[639]

The following day the Bishop returned to the church, this time to conduct the sacrament of confirmation. But almost at once a crisis so shocking broke out among those present, that the newspaper reporting the incident stated: "The details of this scene are too painful to be told." Fortunately one of those present was less reticent and gave this eyewitness account:

> On the 1st of May I went to see the famous "possessed" of Morzine, and I can assure you, my time was not wasted. Never did the idea of so horrible a spectacle come to my mind or my imagination. The ceremony began at 7 in the morning. I hadn't been in the church five minutes before an unfortunate young girl fell at my feet, in horrible convulsions: four men couldn't hold her; she struck the floor with her feet, hands and head with such rapidity that it was like the beating of a drum. After this another, and then another. Soon the church had become an inferno; on all sides were cries, jostling, cursing and blaspheming enough to make your hair stand on end…The entry of the bishop, above all, set everyone shaking: knockings with fists and feet, spitting, abominable contortions, hair loose in the air together with bonnets, clothing torn, hands bleeding; it was so dreadful that everyone was in tears. The elevation and blessing of the sacrament, after vespers, were, along with the bishop's entrance, the most terrifying moment. All the victims, more than a hundred of them, fell rapidly and simultaneously into convulsions, and it was a racket out of this world. I counted eleven around me, within a radius of two metres at the most. Most were girls or young women from 15 to 30 years of age. I saw one girl of ten, five or six old women, and two men. The bishop, as best he could, bestowed confirmation on some of them. As soon as he approached close to them, they entered into crisis, and with the help of gendarmes and nearby men, he confirmed them all the same in the face of the most horrible curses. "Bastard of a bishop," they shouted, "why do you come to torment us?" [using the familiar "tu" instead of the customary respectful "vous"]. They tried to strike him, to bite him, to tear off his official ring; they spat in his face. Only when they were slapped on the face, they let themselves go and fell into a drowsy state which resembled a deep sleep…Near me was a pretty 18-year old married woman, recently a mother, who cried out, "Bastard of a bishop, you force me to go, I who was so happy in this earthly body, you send me back to hell, what a punishment!" I took her by the hand and tried speaking to her in latin and other tongues, but she didn't reply… the gendarmes were terrified… Afterwards, meeting one of the afflicted people by the roadside, I tried to speak with her but she replied only with a handful of gravel…'[640]

The Bishop spoke to them calmly and sensibly, but this only seemed to exasperate the afflicted all the more. "At the moment of the Elevation, the cries of these frenzied creatures dominated everything, and the detonations of fireworks outside the church, the ringing of bells, mixed with the sound of the organ and religious singing inside the church: the confusion was indescribable." Then things got even worse: the relatives of the afflicted children threw themselves at the Bishop, and for about two hours they assailed and cursed him for not allowing them to have the solace – exorcism – which they insisted was the only thing that could save them.

The Bishop's visit had been the last hope of those who believed that only through exorcism could the malady be brought to an end. Now, this hope was denied them. The authorities, for their part, recognized that the methods hitherto pursued were inadequate. The *sous-préfet* estimated the number of afflicted at 150, and noted that many who had been sent away and had returned apparently cured had, at the sight of so many others afflicted, gone into seizures themselves. In his opinion, it wasn't just the afflicted who were sick, it was the entire town. So now he gave orders for spectacles that would distract people's minds – public dances, musical concerts, lectures in the public library. By contrast, the outward manifestations of religion were kept to a minimum, for in the present climate, it took only the mere sound of a church bell or the sight of a priest passing by to trigger a seizure.

These tactics worked, and gradually the town returned to its senses. The Bishop's visit had been the last major outburst. Though the fits didn't altogether stop, they gradually diminished until in April 1868, only 15 still claimed to be possessed – and that claim was no longer accepted, for now they were regarded as victims of superstition or hallucination, imbeciles or hysterics, or liars. And perhaps reclassifying them in this way, according to the new way of the scientists rather than the old way of the church and sorcery, was the saving factor. The malady was no longer a collective affliction but had become an individual one.

Yet long before the authorities managed to deal with the matter, several parents had found a shorter way to control their children. When young Julienne Plagnat went into a crisis, her father grabbed her by the hair, waved a hatchet, and threatened to cut her neck if she didn't stop at once. She stopped then and there, and never tried it again. Another father, who had just lit his furnace, threatened to put his daughter inside it unless she stopped. Another promised his daughter to give her a new dress if she stopped, but threatened to put her in the cellar if she continued; prudently she opted for the dress. Perhaps, if everyone had behaved as forthrightly as these simple folk, the epidemic that gave Morzine seven years of nightmare need never have happened.

COMMENT: The widespread public interest in the affair ensured that suggested explanations were diverse. The *Gazette Médicale of Lyon* attributed it to Protestant propaganda; others blamed the secular authorities.[641] An 1870 encyclopedia classified it as demonomania, while later commentators lined up with Jean-Martin Charcot and attributed it to "*Grande hystérie.*" Charcot's colleague Richer noted that "hysteria is very common in all Savoie, and mental illness is frequent," sharing Dr. Constans' view that hereditary and environmental factors played a significant part. He diagnosed the Morzine affliction as being an intermediary state between the classic possession cases of the 17th century and the clinical observations of grand hysteria made by Charcot at La Salpêtrière in Paris.[642] [643]

A contemporary account observed:

> The medical opinions that have as yet been pronounced on the Morzine evil seem to us remarkably vague. This harlequin malady unites symptoms of hysteria, epilepsy, mania and gastric disturbances; and yet some principal features which usually accompany each of these diseases are wanting. The excellent health of the "possessed" between the seizures seems to indicate that there is no great physical mischief at work. A physician reports of the women whose cases he observed, "They were fat and fresh-looking, enjoying to the full their physical and mental faculties. It was impossible on seeing them to imagine the existence of the slightest illness."[644]

Catherine-Laurence Maire, a later historian of the outbreak, attributed the trouble in part to tensions caused by the fact that the town, hitherto an almost enclosed community, was at this time starting to confront the outer world. For example, the secular authorities were challenging the Church with such measures as introducing non-religious schools. To the tradition-minded residents, all authority apart from the Church – the mayor, the professors, and the doctors – were seen as threats.

MOTOR HYSTERIA

Symptoms include trance-like states, melodramatic acts of rebellion known as histrionics, and what physicians term "psychomotor agitation," whereby pent-up anxiety building over a long period results in disruptions to the nerves or neurons that send messages to the muscles and triggers temporary bouts of twitching, spasms, and shaking. Motor hysteria is prevalent in intolerable social situations, such as strict school, workplace, and religious settings where discipline is excessive. It appears gradually over time and usually takes weeks or months to subside, but only after the stressful cause has been reduced.[645] Presently, motor symptoms are more commonly reported in non-Western settings and common folk theory holds that those affected are exhibiting demonic possession.

See as examples: MASS HYSTERIA, MASS HYSTERIA IN WORK SETTINGS, MASS HYSTERIA IN SCHOOLS, CONVENT HYSTERIA, DANCING MANIA.

MULTIPLE PERSONALITY DISORDER EPIDEMIC

Mainly in United States: 1970s-1990s

Multiple personality (MP) occurs to individuals, but during the latter half of the 20th century the criteria for Multiple Personality Disorder (MPD) was invented and then diagnosed in such numbers that it can reasonably be regarded as a collective behavior. Previous to 1944 there had been an estimated 76 cases: only a handful more were reported until 1970.[646] The situation then changed dramatically, with figures escalating through the 1980s and 1990s. Between 1985 and 1995 nearly forty thousand cases were diagnosed.[647] Ross in 1992 asserted that one percent of the U.S. population fit the criteria for being a multiple personality, which would bring the number to over two million potential cases in that country alone.[648]

Most patients came from the white population of the United States, 92 percent of them women.[649] As with ALIEN ABDUCTIONS, this imbalance may be because reporting and diagnostic facilities were more accessible in that country; or because practitioners were more alert or better informed as to MPD diagnosis; or, since treatment was very costly, because only a certain section of the population could afford to pay for treatment or the high insurance premiums. Alternatively, some cultural factor may have been at work and led to a greater proliferation of cases, whether or not they were what they seemed or were claimed to be.

CONTEXT: The MPD epidemic occurred at a time of convergence of several social trends, each of which favored such a diagnosis. One was a widespread sense that there is more to life than surface materialism; as organized religion lost much of its hold, movements of all kinds sprang up inviting the individual to realize his full potential by following this or that path to self-realization. On a popular level, this often took the form of "New Age" thinking, but it was reflected across society as a whole.[650] While it would be simplistic to think that a person might reason that to possess three personalities would give her three times the opportunity for self-realization, MPD could give that illusion by providing her with a means for self-expression unavailable to her everyday personality.

A second factor was the feminist movement, which sought to end male dominance and oppression by asserting an equal place in society. Not only were most MPD patients women,[651] but the nature of their disorder emphasized in many cases the need for self-assertion: typically, an MPD patient who was timid and subservient in her normal state would develop a secondary personality who was brash, assertive, and sexually liberated. Many books of guidance, written to help possible MPD patients come to terms with their situation, read like feminist tracts.

Most importantly, the MPD epidemic coincided with, and largely overlapped, the repressed memory controversy, in which many thousands of people, particularly women, came or were brought to believe that they possessed "hidden memories." These memories were generally of being abused, particularly sexually, during their childhood. Often, the abuse was thought to have occurred in the context of "satanic" rituals, during which they were forced to undergo and participate in such anti-social practices as incest, rape, murder, and cannibalism. The psychological conflict created by unconscious awareness of these childhood adventures led, it was claimed, to the creation of alternate personalities ("alters") who knew about them even though the individual's conscious primary personality had suppressed the memory.

A British psychologist commented that MPD was clearly not a "culture-free" diagnosis: "A principal reason for questioning the existence of multiple personalities as a discrete clinical entity is their spiralling numbers in the United States contrasted with their virtual absence elsewhere...The United States not only loves its movie stars, it also loves its psychiatrists, psychoanalysts and psychologists...North Americans have integrated psychology into their daily lives as part of personal growth as well as crisis intervention or treating mental illness."[652]

Cynics discerned a further contributing factor, that "in America, psychotherapy is probably a billion dollar a year business with little or no quality control or oversight."[653]

The Problem Of Diagnosis

In 1970, MP was defined as follows: "A rare dissociative reaction in which two or more relatively independent personality systems develop in the same individual...Each of the personalities has characteristic and well-developed emotional reactions, thought processes, behavior patterns, and mannerisms... Usually the personalities are strikingly different and even opposite...The patient changes over from one personality to the other suddenly and without warning, for periods lasting from a few seconds to a few years."[654]

Goldenson emphasized that MP was not a fundamental fragmentation of the individual, but "a gross exaggeration of normal behavior." Those afflicted are people who possess "such acutely incompatible urges that they do not succeed in adjusting their different personality tendencies to each other, and when subjected to stress may unconsciously...cut away the unacceptable side of their personality and mold it into a separate self which appears to act on its own." In 1980, when MPD was first listed in the authoritative *Diagnostic and Statistical Manual of Mental Disorders*, published by the American Psychiatric Association, the criterion was "the existence within the individual of two or more distinct personalities, each of which is dominant at a particular time," which is noticeably more strongly affirmative than Goldenson's definition.

Dissociation has been recognized since the 19th century as a mental phenomenon. In 1880 Pierre Janet interpreted it as occurring when "systems of ideas are split off from the major personality and exist as a subordinate personality, unconscious but capable of becoming represented in consciousness through hypnosis."[655] His patient Léonie, for example, swung from one state to another with sufficient clarity that he could name one as Léontine, another as Léonore.[656] He noted that the mere act of naming a secondary personality tended to reinforce its identity, and the more she was addressed in that personality, the stronger the identity became – an observation that should have carried a warning to the American practitioners of the 1980s that the secondary personalities they "discovered" might be artifacts created by their own suggestions.

Some of the pitfalls of suggestion were foreseen by William James in 1890: "It is very easy in the ordinary hypnotic subject to suggest during a trance the appearance of a secondary personage with a certain temperament, and that secondary personage will usually give itself a name. One has, therefore, to be on one's guard in this matter against confounding naturally double persons and persons who are simply temporarily endowed with the belief that they must play the role of being double."[657] In 1977, before the dramatic proliferation of MPD, Hilgard noted: "Sufficient caution has not always been exercised by the psychotherapist to distinguish between what he discovered and what he produced."[658] The following decade would show the need for such a warning.

Historical Summary

The ability of an individual to present strongly contrasted personalities had been observed long before MP was identified and named. In 1789, when French refugees were fleeing into Germany to escape the Revolution, a 20-year-old German woman of Stuttgart suddenly began alternating her personality with that of a French aristocrat, speaking French perfectly but speaking German with a slight accent. In her French state, she remembered everything she had said and done on other occasions in that state, but in her German state she knew nothing of it.[659]

Twenty years later, in America, Mary Reynolds, who had "fits" as a child, at the age of 18 experienced a prolonged sleeping state from which she emerged as a totally different person who did not recognize her family or surroundings, but who was buoyant and social where originally she had been taciturn and morose. Thereafter she alternated between the two independent personalities, until finally, at about age 35, she remained in her second state for the last 25 years of her life.[660]

A somewhat similar case, Felida X., a French country girl, was investigated by Azam over a 30-year period from 1858. She differed from Mary Reynolds in that her second self was aware of her first self, though the first remained unaware of the other. By 1888 her more social second self was almost always in control; her original self appeared only occasionally.[661]

In 1897 a minister's son, Thomas Hanna, fell from a horse-carriage and lost consciousness. When he recovered, a totally new and richer personality gradually developed. His case, closely studied by Boris Sidis, threw much light on the psychological process involved in switching personalities.[662]

The following year Morton Prince received as a patient Clara Fowler ("Christine Beauchamp" in the report) who set the pattern for subsequent MP studies by seeming to fragment into two and then three persons, one serious and retiring, the second out-going and assertive, then a third who seemed wiser than both and combining their more useful qualities.[663]

In 1929 a man in his fifties was found wandering in Los Angeles, unaware who he was and what he was doing. Identified as Charles Poulting, he was able to account for only part of his past life. Subsequently, he was found to be an Irishman named Poultney, but he had lived a considerable part of his life as Poulting, including military service in Europe and Africa.[664]

In each of these cases the subject seemed to have introduced one or more additional personalities into his life in order to resolve a situation that had become unsatisfactory. Less extreme solutions to such situations might have been fugue, amnesia, or other hysterical behaviors. However, the form of the fragmentation differed one from another in almost every possible way – occasion of onset, periodicity and duration, number and completeness of the personalities, and mutual awareness from one personality to another. Evidently each patient evolved his own strategy to suit his own needs. Furthermore, in most of these cases the dissociation was spontaneous, preceding any medical intervention, and in the exception, Clara Fowler, the secondary personality seems to have emerged spontaneously during hypnosis without any prompting on Prince's part.

Whether such cases should be labeled as a distinct diagnostic category, or included as a variant with other dissociative disorders, has always been and remains a debated question. But the distinction would have been of minor importance had it not been for the MPD mania of the 1980/90s. Hitherto, the relative rarity of the disorder meant that it received little attention from practitioners. This changed in the latter half of the 20th century thanks to two high-profile cases.

The first was that of Christine Sizemore, whose story was first presented professionally in 1954, then three years later in a popular book followed by a film with the same title, *The Three Faces of Eve*.[665] As recounted by therapists Corbett Thigpen and Hervey Cleckley, the alternate personality manifested suddenly and spontaneously, leading to the emergence of a third. The suggestion has been made, however, that the therapists may have unintentionally cued their patient unawares.[666] In 1975, Sizemore revealed her identity to the world: she appeared on television and lecture platforms, and wrote two further books telling her story, revealing that she had in all 21 personalities.

Sizemore's "coming out" may have been triggered by the 1974 publication of *Sybil*, a dramatic account based on New York psychiatrist Cornelia Wilbur's 19-year treatment. Though, as noted below, Wilbur's handling of the case raised serious doubts, but at the time these two books aroused wide interest and inspired others to tell their story. One of many, *When Rabbit Howls*, claimed to be the autobiography of "the ninety-two personalities who share the body of the woman known as Truddi Chase."[667]

At the same time there came a spate of books on the subject of multiple personality from practitioners and other authorities, reflecting all shades of opinion about every aspect of MP, from enthusiastic acceptance to concerned skepticism.[668] Publications on the subject outnumbered those published before 1970 by sixty to one. Together with conferences, these had a snowball effect, which soon spread beyond the professional to the popular media. Talk shows featured therapists and their patients telling their sensational stories; a program on the popular Oprah Winfrey show was entitled, "MPD: the Syndrome of the '90s." Thigpen and Cleckly had tens of thousands of cases referred to them after publishing their account of Sizemore's treatment, (though in all those cases they found only one that they considered genuine).[669] When author Flora Schreiber was negotiating the publication of her book *Sybil*, based on an alleged MPD case of a woman with 16 alters, Herbert Spiegel, who had been in on the case, objected, insisting that Sybil was not an MP case, and that her personalities were artificial fragments created by the therapist. But he learned that the publishers wouldn't accept anything but a multiple: "That's what the publisher wants. That's what will make it sell." Which it did.[670]

In 1980, after considerable lobbying by practitioners, MPD was recognized as a dissociative disorder in its own right, as opposed to just one among many forms of hysteria, in the *Diagnostic and Statistical Manual of Mental Disorders*. This promotion was more than a name-change: as a recognized ailment, MPD now required treatment. There was no other form of treatment than one-to-one sessions with therapists, once or more a week, over months and often years. Moreover, it was covered by health insurance. By diagnosing MP, practitioners acquired a lucrative patient and attracted funding for hospital departments.

In 1992 at Sheppard Pratt Health System, Baltimore, the number of MPD diagnoses increased 900 percent after an MPD expert joined the staff.[671] "A widespread mental disorder that had no accepted drug treatment and that required three to five years of two or three extended [1.5 hours] sessions per week – this was the answer to a prayer....[Diagnosis could] turn a $2,000 eating disorder patient into a $200,000 multiple personality disorder."[672] It was also noted that "the distribution of MPD cases is bizarre...The vast majority of talented, sensitive, observant clinicians have never seen a case at all. A very small number of clinicians report the great majority of case reports."[673]

This dramatic increase in the number of cases was attributed to previous failure to recognize MP as an ailment. "It appears most likely that the modern increase in the diagnosis of DID/MPD patients... is the natural outcome of the mental health professions' increasing sophistication with regard to the diagnosis of this group of patients."[674] Therapists insisted that the MPD cases had been there all the time, they had simply not been diagnosed previously, either because practitioners were unaware of the ailment, or because they were reluctant to diagnose an ailment so rare. Few at this stage were prepared to consider whether some other factor might be at work. But such a factor existed.

Mp And Child Abuse

In the 1980s, widespread rumors seemed to indicate that child abuse, particularly in association with "satanic" rituals, was extremely prevalent in the United States, with tens of thousands of children being kidnapped or murdered for sacrificial purposes, or forced to take part in orgies, or exploited in child prostitution and pornography, supposedly favorite activities of Satanists (see our entry on SATANISM). Cleverly, it was alleged, the ritualists contrived for participants to repress their memories of these activities, with the result that most people were unaware of what they had done, or had done to them, as children.

These rumors were supported by popular books, notably *The Courage to Heal*,[675] and reinforced by television appearances, lectures, and meetings. Police forces were alerted to the danger, and seminars and conferences asserted the existence of a nation-wide, perhaps even international, network of abusers. This was the stuff of which headlines are made, and ritual abuse was widely featured on high-profile television chat shows, creating a climate in which very many, especially women, came to believe that they too had suffered in this way. The reality of the danger seemed confirmed by court cases such as the McMartin trial – the longest and costliest trial in American legal history, and one of the most publicized – in which the managers of a pre-school were accused of sexually abusing their pupils.[676] In 1985, at least one million people in the U.S. were falsely accused of child abuse.[677] Of course, in only a small percentage of these cases did the victims seek treatment, and only a small percentage of those were diagnosed with MPD; nevertheless an estimated 40 thousand cases were so diagnosed. A 1991 survey revealed that more than 10 percent of clinical members of the American Psychological Association had treated patients who "recalled" hidden memories of cult abuse. Virtually all the clinicians believed those memories to be true.[678]

Therapists were not only swept along in this tide of hysteria but contributed to it in their turn. Faced with patients presenting psychological problems for which they could not account, they suspected an inner conflict caused by the possession of hidden memories of childhood abuse. They asked questions such as: "Do you feel different from other people?" or "Do you often feel taken advantage of?"[679] Sometimes such simple questioning was sufficient to bring out the hidden memories, while others had to be coaxed out via hypnosis. It was at this stage that MPD was diagnosed: "The majority of the patients who eventually receive this diagnosis come to therapists with standard psychiatric complaints, such as depression or difficulty in relationships. Some therapists see much more in these symptoms and suggest to the patient...that they represent the subtle actions of several alternative personalities, or 'alters,' co-existing in the patient's mental life."[680] Supposedly, as a survival strategy, the "memories" had been "hidden" by entrusting them to an alter who became their guardian. By encouraging the alters to come out and reveal her childhood ordeal, a therapist could guide the afflicted adult to come to terms with her past and rebuild her life. "During this period, MPD therapists also became incest-resolution therapists, and by the 1980s, the alter personalities of MPD patients began increasingly to be conceptualized as the repositories of memories of sexual abuse that were hidden from the main or host personality. In short, the enactment of MPD came increasingly to involve the recovery of more and increasingly horrendous abuse memories that were 'held' by more and more alter personalities."[681]

It had already been noted that childhood abuse – though not of the "satanic" kind – featured in many MP cases. Psychiatrist Eugene Bliss went so far as to assert that the "evidence suggests that most personalities…are produced by abuse and mistreatment, usually in childhood." Though he described the world of his MP patients as a "land of fairy tales," he insisted that the tales were built on a substratum of fact. In cases in which he had been involved, "all traumas were verified as actual occurrences, with two exceptions."[682] Few therapists, however, went to so much – if any – trouble to verify their patients' claims, insisting that it was sufficient to "believe the patient." By the mid-1980s, one in four MPD patients traced her problems to ritual satanic abuse; by 1992 that figure had doubled.[683]

The therapy sessions were intense and traumatic. The patient would be questioned for hours on end to persuade her to disclose her life history. Any hint she gave would be seized upon as evidence. It didn't even have to be verbal –a body movement could be a "body memory," so that a patient who experienced chronic pain in her arms might recall that she was hung up by the wrists in a satanic ritual.[684] The procedure was uncomfortably reminiscent of the exorcisms of allegedly possessed persons in the 17th century. (See references under CONVENT HYSTERIA.) The patient, already weakened or disoriented by whatever was afflicting her and often numbed by years of treatment, found herself confronted by a professional who was already convinced in her own mind that the MP was there, latent, waiting to be extracted. In such a context, the therapist became an authority figure commanding emotional dependence; more educated than the patient, professionally versed and experienced, supportive and encouraging where the patient's previous social experience may have been indifference or even hostility, it is not surprising that a patient would be anxious to retain this favor by stifling her doubts and giving the therapist what he or she wanted. "Patients in psychological crisis welcome an explanation of their turmoil and inner disarray. Often they long for a reason for their pain, and are vulnerable to the therapist's convictions and beliefs about the causes."[685] Therapists justified themselves by citing Freud: "We must not believe what they say, we must always assume, and tell them, too, that they have kept something back because they thought it unimportant or found it depressing…"[686]

The therapy sessions were also long drawn out. The therapists themselves admitted that "an average of 6.8 years had elapsed between these patients" first mental health assessments and their being diagnosed accurately.[687] Sybil's treatment lasted eleven years and required more than two thousand visits to her therapist. Frequently, treatment ceased only when the patient could no longer afford to pay for it, or her insurance ran out. Even if a fusion of the personalities was triumphantly achieved, post-fusion therapy was required to maintain stability in more than 90 percent of cases, and even then relapse was frequent. Psychologist Richard Kluft, one of MPD's strongest advocates, asserted that a patient's cure frequently left her with "single personality" disorder and that retraumatization led to relapse in virtually every case.[688]

The one-to-one sessions were only part of the process. Once the alters had been coaxed out of their hiding-places, they were welcomed to self-help and support groups, workshops, and reinforcement events of all kinds, as well as given books and newsletters to read. Patients who may have been self-conscious about their histories now felt welcomed and encouraged. They were made to feel privileged rather than persecuted; they were on the high road to self-fulfillment. "Patients often re-create themselves in the mold of the survivor, their beliefs forming the basis of a new identity and world view."[689]

The process of creating an alter was explained to Bliss by one of his patients, speaking as one of her personalities, who said of her: "She creates personalities by blocking everything from her head, mentally relaxes, concentrates very hard, and wishes." Bliss perceptively pointed out: "The crux of the problem is whether patients are consciously playing a role or are someone else."[690]

For the therapist, it was an exciting challenge. "If someone comes into my office and it's kind of a depression and I'm kind of working through their life, it's not as exciting as if I'm in a life-and-death struggle with devil personalities and hooker personalities and little-crying-child personalities."[691] A revealing incident occurred when therapist Cornelia Wilbur, during her treatment of Sybil, had temporarily to entrust her to a colleague. When Sybil came to therapy with Herbert Spiegel, she asked, "'Do you want me to be Peggy, or can I just tell you?' Asked what she meant, she explained, 'When I'm with Dr. Wilbur, she wants me to be Peggy.' Spiegel told her she could be Peggy or not, as she liked. She was relieved, and chose not to assume different personalities when she was with him."[692]

The degree of personalization, and the interplay between the personalities, varied from one patient to the next. Bliss reported that "every gradation of awareness can be found if enough patients are studied."[693] Moreover, they took many forms, which varied from one therapist to another. Bliss confirmed Ernest Hilgard's finding that one of the personalities might be a "hidden observer" who is considerably more intelligent and perceptive than the primary personality. One of his patients produced an alter who described herself as intelligent, enjoying visiting with people of intelligence: "I enjoy quiet evenings, going to places of historic interest. If I had all the time to myself, I'd live in a library." She was able to guide Bliss in his treatment.[694] Psychiatrist Ralph Allison, on the other hand, identified an entity he named the Inner Self Helper; everyone, he claimed, has one of these from birth, "though in a multiple personality, the ISH appears as a separate individual."[695]

Whether "hidden observers," "inner self helpers," or straightforward alters, they came in all shapes and sizes from two-year-old children (who nonetheless had vivid memories of their abuse) to wise old elders. Some patients required huge numbers of alters to express every facet of their nature. Kluft found that one of his patients possessed 4,500.[696] Skeptics mocked such figures, and also the nature of the personalities, which often resembled stock characters from melodrama – the whore, the good-time girl, and the battered child. Though each had its distinctive features, they tended to be two-dimensional, lacking the complexities presented by a real person.

Allison further claimed that many alters were in fact cases of possession – that is to say, not creations of the patient, but invaders from elsewhere who forced their way into suitably vulnerable patients.[697] Possession had been the diagnosis favored by the Catholic Church for many mental afflictions of the medieval and early modern periods (see DEMON POSSESSION), and some early MP cases appeared to support the possibility. In 1919, philosopher Charles Cory described the case of Maria, whose secondary personality claimed to be the spirit of a long-dead Spanish woman.[698] Allison was not the only therapist to revive this approach in the late 20th century. Psychologist James Friesen went further, reaching the conclusion that some of his patients were possessed by demons, and went so far as to perform exorcisms on them.[699] These, however, were exceptions to the general pattern, as were the conspiracy theorists who attributed the proliferation of child abuse to the CIA, which was turning children into "Manchurian candidates" using drugs, electric shock, etc.[700]

What brought the epidemic to an end was the total absence of any convincing factual basis. Official investigations, while not denying that some child abuse did indeed take place, showed that it was almost always a family matter, and not a scrap of evidence for the wilder claims was ever produced.[701] Victims had been advised: "To say 'I was abused,' you don't need the kind of recall that would stand up in a court of law."[702] It was bad advice, as ultimately they did need such evidence. In the early stages of the epidemic, supposed victims not only accused their parents but sued them and were awarded large sums by the courts. Later, the accusations were directed against the therapists. For example, 35-year-old Elizabeth Carlson had been led by her therapist to "remember" that she had been molested as child by some fifty relatives – her parents, grandparents, even her great-grandparents. When she came to realize the absurdity of the charges, she sued her therapist and was awarded $2.4 million in damages.[703] Which was just as well, for the cost of those weekly sessions, year after year, was very high. One innocent family incurred medical costs of over $3 million for therapy, which included the three-year hospitalization of two sons, aged four and five, who provided details of the murder and cannibalism they had performed as members of a satanic cult. Another patient spent two years in a private psychiatric hospital at a cost to her insurers of $1,200 a day. "Her insurance money finally ran out, and when she stopped receiving treatment for MPD, she stopped having MPD."[704]

An important role in the return to reason was played by the False Memory Foundation, created in 1992, supported by several leading psychologists as well as by families falsely accused of abusing their relatives. In a notable experiment to demonstrate how easily false memories can be implanted in a suitably suggestive subject, sociologist Richard Ofshe "fed" a false incest event to an accused father, and the following day the father recalled it as fact, narrating it in florid detail entirely supplied by his own imagination.[705] Gradually the more extreme claims were withdrawn, as more and more therapists were successfully being sued for implanting false memories in their patients. The MPD epidemic had risen and was sustained on the basis of ritual abuse. When it became evident that there was little or no evidence for ritual abuse, the epidemic collapsed.

The effect was to cast doubt on the whole concept of multiple personality. Clearly, MPD had been extravagantly over-diagnosed; if MP fantasies could so easily be created, perhaps the concept of MP was itself a delusion. In the 1994 edition of the *Diagnostic and Statistical Manual of Mental Disorders*, MPD was discreetly replaced by DID – Dissociative Identity Disorder. Referring to the MPD movement, Paul McHugh has commented, "In but a few years we will all look back and be dumbfounded by the gullibility of the public in the late twentieth century and by the power of psychiatric assertions to dissolve common sense."[706]

COMMENT: "What, really, is an ego state, alter, or 'part?' Are these spurious enactments, or do they reflect the deep underlying organization of the client's psyche in a profound way?"[707] The dilemma with which MPD challenged practitioners was neatly summed up at the height of the epidemic by Lisa Uyehara: "Is this a rare disorder that is being over-diagnosed by some who are fascinated by the diagnosis? Is this a common disorder, which has been misdiagnosed or underdiagnosed for decades? Is this a once rare disorder become common today because some confluence of social forces has produced dramatic increases in the prevalence of the most extreme forms of childhood trauma?"[708] Ofshe asserted: "MPD is either a widespread pathology or, like demonic possession, a role that has been forced on vulnerable people in a misguided attempt to cure them."[709]

The history of the MPD epidemic requires that a distinction be made between spontaneous and induced MP. Either way, MP is a fantasy artifact created in the mind of the subject, but there is good reason to believe that this can occur "naturally," as a strategy deliberately chosen unconsciously by the patient. It seems likely that only some people are prone to or capable of this, those who are "naturally dissociative." These may well be the same population as constitute the "encounter-prone" population proposed by Ken Ring[710] and the ASC-prone (altered states of consciousness) population proposed by Hilary Evans.[711] Such people are characterized as being above-average suggestible and good hypnotic subjects.[712] They are liable to report paranormal experiences such as psi incidents, out-of-the-body experiences, and the like.[713] They are likely to readily fantasize and are often unable to distinguish between reality and fantasy. This could be a matter of temperament, or brought about by circumstances such as trauma.

What happened in the 1980s was that therapists came to believe that MP provided the explanation for the "hidden memories" they believed their patients possessed, and which would reveal their involvement in ritual abuse. They set to work in the belief that they were revealing these personalities, unaware that instead they were creating them. This was facilitated by two aspects of mental activity for which insufficient allowance is generally made: on the one hand, the capability for fantasy-creation, vividly illustrated by the Ofshe experiment mentioned above; on the other, the tendency to role-playing which we all share.

There is little doubt that MPD – of a kind – occurs. Whether it should be regarded as a disorder in its own right is questionable. Psychologist Nicholas Spanos suggested that "MPD is a contextually supported social product that is shaped by diagnostic practices and legitimated as a 'real disease' by psychiatric authority."[714] Psychiatrist Harold Merskey asserted, "It is likely that MPD never occurs as a spontaneous persistent natural event in adults."[715] However, MP, as a conflict-resolving strategy, appears to be a genuine psychological process. The danger is that it can be artificially induced, with the horrific results that were seen in the U.S. in the 1980s/1990s.

Case Histories

We have chosen two illustrative cases, one from a hundred years before the American epidemic, the other occurring during its course.

1. Before the epidemic: This case from 1895 took place in northeast London.

At the age of 13, Mary Wood had an attack of meningitis associated with influenza. During the third and fourth weeks of the illness, there was high temperature with delirium bordering on mania; she called people snakes and did not recognize her friends. In the fifth week, during convalescence, she began to give those around her names which were not their own: thus, her father became "Tom," her mother "Mary Ann," etc. About the sixth week attacks of secondary consciousness appeared. She would suddenly turn a somersault on the bed and assume a new character, then return suddenly to the normal and resume what she had been occupied with before the attack. At first the seizures lasted from ten to fifty minutes, but increased to hours, days, and weeks as time went on. The secondary self knew nothing of the primary one, and vice versa; furthermore, the secondary self had apparently lost much of the knowledge the primary self had acquired. Thus, in the second state the patient did not know what her arms and legs were and was childish in her talk. She could write her name, however, but this she did backwards, beginning at the tail of the last letter and writing quickly from right to left – not mirror-writing.

Various others showed themselves from time to time, sixteen in all. In each stage the patient remembered what had happened during previous attacks of the same stage, but knew nothing of what had occurred in any of the other stages, while the primary consciousness remembered only her normal life and knew nothing regarding the incidents that happened in the others. At the end of a year the normal condition rarely appeared, and then only as a flash – sometimes coming to the surface for five or ten minutes, sometimes only for a few seconds.

The following states were noted, most being named by the patient herself:

a. "Thing" was vacant, knew nothing of her past life, could not stand.

b. "Old Nick" was passionate and mischievous.

c. Cataleptic, deaf, mute, but wrote down all she wanted.

d. Forgot not only the incidents of normal life, but apparently also much of the general knowledge acquired during it. In writing, she spelt backwards in the manner described.

e. Characterized by terror.

f. "Good thing" was docile, but usually without power in feet or hands.

g. "Pretty dear" was sweet and amiable, but could not write or spell.

h. "Mamie Wud" recalled the events of childhood better than when awake, but unable to remember anything about her illness.

i. Knew nothing, thought she was just born.

j. "Old Persuader" asked for a stick to strike people if they would not do what she wished.

k. "Tom's darling" was apparently a nice child.

l. Asserted she had "no name" and was violent and unkind.

m. "The dreadful wicked thing" threw her slippers into the fire in a temper, etc.

n. "Tommy's lamb" was blind and idiotic.

o. In December 1896 a further stage developed, which lasted for two months. She constantly repeated the word "picters," and drew beautifully, even when prevented from seeing the paper on which she was drawing. The original self was unable to draw.

In July 1898 she passed into a condition more closely resembling the normal one. She was still, however, childish, and called herself "Critter Wood."

In the spring of 1890, five years after the commencement of her illness, she had apparently settled down into stage (g), but had been taught that "Mary Wood," not "Pretty dear," was her name. She was a fine, healthy, well-developed girl, who helped in the house and was anxious to learn typewriting in order to keep herself. Her character, however, differed slightly from her original one, and she was still somewhat childish at times.[716]

COMMENT: Seen from today's perspective, there is reason to suspect that Mary was often role-playing and perhaps mischievously inventing new roles. However, the initial dissociation seems to have been spontaneous, and genuine enough.

2: During the 20th century epidemic: This case is condensed from her own account and gives some insight into the state of mind of a patient and how she could be drawn into the MPD delusion.

"Nell Charette," a 35-year-old Canadian cleaning woman, went to therapist Milt Kraemer with her psychological problems. "He seemed to be one of the nicest men I'd ever met. Very kind, very understanding…" Under hypnosis, he introduced her to her "inner child," which he named Little Nellie, who was, he told her, "the wounded me." Soon they "discovered" two more parts of her, a 14-year-old boy named Pete, and The Baby who was less than two years old. He instructed her alters to write down their memories, and she began to write "the most horrifying things you can imagine" that her father had done to her. When she took it to Kraemer, she said "This is all garbage" but he insisted that she was angry and in denial. Over the next two years, she filled 15 notebooks. "I couldn't understand why I was writing this crap. It was horrible, it was pornographic."

At subsequent sessions more alters emerged: "There's a whole slew of them, coming out from behind trees… one named Flo, she was 21 maybe, the tart in me. June, she was the spiritual one. Fred, who wanted to die. Sarah, a child about 11…" Each one remembered horrible things her father had done to her.

Though she didn't confront her father, she started alienating herself from her parents. She questioned her mother about her childhood, searching for confirmatory detail. "It wasn't a real truth to me yet. But I did start to take on the feelings of a Sexual Survivor." She joined a support group, where she shared her "memories" with other "victims." "The sicker we were, the better. It was sort of like, Who can top this?" She became really ill, to the extent of hallucinating: "I'd look in the mirror and it wouldn't be me, it would be one of my alters." She began eating compulsively. The voices of her alters carried on conversations in her head. When she began mutilating herself, pulling her toenails off, Kraemer explained it was one of her alters in pain.

Her friends were alarmed at her condition. Things got to the point that she decided to take a break from therapy for a month. The longer she stayed out of therapy, the more she started seeing it for what it was. She went to Kraemer's director, who told her he didn't think she had MPD, that it was being created in her, and gave her a paper on the false memory syndrome to read. She went to an independent psychiatrist who confirmed that she didn't have MPD and never had.

She terminated the therapy and gradually recovered her reason. But her marriage had been destroyed, leaving her with the three children. She told her father that she had believed he abused her. Her parents convinced her that everything the alters had written in those journals were lies. She took Kraemer to court for his treatment.

"In a way being MPD made me feel special and creative. But that discovery isn't worth what I've been through and my ruined marriage. The hunt for sex abuse memories is the con of the '90s. I feel humiliated and stupid to have been so gullible."[717]

MUMMY'S CURSE FAINTING FITS

Turin, Italy: 2001-2002

Starting in March 2001, three fainting episodes occurred while visitors were passing by a pharaoh's mummy exhibited at the Turin Egyptian Museum. In

2001, two teens from Como, Italy, experienced headaches, dizziness, and a feeling of extreme heat while near the mummy. The following month a young girl from Genoa, Italy, was taken to a hospital after suffering similar symptoms. The most recent report occurred on January 16, 2002, when a trio of eight-year-old girls suddenly felt dizzy and ill, with one of them passing out. Italian pediatrician Federico Signorile reported that tests of the girls' blood ruled out carbon monoxide poisoning. Each of the "fits" occurred while the girls were visiting the tomb of the Pharaoh Ini.[718] In all, over a dozen incidents of illness or fainting were reported. Investigators later suggested the cause as poor ventilation.[719]

COMMENT: Archeological excavations, including pharaohs, have attracted more than their share of "curse" rumors. The prevalence of these legends has been widely narrated, perhaps most effectively by Philipp Vandenberg in *Der Fluch der Pharaonen*. However intriguing as folklore, it is unlikely that there is anything more to these tales than popular legend. But this does not rule out psychological effects. The stories have been widely disseminated and might perhaps influence anyone visiting such a museum.[720]

MUSHROOM MADNESS

Papua New Guinea: October 1954 and ongoing

During October 1954, Australian anthropologist Marie Reay was visiting the Southern Wahgi Valley in the Western Highlands of Papua New Guinea, when she observed an outbreak of "mushroom madness" (known as *Komugi Taï* to the locals), after natives began eating a fungus called *nonda*.[721] While the Kuma people eat this fungus all year, on occasion during the late dry season, it appears to develop hallucinogenic properties. Reay observed that 11 males and 19 females, out of a village of 313, began acting in a bizarre manner. The men ran amok, decorating themselves, grabbing bows and arrows or spears, chasing people around, and threatening to kill them. Curiously, many young adults and children seemed to react to the goings-on as a game, as they "dodged behind houses and peeped out, calling the men to incite them to further violence."[722] Women affected remained in their huts, often exhibiting fits of giggling – recounting both real and fantasized sexual escapades. Many of the women had delusions they were not married. In one case, a woman claimed a man had raped her when he obviously hadn't – only to begin flirting with him. The chaos ended after two days. Reay suggested that the episode was an "opportunity for social catharsis" and offered a brief chance each year, to engage in behavior that was ordinarily proscribed.[723]

CONTEXT: The *Komugi Taï*, whatever its stimulus, is highly ritualized and appears to offer natives the temporary opportunity to breach customs and mores, especially married women who are forbidden to have extramarital sexual affairs but whose husbands regularly engage in such behaviors as part of a culture which favors males. Reay observed: "The women feel like dancing; normally they are not permitted to dance, but they are encouraged to do so now. The behaviour of women is a symbolic regression to the... sexual freedom of their earlier years." During episodes, single women encourage men to dance with them, at which point they attempt to seduce them. In Kuma society, there is a double standard when it comes to sexual affairs. While wives are required to stay faithful to their husbands, many men have relationships with single girls and turn their affections to their wives only when they want to father children, resulting in pent-up frustration and resentment by their wives.[724]

In 1963, two botanists, Roger Heim of France and American R. Gordon Wasson, went to the region, met Reay, and together they gathered samples of *nonda* mushrooms that she had identified as being consumed during the "madness." They later determined that the "mushrooms – or at least most of them – do not seem to cause physiological effects leading to madness."[725] As a result of these findings, Reay speculated that the episode was caused by "collective hysteria."[726] Later, based on further analysis, Wasson speculated that one of the mushrooms eaten by the Kuma (*Beletus manicus*) could produce effects similar to those reported during "mushroom madness."[727] More recently, Australian botanist Benjamin Thomas argued that acute nicotine poisoning is the culprit. Based on the symptoms described during the "madness," and analysis of local plants, Thomas identified two types of tobacco commonly ingested by the Kuma during the *Komugi Taï* that could account for the various behaviors described.[728] This hypothesis is supported by Reay's observations that many of the Kuma are seen chewing and swallowing tobacco during episodes of *Komugi Taï*.[729] Thomas also suggested that other forms of "temporary madness" in Papua New Guinea, which have been described by many anthropologists as play-acting, could result from nicotine poisoning. Descriptions of "mushroom madness" are reminiscent of the medieval DANCING MANIA and TARANTISM.

COMMENT: It appears that "mushroom madness" is a brief, annual ritual designed to produce a social catharsis and allow men and women to engage in ordinarily prohibited behaviors with impunity. While the consumption of *Beletus manicus* seems to have some psychotropic effect on those who eat it, Thomas's hypothesis is the most compelling explanation to date. His description of acute nicotine poisoning (shivering, alterations in vision, deafness, mental confusion, tennitus, intermittent aphasia) and the "mushroom madness" are striking. For instance, in addition to these symptoms, researchers have noted the appearance of "Lilliputian hallucinations" in subjects experiencing nicotine intoxication. Consider the following description of a Kuma man observed by Reay. In addition to displaying each of the aforementioned symptoms, the man:

> ...began to experience Lilliputian hallucinations, seeing bush demons flying about his head. The demons were allegedly buzzing about his head when he heard a strange and terrible noise "inside his ears" which he interpreted as a bush demon boxing his ears. The onset of the noise was like a clap of thunder, but it stayed with him throughout his attack and, being loud, deafened him to the ordinary sounds like human voices and the grunting of pigs. His eyesight began to be affected...he was rapidly losing all power to focus his vision. Some reported having double vision, and in any case it was easy for him to lose his way... The disturbance of hearing and eyesight was frightening and confusing. All objects a komugl man saw in front of him while running seemed to him to be rushing towards him...According to men who had been komugl...[they] saw human beings simply as moving objects unless they were very close. The visual sensation of movement in a horizontal direction (like people running or walking) angered him because it irritated his eyes...His eyes were wild and fierce, with a piercing brightness. They began to travel upward until only the whites were showing. The komugl man had periodic rests from his wild running about. In the beginning he would pause, panting, and eat some tobacco as if for refreshment.[730]

Even so, such explanations appear to have a clear social and cultural structuring. Determining what symptoms stem from the ingestion of psychotropic substances and which behaviors are sociocultural are difficult at times to extricate. Both appear to play a role in these events.

Sources

1. Kunitz, Stanley J., and Haycraft, Howard. (1936). *British Authors of the Nineteenth Century*. New York: The H.W. Wilson Company, p. 402-403.

2. Bulgatz, Joseph. (1992). *Ponzi Schemes, Invaders from Mars & More Extraordinary Popular Delusions and the Madness of Crowds*. New York: Harmony Books, p. 2.

3. Bulgatz, op cit., p. 1.

4. *The Economist*, October 24, 1987, p. 75.

5. Fox, Maggie (2003). "'Mad Cow' Diseases Still Baffle Scientists." Reuters News Agency, December 24.

6. Ridgway, Thomas (2002). *Mad Cow Disease: Bovine Spongiform Encephalopathy*. New York: Rosen publishing, pp. 5-6.

7. NewScientist.com. "Timeline: The Rise and Rise of BSE." Http://www.newscientist. com/hottopics/bse/bsetimeline.jsp.

8. Noble, Kate (2003). "Whatever Happened to Mad Cow Disease?" *Time International* 162(4): 44 (July 28).

9. Ratzan, Scott C. (1997). "Don't be Cowed by this Disease." *The Wall Street Journal*, May 11, accessed November 4, 2003 at: http://www.junkscience.com/news/madcow.html.

10. The description of the Virginia 'gasser' is a modified excerpt from Bartholomew, Robert E. and Wessely, Simon (1999). "Epidemic Hysteria in Virginia: The Case of the Phantom Gasser of 1933-34." *The Southern Medical Journal* 92(8):762-769. See pp. 764-766.

11. Pronounced "Bot-ah-tot."

12. Fradkin, E.K. (1934). *The Air Menace and the Answer*. New York: The Macmillan Company, p. 1.

13. See, for example: Kenworthy, J.M. (1930). *New Wars; New Weapons*. London: E. Matthews & Marrot; Lefebure, V. (1931). *Scientific Disarmament*. London: Mundamus; Duffield, M. (1931). *King Legion*. New York: Jonathan Cape and Harrison Smith; Gesner, G.D. (1931). "Morning After." *Forum and Century* 86:240-246 (October); Gilchrist, H.L. (1931). "Effects of Chemical Cases; Research Work of Chemical Warfare Service, U.S. Army." *U.S. Bureau of Labor Statistics Bulletin* 536:293-306; McDarment, C. (1931). "Clouds of Death." *Popular Mechanics* 55:177-179 (February); Mills, J.E. (1932). "Chemical Warfare." *Foreign Affairs* 10:444-452 (April); Anonymous. (1932). "False Faces [Gas Masks] for Everyone." *Popular Mechanics* 57:970-971 (June); Anonymous. (1932). "New Shelter from Poison Gas Tested in France." *Popular Science Monthly* 121:38 (October); Hart, L. (1933). *The British Way of War*. New York: The Macmillan Company; Anonymous. (1932). "Chemicals in Warfare." *Literary Digest* 114:32 (October 15); Anonymous (1932). "Poison Gas." *Review of Reviews* 86:56 (September). Anonymous. (1933). "First Aid for Ghouls." *World Tomorrow* 14:55 (January); Moore, J.M. (1933). "War We Intend to Avoid." *Forum* 89:218-223 (April).

14. "One Gas Victim Seriously Ill. Officers Seek Clues Here With Little Success..." *Roanoke Times*, December 30, 1933, p. 2; "...Girl Still Ill,"

Roanoke Times, January 2, 1933, p. 10.
15. "Gas 'Attack' on Family is Probed. Fumes at Night Fell Girl and Make Others Ill at Haymakertown Home..." *Roanoke Times* [Roanoke, Virginia], December 24, 1933, p. 13.
16. "...Finds Woman's Track," *Roanoke Times*, December 29, 1933, p. 2.
17. "Gas Attacks...Second Reported From Cloverdale," *Roanoke Times*, December 27, 1933, p. 2.
18. "Stealthy Gasser is Active Again. Troutville Man is Latest Victim..." *Roanoke Times*, December 29, 1933, p. 2.
19. "Gas Attacks Appear to have Ceased in Botetourt County," *Roanoke Times*, January 2, 1934, p. 10.
20. "Gasser Busy in West Botetourt. Fourth Attack is Reported..." *Roanoke Times*, January 12, 1934, p. 2.
21. Ibid., p. 2.
22. "...Reports Chlorine Used," *Roanoke Times*, January 21, 1934, p. 15.
23. "Ghostly Gasser Operates Again. Perpetrator Vanishes Again Without Trace After Carvin's Cove Attack. Woman is Made Ill..." *Roanoke Times*, January 21, 1934, p. 15; "...Sees Man Run," *Roanoke Times*, January 22, 1934, p. 2.
24. "...No Motive Known," *Roanoke Times*, January 22, 1934, p. 2.
25. "Four more Homes in Botetourt Visited by Gasser. Shots Fired at Fleeing Suspect..." *Roanoke Times*, January 23, 1934, p. 2.
26. "Gasser Reported in Action. Family, Fearing to Stay in House at Night, Finds Fumes on Return," *Roanoke Times*, January 25, 1934, p. 2.
27. "...Fears Injury to Innocent," *Roanoke Times*, January 31, 1934, p. 2.
28. Ibid., p. 2.
29. Ibid., p. 2.
30. "...Occurs at Customary Hour," *Roanoke Times*, January 24, 1934, p. 2.
31. "Gas Throwing Prompts Bill for Rigorous Penalties. Sponsors Propose Prison Sentence..." *Roanoke Times*, January 24, 1934, p. 2.
32. "...Fears Injury to Innocent," *Roanoke Times*, January 31, 1934, p. 2.
33. "Continue Search for 'Gas' Clues. Officers' Test Eliminates Chlorine–Inhabitants are Highly Keyed," *Roanoke Times*, January 31, 1934, p. 2.
34. "Gas Throwers Make New Foray...Reward of $500 Authorized..." *Roanoke Times*, January 30, 1934, p. 2.
35. "This Gas Attack Less Diabolical Than Real Thing," *Roanoke Times*, January 25, 1934, p. 2; "...Noticed Car Passing," *Roanoke Times*, February 12, 1934, p. 1.
36. "Gasser Suspect Greeted with Buckshot Barrage..." *Roanoke Times*, January 27, 1934, p. 2.
37. "Spirited Pup is Gas Thrower Foe..." *Roanoke Times*, January 28, 1934, p. 2.
38. "...Hoax Angle Taken Up," *Roanoke Times*, January 30, 1934.
39. "...Fears Injury to Innocent," *Roanoke Times*, January 31, 1934, p. 2.
40. "...Sheriff 'From Missouri,'" *Roanoke Times*, February 6, 1934, p. 2.
41. "Mysterious Gas Thrower Visits Home at Vinton," *Roanoke Times*, February 6, 1934, p. 3; "2 New 'Gassings' Puzzle to Police," *Lynchburg News* [Lynchburg, Virginia], February 7, 1934, p. 3.
42. "...Dog Acts Queerly," *Roanoke Times*, February 6, 1934, p. 7.
43. Ibid., p. 7; "Troutville Home Gas Attack...Officers Again Find No Clues," *Roanoke Times*, February 5, 1934, p. 2.
44. "...Latest Call Investigated," *Roanoke Times*, February 6, 1934, p. 2.
45. "Rorer Avenue Home Target of Mysterious Gas Attack..." *Roanoke Times*, February 8, 1934, pp. 1, 4.
46. "...Gas Not Identified," *Roanoke Times*, February 8, 1934, p. 4.
47. "5 Attacks by Mystery Gasser Keep Police Busy. Reports of Nocturnal Visits Come From Widely Separated Spots..." *Roanoke Times*, February 9, 1934, pp. 1, 4.
48. "Seven Suspected Visits of 'Gasser' Reported to Police..." *Roanoke Times*, February 10, 1934, p. 3.
49. Ibid., p. 3.
50. "...Victim Recovering," *Roanoke Times*, February 10, 1934, p. 3.
51. "Bottle of Old Liquid Seen as Clue to Mysterious 'Gassings.' Authorities Investigating Reported Attacks..." *Roanoke Times*, February 11, 1934, pp. 1, 2.
52. "Sample of 'Gas' is Found to be Harmless to Humans..." *Roanoke Times*, February 12, 1934, p. 1.
53. "'Gas Man' takes Full Night Off. Skeptical Police get but One Call and Find Burning Rubber to Blame," *Roanoke Times*, February 12, 1934, p. 1.
54. "Roanoke has No Gasser," *Roanoke Times*, February 14, 1934, p. 6.
55. "Botetourt's Mysterious 'Gassers,'" *Roanoke Times*, February 24, 1934, p. 6.
56. Johnson, Donald Max (1945). "The 'Phantom Anesthetist' of Mattoon: A Field Study of Mass Hysteria." *Journal of Abnormal Psychology* 40:175-186.
57. Smith, Wily (1994). "The Mattoon Phantom Gasser." *The Skeptic* 3(1):33-39.
58. Clark, Jerome (1999). *Unexplained!* Farmington Hills, Michigan: Visible Ink Press; Clark, Jerome (1993). *Encyclopedia of Strange and Unexplained Physical Phenomena*. Detroit, MI: Gale Research, pp. 202-205; Shoemaker, M.T. (1985). "The Mad Gasser of Botetourt." *Fate* 38(6):62-68 (June); Coleman, Loren (1983). *Mysterious America*. Winchester, Massachusetts: Faber & Faber; Smith, Wily (1984). "The Mattoon Gasser: A Modern Myth." *The International UFO Reporter* 9(6):7, 9, 14.
59. Bartholomew, Robert E. (2001). *Little Green Men, Meowing Nuns and Headhunting Panics: A Study of Mass Psychogenic Illness and Social Delusions*. Jefferson, North Carolina: McFarland & Company.
60. Reconstruction of the initial "attack" on Mrs. Kearney is taken from the following sources that include first-hand interviews by Mattoon police and Chicago psychiatrist Harold S. Hulbert. *The Daily Journal-Gazette* (1944). "Anesthetic Prowler on Loose." September 2, p. 1; "Show How They Were Gassed." *Chicago Herald-American*, September 10, 1944, p. 10; Alley, E. "Illness of First Gas 'Victim' Blamed for Wave of Hysteria in Mattoon." *Chicago Herald-American*, September 17, 1944, p. 3; "Chicago Psychiatrist Analyzes Mattoon Gas Hysteria." *Chicago Herald-American*, September 17, 1944, p. 3; Johnson, D.M. (1945). op cit.
61. "Anesthetic Prowler on Loose," op cit., p. 1.
62. The skull cap implies that he was Jewish, possibly reflecting rural mid-western anti-semitism of the time where Judaism was often associated with the "evils" of secularism of big city life. Ironically, during this same period, millions of Jews were gassed to death in Europe.
63. *The Daily Journal-Gazette*, is the paper's popular name and appears on the banner. Its official full title is *The Daily Journal-Gazette and Commercial-Star*.
64. Johnson, Donald Max. (1945). op cit., p. 180.
65. "...Seen by Kearney...", op cit., p. 1.

66. "Mattoon's Phantom 'Suggestive' Fear." *Chicago Herald-American*, September 21, 1944, p. 2.
67. Ibid.
68. Ibid.
69. Ibid.
70. Ibid.
71. "Mattoon's Mad Anesthetist" [Editorial], *The Daily Journal-Gazette*, September 8, 1944, p. 2.
72. Ladendorf, Robert, and Bartholomew, Robert E. (2002). "The Mad Gasser of Mattoon: How the Press Created an Imaginary Chemical Weapons Attack." *The Skeptical Inquirer* 26(4):50-54, 58 (July-August). See p. 53.
73. Smith (1994). op cit., p. 35.
74. Smith (1994). op cit., p. 39.
75. Ladendorf and Bartholomew (2002). op cit.
76. "'Mad Gasser' Adds Six Victims! 5 Women and Boy Latest Overcome." *The Daily Journal-Gazette*, September 9, 1944, p. 1.
77. "Safety Agent to Aid Police in 'Gas' Case." *The Daily Journal-Gazette*, September 6, 1944, p. 6.
78. "Chemists Trace Mattoon Mad Man's 'Gardenia Gas.'" *The News-Gazetter* (Champaign), September 9, 1944, p. 3.
79. "Mattoon Gets Jitters from Gas Attacks." *Chicago Herald-American*, September 10, 1944, p. 1. "Mattoon Gets Jitters from Gas Attacks." *Chicago Herald-American*, September 10, 1944, p. 1. "'Chasers' to be Arrested." *The Daily Journal-Gazette*, September 11, 1944, p. 1. "Sidelights of 'Mad Gasser's' Strange Case." *The Daily Journal-Gazette*, September 12, 1944, p. 4."Safety Agent to Aid Police in 'Gas' Case." *The Daily Journal-Gazette*, September 6, 1944, p. 6. Johnson, D.M. (1945). op cit., p. 181.
80. Ibid.
81. Johnson, D.M. (1945). op cit., p. 181.
82. Ballenger, C. "Mattoon's Gas Fiend Attacks Girl, 11, in Home." *Chicago Daily Tribune*, September 9, 1944, p. 10.
83. "Mattoon Gets Jitters from Gas Attacks," op cit.
84. "Mattoon Gets Jitters from Gas Attacks." *Chicago Herald-American*, September 10, 1944, p. 1.
85. "Mattoon Gets Jitters from Gas Attacks." *Chicago Herald-American*, September 10, 1944, p. 1. "'Chasers' to be Arrested." *The Daily Journal-Gazette*, September 11, 1944, p. 1. "Sidelights of 'Mad Gasser's' Strange Case." *The Daily Journal-Gazette*, September 12, 1944, p. 4. "'Chasers' to be Arrested." *The Daily Journal-Gazette*, September 11, 1944, p. 1.
86. "To All Citizens of Mattoon." *The Daily Journal-Gazette*, September 11, 1944, p. 1.
87. "Sidelights of 'Mad Gasser's' Strange Case." *The Daily Journal-Gazette*, September 12, 1944, p. 4.
88. "'Mad Gasser' Adds Six Victims!..." op cit., p. 1.
89. "...Two Women Believed Victims Examined at Hospital." *The Daily Journal-Gazette,* September 11, 1944, p. 1.
90. "Many Prowler Reports ..." op cit., p. 1.
91. Ballenger, C. "FBI at Mattoon as Gas Prowler Attacks 5 More." *Chicago Daily Tribune*, September 10, 1944, p. 15; "Many Prowler Reports ..." op cit., p. 1.
92. "'Mad Gasser' Case Limited to 4 Suspects." *The Daily Journal-Gazette*, September 12, 1944, p. 1.
93. Johnson (1945). op cit., p. 177.
94 Erickson, G. "Mad Gasser Called Myth." *Chicago Herald-American*, September 13, 1944, p. 1.
95. "'Gasser' Case 'Mistake,'" *The Daily Journal-Gazette*, September 12, 1944, p. 4; "Police Chief Says Sprayer Tales Hoax." *Illinois State Journal*, September 13, 1944, p. 1; "...Cole Amplifies Statement." *The Daily Journal-Gazette*, September 13, 1944, p. 1.
96. "...Police get Two False Alarms During Night..." *The Daily Journal-Gazette*, September 13, 1944, p. 1.
97. "No Gas, Not Even Madman Seen During Night." *The Daily Journal-Gazette*, September 15, 1944, p. 6.
98. "No Gas, Not Even Madman Seen During Night." *The Daily Journal-Gazette*, September 15, 1944, p. 6.
99. "Debunk Mattoon Gas Scare." *Chicago Herald-American*, September 13, 1944, p. 4; Erickson, G. "Mad Gasser Called Myth." *Chicago Herald-American*, September 13, 1944, p. 1; Alley, E. "Illness of First Gas 'Victim' Blamed for Wave of Hysteria in Mattoon." *Chicago Herald-American*, September 17, 1944, p. 3; "Chicago Psychiatrist Analyzes Mattoon Gas Hysteria." *Chicago Herald-American*, September 17, 1944, p. 3; "Study Terror in Mattoon." *Chicago Herald-American*, September 18, 1944, p. 1; Alley, E. "Credulity Seat of Mattoon's Terror." *Chicago Herald-American*, September 20, 1944, p. 4; "Mattoon's Phantom 'Suggestive' Fear." *Chicago Herald-American*, September 21, 1944, p. 2.
100. "The 'Perfumed City' Speaks,'"[editorial] *The Daily Journal-Gazette*, September 20, 1944, p. 2.
101. Anonymous. (1944). "At Night in Mattoon." *Time*, September 18, p. 23.
102. "Letter to the Editor,'" *The Daily Journal-Gazette*, September 26, 1944, p. 2. "Letter to the Editor,'" *The Daily Journal-Gazette*, September 26, 1944, p. 2.
103. "Letter to the Editor,'" *The Daily Journal-Gazette*, September 29, 1944, p. 2.
104. Lindley, E.K. (1943). "Thoughts on the Use of Gas in Warfare." *Newsweek* 22:24 (December 20). Sanders, V. (1945). "Our Army's Defense Against Poison Gas." *Popular Science* 146:106-111 (February). Scott, E.W. (1944). "Role of the Public Health Laboratory in Gas Defense." *American Journal of Public Health* 34:275-278 (March).
105. Marshall, J. (1943). "We are Ready with Gas if the Axis Turns on the Gas." *Collier's* 112:21 (August 7).
106. Brown, F.J. (1968). *Chemical Warfare: A Study in Restraints.* Princeton, New Jersey: Princeton University Press, p. 244.
107. Bartholomew, Robert, and Sirois, Francois (1996). "Epidemic Hysteria in Schools: An International and Historical Overview." *Educational Studies* 22(3):285-311; Bartholomew, Robert E., and Sirois, Francois (2000). "Occupational Mass Psychogenic Illness: A Transcultural Perspective." *Transcultural Psychiatry* 37(4):495-524.
108. Llorente, Juan Antonio (1826). *The History of the Inquisition of Spain.* Translated and abridged from the original Spanish. London: Whittaker, p. 509.
109. Madden, R. R. (1857). *Phantasmata or Illusions and Fanaticisms of Protean Forms Productive of Great Evils.* London: T.C. Newby, volume 2, p. 270.
110. Dupouy, E. (1907). *Psychologie Morbide.* Paris: Librairie des Sciences Psychiques, p. 120.
111. Madden, op cit., volume 2, p. 277.
112. "Mystery Illness Fells 36 at Portland Clothing Factory." *Kennebeck Journal* (Augusta, Maine), May 19, 1972, p. 1 and 2.
113. Bechterew, W.M. [Now spelled Bekhterev, V M] (1910). *La Suggestion.* [Translated from Russian by D P Keraval]. Paris: Boulangé, p. 160 et seq.
114. Quoted by Bekhterev, op cit., p. 186.
115. Bekhterev, op cit., p. 183, quoting Sikorski.
116. Bekhterev, op cit., p. 182.
117. Bekhterev, op cit., p. 179.

118. Bekhterev, op cit., p. 185.
119. Steinbauer, Friedrich (1979). *Melanesian Cargo Cults* (translated by Max Wohlwill). London: George Prior Publishers, p. 59.
120. Steinbauer, op cit., p. 60.
121. Steinbauer, op cit., p. 61.
122. Levine, R. J. (1977). "Epidemic Faintness and Syncope in a School Marching Band." *Journal of the American Medical Association* 238(22):2373-2376, see pp. 2373-2374.
123. Levine (1977). op cit., p. 2376.
124. Levine (1977). op cit., p. 2373.
125. Levine (1977). op cit., p. 2373.
126. Levine (1977). op cit., p. 2376.
127. "Quakes Believed Caused by Mars Bring Panic." *The Daily Gleaner* (Kingston, Jamaica), July 29, 1939, p. 19.
128. Olkinuora, M. (1984). "Psychogenic Epidemics and Work." *Scandinavian Journal of Work, Environment and Health* 10(6):501-515; Hall, E. M., and Johnson, J. V. (1989). "A Case Study of Stress and Mass Psychogenic Illness in Industrial Workers." *Journal of Occupational Medicine* 31(3):243-250.
129. Despine, P. (1875). *De la Folie au Point de vue Philosophique ou Specialement Psychologique Etudiee chez le malade et chez l'homme en Sante* [Madness from the Philosophical Viewpoint, in Particular a Psychological Study of a Sick Person in Relation to a Healthy Person]. Paris: F. Savy.
130. Anonymous. (1888). "Psychic Disturbances in Russia." *Science* 11:178.
131. Sirois, Francois. (1999). "Epidemic Hysteria: School Outbreaks 1973-1993." *Medical Principles & Practice* 8:12-25.
132. American Psychiatric Association (1994). *Diagnostic and Statistical Manual of Mental Disorders* (3rd edition). Washington, DC: APA.
133. Bartholomew, Robert E. (1998). "Dancing with Myths: The Misogynist Construction of Dancing Mania. *Feminism & Psychology* 8(2):173-183.
134. Bartholomew, Robert E. and Wessely, Simon. (2002). "Protean Nature of Mass Sociogenic Illness: From Possessed Nuns to Chemical and Biological Terrorism Fears." *The British Journal of Psychiatry* 180:300-306
135. Bartholomew, Robert E. (2000) "Re: Epidemic Hysteria: A Review of the Published Literature." Correspondence. *The American Journal of Epidemiology* 151(2):206-207 (January 15); Bartholomew, Robert E. (1994). "Tarantism, Dancing Mania and Demonopathy: The Anthro-Political Aspects of Mass Psychogenic Illness." *Psychological Medicine* 24:281-306;Bartholomew, Robert E. (1990). "Ethnocentricity and the Social Construction of 'Mass Hysteria.'" *Culture, Medicine and Psychiatry* 14(4):455-494.
136. Jones, T.F., Craig, A.S., Hoy, D., et al. (2000). "Mass Psychogenic Illness Attributed to Toxic Exposure at a High School." *New England Journal of Medicine*, 342, 96-100.
137. Madden, Richard Robert (1857). *Phantasmata or Illusions and Fanaticisms of Protean Forms Productive of Great Evils*. London: T.C. Newby; Hirsch, A. (1883). *Handbook of Geographical and Historical Pathology*. London: New Sydenham Society; Small, M.H. (1896) The Suggestibility of Children. *Pedagogical Seminary*, 4, 176-220; Burnham, William H. (1924). *The Normal Mind*. New York: D. Appleton-Century; Rosen, George (1968). *Madness in Society*. London: Routledge and Kegan Paul; Markush, R.E. (1973). "Mental Epidemics: A Review of the Old to Prepare for the New." *Public Health Reviews* 4(2):353-442; Sirois, Francois (1974). "Epidemic Hysteria." *Acta Psychiatrica Scandinavica Supplementum* 252:7-46; Bartholomew, Robert E., and Sirois, Francois (1996). "Epidemic Hysteria in Schools: An International and Historical Overview." *Educational Studies* 22:285-311; Boss, Leslie P. (1997). "Epidemic Hysteria: A Review of the Published Literature." *Epidemiological Reviews* 19:233-243; Bartholomew, Robert E., and Sirois, Francois (2000). "Occupational Mass Psychogenic Illness: A Transcultural Perspective." *Transcultural Psychiatry* 37(4):495-524.
138. Wessely, S. (1987). "Mass Hysteria: Two Syndromes?" *Psychological Medicine* 17, 109-120.
139. Calmeil, L.F. (1845). *De la Folie, Consideree Sous le Point de vue Pathologique, Philosophique, Historique et Judiciaire* [On the Crowd, Considerations on the Point of Pathology, Philosophy, History and Justice]. Paris: Bailler; Garnier, S. (1895). *Barbe Buvee, en Religion, Soeur Sainte-Colombe et la Pretendue Possession des Ursulines d'Auxonne* [Barbara Buvee, and Religion, Sister Columbe and the Feigned Possession of the Ursulines at Auxonne]. Paris: Felix Alcan; Loredan, J. (1912). *Un Grand Proces de Sorcellerie au XVIIe siecle, L'Abbe Gaufridy et Madeleine de Demandolx (1600-1670)* [The Grand Process of Witchcraft in the Seventeenth Century, L'Abbe Gaufridy and Madeleine de Demandoux (1600-1670)]. Paris: Perrin et Cie.
140. Davy, R.B. (1880). "'St. Vitus' Dance and Kindred Affection; The Recent Epidemic at the Ursulin Convent in Brown County, Ohio; A Sketch of The Historic Disease." *Cincinnati Lancet and Clinic* 4: 440-445, 467-473.
141. Huxley, A. (1952). *The Devils of Loudun*. New York: Harper and Brothers.
142. Robbins, R.H. (1966). *The Encyclopedia of Witchcraft and Demonology*. New York: Crown, pp. 408-414.
143. Robbins, R.H. (1966). op cit., p. 393.
144. Hecker, J.F.C. (1844). *Epidemics of the Middle Ages* (translated from German by B. Babington). London: The Sydenham Society, p. 127.
145. Darnton, R. (1984). *The Great Cat Massacre and Other Episodes in French Cultural History*. New York: Basic Books.
146. Bartholomew, Robert E. (2000). *Exotic Deviance: Medicalizing Cultural Idioms–From Strangeness to Illness*. Boulder, CO: University Press of Colorado, pp. 192-193.
147. Franchini, A. (1947). "Manifestazioni Isteriche Collettive Interpretate Come Sintomi di Intossicazione da Gas Ignoto" [A Manifestation Interpreted as Collective Hysteria Presenting as Symptoms of Intoxication by Flammable Gas]. *Medicina di Lavoro* 38:57-60.
148. Bouzol, M. (1884). "Relation d'une Epidemie a Phenomene Hysterico-Choreique Observee a Algon (Ardeche) en 1882." [On the Relation of Epidemic Hysterical Chorea Observed at Algon [Ardeche] in 1882]. *Lyon Medical*, 47, 142-148; 174-184; 211-217.
149. Schatalow, N. (1891). "Zur Frage von der Epidemischen Histerie [On the Question of Epidemic Hysteria], *Neurologische Centralblatt*, 10, 405; Bekhtereff V. (1914). "Donnees sur L'epidemie Neuro-psychique Observee Chez les Travailleurs d'usine de Riga et de Petrograd en Mars 1914." [Given on the Neurological Epidemic Observed at the Homes of the Factory Workers at Riga and Petrograd in March 1914]. *Obozrienie Psikhiatrii Nevrologii* (Petrograd) 19:585-613.
150. St. Clare, W. (1787). *Gentleman's Magazine*, 57, 268.
151. Sirois F. (1982). "Perspectives on Epidemic Hysteria." In *Mass Psychogenic Illness: A Social Psychological Analysis*. Colligan, M., Pennebaker, J., Murphy, L. (eds). Pp. 217-236. New Jersey: Lawrence Erlbaum.
152. Bartholomew, Robert E., and Sirois, Francois (2000). "Occupational Mass Psychogenic Illness: A Transcultural Perspective." *Transcultural Psychiatry* 37(4):495-524.
153. Armainguad M. (1879). "Recherches Cliniques sur L'hysterie;

Relation d'une Petite Epidemie d'hysterie Observee a Bordeaux." [Clinical Research on Hysteria and Its Relation to a Small Epidemic of Hysteria Observed in Bordeaux]. *Memoire et Bulletin de la Societe de Medecine et Chirurgie de Bordeaux* 551-579; Hagenbach E. (1893). "Chorea-epidemie [Epidemic Chorea]." Kor-Blatt f Schweit Arzte (Basel) 23:631-632.
154. Regnard, M. and Simon, J. (1887). "Sur une Epidemie de Contracture des Extremites Observee a Gentilly" [On an Epidemic of Limb Contracture observed in Gentilly]. *Comptes Rendus des Seances de la Societe de Biologie* (Paris) 3:344-347, 350-353.
155. Laquer, L. (1888). "Uber eine Chorea-Epidemie" [An Epidemic of Chorea]. *Deutsche Medizinische Wochenschrift* (Leipzig) 14: 1045-1046. Wichmann, R. (1890). "Eine Sogenannte Veitstanzepidemie in Wildbad" [A So-called Epidemic of St. Vitus Dance in Wildbad]. *Deutsche Medizinische Wochenschrift* (Leipzig) 16:632-636, 659-663.
156. Rembold, S. (1893). "Acute Psychiche Contagion in Einer Madchenschule" [Acute Psychic Contagion in a Girls School]. *Berliner Klinische Wochenschrift* 30:662-663.
157. Aemmer, F. (1893). "Eine Schulepidemie von Tremor Hystericus" [A School Epidemic of Hysterical Tremor]. Inaugural dissertation, Basel.
158. Zollinger, E. (1906). "Uber die Padagogische Behandlung des Nervosen Zitterns der Schulkinder" [On the Educational Treatment of Nervous Trembling in School Children]. *Jahrbuch der Schweiz Gesellschaft fur Schulgesundheitspflege*, 7, 20-47.
159. Hirt, L. (1893). "Eine Epidemie von Hysterischen Krampfen in einer Schleisischen Dorfschule" [An Epidemic of Hysterical Cramp in a Village School in Schleisischen]. *Zeitschrift fur Schulgesundheitspflege* 6:225-229. (Summary of an article by L. Hirt in the *Berliner Klinische Wochenschrift*).
160. Schoedel, J. (1906). Uber Induzierte Krankheiten [On Induced Illness]. *Jahrbuch fur Kinderheilkunde*, 14, 521-528.
161. Philen, R.M., Kilbourn, E.M. and McKinley, T.W. (1989). "Mass Sociogenic Illness By Proxy: Parentally Reported in an Elementary School." *Lancet* ii:1372-1376; Selden, B.S. (1989). "Adolescent Epidemic Hysteria Presenting as a Mass Casualty, Toxic Exposure Incident." *Annals of Emergency Medicine* 18:892-895; Cole, T.B. (1990). "Pattern of Transmission of Epidemic Hysteria in a School." *Epidemiology* 1:212-218; Krug, S. (1992). "Mass Illness at an Intermediate School: Toxic Fumes or Epidemic Hysteria?" *Pediatric Emergency Care*, 8, 280-282; Taylor, B.W. and Werbicki, J.E. (1993). "A Case of Mass Hysteria Involving 19 Schoolchildren." *Pediatric Emergency Care* 9:216-217; Small, G.W., Feinberg, D.T., Steinberg, D., et al. (1994). "A Sudden Outbreak of Illness Suggestive of Mass Hysteria in Schoolchildren." *Archives of Family Medicine* 3:711-716.
162. Goh, K.T. (1987). "Epidemiological Enquiries Into a School Outbreak of an Unusual Illness." *International Journal of Epidemiology* 16 2:265-270. See p. 269.
163. Smith, H.C.T., and Eastham, E.J. (1973). "Outbreak of Abdominal Pain." *Lancet* 2:956-958.
164. Araki, S., and Honma, T. (1986). "Mass Psychogenic Systemic Illness in School Children in Relation to the Tokyo Photochemical Smog." *Archives of Environmental Health* 41: 159-162.
165. Amin, Y., Hamdi, E., and Eapen, V. (1997). "Mass Hysteria in an Arab Culture." *International Journal of Social Psychiatry* 43:303-306.
166. Colligan, M.J., and Murphy, L.R. (1979). "Mass Psychogenic Illness in Organizations: An Overview." *Journal of Occupational Psychology* 52:77-90; Boxer, P.A. (1985). "Occupational Mass Psychogenic Illness: History, Prevention, Management." *Journal of Occupational Medicine*, 27, 867-872; Boxer, P.A., Singal, M., and Hartle, R.W. (1984). "An Epidemic of Psychogenic Illness in an Electronics Plant." *Journal of Occupational Medicine* 26:381-385.
167. Stahl, S.M. (1982). "Illness as an Emergent Norm or Doing What Comes Naturally." In M. Colligan, J. Pennebaker and L. Murphy (Eds.), *Mass Psychogenic Illness: A Social Psychological Analysis*. Pp. 183-198. Hillsdale, New Jersey: Lawrence Erlbaum; Stahl, S., and Lebedun, M. (1974). "Mystery Gas: An Analysis of Mass Hysteria." *Journal of Health and Social Behavior* 15:44-50.
168. Alexander, R.W., and Fedoruk, M.J. (1986). "Epidemic Psychogenic Illness in a Telephone Operator's Building. *Journal of Occupational Medicine* 28:42-45.
169. Colligan, M.J., Urtes, M.A., Wisseman, C., et al. (1979). "An Investigation of Apparent Mass Psychogenic Illness in an Electronics Plant." *Journal of Behavioral Medicine* 2:297-309; Colligan, M.J., and Urtes, M.A. (1978). *An Investigation of Apparent Mass Psychogenic Illness in an Electronics Plant*. Unpublished National Institute for Occupational Safety and Health Report.
170. Struewing, J.P., and Gray, G.C. (1990). "Epidemic of Respiratory Complaints Exacerbated by Mass Psychogenic Illness in a Military Recruit Population." *American Journal of Epidemiology* 132:1120-29.
171. Christophers, A.J. (1982). "Civil Emergency Butyl Mercaptan Poisoning in The Parnell Civil Defence Emergency: Fact or Fiction." *New Zealand Journal of Medicine* 95:277-278; David, A.S., and Wessely, S.C. (1995). "The Legend of Camelford: Medical Consequences of a Water Pollution Accident (Editorial)." *Journal of Psychosomatic Research* 39:1-9; Gamino. L.A., Elkins, G.R., and Hackney, K.U. (1989). "Emergency Management of Mass Psychogenic Illness." *Psychosomatics* 3:446-449; Johnson, D.M. (1945). "The 'Phantom Anesthetist' of Mattoon: A Field Study of Mass Hysteria." *Journal of Abnormal and Social Psychology* 40:175-186; McLeod, W. (1975). "Merphos Poisoning or Mass Panic?" *Australian and New Zealand Journal of Psychiatry* 9:225-229.
172. Taylor, L.B., and Taylor, C.L. (1985). *Chemical and Biological Warfare*. Franklin Watts: New York, pp. 23-38.
173. Fradkin, E.K. (1934). *The Air Menace and the Answer*. New York: The Macmillan Company.
174. Bartholomew, R.E., and Wessely, S. (1999). "Epidemic Hysteria in Virginia: The Case of the Phantom Gasser of 1933-34." *The Southern Medical Journal* 92(8):762-769.
175. Johnson, D.M. (1945). op cit.
176. Cantril, H. (1947). *The Invasion from Mars: A Study in the Psychology of Panic*. New Jersey: Princeton University Press, p. 160.
177. Radovanovic, Z. (1995). "On the Origin of Mass Casualty Incidents in Kosovo, Yugoslavia, in 1990." *European Journal of Epidemiology* 11:1-13.
178. Modan, B., Tirosh, M., Weissenberg, E., et al. (1983). "The Arjenyattah Epidemic." *Lancet* ii:1472-1476.
179. Goldsmith, M.F. (1989). "Physicians with Georgia on their Minds." *Journal of the American Medical Association*, 262, 603-604.
180. Wessely, S. (1995). "Hysteria After Gas Attacks." *The Times* (London), July 4, p. 14a.
181. Wessely, S., Hyams, K., and Bartholomew, R. (2001). "Psychological Implications of Chemical and Biological Weapons." *British Medical Journal* 323:878-879.
182. Lellman, L. (2001). "Suspicious Incident Forces Subway's Closing." *Rutland Daily Herald*, October 10, p. A3.
183. Brown, A. (2001). Cable News Network. Special report live with Aaron Brown. CNN headquarters, Atlanta, Georgia, October 16, 10-11pm.
184. Weintraub, M.I. (1983). *Hysterical Conversion Reactions: A Clinical Guide to Diagnosis and Treatment*. Lancaster, UK: MTP Press, p. 5;

Rack, P. (1982). *Race, Culture, and Mental Disorder*. London: Tavistock Publications, p. 141.
185. Kleinman, A. (1988). *Rethinking Psychiatry: From Cultural Category to Personal Experience*. New York: The Free Press, p. 41.
186. Brodsky, C.M. (1983). "Allergic to Everything: A Medical Subculture." *Psychosomatics* 24:731-42; Bardana, E.J., and Montanaro, A. (1986). "Tight Building Syndrome." *Immunology and Allergy Practice* 8:74-88.
187. Bauer, R.M., Greve, K.W., Besch, E.L, Schramke, C.J., Crouch, J., Hicks, A., Ware, M.R., and Lyles, W.B. (1992). "The Role of Psychological Factors in the Report of Building-Related Symptoms in Sick Building Syndrome." *Journal of Consulting and Clinical Psychology* 60(2) 213-19; Ryan, C.M., and Morrow, L.A. (1992). "Dysfunctional Buildings or Dysfunctional People: An Examination of the Sick Building Syndrome and Allied Disorders." *Journal of Consulting and Clinical Psychology* 60(2)220-224.
188. Colligan, M.J., and Murphy, L.R. (1979). "Mass Psychogenic Illness in Organizations: An Overview." *Journal of Occupational Psychology* 52:77-90.
189. Champion, Francis P., Taylor, Robert, Joseph, Paul R., and Heddon, J.C. (1963). "Mass Hysteria Associated with Insect Bites." *Journal of the South Carolina Medical Association* 59:351-53; Kerckhoff, A.C., Back, K.W., and Miller, N. (1965). "Sociometric Patterns in Hysterical Contagion." *Sociometry* 28:2-15; Kerckhoff, A.C., and Back, K.W. (1968). *The June Bug: A Study of Hysterical Contagion*. Prentice-Hall: Englewood Cliffs, New Jersey.
190. Stahl, S.M., and Lebedun, M. (1974). "Mystery Gas: An Analysis of Mass Hysteria." *Journal of Health and Social Behavior* 15:44-50.
191. Wessely (1987). op cit.
192. Kerckhoff and Back (1965). op cit.; Wessely (1987). op cit.; Shepard, R.D., and Kroes, W.H. (1975). "Report of an Investigation at the James Plant." Internal report prepared for the National Institute for Occupational Safety and Health, Cincinnati, Ohio, cited in M. Colligan, J. Pennebaker and L. Murphy (eds.), *Mass Psychogenic Illness: A Social Psychological Analysis*. Hillsdale, New Jersey: Lawrence Erlbaum; Colligan M.J., and Murphy, L.R. (1982). "A Review of Mass Psychogenic Illness in Work Settings." In M. Colligan, J. Pennebaker and L. Murphy (eds.), *Mass Psychogenic Illness: A Social Psychological Analysis* (33-52). Hillsdale, New Jersey: Lawrence Erlbaum; Sparks, P.J., Simon, P.G., Katon, W.J., Altman, L.C., Ayars, G.H., and Johnson, R.L. (1990). "An Outbreak of Illness Among Aerospace Workers." *Western Journal of Medicine* 153:28-33.
193. Anonymous (1983). "Epidemiologic Notes and Reports Epidemic Psychogenic Illness in an Industrial Setting–Pennsylvania." *Morbidity and Mortality Weekly Report* 32(22);287-8, 294 (June 10) [published by the Centers for Disease Control in Atlanta]. Accessed June 18, 2003 at http://www.cdc.gov/mmwr/preview/mmwrhtml/ 00000092.htm.
194. Kerckhoff, Back and Miller (1965). op cit., p. 13.
195. Champion et al., op cit., p. 351.
196. Champion et al., op cit., p. 351.
197. Champion et al., op cit., p. 352.
198. Champion et al., op cit., pp. 352-353.
199. Stahl, op cit., pp. 184-185.
200. Stahl, op cit., p. 185.
201. Stahl, op cit., p. 186.
202. Stahl, op cit., p. 186.
203. St. Clare, W. (1787). *Gentleman's Magazine* 57:268.
204. Smelser, N.J. (1962). *Social Change in the Industrial Revolution*. London: Routledge and Kegan Paul.
205. Ackerman, S.E. (1980). *Cultural Process in Malaysian Industrialization: A Study of Malay Women Factory Workers*. Ph.D. thesis, University of California at San Diego. University Microfilms: Ann Arbor, MI.
206. Bartholomew, Robert E., and Sirois, Francois (2000). "Occupational Mass Psychogenic Illness: A Transcultural Perspective." *Transcultural Psychiatry* 37(4):495-524. See pp. 503-506.
207. Skeat, W.W. (1900). *Malay Magic*. London: MacMillan; Endicott, K. (1970). *An Analysis of Malay Magic*. Oxford: Clarendon.
208. Bartholomew and Sirois (2000). op cit., p. 503.
209. Phoon, W.H. (1982). "Outbreaks of mass hysteria at workplaces in Singapore: Some patterns and modes of presentation." In M. Colligan, J. Pennebaker and L. Murphy (eds.), *Mass Psychogenic Illness: A Social Psychological Analysis* (21-32). Hillsdale, New Jersey: Lawrence Erlbaum, pp. 21-31.
210. Phoon (1982). op cit., p. 23; Colligan M.J., and Murphy, L.R. (1982). "A Review of Mass Psychogenic Illness in Work Settings." In M. Colligan, J. Pennebaker and L. Murphy (eds.), *Mass Psychogenic Illness: A Social Psychological Analysis* (33-52). Hillsdale, New Jersey: Lawrence Erlbaum, p. 36.
211. Phoon (1982). op cit., p. 23.
212. Phoon (1982). op cit., p. 23.
213. Phoon (1982). op cit., p. 31.
214. Bartholomew, R.E. (1990). "Ethnocentricity and the Social Construction of 'Mass Hysteria.'" *Culture, Medicine and Psychiatry* 14:455-494. See p. 476, citing Chan, M., and Wong, C.K. 1983. "Epidemic Hysteria: A Study of High Risk Factors." *Occupational Health and Safety International* 52(3):54-64.
215. The following section is excerpted in part from Bartholomew and Sirois (2000). op cit.
216. Daikos, G.K., Garzonis, S., and Paleologue, A. (1959). "Benign Myalgic Encephalomyelitis: An Outbreak in a Nurses' School in Athens." *Lancet* i:693-6; Pool, J.H., Walton, J.N., Brewis, E.G., Uldall, P.R., Wright, A.E., and Gardner, P.S. (1961). "Benign Myalgic Encephalomyelitis in Newcastle Upon Tyne." *Lancet* i:733-7.
217. Shelokov, A., Habel, K., Verder, E., and Welsh, W. (1957). "Epidemic Neuromyasthenia: An Outbreak of Poliomyelitis-like Illness in Student Nurses." *New England Journal of Medicine* 257:345-55; Poskanzer, D.C., Henderson, D.A., Kunkle, E.C., Kalter, S.S., Clement, W.B., and Bond, J.D. (1957). "Epidemic Neuromyasthenia: An Outbreak in Punta Gorda, Florida." *New England Journal of Medicine* 257:356-64; Albrecht, R.M., Oliver, V., and Poskanzer, D. (1964). "Epidemic Neuromyasthenia: Outbreak in a Convent in New York State." *Journal of the American Medical Association* 187:904-907.
218. White, D.N., and Burtch, R.B. (1954). "Iceland Disease: A New Infection Simulating Acute Anterior Poliomyelitis." *Neurology* 4:506-516; Deisher, J.B. (1957). "Benign Myalgic Encephalomyelitis (Iceland Disease) in Alaska." *Northwest Medicine* 56:1451-1456.
219. Gilliam, A.G. (1938). "Epidemiologic Study of an Epidemic, Diagnosed as Poliomyelitis, Occurring among the Personnel of the Los Angeles County General Hospital during the Summer of 1934." *Bulletin 240*, Washington, DC: U.S. Public Health Service Division of Infectious Diseases, National Institutes of Health, 1-90; Sigurdsson, B.J., Sigurjonsson, J., Sigurdsson, J., Thorkelsson, J., and Gudmundsson, K. (1950). "Disease Epidemic in Iceland Simulating Poliomyelitis." *American Journal of Hygiene* 52:222-238.
220. Acheson, E. (1959). "The Clinical Syndrome Variously Called Benign Myalgic Encephalomyelitis, Iceland Disease and Epidemic Neuromyasthenia." *American Journal of Medicine* 26:569-595; Briggs, M.C., and Levine, P.H. (1994). "A Comparative Review of Systemic and Neurological Symptomatology in 12 Outbreaks Collectively

Described as Chronic Fatigue Syndrome, Epidemic Neuromyasthenia and Myalgic Encephalomyelitis." *Clinical and Infectious Diseases* 18(Supplement 1), S32-42; Chester, A.C., and Levine, P.H. (1994). "Concurrent Sick Building Syndrome and Chronic Fatigue Syndrome: Epidemic Neuromyasthenia Revisited." *Clinical and Infectious Diseases* 18(Supplement 1), S43-48.

221. Shelokov et al., (1957). op cit.; Poskanzer et al., (1957). op cit.; 1957; Albrecht et al., (1964). op cit.

222. Merskey, H. (1979). *The Analysis of Hysteria.* London: Bailliere Tindall.

223. Gilliam (1938). op cit.; Ramsay, A.M. (1957). "Encephalomyelitis in North-west London. An Endemic Infection Simulating Poliomyelitis and Hysteria." *Lancet* ii:1196-2200.

224. Bartholomew, Robert E. (1994). "Tarantism, Dancing Mania and Demonopathy: The Anthro-Political Aspects of Mass Psychogenic Illness." *Psychological Medicine* 24:281-306, see p. 298.

225. Watts, Geoff (2002). "All in the Mind." *New Scientist* 174 (2349):54-55. See p. 55.

226. http://dspace.dial.pipex.com/comcare/chrome/whatis.html. CHROME: (Case History Research on ME), 3 Britannia Road, London SW6 2HJ.

227. Lucire Y. (1986). "Neurosis in the Workplace." *Medical Journal of Australia* 145:323-327; Ferguson, D. (1987). "RSI: Putting the Epidemic to Rest." *Medical Journal of Australia* 147:213; Hall, W., and Morrow, L. (1988). "Repetition Strain Injury: An Australian Epidemic of Upper Limb Pain." *Social Science and Medicine* 27:645-649.

228. Ireland, D.C.R. (1986). "Repetitive Strain Injury." *Australian Family Physician* 15:415-418.

229. Bammer, Gabriele, and Martin, Brian (1988). "The Arguments about RSI: An Examination." *Community Health Studies* 12(3):348-358, accessed July 1, 2003, online at: http://www.uow.edu.au/ arts/sts/bmartin/pubs/88chs.html.

230. Bammer and Martin (1988). op cit.

231. Bammer and Martin (1988). op cit.

232. Bell, D.S. (1989a). "'Repetitive Strain Injury': An Iatrogenic Epidemic of Simulated Injury." *Medical Journal of Australia* 151:280-284; Bell, D.S. (1989b). "'Repetitive Strain Injury': An Iatrogenic Epidemic. In Reply." *Medical Journal of Australia* 151:599-600.

233. Hall and Morrow (1988). op cit., p. 646.

234. Bell (1989a). op cit.

235. Hunter, L. (1989). "'Repetitive Strain Injury': An Iatrogenic Epidemic." *Medical Journal of Australia* 151:598.

236. Bell (1989ab). op cit.

237. Forsyth, J.R.L. (1989). "'Repetitive Strain Injury': An Iatrogenic Epidemic." *Medical Journal of Australia* 151:598.

238. Awerbuch, M. (1985). "RSI or Kangaroo Paw?" *Medical Journal of Australia* 142:376; Sharrod, H. L. (1985). "RSI, Kangaroo Paw, or What?" *Medical Journal of Australia* 142:376.

239. Hall and Morrow (1988). op cit., p. 646.

240. Lucrie (1986). op cit., p. 324.

241. Beard, G.M. (1879). "Conclusions from the Study of 125 Cases of Writer's Cramp and Allied Affectations." *Medical Record* (New York): 224-247.

242. Smith, H., Culpin, H., Farmer, E. (1927). *A Study of Telegraphists' Cramp.* Medical Research Council, Industrial Fatigue Research Board.

243. Anonymous (1911). *Great Britain and Ireland Post Office, Department Committee on Telegraphist's Cramp Report.* London: His Majesty's Stationary Office; Lucire (1986). op cit.

244. Lucire (1986). op cit.

245. Leino, P., and Hanninen, V. (1995). "Psychosocial Factors at Work in Relation to Back and Limb Disorders." *Scandinavian Journal of Work, Environment and Health* 21:134-142. See p. 134.

246. Wessely, S. (1997). "Psychological, Social and Media Influences on the Experience of Somatic Symptoms." Paper prepared for ESF Workshop on "Cognitive Functions as Mediators of Environmental Effects on Health," September 15-17th 1997, p. 9.

247. Wessely, S. (1997). op cit., p. 9.

248. The following sections on the pattern of report incidence and concluding remarks, is partially excerpted from Bartholomew and Sirois (2000). op cit., pp. 512-514.

249. Ackerman, S.E., and Lee, R.L. (1981). "Communication and Cognitive Pluralism in a Spirit Possession Event in Malaysia." *American Ethnologist* 8:789-99.

250. Bell, A., and Jones, A.T. (1958). "Fumigation with dichlorethyl ether and chlordane: Hysterical sequelae." *Medical Journal of Australia* 5:258-263.

251. Sinks, T., Kerndt, P.R., and Wallingford, K.M. (1989). "Two Episodes of Acute Illness in a Machine Shop." *American Journal of Public Health* 79:1024-1028.

252. Yassi, A., Weeks, J.L., Samson, K., and Raber, M.B. (1989). "Epidemic of 'Shocks' in Telephone Operators: Lessons for the Medical Community." *Canadian Medical Association Journal* 140:816-820.

253. Sparks et al. (1990). op cit.

254. Markush, R.E. (1973). "Mental Epidemics: A Review of the Old to Prepare for the New." *Public Health Reviews* 4:353-442.

255. Bartholomew, R.E. (1990). "Ethnocentricity and the Social Construction of 'Mass Hysteria.'" op cit.

256. Sirois F. (1982b). "Epidemic Hysteria." In A. Roy (ed.), Hysteria (101-115). New York: John Wiley; Sirois, F. (1977). Remarques sur l'hysterie collective. *Evolution Psychiatrique* 42:111-24.

257. Inglis, B. (1990). *Trance: A Natural History of Altered States of Consciousness.* London: Paladin, p. 217.

258. Teoh, J. (1972). "Epidemic hysteria in Malaysia." In *Proceedings of the 7th Malaysia-Singapore Congress of Medicine* (August 14-16). The Academy of Medicine of Malaysia, General Hospital, Kuala Lumpur, Malaysia, 73-78.

259. Cornwell, John (1996). *The Power to Harm.* New York: Viking/ Penguin, p. 81.

260. Cruz, C.M. (1990). "Health and Work: The Case of the Gas Emissions at the Industrial Complex of Mayaguez." *Puerto Rician Health Sciences Journal* 9:123-125.

261. A chronological list of reported episodes of mass anxiety hysteria in job settings appears as follows: Parigi, S, and Giagiotti, F. (1956). "Su di una epidemica di isterismo." *Rassegna di Studi Psichiatri* (Siena), 45:1112-1114; Bell and Jones (1956). op cit.; Champion et al. (1963). op cit.; McEvedy, C.P., Griffith, A., Hall, T. (1966). "Two school epidemics. *British Medical Journal* ii:1300-1302; Markush (1973). op cit.; Stahl, S.M. (1982). op cit.; Phillips, P.E. (1974). Internal report prepared for the Division of Health, the State of Missouri. Summarized in: M.J. Colligan and L.R. Murphy. "A review of mass psychogenic illness in work settings." In M. Colligan, J. Pennebaker and L. Murphy (eds.), *Mass Psychogenic Illness: A Social Psychological Analysis* (33-52). Hillsdale, New Jersey: Lawrence Erlbaum; Folland, D.S. (1975). Suspect toluene exposure at a boot factory: Internal report from the Tennessee Department of Health: Tennessee. Summarized in: M.J. Colligan and L.R. Murphy. "A review of mass psychogenic illness in work settings." In M. Colligan, J. Pennebaker and L. Murphy (eds.), *Mass Psychogenic Illness: A Social Psychological Analysis* (33-52). Hillsdale, New Jersey: Lawrence Erlbaum; National Institute of Occupational Safety and Health sponsored study TA-76-102, cited in

Colligan and Murphy (1982); National Institute of Occupational Safety and Health sponsored study HHE-77-27-437, cited in Colligan and Murphy (1982); National Institute of Occupational Safety and Health sponsored study TA-77-35, cited in Colligan and Murphy (1982); National Institute of Occupational Safety and Health sponsored study TA-78-58, cited in Colligan and Murphy (1982); National Institute of Occupational Safety and Health sponsored study TA-78-10, cited in Colligan and Murphy (1982); National Institute of Occupational Safety and Health sponsored study HHE-78-116-557, cited in Colligan and Murphy (1982); National Institute of Occupational Safety and Health Report cited in Colligan and Murphy (1982); National Institute of Occupational Safety and Health Report cited in Colligan and Murphy (1982); Maguire, A. (1978). "Psychic possession among industrial workers." Letter. *Lancet*, i, 376-78; Cunliffe, W.J. (1978). "Psychic possession among industrial workers." Letter. *Lancet*, ii, 44; Cohen, B., Colligan, M., Wester, W., and Smith, M. (1978). "An investigation of job satisfaction factors in an incident of mass psychogenic illness at the workplace." *Occupational Health Nursing* 26:10-16; Murphy, L.R., and Colligan, M.J. (1979). "Mass psychogenic illness in a shoe factory: A case report." *International Archives of Occupational and Environmental Health* 44:133-38; Boulougouris, J.C., Rabavilas, A.D., Stefanis, C.N., Vaidakis, N., and Tabouratzis, D.G. (1981). "Epidemic Faintness: A Psychophysiological Investigation." *Psychiatria Clinica* 14:215-225; Phoon, W.H. (1982). "Outbreaks of mass hysteria at workplaces in Singapore: Some patterns and modes of presentation." In M. Colligan, J. Pennebaker and L. Murphy (eds.), *Mass Psychogenic Illness: A Social Psychological Analysis* (21-32). Hillsdale, New Jersey: Lawrence Erlbaum; Boxer, P.A. (1985). "Occupational mass psychogenic illness: History, prevention, management." *Journal of Occupational Medicine* 27:867-872; Ilchyshyn, A., and Smith, A.G. (1985). "Gum arabic sensitivity with epidemic hysteria dermatologica." *Contact Dermatitis* 13:282-283; Alexander, R.W., and Fedoruk, M.J. (1986). "Epidemic psychogenic illness in a telephone operator's building." *Journal of Occupational Medicine* 28:42-45; Donnell and colleagues used the nondescript title, "Report of an Illness Outbreak at the Harry S Truman State Office Building,"; Hall, E.M., and Johnson, J.V. (1989). "A case of stress and mass psychogenic illness in industrial workers." *Journal of Occupational Medicine* 31:243-250; Sinks et al. (1989). op cit.; Yassi et al. (1989). op cit.; Sparks et al. (1990). op cit.; Struewing and Gray (1990). op cit.; House, R.A., Holness, D.L. (1997). "Investigation of Factors Affecting Mass Psychogenic Illness in Employees in a Fish-Packing Plant." *American Journal of Industrial Medicine* 32(1):90-6; Ford, C.V. (1997). "Somatization and fashionable diagnoses: illness as a way of life." *Scandinavian Journal of Work, Environment and Health* 23 Supplementum 3:7-16; Magnavita, N. (2000). "Industrial Mass Psychogenic Illness: The Unfashionable Diagnosis." *British Journal of Medical Psychology* 73 (Part 3):371-5 (September).

A chronological list of reported episodes of mass motor hysteria in job settings appears as follows: St. Clare (1787). op cit; Seeligmuller, A. (1876). "Uber epidemisches auftreten von hysterischen zustanden." *Allgemeine Zeitschift fur Psychiatrie* (Berlin), 33:510-28; Bouzol, M. (1884). "Relation d'une epidemie a phenomene hysterico-choreique observee a Algon (Ardeche) en 1882." *Lyon Medical* 47:142-148; 174-184; 211-217; Schatalow, N. (1891). "Zur frage von der epidemischen hysterie." *Neurologisches Centralblatt* 10:405; Bechtereff, V. (1914). "Donnees sur l'epidemie neuro-psychique observee chez les travailleurs d'usine de riga et de petro-grad en mars 1914." *Obozrienie Psikhiatrii Nevrologii (Review of Psychiatry and Neurology* (Petrograd) 19:585-613; Franchini, A. (1947). "Manifestazioni isteriche collettive interpretate come sintomi di intossicazione da gas ignoto." *Medicina di Lavoro* 38:57-60; Parin, P. (1948). "Die kriegneurose der Jugoslawen." *Schweizer Arch f Neurol u Psychiat.* 61:303-24; Chew, P.K. (1978). "How to handle hysterical factory workers." *Occupational Health and Safety* 47(2):50-54; Ackerman and Lee (1981). op cit.; Phoon (1982). op cit.; Chan, M., and Kee, W.C. (1983). "Epidemic hysteria: A study of high risk factors." *Occupational Health and Safety* 52:55-64; Ong (1987). op cit.

A chronological list of reported episodes involving the relabeling of mundane symptoms appears as follows: Beard (1879). op cit.; Smith et al. (1927). op cit.; Gilliam (1938). op cit.; Acheson E. (1954). "Encephalomyelitis associated with poliomyelitis virus. An outbreak in a nurses' home." *The Lancet* ii:1044-1048; Acheson (1959). op cit.; Acheson E. (1955). "Letter." *The Lancet* ii, 395; Macrae, A., and Galpine, J. (1954). "An illness resembling poliomyelitis." *The Lancet* ii:350-352; Shelokov et al., 1957; Anonymous. (1955). "Clinical meeting of the Natal coastal branch. The Durban mystery disease." *South African Medical Journal* 29:997; Hill, R.C. (1955). "Memorandum on the outbreak amongst the nurses at Addington, Durban." *South African Medical Journal* 29:344; Hill, R.C., Cheetham, R.W., Wallace, H.L. (1955). "Epidemic myalgic encephalopathy." *The Lancet* 1:689-93; McEvedy, C., and Beard, A. (1970a). "Royal free hospital epidemic of 1955: A reconsideration." *British Medical Journal* i:7-10; McEvedy, C., and Beard, A. (1970b). "Concept of benign myalgic encephalomyelitis." *British Medical Journal* i:11-15; Poskanzer et al. (1957). op cit.; Geffen, D., and Tracy, S. (1957). "Outbreak of acute infective encephalomyelitis in a residential home for nurses in 1956." *British Medical Journal* ii:904; Daikos et al. (1959). op cit.; Ikeda, Y. (1966). "An epidemic of emotional disturbance among leprosarium nurses in a setting of low morale and social change." *Psychiatry* 29:152-164; Albrecht (1964). op cit.; Dillon, M.J., Marshall, W.C., and Dudgeon, J.A., (1974). "Epidemic neuromyasthenia: Outbreak among nurses at a children's hospital." *British Medical Journal* [Clin Res] 1:301-305; Lucire (1986). op cit.

262. For complicated reasons, Robert Bartholomew was unable to study these outbreaks, but they were numerous between 1993 and 1995, none to his knowledge were ever recorded in scientific studies, and only very occasionally did they appear in Malaysian newspaper reports.

263. Sirois, F. (1982). "Perspectives on Epidemic Hysteria." In M. Colligan, J. Pennebaker and L. Murphy L (Eds) *Mass Psychogenic Illness: A Social Psychological Analysis*, pp. 217-236 (Hillsdale, New Jersey, Lawrence Erlbaum).

264. Mackay, Charles. (1852). *Memoirs of Extraordinary Popular Delusions and the Madness of Crowds Volume 2*. London: Office of the National Illustrated Library, pp. 539-540.

265. Bartholomew, Robert E., and Sirois, Francois (1996). "Epidemic Hysteria in Schools: An International and Historical Overview." *Educational Studies* 22(3):285-311, see p. 304.

266. Faust, H.S., Brilliant L.B. (1981). "Is the Diagnosis of 'Mass Hysteria' an Excuse for Incomplete Investigation of Low-Level Environmental Contamination?" *Journal of Occupational Medicine* 23:22-26; Bartholomew, R.E. (1990). "Ethnocentricity and the Social Construction of 'Mass Hysteria.'" *Culture, Medicine and Psychiatry* 14:455-494; Brabant, C., Mergler, D., Messing, K. (1990). "Va te Faire Soigner, ton usine est Malade; La Place de l'hysterie de Mass and la Problematique de la sante des Femmes au Travail." [Go Take Care of Yourself, Your Factory is Sick: The Place of Mass Hysteria in the Problem of Women's Health at Work]. *Sante Mentale au Quebec* 15:181-204.

267. Sirois, F. (1974). "Epidemic Hysteria." *Acta Psychiatrica Scandinavica Supplementum* 252:7-46; Sirois (1982). op cit.; Wessely, S. (1987). "Mass Hysteria: Two Syndromes?" *Psychological Medicine* 17:109-120.

268. Kendell, R.E., Zealley, A.K. (Eds) (1993). *Companion to Psychiatric Studies*, fifth edition (London, Churchill Livingstone).
269. Wessely (1987). op cit.
270. Bartholomew and Sirois, Francois (1996). op cit., p. 293.
271. Schuler, Edgar A., and Parenton, Vincent J. (1943). "A Recent Epidemic of Hysteria in a Louisiana High School." *Journal of Social Psychology* 17:221-235; Teoh, J., Soewondo, S., and Sidharta, M. (1975). "Epidemic Hysteria in Malaysia: An Illustrative Episode." *Psychiatry* 8(3):258-268; Benaim, S., Horder, J., and Anderson, J. (1973). "Hysterical Epidemic in a Classroom." *Psychological Medicine* 3:366-373.
272. Bartholomew and Sirois, Francois (1996). op cit., pp. 293, 296.
273. Moss, P.D., and McEvedy, C.P. (1966). "An Epidemic of Overbreathing Among Schoolgirls." *British Medical Journal* ii:1295-1300.
274. Bartholomew and Sirois, Francois (1996). op cit., p. 296.
275. Moss and McEvedy (1966). op cit., p. 1299.
276. Baker, P., and Selvey, D. (1992). "Malathion-induced Epidemic Hysteria in an Elementary School." *Veterinary and Human Toxicology* 34:156-160. See p. 157.
277. Baker and Selvey (1992). op cit., p. 157.
278. Baker and Selvey (1992). op cit., p. 157.
279. Baker and Selvey (1992). op cit., p. 158.
280. Baker and Selvey (1992). op cit., p. 160.
281. Baker and Selvey (1992). op cit., p. 159.
282. Baker and Selvey (1992). op cit., p. 159.
283. Baker and Selvey (1992). op cit., p. 159.
284. Baker and Selvey (1992). op cit., pp. 159-160.
285. Baker and Selvey (1992). op cit., p. 160.
286. Bhatiasevi, Aphaluck. (2001). "Belief in Ghosts Sparks Hysteria: Students Freak Out at School Camp." *Bangkok Post*, February 4, 2001.
287. Zane, Damian (2003). "Mass fainting hits Ethiopian students." British Broadcasting Corporation, Friday, 14 February, accessed June 27, 2003 at: http://news.bbc.co.uk/2/hi/ africa/2763141.stm.
288. Bartholomew and Sirois, Francois (1996). op cit., pp. 296-97.
289. Bartholomew and Sirois, Francois (1996). op cit., p. 297.
290. Johnson, H. (1908). "Moral Instruction and Training in France." Pp. 1-50. In M.E. Sadler (ed.), *Moral Instruction and Training in Schools: Report of an International Inquiry, Volume 2*. London: Longmans, Green and Company, p. 26.
291. Johnson (1908). op cit., p. 26.
292. Johnson (1908). op cit., p. 27.
293. Dumville, B. (1908). "Should the French System of Moral Instruction be Introduced into England." Pp. 116-117. In M.E. Sadler (ed.), *Moral Instruction and Training in Schools: Report of an International Inquiry, Volume 2*. London: Longmans, Green, and Company.
294. Spiller, G. (1908a). "Moral Education in the Boys' Schools of Germany." Pp. 213-230. In M. E. Sadler (ed.), *Moral Instruction and Training in Schools: Report of an International Inquiry, Volume 2*. London: Longmans, Green and Company, p. 215.
295. Montgomery, J.D. (1908). "The Education of Girls in Germany: its Methods of Moral Instruction and Training." Pp. 231-241. In M. E. Sadler (ed.), *Moral Instruction and Training in Schools: Report of an International Inquiry, Volume 2*. London: Longmans, Green and Company, pp. 237-238.
296. Spiller, G. (1908b). "An Educational Democracy: Moral Instruction and Training in the Schools of Switzerland." Pp. 196-206. In M. E. Sadler (ed.), *Moral Instruction and Training in Schools: Report of an International Inquiry, Volume 2*. London: Longmans, Green and Company, p. 196.
297. Ibid., pp. 199 and 203.
298. Aemmer, F. (1893). *Eine Schulepidemie von Tremor Hystericus* [A School Epidemic of Hysterical Tremor]. Inaugural dissertation, Basel.
299. Zollinger, E. (1906). "Uber die Padagogische Behandlung des Nervosen Zitterns der Schulkinder" [On the Educational Treatment of Nervous Trembling in School Children]. *Jahrbuch der Schweiz Gesellschaft fur Schulgesundheitspflege* 7:20-47.
300. Hirt, L. (1893). "Eine Epidemie von Hysterischen Krampfen in einer Schleisischen Dorfschule" [An Epidemic of Hysterical Cramp in a Village School in Schleisischen]. *Zeitschrift fur Schulgesundheitspflege* 6:225-229. (Summary of an article by L. Hirt in the *Berliner Klinische Wochenschrift*).
301. Schutte, P. (1906). "Eine neue form Hysterischer Zustande bei Schulkindern" [A New Form of Hysterical Conditions in School Children]. *Muenchener Medizinsche Wochenschrift* 53:1763-1764, translated from German by Edgar Schuler and Vincent Parenton and cited in Schuler, E. A., and Parenton, V. J. (1943). "A Recent Epidemic of Hysteria in a Louisiana High School." *Journal of Social Psychology* 17:221-235. Excerpt quoted appears on p. 222.
302. Schuler, E. A., and Parenton, V. J. (1943). "A Recent Epidemic of Hysteria in a Louisiana High School." *Journal of Social Psychology* 17:221-235.
303. Knight, J. A., Friedman, Theodore I., and Sulianti, J. (1965). "Epidemic Hysteria: A Field Study." *American Journal of Public Health* 55:858-865.
304. The follow section on mass motor hysteria in nonwestern settings is exzcerpted from Bartholomew and Sirois (1996). op cit., pp. 297-299, 302.
305. Muhangi, J.R. (1973). "Mass Hysteria in an Ankole School." *East African Medical Journal* 50:304-309; Ebrahim, G.J. (1968). "Mass Hysteria in School Children, Notes on Three Outbreaks in East Africa." *Clinical Pediatrics* 7:437-438; Kagwa, B.H. (1964). "The Problem of Mass Hysteria in East Africa." *East African Medical Journal* 41:560-566; Rankin, A.M., and Philip, P.J. (1963). "An Epidemic of Laughing in the Buboka District of Tanganyika." *Central African Journal of Medicine* 9:167-170.
306. Dhadphale, M., and Shaikh, S.P. (1983). "Epidemic Hysteria in a Zambian School: 'The Mysterious Madness of Mwinilunga.'" *British Journal of Psychiatry* 142:85-88.
307. Dhadphale, M., and Shaikh, S.P. (1983). op cit., p. 87.
308. Ebrahim (1968). op cit., p. 438.
309. Teoh, J.I., and Tan, E.S. (1976). "An Outbreak of Epidemic Hysteria in West Malaysia." Pp. 32-43. In W.P. Lebra (ed.), *Culture-Bound Syndromes, Ethnopsychiatry, and Alternate Therapies, Volume IV of Mental Health Research in Asia and the Pacific*. Honolulu: University Press of Hawaii; Teoh and Yeoh (1973). op cit.
310. Tan, E.S. (1963). "Epidemic Hysteria." *Medical Journal of Malaya* 18:72-76.
311. Selvadurai, S. (1985). *Problems of Residential Students in a Secondary Technical School*. Master's thesis, University of Malaya, Kuala Lumpur.
312. Deva, M.P. (1990). *Psychiatry: A Brief Outline of Clinical Psychological Medicine*. Selangor, Malaysia: Ophir Medical Specialists.
313. Ackerman, S.E. (1980). *Cultural Process in Malaysian Industrialization: A Study of Malay Women Factory Workers*. Ph.D. thesis, University of California at San Diego. University Microfilms: Ann Arbor, MI.
314. Teoh, J., Soewondo, S., and Sidharta, M. (1975). "Epidemic Hysteria in Malaysia: An Illustrative Episode." *Psychiatry* 8(3):258-268. See p. 260.
315. Skeat, W.W. (1900). *Malay Magic*. London: Macmillan; Gimlette,

J.D. (1915). *Malay Poisons and Charm Cures*. London: Oxford University Press; Chen, P.C.Y. (1970). "Indigenous Malay Psychotherapy." *Tropical and Geographical Medicine* 22:409; Endicott, K. (1970). *An Analysis of Malay Magic*. Oxford: Clarendon.

316. Benaim et al. (1973). op cit.

317. Hecker, J.F.C. (1837[1970]). *The Dancing Mania of the Middle Ages*, translated by B Babington. New York, B Franklin; Calmeil, L.F. (1845). *De la Folie, Consideree Sous le Point de vue Pathologique, Philosophique, Historique et Judiciaire* [On the Crowd, Considerations on the Point of Pathology, Philosophy, History and Justice]. Paris: Baillere; Madden, R.R. (1857). *Phantasmata or Illusions and Fanaticisms of Protean Forms Productive of Great Evils*. London: T.C. Newby; Davy, R.B. (1880). "'St. Vitus' Dance and Kindred Affection; The Recent Epidemic at the Ursulin Convent in Brown County, Ohio; A Sketch of the Historic Disease." *Cincinnati Lancet and Clinic* 4:440-445, 467-473; Garnier, S. (1895). *Barbe Buvee, en Religion, Soeur Sainte-Colombe et la Pretendue Possession des Ursulines d'Auxonne* [Barbara Buvee, and Religion, Sister Columbe and the Feigned Possession of the Ursulines at Auxonne]. Paris: Felix Alcan; Loredan, J. (1912). *Un Grand Proces de Sorcellerie au XVIIe siecle, L'Abbe Gaufridy et Madeleine de Demandolx (1600-1670)* [The Grand Process of Witchcraft in the Seventeenth Century, L'Abbe Gaufridy and Madeleine de Demandolx (1600-1670)]. Paris: Perrin et Cie; Huxley, A. (1952). *The Devils of Loudun*. New York: Harper & Brothers; Rosen, G. (1968). *Madness in Society*. London: Routledge and Kegan Paul; Thomas, K. (1971). *Religion and the Decline of Magic*. London: Weidenfeld and Nicolson; Bartholomew, R.E. (1994). "Tarantism, Dancing Mania and Demonopathy: The Anthro-Political Aspects of 'Mass Psychogenic Illness.'" *Psychological Medicine* 24:281-306.

318. Carlisle, Adrienne (1999). "Stress may have Caused 'Mass Hysteria." *South African Dispatch*, May 29, 1999, online at http://www.dispatch.co.za/1999 /05/29/easterncape/CAUSED. HTM.

319. Bridgraj, Ajith (1999). "A Mysterious 'Madness.'" *The Teacher* at http://www.teacher. co.za/9908/demon.html.

320. Bridgraj (1999). op cit.

321. Philen, R.M., Kilbourn, E.M., and McKinley, T.W. (1989). "Mass Sociogenic Illness by Proxy: Parentally Reported in an Elementary School." *The Lancet* ii:1372-1376. See p. 1376.

322. Kerr J. (1907). *Report of the London Medical Officer (Education)*. London: London County Council, p. 32.

323. Levy, D.A., and Nail, P.R. (1993). "Contagion: A Theoretical and Empirical Review and Reconceptualization. *Genetic, Social and General Psychology Monographs* 119 (3):235-283. See p. 270.

324. Levy and Nail (1993). op cit., p. 270.

325. Small, M.H. (1896). "The Suggestibility of Children." *Pedagogical Seminary* 4: 176-220.

326. The following section is excerpted from Bartholomew and Sirois (1996). op cit., pp. 303-305.

327. Wessely 1987, op cit.

328. Aldous, J.C., Ellam, G. A., Murray, V., and Pike, G. (1994). "An Outbreak of Illness Among Schoolchildren in London: Toxic Poisoning not Mass Hysteria." *Journal of Epidemiology and Community Health* 48:41-45.

329. Roueche, B. (1978). *The New Yorker* (August 21) (Interview with Dr. Joel Nitzkin). Nitzkin, J.L. (1976). "Epidemic Transient Situational Disturbance in an Elementary School." *Journal of the Florida Medical Association* 63:357-359.

330. Wong et al. (1982). op cit.

331. Cartter, M.L., MsHar, P., and Burdo, H. (1989). "The Epidemic Hysteria Dilemma." *American Journal of Diseases in Childhood* 143:89.

332. Wessely (1987). op cit., p. 188.

333. See, for example: Bokai, cited in Szego, K. (1896). "Uber die Imitationskrankheiten der Kinder" [About the Imitative Illnesses of Children]. *Jahrbuch fur Kinderheilkunde* (Leipzig) 41:133-145; Legendre (1908). op cit.; Olson (1928). op cit.; Moss et al. (1966). op cit.; McEvedy and Moss (1966). op cit.; "Four-Man Medical Team Visits School: Student Describes Mystery Ghost." *The Straits Times*, November 21 1966, p. 11; Mausner, J. S., and Gezon, H.M. (1967). "Report on a Phantom Epidemic of Gonorrhea." *American Journal of Epidemiology* 85:320-331; Lyons, H.A., and Potter, P.E. (1970). "Communicated Hysteria–An Episode in a Secondary School." *Journal of the Irish Medical Association* 63:377-379; "Hysteria Breaks Out in Another School in Pahang." *The Straits Times*, April 30, 1971, p. 10; "Peace Offering Brings School 'in Hysterics' back to Normal." *The Straits Times*, May 1 1971, p. 20; "'Hysteria' Pupils Out of Hospital." *The Straits Times*, May 7 1971, p. 21; "A Mass Hysteria puts an End to First Aid Course." *The Straits Times*, April 5, 1972, p. 17; "Two Girls Warded for Hysteria Leave Hospital." *The Straits Times*, April 6 1972, p. 4; Goldberg (1973). op cit.; Smith, H.C.T., and Eastham, E.J. (1973). "Outbreak of Abdominal Pain." *The Lancet* ii:956-959; Levine, R.J., Sexton, D.J., Romm, F.J., Wood, B. T., and Kaiser, J. (1974). "An Outbreak of Psychosomatic Illness at a Rural Elementary School." *The Lancet* ii:l500-1503; Polk, L.D. (1974). "Mass Hysteria in an Elementary School." *Clinical Pediatrics* 13:1013-1014; Sirois (1974). op cit.; Sirois (1975). op cit.; Nitzkin (1975). op cit.; Levine, R.J. (1977). "Epidemic Faintness and Syncope in a School Marching Band." *Journal of the American Medical Association* 238(22):2373-2376; Figueroa, M. (1979). "(Related) in Epidemic Hysteria (Editorial)." *British Medical Journal* ii:409; "Mass Hysteria Hits School Kuah." *The Star* (Malaysia), March 27 1978; Forrester, R.M. (1979). "Epidemic Hysteria–Divide and Conquer." *British Medical Journal* (15 September) 2:669; Bebbington, E., Hopton, C., Lockett, H.I., and Madeley, R.J. (1980). "From Experience: Epidemic Syncope in Jazz Bands." *Community Medicine* 2:302-307; O'Donnell, B., Elliot, T.J., and Huibonhoa, C. (1980). "An Outbreak of Illness in a Rural School." *Journal of the Irish Medical Association* 73:300-302; Lee and Ackerman (1980). op cit.; Moffat, M.E. (1982). "Epidemic Hysteria in a Montreal Train Station." *Pediatrics* 70:308-310; Small and Nicholi (1982). op cit.; Wong et al. (1982). op cit.; Tam et al. (1982). op cit.; "Hysteria at Girls' School." *The New Straits Times*, May 18 1982; "School Hit by Mass Hysteria." *The New Straits Times*, September 9, 1982; "Hysterical Schoolgirls Cause Panic." *The Echo*, September 9, 1982; "Hysteria Probe." Bernama, September 10, 1982; Omar A. "Mass Hysteria in Two Johore Schools." *The New Straits Times*, September 21, 1982; Modan et al. (1983). op cit.; Small and Borus (1983). op cit.; Wason, S., and Bausher, J. (1983). "Epidemic Mass Hysteria." *The Lancet* (September 24) ii:731-732; Roback, H.B., Roback, E., and LaBarbera, J.D. (1984). "Epidemic Grieving at a Birthday Party: A Case of Mass Hysteria." *Journal of Developmental and Behavioral Pediatrics* 5:86-89; "'Pontianak' Hysteria." *The New Straits Times*, September 21 1983; Veera, R. V. "Soccer Women Fall Foul to Hysterical Fits." *The New Straits Times*, August 10 1983; "School Closes after 13 Become Hysterical." Bernama (Malaysian News Service) August 22 1983; "School Hit by Hysteria." Bernama (Malaysian News Service), August 26 1983; "Sekolah Ditutup Kerana 15 Murid Sakit Histeria" [School closed because 15 students had hysteria disease]. *Berita Harian*, August 29 1983; Robinson, P., Szewczyk, M., Haddy, L., Jones, P., and Harvey, W. (1984). "Outbreak of Itching and Rash." *Archives of Internal Medicine* 144:159-162; Araki, S., and Honma, T. (1986). "Mass Psychogenic Systemic Illness in School Children in Relation to the Tokyo Photochemical Smog."

Archives of Environmental Health 41:159-162; "15 Pupils Hit by Mystery Itch." *The New Straits Times*, June 6 1984; "Bomoh to the Aid of Hysteria-stricken Pupils." *The New Straits Times*, May 22, 1984; Goh, K.T. (1987). "Epidemiological Enquiries into a School Outbreak of an Unusual Illness." *International Journal of Epidemiology* 16(2):265-270; "Three in Hospital after Bouts of Hysteria." *The New Straits Times*, 22 February, 1986; "9 Pelajar Diserang Histeria" [9 students were stricken with hysteria]. *Utusan*, February 22 1986; "Sembilan Pelajar Diserang Histeria" [Nine students were stricken with hysteria]. *Berita Harian*, February 22, 1986; Elkins, G.E., Gamino, L.A., and Rynearson, R.R. (1988). "Mass Psychogenic Illness, Trance States and Suggestion." *American Journal of Clinical Hypnosis* 30:267-275; "Department Probes Hysteria Outbreak." *The New Straits Times*, September 4, 1987; 11 hit by hysteria. *The Malay Mail*, September 23, 1987; "Hysteria Hits 23 Students." Bernama (Malaysian News Service), October 1 1987; Ruiz, M.T., and Lopez, J.M. (1988). "Mass Hysteria in a Secondary School." *International Journal of Epidemiology* 17:475-476; Cartter et al. (1989). op cit; "Hysteria at School During Blackout." *The Star* (Malaysia), April 30 1988; Gamino, L. A., Elkins, G.R., and Hackney, K.U. (1989). "Emergency Management of Mass Psychogenic Illness." *Psychosomatics* 3(4):446-449; Goldsmith (1989). op cit.; Philen et al. (1989). op cit.; Selden, B.S. (1989). "Adolescent Epidemic Hysteria Presenting as a Mass Casualty, Toxic Exposure Incident." *Annals of Emergency Medicine* 18(8):892-895; Cole (1990). op cit.; Small et al (1991). op cit.; Baker, P., and Selvey, D. (1992). "Malathio-Induced Epidemic Hysteria in an Elementary School." *Veterinary and Human Toxicology* 34:156-160; Desenclos, J.C., Gardner, H., and Horan, M. (1992). "Mass Sociogenic Illness in a Youth Center." *Revue d'Epidemiologie et de Sante Publique* (Paris) 40:201-208; Krug, S. (1992). "Mass Illness at an Intermediate School: Toxic Fumes or Epidemic Hysteria?" *Pediatric Emergency Care* 8:280-282; Rockney and Lemke (1992). op cit.; Taylor, B.W., and Werbicki, J.E. (1993). "A Case of Mass Hysteria involving 19 Schoolchildren." *Pediatric Emergency Care* 9:216-217; Peiro, E.F., Yanez, J.L., Carraminana, I., Rullan, J.V., Castell, J. (1996). "Study of an Outbreak of Hysteria After Hepatitis B Vaccination." *Medicina Clinica* 107(1):1-3; Amin, Y., Hamdi, E., Eapen, V. (1997). "Mass Hysteria in an Arab Culture." *The International Journal of Social Psychiatry* 43(4):303-306; Yasamy, M.T., Bahramnezhad, A., Ziaaddini H. (1999). "Postvaccination Mass Psychogenic Illness in an Iranian Rural School." *East Mediterrean Health Journal* 5(4):710-6; Jones, T.F., Craig, A.S., Hoy, D., Gunter, E.W., Ashley, D.L., Barr, D.B., Brock, J.W., and Schaffner, W. (2000). "Mass Psychogenic Illness Attributed to Toxic Exposure at a High School." *The New England Journal of Medicine* 342(2):96-100; Kharabsheh S, Al-Otoum H, Clements J, Abbas A, Khuri-Bulos N, Belbesi A, Gaafar T, Dellepiane N. (2001). "Mass Psychogenic Illness Following Tetanus-Diphtheria Toxoid Vaccination in Jordan." *Bulletin of the World Health Organization* 2001;79(8):764-70.

334. See, for example: Hirsch, A. (1883). *Handbook of Geographical and Historical Pathology*. London: New Sydenham Society; Regnard, M., Simon, J. (1877). "Sur une Epidemie de Contracture des Extremites Observee a Gentilly" [On an Epidemic of Limb Contracture Observed in Gentilly]. *Comptes Rendus des Seances de la Societe de Biologie* (Paris) 3:344-347, 350-353; Armainguad, M. (1879). "Recherches Cliniques sur l'hysterie; Relation d'une Petite Epidemie d'hysterie Observee a Bordeaux" [Clinical Research on Hysteria and its Relation to a Small Epidemic of Hysteria Observed in Bordeaux] *Memoire et Bulletin de la Societe de Medecine et Chirurgie de Bordeaux*:551-579; Laquer, L. (1888). "Uber eine chorea-epidemie" [An Epidemic of Chorea]. *Deutsche Medizinische Wochenschrift* (Leipzig) 14:1045-1046; Wichmann, R. (1890). "Eine sogenannte veitstanzepidemie in Wildbad" [A So-called Epidemic of St. Vitus Dance in Wildbad]. *Deutsche Medizinische Wochenschrift* (Leipzig) 16:632-636, 659-663; Schatalow, N. (1891). "Zur Frage von der Epidemischen Hysterie" [On the Question of Epidemic Hysteria]. *Neurologische Centralblatt* 10:405; Palmer (1892). "Psychische seuche in der Sbersten Slasse einer Sadchenschule" [A Psychic Epidemic in the Highest Grade of a Girls School]. *Zentralblatt fur Nervenheilkunde und Psychiatrie* 3:301-308; Rembold, S. (1893). "Acute Psychiche Contagion in Einer Madchenschule" [Acute Psychic Contagion in a Girls School]. *Berliner Klinische Wochenschrift* 30:662-663; Hagenbach, E. (1893). Chorea-epidemie [Epidemic Chorea]. *Korrespondenz-Blatt f Schweizer Aerzte* (Basel) 23:631-632; cited in Sirois (1974). op cit.; Leuch (1896). "Eine Sogenannte Chorea-Epidemie in der Schule" [A So-called Chorea Epidemic in the School]. *Korrespondenz-Blatt f Aerzte* (Basel) 26:465-476; Von Holwede (1898). "Eine Epidemie von Hysterischen Anfallen in einer Burgerschule zu Braunschweig" [Hysterical Attacks in a Middle School in Brunswick]. *Jahrbuch fur Kinderheilkunde* (Leipzig). n.f. 48:229-234; Zollinger, E. (1906). op cit.; Schutte, P. (1906). "Eine neue form Hysterischer Zustande bei Schulkindern" [A New Form of Hysterical Conditions in School Children]. *Muenchener Medizinsche Wochenschrift* 53:1763-1764; Schoedel (1906). op cit.; Sterling, W. (1936). "Epidemia dzieciecej histeri religijnej" [Epidemic of Infantile Religious Hysteria]. *Warsz Czas Lek* 13:728-731, 749-752; Schuler and Parenton (1943). op cit.; Michaux et al. (1952). op cit.; Theopold (1955). op cit.; Rankin and Philip (1963). op cit.; Tan (1962). op cit.; Kagwa (1964). op cit.; Knight et al. (1965). op cit.; Helvie, C. (1968). "An Epidemic of Hysteria in a High School." *Journal of School Health* 38:505-509; Olczak et al. (1971). op cit.; Tan S. "50 Girls in School Hit by Strange Hysteria." *The Straits Times*, March 26, 1971, pp. 1, 24; Tan, S. "Girls Hit Again by Hysteria." *The Straits Times*, March 27 1971, p. 15; Muhangi (1973). op cit.; Teoh and Yeoh (1973). op cit. Tan, S. "Hostel Hysterics: 250 Pupils Boycott Classes." *The New Straits Times*, March 13 1973, p. 18; "Hysteria Attacks Shut Down Trade School." *The New Straits Times*, March 16, 1973, p. 6; Adomakoh, C. C. (1973). "The Pattern of Epidemic Hysteria in a Girls' School in Ghana." *Ghana Medical Journal* 12:407-411; Benaim et al. (1973). op cit.; Teoh et al. (1975). op cit.; Ackerman, S.E., and Lee, R.L. (1978). "Mass Hysteria and Spirit Possession in Urban Malaysia: A Case Study." *Journal of Sociology and Psychology* 1:24-35; "Hysteria Attacks Shut Down Trade School." *The New Straits Times*, March 16, 1973, p. 6; Mohr and Bond (1982). op cit.; Dhadphale and Shaikh (1983). op cit.; "New Hostel for Al-Ulum Girls." *The Malay Mail*, July 21 1981; Vijian, K. "Hysteria Hits Estate Classes." *The New Straits Times*, June 26 1982; "Estate School Spirit on the Prowl Again." *The New Straits Times*, August 17 1982; "More Pupils Affected by Hysteria." Bernama News Service (Malaysia), October 26 1986; "12 lagi Murid Perempuan Diserang Histeria" [12 more female students stricken with hysteria], *Utusan*, October 26 1986; "17 Bahu Pupils hit by Hysteria." Bernama News Service (Malaysia), October 22 1986; Rachel, A. "Probing Hysteria Cases in Two schools." *The New Straits Times*, July 4, 1986; Rachel A. (1986). op cit. (second separate episode from the previous citation); "12 Lagi Murid Perempaun Diserang Histeria" [12 more female students stricken with hysteria], *Utusan*, October 26 1986; "More Pupils Affected by Hysteria." Bernama News Service (Malaysia), October 26 1986; "Hysteria Students 'Cured.'" *The New Straits Times*, July 21 1987; "Hysteria Hits 16 Pupils of Residential School." *The New Straits Times*, August, 25 1987; "Hysteria Hit School Closed for Two Days." *The New Straits Times*, July 8 1987; "Outbreak of Hysteria Caused by a Bomoh." *The New Straits Times*, July 9 1987; "Students Still

Hysterical." *The New Straits Times*, July 10 1987; "100 pupils and two Teachers yet to Return." *The New Straits Times*, July 10, 1987; "Hysteria Students to be Transferred." Bernama News Service (Malaysia), May 20 1985; "Hysterical Pupils take Schoolmates Hostage." *The New Straits Times*, May 19, 1987, p. 1; "Hysteria: Schoolgirls 'Confess.'" *The New Straits Times*, May 21 1987, p. 3; "Hysteria Blamed on 'Evil Spirits': School Head wants the Ghosts to go." *The New Straits Times*, May 23 1987, p. 7; "Council to Meet over Hysteria Stricken Girls." *The New Straits Times*, May 24, 1987, p. 4; "Seven Girls Scream for Blood: Hysterical Outbursts Continue." *The New Straits Times*, May 25 1987, p. 4. "Interview: Fatimah, "I Only Fulfilled my Parents Wishes." *The New Straits Times*, May 31 1987, p. 7; "I can't Believe it, says Pupil." *The New Straits Times*, May 31 1987, p. 7; "Transfer Plan for Girls Hit by Hysteria." *The New Straits Times*, July 21 1987; "First Group of Hysteria Girls sees Psychiatrist." *The New Straits Times*, August 11, 1987; "Hysteria: second batch visits 'shrink.'" *The New Straits Times*, August 13 1987; "Parents of 'Hysteria' Girls Agree to Transfer." *The New Straits Times*, July 24, 1987; "Girls Turn Hysterical after Forest Outing." *The New Straits Times*, June 12, 1989; "Hysterics over 'Spirit of the Coin.'" *The New Straits Times*, June 17 1989; Wittstock, B., Rozental, L., and Henn, C. (1991). "Mass Phenomena at a Black South African Primary School." *Hospital and Community Psychiatry* 42:851-853; "Students Hit by Hysteria." *The New Straits Times*, February 24 1989; "100 Factory and College Girls in Hysterical Drama." *The New Straits Times*, September 18 1991; Wahab, A., and Jamaludin, F. "Hysterical 15 Get More Time." *The New Straits Times*, September 27 1991; "Hysteria in Three Schools Under Control." *The New Straits Times*, September 29, 1991; "Hysteria Hits 30 More Students." *The New Straits Times*, October 1 1991; Jamaludin, F. "'Haunted' School Ban Newsmen." *The New Straits Times*, October 3, 1991; "Klang Pupils in a Frenzy: Hysteria Hits School." *The Malay Mail*, July 20 1993; De Paul, V. "Mass Hysteria in Sentul Girls' School." *The Malay Mail*, January 28, 1994, p. 12; Spitlers C., Darcy, J., Hardin, T., et al: (1996). "Outbreak of Unexplained Illness in a Middle School–Washington, April 1994." *MMWR* 45:6-9; Tshala, K., Nunga, M., Pukuta, S., Mutombo, L., Beya, E., Tshoko, K., and Mampunza, M. (1999). "Coexistence of Mass Hysteria, Konzo and HTLV-1 Virus in the Democratic Republic of the Congo." *Medecine Tropicale: Revue du Corps de sante Colonial* 59(4):378-82; Mkize, D.L., and Ndabeni, R.T. (2002). "Mass Hysteria with Pseudoseizures at a South African High School." *South African Medical Journal* 92(9):697-699; Chen, C.S., Yen, C.F., Lin, H.F., Yang, P. (2003). "Mass Hysteria and Perceptions of the Supernatural Among Adolescent Girl Students in Taiwan." *The Journal of Nervous and Mental Disease* 191(2):122-123; Govender, I. (2003). "Mass Hysteria with Possible Pseudoseizures at a Primary School." *South African Medical Journal* 93(1):10.

335. Hecker, J.F.C. (1843). *Epidemics of the Middle Ages* (Translated from German by B. Babingon). London: Sydenham Society.

336. Mackay, C. (1852). *Memoirs of Extraordinary Popular Delusions and the Madness of Crowds Volume 2.* London: Office of the National Illustrated Library.

337. Baillarger, J.G.F. (1857). "Exemples de Contagion d'un delire Monomanique." *Moniteur des Hositaux* (Serie 5) 45:353-354.

338. Despine, P. (1875). *De la Folie au point de vue Philosophique ou Specialement Psychologique Etudiee chez le Malade et chez l'homme en sante.* Paris: F. Savy.

339. LeBon, G. (1879). *The Crowd, A Study of the Popular Mind.* London: T. F. Unwin.

340. Anonymous (1888). "Psychic Disturbances in Russia." *Science* 11:178.

341. Rembold, S. (1893). "Acute Psychische Contagion in einer Madchenschule." Berliner klinische. *Wochenschrift* 30:662-663.

342. Montyel, M. de. (1894). "Des Conditions de la Contagion Morbide." *Annales Medico-Psychologiques* (March):482.

343. Lilienfeld, Paul de. (1896). *La Pathologie Sociale.* Paris: Giard et Briere.

344. Altamira, R. (1898). "L'Homme de Genie et la Collectivite." *Revue Internationale de Sociologie* (June).

345. Rodriques, N. (1901). "La Folie des Foules et Folies Epidemiques au Bresil." *Annales Medico-psychologiques* (May).

346. Friedmann, M. (1901). *Uber Wahnideen im Volkerleben.* Wiesbaden.

347. Dumas, G. (1911). "Contagion Mentale." *Revue Philosophique* 17:225-244, 384-407.

348. Anonymous (1913). *London Daily Mirror*, February 26, 1913.

349. Bleuler, E. (1920). *Lehrbuch der Psychiatrie, 3.* Auflage Belin, Julius Springer.

350. Martin, A. (1923). "History of Dancing Mania; A Contribution to the Study of Psychic Mass Infection." *American Journal of Clinical Medicine* 30:265-271.

351. Fallaize, E.N. (1923). "Some Examples of Collective Hysteria." *Discovery* (London), 4:49-50.

352. Eckert, G. (1940). "Prophetenum und Kulturwandel in Melanesien" (The rise of prophets and cultural change in Melanesia). *Baessler-Archiv Beitrage zur Volkerkunde* 23:26-41.

353. Norman, E.H. (1945). "Mass Hysteria in Japan." *Far Eastern Survey* 14(6):65-70.

354. Simmel, E. (1946). "Anti-Semitism and Mass Psychopathology." In E. Simmel, *Anti-Semitism.* New York: International Universities Press.

355. Page, J.D. (1947). *Abnormal Psychology: A Clinical Approach to Psychological Deviants.* Tokyo: Kogakusha Company.

356. Meerloo, J.A.M. (1949). "Delusions and Mass-Delusion." *Nervous and Mental Disease Monographs.* New York.

357. Gloyne, H.F. (1950). "Tarantism: Mass Hysterical Reaction to Spider Bite in the Middle Ages." *American Imago* 7:29-42.

358. Grosser, D., Polansky, N., and Lippitt, R.A. (1951). "A Laboratory Study of Behavioral Contagion." *Human Relations* 4:115-142.

359. Lefebvre, G. (1954). *Etudes sur la Revolution Francaise.* Paris: PUF.

360. Gruenberg, E.M. (1957). "Socially Shared Psychopathology." In A.H. Leighton, J.A. Clausen and R.N. Wilson (eds.). *Explorations in Social Psychiatry.* London: Tavistock Publications.

361. Taylor, F.K., and Hunter, R.A.C. (1958). "Observation of a Hysterical Epidemic in a Hospital Ward: Thoughts on the Dynamics of Mental Epidemics." *Psychiatric Quarterly* 32:821-839.

362. Meerloo, J.A.M. (1959). "Mental Contagion." *American Journal of Psychotherapy* 12:66-82.

363. Arieti, S., and Meth, J.M. (1959). "Rare, Unclassifiable, Collective, and Exotic Psychotic Syndromes." In S. Arieti (ed.). *American Handbook of Psychiatry.* New York: Basic Books.

364. Lang, K., and Lang, G.E. (1961). *Collective Dynamics.* New York: Thomas Y. Crowell.

365. Kerckhoff, A.C., Back, K.W., and Miller, N. (1965). "Sociometric Patterns in Hysterical Contagion." *Sociometry* 28:2-15.

366. Langness, L.L. (1965). "Hysterical Psychosis in the New Guinea Highlands: A Bena Bena Example." *Psychiatry* 28:258-277.

367. Wheeler, L. (1966). "Toward a Theory of Behavior Contagion." *Psychological Review* 73:179-192.

368. Kumasaka, Y. (1966). "Collective Mental Illness Within the Framework of Cultural Psychiatry and Group Dynamics." *Psychiatric*

Quarterly 40:333-347.
369. Jaspers, K. (1968). *General Psychopathology* (Translated from German by J. Hoenig and M. W. Hamilton). Chicago, Illinois: The University of Chicago Press.
370. Lyons, H.A., and Poter, P.E. (1970). "Communicated Hysteria–An Episode in an Elementary School." *Journal of the Irish Medical Association* 63:377-379.
371. Goldenson, R.M. (1970). *The Encyclopedia of Human Behavior: Psychology, Psychiatry and Mental Health Volume 2*. Pp. 752-754. Garden City, New York: Doubleday.
372. Olczak, P., Donnerstein, E., Hershberger, T., and Kahn, I. (1971). "Group Hysteria and the MMPI." *Psychological Reports* 28:413-414.
373. Turner, R.H., and Killian, L.M. (1987). *Collective Behavior* (Third Edition). Englewood Cliffs, New Jersey: Prentice-Hall.
374. Kiev, A. (1972). *Transcultural Psychiatry*. New York: The Free Press.
375. Page, J.D. (1973). *The Science of Understanding Deviance*. Chicago: Aldine Publishing.
376. Goldberg, E.L. (1973). "Crowd Hysteria in a Junior School." *Journal of School Health* 43:362-366.
377. Sirois, F. (1974). "Epidemic Hysteria." *Acta Psychiatrica Scandinavica Supplementum* 252:7-46.
378. Stahl, S.M., and Lebedun, M. (1974). "Mystery Gas: An Analysis of Mass Hysteria." *Journal of Health and Social Behavior* 15:44-50.
379. Nye, R.A. (1975). *The Origins of Crowd Psychology*. London: Sage.
380. Coleman, J.C. (1976). *Abnormal Psychology and Modern Life*. Glenview, Illinois: Scott, Foresman and Company.
381. Coleman, op cit.
382. Nitzkin, J.L. (1976). "Epidemic transient disturbance in an Elementary School." *Journal of the Florida Medical Association* 63:357-359.
383. Eastwell, H.D. (1976). "Associative Illness Among Aboriginals." *Australian and New Zealand Journal of Psychiatry* 10:89-94.
384. Raschka, L.B. (1976). "Lynching: A Psychiatrist's View." *Canadian Psychiatric Association Journal* 21(8):577-580.
385. Frankel, S. (1976). "Mass hysteria in the New Guinea Highlands: A Telefomin Outbreak and its Relationship to Other New Guinea Hysterical Reactions." *Oceania* 47:105-133.
386. Jilek, W., and Jilek-All, L. (1977). "Mass hysteria with koro symptoms in Thailand." *Schweizer Archive Neurologie Neurochirurgie un Psychiatrie* 120(2):257-9.
387. Cohen, B.G., Colligan, M.J., Wester, W., and Smith, M.J. (1978). "An Investigation of Job Satisfaction Factors in an Incident of Mass Psychogenic Illness at the Work Place." *Occupational Health and Nursing* 26(1):10-6.
388. Mann, J., and Rosenblat, W. (1979). "Collective Stress Syndrome" [Letter]. *Journal of the American Medical Association* 242(1):27.
389. Merskey, H. (1979). *The Analysis of Hysteria*. London: Bailliere Tindall.
390. Tseng, W.S. (1980). "Minor Psychological Disturbances of Everyday Life." In H.C. Triandis and J.G. Draguns (eds.). *Handbook of Cross-Cultural Psychology: Volume 6* (Psychopathology). Pp. 61-97. Boston: Allyn and Bacon.
391. Faust, H.S., and Brilliant, L.B. (1981). "Is the Diagnosis of 'Mass Hysteria' an Excuse for Incomplete Investigation of Low-level Environmental Contamination?" *Journal of Occupational Medicine* 23(1):22-26.
392. Wong, S.W., Kwong, B., Tam, Y.K., Tsoi, M.M. (1982). "Psychological Epidemic in Hong Kong." *Acta Psychiatrica Scandinavica* 65:421-436.
393. Faguet, R.A., and Faguet, K.F. (1982). "La Folie a Deux." In C.T.H. Friedmann and R.A. Faguet (eds.). *Extraordinary Disorders of Human Behavior*. New York: Plenum Press.
394. Faguet and Faguet, op cit.
395. Olkinuora, M. (1984). *Scandinavian Journal of Work, Environment and Health* 10(6):501-515.
396. Nandi, D., and Banerjee, G., Bera, S., Nandi, S., and Nandi, P. (1985). "Contagious Hysteria in a West Bengal Village." *American Journal of Psychotherapy* 39:247-252.
397. Boxer, P.A. (1985). "Occupational Mass Psychogenic Illness: History, Prevention, and Management." *Journal of Occupational Medicine* 27(12):867-872.
398. Alexander, R.W., and Fedoruk, M.J. (1986). "Epidemic Psychogenic Illness in a Telephone Operator's Building." *Journal of Occupational Medicine* 28(1):42-45.
399. Araki, S., and Honma, T. (1986). "Mass Psychogenic Systemic Illness in School Children in Relation to the Tokyo Photochemical Smog." *Archives of Environmental Health* 41(3):159-162.
400. Wessely, S. (1987). "Mass hysteria: two syndromes?" *Psychological Medicine* 17, 109-120.
401. Wessely, op cit.
402. Yassi, A., Weeks, J.L., Samson, K., and Raber, M.B. (1989). "Epidemic of 'Shocks' in Telephone Operators: Lessons for the Medical Community." *Canadian Medical Association Journal* 140:816-820.
403. Yassi, op cit.
404. Coon, Dennis. (1998). *Introduction to Psychology: Exploration and Application* (8th edition). Albany, New York: Brooke/Cole Publishing, pp. 684-685.
405. Coon (1998). op cit., p. 685.
406. Coon (1998). op cit., p. 684-685.
407. Gutman, Jeremiah. (1977). "Constitutional and Legal Aspects of Deprogramming," Pp. 208-215. In H.W. Richardson (compiler). In *Deprogramming: Documenting the Issue*. New York: American Civil Liberties Union and Toronto School of Theology. See pp. 210-211.
408. Conrad, Peter, and Schneider, Joesph W. (1980). *Deviance and Medicalization: From Badness to Sickness*. St. Louis, Missouri: C.V. Mosby, p. vi.
409. Anonymous. (1888). "Psychic Disturbances in Russia." *Science* 11(271):178 (April 13).
410. Anonymous (1896). "Collective Suicide." *British Medical Journal* ii:1181-1182.
411. "33 Bodies Found in Attic," *The Post-Star* (Glens Falls, New York), August 30, 1987, p. A1.
412. Hoffmann, Bill, and Burke, Cathy. (1997). *Heaven's Gate: Cult Suicide in San Diego*. New York: HarperCollins.
413. Locke, Michelle (1997). *South Bend Tribune*, March 31, p. 1.
414. Hoffmann and Burke, op cit.
415. Pope, Frederick E. (1997). "The Psychic Infection of Heaven's Gate." *The Humanist* 57(4):41-42.
416. Gardner, Martin (1997). "Heaven's Gate: the UFO cult of Bo and Peep." *Skeptical Inquirer* 21(4):15-17. See p. 17.
417. Gardner, op cit.
418. Steel, Ronald (1997). "Ordinary People. Heaven's Gate Suicides." *The New Republic* 216(16):25 (April 21).
419. Steel, op cit.
420. Higgins, Alexander G. (1994). "Probe into Cult Spreads to France and Australia." *The Daily Gazette* (Schenectady, New York), October 10, 1994; Davis, Robert. (1994). "Power, Magic and Doom." USA Today, October 7, p. 8A.

421. "Five Cultists Die in Suicide Blaze," *The Post-Star* (Glens Falls, New York), March 24, 1997, p. A2.
422. "...Cult Commit Fiery Mass Suicide." *New York Post*, March 19, 2000, p. 5; "Cult Victims Burned Alive," *Post-Star* (Glens Falls, New York), April 5, 2001; Messing, Philip. (2001). "N.Y. Cult Experts Aid Uganda – 900+ Murders Overwhelming Police." *New York Post*, April 10, p. 20.
423. Melton, J. Gordon (2000). "Cult Mass Suicide/Homicide: Jonesboro/Heaven's Gate Replay?" *The Skeptic* 8(1):17-18 (Winter). See p. 18.
424. Melton, op cit., p. 18.
425. "Another Cult Mass Suicide Bid Aborted!" Africa News Service, April 5, 2000.
426. Rawlinson, G. (1880). *History of Herodotus Volume 3*. London: John Murray, p. 213; Yule, H., & Burnell, A. (1968). *Hobson-jobson delhi*. Munshiram Manoharlal, p. 879; Brooke, W. (1806). *The popular religion and folklore of northern India*. Westminster: Archibald Constable, p. 185.
427. Crosby, K., Rhee, J.O., & Holland, J. (1977). "Suicide by fire: a contemporary method of political protest." *The International Journal of Social Psychiatry* 23(1):60-69. See pp. 65-66.
428. Small, Gary, and Borus, J. (1983). "Outbreak of Illness in a School Chorus: Toxic Poisoning or Mass Hysteria." *New England Journal of Medicine* 308:632-635.
429. Ellis, Havelock (1924). *Studies in the Psychology of Sex* (third edition). Philadelphia: F.A. Davis. Originally piblished 1900-1910, citing volume I, 1900, pages 166 and onwards.
430. Laqueur, Thomas W. (2002). *Solitary Sex*. New York: Zone books, chapter 3.
431. Laqueur (2002), op cit., p. 57.
432. Laqueur (2002), op cit., p. 29.
433. Quoted in Szasz, Thomas S. (1971). *The Manufacture of Madness*. London: Routledge & Kegan Paul, p. 183.
434. Szasz, op cit., p. 184, from Hare's paper.
435. Stengers, Jean, and Neck, Anne van (2002). *Masturbation*. Translated from the French *Histoire d'une Grande Peur, la Masturbation*, by Kathryn Hoffmann. Originally published 1998. English translation: London: Palgrave 2002, p. 197.
436. Stengers, op cit.
437. Szasz, op cit., p. 185.
438. Stengers, op cit., p. 3.
439. Hall, Lesley A. (2003). "It was affecting the medical profession": The History of Masturbatory Insanity Revisited.' *Paedagogica Historica* 39(6): 685-699 (December).
440. Laqueur, op cit., p. 66, 54.
441. Stengers, op cit., p. 107.
442. Rengade, Dr. J. (1881). *La Vie Normale*. Paris: Librairie Illustrèe, pp. 94-95.
443. Stall, Sylvanus (1909). *What a Young Boy Ought to Know*. Philadelphia: Vir Publishing. Originally published in 1897, p. 110.
444. Stall, op cit., p. 114.
445. Stengers, op cit., p. 6.
446. Stengers, op cit., p. 55.
447. Szasz (1971). op cit., p. 191.
448. Stengers, op cit., pp. 111-112.
449. Stengers, op cit., p. 112.
450. Comfort, Alex (1967). *The Anxiety Makers*. London: Nelson, p. 102.
451. Stengers, op cit., p. 114.
452. Stengers, op cit., p. 117.
453. Szasz, op cit., pp. 193-194.
454. Stengers, op cit., p. 125.
455. Kinsey, Alfred C., Pomeroy, Wardell B., Martin, Clyde E. (1949). *Sexual Behavior in the Human Male*. Philadelphia: W B Saunders. Origially publised in 1948, p. 499.
456. Ellis, Havelock (1924). *Studies in the Psychology of Sex* (third edition). Philadelphia: F.A. Davis. Originally published 1900-1910, volume, p. 255.
457. Kinsey (1949). op cit., pp. 499, 513.
458. Kinsey, A. C., Pomeroy, W. B., Martin, C. E., and Gebhard, P. H. (1953). *Sexual Behavior in the Human Female*. Philadelphia, PA: W.B. Saunders, pp. 169-170.
459. Comfort, op cit., p. 95.
460. Szasz, op cit., p. 187.
461. Laqueur, op cit., passim.
462. Klass, Philip (1976). *UFOs Explained*. New York: Vintage books, pp. 85-90.
463. Klass, op cit., p. 86.
464. Klass, op cit., p. 89.
465. Bolt Andrew (2005a). "Hysterical Denial." *Herald Sun* (Melbourne), April 6: 19; personal communication between Robert Bartholomew and Andrew Bolt, April 22.
466. Esplin Bruce. *A Report of the Response to an Emergency at Melbourne on 21 February 2005* [media release]. Melbourne: Emergency Services Commission, State of Victoria, Australia, 2005 Mar 24: 23.
467. Bolt A. (2005a). op cit.; personal communication between Robert Bartholomew and Andrew Bolt, April 22.
468. Personal communication between Andrew Bolt and members of the Melbourne Ambulance Service, February 21, 2005; personal communication between Andrew Bolt and Robert Bartholomew, April 2005.
469. McGrath, K. (2005). Ten News Sydney, February 21.
470. Hatcher, Leigh, McKenzie Sharon (2005). Sky News Australia, February 21.
471. Smith, Alexandra, Milovanovi, Selma. (2005). "Thousands Stranded, 47 Sick as Gas Mystery Deepens." *Sydney Morning Herald*, February 22: 3; Anonymous. (2005). "Virgin Makes Amends." *Sydney Morning Herald*, February 23: 2; Hoare Daniel, and Creedy Steve. (2005). "Mystery gas Hits Passengers." *The Australian*, February 22: 1, 4; Silkstone Daniel. (2005). "Probe over Airport Gas Scare." *The Age*, February 23: 1, 6.
472. Carlyon, Patrick (2005). "Ill in the Mind?" *Bulletin with Newsweek* volume 123, issue 6460 (March 8), page 10.
473. Bartholomew, Robert E., and Wessely, Simon. (2002). "Protean Nature of Mass Sociogenic Illness: From Possessed Nuns to Chemical and Biological Terrorism Fears." *British Journal of Psychiatry*180:300-306.
474. Jones, T.F., Craig, A.S., Hoy, D., Gunter, E.W., Ashley, D.L., Barr, D.B., Brock, J.W., and Schaffner, W. (2000). "Mass Psychogenic Illness Attributed to Toxic Exposure at a High School." *The New England Journal of Medicine* 342(2):96-100.
475. Oliver, Myrna (2002). "Obituaries: A Melin, 77; Introduced Frisbee and Hula Hoop. *Los Angeles Times*, June 30, 2002, p. B-15; Hansell, Saul (2002). "Arthur Melin, 77, Promoter of the Hula-Hoop, Is Dead." *New York Times*, July 1, 2002, p. B-6.
476. "'Mercury Bomb' Fails Fatalist Group in Italy." *Appleton Post-Crescent* (Wisconsin), July 14, 1960, p. A2.
477. McLeod, W.R (1975). "Merphos Poisoning or Mass Panic?" *Australian and New Zealand Journal of Psychiatry* 9:225-229; Christophers, A.J. (1982). "Civil Emergency: Butyl Mercaptan Poisoning in the Parnell Civil Defence Emergency: Fact or Fiction?"

New Zealand Medical Journal (April 28):277-278.
478. Godwin, George (1941). *The Great Revivalists*. London: Watts, p. 5.
479. Knox, Ronald A. (1950). *Enthusiasm*. Oxford University Press, p. 357.
480. Davenport, Reuben Briggs (1976[1888]). *The Death-Blow to Spiritualism*. New York: Arno Press facsimile reprint. Dillingham, 1888, 134 et seq.
481. Wesley, John (1909). *The Journal of the Rev. John Wesley*. Edited by Nehemiah Curnock. London: Culley 1909 [Originally published at various dates from 1739 onwards], volume 5, p. 524
482. Wesley, op cit., volume 2, p. 131.
483. Wesley, op cit., volume 2, p. 180.
484. Wesley, op cit., volume 2, p. 181.
485. Wesley, op cit., volume 2, p. 186.
486. Wesley, op cit., volume 2, p. 187.
487. Wesley, op cit., volume 2, p. 263. The reference to the "Evil One" reminds us that Wesley, for all his open-mindedness, retained the same belief in the Devil as had the witch-hunters of the WITCH MANIA.
488. Cited by Lavington, George (1749). *The Enthusiasm of Methodists and Papists Compar'd*. London: J and P Knapton 1749 (part one), p. 11.
489. Whitefield's Journal, in Lavington 1749: part two 17.
490. Wesley, op cit., volume 2, pp. 221-222.
491. Lavington, op cit., volume 3, p. 177.
492. Wesley, op cit., volume 2, p. 291.
493. Wesley, op cit., volume 2, p. 298.
494. Wesley, op cit., volume 3, pp. 59-60.
495. Wesley, op cit., volume 3, p. 69.
496. Lavington, op cit., volume 3, p. 128.
497. Wesley, op cit., volume 3, p. 63.
498. Lavington, op cit., volume 3, p. 130.
499. Wesley, op cit., volume 4, p. 317 et seq: this section was compiled from other men's journals.
500. Lavington, op cit., volume 2, p. 71.
501. Wesley, op cit., volume 4, p. 336.
502. Lavington, op cit., volume 3, pp. 30 and 295.
503. Wesley, op cit., volume 5, p. 103.
504. Wesley, op cit., volume 4, p. 359.
505. Wesley, op cit., volume 4, p. 539.
506. Wesley, op cit., volume 2, p. 136.
507. Wesley, op cit., volume 6, p. 37.
508. Lavington, op cit., volume 3, p. 174.
509. Dupouy, E. (1907). *Psychologie Morbide*. Paris: Librairie des Sciences Psychiques, p. 115, following Del Rio and De Lancre.
510. Mackay, Charles. (1852). *Memoirs of Extraordinary Popular Delusions and the Madness of Crowds Volume 2*. London: Office of the National Illustrated Library, p. 264.
511. Manzoni, Alessandro (1909). *I Promessi Sposi* (The Betrothed). Published by Eliot, Charles W. (editor). *Harvard Classics, Volume XXI*. New York: P.F. Collier & Son Company, 1909, p. 534.
512. Manzoni, op cit., p. 535.
513. Manzoni, op cit., p. 535.
514. Manzoni, op cit., p. 536.
515. Manzoni, op cit., p. 537.
516. Manzoni, op cit., p. 541.
517. Manzoni, op cit., p. 542.
518. Mackay, op cit., p. 264.
519. Miller Farm website.
520. *Signs of the Times* (Millerite newspaper), January 25, 1843, p. 147.
521. Bekhterev, Vladimir Mikhailovich. (1998)[1908] *Suggestion and its Role in Social Life*, third edition. (translated from Russian by Tzvetanka Dobreva-Martinova). New Brunswick, New Jersey: Transaction Publishers, pp. 97-98.
522. Christian History Institute, accessed January 1, 2004 at: http:// www.gospelcom.net/ chi/DAILYF/2001/10/daily-10-22-2001.shtml.
523. Boyer, Pauyl (1999). "Apocalypse!" Public Broadcasting System program 'Frontline,' accessed January 1, 2004 at: http://www.pbs.org/ wgbh/pages/frontline/shows/apocalypse/ explanation/ amprophesy. html.
524. Housman, A,E. (1936). *More Poems*. London: Jonathan Cape.
525. Lanternari, Vittorio (1963). *The Religions of the Oppressed: A Study of Modern Messianic Cults*. Translated from the Italian by Lisa Sergio. London: Macgibbon & Kee. First published in Italian in 1960 by Giangiacomo Feltrinelli.
526. Scheflin, Alan W., and Opton, Edward M., Jr. (1978). *The Mind Manipulators*. New York: Paddington, p. 91.
527. Scheflin and Opton (1978), op cit., p. 236.
528. Bowart, Walter (1978). *Operation Mind Control*. New York: Dell [London: Fontana/Collins], p. 23.
529. Marks, John (1979). *The Search for the Manchurian Candidate*. New York: Times Books, p. 26.
530. Schefflin and Opton (1978). op cit., p. 131.
531. Bowart (1978). op cit., p. 105.
532. Quoted in Bowart (1978). op cit., p. 153.
533. Quoted in Bowart (1978). op cit., p. 169.
534. Marks (1979). op cit., p. 68.
535. Scheflin and Opton (1978). op cit., pp. 133, 153.
536. Marks (1979). op cit., p. 58.
537. Marks (1979). op cit., pp. 68-69.
538. Marks (1979). op cit., p. 60.
539. Marks (1979). op cit., p. 71.
540. Keith (1997 Keith, Jim (1997). Mind Control, World Control. Kempton IL: Adventures Unlimited, see especially chapter 26.
541. Marks (1979). op cit., p. 116.
542. Bowart (1978). op cit., p. 254.
543. Marks (1979). op cit., p. 204.
544. Scheflin and Opton (1978). op cit., p. 9.
545. Marks (1979). op cit., p. 164.
546. Hoffmann, Frank W., and Bailey, William G. (1991). *Sports and Recreation Fads*. New York: Harrington Park Press, pp. 33.
547. Skolnik, Peter L. (1978). *Fads: America's Crazes, Fevers & Fancies From the 1890s to the 1970s*. New York: Thomas Y. Crowell, pp. 73-75.
548. Panati, op cit., p. 152.
549. Panati, op cit., p. 151; Marum and Parise, op cit., p. 57.
550. "Midget or Colossus?" *Survey* 65:197 (November 15, 1930).
551. "Half-Pint Golf." *Outlook and Independent* 155:656 (August 27, 1930).
552. Trevor, George (1930). "Battle of Lilliput." *Outlook and Independent* 156:194, 199 (October 1, 1930).
553. "Tom Thumb Golf." *The Nation* 131:215-216 (August 27, 1930).
554. Marum, Andrew, and Parise, Frank. (1984). *Follies and Foibles: A View of 20th Century Fads*. New York: Facts on File, p. 57.
555. Marum and Parise, op cit., p. 57.
556. "Even Crazier Hazards on the Tom Thumb Links." *Literary Digest* 108:37 (January 24, 1931); Marum and Parise, op cit., p. 57.
557. Marum and Parise, op cit., p. 57.

558. Monore, Sylvester (1989). "Welcome to Putters Paradise; Miniature Golf, a '20s Fad, Comes Back in Style." *Time* 131(11):73 (September 11, 1989).
559. "Mini Golf: A Hole in One." *Business Week* (August 27, 2001):16.
560. Olson, W. C. (1928). "Account of a Fainting Epidemic in a High School." *Psychology Clinic* (Philadelphia) 18:34-38.
561. Olson (1928). op cit., p. 35.
562. Mackay, Charles. (1852). *Memoirs of Extraordinary Popular Delusions and the Madness of Crowds Volume 2*. London: Office of the National Illustrated Library, p. 261.
563. Kumar, Lalit. "DIG says 'Shoot at Monkeyman' as Panic Spreads." *Times of India*, May 14, 2001.
564. Fathers, Michael (2001). "Monkey Man Attack! Simian assailant sweeps parts of New Delhi – anxious populace is gripped by terror." *Time Asia* (May 28) 157, issue 201, http://www.time.com/time/asia/news/magazine/0,9754,127298,00.html, accessed March 12, 2003.
565. Bartholomew, op cit.
566. Fathers, op cit.
567. "'Monkey' Gives Delhi Claws for Alarm." *The Australian*, May 17, 2001.
568. Chadwick, Alex (Host) (2001). "Analysis: Monkey Man Attacks in New Delhi." Morning Edition of American National Public Radio, May 17, 2001 (Michael Sullivan reporting from New Delhi).
569. Pandey, Prashant. "Cops Step Up Hunt as Panic Spreads." *The Hindu*, May 17, 2001.
570. Maiti, Prasenjit (2001). "India's Monkey Man and the Politics of Mass Hysteria." *Skeptical Inquirer* 25(5):8-9. See p. 9.
571. Palmer, James. Prowling 'Monkey-Man' Causes Panic in Delhi." *The Independent*, May 16, 2001.
572. Bartholomew, Robert E. (2001). "Monkey Man Delusion Sweeps India." *The Skeptic Magazine* 9(1):13.
573. Chadwick, op cit.
574. Verma, S.K., and Srivastava, D.K. (2003). "A Study on Mass Hysteria (Monkey Men?) Victims In East Delhi." *Indian Journal of Medical Sciences* 57(8):355-360 (August). Accessed online at January 1, 2004 at: http://www.bioline.org.br/request?ms03014.
575. Maiti, op cit., p. 9.
576. "Monkey-man morphs into 'werewolf' in Assam villages." *The Indian Express*, May 26 2001.
577. "Monkey-man morphs..." op cit.
578. "Monkey-man morphs..." op cit.
579. "Monkey-man morphs..." op cit.
580. "Monkey-man morphs..." op cit.
581. "Monkeyman finds a Rival." Sapa-AFP news agency, May 26, 2001, accessed January 1, 2004 at: http://www.100megsfree4.com/farshores/indochu6.htm.
582. Monkeyman finds a Rival." op cit.
583. "Rumour of mysterious animal send city in spin." *The Times of India*, May 19, 2001.
584. "Slasher Creates Mass Hysteria." *Waukesha Daily Freeman* (Wisconsin), January 30, 1954, p. 1.
585. Caffrey, Mary (1997). "Freshmen Study Extraterrestrials." *Princeton Weekly Bulletin*, November 24, 1997.
586. "GREAT ASTRONOMICAL DISCOVERIES Lately Made BY SIR JOHN HERSCHEL, L.L.D, F.R.S, &c. At The Cape of Good Hope." *The Sun* (New York), August 25, 1835, p. 2.
587. "GREAT ASTRONOMICAL DISCOVERIES Lately Made BY SIR JOHN HERSCHEL..." op cit., August 26, 1835.
588. "GREAT ASTRONOMICAL DISCOVERIES Lately Made BY SIR JOHN HERSCHEL..." op cit., August 27, 1835.
589. "GREAT ASTRONOMICAL DISCOVERIES Lately Made BY SIR JOHN HERSCHEL..." op cit., August 28, 1835.
590. "GREAT ASTRONOMICAL DISCOVERIES Lately Made BY SIR JOHN HERSCHEL..." op cit., August 29, 1835.
591. "GREAT ASTRONOMICAL DISCOVERIES Lately Made BY SIR JOHN HERSCHEL..." op cit., August 31, 1835.
592. Bulgatz, Joseph. (1992). *Ponzi Schemes, Invaders from Mars & More Extraordinary Popular Delusions and the Madness of Crowds*. New York: Harmony Books, p. 147.
593. Hallett, Vicky (2002). "Extra! Extra! Life on moon!" *U.S. News & World Report*, August 26, 2002:53.
594. Bulgatz, op cit., p. 150.
595. Bulgatz, op cit., p. 150.
596. Bulgatz, op cit., p. 150.
597. Hallett, op cit.
598. Thornton, Brian (2000). "The Moon Hoax: Debates About Ethics in 1835 New York Newspapers." *Journal of Mass Media Ethics* 15(2):89-100.
599. Hallett, op cit.
600. Bekker 1694: volume 4 page 576 et seq. Details are taken from this source unless otherwise indicated. Supplementary information from Mather 1693, Robbins 1959 and Ankarloo 2002. Mather, Cotton (1862 [1693]). *The Wonders of the Invisible World* [originally published in Boston 1693]. London: John Russell Smith; Robbins, Rossell Hope (1959). *The Encyclopedia of Witchcraft and Demonology*. London: Spring Books; Ankarloo, Bengt, and Clark, Stuart (editors) (2002). *Witchcraft and Magic in Europe: the Period of the Witch Trials*. London: Athlone Press.
601. Mather, op cit., p. 169.
602. Mather, op cit., p. 168.
603. Adapted and modified from: Bartholomew, Robert E., Dickeson, Bryan, and Dawes, Glenn (1998). "Expanding the boundary of moral panics: the Great New Zealand Zeppelin Scare of 1909." *New Zealand Sociology* 13(1): 29-61.
604. Cohen, S. (1972). *Folk Devils and Moral Panics: The Creation of the Mods and Rockers*. London: MacGibbon and Key.
605. Cohen (1972). op cit., p. 9.
606. Victor, Jeffrey S. (1998). "Social Construction of Satanic Ritual Abuse andthe Creation of False Memories." Pp. 191-216. *In Believed-In Imaginings: The Narrative Construction of Reality* (edited by Joseph de Rivera and Theodore R. Sarbin. Washingtom, DC: American Psychological Asociation, pp. 192-193.
607. Goode, E. and Ben-Yehuda, N. (1994). *Moral Panics: The Social Construction of Deviance*. Oxford: Blackwell.
608. Barlow, H.D. (1993). *Introduction to Criminology* (sixth edition). New York: Harper Collins, p. 258.
609. Goode and Ben-Yehuda (1994). op cit., pp. 34-35.
610. Goode and Ben-Yehuda, op cit., p. 36.
611. Goode and Ben-Yehuda, op cit., p. 38.
612. Goode and Ben-Yehuda, op cit., pp. 144-184.
613. Baroja, J.C. (1965). *The World of the Witches*. Chicago: University of Chicago Press.
614. Kandel, D., Adler, I. (1981). *The Epidemiology of Adolescent Drug Users in Israel and France*. New York: Columbia University, Department of Psychiatry and School of Public Health.
615. Goode, E. 1990. "The American Drug Panic of the 1980s: Social Construction of Objective Threat." *The International Journal of the Addictions* 25(9):1083-1098.
616. Goode and Ben-Yehuda, op cit., pp. 24-28.

617. Cohen, op cit., pp. 85-86.
618. Becker, Howard S. (1963) *Outsiders: Studies in the sociology of deviance*. New York: Free Press.
619. Hall, S., Critcher, C., Jefferson, T, Clarke, J., and Roberts, B. 1978. *Policing the Crisis: Mugging, the State, and Law and Order*. London: Macmillan.
620. Goode and Ben-Yehuda, op cit.
621. Richer, Paul (1885). *Etudes Cliniques de la Grande Hystérie*. Paris: Delahaye et Lecrossnier, p. 852.
622. Blanc, Hippolyte (1865). *Le Merveilleux dans le Jansenisme &c*. Paris: Plon, p. 279.
623. Maire, Catherine-Laurence (1981). *Les Possédées de Morzine*. Lyon: Presses Universitaires de Lyon, p. 40.
Maire, op cit., p. 40.
624. The basic facts are taken from the *Spiritual Magazine* 1 May 1855; Blanc 1865; Maire 1981.
625. Maire, op cit., p. 41.
626. Richer, op cit., p. 854.
627. Maire, op cit., p. 46.
628. *Spiritual Magazine*, p. 210.
629. Richer, op cit., p. 854.
630. *Spiritual Magazine*, op cit., p. 210.
631. Tavernier, quoted by Maire, op cit., p. 51.
632. Blanc, op cit., p. 289.
633. Maire, op cit., p. 62.
634. Officer of the gendarmerie, cited by Maire, op cit., p. 63.
635. Maire, op cit., p. 61.
636. Richer 855-6.
637. Constans, cited by Richer, omp cit., pp. 855-856.
638. *Spiritual Magazine*, op cit., p. 214 and Maire, op cit., pp. 85-86.
639. Fournier, sous-préfet, cited by Maire, op cit., p. 89.
640. *Le Monde* cited by Blanc, op cit., p. 280.
641. Correspondent in the *Union Médicale* 2 July 1864 cited by Blanc, op cit., p. 280-282.
642. Maire, op cit., p. 20.
643. Richer, op cit., p. 855.
644. *Spiritual Magazine*, op cit., p. 218.
645. Bartholomew, Robert E. and Wessely, Simon. (2002). "Protean Nature of Mass Sociogenic Illness: From Possessed Nuns to Chemical and Biological Terrorism Fears." *The British Journal of Psychiatry* 180:300-306.
646. Spanos, Nicholas P. (1996). *Multiple Identities & False Memories*. Washington DC: American Psychological Association, p. 232.
647. Acocella, Joan (1999). *Creating Hysteria*. San Francisco: Jossey-Bass, p. 4.
648. Ofshe, Richard, and Watters, Ethan (1995). *Making Monsters*. London: André Deutsch [first New York: Scribner's 1994], p. 206.
649. Ross et al quoted in Merskey. H, 'The manufacture of personalities' in the *British Journal of Psychiatry* (1992) 160, p. 327: reprinted in Cohen, Lewis M., Berzoff, Joan N., Elin, Mark B. (1995). *Dissociative Identity Disorder*. Northvale, New Jersey: Jason Aronson, p. 5.
650. Hilgard, Ernest R. (1977). *Divided Consciousness*. New York: John Wiley, p. 3.
651. Simpson in Cohen, op cit., p. 92.
652. Aldridge-Morris, Ray (1989). *Multiple Personality: An Exercise in Deception*. Hove and London: Lawrence Erlbaum, pp. 43, 108-109.
653. Ofshe, op cit., p. xi.
654. Goldenson, R.M. (1970). *The Encyclopedia of Human Behavior: Psychology, Psychiatry and Mental Health Volume 2*. Garden City, New York: Doubleday, volume 2, p. 843.
655. Hilgard, op cit., p. 5.
656. Janet, Pierre (1919[1889]). *L'automatisme Psychologique*. Eighth edition. Paris: Alcan. Originally published in 1889, p. 128.
657. William James, discussing Morton Prince's Dissociation of a personality, quoted by Hilgard, p. 25.
658. Hilgard, op cit., p. 19.
659. Gmelin, cited by Ellenberger, Henri E. (1970). *The Discovery of the Unconscious*. New York: Basic Books, p. 127.
660. Dr. Weir Mitchell's report in the Transactions of the College of Physicians of Philadelphia, 4 April 1888, is reproduced in Funk, Isaac K. (1904). *The Widow's Mite and Other Psychic Phenomena*. New York: Funk & Wagnalls, p. 403.
661. Azam, Dr. (1893). *Hypnotisme et Double Conscience*. Paris: Alcan.
662. Sidis, Boris, and Goodhart, Simon P. (1905). *Multiple Personality*. New York: D Appleton.
663. Prince, Morton (1905). *The Dissociation of a Personality*. London: Longmans Green.
664. Franz, Shepherd Ivory (1933). *Persons One and Three*. New York: Whittlesey House.
665. Thigpen, Corbett H., and Cleckley, Hervey M. (1957). *The Three Faces of Eve*. London: Secker & Warburg; Lancaster, Eveyln, and Poling, James (1958). *Strangers in My Body*. London: Secker & Warburg [USA: McGraw-Hill]; Sizemore, Chris Costner, and Pittillo, Elen Sain (1978). *Eve*. London: Gollancz 1978 [in USA, published as I'm Eve].
666. Pendergrast, Mark (1996). *Victims of Memory*. London: HarperCollins [first New York: Upper Access 1995], p. 157.
667. Troops for Truddi Chase, The. (1987). *When Rabbit Howls*. New York: Dutton.
668. Valuable studies from the pre-epidemic phase: Allison, Ralph (1980). *Minds in Many Pieces*. New York: Rawson, Wade; Bliss, Eugene L. (1986). *Multiple Personality, Allied Disorders, and Hypnosis*. New York: Oxford University Press; Confer, William N., and Ables, Billie S. (1983). *Multiple Personality: Etiology, Diagnosis and Treatment*. New York: Human Science Press; Crabtree, Adam (1985). *Multiple Man*. London: Holt, Rinehart and Winston.
669. Thigpen & Cleckly, op cit., quoted in Cohen, op cit., p. 90.
670. Acocela, op cit., p. 57.
671. Pendergrast, op cit., p. 158: confirmed by Merskey in Cohen, op cit.
672. Acocela, op cit., p. 113.
673. M A Simpson, quoted by Spanos, op cit., p. 234: Merskey in Cohen, p. 5.
674. Kluft, Richard P. (editor) (1985). *Childhood Antecedents of Multiple Personality*. Washington DC: American Psychiatric Press, in Cohen, op cit., p. 354.
675. Bass, Ellen, and Davis, Laura (1988). *The Courage to Heal*. New York: Harper & Row.
676. Eberle, Paul and Shirley (1993). *The Abuse of Innocence*. Buffalo NY: Prometheus Books.
677. Pride, Mary (1986). *The Child Abuse Industry*. Westchester, Illinois: Crossway, p. 166.
678. Ofshe, op cit., p. 4.
679. Bass, op cit., pp. 35, 37.
680. Paul R McHugh. (1992). "Psychiatric Misadventures." *The American Scholar* 61:4:497 (Autumn).
681. Spanos, op cit., p. 9.
682. Bliss, op cit., p. 136.
683. S. Mulhern quoted by Spanos, op cit., p. 271.
684. Spanos, op cit., p. 108.
685. Alan E. Siegel in Cohen, op cit., p. 440.

686. Freud, Sigmund (1955). "The Psychotherapy of Hysteria." In *Studies on Hysteria. Collected Works Volume Two*. London: Hogarth Press [original publication in German 1893-1895], p. 279.
687. Putnam, quoted by Kluft, op cit., p. ix.
688. August Piper Jr in Cohen, op cit., p. 161.
689. Ofshe, op cit., p. 16.
690. Bliss, op cit., pp. 124, 122.
691. Jack Leggett, quoted by Acocela, op cit., p. 116.
692. Pendergrast, op cit., p. 140.
693. Bliss, op cit., p. 140.
694. Bliss, op cit., p. 141.
695. Allison, op cit., p. 131.
696. Pendergrast, op cit., p. 150.
697. Allison, op cit., p. 183.
698. Cory, summarized in Crabtree, op cit., p. 41.
699. Pendergrast, op cit., p. 146.
700. Ofshe, op cit., p. 187.
701. See among others Loftus 1994, Ofshe, op cit., Pendergrast, op cit., Spanos, op cit., Victor Victor, Jeffrey S. (1993). *Satanic Panic: The Creation of a Contemporary Legend*. Chicago, IL: Open Court.
702. Bass, op cit., p. 22.
703. Acocela, op cit., pp. 8, 23.
704. Acocela, op cit., pp. 20-22.
705. Ofshe, op cit., p. 172.
706. Paul R. McHugh, 'Foreword' in August Piper Jr Hoax and reality quoted by Acocela, p. 25.
707. Seth Robert Segall in Cohen, op cit., p. 379.
708. Lisa Uyehara in Cohen, op cit., p. 1985: xvii.
709. Ofshe, op cit., p. 5.
710. Ring, Kenneth (1992). *The Omega Project*. New York: Morrow.
711. Evans, Hilary (1989). *Alternate States of Consciousness*. Wellingborough: Aquarian, p. 28 et seq.
712. Bliss, op cit., p. 124.
713. Michael Simpson, cited in Pendergrast, op cit., p 157.
714. Spanos, op cit., p. 197.
715. Merskey in Cohen, op cit., p. 26.
716. Bramwell, J Milne (1930). *Hypnotism*. Third edition. London: Rider, p. 380.
717. Pendergrast, op cit., pp. 180-186.
718. "Curse Of The Pharaohs Strikes Again In Turin." *The Age* (Australia), January 17, 2002; DPA News Agency, courtesy of Paul Cropper, Telecom, Australia.
719. "Italian Museum Solves 'Mummy Curse' Mystery." http://www.zoomata.com/modules.php?name=News&file=article&sid=885
720. Vandenberg, Philipp (1973). *Der Fluch der Pharaonen* (Vienna, Austria) translated from the German by William Weyr and published as *The Curse of the Pharaohs* (1975) New York: Lippincott.
721. Reay, Marie. (1960). "'Mushroom Madness' in the New Guinea Highlands." *Oceania* 31(2):137-139.
722. Reay, op cit., p. 138.
723. Reay, op cit., p. 139.
724. Reay, op cit., p. 139.
725. Heim, R., and Wasson, R.G. (1965). "The 'Mushroom Madness' of the Kuma." *Botanical Museum Leaflets Harvard University* 21(1):1-36. p. 20.
726. Reay, Marie. 1965. "Mushrooms and Collective Hysteria" Australian Territories 5: 22-24.
727. "Boletus Manicus." Http://www.entheogen.com/boletusm.html, accessed June 5, 2003.
728. Thomas, Benjamin (2002). "'Mushroom Madness' in the Papua New Guinea Highlands: A Case of Nicotine Poisoning?" *Journal of Psychoactive Drugs* 34(3):321-323.
729. Reay, Marie. (1977). "Ritual Madness Observed: A Discarded Pattern of Fate in Papua New Guinea." *The Journal of Pacific History* 12:55-79.
730. Reay (1977)., op cit., pp. 59-60, cited in Thomas, Benjamin, http://www.shaman-australis.com/~benjamin-thomas/Komugl_Tai_and_Acute_Nicotine_Intoxication.htm, accessed June 5, 2003.

N

NAKED CARGO "CULT"

New Hebrides, Eastern Melanesia: 1944-1951

At 35, a native man named Tesk began to preach to the people of the Island of West Espiritu Santo at Nakuvu a message that was almost certainly influenced by meeting European Christians. He preached that the islanders must get back in touch with their original and pure way of life – a utopian time without jealousy, shame, or war. His message was quickly embraced, and in 1945, he sent 30 emissaries on a mission to proclaim his message. He taught that because property quarrels were common, it was important to embrace communal living, and as jealousy often led to rage, marriage restrictions were relaxed. He also claimed that illnesses were the result of disharmony.[1]

Initially, Tesk told his followers to practice open sexual lives and to copulate publicly like fowl and animals in the wild. All men and women were to be sexually available to each other, including girls ages nine and up. This philosophy seemed to backfire however, and near the end of the movement, some of his followers had grown angry with him. (Tesk died of a long, progressive illness in 1951, after which the movement collapsed.) As one person said: "Jack Tesk has spoilt us; he has spoilt our heads; he has spoilt our lives. We know that these things we do now are not right. We don't want to do them any more."[2]

His message had nine basic tenets:

First, people must remove their loincloths and leaf coverings, and necklaces and armbands, as they make people unclean. All people must live naked.

Second, all items taken from Europeans, from money to implements, must be destroyed. Further, bush crafts should be destroyed and people should stop the practice of basket weaving, mat-making, etc.

Third, burn down your homes and build new ones within the following guidelines: each village should have two large community houses, one for the men and another for the women. At night, the men should sleep in their houses, while the women should sleep separately in their houses. A large kitchen should be built next to each community house. This situation was also apparently aimed at getting community members to engage in sexual intercourse in public.

Fourth, no one should cook food at night; all food must be cooked during the morning.

Fifth: working for Europeans is forbidden.

Sixth, kill all animals being kept in villages.

Seven: people from the United States would soon arrive on the island and bring with them everything good. Once this happens, the people of the island would not die.[3]

Eight, people should speak a common language (*Mamara* meaning "bright day"), despite several different languages being spoken by various villages.

Nine, many taboos were eliminated, such as the prohibition on inter-totem marriage, the period of segregation following childbirth, the requirement that one must purchase a bride, and certain burial customs. For instance, in the past, the deceased was buried in the floor of their house. With the new pronouncement, they were to be "buried" exposed to the elements in the bush, on a wooden platform.

In addition to disenchantment by followers, another reason for the rapid demise of the movement after his death was the promise by Tesk to his followers that believers would live forever. As Friedrich

Steinbauer remarked, "his death must certainly have caused doubts in the movement."[4]
See also: THE FILO CARGO CULT, MANGZO CARGO CULT, PRESIDENT JOHNSON CARGO CULT, CARGO CULTS.

NAVAL RECRUIT SMOKE SCARE

San Diego, California: Summer 1988

A naval training center was thrown into pandemonium when a "mysterious illness" swept through the facility, resulting in breathing problems, lightheadedness, and vomiting. At least 119 recruits were taken to the hospital for further examination, but doctors could find no explanation for the incident other than anxiety. Tests for harmful levels of chemicals were negative. The all-male barracks where the incident occurred was inspected by a medical unit, environmental health specialists, and a hazardous materials team. Spokesman Lt. Ken Luchka said, "It could have been that one or two people had a viral infection and got sick, which caused a mass hysteria to the others."[5]

CONTEXT: The episode occurred amid taxing physical exercise, brush fires, an elevated pollution index, and pungent odors. It was exacerbated when some recruits unnecessarily received mouth-to-mouth resuscitation as several medics who had just arrived on the scene believed they were dying. This unusual set of circumstances seems to have generated extreme anxiety among the remaining recruits. A study of the incident found that those observing the resuscitation, or witnessing others exhibit symptoms, were three times more likely to report symptoms. In all, 164 recruits were affected.[6]

NEUROLOGICAL EPIDEMIC

North Carolina: 2002

An outbreak of mysterious seizures in ten girls occurred at a rural high school in the state of North Carolina. The episode began to appear at the beginning of the new school year. Symptoms included bouts of breathlessness, fainting, lightheadedness, headaches, muscle twitching, tingling, and numbness. During their "fits," the school's nurse noted that they were odd, being unlike any epileptic seizures that she had witnessed before. For instance, upon placing smelling salts under the noses of two girls, they actually cringed. Further, two of their mothers said that during "seizures," they could sometimes "talk them" out of it.[7] Most episodes took place either in the hallway between classes, in the schoolyard, or in the cafeteria.

Two physicians living in the area, Steven Roach and Rick Langley, investigated the strange malady and reviewed the tests that had been conducted by themselves and other doctors. When the pair gave four of the girls video EEGs, they concluded beyond any doubt that the seizures were of hysterical origin.[8] Investigators said they could find no obvious stress for triggering the symptoms. However, the first girl to be stricken was a cheerleader. Perhaps the other girls were identifying with a school role model, as four other victims were also cheerleaders or former cheerleaders. It may also have been that once the first girl was stricken, others around her were fearful of "catching it," thus raising tension levels.

This case is unusual in the annals of the mass hysteria literature because only two students were in the same class. While most of the ten girls had just a few "attacks," one student had at least 30. It took four months for the symptoms to subside.

COMMENT: This entry has prompted Hilary Evans to propose a label, "Cheerleader Syndrome," to designate incidents where an Index Case is a community figurehead or role model.

NEW YORK ZOO SCARE

Greater New York City Region: November 9, 1874

As New Yorkers awoke on Monday morning, many became terrified to leave their homes and apartments after picking up their home-delivered copy of the *New York Herald*. The newspaper claimed that a state of emergency had been declared. The headline read: "AWFUL CALAMITY." The story told of how several dangerous animals had escaped from the Central Park Zoo and were terrorizing residents across the city. The paper reported that National Guard troops were patrolling the city in a bid to stop the bloodshed. It claimed that at least 49 people were dead and upwards of 200 were injured in animal attacks.[9]

Timing was a key factor in rendering the story plausible, as the zoo had long been the scene of public safety concerns. For instance, the *New York Times* had noted that such an event "was not altogether unlikely to happen," as the zoo had "the flimsiest cages ever seen."[10]

The accounts were remarkably vivid and gruesome. One witness supposedly said they saw a lion "tugging and crunching at the arms and legs of a corpse, now letting go with his teeth to plant his paws upon the bleeding remains, and snap with his dripping jaws at another beast." Another told of seeing four young children being ripped apart by a lion.

For readers who were diligent enough to read the entire article, the hoax was revealed in the final paragraph. The paper justified the story by arguing that it was necessary to shock readers into taking action about the dangerous state of the Central Park Zoo, before a real tragedy of similar dimensions occurs. Predictably, an editorial in the paper's rival, *The New York Times*, labeled the incident "intensely stupid and unfeeling."[11]

The appearance of the zoo hoax coincided with a series of *Herald* editorials opposing rumors that President Ulysses S. Grant was contemplating a third presidential term, labeling such a move as "Caesarism" (a government ruled by an absolute dictator). In combining these elements in his 1874 *Harper's Weekly* cartoon, Nast drew a donkey in a lion's disguise scaring away other animals. The donkey symbolized the

The scare as depicted in a famous cartoon by Thomas Nast. (Harper's Weekly, 1874).

Herald, the lion costume represented the paper's scare tactic of crying wolf with the possibility of Grant becoming a dictator. The forest animals symbolized the *Herald's* Central Park Zoo hoax.

"One of the animals frightened by the donkey's roar of Caesarism was an elephant – a symbol for Republican voters, who were abandoning President Grant, and in Nast's view, about to fall into the Democrats' trap. Other cartoonists of the time picked up the idea of the timid elephant representing Republicans, and that symbol for the party became widely recognized and accepted by the general public."

While Nast used a donkey to represent a Democrat-biased paper scaring off Republican votes, "his cartoon showing a duplicitous donkey attacking a weak-minded elephant, became a handy symbol for other cartoonists wanting to represent Democrats attacking Republicans. Popular recognition of the image overrode the party's own wishes...the symbol had stuck."[12]

NEW ZEALAND SICK BUILDING

Christchurch, New Zealand: Oct. to Dec. 1999

Health authorities were baffled by a "mystery illness" affecting 17 people, most of them members of the Nurse Maude Association office block. Symptoms included upset stomachs, lethargy, concentration and memory difficulties, headaches, stiffness in the neck and back, sore throats and having a funny metallic taste in their mouths. Tests on the building were negative.[13]

COMMENT: Reports of "sick" buildings, especially schools and work sites, appear to be common. See also: TOXIC BUS CONTROVERSY, TOXIC MOLD, TOXIC COURTHOUSE, SICK PRIMARY SCHOOLS, SICK SCHOOL STAFF SYNDROME, and PARENT HYSTERIA (BY PROXY).

NIJMEGEN CONVENT OUTBREAK

Netherlands: circa 1560

Jean Weyer[14] refers briefly to an outbreak in the convent of St. Bridget at "Hessimonte Neomagi" ("Nieumeghe" and "Mont de Hesse" in the French translation). Unfortunately his location is difficult to identify. The name suggests Nijmegen, in the Netherlands; but Madden identifies it with Odenheym on the Rhine, which he claims was once named Neomagus.[15]

CONTEXT: This outbreak followed soon after those at WERTET and SANTEN, and while the immediate cause was probably internal, it was surely fueled both by these antecedent events and by the unstable religious climate of the time when the witch mania was causing widespread alarm and uncertainty.

The sisters reported that the Devil came into their dormitory at night "like a whirlwind," and then "proceeded to play the lute and the harp so melodiously, that the nuns would willingly have danced to the music. But then he transformed himself into the shape of a dog who jumped into the bed of one of them, whom the others suspected of the sin which they would not name. This and worse things took place, which I will not reveal since the sisters themselves kept them hidden."

COMMENT: The few details we are given hint at an erotic basis for the trouble, and it seems probable that sexual frustration was the cause, conveniently blamed on the Evil One.

See also: CONVENT HYSTERIA, DEMON POSSESSION.

NÎMES OUTBREAK OF POSSESSED NUNS

France: circa 1638

The outbreak at Nîmes had much in common with other 17th century episodes of convent hysteria, in particular the incidents at LOUDUN. However, those who sought to establish the facts of the outbreak adopted a radically different approach, one that signified a change in outlook. Perhaps because at Nîmes there was a strong Protestant presence, instead of the Church being permitted to impose their own interpretation on the matter, medical science was invoked.

CONTEXT: Although Henri IV's Edict of Nantes allowed religious freedom to Protestants and Catholics alike, the pressure on Protestants to convert was very fierce, and this was particularly true of the region around Nîmes. This may be the background to the outbreak, though no specific event is described as setting it off.

An attack of convulsions afflicted women and girls of Nîmes and the surrounding district. The symptoms duplicated those of other outbreaks, notably those at Loudun, and here again the Catholic Church insisted that the devil was responsible for the outbreak. However, in this case others expressed their doubts, and Santerre,[16] the Promoteur of the Bishop of Nîmes, saw fit to consult the medical faculty of the university of nearby Montpellier, which was at that time the leading medical establishment of the country.[17]

The doctors were confronted with a list of symptoms that were an almost total replication of those at Loudun and asked to give their opinion, whether these were truly signs of demonic possession:

- The bending, curvature and movement of the body, the head touching the soles of the feet, with other contorsions and strange postures;
- The rapidity of movement of the head forwards and backwards, against the chest and the back;
- The sudden swelling of the tongue, the throat and the face, with an equally rapid change of hue;
- A "stupid" and abstracted state of mind, and absence of sensation so that they could be pinched without moving the body or changing color;
- The immobility of the entire body when commanded by the exorcist, even when they were being furiously agitated;
- The uttering of cries similar to the yelping of a dog, either in the chest or rather in the throat;
- A fixed stare at some object, without shifting to either side;
- Providing answers in French to questions posed in Latin;
- The vomiting of objects in the same state as they were swallowed:
- The ability to be pricked with a lancet without bleeding.

The faculty of Montpellier was asked if these were truly signs of possession by Satan. The doctors worked their way through the list, showing that each could occur naturally. Prudently, their report concluded that they could not absolutely rule out the possibility of supernatural intervention. But the symptoms presented by the women of Nîmes could be explained without difficulty from their knowledge of physical laws, and nothing proved, in these circumstances, the reality of the intervention of a diabolic power. The failure to reply in Latin they considered to be particularly suspect, for surely the Evil One would be familiar with that tongue.

Once diabolic possession had been eliminated, Dr. Louis Calmeil commented, the professors had to examine whether the young women of Nîmes were afflicted with convulsive melancholia, or if they fell into the class of persons who simulate an affliction which they hope will bring attention on themselves.[18] At that time, they were in an all-or-nothing situation: either the sisters were possessed or they were pretending. The third option, that they were in a pathological state, was not so much as considered as a possibility.

COMMENT: Three hundred years later, researchers would compile similar lists of behavior, and in all seriousness pose the question: did these symptoms indicate that the subject had been abducted by aliens? (See ALIEN ABDUCTION MANIA.)

See also: CONVENT HYSTERIA, DEMON POSSESSION.

NUCLEAR DISASTER HOAX

Springfield, Illinois: circa November 9, 1982

Almost immediately after a scheduled fictional radio drama about a local nuclear power plant disaster was broadcast over WSSR-FM in Springfield, worried residents began calling emergency service agencies to find out if it was true. The program was forced to end just two and a half minutes after it started. During that time, the play claimed "that a nuclear cloud was headed for Springfield." Chuck Jones, of the Illinois Emergency Services and Disaster Agency, said: "I'm still shocked that someone out at that station let that get on the air." The drama was intended to air for half an hour over the public station, which was under the control of Sangamon State University. The nuclear power facility that was mentioned in the drama was located some 25 miles northeast of the city but was not operational at the time of the broadcast.[19]

COMMENT: This is a rare instance in which a "scare" broadcast was actually pulled off the air during transmission.

Sources

1. For an excellent overview of this movement, see: Steinbauer, Friedrich (1979). *Melanesian Cargo Cults* (translated by Max Wohlwill). London: George Prior Publishers, pages 88-90.
2. Miller, J. Graham (1948). "Naked Cult in Central West Santo." *The Journal of the Polynesian Society* 57(4):330-341. Quotation on pp. 331-332.
3. Miller, op cit., pp. 330-341.
4. Steinbauer, Friedrich (1979). op cit., pages 88-90.
5. "Navy Investigates Mysterious Outbreak," *The Valley Independent* (Monessen, Pennsylvania), September 6, 1988, p. 2A.
6. Struewing J.P., & Gray, G.C. (1990). "Epidemic of Respiratory Complaints Exacerbated by Mass Psychogenic Illness in a Military Recruit Population." *American Journal of Epidemiology* 132: 1120-1129.
7. Roach, E. Steven, Langley, Ricky L. (2004). "Episodic Neurological Dysfunction Due to Mass Hysteria." *Archives of Neurology* 61(8):1269-1272 (August). See p. 1270.
8. Roach and Langley (2004). op cit.
9. Sifakis, Carl (1993). *Hoaxes and Scams: A Compendium of Deceptions, Ruses and Swindles*. New York: Facts on File, p. 283.
10. "Practical Jokes" [Editorial]. *The New York Times*, November 10, 1874, p. 4.
11. "Practical Jokes." op cit., p. 4.
12. http://www.c-span.org/questions/week174.asp, accessed June 16, 2008.
13. Langdon, Christine. (1999). "Sick-Building Inquiry Sparks Calls." *The Dominion* (Wellington, New Zealand), December 17, p. 3; "Sickness Remains a Mystery." *The Dominion*, December 22, 1999, p. 8; "Staff Illness Still a Mystery." *The Dominion*, January 6, 200, p. 12.
14. Wier, Jean. [Weyer, Johann] (1885). *Histoires, Disputes Et Discours Des Illusions Et Impostures Des Diables, Des Magiciens Infames, Sorcières Et Empoisonneurs*. Translated from the Latin original, published 1563. Paris: Bureaux du Progrès Médical, volume 1, pp. 530-531.
15. Madden, R. R. (1857). *Phantasmata or Illusions and Fanaticisms of Protean Forms Productive of Great Evils*. London: T.C. Newby, p. 256.
16. Baissac, Jules (1890). *Les Grands Jours de la Sorcellerie*. Paris: Klincksieck, p. 541, wonders if this is the same Santerre who so narrowly escaped the accusations of the nuns of CHINON: if so, the lesson he learned there may have prompted his course of action here.
17. Aubin, Nicolas (1752[1693]). *Histoire des Diables de Loudun*. Amsterdam: 1752, re-issue of a publication in 1693, p. 246.
18. Calmeil, L.F. (1845). *De la Folie, Consideree Sous le Point de vue Pathologique, Philosophique, Historique et Judiciaire* [On the Crowd, Considerations on the Point of Pathology, Philosophy, History and Justice]. Paris: Baillere, volume 2, p. 48.
19. "Radio Hoax Program Halted Early." *Chronicle-Telegram* (Elyria, Ohio), November 10, 1982, p. D2.

OAT BRAN CRAZE

United States: 1980s

During the mid-1980s, oat bran became intensely promoted in the United States as a way to significantly reduce cholesterol levels in the blood after a small study indicated that oat bran dramatic lowered the artery-clogging substance. Soon a flurry of books and magazines were promoting the benefits of oat bran, culminating in the publication of a 1988 article in the prestigious *Journal of the American Medical Association* in which it was claimed that eating oat bran was a "more cost-effective treatment for high cholesterol than any available drug." Sales of Quaker Oats rocketed six-fold and it seemed as though every women's magazine featured oat bran recipes. Stanford professor of statistics Ingram Olkin says that the mania began to subside in 1990 with the publication of a study indicating that common white bread and other baked items could also lower cholesterol levels—while producing a lot less gas. The researchers suggested that it wasn't so much the health benefits from eating oats or refined wheat that lowered cholesterol, but that these goods were replacing more fatty foods.[1]

COMMENT: Recently, the British weekly, *The Week,* has been featuring a "health scare of the week," as this or that nutrient is either demonized or lauded as the next wonder substance. Oat bran is just one of a catalog of foods that briefly become the nutritional answer to health problems, only to fade from the public consciousness as the benefits or negatives are put into perspective when the broader picture is explained.

OHIO CHORUS FAINTING FITS

December 1952

Ohio was the scene of a series of outbreaks of fainting among chorus members. For several days, the chorus girls of Warren High School kept fainting during public performances, with one exception: they were fine when singing in front of classmates. At three separate performances on three separate days within a week, the students fainted. First it was seven girls fainting in front of an Exchange Club luncheon, then six girls fainted at a Rotary Club function, and finally, five collapsed at a meeting of the Kiwanis Club. One reporter noted: "The choir will be singing along when—plop!—down go several girls with a swoon, sometimes six or seven at a time." During this period, not a single member of the school's boy's chorus collapsed.[2]

Several days later in Cleveland, Ohio, a separate fainting epidemic struck members of the Myron T. Herrick Junior High choir. As 70 girls were singing "The Bells of Christmas Morning" before a school assembly on December 19, one collapsed. Before long, many classmates began keeling over "in a wave-like reaction."[3]

OKLAHOMA CHORUS COLLAPSE

Oklahoma State University: November 23, 1959

One of the largest recorded episodes of mass collapse and fainting took place at the Oklahoma State University field house on the evening of November 23rd. An estimated 5,400 members of high school choruses from across Oklahoma were performing at the annual Thanksgiving Song Festival. About halfway through the event, many of the 200 drivers of school busses that were parked around the stadium, started their engines so as to turn on their heaters and ensure that the students would be warm when they boarded the bus for the trip home. Soon a strange smell wafted through the field house. It was the smell of the diesel fumes being sucked into the air intake fans. The mysterious odor scared many of the students who began hyperventilating and fainting. A mass evacuation was soon underway. More than 500 students overwhelmed area hospitals but all the students quickly recovered. Stillwater High School chorus director G.C. Epperly attributed the incident to "a combination of too many hot dogs, a little carbon monoxide and a lot of mass hysteria."[4]

OPERATION FOX RID

Derby, England: circa January 1998

A football club in Derby was having trouble with foxes digging up their soccer pitch, so officers from the Derby Health Department suggested using a harmless chemical that gives off a foul smell in hopes of driving the animals away. The move backfired when the smell wafted over a nearby clothing factory, triggering panic. Upon detecting the odor, a majority of employees reported feeling ill. Some were examined at a hospital for breathing problems. An investigation soon revealed the harmless nature of the odor.[5]

ORSON WELLES MARTIAN PANIC

Across the United States: 1938

Shortly after 8 o'clock on Sunday evening October 30, 1938, many Americans became frightened after listening to a realistic live one-hour radio drama depicting a fictitious Martian landing at the "Wilmuth Farm" in the tiny hamlet of Grovers Mill, a suburb of Princeton, New Jersey, in the town of West Windsor. Those living within the immediate vicinity of the bogus invasion appeared to have been most frightened, although the broadcast could be heard in all regions of the continental United States and no one particular location was immune. The play included references to real places, buildings, highways, streets, prestigious speakers, convincing sound effects, and special bulletins. The drama was produced by 23-year-old theatrical prodigy George Orson Welles (1915-1985) who was accompanied by a small group of actors and musicians in a New York City studio of the Columbia Broadcasting System's Mercury Theatre of the Air. The script was written by Howard Koch, who loosely based it on the 1898 book, *The War of the Worlds,* by acclaimed science fiction writer Herbert George (H.G.) Wells (1866-1946). In the original Wells novel, the Martians had landed in 19th century Woking, England.

CONTEXT: At the time of the broadcast, most Americans were heavily reliant on radio for news and entertainment. Political conditions were tense with Adolf Hitler, having recently annexed Austria, continuing his incursion into Czechoslovakia. With each passing day, Europe was slipping closer to a Second World War that would soon involve the United States. Listeners had grown accustomed to news bulletins interrupting regular programming with live reports from European war correspondents. It was within this context that the Welles drama, interspersed with a series of live field reports, would have appeared highly realistic. Sociologist Hadley Cantril concluded that a

Orson Welles speaks with newsmen after the sensational broadcast of War of the Worlds at the Mercury Theatre.

contributing factor to the panic was the plausibility of the broadcast, as a substantial portion of listeners had assumed that the Martian "gas raids" were actually a German gas attack on the United States that the announcer that misinterpreted as a Martian invasion. One typical respondent said: "The announcer said a meteor had fallen from Mars and I was sure he thought that, but *in back of my head I had the idea that the meteor was just a camouflage.* It was really an airplane like a Zeppelin that looked like a meteor and *the Germans were attacking us* with gas bombs."[6]

The epicenter of fear was in the vicinity of Grovers Mill and nearby Dutch Neck where there was near gridlock as thrill-seekers and rescuers were trying to reach the "crash" site while others were trying to drive away.[7] At Grovers Mill, hundreds of people arrived. Many searched in vain for the imaginary Wilmuth Farm, and instead descended on the Wilson Farm, assuming the reporter was mistaken.[8] Most seriously affected were parts of New Jersey and New York City, which was shrouded in an eerie fog that may have contributed to the scare by reflecting the content of the broadcast, invading Martians attacking both states. On one block in Newark, New Jersey, more than twenty families fled their homes, covering their faces with wet handkerchiefs and draping towels over their heads to protect themselves from the "poison gas."[9] Phone lines were jammed as police were swamped by frantic residents desperate for information on the "gas raids from Mars." Fifteen people in Newark were treated for shock and anxiety at St. Michael's Hospital.[10] At the *New York Times* offices, 875 phone inquiries were logged. At Manhattan Police Headquarters, the 13 telephone switchboard operators could not keep up with calls.[11] Upon hearing the initial reports of a large meteor impact nearby, two Princeton University geologists rushed to the impact site, only to find others like themselves searching in vain for the object.[12]

To a lesser extent, the effects of the broadcast were felt across the country. In Indiana, a woman burst into a church shouting: "New York destroyed; it's the end of the world. You might as well go home and die. I just heard it on the radio."[13] In Lincoln, Nebraska, hundreds of panicky residents jammed the police switchboard wanting to know if it was true and what they should do.[14] In St. Louis, people grouped together in the streets of some neighborhoods to discuss a plan of action in the face of the impending war. In Pittsburgh, a man returned home during the broadcast only to find his wife clutching a bottle of poison, screaming: "I'd rather die this way than like that."[15] In Toronto, radio station CFRB was flooded with inquiries from worried Canadians.[16] In Washington State there was great anxiety as residents also jammed the phone lines of police, fire, and newspaper offices in Seattle. Most terror-stricken were residents of Concrete, 65 miles to the northeast, when a power interruption caused pandemonium. Some loaded their families into cars and headed into the mountains; others fainted.[17] In London, H.G. Wells expressed agitation upon hearing news of the episode, remarking: "I gave no permission whatever for alterations which might lead to the belief that it was real news."[18]

Peoples' minds also played tricks on them, illustrating the extreme variability of eyewitness testimony and suggestibility. One person became convinced that they could smell the poison gas and feel the heat rays as described on the radio; another became distraught and felt a choking sensation from the imaginary gas. In Hamilton, New Jersey, a frantic woman told police she had stuffed wet papers and rags into all of the crevices of her doors and windows, but it was to no avail as the fumes were already seeping in.[19] During the broadcast, several residents reported to police observations "of Martians on their giant machines poised on the Jersey Palisades."[20] Upon hearing descriptions of Martians operating their towering metallic machines on four insect-like legs, several Grovers Mill residents opened fire at a huge outline barely visible through the fog—punching several holes in the community's water tower.[21] A Boston woman said she could "see the fire" as described on the radio;[22] other people told of hearing machine gun fire or the "swish" sound of the Martians. One man climbed atop a roof and told Bronx police: "I could see the smoke from the bombs, drifting over toward New York. What shall I do?"[23] Others created events that never happened, underscoring the subjective nature of human memory reconstruction. An example involved the case of Miss Jane Dean, a devoutly religious woman, who when recalling the broadcast said the most realistic portion was "the sheet of flame that swept over the entire country. That is just the way I pictured the end."[24] In reality, there was no mention of a sheet of flame anywhere in the broadcast. Some who had tuned in from the beginning swore there was never a disclaimer. For instance, Sarah Jacob of Illinois said: "They should have announced that it was a play. We listened to the whole thing and they never did."[25]

The drama appeared in newspaper schedules across the country the day of the broadcast identified as a play, but many listeners did not make the association. An opening announcement clearly stated its fictional nature: "The Columbia Broadcasting System and its affiliated stations present Orson Welles and the Mercury Theatre on the Air in *War of the Worlds* by H.G. Wells."[26] Three other times during the play listeners were reminded of its theatrical origins. Welles also noted that "The Man From Mars" had often been the subject of radio fiction and part of the program was in the form of a past tense memoir.[27] Radio ratings company C.E. Hooper Incorporated estimated that 3.6% of the listening audience tuned in to the Welles broadcast in comparison to the popular *Edgar Bergen and Charlie McCarthy Show* which captured 34.7% of listeners.[28] Listeners commonly tuned back and forth between radio programs, especially near the beginning. In 1937, Welles and actor John Houseman founded the Mercury Theatre, and his radio show by the same name began in mid-September 1938, in relative obscurity. Biographer Barbara Leaming remarked that each week Welles had a small window of opportunity in which to hook listeners. "Each week their one big chance to attract listeners came when Edgar Bergen introduced a guest performer. At that moment, if the performer was not especially good, people across America would quickly turn the dial to hear what else was on before switching back..."[29] Welles planned his script to include live dance music interrupted by special bulletins, in order to grab listeners, especially those switching channels. Leaming suggests that the technique worked beyond his wildest dreams.[30] Two separate listener surveys after the broadcast estimated that between 42 and 61% of listeners to the Welles drama tuned in late, missing the opening disclaimer, many believing it was a live news report.[31]

After the opening announcement, the drama began as a typical radio program of the era. "Good evening, ladies and gentlemen. From the Meridian Room in the Park Plaza in New York City, we bring you the music of Ramon Raquello and his orchestra."[32] The music was interrupted at intervals with special bulletins of increasing length and gravity describing, first, "explosions" on Mars followed by a "meteor" crashing near Grovers Mill. "Live" bulletins from the scene followed. The "meteor" was later identified as a "metal cylinder" that sprouted legs before the announcer's eyes and towered into the air. The cylinder contained hideous beings from Mars who opened fire with "death rays," scorching anyone who opposed them.[33]

Reporter: "A humped shape is rising out of the pit. I can make out a small beam of light against a mirror. What's that? There's a jet of flame springing from that mirror, and it leaps right at the advancing men. It strikes them head on! Good Lord, they're turning into flame!" Shortly after, dead silence and a grave announcement: "Ladies and gentlemen, I have just been handed a message...At least forty people, including six State Troopers, lie dead in a field east of the village of Grovers Mill, their bodies burned and distorted beyond all possible recognition."[34] Later the announcer described a bleak and devastating scene as the Martian machines were marching towards New York City: "All communication with Jersey shore closed...army wiped out..."[35] Soon a voice was heard saying: "I've just been handed a bulletin. Cylinders from Mars are falling all over the country. One outside Buffalo, one in Chicago, St. Louis..."[36]

Immediately following the episode, the Federal Communications Commission (FCC) launched an investigation, publishing its findings on December 5, 1938. Concerned with censorship, the FCC decided not to impose new regulatory controls, noting that the actions taken by CBS since the episode was aired "were sufficient to protect the public interest."[37] In its ruling, the FCC cited a letter from CBS stating that they would refrain from using the technique of live news interruptions and bulletins in any future dramas.[38]

There is a growing consensus among sociologists that the extent of the panic as described by Princeton University psychologist Hadley Cantril in his best-selling book *The Invasion from Mars* was exaggerated. But regardless of the extent of the panic, there is little doubt that many Americans were genuinely frightened and some did try to flee the Martian gas raids and heat rays, especially in the New Jersey-New York area. Based on various opinion polls and estimates, Cantril conservatively calculated that at least six million people heard the drama, 1.7 million of which believed they were hearing a news bulletin, and 1.2 million of those became excited to varying degrees.[39] While some claimed that hundreds of thousands panicked,[40] there is only scant anecdotal evidence to suggest that many listeners actually took some action after hearing the broadcast, such as packing belongings, grabbing guns, or fleeing in motor vehicles. In fact, much of Cantril's study was based on interviews with just 135 people. Sociologist William Bainbridge is critical of Cantril for citing just a few colorful stories from a small number of people who panicked. According to Bainbridge, on any given night, out of a pool of over a million people, at least a thousand would have been driving excessively fast or engaging in rambunctious behavior. From this perspective, the event was primarily a news media creation.[41]

Sociologist David Miller supports this view noting that while the day after the panic many newspapers carried accounts of suicides and heart attacks by frightened citizens, they proved to have been unfounded but have passed into American folklore.[42] Miller also takes Cantril to task for failing to show substantial evidence of mass flight from the perceived attack, citing just a few examples and not warranting an estimate of over one million panic-stricken Americans. While Cantril cites American Telephone Company figures indicating that local media and law enforcement agencies were inundated with up to 40 percent more telephone calls than normal in parts of New Jersey during the broadcast, he did not determine the specific nature of these calls. Miller notes that some callers probably wanted information like which military units were being called up, where they could donate blood, or if casualty lists were obtainable. "Some callers were simply angry that such a realistic show was allowed on the air, while others called CBS to congratulate Mercury Theater for the exciting Halloween program," Miller writes. "It seems... (likely) many callers just wanted to chat with their families and friends about the exciting show they had just listened to on the radio."[43] Sociologist Erich Goode concurs with Miller's view but also notes that to have convinced a substantial number of listeners "that a radio drama about an invasion from Mars was an actual news broadcast has to be regarded as a remarkable achievement."[44]

In 1938, the print media and upstart radio were highly competitive archrivals, with radio viewed as an emerging threat to their advertising coffers. This antagonistic relationship may have prompted journalists to consciously or subconsciously exaggerate the extent of the panic in their press reports.[45] Radio historian Justin Levine notes the conspicuous absence of "independent historical accounts" discussing the panic's severity, with the exception of newspapers. He states: "The anecdotal nature of the reporting makes it difficult to objectively assess the true extent and intensity of the panic."

Science writer Keay Davidson suggests that the exaggerated nature of the panic and failure to correct this oversight reveals how scholars, novelists, and intellectuals have conceived of ordinary working people as a blind, unthinking mob, easily led astray. Panic folklore about the 1938 broadcast reflects an elitist view of "the masses" that has been used to justify unjust social policies and class oppression (i.e., "You can't do that—the people will riot!"). "The implicit message is blunt: most people are irrational and untrustworthy. The covert *political* message is: "Can the masses *really* be trusted to rule themselves? Don't they require a strong leader?" This question seemed urgent in Cantril's era, when the Hitler case suggested that the masses really could be easily manipulated by a charismatic leader equipped with the latest technologies of mass propaganda."[46] Mass panic in reaction to the broadcast has been widely cited since 1938 to support government secrecy of UFO reports.[47] In 1999,

U.S. Senator Christopher Dodd cited the potential of a *War of the Worlds*-type panic in reaction to the Y2K computer scare. "The worst thing the American public could do would be to withdraw funds in excessive amounts from their banks; to hoard medical supplies or...food or products like that in preparation of some—something akin to *The War of the Worlds*... That, in my view today, is the greatest threat that the Y2K problem poses—panic by the American public..."[48]

Widespread panics in response to broadcasts of modified *War of the Worlds* scripts triggered a CHILEAN MARTIAN INVASION PANIC in 1944, the ECUADOR MARTIAN INVASION PANIC of 1949, and the PORTUGUESE MARTIAN INVASION PANICS of 1988 and 1998. Radio broadcasts of regional adaptations of the Orson Welles play have led to small-scale scares in the United States: the BUFFALO MARTIAN INVASION SCARE of 1968 and the RHODE ISLAND MARTIAN INVASION PANIC of 1974.

COMMENTS: It is undeniable that the 1938 panic occurred but the extent remains the subject of debate. The same holds true for Welles' intent. Immediately after the broadcast, Welles vehemently denied having any intention of deceiving listeners, though he later suggested otherwise.[49] It is likely that Welles, intent on boosting his paltry audience share, calculated that some listeners would panic, but grossly underestimated reaction to the broadcast. This view is supported by the proposed script, which was significantly toned down for the broadcast version. Prior to its airing, CBS censors deemed the script too realistic and made 28 amendments. The working script had such phrases as "New Jersey National Guard," "Princeton University Observatory," "Langley Field," and "Magill University," which were changed to "state militia," "Princeton Observatory," "Langham Field," and "Macmillian University." "The United States Weather Bureau in Washington D.C." became "The Government Weather Bureau" and "St. Patrick's Cathedral" was shortened to "the cathedral."[50]

While the realism of the drama may seem implausible to contemporary radio listeners, Mars was the subject of frequent speculation about the existence of intelligent life, and news bulletins about the growing war in Europe were common. It is the modern equivalent of someone tuning in to CNN and being riveted by a catastrophic terrorist-related storyline, assuming it was on all channels. After the initial uproar, Welles' popularity soared; overnight he was world famous, his radio ratings rose three-fold,[51] and Campbell's Soup signed on as a sponsor.[52] In an ironic twist, Welles would become part of a cautionary tale on the dangers of "crying wolf." On December 6, 1941, during a live poetry reading on network radio, Welles was interrupted by a bulletin reporting the Japanese attack on Pearl Harbor. Many listeners refused to believe the report, suspicious of the coincidence.[53]

See also: MARTIAN INVASION SCARE, CHILEAN MARTIAN INVASION PANIC, ECUADOR MARTIAN INVASION PANIC, BUFFALO MARTIAN INVASION SCARE, RHODE ISLAND MARTIAN INVASION PANIC, PORTUGUESE MARTIAN INVASION PANICS.

Sources

1. Anonymous. (1992). "The Rise and Fall of Oat Bran." *Wilson Quarterly* 16(4):128-129, citing Orkin, Ingram (1992). "Reconcilable Differences." *The Sciences* (July-August), The New York Academy of Sciences, 2 East 63rd St., New York, N.Y. 10021.

2. "Choir Hit by Fainting Spells." *The Times Recorder* [Zanesville, Ohio]. December 13, 1953, p. 1.

3. "Mass Fainting Hits Chorus." *Mansfield News-Journal* [Ohio], December 22, 1952.

4. "Exhaust Fumes and Hysteria KO Some 500 Students at Festival." *Stevens Point* [Wisconsin] *Daily Journal*, November 24, 1959, p. 2.

5. Anonymous (1998). "False Alarm over Bad Smell." *The Safety and Health Practitioner* 16(2):3.

6. Cantril, Hadley, Gaudet, Hazel, and Herzog, Herta (1940). *The Invasion From Mars: A Study in the Psychology of Panic.* New Jersey: Princeton University Press, p. 160. Italics in original.

7. "Hoax Spreads Terror Here." *Trenton Evening Times*, October 31, 1938, p. 1.

8. Marvin, Scott. (1975). "The Halloween Radio Spoof that Shook a Nation." *Parade* (October 29):4-5.

9. "Radio Listeners in Panic, Taking War Drama as Fact." *New York Times*, October 31, 1938, p . 1.

10. "Boo!" *Time* (November 7, 1938), p. 40.

11. "Scare is Nation-Wide." *New York Times*, October 31, 1938, p . 4.

12. "Geologists at Princeton Hunt 'Meteor' in Vain." *New York Times*, October 31, 1938, p. 4.

13. "Scare is Nation-Wide." op cit.

14. "Nasty Monsters From Mars Give Radio Listeners Uneasy Moments." *Nebraska State Journal*, October 31, 1938, p. 1.

15. "Scare is Nation-Wide." op cit.

16. "Scare is Nation-Wide." op cit.

17. "Women Faint as Lights Go Out At Concret." *Seattle Post-Intelligencer*, October 31, 1938, p. 1; "Radio 'Invasion' Throws Listeners into Hysteria." *Seattle Post-Intelligencer*, October 31, 1938, pp. 1, 2.
18. "Even Author H.G. Wells Was Deeply Perturbed." *Trenton Evening News*, October 31, 1938, p. 1.
19. "Terror Spread Here by Hoax." *Trenton Evening Times*, October 31, 1938, p. 2.
20. Markush, R.E. (1973). "Mental Epidemics: A Review of the Old to Prepare for the New." *Public Health Reviews* 2:353-442. See p. 379.
21. Scott (1975). op cit., p. 5.
22. "Scare is Nation-wide." op cit.
23. "Radio War Drama Creates a Panic." *New York Times*, October 31, 1938, p . 4.
24. Cantril, op cit., p. 181.
25. Cantril, op cit., p. 55.
26. Cantril, op cit., p. 4.
27. "FCC to Scan Script of 'War' Broadcast." *New York Times*, November 1, 1938: L26.
28. Brady, Frank. (1989). *Citizen Welles: A Biography of Orson Welles.* New York: Charles Scribner's Sons, p. 169.
29. Leaming, Barbara (1986). *Orson Welles: A Biography*. New York: Penguin, p. 198.
30. Leaming (1986). op cit., p. 193.
31. Cantril, op cit., p. 77.
32. Cantril, op cit., p. 5.
33. Uncut version of the original broadcast of Orson Welles' radio adaptation of H.G. Wells novel, *The War of the Worlds*. Distributed by Metacom Incorporated.
34. Cantril, op cit., pp. 18-19.
35. Cantril, op cit., p. 30.
36. Cantril, op cit., p. 31.
37. Levine, Justin. (1999). "History and Analysis of the Federal Communications Commission's Response to Radio Broadcast Hoaxes." *Federal Communications Law Journal* 52(2):274-320. See p. 286.
38. Levine, 1999, op cit., p. 286.
39. Cantril (1940). op cit., pp. 55-58.
40. Milio, James, Peltier, Melissa Jo, and Hufnail, Mark (producers). (1998). "Martian Mania: The True Story of The War of the Worlds" (hosted by James Cameron). First aired on The Science Fiction Channel, USA, October 30.
41. Bainbridge, William. (1987). "Collective Behavior and Social Movements." Pp. 544-576. In Rodney Stark (ed.), *Sociology*. Belmont, California: Wadsworth.
42. Miller (1985). op cit., p. 100; Naremore, James (1978). *The Magic World of Orson Welles*. Oxford University Press: New York.
43. Miller (1985). op cit., p. 107.
44. Goode, Erich. (1992). *Collective Behavior*. New York: Harcourt Brace Jovanovich, p. 315.
45. Brady, Frank (1989). op cit., p. 176; Crook, Timothy. "The Psychological Impact of Radio." Http://www.irdp.co.uk/hoax.html.
46. Letter from Keay Davidson to Robert Bartholomew dated December 12, 2002. Davidson is the science writer for the San Francisco Chronicle.
47. Michell, John, and Rickard, Robert (2000). *Unexplained Phenomena: A Rough Guide Special*. Shorts Gardens, London: Rough Guides Ltd., p. 104.
48. Transcript of remarks by Senator Christopher J. Dodd, Vice Chair, "Committee on the Year 2000 (Y2K) Technology Problem" before the National Press Club, Wednesday, September 8, 1999. Full transcript available at http://www.senate.gov/~y2k/speeches/dodd 990908.htm.
49. Welles, Orson, Bogdanovich, Peter, and Rosenbaum, Jonathan (1992). *This Is Orson Welles*. New York: HarperCollins. The book is comprised of revealing interviews between Welles and his close friend Peter Bogdanovich over a 15 year period, and was published after Welles' death in 1985.
50. Brady, Frank. (1989). op cit., p. 167.
51. Fettmann, Eric. (1988). "'The Martians Have Landed!' In Radio Show 60 Years Ago, America Lost its Innocence." *New York Post*, October 28, 1988, p. 41.
52. Leaming, op cit., p. 198.
53. Levine, 1999, op cit., p. 286.

PADERBORN OUTBREAK

Germany: 1656

In the spring, a hysterical affliction broke out in Paderborn, Germany, that was truly epidemic in character, since it affected the whole bishopric and afflicted men and women, students, girls and children. Insisting that they were possessed, they loudly demanded to be avenged against the sorcerers who had put them in this state. And they named names.

The Burgermaster of Brackel and his servant girl Catherina were accused. Catherina was arrested and her room searched. In a box was found a toad, a small black bird, hair, needles, nut-shells, and white bread – not quite a witch's armory but enough to cast suspicion on her.

Also accused was Vater Egidio, the guardian of the Capuchins. Such were the accusations against his order that the brothers were no longer able to beg for alms in the street, as was their custom, and when they went out of their monastery they carried clubs under their cloaks to defend themselves if attacked.

A feature of the possession was the ability to speak in all languages. When questioned while in ecstasy, the afflicted could answer questions in Hebrew, Greek, or Latin. They also gave intelligent answers, even to difficult questions of theology and philosophy. Unfortunately, few details of this affair are recorded, and the fate of Catherina, and of the afflicted persons, is unknown.[1]

COMMENT: The servant-girl was evidently indulging in some form of domestic magic, which was common enough at this time. The episode seems to have escalated from these humble beginnings.

See also: CONVENT HYSTERIA.

PALESTINIAN POISONING PANIC

Jordan West Bank: March-April 1983

For several months in 1983, the world media spotlight was focused on reports that Palestinian schoolgirls may have been deliberately poisoned by Israelis. Reports of the "poisoning" even appeared in major Israeli newspapers, further crystallizing the popular idea that Jews were behind the sinister series of attacks. Between March and April 1983, nearly a thousand, mostly Arab schoolgirls in the disputed Israeli-occupied Jordan West Bank reported a variety of symptoms: headaches, blurred vision, stomach pain, fainting, blindness, and limb weakness. Following negative medical tests by a variety of investigating agencies, including independent probes by researchers from the World Health Organization and the United States, it became evident that no gassings had occurred.

The episode occurred amid poison gas rumors and a long-standing Palestinian mistrust of Jews. The medical complaints appeared during a 15-day period, coinciding with intense media publicity that poison gas was being sporadically targeted at Palestinians. The episode began in, and was predominantly confined to, schools in several adjacent villages in this bitterly disputed region. The case became widely known as the "Arjenyattah Epidemic" as they occurred in Arabah, Jenin, and Yattah.[2]

CONTEXT: The Israeli military has occupied the Jordan West Bank since 1967, their presence engendering intense hatred. While the occupation is generally viewed as temporary within the Arab World, as one observer notes, "some tend to believe that the Israelis would do anything to perpetuate the status quo."[3] Targeting would-be Palestinian mothers with poison, either by Israeli soldiers or civilian extremists, was a natural suspicion within this long-standing climate of fear and hatred.

The First Wave: Arrabah

The episode occurred in three distinct waves. The first phase began on March 21, during a morning class at the Arrabah Girls' School, when a seventeen-year-old pupil experienced dizziness and breathing difficulties, including headaches and blurred vision. Soon 15 more pupils fell ill. Some of the affected girls said that the symptoms coincided with a rotten egg-like smell from a schoolyard bathroom.[4] By the following day, 61 students and five adults had undergone hospital evaluation. A team of physicians who investigated the incident noted that the "highest rates were observed in 3 upper floor classes nearest the latrine from which most of the odour was reported, and lowest rates in wing [sic] most distant from the latrine."[5]

On March 22, the *Yedi'Ot Ahronot* published a report on the mass illness at the Arrabah school, and though factually correct, the journalist implied the likely presence of poison gas in noting that the pupils "were suddenly afflicted by an attack of blindness, headache and stomach." Also, "blurred vision" was exaggerated and changed to "blindness."[6] The article also stated that "security forces had not used tear gas," seemingly suggesting and anticipating public outcry in reaction to the incident.[7]

The Second Wave: Jenin

On about March 26 and 27, a second wave of illness reports involving similar symptoms swept through six schools in the vicinity of Jenin, including the Elzahra, Burkin, Metalun, and UNRWA schools.[8] About 246 female pupils and some staff were affected. On the evening of March 27, 64 residents in Jenin were rushed to local medical facilities with similar complaints when a cloud of gas was emitted from a passing car.[9]

Descriptions of the episode as an attempt at genocide, appeared in the press by March 26 – even the Israeli press. Israel's *Ma'Ariv*, for example, described the episode as a mass poisoning with absolute certainty, using the sensational headlines: "The Mysterious Poisoning Goes On: 56 High School Girls in Djenin Poisoned." The only uncertainty was the source of the "poison." The report read in part: "The mysterious poisoning of 50 students that took place last week in Arraba...affected 56 additional students yesterday in Djenin. Currently no definite evidence exists as to the source of the poison. Yesterday morning, 29 girl students were admitted to the hospital from Djenin High School with the following symptoms: difficulty breathing, cyanosis, and dizziness."[10] Two days later, a report in another Israeli paper, *Ha'Aretz*, claimed that based on preliminary tests, "nerve gas" had made the Djenin students sick.[11] While the actual cause of the symptoms was not known at the time, the *Ha'Areta* and *Ma'Ariv* discussed the episode as a case of "poisoning."[12]

On March 31, the Israeli Ministry of Health appointed psychiatrist Albert Hafez to investigate the poisoning claims. In visiting the Djenin Hospital on March 31, Dr. Hafez noted that the situation had a melodramatic, soap-opera-like quality as foreign journalists were swarming around, interviewing both the affected girls and hospital staff. Suddenly, an Arab girl was brought in on a stretcher; she was immediately enveloped in a sea of physicians and staff, who push the frightened, bewildered mother aside. Almost instantly, an oxygen mask was forced over the girl's face while someone else administered an intramuscular injection. The mother later told doctors that her daughter was playing near their home when she experienced headache and nausea. Due to the publicity about the mass "poisoning," the mother grew alarmed and rushed her to hospital. Dr. Hafez provided a sense of the chaos at the hospital: "While busy examining the girl amid the surrounding crowd, I became aware of a new turmoil consequent to the arrival of a new group accompanying a second patient...an 18-year-old girl who was quite excited and tried to throw herself off the stretcher while those escorting her tried to restrain her. As with the previous patient, the oxygen mask and intramuscular injection were used instantly. The shouting girl, the excited crowd, the first patient, and her helpless mother together created an atmosphere of utter confusion."[13]

The Third Wave: Yattah

A third wave of reports occurred simultaneously on April 3 in the Tulkarem and Hebron districts, with the epicenter near a girls' school at Yattah. Students affected were attending the Beit Omar, Yattah, Neighbourhood, Nasser, and Anabtah schools.[14] When the schools were closed on April 4, the "outbreak" stopped. In an effort to resolve the reported poisonings, the Israeli government sent their top epidemiologist, Baruch Modan, to investigate.

Modan and his team of medical specialists soon concluded that mass hysteria was the culprit. They traced the "outbreak" to an odorous latrine near the Arrabah school. Later that day a second, larger wave was ignited during recess when friends of the first group affected spread rumors about their possible poisoning. The mass media and rumors were instrumental in spreading the symptoms during the second wave at several Jenin schools and nearby villages. Part of this phase involved the 64 Jenin residents who were reportedly "gassed" by a speeding car. It was concluded that the "poison" was actually thick smoke belched from a faulty exhaust system. The final wave of illness reports were, according to Modan and his investigators, triggered by the continuous spreading of poison gas rumors by the news media.[15]

Modan's report was widely viewed as biased within the Arab World, which dismissed the findings.[16] What followed was a public relations battle between the Israeli government and the Arab World, conducted through the United Nations. On March 30, the Commission on Arab Women, meeting in Tunis, Tunisia, telexed an urgent message to the U.N. Director-General, complaining that "Israeli authorities" were responsible for the "poisoning" and asking the U.N. "to put a stop to this genocide and protect the life of the Palestinian people."[17] In reaction, Israeli authorities described the poisoning claims as a propaganda campaign being fueled by the media and pro-Palestinian politicians.[18]

In an effort to resolve the issue, investigators from the National Institute for Occupational Safety and Health and the Centers for Disease Control, both in the U.S., were invited to conduct their own independent probe. They concluded that there was no evidence of a poisoning agent on the one hand, nor on the other that those affected were feigning symptoms. Their report concluded that the episode "was triggered either by psychological factors, or, more probably, by the odor of low concentrations of H_2S gas [hydrogen sulphide] escaping from a latrine at the school at Arrabah. Subsequent spread was due to psychological factors operating against a background of stress, and it may have been facilitated by newspaper and radio reports."[19] The American investigators, Philip Landrigan and Bess Miller, supported the findings of Modan and his team, noting that without any clear evidence to support their claims, the mass media in the region published and broadcast claims that a toxin was the likely cause.[20] The Americans took air, water, and soil samples and found "no evidence for a toxic aetiology."[21] They also noted the curious pattern of the illness, selectively striking certain groups: "Support for the diagnosis of psychogenic illness was provided here by the preponderance of female patients, particularly of adolescent girls. The relative sparing of infants, adolescent boys, and older adults argues against the presence of a toxin."[22]

"Attack" On Palestinian Fertility

Across the Arab world at this time, a story circulated that a group of Jews perpetrated the poisoning in an effort to counter the Palestinian birth rate, and hence, they "specifically targeted young girls approaching the age of marriage. The poisoning was done to harm this most fertile age group in order to limit Arab demographic growth. They even said they had found medical proof, claiming that urine tests showed a high protein level, which means that something is abnormal in the fertility system."[23] Such test results subsequently proved false. The Palestinian schoolgirl poisoning claims of 1983 are just one in a long list of historical claims of Jews poisoning their "enemies." A similar poisoning claim occurred in 1997, though the episode was devoid of mass psychogenic illness. According to Raphael Israeli, a professor of Islamic civilization at Hebrew University: "In 1997 the Palestinians exposed yet another Israeli 'plot to suppress Arab population growth.' They claimed to have tested packets of strawberry-flavored bubble gum which were found to be spiked with sex hormones and sold at low prices near schoolhouses in the West Bank and Gaza Strip. It was claimed that the gum aroused irresistible sexual appetites in women, then it sterilized them. According to Palestinian Supply Minister Abdel Aziz Shaheen, it was capable of 'completely destroying the genetic system of young boys,' as well."[24]

Physicians treating the schoolgirls often interpreted their medical findings as reflective of their particular worldviews. Hence, Palestinian doctors at the Djenin Hospital tended to assume that different poisons were used to sicken the girls. This assumption was made by doctors without any "laboratory facilities at their disposal and... [who] had to depend solely on their clinical sense and previous experience."[25] In sharp contrast, some Israeli doctors treating "victims" at the country's Tel-Hashomer Hospital were convinced that the girls were faking their symptoms as a political ploy to gain sympathizers for the Palestinian cause. To support this view, they noted that the girls tended to be hostile, aggressive, and uncooperative. Some Israeli press reports also supported this "factitious" position of events. According to Dr. Hafez, "Attracted by such a theory, reporters mobilized their resources and ingenuity to bring in evidence to confirm it. They filmed patients during doctors' rounds and alone, demonstrating the change in behavior from one situation to the other. They even tracked cars that were suspected of "recruiting" new patients and showed these films live on television."[26]

PARANORMAL PHENOMENA

One of the reasons why people behave in an extraordinary way is because they perceive themselves as confronted by extraordinary circumstances, which may range from confrontations with demons and spirits of the dead to supernatural afflictions and catastrophes. Many of the extraordinary behaviors presented in this book have been triggered by what were interpreted by the participants as paranormal or supernatural phenomena, which falls into three categories:

(1) Behaviors Involving Supernatural Entities

Many extraordinary behaviors derive from belief-systems that involve supernatural entities of some kind. The many outbreaks of CONVENT HYSTERIA, for example, presumed a belief in demonic possession, which, to minds brought up in the Christian tradition, provided the only explanation for the convulsions and blasphemies. A similar belief in the existence and activities of the Evil One underlay the WITCHCRAFT DELUSION, and he makes a guest appearance in circumstances as diverse as the WELSH REVIVAL and the TREASURE-DIGGING MANIA. Contemporary examples can be found in numerous school outbreaks of mass hysteria in Asia, Africa, and island settings (see MASS HYSTERIA IN SCHOOLS) where beliefs about supernatural creatures trigger trance states. India's MONKEYMAN SCARE of 2001 coincided with a television series about the popular Hindu monkey deity "Hanuman," who is believed to possess super-human strength and

Elisabeth de Ranfaing (1594-1649) suffered from diabolical possession and, like many other nuns of the period, could reportedly levitate (Nancy, 1619).

the ability to leap incredible distances.

Many behaviors occur because the participants believe their actions to be prescribed by divine authority. This is true of most of the RUSSIAN SECTS: the SKOPTSI who believed themselves beholden to castrate themselves were only one group of many whose actions reflected a celestial mandate. Often the belief spread as the result of the teachings and preachings of one or more charismatic individuals; this was equally true of the METHODISTS of 18th century England or the TAEPING rising in 19th century China. Self-anointed leaders, themselves convinced and in turn convincing their followers that they have been entrusted with a divine mission, make their appearance throughout this encyclopedia, from SABBATAI ZEVI to the DOUKHOBORS. For contemporary examples we need only look to such MASS SUICIDE CULTS as THE PEOPLE'S TEMPLE in Guyana or the ORDER OF THE SOLAR TEMPLE.

Many of these behaviors involve visionary experiences. The many hundreds of claims of APPARITIONS OF MARY have fueled the devotion of many Christians to the virgin mother of Jesus. Alleged miracles, such as the FATIMA SOLAR PHENOMENON and the INDIAN MILK MIRACLE, have reinforced popular faith. The late 19th century Native American GHOST DANCE was prompted by a shaman who claimed he was given instructions in a vision on how and when the sacred dance should be performed.

Belief in the survival, on some other plane of reality, of spirits of those formerly living on Earth underlies many behaviors; our entry on SPIRIT POSSESSION IN INDIA is one of many such, and the belief provided the necessary authorization for such tragic episodes as the XHOSA CATTLE KILLING in South Africa. Such belief was, of course, central to the SPIRITUALIST MANIA that swept through North America in the mid-19th century. Belief in the existence of ancestor spirits watching over the living in Africa is integral in triggering numerous outbreaks of LAUGHING MANIA.

Apart from certain supernatural entities that play leading roles in religious belief-systems, some folklore figures are perceived as intruding on our everyday reality from time to time. Such entities include the PHANTOM GASSER and the PHANTOM SLASHER. Panicking crowds tend to justify their terror with the supposed existence of a hostile entity that personifies the menace. Among the LONDON MONSTERS, for example, a character such as Springheel Jack was thought by some to be a supernatural being of some kind, for how else could his amazing feats be accounted for?

It must be recognized that many of these beliefs are not only sincerely held in popular culture, but are often sustained by informed and intelligent opinion. For many subscribers to the teachings of the Roman Catholic Church, for example, the Devil is a very real being, just as the visits of the Virgin Mary are considered to be veridical events. The thousands who believe that our planet is being visited by extraterrestrial aliens include college professors as well as housewives; for them, ALIEN ABDUCTIONS are terrifyingly real, and in all probability the prelude to an interplanetary invasion to dwarf the WAR OF THE WORLDS panics.

(2) Behaviors Involving Powers or Abilities Transcending Normal Limits

Some instances of extraordinary behavior seem to involve phenomena that go beyond the limits of what today's science regards as possible. The extraordinary self-mutilation feats of ISLAMIC ASCETIC CULTS and those of the CONVULSIONNAIRES DE SAINT-MEDARD seem to go beyond what conventional medicine regards as possible, yet both have been documented with quality testimony that makes it impossible to doubt their reality. Those who take part in such practices, together with observers and commentators, are generally ready to agree that such displays are possible only by virtue of a divinely-bestowed immunity to pain. Skeptics prefer to ascribe them to "hysterical anesthesia" or some such formula, but that does not explain how the human body acquires such a degree of invulnerability. Greater understanding of human potential, especially as regards the interplay between mind and body, may eventually enable us to account for them without having recourse to the supernatural. In the meantime, it is not surprising that such behaviors carry the appearance of the paranormal. Numerous episodes of demon possession during incidents of MASS HYSTERIA involve subjects, typically young girls, who seem to possess superhuman strength and require a half a dozen or more adults to restrain them.

Participants in several extraordinary behaviors noted in this Encyclopedia were members of groups who were led to believe that simply by joining they had acquired supernatural powers. The TAIPING REBELS and the PROPHETS OF THE CEVENNES shared the belief that they were immune to their enemies' weapons. JOHN NICHOLS TOM led his followers into their final fatal battle inspired with a similar delusion. Many followers of the GHOST DANCE were convinced that they were impervious to bullets, only to be felled on the battlefield. Other examples include the obliviousness to cold manifested by those in the throes of PIBLOKTOQ, and of course the seeming immunity to pain displayed by fanatics and martyrs alike in the context of religious or political beliefs of every kind.

(3) Behaviors Related to External Phenomena

In a few cases, external events of an apparently paranormal nature seem to be involved. For most of them, hallucination or misinterpretation of real events is the preferred explanation. Our entry on the FATIMA SOLAR PHENOMENON, regarded by many Christians as miraculous, is susceptible to an alternative explanation in terms of natural phenomena, though it remains true that the circumstances are extraordinary.

Alternative views are equally available for many events supposed to be miraculous by believers but for which others propose a natural explanation. This is notably true of STIGMATA, a category of phenomena chiefly associated with the Christian belief-system, whereby it is claimed that certain privileged individuals reproduce on their bodies the marks of the crucifixion of Jesus. The occurrences are so questionable as to justify skepticism; nevertheless the phenomenon itself unquestionably occurs and has yet to be satisfactorily explained by science.

In many instances it is probable that a psychological explanation will prove sufficient. The extraordinary phenomenon of MOVING IMAGES, regarded as miraculous by many Christians, seems to invite a diagnosis of collective delusion. Nevertheless, the eyewitness reports are not easily set aside and challenge conventional models of collective delusion. The same is true of the luminous phenomena observed by numerous witnesses in the course of the WELSH REVIVAL, which continue to defy simple natural explanation. Mass hallucination – itself a questionable hypothesis – seems inadequate to explain some of these well-documented events.

It may be, therefore, that in a small number of cases, the extraordinary behaviors narrated in this Encyclopedia were initiated, or accompanied, by events that, pending further investigation, must be provisionally assigned to the category of the paranormal. For most of these phenomena, alternative explanations are available, and we would be reluctant to admit any degree of paranormality except as a provisional measure. Nevertheless, the skeptic who doubts, for example, that DEMON POSSESSION involves a real Devil should be aware that there are many rational and intelligent people who are sincerely convinced of his existence.[27] Those who question whether visions of the Virgin Mary take place as a physical reality should recognize that this is considered by many people to be the case not simply as an act of faith or article of doctrine but on the basis of thoughtful evaluation.[28] Those who are skeptical that extraterrestrial aliens are invading Earth should be aware that this view is widely held, not just as an item of popular folklore but in consequence of reasoned evaluation of the evidence. Simple denial of facts for which the weight of evidence is strong is not the way to prevent them inspiring the kind of extraordinary behaviors described in this book.

This is particularly the case when the behavior concerned is practiced by an "exotic" culture. Commentators from western Europe/America, even when they are sufficiently open-minded to recognize that those who practice exotic behaviors such as those of ISLAMIC SECTS are not necessarily mentally afflicted, are apt to evaluate such behaviors from their own perspective.[29] Only by recognizing cultural relativism, and studying each behavior in its own cultural context, can it be fairly evaluated. Thus, what might seem paranormal to some would seem normal and natural to others. In the case of these phenomena, it is ultimately up to the individual to judge, on the basis of the evidence and of inherent probability, how he/she will evaluate them.

The compilers of this Encyclopedia do not presume to take sides in such matters, though we have felt it right to indicate alternative interpretations of ostensibly paranormal events when they help to explain the extraordinary behavior resulting from those events. However, in the long run, just as the diversity of extraordinary behavior we describe in this Encyclopedia will, we trust, result in a widening our ideas of how human beings can behave, so the challenge presented by the extraordinary phenomena that triggered those behaviors may also serve as a challenge to science to broaden its notions of what is possible.

PARENT HYSTERIA (MASS HYSTERIA BY PROXY)

Georgia, United States: 1988

A rare report of what could be described as "mass hysteria by proxy" occurred at an unidentified elementary school near Atlanta. It involved the re-labeling of mundane symptoms that were instigated and maintained by erroneous beliefs among hypervigilant parents. The episode began during a routine social gathering of parents and students in the school cafeteria in early September. The mother of a student commented that, ever since the term began, her child had experienced numerous minor health problems and looked pale. Other mothers at the meeting noted similar signs and symptoms in their children since the beginning of term: pallor, dark circles under the eyes, headaches, fatigue, nausea, and occasional vomiting. They soon suspected that something in the school building was to blame, a view which was confirmed on October 11 when the school was evacuated after a minor natural gas leak occurred during routine maintenance. When intermittent minor gas leaks continued over the next month, concerned parents picketed the school and appealed to the local media, which highlighted their fears. After negative environmental and epidemiological studies, investigators concluded that mothers had almost exclusively redefined common and ever-present childhood illnesses, while the children in question neither sought attention nor were overly concerned with their symptoms, maintaining high attendance levels throughout the term.[30]

Investigators from the Center for Disease Control in Atlanta, and the Georgia Department of Public Health, noted that the episode represented a "sporadic occurrence of common illnesses."[31] Their report noted that one of the affected pupils, a third-grader, had been ill since the first grade with ongoing headaches. Another student had complained of nausea and headaches for two months prior to the gas leak, while still another had a history of headaches for about a year before the leak.[32] Researchers noted that "signs and symptoms of greatest concern to the parents are not consistent with known ill-effects of exposure to natural gas. Most of them were non-specific and could have resulted from a variety of common childhood conditions, and the parents might have mistakenly attributed them to exposure to natural gas. Parental anxiety, interpersonal contacts, and extensive media coverage could have further encouraged this mistake."[33]

The investigators concluded that use of the term mass sociogenic illness seemed inappropriate "because complaints did not come principally from the students and the apparent epidemic illness was not transmitted among them. The term 'mass sociogenic illness by proxy' is proposed to describe this incident, in which transmission in one group (the parents) resulted in reports of an epidemic in another group (students)."[34]

PHANTOM AIRCRAFT WAVES

Worldwide: 1909-1946

Over the past century and a half there have been numerous episodes involving waves of claims and public discourse surrounding the reports of mysterious aerial objects within a specific region over a relatively short period of time. Some UFO researchers view these reported objects as misidentifications of extraterrestrial space vehicles that were interpreted as popular flying machines, reflecting the science fiction of the period. In the case of early airship waves, some speculate that an enterprising inventor had perfected the world's first heavier-than-air flying machine and kept it secret, spurning global fame and fortune. While possible, there is no incontrovertible proof to support either of these or similar claims. In the absence of such compelling evidence, a powerful, plausible explanation can be found in studies of social psychology. It should be pointed out that many of these mis-observations relate to airships that are of course lighter than air, though the term "airships" was sometimes used at the time to describe *any* flying machine.

Mystery aircraft waves can be explained by perceptual psychology, the branch of science that examines how people perceive the world. Humans do not simply receive information; we both perceive and interpret outside stimuli. Numerous social science experiments confirm that a person's mental frame of mind at the time of an incident is highly influential in how they perceive an event and internalize it as reality.[35] In the absence of any incontrovertible proof of the airships having existed, the most compelling evidence is in the form of eyewitness testimony. Yet, human perception is notoriously unreliable.[36] A classic example of this process occurred during the now infamous "War of the Worlds" panic, which led many Americans to believe that a radio drama by Orson Welles on Halloween eve in 1938 (see ORSON WELLES MARTIAN PANIC) was an attack by Martians who had landed in New Jersey. During the panic, several people in New Jersey actually telephoned police and stated that they could see the giant Martian flying machines on the horizon[37] and many even claimed they could feel the heat rays.[38]

Another example of observer distortion occurred on March 3, 1968, in the northeastern United States, when at 8:45 p.m. Central Standard Time, the Zond 4, a Russian moon probe reentered the Earth's atmosphere, creating several fiery "meteors."[39] Numerous people saw the re-entry, some of whom were convinced that they had observed a "flying saucer." One witness was emphatic:

> It appeared to have square-shaped windows along the side that was facing us.
>
> It appeared to me that the fuselage was constructed of many pieces of flat sheets of metal-like material with [a] "riveted-together look..." The many windows seemed to be lit up from the inside of the fuselage... when the craft was flying near us, it did seem to travel in a flat trajectory. I toyed with the idea that it even slowed down somewhat, for how else could we observe so much detail in a mere flash across the sky?
>
> All three of us agreed that we had seen something other than any planes we had seen or read about from our Earth, or that we had seen a "craft from Outer Space."[40]

The human eye and mind do not function like a video tape recorder, passively recording external stimuli; information is interpreted as it is received. This is especially evident in ambiguous situations such as the nighttime sky, as a variety of atmospheric effects can engender misinterpretations. In ambiguous situations, such as scanning the skies at night for the existence of a rumored airship, "inference can perform the work of perception by filling in missing information in instances where perception is either inefficient or inadequate."[41]

Most notable is the "the autokinetic effect." When people stare at a pinpoint of light in a dark environment, the light will appear to move, often a great deal. Psychologist Muzafer Sherif first demonstrated this well-known effect in 1936.[42] In the absence of stable perceptual anchorages, people viewing a common pinpoint of light soon feel uneasy and anxious, and need to either define the light or make sense of it. This process reduces anxiety created by the uncertain situation.

> A viewer in a completely dark room seeing one pinpoint of light experiences a visual stimulus without its normal attendant visual context. Up, down, back, forward, far and near, exist in relation to other stimuli and when this frame of reference is missing, the light is free to roam in one's perceptual field. It is for this reason that considerable random motion will be experienced by anyone viewing the light.[43]

What is remarkable about these sighting waves is how, during times of extraordinary crisis or excitement, humans seem to be trying to make sense of the world by interpreting ambiguous, almost exclusively nocturnal aerial phenomena (stars, planets, meteorological events, illuminated devices sent aloft by pranksters, etc.) as reflecting the *zeitgeist* or spirit of the times. People have a difficult time dealing with chaos. They need to resolve fear and uncertainty by creating an orderly world, even if it is a world that includes the existence of a feared object. During these waves it could be said that the skies had become a projected Rorschach Ink Blot Test of the collective psyche, and the sightings were a sign of the times.

Phantom Zeppelin Scare:
New Zealand, July-September 1909

Between July and September 1909, thousands of people across New Zealand reported seeing German Zeppelins, reflecting a popular folk belief that Germany was conducting flyovers as a prelude to an imminent invasion. The sightings occurred during a tense time in New Zealand history that was dominated by widespread rumors that Germany was intent on invading the country. In reality, an invasion of this small, isolated country in the South Pacific would have been impracticable, representing a huge expenditure of time and resources. And an invasion using Zeppelins would have been technologically impossible. So the sightings appear to reflect the war scare mood of the times as citizens scanned the skies in search of Zeppelins, redefining various mundane objects as airship-related.

CONTEXT: The year prior to the invasion scare, there was a heated debate in the United Kingdom as politicians and commentators questioned whether the Commonwealth had lost its lead as the world's unrivaled naval power. There was much speculation that German leaders might take advantage of England's newly perceived weakness by invading the motherland. At the same time, rapid aeronautical advancements, especially with German Zeppelins, led to fears that bomb-dropping dirigibles would invade England. These fears were unsettling for residents of the scantily defended remote Commonwealth outpost of New Zealand. While in early 1909, the New Zealand press widely discussed the possibility of a German invasion of the British Isles, by the middle of the year there was much speculation that Germany might undertake a surprise attack on an easy target, one of the Empire's more vulnerable outposts. Many New Zealanders naturally thought that their country would be the target, given their rich supply of natural resources: gold, timber, sheep, wool, hides, forestry products, and beef.

Several months before the sightings occurred, British leaders decided to concentrate their naval forces near the motherland. This decision was met with unpopularity and fear in New Zealand, fostering a perception that the country was especially vulnerable. The former commander of British forces in the Pacific region, Admiral Bowden Smith, described the concern: "I think New Zealand and Australia should be awakened to the matter of defence. We have withdrawn our ships...from foreign stations, and concentrated them round...Britain. We all know...[why]. Germany is showing such a feverish haste to build up a big navy...In the event of attack by armed fleets New Zealand and Australia would have nothing to show against them."[44]

In 1909, Germany was at the forefront of aerial technology with its Zeppelin fleet, which, though impractical, was the subject of widespread press publicity and speculation regarding its ability to make long-distance flights.[45] Then on May 19, there came a flurry of reports that German leaders were seriously considering a major strategy shift – away from building naval vessels and instead focusing on the construction of long distance Zeppelins capable of carrying troops and ordnance.[46] The idea of aerial warfare was already a popular science-fiction theme in the early 1900s.[47] For instance, in 1908, H.G. Wells' novel *The War in the Air* both enthralled and horrified readers with descriptions of airships raining bombs on New York City. Many serial magazines of the period reflected this theme. For instance, *Chums* published many stories by Captain Frank Shaw in 1908, "The Peril of the Motherland," depicting a Russian war with England whereby a fleet of airships reek havoc on London. It was within this context that rumors of a Zeppelin invasion of New Zealand took place, and the sightings began as tens of thousands of citizens were not only convinced that a hostile German Zeppelin or Zeppelins were spying and possibly ready to drop bombs under the cover of darkness, but many were certain that they had actually seen the dirigible.[48] While "tens of thousands" may seem like an inflated figure, in many instances, the population of entire towns was reported to have filled the streets to glimpse mysterious aerial lights, typically assumed to have been of German origin.

The Sightings

The sightings began on the night of July 11 on the south island, when several people at Kaitangata reported seeing the mysterious light, possibly from a dirigible, for half an hour. The light was bobbing in and out of view over the Wangaloa Hills.[49] There were widespread rumors at the time that the German ship *Seestern* was off south island and "set the airship free" in order to conduct aerial reconnaissance flights.[50] On July19, a mysterious aerial light was reported in Oamaru, 160 kilometers to the northeast.[51] The most spectacular report occurred in broad daylight on July 24 at Kelso, where nearly two-dozen school children and a teacher said that they watched in amazement as a Zeppelin-style airship swooped low over the town. A local reporter described the incident as "nothing short of dumbfounding."

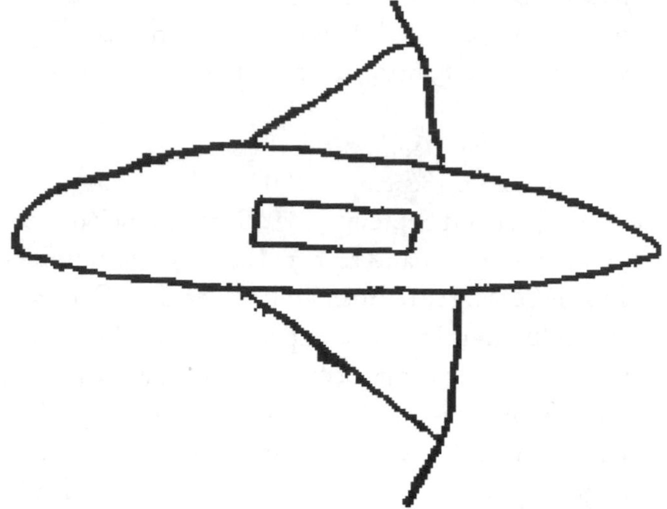

Undercarriage of the "Zeppelin" as described by pupil Thomas Jenkins. Note the cigar-shaped body, suspended gondola, and two large sail-like wings. (Otago Daily Times, August 4, 1909)

> Thomas Jenkins gave a very clear account of the whole incident. He saw the vessel first at 12 o'clock as he was going home from school. It had come over the hill on the east side of the school...and sailed across the plain to the gorge on the other side. He watched it all the time, and saw it altogether about 10 minutes.... As it passed over he saw that it had supports on each side...but these sails did not move. There was a wheel at the rear revolving very rapidly. There was a box beneath the body of the ship...The vessel was entirely black in colour...
>
> Cyril Falconer was with other boys on the school ground when the airship passed over. A big wheel was revolving at the rear. He saw this reversed, and the vessel suddenly turned...This boy drew an angular picture, which appeared to represent the ship as it was turning, with a wheel at the back. Other children saw it but these gave the clearest accounts.
>
> Mrs. Russell, evidently the only adult who saw the phenomenon, said she...saw a streak of blackness shoot over the hill on the left and apparently come straight towards her. Then it suddenly turned and swerved away over some trees out of her sight...In appearance it was just like a boat. It was black in colour. She saw it for just a few minutes. It was travelling very fast at first, but when it turned it came lower and went somewhat slower. She did not notice any wheel at the rear or any sails, but was very flustered, as she thought the end of the world had come.[52]

Side view of the object as seen by Thomas Jenkins. He said the propeller-like wheel at the back was revolving rapidly. (Otago Daily Times, August 4, 1909)

Both locals and police went searching for the vessel's secret launching point.[53] [54] The next day at about 5 pm, another Kelso school student, George McDuff said he saw the vessel near his home. Sixty years after the incident, a reporter for *The Otago Daily Times* tracked down McDuff, asking him about his sighting. He was a farmer living at Weston in North Otago. When asked about the incident, he denied seeing any object and said that it was "imagination, based on what we

Student George McDuff's sketch of the object. (Otago Daily Times, August 4, 1909)

were reading at the time" (magazine articles describing airships). The editors of *The Wanganui Chronicle* were less impressed by the children's drawings of the airship and challenged *The Otago Daily Times* reporter by declaring that "There is nothing convincing to report" about the mass sightings near the Kelso school, and that "the testimony of the children need not be taken very seriously." It was later suggested that they had misidentified a flock of birds. [55]

The Kelso school incident received spectacular press coverage across the country as scores of sightings were recorded over the next 10 days. The next night near Kaka Point, several kilometers from the school, several people reported seeing "a huge illuminated object moving about in the air." Fearing it was a German Zeppelin about to land, the witnesses ran off,[56] vowing that if it returned they would "try to 'prick the bubble' with a bullet."[57]

On July 30, two mining dredge hands were at Gore on the night shift when they said an airship descended into the fog at about 5 a.m. and "that two figures were plainly discernible on board."[58] This incident followed a series of other airship sightings near Gore over the previous several nights.[59]

On the night of August 3, a Waipawa man said that while horse riding near the racecourse, he was startled by the appearance of a large, illuminated torpedo-shaped vessel passing overhead. He could see three passengers in the ship, one of whom "shouted out to him in an unknown tongue." He said that the vessel rose and circled the area before disappearing behind a hill.[60]

The Sightings Wane

Sightings began to wane in early August, with the last known report for the month occurring on the 9th in the gold mining town of Waihi.[61] The reduction in reports during this period coincided with negative press coverage of the sightings, commonly attributing them to over active imaginations. This is in sharp contrast to the beginning of the episode when many newspaper reports of ambiguous aerial lights were commonly described as "airships."[62] But as the sightings continued, in the absence of concrete proof and many obvious misidentifications of stars, planets, and manmade objects, the press began to deride witnesses.

Several newspapers suggested that a stimulus for sightings was alcohol consumption.[63] Another journalist compared the emotional fervor for seeing airships as comparable to religious revivals in which people lose their sense of rationality. "Revival excitements, like airship excitements, are matter for public comment; in neither case is it sacrilege to suggest natural causes... Natural causes? Given a crowd, a speaker that can play upon its emotions, with a singer that teaches it to express them in voluptuous dance rhythms, and you have for your revival excitement some very obvious natural causes."[64]

Beginning in late July, witnesses were often scoffed at and the entire affair was described as an outbreak of "aerialitis"[65] In a letter to *The Otago Daily Times,* one resident described the episode as an irrational "craze," classifying it as a "popular delusion" in an obvious reference to CHARLES MACKAY'S classic book on the topic.[66] "Sir: The airship craze is getting beyond a joke. There is a danger of our level-headed community becoming the laughing stock...[to] the greater world. We do not want to be advertised in that way... The world has had a great many examples of 'extraordinary popular delusions,' such as the South Sea Bubble, the tulip mania in Holland...the persecution of witches... These phenomena arise in times of public excitement, when every whisper and shrug is taken as evidence, and the capacity to weigh matters is for the time submerged by some human passion, such as fear or greed."[67] The writer concluded that the "German scare, the Dreadnought episode, and the conquest of the air" had combined to form a plausible threat, culminating in a popular delusion. In late July there was an upsurge in sales of fire balloons[68] [69] and their remnants were found on the ground near many sightings. As press reports grew increasingly skeptical in early August,[70] more and more reports of mysterious aerial lights were described as stars[71] and fire balloons.[72] The episode was over.

On July 29, the editor of *The New Zealand Herald* savaged witnesses, describing the observations as "Flights of Fancy," while a commentator in *The Evening Post* described the sightings as "Hot-air" ships, noting sarcastically that "the nucleus of an aerial German invasion" resulted from a combination of hoaxes and misperceptions.[73] Following a sighting by several Nelson residents in early August, a reporter commented: "It has come at last. We have been expecting the dread news for weeks..."[74] Another journalist made merry of the Nelson affair:

> Nelson took more interest in astronomy last evening than it has ever done before. People in all directions stood and stared upwards at the sky. An airship had come to Nelson.
>
> There it was, plain enough. Some people could even tell that it had an acetylene lamp at the front of the car [gondola] which was shining so brightly. Others declared that there were lights shining, just as is the case with a motor car.
>
> Attempts, fortunately unsuccessful, were made to break into the Atkinson Observatory and Mr. F.G. Gibbs was literally besieged by telephone and callers. The fact that the light was seen to move was what particularly gave rise to the opinion that the "airship" which was making those night attacks down south, had at last arrived in Nelson, and was skimming about in the air above the town.[75]

The *Timaru Post* used the term "airship fever."[76] Other papers linked sightings to "the silly season," a term describing the tendency of journalists to write stories on trivial topics during "slow" news periods.[77] When the Zeppelin sightings were recorded in the capital city of Wellington, the *Southland Times* proclaimed: "Wellington Bitten at Last."[78]

The last known reports from the episode occurred in one grand finale during early September. A remarkable series of sightings was reported at Gore as hundreds of citizens swore to seeing the clear outline of a cigar-shaped object floating near the Tapanui Hills. The observations were recorded between 4:30 and 6 p.m. on the first two days of September.[79] A newspaper correspondent for *The Southland Times* reported on September 4th that he traveled to the site and identified the cause – "repeated flights of thousands of starlings, which, prior to nesting season, were making their temporary homes in a clump of pine trees" at Holland's farm. He continues: "About 5:00 p.m. movements from the pine trees commenced. The birds would rise up in one thick black mass and circle round in the sky. Their evolutions were wonderful to behold. At first they would look like a dark cloud; then they would assume the shape of a very long strip, darting up into the air and then descending with very great rapidity." He said there were so many birds that their wings made a loud whirring sound, similar to that of machinery in motion.

The Australian Airship Mania: August 1909

During an approximately one-week period in 1909, a fascinating social delusion swept across parts of Australia, as scores of citizens became convinced that an Australian had perfected the world's first practical heavier-than-air flying machine. What is even more extraordinary is that many people not only believed the rumors but actually claimed to have spotted the craft motoring through the nighttime sky! At the time, a practical heavier-than-air ship did not exist.

CONTEXT: From about 1880 to the early twentieth century, a massive popular literature appeared on the theme of science and inventions. Aeronautical developments were a prominent feature of these accounts as "this literature fed the public a steady diet of aeronautical speculation and news to prime people for the day when the riddle of aerial navigation finally would receive a solution."[80] The general mood of this literature was positive, trumpeting the wonders of science and technology.[81] In the years immediately preceding the episode, intense excitement was experienced worldwide in anticipation of the first practical, mechanically-powered heavier-than-air flight.[82] With the dawn of the twentieth century there were rapid, dramatic aeronautical advances coupled with heavy newspaper coverage of powered flight attempts, leading to a spectacular climax just prior to the Australian airship delusion.

During the first two weeks in August, a brief spate of sightings occurred over Australia, being mainly confined to the east coast region of New South Wales. Between August 5 and 9, there were scores of sightings at Goulburn. On Saturday night August 7, a clergyman and several eyewitnesses saw strange lights above the Dandenong Ranges. They said the lights changed color from blue to red to white and then "slowed down, dipped, and rose again."[83] On the evenings of the 8th and 9th, people living between Mittagong and Wollongong reported seeing a possible airship light. Numerous residents near Moss Vale saw what appeared to be an airship or balloon hovering some 2,000 feet above the highlands on the 9th. On Tuesday evening August 10, it appeared near Sydney *and* all the way across the country at Perth.

To provide readers with a flavor of the sightings, consider the following excerpt from the *Goulburn Evening Penny Post* of August 14, 1909, under the headline "The Mysterious Light."

> Thomas Apps, Breadalbane Hotel, writes under date Friday 13th:--"A mysterious light was seen here tonight about 7:30 in the west from Breadalbane. It was seen by myself and several other people staying at the hotel."
>
> *Sights Visible in Sydney*
>
> Considerable excitement was occasioned in all the coastal suburbs on Friday night between 7 and 8 o'clock, when residents were afforded an excellent view of the nocturnal mystery of the air at present creating such a stir in all parts of the State. The lights were plainly visible in the north-west, and after several sharp movements to the east they slowly disappeared south.
>
> *More Reports*
>
> Bathurst, Friday.--The mysterious light observed at about 9 o'clock last night was floating in an easterly direction. At times the light had a bluish appearance.
>
> Helensburgh, Friday.--An illuminated body was observed here on Tuesday night. At about 10 o'clock the object appeared to be about a mile east of the town, and to be moving in a northerly direction. The brilliancy of the light was continually varying, and at times swaying movements could be plainly detected...
>
> Sutherland, Friday.-- At about 10 o'clock what appeared to be a light blue light steadily ascended from the east, and when at a certain height appeared to circle about for 20 minutes...
>
> Zeehan (Tas.). Friday.-- A number of residents at Zeehan report today having seen mysterious lights in the sky. Shortly after seven o'clock last night there were two lights, white and brilliant, which seemed to be travelling rapidly in a north-westerly direction, against the wind, and soon disappeared behind the clouds. As the lights travelled one appeared to grow smaller and the other larger...

In Western Australia, the Perth area sightings were first reported at Pingelly, halfway between Perth and Albany, at about 7:30 p.m. on the 10th when "residents saw two mysterious lights, a few feet apart, rapidly passing southwards over the township." On the morning of the 12th, an airship was sighted in the northeastern Perth suburbs and on the evening of the next day a large crowd gathered in Victoria Park to gaze at the mysterious lights that some took to be the airship. "Quite a crowd of people gathered [at Victoria Park], focussing the sky through binoculars, and seeing red and blue lights in familiar stars. A practical experiment convinced the pressmen that, if looked long enough at, any star could be seen to show red, blue, and other lights, and that if viewed through the fleeting clouds it could easily be imagined that the lights moved. Previous witnesses, however, were emphatic that they had seen not only red and blue lights, but clusters of lights 'shaped like a boat,' passing over Mount Eliza, low down on the horizon."[84]

Most of the sightings correspond with the appearance times and sky positions of Mars, Venus, and Jupiter. Near the end of the episode, two residents who pointed out a strange light contacted Mr. W.E. Raymond, the officer in charge of the Sydney observatory. Raymond said they were pointing at Venus and Jupiter, which were approaching each other and nearly in the same line of vision at the time of the evening they observed it. Further, Mars was nearing opposition and was strikingly brilliant in the eastern sky a few hours after sunset. We also know from press accounts that many shopkeepers reported brisk sales of fire balloons during early August. Fire balloons were available in Australia during this period and typically sold at shops selling pyrotechnics. They were also referred to as tissue balloons and consisted of paper balloons with candles attached near the mouth and made buoyant by the generation of heat. Another common prank at this time was to send up a kite at night with Japanese lanterns attached.

Great New England Airship Hoax: December 1909 to January 1910

During December 1909 and January 1910, thousands of residents in the New England region of the northeastern United States were convinced by a series of hoax newspaper interviews that a Massachusetts businessman had invented the first practical heavier-than-air flying machine. What's more, he claimed to be piloting the vessel at night on test flights. In response to the press claims, many people reported seeing the vessel, almost exclusively at night. As a result, journalists from across the country soon converged on Boston and Worcester, Massachusetts, where the sightings were concentrated. Foreign governments even sent representatives to assess the potential military and commercial applications of such a machine.

CONTEXT: The year of the hoax, there were rapid, spectacular advancements in aeronautics, prompting aviation historian Charles H. Gibbs-Smith to remark that 1909 was the year "the aeroplane came of age" though flight remained very crude. Historian R. E. Bilstein notes that 1908 and 1909 were huge years for aviation publicity and acclaim. "Orville's tests for the War Department...and Wilbur's flights in Europe before enthralled crowds, including the kings of Spain and England, became...front-page news. Meanwhile, the flights of other pioneers, like Glen Curtiss, stirred additional interest in aviation."[85] It was during 1909 that the British accepted the aeroplane as a practical vehicle for two reasons. A major event of the year was the English Channel crossing by Louis Bleriot's monoplane on July 25, followed by an aviation meeting in France during late August – the first gathering of its kind. Gibbs-Smith states: "If the Channel crossing made the greatest impact on the public, it was the Reims aviation week which provided the greatest technical and governmental stimulus to aviation, and proved to officialdom and the public alike that the airplane had indeed 'arrived.'" Furthermore, the Reims meeting "marked the true acceptance of the airplane as a practical vehicle, and as such was a major milestone in the world's history."[86] To give an idea as to how the world was "bitten" by the aviation bug, in 1900 *The New York Times Index* listed one article under the heading of "aeronautics." By 1905, this number was 58; it was 466 in 1908 and 964 in 1909.

The Hoax Begins

On December 13, 1909, the *Boston Herald* published an interview with prominent, colorful Worcester businessman and entrepreneur Wallace E. Tillinghast,[87] in which he made his remarkable claims about making experimental airship flights. The account was afforded dramatic, front-page headlines:

TELLS OF FLIGHT 30 MILES IN THE AIR
Engineer says he sailed from Worcester to New York
to New York Harbor at Night in Aeroplane of his Own Invention
CLAIMS CIRCLING STATUE WHEN 4000 FEET UP
Wallace E. Tillinghast says He Invented Machine Under Cover
and is Going to Smash International Records

WORCESTER, Dec. 12--Wallace E. Tillinghast of this city, vice-president of a manufacturing company here, made public a story today...[that] he invented, built, and tested an aeroplane capable of carrying three passengers with a weight limit of 600 pounds, a distance of about 300 miles with a stop to replenish the supply of petrol, at a rate of 120 miles an hour.

He refuses to say where his flying machine is...as he wants to enter into Boston contests next year as a sure winner. He says that on Sept. 8 he made a night trip to New York and return, at which time the machine was thoroughly tested...

In describing his machine, Mr. Tillinghast says: "It is one of the monoplane type, with a spread of 72 feet, a weight of 1550 pounds, and furnished with a 120-horsepower gasoline engine made under my own directions and specifications. It differs from others in the spread of the canvas, the spread of the plane and in stability features. Special attention is given in making it adaptable for high speed. All the important parts are covered by patents.

"Other distinguishing features are that it cannot be capsized, is easily controlled and the occupants ride on the body of the machine instead of having the body of the machine behind them. The headlight is made by the use of acetylene gas generated on the machine. I decline to say where the machine was built or is stationed, because it is the business of no one but myself and my mechanics.

"I also decline to say what is the limit of speed of the aeroplane or the highest altitude that I can reach, because I wish to enter the international races in a fair trial and without rivals knowing what speed reported at the recent meeting at Reims that I feel sure the result will be that the Tillinghast aeroplane is more than an 'also ran.'

"....The machine is no experiment, as it has been thoroughly tested. All of the tests have been under the cover of night and have been considered successful."

Among Tillinghast's outrageous claims was that he had not one but four vessels built at a secret workshop. At the time of his interview, it was well known that a couple of weeks earlier, a Fire Island lifeguard, William Leach, claimed to have heard a noise like the rumbling of an aeroplane engine "pass high above him while he was doing patrol duty."[88] The opportunistic and cunning Tillinghast claimed that it was his vessel that was heard, as an engine cylinder was malfunctioning that forced him to fly over the beach and the lifeguard as a precaution.

Over the next several days, several area residents began redefining recent events and circumstances as airship-related. The day after his sensational interview, Mr. E. B. Hanna of Willimantic, Connecticut, came forward to claim that he too had seen Tillinghast and his vessel on the same night as the lifeguard sighting. He said the vessel appeared as a "bright light" that was in view for an hour.[89] In spite of the vague nature of the report, the *Willimantic Chronicle* printed the headlines: "What Mr. Hanna Saw May Have Been the Worcester Airship!...Now Thinks That it may have been the Aeroplane in Which Wallace E. Tillinghast Claims to Have Made a Flight from Boston to New York and Return."[90]

A third sighting claim was made by Massachusetts immigration inspector Arthur Hoe early on the morning of December 20, above Boston Harbor.[91] His observation of a circling airship was later discredited after it was evident that he had mistaken the masts of a steamship for the flying machine.[92] Yet at the time of his sighting, the *Boston Globe* described Hoe's report as most likely that of Tillinghast's vessel.[93] Soon people began redefining events months earlier as having been Tillinghast and his marvelous vessel. One of those was Cyril Herrick who wrote to the *Boston Globe*, describing a sighting of what he thought at the time was a "Double Meteor" in 1908, but was now convinced it was the Tillinghast airship:

> ...I [would like to] recount the following, seen while in camp on the shores of Lake Winnipesankee last August. Shortly after dark one evening we saw approaching from Meredith way, two bright lights in the sky a fixed distance apart, high in the air and drawing near with lightning speed. Passing our camp, whatever it was, disappeared over toward the Ossipee hills. Only the great speed of the lights marred our belief that it was an aircraft. All doubt was dispelled the next morning by news received from two vacation people a half-mile distant – Dr. Frank Chapman of Grovetown, N.H., and Dr. Walter Westwood of Beachmont, saw them [the lights] returning about an hour later. Thus the meteor theory is disposed of, and this news from Worcester as to Tillinghast offers itself as a refreshing possible hypothesis in explanation of the strange sight we saw that night.[94]

Just before Christmas, the floodgates opened. On the evening of December 22, upwards of 2,000 people reported seeing an airship "circling" Boston several times. The "craft" was reportedly visible for over three hours. The "show" began at about 5:40 p.m., when several police officers noticed a strange light in the sky.[95] By 6:30 p.m., Christmas shoppers and policemen reported that the light was growing bigger and seemed to be about a thousand feet (about 300 meters) above the ground. At about 7 o'clock, the "ship" appeared to fly over the city before hovering stationary over the State Mutual Life Insurance Building, then flying off.[96] That same evening, an "airship" was seen at about 6 o'clock in nearby Marlboro, traveling northwest.[97] Other reports were made by hundreds of citizens in nearby Worcester, Greendale, Nahant, Maynard, Marlboro, Cambridge, Revere, Fitchburg, Leominster, and Westboro. Word of the sights spread quickly over the telephone.

The most spectacular sighting occurred on December 23, as the ship was seen flying over Worcester and several nearby towns between 6:00 and 7:30 pm. An estimated 50,000 residents poured into the streets, bringing Worcester to a temporary standstill.[98] One reporter wrote: "In the main thoroughfares people with bundles stood agape... Men and boys poured from the clubrooms and women rushed from the houses to view this phenomenon. The streets were thronged."[99] The *Boston Herald* proclaimed: "Mysterious Air Craft Circles About Boston for Nearly Six Hours."[100] One man, Alex Randell of Revere, swore that he could distinguish "the frame quite plainly."[101] P.D. Donahue of Baltic said there were two men in the vessel as it flew by.[102] Even the Mayor of Williamantic, after a sighting in his city, said "there was no doubt but that it was an airship."[103]

On Christmas Eve, "thousands upon thousands of people" in Boston "stood on sidewalks, street corners and squares from soon after dark till well on toward midnight" hoping to spot the airship. Few were disappointed.

> Lower Washington st, Dock sq, Scolay sq, Tremont row, Court st, Bowdoin sq, Court sq, Tremont st and the Common were haunted by large groups of more or less excited and awe-struck belated Christmas shoppers, many of them laden with bundles, all gazing well up into the zenith at the gleaming lights...
>
> At the corner of Washington and Summer sts the elevated roads starter had the hardest job he had since the last big fire in his district, all owing to the crowd of sky gazers that would persist in obstructing the car track.
>
> On the Common a policeman got extremely angry at a bystander who undertook to argue against the genuineness of the airship and to suggest that the signal lanterns might be stars. "Haven't I seen the airship standing here?" demanded the bluecoat with an asperity that discouraged argument to the point...
>
> Another man plainly distinguished that one of the twin lights was green, the other red, as they should be to conform to the rules of navigation, and he flatly told an observer at his elbow that he must be blind not to be able to see the difference in the color of the lights.
>
> Another man expressed doubt whether the airship was really moving but he was assured in gentle but firm tones by another that undoubtedly the operator had temporarily shut off his power, but that the machine had been moving unmistakably a few minutes before.
>
> A large majority of observers commented on the frequent ascent or descent...Now it appeared to be gliding higher in space, then taking a chute downward in a gradual and graceful plane.
>
> A large group at the corner of Bromfield and Tremont sts showed the most marked agitation seen during the evening, for at one time, from that point, the airship appeared to be a few feet lower than the top of Park-st church steeple and so near that everybody felt sure that it was certain to crash into the steeple.
>
> Just when the nervous tension had reached its most critical stage, apparently, the operator appeared to see his danger, for the machine approached no nearer and appeared to be at a standstill as the crowd uttered a concerted sigh of relief and dispersed, to be succeeded by another a moment later.[104]

While Tillinghast continually insisted that he shunned publicity and was sought out for his initial

Boston Herald interview, a rival reporter from the *Boston Globe* later found out that the reporter who interviewed Tillinghast "didn't have to spend any sleepless nights running down Mr. Tillinghast" as the day before the interview, Tillinghast had set up the interview himself, saying that "he had an item to get out."[105]

The Episode Ends

The sightings waned dramatically from Christmas through the end of the month, except for six sightings on December 2, as reporters and residents grew increasingly skeptical. During the last week in December, the *Boston Globe* expressed concern that those living in the vicinity of Worcester would become laughing stocks if the "fantastic stories" didn't stop.[106] That very day C. D. Rawson of Worcester admitted to attaching small lanterns and a reflector to the legs of large owls.[107] Another resident noted that most sightings coincided with the appearance of Venus, which was conspicuous in the Western sky during early evening.[108] By Christmas, most residents had become leery of the reports in the absence of physical proof. One newspaper correspondent sent a wire to his home office in West Virginia, noting the growing number of doubting residents.: "Go where you will in New England today and you will hear them talk about Tillinghast and his mysterious airship. The majority of New Englanders don't believe in Tillinghast."[109] Some press correspondents hyped the story in an effort to keep the excitement going so as to earn more money. While one editor observed that the airship had appeared in the same area of the sky over three straight nights and was undoubtedly Venus, he observed that "One ambitious news writer...sent long dispatches to two New York papers, telling how hundreds had stood out and watched the airship maneuver, and the metropolitan papers printed the story along with the story of Tillinghast's ship, giving the impression that it was the Worcester man..."[110] There were only a few sightings in January, each met with incredulity.[111]

The British Zeppelin Scare: 1912-1913

Between mid-October of 1912 and early March of 1913, thousands of British citizens reported seeing phantom Zeppelins far exceeding the technology of the period and reflecting popular folk beliefs that German dirigibles were conducting reconnaissance missions above England prior to an invasion. The episode reflected a German military buildup of Dreadnought-style battleships and Zeppelins. Britain's susceptibility to an aerial attack was recognized and its long-standing complacency as the unrivalled sea power was suddenly questioned,[112] resulting in a feeling of "hysteria germanica."[113] In mid-1912, British Prime Minister Arthur Balfour also worried that Germany would soon eclipse Britain's long-held status as the world's most powerful navy.

CONTEXT: Rapid aeronautical progress during this period, and the ascendancy of Germany as the unrivaled leader in dirigible technology, only fueled invasion fears and lent credence to rumors that the Germans were planning an aerial invasion. During this time the British were preoccupied with the possibility of a Zeppelin invasion of the motherland. This fear had been the subject of many science fiction novels for decades prior to this time.[114] The central theme in many of these books was the need for "higher budgets and a stronger war machine."[115] However, with rapid progress in aerial technology during the early years of the twentieth century, many magazines and nonfiction books expressed concern over Britain's poor standing in this field, including H.G. Wells in his novel *The War In The Air* (1908).[116] It was within this context of German xenophobia that phantom Zeppelin sightings occurred.

The Zeppelin Wave Begins

The wave of Zeppelin sightings over Britain began on October 14, 1912, when several people at Sheerness, including Lieutenant Raymond Fitzmaurice, reported hearing the sound of an aerial ship in the early evening. Some of those present said they could discern an aerial light thought to belong to a dirigible. The incident went relatively unnoticed until November 21, when a British Member of Parliament made inquiries to Winston Churchill concerning rumors of the report, which had become known as "the Sheerness Incident." When asked if the object with an estimated speed of 60 miles per hour could have been a

British dirigible, "Mr. Churchill replied in the negative."[117] Despite this denial, the minutes of the 120th Meeting of the Committee of Imperial Defence taken on December 6, reveal that Churchill privately was of the opinion that what the Sheerness witnesses saw was a Zeppelin.[118] A few days later, the editors of the respected publication *The Aeroplane* reached a similar conclusion, noting that "Never was the 'Wake up England' spirit more immediately of importance."[119] This story triggered an avalanche of British press reports suggesting the likelihood that Zeppelins were spying on England. As residents began scanning the skies for evidence of the Zeppelin, starting shortly after the New Year, sighting reports became epidemic.

Early on the morning of January 4, 1913, a road inspector named John Hobbs reported seeing a brilliant light above Dover, expressing his view that it was an airship. In describing the sighting, several newspapers reported the existence of the airship as a fact.[120] On the 18th, the Chief Constable of Glamorgan, Captain Lionel Lindsay, reported seeing an airship emitting a smoke trail.[121] While some papers reported the possibility that Lindsay may have seen an airship,[122] many others described his fleeting, distant observation as reality.[123] Over the next week, many other people said that they too had seen an airship light that evening,[124] or in the days before Captain Lindsay's sighting.[125] Zeppelin sightings were recorded nearly every night through March 7, when the wave ended suddenly. It is difficult to describe the widespread, intense nature of the wave. The following press report summarizes sightings during a single week in late February:

Everyday new reports arrive of more Airships…
FRIDAY. Scarborough (searchlight seen and engine heard). Bridlington (lights and dim shape seen). Selby (long cigar-shaped body, searchlight...other lights...noise of motor heard). Hunstanton (rapidly moving lights seen).
SATURDAY. Scarborough (lights and dim shape seen). Corbridge-on-Tyne (lights seen).
MONDAY. Sunday, Orkney Isles (airship seen). Witherness (lights and...body of the vessel seen). Portsmouth (lights seen). Ipswich (ordinary lights, powerful searchlight, and body of the vessel seen; throb of engine heard).
TUESDAY. Horsea (white and red lights and cone of airship seen). Hull (lights seen). Grimsby (lights and dim shape seen). Leeds (bright light and dim shape seen). Seaforth, Liverpool (bright light and outline of vessel...whirring of propeller and throb of the engine heard). Portishead, Somerset (lights and outlines of airship seen). Castle Donington, Derbyshire (lights seen; engine heard). Dover (lights seen; engine heard). Hunstanton (bright lights seen).
WEDNESDAY. Portland Harbour (dazzling searchlight and clear outline of airship seen; sound of propeller heard). Hyde (flashing lights and long, dark moving object seen). Romiley (...vivid searchlight seen). Avonmouth, Bristol (two lights seen).
THURSDAY. Hucknall, Nottinghamshire (airship and powerful searchlight seen). Kirkcaldy and Rosyth (brilliant light and dimly outlined airship seen). Liverpool and New Brighton (bright lights and dim shape seen). Ardwick, Manchester (two head lights and a tail light seen).[126]

As the reports mounted, more and more citizens began to speak out against the state of military preparedness, which was widely viewed as vulnerable, especially defenses against an aerial attack. Said one Manchester resident: "The country will not be satisfied with a reassurance that the Admiralty has the matter in hand."[127] An ex-naval officer called for the bolstering of coastal defenses, noting that there were many advantages of a foreign power being familiar with the nocturnal geography.[128] One of the most ominous warnings came from a British correspondent in Germany, who issued the chilling warning that "England's maritime superiority [had] lost its whole significance, as superiority in the air [now] brings mastery of the world."[129]

From about February 6 onwards, newspaper reports were more skeptical of sighting claims, often attributing them to misperceptions of Venus[130] that was a prominent feature in the evening sky during this period. An equally popular explanation was that of fire balloons, the remains of which were found near several sightings and suspected in several others.[131] More novel theories included rubber balloons with an attached battery and light[132] and atmospheric illusions.[133] As for the mysterious distant aerial noise that was so often heard in association with the aerial light, "flocks of wild geese" were suggested.[134]

South African's Mystery Monoplanes: August-September 1914

Between August 11 and September 9, 1914, thousands of residents in British South Africa spotted a mysterious object or objects in the skies, which was assumed to have been a German monoplane on a reconnaissance mission. It was spotted mostly at night and at a distance; its appearance coincided with the outbreak of World War I in Europe. Only three German monoplanes were known to be in adjacent German South-West Africa during this time, and none were capable of the sophisticated maneuvers observed, including staying aloft for many hours and traveling great distances without refueling –not to mention the dangers of night flight.[135] Only after the sighting wave had ceased was it revealed that two of these three planes had been disabled during the episode, while the third was of little practical use.[136] [137]

A reporter for the *Natal Advertiser* in Durban summed up the mystery: "Whether it is a British or German aeroplane nobody knows. Where it comes from is equally a mystery. Where it goes to we cannot guess. How it lands for re-petrolling and where the pilot gets his food are insoluble mysteries...Why it should carry headlights is hard to say...Why, too, should it fly by night. Much more useful and interesting observations could be made by daylight.... And why, if it dare not appear by day, does it advertise its whereabouts...after dark?...There is a baffling mystery about it all."[138]

CONTEXT: Sociologist Robert Bartholomew views the episode as a form of social delusion triggered by a confluence of factors. He notes the sightings coincided with widespread anxieties due to the onset of the Great War and uncertainty as to whether hostilities would occur in British South Africa. A survey of seven South African newspapers during this period reveals concerns over a possible German invasion of British held territory, including a widespread belief that any such attack would involve bomb-carrying German monoplanes. Amid this atmosphere of fear, rumors were spawned about the existence of a German monoplane carrying out spy missions as a prelude to an eventual attack that would involve aerial bombing. Under these circumstances, people began scanning the skies in order to confirm or deny the reality of the planes. In doing so, "Natural phenomena such as stars, planets and manmade phenomena such as fire balloons or illuminated kites became redefined as a hostile German monoplane."[139]

The first scattered sightings of a mysterious monoplane were recorded in early August on the Cape Peninsula. Despite the vague nature of these reports, one major newspaper lent credibility to the claims by remarking: "There is no reason to suppose that their information is incorrect, as wholly independent reports seem to establish the fact."[140] Within a few days there were numerous monoplane sightings in widely separated areas across British South Africa, and the press reported on observations as if they were fact. For example, when some people living near Vryburg reported seeing a strange nocturnal light near several farms,[141] one newspaper published the sensational headline: "Aerial Scouts! German Aeroplane Near Vryburg."[142]

Press accounts like this were instrumental in spreading the aeroplane scare by lending credence to the initial rumors that a German aeroplane was flying about. By August 22, six British South Africa newspapers had all published stories describing the existence of hostile German monoplanes as absolute fact.[143] As is typical of war scares, once residents defined the situation as real, a variety of pedestrian events and circumstances became redefined as monoplane-related. In one instance in the Durban district, a farmer's sugar, burned under mysterious circumstances, was attributed to the monoplane. According to the *Cape Argus* of September 9, "Reports as to the passage of aeroplanes over the Natal coast districts persist, and one statement, with apparently some authenticity behind it, is that soon after the appearance over his plantation of this supposed object, a considerable quantity of a planter's growing sugar had been found to have been burned during the night."[144]

Some residents even began redefining past observations of vague stars, as monoplane related. For instance, during the wave the *Johannesburg Star* published a letter from a resident about what was interpreted as a "shooting star" near Pretoria earlier in the year but in the wake of the monoplane reports was redefined as a German plane. "In regard to the presumed German aeroplane said to have been seen over Pretoria, I should like to relate to you a little experience of my own while in that town. One evening in January, between 9 and 10 p.m., the children called me to the verandah to see a shooting star. We all went to the gate and watched. The supposed star proved to be a powerful light or lamp attached to what appeared to be an aeroplane in shape. For some time the machine circled over the town and then descended about

11:30 p.m. as far as I could guess on to the roof of the Law Courts, not far from where we were. As the machine circled in the air it made a loud swishing kind of noise. I spoke of the matter next day, yet, strange to say, the only one who had noticed it was an old native man."[145]

On August 27, many natives in Durban began fleeing their villages, fearing aerial bombs "about to deal death and destruction from on high."[146] Some companies posted extra security guards in an attempt to stop their workers from deserting. In many instances, however, the workers managed to leave, as in the case of a whaling company that lost nearly 60 young black men.[147] During late August the sightings peaked across the country.[148] It was at this juncture at the very end of the month that a wave of skeptical press reports began to appear, and the number of sighting reports quickly subsided, ceasing altogether by mid-September.[149] For instance, the editor of the *Natal Advertiser* wrote that he was getting increasingly impatient with the subject matter, which was continuing to be discussed "with nauseating frequency." Furthermore, he said: "A man comes up to you and says, with all the solemnity of a judge, that he has seen what he calls 'the aeroplane.' You know that he has not, but you cannot very well tell him that he is a blithering idiot."[150]

Astronomers pointed out that most sightings happened at night and involved the observation of a bright "headlight" that corresponded to the approximate sky position of Venus.[151] Other professionals, including meteorologists[152] and journalists,[153] concurred with the assessment that people were misidentifying stars and planets. One humorous account of how residents overreacted to nocturnal lights that were mistaken for bomb-carrying monoplanes happened in East London near the end of the wave in late August:

> East London, and particularly Oxford-street, was agog with excitement on Saturday evening. At every corner...were...groups of men, women and children, with eyes goggling, fingers pointing heavenward, and tongues going twenty-four to the dozen as they gazed at an alleged aeroplane in the western heavens. There it was sure enough, visible to all but the blind: at least, a very brilliant light was visible. An aeroplane it was, and of that there was no doubt, for according to various observers it went through all the tricks in an up-to-date airman's repertoire. It looped the loop, squared the circle, spiralled up and spiralled down, volplaned, tangoed to the right and one-stepped to the left, advanced, retired, set to partners, hands down the middle, did everything except...descend in the Recreation Ground of the Market Square. And that searchlight, what did that not do? It waxed and waned, appeared and disappeared, twinkled, winked the other eye, and signalled in the Morse code in English, French, Dutch, German...and Pitman's shorthand. And all the time it was getting further and further away, though never diminishing in brightness, so that it must have been carried in the tail of the machine.
>
> And oh, the theories that were advanced. Men laid down the law... Ladies became alarmed and wanted to go home and protect their babies from bombs... And it was not until it disappeared behind a heavy bank of clouds in the west that East Londoners breathed a sigh of relief at another happy escape, and went home to dip their pens in the candle and write to the "Daily Dispatch" to describe in letters of fire and words of flames the dastardly attempt to blow up an undefended city.
>
> ...[T]he same aeroplane appeared yesterday in about the same place. However, it is safe to predict that it may be looked for again tonight and for several following nights. As a matter of fact what was seen was the evening star, Venus, which happened to be particularly brilliant. A heavy bank of clouds fringed with flying scud and aided by vivid imaginations accounted for all the evolutions and manoeuvres, and we have to hesitate in assuring everyone that they may sleep in peace, for if it depends upon this particular aeroplane, no bombs will be dropped on East London.[154]

Phantom German Air Raids On Eastern Canada: 1915-1917

In August 1914, Canada entered World War I following the unanimous vote of a special session of Parliament.[155] This event occurred amid great exuberance and unanimity and was marked by "parades, decorations, cheering crowds and patriotic speeches."[156] Canada was situated far from the European front lines, and its distant, vast land mass and cold climate also contributed to a feeling of insulation from attack or invasion. However, despite an initial enthusiasm to enter the war, and a general feeling of distance from its unfolding events, there was a rapidly growing real-

Bleriot monoplane owned and flown by Delagrange.

ization that German sympathizers and enemy agents might pose a more immediate threat.

During World War I, a series of espionage dramas unfolded among the protagonist countries. Canada and the United States had their share of confirmed spy scandals, acts of subversion, and sabotage, and there was considerable concern among Canadians that German-Americans and sympathizers acting on orders from Berlin or independently might cross the border intent on crippling Canada's war efforts. In reality, the acts of espionage, sabotage, and subversion that took place had relatively little impact on everyday life in the U.S. or Canada – or the war's outcome. The few successful incidents that did occur only heightened fears and suspicions surrounding the intentions of German sympathizers in Canada, and especially the United States. It is difficult to give an exact figure to the number of enemy acts in Canada during the war as "there was hardly a major fire, explosion, or industrial accident which was not attributed to enemy sabotage," and by the time an incident had been thoroughly investigated, it "invariably led elsewhere."[157] Beginning in 1914, an anti-German hysteria steadily rose in North America and would not subside until well after the Armistice agreement ended the war on November 11, 1918.

During The Great War vivid imaginations and wild rumors were the order of the day, and politicians did little to ease fears. For instance, in the U.S., President Woodrow Wilson told Congress that Germans "filled our unsuspecting communities with spies and conspirators."[158] In America, the German scare reached such proportions that foods, streets, schools, businesses, and cities with Germanic names were renamed; communities prohibited German music or theatre performances; and suspected traitors were occasionally assaulted, tarred and feathered, or hanged by vigilantes.[159] A similar social paranoia swept across Canada as schools and universities stopped teaching German as a language, the city of Berlin was renamed the town of Kitchener, and The Anti-German League was formed to rid Canada of all German influence, including products and immigrants.[160] In August of 1915, miners in Fernie, British Columbia, refused to work until alien employees at the Crow's Nest Pass Coal Company were dismissed, after which they were promptly placed in a makeshift internment camp.[161] As in the U.S., Dominion politicians further stoked the fires of public hysteria. For instance, the former Saskatchewan lieutenant governor made the sensational claim that 30 percent of Canada's newer provinces were comprised of "alien enemies, who made little secret of their desire to see the flag of Germany waving over the Canadian West."[162] Between 1914 and 1918, 8,579 German and Austro-Hungarian-Canadian men were placed in internment camps.[163] But clearly, Canadians viewed the greater threat as coming from the U.S., where in 1910 there were nearly 10 million German-Americans.[164] Initially, the German scare was more intense in Canada as they entered the war in 1914, while the U.S. remained neutral in the conflict and did not officially join the war effort until April of 1917.

Of the many rumors to circulate across Canada during the war, one was particularly persistent and widespread. From the very onset of hostilities, it was widely rumored that German-Americans sympathetic to the Kaiser had been secretly drilling to conduct large-scale military raids or an invasion into Canada.[165] During January 1915 alone, the British consul in Los Angeles warned Canadian authorities that German sympathizers were planning attacks on Port Arthur, Fort William, and Winnipeg.[166] Meanwhile, the consul general in New York, growing increasingly agitated, claimed that a raid on Canada was imminent and that the Germans had mustered five thousand men in Chicago and up to four thousand in Buffalo. The foreign office in London [claimed]...that a "reliable source" had reported that a group of eight thousand men had been formed in Boston and that bombing raids on Halifax and St. John's could be expected.[167]

As "imaginations ran wild, and on the flimsiest of what passed as evidence," there were scores of false accusations about scheming Germans on both sides of the border.[168] British consul-general Sir Courtney Bennett, stationed in New York, held top honors for being the worst offender.[169] During the war, Bennett made several sensational claims, in the early months of 1915, about a plan in which as many as 80,000 well-armed, highly trained Germans, who had been drilling in Niagara Falls and Buffalo, New York, were planning to invade Canada from northwestern New York State. Incredible as his assertions were, it was a testament to the deep anxiety and suspicion of the period that Prime Minister Sir Robert Borden requested a report on the invasion stories, which Canadian Police Commissioner Sherwood assessed to be without any foundation.[170]

In conjunction with the German scare, recent rapid advances in aeronautics contributed to a growing insecurity among Canadians that they could be vulnerable to an aerial attack. Amid these concerns, rumors circulated that German sympathizers from within Canada or the adjacent United States, and almost exclusively the latter, were planning to launch surprise bombing raids or espionage missions using aeroplanes flown from secret, remote airstrips.[171]

It was within this context that a series of phantom aeroplane scares swept across Ontario and Quebec provinces between 1914 and 1916. Aeroplanes of the period were crude affairs, very limited in maneuverability, and risky to fly at night; the first nocturnal flight did not occur until 1910 and lasting just 20 kilometers.[172] Sightings over Canada during the war were almost exclusively confined to observations of nocturnal lights.

The first reports were confined to southeastern Ontario and began in the village of Sweaburg, six miles south of Woodstock, on Wednesday evening, August 13, 1914, when High County Constable Hobson and numerous residents reported seeing "two large aeroplanes" pass from east to west at about 7:30.[173] Sporadic sightings of mysterious aeroplanes continued over the next two weeks, being reported by many farmers in the region, and in such places as Aylmer, Tillsonburg, and Port Stanley.[174] As a result, a special guard was placed at the wireless station in Port Burwell on Lake Erie.[175] The next major incident occurred at about 9 p.m. on September 3, when three aeroplanes were observed in the oil town of Petrolea [176] with powerful searchlights sweeping the countryside. Scores of residents watched the spectacle for hours as "every field glass in Petrolea was brought into requisition."[177] The "aeroplanes" were widely thought "to have some connection with Great Britain's war against Germany."[178] One "plane" was observed to fly in the direction of Oil Springs, while a second hovered near Kingscourt, and a third appeared to travel eastward toward London along the Grand Trunk, "evidently scanning the line carefully."[179] Petrolea police chief Fletcher was in communication with nearby communities and immediately began conducting witness interviews.[180] Meanwhile, military authorities attempted to allay fears and suggested the possibility that they were privately owned aircraft.[181] There were also reports that an American pilot crossing the border at night may have owned the planes.[182]

Several observations of "a mysterious aeroplane" were reported near Hamilton during early September and prompted military personnel to investigate.[183] After a spate of sightings between September 8-10 at Springbank, residents were described as "greatly stirred."[184] One witness was Fred Bridge, who urged Canadian authorities to take the reports seriously.

> With my neighbor, I have seen the flashlights which swept the countryside and have heard the roar of the motors. Last night three of them came down over Springbank...
>
> The people of London [Ontario] are not taking this matter seriously enough. Some of those fellows will drop something in the reservoir and cause no end of trouble. I am a time-expired man of the British army...[and if] the call is urgent I am prepared to respond. ...every farmer in the community should be given a rifle and service ammunition by the department of militia, that these spy aviators might be brought down.[185]

By mid-September, the military had issued orders to fire on aeroplanes seen within 14 miles of any wireless stations,[186] and one American plane was even shot at near the border.[187] As war tension continued, a short-lived panic occurred in Toronto on Saturday morning October 10, when a large fluttering kite flown in the city center caused a traffic jam as anxious crowds gathered to try to identify the object. Some residents even dove for cover. The incident exemplified the "nervous state into which even Toronto is thrown by the talk of war and of raiding aeroplanes."[188] During mid-October, several residents on the outskirts of Sault Ste. Marie, claimed to have observed an illuminated aeroplane rise into the sky from the American side of the border near Soo Locks, and sail over the river above the Canadian locks, which were under close guard by militiamen.[189]

Considerable alarm was caused in the city of London on the morning of October 21, when several soldiers reported that an aeroplane carrying a powerful spotlight flew directly over the Welseley Barracks and nearby ordnance stores at about 5:50 a.m. Sergeant Joseph who was on guard duty stated: "It was an aeroplane all right... I and three members of the guard were sitting around the camp fire when we heard the purr of engines and looking up saw the aeroplane coming from the northeast of the barracks. It had a bright light and was traveling rapidly. It came practically over us and the ordnance stores and then turned to the east and south. There was no use firing at it for it flew too high and at too rapid a rate. It was an aeroplane, of that we are sure."[190] This incident followed a series of aeroplane sightings and reports of aerial motor sounds in the vicinity of London over the previous several weeks, but which investigations had traced to causes such as toy balloons or boat engines.[191] Meanwhile, shortly after the barracks sighting at London, Canadian military authorities once again reiterated the unlikelihood of a spy or warplane flying overhead, since, it was argued, they could travel the city unmolested in broad daylight and achieve similar results. They also wondered why planes on a secret mission would use brilliant searchlights that would surely attract attention.[192]

Scattered sightings continued during November. On the Canadian portion of Niagara Falls, guards watching over the Toronto power plant reported seeing what appeared to be signal lights being flashed from the American side of the border across Lake Ontario. The lights would appear during the early morning hours and consisted of red, yellow and green colors. The militiamen believed the lights were held in order "to form different combinations. A close watch is being kept for spies."[193] During this period there were also rumors of sightings in numerous Canadian villages including Forestville, Quebec.[194]

In the early morning hours of December 3, a major scare occurred in Toronto as a series of ambiguous rumbling noises were widely thought to have been an aeroplane raid. It was later suggested that the city's cyclone dredge, in conjunction with war jitters, was responsible for the scare. In the light of day, when it was realized what had happened, The *Toronto Daily Star* somewhat sarcastically described the episode as follows:

Aeroplane Raid Robs Citizens of Slumber
Ominous Rumbling, Apparently Coming From Sky, Caused Widespread Uneasiness

> Half of Toronto sat up in bed last night and held its breath, listening to the Germans in aeroplanes flying about over the roof. Towards five o'clock...the Star office was deluged with reports that included window and picture rattling, purring noises and everything but bombs. From their reports it was learned that the Germans had investigated Bleecker street at 12 p.m., Indian road and Clinton street at 4 a.m., and had stood directly over 45 St. George street at 4.30 a.m.[195]

The sightings were sporadic until mid-February, with reports of aeroplanes near Niagara Falls on December 10,[196] and Montreal during the early morning hours of January 11.[197]

The biggest scare began on Sunday February 14, 1915, at 9:15 p.m., at Brockville, a community on the U.S. border, nestled along the St. Lawrence River. Constables Storey, Thompson, and Glacier, along with several residents, became convinced that three or four aeroplanes had passed by the city to the northeast, heading in the direction of Ottawa, situated about 60 miles due north. The actual observations were vague, with the exception of "light balls" falling from the sky.[198]

"The first machine was flying very rapidly and very high. Very little could be seen, but the unmistakable sounds of the whirring motor made the presence of the aircraft known."[199] Five minutes later a second machine was heard, then suddenly three balls of light descended from the sky, plunging several hundred feet and extinguishing as they hit the river. A few minutes thereafter, vague observations of two more aeroplanes were reported to be passing over the city.[200]

As word of the sightings spread throughout Brockville, its inhabitants became "wildly excited."[201] At 10:30 p.m., the Brockville Police Chief sent an urgent telegram to Premier Sir Robert Bordon, who summoned Colonel Percy Sherwood, Chief of Dominion Police, and after consultation with military authorities, all lights in the Parliament buildings were extinguished and every blind was drawn.[202] Marksmen were posted at several vantage points on Parliament Hill, while the Premier and Cabinet Ministers kept in close communication in the event of an attack during the night. News of the possible attack spread rapidly, and several Members of Parliament rushed to the roof of the main building to see if they could spot any aircraft.

The scare in Canada was intensified the following morning, when the *Toronto Globe* implied that the incident had actually happened. Its banner, front-page headlines stated: "OTTAWA IN DARKNESS AWAITS AEROPLANE RAID. SEVERAL AEROPLANES MAKE A RAID INTO THE DOMINION OF CANADA. Entire City of Ottawa in Darkness, Fearing Bomb-Droppers. Machines Crossed St. Lawrence River...Seen by many Citizens Heading for the Capital – One was Equipped with Powerful Searchlights – Fire Balls Dropped." On the American side, the description of the incident by *The New York Times* the next morning was much more cautious, with its headlines stating in part: "Scare in Ottawa Over Air Raid...but Police Chief's Report is Vague." The same paper also noted that the police chief in Ogdensburg, New York, just 12 miles down the St. Lawrence River from Brockville, stated that no one had reported seeing or hearing anything at the time the aeroplanes were said to have passed near Brockville. In addition, flying machines were also sighted at Gananoque, in Ontario,[203] and other observations of unusual aerial objects were redefined. For instance, once the news of the sightings spread, an Ogdensburg farmer told police that he had seen an aeroplane on February 12 flying toward Canada.[204]

It is important to note that within the context of the outbreak of World War I and Canada's involvement, the aeroplane raid appeared plausible. One press account stated: "The fact that the country is at war and the Germans and pro-Germans abound across the border renders it quite within the bounds of possibility, if not probability, that such a raid might occur."[205]

On the night of February 15, and the early morning hours of the following day, the Parliament buildings again remained dark, and marksmen were posted at strategic locations.[206] This appears to have been both a precautionary and face-saving measure, as information was rapidly coming to hand, indicating that a series of toy balloons had been sent aloft the previous night on the American side and mistaken for enemy aeroplanes. In Parliament, Premier Robert Borden was defensive, and when asked for information on the "invasion," replied that when informed of the reports, he had left the matter to the judgment of the chief of staff and chief of Dominion Police.[207] The Canadian press, such as the *Toronto Globe*, was also left embarrassed, as it had reported the aerial incursion as a certainty in its previous edition. However, in its next edition, it blamed the affair on "hysterical" residents in Brockville.[208] Meanwhile, the charred remains of two large toy balloons[209] had been found in the vicinity of Brockville, which local residents, in turn, blamed on boys from nearby Morristown. A number of toy balloons in other locations had also been sent aloft by Americans on February 14-15, in commemoration of the centenary of peace.[210] An adviser for the Canadian Aviation Corps, Mr. J. D. McCurdy, stated that a mission by German sympathizers from northern New York was highly improbable, especially given the difficulty in night flying.[211]

The last major sighting wave during World War I occurred during mid-July. In the first week of the month, an aeroplane reportedly landed in a field near Nolan Junction, Quebec. It was claimed that two men carrying plans and papers disembarked, then shortly after flew off toward Montreal.[212] On July 16, an illuminated aeroplane was seen by blacksmith Silvanus Edworthy in London,[213] while on the morning of the 17th a craft was seen near Massena, Ontario.[214] During mid-month, aeroplanes were widely reported by numerous residents flying in the vicinity of Quebec City[215] and Montreal.[216] When the craft was seen near a factory in Rigaud, the lights were extinguished and precautions "taken to protect the place from possible attack."[217] On Sunday night the 18th, a military guard at the Point Edward wireless station fired five shots at what he took to be aeroplanes, and two large paper balloons plummeted to earth.[218]

At 11 p.m. on Tuesday night July 20, when a mysterious aircraft was sighted by several citizens of Chateauguay near Montreal, speculation became rifle that a five-year German resident of that town was believed to have secretly flown across the border to the U.S. The man had been closely watched since the outbreak of hostilities and disappeared the night the plane was sighted.[219]

Widely scattered nocturnal aeroplane sightings continued until July of 1916, including sightings at Tillsongburg on July 22,[220] and London on August 8 of 1915.[221] On February 5, 1916, a railway worker spotted two aeroplanes near Montreal. There was thought to be a connection between this sighting and a suspicious man who was seen at about the same time under the Victoria Bridge. Fearing an attempt to blow up the bridge, guards on the structure opened fire on the figure, who then fled.[222] Several days later on February 13, a rare configuration of Venus and Jupiter resulted in a brilliant light in the western sky that was mistaken by hundreds of residents of London as an aeroplane about to attack.[223] Finally, the last known scare during the war occurred at Windsor, when a biplane was sighted by hundreds of anxious residents for about thirty minutes on July 6. Several persons using binoculars actually claimed "to distinguish the figure of the aviator."[224]

The outbreak of World War I generated extraordinary anxiety in Canada, as did concerns about the allegiance of German-Canadians and German-Americans, which was unclear. It was not known whether they possessed the motivation, means, and resources to launch aerial missions. Recent advances in aviation technology lent plausibility to the rumors. The ambiguous nighttime sky was ideal for fostering misperceptions of stars, planets, and other natural phenomena.

It is difficult to imagine Canadian military authorities handling the sporadic sightings more successfully than they did, short of censoring press accounts. While realizing a responsibility to investigate reports, they simultaneously issued confident, reassuring press statements that helped to contain the spread of each episode and avoid public panic. Ironically, the very act of conducting an investigation may have lent credence to public perceptions that there was something to the sightings. The Canadian press was more influential in triggering episodes. On several occasions the language of their accounts treated the existence of a hostile aeroplane as a certainty, and the publication of eyewitness reports intermittently rekindled public attention on the issue and lent legitimacy to the rumors of their existence.

The Capitol Area War Scare Of 1916

In early 1916, tensions in America were running high over World War I. Until this point, America had remained neutral, despite Canada already being at war for some time. Anxieties were further heightened about how to handle the delicate problem of German-Americans, many of whom were publicly expressing their support for the U.S. to enter the war, but on the side of the Germans! What would happen if America entered the war? The issue of how loyal German-Americans were, and whether they might carry out acts of subversion or sabotage against strategic military sites on U.S. soil, was a highly emotional one,[225] and a good deal of mass media discussion was devoted to it. A number of books were in circulation by this time that could only have heightened suspicions. Among them were *German-American Conspiricies in America* by William Skaggs and Frederic Wile's *The German-American Plot*.[226] A prime target for such activities was widely held to be Atlantic coast military installations due to their close proximity with Europe compared with the rest of the country.

It was against this historical-political backdrop that during early 1916 a flurry of mysterious aeroplane sightings occurred in the greater capitol area of the United States. The scare began in January amid fears that German sympathizers might attempt air raids on the DuPont gunpowder mills in Delaware and New Jersey. During this month, phantom aeroplanes were spotted in several towns in the vicinity of Pennsgrove, New Jersey. At Paulsboro, residents and several workers at the dynamite plant in Gibbstown were certain they "heard the whirring of an aeroplane propeller over the town and plant, and they say a machine sailed over the works the night of the explosion when five men were injured recently."[227] Shortly after press reports of these sightings appeared, a Mrs. Zahner of Kensington told journalists that near dusk on January 15, she saw from her house "a big black dot" in the sky and thought she could discern "the framework and the engine."[228] On Monday afternoon January 31, a shoe salesman in Tacony excitedly told how a "big aeroplane" swooped to within 250 feet of his home and headed toward the Frankford Arsenal.

A spokesman for the Arsenal was adamant that it was "Nothing more than blackbirds."[229]

That evening, tensions quickly escalated as a mysterious flying machine was spotted near the large gunpowder plants owned by the DuPont Company at both Carney's Point and Deep Water Point, just across the Delaware border in New Jersey. Company employees, including guard Captain Albert Parsons told reporters that the aeroplane was about 1,500 feet up in the sky and was lost to sight to the southeast after 15 minutes.[230] "The light and the blurred object about it hovered about the powder plant… [moving] at times and then appeared to be still and then it seemed to be going up and down or moving in a semi-circle."[231] The company quickly issued a statement that said, in effect, all Mr. Parsons saw was a light and there was no evidence of an aeroplane. This did little to quell anxieties and there was considerable press speculation that the plane was spying or on a practice bombing mission.[232] While *The Philadelphia Evening Bulletin* reported the observations as improbable, the Wilmington *Every Evening* reported the sightings as fact. It began: "An aeroplane, the identity of which has not been established, on some mysterious mission, has been reconnoitering over the Carney's Point, N.J. powder plant of E.I. du Pont…"[233] A report in the *Philadelphia Inquirer* of April 4 also suggested that Captain Parsons probably saw an aeroplane.[234]

> During the first week of February, many town folks in the Delaware, New Jersey, Maryland area were on edge. One town affected was Woodbury, New Jersey. Like a Zeppelin-threatened city, Woodbury has become a sleepless town, at least for the more timid of the residents, who fear that an aeroplane, phantom or real, which a score of persons claim to have seen the past two nights, is bent on raiding a town unprotected by aircraft guns. Aeroplane is a plain name for the aerial machine, according to those who have seen it for they declare that it appears to be some foreign war contrivance, never seen before on this side of the Atlantic.[235]

Meanwhile, the morning after the sighting by Captain Parsons, recent nocturnal aeroplane sightings were described by people claiming to have seen it hovering near the DuPonts' Hagley Yard, about three miles from Wilmington, Delaware, and at Coatsville, Pennsylvania, near the large steel and iron plant owned by the Lukens Company.[236] A few days later an illuminated aeroplane was seen by several residents near Fenton Beach where "one man declared that his wife started praying that a bomb would not be dropped close by."[237] When an astronomer correlated their sighting with the positions of Jupiter and Venus, the Fenton Beach witnesses steadfastly refused to believe it.[238]

On Saturday night February 12, the aeroplane was seen over Dover, Delaware, by two citizens,[239] while on evening of the 15th, at least two dozen residents at Middletown reported seeing the aeroplane in the eastern sky carrying three lights – one red, one white, the other bluish green. It was first spotted hovering above the Delaware River by Mr. and Mrs. Norman Beale before it moved in the direction of Odessa. Mr. Norman rang the telephone exchange of the news and word quickly spread. One of those alerted, town druggist Ernest A. Truitt, claimed that he could not only see the object from his Cochrane Street home but was "positive he heard a whirring noise, like the noise of a gasoline engine."[240]

A major scare occurred in Wilmington on Sunday evening, February 13, as residents were greatly excited by the appearance of what was thought to have been a German aeroplane between 8 and 9 p.m. During the sighting, the *Wilmington Morning News* received more than 100 telephone calls by anxious citizens who gathered in crowds across the city to gain a better vantage point.

> The first report received at this office stated that the airship was… hovering…over Ninth and Broome streets, and it was "just floating, with practically no motion." Roofward went the entire office force…
> …in a few minutes…[it] was reported as having circled the Baltimore and Ohio railroad station at Delaware avenue and DuPont streets, flying low, and then had sheered off toward the Rockford water tower…
> …But there was no time for speculation before, according to the next call…which came from the Pennsylvania station, the mysterious aircraft was seen slowly circling over the center of the city…
>
> Another caller said it was floating, apparently only a few hundred feet in the air, over Richardson Park.[241]

On the same evening, shortly after the 8 o'clock services began in the Lyon Tabernacle, several persons seated in the edifice thought they heard an aeroplane, as police officers and ushers promptly left the building to look for the flying machine.[242] Witnesses said it appeared to drift along Brandywine Creek, then hovered over the Washington Street Bridge, before slowly turning and flying out of sight to the southwest.[243] It was also spotted by groups at Queens Anne in Maryland, and Clayton and Dover, Delaware.[244]

The sightings quickly died down when several regional newspapers reported that, after an examination of the reports, their times of appearance and location in the nighttime sky, it was evident that Venus and Jupiter in near conjunction, had created an unusually brilliant light on the horizon – a light that was interpreted according to the predominant concerns of the day.[245] It is likely that other astronomical bodies were also mistaken for a German aeroplane.[246]

The German "Invasion" Of New Hampshire: 1917

During The Great War, Germans operatives in the United States were only able to manage a few acts of sabotage and espionage on American soil. These acts were relatively minor and had little influence on the outcome of the war or on the person on the street. In reality, intelligence reports pieced together soon after the war's end depict this small lot of spies and saboteurs in a Keystone cop fashion, fumbling and bungling their way through mostly failed missions because of their incompetence and ineptitude. In spite of this reality, widespread perceptions of spies and saboteurs lurking in every community were common, culminating in a "spy mania" in April of 1917 when America officially entered the war. In his book on spy scares, *Insidious Foes*, Francis MacDonnell documents how the German scare reached such proportions during this period that streets, schools, cities, and foods with Germanic names were renamed, and communities forbade German music, fearing the passing of secret coded messages during performances. There were even rumors that German submarine captains would embark from their vessels in secret coastal locations to attend the theatre in order to spread influenza germs.[247]

Within this tense atmosphere, people began to exercise their imaginations and rumors soon spread that German sympathizers were planning to conduct nighttime bombing raids or spy missions on U.S. targets by piloting aeroplanes flown from secret, isolated airstrips along the New England-Canadian border.[248] The prime target for such activities was widely held to be military installations on the Atlantic coast, due to their close proximity to Europe. Naturally, there was much speculation that the planes were spying on the major strategic naval base at Portsmouth, New Hampshire, as a prelude to a possible bombing raid. It must be remembered that the aeroplanes of 1917 were crude and treacherous to fly. That they could perform sophisticated maneuvers at night and in rough terrain, taking off and landing from a secret base in the mountains, and remaining aloft for several hours at a time, was simply impossible. Yet, that is exactly what happened – or many residents thought they saw.

While stress can have a strange effect on the body, it can also do strange things to the mind. For it was within this war scare climate that during the early morning hours of April 13, 1917, one week after America declared war, two National Guardsmen from Company L of the Sixth Massachusetts Infantry were stationed on the bridge linking Portsmouth, New Hampshire, and Kittery, Maine, when they heard something like the noise of an aeroplane. While watching the distant object, one guard panicked when he said that it looked like a plane that was starting to descend to make a pass over the bridge. He immediately fired his rifle at the object, at which point it moved off and soon disappeared in the distance.[249] On the same night, two soldiers guarding a railway bridge at Penacook reported that two mysterious intruders fired four shots in their direction before fleeing into the night. Not a single clue as to the identity these "attackers" was found.[250] It was later thought to have been a backfiring motor or firecrackers in combination with war jitters.

Despite the vagueness of these two reports, they generated great anxiety across the state. While the Penacook incident was dismissed for lack of evidence, the aeroplane reports raised eyebrows in military circles and further excited the public.[251] While the possibility was discussed that the aeroplane had been launched from an enemy vessel situated off the coast, it was widely believed to have taken off from a secret remote airstrip nestled in the nearby mountains and circled the area before returning to its point of departure. Naval authorities ordered an investigation into the sightings and issued an urgent appeal to the public in an attempt to determine the identity of the pilot, which they hoped was a local aviator. In the wake of the Portsmouth publicity, a night police officer on duty at Rochester, New Hampshire, claimed that while on patrol, he also had heard an aerial noise, which he assumed to have been the "Portsmouth aeroplane" as it passed overhead.[252] Another report on the same night came from James Walker, a motorman on the Dover, Rochester, and Somersworth railway. He stated that the craft was "plainly visible" over Gonic and was "flying high and headed north."[253] By Tuesday, April 17, in the wake of great press publicity, several residents of East Manchester reported that they, too, had observed the aeroplane or heard the whirring of its propeller on Saturday night, as it traveled in a northeasterly direction at about 10 p.m.[254]

The phantom aeroplane sightings abated until the night of April 23, when several residents of North Conway, New Hampshire, observed mysterious lights near Kearsarge Mountain. There was speculation that "an aviator was maneuvering about the summit."[255] Just prior to the sightings, rumors had been circulating in area that "a small party of strangers" was observed recently east of Kearsarge, and speculation was rife that they may have been German aviators.[256] On April 30, prominent Deerfield horseman Charles Churchill was awakened by a peculiar noise and observed an aeroplane hovering in the distance that appeared to be flashing signals towards Portsmouth.[257] About an hour earlier, Mrs. Edson Roberts of Wolfeboro also reported hearing the craft above her house, near the East Alton line.

By May 2, the aeroplane war scare had subsided, no doubt helped by the stark absence of tangible evidence to support the rumors that German sympathizers were engaged in secret reconnaissance missions over the Portsmouth naval base. Another reason for the decline in reports was an embarrassing disclosure about the aeroplane sightings of the previous night. The press reported that the "aeroplane" heard whirring above Deerfield was actually a large truck rumbling through the community in the middle of the night. There is also little doubt that the media's ridicule of this incident discouraged further reports of enemy aeroplanes.[258] Typical was the reaction of the *Manchester Union*, which on May 2 reported on the mysterious light and noise that were widely assumed to have been a German plane. "'Airships,' said one resident, and at once the farmers' phone lines became active. All agreed...that Deerfield was menaced by hostile aircraft. All...would doubtless continue to agree, except for the fact that somebody always has to take the joy out of life." The reporter noted that "In this case it is E.E. Holmes, Manchester truckman, who comes to bat as The Union goes to press, and announces that the strange Zeppelin was his big motor truck, which went through Deerfield with a heavy load in the dead of the night."

Anxiety over America's involvement in World War I, concerns that German sympathizers might attempt to spy on or attack the strategic Portsmouth Naval Base, and rumors, appear to have resulted in a variety of natural phenomena such as stars, planets, and vague noises, being redefined relative to prevailing fears. The phantom German aeroplane sightings over New Hampshire reflected the prevailing state of mind of many citizens as America entered the war.

The Ghost Flier Sightings: Scandinavia 1933-34

Between November 15, 1933, and February 11, 1934, tens of thousands of Scandinavians, often entire villages, reported observing "ghost planes"[259] with the heaviest concentration of sightings occurring over Sweden. The objects were described as gray monoplanes without identifying insignias or markings. On several occasions pilots were perceived. The "ghost flier" or "Flier X," as it became popularly known, was frequently observed or heard during fierce blizzard conditions, occasionally alighting and taking off, always in remote areas. The "plane" was almost exclusively nocturnal and typically illuminated by a "searchlight." Despite the pervasive folk belief in the existence of the ghost flier, no verification of a plane or secret airfield was ever found, and aircraft of the period were incapable of operating under blizzard conditions for several hours.[260]

CONTEXT: Two folk theories prevailed during this time. One was that liquor, silk, or narcotics smugglers had contracted a highly skilled, daring pilot to undertake flights to avoid customs officials.[261] Alternatively, it was held that aviators from Russia,[262]

Japan,[263] or Germany[264] were engaging in reconnaissance missions with potentially sinister intentions. The ghost flier's existence was legitimized through the press in the form of suggestive stories and the reporting of statements and actions by Swedish military authorities. The initial sighting reports appeared in the *Vasterbotten-Kuriren,* which serves the vicinity of Umea; they described perceptions of an ambiguous nocturnal light that may have been a "flying machine." It was not disclosed until near the end of the episode that details of this report, which had prompted so much intense newspaper coverage, were either fabricated or grossly misunderstood.[265] Newspapers were instrumental in the creation and diffusion of the generalized belief in the phantom flier, as voluminous speculation was published supporting the flying machine hypothesis.

The predominant circulating rumors held that the ghost flier represented Soviet incursions into Swedish airspace. Given the long history of Soviet invasion fears in Scandinavia,[266] and the ambiguous nocturnal nature of the observations, such speculations were plausible and of perceived importance since a consensus prevailed that Sweden's aerial defense was inadequate.[267] Newspaper speculation and exaggeration of this fear significantly contributed to a redefinition of the situation. One typical headline proclaimed: "Air Force powerless to Expose the Ghost Flier. Equipment and Outposts Insufficient. Swift Machines... Called for..."[268]

As sightings continued amid persistent rumors of the ghost flier's potentially hostile intentions, Swedish military officials actively investigated reports and issued public statements as to their likely foreign-power origin.[269] By December 28, in a highly publicized event, the Swedish Flying Corps Number 4 was dispatched to Tarnaby to probe the reports. By early 1934, 24 Swedish Air Force biplanes were searching northern districts where the sightings were concentrated. Several "ghost plane" sightings by military personnel during this period further legitimized its reality. These observations were reinforced by press accounts detailing opinions as to the ghost flier's existence by high-ranking military officials, such as those of the northern Swedish commanding general, C.P. Reutersward,[270] a position that he continued to publicly espouse even after the reports ceased.

The popular press usage of such terms as "ghost flier," "ghost plane," and "Flier X" provided a convenient means for residents to define unfamiliar stimuli within familiar terms, further legitimizing its existence.[271] From a labeling theory perspective, once the ghost flier became a part of taken-for-granted reality, citizens acted within a different frame of meaning, redefining various objects, events, and circumstances relative to the newly ascribed reality. On February 5, 1933, several residents observed a "flying machine" crash-land during a violent snowstorm on Norway's Mount Fager. Peering through telescopes, residents could discern the plane and its two-man crew shoveling snow away from the craft, which rested on a plateau.[272] Two days later one of several search parties reported finding apparent airplane tracks and curious footprints nearby. A subsequent investigation by Norwegian marine and police personnel determined that "it was impossible for an airplane to start up from the stated place," and that the "tracks" were furrows created by the storm.[273] Separate police search parties scoured the area, determining that the "plateau" where the plane reportedly landed was actually "a moderately steep hill" and the ghost plane was a large rock.[274] Even mundane audio stimuli were redefined. Several residents near Bjurholm heard eight "shots" while observing an ambiguous nocturnal object. The sounds were presumed to have emanated from the flier's "backfiring motor."[275] Residents in Dorotea, who had on several occasions "heard noise among the mountains," attributed it to "Flier X."[276]

During the Flier X sightings, numerous events were labeled as deviant and suspicious that just prior to or after the episode would have been labeled as prosaic. For instance, during early January 1934, a theory that the mysterious objects may have represented Soviet military planes on training or reconnaissance flights received prominence in the Scandinavian press. During this period, a "mysterious Russian steamer" became the focus of much interest in the northern Norwegian district of Tronlelagen. By February 24, the Oslo correspondent for the *Svenska Dagbladet,* described ambiguous associations that had been drawn between the vessel and Flier X, exemplifying how the press fostered and legitimized the pervasive taken-for-granted existence of the plane. "Fourteen days ago it steamed low for two days off Brekstad but did not try to make contact with land... later...at Hestvik the Russian cargo ship Kola...laid by the side of the vessel. The two steamers laid side by side for a day...The steamer has been observed many times in the waters where ships never usually go. When the mysterious airplane was seen out there some time past, the Russian steamer was also there, and when any kind of telegraphing took place involving disturbed radio contact, it was around."[277]

Once the ghost flier's existence was widely accepted by a populous preconditioned by the press and authority figures, numerous experiences occurring before the episode began were also reinterpreted.[278] The following account is typical:

> Some time past it was reported that a British trawler informed...[a Norwegian coast guard ship at a secretly confided position] that it was in contact with a Japanese support cruiser and sold fish to them. According to the *Tidens Tegn* the meeting of the trawler took place back at the beginning of November, [while] the first ghost flier was not reported before the end of the month...we have reason to believe that the trawler belongs to the British Admiralty.

There is speculation that "something happened up in Ishavet" and that the British trawler had a mission to investigate and assess the potential threat.

The ghost flier may have been a barometer of the social climate of the period, reflecting popular stereotypes and fears.[279]

See also: FLYING SAUCERS, GREAT AMERICAN AIRSHIP WAVE, GHOST ROCKET SCARE, EDISON STAR SIGHTINGS, RUSSIAN POLAND BALLOON SCARE, ANDREE BALLOON MANIA.

PHANTOM FLORIDA GAS POISONING

Dade County, Florida: May 1974

Monday, May 13, 1974, was a typically calm, sunny morning in southern Florida, when emergency personnel in Dade County responded to a fairly common occurrence. A student had reportedly fainted at an elementary school.[280] The time was about 9:30 a.m. The fainting incident took place at the Bay Harbor Elementary School as 169 pupils from the 4th, 5th, and 6th grades were assembled in the cafetorium, rehearsing an upcoming musical. The students had been singing for about 25 minutes, when "Sandy," an eleven-year-old 5th grade girl began to experience headache and faintness. As the music teacher looked in another direction, the girl managed to slip away to the nurse's office just down the hall, where she collapsed. While the teacher was oblivious to these goings-on, most of the group was aware of the situation. As Sandy was unresponsive to smelling salts, local rescue personnel were summoned.

Just as the rehearsal was breaking up, uniformed rescue squad members were passing through the hall, wading through the departing students. They entered the clinic and soon emerged with the unconscious Sandy "on a stretcher for all to see."[281] At this point, several of the students exiting the rehearsal began to complain of feeling unwell. As word of the "gas leak" poisoning students spread throughout the building, pupils in different parts of the school reported feeling ill in the hour that followed. Symptoms included difficulty breathing, headache, nausea, stomach pain, and chills. Shortly thereafter, the school was besieged by police, fire and rescue personnel, politicians, community leaders, and scores of representatives from the south Florida news media.[282]

CONTEXT: The lengthy exposure of cafetorium rehearsal students to Sandy's collapse, and the presence of a strange odor, generated anxiety and concern. Combined with the chance meeting of ambulance squad members, the departing rehearsal group appears to have grown over-anxious. The subsequent spread of illness symptoms among students throughout the school seems to have been exacerbated by the presence of politicians, the media, and emergency workers.

By 10:30 a.m. County Health Department officials were asked to go to the school to help treat those children sickened by the "poison gas." By the time epidemiologist Dr. Joel Nitzkin of the Dade County Public Health Department reached the school at 11:15, 34 pupils had either been sent to the hospital or home after complaining of symptoms – 11 male, 23 female. Dr. Nitzkin described the situation: "The scene was complete pandemonium. It had the *look* of a disaster." Nitzkin said that he and two colleagues could not park near the school as the parking area was jammed with all types of vehicles haphazardly parked in all different directions. "Ambulances. Fire equipment. Police cars. All with their flashers flashing. And the media – they were swarming. Newspaper reporters and photographers. Radio people with microphones. Television cameras from four local stations...Members of the Dade County School Board. Members of the Bay Harbor Town Council. And neighbors and passersby and parents all rushing around. I had never seen anything like it..."[283]

Nitzkin stood out even amid the chaos, towering over the crowd at 6 feet, 9 inches tall. After several minutes he assessed the situation, then phoned the hospital, learning that the series of tests on the children were all negative, including urinalyses, electrolytes, blood counts, and blood gases. None of them appeared seriously ill; one was clearly hyperventilating, and one seemed to be suffering from a mild virus.[284] Due to the presence of nausea and headache in conjunction with reports of a strange odor in the school, an emergency room doctor complicated matters by informing emergency personnel, parents, children, and media representatives "that the children must have been exposed to a toxic gas."[285] Based on a subsequent survey, 39 students reported experiencing mild symptoms that morning, but they stayed in school.

An abbreviated search and survey of the building was conducted for a possible source of the illness agent. Bacteria and viruses were eliminated as possible causes "on the basis of the extremely short incubation period and clinical syndromes observed."[286] The strange odor that had been reported by many students was pinpointed as a carpet adhesive in the library. While the substance gave off a distinctive, solvent-like smell, it had been in the school for the previous two weeks when the carpet was installed. Further, none of the ill children had visited the library that day. Dr. Nitzkin made another interesting observation: "Minutes after dismissal of the class in question from the cafetorium, another group of children entered through a separate door and spent the next 30 to 40 minutes in musical rehearsal similar to the class before. No one in this second group, including the teacher, was aware of the commotion from the previous class immediately outside the door. No one in this second group experienced illness despite exposure to the room in question."[287]

At 11:40 a.m., Dr. Nitzkin announced to the news media that there was no evidence of any poison gas or fumes in the building. He said the cause was "mass hysteria with hyperventilation."[288] Nitzkin later admitted that he feared others might challenge the diagnosis, and he tried to act as calm and confidently as he could. The immediate reaction was surprising – silence. However, their body language told another story. Dr. Nitzkin would later recall what happened next: "The public health nurses looked stunned. I saw Dr. Enriquez smiling and nodding. The parents of the sick children looked horrified and insulted – I was telling them their children were crazy. But most of the others – the teachers and school board people and the firemen and the head secretary – just stood there looking thoughtful."[289] Nitzkin then carefully explained his reasons for his diagnosing hysteria, after which a collective sigh of relief seemed to sweep over his audience as "the tension dissolved. The firemen and the police just sort of disappeared. People began to turn to each other and talk. The sick kids stopped looking so sick."[290] The Health Department performed far more thorough environmental tests of the building the following day; the results fully supported Dr. Nitzkin's initial impressions. By noon, the "crisis" at the school had resolved, no further pupils were sent home due to illness, and attendance rates remained normal.[291]

Dr. Nitzkin's bold, decisive handling of the crisis created a firestorm of criticism by many angry parents, who were furious at his quick diagnosis that their children had succumbed to their own imaginations. The actions he took to stem the spread of the episode are very rare in the mass hysteria literature. Nitzkin's prescription for controlling the situation was a prompt but careful diagnosis of psychogenic illness, after which he quickly imposed measures to control the crisis – that is, to announce epidemic hysteria as the culprit and to return the school to a state of normal operations as soon as possible.[292] However, most investigators are hesitant to make such announcements so early in episodes, erring on the side of caution until more detailed tests of the premises can be conducted. However, Dr. Nitzkin argues that the presence of certain key elements allowed for an early diagnosis. These include: initial laboratory tests within normal limits except for values that have been altered by over-breathing; the rapid cessation of transient, benign symptoms; the conspicuous absence of illness in adults sharing the identical environment; a preponderance of young females; and symptom transmission by sight or sound.[293]

In addition to Sandy, seven students were hospitalized. Dr. Nitzkin conducted a study of these students, which revealed a curious pattern. Five were girls – one of whom was a known hypochondriac. Another always seemed to be sick. Another was known to hyperventilate at stressful times. And of the remaining two girls, one described herself as one of Sandy's best friends, while the other came to school with vague feelings of illness. As for the boys, one had a long history of discipline problems, while school officials described the other boy as "highly excitable."[294] Sandy also fit the profile of a classic trigger who is usually a strong group leader: popular, attractive, precocious, and a good student.

PHANTOM HAT PIN STABBER

France: circa 1923

A man told of being "pricked with a long hat pin or the like." As the story spread, many other residents reported that they too had been pricked. One person was arrested and put on trial but let go on insufficient evidence. Police later determined that the assailant was imaginary.[295]

See also: PHANTOM SLASHER OF TAIPEI, HALIFAX SLASHER.

PHANTOM PREGNANCY ATTACKS

England: circa 1971-72

Epidemic fainting, trance-like states, and histrionics struck a single classroom of sixteen- and seventeen-year-old females at a girls' school in a London suburb. In all, eight students of a class of 24 were affected over seven months, including a teacher. Dr. Silvio Benaim and his colleagues determined that accumulating tension triggered the outbreak, which transpired amid serious ongoing interpersonal and sexual conflicts after the death of a former schoolmate and lesbian advances by a teacher. They concluded that the school served as a stage where the girls' personal problems appeared in the form of hysterical dramas.[296]

The episode began around Christmas when the class was taking practice "O" level examinations. Louise, 17, began to experience "fainting attacks" in class.[297] After the Christmas break, she continued having "falling" or "drop attacks" when school resumed in January. In late February, another pupil in the class, Margaret, had fainting spells. Shortly after, a third pupil, Rosemary began to have similar "drop attacks." Soon five other classmates and a young teacher began to fall, at which point school officials decided to disband the class and sent the group home a week early for the spring vacation.[298] While most of the girls affected "dropped" or "fell," Louise, the first one afflicted, was the most severely impaired and would reportedly curl up and appear to sleep or "to have been very dramatic, rolling her eyes, flinging her arms about, and always claiming a complete retrograde amnesia for the attacks."[299]

As the term continued, Louise and Margaret received psychiatric counseling but remained in the class. The symptoms were confined to the classroom except for Louise and Margaret who reported "drop attacks" both at home and occasionally while walking on the street.

The episode ended in July when the class split up for the summer recess. When school started up again in September, most of the affected students had either left school or been scattered in different classrooms. There were no more reports of "attacks."[300] Interviews by psychiatrists later revealed that the first "attacks" in Louise began about the time she learned that her best friend, Anne, who had left her class the previous May, was pregnant. Anne gave birth in February at which time she died of a cerebral hemorrhage. At this point the "attacks" spread and became more severe. The psychiatric team who investigated the case remarked: "Perhaps it was anxiety about the dangerous results of sexual experience which was communicated by Louise and Margaret to the rest of the form (class)."[301] They continued: "If one assumed that Louise's falling was a form of identification with her pregnant friend, Anne, one would not be surprised at the epidemic ending after a period of nine months!"[302] Louise was described as a seductive, intelligent girl with a charismatic personality. Her home situation was poor, having recently had an affair with a brother-in-law, and an incestual relationship with her bisexual brother, and after that ended, his bisexual partner, whom she eventually married.[303]

Later, Louise "confessed" to psychiatrists that after the first month of uncontrollable fainting, she relished the attention and began to fake "drop attacks." "At first, I would not admit to myself that it was not genuine: I was convinced that, because I really had fainted several times, that I was still doing so. When I did face up to the fact that it was false, I still couldn't stop."[304] Louise also said: "I was extremely ashamed of my deceitfulness ... and I found it impossible to stop. I used it as an escape from the problems I could not face at home and at school, and became completely wrapped up in it. It was the only thing from which I gained pleasure."

Phantom Pregnancy "Epidemics"

During one of her hospital admissions for psychiatric treatment, Louise was credited with triggering a phantom pregnancy "epidemic" in her ward. As some of her hysterical symptoms corresponded with the possibility of pregnancy, Louise had requested a pregnancy test. A few days later, several women, especially "the younger patients, at least one of whom had no sexual experience whatsoever, began to complain of the same symptoms and needed to be reassured that they were not pregnant."[305]

A similar phantom pregnancy "epidemic" spread through a 24-bed hospital psychiatric ward in the U.S. during the 1950s. Psychotherapists Taylor and Hunter saw the patients 3-to-5 times weekly, recorded their interviews, and later determined that the episode began when one of the patients – a professional woman of high prestige – had a dream which she discussed with other patients who became excited about the notion. Soon several other women reported symptoms associated with birth and rebirth.[306]
See also: MASS HYSTERIA IN SCHOOLS.

PHANTOM SLASHER

Taipei, Taiwan: 1956

During the first two weeks of May 1956, residents in the vicinity of Taipei, Taiwan, and Keelung 40 miles (60 kilometers) to the north, lived in fear that their children would be the next targets of a demented villain who was prowling the streets in broad daylight and boldly slashing people, mostly unsuspecting youths, at random with a razor-like weapon. At least 21 attacks were reported to police. Norman Jacobs of the University of Kansas was teaching in Taipei at the time and surveyed local press coverage after authorities prohibited him from interviewing the alleged victims. Opinions as to a motive varied from slashing to divert attention while stealing jewelry to sexual sadism. Another theory held that a blood ritual was involved, based on local folklore that drawing blood from children brings luck.[307] Some said the slasher was a woman, others a man; still others said it was a "teenager with a sad smile."[308] Soon various mundane events, situations, and circumstances were being redefined as slasher-related. Yet, no one ever saw an actual slashing.

CONTEXT: The episode occurred amid widespread xenophobia and invasion fears from the communist People's Republic of China on the mainland, whose leaders vowed to reunite the island. The local folk theory associating bloodletting and good fortune among non-Chinese indigenous Taiwanese enhanced the plausibility of slasher-related press reports and rumors.

Jacobs found that since February rumors circulated throughout Taipei that a serial slasher was attacking children between the ages of six months and eight years. On May 3, police began a formal investigation, triggering intense publicity and speculation. On May 4, the Taiwanese press began reporting on the claims, publishing a flurry of often unsubstantiated, sensationalized accounts of slashings. For instance, both the *China Post* and *Hong Kong Standard* reported that one child died from castration.[309]

By May 4, the city was gripped by fear as two children were reportedly slashed under vague circumstances: an eleven-year-old boy sustaining a cut to his left arm but unable to recall the circumstances, while a two-year-old boy in a northern suburb noticed a mysterious leg cut while playing. Widespread rumors swept through Taipei of numerous young girls being slashed at various primary schools. The terror grew as one paper erroneously reported that some victims had died.[310] Small children were being kept indoors while older ones were escorted to school and back. The crisis peaked on May 11 as police thought they had solved the case with the arrest of the "woman in red" for the razor slashing of a nine-month-old. A mother holding a baby in her arms was walking on the street when the baby was hit by an object from behind and began bleeding and crying. The mother turned and screamed as she noticed a girl walking behind in a red jacket and started chasing after "the slasher." Bystanders joined in the chase, during which the "woman in red" was seen tossing a package away. She was soon arrested by police who fended off the angry mob. The parcel was retrieved and found to contain a razor blade. An investigation revealed that the woman was opening her umbrella when it caught on the baby's sleeve and she panicked. The woman feared for her life knowing she was carrying a razor and could be mistaken for the slasher. The woman was a seamstress and used the razor in her work. She pointed out that the blade was wrapped in paper and couldn't have been used as a weapon. A doctor summoned to examine the child stated that an umbrella and not a razor was the likely cause.[311] The woman, in the wrong place at the wrong time, was released.

Police later concluded that the "slashings" had resulted from inadvertent, everyday contact in public places that ordinarily would have gone relatively unnoticed. One man told police in detail how a man carrying a mysterious black bag had slashed him. When a doctor determined that the wound was made by a blunt object and not a razor, the "victim" admitted that he could not recall exactly what had happened but assumed that he had been slashed "because of all the talk going around about razor slashings."[312] In another incident, it was not the supposed victim but a physician who was responsible for creating an incident, as an elderly man with a wrist laceration sought medical treatment. The attending doctor grew suspicious and contacted police when the man casually noted that a stranger had coincidentally touched him at about the same time when he first noticed the bleeding. A more thorough examination led to the conclusion that the "slash" was an old injury that had been re-opened after inadvertent scratching.[313]

On May 12, police announced the results of their investigation: the episode was entirely psychological in origin. Of the 21 slashing claims examined by their office, they determined that "five were innocent false reports, seven were self-inflicted cuts, eight were due to cuts other than razors, and one was a complete fantasy." In one case, police determined that a baby thought to have been slashed while waiting for a bus had been accidentally scratched by one of several umbrella peddlers at the bus depot.[314] Rumors, amplified by sensational press coverage treating the slasher's existence as real, served to foment the scare by altering the perceptual outlook of residents to include the reality of a daring slasher, resulting in a self-fulfilling prophesy.

COMMENT: The Taiwanese press was instrumental in spreading the existing rumors and generating undue fear by exaggerating the extent of the threat and engaging in speculative, sensationalistic journalism.

See also: THE HALIFAX SLASHER, PHANTOM HATPIN STABBER.

PHILIPPINE DEVIL HYSTERIA

Manila, Philippines: January 1994

An elementary school in Manila was temporarily closed after about 20 Filipino students went into an emotional frenzy after claiming to see "the devil" standing under a schoolyard tree. Afterwards, six female students fainted, including Joy Bolante, 12, who kept screaming out, "There is no God" as she struggled against several adults who were trying to calm her. The affected students were later taken to a nearby Roman Catholic church where a priest dabbed them with Holy Water and said prayers for their recovery. According to another twelve-year-old pupil, Marilyn Umpat: "He is a gigantic man who has horns and a tail."[315]

PHILLIP KNIGHTLEY'S HOOK HOAX

Eastern Australia: 1954

Australian-born journalist and spy expert Phillip Knightley's memoir, *A Hack's Progress*, is a delightfully candid look behind the scenes of his life as a writer for several prominent Fleet Street tabloids. While working as the news editor for the *Truth* newspaper in Australia, Knightley said that although the bulk of the paper was easy to fill with divorce cases and sports, finding a riveting front-page story was more challenging. This being the case, Knightley said, and unlike the other British Sunday papers, "no one on *Truth* began working on a major news story until Friday or Saturday and if nothing sensational had emerged by Saturday afternoon, panic followed."[316]

One particular week, Knightley assigned two reporters to a planned expose of Sydney milk suppliers, based on strong suspicions that milk was being watered down. Bottles were gathered from across Sydney and their contents analyzed. Knightley was sure that some of the bottles would be under the legal requirement for buttermilk fat content – and *voila*– he would have a front-page story. Late on Friday afternoon the results came back normal, forcing Knightley to scramble to find a last-minute replacement story.

With the deadline rapidly approaching, Knightley recalls that his boss, Jack Finch, told him: "For Christ's sake, find something...You're an imaginative fellow. Use your fucking imagination."[317] He scanned various newspapers and came upon a story in *The Sydney Morning Herald* about a young man convicted of indecently assaulting a girl on a crowded commuter train by pressing his groin against her. Said Knightley: "To my everlasting professional shame – I can only plead that I was just twenty-four and very ambitious – I obeyed Finch and used my imagination. I invented a story about a pervert known only to his victims and the police as 'The Hook.'" Knightley's sex pervert supposedly traveled the Sydney rail network, armed with a wire hook made from a coat hanger that ran from his right shoulder to his coat sleeve and stopping just under the cuff. "The Hook" would wait for the train to become crowded, then maneuver next to an attractive female and pretend to be reading the newspaper. Dropping his shoulder, the hook would then extend the wire outward, at which point he would slip it under her skirt and lift it in order to see her stocking tops. The device was quickly retracted, as "The Hook" appeared to be innocently reading the paper.

Knightly also imaginatively created quotations. One woman vowed never to ride the train again until the pervert was caught. Another anonymous source, a police officer, said he had been overwhelmed with complaints. Knightley even had a staff artist draw a sketch of The Hook at work. Knightley said, "The more I worked on my fairy story, the more I enjoyed it. There were no inconvenient facts to get in the way of a perfect narrative. Like Lionel Hogg said – it was how it should have happened."[318] Knightley said that Finch read the story with glee, changing only one part – that The Hook had been actively plying his fiendish trade across Sydney on that very Saturday night. Finch then added the headline: "HOOK SEX PERVERT STRIKES AGAIN."

Knightley later learned that rival reporters had spent hours phoning Sydney police stations trying to confirm the *Truth*'s claim or brand the story a fabrication. All that the duty officers could say was that it had not happened in their district but couldn't vouch for the others. Come Monday morning, Knightley came to work confident that he had succeeded in perpetrating his hoax. Besides, the *Truth* didn't use bylines, so it would be difficult to determine who had actually written the story. Then, his telephone rang. "'Sergeant Williamson here. Did you write that stuff about The Hook?' He obviously knew, so there was no sense in lying. 'Yes,' I said. 'Right. Well, I just want to thank you and let you know that we got the bastard this morning.' Had I heard right? 'Got him?' Yeah. Arrested him at Punchbowl station. Caught him in the act. You might want to write about it."[319]

Knightley called the police roundsman and confirmed that the officer was not having a joke at his expense. For several weeks, a curious and somewhat befuddled Knightley waited for The Hook to appear in court, but it never happened. Knightley didn't want to press his luck by making further enquiries, so he let the matter rest.[320]

Decades later, and after giving the matter considerable thought, Knightley came up with three possible theories.

1. Through a remarkable coincidence, there really had been a Hook.
2. A *Truth* reader had seen the story and decided to be a copycat.
3. The most likely conclusion, Knightley said, was that Sydney police, "who had a reputation for massaging crime statistics to polish their public relations, got rid of a case which promised to be a PR disaster by arresting some pathetic minor sex offender and nominating him as The Hook."[321]

PHOTOCOPIED GHOST SCARE

Malaysia: August 2001

The circulation of photocopies of a supposed ghost photograph sent waves of fear through students in several Malaysian schools at such locations as Kuala Kangsar and Pantai Remis. The picture depicted a ghostly figure lurking behind a boy. Primary school children were especially fearful – to the extent that many refused to use the bathrooms. Malaysia's National Union of the Teaching Profession called on parents and teachers to discuss the matter with the children and explain that there were no real ghosts. Union president Ms. Tengku Habsah Tengku Petera said the scare may have been a deliberate attempt by irresponsible parties to frighten students.[322]

CONTEXT: Throughout Malaysia there is a widespread belief in the reality of a variety of supernatural beings, including ghosts and spirits. It is likely that many of the teachers may have contributed to the episode by expressing their views in the existence of ghosts and the reality of the authenticity of the ghost photograph.[323]

PIGSTY HYSTERIA

Hazlerigg, England: July 8, 1972

A juvenile jazz band was performing at a children's gala in the village of Hazlerigg near Newcastle upon Tyne, when more than 130 children and a few adults suddenly became ill.[324] The main complaint was epigastric pain (stomach ache). Other symptoms included nausea, dizziness, headache, feelings of hot and cold, shivering, and tingling or numbness of the hands and feet. The episode happened at the Hollinwell showground about 15 kilometers north of Nottingham.

CONTEXT: Concerns that odor from a pigsty may have been a toxic spray from a nearby farm field, and mass media sensationalism, appear to have combined to trigger a case of mass psychogenic illness.

Six children's jazz bands from across the region converged on Hazlerigg for the annual event, which was attended by about 1,200 people – some 400 band members, 300 well-wishers among whom were many adults, and an estimated 500 local children and adults. Gala organizers offered no food and most children ate home lunches before the event got underway. The hour-long gala parade began at 1 p.m., with the six bands leading the way, followed by local children in fancy attire, and ending at a nearby sports field. Band members ranged in age from 5-to-16, and nearly all were girls. The route was about 1.6 kilometers long. Most band members played kazoos, though some had cymbals or drums, and the youngest children carried banners.

The first sign of illness occurred when a 16-year-old bass drummer fainted. Within minutes, up to six more girls collapsed, exhibiting dizziness and stomach pain. Many were clutching their abdomens and weeping. By 6 p.m., four grown-ups and 168 children were being examined at one of five hospitals. During the initial chaos, authorities thought they were dealing with a food poisoning event. However, this made little sense as they hailed from different regions and consumed their own food. Investigators were also curious to note that upon examination at their respective hospitals, "the vast majority of children had few physical complaints and said they were feeling better. They were all...very frightened and bewildered, many of them believing they had been poisoned and several spontaneously said they had thought that they were dying."[325] A few of those treated in hospital exhibited anxiety-generated muscle twitching, while many more were diagnosed as hyperventilating. Another oddity also stood out to investigators – not a single adult or child from Hazlerigg was affected.[326]

In their final report on the episode, two local physicians who treated those affected, H.C.T. Smith serving Northunberland, and E.J. Eastham of Newcastle University Hospitals, noted that the local press refused to accept their initial diagnosis of psychogenic illness. This had the effect of undermining their credibility and authority. They stated: "A bacteriological or viral cause can be ruled out. The children came from different areas and only assembled three to five hours before most of the cases occurred. No known virus or bacteria has as short an incubation period as this. We were singularly unsuccessful in persuading the Press of this elementary fact and 'Mystery Bug K.O.s Children' was the favorite headline."[327]

Immediately after the incident, investigators scoured the area in search of a probable cause, without success. Everything from ice pops and ice cream sold nearby to the possibility that weed killer sprayed on the field 10 days prior to the event were thoroughly investigated. Grazing fields surrounding the gala had not been sprayed and there had been no gas leaks – and indeed, there were no pipes under the field. Weather also did not seem to be a factor, as by midday the temperature only reached a cool 16°C and the humidity was a comfortable 57 percent.[328]

Based on responses to questionnaires returned by most of those affected, many noted a foul smell while making their way to the sports field, a smell from a recently cleared pigsty. It's likely that locals were aware of the odor's origin – and perhaps even accustomed to it – but "outsiders" were left guessing as to its cause. Many of those who fell ill described the smell "in most melodramatic terms."[329]

Symptoms quickly resolved, with a third reporting no symptoms after only four hours, and within a day more than half said they felt fine. Symptoms gradually subsided over the next week. Investigators reported that during the incident a television film crew arrived on the scene, heightening the drama. But that was just the beginning. "Subsequently there was intense Press and television coverage out of all proportion to the medical significance of the event. It was implied that the children had a mysterious illness baffling medical science. It was not surprising, therefore, that in some children the symptoms tended to persist."[330]

A BBC investigation in 2003 by members of their "Inside Out" documentary team suggested that fungicide poisoning may have been responsible. Investigators say they found that tridemorph had been sprayed on the nearby fields at the time of the episode. Tridemorph was banned from use in the United Kingdom in 2000 due to its detrimental effects. The fungicide was applied to cereal crops and is capable of causing skin and eye irritation. One of the rescue squad members who treated victims at the scene, Steven Mitchell, supported the fungicide theory, saying: "There were a lot of young people very distressed – their eyes were very sore and had severe breathing difficulties – there was a smell in the air... With the bands marching up and down, they were dispersing the chemical into the air – and I am sure it was inhaled by the young children."

Other possible explanations for the incident include food poisoning, water pollution, nerve agent, and radio waves, though the most widely accepted explanation is mass hysteria given the lack of evidence for these theories.[331]

PITTSBURGH FURNACE SCARE

Pennsylvania: May 23, 1939

An eerie pillar of light towering into the night skyline prompted "a flood of phone calls to Pittsburgh's newspapers and observatories inquiring if the world was coming to an end…" Authorities explained the strange sight as "the reflection of steel furnace lights on sleet storm clouds in the northern sky."[332]

PLÉDRAN DEMON ATTACKS

Northern Brittany, France: 1881

This outbreak was confined to the seven children of a single family, so it barely qualifies as social behavior. However, the case is interesting in two respects: it illustrates how such maladies, though confined to a family group, can present just the same symptoms as, say, those which affect nuns in a convent; also, how such an ailment can spread within a restricted milieu.

CONTEXT: The Morcet family lived in the Hôtel Morin, a farm in the village of Grand-Hirel, 4 km from Plédran in northern Brittany. A Dr. Baratoux observed: "It must be said that the inhabitants lead a very primitive life, they are ignorant, credulous and naïve. Their chief and indeed only distraction in the winter is the *veillée* [literally, "watching"] where they take turns telling stories of witchcraft and magic. [The same is reported of the outbreak at MORZINE] This explains why, when anything unusual occurs, their easily struck imagination attributes it to occult influence. Needless to say these people are under the almost exclusive domination of the village priest."[333]

The first to be afflicted was Marie-Jeanne, 15. On February 23, she complained of headaches and wished to vomit. The following day she had contractions of the arm over a period of several days. Then followed convulsions and loss of consciousness. These are, of course, classic symptoms of CONVENT HYSTERIA. When the parish priest was called to the farm, he found Marie-Jeanne on the roof. When he asked her to come down, she replied angrily and insultingly.

After two weeks the seizures stopped for a while, apart from headaches and a sense of choking. On April 21, they started up again, and the following day her eleven-year-old brother Pierre suffered a similar attack, which lasted four hours. Twelve days later he had another. After these attacks he remained agitated, nervous, and irritable, breaking anything that came to hand.

On April 23, the second sister, thirteen-year-old Louise, had a seizure just like her sister's. The following day, six-year-old Anne-Marie fainted but without convulsions. She had several further attacks, but they were always milder than her older sisters'. Two days later, four-year-old Toussaint had a contraction of the arm that lasted two days, and he remained very nervous. His eight-year-old brother Jean, working on a nearby farm, became very fatigued and had to stay in bed; from being a well-behaved boy he became quite the contrary, refusing to mind the cows, which was his job.

It was also said that the seven-month old baby, still in its cradle, became very agitated and would have been thrown onto the floor if there had been no one watching. But it was generally felt that this was a normal accident unless the infant had been more than usually agitated or trying to imitate the contortions of its sisters.

During their crises, which happened mostly around 1 p.m., the children would often climb trees, or run down the interior steps of the well of the farm, or onto the low roof of the single-story house where they would perch on the chimneys or dance there while uttering savage cries. Their grimaces, their contortions, their frenzied dances, their irrational irritability, which drove them to insult the parish priest and to throw stones at strangers, all these seemed to be the effects of a demonic attack to the simple-minded locals. In addition they manifested hemianesthesia, hallucinated, and did not seem masters of themselves.

By chance Dr. Baratoux, who was a collaborator with Charcot at La Salpétrière in Paris, happened to be spending his vacation at nearby Saint-Brieuc. Accustomed to observing hysterics in a clinical situation, he took the opportunity to observe them in vivo. Baratoux supplied this detailed description of Marie-Jeanne in one of her seizures:

> Towards one o'clock Marie-Jeanne became extremely excited: her face was animated, her eyes gleaming and injected, she was panting. She pushed away people who came near her, her fingers were continually moving, she pulled nervously on the sleeve of her dress and violently threw her shoes at the horse who was lying nearby. She felt as though there was a ball in her throat and a pain in her stomach. She soon lost consciousness. She was overtaken by circular movements of her upper limbs, then an instant later, a tetanic immobility of her whole body, which lasted a few seconds, then her limbs and body were agitated again with rapid movements, to which succeeded a complete resolution. But almost at once, she had bizarre contortions, rolled on the ground and knelt to grab a sack of corn, under which she hid her head. In vain we tried to maintain her in this state, for she struggled vigorously, agitating her limbs in all directions. It is very difficult to describe these uncoordinated movements, so violently did she move on the floor, so much did she shake her head. She was panting, interrupted by piercing shrieks as she drew breath; at times she would tear her clothing, at other times she would carry her hand to her throat, as though to remove a body which

seemed to be stifling her.

When her convulsive movements diminished, her face, which was covered with saliva, became calmer; she took various poses; sometimes she leant and seemed to be listening to a distant sound, that she told us later was a drum; sometimes she shivered, adopted a frightened air, hid her head under her clothes; she told us she heard a sound of chains being dragged and a salvo of gunfire; she saw the Devil escorted by an army of demons. She called on her father and her grandmother who were dead "I want to go with you." She also thought she saw the sea full of red fish. This is what she told us of the visions which she had seen during her fit which lasted about one quarter of an hour.

But after a moment of repose she went into her fits again. We pressed her left ovary; her attack ceased and soon after the sick girl recovered consciousness, crying profusely. It was now that she recounted her visions; she felt pain in the part of the belly we had pressed, hurling at us a series of insults which witnessed to her displeasure.

Towards the end of this seizure, her sister Louise felt her own coming on, so she took a bowl of water which she poured over her head, which calmed her. The children's parents habitually used this means when they had warning that one or other of their children was about to have an attack.[334]

COMMENT: Thomas de Cauzons, a French historian of witchcraft and religion, observed: "It's hardly surprising that simple peasants should see in these strange phenomena of grand hysteria the influence of the Evil One and the characteristics of demoniacal possession."[335] Baratoux, of course, recognized symptoms similar to those of grand hysteria and Paul Richer, Charcot's colleague, confirmed this, saying, "We could not find a more classic example of the crisis of grand hysteria."[336]

What is noteworthy, in the context of this Encyclopedia, is how the behavior of these peasant children duplicates that of the sophisticated nuns of AUXONNE and LOUDUN, not simply in physical characteristics such as the posture of the body and violent agitations, but also in behavioral patterns such as climbing on roofs and going down wells. Unless conscious imitation was involved, which hardly seems likely, it would seem that these actions are symptomatic of a certain psychological pattern that can manifest either in religious terms or, as in this case, in circumstances where the only religious element is belief in the devil, which in any case could as well be ascribed to folklore as to religious teaching.

POKÉMON ILLNESS

Japan: December 16-17, 1997

More than 12,000 Japanese children reportedly became ill after watching a single episode of a popular animated cartoon, *Pokémon*. Symptoms included convulsions, altered levels of consciousness, headache, breathlessness, nausea, vomiting, blurred vision, and general malaise. While a minuscule fraction of those affected were diagnosed with photosensitive epilepsy, this explanation cannot account for the breadth and pattern of the events. Media coverage of the few initial cases appears to have been instrumental in spreading the symptoms. The characteristic features of this event are consistent with the diagnosis of epidemic hysteric triggered by sudden anxiety after dramatic media reports describing a relatively small number of genuine photosensitive epilepsy seizures.[337]

Pokémon comes from the term "Pocket Monsters," or what the Japanese refer to as *Poketto Monsuta*. It is a popular video game created in 1996 by Satoshi Tajiri. The game's success spawned an array of spinoffs: magazines, trading cards, internet sites, comic books. By 2000, Pokémon-related products were generating more than a billion dollars per year. One of the most popular aspects of Pokémon is a major cartoon by the same name debuting on Japanese television on April 1, 1997. Each of the over 150 different Pokémon cartoon characters has its own unique personality and powers. One of the most popular characters is Pikachu, a friendly yellow mouse with the ability to move with exceptional speed and agility and to disable opponents with electric shocks.

The episode in question was broadcast on Japanese television at 6:30 p.m. on Tuesday, December 16. The particular show was entitled "Dennou Senshi Porigon" or "Computer Warrior Polygon." At the time of the broadcast, the cartoon was extremely popular, with a 15% market share. During the program, Pikachu goes on an adventure inside a computer, accompanied by his companions Satoshi, Kasumi, and Takeshi. Near the 20-minute mark, a battle ensues, forcing Pikachu to use his powers of electricity. Animators depict Pikachu's attack with a sequence of rapidly flashing lights.

Millions of citizens viewed the program, especially children. The show is so popular with children that in Toyohashi, it was estimated that 70 percent of the city's 24,000 elementary students were tuned in.

Twenty-one minutes into the program at 6:51 p.m., Pikachu's "attack" began to send flashes across computer screens. Japan's Fire-Defense agency reported that within 40-minutes of the flashing sequence airing, 618 children had been taken for hospital evaluation with a variety of complaints. The illnesses were headline news across the country during the evening. Several TV stations aired replays of the flash sequence, after which more children reportedly became sick and required medical evaluation.[338]

While the light flashes have been blamed for the symptoms, the same flashes had been used on numerous occasions during animation, without incident. The technique used, *paka-paka*, features different flashing colored lights. Curiously, Japanese animators use the same technique in other cartoons. Examples include *Sailor Moon* and *Speed Racer*. Episode 38 seemed no different than any of the previous shows, including the use of nearly identical *paka-paka*.

Six days after the episode, a team of researchers led by Yushiro Yamashita investigated 80 elementary schools on Kyushu Island. Teachers were prompted to ask their students who had watched the show and if they could recall experiencing symptoms. A series of questionnaires were also mailed to surrounding medical facilities. Just one of 32,083 enrolled students had exhibited convulsions; 1,002 others, or just over six percent of the children, reported "minor symptoms."[339] A separate survey of a dozen hospitals in the same prefecture found that 17 children were treated for convulsions. Of course, this doesn't mean that they had convulsions but only that they were treated for them. The man who headed this investigation, S. Tobimatsu, studied four children who had been affected by *Pokémon* and diagnosed all with photosensitive epilepsy.[340] He and fellow researchers suggested that "the rapid color changes in the cartoon thus provoked the seizures." The researchers believe that the children's sensitivity to color, in particular rapid changes between red and blue, may have played an important role in triggering the seizures.

In their study of the episode, Benjamin Radford and Robert Bartholomew concluded that the vast majority of subjects reporting symptoms exhibited mass hysteria. The anxiety was spread primarily through either the mass media or word of mouth, or seeing a student experience a genuine seizure. Other than the few verified seizure cases, the *Pokémon* incident has several characteristic features of epidemic hysteria such as minor, short-lived symptoms with no organic basis, and near exclusive confinement to persons in early adolescence. There was also the clear presence of anxiety generated from seeing the dramatic media reports describing the first wave of cases. Most of the symptoms were more typical features of mass hysteria outbreaks than of seizures (e.g., headache, lightheadedness, vomiting). Conversely, symptoms such as body stiffness and tongue biting, which are common features of seizures, were conspicuously absent in the *Pokémon* victims.[341]

COMMENT: While a relatively small number of children who exhibited symptoms were actually diagnosed with photosensitive epilepsy, most clearly were not. Photosensitive epilepsy is rare at 1 per 5,000. There are no known previously reported outbreaks of mass illness symptoms in conjunction with viewing television programs. The massive number of children who were reportedly affected, and the rapid onset and recovery of symptoms, are suggestive of anxiety.[342]

POPISH PLOT, THE

Great Britain: 1678-1679

For nearly four centuries after Henry VIII severed England's subservience to the authority of the Pope, the British people nourished fears that the Roman Catholic Church would seek to recapture their allegiance. After the Restoration of the monarchy in 1660, it was widely believed that England was in real danger of a Catholic conspiracy, both from within and from without, that would bring this about. Consequently, when in 1678 informers asserted that a "Popish plot" was actually taking place, wild rumors swept the country and led to extraordinary behavior, often with fatal consequences for innocent victims.[343]

CONTEXT: Though only one Briton in twenty was Catholic, the other nineteen lived in fear of Catholic attempts to force Britain back into the Church's fold. These fears were not groundless. The marriage of Mary Tudor with the Catholic Philip II of Spain had brought about a brutal reversal of Henry's policy: nearly 300 Protestants were burnt at the stake during her brief reign. When her Protestant sister Elizabeth took the throne, she became the target of a series of Catholic schemes – the Ridolfi, Throckmorton, and Babington plots. In 1588, the Spanish Armada was sent with the Pope's blessing to attack England. The discovery of the Gunpowder Plot of 1605, intended to blow up the Houses of Parliament and the government with it, was the occasion for annual celebrations. The Stuart kings were suspected, with good reason, of Catholic sympathies. In 1641, fears of a Catholic uprising were so strong that the militia was called out. Fortunately for England, the civil war did not divide the country along religious lines, as had been the case in France, as the royalist "Cavaliers" included Protestants and Catholics alike. However, there was a sufficient correlation between Royalists and Catholics to make people watchful. When the monarchy was restored in 1660 after a brief flirtation with something like a republican form of government, the hopes of the Catholics rose and the fears of the Protestants also. "So long as the Church of Rome was of a warring disposition, it was vain to expect that the English people would see in it other than an enemy."[344] Charles II, though married to a Catholic, knew on which side his bread was buttered, and staunchly professed himself Protestant, but the populace was nevertheless uneasy, and the informers who triggered the "Popish Plot" in 1678 found a ready audience for their alarming assertions.

On August 12, 1678, Charles II, walking his spaniels in St James' Park near his palace of Whitehall, was informed by a gentleman named Kirkby that a priest named Titus Oates had information about a Catholic conspiracy to murder him and raise rebellion throughout the country. Oates, a 29-year-old priest, had converted to Catholicism the previous year, but explained that this was a contrivance to infiltrate the Jesuits, who were widely seen as the most dangerous conspirators. He claimed to have been employed as a special messenger by the Jesuits, in which capacity he had learned of the conspiracy. He named 99 alleged conspirators, together with their supporters on the Continent; also listed were prominent men who would be killed along with the king.

Oates' personal history was hardly to his credit. A popular ballad of the day called him:

> … an Instrument fit for the Devil,
> Whose mind had been train'd up to all that was evil…
> Though his Tale was ill told, it serv'd to give fire,
> Dispis'd by the Wise, whilst Fools did admire.[345]

His career to date had not been one to inspire confidence – expulsion from school, ejection from university without a degree, and imprisonment for false pretences. His account of his relations with the Jesuits had some slim basis in fact, but was twisted where true, and largely untrue. Thus he styled himself Doctor of Divinity on the strength of a stay in the Jesuit Collegio de los Ingleses at Valladolid in Spain, but though it was true he had entered the College, it was no less true that he had been expelled for scandalous behavior. Nor was the story he had to tell a convincing one. It lacked in substance and proven fact, failed to present a coherent conspiracy, and provided no satisfactory corroborative documentation. It was full of falsities; to name but one, Pope Innocent XI, accused by Oates of approving the plot, was in fact opposed to the Society of Jesus, and it was unthinkable that he would back a Jesuit conspiracy. Only on minds previously conditioned to receive Oates's wild story could such a farrago of nonsense carry any weight.

Charles learned that two men, Pickering and Grove, were watching for an opportunity to shoot him. If no opportunity offered, he would be poisoned by Sir George Wakeman, his wife's physician, with her approval. When no attack took place, the informers explained that one of the assassins had caught a cold. Then, when they were supposed to travel by coach to kill the king at Windsor, an accident is said to have delayed them. Two days later, it was alleged that the two assassins had been out riding and that one had been hurt in the shoulder by his horse. When they had tried to shoot the king in London, the flint of Pickering's pistol was loose, and he dared not fire. On another occasion, he had loaded the pistol with bullets only and forgot the powder. Confronted with such a recital of incompetence, Charles was understandably skeptical, and was to remain so throughout the entire episode, though he was cautious not to take sides too openly when public opinion was so volatile.

On September 6, Oates made a formal deposition, comprising 81 articles, before a magistrate, Sir Edmund Berry Godfrey. On September 28, Oates repeated his story to the Privy Council, with further embellishments, and now the story leaked out to the public. Oates went about the town with a posse of men, arresting some of those he had accused, including Sir George Wakeman, the Queen's Physician, who was accused of plotting to poison the king if the assassins failed in their enterprise.

Three weeks later, on October 17, Godfrey was found dead, strangled and stabbed with his own sword – though not robbed. As a magistrate, he may well have made enemies, and he certainly had some unusual friends. But to this day the identity of his murderers, and the motive for his murder, remains a subject of scholarly debate, though Pollock's theory is perhaps the most plausible: that Godfrey, in taking Oates' testimony, false though it was, had learned facts detrimental to the king's brother (the Catholic Duke of York, later James II) and so endangering his succession, and that he was killed to ensure his silence. At the time, however, it was claimed, and was widely believed, that the killing was part of the Catholic plot. Three men, Green, Berry, and Hill, were accused, convicted on dubious circumstantial evidence and hanged – three of the many innocent people who were to die as a result of the informers' lies.

Godfrey's funeral was made the occasion for a massive popular anti-papal demonstration, clearly orchestrated by persons anxious to stir up public feeling against the Catholics. Souvenir replicas of the fatal dagger were made and sold by an enterprising cutler; ladies carried these about with them and slept with them beneath their pillows. The Countess of Shaftesbury had a set of pocket pistols made, which she carried in her muff lest she be attacked in the street. Dr. Stillingfleet's sermon preached at the funeral was printed and sold 10,000 copies. Godfrey's ghost was said to have appeared above the altar in the Queen's Catholic chapel at Somerset House.

The murder fueled the panic. "Without the mystery of Godfrey's death it is possible that the agitation of the plot would have burnt itself out in the course of a few months. As it was, the fuel was fanned into a blaze of unexampled fierceness, which did not die down until nearly three momentous years in English history had passed."[346] "Hell was let loose," declared the Earl of Peterborough, himself involved in the proceedings, "malice, revenge, and ambition were supported by all that falsehood and perjury could contrive… it was the most deplorable time that was ever seen in England."[347]

Households stocked arms to defend themselves. Posts and chains barricaded the streets of London, with the City Chamberlain, Sir Thomas Player, justifying this act, saying "he did not know but the next morning they might all rise with their throats cut."[348] On October 26, the Commons were warned that another Gunpowder Plot was rumored, and a deputation was at once sent to search the cellars. When, in November, "a noise of knocking and digging" was heard at night in Old Palace Yard, near to the Parliament buildings, there was great alarm. Sir Christopher Wren and other experts inspected the cellars and reported the lower structure of the house to be very vulnerable to attack, containing many secret places where gunpowder could be introduced. Sentinels were set to patrol them day and night. A French Catholic was indeed found to be storing gunpowder in a nearby house, but he turned out to be the official fireworks-maker to the King. Funeral processions were halted and the coffins searched in case they were carrying arms. Locks were changed on the doors of Whitehall palace, the king's residence, and twenty doors leading into St James' Park were blocked in case conspirators had obtained keys.

A general fast day was appointed for November 13. A reward of £20 was offered to any who should discover and apprehend a Catholic priest or Jesuit. Warrants were issued for 26 prominent Catholics named by Oates, including several peers of the realm. Further rewards up to £200 – a sum equivalent to more than £20,000 today – were offered for further information, and numerous new informants appeared as a result. As accusations poured in, the atmosphere of panic grew, and the fact that they contained an admixture of truth encouraged people to believe them in their entirety. The papers of Edward Coleman, a known Catholic sympathizer, were seized, examined, and found to contain inflammatory remarks that could be construed as conspiratorial. He would be hanged on December 3, guilty of little more than foolish ideas. But so high were feelings running that a contemporary commentator, Roger North, observed that "people's passions would not let them attend to any reason or deliberation on the matter... so as one might have denied Christ with more content than the Plot."[349]

Oates's claims were the first of many such revelations, but the others – Bedloe, Prance, Dugdale, and countless lesser individuals – acting independently of one another, told stories which, while they corroborated Oates in general terms, frequently conflicted in detail. Specific details were blatantly wanting. Bedloe said that the King was to be deposed and confined in a convent, while the government would be handed over to some lords appointed by the Pope. In another version, Charles was to be assassinated while walking, as was his custom, at Newmarket.

Though it was common knowledge that Oates and Bedloe had made statements, their specific contents were not made public until April of the following year. The public had only a general notion of the accusations, but all could see from the actions of the government that something serious was afoot – the disarming of Catholics, the arrest of all Catholic priests, all suggested a crisis situation. Roger North recalled:

It was not safe for anyone to show scepticism...What, replied they, don't you believe in the Plot? (As if the Plot were turned into a creed.)... That must be admitted, that the papists ever since the Reformation have had designs by all means possible to bring in their persuasion again, and so have the rest of the sectaries, not one of which are quiet a moment in their Plot to subvert the Church and Monarchy, and to introduce their model in Church and State. But what is all this to Oates? Nay, said they, if you will allow there is a Plot, we will make no doubt but this is it. And this sort was the reasoning at that time even amongst the better sort of people who should know better.[350]

Now Catholics were being suspected, and actually harassed, everywhere. The Queen's Portuguese servants were sent home, and Catherine herself was accused of being a party to the plot, much to Charles's indignation: "I will not see an innocent woman abused." The City of London was patrolled every night by a regiment of the trained bands in arms – 2,500 men in an area of two square miles, and even in daytime passers-by were apt to be challenged. It was suggested in Parliament that those in charge of the city's water supply be screened for papist sympathies, lest they seek to gain their ends by poisoning the water. In November a reckless young goldsmith, William Stayley, a Catholic, while drunk in a pub, was overheard to say the King was a heretic and to speak of killing him. He was found guilty and hanged, drawn, and quartered on November 26.

False rumors abounded. A report came to London that St John's College at Cambridge had been burned down and three priests taken with fireballs in their possession. Some Catholic priests imprisoned there had set Clerkenwell Prison on fire. Wealthy papists were suspected of storing arms in cellars or in underground rooms – the Bishop of Winchester's house alone was said to contain an arsenal of 200 muskets. Somerset House, home of the Catholic queen, was supposedly searched and a hundred thousand fireballs and grenades discovered. Ships were seen standing off the coast – with what purpose could only be surmised. Priests were said to be disembarking with every ship that arrived on English shores, disguised as merchants. Cartloads of arms were being carried about the country.

The most frequent claims were sightings of armed men, on horse or on foot, traveling about the country. Thus at Whitby, Yorkshire, forty horsemen were heard and seen marching in the dead of night. Figures from folklore, these "night riders" were reported all over England. "In Wiltshire they were seen riding north every night between twelve and two, in parties of twenty or thirty men, over the bridges at Hannington, Castle Eaton and Cricklade. On 14 November the House of Lords heard of them in south Yorkshire, and by the 20th they were in Buckinghamshire. The Chancellor told the Commons they had been seen in Gloucestershire...the order was given for regular garrisons throughout England to mount night patrols."[351]

A crucial ingredient of the plot was to be the arrival of foreign troops from Catholic countries, France and Spain, and rumors of such landings abounded – a Spanish force in Ireland, which was still mainly

Catholic, another in Wales, and a French force in Scotland, where many cherished the memory of the Catholic Mary Queen of Scots. Tynemouth Castle in Northumberland was reported blown up by gunpowder, the prelude to a predicted uprising in the northern counties; the arsenal at Hull would be seized, and the weapons handed to ten thousand men from Flanders who would land at Bridlington Bay. Another uprising would take place in the West, Chepstow Castle would become a rebel stronghold, an army of 20-30 thousand Spaniards would land at Milford Haven, and 40 thousand Catholics would be recruited locally. All this at a time when the English standing army was under ten thousand men![352]

In December there seemed to be some reality behind these rumors. A great body of men, both horse and foot, were seen on the Isle of Purbeck on the night of December 9-10 and this was taken to be a French invasion. The local militia went to investigate, but found nothing. Nonetheless the rumor spread to Bristol, where the mayor "in a state of horrible fear" called out the militia. The rumors were denied, but they carried as far north as Yorkshire, where a justice of the peace at Leeds reported:

> On the breaking up of the great Popish Plot the crack and noise filled us with great visions and the apparition of armed men assembled and riding by night, on which strong, strict watches were set, our militia drawn out, all popish houses searched, and all in great rumor and expectation for ten or twelve days; and I, hearing of such rides, made my best enquiries, but could not find one word of truth in any of these reports, nor person nor thing of danger met with, no arms of danger nor ammunition in any popish house.[353]

Any accidental fire was interpreted as the start of another Great Fire of London – which many believed had itself been started by the Papists. These rumors were not altogether without substance, as on April 10, 1879, a house in Fetter Lane belonging to a Mr. Bird was discovered in flames. His servant-girl, Elizabeth Oxley, confessed that "she had been employed to do it by one Stubbs, a Papist, who promised her five pounds" (£500 in today's money). Stubbs admitted this, saying that his confessor, Father Giffard, had put him up to it. Both affirmed that the Papists were imminently expected to make an insurrection, and that an army of sixty thousand men was daily expected from France. In consequence of their ready confession, the Commons pardoned Oxley and Stubbs: "Plainly it was a got-up case, to suit the purposes of the intriguers."[354]

As more and more accusations were made, conflicting with one another, and all devoid of any factual basis, the credibility of the informers gradually crumbled. The attitude of those in authority varied, but one significant comment was that of Lord Halifax, who said that "the Plot must be handled as if it were true, whether it were so or not."[355] Consequently many Catholic priests were arrested and executed, despite the lack of any hard evidence of their guilt.

During the early months of the "plot," the informers were well rewarded. Oates received a generous, albeit fluctuating weekly income plus lavish expenses. For a while he was a privileged creature, popular wherever he appeared, feted in society, and provided with a bodyguard against vengeful Catholics. Bedloe received a generous reward for denouncing Godfrey's alleged murderers. But as the months went by and nothing of any substance materialized, the credibility of the informers gradually deflated.

The turning-point came on June 18, 1679, when Sir George Wakeman, the Queen's physician, was cleared of the charge that he had received £8000, with a further £7000 to follow when the deed was done, to poison the king. Judges who had previously been active in condemning the supposed conspirators also acquitted several other Catholics pointed out by Oates. "The acquittal of all these was the first clear token that juries were becoming disgusted with the Sham-Plot prosecutions and butcheries."

The acquittal was very unpopular. The public had been worked up into a frenzy of anti-Catholic feeling, and they wanted to see tangible signs of the conspiracy. But the verdict turned the tide. A ballad of the day had Oates confessing:

> I swore that the Queen would poyson the King,
> That Wakeman had moneys the Poyson to bring,
> When I knew in my Heart there was no such thing.
> I now must be pillori'd, and after be hang'd.[356]

In 1684 Oates was arrested and put on trial. The Solicitor-General, Heneage Finch, said:

> Gentlemen, when we consider the circumstances of this case now, I do verily think it will appear to be a very strange and wonderful thing to us, that ever any man should have believed him. And it is a strange

consideration to reflect upon, to think what credit he had at that time. But withal consider, gentlemen, could anyone imagine that it were possible for any man on earth to become so impudent, as to dare expose himself before the high court of Parliament, the great courts of justice, and there tell a most infamous lie for the taking away of lives of men? The greatness of the attempt was a great inducement to the belief of it, because no man could be presumed to dare the doing of such a thing, if he had not had a foundation of truth to build upon.[357]

Oates was unfrocked, fined, condemned to the pillory, whipped, and imprisoned for life. These were severe punishments, he was not expected to survive the flogging, and indeed it was widely believed that the intention was that he should not survive. But survive he did. He was not hanged but imprisoned, and in time, after the accession of William III, he was actually pardoned, and lived till 1705.

The controversy, as to how much reality, if any, there had been in the accusations of a popish plot, continued to foment controversy, until with cool hindsight men came to their senses and it came to be generally admitted that the Popish Plot had been a fabrication from start to finish.

COMMENTS: The panic produced by the accusations of Oates and others did not spread directly to the populace. It came via the authorities, whose reticence in not revealing the conspiracy charges only alarmed the ordinary people and allowed rumors to spread. With some justification, it can be said that the authorities themselves were greatly perplexed as to the credibility of the stories they were told. "Told nothing except the fact that there had been a conspiracy against the king's life, the people can be forgiven for thinking, first, that it was entirely proved, and second, that it was much more serious than it was."[358] The motives of Oates and the other informers seem to have been solely of personal advancement; none seems to have acted from any kind of political or religious incentive, whatever their personal beliefs may have been. Since there was no real foundation for any of their accusations, they were deliberately lying – it was not a question of misinterpretation, but the manufacture of mischievous lies. This self-aggrandizing opportunism is exemplified in the case of one of the minor informers, a Welshman named John Arnold, a notorious anti-papist, who claimed to have been attacked off Fleet Street, London, by Catholics. The evidence is clear that the attack was staged, and that the wounds, though severe, were actually self-inflicted, with Arnold hoping to emerge as a popular victim.

Echo In America

What has been described as "a frontier skirmish of England's wider war"[359] occurred across the Atlantic in England's American colony of Maryland. Although a "Popish plot" was the focus of the trouble, the motives were more overtly political and economic than religious. Whereas in England, what was feared was a return to submission to governance from Rome, the dissenters of Maryland were concerned with the realities of having to live under Catholic dominance.

Maryland was the first American state to achieve religious tolerance, yet by the 1670s it was dominated by a Catholic governor, Lord Baltimore, who ran the state virtually as his own fiefdom, placing his own appointees in virtually every high office. The Protestants, with some reason, felt oppressed, and in a series of rebellions of increasing violence from September 1676 through March 1689, they sought to remedy matters, until with the outing of the Stuarts in England, they asserted themselves to such an extent that throughout the remainder of the colonial era Maryland was firmly supportive of the Church of England and it was the Catholics who were harassed.

What distinguished these rebellions, from the viewpoint of this Encyclopedia, were the exaggerated fears of the Protestant settlers, who became convinced that the Catholics were intent on eradicating them altogether. It was rumored that the priests would earn a bounty of £5 sterling for every Protestant they converted to Rome, with the ultimate intention "to propagate the Pope's interest and supremacy in America." But if the Protestants would not yield to persuasion, they would simply be eradicated. The government was said to be encouraging [Catholic] Irish settlers to settle in Maryland, the vanguard of an Irish army who, it was intended, would in time cut the Protestants' throats. To this end, the governor and his Catholic Council were said to be forming an alliance with French Canadians – predominantly Catholic – and Native American tribes hired for the purpose, who between them would slaughter the Protestant community. Rumors proliferated of Seneca warriors and

Canadian troops moving into Maryland in the thousands, and a [Catholic] Councilman was said to have expressed the hope that before Easter Day he would wash his hands in the Protestants' blood. June 1681, when Native Americans at Point Lookout murdered several settlers, was perceived as the beginning of the massacre. The rumor even spread that the killers were not natives at all, but "People of their own Physiognomy or complexion dressed up in Indian habit."

Though all these rumors proved false, so widely were they believed that they re-surfaced time and again, until in the end the Protestant settlers were sufficiently aroused to raise an army from amongst themselves, who would ultimately overthrow the existing establishment.

As in England, so in America: the rumors and conspiracy theories reflected the deep concern of the people, that their cherished independence was threatened by "England's national foe – which was always Rome, no matter what particular national intermediary (Spain, France) it happened to be working through at a given time." Both in England and in America, a very real fear led to exaggerated fears, wild rumors, and extraordinary behavior.

See also: CATHOLIC SCARE.

PORTUGUESE MARTIAN INVASION PANICS

Portugal: 1988 and 1998

On Sunday October 30, 1988, Radio Braga in northern Portugal caused hundreds of residents to become frightened after airing a drama about invading Martians. Intended as a tribute to the original 1938 *War of the Worlds* broadcast on its 50th anniversary, it inspired hundreds to inundate police and fire agencies with telephone inquiries. While some got into their motor vehicles and sped away from the area, others actually headed toward the landing site near the town of Braga.[360]

On Friday morning October 30, 1998, Antena 3 (a subsidiary of Portuguese National Radio) in Lisbon, Portugal, aired a radio drama about invading Martians, triggering a regional panic. Broadcast in commemoration of the sixtieth anniversary of the infamous 1938 production by Orson Welles, which triggered panic in the United States, the modified version of the Welles script (translated into Portuguese) was highly realistic. Hundreds of anxious residents deluged the radio station with phone calls. Some left work, while others felt sick in response to the news. While an announcer cautioned listeners at 7 a.m. that the drama would start in an hour, many did not hear the announcement. The play began with the report of a UFO landing in the town of Palmela, 21 miles south of Lisbon, followed by a series of news bulletins describing Martians heading toward Lisbon after destroying military units sent to stop them.[361]

See also: ORSON WELLES MARTIAN PANIC, MARTIAN INVASION SCARE, CHILEAN MARTIAN INVASION PANIC, ECUADOR MARTIAN INVASION PANIC, BUFFALO MARTIAN INVASION SCARE, RHODE ISLAND MARTIAN INVASION PANIC.

POSSESSION

Possession is supposed to occur when an individual is "invaded" by a "personality" not his or her own: either that of another human, living or dead, or by a non-human entity such as a demon, or even by an animal. The circumstantial evidence that such events ostensibly occur is very abundant, but conclusive evidence is lacking, and there are several alternative explanations for what may be happening. Possession is a part of many belief-systems and has been institutionalized into several religious practices such as voodoo. It is also relevant to concepts such as reincarnation, where a living person – usually a child – seems to be possessed by a dead person; to multiple personality, where some of the patient's alter personalities are not, as is generally the case, internally co-existing personalities, but said to be invading personalities from outside the patient; and to spirit mediumship in which the medium is ostensibly possessed on a temporary basis by a "control" and/or the spirit of a dead person.

Possession is, by definition, an ALTERED STATE OF CONSCIOUSNESS, which may be entered voluntarily or which may overtake the individual without his realizing what is happening. A person can believe himself possessed, or others can diagnose him as being possessed. It is something that mostly happens to individuals, and so most forms of possession fall outside the scope of this Encyclopedia. However, there are some forms that do have a social dimension:

Epidemic possession occurs when a number of people become persuaded that they are possessed, either as a cultural group or as a community. For example, the *mpepo* sickness would periodically afflict certain tribal communities in East Africa:

> The malady breaks out in epidemic form, descends upon whole regions, and even spreads from the coast into the interior... This malady particularly affects women, and is considered as a noble and distinguished affliction... After the arrival of the "spirit," the people speak of *mpepo ya mzuka*, possession by the vampire, *ya-ijeni* by a kind of spirit related to the mzuka, *ya Msuaheli*, by the male of the Swaheli, *ya Mringa*, by the Masai, *ya Msungu*, by the Europeans, and also *ya nkoma*, generally by the spirit of a dead person.[362]

The more notable cases of epidemic possession are dealt with separately in this Encyclopedia: see HYSTERIA, MASS HYSTERIA IN SCHOOLS, MASS HYSTERIA IN JOB SETTINGS, MASS MOTOR HYSTERIA, THEORIES OF MASS HYSTERIA, THE GHOST DANCE, UGANDAN RUNNING SICKNESS, LAUGHING EPIDEMICS, DANCING MANIA, DANCE FRENZIES IN JAPAN, FORCED MARRIAGE SYNDROME.

Trance possession as a religious practice. Voodoo is the best known of many belief systems in which voluntary possession by deities is common practice.[363] In some religions, possession is open to all members of the community; in others it is restricted to an elite. Thus in many cultures a shaman claims to be possessed by divine entities in order to act as an intermediary between the gods and his own people. During the Native North American Ghost Dance of the late 19th century, some dancers stood motionless for several hours while in trance states. Sociologist David Miller reports that upon awakening, dancers gave descriptions of having visited the "Happy Hunting Ground" where they conversed with their ancestors. Some dancers gave accounts of a dawning utopian world.[364]

Writing about possession trance in sub-Saharan Africa, Greenbaum noted:

> Possession trance may be an individual or a group phenomenon. It may be induced by drugs, music, or other methods external to the individual, or it may be a spontaneous manifestation by the person possessed. It may be a phenomenon restricted to a particular status or role (for example, a diviner, medium, priest) or it may occur at random in the society. In all cases, however, the phenomenon is accepted within the society as a trance induced by a spirit entering the person possessed, and not as an individual psychological aberration....
>
> During this "possession" by a spirit other than his own, the person is in an altered state of consciousness, evidenced by one or more of the following: talking and acting like the inhabiting spirit, lapsing into a coma-like state, speaking unintelligibly, exhibiting physical symptoms such as twitching, wild dancing, frothing at the mouth, and so on. Upon regaining his original identity, the person generally retains no conscious memory of the activity of the spirit.[365]

Such behavior is common practice in some religions, and as such does not qualify as "extraordinary" for the purpose of this Encyclopedia. But the similarity to other forms of behavior is significant, providing further evidence that – irrespective of whether he or she is truly possessed or simply deluded into thinking so – when in an altered state a person can transcend his normal waking potential.

Possession by demons. Involuntary possession by malevolent demons is far more prevalent than possession by benevolent entities. It is the most widespread form of possession and is known to have occurred in virtually every culture throughout human history. Traugott Konstantin Oesterreich has shown that possession, though it takes many forms, remains remarkably similar wherever it occurs and whatever the beliefs held by the community.[366] See entries DEMON POSSESSION and CONVENT HYSTERIA.

Despite its long history and widespread prevalence, the evidence that possession takes place is far from conclusive. The alternative explanation of choice is dissociation in the form of role-playing: the individual unconsciously assumes the characteristics of the possessing entity or person. Such an explanation is not difficult to accept in the case of a religious practice such as voodoo, where the subject assumes the general characteristics of a deity, or demon possession where the supposed characteristics of demons are a matter of popular folklore and easily simulated. There have been, however, individual cases where familiarity with the possessing person is so detailed, not simply in matters of fact but also in characteristics of behavior, speech, and attitude, that there seems to be no way in which it could have been acquired by any normal means.

PRESIDENT JOHNSON "CULT"

Papua New Guinea: latter 20th Century

In 1964, tiny New Hanover Island (population 7,000), in Australian-controlled Papua New Guinea, made worldwide headlines with news reports of a fantastic story involving then United States President Lyndon Baines Johnson. According to press accounts, government officials were arresting members of the so-called President Johnson cult for refusing to pay taxes. What they were really doing is collecting the money in order to entice United States President Lyndon Johnson to come to the island and rule it.[367] During the February election about 3,500 inhabitants refused to vote for any of the candidates on the ballot and instead wrote in "Johnson of America."[368]

CONTEXT: The Johnson cult emerged during a time of political unrest and dissatisfaction with the ruling Australian administrators of New Hanover. From a historical perspective, it appeared within a decade of several natives having a positive and memorable encounter with a team of U.S. Army surveyors who reportedly were generous, sharing their food and other items. From a cultural standpoint, it may reflect the islander's sophisticated system of gamesmanship.

Shortly after the election, about $1,000 had been collected for Johnson's travel expenses.[369] By November, when Johnson had still not come to the island, the natives pledged to exercise patience as they knew that Johnson was very busy and preoccupied with the Vietnam war. Near the end of 1964, Australian officials attempted to intimidate "tax defaulters" into paying their taxes, and native police were dispatched to New Hanover. In a show of strength, "a coconut was shot off a tree; a smoke bomb was tossed on the beach and a young boy sent to stand in the smoke; one fleeing native was shot and wounded, though not seriously."[370] When several hundred natives continued to defy the Local Government Council, they were jailed. Similar jailings took place in 1965 and 1966, diminishing in number over time.

On the surface, the episode seems to be a classic example of irrational, backward thinking in a "primitive" culture, naively misunderstanding the political dynamics of Western society. This is certainly the way the Johnson cult has been portrayed in the Western mass media. The reports captured the attention of anthropologist Dorothy Billings who has conducted fieldwork on the island and visited numerous times beginning in February 1967. Billings contends that the episode was an illustration of a complex native symbol system, and that the affair was actually a form of political performance intended to embarrass the Australian government, which ruled over the island and eastern Papua New Guinea until 1974.[371] "What made me understand that this was street theater was that when (locals) told me about buying LBJ they would laugh ... [knowing] the Australians would be embarrassed. It was a way of expressing a demand. People who resist oppression are often thought to be crazy."[372]

The episode corresponded with the beginnings of a separatist movement across the region as natives began voicing their desire for independence from Australian control of Papua New Guinea. During an early phase of the independence movement, a national House of Assembly was created, and on New Hanover many locals tried to elect Johnson. When Australian officials told natives that Johnson was not a candidate, some collected money for Johnson's plane ticket.[373]

Billings observes that the New Hanover natives have a complex system of game-playing and the Johnson cult appears to have been enjoyed by the natives

Anthropologist Dorothy Billings with Walla Gukguk, head of the Tutukuval Isukal Association, successor to the "President Johnson Cult."

as a test of wits. The one exception was the jailings, which were not part of the game. Billings notes that the New Hanoverians "enjoy dramatic quarrels both as participants and as spectators."[374] Even though participants may win or lose, the act of playing "implies a kind of equality and intimacy between the parties. A display of anger seems to promote intimacy ... [and] New Hanoverians seem to feel that you cannot trust a person until you have seen his anger – then you know him and are at ease. Provoking a quarrel is also a way of gaining attention."[375]

COMMENTS: Similar systems of complex performance and political theatre have been reported elsewhere in the Pacific. In other parts of Papua New Guinea, in the Highlands, natives will occasionally appear mentally disturbed to outsiders, engaging in such behaviors as pseudo-aggression, bluffing, and play-acting (so-called "WILD MAN" behavior),[376] and have been labeled as psychological disorders by outsiders unfamiliar with the conduct code.[377] Sociologist Robert Bartholomew describes a similar ritual in that region in Malayo-Indonesia called *latah*.[378]

> One form of "wild man" acting known as *negi-negi* among the Guramumba, has been interpreted as theatre.[379] The "wild man" often brandishes a weapon and appears to enter a state of uncontrollable rage against people and property. When he "regains his senses," claims of amnesia and spirit possession deflect the attribution of blame. Those affected are typically young males who are socially and/or politically weak, grow impatient and feel aggrieved by excessive dowry stipulations from relatives of the betrothed. Performances allow for a re-negotiation of marriage compensation terms, explaining the "disproportion between the injury threatened and actually inflicted,"[380] and why natives appear composed and casual during episodes. Hence, Anthropologist Marie Reay observes that among the Kuma, "wild man" episodes never result in death or serious injury, despite threatening behavior.[381] P.L. Newman states that people come from nearby villages just to watch the spectacle, and while "spectators are prone to keep their distance because of the potential danger," they "obviously enjoy the instances when the wild man turns on the group and chases one after another of them in erratic, and seemingly comic pursuit...the community can be regarded as an audience to a performance."[382]

There are numerous examples of anthropologists mistranslating eccentric conduct codes or simply being deliberately fooled by their subjects. New Zealand anthropologist Derek Freeman later challenged the accuracy of Margaret Mead's classic, *Coming of Age in Samoa*, contending that she had been duped by her female subjects who fed her false tales about their sex lives.[383]

PROFANITY AND BLASPHEMY

A good many entries in this Encyclopedia involve behaviors of which profanity is a conspicuous feature. This is notably true of DEMON POSSESSION and CONVENT HYSTERIA and similar incidents in which Demon Possession was diagnosed. Time and again we are told of possessed nuns such as Suor Costante Maria (1670-1726), an Italian stigmatic, who "wanted to say Office properly, but for more than a month together her lips could only frame profanities and curses."[384]

When such outbursts of profanity occurred in a religious context, it was attributed to the Evil One, since it was unthinkable that a nun would utter such horrors. From demons, on the contrary, they were to be expected. But the Devil could possess lay people, too. The afflicted women of MORZINE, in the 1850s, assailed the visiting archbishop with curses, blaming him for their state.

The blasphemies were frequently accompanied with obscenity. This was particularly true of outbreaks in a religious setting. It is significant that neither at Morzine nor at VERZEGNIS, where the victims were secular, was there any sign of erotomania. By contrast, obscenity almost always accompanied profanity in cases of convent hysteria. When the sisters at AUXONNE were afflicted in 1662, their wild accusations against the innocent Buvée included all kinds of sexual acts, some performed with the male confessors, others with the sisters, and yet others with demons. Not only was she said to perform the sexual act with two apostate priests, but they added sacrilege to impurity by placing consecrated hosts in her vagina. She was accused of misbehavior with other sisters – impure kisses and touching, and mutual masturbation. One of them, Sister Marguerite, was assailed by demons that tried to rape her with batons of rolled linen. Sister Françoise Borthon confessed that she had been raped by a demon. When she became pregnant, however, the demons aborted the birth to save her honor. Needless to say, there was no substantive evidence for any of this, but there was no doubt that the moral state of the convent was less than ideal, and some minor naughtiness may have been at the bottom of the accusations.

For the rest, they can reasonably be ascribed to wishful fantasy on the part of the cloistered sisters. It is important to bear in mind that these were often young women in their 20s or even younger. During their seizures, when they were supposedly possessed by demons, they were "authorized" to indulge in role-playing, releasing their pent-up natural urges while avoiding responsibility for their words or actions. Many of the sisters had been constrained to the monastic life not through any pious vocation but because marriage was for one reason or another barred to them. Under such conditions it is not surprising if they were troubled by erotic fantasies leading to solitary or mutual lesbian practices. Nor is it surprising that when they were afflicted with hysterical trances in which they were speaking as demons, they dropped all inhibitions and gave full rein to their frustrated urgings.[385]

This was notably the case at LOUDUN in 1632, where the oldest of the afflicted sisters was only 36, the youngest 18. Most were in their twenties, and the prioress herself was only 25 when she took office. Their passionate lusting after Grandier, which turned to hatred when it was thwarted, was evidence enough that they were afflicted with something approaching erotomania. Under exorcism they shocked the spectators with their obscene body movements and utterances: masturbation with a crucifix was a manifestation here as it was also at LOUVIERS in 1642.[386] There, one of the sisters' accusations was that Father David, their spiritual director, preached in the nude, and encouraged the nuns to strip in order to emulate the innocent state of Adam and Eve before they ate the apple. They even claimed that he encouraged them to mutually masturbate. Whether there was any foundation for these accusations, or whether it was simply lustful wishing, is impossible to establish, but in any case, what is significant is that the nuns were prepared to make this kind of accusation in public.[387]

Bechterev observed similar behavior in Russia, referring to the KLIKOUSCHESTVO sect (1861) in particular and to this type of popular movement in general.[388] Wherever it occurs, there can be no doubt that the underlying motivation is defiance of authority. Supporting this is the observation that it is frequently accompanied by disrespectful FAMILIARITY, for instance employing the familiar *tu* instead of the polite *vous*, a trait that also manifested among the children in the SWEDISH PREACHING EPIDEMIC and at Morzine.

Nowhere is this anti-authority motivation seen more clearly than in the LANDES outbreak (1732), where the afflicted girls of the Laupartie household, believing themselves possessed by demons, combined the utterance of every kind of blasphemy and obscenity with a virulent antagonism to their parents:

> They frequently and suddenly display an aversion and an inconceivable hatred towards God, and particularly against the holy sacrament… You would need to see it to credit the extent of their hatred and spite against their fathers and mothers. Often they can't bear to see them or speak to them: they refuse to use the terms 'father' and 'mother,' for which they substitute the most injurious and spiteful terms. There is no insult they have not applied to their parents, no evil they have not wished on them. They do everything in their power to cause them distress and irritation. They even urge the servants to behave in the same way.[389]

See also: RUNNING AND CLIMBING.

PSYCHOSOMATIC ILLNESS

Although illnesses by definition affect individuals, it is a matter of common observation that certain ailments occur from time to time in a widespread manner. That this should be true of epidemic diseases, spread by infection or contagion, is to be expected, but the same is true of other ailments that are pseudo-diseases, resulting from erroneous diagnosis by doctors and/or erroneous self-diagnosis by those who suppose themselves to be afflicted. Edward Shorter, who has chronicled the history of psychosomatic illness in the modern era, sees it above all as a cultural phenomenon operating in a cyclical manner.[390] A doctor offers his own diagnosis of his patient's trouble, other doctors concur and diagnose their patients in the same way, and soon the patients themselves present with symptoms appropriate to the supposed ailment. These may include loss of hearing or sight, paralysis, hypersensitivity etc., where it is often difficult to distinguish the pseudo-condition from a genuine organic illness. In this way, a succession of pseudo-illnesses makes their appearance, flourish for a while, then fade away. Examples have included Spinal Irritation. Reflex theory,

Neurasthenia, and Chronic Fatigue Syndrome.

Psychosomatic illness is relevant to this Encyclopedia because many extraordinary behaviors seem to manifest in the same way as individual illnesses; that is, the perception of the ailment leads to a conviction that there is something organically wrong, whereas this is not the case. Such ailments are often culturally defined; *latah* and PIBLOKTOQ are clear examples, and Shorter provides another example, that of *susto*, experienced by Mexicans as a reaction to fright. "Suddenly alarmed, they might experience nausea, stomach cramps, and difficulty in breathing…These extreme psychophysiological reactions are said to lead even to death. For Mexicans the symptoms make sense as an expression of the breakdown of one's internal strength, or *consistencia*. If one's *consistencia* has crumbled, naturally one will be vulnerable."[391]

COMMENT: In Shorter's view, "the process of becoming ill without being organically sick occurs as an interaction between the genetically driven brain and the socially conditioned mind."[392] That is to say, the disposition to become a victim of a psychosomatic ailment may exist within the individual as an underlying genetic influence, but the form it will take depends on the prevailing circumstances and the cultural context.

The ability of the subconscious mind to create ostensibly physical symptoms has long been recognized, and there are many examples in this Encyclopedia, like the symptoms supposed to be of DEMON POSSESSION, which were widespread in Western Europe during the 16th and 17th centuries, and which enjoyed a somewhat surprising revival in 20th century America in the context of fundamental Christianity. The fact that the victims presented the same symptoms in almost every case confirmed, in the view of authorities, that their affliction was authentic.

PURITANISM

Puritanism in its broadest sense is much the same as fundamentalism – a return to the perceived purity of the primitive Christian church, before it was corrupted by priestcraft and theology. In this sense, several communities described in this Encyclopedia manifest puritan principles, notably the RUSSIAN SECTS, the ADAMITES, and ANABAPTISTS.

However, the term is more particularly used to define those sects in Britain that sought the same ideal (and later carried it to the Americas). Though this Puritanism itself was only occasionally responsible for the kind of extraordinary behavior described in this Encyclopedia, it led to a great many sectarian movements whose members tended towards extreme beliefs and behavior, which were liable to be denounced as ENTHUSIASM EPISODES.

The Puritan movement reached its high point during the years of the Commonwealth, when England briefly managed to free itself from monarchist government. The context is well summed up by George Godwin:

> The Puritans considered that the work of reformation had not been carried out with sufficient enthusiasm and thoroughness; that the reformed Church still had a popish taint. Believing that the reformed Church still bore many marks of its former affiliation, they pressed for far more drastic changes. In particular, the party disliked the Church's hierarchy, the use of ceremonial, prescript prayer, and the loss of a simplicity believed to have been characteristic of the Christianity of the first century, a return to which was desired. Ritual and ceremonial, fine music, a sonorous liturgy, and the "vain repetitions" of the ordered service: all these they opposed, asking in their place plain services, long sermons, extemporaneous prayer.[393]

Under the Commonwealth, freedom of conscience was in principle extended to all. When, as inevitably happened, some sects interpreted this as permitting any kind of behavior, the authorities felt constrained to act against them, though rather in the name of disturbing public order than for their beliefs as such. The fondness of many sectarians for wandering around the country proclaiming their beliefs was offensive in itself, the more so when the preachers wore only sackcloth and ashes or, as tended sometimes to be the case with the QUAKERS, nothing at all.

For a decade after the execution of Charles I, Puritans ruled England, but the reasons that took them to power were political rather than religious. Theirs was by no means a religious coup purposed at creating a theocracy, though this was what many of them wished. Extremists were not encouraged, and those who counted on a sympathetic ear from Cromwell's government were disappointed.

Reestablished in the American colonies, however,

Puritans for the first time had the upper hand. Here, fleeing from persecution in Europe, they in their turn sought to impose their views on any that happened to interpret God's word differently than themselves.[394] This intransigence led to the tradition of fundamentalism in American religion, which found expression in the episodes of AMERICAN REVIVALISM.

Puritanism is popularly associated with intolerance and a holier-than-thou attitude. The historian Thomas Babington Macaulay commented: "The Puritan hated bear-baiting, not because it gave pain to the bear, but because it gave pleasure to the spectators."[395] The 17th century Puritan Richard Baxter told how his father had been dubbed a Puritan because he preferred to spend his Sundays at home reading the Bible rather than dancing round the maypole as was the village custom.[396]

Puritans tend to be remembered for their exaggerated attitudes, which could lead to such absurdities as hanging a cat for killing a mouse on the Sabbath Day. Generally speaking, however, apart from the references above, the views of the Puritans did not lead them to extraordinary behavior.

Sources

1. Lea, Henry Charles (1957). *Materials Toward a History of Witchcraft*, Volume 3. New York: Yoseloff, p. 1040.
2. Modan, Baruch, Tirosh, Moshe, Weissenberg, Emil, Acker, Cilla, Swartz, T.A., Coston, Corina, Donagi, Alexander, Revach, Moshe, and Vettorazzi, Gaston (1983). "The Arjenyattah Epidemic." *The Lancet* ii:1472-1474.
3. Hafez, A. (1985). "The Role of the Press and the Medical Community in an Epidemic of Mysterious Gas Poisoning in the Jordan West Bank." *American Journal of Psychiatry* 142:833-837. See pp. 834-835.
4. Modan et al., op cit., pp. 1472.
5. Modan et al., op cit., p. 1472.
6. Hafez, op cit., p. 834.
7. Hafez, op cit., p. 834.
8. Modan et al., op cit., pp. 1472-1473.
9. Modan et al., (1983), op cit., p. 1472.
10. Hafez, op cit., p. 834.
11. Hafez, op cit., p. 834.
12. Hafez, op cit., p. 834.
13. Hafez, op cit., p. 834.
14. Modan et al., op cit., pp. 1472-1473.
15. Modan et al., op cit., p. 1473.
16. Modan et al., op cit.
17. Report issued by the United Nations Educational Scientific and Cultural Organization (UNESCO) Executive Board, June 13, 1983 (116th Session) 116 EX/16 Add., Paris, 9 June 1983, Item 5.1.5 of the agenda: "Implementation of 21 C/Resolution 14.1 Concerning Educational And Cultural Institutions in the Occupied Arab Territories: Report of the Director-General: http://domino.un.org/UNISPAL.NSF/0/1198eaeac7114c0585256970005642d8?OpenDocument.
18. Report issued by the United Nations Educational Scientific and Cultural Organization (UNESCO) Executive Board, June 13, 1983, op cit.
19. Landrigan, Philip J., and Miller, Bess (1983). "The Arjenyattah Epidemic: Home Interview Data and Toxicological Aspects." *The Lancet* ii: 1474-1476. See p. 1475.
20. Landrigan et al., op cit., p. 1474.
21. Landrigan et al., op cit., p. 1475.
22. Landrigan et al., op cit., p. 1475.
23. Israeli, Raphael (2002). "Poison: The Use of Blood Libel in The War Against Israel." *Jerusalem Letter* (Number 476), April 15, 2002, p. 2 of 6, accessed at http://www.jcpa.org/jl/vp476.htm.
24. Israeli, op cit., p. 4 of 6.
25. Hafez, op cit., p. 836.
26. Hafez, op cit., p. 837.
27. For example: Goodman, Felicitas D. (1981). *The Exorcism of Anneliese Michel.* Garden City NY: Doubleday.
28. For example, Bouflet, Joachim (1999). *Medjugorje, ou la Fabrication du Surnaturel.* Paris: Salvator.
29. Bartholomew, Robert E. (2000). *Exotic Deviance: Medicalizing Cultural Idioms–From Strangeness to Illness.* Boulder, CO: University of Colorado Press.
30. Philen, R.M., Kilbourn, E.M., and McKinley, T.W. (1989). "Mass Sociogenic Illness by Proxy: Parentally Reported in an Elementary School." *The Lancet* ii:1372-1376.
31. Philen et al., p. 1372.
32. Philen et al., p. 1373.
33. Philen et al., p. 1375.
34. Philen et al., p. 1372.
35. Buckhout, R. (1974). "Eyewitness testimony." *Scientific American* 231:23-31.
36. Borchard, E.M. (1932). *Convicting the Innocent: Errors of Criminal Justice.* New Haven, CT: Yale University Press; Loftus, E. (1979). *Eyewitness Testimony.* Cambridge, MA: Harvard University Press; Buckhout, R. (1980). "Nearly 2000 witnesses can be wrong," *Bulletin of the Psychonomic Society* 16:307-310; Wells, G., & Turtle, J. (1986). "Eyewitness identification: The importance of lineup models," *Psychological Bulletin* 99:320-329; Ross, D.F., Read, J.D., & Toglia, M.P. (1994). *Adult Eyewitness Testimony: Current Trends and Developments.* Cambridge: Cambridge University Press.
37. Markush, R.E. (1973). "Mental epidemics: a review of the old to prepare for the new." *Public Health Reviews* 4:353-442.
38. Ward, Philip (1980). *A Dictionary of Common Fallacies.* Cambridge, UK: The Oleander Press, p. 97.
39. Klass, P. (1976). *UFOs – Explained.* NY: Random House, pp. 14-15.
40. Bullard, T. (1982). op. cit., pp. 10-11.
41. Massad, C.M., Hubbard, M., & Newston, D. (1979). "Selective perception of events." *Journal of Experimental Social Psychology* 15:513-532
42. Sherif, M. (1936). *The Psychology of Social Norms.* NY: Harper & Row.
43. Beeson, R. (1979). "The improbable primate and the modern myth." pp. 166-195. In G. Krantz & R. Sprague (eds.), *The Scientist Looks at the Sasquatch II.* Moscow, Idaho: University Press of Idaho, p. 180.
44. *Wellington Dominion*, May 8, 1909, p. 5.

45. Gibbs-Smith, C. (1985). op. cit., 1985, pp. 145-146.
46. The following headline typified press reaction: "Military airship preferred to dreadnoughts... A remarkable agitation is going on in Germany to build a huge aerial fleet, instead of many dreadnoughts," *Wellington Dominion*, May 19, 1909, p. 7.
47. Clute, J. (1995). *Science Fiction: The Illustrated Encyclopedia*. New York: Dorling Kindersley, pp. 44-45.
48. It is notable that just prior to and encompassing the New Zealand sightings, a spate of phantom airships, typically described as Zeppelins, were observed across England, accounts of which appeared widely in the dominion press. See "Airships and scareships," *Evening Star*, July 7, 1909, and numerous other New Zealand newspapers. The following is an excerpt from this account: "The people who are always discovering German spies in England disguised as waiters or tourists have found a new occupation of apparently absorbing interest. They are writing to the papers to report having seen mysterious airships making midnight voyages over various parts of England. The ghostly vessels have been seen at spots as distant from each other as Belfast and East Ham, but the most numerous reports are from the eastern counties. The 'Daily Express' is full of dark tales of a long, cigar-shaped craft dimly visible through the night air, passing overhead with a whirring noise. Those watchers who are particularly lucky espy searchlights and hear 'foreign sounding' voices." For similar accounts in the New Zealand press, see "Mysterious airships," *Timaru Herald*, July 23, 1909; "Real scareship," *Timaru Herald*, August 14, 1909.
49. *Otago Daily Times*, July 16, 1909, p. 10; "A mysterious light. Was it an airship? Excitement in the south," *The New Zealand Herald*, July 27, 1909.
50. The following account appeared in the *Evening Star*, July 27, 1909. "The explanation that is finding favor with those who have put two and two together is that the fact that German vessels are in New Zealand waters is responsible for it. They aver that the German Government yacht Seestern, for which the German warship Condor, which left Auckland on Sunday, is "supposed" to search for (the Seestern being said to be considerably overdue at the Island from Brisbane), is, they state, in reality off the New Zealand coast. They are not backward in advancing the theory that the Seestern set the airship free somewhere in the neighborhood of the Nuggets, where it was first observed. ...A thorough elucidation of the whole mystery is awaited with keen interest." For similar discussions of the German origin of the mysterious lights, refer to: "The 'German' theory," *Evening Star*, July 29, 1909; "The German scare," *Timaru Post*, July 28, 1909; "Airship mysteries," *The New Zealand Herald*, July 27, 1909.
51. Brunt, A. (1975). "The New Zealand UFO wave of 1909." *Xenolog*, Number 101, p. 2.
52. "The airship mystery. Stories of mysterious lights," *Otago Witness*, August 4, 1909.
53. "The mysterious lights. Seen in widely separated districts," *Otago Daily Times*, July 30, 1909.
54. "Searching at Kelso," *Evening Star*, July 29, 1909.
55. Bartholomew, Robert E. (1998). "The Great New Zealand Zeppelin Scare of 1909." *New Zealand Skeptic* 47(Autumn): 1, 3-5.
56. *Clutha Leader*, July 27, 1909.
57. *Clutha Leader*, July 27, 1909.
58. "Two miners see the 'ship,'" *Dominion*, July 31, 1909; "Airship seen by two dredge hands. At close quarters. Two persons on board," *Evening Star*, July 30, 1909; "Close view of the craft," *The Auckland Star*, July 31, 1909. The time and location of this sighting suggests that they misidentified the moon.
59. "In the Gore district," *Evening Star*, July 29, 1909.
60. *Hawkes Bay Herald*, August 6, 1909.
61. Brunt, A. (1975). op. cit., p. 7, quoting a New Zealand Broadcasting Service documentary from 1961; "The mysterious lights," *Geraldine Guardian*, August 12, 1909.
62. "The airship mystery seen at Dunedin," *Evening Star*, July 28, 1909, p. 4; "Clear evidence," *Evening Star*, July 29, 1909, p. 4; "The Kelso airship. Cumulative evidence," *Otago Daily Times*, July 29, 1909, p. 7; "The airship, seen in North Otago," *Otago Daily Times*, July 30, 1909, p. 8; "What the dredge-men saw," *Auckland Weekly News*, August 5, 1909, p. 21; "The airship. Further evidence from Kelso. Statements by eye-witnesses," *Otago Daily Times*, August 6, 1909, p. 5.
63. *Wellington Dominion*, July 28, 1909, p. 6; "The mysterious lights. Seen in widely separated districts," *Otago Witness*, August 4, 1909.
64. *Otago Daily Times*, August 7, 1909, p. 6.
65. *Dunedin Evening Star*, August 4, 1909, p. 5; *Wellington Dominion*, August 11, 1909, p. 8.
66. Mackay, Charles (1852). *Memoirs of Extraordinary Popular Delusions and the Madness of Crowds, Volume 2*. London: Office of the National Illustrated Library. In the preface to his book, Mackay remarked that, "We find that whole communities suddenly fix their minds on one object, and go mad in its pursuit... Men, it has been well said, think in herds, it will be seen that they go mad in herds, while they only recover their senses slowly, and one by one" (pp. vii-viii).
67. Letter to *The Otago Daily Times*, August 3, 1909, p. 10.
68. Fire balloons were widely available in New Zealand at this time and commonly sold at shops selling pyrotechnics. They were paper balloons with candles attached underneath near the mouth and made buoyant from the heat. The stimulus for many other sightings was likely to have been kites, which were more popular and less expensive.
69. "Possible explanations," *Otago Daily Times*, August 30, 1909; "Fire balloons suggested," *Evening Star*, July 29, 1909; "A fire balloon found in Dunedin," *Garaldine Guardian*, July 31, 1909.
70. On the evening of August 10, four reports of 'mysterious lights' (but not airships) were recorded in the *Southland Times* of August 11. The first two were from Goulburn and Moss Vale in Australia, the others from Waihi and Stony Creek in New Zealand. The reports were limited to no more than four sentences and appeared as follows: "In the air. Glimmers at Goulburn;" "Visions in Victoria;" Wonder at Waihi," and "Stony Creek Stratagem."
71. "A remarkable sight. Strange movements of a star," *Dominion*, August 7, 1909.
72. "A fire balloon. Found in York place," *Otago Daily Times*, July 30, 1909; "Fire balloons," *Tapanui Courier*, August 4, 1909.
73. "Hot-air ships," *Evening Post*, August 2, 1909.
74. *Thames Star*, July 31, 1909.
75. *The Nelson Mail*, August 3, 1909.
76. "The supposed airship. Nelson people hoaxed," *Timaru Post*, August 3, 1909.
77. "The 'airship,'" *Tapanui Courier*, August 4, 1909.
78. *Southland Times*, August 4, 1909.
79. "More seeing at Gore," *The Southland Times*, September 2, 1909; *The Southland Times*, August 3, 1909.
80. T.E. Bullard. *Mysteries in the Eye of the Beholder: UFOs and Their Correlates as a Folkloric Theme Past and Present*. Doctoral dissertation, Indiana University Folklore Department, 1982.
81. I.F. Clarke (1986). "American Anticipations: The First of the Futurists." *Futures* 18: 584-596.
82. Hot air balloons are not encompassed under this definition of successful flight. However, such modes of transport are unlikely to be mistaken for an airship. Balloons of the period were highly unstable,

clumsy, sensitive to even slight wind shifts, dangerous to fly at night, and could not remotely perform the sophisticated maneuvers reported by "airship" observers. These same proscriptions applied to airships of the period, which were bulky and impractical.

83. "Mysterious Lights," *Taranaki Daily News*, August 10, 1909, citing an Australian Press Association cable from Melbourne.

84. "The Lights in the Sky. West Australia Falls into Line," *Goulburn Evening Penny Post*, August 17, 1909.

85. Bilstein, R.E. (1984). *Flight in America 1900-1983: From the Wrights to the Astronauts*. London: John Hopkins University Press, p. 15.

86. Gibbs-Smith, C. (1985). op. cit., pp. 145-146.

87. "Tillinghast to his story clings," *Berkshire Evening Eagle*, December 14, 1909.

88. "Noise like an aeroplane. Fire Island surfman heard it in air; sure it was not geese," *Boston Herald*, December 13, 1909, p. 1.

89. "What Mr. Hanna saw may have been the Worcester airship!" *Willimantic Chronicle*, December 14, 1909, p. 8.

90. "What Mr. Hanna saw..." *Willimantic Chronicle*, December 14, 1909, p. 8.

91. "Sailed over the harbor. Unknown airship makes a flight in night... Immigration inspector Hoe able to distinguish part of framework of craft," *Boston Globe* Evening Edition, December 20, 1909, p. 1.

92. "Boston airship a boat's masts. Inspector Hoe mistook towering sticks of the James S. Whitney for framework of mysterious night flier," *Boston Herald*, December 21, 1909, p. 12.

93. "Sailed over the harbor..." *Boston Globe* Evening Edition, December 20, 1909, p. 1.

94. "Air ships seen at night," *Boston Globe*, December 23, 1909, p. 6.

95. "Worcester agape at airship lights. Wallace E. Tillinghast may have been flying above city. Business at standstill while people watch..." *Boston Herald*, December 23, 1909, p. 1.

96. "Worcester palpitating. All excitement today over that airship. Tillinghast generally given credit for being the man. So many people saw it that no question is raised of some craft making flight," *Boston Globe* Evening Edition, December 24, 1909, p.1.

97. *Boston Herald*, December 23, 1909, p.1.

98. "Mysterious air craft circles about Boston for nearly six hours. Some declare they discern outlines of monoplane bearing two men..." *Boston Herald*, December 24, 1909, p. 1.

99. Airship is just Venus," *Boston Globe*, December 24, 1909, p. 1.

100. "Mysterious air craft circles about Boston..." *Boston Herald*, December 24, 1909, p. 1.

101. "Skyship of mystery flies above Boston. Revere man gets close enough to see framework and hears the engine..." *Boston Journal*, December 24, 1909, p. 1.

102. "Mystery airship just like Venus. Machine hovers over Willimantic," *Daily Times*, December 24, 1909, p. 3.

103. "Mystery airship just like..." *Daily Times*, December 24, 1909, p. 3.

104. "Certain as the stars. Airship again on route. Even skeptics see its charging lights," *Boston Globe*, December 25, 1909, p. 1.

105. "Tillinghast very modest," *Boston Globe*, December 20, 1909, p. 14.

106. "Airship story worries them..." *Boston Globe*, December 26, 1909, p. 14.

107. "Airship owl is Worcester tale. C.D. Rawson says he hitched lights to birds and let them fly on nights skycraft was seen," *Boston Sunday Herald*, December 26, 1909, p. 15.

108. "Venus and the public eye," *Providence Sunday Journal*, December 26, 1909, Section 2, p. 5.

109. "Tillinghast in his shop, Not in his airship. New Englanders probably mistake Venus for a soaring flying machine and get excited," *Wheeling Register*, December 26, 1909.

110. "Willimantic laughs at the airship faking," *Hartford Daily Times*, December 27, 1909, p. 11.

111. "The inky sky, and not a star in sight," *Willimantic Daily Chronicle*, January 7, 1910, p. 1; "Willimantic men see things again," *Hartford Courant*, January 8, 1910, p. 1; "The inevitable airship," *Rutland Daily Herald* [Vermont], January 10, 1910, p. 4; "Fair Haven sees phantom airship...astronomer has solution," *Hartford Daily Times*, January 19, 1910, p. 9.

112. Gollin, A. (1984). *No Longer an Island: Britain and the Wright Brothers, 1902-1909*. London, p. 433.

113. Gollin, op. cit., p. 437.

114. Watson, N., Oldroyd, G., & Clarke, D. (1988). *The 1912-1913 British Phantom Airship Scare*. Fund for UFO Research: Mount Rainier, MD.

115. Suvin, D. (1984). The extraordinary voyage, the future war, and Bulwer's 'The coming race': Three sub-genres in British science fiction, 1871-1885. *Literature and History* 10.

116. Watson, et al., op. cit., p. 3.

117. "The alleged visit of a foreign airship," *London Times*, November 22, 1912, p. 8.

118. Watson et al., op. cit., p. 10.

119. *The Aeroplane*, November 28, 1912, p. 497.

120. "Unknown aircraft over Dover. Reported night visits of a lighted machine," *The Times of London*, January 6, 1913, p. 6; "Aircraft from the sea. Mysterious flight before daybreak," *London Daily Express*, January 6, 1913, p. 7; "Mysterious airship. Flight over Dover," *London Daily Telegraph*, January 6, 1913, p. 10; "Dover airship mystery," *Bristol Evening News*, January 7, 1913, p. 4; "Mystery airships," *London Daily Times*, January 7, 1913, p. 5; "Airship mystery. Was it a Zeppelin? The Hansa at Sheerness," *Bradford Daily Telegraph*, January 14, 1913.

121. "An airship over Cardiff," *Times of London*, January 21, 1913, p. 10.

122. "Airship mystery. Cardiff story of unknown vessel's night flight," *Nottingham Daily Express*, January 21, 1913; "A mystery of the sky. Chief constable's vision of an airship," *Yorkshire Post* [Leeds], January 21, 1913.

123. "Mysteries of the air. Unknown craft seen over Cardiff. Third in a month," *South Wales Daily Post*, January 21, 1913, p. 6.

124. "The airship at Cardiff," *Times of London*, January 22, 1913, p. 10; "Cardiff airship mystery. Chief constable's story supported by other eye-witnesses," *Nottingham Daily Express*, January 22, 1913; "Airship mystery," *Western Mail* (Cardiff), January 22, 1913, p. 6; "The mysterious airship," *Yorkshire Post*, [Leeds], January 22, 1913. "Seemed to carry a searchlight" (letter), *Western Mail*, January 25, 1913; "That mysterious airship. Seen at Foxwood, Rogerstone, near Newport, Jan. 23" (letter), *Monmouthshire Evening Post* (Newport), January 25, 1913, p. 5.

125. "Two mysterious aircraft," *London Daily Express*, January 22, 1913, p. 5.

126. "Seeing airships. Everybody's doing it," *Manchester Guardian*, March 1, 1913, p. 9.

127. "Germany's aerial fleet..."menace" to our navy," *Manchester Guardian*, February 27, 1913, p. 8.

128. "Airships or scareships," *The Aeroplane*, January 30, 1913, p. 111.

129. "The English phantom airship," *Berliner Tageblatt* [Berlin] February 25, 1913.

130. "The planet Venus responsible," *Manchester Guardian*, February

27, 1913, p. 8; "Mystery airship. Excitement at Newport," *The South Wales Argus*, February 6, 1913, p. 6; "Did you see it? Some reflections on the 'light' in the sky. Venus the beautiful," *The Cambria Daily Leader*, [February 6, 1913, p. 7; "The mysterious airship. Seen over Wells and Shepton Mallet," *The Western Gazette* [Yeovil, Somerset), February 7, 1913, p. 2; "Day by day," *Bath Herald*, February 8, 1913, p. 3; "Notes & comments," *The Blackburn Times*, February 8, 1913, p. 7; "Venus of an airship? Attempt to explain the mysterious lights," *The Evening News* [London], February 8, 1913, p. 2.

131. "Airship hoax," *London Daily Telegraph*, March 1, 1913, p. 9; "Airship mystery. A gamekeeper's find. Fire balloon in a moor," *Manchester Guardian*, February 28, 1913, p. 7; "Swansea's 'airship.' An explanation," *South Wales Daily Post*, January 22, 1913, 5; "Mysterious airships," *Neath and County Standard*, [Neath, Glamorganshire], January 25, 1913, p. 4; "The airship rumours. Fire balloon found in Yorkshire," *London Times*, February 28, 1913, p. 5; "Strange lights in the sky. Fire balloon discovered," *Manchester Guardian*, February 28, 1913, p. 7; "Airship hoax," *London Daily Telegraph*, March 1, 1913, p. 9.

132. "The explanation of the phantom airship (ghost balloon). Glowing in a rubber balloon," *Berliner Tageblatt* [Berlin], February 28, 1913.

133. "E. J. P. writes" (letter), *Manchester Guardian*, February 27, 1913, p. 8; "Is it auroral light," *Manchester Guardian*, March 1, 1913, p. 9.

134. "Airship or geese? Midnight mystery..." *London Daily Express*, January 27, 1913, p. 7.

135. "Once a week," *Natal Advertiser* [Durban], August 29, 1914, p. 7; "Our aeroplnes," *Pretoria News*, September 2, 1914, p. 5; "Aviator discusses air visitors. John Weston's views," *Cape Times*, September 5, 1914, p. 5.

136. "Defense department and aeroplanes. No union machines," *Cape Times*, August 29, 1914, p. 8; "Those aeroplanes," *Rand Daily Mail* [Johannesburg], August 29, 1914, p. 5.

137. "Aeroplanes in German south-west. Only one efficient," *Cape Times*, September 21, 1914, p. 8.

138. "Once a Week." *Natal Advertiser* [Durban], August 29, 1914, p. 7.

139. Bartholomew, Robert E. (1989). "The South African Monoplane Hysteria: An Evaluation of the Usefulness of Smelser's Theory of Hysterical Beliefs." *Sociological Inquiry* 59(3):287-300, see p. 294.

140. "Cape Town and Peninsula. Mysterious airplane flight," *Cape Times*, August 15, 1914, p. 7.

141. "Aeroplane seen at Vryburg," *Cape Times*, August 19, 1914, p. 5.

142. "Aerial scouts!..." *Rand Daily Mail* [Johannesburg], August 19, 1914, p. 5.

143. "The aeroplane...On Table Mountain," *Cape Times*, August 20, 1914, p. 5; "The aeroplane. Seen at Porterville," *Cape Argus*, August 21, 1914, p. 5; "At Ashton," *Johannesburg Star*, August 21, 1914, p. 4; "That aeroplane," *Rand Daily Mail* [Johannesburg], August 21, 1914, p. 5; "The mysterious aeroplane," *Natal Advertiser* [Durban], August 22, 1914, p. 1; "The mysterious aeroplane," *Rand Daily Mail* [Johannesburg], August 22, 1914, p. 5.

144. "Mysterious aeroplanes. A Natal report," *Cape Argus*, September 9, 1914, Second Edition, p. 5.

145. "Something Seen in January." *Johannesburg Star* [Johannesburg], Union of South Africa, August 26, 1914, second edition, p. 4.

146. "Native restlessness. The folly of wild rumors," *Natal Advertiser* [Durban], August 27, 1914, p. 8.

147. "Alleged native restlessness. What the officials have done," *Natal Advertiser* [Durban], August 2, 1914, p. 14.

148. "The aeroplane again," *Cape Argus*, August 25, 1914, p. 3; "That aeroplane! Return visist to the east," *Cape Times*, August 25, 1914, p. 5; "...Seen at Hoetjes Bay," *Cape Argus*, August 26, 1914, Second Edition, p. 5; "Aeroplane reports," *Cape Times*, August 26, 1914, p. 5; "Sea Point aeroplane," *Cape Argus*, August 28, 1914, p. 4; "Day by day," *Pretoria News*, August 29, 1914, p. 5; "'Aeroplanes' in Natal," *Rand Daily Mail*, August 29, 1914, p. 5; "Headlight," *Cape Argus*, August 31, 1914, p. 3; "The mysterious aeroplane," *Natal Advertiser*, September 31, 1914, p. 1; "Cape Argus. The aeroplane again." *Natal Advertiser*, August 31, 1914, p. 5; "Aeroplane at Skinner's Court," *Pretoria News*, August 31, 1914, p. 5.

149. "That aeroplane. Natal reports," *Cape Argus*, September 5, 1914, p. 7; "That aeroplane!" *Natal Advertiser*, September 7, 1914; "That aeroplane seen at Warmbaths," *Rand Daily Mail* [Johannesburg], September 10, 1914, p. 2.

150. *Natal Advertiser* [Durban], September 5, 1914, p. 7.

151. "Aeroplane or planet?," *Johannesburg Star*, August 28, 1914, Second Edition, p. 5.

152. "Aeroplane problem. Maritzburg optician's solution," *Cape Times*, September 10, 1914, p. 5.

153. "Coloured planet," *Johannesburg Star*, August 31, 1914, p. 3.

154. "The mysterious aeroplane. What East London saw," *Cape Argus*, August 27, 1914, Second Edition, p. 5.

155. Portions of this entry are excerpted from: Bartholomew, Robert E. (1998). "Phantom German Air Raids on Canada: War Hysteria in Quebec and Ontario during World War I." *Canadian Military History* 7(4):29-36 (Autumn 1998).

156. Creighton, D. (1958). *Dominion of the North: A History of Canada*. London: Macmillan & Company, p. 437.

157. Morton, D. (1974). "Sir William Otter and Internment Operations in Canada during the First World War." *The Canadian Historical Review* 55(1):32-58. See p. 36.

158. MacDonnell, F. (1995). *Insidious Foes*. New York: Oxford University Press, p. 23.

159. MacDonnell, F. (1995) op cit., pp. 25-26.

160. Morton, op. cit.

161. Morton, op. cit., p. 46.

162. Morton, op. cit., pp. 48-49.

163. Morton, op. cit., p. 33; Keyserlingk, R.H. (1985). "Agents within the Gates'" The Search for Nazi Subversives in Canada during World War II. *Canadian Historical Review* 66(2):211-239.

164. MacDonnell, op. cit., p. 21.

165. Kitchen, M. (1985). "The German Invasion of Canada in the First World War." *The International History Review* 7(2):245-260.

166. Kitchen, p. cit., p. 246.

167. Kitchen, op. cit., p. 246.

168. Kitchen, op. cit.

169. Mount, G.S. (1993). *Canada's Enemies: Spies and Spying in the Peaceable Kingdom*. Toronto: Dundurn Press, p. 40.

170. Mount, G.S. (1993). op cit., p. 40.

171. Throughout this article I will refer to aircraft of the period as "aeroplanes" instead of the present spelling "airplane," as the former spelling was the standard usage at the time.

172. Gibbs-Smith, C.H. (1985). *Aviation: An Historical Survey from its Origins to the End of World War II*. London: Her Majesty's Stationary Office, p. 152.

173. "Reports aeroplanes over Oxford village," *London Free Press* [Ontario], August 13, 1914, p. 2.

174. "Airship in Western Ontario," *Toronto Star*, August 31, 1914, p. 5.

175. "Airship in Western Ontario." op cit., p. 5.

176. Presently spelled "Petrolia."

177. "Three aeroplanes scan topography of the province," *London Free Press*, September 5, 1914, p. 8.
178. "Three aeroplanes scan topography of the province." op cit., p. 8.
179. "Three aeroplanes scan topography of the province." op cit., p. 8.
180. "Petrolea planes...Military men say, 'We shouldn't worry," *London Free Press*, September 5, 1914, p. 2.
181. "Why get excited?" *London Free Press*, September 5, 1914, p. 16.
182. "Believe 'aeroplane' is an American one," *London Free Press*, September 5, 1914, p. 16.
183. "Mysterious flyer now at Hamilton," *London Free Press*, September 12, 1914, p. 5.
184. "Pipe line road saw three aeroplanes. Mr. Fred Bridge...and other people say they saw spies," *London Free Press*, September 11, 1914, p. 9.
185. "Pipe line road saw three aeroplanes." op cit., p. 9.
186. "Airships restricted in flights in Canada," *Toronto Globe*, September 18, 1914, p. 7; "Asks permission to fly over Ontario..." *London Free Press*, September 28, 1914, p. 3.
187. *Niagara Falls Gazette*, September 17, 1914, p. 1.
188. "Had an aeroplane scare," *Toronto Star*, October 10, 1914, p. 10.
189. "Aeroplane reported hovering over Soo Locks. Residents claim to have seen craft rise from south of American canal," *Toronto Globe*, October 20, 1914, p. 9.
190. "Soldiers claim they saw airship over barracks... Flew directly over the ordnance stores department. Men are emphatic there was no mistake," *London Evening Free Press* [Ontario], October 21, 1914, p. 1.
191. "Many reports," *London Evening Free Press*, October 21, 1914, p. 1.
192. "Still see them, but military authorities are not worrying," *London Free Press*, October 23, 1914, p. 2.
193. "Signal across river?" *Buffalo Express* [Buffalo, New York], November 19, 1914, p. 7.
194. "Seeing things in air. Forestville man says two aeroplanes went over town in dark," *Buffalo Express*, November 21, 1914, p. 7.
195. "Aeroplane raid..." *Toronto Daily Star*, December 4, 1914, p. 6.
196. "Saw an aeroplane," *Niagara Falls Gazette* [Niagara Falls, New York], December 12, 1914, p. 9.
197. "Strange aeroplane appears six miles from Montreal. Ottawa officials...will investigate matter immediately," *London Evening Free Press*, January 11, 1915, p. 2.
198. "Brockville's story of the air craft. Dropped fireballs as they crossed river..." *Toronto Globe*, February 15, 1915.
199. "Brockville's story of the air craft..." op cit.
200. Brockville's story of the air craft..." op cit.
201. Brockville's story of the air craft..." op cit.
202. "Scare in Ottawa over air raid. Parliament buildings darkened on report that three aeroplanes crossed the border," *New York Times*, February 15, 1915, p. 1.
203. "Were also seen at Gananoque," *New York Times*, February 15, 1915, p. 1; "Brockville's story of the air craft..." *Toronto Globe*, February 15, 1915.
204."Ogdensburg heard of this Friday," *New York Times*, February 15, 1915, p. 1.
205. "Police force augmented," *London Evening Free Press*, February 15, 1915, p. 1.
206. "Ottawa again dark..." *New York Times*, February 16, 1915, p. 4.
207. "Parliament Hill in darkness," *Toronto Globe*, February 16, 1915, p. 2.
208. "Were toy balloons and not aeroplanes! Brockville's latest on Sunday night's scare..." *Toronto Globe*, February 16, 1915, p. 1.
209. Toy balloons were also popularly referred to as "fire balloons," and commonly available at shops selling fireworks. They were composed of paper with candles attached near the mouth and made buoyant through the generation of heat.
210. "Ottawa again dark..." *New York Times*, February 16, 1915, p. 4; "Were toy balloons..." *Toronto Globe*, February 16, 1915, pp. 1-2.
211. "Air raid from the states improbable..." *Toronto Globe*, February 16, 1915, p. 7.
212. "Saw aeroplane...after landing, took flight towards Montreal," *London Free Press* [Ontario], July 6, 1915, p. 1.
213. "Saw an aeroplane...passed over the southern part of city," *London Evening Free Press*, July 17, 1915, p. 3.
214. "...People near Massena, Ont., spy strange lights in Heavens," *London Evening Free Press*, July 20, 1915, p. 9.
215. "Saw aeroplanes hovering over city of Quebec. Fully creditable persons reported to have noticed mysterious aircraft," *London Evening Free Press*, July 21, 1915, p. 1.
216. "Strange airships seen hovering near Montreal," *London Evening Free Press*, July 19, 1915, p. 7.
217. "Strange airships seen hovering near Montreal." op cit. p. 7.
218. "Point Edward guard brings down balloons. Were at first thought to be aeroplanes..." *London Evening Free Press*, July 21, 1915, p. 7.
219. "French believe German officer 'flew the loop,'" *London Evening Free Press*, July 22, 1915, p. 1.
220. "Mysterious light passes Tillsonburg," July 23, 1915, p. 2.
221."Another aeroplane seen over the city," *London Free Press* [Ontario], August 9, 1915, p. 2.
222. "Two aeroplanes...close to Montreal," *London Evening Free Press*, February 7, 1916, p. 1.
223. "Display in sky mistaken for an aerial invasion," *London Evening Free Press*, February 14, 1916, p. 12.
224. "Unknown aviator surveys Windsor," *London Evening Free Press*, July 7, 1916, p. 14.
225. Shores, L. (editor) (1965). "World War I," in *Collier's Encyclopedia*, Volume 23. NY: Crowell-Collier Publishing, p. 599.
226. For a good summary of Anti-German-American literature during this period, see Francis MacDonnell (1995). *Insidious Foes*. Oxford: Oxford University Press, pp. 20-25.
227. "Guard 'Planes to Avert Powder Raids Following Reports of Airship over DuPont Plants..." *Evening Bulletin* (Philadelphia, PA), January 24, 1916, p. 2.
228. "Aeroplane or Blackbird?" *Evening Bulletin* (Philadelphia, PA), January 24, 1916, p. 2.
229. "Another Aeroplane Sighted," *Evening Bulletin* (Philadelphia, PA), February 1, 1916, p. 3.
230. "Mystery airship hovering over powder plants...mission unknown; rouses suspicion," *Every Evening* [Wilmington, Delaware], February 3, 1916, pp. 1 and 6.
231. "Powder guard says he saw airship," *The Wilmington News*, February 4, 1916, p. 1.
232. "Powder guard says he saw airship," *The Wilmington News*, February 4, 1916, p. 1.
233. "Mystery Airship Hovering Over Powder Plants..." *Every Evening* (Wilmington, DE), February 3, 1916, p. 1.
234. "Asserts that He Saw Machine..." *Philadelphia Inquirer*, February 4, 1916, pp. 1 and 6.
235. "Aircraft, Phantom or Real, Stirs Woodbury," *Philadelphia Inquirer*, February 7, 1916, p. 1.
236. "Doubt by Du Ponts that Airship Flew over Powder Mill," *Evening Bulletin* (Philadelphia, PA), February 3, 1916, p. 1.

237. "Still sky gazing at Fenton Beach," *Delmarvia Star* [Wilmington, Delaware], February 13, 1916.
238. "Studying astronomy with a searchlight," *Sunday Morning Magazine* [Wilmington, Delaware], February 20, 1916, part 3, p. 1.
239. "Air ship..." *Every Evening*, February 19, 1916.
240. "Are sure they saw an aeroplane," *Every Evening*, February 16, 1916.
241. "Citizens declare they saw airship," *Wilmington Morning News*, February 14, 1916, pp. 1 and 2.
242. "They heard something," *Every Evening*, February 14, 1916, p. 7.
243. "Honest, now, did you yourself see that aeroplane?" *Every Evening*, February 14, 1916, p. 7.
244. "Kent county reports seeing an airship," *Every Evening*, February 14, 1916, p. 7.
245. "To Arms, Annapolis! Zeppelins Coming!" *Every Evening*, February 15, 1916, p. 2.
246. Excerpts from this entry first appeared in Bartholomew, Robert E. (1998). "War Scare Hysteria in the Delaware Region in 1916." *Delaware History* 28(1):71-76 (Spring/Summer 1998).
247. MacDonnell, F. (1995). *Insidious Foes*. New York: Oxford University Press.
248. Excerpted from Bartholomew, Robert E. "German Invasion of New Hampshire." *New Hampshire Magazine* (June 1998). Published online http://www.nhcentury.com/portsmouth/porcen/thegerinv.html.
249. "Hunt for aircraft base. Fire at aircraft near Portsmouth. Effort now to trace its course--shots aimed at Penacook sentries," *Manchester Union*, April 14, 1917, pp. 1, 3; "Portsmouth guards fire at plane--course is changed at once," *Manchester Union*, April 14, 1917, pp. 1, 3.
250. "Hunt for aircraft..." *Manchester Union*, April 14, 1917, pp. 1, 3.
251. "Portsmouth guards..." *Manchester Union*, April 14, 1917. pp. 1,3.
252. "Strange aeroplane heard and seen by Rochester people," *Manchester Union*, April 14, 1917. pp. 1,3.
253. "Strange aeroplane heard and seen..." op cit.
254. "Aeroplane heard over East Side. Darkness prevents clear view of it...," *Manchester Union*, April 17, 1917, p. 14.
255. "Lights hover over Kearsarge. Movements suggest airplane--close watch kept on mountain," *Manchester Union*, April 26, 1917, p. 1.
256. "Lights hover over Kearsarge..." op cit., p. 1.
257. "Aeroplane seen at Deerfield. Awakened resident observes flashing of lights--Report from Wolfeboro," *Manchester Union*, May 1, 1917, p. 1.
258. For instance, the next report of a phantom aeroplane over New Hampshire occurred on May 20th and consisted of a tiny article 3 short sentences in length, on page 2 of the *Manchester Union*. The account simply described the report of Dover resident Mrs. Arabella R. Mason who claimed to see an aeroplane fly over her farm on Middle Road. See, "Airship seen above Dover," *Manchester Union*, May 21, 1917, p. 2.
259. Despite minor intermittent ghost flier sightings over Scandinavia between 1934 and 1937, none of these episodes compares with the 1933-34 wave in terms of pervasiveness and volume of reports.
260. Keel, J.A. 1970. *Why UFOs?* New York: Manor, p. 118.
261. "The mysterious light still haunts. Airplanes seen in Norway and in the north. What's the truth? Liquor traders attend their customers in a modern way?" *Vasterbottens Folkblad*, December 27, 1933, p. 1; "Liquor by air from a depot outside Norway. The mysterious airplane in the mountains receives its explanation..." *Svenska Dagbladet*, December 28, 1933, p. 6; "The giant airplane goes with liquor over Norrland. A regular smuggler's line between Vasa and Mo in northern Norway," *Stockholm-Tidningen*, December 28, 1933, p. 1; "Liquor smugglers use the air for their own purposes..." *Vasterbottens Folkblad*, December 28, 1933, p. 1; "Finnish customs convinced that smugglers fly the Atlantic - the Gulf of Bothnia. Transport cost would be almost three crowns per litre through the air," *Norrlandska Social-Demokraten*, December 28, 1933, p. 1.
262. "The 'sawfilers' of the air guilty of the disorder by mountains and coasts?" *Vasterbottens Folkblad*, January 10, 1934, p. 1; "The ghost fliers of Norrland Soviet-Russian military experts!..." *Nya Dagligt Allehanda*, January 10, 1934, p. 1; "Soviet machines that haunt us..." *Umebladet*, January 11, 1934, p. 1; "Systematic military espionage is the mission of the ghost flier in Norrland..." *Aftonbladet*, January 13, 1934, p. 1; "Soviet machines that cross over Swedish areas? The Boden fort a taboo for strangers. Both Swedish and Norwegian government take on special measures," *Umebladet*, January 15, 1934, p. 1; "The flying X's Soviet-Russian planes in spite of denials..." *Norrbottens-Kuriren*, January 16, 1934, p. 4; "The night fliers Soviet-Russian..." *Umebladet*, January 18, 1934, p. 1; "The ghost flier over Kemi was a Russian. Finnish authorities confirm..." *Norrbottens-Kuriren*, January 27, 1934, p. 15; "The ghost fliers...Base and depot in the vicinity of Boris Gleb..." *Aftonbladet*, January 27, 1934, p. 18; "Do Finnish authorities have a solution? Mysterious light on the ice outside Kemi. Is the flier of Russian nationality?" *Svenska Dagbladet*, January 28, 1934, pp. 3, 6; "Is weapons transport the ghost flier's main purpose...Russian base, thinks Finnish expert," *Svenska Dagbladet*, January 30, 1934; "Do the Russians want to intimidate Scandinavia? The ghost raids Russian war plans, says Finnish air expert," *Aftonbladet*, January 30, 1934, p. 1; "Base of the ghost flier..." *Nya Dagligt Allehanda*, February 12, 1934, p. 8; "The secretary of defense, 'the ghost fliers' and the mysterious radio signals..." *Nya Dagligt Allehanda*, April 17, 1934.
263. "The ghost flier a Japanese machine..." *Umebladet*, January 23, 1934, p. 3; "The Japanese warship near Lofoten?..." *Umebladet*, January 24, 1934, p. 1; "The ghost flights now directed from the White Sea coasts?..." *Vasterbottens-Kuriren*, January 25, 1934; "Japanese help cruiser confirmed off the coast of northern Norway," *Norrbottens-Kuriren*, January 31, 1934, p. 7.
264. "The fliers German front pilots," *Stockholms-Tidningen*, December 29, 1933, p. 20; "The haunting arranged to motivate the demand for new bombers. Has the Nazi junker works and air administration arranged the matter together..." *Ny Dag* [communist daily], January 17, 1934, p. 1; "New theory on the ghost. German rockets..." *Hufvudstadsbladet* [Helsinki, Finland], February 9, 1934, p. 3; "Crossmarked airplane seen at low level over Jokkmokk...Only German machines carry crossmarks," *Social-Demokraten*, March 16, 1937.
265. *Svenska Dagbladet*, January 16, 1934:3, 20.
266. Orvik, N. (1982). *Europe's Northern Cap and the Soviet Union*. Boulder, CO: Westview; Vayrynen, R. (1972). *Conflicts in Finnish-Soviet Relations: Three Comparative Case Studies*. Tempere University.
267. *Svenska Dagbladet*, January 15, 1934, p. 4.
268. *Svenska Dagbladet*, January 29, 1934.
269. "Aerial searchers do not Doubt Flier X," *Svenska Dagbladet*, January 18, 1934, p. 13; "Is Weapons transport the ghost flier's main purpose?...Russian Base Thinks Finnish Expert," *Svenska Dagbladet*, January 6, 1934, p. 3.
270. *Svenska Dagbladet*, January 27, 1934, p. 3.
271. The following accounts typify press coverage during this period: "Flier X at 30 meters over Robertsfors," *Svenska Dagbladet*, January 29, 1934, p. 20; "Ghost Flier Seen and Heard over Transtand. Passed off over the Norwegian Coast, was Observed by Reliable People," *Svenska Dagbladet*, February 6, 1934, p. 3; "Ghost Flier makes Emergency

Landing on Norwegian Mountain, Flies but Disappears Again," *Svenska Dagbladet*, February 7, 1934, p. 3.
272. *Svenska Dagbladet*, February 7, 1934, p. 22.
273. *Svenska Dagbladet*, February 9, 1934, p. 22.
274. *Svenska Dagbladet*, February 10, 1934, p. 6.
275. *Svenska Dagbladet*, January 15, 1934, p. 3.
276. *Svenska Dagbladet*, January 9, 1934, p. 10.
277. *Svenska Dagbladet*, February 24, 1934, p. 5.
278. *Svenska Dagbladet*, February 1, 1934, p. 16.
279. We wish to thank Professor Thomas Bullard, Department of Folklore, Indiana University at Bloomington, who supplied many of the press accounts used in this entry.
280. Nitzkin, J.L. (1976). "Epidemic Transient Situational Disturbance in an Elementary School." *Journal of the Florida Medical Association* 63:357-359.
281. Nitzkin (1976). op cit., p. 357.
282. Nitzkin (1976). op cit., p. 357.
283. Roueche, B. (1978). "Annals of Medicine. Sandy" [Interview with Dr. Joel Nitzkin] *The New Yorker* 21:63-70. See p. 63.
284. Nitzkin (1976). op cit., p. 357.
285. Nitzkin, op cit., p. 358.
286. Nitzkin, op cit., p. 358.
287. Nitzkin, op cit., p. 358.
288. Nitzkin, op cit., p. 358.
289. Roueche, op cit., p. 68.
290. Roueche, op cit., p. 68.
291. Nitzkin. op cit., p. 358.
292. Nitzkin. op cit., p. 359.
293. Nitzkin. op cit., p. 359.
294. Roueche, op cit., p. 70.
295. Burnham, William H. (1924). *The Normal Mind.* New York: D. Appleton-Century, pp. 337-338.
296. Benaim, Silvio, Horder, John, and Anderson, Jennifer (1973). "Hysterical Epidemic in a Classroom." *Psychological Medicine* 3:366-373.
297. Benaim, et al., op cit., p. 367.
298. Benaim, et al., op cit., p. 368.
299. Benaim, et al., op cit., p. 368.
300. Benaim, et al., op cit., p. 368.
301. Benaim, et al., op cit., p. 368.
302. Benaim, et al., op cit., p. 371.
303. Benaim, et al., op cit., p. 369.
304. Benaim, et al., op cit., p. 369.
305. Benaim, et al., op cit., p. 369.
306. Hunter, F.K., and Hunter, R.C.A. (1958). "Observation of a Hysterical Epidemic in a Hospital Ward." *Psychiatric Quarterly* 32:821-839.
307. Jacobs, Norman. (1965). "The Phantom Slasher of Taipei: Mass Hysteria in a Non-Western Society." *Social Problems* 12:318-328. See p. 320.
308. Jacobs, op cit., p. 320.
309. Jacobs, op cit., p. 319.
310. Jacobs, op cit., pp. 320-321.
311. Jacobs, op cit., p. 325.
312. Jacobs, op cit., p. 322.
313. Jacobs, op cit., p. 322.
314. Jacobs, op cit., p. 324.
315. "Schoolchildren Possessed by 'Devil' in Manila." Reuters News Service report dated January 28, 1994.
316. Knightley, Phillip (1998). *A Hack's Progress.* London: Vintage Random House; personal communication between Robert Bartholomew and Philip Knightley, August 2005.
317. Knightly, op cit., p. 51.
318. Knightly, op cit., p. 52.
319. Knightly, op cit., p. 52.
320. Knightly, pp. 52-53.
321. Knightly, op cit., p. 53.
322. Kalai, K. (2001). "Photostated 'Ghost' Creates Chaos." *New Straits Times* (Kuala Lumpur, Malaysia), August 10, 2001.
323. Co-author Robert Bartholomew conducted anthropological fieldwork in Malaysia during the early 1990s, and taught effective writing and speaking skills to new school teachers. The vast majority believed in the existence of ghosts and other supernatural entities. It is difficult to imagine that these beliefs did not "rub off" on their students.
324. Smith, H.C.T., and Eastham, E.J. (1973). "Outbreak of Abdominal Pain." *The Lancet* 2:956-958.
325. Smith and Eastham, op cit., p. 957.
326. Smith and Eastham, op cit., p. 957.
327. Smith and Eastham, op cit., p. 958.
328. Smith and Eastham, op cit., p. 958.
329. Smith and Eastham, op cit., p. 958.
330. Smith and Eastham, op cit., p. 958.
331. "New theory on 'mass hysteria.'" BBC News, 23 September, 2003, online at: http://news.bbc.co.uk/1/ hi/england/nottinghamshire/ 3128402.stm.
332. "Ghostly Lights of Furnaces Shining." *The Charleroi Mail and Mirror*, May 23, 1939, p. 4.
333. Richer, op cit., p. 860.
334. The primary source is a letter by a Dr. Baratoux published in *Progrès médical* July 1881, and reprinted in Richer, Paul (1885). *Etudes Cliniques de la Grande Hystérie*. Paris: Delahaye et Lecrossnier, p. 859.
335. Cauzons, Th. de. (1901-1912). *La Magie et la Sorcellerie en France*. Paris: Dorbon-Ainé, volume 4, p. 588.
336. Richer (1885). op cit., p. 863.
337. "Pocket Monsters' Shocks TV Viewers into Convulsions." *Japan Times*, December 17, 1997; "Govt Launches Probe of 'Monster' cartoon." *Yomiuri Shimbun*, December 18, 1997; "Psychiatrists Seek Animation Probe." *Yomiuri Shimbun*, December 19, 1997; Yamashita, Y., Matsuishi, T., Ishida, S., Nishimi, T., and Kato, H. (1998). "Pocket Monsters Attacks Japanese Children via Media." *Annals of Neurology* 44(3):428; Hayashi, T., Ichiyama, T., Nishikawa, M., Isumi, H., and Furukawa, S. (1998). "Pocket Monsters, a Popular Television Cartoon, Attacks Japanese Children." *Annals of Neurology* 44(3):427; Tobimatsu, S., Zhang, Y.M., Tomoda, Y., Mitsudome, A., and Kato, M. (1999). "Chromatic Sensitive Epilepsy: A Variant of Photosensitive Epilepsy." *Annals of Neurology* 45(6):790.
338. Snyder J (1997). "Cartoon Sickens Children." Reuters report on American Broadcasting Corporation News, December 17, 1997a; Snyder J: "'Monster' TV Cartoon Illness Mystifies Japan." Reuters report, December 17, 1997b; "Govt Launches Probe of 'Monster' Cartoon." *Yomiuri Shimbun*, December 18, 1997.
339. Yamashita, Y., Matsuishi, T., Ishida, S., et al. (1998). "Pocket monsters attacks Japanese children via media (letter)." *Annals of Neurology* 44:428.
340. Tobimatsu S., Zhang, Y.M., Tomoda, Y., et al. (1999). "Chromatic sensitive epilepsy: a variant of photosensitive epilepsy." *Annals of Neurology* 45:790.
341. Radford, Benjamin, and Bartholomew, Robert E. (2001). "Pokémon Contagion: Photosensitive Epilepsy or Mass Psychogenic

Illness?" *The Southern Medical Journal* 94(2):197-204 (February).
342. Radford and Bartholomew (2001). op cit.
343. This account is summarized from Pollock (1903) and Kenyon (1972) unless otherwise indicated. Pollock, John (1903). *The Popish Plot.* London: Duckworth; Kenyon, John (1972). *The Popish Plot.* London: Heinemann.
344. Pollock, op cit., p. 19.
345. "A Ballad upon the Popish Plot' by a Lady of Quality," in Ebsworth, Joseph Woodfall (editor) (1878). *The Bagford Ballads.* Hertford: The Ballad Society, p. 688.
346. Pollock, op cit., p. 85.
347. Lord Peterborough, quoted by Pollock, op cit., p. 80.
348. Sir Thomas Player, quoted by Kenyon, op cit., p. 81.
349. Roger North, quoted by Kenyon, op cit., p. 85.
350. Kenyon, op cit., p. 97.
351. Kenyon, op cit., pp. 101-102.
352. Kenyon, op cit., pp. 94-95.
353. Kenyon, op cit., p. 108.
354. Ebsworth, op cit., p. 986.
355. Kenyon, op cit., p. 166.
356. Ebsworth, op cit., p. 701.
357. Kenyon, op cit., p. 248.
358. Kenyon, op cit., p. 238.
359. This phrase, and all details of the Maryland incident, are taken from: Graham, Michael (1993). "Popish Plots: Protestant Fears in Early Colonial Maryland, 1676-1689." *Catholic Historical Review* 79(2):197-216 (April).
360. "A 50th Anniversary Recreation." *The Post-Star* (Glens Falls, New York), October 31, 1988, p. 2.
361. Dispatch in French from l'Agence France Presse, October 31, 1988.
362. Oesterreich, T.K. (1930[1921]) *Possession.* [Originally published in German 1921]. London: Kegan Paul, Trench, Trubner, p. 137, quoting Dannholz.
363. Deren, Maya (1953). *Divine Horsemen.* London: Thames & Hudson.
364. Miller, David L. (2000). *Introduction to Collective Behavior and Collective Action.* Prospect Heights, Illinois: Waveland Press, p. 423.
365. Bourguignon, Erika (editor) (1973). *Religion, Altered States of Consciousness and Social Change.* Columbus: Ohio University Library 1973, p. 42, citing Lenora Greenbaum.
366. Oesterreich, T.K. (1930[1921]). op cit.
367. *The New York Times,* August 23, 1964, cited in Cotlow, Lewis. (1966). *In Search of the Primitive.* Boston: Little, Brown and Company, p. 370.
368. Billings, Dorothy K. (1969). "The Johnson Cult of New Hanover." *Oceania* 40(1):13-19. See p. 13.
369. Billings, op cit., p. 13.
370. Billings, op cit., p. 14.
371. Billings, Dorothy K. (2002). *Cargo Cult as Theater: Political Performance in the Pacific.* Lanham, Maryland: Lexington Books.
372. Geiszler-Jones, Amy (2002). "Billings Studies Pacific 'Cult.'" (2002). *Inside Witchita State University Online Edition,* November 06, 2002, http://www.wichita.edu/insidewsu.
373. Geiszler-Jones, op cit.
374. Billings, 1969, op cit., p. 17.
375. Billings, 1969, op cit., p. 17. For a more detailed discussion of this performance, see, Billings, Dorothy K. 2002, op cit.
376. Clarke, W. C. (1973). "Temporary Madness as Theatre: Wild-Man Behaviour in New Guinea." *Oceania* 43(3):198-214; Newman, P. L. (1964). "'Wild Man' Behavior in a New Guinea Highlands Community." *American Anthropologist* 66:1-19.
377. Bartholomew, Robert E. (2000). *Exotic Deviance: Medicalizing Cultural Idioms--From Strangeness to Illness.* Boulder, Colorado: University Press of Colorado.
378. Bartholomew, Robert E. (1999). "The Conspicuous Absence of a Single Case of *Latah*-Related Death or Serious Injury." *Transcultural Psychiatry* 36(3):369-376; Bartholomew, R. E. (1997). "The Medicalization of the Exotic: Latah as a Colonialism-Bound Syndrome." *Deviant Behavior* 18:47-75; Bartholomew, R. E. (1994). "Disease, Disorder or Deception? Latah as Habit in a Malay Extended Family." *Journal of Nervous and Mental Disease* 182:331-338.
379. Newman, op cit.
380. Littlewood, R., and Lipsedge, M. (1985). Culture-Bound Syndromes. Pp. 105-142. In K. Granville-Grossman (ed.), *Recent Advances in Clinical Psychiatry.* London: Churchill Livingstone, p. 119.
381. Reay, M. (1965). "Mushroom Madness and Collective Hysteria." *Australian Territories* 5(1):18-28. See p. 26.
382. Newman, P. L. (1964). "'Wild Man'" Behavior in a New Guinea Highlands Community." *American Anthropologist* 66:1-19. See p. 7.
383. Freeman, Derek (1983). *Margaret Mead and Samoa: The Making and Unmasking of an Anthropological Myth.* Boston, MA: Harvard University Press.
384. Thurston, Herbert (1952). *The Physical Phenomena of Mysticism.* London: Burns & Oates, p. 107, quoting Buti, Vita della Maria Costante Maria Castreca.
385. For references, see entry on AUXONNE.
386. See entry on LOUDUN.
387. See entry on LOUVIERS.
388. Bechterew, W.M. [Now spelled Bekhterev, V M] (1910). *La Suggestion.* [Translated from Russian by D P Keraval]. Paris: Boulangé, p. 143.
389. Calmeil, L.F. (1845). *De la Folie, Consideree Sous le Point de vue Pathologique, Philosophique, Historique et Judiciaire* [On the Crowd, Considerations on the Point of Pathology, Philosophy, History and Justice]. Paris: Baillere, volume 2, p. 400.
390. Shorter, Edward (1992). *From Paralysis to Fatigue.* New York: The Free Press. Shorter, Edward (1994). *The Cultural Origins of Psychosomatic Symptoms.* New York: Maxwell Macmillan International.
391. Shorter, op cit., p. 91.
392. Shorter, op cit., p. vii.
393. Godwin, George (1951). *The Great Revivalists.* London: Watts, p. 98.
394. An account of Puritanism in the American colonies can be found in Lovejoy, David S. (1985). *Religious Enthusiasm in the New World.* Cambridge, MA: Harvard University Press.
395. Macaulay, Thomas Babington (1887). *The History of England from the Accession of James II.* Philadelphia, PA: Porter & Coates.
396. Richard Baxter quoted in Hastings, James (1908). *Encyclopaedia of Religion and Ethics, Volume 10.* Edinburgh: T & T. Clark [published by volumes], p. 507.

QUAKERS

England: 1653

Though the Society of Friends is today the most decorous of religious communities, it was not always so. Their early history includes manifestations of extraordinary behavior that are characteristic of the revivals of the 18th and 19th century.

CONTEXT: The mid-17th century in England was a free-for-all for new religious and millennarist groups. "During the years from 1643 to 1649 London became a cauldron of seething Puritan causes… in the opinion of [some] it became a hot-bed of pernicious and heretical sectaries."[1] Along with most religious breakaway communities, the Quakers rejected not simply the Papism from which England had freed itself, but also the Presbyterianism that had widely replaced it. Persecuted and often self-exiled under James I and Charles I, they emerged under the Commonwealth as independents. England teemed with groups large and small who sought total freedom of conscience, often going to extremes in their search, extravagant both in their policies and their behavior. Most of these – the Fifth Monarchy men and the Family of Love, the Ranters and the Seekers – either disintegrated or faded away. If the Quakers survived, it was only by changing their ways, renouncing extravagance and adopting simplicity. But the respectable adulthood of the Friends sprang from a turbulent adolescence that earned them, not without cause, the nickname of Quakers.

The sect that came to be called Quakers originated about 1647 in the northern counties of Yorkshire, Lancashire, Cumberland, and Durham. The two principal leaders were James Naylor and George Fox, both of whom, though unquestionably sincere in their motivation, behaved in ways perceived as bizarre and even anti-social by outsiders. Indeed, the extravagant behavior of Naylor was so extreme that in the course of time he was repudiated by Fox and his friends, and soon crossed the law not simply in the minor infringements, thereby bringing many Quakers into the courts and frequently into the jails. His followers all but worshipped him, calling him the Everlasting Son and the Prince of Peace, but the scandalous behavior of himself and that of his disciples led to his being imprisoned, pilloried, whipped at a cart's tail, his tongue bored through with a hot iron, and his forehead branded. After a spell in prison he recanted and was subsequently readmitted into the Society.

His colleague Fox was hardly less extreme in his behavior as he walked the countryside, preaching salvation and denouncing injustice and oppression. Famously, but not untypically, in the winter of 1650 he was suddenly inspired by the sight of the three

George Fox, founder of the Society of Friends, sees the streets of Lichfield running with blood.

spires of Lichfield Cathedral to walk over hedge and ditch until within a kilometer or so of the city, he left his shoes with some shepherds and walked barefoot through the city – which was exceptionally busy, it being market-day – crying, "Woe unto the bloody city of Lichfield!" – bloody, because "there seemed to me to be a channel of blood running down the streets and the market-place appeared to be a pool of blood."[2] He was liable to strip off his clothes and walk naked through towns and villages "as a sign amongst you before your destruction cometh, that you might see that you were naked and not covered with the truth."[3] In this practice he was imitated by a good many of his followers, and one woman went so far as to strip in Whitehall Chapel in the presence of Cromwell.[4] In 1655 one Richard Sale walked through the streets of Derby, "barefoot and bare-legged, dressed in sackcloth, with ashes on his head, sweet flowers in his right hand and stinking weeds in his left… the people struck into astonishment, though some set their dogs at him."[5]

Such excesses were generally disapproved of, and in the unsettled state of the country between 1651 and 1657, it is not too surprising that some two thousand Quakers were at one time or another imprisoned for disturbing the peace. Fox himself set the example by being imprisoned for "brawling" in 1651. In 1652, a number of Lancashire ministers and justices petitioned Parliament against these troublesome folk who "have drawn much people after them; many whereof (men, women and little children) at their meetings are strangely wrought upon in their bodies, and brought to fall, foam at the mouth, roar and swell in their bellies."[6] They also offended many by refusing such common courtesies as doffing the hat when greeting, and by using the familiar "thee" and "thou" to social superiors. Apart from actions taken by the authorities, they were often physically attacked by the populace they were trying to convert, and Fox came close to being lynched on more than one occasion.

The young sect called themselves by various names, but soon accepted the name popularly bestowed on them, first applied formally by Justice Gervase Bennet of Derby, when ordering Fox to prison. The term "quakers" had been used previously by a sect of women at Southwark, London, who swelled, shivered, and shook before commencing to preach, but after 1650 the term was reserved for the Society of Friends.[7] Fox himself made shakings part of his ritual, and exhorted his followers to follow his example. Evidently they did so, for a contemporary commentator speaks of "a people called Quakers" who "fell into strange fits of quaking and trembling."[8]

The kind of behavior that gave rise to the name is illustrated in this account from 1653:

Some Quakers came out of the North into Wales about Wrexham; at their Meetings after long silence, sometimes one, sometimes more, fell into a great and dreadful Shaking and Trembling in their whole Bodies, and all their Joynts with such Risings, and Swellings in their Bellies and Bowels, sending forth such Shriekings, Yeaulings [sic], Howlings, and Roarings, as not only affrighted the Spectators, but caused the Dogs to bark, the Swine to cry, and the Cattel to run about; to the astonishment of all that heard them. By these Artifices one William Spencer was drawn by them to leave the Church, and to follow them, whereupon several times he fell into the same quaking Fits; and lying with one of them three several Nights, the last Night being much troubled, and not able to sleep, upon a sudden he heard something buzzing and humming about the Quakers Head like an Humble-Bee, which did sore affright him, whereupon he sought to rise, but the Quaker persuaded him to lie still; and immediately there arose a great Wind and Storm, which shook the House wherein they lay.[9]

The following year, an Anglican priest was persuaded by some friends to attend a meeting of the Quakers at Benfield-side, in County Durham…

…where I found about twenty Persons siting all silent. And after we had sate a while, all being mute, the Lord moved me to arise and call upon his Name by Prayer; I was no sooner up, but my Legs trembled greatly, so that it was some difficulty to me to stand; but after I had Prayed a short space the trembling ceased. While I prayed to God as a Creator, there was but little disturbance; but when I cryed in the name of Jesus Christ my Mediator, God in my Nature in the highest Glory appearing, and interceding for his Saints, then the Devil roared in the deceived Souls, in a most strange and dreadful manner, some howling, some screeching, yelling, roaring, and some had a strange confused kind of humming and singing Noise. Such a representation of Hell I never heard of; there was nothing but Horror and Confusion.

After I had done Praying, (not opening my Eyes before), I was amazed to see about the one half of those miserable Creatures so terribly shaken, with such strange, violent, various Motions, that I wondered how it was possible for some of them to live. In the midst of this Confusion one of them asked me, if I was come to torment them… After two Hours, as we were departing out of the House, one of them cursed me with these words, All the plagues of God be upon thee; whereupon I return'd and pray'd for such of them as had not committed the unpardonable sin.[10]

After the Restoration, stricter laws were passed against the Quakers, nominally for such actions as refusing to take the oath of allegiance to the restored monarchy on the grounds that it was against their principles. In 1665 or so two of them – one of them being William Penn, the future founder of Pennsylvania, who had joined the Society in 1666 – were imprisoned for causing a riot. But by this time a great change was coming over the Society, and from being one of the most extravagant of sects they became one of the most well-behaved. Baxter noted the change as early as 1664: "At first they did use to fall into violent Tremblings and sometimes Vomitings in their meetings, and pretended to be violently acted by the Spirit; but now that is ceased, they only meet, and he that pretendeth to be moved by the Spirit speaketh, and sometimes they say nothing, but sit an hour or more in silence, and then depart."[11]

COMMENT: The Society of Friends is proof that it is possible for a community to progress from extravagant behavior to a more tranquil style of worship without compromising their principles. Moreover, whereas sects such as the Mennonites and Amish have survived by isolating themselves from mainstream society, the Quakers not only survived but went on to play a distinguished part in public life.

Sources

1. Braithwaite, William C. (1955). *The Beginnings of Quakerism.* Cambridge: University Press, pp. 11, 13.
2. Braithwaite, op cit, p. 16, quoting Fox's journal.
3. Braithwaite, op cit., p. 148, quoting a letter by Fox to the people of Ulverston.
4. Blunt, John Henry (1874). *Dictionary of Sects, Heresies, Ecclesiastical Parties and Schools of Religious Thought.* London, Oxford & Cambridge: Rivingtons, p. 464 et seq.
5. Braithwaite, op cit., p. 126.
6. Quoted by Braithwaite, op cit., p. 108.
7. Braithwaite, op cit., p. 17.
8. Braithwaite, op cit., p. 72.
9. Turner, William (1697). *A Compleat History of the Most Remarkable Providences.* London: Dunton, Part II, p. 131.
10. Turner, op cit., p. 131.
11. Knox, Ronald A. (1950). *Enthusiasm.* Oxford University Press, p. 150, citing Baxter.

R

RAILWAY SPINE

United States and United Kingdom: 19th century

As railroads revolutionized transportation and people flocked to ride the rails, a new medical condition arose in Great Britain and later spread to the United States. "Railway spine" or "spinal irritation" was supposedly caused by railway mishaps. The symptoms were as bizarre as they were vague – everything from menstrual pain to temporary blindness, paralysis, and drooling were attributed to this new condition. The treatments were equally varied and included applying leeches, caustic substances, or magnets. During the 20th century, the diagnosis was discarded. Railway spine was steeped in controversy, as many physicians believed that the "victims" were practicing deception for financial gain. As William Osler once noted: "In railway cases, so long as litigation is pending and the patient is in the hands of the lawyers, the symptoms usually persist. Settlement is often the starting-point of a speedy and perfect recovery."[1] Other physicians of the era considered the symptoms to be of psychogenic origin.

RAILWAY AND OTHER INJURIES

OF THE

NERVOUS SYSTEM.

BY

JOHN ERIC ERICHSEN,

FELLOW OF THE ROYAL COLLEGE OF SURGEONS,

PROFESSOR OF SURGERY AND OF CLINICAL SURGERY IN UNIVERSITY COLLEGE;

SURGEON TO UNIVERSITY COLLEGE HOSPITAL;

EXAMINER IN SURGERY AT THE UNIVERSITY OF LONDON;

AND FORMERLY SO AT THE

UNIVERSITY OF DURHAM, AND THE ROYAL COLLEGE OF PHYSICIANS.

"JE RACONTE, JE NE JUGE PAS."

MONTAIGNE.

Work stress can lead to confusion and cause accidents.

RED SCARES

United States: 1918-1921 and 1946-1955

THE FIRST COMMUNIST RED SCARE

Fear of "Reds" or "Outside Foreign-Born Radical Agitators" swept across America at about the same time as World War I was ending. This chapter in American history is sometimes referred to as "The Big Red Scare." While "Red" refers to Communists, who were viewed as the primary threat, it also involved a growing intolerance for many foreigners.

CONTEXT: Historians Landis Heller and Norris Potter remark that this was a period of widespread xenophobia, as fear and prejudicial sentiments were displayed not just against Communists but Socialists, African Americans, Jews, and other minorities.[2] These unpopular groups served as scapegoats for prevailing fears. A similar episode during the late 1940s and early 1950s coincided with Cold War anxieties of Communists and other "subversives."

The Red Scare was characterized by a series of bitter union strikes for better wages, and a fear that Russian radicals were infiltrating American unions. The March 1917 Bolshevik Revolution and the ascendancy of Soviet communism had made many citizens fearful of a communist overthrow of the U.S. government. Russian leader Vladimir Ilyich Lenin had asked for workers across the planet to unite in the Communist cause and revolt. "Many Americans saw the strikes that swept the nation as the start of a Communist revolution."[3] British historian M.J. Heale wrote that during this period, the U.S. Justice Department arrested about 6,000 "suspected radicals," while in Washington State, about 249 labeled as "dangerous Reds" were placed on a ship bound for Russia. Heale said that throughout the country there were "countless official and vigilante actions, strikers were beaten and sometimes killed, socialist meetings were broken up, radical newspapers were suppressed, allegedly unpatriotic teachers were fired, and men and women suspected of disloyalty were assaulted, arrested, or forced to kiss the flag."[4]

The Second Red Scare

Between 1946 and 1950, several people were arrested in the U.S. for being Soviet spies, most prominently Ethel and Julius Rosenberg, who were convicted of giving secrets of the atomic bomb to the Soviet Union. Soon there was a great fear that other seemingly ordinary citizens could also be Russian spies. These events set the stage for the Red Scare of the early 1950s. A statement in 1947 by the U.S. Attorney General under President Harry Truman captured the mood of this period: "American Reds are everywhere – in factories, offices, butcher stores, on street corners, in private businesses – and each carries in himself the germ of death for society."[5]

Communists depicted as a pack of destructive wolves in 1918.

There was also concern during the late 1940s over the infiltration of radio and television programs by "Reds." In 1947, public hearings were held by the House Un-American Activities Committee to determine the extent of the communist influence among various actors, writers, and directors. Soon thousands of innocent people suspected of supporting communism were fired from their jobs, and many actors, writers, and directors of radio, television, and movies were blacklisted from their professions. The publication *Red Channels*, which provided lists of radio and television employees who were suspected of being or supporting communist activities, became popular during this period. Actor Lee Grant offered firsthand insights into the mood in Hollywood at the time, observing that the few Communists in the film industry were not trying to overthrow the government but simply earning a living. After the anti-Communists had neutralized these so-called "real Communists," they began to cast a wider net of suspicion.[6] Grant stated that soon "they started picking on people who had given money to certain organizations, people who had shown up at the 'wrong' party, or people who voted for the 'wrong' person – people who weren't even political at all, like me. And the entertainment industry buckled under the pressure."[7] Grant also noted how *Red Channels* was highly influential for TV actors and making the list was not difficult. He said that if someone publicly complained about the practice of blacklisting during a union meeting, "somebody from the union board would write your name down, and the next day you'd be on the list. The Screen Actors Guild, run by Ronald Reagan, did the same thing. And once you were blacklisted you were out of work unless you got up in front of the union and said, 'I'm sorry...'"[8]

The exaggerated fear of a Communist-led takeover of the U.S. began gaining even greater momentum in 1950, sparked by a reference made by Republican Senator Joseph McCarthy of Wisconsin who claimed to be aware of a list containing the names of many State Department employees who were supposedly Communists. McCarthy's speech before a Republican woman's group in Wheeling, West Virginia, was dramatic, chilling, and made simplistic references between good and evil: "Ladies and gentlemen, can there be anyone here tonight who is so blind as to say that the war is not on? Can there be anyone who fails to realize that the Communist world has said, 'The time is now' – that this is the time for the show-down between the democratic Christian world and the Communist atheistic world..." McCarthy then told the crowd: "In my opinion the State Department, which is one of the most important government departments, is thoroughly infested with Communists. I have in my hand fifty-seven cases of individuals who would appear to be either card-carrying members or certainly loyal to the Communist Party, but who nevertheless are still helping to shape our foreign policy."[9] In later speeches, he gave varying numbers. In reality, there was no list, but he realized that his initial mention of such a list was a magnet for attracting mass media coverage to his cause.[10]

In 1952, McCarthy was assigned to chair the new, seemingly insignificant Committee on Government Operations. The committee soon held great influence as it "carried in its wake an investigative subcommittee with authority to scrutinize 'government activities at all levels,' and McCarthy determined to use it to pursue his crusade against communism."[11] McCarthy's committee chairmanship gave him access to vital resources, as he headed "a federally funded staff and budget and a kind of quasi-legitimacy in employing his extensive network of bureaucratic informants."[12] McCarthy's public stature and recognition continued to grow in 1953 during a series of hearings held by his committee. During the spring and summer of 1954, the scare reached a fever pitch with televised hearings beginning in April. Millions of Americans were able to watch McCarthy on national television, and by the time the hearings ended in June, his favorable ratings in opinion polls were eroding, his image as a hero was shattered, and he was widely condemned as a bully who was unable to substantiate his many allegations. American journalists Peter Jennings and Todd Brewster described McCarthy as a "buffoon" whose charges were typically comprised of innuendo, suggestion, and diversion, as well as direct attack.[13] By December, the Senate voted 67 to 22 to censure McCarthy. During the mid-1950s the scare gradually subsided.

The absurdity of McCarty's methods was such that word McCarthyism is now synonymous with Red Scare and bigotry. The word entered the political lexicon in the early 1950s and refers to anyone engaging in the public practice of making indiscriminate, unsubstantiated accusations of political subversion with the intention of suppressing opposition. Some scholars consider the U.S. government's reaction following the September 11, 2001 terrorist attacks on the United States, and the U.S.-Iraq War of 2003, as forms of neo-McCarthyism. These events coincided with a widespread demonization of Arab-Americans as terrorists or subversives, accusations that were supported by little evidence. Following the September 11th attacks, many civil rights organizations were critical of actions taken by the U.S. government, including the detaining of illegal immigrants. A U.S. government investigation later supported such claims, including "failure to promptly tell detainees why they were being held; hindering their ability to secure legal counsel and bond hearings; a denial of bail for many detainees; physical and verbal abuse; and sometimes harsh conditions of detainment."[14]

During the 2003 Iraq War, "intolerance arose against those in the film and television industry and elsewhere who opposed war with Iraq. Many were accused of being 'anti-American' or 'unpatriotic' for taking public stands on matters of conscience, or simply for stating views that were opposed to that of the government."[15]

REVIVALISM

A catch-all term for a variety of religious manifestations, revivalism implies attempts to breathe new life into religious faiths, beliefs, and practices by means of a campaign of vigorous propaganda and preaching. Implicit is the assumption that there is something to be revived. As opposed to missionary work directed towards adherents to other beliefs, revivals are addressed to those who are nominally fellow-believers but who are not active or are perceived as backsliding in their beliefs.

Revivalism can take place within any religion, but as a recurrent practice it is confined most notably to Protestant Christian churches in North America and Great Britain. In Britain, the METHODIST REVIVAL (commenced circa 1739), and in America, the Great Awakening from the same period (see AMERICAN REVIVALISM) set the tone for future manifestations. John Wesley's huge outdoor gatherings and the camp meetings of rural America brought to ordinary people a quite different kind of religious involvement than that offered by the traditional churches. While purporting to restore the principles of true Christianity, they seemed to open up new dimensions of personal spirituality. In so doing, they aroused the suspicion, and often the hostility, of critics who then and subsequently have disparaged the emotionalism of revivals as shallow and transitory. While their short-term achievements are often impressive, the long-term benefits are less so, and many opponents consider the overall psychological damage far outweighs any benefits.

Camp meetings were often the occasion for outbreaks of collective enthusiasm.

Critical comment has come from many quarters, notably from Church establishments that have perceived revivalism as undermining rather than reinforcing their own regular efforts. (See METHODISM for Bishop Lackington's vigorous contemporary riposte to Wesley.) Criticism of a different kind has come from sociologists, who consider revivalism as a harmful social activity. As early as 1905, Frederick Davenport, for example, accused revivalists of appealing to primitive elements in their congregations.[16] Robert Thouless, in 1923, concluded: "Although even emotional violence may be used to produce desirable changes in people's hearts, it should be clear that [such] methods have great dangers. The jerks and other morbid symptoms, even when they are only temporary, are undesirable. But they may also, although perhaps rarely, end in permanent insanity. The weakening of moral control tends to result in immorality. In addition to this there is a danger of revivals losing their beneficial effect on conduct, and becoming a kind of emotional debauch."[17]

It is precisely this aspect of revivalism that earns it a place in this Encyclopedia. The revival meeting is par excellence the occasion to observe suggestion and imitation occurring in a crowd situation, because, for all the tumult, the gathering is relatively coherent and, in all respects other than its behavior, well controlled. The participants are self-defined as sharing a common purpose, and their behavior is the expression of that purpose. For that reason, the manifestations are not simply tolerated but positively welcomed as the outward signs of the inner process in which all those present are involved.

These behaviors, described in our individual entries, comprise, inter alia, the uttering of cries and animal noises, convulsions leading to collapse, and compulsive movements known as "jerks." Commencing with a few individuals, these behaviors spread rapidly through the assembly and frequently involve simultaneous actions by hundreds of participants.

The preachers and other leaders do not purposefully instigate these manifestations; they arise spontaneously among the assembly. Nevertheless, it is the preachers who create the necessary conditions. Underwood noted: "When the revivalist confronts his audience, his first business is to transform it from a mere aggregate of individuals into a psychological mass – into a genuine crowd with its interest and attention fixed in a common direction. At first the audience is not homogeneous. Many may be in a mood of expectation, but not all. Some are preoccupied, some indifferent, some prejudiced or even antagonistic. The revivalist's efforts will fall short of full success if these people are not welded into a sympathetic unity. Singing in chorus is one of the chief means used for securing this unity. In the Torry-Alexander mission in London in 1904, Alexander was most insistent that everybody should sing. He would say, those who have never sung before in their lives must sing today."[18]

Having broken down any tendency to individual action, the preacher works on the emotions of his audience, particularly by addressing himself to their fears rather than their hopes. Edwin Starbuck, in his landmark study of religious conversion, noted that "Fear of Death and Hell" easily outranked any other motive in those who converted as a result of attending a revival meeting.[19] Jonathan Edwards, in the course of the American "Great Awakening," scared his hearers with terrifying warnings: "All are by nature the children of wrath and heirs of Hell...Everyone that has not been born again, whether he be young or old, is exposed, every moment, to eternal destruction, under the wrath of Almighty God...As innocent as children seem to be to us, if they are out of Christ, they are not so in God's sight, but are young vipers and are infinitely more hateful than vipers..."[20]

The effect of such sentiments on an uncritical audience for whom the preacher represented unquestioned authority was to arouse feelings to such an extent that they translated into physical expression. Though some preachers deplored the excesses, others welcomed them as the outward signs of inward conversions, an emotional catharsis which they regarded as equivalent to a second birth. Wesley himself, at whose meetings these manifestations first took place in the context of religious revival, hesitated to think them ultimately beneficial, and his Methodists, like the QUAKERS, outgrew their early enthusiasm. Although revivalism continues to be marked by emotionalism and collective fervor, even the histrionics of a Billy Sunday or an Aimée Semple McPherson did not inspire their audiences to the extremes of behavior which characterized it in the 18th and 19th centuries.

See also: ANIMAL NOISES, DEMON POSSESSION, ENTHUSIASM EPISODES.

RHODE ISLAND MARTIAN PANIC

Providence, Rhode Island: October 30, 1974

Between 11 p.m. and midnight on Wednesday, October 30, 1974, a local adaptation of the original 1938 *War of the Worlds* script was broadcast over radio station WPRO, Providence, frightening listeners in the tiny New England coastal state of Rhode Island. The play had an opening storyline similar to the Welles drama, and the script was vivid and localized with WPRO reporters covering a series of explosions near Jamestown, the purported Martian landing site. Included was a description of a "blue flame from Mars." This was followed by reports of traffic jams and several fatalities, and a dramatic announcement that Governor Philip Noel was mobilizing the National Guard. WPRO reporters were sent to the scene, only to be vaporized by Martian ray guns. Prominent landmarks such as the two-mile long Newport Bridge were "blown up" in the alien attack.

The drama aired during the Holland Cook show, a nightly feature between 7 p.m. and midnight. At 11 o'clock, Cook, a local disc jockey who had only been working for about a month, began by playing the taped invasion, which opened with a continuation of his regular music program. Suddenly there was a bulletin about a meteor impact near Jamestown. The prerecorded program was produced by Jake Pacquin, but unlike the 1938 Welles broadcast, there was no opening disclaimer about the fictional nature of the program listeners were about to hear.[21] WPRO did not begin to promote the Halloween show until 12:45 p.m. the day of the broadcast, airing them about one per hour.[22] Station management had notified various police agencies within the primary listening area prior to the broadcast and told listeners there would be "a Halloween spoof" at 11 p.m.

Area police departments logged more than 80 telephone inquiries about "the disaster," while the city fire stations and other radio and TV outlets reported being inundated with inquiries from anxious callers, as was WPRO, which received more than 100 calls.[23] Police switchboards statewide were jammed with calls from panic-stricken or angry listeners.[24] The impact of the broadcast was not nearly on the scale of the Orson Welles drama, as it was not broadcast over a syndicated network of stations but on a station with a modest signal. Another factor in reducing the panic was the late hour at which it aired.[25] By 11 o'clock, many listeners were already asleep and many others were tuned in to their local TV news. The *Providence Journal-Bulletin* received about 500 calls within the period of an hour.[26]

The Federal Communications Commission (FCC) received letters of complaint protesting the broadcast, including accounts of frightened citizens speeding through the streets in an effort to reach home to protect their families. Some people altered their travel routes in an effort to bypass areas that the announcer told people to avoid. One letter writer conveys the depth of the scare: "We are not alarmists or gullible people but in the hour that we listened we were so afraid we called neighbors and our parents to warn them."[27] One man left work after receiving a phone call from a friend telling him that his family, living near Jamestown, was in danger. A number of people were frightened and disoriented after being awakened by others and hearing disturbing details of the "disaster."[28] Even Providence Democratic Congressman William Babin heard the broadcast, noting that his 19-year-old daughter woke him after being "really scared" by the show.[29] In East Providence, some residents began "crying and throwing up."[30] Another caller told a reporter, their voice shaking: "I was scared to death, running around the house with a gun. I can understand replaying the Orson Welles' thing. But I listen to WPRO at morning and night [sic], and I never heard them advertise that program."[31] The station did not air a disclaimer until 35 minutes into the show.[32]

Following its probe of the event, the FCC issued a reprimand to WPRO but did not suspend or revoke their license. In doing so, it cautioned against using "'scare' announcements or headlines which either are untrue or are worded in such a way as to mislead and frighten the public..."[33] An attempt to downplay the extent of the public reaction turned comical when station officials pointed out to the FCC that there was no public gathering at the "landing site," as happened in the 1938 Orson Welles episode. The Commission replied that "it would be reasonable to assume that the last place that those people misled by the broadcast would want to gather is at the Martian landing site."[34] Despite the initial concern over the possibility of the station losing its license, "It was a powerful boost to our sales staff and boosted advertising revenues," Cooke said.[35] "The program showed just how easy it is to fool the public."[36]

COMMENT: As is evidenced by the public reaction to earlier radio broadcasts of Martian invasion scares, disclaimers, even those played during the broadcast, are not always adequate to counteract the use of local announcers and live bulletins. The editors of the *Providence Bulletin-Journal* summarized this point well: "There is no way in which any radio station or television can be sure that its early warnings about hoaxes will be heard by all those persons who may tune in on broadcasts at later hours of the day or evening. For that reason...full explanations ought to be offered as the show opens and at frequent intervals during productions."[37]

See also: ORSON WELLES MARTIAN PANIC (1938), MARTIAN INVASION SCARE (1939), CHILEAN MARTIAN INVASION PANIC (1944), ECUADOR MARTIAN INVASION PANIC (1949), BUFFALO MARTIAN INVASION SCARE (1968), PORTUGUESE MARTIAN INVASION PANICS (1988 and 1998).

RIOTS

Perhaps the most feared form of social chaos is the riot. Riots are the relatively spontaneous gathering of people who blatantly break traditional norms and usually engage in destructive behavior to people or property. They typically last from a few hours to several days and, occasionally, intermittently for weeks or months. Contrary to popular belief, rioters are not necessarily made up of mostly the riff-raff and criminal element. When Anthony Oberschall analyzed the Los Angeles race riots of August 1965, he found that the 4,000 or so people arrested came from various segments of the population, although most were from lowest rungs of the economic and social ladder.[38]

Why do some people go on rampages, destroy property, loot stores of their valuables, and beat or kill innocent victims? Riots may be viewed as a problem-solving exercise whereby frustration, tension, and anger over what are perceived to be unjust social conditions foster a need for action by challenging authorities and attacking the existing social order. However, this is not always true. In some instances joyous crowds may become so excited as to riot, after a team wins a big game or championship, for example.

Riots can be broken down into two categories. *Uncoordinated riots* involve random destruction, looting, and pilfering with no specific target group in mind; it is an expression of general dissatisfaction. *Coordinated riots* are purposeful when the anger is vented with a specific goal or direction in mind such as a person, group, or commodity. Included are race riots and revolutionary crowds, such as the storming of the French Bastille on July 14, 1789, when an enraged mob freed the prisoners in this huge fort. Lynchings also qualify as a coordinated riot. More than 3,000 people are known to have been lynched in the United States between 1900 and 1950 – of which less than a tiny fraction were white. Triggering events included acting in a boastful manner, riding with white passengers on a train, and asserting one's right to vote.[39]

During a prison riot in Montana, an officer is murdered before the leaders kill themselves and others surrender.

Ralph Conant has identified the four phases that all riots pass through.[40] First is *the precipitating incident*. This is a situation, act, or event that those rioting view as proof that they are the victims of social injustice. After studying 76 race riots spanning 50 years, Stanley Lieberman and Arnold Silverman listed various triggers. These include reports of interracial fights, murder, or shootings; desecrating the American flag; violations of civil liberties; and the murder, attack, rape, or hold-up of white women by black men.[41] Precipitating events can be either real or imagined. For instance, in 1780, the Gordon Riots were triggered in part after the passage of Parliamentary legislation extending Catholic rights, which confirmed the widespread belief among Protestants that they were second-class citizens.[42] Protestants were also fearful that such acts as the proposed restoration of privileges to Catholics might rekindle attempts to restore the Pope's authority. Sociologist Reid Luhman remarked that "riots form around some kind of precipitating event, or spark, that sets things off. As with checking a gas tank with a lighted match, the cause of the conflagration is more the gas than the match, but both are necessary."[43]

The second phase is *the confrontation*, where potential rioters are incited to right the perceived injustice. This commonly occurs when outraged group members have gathered publicly and vocalize injustices (real or imagined), heightening emotions and the urge to take immediate action. Often, the confrontation develops after police arrive at the scene immediately after the precipitating incident, become the subject of taunts, and cause an increase in violence as they try to disperse or arrest members of the crowd.

Conant's third stage is the *Roman holiday*, where authorities lose control of the situation and "all Hell breaks loose." This is the most dangerous, violent, and destructive part of any riot. On November 30, 1946, police arrested 600 street vendors in parts of Shanghai, China, for illegally selling their goods. That evening after unsuccessful attempts to end the protest, police used machine gun fire and a show of bayonets to disperse the infuriated crowd. Chaos followed as the mob rampaged through the city, smashing and overturning cars, burning buildings, attacking foreigners, and shouting pro-communist slogans. Within a few short hours a semblance of order was restored, but 221 persons were under arrest and parts of the city were in shambles.[44]

The final stage is *the siege*, where most of the looting has ceased, reinforcements have arrived, and authorities must regain control, or in some cases of deep, widespread dissatisfaction, risk a government overthrow. Here martial law is often declared, the battle lines are clearly drawn as snipers may prevent firefighters from doing their job and fire-bombings may continue. A classic example of riots bringing down a government is the French Revolution.

Sociologists commonly discuss four categories of riots. *Communal riots* (sometimes called *race riots*) usually involve violent clashes between opposing groups that are split along religious or racial lines. They tend to be turf wars in which control of a particular neighborhood, such as a park, a beach, or even part of a prison recreational area, is contested. Between June 3-9, 1943, Los Angeles was ravaged by race riots after a fight broke out between a group of U.S. sailors and young Mexican-American gang members flashily dressed in "zoot suits" (a men's suit fashion at the time, consisting of a long, loose-fitting jacket with padded shoulders and high-waisted pants). The turf in dispute was downtown L.A. While the initial altercation was relatively minor, it served to foment stereotypes and prejudice against Hispanics, who were widely viewed as mentally inferior and prone to commit crime. Indeed, the public, press, and police all backed the servicemen who were viewed as heroic patriots, as World War II was raging. Soon, uniformed members of the various armed forces were roaming the city in taxicabs, spotting and attacking zoot-suiters, and eventually targeting anyone of color. Many of those arrested were zoot-suiters whose crime was to have been beaten up by the servicemen. The rioting did not end until the City Council proclaimed the wearing of zoot suits was a misdemeanor, and the military declared the city off limits to service personnel.[45]

Commodity Riots involve civil disorder where the target of attack is not directly people but property, especially buildings, goods, and equipment. While violence often occurs, it is usually in the course of authorities trying to stop the looting or destruction of property. Commodity riots, especially over food, are common in parts of impoverished Africa. Periodic bread riots were part of the political landscape across Europe, notably in England, France, and Italy in the 18th and 19th centuries. Bread is the commodity par excellence, and its shortage was a disaster for those living near the subsistence level.

Protest Riots are a reaction to a particular government policy. Episodes usually involve civilians who refuse to obey an official directive and who often physically or verbally attack government agents. On the other side stand the police or military, which are called in to restore order and stop the unrest from spreading. Sometimes citizens hurl objects at authorities – stones, bottles, and sticks. Such acts were common in the late 1960s and early 1970s during many Anti-Vietnam protests of the U.S. government policy of sending troops to fight against communism in Indo-China. David Miller noted that during protest riots, citizens rarely use weapons such as firearms or Molotov cocktails, and most of the casualties are inflicted by the authorities in their crackdown to reestablish control.[46] At Kent State University in Ohio, four students were shot dead on May 4, 1970, after National Guardsmen fired into a group of unarmed demonstrators. The protesters were upset with the Vietnam War, had broken windows, thrown rocks at the troops, and burned down a military recruitment office. In the "Boston Massacre" of March 5, 1770, a mob of angry American colonists gathered near the Boston customs house where unpopular taxes were collected. They shouted inflammatory names at the British Red Coats who guarded the building, tossing oyster shells and snowballs at the frightened soldiers, daring them to fire. Shortly thereafter, musket balls struck down five colonists while no soldiers were hurt.

Perhaps the worst protest riot in U.S. history occurred in response to a draft. On March 3, 1863, Congress passed the Conscription Act requiring all able men between 20 and 45 to report for military service in the Civil War if called upon. Many people were furious because the law stipulated that anyone could avoid the draft by paying $300 to Uncle Sam or hiring someone to fight for him (substitute soldiers). The northern states erupted in riots, the worst of which occurred in New York City, where those who could not afford to pay $300, especially poor Irish Americans, went on a rampage in July 1863. They attacked wealthy citizens who had paid to get out of the draft, as well as Negroes who were resented for causing the Civil War to begin with. The Colored Orphan Asylum was even torched, as were government buildings, including conscription offices. At least 70 people were killed.[47]

Celebration Riots are perhaps the most common type of riot and involve mass joys and exuberance, usually after sporting events when one team wins a championship or upsets another team especially against long odds. During such outbreaks, fans may rock, pound on, or push over vehicles; start fires; break items such as windows or bottles; and even loot.[48] In October 1971, the Pittsburgh Pirates baseball team beat the Baltimore Orioles to win the World Series. Excited fans reacted by flipping over cars, breaking store windows, and setting fire to a police motorcycle. In addition to about 100 people being arrested, one reporter wrote: "As for eyewitness accounts of love-making in the park, the police chief conceded that some people 'got a little out of hand.'"[49] An incident not involving sports occurred in March 1986, when thousands of college students descended upon the vacation community of Palm Springs, California, to have fun during spring break. Many students became so excited and high-spirited that they began tearing clothing off women and tossing bottles and rocks at cars. Before order was restored, a hundred students had been arrested.[50]

See also: ZOOT SUIT RIOTS.

RIVETER'S OVARIES

United States: World War II

In his book *The Natural History of Nonsense*, Bergen Evans recounts that during the summer of 1943, sexual fears developed among American female factory workers who were aiding the war effort on the home-front. Absenteeism rates were so high that the FBI investigated the possibility of sabotage. "Their findings, confirmed by other government and private agencies, was that women were being driven from the lathes and benches by strange sexual fears. Some feared that riveting caused cancer of the breast. A wholly new and fictitious female disorder – 'riveter's ovaries' – had been invented. And scores of women engaged in filling fire-extinguishers for airplanes had quit in panic when it was rumored that the material they were handling, carbon tetrachloride, caused pregnancy."[51]

CONTEXT: War-time stress and fears by women, who were widely believed to be physically and emotionally inferior to males, may have led to exaggerated concerns over the harm of workplace devices and chemicals in a setting a where women were traditionally not used to working.

ROLLING STONES MANIA

Glasgow, Scotland: June 15, 1965

Twenty-five girls collapsed and fell unconscious inside a hall during a Tuesday evening singing appearance by the popular rock group The Rolling Stones.[52]

COMMENT: This reaction to the Rolling Stones was typical of pop-music-inspired incidents. Mass swooning by adoring crowds occurred at concerts of such singing idols as Frank Sinatra, Elvis Presley, and The Beatles. Similar reactions resulted from the sudden, unexpected death of music and film stars. In August 1926, silent film star Rudolph Valentino, who died in New York at the age of 31 from complications from a ruptured appendix, triggered mass fainting and weeping, mostly among female fans. There are also press reports of female theatergoers fainting during screenings of his 1921 film, *The Sheik*.

RUMORS

A rumor is typically defined as the spread of an unverified but plausible story of perceived importance that may possess a "kernel of truth" but lacks substantiating evidence. Rumors are spawned during periods of uncertainty and anxiety. They are dynamic and change continuously, reflecting popular and personal beliefs. They typically last from a few days to a several months. Rumors are essential components of mass scares and hysterias. While rumors do not always precede panics, they almost always follow them. Rumors take root in the fertile soil of plausible, ambiguous situations of perceived importance as people unconsciously construct stories in an attempt to gain certainty and reduce fear and anxiety. In other words, "rumor is most likely to occur when people are intensely interested in a topic and little definite news or official information is available."[53] Conversely, when there is little interest in a topic and authoritative information is abundant, a rumor is unlikely to sprout. In his classic study of rumor, Tamotsu Shibutani described it as "improvised news" when the demand for a certain piece of news exceeds the supply.[54] The more ambiguous or unclear the situation, and the greater perceived importance of the story, the greater the likelihood and number of rumors. This is why there are so many rumors surrounding the stock market or during periods of war and crises.

Gordon Allport and Leo Postman were pioneers in the study of rumor. They monitored their formation in controlled laboratory experiments, observing that rumors change with retelling and undergo three processes. The first is *leveling*, which refers to the tendency for a story to become shorter, more concise, and more easily understood. A second process is *sharpening,* whereby key details become more prominent while other details are reduced or disappear altogether. Finally, *assimilation* refers to the tendency for stories to be sharpened and leveled in ways that reflect cultural themes, biases, and stereotypes. An example of this latter process occurred after the Japanese attack on Pearl Harbor on December 7, 1941, when wild rumors abounded. The loyalty of Japanese-Americans, long under suspicion, became the subject of intense speculation, especially the 160,000 Hawaiians with Japanese ancestry. Among the rumors:

> ... a McKinley High School ring was found on the body of a Japanese flier shot down over Honolulu; the water supply had been poisoned by the local Japanese; Japanese plantation workers had cut arrows pointing to Pearl Harbor in the cane field of Oahu; the local Japanese had been notified of the attack by an advertisement in a Honolulu newspaper on December 6...automobiles driven by local Japanese blocked the roads from Honolulu to Pearl Harbor; Japanese residents waved their kimonos at the pilots and signaled to them; some local men were dressed in Japanese Army uniforms during the attack...[55]

Even well after the attack, American newspapers and magazines, especially on the mainland, continued to perpetuate these tales. A spate of alarming rumors that

An American World War II poster: "No Room For Rumors."

the Pacific fleet was destroyed in the attack circulated across the country, eroding homeland confidence and morale. When the rumor continued to persist two and a half months after the incident, President Franklin Roosevelt decided it necessary to restore public confidence by holding a fireside radio chat, in which he accurately detailed the damage.[56]

Rumors are common under the stress, uncertainty, and ambiguity of wartime. Another example of this type occurred when Canada entered World War I in 1914, but the United States did not declare war until April 1917. During much of this interim period, rumors circulated across Canada that German-Americans, owing their allegiance to the Kaiser, were planning to launch surprise bombing raids or espionage missions on their unsuspecting northern neighbors. At the time there were nearly 10 million German-Americans living in the U.S. As accusations were made on the flimsiest evidence, there were scores of false claims about scheming Germans in both the U.S. and Canada. The British consul-general who was stationed in New York, Sir Courtney Bennett, was notorious for spreading unsubstantiated rumors. In early 1915, Bennett made several wild claims about a plot involving upwards of 80,000 armed, highly trained German-Americans who he said were secretly training in Western New York. The group was supposedly intent on invading Canada from the northwestern border of New York State. Despite the incredible, unfounded nature of his assertions, it was a reflection of the deep tension and suspicion of the period that Canadian Prime Minister Sir Robert Borden asked his Police Commissioner to issue a report on the stories, which were assessed to be without foundation.[57] (See also the section, "Phantom German Air Raids on Eastern Canada: 1915-1917" in the entry on PHANTOM AIRCRAFT WAVES.)

Recent research also identifies anxiety relief as a central element in rumor formation, a factor not identified in Allport and Postman's law of rumor.[58] Rumors are also a social barometer of a particular society at any given time. "Rumors...pass over many tongues, changing and enlarging in the process. The individual's ability to (re)shape the rumor multiple times transforms it into a collective representation of fears and anxieties."[59] Rumors also function as entertainment and elevate the teller's status.[60]

Jean-Noel Kapferer viewed rumor as a collective problem-solving activity through which "in the course of successive exchanges, the group tries to reconstruct the puzzle made up of scattered pieces gathered here and there. The fewer the pieces they have, the greater a role the group's unconscious plays in their interpretation; the more pieces they have, the closer their interpretation is to reality."[61] While Allport and Postman viewed rumor as growing increasingly distorted as it passes from person to person, viewing rumor as a collective activity poses a very different model of rumor transmission. Hence, if rumors are transmitted collectively, they may pass quickly to large numbers of people.[62] "In fact, the same person might expect to hear the same rumor, or some variation of it, among more than one source. Rumors travel back and forth, perhaps many times, from an entire network of people who know or are in contact with one another."[63]

Sociologists and social psychologists have devised categories for the many types of rumors. These include *bogy rumors,* which discuss an imminent disaster like a stock market crash. *Pipe-dream rumors* are sometimes called magical or wishful thinking rumors and involve stories that people hope are true. For instance, shortly after the collapse of the World Trade Center on September 11, 2001, it was rumored that a group of victims had been found in a small pocket of debris and pulled alive from the rubble. Once the U.S. bombing of the Taliban in Afghanistan began, there were a series of rumors that terrorist leader Osama bin Laden had been killed in the bombing. Another story claimed that he died of kidney failure. Still another had him succumbing to a lung ailment. There were even rumors of bin Laden hiding in a place people would never suspect – the United States. *Scapegoating* rumors involve blaming an innocent person or group. Shortly after September 11th, it was widely reported in the Arab-Muslim world that the Twin Towers attack had been orchestrated by the Israeli secret service in a cunning, ruthless attempt to foster anti-Islamic sentiment against Middle Eastern countries. Some researchers talk of *creeping rumors,* which are slow to build; *impetuous rumors,* which spread like wild fire;

and *diving rumors,* which disappear/reappear periodically. HEAD-HUNTING SCARES in Southeast Asia fall under this latter category, cropping up periodically over several centuries.

There are a number of specific types of rumors. *Product rumors* center on products that people commonly use. In the 1950s a rumor spread across the U.S. that a worker at a Coca-Cola plant had suddenly disappeared. After several days it was determined that he had fallen into a vat of Coke and the acid had completely dissolved his body. The story claimed that the tainted Coke had already been distributed to stores across the country.[64] *Atrocity rumors* are common during times or war or civil unrest and portray "the other side" as evil. During the 1943 Detroit race riots rumors circulated among the black community that a group of white sailors had pushed a black woman, who was holding her baby, off the Belle Isle Bridge. Yet, among the white community, the story spread that a black man had raped and murdered a white woman at Belle Island.[65] *Conspiracy rumors* often center around government cover-ups, such as claims surrounding the assassination of John F. Kennedy in Dallas, Texas in 1963, for instance, that there was a second shooter on the grassy knoll. Another common conspiracy rumor claims that the government is holding wreckage of an alien spaceship that allegedly crashed in Roswell, New Mexico in 1947. According to the story, the government won't release this information for fear of public hysteria.[66]

Psychoanalyst Carl Jung referred to rumors that are exclusively grounded in fantasy as *visionary rumors*. Jung used the example of a rumor at a girl's school that involved a teacher having sex with a student; the story had originated after a girl told friends of a dream. Jung also viewed UFOs as visionary rumors.[67]

It is sometimes alleged that "so and so" was guilty of spreading rumors about them. In reality, rumors are impossible to control since the content often changes in unexpected directions. A classic example of this point occurred during the 1930s when an advertising agency hired actors to spread rumors about certain products in the expectation that they could boost sales. In one case, two actors would board a crowded commuter train, one posing as a rich businessman, the other as a chauffeur. The latter – who presumably should know tires – would start a loud conversation with his counterpart, vigorously recommending a certain brand. Perhaps fortunately, the charade more often than not backfired as the story either did not spread, or worse, consumers mixed up the brands. At any rate, the scheme was a failure.[68] Most rumors are generated spontaneously and spread without ulterior motivations.[69]

During January 1983, the "Great Smurf Scare" swept across Houston, Texas, as scores of junior high school students refused to attend classes after a rumor circulated that a group of blue Smurfs from the popular TV cartoon were carrying guns and knives into local schools and killing people. The panic abated after several days, helped by the appearance of a principal who had supposedly been killed by the Smurfs. The story may have been triggered by a local TV broadcast of the arrest of 40 members of a youth gang, The Smurfs, for relatively minor crimes.[70]

The Paul McCartney Is Dead Rumor is classic, appearing in 1969, when stories circulated that musician and Beatle rock star Paul McCartney had died, but the band was keeping it secret. It was claimed that McCartney had died in an auto mishap in November 1966, and had been replaced by a look-alike by record company executives fearing that release of the "truth" might result in plummeting album sales.

The first known published account of the story appeared on September 23, 1969, in Illinois University's *Northern Star* newspaper, where it was noted that "there has been much conjecturing on the present state of the Beatle Paul McCartney."[71] On October 12, 1969, a man identifying himself only as "Tom" telephoned disc jockey Russ Gibb at Detroit, Michigan radio station WKNR-FM and began pointing out a series of coincidences to explain why McCartney had made few recent public appearances. "Tom" claimed that there were hidden clues to McCartney's death in a number of their songs. For instance, at the end of the song "Strawberry Fields Forever," it sounds like someone is saying, "I buried Paul."[72] On October 14, the *Michigan Daily,* published by students at the University of Michigan, carried an article entitled: "Mc-

Cartney is Dead." The lengthy article added more coincidences, and suggested that "Paul McCartney was killed in a car accident in early November 1966 after leaving the EMI studios tired, sad, and depressed."[73] The author, Fred LaBour, then made the astonishing claim that a double had taken McCartney's place. The *Chicago Sun-Times* published the story on October 21, 1969, lending further credence to the rumor.[74]

Over the ensuing weeks and months, fans began scrutinizing Beatle records and album covers for clues. On the "Sergeant Pepper" album, McCartney sports an armband with the letters "OPD," which some interpreted to mean "Officially Pronounced Dead." On their "Abbey Road" album, the Beatles were crossing a road in single file. Some speculated that it was a funeral procession as John Lennon, who led the pack, was dressed in white (the priest). Next came Ringo Starr dressed in black (the undertaker). Third was McCartney, who was dressed but barefooted (the corpse), followed by George Harrison, who was in street clothes (the grave digger). If that weren't enough, a car in the background has the plate "28IF." This was interpreted to mean that McCartney would have been 28 if he hadn't died. In the "Magical Mystery Tour" album, McCartney was wearing a black carnation – signifying death. There seemed no end to the speculations. People – especially teenagers – began scrutinizing their records and found hidden meanings everywhere. On the song "Revolution No. 9," some claimed to hear a faint voice in the background saying, "Turn me on, dead man."[75]

Even when McCartney denied the rumor in a *Life* magazine interview, some fans were suspicious, noting that "on the back of the page upon which McCartney's picture appeared, there was an advertisement for a car – if one looked through the page, the car could be seen cutting McCartney's head off."[76] In denying his death, McCartney stated: "It is all bloody stupid. I picked up that O.P.D. badge in Canada. It was a police badge. Perhaps it means Ontario Police Department... I was wearing a black flower because they ran out of red ones. It is John, not me, dressed in black on the cover and inside of 'Magical Mystery Tour.' On 'Abbey Road' we were wearing our ordinary clothes. I was walking barefoot because it was a hot day. The Volkswagen just happened to be parked there."[77]

RUNNING, JUMPING AND CLIMBING

A conspicuous feature of many of the collective disorders described in this Encyclopedia is the propensity for persons afflicted by them to run, jump, and climb. In case after case we find similar behaviors reported, whether of young nuns at WERTET, of orphans at HOORN, of Scottish village children at BRECHIN, or of French country children at MORZINE.

For example, in the Brechin outbreak of 1763, we are told

> They start up, and jump ten, fifteen or twenty times together, straight upward two, three or more feet from the ground. Then they start forward, and run with amazing swiftness two, three, or five hundred yards. Frequently they run up, like a cat, to the top of a house, and jump on the ridge of it as on the ground. But wherever they are, they never fall or miss their footing at all.[78]

And in the outbreak at Forfarshire, circa 1770:

> Sometimes they run with astonishing velocity, and often over dangerous passes, to some place out of doors, which they had fixed on in their own minds, or, perhaps, even mentioned to those in company with them, and then dropped down quite exhausted. At other times, especially when confined to the house, they climb in the most singular manner. In cottages, for example, they leap from the floor to…the beams…springing from one to another with the agility of a cat, or whirling round one of them, with a motion resembling the fly of a jack…but when the fit of dancing, leaping, or running came on, nothing tends so much to abate the violence of the disease, as allowing them free scope to exercise themselves, till nature be exhausted…and I have heard of one [house], in which a horse was always kept ready saddled, to follow the young ladies belonging to it, when they were seized with a fit of running.[79]

Whereas we should not be too surprised to find purely physical symptoms, such as the characteristic features of ecstatic trance recurring in diverse instances, these distinctive behaviors, which seem to have no intrinsic link with the disorder, are more puzzling.

The behavior is clearly compulsive, and nowhere is this more clearly seen than at Amsterdam in 1566, where the orphans climbed walls and rooftops as if they were cats, without coming to any harm. They had a particular habit of running towards a piece of water that was nearby as if intent on drowning themselves, then stop abruptly at the brink, explaining "The big man [meaning God] does not permit it."[80] If this had happened only at Amsterdam, one might suppose it to have been a game that these particular children had invented, but the sisters at WERTET, for example, were driven by the same impulse. Some scrambled up trees, clambering with their feet like cats and coming down again head foremost.[81]

The children at MORZINE, four hundred years later, behaved in the same way. One father reported:

The youngest of my daughters, 9 years old, was taken [by the epidemic]. When the crises took her, she ran out of the house and started climbing trees. She was ill for 18 months, and it was I who cured her. One day when she was in the highest branches of a plum-tree, I climbed after her and pretended to be very angry with her, saying "I've had enough of these sick girls, I want to rid the district of this one, I shall have to kill her." Thereupon she replied – or the devil did through her mouth – "I don't give a fuck for you, you filthy pig!" I grabbed her by the foot and tugged at her as if I was going to throw her down; then she cried out "Don't hurt the girl: I will loose hold of her, I won't torment her any more, and she won't climb trees any more." And since then, she has stayed cured.

Another boy, 12-year-old Joseph Plagnat, described as healthy and intelligent, began to experience the seizures on the way home after his father's funeral:

He climbed an enormous pine tree. Arriving at the very top, he broke off the highest twig and positioned himself there with his head down, singing and waving. His brother told him to be quiet and come down, saying this wasn't a good occasion to be playing games, when they had just buried their father. At this injunction, the child seemed to awaken; when he realized where he was, he was overtaken with great terror, and called for help. His brother then changed his tactic and shouted, "O Devil, possess this child again so that he can come down." The boy instantly went back into his trance, stopped shouting, lost his fear, and came down head foremost with the speed of a squirrel.[82]

Whatever the nature of the boy's trance may have been, it was clearly capable of taking away his normal fear of heights and thus made it possible for him to indulge in this remarkable behavior. But that does not help us find the motivation for behaving in this way in the first place.

That climbing is a characteristic of certain altered states of consciousness is evidenced by an interesting parallel. An unnamed Parisian architect displayed a similar inclination:

While overlooking the erection of one of the many palaces for which that city is noted, suddenly, with a cry, the man would rush from scaffold to scaffold, up and down steep inclines, never falling, passing with a steady head over places where he dare not go when conscious. There was an apparently purposive action, and yet when the man came to himself he had no memory of what he had done, and during the time of the attack he did not respond to irritation.[83]

If the phenomenon were confined to children, one might look for the motivation in a bid to escape from adult authority. The girl's father at Morzine was a rarity among grown-ups in being willing to pursue her up a tree. But the nuns at Wertet and the Paris architect point to something more general, perhaps some atavistic trait. They raise the question whether this type of behavior is essentially an individual symptom, manifesting in a group situation propagated by suggestion, or imitation.

The clearest parallel is with somnambulism. It is notorious that sleepwalkers are prone to walk on rooftops and high walls, in places where they would never go in their normal state. Yet accidents are rare, and when others perceive them in such a situation they forbear to wake them in case, like the boy at Morzine, they are overcome by terror. Somnambulists, like those afflicted with these behaviors, are able to perform prodigious feats, which they would certainly be incapable of in their normal state, without coming to any harm.

While the physiological aspects of somnambulism are recognized, the psychological aspects have rarely been addressed, let alone satisfactorily explored.[84] "Psychiatrists have considered sleepwalking the result of unresolved Oedipal conflicts, the enactment of sibling rivalry, or hysterical reactions to deep conflicts within the personality. There have been almost as many conjectures as sleep walkers, many of them postulating emotional disorder and the reenactment of significant events."[85] While it is recognized that "some degree of awareness of the environment is apparent, as often objects of furniture are bypassed or stairs negotiated safely," this falls a long way short of explaining why the sleepwalker chooses what he will do, and especially, why it should take the form of venturing into dangerous places.[86] It could well be that the sleepwalker is making some kind of gesture, perhaps simply effecting a symbolic escape from the literally down-to-earth restrictions of his waking life.

The fact that the same kind of behavior is engaged

by somnambulists points clearly to the likelihood that all those who behave in this way are driven by the same psychological impulses and suggests that this is the direction in which to look for an explanation. It seems certain that climbers are in some altered state of consciousness, as of course somnambulists are. But the process whereby they enter this state and what force sustains them while they are in it remain to be explored.

RUSSIAN POLAND BALLOON SCARE

Poland: 1892

Between late February and early April 1892, a wave of phantom military balloon sightings were reported above Russian Poland, engendering a common folk theory that steerable German military balloons were being used to conduct reconnaissance and espionage missions. Based on eyewitness descriptions, the objects sighted exceeded the aeronautical capabilities of the period.

CONTEXT: The wave began amid border tensions between Russia and Germany. This period was characterized by spy scares and fears of a Russian invasion.

Russian psychiatrist VLADIMIR BEKHTEREV attributes the episode to rumors fueled by war anxieties. "There were legions of witnesses who positively affirmed that they had seen them, simultaneously and at a specified time, even though the progress of aeronautics at the time did not encourage belief in their statements."[87] Bekhterev considered the phantom balloon flights to be "collective hallucinations" that were "born of the tendency of certain minds to impute to Germany acts of hostility against Russia."[88] Folklorist Thomas Bullard concurred with Bekhterev's assessment that the mysterious "balloons" far exceeded the aerial technology of the period, such as purportedly flying over 140 miles [225 kilometers] in a single night.[89] The object was also occasionally reported flying "against the wind at a time when experimental airships barely could maneuver in calm air."[90]

The earliest known report of the wave occurred at 5:30 p.m. on February 26, when a mysterious "globe" or "balloon" was sighted over the Polish community of Dabrowa. Witnesses said the 'balloon' was traveling northward against the wind and performing complex maneuvers, prompting an observer to state that the balloon must have been equipped "with the most up-to-date aeronautic equipment, operated by an experienced crew..."[91] Meanwhile, despite the allegations against them, the Germans were also reporting military balloons, which were assumed to have been carrying Russian spies. According to a reporter in the Volyn province, "Local inhabitants see in these events the hand of the Germans; but in all probability, these balloons belong to the Russian army, being launched from local fortresses for test purposes in anticipation of a possible war."[92]

In March, Russian War Minister P. S. Vannovskiy ordered the Russian Technological Society's Aeronautical Section to investigate the reports. On April 14, the group convened and two esteemed aeronautical experts, M. M. Pomortsev and A. M. Kovan'-ko, presented their findings in "About Flights of Balloons on our Western Frontier According to Existing Data."[93] Pomortsev stated that most reports "were due to pure fantasy and mistakes," while Kovan'-ko concluded that "the information sent in by correspondents should be ascribed to errors of observation."[94]

See also: EDISON STAR SIGHTINGS, ANDREE BALLOON MANIA, PHANTOM AIRCRAFT WAVES, FLYING SAUCER, GREAT AMERICAN AIRSHIP WAVE, GHOST ROCKET SCARE.

RUSSIAN SECTARIANISM

Throughout their history, the Russian people have displayed as much resistance as conformity to the religious establishment imposed on them by the authorities. "From the earliest times down to to-day, dissent has existed, now burning up fiercely, now dropping almost out of the ken of history, now reappearing in fresh forms, but always there, ready to make itself felt when circumstances favoured it."[95]

Such an occasion arose in 1654 when the Patriarch Nikon carried out reforms in the Russian Orthodox Church. The reforms in themselves were outwardly trivial, relating to questions of ritual without affecting fundamental beliefs: how the name Jesus should be spelt, whether two fingers or three should be extended when the priest uttered his blessing, and whether "Hallelulia" should be uttered once or twice. But of such trivia are theological disputes made, and these questions were perceived as fundamental by those who held to traditional forms and practices, and the changes led to a major split in the religious population.

The breakaway sects were known as *raskolniki* (schismatics). Those who harked back to the pre-reform ways were known as Old Believers or Old Ritualists. However, many of them, while they believed they were reverting to an age of innocence, were in fact very innovative in their ideas, since no such simplicity of ideas had ever in fact prevailed.

The *raskolniki* sects held a variety of views and fell into two classes. The conservative sects comprised the *popovtsi* (priestists), who clung to the old ways, and adhered to the traditionally anointed priesthood of the pre-Nikon period. The more radical considered themselves *bespopovtsi* (priestless), holding that God exists in spirit and truth, that man is his own church, and no intermediaries are needed between man and his god. However, in practice, most if not all of these sects followed leaders who prescribed their beliefs and practices and who often considered themselves to be new incarnations of Christ or the equivalent, and were so regarded by their followers.

The *raskolniki* were not only anathematized by the Orthodox Church but attacked vigorously by the secular authorities. The Tsarina Sofia, regent during the minority of Peter I (the Great), desired to see them exterminated. The Orthodox Church acted with the ruthlessness associated with the Inquisition of the Roman Catholic Church in the west. The dissenters were arrested, tortured, flogged, and burned alive.

As always, repression was counterproductive and sectarianism spread throughout the Russian territories. One estimate is that between 1667 and 1700 more than 8,000 *raskolniki* chose voluntary suicide rather than give up their beliefs. In one instance, the monk Danilo, when it was obvious that he and his followers could not hope to escape capture by the authorities with all that that entailed in torture and execution, persuaded his 300 followers to enter with him into a big wooden shed where they burned themselves alive.[96]

Matters were complicated by the fact that many of the sects held beliefs that ran counter to the law. Thus the DOUKHOBORS, who were opposed to killing people under any circumstances, refused to perform military service. Many sects were characterized by extreme beliefs and behavior. Some of these dictated simply the way they behaved at their meetings – singing, shouting, falling into ecstasies, and so on. In the more extreme cases, these were incorporated in their teachings – for example, castration among the SKOPTSI, free love among the SOUPONIEVO sect.

Encouraging the formation and spread of these sects were the living conditions of the Russian people, which were generally at subsistence level and frequently below. "Popular misery feeds the spirit of rebellion, giving it birth and sustaining it. There are religious sects based almost wholly on social discontent." Jean

Russian pilgrim, circa 1900. Any occasion, from celebration to bereavement, might inspire a pilgrimage.

Finot pointed to the *biegouny* (fugitives) who during the 19th century traversed the country from one end to another, without regard where they lodged. Initiates into the sect destroyed their passports, which they considered as a device of Satan. Indeed, the entire machinery of State and Church was considered of Satanic origin. They rejected the idea of marriage, taxes, or submission of any kind to authority. One of their icons showed the Devil holding out a candle to the Tsar, inviting him to be administrator of his works on Earth. From time to time their frustration would erupt in acts of violence, when a *biegoun* would strike a priest or interrupt a religious service. On one occasion a peasant named Samarin threw himself at the priest who was conducting a service, forced him to quit the altar, and threw the sacraments onto the floor and trampled them, while crying out that he was treading on the handiwork of Satan. Condemned to a lifetime of hard labor, Samarin complained that he had not been executed, in which case he was sure to have gone directly to Heaven.[97]

Often, a sect would grow around the activities of an inspired individual. A humble workman of Tver named Soutaiev, around 1880, attracted followers when he threw into a fire the money he had earned as a mason at Saint Petersburg and wandered the countryside declaring that true Christianity consisted in loving one's neighbor, and that the apparatus of theology, with its priests and churches, angels, and devils, were inventions to be rejected if the Earthly Paradise was to be created. Like most of the sects, the Soutaievtzy held that private property was the source of all unhappiness, and that violence should be renounced.[98]

Countless sects of this kind proliferated among the Russian populace, often on a limited, local basis. The spiritual hunger of the people, dissatisfied with the established church, was shown by the rapidity with which a prophet could attract a following. Typically, in 1893 a carpenter named Mikhail Raboff came to St. Petersburg and began preaching what he named "Mysterious Christianity." Suspicious, the police exiled him and his apostle Nicolas Komiakoff to a distant province. There, his teachings soon attracted followers, including his employer Borykine together with his wife and all his fellow-workers. The teachings were a seemingly innocuous expression of simple faith: the *rabofzi* eschewed the consumption of meat, alcohol, and tobacco, and were sexually chaste. Along with these innocent austerities, however, went a defiance of authority in the form of a refusal to pay taxes or perform military service, and the police felt obliged to interfere, closing the workshop. Borykine, taking employment with a certain Grigoriev, converted all his new colleagues, and the factory was transformed into a chapel. An illiterate woman, Wasilisa Grigoriev, presumably the wife or a relative of the factory-owner, was carried away by the general enthusiasm and hailed as the sect's prophetess. She would go into ecstasy and utter extravagant and incomprehensible preachings, while the members of the sect wept, cried out, and danced. A typical gathering would start soberly enough with a reading from the scriptures, followed by a commentary on the reading. As the preacher's enthusiasm grew, so did that of his congregation:

> His voice animated little by little, the preacher ended by falling into ecstasy which was communicated to the assembly. Everyone cried out, gesticulated, tore their hair. The congregation threw themselves onto the floor. Some foamed at the mouth, others gnawed the wooden floor, tore their clothing, prey to the most violent contortions. Suddenly, one of them would start to sing a pious song; beginning with well-known words, it gradually changed to incoherent phrases, the true language of illumination, which the assembly took up in chorus, singing while they covered with kisses the feet of their "spiritual mother."[99]

Such behavior was characteristic of innumerable sects of this kind, which proliferated throughout Russia, almost all of them subscribing to simplistic doctrines perceived as a return to the spiritual values of Christianity that had been abandoned by the established church. Common to all was a call for the rejection of private property, a defiance of authority and priesthood, and a reversion to a simpler and more egalitarian way of life. In many respects, such sentiments anticipated and facilitated the growth of Communism on Russian soil in the 20th century.

The more notable of these sects have individual entries: BEZPOPOVSKY, DOUGHITELI, DOUKHOBORS, KLIKOUSCHESTVO, MALIOVANNY, SKOPTSI, SOUPONIEVO.

Sources

1. Bynum, Bill (2001). "Railway Spine." *The Lancet* 358 (July 28):339. See also: Shorter, Edward (1992). *From Paralysis to Fatigue: A History of Psychosomatic Illness in the Modern Era.* New York: The Free Press, pp. 25-39, 114.
2. Heller, Landis, and Potter, Norris (1966). *One Nation Indivisible.* Columbus, Ohio: Charles E. Merrill books, p. 478.
3. Davidson, James W., Castillo, Pedro, and Stoff, Michael B. (2000). *The American Nation.* Upper Saddle River, New Jersey: Prentice-Hall, p. 694.
4. Heale, M.J. (1990). *American Anti-communism: Combating the Enemy Within 1830-1970.* Baltimore, Maryland: The John Hopkins University Press, p. 60.
5. Davidson et al. (2000). op cit., p. 772.
6. Jennings, Peter, and Brewster, Todd (1998). *The Century* [photographic editor Katherine Bourbeau]. New York: Doubleday, p. 315.
7. Jennings and Brewster, op cit., p. 315.
8. Jennings and Brewster, op cit., p. 315.
9. Excerpt of speech made by McCarthy made to the Woman's Club of Wheeling, West Virginia in 1950, accessed July 21, 2003 at: http://www.turnerlearning.com/cnn/coldwar/reds/reds_re3.htm, citing the Congressional Record of the 81st Congress, 2 Sess., pp. 1952-1957.
10. Jennings and Brewster (1998). op cit., p. 313.
11. Heale, op cit., p. 179.
12. Heale, op cit., p. 179.
13. Jennings and Brewster, op cit., p. 313.
14. Donovan, Jeffrey. (2003). "U.S.: Government Probe Criticizes Arrests Of Immigrants After 11 September." Accessed July 21 at: http://www.rferl.org/nca/features/2003/06/050620 03152917.asp.
15. http://www.wikipedia.org/wiki/McCarthyism, accessed July 21, 2003.
16. Davenport, Frederick Morgan (1905). *Primitive Traits in Religious Revivals.* New York: Macmillan.
17. Thouless, Robert H. (1924). *An Introduction to the Psychology of Religion.* Cambridge: University Press, pp. 157-158.
18. Underwood, Alfred Clair (1925). *Conversion, Christian and Non-Christian.* London: Allen & Unwin, p. 205.
19. Starbuck, Edwin Diller (1901). *The Psychology of Religion.* London: Walter Scott, p. 54. First published in 1899.
20. Jonathan Edwards, quoted by Godwin, George (1941). *The Great Revivalists.* London: Watts, p. 21.
21. Telephone interview between Holland Cooke and Robert Bartholomew on January 2, 2003. Mr. Cook is a talk radio consultant living in Block Island, Rhode Island. Holland Cooke is his stage name; his real name is Robert Cooke.
22. Reid, David. (1974). "'Halloween Hoax' Broadcast by WPRO is Studied by FCC." *The Evening Journal-Bulletin* (Providence, Rhode Island), October 31, 1974, p. B8.
23. Levine, Justin. (1999). "History and Analysis of the Federal Communications Commission's Response to Radio Broadcast Hoaxes." *Federal Communications Law Journal* 52(2):274-320. See p. 288.
24. "Broadcast Jams Police Switchboards." *The Evening Journal-Bulletin* (Providence, Rhode Island), October 31, 1974, p. A1.
25. Levine, op cit., p. 288.
26. "Broadcast Jams Police Switchboards." op cit.
27. Levine, op cit., p. 288.
28. "Broadcast Jams Police Switchboards." op cit.
29. Reid, op cit.
30. Reid, op cit.; "Broadcast Jams Police Switchboards." op cit.
31. "Broadcast Jams Police Switchboards." op cit.
32. Reid, op cit.
33. Levine, op cit., p. 289.
34. Levine, op cit., p. 288.
35. Telephone interview with Holland Cooke, op cit.
36. Telephone interview with Holland Cooke, op cit.
37. (Editorial). (1974). "Radio Hoaxes Must Carry Warnings." *The Evening Bulletin* (Providence, Rhode Island), November 3, 1974, p. F16.
38. Oberschall, Anthony. (1968). "The Los Angeles Race Riot of August 1965." *Social Problems* 15:322-341.
39. Robertson, Ian. *Sociology* (third edition). New York: Worth Publishers, p. 540.
40. Conant, Ralph W. (1972). "Phases of a Riot." Pp. 108-110, in Ralph Turner and Lewis Killian (eds.). *Collective Behavior* (second edition). Englewood Cliffs, NJ: Prentice-Hall.
41. Lieberman, Stanley, and Silverman, Arnold. 1965. "Precipitants and Conditions of Race Riots." *American Sociological Review* 30:887-898.
42. Rude, George. (1964). *The Crowd in History, 1730-1848*, New York: John Wiley, pp. 57-59.
43. Luhman, Reid. (1989). *The Sociological Outlook* (second edition). San Diego, California: Collegiate Press, p. 435.
44. Lang, Kurt, and Lang, Gladys. 1961. *Collective Dynamics.* New York: Thomas Y. Crowell, p. 129.
45. Marden, Charles F., Meyer, Gladys, and Engel, Madeline H. (1992). *Minorities in American Society* (sixth edition). New York: HarperCollins, pp. 272-273; Wallechinsky, Davis and Wallace, Irving (eds.) (1975). *The People's Almanac.* Garden City, New York: Doubleday, p. 233.
46. Miller, David L. (2000). *Introduction to Collective Behavior and Collective Action* (second edition). Prospect Heights, Illinois: Waveland Press, p. 317.
47. Davidson, James, Castillo, Pedro, and Stoff, Michael. (2000). *The American Nation.* Upper Saddle River, New Jersey: Prentice-Hall, p. 464; Wallechinsky, Davis and Wallace, Irving (eds.) (1975). *The People's Almanac.* Garden City, New York: Doubleday, p. 183.
48. Miller, op cit., p. 317.
49. "Behavioralists Ask: Why Did Pittsburgh Fans Go Berserk?" *Seattle Times*, October 24, 1971, p. 17.
50. DeMott, John S. (1986). "Wreaking Havoc on Spring Break," *Time* 127(14):29 (April 7).
51. Evans, Bergen (1946). *The Natural History of Nonsense.* New York: Vintage Books, 1958, p. 98.
52. "Rolling Stones Shake 'Em Up." *Burlington Daily Times-News* (North Carolina), June 16, 1965, p. 6B.
53. Miller, op cit., p. 95.
54. Shibutani, Tamotsu. (1966). *Improvised News: A Sociological Study of Rumor.* Indianapolis, IN: Bobbs-Merrill.
55. Shibutani, op cit., pp. 133-134.
56. Miller, op cit., p. 95.
57. MacDonnell, F. (1995). *Insidious Foes.* New York: Oxford University Press; Mount, G.S. (1993). *Canada's Enemies: Spies and Spying in the Peaceable Kingdom.* Toronto: Dundurn Press, p. 40; Kitchen, M. (1985). "The German Invasion of Canada in the First World War." *The International History Review* 7(2):245-260.
58. Bordia, P., and Rosnow, R. L. (1998). "Rumor Rest Stops on the Information Highway: Transmission Patterns in a Computer-Mediated Rumor Chain." *Human Communication Research* 25:163-179.
59. Samper, David (2002). "Cannibalizing Kids: Rumor and Resistance in Latin America." *Journal of Folklore Research* 39(1):1-32, see p. 5.
60. Rosnow, Ralph L., and Fine, Gary Allen. (1976). *Rumor and Gossip.* New York: Elsevier, p. 20.

61. Kapferer, Jean-Noel (1990). *Rumors: Uses, Interpretations, and Images*. New Brunswick, Connecticut: Transaction publishers, p. 24.
62. Levin, Jack, and Arluke, Arnold (1987). *Gossip: The Inside Scoop*. New York: Plenum Press, p. 43.
63. Levin and Arluke, op cit., pp. 44-45.
64. Miller, op cit., p. 86.
65. Miller, op cit., p. 87.
66. Miller, op cit., pp. 87-88.
67. Jung, C.G. (1959). "A Visionary Rumour." *Journal of Analytical Psychology* 4: 5-19; Jung, C. G. (1959). *Flying Saucers: A Modern Myth of Things Seen in the Sky*. New York: Harcourt, Brace & World; Kapferer, op cit., p. 29.
68. LaPiere, Richard T. (1938). *Collective Behavior*. New York: McGraw-Hill, p. 199.
69. Kapferer, Jean-Noel (1992). How Rumors are Born." *Society* 29(5):53-60 (July-August).
70. Rickard, Robert, and Michell, John. (2001). *Unexplained Phenomena: A Rough Guide Special*. London: Rough Guides Limited, p. 113.
71. Morgan, Hal, and Tucker, Kerry (1984). *Rumor!* New York: Penguin, p. 82.
72. Kapferer, op cit., p. 22; Rosnow and Fine, op cit., p. 14.
73. Rosnow, Ralph L., and Fine, Gary Allen. (1976). *Rumor and Gossip*. New York: Elsevier, p. 14; Kapferer, op cit., p. 22.
74. http://www.beatles.ws.
75. Rosnow and Fine, op cit., pp. 14-20; Kapferer, op cit., pp. 22-23.
76. Kapferer, op cit., p. 23.
77. Morgan and Tucker, op cit., p 87.
78. Wesley, John (1909). *The Journal of the Rev. John Wesley*. Edited by Nehemiah Curnock. London: Culley 1909 [Originally published at various dates from 1739 onwards], volume 5, p. 73.
79. Hecker, Justus Friedrich. (1844). *Epidemics of the Middle Ages* (translated from German by B. Babington). London: The Sydenham Society, p. 157.
80. Görres, Johann Joseph von (1845). *La Mystique Divine, Naturelle et Diabolique*. Paris: Poussielgue-Rusand, 1855, translated from the German Christliche Mystik, volume 5, p. 231.
81. Wier, Jean. [Weyer, Johann] (1885). *Histoires, Disputes Et Discours Des Illusions Et Impostures Des Diables, Des Magiciens Infames, SorcièRes Et Empoisonneurs*. Translated from the Latin original, published 1563. Paris: Bureaux du Progrès Médical, volume 1, p. 529.
82. Blanc, Hippolyte (1865). *Le Merveilleux dans le Jansenisme &c*. Paris: Plon, p. 291.
83. Wood, H C. (1890). "A Study of Consciousness." *Century Magazine* (May), page 73, taken from the French writer Trousseau.
84. For example, Hobson, Allan (1989). *Sleep*. New York: Scientific American Library.
85. Luce, Gay Gaer, and Segal, Julius (1967). *Sleep*. London: Heinemann, p. 102.
86. Carskadon, Mary A. (Editor) *Encyclopedia of Sleep and Dreaming*. New York: Macmillan, p. 578.
87. Bekhterev, Vladimir Mikhailovich. (1910). *La Suggestion* (Translated from Russian by D P Keraval). Paris: Boulangé, p. 76.
88. Bekhterev, op cit., p. 76.
89. Bullard, Thomas E. "Newly Discovered 'Airship' Waves over Poland." *Flying Saucer Review* 29(3):12-14. See p. 13.
90. Bullard, op cit., p. 13.
91. Gershtein, Mikhail B. "A Thousand Years of Russian UFOs (Part II). The Wave of 1892." *RIAP Bulletin* 8(1-2):2-8 (January-June 2002). Quote appears on p. 5, citing: "Sensational News." *Kievskoye Slovo*. Kiev, March 4, 1892. The *RIAP Bulletin* is a quarterly publication of the Research Institute on Anomalous Phenomena, P.O. Box 4542, 61022 Kharkov-22, Ukraine.
92. Gerstein, op cit., citing "The Balloons." *Kievlianin*, Kiev, March 24, 1892.
93. Gerstein, op cit., p. 5, citing "Modern Aeronautics." *Peterburgskaya Gazeta*, St. Petersburg, April 15, 1892.
94. Gerstein, op cit., p. 5, citing "Modern Aeronautics." *Peterburgskaya Gazeta*, St. Petersburg, April 15, 1892.
95. Maude, Aylmer (1905). *A Peculiar People*. London: Constable, p. 79.
96. Maude, op cit., p. 98.
97. Finot, Jean (1918). *Saints, initiés et Possédés Modernes*. Paris: Charpentier, pp. 23-24.
98. Finot, op cit., pp. 25-29.
99. Finot, op cit., p. 40.

SABBATAI ZEVI THE MESSIAH

Eastern Mediterranean: 1626-1676

"All the world has been informed of the impostures and extravagances of this man, and the follies of an infinite number of Jews who ran after him."[1] The remarkable feature about this affair is that the vast majority of those in whom it excited extraordinary behavior lived at a considerable distance from the individual responsible for it and never set eyes on him. What set them off was not the man himself but the myth he professed to incarnate.

Izmir-born Sabbatai Zevi (variously spelled: Sabbathai, Zwi, etc.) was one of many who at various times have believed themselves to be the Messiah for whom the world was waiting to be reborn. His claims were accepted by tens of thousands of Jews, scattered in many parts of the world, who proceeded to act in the firm belief that Paradise was about to be reinstated in Palestine. Sabbatai's own belief in himself was typical as self-anointed spiritual leaders go; it is the behavior of those who believed in him which was exceptional.

CONTEXT: The expectation that a Messiah would come to restore the Jewish people to their privileged position in God's plans for mankind has been part of Jewish belief from Old Testament times. (See MESSIANISM.) Jesus of Nazareth was one of the earliest candidates, but he was rejected, as were numerous others who followed him through the ages. In the early 17th century expectation was running particularly high since a number of prophecies could be interpreted (usually by replacing letters with numbers) as presaging the coming of the Messiah at this time. Rumors and false reports proliferated. In 1642 it was said (mistakenly) that the Sultan of Turkey had fled to Mecca from his capital at Constantinople (Istanbul), and legends circulated concerning the "lost tribes" who dwelt on the eastern bank of the mysterious (indeed, mythical) river Sabbation in Arabia, which they would cross to greet the Messiah when he appeared.[2]

Sabbatai Zevi was born on August 1, 1626, the son of a well-to-do poultry merchant at Izmir (Smyrna), then a Greek port on Turkish territory. His birthday, in the Jewish calendar, was the anniversary of the Destruction of the Temple, one of many dates earmarked for the new Messiah's birth. His father destined him for study, and by age fifteen he was well versed in Jewish and Islamic teachings. Already he attracted followers who admired his learning and ideas.

Early marriage was prescribed in his community. First one bride, then a second eminently suitable one, was found for him, but in both cases the girl complained that he had not consummated the marriage, and twice he was divorced. He explained that the Holy Spirit had announced to him that neither of his wives was the woman destined for him by Heaven.

A Kabalistic calculation suggested that 1648 would be the year when the Messiah would make his appearance, and in this year the 22-year-old Sabbatai again heard a voice from heaven, this time to inform him that he was indeed the Messiah, whose mission would be to bring together the twelve tribes of Israel, currently scattered round the world. His knowledge of the scriptures enabled him to provide textual confirmation of his candidacy. Emboldened by his new rank, he called for a re-think on sexual morality, replaced the Ten Commandments of Moses by eighteen of his own, rearranged the Jewish Holy Days, and presumed to pronounce openly the name of God, Yahveh, which hitherto only the High Priest had dared to utter, and then only in a whisper on special occasions. Some of his ideas were sensible, such as to allow women to study the Judaic scriptures; others, such as his mystical marriage ceremony with the Torah (Jewish sacred scriptures), were considered shocking.

The church authorities of Izmir, while acknowledging both his knowledge and his piety, supposed him mentally ill, apart from his defiance of religious law, stories of visions, and claims to levitate led to accusations of sorcery. In 1651 he was banished as a disturber of the peace, under a solemn curse that forbad any man to have anything to do with him or show him favor or hospitality. He left Izmir and spent the next few years wandering through Greece, Turkey, and Syria, seeking to establish his Messianic claim. Few took him seriously and when in 1658 he went to Istanbul, where he had high hopes of recognition, he was banished from there also. He left the city predicting it would be struck by a terrible awakening, and the following year it was partially destroyed in a fire that hit the Jewish quarter in particular.

The turning point came in May 1665, when he met the influential Nathan of Gaza, in Palestine, to whom he confided his self-doubts; there were moments when he wondered if he was possessed by demons. Nathan, a brilliant scholar who himself claimed to be the re-incarnation of the prophet Elijah, did not simply accept Sabbatai's claim to be the Messiah but became his most enthusiastic and active supporter. He had a vision, after which his friends found him foaming at the mouth like a madman, that brought him divine foreknowledge that he would see the kingdom of the Messiah established on Earth within little more than a year. At once he set to work to pass along the wondrous news to Jews all over the world. Letters were sent to Amsterdam and Hamburg, Venice and Istanbul, Paris and London. Sabbatai's erratic behavior, Nathan reassured them, was due to his divine nature. Within a short time the great majority of Jews, not only locally but in Europe, Africa, and America, were persuaded that the 2000-year-old dream of the Jewish people was about to become reality.

Meanwhile, Sabbatai, after three indecisive years in Jerusalem, went on a mission to Cairo where he chanced to meet – insofar as anything in his career can be attributed to chance – a Polish Jew named Sarah who, in 1648, had received a vision telling her that she would one day be the Messiah's wife. Educated in a Christian convent, her subsequent career had been a lurid progress from one wealthy lover to another, travelling eastwards from Amsterdam in search of her destined spouse. Even before meeting her, Sabbatai recognized her as his predestined bride, and when she reached Cairo, they were married, though, like his previous marriages, was not consummated either.

The couple returned to Izmir, where they were received in triumph. Though the religious establishment remained hostile, scholars came to meet him from all over the Jewish world, and he promised them that next year they would meet in Jerusalem. Legends and rumors abounded, rich in hopes and expectations. It was prophesied that within a few months he would take over the dominion of the Turkish sultan, and do so without waging war but simply by the power of hymns and praises which he would utter. The sultan would become his servant, and all kings would pay tribute to him. A resurrection would take place of all the dead who had died in Palestine, to be followed forty years later by a general resurrection of all the dead of whatever faith.

Sabbatai returned to Jerusalem, now hailed as king by the populace. Here, as at Izmir, the rabbis were less than enthusiastic about his high-handed changes to the Law, which had been honored for more than a thousand years. He defied regulations about clothing, diet, and feast days. Though he had not yet formally proclaimed himself to be the Messiah, he was everywhere hailed as such, and when he passed through Aleppo the people danced for joy, many falling to the ground with convulsive seizures, which from this time on would occur wherever he made a personal appearance. Others saw visions of Sabbatai, wearing the triple crown of the Messiah, subduing all the nations of the world. Letters poured into Istanbul, and although their exaggerations and absurdities revealed many of them to be forgeries, the excitement for Sabbatai did not diminish. At Izmir, Sabbatai now began to appear in regal state. When he walked down a street, banners were carried by a procession of devoted followers. Citizens would emerge from their homes and lay costly rugs for him to walk on (though he humbly avoided treading on them). He made noisy torch lit processions at night, though this was forbidden, and entered the synagogue where at last he proclaimed that he was, indeed, the Messiah. Now he held royal levees where devotees came to do obeisance. He received lavish money gifts and won hearts by using much of it to buy the freedom of galley slaves.

His closest followers were rewarded with crowns. His brother Elijah was made ruler of Turkey, his brother Joseph emperor of the Romans. (Bockelson at Münster had similarly distributed empty titles: see ANABAPTISTS.) A public display was made of the royal bed sheets, showing that Sarah had been a virgin and that Sabbatai had performed a husband's duty. Though neither was in fact the case, the people expected no less.

Meanwhile the church authorities debated what they should do and finally reached the conclusion that he should be sentenced to death as an impostor. Unfortunately there was no one among them willing to be the executioner. The populace was completely on Sabbatai's side. When a merchant expressed skepticism, his house was attacked and he barely escaped with his life. There were other violent incidents, many of them incited by Sabbatai himself who was furious that anyone should doubt his authority. Another skeptic came home to find his two daughters lying on the floor, writhing in agony and foaming at the mouth. When one of them claimed to see a vision of Sabbatai crowned on a heavenly throne, her father converted on the spot and hailed Sabbatai as the true Messiah.[3] She was just one of four hundred people who were said to have enjoyed similar visions and prophecies; wonders were seen in the skies – pillars of fire, stars that fell and rose again, the moon enveloped in flames. It was rumored that a ship named "The twelve tribes of Israel," with silken sails and ropes, had landed in Scotland, and that her crew spoke no other tongue but Hebrew.[4] All were taken as signs of Sabbatai's claim. With such evidence to authorize them, the populace believed that a new life lay just ahead of them and abandoned all restraint, feeling free to dance, sing, feast, and fornicate without fear of retribution.

The Jews of Izmir now lived only in expectation of the great event. Commerce was at a standstill. Shops were opened only to empty the shelves and private homes got rid of superfluous furniture. This they could do with an easy mind, since in the national home God was about to bestow on them, they would inherit all the possessions of the infidels. Families married off their daughters as rapidly as possible, even girls of ten or less. The money that accrued from all this went to Sabbatai who, a wealthy man, gave it away to the poor and needy, winning further stores of adulation.

News of these events spread from one Jewish community to another, wherever Jews were dispersed throughout the world. Agents and diplomats sent reports back to their superiors in Venice, Dresden, and Paris commenting on the fall in business. Throughout Europe, Jewish merchants played a crucial part in international commerce. Now, with the advent of the Messiah, they grew disinclined to business. They made no new undertakings and began to wind up their current ventures. Rumors fueled their hopes. When they heard that the Sultan was about to hand over Palestine to Sabbatai as a new promised land, many prepared to migrate there. The number of pilgrims swelled, journey fares rose as the demand increased.[5] And as the great event drew closer, the Jews began to indulge in remarkable behavior:

> All the Jews of the Levant believed firmly that he was their King and the veritable Messiah who would deliver them from servitude. In this belief they honoured him, fasted, and did penance to win favor. Most of them went beyond what natural forces could withstand; some were seen to fast for seven days without taking any nourishment, others till they died of hunger. Some buried themselves in their gardens, covering their naked bodies with soil up to the neck: others slept in beds of mud until they were rigid with cold. Some had molten wax poured over their shoulders, others rolled in the snow or plunged naked into the sea or other icy waters when winter was at its coldest. But their most common form of mortification was to prick their back and sides with thorns, followed with scourging.[6]

"Traffic in the greatest commercial centers came to a complete standstill: most of the Jewish merchants and bankers liquidated their affairs."[7] In spring 1666, at Avignon, the Jewish community prepared to emigrate to Palestine. In England, Jews had hardly been readmitted to the country when they learned that the Diaspora was at an end, and that they would soon return to the homeland God had prepared for them. They were confirmed in their hopes by the fact that the year 1666 was expected by English sects to be a special year, though many Christians interpreted this as meaning that this would be the year when the Jews would be converted to Christianity.[8] In Persia Jewish husbandmen refused to work in the fields. In Hungary the Jews removed the roofs from their houses. In Amsterdam, Jews took to the streets, dancing to the sound of drums. Special feasts were held, Messianic texts poured off the printing presses. One eyewitness wrote at Hamburg: "Many of them sold their homes and houses and all they possessed and were expecting salvation every day...My stepfather sent to his children in Hamburg a number of boxes packed with linen and dried foodstuffs, as he took it for granted they would all travel direct to Palestine from there. Many months afterwards when all was over, the boxes were at last unpacked to prevent their contents from rotting."[9] One prominent Hamburg Jew, Sasportas, declared that his was the only sober mind in a world of drunkards. "And when I saw all these things happening, although the farce was worthy of laughter, I shed silent tears full of anguish for the credulity of these people from whose spirit all memory of our true prophets and traditions had vanished."[10]

But skepticism could not stop the flow of wonderful rumors. The Jews had risen up and taken Mecca; the prophet Zechariah had risen from the grave; a mysterious light was shining continually over Jerusalem; and much more.

It was on the swell of this tide of enthusiasm that Sabbatai set off to Istanbul to confront the Turkish sultan face to face. Even though it was too much to hope that Mehmed IV would invite him to take his throne, at least he would give the Jews a homeland in Palestine. But Mehmed didn't even do that. Without giving him an audience, he commanded that Sabbatai be detained in the fortress of Abydos in the Dardanelles. There, though technically a prisoner, he continued to hold court like a ruler, receiving money and gifts of all kinds, messages of goodwill, and devotion from round the world; a stream of delegations and visitors were ferried across from the mainland. "The bare rooms of the fortress were fitted out with all the solemnity and luxury of royal apartments. The prisoner's warders became a guard of honor... The Jews were exultant and declared that the pit into which their enemies had tried to cast the Messiah had become a throne."[11] Nathan explained to doubters that Sabbatai's incarceration was part of a divine process. When devoted followers raised a vast sum to purchase his liberation, he refused, for he was confident that the sultan would recognize his claims.

He was mistaken. When on the September 16, 1866, he finally met the sultan at Edirne (Adrianople), he was offered three options: to perform a miracle that would prove beyond doubt that he was the Messiah; to be executed; or to convert to Islam. By way of miracle, he would be taken into the palace garden and suspended naked from a gallows, where bowmen would loose three poisoned arrows at him. If he were indeed the Messiah, the arrows would surely bounce off him, whereupon the sultan would declare his readiness to convert to Judaism and acknowledge Sabbatai as the Messiah. Alternatively, if he preferred execution, and since he delighted in processions, he would be led through the streets of Istanbul with a burning torch tied to each limb, and thus the spiritually illumined one would be physically illumined also, until such time as the flames consumed him.

The news that the Messiah, on whom rested all their hopes, had converted to Islam stunned the Jewish community throughout the world. Nathan of Gaza and other loyal followers yet again justified the decision by presenting it as part of his divine mission. Sabbatai had first to descend into the kelippah, the domain of evil, to rescue Christians and Moslems from their false beliefs. (In Christian legend, Jesus also is supposed to have descended to Hell, and classical heroes also visited the Underworld.) Which was all very well, but it no longer seemed likely that the Jews would enter their Earthly Paradise during their lifetime. Even for a community accustomed to misfortune and harassment, this was disillusion on the grand scale.

A good number of his close followers accepted the scholars' explanation, and some of them followed his example and publicly converted, while privately remaining true to their Judaic beliefs. Others denied the facts: Sabbatai himself had been taken up to heaven, the supposed convert was simply a ghost left on Earth to fool the Turks.[12] For a while he retained considerable popularity, so much so that his enemies demanded that, Muslim or no, he be banished. Yet even exiled to Dulcigno (now Ulcinj) in Montenegro, wearing a turban and naming himself Aziz Mehmed Effendi, he continued to receive loyal visitors until he died in 1676. Even after his death, some maintained their beliefs. In the 1750s, a Polish candidate for the role of Messiah, Jacob Frank, claimed to be a reincarnation of Sabbatai, and a small Sabbatean community survives to the present day in Iran.

But for the great majority of Jews, for those in Izmir or Amsterdam who had closed down their businesses, for those in Hamburg or Poland who had sold their homes, all in the expectation of a new life in a Jewish state in Palestine personally vouchsafed by God through his elected emissary, the apostasy of Sabbatai was one more disappointment in the chronicle of false Messiahs.

COMMENT: This extraordinary event was built on a myth, the Messianic myth. Sabbatai's career was raised on the hopes and expectations of the Jews scattered across the world. While he seems to have had a certain amount of personal charisma, he also showed himself weak and indecisive. He was sustained more by the beliefs of others than his belief in himself, which seems to have been fragile and wavering. He was subject to violent mood swings, which Christphe Bourseiller suggests supports Scholem's diagnosis of a bipolar disorder: "a manic-depressive psychosis, to which were probably added certain elements of paranoia."[13]

Jurist and biographer Joseph Kastein speculates how things might have been if the pretender had possessed a stronger personality: "What might have happened if Sabbatai had really availed himself of the forces at his disposal? He would certainly have created an epoch-making situation in history. But he could not rise to it. He had never been able to brace himself to anything more than speech and symbolic acts, and his powers were always limited to stimulating others and inciting them to action."[14]

The most remarkable aspect of this episode is the credulity of shrewd merchants and businessmen throughout Europe who accepted Sabbatai's messiahship without, as it were, seeing the goods with their own eyes. This Encyclopedia contains few more striking instances of the power of myth to direct men's lives.

SAINT-MEDARD CONVULSIONNARIES

Paris: 1730s and later

In 18th century Paris, miraculous cures were reported at the tomb of a priest in the graveyard of Saint-Médard. These were generally accompanied by convulsions, which came to be experienced in their own right, spreading by contagion. Official attempts at suppression had the effect of reaffirming the phenomenon, which persisted clandestinely through most of the century. The "convulsionnaires," who numbered several hundred, demanded *soulagement* (relief) in the form of extreme physical action, begging for relief by blows, trampling, and so on, to a degree which would seem to exceed the limits of human endurance.

CONTEXT: The affair was triggered by the burial of François de Paris, a priest who favored Jansenist teachings. While devoutly Christian, these teachings were considered heretical by the Catholic establishment despite being held by many reputable people including the philosopher Pascal. When their monastery of Port-Royal was razed to the ground, their leaders emigrated to the Netherlands.

François de Paris was manifestly a good and pious man, whose death at age 37 in 1727 was brought on by the austerities he suffered while caring for the poor and needy. His exemplary life had earned him the reputation of a saint. Those who shared his views perceived him as a symbol of their cause and erected an elaborate tomb in the churchyard of Saint-Médard. So feelings were already running high when admirers came to pay their devotions at the dead priest's tomb, and when a visitor reported that she had miraculously been healed, the news set off a series of remarkable cures.[15]

The Start Of The Convulsions

From the start, visitors claimed physical as well as spiritual benefits. But in August 1731, by which time thousands were flocking to the cemetery, the character of the cures changed. A woman named Louise Hardouin, who came in hope of a cure, suddenly went into convulsions, losing all control over her jerking, twitching body. Other visitors found themselves in a strange state: "God was pleased to work his miracles in a different manner; violent pains, agitations of the body, extraordinary convulsions, were the means by which the sick were healed, not all at once, but gradually."[16]

It has been suggested that among those who presented themselves at the tomb were some epileptics and that Louise and others unconsciously imitated them. But there is no evidence for this, and it may equally be that the outbreak of convulsions was spontaneous. Soon it was accepted that sufferers could not hope for a cure without passing through a convulsive phase, signifying that the subject was being filled with the divine grace that would bring about the cure. "From the first moment that la demoiselle Duchenne was placed on the tomb, all her members were agitated with an inconceivable force: and it must be admitted that nothing could be less likely than these violent agitations to repair the broken veins in her chest and stomach. Nonetheless it was during the course of these impetuous shakings that it pleased the Almighty to rejoin them, to restore her stomach and chest, and cause her awful hemorrhages to cease for ever."[17]

Marguerite Francoise du Chene is one of the convulsionnaires who is cured of haemorrhage and fever, at the tomb of M. de Paris.

The title of Carré de Montgeron's monumental history of the affair is *La Vérité des Miracles*, and the testimony he produces in such abundance is intended to prove the miraculous nature of the convulsions. Even if they can be explained in medical and/or psychological terms, the specific circumstance of the cures is what enabled them to take place. If they had not been perceived as miraculous, they would not have happened.

It became a fashionable spectacle to visit Saint-Médard and watch the convulsionnaires. Observers were astonished, as men and women went into violent spasms, thrashing around among the gravestones, oblivious of their surroundings, and without respect for modesty. Simply to touch the tomb was sufficient to provoke the convulsions, and indeed it was not necessary for the sufferer to actually visit the cemetery, for sachets of soil from the ground near the tomb, taken to them, would do the trick. In January 1732, the authorities, ostensibly in the interest of public order but also concerned that the Jansenists were winning too much sympathy, closed the cemetery, provoking a famous graffito: *By the king's command, no miracle may be performed in this place*. For a while, the faithful got round this by waiting till a burial took place, then crowding in along with the coffin. The authorities then banned all burials in the cemetery.

The effect was not to deter the convulsionnaires, but to drive them elsewhere. Those whose "treatment" had been cut short by the official ban continued it in cellars and attics, and soon these private demonstrations attracted spectators just as the public manifestations in the cemetery had done. After a while, the character of the phenomena changed. Though cures of specific ailments continued to be reported, many of the convulsionnaires were craving *secours* (help, relief, aid) as a kind of physiotherapy. They begged for physical treatments of an extreme kind. The girl Giroux, who was cured through convulsions in August 1732, insisted on being carried about on a man's shoulders for ten hours at a stretch.[18] Another convulsionnaire had herself hung up by the heels and remained in that position three-quarters of an hour. On another occasion, while she lay on her bed, two men held a cloth behind her back with which they violently threw her forward 2,400 times, while two others threw her back onto the mattress, no less violently.

Accompanying the performances were a variety of manifestations, some physical, others psychological, which added to their perceived supernatural character:

> The convulsionnaires exhibited, not only occasionally but frequently, all the phenomena which are ascribed by mesmerists to animal magnetism – somnambulism, ecstasies, raptures, insensibility to pain, rigidity of muscles, submission of the will and the senses to the volition of another person...Increased subtility of thought, quickness of perception, heightened powers of imagination, a vivid energising influence, fraught with enthusiasm and even eloquence; claims to clairvoyance, to communion with another world, to "spirit life"; all these phenomena were to be found.[19]

Montgeron notes:

> In the state of convulsion, the patients generally showed a much higher degree of intelligence and penetration than was natural to them. Girls who were extremely timid, of low birth, and without talent, spoke under the excitement of their state with eloquence, accuracy, and elegance. A young girl who, in her ordinary state, was so stupid and rude as almost to pass for an idiot, when in convulsions showed so much penetration, and answered questions so ably, that she might have passed for a person of excellent education, and great natural talents.[20]

This feature is found in other types of extraordinary behavior, such as the CEVENNES PROPHETS and MORZINE. Other types of behavior that match others in this Encyclopedia include animal-like behaviors. Some convulsionnaires, known as *sauteuses*, were given to jumping. There were *aboyeuses* who barked like dogs, and *miaulantes* who meowed like cats. The girl Lopin, when in the hysterical fit, barked, as did the witches of the south (LANDES), and was named *l'aboyeuse* ("the Barker"). The widow Thevenet, during her convulsions in 1734, uttered a torrent of unintelligible words belonging to no known language.[21] (GLOSSOLALIA)

Another frequent characteristic, found also for instance in American camp meetings (AMERICAN REVIVALS), is contagion. For example, when the same widow Thevenet went into convulsions, a woman who held her experienced a long nervous shivering. Montgeron reported such incidents time and time again.

In 1735, even the private exhibitions were banned, and those who persisted ran the risk of being raided by the police. From then on, the performances took place clandestinely in private homes – in small, crowded upstairs rooms in the narrow streets of Paris. Arrests were frequent – at least Louis XV's jailers imprisoned 200 – but the authorities were clearly at a loss how to deal with behavior that appeared to harm no one and which was so enthusiastically indulged in. The arrests did little to discourage the activity. The convulsionnaires were reliably estimated at between five and six hundred, supported by three or four thousand men who provided the *secours*.[22] These secouristes played an essential role; since the victims craved pain, someone had to inflict it, and their part in the phenomena was second only to the convulsionnaires themselves.

THE PHENOMENA

The most important commentator on these happenings was Louis Carrè de Montgeron, a *Conseiller au Parlement*. Initially a thorough skeptic, he determined to witness these impostures for himself. Then, realizing that the convulsionnaires were sincere and devout, he became a fervent partisan of the movement. In 1737 he produced a report entitled *La veritè des Miracles operès par l'intercession de M. Paris*, which he personally presented to the king. Louis XV's response was to have him taken at once to the Bastille, and he spent the rest of his life in prison, where he wrote two more monumental volumes, published in the Netherlands, before his death in 1754.

He recounts how he himself acted as a secourist, albeit somewhat ineffectually. The patient, Jeanne Moler, a young woman of some 23 years, leaned against a wall while he hit her in the pit of the stomach with a firedog:

> I began by giving relatively light blows. However, excited by her complaints which left me in no doubt that she wanted harder blows, I redoubled my efforts; but in vain I employed all my strength. She continued to complain that the blows I was giving her were so feeble, that they didn't give her any solace, and she made me hand the iron to a stronger man. Having watched me, he realised that no blows that he could give her would be too violent, he discharged terrible blows, always in the pit of the stomach. The girl received 100 from him, over and above the 60 I had given her which she found so feeble. Only then did she

cry out with joy which was reflected on her face and in her eyes: "Ha! that's so good! Ah, that does me such good! Take heart, my brother, double the force, if you can."[23]

If Montgeron's testimony stood alone, we might suspect him of both partiality and exaggeration, but others abundantly confirm it. Several doctors, skeptical at first, expressed astonishment when faced with the phenomena. Louis Sivert, master surgeon, declared he had seen convulsionnaires make movements so singular that it was not possible for a person to make them voluntarily, such as moving the head rapidly and to such a degree that the nose was between the shoulder-blades.[24]

Many medical observers started from the viewpoint that the convulsionnaires were faking, but they were invariably convinced that the phenomena were genuine even if their miraculous nature was open to question. When the police arrested Denise Régnier, known as Nisette, a volunteer claimed that anything she could do, he could do better. He started out bravely enough, imitating the jerking and twitching, but he complained that the hot coals he took into his mouth, as Nisette had done, burned him. Finally, when the time came for him to be crucified, even though it was with bonds rather than the nails driven through Nisette's hands, he had to confess that he could not match her feats.[25]

It became customary to give money to the family of the convulsionnaires, so "star" performers like Gabrielle and Marie Moler must have found it in their financial interest to continue. It could be argued that after a while the convulsions became mere spectacles, serving the interests of both performers and spectators. Yet there seems no reason to doubt the sincerity of the convulsionnaires. An officer of the royal court testified: "I observe that it is always in the name of Jesus-Christ that the Convulsionnaires demand the *secours*. They start by arming themselves with the sign of the Cross, and the Secourists also."

There was no simulation as regards the ailments that were treated. The cure of Charlotte La Porte (born in 1681) was conducted under controlled conditions, with medical examination before and after. She had come into the world with a deformed spine and misplaced hips, with no legs or feet but in their place pieces of soft flesh with no feeling, yet where one could discern half-formed feet, turned inwards. Her unformed limbs had not grown since she was 5, fifty years before, and she was carried about like an amputee.

On August 11, 1731, she had herself carried to the tomb. No sooner had she been placed there, than her "legs" began to move, and for the very first time she had feeling in them. From this moment she was convinced that her legs would be re-formed. But first, she had herself carried to a doctor, who had known of her condition at birth; he testified that he found her in the same state as she had been in 1686. An interested person sent a famous surgeon named Sauret to examine her. He reported that her legs were incapable of supporting her, had no feeling, and were no larger than a child's, and that at her age there wasn't the slightest possibility that her legs could form.

Yet, thanks to the *secours*, her legs lengthened by one-third, to their natural length; and her legs and feet gradually acquired for the first time their natural form. Cords were attached to her legs, and eight to ten men pulled on them with all their strength. As Montgeron observes, "consider how many different parts – bones, nerves, guts and organs of every kind had to be created in order that her unformed flesh could turn into legs and feet?"

When last reported on, Charlotte enjoyed the use of her legs for more than seven years, without relapse.[26]

Apart from the quality of the testimony, there is its quantity; Montgeron and others recount scores of cases in detail. Besides the published literature there is a vast quantity of police reports in the public archives, covering many thousands of individual cases.[27] Astonishing as the phenomena were, it is hard to quarrel with the verdict of Dr. Douglas, Bishop of Salisbury: "Whoever attentively weighs the evidence…must own that few matters of fact ever were confirmed by more unexceptionable testimony. They were performed openly in the sight of the whole world; in the heart of one of the greatest cities in the universe; on persons whom every body could see and examine."[28]

Individual Cases

While the convulsions themselves conformed generally to a stereotype, they took many particular forms. Those quoted here illustrate by no means exhaust the diversity of the phenomena.

Marguerite-Catherine Turpin (aged 27), July 1732

Described as a simple girl of exemplary piety, her body had been hideously deformed since a childhood fall at age six. Her condition was regarded as incurable, but her mother, hearing of the miracles occurring at Saint-Médard, took her there and laid her on the tomb. She was seized by convulsions so fierce that, although her state of illness made her extremely feeble, it took several people to restrain her movements.

Back home, she begged for *secours*. At first they were mild, but she implored them to try harder. People would pull her arms as forcibly as possible, and as a result her arms stretched to those of a normal person of her age, and she was able for the first time to use her hands to work.

Encouraged, she begged for even stronger secours, asking to be hit on her loins and hips, where the bones were monstrously deformed. It reached a point where she was being struck as hard as possible with an oak club which the secourist held above his head before letting it fall with all his strength on her body. Every day she received thousands of these blows, without feeling the least harm though they would have shattered an iron statue. Far from injuring her, the effect of these secours was that her hip-bones gradually shrank to a normal size by early in 1733, and she was able to walk normally, which previously she couldn't.[29]

Marie Sonnet, May 12, 1836

Marie's specialty was her resistance to fire. Montgeron invited eleven reliable citizens, including two doctors from the Sorbonne and a *Conseiller au Parlement*, to witness her performance. They signed an account:

We the undersigned certify that we have seen today, between 8 and 10 hours of the evening, Marie Sonnet go into convulsions, her head on one stool and her feet on another, which stools were entirely in the two sides of a large chimney-piece and beneath the mantelpiece in such a way that her body was in the air above the fire which was of extreme violence, and that she there rested for 36 minutes in this situation, on four separate occasions, while the sheet in which she was wrapped, having no clothes on, was not burned even though the flames sometimes passed above her; which seemed to us supernatural.

Moreover we certify that while we were signing this document, Sonnet placed herself back over the fire in the way described, and stayed there 9 minutes, seeming to be sleeping over a brazier which was very ardent.[30]

Sister Sara, April 27, 1745

On April 21, Sara was severely injured by a runaway carriage. For four days she lay in great pain, hardly able to eat or drink; she threw up her food and began spitting blood. A friend persuaded her to try the *secours*:

She lay down in her room, and after praying for a while, "j'entrai en état d'Enfance" ("I entered an infantile state": a technical term meaning a childlike trance). In this state she said "Elijah says that when I am back in my normal state, I must be given 100 blows on my injured parts and then some [holy] water from the house of M de Paris."

Back in her natural state, she was told she would be cured with 100 blows on her stomach. Unaware of what she had said in her altered state, she exclaimed "Are you joking? Surely my condition is bad enough without your making fun of me!"

But then I saw Brother Lévi approaching with a log of wood in his hand, and I was seized with fright. I trembled and cried, as though I was really going to be attacked. But everyone around me begged me to receive the blows, telling me it was the only way I could be cured.

I started praying, and I was still praying when the sister took hold of me and laid me on the floor on my back. The first blow was extremely painful, and I felt like a criminal receiving the finishing stroke: but I didn't feel any of the other blows, being hardly conscious and feeling almost nothing. It seemed to me that as they struck me with the stick, it took and carried away my sickness…so it seemed at the time, and so it seems to me now.

When I had received the 100 blows, it was as though I awoke from a deep sleep. I got up full of joy, and felt absolutely no pain whatsoever…I ate some supper, with a good appetite, like someone who has not been fed in several days.

Since then, my pain has completely gone, my appetite has fully returned, I breathe easily, I walk without difficulty, I sleep better than ever before.[31]

Gabrielle Moler (sister of Jeanne, aged 12-14)

Gabrielle's *secours* were witnessed, amongst others, by 21 persons who signed a Procès-Verbal; they included persons of distinction including a Scottish visitor, Lord Drummond of Perth, the Comte de Novien, magistrates, officers of His Majesty's Household, military officers and ecclesiastics.

She would normally start by having assistants strike her with their fists, and a hostile witness testified to seeing her receive 30,000 blows of this kind. Far from causing her pain, they rejoiced her marvelously.

Her cure involved four bars of iron, about the thickness of the little finger, about half a meter in length, with a head. Gabrielle would lie on the ground, and four persons pushed the points with all their force into her stomach, which they would enter to a depth of 7 cm, through her clothing.

After this *secours*, she herself directed the point of one of these bars to the hollow of her throat beneath her chin, and one would push with all their force, several times; then she got to her knees and had one person push at her throat from in front, and another from behind, both with all their strength. This caused her no pain, and left no mark afterwards.

Moreover she ordered spades to be brought, whose base was sharper than ordinary spades; two were straight, two others were rounded. She herself placed one of these rounded spades immediately below one of her breasts, another above, the two others to either side, so that her breast was enclosed on four sides, Then four assistants were required to push with all their strength, but none penetrated her breast which was as if made of iron. Immediately afterwards, some of the ladies present inspected her body, and testified that it was as hard as stone.

Lying on her back, she placed the blade of one of the spades against her larynx, and obliged one of the assistants to push with all his strength against her throat, perpendicularly. She received only an agreeable and beneficial impression, and asked for more.

Then she stood up and, leaning against a wall, had herself thumped with a bar of iron in the stomach. It seemed impossible to strike her hard enough. Even though the assistant was using all his strength, she cried unceasingly: Harder, harder!

Also she would lie on her back and ordered the assistant to throw a big stone, weighing nearly 30 kg, onto her chest and stomach, adding his strength to the weight of the stone. The assistant was soon exhausted, so had to rest from time to time, or hand over to someone else.[32]

Sister Dina, July 1743

She would lean on swords fixed into the wall, or lay her body on them when fixed in the floor, without feeling pain, yet she pressed on them with sufficient force to bend the blades, and on one occasion to break one. Examining her, women found no protective clothing beneath, no underclothes beneath her chemise except a simple cloth garment over her stomach; these garments were frequently pierced through by the swords, but her skin was untouched.

One observer watched as six people press the swords into her body:

> She held a large chain round her hips, whose links were big enough that the swords could pass through; six swords were thus held in place; also a ninth against her stomach, and two more against her breasts, one of which I myself held. When she gave the signal, the nine secourists began pushing: gently at first, till she cried out to press more strongly. When we were all pressing with all our strength, she still wanted more, so others came and pushed us from behind. Afterwards she complained that one of the swords – the one I was holding – hadn't been pressed hard enough; yet I was pushing so hard that the pommel was pressed painfully into my hand.[33]

La Fontaine, 1733

M. Fontaine was secretary of state to Louis XV, a high official of impeccable social standing. Nevertheless, in 1733, "being in a house where he had been invited to dine with a large company, he felt himself all at once compelled by an invisible power to turn round and round on one foot with prodigious swiftness, which gyrations lasted upwards of an hour without a moment's intermission. "Observers counted as many as 60 turns in a minute. He cried out for a book of prayer, and – still turning with a dazzling rapidity – read aloud from the Moral Reflections of Père Quesnel, a Jansenist writer, though hitherto Fontaine had opposed Jansenism. For six months or more, he experienced these convulsions morning and afternoon, each session lasting up to two hours."[34]

Convulsions As Therapy

Theories abounded. Montgeron himself favored the view that divine emanation from the dead priest brought about both the convulsions and the cures. La Taste, a Benedictine from Bordeaux, opposing him from the standpoint of orthodox Catholicism, thought they might be the work of the devil. Others, notably Hecquet, looked for a natural explanation.

The difficulty is to establish how far "natural" explanations can be extended. As Montgeron points out, the challenge to understanding is the sheer improbability that a cure of any kind could be affected, let alone by such crude and violent means that ostensibly would aggravate rather than alleviate the ailment.

Noted French physician and medical historian Louis-Florentin Calmeil attributed the remarkable immunity to "...the rigid state of the muscles, the powerful contraction of all their fibres, the turgescence of all the tissues which cover and protect the abdomen and thorax, the principal vascular trunk, and surfaces of bone in the vicinity of those parts."[35] However, this falls far short of being an explanation, for it fails to account for the process whereby these conditions came about in the first place.

Moreover, the physical phenomena were accompanied by a number of other features, ranging from glossolalia and animal sounds at one extreme, to eloquence and intelligence displayed by people described as simple to the point of idiocy. These make it evident that the phenomenon of the convulsions was at least as much psychological as physical.

"By accumulating these incredible wonders before our eyes," insisted Lepaige, a contemporary commentator, "God is pleased to overturn nature." The feats of the convulsionnaires may not have overturned nature, but they certainly stretch to the limit our understanding of what nature can do.

SALEM WITCH-HUNTS

Massachusetts Bay Colony: 1692

While the Salem witch-hunts of 1692 constitute the most famous episode of witchcraft persecution in North America, it pales in comparison to the European witchcraft holocaust that claimed between 100,000 and half a million souls. In contrast, fewer than fifty people are known to have been executed as witches in North America.[36] Accusations and executions for witchcraft were primarily confined to the New England colonies in areas under strict Puritan control; more tolerant religious groups settled the southern colonies.[37]

On May 26, 1647, Alse Young became the first recorded witch execution in North America when she was hanged at the Puritan village of Wethersfield.[38] In 1648, Boston in the Massachusetts Bay Colony, was the site of the hanging of Margaret Jones. A midwife from Charlestown who used native plants to cure the sick, Jones had the misfortune of exchanging angry words with some neighbors, and shortly thereafter they experienced misfortunes attributed to her casting spells.[39] The Colony's Governor, John Winthrop, kept a journal of the episode, noting the evidence against her. She apparently had many enemies and was not reticent in making her opinions known. She had also been caught stealing on several occasions, tainting her reputation.[40] Among the accusations at her trial: touching people who shortly thereafter became sick, foretelling future events, and having a witch's teat "in her secret parts as fresh as if it had been newly sucked and after it had been scanned, upon a forced search, that was withered, and another began on the opposite side."[41] Eight years later, two neighbors accused an outspoken Boston widow, Anne Hibbins, of being a witch. The women charged that they had been talking about Hibbins when she walked to them, recounted for them their conversation, word for word, exactly as it had occurred, then walked away muttering curses.[42] Other villagers stepped forward to with similar accusations. Despite being the sister of Governor Richard Bellingham, Hibbins was tried in court, found guilty, and hanged at Salem on June 19, 1656.[43] In Boston in 1688, four children of mason John Goodwin were seized by strange fits. Suspicion of bewitchment fell on an Irish cleaning woman, a Mrs. Glover, who was hanged for witchcraft.[44]

CONTEXT: Any evaluation of the events in Salem must be viewed in relation to the socio-cultural context and the role of the *zeitgeist* or spirit of the times. According to historians Paul Boyer and Stephen Nissenbaum, "when the roles assigned to the actors of 1692 are shaped by a script not of their own making...[it] cannot rise above the level of gripping melodrama. It is only as we come to sense how deeply the witchcraft outbreak was rooted in...everyday lives and how profoundly those lives were being shaped by powerful forces of historical change...the more we have come to...realize how profoundly they were shaped by the times in which they lived. For if they were unlike any other men, so was their world unlike any other world before or since..."[45]

The Witch Trials

In 1692, Salem Village, in the British colony of Massachusetts, was the scene of a great witchcraft fear that spread throughout the region. During the scare, at least 200 people were arrested on suspicion of bewitching others and put in jail to await trial. Some were tortured into confessing while waiting for their day in court; others died before ever going on trial. At least 20 residents were executed – 19 by hanging. All of those executed were convicted on "spectral evidence" whereby accusers claimed that spirits of the accused had left their bodies and visited them, especially at night, causing torment or misfortune. It was nearly impossible to refute such claims. In 1692, it was widely believed that witches could take any shape or form, adding to the anxious atmosphere, as potential witches were everywhere. Two dogs were even accused and executed.

At the time of the outbreak, the Puritans controlled Salem Village. Also known as Separatists, the Puritans were at odds with teachings of the Church of England, taking a more "pure," strict interpretation of the Bible. They opposed priests elevating their status by wearing special clothing. They also condemned church services that included written prayers, the playing of organ music, and the use of pictures and statues. Politically and economically powerful, the well-educated Puritans had members who sat in the House of Commons and posed a growing threat to the Church of England. In September 1620, a group of about 100 Pilgrims embarked on a two-month voyage aboard the Mayflower after being granted a charter to settle in the Virginia colony. The Puritans who remained in England faced continued persecution under Charles I, expelling them from universities, canceling business charters, and jailing dissidents. By 1629, many Puritan leaders had given up on reforming the Church of England and successfully lobbied royal authorities for the right to form their own colony in the New World under The Massachusetts Bay Company.[46] Beginning in 1629, many Puritans sailed to the New World to practice their beliefs free from religious persecution by the Church of England. Ironically, the Salem witch-hunts that would follow were fostered by Puritan religious intolerance.

The Salem witch scare began in December 1691, at the home of the ordained minister of the Salem Village church, Samuel Paris and his wife, Elizabeth Elridge Paris. Inside the house were four young girls, including his daughter Elizabeth, 9, and niece Abigail Williams, 11. An elderly Barbados slave named Tituba Indian did the household chores, while her husband John Indian, also a slave, worked outside with The Reverend Paris. In January 1691, a strange affliction struck young Elizabeth. She became confused, forgetful, and made animal-like sounds. This would be followed by fits of screaming and crying.[47] Soon Abigail exhibited similar symptoms. Their bodies would convulse and shake, and they would speak incoherently.

Soon other young girls in the community began having other fits of strange behaviors: disordered speech, convulsive movements, and bizarre conduct. Village physician Doc Griggs deduced that they had been bewitched. Many of the girls were friends with the Barbados servant Tituba who would meet secretly with them and tell scary tales of Caribbean voodoo

"THERE IS A FLOCK OF YELLOW BIRDS AROUND HER HEAD."

At a Salem witch trial the accusing girls point at the victim.

and magic. Overexcited, the girls had difficulty sleeping and had nightmares about demons and witches. At the time, it was well established among the Puritans that the Devil could not act directly on humans but used intermediaries in the form of witches to do their bidding. As a result, the afflicted girls were constantly pressured to give the names of their tormenting witches.[48] Soon the affected girls accused two elderly women and Tituba of bewitching them. On February 29, warrants were issued and they were arrested. The trio were social deviants and made easy targets. Sarah Osburn was a cross woman who had stopped going to church; Sarah Good was a pipe smoker, suspected of sexual promiscuity, rarely bathed, was poverty-stricken, and forced to beg for survival. Tituba, of African-Carribean descent, possessed odd customs and appearance, and spoke of voodoo.[49] While Good and Osburn vehemently protested their innocence, Tituba confessed to being a witch, sought forgiveness, was eventually let go and left the village after being sold to another master. In fact, all anyone accused had to do to go free was confess to being a witch and show remorse.

Those who would die steadfastly refused to confess guilt, as it would constitute living in sin; the Puritans were devoutly religious and many believed that falsely confessing would condemn them to an afterlife in hell. During her "confessions," Tituba said that she had been forced to serve the Devil and hurt the afflicted girls, but she was now deeply remorseful and sought God's forgiveness. While Tituba testified, at a nearby inn, her husband John Indian went into fits of demonic possession, which authorities took as proof of his innocence.[50]

As word quickly spread of the "bewitchment," other young females were afflicted with the fits: neighbor Mary Walcott, 16, a maidservant named Mary Warren, 20, and Griggs' own niece, Elizabeth Hubbard, 17.[51]

Events quickly spiraled out of control and soon more than 200 people were accused of witchcraft and held for trial. On May 10, 1692, Sarah Osburn became the first victim of the witch-hunt, dying in a Boston jail cell while awaiting trail.[52] On June 10, Bridget Bishop was the first to be hanged. By all accounts she was a fun-loving woman who enjoyed playing shovelboard and wearing colorful, flamboyant attire that did not endear her to her fellow Puritans. She had long been rumored to be a witch, and in 1680 she was tried and acquitted of witchcraft.[53]

On June 16, Roger Toothaker passed away in jail. On July 19, five more swung from the gallows: Sarah Goode, Elizabeth How, Susanna Martin, Rebecca Nurse, and Sarah Wildes. One month later on August 19, five more were hanged: George Burroughs, Martha Carrier, George Jacobs, John Proctor, and John Willard. Eight more suspected witches were hanged on September 22: Martha Corey, Mary Easty, Alice and Mary Parker, Ann Pudeator, Margaret Scott, Wilmot Redd, and Samuel Wardwell.[54]

When a feisty 80-year-old farmer named Giles Corey was accused of consorting with Satan, he defied the court by refusing to enter a plea. In an effort to get a confession, on September 17, he was brought to a field near the courthouse and a plank was placed on him. One by one, heavy stones were placed onto the plank in a vain effort to get the stubborn man to confess to being a witch. Corey never did, and prior to his death two agonizing days later, he reportedly muttered, "More weight!"[55]

By October 1692, there was a rapid shift in public opinion as the circle of accusations grew ever wider and implausible, implicating more and more people of wealth and influence. Among the accused was the wife of the Reverend Increase Mather, a prominent Boston minister and president of Harvard University. On October 3, Mather delivered a powerful rebuke of spectral evidence entitled: "Cases of Conscience Concerning Evil Spirits Personating Men."[56] Mather cautioned against the use of such evidence, including the claims of the "visionary girls": "It were better that ten suspected witches should escape, than that one innocent person should be condemned."

At about the same time, influential Boston resident Thomas Brattle circulated a letter containing a series of embarrassing observations. Why was it that some accused witches – members of high society – were not prosecuted in court, while their poorer counterparts were? Why should the court accept the testimony of confessed witches who have conspired with the Devil, when they sought to implicate Christians?[57] Brattle forcefully and eloquently destroyed the credibility of the court, pointing out so many inconsistencies, contradictions, and illegalities that the court members themselves felt compelled to published an apology. Brattle concluded: "The witches' meetings, the devil's baptisms and mock sacraments, which the accusing and confessing witches oft speak of, are nothing else but the effect of their fancy, depraved and deluded by the devil, and not a reality to be regarded or minded by any wise man."[58]

At about this time, the popular public perception of those accused of witchcraft was changing from that of a willing participant in cahoots with the Devil to having had the misfortune of being possessed against their will.[59] On October 12, Massachusetts Governor Sir William Phips (who's own wife was under suspicion of witchcraft),[60] issued a moratorium on further witch trials, and on October 29 he dissolved the Court of Oyer and Terminer (from Old French meaning "To Hear and Determine").[61] However, many suspects continued to be held, and on December 3, Ann Foster died in jail.

On January 3, 1693, a new Superior Court was convened to continue the witch trials, but this time spectral evidence was rejected. Of the 52 accused witches before the court, three were ordered hanged and five others who were previously sentenced were ordered to continue being held. Phips ordered reprieves for all eight, and in May, ordered all suspects to be released.[62] However, to add insult to injury, they were only set free after paying their jailing costs.[63] Phips' reprieve did not come soon enough for the last person to die from the witch-hunt. Linda Dustin succumbed in jail on March 10, 1693.

Theories For The Witch-Hunts: Ergot Poisoning

Psychologist Linda Caporael argued that the "fits" and strange behaviors are characteristic of ergot poisoning of the food supply. Ergot fungus is a chemical relative of infamous 1960s psychedelic drug lysergic acid diethylamide, or LSD, and can cause hallucinations, convulsions, confusion, disorientation, depression, and sensations of crawling and pinching on the skin. Nicknamed St. Anthony's Fire, ergotism is known to coincide with floods and wet growing seasons which foster the growth of the fungus *claviceps purpura,* which thrives after a cold winter and a damp wet summer. Ergot forms on cultivated grains, especially rye. Just prior to the outbreak there had been a wet growing season and ideal conditions for the development of ergot.[64] Most of those afflicted were living near farms that were growing grains in swampy marshlands – ideal for the promotion of ergot.[65] The month after Abigail Williams and Betty Parris began having "fits," on February 25, a "witch cake" was baked to determine if the girls were truly bewitched. A "witch's cake" consisted of batter mixed with the girl's urine which was then fed to the dog in order to determine the presence of a spell if the animal changed into a "familiar" or began acting strangely.[66] It was suspected that the dog might have been a familiar, that is, a demon in animal form that was provided by the Devil to do the bidding of someone who had made a pact with the Devil (a witch).[67] Caporael assumed that the dog must have begun to act strangely from the ergot residue in its urine, as within hours of this incident, the girls began accusing others of witchcraft for the first time.[68]

Despite Caporael's speculation, there is no record of the dog's reaction. If the dog had acted strangely or died, one might expect to find more references to this sensational incident in the substantial records of the Salem events. It is also known that when the Reverend Parris learned of the baking of the witches' cake, he became furious to think that anyone would consider using witchcraft in his house. This may have motivated the girls to divert attention away from themselves and onto others – instead of hypothesized reactions to eating witch cake by the dog. In the absence of any concrete evidence that the dog went crazy after eating the cake, Salem historian Peggy Saari speculates: "Terrified by their own 'crimes' – such as mixing the egg-white potion – would be discovered, the girls began pointing fingers."[69]

Also, if ergot was to blame, why did it affect mostly young girls in Salem Village – the very group that historically has been the target of hysterical fits? Presumably, adults would have eaten the contaminated bread as well but few were affected. If the young girls were susceptible to the poisoning because of their low body weight, why weren't young boys similarly afflicted? Further, the symptoms of the "visionary girls" "could be turned on and off, depending on the audience, unlike the toxidrome of convulsive ergotism."[70] Such actions are impossible with victims of ergot poisoning and would be the equivalent of having a drunk suddenly turn sober or a psychotic suddenly stop hallucinating. Also, between 1638 and 1699, apart from Salem, at least 141 persons went on trial for witchcraft in New England. It is highly unlikely that all were afflicted with ergotism. Toxicologist Alan Wolf observes that in Salem, "There were none of the constitutional, residual effects typical of ergotism, such as weakness, strictures, or dementia. The afflicted were hale and hearty."[71]

There are two main types of ergot poisoning – gangrenous ergotism and convulsive ergotism. Contemporary reports of the former have been reported in England and Ethiopia. In 1927, over 200 people were afflicted with ergotism in Manchester, England, after eating contaminated rye bread. Most victims had signs of gangrene.[72] In a 1978 outbreak involving contaminated barley in Ethiopia, gangrene was also prevalent and nearly half the patients died. Gangrene was not a symptom in Salem.[73] Therefore, if ergotism was involved it Salem, it would have to have been of the convulsive variety, which is typified by delirium, auditory and visual hallucinations, mania, muscle seizures, and headaches. But the appearances of these standard symptoms in convulsive ergotism do not suddenly manifest and subside across a scattered population as occurred in Salem. Indeed, not a single "bewitched" Salem resident is known to have exhibited the full range of signs and symptoms that typify ergotism.[74] The pattern of accusations and bewitchments closely parallel the social, economic, and political divisions between the town and village residents, suggesting a cause other than ergot.[75]

Hysteria

Most of those exhibiting fits of strange behavior were young repressed girls – the exact group that historically has been prone to experiencing individual HYSTERIA and MASS HYSTERIA. Hysteria is a condition whereby people under extreme stress in intolerable social settings and seemingly with no way out begin to experience screaming, crying, shaking, twitching, fainting, visions, trance-like states, and hallucinations. Histrionic melodrama, attention seeking, and exaggeration are integral parts of the syndrome. The symptoms usually go away once the stress subsides. In Puritan Salem, young girls lived a monotonous existence, especially during winter months, when the "bewitchment" began. Conversely, young boys would practice shooting their musket, hunt for wild game, and ice fish. The young girls would remain cloistered inside and perform endless hours of tedious drudgery.[76] The life of a young girl was filled with restrictions – even singing and dancing were prohibited. Any spare time was usually spent studying the Bible. The strange "fits" that the girls would exhibit are consistent with scores of historical outbreaks of MASS HYSTERIA in long-term repressive environments, including CONVENT HYSTERIA. Occasionally during their fits, the girls would exhibit exceptional strength and require several grown men to subdue them. Similar examples are commonplace in the hysteria literature. At times some of the girls seemed to be purely playacting, such as when several were taken to a neighboring town to identify other witches. Upon meeting several strangers on the road, the girls displayed strange, seemingly uncontrollable fits, including convulsing on the ground. When the group paid little attention to them, the girls simply stood up and continued walking down the road.[77]

Social Economic Explanations

An analysis of a map of Salem based on old land deeds shows that the overwhelming majority of those making witchcraft accusations resided in central and western Salem Village. Conversely, the accused lived mostly in eastern Salem.[78] Upon noting this conspicuous pattern, Boyer and Nissenbaum examined various legal records and uncovered a long-standing feud between the town and village that had been simmering for at least two decades prior to the witch-hunts.[79] Most of those residing on the east side were prosperous businessmen and merchants; most of those living on the west side were subsistence farmers who attributed their steady economic decline over the years to overtaxing by the townsfolk. Petitions protesting their burden fell on deaf ears. As the years passed, the resentment and tension festered and the rift grew wider and wider.[80] The witch-hunts essentially pitted the more prosperous, liberal Salem Town against the inhabitants of the more conservative, traditional Salem Village. The affluent town was a busy urban center located closer to the Atlantic Ocean and commerce; the village was a sparsely populated agricultural region with scattered farms and houses. A separatist movement had also developed as many villagers expressed a desire for separation from the town's political and religious dominance.[81] Further fueling the rift was a long-standing dispute between the town and village over who should pay for the local minister.[82]

Feminist Views: Misogyny And Power

As the overwhelming majority of victims were women, Fred Pelka contends that the witch-hunt was the "woman's holocaust" perpetrated by Puritan misogynists out of fear of female independence and sexuality, and serving as a means to control deviant women who were not under direct male control.[83] In *The Devil in the Shape of a Woman*, Carol Karlsen argues that the persecutions had the effect of controlling females who threatened the traditional social order by challenging the long-standing practice of males inheriting property from their fathers. Most of the accused women either had inherited property or stood to inherit property.[84]

The Demoniziation Of Native Americans

Historian Mary Beth Norton takes a more novel, provocative approach, viewing the witch-hunts as an extension of the conflict between the Puritans and Native Americans (specifically the Wabanaki "Indians") in the Maine-New Hampshire frontier. Many of the accusers and the accused had settled in Salem after experiencing unspeakable frontier horrors. Norton argues that many of those involved in the interrogation and subsequent trial of suspected witches had played integral roles in the war in which the Massachusetts soldiers in Maine were being trounced.[85] Reeling from the failure of male leaders to adequately protect Salemites against the feared and demonized Wabanaki, "the afflicted rose to the challenge of defending the colony from its invisible enemies," in the process deflecting attention from their inability to protect the colonists from this outside threat.[86]

COMMENTS: Any explanation of the events at Salem must account for a variety of factors: settling old scores; hysterical symptoms among repressed girls who had been exposed to scary tales during the monotonous, gloomy winter months; Puritan piety; political instability; the fragility and anxiety of Puritan New England life in 1692, which could be quickly snuffed out by unfriendly Natives; hurricanes, drought, harsh winters – and spells by "witches."

SANTEN CONVENT OUTBREAK

Germany: circa 1560

Near Santen (also spelled Xante and Zante), which at that time was in Flemish territory though subsequently it was absorbed into Prussia, there was an outbreak of hysteria in a convent of nuns of Saint Bridget.

CONTEXT: This was the third notable outbreak that disturbed convents in Western Europe during the 15th and 16th centuries. While each incident seems to have been independent of the others, the occurrence of three such incidents sharing common features, close in time and quite close in location, suggests that a shared emotional climate favored such manifestations, and that news spread easily from one location to another.

The sisters were taken with convulsions, followed by breathlessness and spasms of the throat that persisted for several days, so that the victims had to be force-fed. "They were diversely and strangely tormented," Jean Weyer reported, "now they shuddered, now they baaed like sheep and uttered horrible noises. Sometimes they were thrown from their chairs in the church and their veils were torn from their heads: sometimes their throats were blocked so that they could not swallow any meat."[87]

As was customary, a search was made for whoever was responsible for bringing the demons into the convent, and the troubles were attributed to a young nun who had entered the community not out of any religious vocation, but as a consequence of love difficulties. When her parents opposed her marriage to a young man on the grounds of too close affinity, she was very distressed. Consequently, when the devil appeared to her in the form of her lover and advised her to become a nun, she did so straight away. But once enclosed in the convent walls, she became very restless and everyone witnessed her uncontrolled behavior. This in turn set off some of the other sisters.

The authorities quickly concluded that this must be the work of a demon, and that it was the lovelorn nun who had brought the demon with her into the convent. Consequently she was placed permanently in the prisons of another church. There, she twice gave birth to a child, thanks to the kindly attention of her jail keeper. After that, she was set free, and, said Weyer, with evident satisfaction that for once something like justice had been done, "I think she lived a long time after that without anyone supposing her to be a sorceress."[88]

However, isolating the reluctant novice did not, alas, resolve the matter. The sisters of St Bridget's were troubled with their affliction for ten years before it finally ceased.

COMMENT: Weyer's narrative, from which all other accounts are drawn, provides few details. We do not even know for sure that the sisters were exorcized, though this was the standard practice in such cases and was probably performed here. As always, the Evil One was blamed for the attacks. But we may well go along with Madden's conclusion: "It is sufficient for us to believe that there may have been good grounds for the statement that the young lady referred to had been in love, had been refused in marriage, had been compelled by her parents to enter a convent, had pined in its cloisters, sickened in its seclusion; and, having lost all hope, and health, and spirits, she became a monomaniac, labouring under hysterics, convulsions and delirium."[89]

See also: CONVENT HYSTERIA, DEMON POSSESSION.

SARDINE PACKING HYSTERIA

New Brunswick, Canada: August-November 1992

In late August, workers at a sardine packing plant in a small community in Northeastern Canada began to develop mysterious symptoms: eye and throat irritation, headaches, chest tightness, and weakness. Most of those affected were women working on the packing line. Over the next four months (August to November) other symptoms began to appear: dizziness, poor coordination, and bouts of laughing followed by fits of weeping. The symptoms became so prevalent and severe that the line was forced to temporarily close. Eventually, symptoms spread to other parts of the plant. Both private and government specialists in industrial health were called in to investigate and several potential exposure sources were pinpointed, though the levels of these sources were not in high enough quantities to cause illness. Small amounts of carbon monoxide and sulfur dioxide were found leaking in the boiler room near the packing line and were fixed. Another source of minute quantities of carbon monoxide were propane-burning forklifts that were fitted with catalytic converters. Once it was announced that these changes had been made, the illness symptoms stopped, but then resumed. Environmental tests of the factory were within normal limits, and although some physical causes may have contributed to or triggered the outbreak, the symptoms were deemed to have been psychological in nature. A total of 208 out of 270 employees were affected.[90]

SARS SCARE

Worldwide: 2003

Severe Acute Respiratory Syndrome, or SARS, is a new type of atypical pneumonia that was first identified in November 2002, in Guangdong Province, southern China. It soon spread to many Asian countries and Canada. The World Health Organization reports that between November 1, 2002, and July 31, 2003, there were 8,437 cases and 813 deaths.[91] During 2003, a worldwide scare erupted over the possible spread of SARS, into a pandemic. These fears proved exaggerated.

American physician Theodore Dalrymple said the

media contributed to the scare: "A single death from Sars, even one that takes place ten thousand miles away, is more real to us than the 600 deaths that take place daily from cardiovascular disease in our own country. We are used to people keeling over and dying of heart attacks and strokes, as half of us will do; but a picture of a Chinese child with a face mask causes us to quake in our boots."[92]

British doctor Clare Gerada was more fearful of the public reaction: "The fear of it is gong to create more problems than the disease itself. We have got to get some sense into this – this is not Ebola and not smallpox."[93]

Canadian medical historian Edward Shorter said the mass media exaggerated the SARS danger and should shoulder much of the blame for the unnecessary fear: "What hasn't been contained is the mass psychosis surrounding it. It's entirely the working of the media; this need never have happened."[94] Science writer Michael Fumento concurred with this assessment but said the public health sector was also responsible for the scare.[95]

CONTEXT: The fear of SARS was clearly exaggerated by alarmist media reports and emotional remarks by some public health officials. Labeling the scare as "mass psychosis" is inaccurate. The episode is best described as a media-driven collective delusion that is perhaps best summed up by California physician David Safir, who said that "the level of fear generated is far out of proportion to the actual danger," noting that each day thousands of people die "of pneumonia in which the organism is not identified."[96]

SATANIC CULT AND RITUAL ABUSE SCARE

Mid-1980s to mid-1990s

The Satanic Ritual Abuse (SRA) scare can be traced back to 1980 with the publication of *Michelle Remembers*.[97] Set in Canada, the book purports to be a true account of Michelle Smith's childhood nightmare of abuse at the hands of a satanic coven. Written with her psychiatrist Lawrence Pazder, *Michelle Remembers* is the first known story of a "repressed memory" involving Satanic Ritual Abuse. Michelle describes a horrific childhood in which both parents were alcoholics. Her mother died when she was just 14; her father then left the family and she was raised by her grandparents. At the end of the 1970s, Smith began attending therapy sessions with Dr. Pazder, whom she was to later marry. Dr. Pazder placed her under hypnosis in order to release "repressed" memories of her abuse. Smith told an intriguing story of having been mistreated by a group of Satan worshippers, her mother among them.

Over the course of several months, Michelle's "repressed" memories flooded back in vivid detail. Among her disclosures, Michelle told of being stripped naked and placed in a cage filled with snakes. Investigative journalist Mark Pendergrast summarized her claims, including the account of butchering and burning "stillborn fetuses in her presence, killed kittens and forced her to perform lurid sexual acts. At one point, they surgically attached horns to her head and a tail to her spine. Finally, Michelle supposedly was allowed to go home with her mother and promptly repressed the memory..."[98] Smith's claims are as unbelievable as they are dubious. For example, neither of her two sisters could recollect the "abuse."[99] David Alexander of *The Humanist* concurred: "As for bringing Smith's tormentors to justice, it should be relatively easy to identify them, even years later, since the members of this 'cult' reportedly cut off the middle fingers of their left hands as a sign of obedience to the Prince of Darkness. Unfortunately, no independent evidence has surfaced to corroborate any of the claims made by Smith."[100]

From about 1983 to 1993, stories began to circulate widely around the world about the existence of a network of satanic cultists kidnapping, murdering, or torturing children during ritual sacrifices. At least sixty rumor-panics were triggered in various sections of the United States during this period. Since 1993, the claims have continued, but in a more sporadic fashion. Most social scientists studying these episodes classify them as MORAL PANICS that coincide with the breakdown of the traditional family and a desire to find scapegoats. They are viewed as performing a function as cautionary tales – a metaphor for prevailing concerns over the weakened family and its diminished capacity to protect children.[101]

The Moral Panic About Satanic Ritual Abuse

American sociologist Jeffrey Victor, arguably the most prolific researcher of Satanic Ritual Abuse, has traced its history as a moral panic, identifying four factors that engendered the Satanic cult scare. Building on research on false criminal accusations by Klemke and Tiedeman, Victor outlined four major causes.

The first factor is *the existence of a new, significant group of moral deviants who pose a direct threat to children.* First, was the widespread appearance of beliefs within segments of American society, of the existence of a new type of deviant – dangerous Satanic cultists – and the serious and growing threat they purportedly posed to American children. The "panic" began with sporadic rumors and claims by authorities such as clergy, law enforcement, cult experts, and psychotherapists warning of the widespread threat. While the mass media did not start the scare, they did help to spread the claims.[102] The ritual abuse scare was a schism of the child sex abuse fear prominent during the 1980s, as there was a growing perception that the sexual abuse of children was a hidden epidemic. Victor stated: "In the 1980s, there was...already a moral panic over crimes against children. Claims were being made that thousands of children were being kidnapped, sexually assaulted, and murdered...As a result, the general public was more receptive to the self-appointed authorities who lent credibility to SRA stories."[103]

The second factor in the SRA epidemic is *the expanding role of different authorities in social control.* Authorities are important for their role in not only defining what constitutes deviant behavior, but also in evaluating and legitimating emerging claims about supposedly new societal threats. If these new claims are not deemed credible by authorities, they fail to gain a foothold in society. However, new authorities, especially from the medical community, are being increasingly relied upon by law officers, justices, legislators, and court juries due to their specialist knowledge and present their interpretations of information and evidence that are often viewed as "scientific facts."[104] Victor argues that at the time of the SRA epidemic in the early 80s, psychotherapists and social workers "were struggling to gain greater recognition and respect within their larger community of professionals. The discovery of the SRA of children thrust these marginal specialists into the spotlight of mass media attention...If this important discovery could be confirmed in the courts of law and science, these specialists could obtain well-deserved recognition and respect for their work."[105] These same psychotherapists and social workers spread the SRA message initially through conferences and seminars, and subsequently gained widespread media attention and became part of the broader child molestation scare.[106]

A third reason for the sudden proliferation of SRA reports during the 1980s concerns the use of *flawed investigation methods for evaluating reports of deviant acts.* These are the same controversial techniques outlined earlier in this Encyclopedia under False Memory Syndrome. Techniques such as hypnosis, dream interpretation, and guided imagery have been linked to the production of false memories,[107] in addition to the use of leading questions, implanting ideas in children's minds.

A fourth factor engendering the SRA scare is what Victor calls "symbolic resonance" of the perceived threatening agent within a broader ideology in American society, namely *an evil force that threatens the American moral fabric.* The SRA "epidemic" was fostered by three groups in particular whose "demonologies" resonated closely with belief systems. *Traditionalist Christians* have a moral worldview attributing the cause of evil acts to Satan [see SATANISM]. This perspective views Satanists as literal agents of the Devil whose intentions are "to spread immorality of all kinds in order to destroy the moral order of American society and hasten Satan's takeover of the world."[108] A second major group who helped to fuel the SRA cause were *social conservatives,* such as certain "feminist" and "Christian" psychotherapists, concerned with the decline in American morality.[109] A third group contributing to the scare is what Victor terms *radical feminists* who have a demonological view of patriarchy and its many sexual aggressions against women and children, including incest and rape. "Skepticism about accusations of SRA is regarded as being one more attempt by men to discredit women and children's testimony about their sexual victimization. The anomaly that many of the people accused of SRA are mothers or female child care workers is ignored or is attributed to male manipulators."[110]

The Functions Of The Sra Scare

Accounts of organized satanic ritual sexual abuse serve a function in contemporary society as a form of scapegoating. All cultures have a concept of evil, and Satan typifies it in modern Western society heavily influenced by Christianity. For most of the second half of the twentieth century, Communists have filled this niche quite nicely. The rise of the satanic cult threat is an "invented" evil that conspicuously coincides with the breakup of the Soviet Union and the Communist Block as a new evil was able to fill the void.[111] Victor stated that the creation of moral scapegoats promotes social stability: "A search for internal enemies can also serve the same functions – providing a target for displaced aggression and unifying the conflicting elements within a society – by defining some category of people as being traitors to, or deviant from, the overarching moral values of that society."[112] On a different level, the creation of devil cultists violating America's youth reflects widespread anxieties about internal conflicts among parents. "There is a great deal of parental guilt today; many parents feel guilty about leaving their children at day-care centers or about having little time to spend with them or about being reluctant to use their authority to guide their children's choice of entertainments and friends or about feeling unable to guide the moral values of their children."[113]

See also: FALSE MEMORY SYNDROME.

SATANISM

The term Satanism suggests a formal, structured religion in which adoration of Satan is the most prominent feature. No such religion has ever existed, nor could it exist. At most, Satanism comprises a variety of principles and practices in which the mythological figure of Satan is treated as though he were a god rather than a theological abstraction, a convenient personification of the force of evil.

Satanism and demonism: The Church did not invent Satan. A belief in demonic entities is well nigh universal. It is found in the oldest literature and in the most remote cultures. However, these entities are generally regarded as amoral, rather than outright evil; they are rarely honored, let alone worshipped. Anthropologist Philip Stevens has pointed out that "most of the world's religions have no counterpart to Satan or to Hell."[114] These entities are feared and propitiated, and avoided wherever possible. It is often believed that they can be constrained – they can be invoked and compelled to do the bidding of someone sufficiently adept. And should they become obstreperous, they can be exorcized, for man can always call upon even more powerful entities, except when he has chosen to abdicate his rights by signing a pact with the devil in exchange for short-term rewards.

Insofar as Satan is considered demonic, there is an inevitable overlap between demonism and Satanism, but they are quite different. Demonism is a perception of demons as part of the natural order of things and the development of means of coping with them. Satanism is the result of a choice to honor and even worship one particular demon.

The Satan myth: The Satan of Christian doctrine is the result of a mythmaking process by the Church; the Satan of Satanist teaching is the result of a counter-process by those who find the Church's myth unacceptable or inadequate.

Satanism can be said to have its origin in Persia BCE, where Zoroastrian beliefs made a clear distinction between light and darkness, good and evil. Judeo-Christian doctrine perpetuated this notion, embodying it in the myth of the rebel angels who defied God and were expelled from Heaven in consequence. The church fathers took over the myth and involved themselves in labyrinthine argument as they sought to fix Satan's role in their scheme of things. Greek dualism, in which spirit is good, matter bad, contributed to the debates whose outcome was that Satan came to be defined as God's adversary, who encourages and embodies all evil tendencies in human behavior. Christian theology regards sexual activity as a regrettable necessity, relegating women to an inferior rank in God's creation and honoring celibacy; it also regards all magic as black magic, and constructed its own idea of Satan as the personification of all evil. Richard Cavendish pointed out: "By itself dualism does not imply devil-worship, but it creates a favourable background for it. There is more incentive to enlist in the Devil's ranks if he is on more or less equal terms with God than if he is subordinate to God and acts only on God's sufferance."[115]

By creating this monster, the Church can be said to have brought Satanism upon itself, for it thrives on the shortcomings of Church teaching. From the earliest years of the Church there were differences of interpretation on many aspects of doctrine. The role of the Evil One, in particular, was perceived very differently by all kinds of dissident sects. As the Roman Catholic Church gained power, it was able to categorize all these dissidents as heretics. So Gnostics, Cathars, Waldenses, and countless smaller sects, branded as heretical, came to be accused of Satanist practices despite standards of conduct and morality that often shamed the established Church. They were harassed, persecuted, crusaded against, and largely destroyed.

Having created a Satan bogeyman to frighten itself, the Church was duly frightened. Around the year 1000, a chronicler named Guérard, of the abbey of Saint-Pierre at Chartres, reported on a sect comprising persons of both sexes, who met clandestinely in a big house in the suburbs of Orléans, where sabbats were held which terrified the populace for a hundred leagues around. Each attendant arrived with a burning torch. Once gathered, they uttered long litanies that had nothing Christian about them, until there appeared a being, sometimes in the form of a dog, sometimes a wolf, sometimes a serpent, with a putrid smell and a cloud of white smoke. Whereupon the torches were extinguished and each man embraced the nearest woman to perform a sexual rite. Many such unions were incestuous. If a child was subsequently born, it would be killed when it was eight days old, the body burnt, then the ashes kept and venerated.[116]

20th century "black mass" performed by Parisian decadents.

Since a churchman penned this farrago of nonsense, we are under no obligation to believe it. The accusations are similar to those leveled at almost any group the Church wished to disparage, be they Gnostics, Cathars, or Waldenses. What is significant is that Guérard considered it worth reporting. Whether or not anything meriting the label of Satanism was being practiced, the Church was convinced that it was.

The rarity of such accounts suggests that there was little, if any, Satanism at that time, and certainly no organized anti-Christian movement. At most, there existed an attitude of mind underlying a wider dissatisfaction, which might from time to time find expression in some such gesture. Satan, created by the Church to embody all that is evil, came to be favored by those who wish to emphasize the self-assertive, self-indulgent aspect of humanity rejected by the Church. In Milton's *Paradise Lost*, Satan is presented as a near-heroic figure, prompting William Blake to observe that he was of the Devil's party without knowing it.[117] It was this aspect of Satan that in the 19th century would appeal to Baudelaire and his generation; they recognized in him the qualities that Christian doctrine sought to disparage.

Satanistic practices: A great many practices, over the centuries, can be described as "Satanic," and no clear line can be drawn between magic, witchcraft, and Satanism. Witches perform magic and may invoke the name of Satan when they do so. Generally, however, magic is for witches the means to an end, and if they invoke Satan it is to get him to do their will. There need be no question of worship or even respect. Satan is their servant who obeys them because of their superior power. Lucifer, as bringer of light, is no concern of theirs.

With Satanists it is quite otherwise. Satan is their god, and their practices are performed in his honor, and to the dishonor of his adversary, God. This is why present-day witches are appalled to be confused with Satanists and do their best to distance themselves from Satanist practices.

Nevertheless, there is considerable confusion. In the Middle Ages, individual acts of defiance would take place in which Satan was honored rather than God. On May 28, 1574, at Vincennes, France, a black mass was held in hope of curing king Charles IX of a mysterious malady. A small Jewish boy, who had been converted to Christianity and baptized, was beheaded; his head was then placed on a sacramental wafer consecrated to Satan and was asked to indicate the king's illness. But when the head began to speak, the king took fright and cried out for it to be taken away. He died two days later.[118] By the sound of it, this was a pantomime devised by the court magicians. A more notorious mass was held a hundred years later, January 1678, where Louis XIV's mistress, Madame de Montespan, played the part of the altar for a mass whose intention was to confirm her place in the royal favor. A scandal followed when word of the affair was leaked. Neither of these events, however, can be categorized as Satanism. They were black magic, not Satan-worship; Satan's power was invoked as a servant, not as a deity.[119]

Satan was invoked, too, by the notorious "Hellfire clubs" of the 18th century, but by now the image of Satan had changed. "The Seventeenth Century believed with passion and terror in the reality of witchcraft and the palpable presence of the Arch-Fiend. The Eighteenth Century dabbled in diabolism and played with hell-fire."[120] Sir Francis Dashwood and his fellow Friars of Medmenham could be serious on occasion, but not about Satan. For these depraved bucks, profanity and sex were the driving motifs. Nothing is known about what went on in their meetings, for any records have been destroyed. Mostly it was drinking, profanity, and sex; the girls dressed as nuns and doubtless black masses were held but serious Satan-worship played no part in their activities.

During the 19th century, the image of Satan changed further, and it was at this stage that a distinction came to be drawn, distinguishing Satan from Lucifer. "The unorthodox Satan got rid of his goat skin, and took on a more respectable appearance. Lucifer the Lightbringer becomes an athletic young man with picturesque wings and well-developed muscles."[121] Writers such as Hugo and Baudelaire praised Satan/Lucifer as a force in his own right, embodying qualities that deserve respect. "For some Romantics, Satan was a redeemer who bought human liberty at the cost of his own ruin."[122]

Writing of the Satanist cults that operated in Paris in the fin de siècle and through to the 1930s, Geyraud stressed the importance of distinguishing between the followers of Satan and those of Lucifer. Satan was seen as purely negative force that pursues evil for its own sake out of defiance against God, whereas Lucifer – embodied in the serpent of Genesis – is as his name suggests the bringer of light and wisdom to mankind. It was this that attracted serious believers who were sometimes styled "Palladists," implying a dedication to Satan-Lucifer.[123]

Geyraud described a meeting with a priest who had become disenchanted with Christian hypocrisy. The Judeo-Christian god seemed to him no better than a tyrant, whereas the rebel angels were manifesting a legitimate dignity when they refused to submit to his authority: "Satan expiates by his perpetual damnation his noble pride and his disinterested love for mankind." The priest periodically celebrated the black mass "in the name of our Lord God Satan-Lucifer, the All-Highest" at which everything that can be, is reversed. "Oh sinful Adonais, who art in heaven, blasphemed be thy name, may thy reign come to an end, may angels and men rise against thy will, on earth as in heaven. Perish, accursed one, as thy son the Christ perished on the cross. May thy name be forgotten, now and forever."[124]

The disillusioned priest seemed to have been a loner, but Geyraud also gave an account of a Palladist initiation, in which the participants were 11 brothers and 11 sisters, masked and robed. The initiate was given a new identity and assigned a beautiful young woman as guide. A black mass was celebrated, in Latin, on the naked body of a female, who went into ecstatic seizure. The congregation, many if not all of whom had taken drugs, became very excited, and a considerable amount of uninhibited sexual activity followed.[125] Though records are understandably rare, there is little doubt that such practices, clandestine, elitist, and on a very limited scale continued intermittently throughout the 19th and early 20th century in France and elsewhere, and they certainly qualify for the Satanist label.

Modern Satanism: Current interest in Satanism is evidenced by the fact that an internet search on Google produces some 157,000 responses. Clearly, the idea of Satanism continues to have considerable appeal for today's generation.

Satanism, as practiced today, is an artificial amalgam in which traditional practices such as the black mass are combined with do-it-yourself rituals drawn from 20th century occultists such as Aleister Crowley, Gerald Gardner, and those associated with the Golden Dawn. Whether these "authorities" have any claim to be authoritative is a matter of opinion. For their followers, they are the torchbearers of a traditional arcane wisdom; for skeptics, they are either self-deluded fools or outright charlatans. David Bromley sums up the public manifestations that cumulatively provided the anti-Satanists with their raison d'être:

> What is referred to as satanism in the mass media and by the Antisatanism Movement involves a number of distinct elements: local incidents e.g. church and grave desecrations, animal mutilations, and community or regional rumors of impending abductions and ritual sacrifice of children; claims that heavy metal rock music (or fantasy games) containing occult themes or satanic messages caused homicides and suicides; confessions by convicted murderers attributing their crimes to involvement in satanism; and accounts by "ritual abuse survivors" who claimed to have participated in satanic rituals involving human sacrifice and even cannibalism. The Antisatanism Movement links these phenomena through an assertion that a nationally organized, underground, hierarchically structured cult is the ultimate source of these forms of deviance.[126]

No evidence for any such organization has been found, nor for any link between these happenings beyond the idea of Satanism per se. The barrenness of current Satanist "thinking" is demonstrated by the most prominent attempt to present Satanism as a coherent "philosophy" – the 1966 Church of Satan created by the flamboyant and charismatic entrepreneur Anton Szandor LaVey (born Howard Stanton Levey) (1930-1997). He presented himself to the world with a colorful public image, including gipsy origins, lion-taming in a circus, playing oboe in an orchestra, and an affair with Marilyn Monroe. All of this has been shown to be bogus, and the persona he projected on countless talk-show appearances was equally deceptive. His daughter, formerly a High Priestess in his Church, revealed him as a cruel and violent liar, who beat his wife Diane throughout their marriage and was equally violent towards the female disciples whom he forced into prostitution, collecting their earnings.[127]

The title of his book *The Satanic Bible*[128] demonstrates the anti-Christian basis of his creed. Apart from defying the Church, his "philosophy" is a naïve endorsement of selfishness and self-indulgence, in which consideration for others is seen as a weakness. In no sense does his Church of Satan constitute a church; its doctrines are little more than a loose collection of principles, some of them positive, others crudely negative as regards establishment religion. ("Blessed are the bold, for they shall be the masters of the world.")

For LaVey, Satan was "the spirit of progress, the inspirer of all great movements that contribute to the development of civilization and the advancement of mankind. He is the spirit of revolt that leads to freedom, the embodiment of all heresies that liberate."[129] However, in his introduction to *The Satanic Bible*, Burton H. Wolfe, one of the church's priests, admitted that "Satanism is a blatantly selfish, brutal philosophy. It is based on the belief that human beings are inherently selfish, violent creatures, that life is a Darwinian struggle for survival of the fittest, that only the strong survive and the earth will be ruled by those who fight to win the ceaseless competition that exists in all jungles – including those of urbanized society."[130]

Despite his enthusiasm for unrestrained self-indulgence, most of what LaVey's followers do is harmless, gathering to perform rituals borrowed or re-worked by him. "The rites that LaVey worked out, while still maintaining some of the trappings of ancient ceremonies, were changed from a negative mockery to positive forms of celebrations and purges: Satanic weddings consecrating the joys of the flesh, funerals devoid of sanctimonious platitudes, lust rituals to help individuals attain their sex desires, destruction rituals to enable members of the Satanic church to triumph over enemies."[131] Satanic crimes, such as those described in our case histories below, are more likely to be perpetrated by lone individuals or very small groups, acting independently of the larger groups.

While as an institution the Church of Satan is highly visible, thanks to LaVey's charisma and showmanship, the number of his followers never approached the hundreds of thousands he claimed. His daughter and first wife affirmed that "the membership never exceeded 300 individuals, several of whom were nonmember subscribers or friends receiving complimentary mailings."[132]

If this is true of LaVey's church, it is even more likely to be true of other groups. The Process, which had a considerable vogue from in the 1960s, sought to comprise Satanist elements in a wider scheme that purported to draw in the best from a diversity of religious and philosophical systems. These high-sounding claims were somewhat undermined by its bombastic utterances and flamboyant self-image (see below). As with all such groups, its original good intentions fragmented and The Process eventually disintegrated.[133]

Michael Aquino, a military officer, founded the Temple of Set, a breakaway from LaVey's Church, which promulgated an intellectual hedonism achieved through the empowerment conferred by Black Magic. Writing of Aquino and LaVey, two researchers concluded: "Both men have less influence than perhaps they themselves would like to believe. Of the two, Anton LaVey is the more important on a national scale. His *Satanic Bible* and the showmanship that has made him famous have encouraged many people, some of whom are deranged, to begin acting in the name of Satan. He has made the socially unacceptable more acceptable. He has helped make Satanism and Devil worship a topic for home conversation. No matter how serious he may be, no matter what powers he may have developed, it is the image even more than the substance that has had such a strong influence on individuals throughout the nation." Michael Aquino's place in the contemporary Satanism movement is considered to be less obvious. "From his writings, he must be considered the most important representative of Satan/Set on earth. Yet his followers are few, his name not widely known. The number of people practicing Satan worship in any form, whether organized or by a few individuals, is fairly small. Some are serious members of a group such as the Church of Satan or the Temple of Set. Some form their own groups, some are loners, and a few use their version of Devil worship to justify perverted and/or illegal acts. Some are obvious deviates, but most are ordinary individuals, perhaps your friends or neighbors."[134]

Satanist practices are always clandestine, and hard facts as to the number of practicing Satanists are simply unavailable. Guesses range widely according to who is doing the guessing and how Satanism is defined. If Parker is correct in asserting that "worldwide there are dozens of active and well-organized satanic groups,"[135] they do not seem to constitute much of a threat to society. On the other hand, noted talk-show host Geraldo Rivera has asserted that "there are over one million Satanists in this country [the USA]. The majority of them are linked in a highly organized, very secret network...The odds are that this is happening in your town."[136]

Satanism and the Satanic Ritual Abuse mania: This mania of the 1980s/1990s is treated elsewhere in this Encyclopedia (SATANIC CULT AND RITUAL ABUSE SCARE). Millions in the U.S. have accepted the assertions of people like Rivera that Satanism was rampant in their country and involved untold criminal acts. The perception of Satanists as child-abusers was widely accepted, until ultimately, it was established that no such connection exists. "In Britain and America between 1985 and 1991, well over 10,000 cases of such alleged ritual abuse were investigated. Thousands of man hours involving police and social workers were expended, thousands of children largely under the age of eight were subjected to the trauma of being questioned about devils and snakes and horrible things. But at the end of the day only four known cases where ritual abuse was specifically on the charge sheet were brought to court – and two of these failed."[137]

Given the confusion between Satanism, magic, and witchcraft, such a misperception is not too surprising. The clandestine, cloak-and-dagger activities of Satanists, like the secret goings-on of the Freemasons, are always liable to incur suspicion, misperception and accusation of anti-social behavior.

One investigator of Satanism reached this conclusion:

The question is whether such a thing as satanic ritual abuse actually exists. Let's be clear about what we mean. There certainly are satanists, who sometimes commit crimes, although they are usually loners or small groups of disaffected teenagers. And without doubt there is child abuse on an appalling scale. But as for satanic ritual abuse as it has been defined – usually via American television talk shows – as multi-generational cults, within families, who use their daughters as breeders, who sacrifice infants on ceremonial altars, who belong to a widespread, all-powerful satanic conspiracy – there's simply no evidence that anything like that exists. Indeed, the FBI has examined thousands of reports over the years and never found a single incident of that nature.[138]

COMMENT: Whatever form it takes, Satanism is necessarily contingent and derivative, since regardless of how Satan is perceived, he remains the negative force in a belief-system where "God" is the positive force. Even if Satanism is categorized as a religion in its own right, it is a kind of counter to, or parasite on, the Judeo-Christian religions, to which it presents a rather naïve defiance, rather than a religion *sui generis* founded on revelation.

Countless attempts have been made to organize Satanism as a belief system with intricate rituals and practices that tend to obscure the fact that there is no basis for any of it except in the minds of those who create it. Many Satanic practices involve the invocation of individual demons, and dictionaries of demons, each with his or her own attributes, have been compiled. Fred Gettings lists more than 3000,[139] not one of whom has any existence outside human fantasy.

Satanism as performance: The theatrical character of most Satanic practices is strikingly evident. Even when they are the only audience, Satanists get themselves up for their ceremonies as though for a theatrical production. Dress is very important. Satanists alternate between stripping off their clothes altogether, or covering themselves with masks and cowled robes. The words of their rituals, expressed in florid prose, are repetitious incantations of impressive-sounding names and phrases. Often Latin is used, though there is no reason to suppose this to be the Devil's native tongue and the only reason for its use is to impose a kind of spurious validity. The Satanists excuse such usages as being powerful symbols whose very use gives it force, but the Devil must be very naïve if he is convinced by such a charade. There is a somewhat old-fashioned feel to the idea of using a naked female as an altar and ejaculating onto her body as a religious act. "The Beings of the Process stalked Europe and America in the late 1960s and early 1970s, dressed in sinister black uniforms with flowing cloaks, accompanied by huge Alsatian hounds, bearing on their chests the sign of the Devil, the red Mendes Goat badge… An outsider observing a Sabbath Assembly would have had no doubt that this was a real Satanic cult. Through the haze of heavy incense he would have seen swastika-like symbols carved in a wooden altar…But of course first impressions are often wrong. The Process was easy to misunderstand because it was complex and highly metaphoric…It was a Satanic cult, but Satan had a very special meaning for its members that no outsider could easily grasp."[140]

The impression given is that it is the Satanists who need to convince themselves, and it is likely that the whole effect is directed inwardly at the practitioners rather than outwardly at the world outside. The psychological effect of the *mise-en-scène* – robes, daggers and other artifacts, altars, candles, incense, chanting, the nudity, and drugs – is intended to produce a state of mind in the participants whereby they are released from the inhibitions of their everyday selves and enter a higher level of self-expression. How much of this is self-delusion is another matter.

Unfortunately, what is role-playing for some is reality for others, and Christian fundamentalists, who perceive such practices as inherently evil, find it easy to believe that from black masses and such nonsense Satanists proceed to more serious crimes. And indeed, as our case histories show, this undoubtedly happens. But it seems likely that it happens on an individual basis, and that larger group activities are relatively harmless to society as a whole. "To dabble in demonology is a favourite occupation of repressed and imaginative undergraduates: and all Sir Francis' decorated urns, his indelicate satyrs and his mockeries of religion are drearily reminiscent of the nursery."[141]

The comment by Ronald Fuller, who was Sir Francis "Hell-Fire" Dashwood's biographer, applies to a great many Satanist practitioners. The followers of Lucifer, the bringer of light, are probably in a minority. LaVey's naïve "philosophy" displays no depth. Without question, some of those who proclaim themselves Satanists seriously believe that by following this path they will open themselves to a greater self-knowledge and discover a new and freer life. But for others, probably the majority, self-indulgence as an end for its own sake is the strongest motivation.

Case Histories

Many cases have come before the courts in which Satanic practices are alleged, notably in America but sporadically worldwide. Whether or not the charges and the subsequent court decisions are correct is often debatable, but in some cases at least it seems clear that some kind of ritual has been performed and that some form of Satanism is being practiced. These cases, taken from the internet, are representative:[142]

December 1995: Jimmie Lee Penick v. State of Indiana

Four practitioners of Satanism conspired to murder William Ault, a prospective member of their Satanic Church, who knew about a previous murder. They took him to what he believed was an initiation. He lay down on a door that was being used as an altar. Keith Lawrence read an invocation to Satan. Goodwin and the Lawrences made cuts on Ault's chest and abdomen in the form of an inverted cross. Goodwin tried to cut out the victim's heart before he died; the victim remained conscious throughout and responded to questions. Penick dismembered the victim's head and hands, with the intention of giving the skull to a friend. His defense was that he acted under the influence of his strong beliefs in Satanism.

August 1985: Edward Bennett v. State of Nevada

Bennett was arrested for killing a girl. At his home, writings were found, showing that the murder was "ritualistic and Satanic." They included such statements as: "I need to kill somebody or tear someone apart. I got to satisfy my need, cure this thirst for blood. So as I make the sacrifice and kill this child, for it is a first-born, I'm giving you my soul, Satan. My power is so strong I need to cause some death. For Lucifer's inside of me, and I don't want to let him out. I look in the mirror. I see him in my eyes. I feel his heart beating in my chest, and I know it is not mine. I'm so fucking strong for I am the devil's right hand man. I make this sacrifice in his name, Lucifer the Great." Bennett was sentenced to death.

December 1990. People v. Cliff St. Joseph, San Francisco, California

A body, whose identity was never established, was discovered with multiple stab wounds, genital injuries, and a pentagram carved in the chest. Forensic studies revealed evidence of whipping with a chain, slashing the victim's lips, dripping wax into his eyes, burning and carving the flesh with a knife, multiple stabbings, genital mutilations, etc. Cliff St. Joseph was revealed as the perpetrator after a later incident in which four people were arrested in connection with satanic worship. One of those arrested testified that he had been present at the earlier killing and had helped St. Joseph dispose of the body. The court found that there was sufficient evidence that the injuries had been inflicted while the victim was alive, and that the manner in which the victim was murdered, along with inferred intent, indicated that this was a ritualistic sacrifice.

It is noteworthy that none of these crimes involved a large organization; all were committed by one or a few individuals acting on their own initiative. Clearly the perpetrators were driven by Satanist ideas. Equally clearly, they were not representatives of a nation-wide, let alone worldwide, Satanist conspiracy.

SAUDI TEACHER FITS

Saudi Arabia: 2000

Several teachers at the Al-Fikriyah Institute of Education reported experiencing epileptic-like fits. Investigators could find no environmental cause for the strange seizures and labeled the episode mass hysteria. Many of the teachers believed the school was inhabited by *Jinn* creatures mentioned in the Islamic Holy Koran. Ali Faqeeh from the Al-Amal Hospital, blamed the episode on low morale and depression. Sheikh Ibrahim Al Guaid of Imam Muhammad ibn Saud Islamic University was critical of the teachers for adhering to "silly beliefs" and "superstitions." He then went on to conclude that "the devil" was responsible for frightening them by encouraging their imaginations to run wild with speculations about the *Jinn*. Several of the affected teachers were reportedly distressed after having miscarriages the pervious year.[143]

CONTEXT: Folk beliefs about the reality of Jinn creatures, combined with low teacher morale and several coincidental miscarriages, may have culminated in stress-induced psychological reactions.

SCHOOL FAINTING FLURRY

Oswego, New York: May 1987

A gas station near the Bishop-Cunningham Junior-Senior High School was the scene of intense interest after 3,000 gallons of gasoline leaked from a storage tank. Two days later, fire and rescue personnel converged on the school shortly after 9 a.m. after five students fainted. The incident happened as the pupils were gathered in the gym for an Ascension Mass. School officials released a statement attributing the episode to "high humidity and students not having eaten lunch." The students quickly recovered in the hospital. Three other students, who said they felt ill at the time, were not examined at the hospital. While authorities were confident there was no direct relationship between the two incidents, Oswego Fire Chief Donald Beauchene said the prevailing southerly winds "would have blown vapors away from the school," though "knowledge of the vapors among students may have contributed to a psychologically-induced rash of fainting." Beauchene said the emergency room physician reported that he could find "nothing physically wrong with the students."[144]

SCHOOL VAMPIRE SCARE

Detroit, Michigan: September 1970

Rumors that a vampire had attacked a nine-year-old schoolgirl sent waves of fear through the Stephens Elementary School. On Wednesday, September 23, the girl told police that while walking home for lunch, "a tall man in a black dress carrying a knife and a gun" chased her for a block. The story of the "vampire attack" spread like wildfire through the school as 500 students were absent the next day, apparently too frightened to attend classes. The total school population was 900. Police soon traced the scare to a 21-year-old man who tried to hang himself after drinking liquid bleach. Police said that a black velvet dress, knife, and bullets were nearby, leading to the conclusion that the man had inadvertently triggered the vampire scare.[145]

See: VAMPIRISM.

SCHOOL WRITING TREMORS

Europe: Late 19th century

In Europe during the late nineteenth century, an influx of epidemic hysteria reports involving a dysfunction of motor coordination (see MOTOR HYSTERIA) appeared in numerous science journals describing episodes of shaking, twitching, and abnormal movements in schools located in Germany, Switzerland, and France. Outbreaks corresponded with those institutions requiring the most rigid academic discipline. One distinct sub-type of case involved pupils engaged in meticulous, lengthy, tedious, often repetitive handwriting assignments. A representative sample of cases follows.

CONTEXT: Outbreaks of psychogenic writing tremor in European schools during this period were almost exclusively confined to school districts where administrators and instructors set extremely high performance standards. Instruction was characterized by monotonous, repetitive drills in memorization, repetitive writing and mathematics, and a notorious lack of imagination and individuality.[146]

German Writing Tremor Of 1892 And 1906

Between June and September 1892, a writing tremor affected numerous pupils at a village school in Gross-tinz near Liegnitz, Germany. The episode began on June 28, when a 10-year-old girl suddenly experienced trembling in her right arm. Soon her whole body was affected, but the trembling subsided after some 30 minutes. The outbreak lasted until mid-October 1892, but the initial hand tremors soon affected the entire body. The following day several other girls experienced trembling lasting for up to an hour. With each passing day the trembling lasted longer and longer so that the girls could not write. In early July one of the trembling students began to exhibit sudden, involuntary muscle contractions and irregular movements. These convulsive movements soon affected 20 students by July 20. Soon 8 of the 20 were experiencing altered states of consciousness and amnesia. After school vacation through August 19, classes resumed, the trembling and convulsions stopped, but several girls reported severe headaches. The outbreak ended on October 20th.[147]

During February 1906, in Chemnitz, Germany, school physician Johannes Schoedel of the People's School observed arm and hand tremors in female elementary students ages 9 and 10 during their writing exercise hour. The symptoms began in two pupils on February 7, but gradually spread to 21 of 35 females over four weeks. The students performed all other manual tasks normally, including gymnastics exercises, and were affected only during written schoolwork. Schoedel's treatment was to administer electric shocks to those affected, not as punishment but to render them suggestible. While the shocks were given, he suggested that their tremors stop. Also, he instructed that during their writing period, demanding drills in mental arithmetic be administered and the students told that since they cannot write they must regrettably have mental arithmetic again.[148]

"Trembling" Schoolgirls In Basel, Switzerland, 1892 And 1904

In 1892, "infectious" trembling and convulsions were recorded at a girls' school in Basel, Switzerland. Twenty pupils were unable to complete in-school writing assignments. Symptoms subsided after school hours, only to relapse upon re-entering school grounds. The tremor began in a single classroom and soon spread to other rooms.[149] "The disorder frequently appeared among children who had before been healthy when one of the sufferers had an attack in the immediate neighborhood; and when one child had an attack others did so."[150]

Nearly a decade after the previous report, in 1904, the same girls' school in Basel, Switzerland, was swept by fits of trembling and convulsions affecting 14 classes of pupils ages 11 to 15. The primary symptom, a vibrating tremor in the right hand and forearm, were first observed in a pair of students on June 11. The outbreak coincided with rumors that the tremor would result in the school being closed for six weeks. While this did not happen, over the next several weeks the symptoms gradually spread until 27 pupils were affected, amid rumors that the school would be closed for six weeks if the number of pupils with tremors rose to 300. The administrators refused to close the school and instead announced that not only would academic sessions continue, but the affected pupils were ordered to meet in a special classroom with the same teacher who instructed them for the next month. Instead of feeling they were being punished, an opposite approach was taken. Their workload was reduced, they were well fed, and the teacher and administrators were careful not to project any sense of blame for the student's inability to complete written work resulting from their tremors. In spite of some initial disruptions in their math and handwriting performances, the symptoms slowly diminished. There were six cases of relapse, but the outbreak soon ended.[151]

A case description of one of the afflicted girls, a 13-year-old identified as E.S., tells how her mother scolded her after coming home on June 17 with violent trembling of her right hand. In reaction, over the next hour, she experienced facial twitching as well. The following day the girl was brought into the special class for those exhibiting tremors. "She trembled so violently that writing was impossible for her. She was unable to answer the easiest questions and could not work with one-place numbers in arithmetic. On Monday, the 20th of June, during a conversation at the ten o'clock recess her arm was unobtrusively massaged by the teacher, whereupon the movements became weaker. On Tuesday, the 21st of June, toward evening the tremor ceased."[152] She was dismissed from the special class on the 24th, free from any symptoms.[153]

COMMENT: Episodes of hand tremor coinciding with intense writing assignments appear to be classic examples of CONVERSION DISORDER, whereby pupils are socialized into staying in school and achieving a high standard, yet are in conflict with the excessive, repetitious, monotonous workload. In such cases, the long-term anxiety slowly builds and is unconsciously converted into hand tremors, allowing the students to receive attention for their plight, and often a temporary respite from their assignments. The mechanism has parallels in military cases whereby a soldier with a deep moral philosophy against killing, when placed in a combat situation, is unable to move their hand to fire a weapon.

See also: MASS HYSTERIA IN SCHOOLS.

SCOTTISH AND WELSH RELIGIOUS EXCITEMENT

1740-1790s

The 18th century in the British Isles saw numerous outbreaks of exceptional behavior. Many of these, such as the JUMPERS, were clearly religious in character, manifestations of the religious movements of the day, notably METHODISM, which stressed personal salvation through faith rather than institutionalized salvation through work. In others the religious aspect is not so evident, raising the possibility that their roots were in the social and even the economic condition of those affected, the religious aspect being only secondary.[154]

CONTEXT: It is noticeable that these outbreaks tended to occur in relatively isolated communities: the Shetland Islands and Anglesey, like Cornwall and Wales (see JUMPERS) and MORZINE in France, were remote from mainstream culture and dependent on their own cultural resources. This is hardly an explanation, but it does point towards the conditions that enabled and perhaps encouraged the outbreaks to occur.

The Shetlands Outbreak

A "convulsive disease" broke out in the Shetland Islands in about 1740. At first the "distemper" was confined to a single female but spread when she was seized at church. From then on, it seems to have spread rapidly, especially among young women. The malady was said to resemble epilepsy. The locals named this condition "convulsion fits" and episodes typically began "with a palpitation of the heart, of which the victims complained for a considerable time; this was followed by swooning fits, in which those who were seized would lie motionless for upwards of an hour. At length, as the distemper gathered strength, seized with a violent passion or on a sudden surprise, they would all at once fall down, toss their arms about, twisting their bodies into many odd shapes, crying out all the while most dismally, throwing their heads about from side to side, with their eyes fixed and staring. Public assemblies, especially at church, were much disturbed by these demonstrations." These happenings were reportedly more violent during the summer.

A feature of the malady was that, as soon as a fit ceased, those stricken would mingle with their companions and continue as if nothing had happened. Most of those affected were female. By the 1770s the malady seemed to be declining, and in some parishes where it once thrived, not a single case was recorded. At Northmaven, those affected were said to have been cured by tossing the afflicted person into a ditch of water.

> Convulsion fits of a very extraordinary kind seem peculiar to this country. The patient is first seized with something like fainting, and immediately after utters wild cries and shrieks, the sound of which, at whatever distance, immediately puts all who are subject to the disorder in the same state. It most commonly attacks them when the church is crowded, and often interrupts the service in this and many other churches in the country. On a sacramental occasion, fifty or sixty are sometimes carried out of the church, and laid in the church-yard, where they struggle and roar with all their strength, for five or ten minutes, and then rise up without recollecting a single circumstance that happened to them, or being in the least hurt or fatigued with the violent exertions they had made during the fit. There is one observation which may be significant, that during those years when harvests were poor and food scarce, outbreaks were very uncommon: whereas during the years of plenty such as 1791 it has appeared more frequently.

The Lanarkshire Outbreak

It is hard to say to what extent the outbreak in the Shetlands was religious in character. The fact that the first and most subsequent manifestations occurred in church is not necessarily conclusive because, church services being one of the few opportunities where the community could foregather, they were as much social meetings as occasions for worship. However, the outbreak in Lanarkshire, similar in its character, was certainly fueled by religious enthusiasm.

In January 1742, about 90 people in Cambuslang parish, in Lanarkshire, petitioned their minister for weekly religious lectures. The first two presentations were unremarkable, but during the third sermon, during his last prayer when he said, "Lord, who hath believed our report, and to whom is the arm of the Lord revealed? Where are the fruits of my poor labours among this people?" several congregants cried out, and later about fifty men and women visited the minister's home, seeking help, convinced of their sin and apprehensive of punishment.

After this period, so many people from the neighborhood visited Cambuslang that the minister felt obliged to offer daily sermons or "exhortations" and kept it up for seven or eight months. One observer described the scene as follows:

> They were seized, all at once, commonly by something said in the sermons or prayers, with the most dreadful apprehensions, concerning the state of their souls, insomuch that many of them could not abstain from crying out, in the most public and frightful manner, bewailing their lost and undone condition by nature; calling themselves enemies to God, and despisers of precious Christ; declaring that they were unworthy to live on the face of the earth; that they saw the mouth of hell open to receive them, and that they heard the shrieks of the damned. But the universal cry was, "What shall we do to be saved?"

> The agony under which they laboured, was expressed, not only by words, but also by violent agitations of body; by clapping their hands and beating their breasts; by shaking and trembling; by faintings and convulsions; and sometimes by excessive bleeding at the nose. While they were in this distress, the minister often called out to them, not to stifle or smother their convictions, but to encourage them: and, after sermon was ended, he retired with them to the manse [the minister's house], and frequently spent the best part of the night with them in exhortations and prayers. Next day, before sermon began, they were brought out, and, having napkins tied round their heads, were placed altogether on seats before the tents, where they remained sobbing, weeping, and often crying aloud, till the service was over. Some of those who fell under conviction were never converted; but most were converted in a few days, and sometimes in a few hours.

> In most cases their conversion was as sudden and unexpected as their earlier conviction. They were raised all at once from the lowest depth of sorrow and distress, to the highest pitch of joy and happiness; crying out with triumph and exultation, that they had overcome the wicked one; that they had gotten hold of Christ and would never let him go; that the black cloud which had hitherto concealed him from their view, was now dispelled; and that they saw him, with a pen in his hand, blotting out their sins. Under these delightful impressions, some began to pray, and exhort publicly, and others desired the congregation to join with them in singing a particular psalm, which they said God had commanded them to sing. From the time of their conviction to their conversion, many had no appetite for food, or inclination to sleep, and all complained of their sufferings during that interval.

The Forfarshire Outbreak

Another outbreak known as "the leaping ague" was localized to Forfarshire. It was first observed in Kenmuir parish about 1770, and prevailed periodically and in the nearby parishes for about seventy years. Those affected first complained of a head pain, or lower back discomfort, followed by convulsive fits, or dancing fits, at certain periods. During paroxysms they distorted their bodies, leaping and springing, giving the malady its popular name. Sometimes they would run with astonishing speed, and often over dangerous passes, to some place outdoors, which they had fixed on in their own minds, and then dropped exhausted. At other times, often when confined to a house, they would climb. Indoors, in their cottages, they would leap from the floor to the beams, "springing from one to another with the agility of a cat."

Cold baths were found to be the best remedy, "but when the fit of dancing, leaping, or running came on, nothing tended so much to abate the violence of the disease, as allowing them free scope to exercise themselves, till nature be exhausted." No mention is made of its being peculiar to any age, sex, or condition of life, although it was most common before puberty. In some families it seems to be hereditary; "I have heard of one, in which a horse was always kept ready saddled, to follow the young ladies belonging to it, when they were seized with a fit of running." By 1840, though it was sporadically reported, it was not nearly so frequent as in prior years.

Anglesey Outbreak

In 1796, on the estates of the Earl of Uxbridge and a man named Holland Griffith, 23 females, ages 10 to 25, and a young man aged about 17 years, all of whom were socially acquainted, were seized with convulsions, affecting their upper extremities. Dr. Haygarth describes the symptoms that he observed:

> It began with pain of the head, and sometimes of the stomach and side, not very violent; after which there came on violent twitchings or convulsions of the upper extremities, continuing, with little intermission, and causing the shoulders almost to meet by the exertion. In bed the disorder was not so violent: but, in some cases at least, it continued even during sleep. Their pulse was moderate, the body costive, and the general health not much impaired. In general they had a hiccough; and, when the convulsions were most violent, giddiness came on, with the loss of hearing and recollection. During their convalescence, and they all recovered, the least fright or sudden alarm brought on a slight paroxysm.

Dr. Haygarth successfully treated those affected with "antispasmodics." He also stipulated that all of the girls and young women should be prevented from communicating in any way with those affected, and that the convulsing females should be isolated as much as possible.

COMMENT: Although in the Lanarkshire outbreak the religious context is manifest, this is not so clearly evident in the others. In the Forfarshire and Anglesey outbreaks no indication is provided of any circumstances that may have brought the behavior about. Dr. Haygarth seems to have concerned himself only with the physical aspects of the affliction, as indeed almost any medical man would have done at this period. The persistence of the affliction in the Shetlands, and particularly in Forfarshire, excludes any immediate cause, and raises the possibility of a cultural tradition of such behavior in a limited community, of the kind which seems to have affected the people of BRECHIN, and also the KLIKOUSCHESTVO seizures in Russia. Though each of the outbreaks described above presents individual features, they possess a general resemblance which suggests that what was involved was a generic form of hysterical behavior which adapted to local conditions. If so, the religious context, where it existed, may have been no more than a pretext for the expression of a personal condition.
See also: JUMPERS; RUNNING, JUMPING AND CLIMBING.

SCOTTISH END-OF-THE-WORLD SCARE
September 25, 1950

In eastern Scotland, when the Sun appeared as a "perfect pale blue sphere in the western sky," thousands of excited inhabitants became fearful that the world was ending or that there had been a nuclear attack. Phone lines were jammed for much of the day as residents called newspapers, weather bureaus, and observatories. Some meteorologists attributed the strange sight to smoke from forest fires in Alberta, Canada, which swept across the Atlantic Ocean.[155]

SCOWERERS AND MOHOCKS
London: 1711-12

Who has not heard the Scowerer's midnight fame?
Who has not trembled at the Mohock's name?

So John Gay, author of *The Beggar's Opera*, wrote in 1712. Indeed, in that year all London had been thrown into panic by the Scowerers (= Scourers) and their successors, the Mohocks (= Mohawks).

Street crime was nothing new in the streets of London. In 1598, Captain Bobadill, in Ben Jonson's *Every Man in his Humour*, speaks of "brave fellows indeed; in those days a man could not go from the Rose Tavern to the Piazza [in Covent Garden] once, but he must venture his life twice." During the following century, those who walked the streets had to beware of the Hectors, the Muns, and other gangs, one rising to notoriety as another ceased its activities.

In 1712, however, the assaults of the Mohocks threatened to raise the customary level of street violence to new heights. Their favored activity was said to be "Tipping the Lion," a euphemism for crushing the noses of their victims and gouging out their eyes with the thumbs. They slit the ears and distend the mouths with peculiar instruments of iron.[156]

On the 6th of June 1712, Sir Mark Cole and three other gentlemen were tried at the Old Bailey for riot, assault and beating the watch. A paper of the day asserts that these were "Mohocks," that they had attacked the watch in Devereux Street, slit two persons' noses, cut a woman in the arm with a penknife so as to disable her for life, rolled a woman in a tub down Snow Hill, misused other women in a barbarous manner by setting them on their heads, and overset several coaches and (sedan) chairs with short clubs, loaded with lead at both ends, expressly made for the purpose. In their defence the prisoners denied that they were Mohocks, alleging that they were "Scourer," and had gone out, with a magistrate's sanction, to scour the streets, arrest Mohocks and other offenders, and deliver them up to justice. On the night in question they had attacked a notorious gambling-house, and taken thirteen men out of it. While engaged in this meritorious manner, they learned that the Mohocks were in Devereux Street, and, on proceeding, found three men, desperately wounded, lying on the ground; they were then attacked by the watch, and felt bound to defend themselves. As an instance of the gross misconduct of the watch, it was further alleged that they, the watch, had on the same night actually presumed to arrest a peer of the realm, Lord Hitchinbroke, and had latterly adopted the practice of going their rounds by night accompanied by savage dogs. The jury, however, in spite of this defence, returned a verdict of guilty; and the judge fined the culprits in the sum of three shillings and fourpence each.[157]

Clearly the jury was not deceived by the attempt to lay the blame on others. John Bouch, the watchman, told how he had been threatened by a gang of twenty Mohocks who proposed to nail him in his watch-box and trundle him down the pavement. He had arrested three of the ringleaders and driven off the remainder with his sword. Gay, quoted above, refers to this incident and wrote a play, entitled *The Mohocks*, which was printed that year though apparently never performed.

Steele's *Spectator* refers to "the late panic fear" inspired by a roaming bands of men, known as Mohocks, who attacked people in the street. The motive does not seem to have been robbery. Lady Wentworth declared that "they are said to be young gentlemen: they never take any money from any."[158] Instead, what amused them was inflicting physical harm – disfiguring the men, sexually assaulting the women. Understandably, this so alarmed the populace that in 1712 a royal proclamation offered £100 – equivalent to £11,000 today – for their apprehension.

The watchman incident seems to have been the climax of the Mohocks' reign of terror, for in March Jonathan Swift felt able to write in a letter to his friend Stella that "our Mohocks are all vanished." But if the Mohocks quit the scene, the stage was soon filled by other gangs. Some were out-and-out criminals, such as "Lady Holland's Mob," which terrorized Bartholomew Fair. Others were clubs of aristocratic rakes such as the Hell-Fire Club, more interested in amusement (at the expense of others) than in mere crime.[159]

However, of all the London street gangs, it was the Mohocks who lived most vividly in the memory of Londoners. Nearly three centuries later they were

Getting the best of a Charley (night watchman), by emptying his sentry box.

still sufficiently remembered to inspire an episode of the classic television series *The Avengers* in which Steed and Mrs. Peel are confronted by a reincarnation of the 18th century fiends, imitating the originals and even speaking what they supposed to be an 18th century style of speech. As for the "Scourers," the term was still in use at the close of the 20th century. Novelist Michael Dibdin refers to "the 'scourers,' men who infiltrate themselves into the crowds attending papal appearances with the aim of touching up as many distracted females as possible."[160]

SELF-FLAGELLATION MANIAS

Medieval Europe: 12th to 15th centuries

Between the 12th and 15th centuries, self-flagellation – the practice of flogging oneself with sharp objects – swept across Europe.

CONTEXT: Self-flogging was a new form of penance, adopted from 11th century monastic hermits of Camaldoli and Fonte Avellana, and spread rapidly throughout Europe during this period, as groups of people tried proving their worthiness to God and imposing self-punishment for their sins.

Self-flagellation gained widespread acceptance during 12th century Europe, not only becoming a "normal feature" of monastic Latin Christendom, "but one of the commonest of all penitential techniques."[161] Historian Norman Cohn cited a first-hand description of a 14th century flagellant: "[He] shut himself up in his cell and stripped himself naked...and took his scourge with the sharp spikes, and beat himself on the body and on the arms and on the legs, till blood poured... One of the spikes...was bent crooked, like a hook, and whatever flesh it caught it tore off. He beat himself so hard that the scourge broke into three bits and the points flew against the wall. He stood there bleeding and gazed at himself. It was such a wretched sight that he was reminded in many ways of the appearance of the beloved Christ, when he was fearfully beaten. Out of pity for himself he began to weep bitterly. And he knelt down, naked and covered in blood, in the frosty air, and prayed to God to wipe out his sins from before his gentle eyes."[162]

In 1266, there was an extraordinary outbreak

starting in Italy and spreading across Europe. One historian described the flare up as follows: "A salient spirit of self-blame suddenly seized the minds of the people. The fear of Christ came over all the people, noble and common, old and young. Even five-year-olds were wandering in the streets without clothes, with only a waistband. Everybody had a whip of leather straps with which they so cruelly lashed their own limbs, with tears and sighs, such that blood was running from their wounds."[163]

While the self-flagellation movement began to subside in the 1500s and 1600s and never regained its prevalence, scores of prominent flagellant sufferings have been recorded after its heyday. For instance, Vincentio Puccini provided a description of Florence-born Italian flagellant Maria Maddalena de' Pazzi in a 1619 biography of the woman who would gain sainthood for her piety. On September 8, 1587, she entered a room, bolted the door, piled up jagged sticks and thorns onto which she fell. She would also gird her body with very coarse canvass containing sharp nails. This description is tame in comparison to other accounts.[164] Religious scholar Ariel Glucklich noted that on other occasions before retiring to sleep Maria would tightly wind and tie thorny stalks around her head to imitate the sufferings of Christ. "Maria on various occasions had herself tied to a post, hands bound behind her back. At other times she lay on the ground for members of the congregation to step on her body. She slept on rough straw, walked barefoot in the winter, dripped hot candle-wax on her own body, and dressed in a coarse and irritating garment. These and other forms of torment, when not conceptualized as an imitation of Christ, were described as ways of testing and fighting bodily temptation (like Daniel in the lion's den), fighting the urge to eat too much, or battling the pleasures of comfort and sexual desire."[165]

Two men, bare to the waist, flagellate themselves with whips.

Cohn offers an underlying collective psychopathological interpretation of medieval flagellants, viewing them as mass "paranoid phantasies."[166] Similar forms of "self-torturing" in expectation of spiritual reward have occurred in northern New Mexico among the *Los Hermanos Penitentes de Sangre de Christo*,[167] and have also been classified by psychiatrists as "collective mental disorders."[168] The ranks of members experienced a resurgence in the late 1980s.[169] Self-flagellation continues to be a feature of certain Islamic groups.[170] More recent interpretations of self-flagellation hold a more culturally relativistic position, typifying it as just one of many forms of religious expressions of devoutness.[171]

COMMENT: Flagellation is also known to occur as a "perverse" sexual proclivity. We note this in order to distinguish between those who engage in such acts to please themselves and those who do it to please "God."

SEXUAL MORES

Most human societies have constructed codes of what is acceptable and what is unacceptable conduct in matters of sex. These codes are generally given a religious coloring and are supposed to be divinely ordained. Any deviation is regarded as at least sinful and frequently criminal as well; a person who strips off his or her clothes in Piccadilly Circus, for example, offends both God and Man.

How this state of affairs has come about is a complex issue of social mores, ethical concerns, practical eugenics, and property law, which have been debated throughout human history. Because prevailing standards are culture-specific, evaluation of what constitutes extraordinary behavior are inevitably contingent on their context. To give a simple example, the image library that supplied most of the illustrations in this Encyclopedia was asked by a leading American publisher to provide depictions of Livingstone's explorations in Africa; the pictures were rejected on the grounds that the female natives in the pictures had bare breasts.

When Christians assert that their God is offended by the sight of a woman attending church service with bare arms or uncovered head, let alone baring her breasts, it is evident either that the Church authorities have received a divine instruction to that effect, or that human interpretation of God's preferences has taken place. We, the authors of this Encyclopedia, do not presume to take sides in such a matter. Consequently, our examples of extraordinary behavior in sexual affairs are limited to those cases where the behavior is either shown to be based on fallacious premises, or is at odds with consensus standards prevailing at that time and place. Any evaluation can only be relative.

All human societies regulate sexual conduct to a greater or lesser extent. For complex and controversial reasons, most societies have developed attitudes to sexual activity that run counter to basic instinct, with the result that it is restricted, repressed, and even demonized. Consequently, most extraordinary behavior in matters of sex comes about as a result of conflict between individual instinct and society's requirements. The history of the MASTURBATION DELUSION perfectly exemplifies this conflict.

The conflict is an operative factor in a great many of our entries. The outbreaks of CONVENT HYSTERIA in 17th century Europe, for example, occurred when the nuns – who were often young women incarcerated against their will: Gertrud, the primary victim of the 1564 Köln outbreak, was only 14 – responded to circumstances by manifesting repressed sexual urges. Claiming that the Devil was speaking through them, they uttered blasphemies and obscenities. They mimed or indulged in sexual activity, either solitarily or with their companions; they accused priests of seduction and rape, and confessed to sexual encounters with demons. Often, as with Marie de Sains at Lille in 1608, their claimed misdeeds were physically impossible.

Only a few entries in this Encyclopedia are explicitly concerned with overt sexual behavior. A clear example are the outbreaks of PENIS LOSS SCARES that occur in several cultures, suggesting a universal fear. While penis loss does not seem to carry any religious connotation, the impulse to castration, displayed notably by the Russian SKOPTSI sect, exemplifies a confusion of thought that mingles sexual guilt with religious ascetism. A more widespread behavior, the compulsion to take off one's clothes, is seen in a wide range of behaviors, from the victims of PIBLOKTOQ to the ADAMITES, from nuns at Toulouse to schoolgirls in Uganda. The DOUKHOBOR sect notoriously employed it as a weapon in their struggle with the Canadian authorities.

Often, the leaders of sects and cults are activated by sexual urges. Such a leader may proscribe unrestricted sexual activity in the name of "free love," which is presented as a divinely sanctioned and natural activity. The ADAMITES, for example, were accused of indiscriminate orgies, though perhaps falsely. Among the ANABAPTISTS of 16th century Munster, as among the Latter-Day Saints of 19th century Utah, polygamy was encouraged. Alternatively, the leader may abrogate sexual privileges to himself as a mark of his divine status. Thus Ossip, the charismatic leader of the SOUPONIEVO sect, successfully persuaded his female followers that to have sex with him was a religious duty.

In many cases, the sexual dimension, though unquestionably present, is only secondary. This is true of SATANISM, for example. Religion is attacked through blasphemy, and for Christians there can hardly be any greater blasphemy than to parody the sacrament of the Mass using the body of a naked female as an altar, onto which the officiating priests ritually ejaculate. Here, as in so many extraordinary behaviors, sex is just one thread among a tapestry of urges that only a psychiatrist could unravel.

SHARED PSYCHOTIC DISORDER

Commonly referred to as *folie a deux* (from the French *folie* or insanity, and *deux*, two), shared psychotic disorder is also known by a variety of other terms: communicated insanity, double insanity, infectious insanity, imposed psychosis, psychosis by association, induced psychotic disorder, shared paranoid disorder, and *folie induite*. Some terms are used to denote the specific number of subjects involved. For example, *folie a trois* refers to the presentation of identical delusions in three family member. *Folie a quatre* would be the same delusion in four family members, and so forth.[172]

Shared psychotic disorder is rarely reported in the scientific literature and is almost exclusively found in the form of case studies. A characteristic feature of the disorder is the transfer of psychotic delusions from one person to others. It commonly involves just two people. Those involved typically have a long, close association, usually having lived together in "relative social isolation." *Folie imposee* is the most commonly reported type, whereby the primary subject who has the initial delusion "is often chronically ill and typically is the influential member of a close relationship with a more suggestible person (the secondary case) who also develops the delusion. The secondary case is frequently less intelligent, more gullible, more passive, or more lacking in self-esteem than the primary case."[173]

Most cases involve members from the same family, with the most frequent relationships being that of husband-wife, mother-child, and two sisters. There is an ongoing debate among psychiatrists as to whether the secondary subject is experiencing psychotic delusions or is simply impressionable.[174]

COMMENT: Shared psychotic disorder by definition involves psychosis. However, it is important to make the distinction with *folie a deux*, which involves a shared delusion that may, or may not, involve psychotic delusions.

See also: SMALL GROUP SCARES.

SHEEP PANIC, THE GREAT

United Kingdom: 1888

At approximately 8 p.m. on Saturday evening November 3, the "great sheep panic" occurred in the vicinity of Reading, Berkshire, England, as farmers awoke to find their sheep scattered across an area measuring 25 by 8 miles (40 x 20 km). According to a report in the *Times* of London, "thousands of sheep folded in the large sheep-breeding districts north, east and west of Reading were taken with a sudden fright, jumping their hurdles, escaping from the fields, and running hither and thither..."[175] Early the next morning, shepherds found their sheep "under hedges and in the roads, panting and frightened as if they had been terror-stricken."[176] Observers from Reading report that "We have not heard, nor can any of the farmers give, any reasonable explanation of what we have described." While no cause was ever found,[177] some have suggested that a mild earthquake may have been the stimulus in this instance.[178]

COMMENT: The earthquake explanation seems plausible given the association between unusual animal behavior and seismic events, although there is insufficient information with which to base any firm conclusions.

SHOWALTER, ELAINE

A Princeton University feminist, historian, and English literature scholar known for her studies of hysteria, Elaine Showalter is perhaps best known for her contentious book, *Hystories: Hysterical Epidemics and Modern Media*.[179] Born in Cambridge, Massachusetts, on January 21, 1941, Showalter contends that a variety of so-called modern "illnesses" or disorders are really forms of hysteria that are psychological in origin and unwittingly propagated and legitimized by the mass media. These include Chronic Fatigue Syndrome, Gulf War Syndrome, Satanic Ritual Abuse, recovered memories, Multiple Personality Disorder, and UFO abductions.

Much of the controversy surrounding *Hystories* involves the recasting of Chronic Fatigue and Gulf War Syndromes. Showalter says that it is accurate to call these experiences syndromes, as the people supposedly affected experience "a cluster of symptoms and signs rather than a disease which is something for which we have a medically established cause. In the case of Chronic Fatigue advocacy groups are very eager to get the name of the disease, the disorder, the syndrome legally, officially changed in this country. They call fatigue the F word, and they're very concerned that...if they can get another name for this syndrome that everybody will take it more seriously.."[180] While Showalter notes that many people are convinced that Chronic Fatigue and Gulf War Syndromes are real because of the large numbers of claimants reporting similar symptoms, she points to powerful social factors at work. These include the influence of self-help networks, internet bulletin boards, and dissemination of what symptoms to look for in these "disorders" by the mass media that only encourages more patients. Soon after publication of the book, Showalter reported receiving a number of threatening or obscene letters from people claiming to be suffering from these conditions, especially chronic fatigue.[181]

Hystories continues to be polarizing among academics. Prominent British psychiatrist Simon Wessely takes a moderate approach, agreeing with Showalter's thesis of culture shaping illness, but disagrees with her broad interpretation of hysteria, which he says is not shared by most psychiatrists in academia. "The book is very much a literary historian's account. She's obviously not done clinic, seeing people with these various syndromes. I can't see any link at all, for example, between multiple personality disorder and Gulf War syndrome, other than that there is media interest in them, and they are spread to a certain extent by the media."[182]

SICK PRIMARY SCHOOLS

Jamaica: 2004; Australia: 2003

Manchester, Jamaica: Sept.- Oct. 2004

The Jamaican Education Minister ordered the Pratville Primary and Infant School closed following a mysterious illness to 60 sixth grade students, while the principal was vowing not to return to the building until the mystery was solved. On Monday, September 20, several students reported feeling unwell, but as they weren't severely ill, school officials downplayed the claims. Two days later at about 11 a.m., the situation got worse as students reported nausea, stomachache, listlessness, and dry throat. Some vomited.

The school's 20-year principal, Valda Buckle said it was her responsibility to keep the school closed until the threat had passed, noting: "We know that there is an environmental problem. We can't just go back in there into the same situation."[183] The malady also affected the principal and two teachers. The Ministry of Education, Youth and Culture closed the school in late September. The Manchester Health Department conducted a thorough examination of school premises, giving it a clean bill of health. The department's chief public health inspector, George Sloley, was emphatic that the school was safe to return to: "We inspected the facility. We did some blood tests, urine tests and tests for traces of any chemical and the tests have shown nothing unusual." In response to the principal's claims that the threat remained, Sloley said that as nothing was found, "Whatever it was, it must have gone."[184]

Forrestdale, Perth, Western Australia circa 2003

After being the subject of an intensive investigation by health officials, the Forrestdale Primary School was declared to be safe by a special panel of independent health experts who were convened by the Western Australian government. The school had been the scene of a spate of mysterious health issues among students. The panel's conclusions were revealed amid public fears and outcry that the school grounds contained a variety of toxic substances. High lead levels were found at the school in June 2002, raising fears that the school grounds had been tainted by toxic agents from the nearby Brookdale industrial waste facility. The panel determined that the high lead readings were the result of a flawed collection method.

Professor D'Arcy Holman, chair of the University of Western Australia's population health department and a panel member, said that he was confident that the school was safe. As for the mysterious ailments that had been reported by students such as nose bleeds, high rates of Attention Deficit Disorder and fainting spells, he said it was unrelated to the nearby plant. "Whatever other health issues may occur in this community or any other community, as far as this expert panel is concerned we could not attribute anything of that nature to heavy metal contamination or atmospheric soil contamination at the school site."[185]

SICK SCHOOL STAFF SYNDROME

Illinois: 1986-87; New York: 1989-90

Reports of mass psychogenic illness in school settings are usually dominated by health complaints that are initiated by students and remain mostly a student event. However, there are cases where the symptoms begin with school staff and spread predominantly among staffers.

Carpersville, Illinois

Many parents, teachers and administrators at the Sunny Hill School in Carpentersville were under the belief that about 180 reports of illness at the school over the previous four months were the result of something in the building, despite tests indicating no harmful agents.[186]

The health scare began on December 10, 1986, when teacher Janet Katzel began feeling unwell due to what she suspected was either poor air quality or mold contamination. Her illness and concerns were conveyed to school district officials, and concern quickly mounted over the safety of the school. Meanwhile the assistant superintendent made a check of the building but found no obvious cause. On December 18, 1986, a petition was turned into school officials by staff members, seeking something be done about the mystery ailments at the school. All 36 full-time staffers signed a petition that was handed to administrators, complaining over "questionable health and safety conditions" that they said had been plaguing the building for years. Among the supposed ongoing symptoms by those working in the building were itchy and/or puffy eyes, headaches, and breathing problems. Soon students were recording similar complaints, including nausea, vomiting, dizziness and feeling sleepy, irritability, lack of interest in playing with classmates, and depression.

On December 31, the building's heating and ventilation systems were tested and given a clean bill of health. After retesting in mid-February, it again appeared to be fine. On February 27, a series of ongoing tests of the school's air quality were begun, but no abnormal readings were found. On March 3, after eight parents met with the principal about the mystery ailment, the ventilation was again tested with unremarkable results.

A local physician's suggestion that a toxic contaminant might be the culprit only served to solidify the sick school belief in the community. Dr. Mark J. Round said that after examining five staff members, and seeing the similarity in symptoms, he was of the opinion that a mixture of chemicals – either inside the building or nearby – were interacting to cause the illnesses. He suggested the possibility of either cleaning fluids or pesticides.

The vice president of a private company hired to conduct a series of tests on the school, Gary N. Crawford, said he believed that most of the symptoms were the result of anxiety from the public interest in the "mystery illnesses." He said: "This fear has grown so intense in recent weeks that many teachers, students and parents are exhibiting definite signs of stress, anxiety and tension."[187] He noted that anxiety and stress were notorious for triggering an array of physical complaints – the same complaints being reported at the school.

By late March, school superintendent Clyde W. Slecum was sounding a note of caution about the entire affair in response to concerns over the "sick school." He said: "We have not concluded that there is a problem."[188]

Oswego County, New York

Starting in October 1989, several employees of Mexico High School near the New York State-Canadian border reported an array of ailments while in the school, leading to the conclusion that the building was responsible. However, tests on the building were negative. School officials even tested the carpet, removed a photocopier, and installed an air cleanser, but the illness continued. Principal John Proud said that while he was one of those who got ill when coming to work, he had not missed a single day at school because of it. Proud said that within 10 minutes of arriving at school and shutting his office door, his sinuses became congested. Secretary Anne Edwards reported suffering from fatigue, laryngitis, and throbbing headaches within two hours of being at the school. A series of doctors' visits and blood tests turned up nothing. Clerk Janice Runkles also complained of occasional sinus problems while at the school.[189]

SINGAPORE FACTORY HYSTERIA

Southeast Asia: 1970s

During the 1970s, a series of mass hysteria episodes swept across factories in the tiny Island city-state of Singapore in Southeast Asia. W.H. Phoon of the Singapore Labour Ministry documented six episodes.[190] We will describe the first two "outbreaks."

CONTEXT: Episodes almost exclusively strike female Malays, reflecting their belief in an array of supernatural spirits and the common Malaysian folk belief that Malay women have weaker mental strength, rendering them vulnerable to spirit "attacks."

The first incident occurred at a television assembly plant during January 1973. On the evening of Saturday, January 13, a female employee began screaming and fainted. As her supervisor and several colleagues carried her to the medical clinic on a different floor, she screamed out and struggled against them. Before long, other female workers exhibited similar symptoms, and plant officials closed the factory later that night, reopening the following Tuesday. Of the plant's 899 workers, just 97 were male, and most of the workers were Malays. Curiously, of the 84 workers stricken with "spells," all were female Malays. During the two days the plant was shut down, management hired a *bomoh,* or Malay "medicine man," to exorcize the evil spirits. The day the factory reopened, more women had spells.[191]

The episode soon spread to two nearby factories. On January 17, a nearby electrolytic capacitor factory reported that 16 female employees were having similar spells. Several days later, another nearby factory reported a single case. Most of those affected in these two additional factories were female Malays. Phoon and his colleagues identified three distinct types of cases. First were "hysterical seizures" which were typified by screaming, fierce struggling, and violence. Many of those affected showed extraordinary strength and often required several men to restrain them. Injections of tranquilizers, such as valium, were ineffective. Those affected would ignore attempts to reassure them, or not respond to any questions posed to them, or would scream even more after inquiries were made. Between screams and shouts, some would break out in laughter, interspersed by more screaming. Some said they could see "a dark figure" who was about the strangle them.[192] A second category of affected worker were those who seemed to exhibit trance states. "While being violent, or before becoming violent, a worker would suddenly speak as though she was someone else, and claim that a "jinn" or spirit was speaking through her. Such states persisted for no more than several minutes. A third presentation type were those exhibiting "frightened spells." These are workers who "expressed a feeling of unexplained fear, and might complain of feeling cold, numb, or dizzy."[193]

A second "outbreak" was reported in a dried cuttlefish factory on September 29, 1973, when a female employee began to suddenly scream and cry. When she became violent, she had exceptional strength and several men were needed to restrain her. Two more women soon followed with similar outbursts. The "attacks" resumed on the morning of Thursday, October 4, when ten workers were stricken including three repeat cases from the 29th. The scene was one of chaos and confusion, and plant officials closed the plant that afternoon. In all, 28 females and two males were affected out of a total of 350 workers. The main symptoms were screaming, weeping, and violence. Some employees claimed to see visions of a dark-skinned man with hairy arms. Like the previous outbreak, all those involved were Malays. While management brought in a *bomoh* to rid the premises of evil spirits, sporadic cases continued to be recorded even after the exorcism. Some workers reported as many as five separate "attacks."

See: MASS HYSTERIA IN JOB SETTINGS.

SKOPTSI CASTRATION SECT

Russia: 18-20th Century

Among the proliferation of Christian sects that sprang up in 18th century Russia, the Skoptsi were one of the most extreme and the most long-lived. Their persistence, for more than two hundred years, was no doubt partly because of their extreme views, yet also in spite of them; for central to their creed was that the males should undergo a "second baptism" of castration, thus preventing reproduction. The females were somewhat less drastically subjected to mutilation. Remarkably, they attracted a sufficient number of new adherents for the sect to survive.

CONTEXT: In mid 17th century, the Patriarch Nikon initiated a reform of the Russian Orthodox Church, involving many innovations. These were fiercely resented and resisted by many, and a great number of groups of "Old Believers" broke away from the established church in what was known as the raskol (= schismatic) movement. While the ostensible motivation of the raskolniki was religious, social factors also contributed; the overwhelming majority of them were serfs, whose living conditions were deplorable. The historian Tsakni gave this description:

> The peasant who lives under the yoke of unrelieved misery, hardships of every kind, exorbitant taxes, deprived of the benefits of civilization and science, seeks his salvation and moral truth in a religion which is appropriate to his lifestyle and which, while securing his soul, can procure for him peace, happiness and well-being on this Earth.[194]

Consequently, to become a raskolnik was to express defiance of authority, and this attracted those who considered themselves to be persecuted victims of the social system. It is estimated that there were at any time some 15 million individuals aligning themselves with breakaway sects, many moving from one to another in their search for spiritual satisfaction.

From Khlysti to Skoptsi: The Khlysti sect was the creation of Danille Philippovich, whose central teaching was the rejection of all dead book-engendered theology in favor of a living religion of the heart. His followers called themselves "Men of God." The word *khlysti* seems to be a corruption of "Christ," but it was also the word for whip, and flagellation was a conspicuous feature of the sect. According to contemporary witnesses, the member of the sect achieved a collective ecstasy through flagellation, which carried the gathering to religious fervor. They were fiercely ascetic, and abstained from reproduction. Those unfortunate enough to be married were urged to live with their wives "as with a sister."[195]

Accusations were leveled at them, alleging religious ceremonies that moved from giddy dances and flagellation to orgies that were far from sisterly. These should be received with some skepticism, since they were made by defectors who left the sect, but it is easy to believe that some found chastity difficult to sustain. Thus it came about that some members formed a sect within a sect, the skoptsi, which means the castrated. A skopets voluntarily chose to be castrated, by way of making sure that he was not tempted to abandon his principles.

It is not clear whether the creation of the skoptsi can be credited to the man who became their leader, Kondrati Selivanov, but in July 1772 a certain Andrei Ivanov was among thirteen peasants who were arrested and found to be castrated. This was the first time the sect had been brought to public notice, and the authorities immediately began to make inquiries. It was not clear of what crime, if any, the skoptsi were guilty, but Laura Engelstein noted: "In the enlightened reign of Catherine the Great, what crime or transgression had these miscreants been charged with committing? Because secular and ecclesiastical authority were tightly entwined, it is not surprising that grounds for prosecution were mixed...To martyr oneself in the name of 'false belief' was a form of political insubordination, akin to soldiers' rushing into battle without an officer's command."[196]

Considered to be their chief, Ivanov was punished by the knout (a scourge so severe that it frequently caused death) and then exiled to Riga. Though historians differ on the matter, it is plausible that Ivanov was Selivanov under another name. Originally from the Orel district, he had previously been a serf on a princely estate before joining the khlysti where he was dismayed to find that the principle of chastity was widely ignored. Though many of the khlysti opposed his extreme views, many others followed him into a stricter inner elite, which eventually separated entirely.

Selivanov succeeded in escaping from Riga, but in 1775 he was recaptured, again punished with the knout, and exiled, this time to Siberia. By now his followers had accepted him as the second incarnation of Jesus Christ, and he seems to have had no difficulty in persuading them that castration was the only true baptism. Hardly less remarkably, his punishment and exile actually strengthened his leadership, conferring on him a martyr's crown. The sect not merely survived but flourished during his twenty-year absence in exile. He seems to have obtained considerable freedom of action in Siberia and was able to communicate and direct the sect from Irkutsk. His followers erected a church on the spot where he had been flogged, and membership grew rapidly throughout Russia, Finland, and Romania.

In 1795-6 Selivanov returned from Siberia to Moscow. His followers claimed he once again escaped, though other accounts suggest Tsar Paul released him on his accession in 1796. Legend attributed to him a meeting with Tsar Paul I, who, affronted by Selivanov's claims of divine authority, had him confined to a lunatic asylum. From there he continued to direct the sect, and after Paul's assassination in 1801 influential followers obtained his release from the moderate Tsar Alexander I and his transfer to a monastery.

Skoptsi rites: Since castration was illegal, the Skoptsi were understandably secretive about their practices and only a sketchy account was ever revealed. Moreover, we should not suppose that the practices continued the same throughout two centuries, or were the same in different parts of the country. Minor ceremonies were held periodically, and some four times a year there were the *radenije,* when the group – the men in baggy pants and floor-length shirts, the women in long skirts and chemises, all barefoot – would commence by singing hymns in chorus. This led to enthusiastic dancing which was continued until the faithful fell exhausted, pouring with sweat, in a state of drunken vertigo to which they themselves gave the name "spiritual beer." They believed that their dancing brought them into a state of ecstasy in which they achieved direct contact with the divinity. Sometimes, when in this state, neophytes would castrate themselves without waiting to have it done to them.

Castration represented a baptism that marked the initiation of the subject as a fully fledged member of the sect. In the early years of the skoptsi, castration took place generally at 18-to-20 years of age; later a change was introduced, whereby men were permitted to marry and obtain one or two sons before the operation, thus ensuring another generation to secure the continuance of the sect. Indeed, to undergo castration after becoming a parent was regarded as more meritorious than undergoing it before fatherhood, for now the individual knew what he was renouncing.

Little is known about how the castration took place. No initiate ever revealed what happened, so we have only the word of observers. There are indications that in the early days of the sect it was a public ceremony, the community singing and dancing round the initiate as he underwent his ordeal. Later, though, there is general agreement that it took place in private and with little or no ceremony. One authority went so far as to declare that it was carried out in any old place and any old how.[197] The initiate and the castrator (who might be a butcher or a surgeon) and perhaps the chief of the chapel might be the only ones present.

The new adept had fasted for three days that he spent in prayer. Some have suggested that the victim was numbed with alcohol or other stupefiants. Against this is the fact that the skoptsi strictly forbade the use of alcohol, but perhaps an exception was made for this one and only occasion. All agree, however, that everyone concerned was in a state of high arousal when the operation was carried out, so it may be that no anesthetic was needed. The cut was effected by the operator kneeling on one knee before the initiate, one hand holding the parts to be cut off, the other wielding either a red-hot iron or a knife, razor, or even scissors. The change from the iron to the knife is supposed to have come about between 1806 and 1819. The testes and scrotum were cut off, the initiate was sprinkled with water and, unless, as happened more often than not, he fainted, he uttered the ritual formula "Christ is reborn."

A ligature was rapidly tied round the wound, which was cauterized and bandaged. He was laid on a bed and the company danced round him singing. The cut-off parts were displayed for all to see with the words "See the serpent trampled," then thrown into a stove. The initiate had to fast for another three days, taking in only a little water, while medicines were applied to his wound for about five weeks.

In 1816, some members came to the conclusion that cutting off the testes – "the keys of damnation" – was not enough, and that the penis too – perceived as "the key to the abyss" – should be removed. This seems to have been accepted in principle, though how many went through the second stage is not known. One medical authority states that out of 1422 castrated Skoptsi he examined, 588 had lost their penis also,[198] but those he saw included many Finns who tended to be more extreme in their fanaticism, so overall the proportion was probably lower. Removal of the penis was carried out a few years after the first operation; the penis was laid on a block, a sharp knife placed on it, then it was struck sharply with the fist.

As for the women, the operation was less radical, but could entail the mutilation and ablation of one or both breasts, the re-section of the clitoris, and amputation of the labia – all done with knife or scissors. The aim was to reduce sexual pleasure to a minimum while permitting impregnation and childbirth.[199]

Accounts by hostile witnesses may have had their foundation in fact, but exaggeration may be suspected. One such described a young virgin placed in a warm bath where one of her breasts would be cut off, cut up, and eaten by the assembly, after which she was seated on a pedestal and the gathering would dance round her singing. This may be invention, but mutilation undoubtedly took place.

Male or female, once they had submitted to the operation, they were admitted to the elite. The skoptsi believed that when their number reached 144,000, Selivanov would rise from his tomb and ascend the throne of Russia. There, he would conduct the Last Judgment, all humankind would be castrated, and our Earth would be transformed into an eternal paradise.

The golden age of the skoptsi: The first decades of the 19th century saw the skoptsi at their most prosperous. Powerful friends in high society protected them; in Moscow they were given a fine house, which the police were forbidden to enter. There were communities throughout the empire, a thousand members in Moscow alone. The sect had its relics – the community at Riga boasted the actual shirt Selivanov had been wearing when he was punished with the knout back in 1775. And it had its pilgrims – his followers came from all over Russia to visit their leader. Things reached the point where a powerful follower put forward a plan whereby Selivanov and the skoptsi would become official advisers to the government – but the man who proposed the scheme was sent, instead, to a lunatic asylum.

Hostility towards the skoptsi was growing. The government became alarmed at the number of officers who had joined the movement; two nephews of the governor of St. Petersburg castrated themselves. In 1820, Selivanov was once again arrested and taken in the private carriage of the chief of police to a cloister where he was confined for the remaining 12 years of his life. He was said to be 100 years old when he died.

The sect survived his death, though its procedures became more and more clandestine. From time to time the authorities would uncover groups who would be punished, usually by exile to Siberia. Investigation by the police revealed that a good many of those who went to church dutifully were in fact skoptsi, hiding their true adherence. They showed themselves at theaters, where, since it was common knowledge that the skoptsi avoided public entertainments, they hoped to put informers off the scent. With the same intention they changed their homes, their towns, their names. Nonetheless, arrests continued. In 1851, fifty were rounded up, and in 1865 a wealthy patron of the sect escaped exile only by fleeing by steamship to San Francisco. The authorities realized they had seriously underestimated their number. An official estimate in 1875 put their numbers between 30,000 and 40,000, though not all were castrated. There were about four men for every woman.

From this date on, the authorities tended to close their eyes – in part because they were bribed to do so, as the skoptsi had wealthy protectors. Some of their money went into the recruitment of new members. Since they were prevented from reproducing in the usual way, they would purchase children as servants, whom they would persuade to join them. A parent might be paid a thousand roubles to place a child with them.

From time to time, disputes would break out within the sect. Some related to the practices, proposing other forms of castration such as a surgical operation, which left no outward trace, so if one was arrested and stripped it would be undetectable. Other disputes were about leadership. Although Selivanov had proclaimed himself the second and last Christ, in 1872, a fanatical peasant named Lisin proclaimed himself the new Messiah. The following year he and 162 neo-Skoptsi were arrested. In prison they danced and sang, and those who had not yet castrated themselves did so; those who survived the castration were sent to Siberia where the skoptsi were established in large communities, and there Lisin faded from view.

Arrests, trials, and deportations continued periodically until the uprising of 1905. Though religious tolerance was one of the measures of reform that followed the uprising, there were further arrests every year until the outbreak of World War I. After the revolution, the exiles in Siberia returned to Moscow but found the climate did not favor religion of any kind, let alone religious fanaticism.

Nevertheless, even under Stalin, they continued their clandestine activities despite official disapproval. In 1930, there were nearly a thousand members still active in Russia. But the remaining skoptsi flourished most outside Russia, especially in Romania where in 1913 there were estimated to be between 2,000 and 3,000, plus a number of "spiritual" skoptsi who abstained from castration.

COMMENT: As indicated in the general entry CASTRATION, this remarkable act has been performed in many parts of the world at many periods of history. Why it should have caught on so in 18th century Russia, and even more remarkably have survived until well into the 20th century, makes the skoptsi a special case.

Even if not all the skoptsi adhered in full to the teachings, there can be little question of the sincerity of their piety. Voluntary castration and mutilation on such a scale can hardly be attributed entirely to psychosocial pressure. Moreover, these extreme deprivations were accompanied by many other ascetic practices; most skoptsi, if not all, renounced meat, alcohol and tobacco, card playing, and attendance at theatres and other public amusements.

SKUNKED WORKERS

Dayton, Ohio: July 15, 1948

Nine female office workers at the Univis plant who crossed a picket line during a strike, fell ill and were taken to nearby hospitals for treatment after they were sprayed with a foul-smelling chemical. The incident happened as the women passed by a picket line set up by the CIO United Electrical Workers union. Several of the women fainted after the incident. The chemical turned out to be "skunk oil." Other office workers who said that they too were sprayed with the oil, apparently suffering no ill effects.[200]

SMALL GROUP SCARES

In *A Midsummer Night's Dream*, William Shakespeare perhaps best captures the flavor of this category when he wrote: "Or in the night, imagining some fear, How easy is a bush suppos'd a bear!" Small group scares are a type of social delusion that was formally identified by sociologist Robert Bartholomew and psychologist George Howard in 1998.[201] Episodes occur to persons who are in close physical proximity and in settings that are temporarily closed so that escape routes are either impossible or inhibited. The site of the scare is isolated and usually takes place in a house or car. Participants grow fearful after perceiving an agent that is interpreted as posing an immediate personal threat. Members of the group become emotionally unstable, often as a result of fear, fatigue and lack of sleep, and begin to redefine various mundane objects, events and circumstances within the emerging definition of the situation. Such interpretations reinforce suspicions that they are potential victims of a dangerous attacker. It is within this context that the rustling of bushes may be perceived as Sasquatch or a car backfiring, a gunshot. Of the 15 examples of small group attacks, pursuits and sieges that were originally identified by Bartholomew and Howard, most involve observations of unidentified flying objects and mysterious creatures. While there are hundreds of reports throughout history, they chose to examine cases in which the investigators were either police officers, held doctorates or the participants were personally known to them.

Each of the 15 small group scares analyzed by Bartholomew and Howard transpired in an isolated environment and under the cover of darkness. Often the dominant social figure made remarks about their being mentally or physically fatigued at the time. Such circumstances are likely to enhance suggestibility and inhibit their powers of critical thinking. Dark, isolated environments are associated with an extensive folklore pertaining to nefarious creatures or agents, the content of which correspond to the phantom attack scenarios. Another common factor was that each participant was a close friend or relative. Bartholomew and Howard note: "The primary witness (the first to draw attention to the unusual agent, to initiate detailed discussion as to its origin, or to panic), almost always holds an influential social position (is the oldest in the group, household head, vehicle driver or group leader), and interprets the stimulus as a potential threat. In each case, a bogus consensus is soon reached that the object or agent is pursuing the group. The ambiguous stimulus is rapidly redefined within popular cultural labels (Bigfoot, extraterrestrial spacecraft, drug dealers...)."[202]

Many participants experience over-breathing, headache, nausea, lightheadeness and skin rash in response to the episode. After the incident is over, many of those involved report "lost" or "missing time" that they cannot account for. In each case, there is an absence of physical evidence that could be used to confirm the existence of the attackers. All that investigators are left with is eyewitness testimony from a small number of socially cohesive people, and no confirmation of the event from independent observers who are outside of the particular social dynamic. Further, the reliability of human perception and memory reconstruction are well known, and time estimates in subjects under extreme stress are notoriously inaccurate.[203]

In five cases, the primary social figure exhibits symptoms of acute stress disorder. In four of these cases, a panic ensued among the occupants of a motor vehicle when the driver appears to have entered a stress-induced trance-like state after believing that an alien spaceship was pursuing the vehicle. The driver became unresponsive to others in the vehicle, pressing the accelerator and further heightening anxiety among the passengers.[204]

Examples: The Kentucky Farm Encounter Report

During the early evening of August 21, 1955, a farm family in the southeastern U.S. state of Kentucky, made national headlines after reporting a fantastic story to authorities, of being terrorized by strange beings from outer space. Members of the Sutton family, comprised of seven adults and three children, were living in the rural community of Kelly. The episode began at about 7 o'clock, during a visit by their landlord William Taylor. Taylor left the house to fetch water from a nearby well and upon returning, he told the others that he saw a glowing "flying saucer" appear to land in a gully near the house. Family members were incredulous and thought that Taylor had probably overreacted to seeing a "falling star." By 7:30, a pet dog began barking frantically. Taylor and Lucky Sutton went to the back door to look around and spotted a faint glow in a field. The glow seemed to be to approaching the house. As it got closer, they perceived what appeared to be a three-and-a-half-foot-tall creature with a huge head, extended arms and

At Kelly, Kentucky, the Sutton family see small figures around their farm, fire on them, and report in panic to the police.

elephant-like ears. The pair panicked, withdrew inside the house, grabbed their guns and began shooting. The commotion sent fear rippling through the rest of the household. Over the next three and a half hours, various family members glimpsed creatures either on or near the house, sometimes peering through windows, with intermittent bursts of gunfire in response. At times the frightened pair actually shot through a window screen at the "creature."

The Sutton's didn't have a telephone, so at about 11 o'clock, they decided to flee, piling into two cars and racing into the night to summon help. Police arrived, searched the area and found nothing unusual. Soon after the last officer left at 2:15 am, the family's mother was still anxious, lying in bed and staring at a window. She soon became convinced that one of the creatures was looking in, and duly alerted the family. More sightings and sporadic gunfire continued for the next three hours until just before sunrise. Everyone in the house said that at sometime during the ordeal, they had actually seen at least one creature. When police again arrived, they thoroughly combed the area but found no evidence of extraterrestrial beings—only a terrified family and a house riddled with bullet holes.[205]

Phantom Drug Siege in Michigan

Between November 7 and 8 of 1978, what could be described as a phantom drug siege took place near Lowell, Michigan. The description of the episode was reconstructed by Harvard-educated sociologist Ron Westrum who interviewed those involved and investigated the scene.[206] The remarkable series of events occurred at a house. The first man, "Masters," was 24 years of age and suspected of being a drug dealer. The other man, "Cordell," was 29. It appears that the pair gradually became suspicious of a series of mundane events outside the house, with each new event "feeding on itself," fostering more anxiety and further suspicions. To give an idea as to the suspicious mindset that the two men were in on the afternoon of the 7th, in one incident great significance was given to finding a piece of grape bubble gum wrapper on the roof, the other half near a wood pile. They also grew certain that people were lurking about the house, peering through the windows.

During the afternoon of the 7th both were "on the lookout" for intruders. Correspondingly, they reported seeing fleeting glimpses of shadowy figures outside. Near dusk, they thought they may have spotted a "kid" wearing a camouflage outfit. Cordell chased after the figure but to no avail. Then he shouted a warning to "the people he felt were hiding but could not see that if the nonsense did not stop somebody was going to get shot." A short time later they thought they could hear people near a back door. At this point events spiraled out of control as anxiety levels rose dramatically. Cordell fired a warning shot to scare away the people he thought were there. Fearful that they may be under siege, Masters telephoned a friend and asked him to bring over a variety of weapons. Soon, a 23 year-old named "Hamby," joined them. The trio kept a watchful eye on the house until about 1:30 a.m. when Cordell and Masters thought they saw shadowy figures near the house and they fired off some ten shots. Meanwhile, Hamby was adamant that he saw and heard no one.

Over the next three and a half hours, the trio said they heard more noises and distant figures. Then, as the clock was nearing 5 a.m., physically and emotionally exhausted, the episode reached a climax as the men themselves became terror-stricken and lost their composure. Thinking the house was under assault, they began firing their weapons indiscriminately. Cordell was sure he saw someone hanging in a window and that he shot the figure but later no body or blood were found. Ron Westrum continues: "Hamby fired a .44 magnum through a refrigerator—I saw the hole myself—at a person in the kitchen, whom he heard slam against the sink, fall on the floor, and make gurgling noises, as if critically wounded. ...All three were extremely scared; Masters to the point where he was re-loading spent cartridges into the revolver. At 5:30 a.m., they called the sheriff's department. Because one of them was on parole, and had a real interest in not being associated with firearms or drugs, it demonstrates the degree of their desperation."[207] One of the men, Hamby, was so anxious to get the attention of a police car that he fired off a shotgun, inadvertently striking the windshield and later being charged with attempted murder, though the charge was later reduced to misuse of a firearm. Police conducted a thorough investigation of the scene and found no evidence of any intruders. The only clear physical evidence of a confrontation was the damage left behind by the three men. Police found a bullet-ridden home that was littered with empty gun cartridges and three petrified men

An Incident at Mundrabilla, Australia

On January 19, 1988, a domestic argument took place between members of the Knowles family in Perth, Western Australia. As a result, Mrs. Faye Knowles decided to drive her Ford Telstar across the entire continent to stay with relatives in Melbourne. Accompanying her were three sons: Wayne, Sean and Patrick, ranging in age from 18 to 24. They traveled virtually non-stop for 13-hours, at which point they were somewhere between the tiny outposts of Madura and Mundrabilla in the remote Western Australian desert. The time was just before dawn.

Sean, who was driving and the only occupant who seemed to be fully awake, noticed a mysterious light in the distance and became convinced it was a "spaceship." He alerted the others to what he saw but the brilliant illuminated light soon disappeared. A short time passed before another strange light was seen to their rear. Sean became frightened that the object was pursuing them and he pressed the accelerator as the car roared down the remote highway at high speed.

The group later told authorities that as they were trying to get away, a beam raised the vehicle into the air, then dropped it. The impact reportedly caused the tire to burst and the car became disabled on the roadway. The nervous occupants changed the tire and drove on the Mundrabilla. Two truck drivers who encountered the family there said they looked visibly upset. One of the truckers said that the Knowles car was laden with a strange "black ash;" the other truck driver said that it looked like normal road grime to him. When they reached South Australia, police interviewed the family who by now were making worldwide headlines after claiming that their car had been picked up by a "UFO." They also told authorities that during the encounter, a mysterious ash was deposited on and in the vehicle. South Australian police inspected the car and found only typical road grime. An investigation of the car and blown tire were conducted by The Australian Mineral Development Laboratory. Their findings were unremarkable as samples of the substance revealed particles of clay and salt. This is consistent with what one should expect to find in a vehicle that had recently crossed the sand-laden Nullarbor Plains near the Great Southern Ocean.[208]

COMMENT: The dynamics of small group scares require further study. Episodes may be responsible for initiating new folklore motifs or reinforcing existing themes and beliefs. To the participants, they really happened. In this sense, they can be viewed as living folklore.

SNAKE HANDLER SECT

United States: 1909 to the present

The Church of God with Signs Following seeks to put into practice what it perceives as an injunction given by Jesus to his disciples after his resurrection. For nearly two thousand years, no one gave his words this literal interpretation. Then in the early 20th century, in rural Tennessee, Alabama, and perhaps elsewhere, fundamentalist ministers turned the words into actions and laid the foundation of a religious practice that made a strong, if local, appeal. Though confined geographically to some southern states, and to a small and demographically restricted population, the practice has survived, more or less clandestinely but with occasional outbreaks of publicity, until the present day.[209]

CONTEXT: Snake-handling is exclusively a practice of American Protestant Christians of a fundamentalist outlook, generally living in remote country areas. In the early 20th century the population of rural Kentucky and Tennessee was largely illiterate but well acquainted with the Bible. It came quite naturally to them to accept a literal interpretation of the reported words of Jesus, and to ascribe to them an authority above question. They believed they were reviving the practices of the earliest Christians; commenting on current activities in 1916, the General

Overseer wrote, "I leave it with any honest thinker to say if it does not read like Bible times."[210] Though some commentators have probed for underlying significance that might account for the popularity of the practice, the fact that snake-handlers believe they are carrying out Jesus's wishes seems to be the entire motivation for a practice that offers no rewards except personal satisfaction.

The inspiration to handle snakes was derived from words allegedly spoken by Jesus after his resurrection, according to the gospel of Mark: "And these signs shall follow them that believe: In my name shall they cast out devils; they shall speak with new tongues; They shall take up serpents; and if they drink any deadly thing, it shall not hurt them; they shall lay hands on the sick, and they shall recover."[211] In 1909, George Went Hensley (circa 1877-1955), a preacher in Tennessee, decided that these words constituted an injunction that should be taken literally, so he went out into the countryside, caught a rattlesnake, and produced it at a religious meeting, inviting all present to take it up as evidence of their faith.[212]

This was a sparsely populated region, and there were few converts to start with. But little by little the numbers grew. After about a year of such meetings, a large rattlesnake bit one of the participants. Though he survived, this was seen as evidence that he was insufficiently anointed, and the movement halted for a while. Hensley moved to the neighboring state of Kentucky, where he introduced snake handling at the Church of God of Pine Mountain. Though the practice continued through the 1920s and 1930s, it did so only in a more or less clandestine manner. A report of a service in 1914 shows that it was one of many activities:

> The Word was given out with love and power and it had its effect. The saints [members of the congregation] were greatly edified and God showed His mighty power of healing. We prayed for a baby with the small pox and God immediately healed the child. The saints danced, talked in tongues, handled a hot lamp chimney and some live coals. Serpents were also handled without injury.[213]

In 1938 the Pine Mountain church was thought to be only one church where snake-handling was practiced, but it was certainly taking place more widely, albeit clandestinely. In the 1940s there was something of a revival, headed by Raymond Hayes, one of Hensley's converts, with the foundation of the Dolly Pond Church of God with Signs Following.

The Pine Mountain church is a primitive building, plainly furnished, in a remote and sparsely populated rural area. Its congregation is largely made up of farming or mining families. Taking their cue from the Bible, they believe in the gift of tongues, the gift of spirit healing, the gift to handle snakes, the gift to withstand heat, and to drink poison without ill effect. Their life-style is austere: no theatre-going and suchlike entertainment, no smoking or drinking, no dancing. Dress is modest and women do not wear make-up or cut their hair. They rarely patronize professional doctors and hospitals, believing that God will heal if he sees fit.

The services take place in an atmosphere of intense enthusiasm. One at Carson Springs, Tennessee, in 1973, is described thus:

> While the heavy morning grayness spread an intermittent drizzle over the worshippers, the whole hollow was aglow with excitement and zeal. Sweat poured down the faces and soaked the clothing of believers as they jumped and shouted, "Praise God! Praise Jesus!" Hands were thrust into the now open wooden boxes and a multitude of writhing serpents were hastily pulled forth. Men and women excitedly surrounded the ecstatic handlers, clapped their hands in unison, and uninhibitedly sang old-time gospel songs...Many in the congregation responded with their own praises to the Lord. The excitement steadily heightened. A great number of people felt the Spirit enter, as was evident in the screams of exuberance accompanied by wild, uninhibited dancing in the pews and aisles. Handclapping and a variety of tongues added to the mood of the moment. The very air seemed charged with a flow of electrical energy. The atmosphere in and around the building was voltaic. Everyone felt the galvanic effect of the magnetic musical beat. A spiritual blanket fell over the packed house, enveloping the brothers, sisters, and most visitors. There was pure bedlam in the little church.[214]

Just how much their practices mean to the participants can be judged from this comment: "One night there was a big black diamond rattler, five feet long... God gave us power to handle it, Praise his dear name. The Lord surely did bless during the time. It was really a foretaste of heaven. The saints remarked about the sweet spirit."[215]

Excitement is further increased by the preaching, though it is doubtful if the congregation takes in much of the content beyond the ritual phrases. Brother Buford Pack, a 30-year-old former paratrooper, preached to a frenzied congregation on a night when he and another follower died from strychnine. He had already drunk a glass of the poison when he began preaching

– some called it testifying – which is to say that he was already a dying man, though neither he nor anyone present knew it.

Whooping, yelling, praises to God, and amens poured forth from all corners of the church. Brother Buford then began talking seriously to the congregation…Most of his speaking was unintelligible, as the clamor again submerged him…Bedlam reigned supreme. Pack was now really beginning to "get with it." He was becoming anointed to preach. He raised his voice noticeably as he continued above the pandemonium. He yelled louder – the people responded louder in turn. His ardorous ecstasy picked up the already frenetic pace. Pack was now shouting his sermon. A woman shrieked shrilly above the thunderous rumble, as Brother Pack punctuated his sentences with numerous hallelujahs. "When I get talking about Jesus, I can't be quiet…You gotta love for Him all the time – every day… and every night…It's seven days a week, twenty-four hours a day, and 365 days a year…"

Soon after, he left the church and walked to his car. "Boy, I feel really good!" he said to his brother there: within hours he was dead.[216]

Whatever Brother Hensley may have intended back in 1909, the handling of the serpents is emphatically not perceived as a test of faith. Brother Bob Fraley comments: "All the newspapers print that it's a demonstration of faith. But you'll find very few people around here [Tennessee and Virginia] that will take up a serpent on the faith, that way…It's not testing or tempting God. It's just a sign confirming the Word of God."[217] So snake handling is performed only when the individual feels an "anointing," a condition in which he or she feels to be the recipient of a divine power. Sister Lida Davis, from West Virginia, states, "I know when He [God]'s a-moving on me to get the serpents. It's through the Holy Ghost that I know exactly what to do and when to do it. I am led to do it. I know exactly what the Spirit of God is bidding me to do. It wouldn't be possible to make a mistake because God tells me what I must do."[218]

Sister Ruth Dillon, also from West Virginia, explains: "The anointing moves as fast as lightning when it comes on me. I can feel the Spirit in my hands and feet. My entire body feels it when the anointing comes for me to take up serpents. I always know exactly what I am doing all the time the anointing is on me. I speak in tongues some, but not all the time when I'm handling serpents. Most of the time I have a quiet, calm spirit, for I like to listen for the voice of God."[219] The handling of the snakes is not formalized or ritualized, as each handler does it in his or her own way, and only when they feel the time is right. "You should pick up the serpents only when you're under God's anointing. I never go near them, or even try to touch one unless I feel the Holy Ghost come down on me. You've got to go and take them up in the right spirit, or they'll bite you and hurt you."[220] If it should happen that a person is bitten – which occurs surprisingly seldom – this was in the past attributed to the fact that he had insufficient faith or was "in sin." Today it is more likely to be regarded simply as God's will.

The snakes are generally pit vipers – rattlesnakes or copperheads – whose bite may be fatal, though not necessarily. By the time anyone starts to handle the snakes, the emotional climate of the church is generally very intense, with people singing, dancing, perhaps speaking in tongues or in some frenzied state, led by the preacher who leads the service and exhorts the congregation. Those who feel the urge take one or more snakes from the container, and proceed to simply hold them or to twine them about in all kinds of ways. Many of their actions reflect their belief that the snakes represent the devil, so they will be addressed as such. Some snake-handlers, overcome with emotion, go into an altered state of consciousness, their eyes rolling, they spin, jerk, or dance, or speak in tongues. Psychiatrist Berthold Schwarz suggests that the state of exaltation achieved by the "saints" in some way modifies the effects of what would otherwise be dangerously toxic hazards.[221] When 35-year-old Murl Bass was bitten by a rattlesnake on July 1, 1973, he "commenced jumping straight up and down in an apparent effort to retain the protection of the Spirit. He raised his hands and eyes to Heaven. He was inebriated with pure pleasure and joyousness. 'Thank you, Jesus!… He continued his wild dancing, hand clapping and uninhibited shouting for about three minutes before the destructive venom finally took its toll. He began to stagger blindly." Though he resisted medical help, he was taken to hospital where his life was saved.[222]

On the same day, Brother Clyde Ricker handled a cobra, "It immediately went limp as if it were itself in a trance. Brother Clyde danced in ecstasy. His body jerked spasmodically, his breathing became heavy. He jumped, he shouted, he sweated. And then he began to speak in tongues – 'muma-mu-mamuma-

mamuma-mamuma, glory to God! Hallelujah!' The crowd went absolutely wild...He was at the height of his euphoria. He almost carelessly draped the shiny black creature around his neck and held its wicked-looking head close to his face and lightly kissed it on the mouth."[223]

Those who feel an anointing to follow the fire-resistance sign generally do so by using a bottle containing flaming material, for example a Pepsi bottle filled with kerosene. Strychnine is the poison of choice for those who feel an anointing to follow this sign. The concentration is entirely at hazard, but that the dose is potentially lethal is shown by the fact that people occasionally die of it.

In 1945 a death by snakebite attracted wide media attention, and led to state legislation in Tennessee making snake handling illegal. Moreover, the widow was not entitled to accident compensation since her husband had deliberately incurred the risk. During the following years there were periodic police raids on services, and occasional arrests. These had the customary effect of attracting interest, and snake-handling seems actually to have spread as a result.

In 1947, a death by poison occurred in Georgia, when a 34-year-old farmer died five days after drinking a "salvation cocktail" with a strychnine base. This was not considered a crime. That same year a snake-handling group at Durham, North Carolina, came up against the law since it was forbidden in that state. Police interrupted a service that was marked by fervent behavior – "people jerking their necks, dancing, waving their arms, and collapsing onto the floor."[224]

By the 1950s, laws had been passed in Kentucky, Virginia, and Tennessee against handling snakes in public religious services. The effect was to disperse the cult. In 1951, a farm woman brought a snake to her local church in Alabama; unfortunately the rattlesnake bit her four times and she died. Since snake handling was not illegal in Alabama, the death was ruled an accident. In 1954, snake handling was reported elsewhere in Alabama and Georgia, also in far-off Long Beach, California. In 1955 Hensley, now aged 70, was fatally bitten in Florida after handling a snake for fifteen minutes. He refused medical aid and died next morning. He is said to have claimed to have been bitten four hundred times "till I'm speckled all over like a guinea hen."[225] It is estimated that present-day practitioners number around 5,000, worshipping in a few hundred churches mainly located in the states where the practice grew.

Although the innovation of snake handling is widely attributed to Hensley in Tennessee, other manifestations occurred at about the same time and may even have preceded him. A snake-handling group is said to have existed in Cherokee, North Carolina, in 1903, but no further information is available, so it is not certain whether it occurred in a Christian religious setting, nor in what ethnic context. A snake-handling cult is said to have existed at Los Angeles, California, in 1906, and a certain James Miller is thought to have brought snake handling to Sand Mountain, Alabama, around 1912.

COMMENT: Snake-handling does not appear to have any prehistory, and its origins are obscure. Snakes play a symbolic role in many belief-systems, but snake handling as practiced by these American fundamentalist congregations is not replicated in other cultures, Christian or otherwise.

Behavioral scientists have found snake handling a fascinating field of study, and various approaches have been pursued. The psychological approach of La Barre, on largely Freudian lines, has been received with respect but not with widespread acceptance. His contention that snake-handlers are displaying a psychopathic behavior is at odds with their manifestly positive and affirmative attitudes. The serpent, far from representing "one's own projected, hysterically unacknowledged, and unadmissible desires"[226] is, quite simply and openly, the Evil One, which the snake-handlers confront in this simple and open way. Psychological tests show snake-handlers to be well adjusted and health minded.[227]

Another approach is the socio-economic: "Sociological research suggests that the Snake Handlers are sending a defiant socio-economic message...that though they may not be economically powerful, they are spiritually powerful."[228] Burton gives several reasons for rejecting this view, and so do the snake-handlers themselves: "We just want the world to know that Brother Charles didn't die in a one-room shack or that he was being cared for by a bunch of unlearned, backwoodsy, bare-footed people who don't belong in the 20th century. As you can see, we have electricity. We are college educated. Most of us here have been in the coal-mining business. We think we're doing all right. The banks do too."[229]

Though psychological and socio-economic factors doubtless play their part, they do not seem to be more than secondary or enabling factors. Burton is surely correct to comment that "the validity of a spiritual experience…is not negated by its fulfilling other psychological needs. To show that serpent-handling satisfied a number of individual as well as social needs does not repudiate in any way its manifestation of a divine or psychic event."[230] To the snake-handlers themselves, their practice is no more exceptional a form of worship than the dervish dancing or self-mutilation of Muslims, the penances of Christian mystics or the voluntary afflictions of Hindu ascetics.

SOCIAL MOVEMENTS

A social movement is an organized effort by people to foster change either in individuals or members of society. All social movements share three common elements: a *dissatisfaction* with unwanted conditions in the social system, a *shared identity* among its members, and the appearance of being *organized.* Sociologist Lewis Killian noted the power of social movements as a force for societal change, observing that "The study of social movements reminds us of the irrepressible conviction...that they [human beings] can collectively, if not individually, change their culture by their own endeavors,"[231] and perhaps seek to modify or even reverse a particular policy.

Several different types of social movements have been identified. There is no universal agreement as to how to classify them, but many sociologists use all or part of the following scheme. In *reformist movements* members are basically happy with the system in general but are intent on changing certain parts of society. This could also be called the "Don't throw out the baby with the bath water" view. An example would be a group advocating a ban on whaling. They don't want to overthrow the American government, but they are not happy with certain aspects of the existing system. *Resistance movements* contain members who resist change and want to keep the status quo. Also known as regressive or conservative movements, they support "turning back the clock" in an effort to retain old-fashioned values. The Moral Majority religious organization is one example, advocating prayer in schools, opposing same sex marriages, and abortions. *Expressive movements* hold a goal of changing the emotional state or mental outlook of individuals but not society. Examples include the Jehovah's Witnesses who do not vote in elections, run for political office, or pledge allegiance to the flag of any country. While some of the cases in our catalog have some elements of reformist, resistance, or expressive social movements, none clearly fits wholly under any of these categories.

Revolutionary groups are composed of members who seek radical changes throughout a society. They often advocate overthrowing governments entirely, as in the case of the American and French revolutions. At the very least, they desire dramatic, sweeping changes. The bloody and gruesome crusades could fall under this umbrella. Groups of zealous Christians traveled to the Middle Eastern Holy Land between 1095 and 1272, intent on wiping out Muslim Turks and regaining control of the Holy City of Jerusalem. Problems had begun to emerge in 1009 when the Islamic leader, Caliph Umar, who controlled Jerusalem, began persecuting Christians and demolishing holy sites. In response, Christians in Europe organized the first of nine Crusades. The Crusaders were an especially abhorrent revolutionary group, and many committed the most horrific atrocities in the name of god: rape, torture, massacres, and the killing of innocent women and children. Name an atrocity and it probably happened during one of the Crusades. In the end, the Crusade movement failed and Jerusalem remained under Muslim control.

See: CHILDREN'S CRUSADES.

SORORITY MYSTERY ILLNESS

Winston-Salem, North Carolina: January 15, 2001

Some 50 students experienced nausea and dizziness

while attending a Monday evening sorority recruitment gathering at the Benson Center on the campus of Wake Forest University. The first hint of trouble began at about 7:30 when police received a report that a female student had collapsed. Soon more students fell ill. Two food service workers in the building were also stricken and taken to the hospital along with one student who fainted. Their examinations were unremarkable and they were soon released. Just prior to feeling ill, some students said they recalled smelling a gaseous ordor.

The building was evacuated and a hazardous materials team conducted an extensive search in an effort to pinpoint the cause. Investigators checked the air for hazardous materials and found nothing out of the ordinary. University staff also examined the building with their own air monitoring equipment. Again, all readings were normal. Of the several hundred female students in the Benson Center that evening, about 300 were attending one of two sorority recruitment gatherings on the fourth floor. At one function, none of the sorority members became ill, while just down the hall, about four dozen fell sick.[232]

SOUPONIEVO OUTBREAK

Russia: 1903

Though a relatively minor episode, the outbreak of religious mania among a community at Souponievo, in Russia's Orel district, is interesting in two respects. First, it shows how a quite innocuous activity can escalate to more serious behavior; and second, it also shows how the force of suggestion can lead people to set aside their most fundamental standards of conduct.[233]

CONTEXT: The community affected seems to have been backward and deprived, comprised of ignorant and culturally impoverished folk. The political climate in Russia was at this time very unstable, and this may have contributed to a state of unease in which any suggestion of divine intercession would be welcome.

Things began with simple bible-reading meetings, accompanied by commentaries, which led to discussions of Lutheranism. Vassili D., whose enthusiasm initiated the movement, would launch into impassioned sermons that had a strong effect on his auditors. They found the force of his words impossible to resist and felt an overpowering urge to attend his meetings and to accept his every word. Their will was wholly subjected to the preaching of the man whom they quickly acknowledged as their master. Dr. Jacobi, reporting on the case, observed: "Basically, at this stage it was no more than a fairly ordinary explosion of religious exaltation, due to the action of a hysterical and perhaps already delirious personality on a population no less neurotic and hysterical than himself."[234]

But the initial suggestion was not slow to escalate, developing all the more rapidly since the movement, which seemed from the outside to be purely ethical in character, encountered no opposition from the local Orthodox clergy. In contrast, the local secular authorities were on their guard, alerted by certain people whose incomes were threatened by the policy of abstinence adopted by the new sect. The result was that a minor conflict broke out, which had the further effect of exciting the population as a whole and particularly affecting the more nervous and unstable among them.

When this happened, Vassili left by boat for the south, where he spent the winter. Another member of the sect, Ossip Potopkin, left with his wife Pelagia for the Caucasus, where they met an exiled group of flagellants. (Many awkward sects, including the DOUKHOBORS, were exiled by the authorities to the Caucasus, thereby distancing them from the cities to a remote region where it was felt they could do little harm.) There Ossip had a symbolic vision, shared with his feeble-minded wife, followed by prophetic dreams, whereby he was led to believe that he had received from heaven the gift of interpreting the holy scriptures. Finding that the climate of the Caucasus didn't suit him, Ossip and his wife, filled now with the teachings of the flagellants, returned to Souponievo.

Until now, he had accepted the teachings of Vassili D. as a submissive disciple. Now, however, he broke with him and began to interpret the scriptures of his own accord, adding his own speculations. These included direct access to the Holy Spirit, and with it a doctrine of automatism. He claimed that "every man can call unto himself the Holy Spirit, who enters into his person and governs him like a machine, annihilating his own will. The man ceases, in consequence, to be responsible for his acts: everything he does, however shameful and depraved, becomes sanctified and blameless because it is the Holy Spirit who performs it."

This was accompanied by teachings with regard to purity and chastity of a kind that recurs over and over again in such sects. Relations between spouses are perceived as an abomination, an obscenity. Those who have discovered for themselves the sublime truth will find themselves united by new links, spiritual links of fraternity and love. This love binds equally the "brothers" and "sisters" of the sect, who can, and indeed should, by virtue of this love, perform the sexual act with one another. This act of sexual communion binds the members of the community together in the new truth: it is a symbolic and obligatory ceremony.

This seems to have been the one teaching that emerged clearly and unambiguously from Ossip's teaching. For the most part, his doctrine was inconsistent and incoherent, insofar as it could be understood at all. His preaching took the form of absurd affirmations, interspersed with biblical quotations and mystical formulas. Nonetheless, this sufficed to seduce a community thirsty for an ideal of which it was totally deprived.

Ossip had converted to flagellant principles not only his wife but her sister Eudoxia, who lived under the same roof, and Matriona Morozova. These and several other women, led to believe that performing the sexual act was a religious ceremony, had already communicated carnally with Ossip. Others, without going so far, took part in the reunions. Abandoning themselves to rhythmic movements, singing and hand-clapping, stamping their feet, exchanging kisses, calling on the Holy Spirit, they plunged into a state of ecstasy. This exaltation rapidly became for them a necessity. They burned with desire to go to these meetings; incapable of staying at home, they were drawn irresistibly to them, and declared they could not live if they were prevented from participating in these Orphic excitements. Even though their fathers, husbands, or brothers forbade them, and despite the sarcasms and reproaches of their neighbors, they escaped at night to join Ossip, staying in his house till dawn.

One of the women said later that if Vassili had not returned, they would all have prostituted themselves to Ossip. The women rose and walked about without ceasing, uttering predictions, exchanging kisses, singing, taking off their caps, and shaking their hair loose. Almost all of them sobbed or uttered cries of joy; many fell to the floor in convulsions, while others manifested hysterical phenomena.

Of those who had sex with Ossip some openly confessed it, but others admitted only to their participation in the ceremonies and kept quiet about performing the act itself. Pelagia, the weak-minded woman, was driven further into madness by these sexual ceremonies, and one day, after the sect had disintegrated, she began to recount stories of these erotic couplings with Ossip, describing how her fellow "sisters" watched the spectacle. Their reaction: silence and hostile looks. Others turned away, visibly ashamed of the memory of this period of their lives. Their shame became all the greater when Ossip was officially certified as insane, and taken away by the Tribunal investigating the affair. From the insane asylum of Orel, he continued to write rambling, incoherent letters in which he insisted he was the risen Christ, reproaching the doctors who confined him to these stone walls, and issuing demands for his release and recognition.

COMMENT: Vassili D., in his turn, was subsequently diagnosed by doctors as a hysteric tainted with delirious paranoia. But Vladimir Mikhailovich Bekhterev, commenting on the affair, is less surprised by the patent megalomania of the leaders than by the willingness of their followers to believe their "ridiculous" claims and follow teachings that diametrically contradicted their notions of acceptable conduct.

SOUTH CAROLINA MARTIAN PANIC

South Carolina: October 27, 1939

According to an Associated Press report dated October 28, "Charleston and its environs had a 'Men from Mars' scare last night."

The report continued: "A radio broadcast told of a

death-dealing anti-aircraft ray which got beyond control in the Santee-Cooper area...It was one of a series of 'palmetto fantasies,' broadcast once a week" and dedicated to Orson Welles, who was credited with producing a similar broadcast the pervious year, causing widespread anxiety and limited panic across the continental United States.

"Several times during last night's broadcast over Station WCSC here, announcement was made that the program was fictitious. However, scores of persons called the radio station, the morning paper, and the police station, inquiring about the disaster."[236]

See also: ORSON WELLES MARTIAN PANIC (1938), CHILEAN MARTIAN INVASION PANIC (1944), ECUADOR MARTIAN INVASION PANIC (1949), BUFFALO MARTIAN INVASION SCARE (1968), RHODE ISLAND MARTIAN INVASION PANIC (1974), PORTUGUESE MARTIAN INVASION PANICS (1988 and 1998).

SPACE ALIEN SCARE

Romania: Early October 2004

The small community of Cristinesti in eastern Romania became a temporary ghost town after terror-stricken residents fled, fearing they were in the midst of an invasion by space aliens. The inhabitants left their homes after seeing strange colored lights in the sky. A police investigation quickly identified the source of the bright lights – a disco from the nearby town of Herta on the Ukrainian border. Police eventually persuaded the villagers that it was safe to return home. Villager Costel Roman said: "Everybody was out on the streets and wondering what to do if the aliens landed. We believed we were seeing UFOs and some old legends from around here about clocks stopping, animals going crazy and a previous UFO landing in the area suddenly came to our minds. We were terrified."[237]

SPIRIT INFESTATION AS MASS PSYCHOGENIC ILLNESS

Psychiatrists James Houran and V.K. Kumar, and psychologists Michael Thalbourne and Nicole Lavertue, believe that certain poltergeist and haunting experiences may be forms of mass psychogenic illness. Writing in the journal *Mental Health, Religion & Culture*, they set out to test this theory on a sample of 314 undergraduate students from West Chester University in Pennsylvania, who were given a number of questionnaires and surveys, hoping to find if there was a link between students reporting paranormal experiences and those with somatic and hypochondriacal tendencies. They found that certain tendencies correlated with specific paranormal experiences. There was a relationship between autonomic sensations and spirit infestation; perceptions of paranormal ability and cognitions of catastrophes; and general paranormal experiences and somatic traits.

Houran and his colleagues stated that while research into this area is still in the pioneering stages, there is an emerging picture that some "spirit infestation" experiences are the result of "misattributions of internal experience (apparently shaped partly by the immediate physical environment) to external" stimuli.[238] On the other hand, those thinking they had paranormal abilities were much more likely to believe they were having "catastrophizing cognitions" (CCs). The researchers believe that those experiencing CCs attend and give substantial credence to sudden changes in the body such as pains, sweating, and tingling sensations. "[It may be that] ambiguous events are explained automatically and without much reflection. Thus, bodily complaints are always interpreted as threatening. Since the concepts of chance and random fluctuation probably hold little meaning for these individuals, it is easy to see how beliefs in their own paranormal abilities arise. That is, occasional involuntary thoughts might be perceived as cases of ESP, associations and coincidences masquerade as synchronicity, and occasional physical incidents might be seen as evidence for psychokinesis."[239]

The researchers noted that reports of poltergeists and hauntings are likely to be under reported due to the stigma associated with them, thus posing a challenge to future research.[240]

While Houran and his colleagues cautioned that while there is no conclusive proof that poltergeist and haunting experiences are forms of mass psychogenic illness, they felt they had established a clear link between spirit infestation experiences and hypochondriacal and somatic tendencies. They also highlighted the importance of context in mass psychogenic illness reports. For instance, "symptoms experienced in a cafeteria setting are likely to be explained automatically in terms of 'food contaminants,' whereas somatic complaints perceived in an office complex might be regarded as a consequence of poor 'air quality.'" If seemingly conventional explanations for psychosomatic phenomena are absent, paranormal beliefs can be adaptive. Hence, a person with a paranormal belief system "may be more motivated to interpret any unusual perceptual experiences or thoughts in the context of such beliefs, especially in a culture that readily accepts these beliefs."[241]

SPIRIT POSSESSION IN INDIA

20th century

From time to time Indians may be afflicted with a state that is claimed to be the consequence of possession by the spirit of a dead person. Though this occurrence affects individuals, it does so in a formalized manner recognized by the community, and may therefore be regarded as a collective phenomenon.

CONTEXT: The idea that a living person can be possessed by the spirit of a person who is no longer living is, on the face of it, absurd. Nevertheless the belief that it can happen, and does happen, has been, in one form or another, an element in almost every human culture, and continues to be widely accepted. This is all the more surprising because the concept is not a simple one, but is contingent on a set of underlying beliefs: that a living person incorporates a spirit that survives his or her physical death, that there is a part of him or her that is capable of being possessed, and that the possession of one person by the spirit of another is a viable procedure. None of these is self-evident.

Nevertheless it is taken-for-granted by these Indian villagers that the ghosts are indeed what they claim to be, spirits of the dead, who usually have died a violent death. The Indian spirit possession described here is representative of practices that can be observed, in one form or another, throughout the world. T. K. Oesterreich's classic study bears witness to the universality of the concept and the diversity with which it is expressed in different cultures.[242]

There is one respect in which this particular instance of a possession culture is distinctive: the identification of the possessing spirit with a deceased individual. This is by no means universal; possession by non-human demons or malign spirits is more common, as many entries in this Encyclopedia testify. In the case history given here, the patient identifies first one person, then another, as the invading ghost, while other victims made similar claims. Evidently, in this particular culture, this was the standard expectation. Whereas the hysteria of a 17th century French nun would immediately be ascribed to a non-human agent of Satan, in India it is generally the malign ghost of a human person who died in violent circumstances.

"The possession of a person by a ghost or godling which results in somatic or psychological illness is widespread in India," stated American anthropologists Stanley and Ruth Freed in their study, which, while it focuses on a few individuals, recognizes that they are representative of a considerable number of victims, so that their affliction can fairly be described as epidemic.[243] That is to say, like *latah*, PIBLOKTOQ and many other extraordinary behaviors described in this Encyclopedia, the individual experience conforms to a model that has been culturally established and from which the individual departs only in personal details derived from his/her personal circumstances.

The cultural character of the outbreaks is confirmed by the fact that the nature of the spirit possession varies from one district to another. In the district studied by the Freeds, the possession was relatively benign, in that the patient did no damage to herself or to others. By contrast, in the district studied by M. R. Opler, "attacks are characterized by aggression and threatened or actual physical violence."[244] The patient may hurl abuse at those around him and even strike them; in one case a wife tried to strangle her husband. It is as though each community draws up its own agenda and creates its own model of what is socially acceptable, to which members of that community unconsciously conform.

Despite these variations, however, the motivation seems everywhere to be much the same, for in both districts the attacks have their origin in domestic circumstances. It is clear that they serve the function of social control, enabling the individual to proclaim his/her problem, draw attention to their predicament, and hopefully, obtain some kind of remedy or redress. As in so many examples of extraordinary behavior, it is a coping strategy. What is interesting, however, is that it is accepted as such by the community, which recognizes the individual's prerogative to be afflicted with spirit possession, and that some kind of appropriate remedy must be sought.

Either men or women, of any age, can be possessed. Of five cases investigated by the Freeds, only one was an adolescent. What all the cases had in common, however, is that they seemed to be caused by domestic circumstances – difficulties with relatives, adjustment to marriage, rivalries between relatives, and the like.

Typically, an afflicted person will go intermittently into a trance-like state, during which he – or rather, the spirit supposedly possessing him – can be interrogated as to its identity and motive. Others recognized the various preliminary symptoms indicating the onset and progress of the ailment. Treatment of the possessed person can be carried out, to some extent, by the patient's relatives, neighbors, village elders, and the like. The methods prescribed by custom are shock treatments directed towards driving the ghost away, and so tend to be physically unpleasant, ranging from the smoke of burning pig's excreta, which ghosts dislike, to beating the girl until the ghost takes itself off. Should these simple remedies fail to prove effective, one or more shamans will be called in.

Shamans, who exist in every community, are usually the mediator whereby the individual is relieved of her possession. The shaman interrogates the ghost and will try to do a deal – persuading the ghost to depart either with threats or with promises of reward. He may perform a form of exorcism, such as reciting sacred mantras, or cutting a piece of the patient's hair and throwing it in a fire. The ghost may be invited to take up residence elsewhere, often within the shaman himself. However, when questioned by the Freeds, the shaman who treated Daya (see case history that follows) acknowledged that his public performance was a sham: "the real process of catching the ghost goes on in the heart."[245]

Sooner or later, a cure is generally obtained. The Freeds observed cures in all but one of their cases while they were there.

COMMENT: The diagnosis formulated by the Freeds as a result of their investigation is as follows: "The basic condition of spirit possession is psychological. The precipitating conditions are cultural events or situations that exhibit two general characteristics: (1) the victim of spirit possession is involved in difficulties with relatives within the nuclear or joint family, and (2) he is often in a situation where his expectations of aid and support are low."[246] They found that "spirit possession as illness is a basically uniform pattern in northern India, although regional variations do occur."

The question arises, why do the individual's private difficulties manifest in this public and collectively formalized way? To this the answer surely is that, by exteriorizing the problem along lines recognized by the community, the individual is not only making a public appeal for something to be done about her plight, but also emphasizing its serious nature by pointing to the intervention of a higher power. This way, the subconscious argument runs, the community will have to do something about it. An individual cry for help would not receive the same degree of attention. By conforming to a model that is generally accepted by the community, the individual affirms her standing in that community and, in a sense, claims her right to a hearing.

Case History

Daya is 15, recently married, a member of the leatherworking caste, one of the lowest social levels. She lives with her husband's extended family in a small village near Delhi. Within the family the relationships are complex and intricate, dictated by traditional protocol. By way of example, only her husband's younger brothers would be permitted to make fun of her, so that when his older brother teases her, it is a breach of custom that she would inevitably find disturbing.

The first signs of Daya's possession show when she starts to shiver and complains of feeling cold, though the weather is warm. She moans and breathes heavily. These signs are instantly recognized by her mother-in-law, who is fond of her. Daya is made to lie down and quilts are piled upon her. She loses consciousness, at which point she is considered to be possessed by a ghost. For some hours she alternates between sleeping and a semi-conscious trance state. While she is in trance, the family do their best to prevail upon the ghost to depart. It claims to be Chand Kor, a woman from Daya's mother's brother's village with whom she had lived for a while and became close friends. Chand Kor had drowned in a well, almost certainly an enforced suicide as a result of a shameful extramarital pregnancy. This violent death explains why she has returned to Earth. The ghost declares that it will not leave without taking Daya away with it.

Although the mother-in-law is distressed by these goings-on, neither she nor any of the other relatives present behave as though they consider Daya's behavior strange or unusual. All recognize her state. During the lulls, they speculate as to the authenticity of the ghost's identity, and discuss ways of getting it to go away.

Daya's possession lasts for about two weeks, during which she has long periods of unconsciousness. A succession of shamans are called in, and eventually one of them succeeds in banishing the ghost, which now claims not to be Chand Kor but a girl named Prem from Daya's village who had recently died of illness. This, however, is probably a subterfuge, intended to confuse identification and, perhaps, to increase the interest in her case.

Daya's state is rooted in her domestic relationships: the strain of living with a new family and her fears regarding the sexual relationship to which she is not yet accustomed. Though her husband treats her gently and understandingly, and though her mother-in-law and other relatives are welcoming and helpful, she still has to adjust to the restraints of her life as a married woman compared with the freedom she recently enjoyed as an unmarried girl.

Had the spirit-possession model not been available to her, Daya would have had to resort to some other way of expressing her feelings, perhaps in the form of depression, perhaps in the form of some aggressive behavior. Thus the possession, though it is described by the Freeds as an "illness," can be seen more favorably as a form of therapy.

Such practices are far from being exclusive to Indian village life, as anthropologists have noted similar behavior in many other cultures. Thus:

> Lewis studied Somali [African] communities where women, unable because of their inferior status to express their demands explicitly and effectively in secular terms, resort to what he calls "mystical modes of ventilating grievances." They claim to be possessed by spirits, and in this state they soundly denounce their husbands' shortcomings.[247]

This would seem to account for Daya's behavior.

SPIRITUALIST MANIA

United States and Europe: 1850s

The concept that inspired the spiritualist mania, which swept through the United States in the 1850s, thereafter spreading to other parts of the world, was not a new one. The possibility of contact with spirits of the dead has teased humanity throughout its history. Ghost stories involving reciprocal communication are centuries old, and in 17th century France charlatans made a precarious living by pretending to put their clients in touch with the departed. Throughout the early 19th century, American visionaries believed themselves to be in touch with spirits; these included groups such as the Shakers and individuals such as Andrew Jackson Davies. The Fox sisters, who are generally credited with the creation of modern spiritualism, were far from being innovators. What was new about the movement they inspired was that it offered to make spirit communication accessible to everyone. While some individuals were more effective than others at making contact with the dead, in principle this was something that anyone might find themself able to do. Though many factors contributed to the spiritualist mania of the 1850s, this was unquestionably the principal one.

We are not here concerned with the veridicality or otherwise of the ostensible communication with spirits; our concern is simply with the social response to the claims. But the question is relevant, just as the reality or otherwise of DEMON POSSESSION or UFO ABDUCTION is relevant to our understanding of these alleged phenomena. An open-minded reading of the original witness accounts of American spiritualism makes it difficult to maintain that the entire episode was based on simple fraud perpetrated on gullible would-be-believers by untrained children and sustained by the self-deception of millions. There were countless instances of extraordinary phenomena reported by credible observers. Yet at the same time, many of the claims were so ludicrous that it is hard to believe they were made by people with their wits around them. Credulity is challenged, too, by the "parlor-trick" character of the spirits' performances – floating guitars and luminous tambourines – and by the content of the alleged communications, which for the most part were trivial and childish. Even when there is evidence to support the view that something paranormal was occurring, the evidence for its supramundane origin is weak.

CONTEXT: The social, religious, and intellectual climate in the United States in the 1840s was admirably suited to the outbreak of the spiritualist mania. For the great majority of Americans, religion was a central element in their lives, and this was periodically reinforced by revivals (see AMERICAN REVIVALISM). This is true to such an extent that New York State, where the spiritualist mania originated, became known as the "burned-over district." At the same time, there were numerous sects and communities whose practices incorporated visions, ecstasies, and purported communication with otherworldly entities, including spirits of the dead. This was the period when the Mormon religion was created, thanks to divine revelation vouchsafed to New England country folk; individual prophets such as Andrew Jackson Davis were spreading ideas linking this world to the next. In 1850 "in Providence [Rhode Island] there was an unusual number of fanatics on the subject of spiritualism, and I observed that the fanaticism took mostly a religious turn, and was exhibited by persons who had been over-zealous in religious enthusiasm."[248]

The Fox sisters: The mania was triggered by happenings in the home of the Fox family, in Hydesville, New York, a house which had for some years been the scene of unaccountable shakings of the walls and furniture, and the sound of footsteps and knockings. Only two of the seven sisters were living at home at the time, Margaretta, aged 14, and Kate, 12. The family went to bed early on the night of Friday, March 31, 1848. Frightened by the sounds, the two girls took their bedclothes into their parents' room. The mother reported in a sworn statement made a few days later:

> The girls heard the noise and tried to make a similar noise by snapping their fingers. The youngest girl is about twelve years old. She is the one who made her hand go. As fast as she made the noises with her hands or fingers, the sounds followed up in the room…It made the same number of raps the girl did. The other girl, who is in her fifteenth year, then spoke, in sport, and said, "Now, do just as I do. Count one, two, three, four." etc., at the same time striking one hand in the other. The blows which she made were repeated…Then I said to the noise "Count ten," and it made ten strokes or noises. Then I asked the ages of my different children successively, and it gave the number of raps corresponding to the ages of each of my children.[249]

From these simple beginnings they moved on to questions, to which the raps replied after an alphabetical code had been established. (It is noteworthy that, from the very start, the Fox family was mentally prepared for otherworldly communication and was quick to improvise procedures to achieve it.) As the questioning became more elaborate, the family learned that the rappings were done by a spirit, who eventually identified himself as a 31-year-old peddler who had been murdered, his body buried under the house.

Neighbors were invited to verify the proceedings. They too heard the raps, asked questions of their own, and received satisfactory answers. Many of them signed detailed eyewitness statements.[250] "Hundreds flocked to the house to see the wonders," and life became so difficult that the two girls were sent away. Margaretta went to stay with their older sister Leah in Rochester, Kate was taken in by Capron, the level-headed historian of the early days of the movement, in his household at Auburn for several weeks, where she was tested in every conceivable way.

> She slept with the ladies of the house – different ones – and was tested by them, as well without a dress as with. No kind of device was left untried to discover if there could be any trick, or any way of accounting for the strange occurrences on any known laws, applicable to mundane phenomena. It was at this time that the matter was finally settled, in my mind, in regard to the spiritual origin of the sounds.[251]

Interest spread with extraordinary rapidity. The

demand to sit with the girls became so great, and their expenses so heavy, that they felt justified in requesting payment. "Our regular charge was $1 per person, and, for a private séance of an hour, $5 for two or more persons. These figures had been prescribed to us [by the spirits]."[252]

While staying in Rochester, Margaretta was instructed, again by the spirits, to hire the largest hall in the town to demonstrate their powers. On November 14, 1848, a meeting was held at the Corinthian Hall, and public opinion was at once sharply divided between enthusiasts who welcomed and believed in the phenomena, and skeptics who deplored and denied them. The opposition was vigorous: "They were denounced by the bigoted and superstitious as impostors; or, if they could not dispute the facts, they were charged with being in league with the devil."[253] Others took a different approach: a newspaper in Auburn claimed that "Mr. Fox himself, at whose house the miracles were performed, had contrived the whole matter by an ingenious arrangement of wires, springs etc, and was enabled to make a great variety of supernatural sounds, and to get up many wonderful sights, such as the locomotion of chairs, tables, books and other household fixtures."[254] However, no springs or wires were noticed by the hundreds of people who swarmed into the house, many of them looking out for just such evidence of imposture.

After the public demonstration, a committee was formed to investigate, and when it failed to produce any evidence of imposture, a second was formed, which likewise failed. Though this only further angered the skeptics, it encouraged the girls' supporters. "The public meetings had done their work, and set a ball in motion which has already rolled over the whole Union, and much of the civilized world besides. The attention of the public was called to it. The press commenced its comments generally in ridicule, but still in a way that aroused the curiosity of people to know what it was."[255]

The sisters moved from one friend's place to another, finally ending up in New York in June 1850, taking rooms at Barnum's Hotel where they were visited by hundreds of curious people and besieged by reporters who on the whole treated them kindly. One of the most famous was the redoubtable journalist Horace Greeley, who while withholding any commitment as to the implications of the phenomena, was persuaded that the sisters were not impostors and became a kind of patron. Other visitors were less enthusiastic. A Mr. Elliott, after receiving a quantity of false information from the spirits, concluded "that the three women were shallow and simple cheats and tricksters."[256]

In 1851, Ruth Culver, a relative by marriage of the Fox sisters, publicly stated that, after at first believing in the girls' sincerity, she had developed doubts. To test them, she had offered to help the girls in their manifestations. They had welcomed her offer and showed how they produced the raps by using their toes. After about a week's practice, she herself learned how to do it. While her statement has a ring of plausibility, it contained substantial errors of fact. Even if there was any truth in it, it can hardly have been the entire truth. The sisters were tested time and time again, by competent and intelligent people many of whom were eager to expose imposture, yet they were never detected in any fraudulent conduct.[257]

Although by this time many others had manifested mediumistic powers, the sisters continued to be the leading lights of the movement, as it had then become. They visited Europe where they gave successful demonstrations and emerged unscathed from investigations. Both married – Kate to an English businessman, Margaretta to the Arctic explorer Elisha Kent Kane – but both lost their husbands prematurely.

On October 21, 1888, a huge crowd gathered at the New York Academy of Music to hear the sisters confess that their mediumship had been a fake from start to finish. "'It's a fraud!' Margaretta insisted, 'Spiritualism is a fraud from beginning to end! It's all a trick! There's no truth in it!'" Her confession was greeted with a whirlwind of applause.[258] That same year, in a book authorized by Margaretta and Kate, they detailed their long life of deception.[259]

That book, however, suffered from serious inaccuracies. Margaretta states she was age 8 when the Hydesville knockings occurred, when in fact she was 14. Verbatim transcripts of interviews with the sisters are evidence that they were in a highly emotional state, enhanced by alcohol abuse (both were to die of alcoholism[260]). Despite their fame, both sisters were now widows living in near-poverty without support, so there is the possibility that they yielded to pressure – a possibility strengthened when, within a year, Margaretta retracted her confession. She told the *Celestial City*, a New York spiritualist periodical, "Would to God I could undo the injustice I did the cause of spiritualism, when, under the strong psychological influence of persons inimical to it, I gave expression to utterances that had no foundation in fact."[261]

Even if Margaretta's first confession is accepted, this by no means conclusively establishes that the entire spiritualist movement was built on a deliberate fraud. The Fox sisters were not alone. Throughout the United States, and subsequently farther afield, thousands of others were producing similar phenomena within a few weeks of the Hydesville episode. Many of them, doubtless, were deceiving themselves or knowingly cheating, but the best of the testimony was impressive. The neighbors who crowded into the Fox's home may have been happy to believe the phenomena were genuine, but reading their signed statements, it is evident that they were unlikely to allow themselves to be duped by two adolescent girls, and that they made every effort to detect imposture if it existed.

The Fox sisters provided the model for the millions who participated in the spiritualist mania, yet they were never in any sense the leaders of the movement. They were its figureheads at most. They were, after all, two adolescent girls of limited education and no knowledge of the world beyond the small-town life of provincial America. But they won the respect of many reputable and intelligent people, and so people flocked to see them perform, and left wondering if they, too, might have, in however lesser degree, the same gift. The spiritualist mania was a self-propagandizing movement, not imposed from above as a divine revelation, but growing of its own accord by the response it provoked from those it touched.

The spread of the movement: The rapidity with which the spiritualist mania swept across the United States astonished all contemporary observers. A great many of those who witnessed the demonstrations of the Fox sisters resolved, when they were back in their homes, to see whether they could reproduce the same effects, and many found they could. Capron reports that in the summer of 1850 there were about a hundred mediums performing in his hometown of Auburn. In 1851 between fifty and sixty circles were active in Philadelphia "composed of Presbyterians, Quakers, Unitarians, Baptists, Methodists, Come-outers, Infidels and Atheists."[262] In the same year it was calculated that there must be some 1,200 practicing mediums in Cincinnati.[263] By 1853 the number of spiritualists in New York was estimated at 40,000, meeting in about 300 "magnetic circles," and twice that number in Brooklyn and outlying suburbs. Even in distant San Francisco, already sufficiently excited by the gold rush, twenty mediums were plying their

British illusionist William Marriott, circa 1910, shows how easy it was to fake ghostly pictures. He was known for investigating and exposing fake mediums.

trade – for a trade it had now become, with professional mediums charging for their services, which they advertized in local newspapers. This example is from the *Boston Herald*:

SPIRITUAL MANIFESTATIONS. – Mrs. A L Coan, declared to be the best medium for rapping and writing by the influence of departed spirits in Boston, will receive company for sittings every day in the week, from nine o'clock A.M. till ten P.M. Sittings, fifty cents each. Mrs. Coan will give sittings in the house of any person who may apply.[264]

But the professionals were a small minority compared with the tens and perhaps hundreds of thousands of domestic practitioners, who found that some member of the family was gifted, or who exchanged visits with neighbors who numbered a medium among them. Throughout small-town and rural America, the mania flourished without professional help. James Sargent, a Boston author, in 1853 found spiritualism being practiced even in log cabins whose inhabitants dwelt "in a state but little removed from barbarism." Though he could not imagine how they had spread to these people, he found that "rappings and all the other spiritual manifestations were of common occurrence." He describes entering a cabin to find the villagers occupied in communicating by raps; he witnessed tables and chair being moved and tipped over, "and many other Puck-like gambols."[265]

Indeed, what adds to the extraordinary character of the mania is the fact that there was no active proselytizing. Though the Fox sisters, and a handful of other renowned mediums, caught the newspaper headlines, there were no charismatic figures directing individuals with eloquent urgings, no missionaries going from town to town drumming up support. The excitement seemed to spread of its own accord, driven only by its inherent appeal, from one home to another. Demonstrations by the Fox sisters certainly played their part at first, but clearly only a relatively small number could attend their séances in person. Public meetings contributed, but these too were the expression of local interest rather than part of an organized campaign. "A great variety of gifts in the direction of physical writing, healing, seeing, and trance mediumship also became rapidly manifest in various families of the highest respectability, and the great majority of these developments took place irrespective of Miss Fox's presence, although her visit first called the attention of the community to the subject."[266] A factor that doubtless contributed to the widespread popularity of the phenomenon was that, while visits to professional mediums were expensive, home séances cost nothing.

Conditions at the early séances, even as described by their supporters, were fairly wild. The following description comes from a commentator who, though one of the movement's most enthusiastic members, could deplore its extravagances:

In some of the circles where entranced clairvoyant or impressional media presided, the wildest scenes of confusion would often prevail. Two or three of "the prophets" would be jabbering in unknown tongues at once, while others would be shouting the war whoop of the Red Indian. "Apostolic" letters, in miserable grammar and worse spelling, were palmed off as genuine productions from the seventh sphere; and all the crudities of impressible minds, stimulated half to frenzy by the contagious excitement of the times, were set down as direct communications from exalted ancients whose authoritative teachings no doubt emanated from the fantastic imaginings of self-psychologized persons.[267]

Nevertheless, extraordinary phenomena were being reported, often vouched for by people who were unquestionably sincere. The most common were, of course, communications with the spirits of the dead. Understandably, curiosity as to what we may expect in the next world was a predominant theme. Sitters were delighted to learn that when they went to the next world they would be received at a welcoming party, arranged by their relatives who had preceded them; there would be music and dancing. Many were no doubt relieved to learn that there is no marriage in the next world, but that "every spirit has its partner of the opposite sex." For the serious-minded, there will be lectures: for the frivolous, whist-parties.[268]

Information about living conditions in the next world came flooding in, often contradictory, but always optimistic. Whole books of revelations were written by the spirits themselves to enlighten the living. The freethinker Thomas Paine, for example, described his progress through the concentric spheres of the spirit world, helpfully supplying a diagram. His guide, the Virgil to his Dante, was the Quaker William Penn. The book-length account was transcribed through automatic writing by the Reverend Charles Hammond.[269]

Meanwhile, there were marvels a-plenty to excite

the wonder of those on Earth. Emma Hardinge [Britten], spiritualism's most diligent supporter, reported in 1870:

> ...upwards of five thousand portraits of deceased persons have been executed under circumstances that rendered deception or mistake as impossible as to mistake the light of the midday sun for the glaring lamps of the city gas; thousands and thousands of heavy, ponderable bodies have floated in space without human contact; spirit hands have been formed and melted in the grasp of the examinant; pages, even to the amount of volumes, have been written by spirit hands alone; millions of forms have been seen, described and recognized as well-remembered friends, through the mediumship of total strangers; hidden things have been dragged to light; secret crimes revealed; thousands of darkened souls have been convinced of their immortal destiny by facts tested through the severest and most exhaustive scrutiny, and the few hundreds of "credulous, gullible" believers... have swelled to a mighty army of eleven millions of persons![270]

Other phenomena included healing of various kinds, including diagnosis; a twelve-year-old child prescribed cures, which proved efficacious.[271] The playing of spirit music on instruments seemingly untouched by human hands was a favorite feature of séances, and a whole repertoire of "parlor tricks" were reported which, even though they seemed hardly relevant to the serious matter of spirit communication, certainly impressed the sitters.

A curious phenomenon that links spiritualism to other forms of extraordinary behavior was the dancing impulse, which overtook some of those who attended meetings. "The dancing mediums are old and young, and of both sexes. Sometimes the dance is performed in a circle of three or four persons, but not always. The movements are very eccentric, yet often exceedingly graceful...There was a peculiar feature in this display of spirit-power which arrested my attention. No one who danced desired it, neither could they stop it. They sometimes made an effort (for they were conscious) to sit down or fall down, but they could not do either."[272]

There was little attempt at scientific investigation. For the believers, the evidence of their own senses sufficed; for the unbelievers, the whole matter was undeserving of serious attention. An exception was Robert Hare, an engineer who reasoned that it should be possible to determine "if the manifestations attributed to spirits could be made without mortal aid" and constructed a device for this purpose, which he named "The Spiritoscope." Though insisting that "it were impossible for any one to be more incredulous than I was when I commenced my investigations... by deciding the question affirmatively they led to the author's conversion." He went on to build a second machine to enable the spirits to move furniture independently of the medium, but the spirits were unable or unwilling to use it effectively.[273]

Spiritualists of an inquiring mind would question the spirits, who would sometimes satisfy their curiosity. They explained how spirit writing was done: "The spirit who was best adapted to this purpose, approached the medium whose hand and arm were to be employed, at a distance of about two miles from the earth; then he breathed out the spiritual atmosphere which he inhaled towards the individual who was writing and in this manner caused a complete chain of spiritual substance to be established between the directing spirit and the system of the medium, by which chain a perfect connection was formed."[274]

Anna Blackwell, subsequently the translator of French spiritist Kardec into English, reported a séance where there was some delay in establishing communication with the spirits. One of the mediums "told us that we must be patient, for they would soon have prepared 'the battery,' and that already a crowd of our friends were there, and ready to communicate as soon as the telegraph could be in a state to act."[275] A good many people volunteered explanations for the rappings, which had sparked off the mania and which continued to be a staple feature of séances. The source was generally supposed to be the ankle and knee bones, which could be made to produce a variety of sounds. New York journalist Chauncey Burr, after attending séances with the best professionals, claimed, "I can now produce 'mysterious rapping' seventeen different ways, which tricks I have learned by the detection of so many mediums."[276]

Hardly less remarkable than the enthusiasm of the believers was the violence of their opponents. The antagonism shown towards the spiritualists was frequently as exceptional as the fervor of the believers. Margaretta Fox was staying with friends in Troy, near Albany, where a group of Irish Catholics determined that she must be destroyed, and repeated attacks were made on her or her friends or the house where she was staying; even her murder was planned, until the authorities were persuaded to intervene.[277] This was, no doubt, an extreme case, but Britten describes how "many of the houses where circles were being held were disturbed by crowds, who would gather together after night-fall, and with yells, cries, whistles and occasionally with the breaking of windows by stones and other missiles, endeavor to molest the quiet investigators in their 'unholy work of waking the dead.'"[278] Capron records that many spiritualists suffered in their business lives from being known to be believers. "More than this: men have been seized, kidnapped, and conveyed to distant states, and incarcerated in lunatic asylums, and their property as nearly confiscated as grasping relatives could make it, for no other reason than that they believed in spiritualism. Women have been declared insane, and taken from their homes..."[279]

Although the Spiritualists constituted no formal body, still less an organized church, for most people the spiritualist experience was a religious experience, as their accounts refer continually to the heavenly origin of the phenomena. Typically, Josiah Gridley, a farmer of Southampton, Massachusetts, told in a self-published book how his family held séances at home to which the spirits of his dead relatives came, and gradually constructed a whole cosmic system of concentric spheres, thus reconciling his Christian beliefs and his spirit revelations.[280] Capron, generally sympathetic, decried those spiritualists who sought to use the manifestations as support for extreme religious beliefs. On a private circle at Providence, Rhode Island, where the messages intimated that the Second Coming of Jesus was at hand, he commented: "I have never known an instance where a medium or circle claimed to have great dignitaries for their instructors, that the communications did not consist of the most senseless twaddle, full of ranting and sheer nonsense."[281]

Such beliefs contradicted those of the established churches who were quickly up in arms against their new competitor. On June 19, 1852, a Methodist periodical reprinted an article from a Catholic paper, indicating that whatever their other differences, the churches were united against spiritualism:

> Spiritual Rappings...Our readers will hardly believe that this delusion has so spread over New England, and towns in other States, that scarcely a village can be found which is not infested with it. In most small towns several familes are possessed, the medium between the erratic ghosts and the crazy fools being, in some cases, a weak and half-witted woman, but in most instances a little girl whom her parents and friends have prostituted to this wicked trade. Most of the mediums, who are sometimes, but not always, put into a mesmeric sleep before starting in search of the ghosts, become stark, staring mad, and so do many of the believers. Not a week passes that does not see some one of them commit suicide or go to the mad-house. All of the mediums give unequivocal signs of some abnormal, unnatural, disturbance of their bodily and mental functions. Some of them discover indications of what looks like genuine possession by a devil.[282]

The press almost gleefully reported insanity and suicide linked to spiritualism. In April 1853 the *New York Herald* told of a Mr. Junius Alcott whose brain had been deranged by spiritual rappings and had thrown himself onto the wheel of a water mill. The following month the *Courier and Inquirer* reported that six people had been admitted to the lunatic asylum of the state of Indiana, the only cause of their derangement being spirit rappings. The *Cleveland Herald* reported that a young man named Peabody hanged himself in a barn as a result of absorbing himself in spirit rappings. *The New York Times* reported the self-destruction of a 38-year-old printer named Langdon in consequence of attending the Fox sisters' circle.[283]

Opposition of a different kind came from intelligent skeptics, who investigated the phenomena, or gave it a decent hearing, before concluding that there was no need to have recourse to the spirits of the dead. Asa Mahan, president of Cleveland University, conducted his own first-person investigation. While unable to dismiss the phenomena, he felt justified in concluding: "Such is Spiritualism. We have examined its high claims, and found them empty and vain. We have handled the spirits and found them absolute insubstantialities. We have scrutinized the facts set forth as the basis of the system, and found them wholly mundane in their character, and presenting no evidence whatever of a super-mundane origin."[284]

Capron, the sympathetic chronicler who housed and studied Kate Fox for several weeks in 1848, recognized in 1852 that there was much chaff along with the wheat, much of it "unworthy of a child of half-a-dozen years...It will be found that there is much, not only in Rochester but in every place where these phenomena have prevailed to any great extent, that is the result rather of a peculiar nervous sensibility and susceptibility, than of any intelligent agency operating out of or independent of, the individuals exercised in various ways, which a too credulous class of individuals have attributed to the influence of spirits...Great care should be exercised in the investigation of this subject, and, while all due weight is given to the claims and influences of superior intelligences, we should be cautious about adopting every singular exercise of the nerves or body as an emanation from spirits."[285]

Spiritualism in Europe: News of the events in America rapidly spread to Europe, and though nothing approaching the American mania occurred beyond its shores, considerable excitement was generated. Maria Hayden was the first professional American medium to take her business to Europe, arriving in England in 1852 accompanied by her husband and a Mr. Stone, a lecturer in "electro-biology," and she was soon followed by others, though whether from a desire to spread the good news or to tap a market which back in America was saturated is a matter of opinion. In 1855 one of Mrs. Hayden's clients passed on his findings in a book significantly entitled *Mesmerism and Media*, with full instructions how to develop the alleged spiritual findings in every family."[286]

Spirit circles quickly established themselves in London, Paris, and other cities, and spread into the provinces, but without the fervor and intensity displayed in America, and on the whole without any religious connotations. It became highly professional, the mediums vying with one another for customers. In 1853, clients of Mrs. Roberts in London were warned by her attendant spirits: "Wo be to those who believe in these people named Haydens! They are not words and responses from God, but from the devil."[287] No doubt Mrs. Hayden's spirits were equally outspoken about Mrs. Roberts's.

Above all, it was table-turning and table-speaking that caught the European public's fancy. The *Augsburger Zeitung* for March 30, 1853, reported: "Since about eight days ago, our town has been in a state difficult to describe. It is completely absorbed in a marvel which no one had dreamt of until the arrival of the steamship Washington from New York. Instead of discussing the price of tobacco or the new Ericsson machine, everyone is talking about the moving table or the dancing table. There isn't a household hereabouts where everyone isn't preoccupied with this fantastic promenade."[288]

Known as the *Tischbruken* or the *Klopfgeister*, the dancing table or the gymnastic spirit took the fancy of the German populace in the spring and summer of 1853, giving rise to an epidemic briefer and less intense than in the United States, but equally pervasive while it lasted. On the April 13, Dr. Schauenberg, a professor at Bonn, went with his wife to visit some friends to observe the manifestations, which he supposed an amusement for women and children. "I agreed to go with a certain repugnance to be involved in this foolishness...but I saw and I was convinced. For five hours we made experiments of every kind, all admirably successful, and of a nature to tame the most recalcitrant skepticism." With admirable thoroughness, he describes how the assembled company formed a circle, touching hands round a small three-legged table, which after a wait of about half an minute began to move this way and that, following the commands of one or other of the company turning clockwise or anti-clockwise, directing itself towards a nominated person, moving faster or slower, stopping then starting again. The professor was convinced that no one was exerting any pressure on the table either then or during the period of question-and-answer when the table would tip the requisite number of times to correctly answer questions such as the age of the sitters, the number of children they had, and so on. Further experiments, equally successful, were carried out with a larger table and a mahogany commode.[289]

Similar performances were taking place in France, where the popular magazine *L'Illustration* reported, "Go where you will, all you'll hear is talk of table turning!" Count Théobald Walsh described many séances; at a friend's house, two children placed their hands on a stool that proceeded to dance in perfect tempo accompanying their music-teacher's playing, switching from waltz to polka, from mazurka to an Alsatian folk-dance with which the children could not have been familiar.[290]

Incidents equally remarkable were reported in England. A skeptical observer decided to see for himself what this business was all about, and experimented with a Catholic priest and a lawyer who seemed to be in touch with the spirit of a foul-mouthed bargee. Sitting round a table, they contacted a spirit who claimed to be the devil. They asked for evidence: "We were sitting with only the tips of our fingers on the table, but it forthwith rose up quite perpendicularly, and came down with a crash that completely shivered it to pieces. I have not the slightest idea how it was done – but it certainly was done. A large portion of the table was reduced to a condition that fitted it for a match factory."[291]

The question – How is it done? – was put to scientists, who generally responded with some version of the "unconscious pressure" explanation. The chemist Michael Faraday was able to show that unconscious muscular action could produce many of the effects, and a committee of scientists endorsed this in 1853, though it could not explain Davies' adventure with the splintering table. Lord Macaulay was disgusted when his family insisted on experimenting at his own breakfast table, but he could not deny what all his guests had seen: a long, heavy table moving about of its own accord. In Paris, the Emperor and Empress had to believe the evidence of their own eyes when in 1855 the celebrated medium Home caused a massive wooden table to rise more than a meter into the air.[293] Even if trickery was possible in so public a place as the Tuileries palace, what mechanism could have produced such an effect?

Many were concerned that these practices could be dangerous. A Leipzig doctor warned that ailments could be transmitted by the fluid, which, passing from hand to hand, made the tables move. At Roth, a Jewish tradesman died while taking part in a table-turning séance, as did a 16-year-old boy in Vienna. At Liège, a shoemaker went out of her mind when she asked the table how long she had to live and received just two raps in reply.[293]

Agénor de Gasparin, a Swiss count, conducted impressive experiments in 1854. No spiritualist, he was persuaded that whatever was moving the tables was something natural, not supernatural. But like many observers, he considered Faraday's explanation inadequate, for his experiments showed that the table would often move even when no one was touching it.[294]

The table-turning mania was intense while it lasted, but it did not last long. Spiritualism became an established belief-system, with its own organizations and periodicals. In France it took the form of *Spiritisme* under the leadership of Allan Kardec, in which form it was exported to Latin America where it rapidly took root. Interested researchers such as Agénor Gasparin continued to study the phenomenon, and psychical research established itself as a form of scientific inquiry. But as a collective activity the spiritualist mania gradually lost the broad popular appeal of its heyday, and became a minority pursuit.

COMMENT: Some idea of what the spiritualist movement meant to Americans of the 1850s comes across in this extract from a Philadelphia report:

> For the first time their ears had been saluted with sounds from the other world; the dark and impenetrable gulf, hitherto existing between them and the eternal future, had been annihilated as if by magic; that awful veil, through which their mental vision had never before penetrated, was at once withdrawn, and they were enabled to inhale through their physical senses sweet and soothing intelligence from the celestial spheres. Long absent friends stood in their midst, old associations were revived, and interesting conversations were held. Parents met children; children met parents; brothers and sisters, husbands and wives, after what they had supposed an eternal separation, greeted each other in sweet and holy communion.[295]

By contrast, in April 1854, a memorial was presented to the United States Senate, signed by 13,000 persons, petitioning the U.S. government to set up a scientific commission to investigate the matter of spirit communication. The petition was presented soberly by Senator James Shields, who then added his personal comments: "Having discharged this duty, I may be permitted to say, that the prevalence of this delusion at this age of the world, among any considerable portion of our citizens, must originate, in my opinion, in a defective system of education, or in a partial derangement of the mental faculties, produced by a diseased condition of the physical organization."[296]

The dichotomy of these two viewpoints was part of the explanation for the mania. The virulence of the skeptics only served to rouse the believers to greater enthusiasm.

Case History

The Spiritualist mania took so many forms, from sober investigation to wild extravagance, from scientific inquiry to erotic displays,[297] that there can be no question of presenting a typical example. But the performances at the Koons "spirit-rooms" in Milfield, Athens County, Ohio, in 1855, give some idea of the sensational manifestations that encouraged the believers and discouraged the skeptics:

I attended three public circles in the spirit-house of Mr Koons. The presiding spirits, King, claim to be father and son, and to have lived on this earth 14,500 years ago.

These rooms will seat 25-30 persons each, and are usually full. After the circle is formed, the doors and windows are shut, the light is usually extinguished, and almost instantaneously, a tremendous blow with the large drumstick is struck on the table, when immediately the bass and tenor drums are beaten rapidly, like the roll-call for parade, waking a thousand echoes. This is continued five minutes or more, and when ended, King usually takes up the trumpet and salutes us with "Good evening, friends," and asks what particular manifestations are desired. If none are especially asked for, King often asks Mr Koons to play on the violin, the spirit-band playing at the same time on the drums, triangle, tambourine, harp, accordion, harmonica etc; the spirits perform scientifically, in very quick and perfect time. After the introductory piece on the instruments, the spirits often sing. They spoke to us, requesting us to remain perfectly silent. Presently we heard human voices singing, apparently in the distance; the sounds gradually increased, each part relatively, until it appeared as if a full choir of human voices were in our small room, singing most exquisitely. I think I never heard such perfect harmony. I don't know that the spirits attempted to utter words with their song; if they did, they succeeded in this particular no better than modern singers. But it was hardly necessary for the spirits to articulate, for every strain and modulation seemed pregnant with holy sentiments.

Spirits reconstruct their physical bodies, or portions of them, from similar elements, apparently, as those which constitute our mortal bodies. Spirits' hands and arms were reorganised in our presence, and that we might see them more distinctly they wet their hands with a weak solution of phosphorus...at one of these circles there were three hands which had been covered with this solution, and we saw them passing swiftly round the room over our heads, carrying the instruments, and playing upon the violin, accordion, triangle, harmonica and tambourine, keeping perfect time. These instruments were moved so swiftly, and near the faces of the audience, that we felt the cool atmosphere in different parts of the room. I have seen the best performances in the country, but they cannot perform equal to these spirits.

I put out my hands, and asked the spirits to shake hands with me: they did so almost instantly. I then asked them to let me examine their hands; and they placed them in mine, and I looked at them and felt them until I was entirely satisfied. The spirit-hand took a pen, and we all distinctly saw it write on paper which was lying on the table; the writing was executed much more rapidly than I ever saw mortal hand perform. At the close of the session the spirit of King took up the trumpet and gave a short lecture.[298]

SPOUSE DROPPING REVIVAL

Western New York: 1832

The Great American Revival of 1832 was especially strong in parts of Western New York along the shore of Lake Ontario in Madison and Oneida Counties. One of the leaders advocated that with the end of the world near, a man should seek their "Paradise" and their "Eve." Finding neither Paradise in their own homes or partners, they sought to find it with new relationships. People no longer felt obligated to follow traditional rules and many adults began choosing heavenly companions without regard to existing marriages. While initially such unions were supposedly purely spiritual and Platonic, soon many sexual unions took place. After a relatively short period, many men and women went back to their spouses and the religious fervor quickly faded.[299]

CONTEXT: Believing in the second coming of Christ and the imminent apocalypse, encouraged by a revival leader and perhaps in a state of hypersuggestibility from observing emotional religious meetings, many zealots began to temporarily ignore existing rules and obligations.

SPRING BREAK RIOT

Palm Springs, California: March 1986

Police moved in and arrested at least 100 students after they traveled to Palm Springs, California, on spring holiday break from college. Some of the male students became overly excited and started ripping the clothes off women, and pelting cars with bottles and rocks.[300]

SPRINGHEEL JACK SCARE

London: 1837-1838

In September 1837, three girls on Barnes Common, southwest London, reported that a man in a dark cloak, vaulting the railings of a churchyard, had torn off their clothes, then run off laughing loudly. In October, a strange account was reported from nearby Streatham, in which the drivers of a coach said that a huge creature had frightened their horses, "whether man or bird or beast they could not say." Further reports of attacks came in. On one occasion footprints were left that seemed to show that the mysterious being had "machines or springs" on his shoes, and this led quickly to the mystery predator being dubbed "Springed-heel" or "Springheel Jack."

Further events followed in quick succession. On October 11, a barmaid attending Blackheath Fair was twice molested. On the first occasion her shawl was simply pulled from her shoulders, but later, as she was going home, a laughing man "who looked like a nobleman" bounded after her in great strides and ripped her clothes with what seemed to be iron claws. An observant girl, she couldn't help noticing that he was spitting blue flames, which together with his fiery eyes and a smell of sulfur caused her to faint.

Through the closing months of the year, similar reports spread throughout southwest London as far as Kingston. In February 1838, further off in Limehouse, Lucy Scales was pounced on by a tall-cloaked man who, again, spat blue flames at her. Nor was it only women in open places who were attacked. Jane Alsop in Bow opened her door to a man who claimed to be a police officer in chase of Springheel Jack, but who then attacked her, tearing at her clothing and hair until she was rescued by members of her family. "He was wearing a kind of helmet, and a tight-fitting white costume like an oilskin. His face was hideous, his eyes were like balls of fire. His hands had great claws, and he vomited blue and white flames." On another occasion, a maidservant who answered the door was confronted by a figure so terrifying that she took leave of her senses.

Though descriptions of the monster varied in detail, they generally conformed to the description of a tall, athletic figure, dressed in a long cloak and high-heeled boots. A helmet was mentioned by some, a coat of mail by another. He had fiery eyes and claw-like fingers. Some credited him with pointed ears. A servant girl in Forest Hill was scared into fits by a figure resembling a bear.

The attacks were frightening but seldom serious. There was no attempt at rape and no serious wounding. As with the LONDON MONSTER, the intention seemed to be to cause a fright, to rip or slash clothing, and perhaps inflict superficial wounds.

Though all but a few of the incidents took place in southwest London, rumors proliferated throughout the city, and the number of attacks led to the Lord Mayor of London expressing his concern. Admiral Codrington organized a fund to offer a reward for the apprehension of Jack, personally contributing £100 – no small sum at the time. The fund eventually reached £1,000 but the reward was never claimed. Another eminent figure to take the menace seriously was the Duke of Wellington. The Victor of Waterloo, now in his sixties, set out on his horse several nights running, armed with pistols, but never caught sight of Jack.

Although many of the accounts pointed towards a supernatural being, opinion generally favored the idea that a human being was responsible. If so, the most eligible candidate was Henry de la Poer Beresford, Marquis of Waterford, a wealthy 27-year-old Irish peer, educated at Eton, who indulged himself in travel, sport, and riotous living. He was notorious for wild escapades and cruel practical jokes, and for his readiness to bet on anything. It was supposed that he was performing the role of Springheeled Jack in consequence of such a bet. Two boys, whose mother was attacked in Clapham churchyard, described the attacker as a tall, slim young man wearing dark clothing and a cape and a hat. E. Cobham Brewer[301] takes it as certain that Waterford was to blame, and Peter Haining has made out a very persuasive case for his responsibility though the evidence is admittedly only circumstantial.[302] His character was certainly in keeping, and he is known to have been resident in London at the time of many of the incidents.

However, the sheer number of assaults means that no one person could possibly have been responsible for all of them. This may be because many were purely imaginary – as was almost certainly the case – or because Jack's deeds inspired copycat attacks. Though the original Springheel Jack was never caught or even positively identified, his exploits diminished in 1838 and the panic died down in consequence. But in 1845 a Mr. Purdy of Yarmouth, wandering delirious in his nightshirt, alarmed a neighbor who called for help; he was attacked by a young man on suspicion of being "Spring-heeled Jack," though his death was attributed to natural causes.[303] Occasional reports continued to be made long after there was any chance that Waterford could have been responsible, thus Brewer reports that "even so late as 1877-1878 an officer in her majesty's service caused much excitement at Aldershot, Colchester and elsewhere by his 'spring-heel' pranks. In Chichester and its neighbourhood the tales told of this adventure caused quite a little panic, and many people were afraid to venture out after sunset…I myself investigated some of the cases reported to me, but found them for the most part Fakenham ghost tales" [natural causes misinterpreted]. By this time Jack had become a folklore figure. Folklorist Jacqueline Simpson reported that in 1887 maids who had just received their wages were afraid to go out because "there are so many of these spring-heeled jacks about," and the name was used as a popular bogey to frighten naughty children.[304]

Winged man-monster who terrified residents of Blackheath and other London suburbs from 1837 for many years but was never caught.

STARPOINT HIGH MYSTERY ILLNESS

Western New York State: 2004-2005

In 2004, Starpoint High School, in suburban Buffalo, gained a reputation for being a "tainted" school after a series of health scares. In February, a Spanish classroom was closed for over a week after parent complaints that one of the students was made ill by a substance smelling like rotten eggs. Others theorized that it was mold contamination. No cause was ever found. In September, a math classroom was shut down after students and teachers reported smelling an ammonia-like substance. Again, nothing harmful was found though rumors began to abound that there was "something in the school."[305]

Within this backdrop of fear and uncertainty, by mid-December events began to escalate. On Tuesday morning, December 14, 52 chorus members were rehearsing Christmas carols in the auditorium, preparing for a big holiday concert that evening. At 9:20 a student felt ill. Before long, more and more chorus members began to feel unwell. Within an hour, 31 were complaining of an array of symptoms including dizziness, headache, nausea, and feelings of flushness and lethargy. At least one student vomited. Some students noted a strange odor. Amid concerns of a possible bio-terror attack, an army of response teams converged on the school: State Police, FBI agents, officials from the State Department of Environmental Conservation, firefighters, ambulance personnel, and first responders. Hazardous Materials specialists donning "space suits" and breathing apparatus were also called in. The students were rushed to local hospitals as the rest of the school was locked down and eventually evacuated. Those affected quickly recovered and were released within hours. Environmental tests at Starpoint were conducted by a private firm and a separate team of experts on hazardous materials from Niagara County. All tests were negative. When the school re-opened Friday, December 17, there was tension in the air as no cause for the illnesses had been pinpointed. As a result, there were 308 absentees.[306]

On January 10, press reports cited local fears

that Starpoint was wedged between two former toxic dumps that may be responsible for the "mystery illnesses."[307] On the 13th, there was another health scare as an ammonia-like odor was detected in three classrooms. More tests were conducted – all negative.[308] Then on Friday, January 28, bus diesel fumes were blamed for a rash of nausea and headaches among students. Superintendent C. Douglas Whelan theorized that the fumes didn't dissipate in the near zero temperatures and were sucked back into the building through the air flow system.[309] But surely on cold mornings, hundreds of schools in northern states and in Canada, let their busses idle so they don't stall – and no one reports mass illness. Why Starpoint?

Folk Theories Abound

When pressed for an explanation, Starpoint school officials initially began to speculate that the chorus members "were overcome by the heat of the lights in the auditorium."[310] Again, why Starpoint? Why the chorus? Thousands of chorus rehearsals are held across the U.S. and Canada each year during which students practice for their upcoming concerts under hot lights? Young, fit chorus members stand under hot lights all the time and they don't fall ill in droves. When the "hot lights" theory proved untenable in light of other incidents at the school, the "stale air" hypothesis was evoked.

The Scare Spreads

A week after the Starpoint choral incident, 26 pupils and four teachers at another suburban Buffalo school, North Park Middle School in Lockport, suddenly fell ill with similar symptoms, only to recover quickly. Under pressure to explain what happened, school officials suggested that low levels of carbon monoxide were given off by the boiler, and the weather conditions being just right (or wrong), the gas hung around and was sucked back through the ventilation system. Lockport Superintendent Bruce Fraser remarked: "It was caused by an unusual set of circumstances...It was extremely cold, and the outside air was very still. Normally, carbon monoxide goes up the smokestack and dissipates, but the very cold temperatures and very still air created an almost inversion type condition...Instead of dissipating, conditions tended to force the carbon monoxide down and may have built up carbon monoxide levels in the (two) courtyards and areas surrounding the building." Vents in these courtyards send fresh air back through the school, supplying fresh air to the boiler system.[311]

While it's common to have very cold, still conditions in Buffalo and across North America during December, there are thousands of schools operating under similar conditions every day in North America during winter, and there are no outbreaks of sudden illness. Every one of the 30 treated at area hospitals after the incident had carbon monoxide levels within the normal range. Fraser seized on the claim that some carbon monoxide levels were slightly elevated but "well below the level of a smoker."[312] Yet, people are exposed to slightly elevated carbon monoxide levels all the time and nothing happens – crossing the road in traffic, walking in an underground car park, even standing next to the idling school busses. The carbon monoxide theory is wishful thinking. Mr. Fraser is quoted as saying that the flu situation may have worsened the students' reaction to the carbon monoxide. But what school doesn't have some illness going around at any given time?

Mr. Fraser concedes that some of the affected students "may have had their own situations aggravated when they saw other kids get sick."[313] Given the negative test results, it may have been *all* anxiety – fed by rumors.

The Power Of The Mind

Mass hysteria is the best explanation for the events at Starpoint and Lockport, but does not mean that their students are crazy or are the "nervous type" or even prone to imagination. It is not to say that it was "all in their heads." If one accepts this explanation, it means the reactions were real but were generated by anxiety.

CONTEXT: Starpoint had developed a reputation for being a "sick" school. The earlier "outbreaks" of mysterious illness at Starpoint served as proof and kept the issue alive. The Lockport incident occurred just a week after the Starpoint "mystery illness" and the prominent newspaper and television coverage that ensued.
See also: MASS HYSTERIA IN SCHOOLS.

STEVENAGE MYSTERY ILLNESS

England: September 2004

Thursday, September 9, began like any other day at Collenswood School in Stevenage, Hertfordshire, north of London. But before it was over, what happened that day would make headlines across England. Suddenly a call went out to local emergency services – there had been a "hazardous incident" at the school. Before long, ambulances and emergency personnel were rolling to the scene. In all, 55 people, all but 13 of them children between the ages of 11 and 13, were treated at the hospital with headaches and general illness. Police took no chances and soon evacuated the school's 820 students and staff.[314] After authorities searched the building, nothing was found.

Meanwhile back at the hospital, doctors could find nothing wrong with those who were taken for treatment, and they were all discharged later that day. The Hertfordshire police issued a statement that suggested a psychological cause: "After detailed examination, environmental and public-health experts have confirmed that the school poses no risk to the health of pupils and staff. Despite detailed investigations, no identifiable cause for the incident has yet been established. It is, however, clear that a number of unrelated incidents involving the health of some pupils could have contributed to a general feeling of concern at the school on Thursday."[315]

STIGMATIZATION

Stigmata can take many forms, but as a social manifestation they imply the appearance on an individual's body of wounds corresponding to the alleged wounds on the body of Jesus when he was crucified by the Romans, circa 30 CE. The phenomenon as a rule affects only individuals, but it is included here for two reasons. First, there are occasional instances of stigmata manifesting collectively, notably during the ULSTER REVIVAL. And second, although they manifest individually, they do so in conformity with existing models, that is to say, most people experience them in much the same way.

As with ALIEN ABDUCTIONS and RELIGIOUS VISIONS, a consensus protocol seems to be established for the behavior, to which the individual conforms subconsciously. Thus a manifestation of stigmata is immediately recognized and the recognition serves to validate their authenticity.

Stigmata, in this sense, are contingent on Christian belief, and consequently stigmatics are almost always Christians, and almost always Roman Catholics. A high proportion, particularly during the early centuries, were religious professionals, and those of more recent times have usually been persons noted for their piety. These generalizations, however, are not without exceptions.

The problem presented by many possibly miraculous manifestations, such as visions and possessions – are they of divine or demonic origin? – does not arise with stigmata, for if they are a miracle, it can safely be assumed that they are divine. Instead the debate is: are they of natural or supernatural origin? For this reason, the attitude of the Catholic Church has been cautious, and of the many hundreds of people who have presented stigmata, only about 60 have been officially recognized. In the remaining cases, while the reality of the signs may not be disputed, their supernatural origin is questioned.

It has been suggested that some enigmatic words of Saint Paul in his letter to the Galatians imply that he was a stigmatic: "I bear in my body the marks of the Lord Jesus." However, this is not generally accepted, and the earliest mentions of stigmatization date from the 13th century. The idea of reproducing Jesus's wounds was already in existence previous to the first detailed account relating to Francis of Assisi, who is said to have received the stigmata in 1234.[316]

Francis's stigmata seemed to set off an explosion, including nine Dominican nuns in Germany. Several further cases were reported, and since the 13th century, several hundred cases are known, and they continue to occur. In 1894, Imbert-Goubeyre published his massive catalog of 321 accounts, though he included some in which the stigmata were not visible but only sensed.[317] Since then many further cases have been revealed or have occurred.

The Nature Of Stigmata

Stigmata can take a variety of forms, but virtually all of them correspond to the wounds supposedly incurred by Jesus in the course of his crucifixion, and they have little meaning unless the crucifixion took place as alleged. A complete set of stigmata includes: wounds piercing hands and feet where he was nailed to the cross, a wound in his side where he was pierced by a soldier's spear, injuries to his back resulting from scourging, and to shoulders from carrying the cross, and bleeding on the brow caused by a crown of thorns. An additional feature is weeping bloody tears, which trickle down the cheeks. Stigmata reflect some differences of opinion as to the manner in which the crucifixion and other actions were carried out. Some stigmatics locate the side wound on the left, others on the right. This, and the fact that in some cases the manner of the stigmata corresponds to an image of the crucified Jesus with which the stigmatic is familiar, supports the view that stigmata are modeled not on direct knowledge divinely transmitted, but in conformity with a perceived model. Though they are usually very painful, stigmata are welcomed by the stigmatic because it is perceived as participating in the sufferings of Jesus and thus helping to redeem sinful mankind.

Stigmata vary greatly in their duration. Padre Pio (1887-1968) had them more or less permanently from 1918 till his death. Others had them once only, or once a year like Christine Marie de la Croix who had them each Good Friday. Others, like Stefania Quinzani of Soncino (1457-1530), had them every week over a period of years.

Stigmata rarely present independently from other symptoms. A majority of stigmatics are medically sick, some almost extravagantly so. "We know of no case affecting a completely healthy and robust body from a biological point of view, or of an exuberant vitality. So far as we know, stigmata appear only on enfeebled bodies, whether by illness, fasting, ascetic practices or mortifications. We will go further: it seems that it is a question of individuals whose nervous system is enfeebled, irritable, hypersensitive and particularly open to suggestion."[318] While it is open to question whether Dom Alois Mager's finding is entirely true, it is certainly largely so, as the life of the Dutch stigmatic Lydwine van Scheedam (1380-1433)[319] provoked the comment that she was "like a museum of pathology,"[320] and there are many accounts of stigmatics suffering from such an accumulation of internal ailments and external afflictions that it would seem no one could survive them. Several claimed to live without food over long periods, including Theresa Neumann (see case history that follows). Bleeding, particularly from the eye sockets, is common. The Cistercian nun Lutgardis de Tongres (1182-1246), in ecstasy while meditating on the Passion of Jesus, was inundated with blood that flowed from her hands and face. Louise Lateau (1850-1883) produced profuse streams of blood, under close medical observation. A great many were subject to ecstasies and visions, but also with seizures similar to those afflicted with CONVENT HYSTERIA, provoking the Jesuit commentator Herbert Thurston to inquire, "Is this disease, or are these the strange ways in which the soul is led on to higher union with God?"[321]

Stigmata can manifest on quite young children. In 1744 Magdeleine Morice, a dressmaker of Brittany, experienced them when she was eight, and Angèle de la Paix in 1619 at age 9, Agnes de Jésus at 12, and so on. And they can manifest late in life; Christine Marie de la Croix had them in 1307 when she was 65, and Delicia di Giovanni had stigmata for 75 years till her death in 1632.

The fact of stigmatization is uncontested. Padre Pio, one of the most venerated but also most controversial of stigmatics, was examined on many occasions by qualified medical people, who were in no doubt that the lesions existed. "Nonetheless, the sacred tribunal [Congregation of the Holy Office] has decided that these marks are not necessarily supernatural in their origin, a pronouncement which must give pause to many over-enthusiastic believers in the marvellous."[322] Other well-observed cases include three 20th century stigmatics, Jane Hunt and Dorothy Kerin (both Anglicans), and Eva McIsaac.[323] There is, therefore, sound medical evidence that stigmatization occurs, that physical wounds are simulated, that blood flows. Louise Lateau (1850-1883), for example, was estimated to lose an average of 250 grams, that is, a large tumblerful – each time she bled.[324]

Catholic commentators recognize that stigmatization can take place in a number of ways and are not necessarily supernatural.[325] So long as the symptoms can occur in some other context, there is a possibility of a natural explanation. Catholic theologians distinguish between mystical stigmatization, which occurs in association with mystical activity; charismatic stigmatization, which is bestowed as a divine gift; and natural stigmatization, which occurs as the result of hysteria and auto-suggestion. But there is no consensus as to the criteria whereby these can be distinguished.

Stigmatization occasionally occurs to Protestant Christians. Besides the two Anglican cases mentioned above, Cloretta Robinson, a young Afro-American Baptist girl in California, presented classic stigmata before Easter 1972.[326] In 1993 psychologist Stanley Krippner investigated Amyr Amiden, a 52-year-old healer and psychic raised as a Muslim who told Krippner that "all religions are the same to him now." In the presence of several qualified observers, though in informal circumstances, Amiden presented stigmata resembling those of Christian stigmatics, apparently triggered by the mention of "Christ" in the conversation. Krippner also states that devout Muslims have reproduced the battle-wounds of Mohammed.[327]

Nearly all stigmatics report visions, in which they often seem to be directly involved. Anna-Katharina Emmerich (1774-1624) and Theresa Neumann (see case history that follows) are two notable examples, and the reports of people present at Teresa Higginson's participation in the Passion of Jesus testify to her seeming participation in the events as they unfolded.[328] Though these visionaries were ostensibly playing a part in the events, the errors and improbabilities leave no doubt that their visions, however intensely experienced, were imaginative fictions based on their reading and meditation. Their emotional involvement in these fantasies goes hand in hand with the powers of visualization that result in their stigmata.

Dermographism is a well-established psychosomatic process. Indeed, being so visible, it is probably the clearest example of the mind influencing the body. Toussaint Barthélémy cites this striking case:

> A mother is arranging china in a cupboard while her small child is playing near an unlit stove at the far end of the room. Suddenly, with her hands full of china, she turns to see that her child has accidentally touched the mechanism which brings down the screen; the child is in such a position that the screen would drop onto its neck like a guillotine. Though she rescues her child in time, there forms on the back of her own neck a raised mark at the point where the child would have been hit: it is there some hours later when her doctor pays his visit.[329]

The woman is described as nervous and impressionable, as is the case with virtually all stigmatics. The fact that such cases can occur outside the Christian context justifies D. Georges Wunderle when he wrote: "One can, from a psychological point of view, regard the process of stigmatisation as a typical case of ideoplasty."[330]

Bleeding from the eyes, which frequently accompanies stigmatization, is also reported in non-religious contexts. Professor Magnus Huss of Stockholm had a patient, Maria K., diagnosed as hysterical, who produced a flow of blood from the eyes, ears, and mouth. She became an object of curiosity, attracting visitors who left presents for her. And perhaps encouraged by the presents they left, she reached the point where she could produce a hysterical attack in the course of which she hemorrhaged at will.[331]

COMMENT: Stigmatization is predominantly a Christian experience, experienced mostly by Roman Catholics. For true believers, it is a miraculous event, a gift bestowed by God on favored subjects, who though they feel intense pain, accept it gratefully as a gift from God. For others, including many devout Catholics, a psychological explanation is more plausible.

The abundance of testimony, much of it made under oath, lead many to agree with the noted Jesuit researcher Herbert Thurston when he stated, "We can certainly assert with confidence that the wounds could not possibly have been self-inflicted either consciously or unconsciously, and the material conditions have nearly always been such that collusion or fraud are unthinkable."[332]

The primary process is generally held to be auto-suggestion, and this is Thurston's view. He sees stigmatics as especially devout persons who develop an obsession, which he designates as a "crucifixion complex."[333] Intense meditation on the crucifixion story results in the body simulating the outward signs of the experience, while also experiencing the pain, which they are willing to accept because it makes them feel as though they are participating in the sufferings of Jesus. This accounts for the fact that the great majority of stigmatics are devoted Christians, and predominantly Catholics, but it also explains the fact that a small number of stigmatics are Protestants, or not even Christians at all. The common factor is not so much the belief itself, as the intensity with which it is held and concentrated upon. If the individual is sufficiently impressionable, suggestion or auto-suggestion will complete the process.

A feature which supports the auto-suggestion hypothesis is that the nature of the wounds varies greatly from one stigmatic to another. If the stigmata were indeed a divine infliction, we would expect them to be consistent, whereas in practice we find wide differences as to where they are located on the body and in the form they take. Some are hardly more than superficial scratches, though bleeding nonetheless, while others are deep incisions that appear to perforate the hand or foot from front to back. In yet others, the blood seems to well up through the skin without any wound as such. In some stigmatics the stigmata disappear between manifestations, while in others there is a permanent mark, albeit it may be dormant between eruptions. These differences point to a process whereby the subconscious creates the stigmata in accordance with preconceived ideas.

Further support for the auto-suggestion hypothesis comes from the 1932 experiment of Alfred Lechler, who by suggestion induced a 29-year-old patient Elizabeth, a Lutheran protestant, to reproduce stigmata on hands and feet, on the forehead, also bloody tears, after attending a cinema show of Jesus's crucifixion which strongly affected her.[334] Another interesting feature is the fact that many stigmatics, embarrassed by their stigmata, pray that they would go away, not wishing to be seen to be favored. Thurston comments: "Whether this withdrawal of the external manifestations ought to be described as miraculous, or whether it was the natural result of concentration upon the fixed idea that all such outward marks of God's favour were dangerous to the soul and ought to be repressed, is perhaps not the least perplexing of the many problems which beset the inquirer into these psycho-physical phenomena."[335]

A further consideration is the fact that stigmatics are far from being a typical cross-section of mankind. Not only are they overwhelmingly female, but they are frequently sufferers from ailments, have a history of accidents, or have some other circumstances which could predispose them. Even Lechler's patient Elizabeth had a history of abuse and illness.

If auto-suggestion is part of the explanation, then the question arises, are stigmatics modeling themselves unconsciously on previous stigmata, or is it a direct result of intense meditation? Tests would probably show that stigmatics are found among the more suggestible sections of the population, but there has not been sufficient testing for this to be more than a hypothesis. In the early days of scientific stigmata research it was often proposed that stigmatics were hysterics. But even using the term loosely, this is not a very helpful suggestion. Thurston comments: "However little we may be disposed to admit that the physical phenomena of mysticism can be reduced to hysteria, still it cannot be disputed that the ecstasy of the mystic and the trance of the hysterical patient are very closely allied and cannot always be readily distinguished. The mimetic tendencies of the hysterical diathesis are the commonplace of all writers on the subject."[336]

If the auto-suggestion/hysteric explanation is accepted, however, it leaves us, as the Catholic psychologist Lhermitte reminded us, with a problem: why does this natural process almost invariably take this particular form?[337] The answer is suggested by other entries in this Encyclopedia, such as UFO ABDUCTION MANIA, CONVENT HYSTERIA, etc. For such a belief to become epidemic and recurrent, an "authorized myth" must be created which, because it is widely recognized and accepted, provides a model for the individual and a point of recognition for the observer.

In the case of stigmata, the wounds of Jesus are the only model that has achieved sufficient status to inspire auto-suggested imitation combined with the intensity of feeling required to trigger the process.

Case History

The case of Theresa Neumann (1898-1962) is the best observed and most discussed of all stigmatization cases. A huge literature has been devoted to her, mostly taking the view that she was supernaturally gifted. Yet even within the Catholic Church there were many who concluded that her stigmata were a natural phenomenon.

A Catholic peasant girl from Konnersreuth in Bavaria, Germany, Theresa was noted for her piety as a child. Her greatest wish was to become a missionary, and she put aside her savings to provide a dowry to enter a religious order for this purpose. Like most girls of her station, she was employed as a servant on a neighboring farm. In March 1918, while helping to put out a fire, she was afflicted with some kind of internal pain and collapsed. In hospital, this led to other afflictions, she became temporarily blind and deaf, and her legs were paralyzed, though the symptoms – and her state of health generally – fluctuated continually, so that she would be cured of one ailment only to be afflicted by another.[338] However, in 1920, when she applied for an invalid's pension, four doctors examined her and diagnosed "very grave hysteria, with blindness and partial paralysis." Had there been any organic illness, they would surely have offered this as it would have provided stronger grounds for a pension. There followed five years at home in continual pain, alleviated by religious meditation. During this time she had four serious falls, not to mention such minor accidents as falling out of bed while playing with her younger brothers. Each of these might leave her unconscious, sometimes for days on end. Up to this time, however, nothing allegedly supernatural had occurred. "Before approaching the period in which extraordinary phenomena begin to appear, the results of our preliminary investigation are: on the physical plane, a series of illnesses attributed to grave hysteria; on the moral plane, no visible outstanding virtues, but several imperfections combined with the sincere piety of an ordinary Catholic peasant girl."[339]

On April 29, 1923, the day of the beatification of Thérèse of Lisieux to whom Theresa had a particular devotion, she recovered her sight. She also claimed a miraculous cure of her foot, saving it from amputation, thanks to rose leaves from Thérèse's tomb. Two years later, when Thérèse was canonized, a divine voice told Theresa she would walk, and so she did.

In March 1926, she had a series of visions relating to the passion of Jesus, and became aware of wounds in her left side, near her heart, and on her hands and feet. She did not receive the stigmata all at once, but over a period. On March 4, 1926, she received a wound in her side;[340] later in March on the back of her left hand; on April 2, the back of the right hand and the upper surfaces of her feet; but not until Good Friday 1927 were the undersides of her feet and the palms of her hands affected. They reappeared every Thursday night and disappeared on Saturday. The wounds did not always appear the same but were modified over the years.

The parish priest realized immediately that Theresa's wounds were the classic stigmata. Each week she would meditate on the Passion of Jesus, the wounds

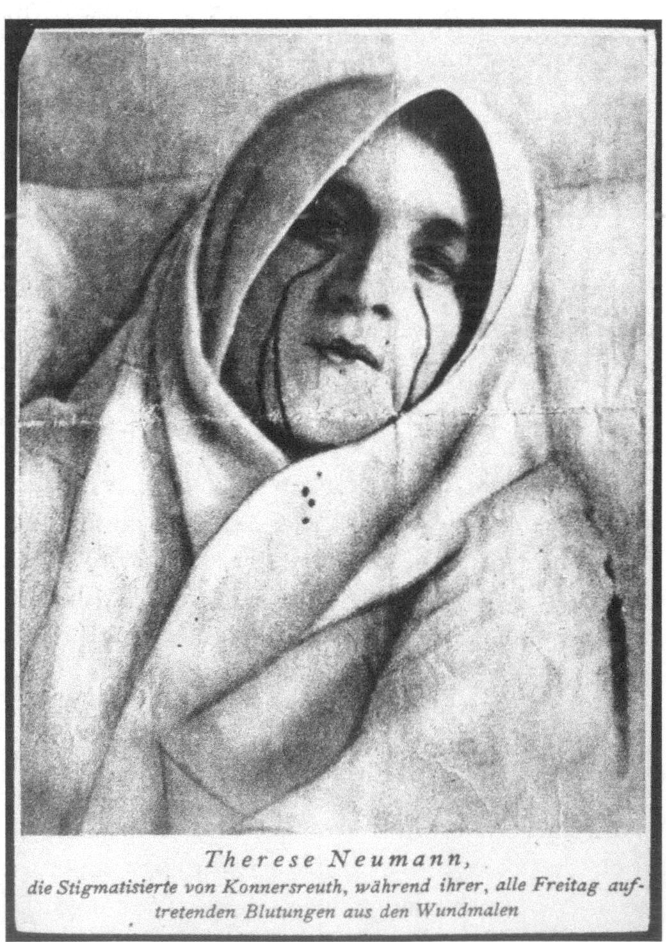

Therese Neumann, the German stigmatic of Konnersreuth, weeps blood on Good Friday, every year.

in her hands and feet would bleed, blood would flow from her eyes, and she had detailed visions that constituted a step-by-step reconstruction of Jesus's trial and crucifixion. However, these visions were not always in conformity with known or generally accepted facts. Moreover, she herself was a participant – on one occasion, Jesus actually saw her from the cross and looked at her as though to thank her! She heard the voices of the people, and those of Jesus, in Aramaic. These visions of Jesus's passion were in addition to the visions and voices that she received on a more or less everyday basis.

At Christmas 1922, she reportedly ate only a few teaspoons of coffee, tea, or fruit juice, and from Christmas 1926, claimed to stop taking any nourishment.

She had apparent out-of-body experiences and seemed to have clairvoyant powers. Pilgrims flooded to Konnersreuth, though discouraged by the Church, which never gave her any official recognition. During the Third Reich she continually opposed the Nazi regime but escaped serious harassment, presumably for fear of alienating popular opinion.

There is no doubt that Theresa was a pious person, good-natured, and friendly. Equally, there is no doubt that she suffered appallingly, and that her stigmata were physically real. On the other hand, there are circumstances that trouble the critic. Poray-Madeyski takes us step by step through Theresa's early ailments showing that all could be attributed to post-traumatic hysteria. His view is corroborated by the Catholic psychologist Lhermitte, who commented: "The manifestations presented by Theresa from 1918 to 1923 possess all the characteristics of hysterical accidents: we have the right to ask ourselves if the visions, the ecstasies, the stigmata, the sweating and weeping blood, do not draw their cause from the same source."[341]

Some rudimentary tests were carried out March 22-23, 1928, by Professor Martini, director of the medical clinic of Bonn University, in the presence of the Bishop of Regensburg and a colleague, and three other scientific colleagues. This was the nearest thing ever known to a clinical examination of a stigmatic, but they left much to be desired. Theresa's father refused to let her be taken to a clinic where examination would be facilitated. Instead, the observations were carried out in her bedroom, under the strict supervision of her family who behaved angrily and uncooperatively despite the presence of the bishop. Theresa would complain of the heat and lift her bed-covers, largely blocking her from view; her parents prevented the investigators from moving to where they could observe her.

"During these intervals, where the parents explained that Theresa needed to cool herself, I was struck by the strange and intensive movements that she made with arms and legs, movements which seemed excessive for the simple purpose of cooling her, and which left me with an unfavourable impression…" During the night the doctors went out for a short space: "It was precisely during this interval that a fresh afflux of blood occurred. The fact that on two or three occasions the observers were made to leave the room just at the time that a new flow of blood opened the wounds, wakes the suspicion that during this time something happened, which it was necessary to conceal from observation." When she displayed symptoms of her internal disorder, the signs were sometimes inappropriate. "The ensemble gave me the impression of a *mise en scène* produced arbitrarily without a true knowledge of the way in which asphyxia presents." Altogether, "I did not find any proof of the spontaneous flow of blood from the skin, and I was struck by a whole series of facts which made it my duty to preserve a very critical attitude. While I am not convinced that it is the case, my reasoning instructs me that, for psychological reasons, one cannot exclude the possibility of pious fraud."[342]

The most prominent explanations for stigmata are psychosomatic conditions versus fraud. Which explanation fits the majority of cases is open to debate.

STRAWBERRIES WITH SUGAR VIRUS

Portugal: May 2006

At least 300 Portuguese children from various schools developed a mysterious ailment characterized by breathing problems, dizziness, and rashes. Physicians have concluded that the outbreak was a case of mass suggestion and dubbed it the "Strawberries with Sugar Virus" – after the popular teen television soap opera blamed for triggering the malady. The symptoms appeared within days of an episode depicting characters coming down with similar symptoms as those caused by an imaginary virus that swept through a school. "What we concretely have is a few children with allergies and apparently a phenomenon of many other children imitating."[343] Another physician, Mario Almeida, said: "I know of no disease which is so selective that it only attacks school children.[344] Anxiety levels may also have been high as the illness coincided with final exams.

STREAKING FAD

Worldwide: 1973-1974

Streaking—running nude in public – appeared suddenly on college campuses across the United States between the late Fall of 1973 and May 1974, and soon around the world. Within a few weeks it had spread to all aspects of American life and numerous variations appeared. Soon it wasn't enough to simply streak, but people began doing it on bicycles, roller skates, motorcycles, and skis. At the University of Georgia, students even parachuted naked – though some miscalculated, alighting in a cesspool. They streaked on busy public streets, at shopping malls, and at state legislatures. In some instances, they wore only tennis shoes or ski masks. From Africa to South America, New York to Paris and St. Peter's Square in Rome, people stripped off their clothes and ran in public. While most were college students, streaking was reported among those as young as 11 and as old as 65.[345] Soon there were organized streaks on campuses to outdo rival institutions and set a new record. At one point, the University of South Carolina held the record at 520. Students at the University of Maryland soon topped this with 550. The number eventually climbed to 1,200 at the University of Colorado.[346]

CONTEXT: There is no obvious context for the streaking fad. While it did conspicuously occur shortly after the Watergate scandal and in the wake of widespread American disrespect for politicians, any association seems tenuous and speculative at best.

How widespread was streaking? Of 1,016 schools surveyed by sociologist Benigno Aguirre and his colleagues, 78 percent were estimated to have had at least one episode.[347] Then by mid-May, it ended as suddenly as it began, except for a few occasional incidents at sporting events that have become something of an institution, are usually frowned upon, and met with arrests and fines. During the streaking fad, very few people were arrested and most authorities, although perplexed by the behavior, looked upon it as humorous and harmless.[348] Even at the U.S. military academy in West Point, New York, known for its discipline and rigidity, a streaking incident involving several dozen cadets was not met by any punishment by superiors.[349]

Sociologists Robert Evans and Jerry Miller identified a pattern in college streaking episodes, starting with a small-scale incident involving one or several bold college students, typically at night. By the next day, news of the event had spread rapidly across the campus, often assisted by the local mass media. Other streaks would quickly follow, culminating in a major pre-announced incident (often referred to as a "streak-in"), attracting large crowds and local reporters, during which participants would not only streak but exhibit innovations such as the use of roller skates or bicycles, stripteases or "moonings" (baring one's buttocks in public). Several days later another streak-in would occur, and by typically the third cycle, students lost interest.[350]

Annual ritualized streaking events persist on certain college campuses. For instance, each April at the University of Michigan in Ann Arbor, upwards of 1,000 students participate in "The Naked Run" where members of the student body run in the nude to mark the end of classes for the school year.[351]

COMMENTS: As for why people engaged in streaking, sociologist David Miller observed that there are no convincing explanations and it may have been that people were simply taking the opportunity to partake in "naughty fun."[352] Stanford University social psychologist Philip Zimbardo suggested that streaking represented "an attack on dominant social values," while Michael Nichols of Emory University contended that streaking is "an impulse that comes to

frustrated persons who are afraid of being conformists."[353] The end of the fad coincided with the end of college classes – perhaps students began focusing on final exams and the upcoming summer break.
See also: FADS.

STREET FAINTING SCARE

Zetel, Germany: December 1921

On a street, someone fell unconscious. Soon several others fainted on the street. No cause was found.[354]

SUICIDE CLUSTERS

Outbreaks of collective suicide are of two kinds. One, which may be termed the "collective decision" kind, occurs when a coherent group of people – usually though not invariably members of a religious "cult" – make a communal decision to kill themselves together. While the decision is instigated, and sometimes imposed, by the leaders of the "cult," in principle at least the individuals involved acquiesce in the decision and their action is supposedly voluntary. Events of this kind range from the mass suicide of 960 Jewish Zealots at Masada in 74 BCE to that of 408 American members of The People's Temple in Guyana in 1978. Many are treated elsewhere in this Encyclopedia.

The other kind, the "individual decision" kind, occurs when a statistically anomalous number of persons separately take their lives within a limited timespan, geographical area, or community. Individual suicides generally have a rational cause. It is easy to understand why the victim of an incurable illness or a financial catastrophe might be driven to despair. Unhappy love affairs, as in the case of Romeo and Juliet, seem sufficiently justified to the protagonists, if not to others. Suicide clusters, on the other hand, are rarely so easily understood.

Suicide clusters may be characterized by a wide variety of shared features.

Old age or incurable illness have led to many suicides, including suicide pacts such as that of French socialist Paul Lafargue and his wife Laura (Marx) on November 11, 1911, and author Arthur Koestler and his wife in 1983. But plague and epidemic can also lead to mass suicide. In 1887 an outbreak of cholera in Sicily inspired hundreds to anticipate the disease itself, yielding to despair and throwing themselves from windows, hanging themselves, or blowing their brains out. For many young people, simply the menace of being disfigured by the disease was sufficient cause.[355]

Socio-economic factors evidently lead to many suicides. Farmers are particularly vulnerable to hard times, but that hardly accounts for the disproportionate numbers who kill themselves, as noted by Loren Coleman.[356] The Wall Street financial panic of 1929 is popularly associated with ruined speculators throwing themselves out of windows, and statistics bear out the popular image, inspiring such legends as the client who on October 24 presented himself at the Waldorf-Astoria Hotel and requested a room on the upper floor. Is it to admire the view, sir, inquired the receptionist, or to jump out of the window?[357]

Certain professional groups seem particularly liable. In 1969 French sailors and fishermen killed themselves in unusual numbers, for no evident reason.[358] Equally puzzling is the remarkable number of suicides in the 1980s noted by Coleman among police in Boston and New York.[359]

Obedience, loyalty, and perceived dishonor are responsible for many notable clusters. Until today's SUICIDE BOMBERS (see entry) the best-known "duty" suicides were those of the Japanese kamikaze pilots who posed a serious threat to the American Navy during World War Two by flying their bombers (often designed for this precise purpose) into the enemy vessel.[360] There is abundant testimony to the fact that these men gave their lives voluntarily and heroically, dedicated to the glory of their homeland.

Military defeat often leads to suicide among those who feel themselves disgraced. After their rout during the Six Day War against Israel in 1967, several Egyptian officers killed themselves. When the communists of North Vietnam entered Saigon in 1975, 14 South Vietnam generals blew out their brains, preferring death to dishonor.[361]

Other clusters are motivated by *ideologies and beliefs*. The Russian BEZPOPOVTZY sect in 1896 felt obliged by their principles to choose death rather than submit to government demands. On June 11,

1963 the Buddhist bonze Thich Quang Duc set himself on fire in the streets of Saigon in protest at political events. There had been five cases of self-cremation in the previous six years: in the following six years there were 105.[362]

Certain *locations* attract suicide clusters, often for no apparent reason. At Versailles, France, there was an outbreak of 1,300 suicides in 1793; true, the Revolution was then at its height, but why was this town so afflicted?[363] When in 1933, a Japanese student Kiyoko Matsumoto jumped to her death in the volcano at Oshima, 90 km from Tokyo, her example was followed by 982 imitators, not to mention 3,208 who were prevented at the last moment. Nearby hotels required guests to pay in advance, in case they never returned to settle their bills.[364]

Some of the most extraordinary suicide clusters seem to be expressions of the prevailing *zeitgeist*. The romantic movement of the late 18th/early 19th centuries saw a vast surge in suicide expressive of what Mario Paz termed "the romantic agony." Deaths reached a crescendo with the publication of Goethe's novel *The Sorrows of Young Werther*, whose protagonist's suicide, brought about by his passionate love for another man's wife, led to countless imitations. In London alone, between 1772 and 1835, police found that 42 suicides possessed a copy of the book. As Martin Monestier commented, "Werther was no longer a character in a novel, he had become a lifestyle icon."[365]

In the 1920s the body of a young woman, never identified and known only as "L'inconnue de la Seine" was dragged from the river in Paris. Her death mask became a cultural icon like that photo of Che Guevara, and German novelist Conrad Muschler wrote a best-selling novel providing her with a fictitious history; many suicides were found with a copy of the book in their possession. Much the same happened in 1936 in Hungary with a song called *Sad Sunday*; after its gloomy sentiments had driven more than 20 to kill themselves, the Budapest authorities banned its performance, but suicides continued to be found with copies of the words in their pockets.[366]

In such cases, it seems that the mere idea of suicide is sufficient incentive, and this is further exemplified by the periodic formation of "suicide clubs." Robert Louis Stevenson's fiction *The Suicide Club* has had several real life counterparts, generally made up of well-to-do people, bored with everyday existence and seeking an extra frisson. One such was active in Paris during the Revolution; another flourished in the late 19th century in Craiova, Romania. In Berlin in 1907 a "Circle of Death" was founded. Typical was a London club, whose members were notified of their death days by lot, and then suffered an "accident" – a hit-and-run car, a stone falling from a building, organized by their fellow-members. Police broke up the club in 1931 after being denounced by a member who had changed his mind after a woman had restored his will-to-live. In 1930 in Yugoslavia the club of "Those who know" operated in a similar fashion.[367]

Teenagers and students seem to be particularly prone to killing themselves, often leaving notes saying that nobody understands them or similar pleas. In his book on the subject, Coleman devotes more than four pages to teen suicide clusters of the 1980s alone.[368]

These and other circumstances may provide the context and the immediate trigger, but all authorities on suicide agree that *imitation* is the key factor in the great majority of self-inflicted deaths. A celebrity suicide often attracts copycats. When Lord Castlereagh in 1824 jumped into the crater of Vesuvius, several others followed his example in the days which followed. In 1889 Archduke Rudolph of Austria killed his mistress Marie Vetsera and himself in a hunting lodge at Mayerling; the widely reported event triggered numerous suicides all over Europe. After the deranged Ludwig II of Bavaria drowned himself in the Starnsee in 1886, a forester and his wife traveled to the same spot, to kill themselves in the same manner.[369]

A different kind of imitation was displayed following the 1978 release of the film *The Deer Hunter,* which contains a scene of Russian roulette. Dr. Thomas Radecki, psychiatrist at the University of Illinois School of Medicine, listed 37 deaths apparently attributable to the film, as well as many more attempts. In 1985, eight years later, "another death inspired by the Russian roulette scene was reported in Dallas, Texas, where a 37-year-old man shot himself in the head while still watching the program on TV."[370]

COMMENT: According to the Centers for Disease Control in Atlanta (CDC), suicide clusters or contagion refer to "a process by which exposure to the suicide or suicidal behavior of one or more persons influences others to commit or attempt suicide."[371] The mass media appear to play an influential role in triggering suicide clusters that may be spread across a wide geographical area. Specifically, newspaper and television reporting of suicides is linked to statistically significant increases in more suicides. The effect is the most profound among adolescents.[372]

The CDC has issued several recommendations for reducing the impact of news reports on the suicide rate. A reading of these guidelines suggests some of the reasons for the link between the media and suicide. These include giving specific details as to how the person committed suicide, showing photographs from the scene, and offering simplistic explanations for what is seldom a simple event. They also recommend against suggesting that suicide can be used as a means to accomplish certain ends. "Suicide is usually a rare act of a troubled or depressed person. Presentation of suicide as a means of coping with personal problems (e.g., the break-up of a relationship or retaliation against parental discipline) may suggest suicide as a potential coping mechanism to at-risk persons. Although such factors often seem to trigger a suicidal act, other psychopathological problems are almost always involved. If suicide is presented as an effective means for accomplishing specific ends, it may be perceived by a potentially suicidal person as an attractive solution."[373]

When clusters of suicide or attempted suicide occur in a specific geographic region, they are commonly preceded by one or more intended or unintended traumatic deaths among community youth. The CDC provides the following example of a local suicide cluster: "In the 9 months preceding one cluster of four suicides and two suicide attempts among persons 15-24 years of age, there were four traumatic deaths among persons in the same age group and community – two from unintentional injuries, one from suicide, and one of undetermined intentionality. One of the unintentional-injury deaths was caused by a fall from a cliff. Two of the persons who later committed suicide in the cluster had been close friends of this fall victim; one of the two had witnessed the fall."[374]

Suicide clusters may account for up to five percent of all teen suicides in the United States.[375] According to American researcher Simon Stack, the so-called "copycat effect" was 14 times more likely to occur after the reporting of celebrity suicides than non-celebrities. He also found that real life accounts of suicide, by contrast with fictional accounts, were four times as likely to result in copycat behavior. Stack notes that suicides depicted on television were 82 percent less likely to trigger copycat acts in comparison to similar reports in newspapers. A possible explanation for this pattern may be because television coverage of such events tends to be broadcast for 20 seconds or less, "while a newspaper can be saved, re-read, and digested." As for the best way to reduce the incidence of suicide clusters, Stack stated that "it appears that the greatest reduction in copycat suicide may sometimes come from reducing the sheer quantity of news on suicide, as opposed to the perceived quality of news reporting."[376]

See also: COPYCAT EFFECT, DEFENCE INDUSTRY SUICIDE CLUSTER, MASS SUICIDE CULTS, RUSSIAN SECTS, BEZPOPOVTSY.

SWEDISH PREACHING EPIDEMIC

Sweden: 1841

In December 1841, a form of collective behavior swept through certain country districts of Sweden, involving many thousands of persons, mainly women and children, in trances, hallucinations, and convulsions. Because a conspicuous symptom was a tendency to religious preaching, the outbreak became known as "The Preaching Epidemic."

CONTEXT: There does not seem to have been any particular occasion for the outbreak, but there were signs of unrest in the established church. The Archbishop of Uppsala, Primate of all Sweden, declared: "We do not deny the possibility that circumstances connected with the Church in our country, and more particularly in that province in which the epidemic first broke out, might have caused the first impulse."[377] It is plausible that local religious differences created some kind of tension in these country districts. The puritanical sentiments of the preaching suggest one of those swings against perceived decadence that periodically sweep through pious communities.

Dr. Souden, director of the Stockholm lunatic asylum, declared that the ground had been prepared by the fanaticism of the population, by religious pamphlets that circulated at this time in great numbers among the people, and finally by the credulity and ignorance of the people themselves.[378]

The end of the world: In September 1841, a 16-year-old girl, Lisa Andersdocter, complained of pains in her chest and head. Some time later, she had an irresistible impulse to sing throughout the day. At first, she uttered inarticulate sounds, but these changed after a few days into psalms and litanies. This led to her preaching on religious themes. These crises didn't occur every day, but on average every ten days. Then she began to fall into ecstasies in the course of which she seemed to receive divine inspiration. These ecstasies were nearly always followed by crises that were at first light, but gradually escalated into seizures of her limbs. Then she would begin to prophesy, almost always announcing the end of the world, the Last Judgment, and the exact date of her death. Her prophetic crisis was often far from calm, she spoke with great volubility, sweat poured down her forehead testifying to the ardor of her excitement. She claimed that it was the Holy Spirit who inspired her and spoke through her mouth.[379]

News of this "miracle" spread rapidly, and so did the impulse to replicate Lisa's performance. In December 1841, at the parish church of Hjelseryd, four country girls announced the imminent end of the world, and urged all to repent and prepare to meet their God. Almost simultaneously, a number of other prophetesses – children aged from 6 to 12 years old, echoed the warning in nearby parishes. In the village of Hornborga, six boys, aged between 8 and 18, issued the same message. The young prophets became known as "repentance criers."

The outbreak benefited from a personal investigation by Dr. Butsch, the archbishop of the district most affected, Skara in southwestern Sweden. He reckoned that in his diocese there were somewhere between 2000 and 3000 afflicted, and personally examined about 200 of them. He listed the characteristic symptoms as follows:

> Heaviness in the head; a burning heat in the orifice of the stomach; a sensation of crawling and pricking in the extremities; convulsions and quakings in various parts of the body; copious perspiration (sometimes with the smell of sulphur); dropping down and fainting, sometimes with a heavy groan, after which the patient for some time remains in such an insensible state as not to seem to feel the least impression of a loud voice speaking to him, or a needle which is thrust deeply into his body, and so on; but sometimes he both hears when spoken to, and answers questions put to him, in doing which he addresses everyone, regardless of their status, by the word "thou" [i.e. not employing the polite "you"]; his power of speech in this state is often more coherent, more lively and in a purer language than might have been expected; his generally unceasing assurance that he is exceedingly well, and that he has never before been so happy; his assertion that the words are given to him by some one else; his pious and quiet disposition of mind; his inclination for fixed ideas, visions and predictions; his dislike of certain words and phrases; and lastly, that the afflicted persons like to be together, and feel a particular affection towards each other.[380]

During their ecstasies, the afflicted persons had visions of God, of angels, the Table of the Elect presided over by God in person, and also demons and Hell. In contrast to many afflicted in other such outbreaks (such as the convent hysterics of the 17th century), they were able to tell, when their ecstasies terminated, what they had seen. Both sexes and all ages were affected, but women and children more frequently than men or older people.

The behavior followed a specific pattern, so that observers could say: "This or that person has begun to quake, but he has not yet dropped down, nor has he had visions, or been preaching."[381] One boy was reported to drop down three times within the space of one or two hours, without either before or afterwards having any symptoms of the disease. By far the most distinctive feature of the epidemic was the prophetic delirium, characterized by an irresistible loquacity. The preaching and prophesying were sometimes performed standing, with the eyes open, sometimes lying down with the eyes closed.

Shortly before Christmas 1842, Butsch visited a family with three preaching girls, aged 8 to 12, who "were advanced to one of the highest stages of the disease." He observed them on two occasions, for seven hours in all. They had a tolerably good religious knowledge, and also a readiness in reading. He watched while they went into trance, and heard them preaching, observing their behavior in each state. "The more severe and distinct symptoms of the disease manifested themselves in the children, first, when they were in the act of dropping down, and then during the trance, after they had fallen. The fall was preceded by tremblings, shakings and quakings in the arms and legs. They always fell backwards, in whatever direction they happened to be, when the trembling first came on; and it was often connected with such a force, and with such a rattling noise, by the knocking of the head against the floor, that no person present could help feeling a painful sensation."[382]

One particular aspect of the children's behavior makes it plain that, unconsciously, they were echoing adult concerns about dissolute behavior. While in trance, they would mime certain behaviors of which they disapproved – pouring liquid into a glass, shuffling a pack of cards, firing a gun, dressing in fine clothes to go dancing. Some would bend their body back till their head nearly touched their feet; this was taken to represent the wreath placed at the top of a maypole, another focus of disapproval. Sometimes a child would mimic a fight, taking the turn of each of two protagonists, performed with the utmost vigor, hitting herself repeatedly very hard, panting and exclaiming all the time. Then she would become calm, and start to preach. It was said that 70 distillers closed their business after hearing the messages.

As with the CEVENNES PROPHETS, the words of the "sermons" echoed pious sentiments, which the children had doubtless heard from the adults. But if cryptomnesia was involved, it was combined with a remarkable fluency, giving the impression of a spontaneous homily. The archbishop heard one of his girls speak in this manner: "Let us now, dear friends, raise a sigh, a good sigh, which penetrates through the clouds up to the Saviour. Let us go in the narrow way, let us go in the thorny path? Will you not go there? Then I will go there myself alone. And you shall believe my little words. Although they are little, still they are well-meaning..." However the prophets do not seem to have displayed the oratorical powers of the Cevennes prophets. "There is no superior intellectual activity here: the discourse of the inspired persons is totally lacking in eloquence, and the substance is childish,"[383] commented Maurice Prouvost, who said this was no doubt because the epidemic found most of its victims among the common people.

Believing the children when they stated they were inspired by some higher power, thousands thronged to hear them preach. In February 1842, one peasant girl spoke to an audience of three or four thousand people. Those afflicted had no wish to form a sect, or to depart in any way from conventional religious practices. On the other hand, they seemed to share some kind of bond, which made them answer "we" to questions where an individual response would be expected.

There were minor differences in behavior from one part of the country to another. In Eltsborg, groups of children went around singing hymns, but the archbishop did not hear of this in Skara. He heard that in some districts the afflicted people tended to break the seventh commandment, relating to adultery, and the eighth, which relates to stealing.

COMMENT: Following his first-hand investigation, Dr. Butsch declares it to be "a subject which, so far as I can judge, requires the insight and experience of a natural philosopher [i.e. a scientist] and of a phy-

Mora, Sweden. Witches gather at Blokula, the assembly point for the Sabbat.

sician, rather than of a theologian and a clergyman."[384] However, he recognized that there were many different opinions regarding the origins of the epidemic, ranging from "divine miracle" to "an operation of the devil" by way of "intentional deception" or "self-deception." He himself, however, was disposed to prefer a natural rather than a supernatural one: "I for one belong to that minority who consider the preaching epidemic to be a disease, originally bodily, but in a peculiar manner affecting the mind."[385] This he inferred from the fact that an internal bodily disorder and pain preceded, or were at any rate contemporary with the religious excitement, which those affected considered to be the commencement, and that "there are persons who have against their own will been affected by the quakings, without any preceding or subsequent religious excitement."

Butsch asserts that the disease has often been cured by the use of medicine. In other cases, "severe words and the application of a cane" did the trick. In such a case, he supposed that "the fright and the physical pain served as a check to follow the impulses of the disease."[386] Prouvost stated: "The afflicted persons did not all emerge unscathed, and often serious brain disorders manifested, such as mania, melancholia, and other forms of psychopathology."[387]

SYRACUSE FOG SCARE

Western New York: December 29, 1950

According to the editor of the respected *Post-Standard* newspaper published in Syracuse, New York, on Friday, a thick ground fog triggered "a case of public hysteria because far from a few persons thought we were under bombardment, were being gassed, or at least that the 'enemy' had caused the fog as some kind of a camouflage." The incident was compared to the 1938 ORSON WELLES MARTIAN PANIC.[388]

CONTEXT: The incident coincides with the fear of communists, the Korean War, and early Cold War years between the United States and the former Soviet Union, less than a decade after the Japanese sneak attack on Pearl Harbor. Within this milieu of fear and suspicion, and in conjunction with the appearance of unusual meteorological conditions, the possibility of a foreign attack was rendered plausible.

Sources

1. Rocoles, Jean-Baptiste (1728). *Les Imposteurs Insignes.* Brussels: Vlaenderen, volume two, p. 249: our account draws on this source and on Kastein (1931) except where otherwise indicated.
2. Kastein, Joseph (1930[1931]). *The Messiah of Izmir.* [Original German *Der Messias von Izmir,* 1930] New York: Viking, p. 78 et seq.
3. Kastein, op cit., p. 169.
4. Rocoles, op cit., p. 260.
5. Kastein, op cit., p. 189.
6. Rocoles, op cit., p. 261 et seq.
7. Sidis, Boris (1911). *The Psychology of Suggestion.* New York: Appleton, p. 329.
8. Rocoles, op cit., p. 249.
9. Kastein, op cit., p. 207, quoting from a memoir of the Glückel family of Hameln.
10. Kastein, op cit., p. 208, quoting Sasportas.
11. Kastein, op cit., p. 243.
12. Collin de Plancy, J. (1861). *Légendes de l'Ancien Testament.* Paris: Plon, p. 285.
13. Bourseiller, Christophe (1993). *Les Faux Messies.* Paris: Fayard, citing Scholem.
14. Kastein, op cit., p. 259.
15. Carré de Montgeron, Louis-Basile (1737). *La Vérité des Miracles Opérés à L'intercession de M. de Paris &c Utrecht,* volume 1, section relating to Hardouin.
16. Picart, quoted by Madden, R. R. (1857). *Phantasmata or Illusions and Fanaticisms of Protean Forms Productive of Great Evils.* London: T.C. Newby, volume 2, p. 544.
17. Carré de Montgeron, op cit., idée 26.
18. Madden, op cit., volume 2, p. 555.
19. Madden, op cit., volume 2, p. 541.
20. Carré de Montgeron, op cit.
21. Madden, op cit., volume 2, p. 557.
22. Carré de Montgeron, op cit.
23. Carré de Montgeron, op cit., volume 3, p. 692.
24. Mousset, Albert (1953). *L'étrange Histoire des Convulsionnaires de Saint-Médard.* Paris: Editions de Minuit, p. 60.
25. Carré de Montgeron, volume 2, p. 49.
26. Carré de Montgeron, volume 3, p. 555.
27. Mousset, op cit., p. 122.
28. Quoted by Madden, op cit., p. 542.
29. Carré de Montgeron, volume 3, p. 7.
30. Carré de Montgeron, volume 2, p. 31.
31. Carré de Montgeron, volume 3, p. 635.
32. Carré de Montgeron, volume 3, p. 700.
33. Carré de Montgeron, volume 3, p. 708.
34. Carré de Montgeron, volume 2, p. 120.
35. Calmeil, L.F. (1845). *De la Folie, Consideree Sous le Point de vue Pathologique, Philosophique, Historique et Judiciaire* [On the Crowd, Considerations on the Point of Pathology, Philosophy, History and Justice]. Paris: Baillere, volume 2, p. 386.
36. Robbins, Peggy. "The Devil in Salem." *Annual Editions Readings in American History, Volume 1.* Guilford, Connecticut. Dushkin Publishing, pp. 556-65. See pp. 519-520.

37. Robbins, op cit., p. 519.
38. Saari, Peggy. (2001). *Witchcraft in America*. Boston, Massachusetts: UXL, pp. 26-27.
39. Robbins, op cit., p. 529.
40. Saari, op. cit., p. 27.
41. Rice, Earle Rice, Jr. (1997). *The Salem Witch Trials*. San Diego, California: Lucent Books, quoting the personal journal of Governor John Winthrop.
42. Saari (2001). op cit., p. 28.
43. Robbins, op cit., p. 520; Saari, op cit., p. 28.
44. Robbins, Peggy. op cit., p. 557.
45. Boyer, Paul, and Nissenbaum, Stephen (1974). *Salem Possessed: The Social Origins of Witchcraft*. Cambridge: Harvard University Press, pp. xii-xiii.
46. Davidson, James West, Castillo, Pedro, and Stoff, Michasel B. (2000). *The American Nation*. Upper Saddle River, New Jersey: Prentice-Hall, pp. 88-95.
47. Zeinert, Karen. (1989). *The Salem Witch Trials*. New York: Franklin Watts, pp. 31-32.
48. Upham, Charles W. (2000[1867)]. *Salem Witchcraft*. Mineola, New York: Dover, p. 323.
49. Robbins, op cit., p. 60; Rice, op cit., pp. 31-32.
50. Robbins, op cit., p. 61.
51. Robbins, op cit., p. 60.
52. Upham, Charles W. (2000[1867]). *Salem Witchcraft: With an Account of Salem and a History of Opinions on Witchcraft and Kindred Subjects*. Mineola, New York: Dover Publications, p. 338.
53. Upham, op cit., p. 128.
54. Rice, op cit., p. 102.
55. Rice, op cit., p. 96; Robbins, op cit., p. 64.
56. Rice, op cit., pp. 96-97.
57. Robbins, op cit., p. 440.
58. Robbins, op cit., p. 441.
59. Saari, op cit., pp. 64-65.
60. Rice, op cit., p. 97.
61. Saari, op cit., p. 56.
62. Robbins, op cit., p. 442.
63. Rice, op cit., p. 97.
64. Caporael, Linda. (1976). "Ergotism: The Satan Loosed in Salem?" *Science* 192:21-26
65. Lewis, Mark (producer) (2001). "Witches Curse." A Mentorn Barraclough Carey Production in association with the Educational Broadcasting Corporation production for WNET, New York.
66. Rice, op cit., pp. 30-31; Saari (2001). op cit., pp. 39-40.
67. Robbins, op cit., p. 190.
68. Lewis, Mark (producer) (2001). op cit.
69. Saari, op cit., p. 40.
70. Wolf, Alan. (2000). "Witchcraft or Mycotoxin? The Salem Witch Trials." *Clinical Toxicology* 38(4):457-460. See p. 460.
71. Wolf, Alan. (2000). op cit., p. 460.
72. Morgan, M.T. (1929-30). "Report on an Outbreak of Alleged Ergot Poisoning by Rye Bread in Manchester." *Journal of Hygiene* 29:51-61.
73. Demeke, T., Kidane Y., & Wuhib, E. (1979). "Ergotism: a Report on an Epidemic." *Ethiopian Medical Journal* 17:107-113.
King, B. (1979). "Outbreak of ergotism in Wollo, Ethiopia." *The Lancet*, 1: 1411.
74. Spanos, N.P. (1983). "Ergotism and the Salem Witch Panic: A Critical Analysis and an Alternative Conceptualization." *Journal of the History of the Behavioral Sciences* 19:358-369.
75. Spanos, N.P. and Gottlieb, J. (1976). "Ergotism and the Salem Village Witch Trials." *Science* 914:1390-1394.
76. Rice, op cit., pp. 16-17.
77. Zeinert, op cit., p. 76.
78. Zeinert (1989). op cit., pp. 81-83.
79. Boyer and Nissenbaum, op cit.
80. Boyer and Nissenbaum, op cit.
81. Saari (2001). op cit., p. 35.
82. Zeinert (1989). op cit., pp. 81-83.
83. Pelka, Fred. (1992). "The 'Women's Holocaust.'" *Humanist* 52(5): 5-9.
84. Karlsen, Carol F. (1987). *The Devil in the Shape of a Woman: Witchcraft in Colonial New England*. New York: W.W. Norton.
85. Norton, Mary Beth. *In the Devil's Snare: The Salem Witchcraft Crisis of 1692*. New York: Alfred A. Knopf.
86. Brown, Kathleen M. (2002). "Raising the Devil." *Chicago Tribune*, October 13, section 14, pp. 1, 4. See p. 4.
87. Wier, Jean. [Weyer, Johann] (1885). *Histoires, Disputes Et Discours Des Illusions Et Impostures Des Diables, Des Magiciens Infames, SorcièRes Et Empoisonneurs*. Translated from the Latin original, published 1563. Paris: Bureaux du Progrès Médical, volume 1, p. 530.
88. Wier, op cit., p. 531.
89. Madden, R. R. (1857). *Phantasmata or Illusions and Fanaticisms of Protean Forms Productive of Great Evils*. London: T.C. Newby, volume 2, p. 256.
90. House, Ronald A., and Holness, D. Linn (1997). "Investigation of Factors Affecting Mass Psychogenic Illness in Employees in a Fish-Packing Plant." *American Journal of Industrial Medicine* 32(1):90-96.
91. Health 24.com, accessed March 31, 2005 at: http://www.health24.com/news/Respiratory/ 1-942,26937.asp.
92. Dalrymple, Theodore (2003). "Apocalypse Probably Postponed." *New Statesman* 132:30 (April 28).
93. Anonymous (2003). "GP Condemns the Hysteria Over SARS." *Pulse* 63(17):1, 8 (April 28).
94. Fumento, Michael (2003). "SARS Hysteria Must End." Scripps Howard News Service, May 8. Accessed March 31, 2005 at: http://www.fumento.com/disease/scrippsars.html
95. Fumento, Michael (2003). op cit.
96. Safir, David E. (2003). "Put SARS 'Epidemic' in Perspective." *USA Today* (April 9): 12.
97. Smith, Michelle, and Pazder, L. (1980). *Michelle Remembers*. New York: Congdon & Latte.
98. Pendergrast, Mark (1995). *Victims of Memory: Incest Accusations and Shattered Lives*. Hinesburg, Vermont: Upper Access, Inc., p. 49.
99. Pendergrast, op cit., p. 49.
100. Alexander, David (1990). "Giving the Devil More Than His Due." *The Humanist* 50(2): 5-14. (March/April), accessed at: http://users.cybercity.dk/~ccc44406/smwane/Devildue.htm.
101. Victor, J.S. (1993). *Satanic Panic: The Creation of a Contemporary Legend*. Chicago, IL: Open Court; Victor, J.S. (1991). The Dynamics of Rumor-panics about Satanic Cults. Pp. 221-236. In James Richardson, J. Best and D. Bromley (eds.). *The Satanism Scare*. New York: Aldine de Gruyter; Hicks, R. (1990). "Police Pursuit of Satanic Crime Part II: The Satanic Conspiracy and Urban Legends." *The Skeptical Inquirer* 14:378-389; Victor, J.S. (1989). "A Rumor-Panic about a Dangerous Satanic Cult in Western New York." *New York Folklore* 15:23-49.
102. Victor, Jeffrey S. (1998). "Social Construction of Satanic Ritual Abuse and the Creation of False Memories." Pp. 191-216. *In Believed-In Imaginings: The Narrative Construction of Reality* (edited by Joseph de Rivera and Theodore R. Sarbin. Washington, DC: American Psychological Association, p. 200.

103. Victor, 1998, op cit., p. 201.
104. Victor, 1998, op cit., pp. 201-202.
105. Victor, 1998, op cit., p. 203.
106. Victor, 1998, op cit., p. 203.
107. Victor, 1998, op cit., pp. 204-205.
108. Victor, 1998, op cit., p. 206.
109. Victor, 1998, op cit., p. 206.
110. Victor, 1998, op cit., p. 206.
111. Victor, Jeffrey S. (1992). "The Search for Scapegoat Deviants." *The Humanist* (September/October):10-13.
112. Victor (1992). op cit., p. 11.
113. Victor (1992). op cit., p. 13.
114. Richardson, James T., Best, Joel, Bromley, David G. (compilers) (1991). *The Satanism Scare.* New York: Aldine de Gruyter, p. 35.
115. Cavendish, Richard (1967). *The Black Arts.* London: Routledge and Kegan Paul, p. 291.
116. Frere, Jean-Claude (1972). *Les Sociétés du Mal.* Paris: Culture.Art. Loisirs, p. 26.
117. William Blake, The marriage of Heaven and Hell.
118. Geyraud, Pierre [nom-de-plume of Abbé Guyades] (1937a). *Les Petites églises de Paris.* Paris: Emile Paul Frères, p. 139.
119. Rhodes, Henry T.F. (1954). *The Satanic Mass.* London: Rider, p. 112.
120. Fuller, Ronald (1939). *Hell-Fire Francis.* London: Chatto & Windus, 138.
121. Rhodes, op cit., p. 163.
122. Jeffrey Burton Russell in Richardson et al: 47.
123. Geyraud, Pierre [nom-de-plume of Abbé Guyades] (1937b). *Les Religions Nouvelles de Paris.* Paris: Emile Paul Frères, p. 159.
124. Geyraud, 1937a, op cit., p. 141.
125. Geyraud, Pierre [nom-de-plume of Abbé Guyades] (1937b). *Les Religions Nouvelles de Paris.* Paris: Emile Paul Frères, p. 165.
126. Richardson et al., op cit., p. 49.
127. Zeena LaVey [his daughter] and Nikolas Schreek, 'Anton LaVey: legend and reality' on www.churchofsatan.org.
128. LaVey, Anton Szandor (1969). *The Satanic Bible.* New York: Avon Books.
129. LaVey, op cit., p. 5.
130. LaVey, op; cit., p. 10.
131. LaVey, op cit., p. 6.
132. Zeena LaVey, in LaVey, 1969, op cit., p. 6.
133. Bainbridge, William Sims (1978). *Satan's Power.* Berkeley: University of California (the group is named 'The Power' in his account).
134. Schwarz, Ted, and Empey, Duane (1988). *Satanism.* Grand Rapids, Michigan: Zondervan, pp. 117, 193.
135. Parker, John. (1993). *At the Heart of Darkness.* London: Sidgwick & Jackson, p. 242.
136. Cited by Joel Best in Richardson et al., op cit., p. 104.
137. Parker, op cit., p. viii.
138. Wright, Lawrence (1994). *Remembering Satan.* New York: Knopf, p. xiii.
139. Gettings, Fred (1988). *Dictionary of Demons.* London: Century Hutchinson.
140. Bainbridge, op cit., pp. 3-4.
141. Fuller, op cit., p. 39.
142. Posted by Diana Napolis aka Karen Jones on www.newsmakingnews.com.
143. Al-Matrafi, Saad B. (2000). "Mass Hysteria Behind Scared Teachers at 'Haunted' School." *Arab News* (Jeddah). November 5; Abuljadayel, Sarah (2000). "Two More Teachers have fits at 'Haunted' School." *Arab News*, November 7.
144. Sweeney, Michael (1987). "Students Faint During School Mass." *Syracuse Herald-Journal* (New York), May 29, p. B1.
145. "Suicide Attempt Causes 'Vampire' Scare in School." *The Holland Evening Sentinel* (Michigan), September 25, 1970, p. 8.
146. Montgomery, J. D. (1908). "The Education of Girls in Germany: its Methods of Moral Instruction and Training." Pp. 231-241. In M. E. Sadler (ed.), *Moral Instruction and Training in Schools: Report of an International Inquiry, Volume 2.* London: Longmans, Green and Company; Spiller, G. (1908a). "Moral Education in the Boys' Schools of Germany." Pp. 213-230. In M. E. Sadler (ed.), *Moral Instruction and Training in Schools: Report of an International Inquiry, Volume 2.* London: Longmans, Green and Company; Spiller, G. (1908b). "An Educational Democracy: Moral Instruction and Training in the Schools of Switzerland." Pp. 196-206. In M. E. Sadler (ed.), *Moral Instruction and Training in Schools: Report of an International Inquiry, Volume 2.* London: Longmans, Green and Company.
147. Hirt, L. (1893). "Eine Epidemie von Hysterischen Krampfen in einer Schleisischen Dorfschule" [An Epidemic of Hysterical Cramp in a Village School in Schleisischen]. Zeitschrift *fur Schulgesundheitspflege* 6:225-229. (Summary of an article by L. Hirt in the *Berliner Klinische Wochenschrift*).
148. Schoedel, Johannes (1906). "Uber Induzierte Krankheiten" [On Induced Illness]. *Jahrbuch fur Kinderheilkunde* 14:521-528.
149. Aemmer, Fritz. (1893). *Eine Schulepidemie von Tremor Hystericus* [A School Epidemic of Hysterical Tremor]. Inaugural dissertation, Basel.
150. Burnham, William H. (1924). *The Normal Mind.* New York: D. Appleton and Company, p. 329.
151. Zollinger, E. (1906). "Uber die Padagogische Behandlung des Nervosen Zitterns der Schulkinder" [On the Educational Treatment of Nervous Trembling in School Children]. *Jahrbuch der Schweiz Gesellschaft fur Schulgesundheitspflege* 7:20-47; Brunham (1924). op cit., p. 329-331.
152. Burnham, W.H. (1924). *The Normal Mind.* New York: D. Appletin, p. 331.
153. Burnham, op cit. , p. 331.
154. Hecker, Justus Friedrich. (1844). *Epidemics of the Middle Ages* (translated from German by B. Babington). London: The Sydenham Society. All information and quoted passages are from this source, which itself drew on contemporary reports from several sources.
155. "Alberta Smoke in East Scotland," *The Lethbridge Herald*, September 26, 1950, p. 3.
156. Fuller, Ronald (1939). *Hell-Fire Francis.* London: Chatto & Windus, p. 18.
157. *Chambers Book of Days*, volume 1, page 743.
158. Quoted from the Wentworth Papers on wikipedia.org/wiki/Mohocks.
159. Fuller, op cit., p. 22.
160. Dibdin, Michael (1992). *Cabal.* Faber, p. 20.
161. Cohn, Norman (1957). *The Pursuit of the Millennium.* Fair Lawn, New Jersey, Essential Books, p. 127.
162. Cohn, op cit., p. 127.
163. Bekhterev, Vladimir Mikhailovich. (1998)[1908] *Suggestion and its Role in Social Life*, third edition. (translated from Russian by Tzvetanka Dobreva-Martinova). New Brunswick, New Jersey: Transaction Publishers, p. 74.
164. Glucklich, Ariel (1999). "Self and Sacrifice: A Phenomenological Psychology of Sacred Pain." *Harvard Theological Review* 92(4):479-506, accessed July 20, 2003, at: http://www.findarticles.com/cf_dls/

m2399/4_92/58617490/p3/article.jhtml?term=self-injury.
165. Glucklich (1999). op cit.
166. Cohn, op cit., p. 73.
167. Menninger, K.A. (1938). *Man Against Himself.* New York: Harcourt, Brace & World.
168. Faguet, R. A., and Faguet, K. F. (1982). "La Folie a Deux." Pp. 1-14. In C.T.H. Friedmann and R. A. Faguet (eds.), *Extraordinary Disorders of Human Behavior*. New York: Plenum Press, p. 11.
169. Larson, W. (1989). *Larson's New Book of Cults*. Wheaton, IL: Tyndale House Publishers.
170. Cardoza, R. (1990). "The Ordeal of Moharram." *Natural History* (American Museum of Natural History, New York), 99:50-57 (September).
171. Bartholomew, Robert E., and O'Dea, Julian (1998). "Religious Devoutness Construed as Pathology: The Myth of "Religious Mania." *The International Journal for the Psychology of Religion* 8(1):1-16.
172. Campbell, Robert Jean (1996). *Psychiatric Dictionary*, seventh edition). New York: Oxford University Press, pp. 283-284.
173. Kaplan, Harold I., and Sadock, Benjamin J. (eds.) (1995). *Comprehensive Textbook of Psychiatry VI, Volume 1* (sixth edition). Baltimore, MD: Williams and Wilkins, p. 1044.
174. Kaplan and Sadock (1995). op cit., p. 1044.
175. "Extraordinary Phenomenon." Letter dated November 17. *London Times*, November 20, 1888, p. 13.
176. "Extraordinary Phenomenon." op cit.
177. Rickard, Robert, and Michell, John. (2001). *Unexplained Phenomena: A Rough Guide Special.* London: Rough Guides Limited, p. 100, citing several unnamed reports in British newspapers shortly after the event.
178. "Extraordinary Phenomenon." op cit.
179. Showalter, Elaine (1997). *Hystories: Hysterical Epidemics and Modern Media*. New York: Columbia University Press. In some later editions the subtitle was changed to "Hysterical Epidemics and Modern Culture."
180. Crossfire Sunday, "Discussion on the Causes of the Gulf War Syndrome." Aired April 20, 1997 - 7:30 p.m. Eastern Time. Acessed April 30, 2005 at: http://www.cfs-news.org/show-cnn.htm.
181. Larkin, Marilynn (1998). "Elaine Showalter: Hysteria's Historian." *The Lancet* 351(9116): 1638 (May 30).
182. Larkin, Marilynn (1998). op cit.
183. Rose, Dionne (2004). "Pratville Primary to Reopen After Mystery Illness." *The Gleaner*, October 6, p. A2.
184. Rose, Dionne (2004). Op cit.
185. "'Toxic' School Declared Safe," *The Australian*, January 24, 2003, p. 4.
186. Carreon, Joan (1987). "What's Ailing Sunny Hill? Sleuths Coming up Empty-Handed." *Daily Herald* (Chicago, Illinois), March 30, 1987, pp. 1, 9.
187. Carreon, Joan (1987). op cit., p. 9.
188. Carreon, Joan (1987). op cit., p. 9.
189. Arnold, Jacqueline (1990). "Mexico Seeks Cause of Illness at School." *Post-Standard*, (Syracuse, New York), April 16, p. B3.
190. Phoon, W.H. (1982). "Outbreaks of mass hysteria at workplaces in Singapore: Some patterns and modes of presentation." In M. Colligan, J. Pennebaker and L. Murphy (eds.), *Mass Psychogenic Illness: A Social Psychological Analysis* (21-32). Hillsdale, New Jersey: Lawrence Erlbaum, pp. 21-31.
191. Phoon (1982). op cit., p. 23; Colligan M.J., and Murphy, L.R. (1982). "A Review of Mass Psychogenic Illness in Work Settings." In M. Colligan, J. Pennebaker and L. Murphy (eds.), *Mass Psychogenic Illness: A Social Psychological Analysis* (33-52). Hillsdale, New Jersey: Lawrence Erlbaum, p. 36.
192. Phoon (1982). op cit., p. 23.
193. Phoon (1982). op cit., p. 23.
194. Tsakni (1888). *La Russie Sectaire*. Paris, quoted in Rapaport, L. (1949). *Introduction à la Psychopathologie Collective*. Paris: Editions Erka, p. 44.
195. Except where otherwise indicated, the information in this entry derives from Rapaport.
196. Engelstein, Laura (1999). *Castration and the Heavenly Kingdom*. Ithaca: Cornell University Press, p. 29.
197. Volkov, a Soviet writer, cited by Rapaport, p. 100.
198. Pelikan, cited by Rapaport, p. 108.
199. Hastings, James (1908). *Encyclopaedia of Religion and Ethics*. Edinburgh: T & T Clark [published by volumes], volume 3, p. 667.
200. "Scent is Upsetting." *The Independent* (Helena, Montana), July 16, 1948, p. 3.
201. Bartholomew, Robert E., and Howard, George S. (1998). *UFOs and Alien Contact: Two Centuries of Mystery*. Buffalo, New York: Prometheus Books.
202. Bartholomew and Howard (1998). op cit., p. 228.
203. Buckhout, R. (1974). op. cit., p. 25.
204. Story, R. (1980). op. cit.; Johnson, F. (1980). op. cit.; Hind, C. (1982). op. cit.; Schwarz, B. (1983). op. cit.
205. Davis, Isabel, and Bloecher, Ted. (1978). *Close Encounter at Kelly and Others of 1955*. Evanston, IL: Center for UFO Studies; Hynek, Josef Allen, and Vallee, Jacques. (1975). *The Edge of Reality: A Progress Report on Unidentified Flying Objects*. Chicago: Henry Regnery; Rickard, Robert J.M. (1985). "More Phantom Sieges." *The Fortean Times* (Winter):58-61.
206. Westrum, Ronald. (1985). "Phantom Attackers." *The Fortean Times* (Winter):54-58; undated letter from Westrum to Robert Bartholomew circa 1994.
207. Westrum, R. (1985). op. cit., p. 55.
208. Personal communication between Robert Bartholomew and South Australian resident Keith Basterfield who investigated the case and interviewed both the witnesses and police. Robert Bartholomew was living in South Australia when the incident occurred.
209. The historical details are drawn mainly from Burton, Thomas (1993). *Serpent-Handling Believers*. Knoxville: Tennessee University Press; La Barre, Weston (1962). *They Shall Take up Serpents*. Minneapolis: University of Minnesota Press.
210. A J Tomlinson, quoted by Burton, op cit., p. 71.
211. The New Testament: Mark chapter xvi, verses 17-18.
212. Burton, op cit., p. 41 et seq.
213. 'The Church of God Evangel' (1914) quoted by Burton, op cit., p. 64.
214. Carden, Karen W., and Pelton, Robert W. (1976). *The Persecuted Prophets*. South Brunswick: A S Barnes, pp. 25, 85.
215. 'The Church of God Evangel' (1914) quoted by Burton, op cit., p. 64.
216. Carden, op cit., pp. 92-94.
217. Carden, op cit., p. 65.
218. Carden, op cit., p. 53.
219. Carden, op cit., pp. 55-56.
220. Carden, op cit., p. 23.
221. Berthold Schwarz (1979). "Ordeal by Serpents." In Ebon, Martin (editor). *The World's Wierdest Cults*. New York: Signet.
222. Carden, op cit., p. 28.
223. Carden, op cit., p. 34.

224. La Barre, op cit., p. 36.
225. La Barre, op cit., p. 46.
226. La Barre, op cit., p. 170.
227. Burton, op cit., p. 129.
228. J. Kenneth Moore, quoted by Burton, op cit., p. 130.
229. Bob Hurley, writing in the *Greenville Sun*, 26 August 1985, quoted by Burton, op cit., p. 132.
230. Burton, op cit., p. 132.
231. McKee, James B. (1974). *Introduction to Sociology*, second edition. New York: Holt, Rineharrt and Winston, Inc., p. 438.
232. Cox, Kevin P. (2005). "Investigation Reveals No Source for Illness Reported by Students." Published January 16, 2001 at: http://www.wfu.edu/www-data/wfunews/ 2001/011601i.htm.
233. All the information is from Bechterew, W.M. [Now spelled Bekhterev, V M] (1910). *La Suggestion*. [Translated from Russian by D P Keraval]. Paris: Boulangé.
234. P Jacobi, cited by Bechterev, op cit., p. 202.
235. Bechterev, op cit., p. 207.
236. "Martian." *Indiana Evening Gazette*, October 28, 1939.
237. "Fleeing Villagers Mistook Disco Lights For Aliens." October 4, 2004. http://www.ananova.com/news/story/sm_1128290.html, accessed October 8, 2004,
238. Houran, James, Kumar, V.K., Thalbourne, Michael, and Lavertue, Nicole (2002). "Haunted by Somatic Tendencies: Spirit Infestation as Psychosomatic Illness." *Mental Health, Religion & Culture* 5(2):119-133.
239. Houran et al. (2002). op cit, p. 127.
240. Houran et al. (2002). op cit, p. 129.
241. Houran et al. (2002). op cit, p. 128.
242. Oesterreich, T.K. (1930[1921]) *Possession*. [Originally published in German 1921] London: Kegan Paul, Trench, Trubner.
243. Freed, Stanley A and Ruth S. (1966). "Spirit Possession as Illness in a North Indian Village." *International Journal of Parapsychology* VIII:1 (Winter).
244. Freed, op cit., p. 126.
245. Freed, op cit., p. 110.
246. Freed, op cit., p. 105.
247. Lewis, Ioan M. (1967). "Reply to Wilson." *Man* (2):626-7, quoted by Wells 1999.
248. Capron, Eliah Wilkinson (1855). *Modern Spiritualism*. Boston: Bela Marsh, p. 231. The account of the Fox family manifestations is taken from Capron, unless otherwise indicated.
249. Margaret Fox, reproduced in Capron, op cit., pp. 39-43.
250. Capron, op cit., pp. 43-56.
251. Capron, op cit., p. 101.
252. Davenport, Reuben Briggs (1976[1888)]. *The Death-Blow to Spiritualism*. New York: Arno Press facsimile reprint. Dillingham, 1888, p. 120.
253. Capron, op cit., p. 55.
254. Capron, op cit., p. 102.
255. Capron, op cit., pp. 95-96.
256. Anonymous (1853). *Spirit Rapping in England and America; its origin and history, including descriptions of the spheres, the spirits and their pursuits, and the various classes of mediums; also records of numerous interviews with spirits and mediums*. London: Vizetelly, pp. 31-33.
257. Capron, op cit., p. 421 et seq.
258. *New York Herald* reported in Jackson 1972: 203-4.
259. Davenport, op cit., 1888 passim.
260. Brown, Slater (1970). *The Heyday of Spiritualism*. New York: Hawthorn Books, p. 204.
261. *The Celestial City*, quoted in Pond 1947: 405.
262. Capron, op cit., p. 251 quoting a pamphlet, *A History of the recent Developments in Spiritual Manifestations*, dated 1850.
263. Capron, op cit., p. 306.
264. *Spirit Rapping*, op cit., p. 156.
265. [Britten], Emma Hardinge (1870). *Modern American Spiritualism*. New York: The author, p. 104.
266. Britten, op cit., p. 57.
267. Britten, op cit., p. 52.
268. *Spirit Rapping*, op cit., pp. 56-57.
269. Hammond, Charles (1852). *The Pilgrimage of Thomas Paine and Others to the Seventh Circle of the Spirit World*. New York: Partridge & Brittan.
270. Britten, op cit., p. 68.
271. Britten, op cit., p. 105.
272. Charles Hammond, op cit., quoted in *Spirit Rapping*, p. 77.
273. Hare, Robert (1855). *Experimental Investigation of the Spirit Manifestations*. New York: Partridge & Brittan, p. 166.
274. *Spirit Rapping*, op cit., p. 70.
275. *Spirit Rapping*, op cit., p. 219.
276. Chauncey Burr, quoted in *Spirit Rapping*, op cit., p. 253.
277. Capron, op cit., p. 270 et seq.
278. Britten, op cit., p. 86.
279. Capron, op cit., p. 377.
280. Gridley, Josiah A. (1854). *Astounding Facts from the Spirit World*. Southampton, MA: The author, passim.
281. Capron, op cit., p. 231-234.
282. Ballou, Adin (1852). *Spirit Manifestations*. London: H Baillière 1852 [first published in USA same year], p. 145, reprinting the *Olive Branch* which in turn is reprinting the *Boston Pilot*.
283. Cited in *La Table Parlante* (1854): 122, and *Spirit Rappings*, 266.
284. Mahan, Asa (1855). *Modern Mysteries Explained and Exploded*. Boston: Jewett, p. 344.
285. Capron, op cit., p. 100.
286. Reviewed in *The Spiritual Herald*, April 1856, p. 79.
287. *Spirit Rapping*, op cit., p. 229.
288. Quoted in Guillard (apparent pen name of Schauenburg, Karl Hermann) (1853). *Table qui Danse et Table qui Répond, Expériences à la Portée de tout le Monde*. Paris: Garnier Frères, p. 7.
289. Guillard, op cit., p. 16.
290. Walsh, Le comte Théobald (1858). *Dunglas Home et le Spiritualisme Américain*. Paris: Claye, p. 21.
291. Davies, Charles Maurice (1875). *Mystic London*. London: Tinsley, p. 305.
292. Home, Madame Dunglas (1888). *D.D.Home, His Life and Mission*. London: Trübner, p. 73.
293. Silas, Ferdinand (1853). *Instruction Explicative et Pratique des Tables Tournantes*. Paris: Houssiaux, pp. 22-23.
294. Gasparin, Comte Agénor de (1892). *Du Surnaturel*. Paris: Calmann Lévy, p. 34 et seq.
295. Capron, op cit., p. 254 quoting a pamphlet, *A History of the recent Developments in Spiritual Manifestations*, dated 1850.
296. Capron, op cit., p. 365.
297. Margaret Fox, cited in Davenport 1888: 50-51.
298. *The Spiritual Herald*, May 1856, 125, from *The Spiritual Telegraph*, 21 July, 1855.
299. Bekhterev, Vladimir Mikhailovich. (1998)[1908] *Suggestion and its Role in Social Life*, third edition. (translated from Russian by Tzvetanka Dobreva-Martinova). New Brunswick, New Jersey: Transaction Publishers, pp. 96-97.

300. DeMott, John S. (1986). "Wreaking Havoc on Spring Break." *Time* 127(14):29 (April 7).
301. Brewer, E. Cobham (1925). *The Reader's Handbook*. London: Chatto & Windus [revised edition].
302. Haining, Peter (1977). *The Legend and Bizarre Crimes of Spring Heeled Jack*. London: Frederick Muller.
303. *Illustrated London News*, 27 September 1845.
304. Jacqueline Simpson (2001). "Spring-Heeled Jack." *Foaftale News* 48 (January).
305. Lindsay, Mark (2005). "A Familiar Situation at Starpoint." *Lockport Journal*, January 29.
306. Lindsay, Mark (2004). "Evacuation Scene had Surreal Calm." *Tonawanda News*, December 15, 2004; WBEN newsroom (2004). "Mystery Illness at Starpoint Schools." December 14 at 12:10 pm; Besecker, Aaron, and Lindsay, Mark (2004). "Scare at Starpoint." *Lockport Journal*, December 15, 2004; Nemeth, S. (2004b). "Starpoint Reopens, but with 308 Absentees." *Lockport Journal*, December 18.
307. Nemeth, S. (2005a). "Starpoint Takes Paper to Task Over Story." *Lockport Journal*, January 11; Nemeth, S. (2005b). "A Chemical Link?" *Lockport Journal*, January 10.
308. Nemeth, S. (2004a). "Starpoint Students Complain about Ammonia-like Smell." *Lockport Journal*, January 14.
309. Lindsay, Mark (2005). "A Familiar Situation at Starpoint." op cit.
310. Michelmore, Bill, with Kowalik, Pam (2004). "Teachers, Pupils Fall Ill in Lockport." *Buffalo News*, December 22, 2004.
311. Westmoore, Paul (2005). "Lockport Schools. Unusual Weather Conditions Apparently Led to Illnesses." *Buffalo News*, January 1, 2005.
312. Westmoore, Paul (2005). op cit.
313. Westmoore, Paul (2005). op cit.
314. Hayes, Dominic (2004). "School Illness 'was Mass Hysteria.'" *The Evening Standard* (London, England), September 13.
315. McCartney, Margaret (2004). "Don't panic! Could 'Mass Hysteria' Explain why 55 pupils and Staff from Collenswood School in Hertfordshire Fell Mysteriously Ill Last Week?" *The Guardian* (London), September 14.
316. Thurston, Herbert (1952). *The Physical Phenomena of Mysticism*. London: Burns & Oates, p. 32 et seq. This, like virtually all the references quoted, is written by a Catholic and the book has received official authorization from the Church.
317. Imbert-Goubeyre 1896.
318. Dom Alois Mager. *Le Problème Scientifique de la Stigmatisation*. Etudes Carmelitaines: Douleur et Stigmatisation.
319. Huysmans, Joris-Karl (1901). *Sainte Lydwine de Schiedam*. Paris: Stock.
320. Biot, René (1955). *L'énigme des Stigmatisés*. Paris: Fayard, p. 66.
321. Thurston, op cit., p. 77.
322. Thurston, op cit., p. 101.
323. Wilson, Ian (1989). *Stigmata*. New York: Harper & Row, pp. 54-57.
324. Bourneville, Dr. Louise (1875). *Lateau*. Paris: Aux bureaux du Progrès Médical, p. 13.
325. Lhermitte, Jean (1934). "Konnersreuth." *Etudes Carmélitaines*, April 1934, p. 211 et seq.
326. Wilson, op cit., p. 58.
327. Krippner, Stanley (2002). "Stigmatic Phenomenon: An Alleged Case in Brazil." *Journal of Scientific Exploration* 16:2, 207.
328. Kerr, Cecil (1927). *Teresa Helena Higginson*. London: Sands. Kerr 1922: 72 et seq.
329. Barthélemy, Toussaint (1893). *Etude sur la Dermographisme*. Paris: Société d'éditions scientifiques, p. 82.
330. Wunderle, D Georges (1936). "Psychologie et la Stigmatisation." *Etudes Carmélitaines* (October), p. 162.
331. Poray Madeyski, Boleslas de (1940). *Thérèse Neumann de Konnersreuth*. Paris: Lethielleux, p. 242.
332. Thurston, op cit., p. 56.
333. Thurston, op cit., p. 122.
334. Thurston, op cit., p. 204 et seq: Lechler's experiments are referred to in most histories of stigmatization.
335. Thurston, op cit., p. 60.
336. Thurston, op cit., p. 40.
337. Lhermitte (1936). "Le Problème Médical de la Stigmatisation." *Etudes Carmélitaines* (October).
338. Theresa's medical history is narrated in some detail in Poray-Madeyski, op cit.
339. Graef, Hilda C. (1950). *The Case of Therese Neumann*. Cork: Mercier Press, p. 19.
340. Poray-Madeyski, op cit.
341. Lhermitte, Jean, op cit., p. 219.
342. Professor Martini, quoted in Poray-Madeyski, op cit., pp. 126-130.
343. San Antonio Express-News, May 22, 2006, accessed May 24, 2005 at: http://www.my sanantonio.com/opinion/editorials/stories/MYSA052206.1O.soaps3ed.1c6e953.html.
344. "Teens Suffer Soap Opera Virus," Reuters report accessed May 25, 2006 at: http://go.reuters.com/newsArticle.jhtml?type=oddlyEnoughNews&storyID=12254563&src=rss/oddlyEnoughNews.
345. Evans, Robert R., and Miller, Jerry L. (1975). "Barely an End in Sight," in Robert R. Evans (ed.), *Readings in Collective Behavior*. Chicago: Rand McNally, pp. 401-415; Anderson, William A. (1977). "The Social Organization and Social Control of a Fad." *Urban Life* 6:221-240; Marum, Andrew, and Parise, Frank. (1984). *Follies and Foibles: A View of 20th Century Fads*. New York: Facts on File, pp. 178-180.
346. Marum and Parise, op cit., p. 178.
347. Aguirre, B., Quarantelli, E., and Mendoza, J. (1988). "The Collective Behavior of Fads: The Characteristics, Effects, and Career of Streaking." *American Sociological Review* 53: 569-584.
348. Evans and Miller, op cit.
349. Schwarz, Frederic D. (1999). "Twenty Five Years Ago (Watergate and Streaking Filled the News)." *American Heritage* 50(2):130.
350. Evans and Miller, op cit.
351."The Streaking Phenomenon." Http://www.historychannel.com/speeches/archive/speech _368 .html, accessed March 14, 2003.
352. Miller, David L. (2000). *Introduction to Collective Behavior and Collective Action*. Prospect Heights, Illinois: Waveland Press, p. 180.
353. Hoffmann, Frank W., and Bailey, William G. (1991). *Sports and Recreation Fads*. New York: Harrington Park Press, p. 352.
354. *The Complete Books of Charles Fort*. New York: Dover Publications, p. 853, citing the *London Daily News*, January 2, 1922.
355. Monestier, Martin (1979). *Ils ont Choisi de Mourir Ensemble*. Paris: Encre Editions, p. 77.
356. Coleman, Loren (1987). *Suicide Clusters*. London: Faber, p. 35.
357. Monestier, op cit., p. 45.
358. Monestier, op cit., 1979, p. 20.
359. Coleman, op cit., pp. 31+.
360. Monestier, op cit., p. 115.
361. Monestier, op cit., p. 85.
362. Monestier, op cit., p. 31.
363. Monestier, op cit., p. 22.
364. Monestier, op cit., p. 29.

365. Monestier, op cit., p. 33.
366. Monestier, op cit., p. 37.
367. Monestier, pp. 102+.
368. Coleman, op cit., pp. 115-120.
369. Monestier, op cit., p. 23.
370. Coleman, op cit., p. 126.
371. O'Carroll, Patrick W., and Potter, Lloyd B. (1994). "Suicide Contagion and the Reporting of Suicide: Recommendations from a National Workshop." *Morbidity and Mortality Weekly* 43(RR-6);9-18. Accessed January 23, 2004 at: http://www.phppo.cdc.gov/cdcRecommends/showarticle.asp?aartid=M0031539&TopNum=50&CallPg=Adv.
372. Davidson, L.E., Rosenberg, M.L., Mercy, J.A., Franklin, J., Simmons, J.T. (1989). "An Epidemiologic Study of Risk Factors in Two Teenage Suicide Clusters." *Journal of the American Medical Association* 262:2687-2692.
373. O'Carroll and Potter (1994). op cit.
374. No author. (1988). "CDC Recommendations for a Community Plan for the Prevention and Containment of Suicide Clusters." *Morbidity and Mortality Weekly* 37(S-6);1-12, accessed January 23, 2004 at: http://wonder.cdc.gov/wonder/PrevGuid/p0000214/p0000214.asp.
375. Gould, Madelyn S. "Suicide Contagion (Clusters)." Accessed Januiary 24, 2004 at: http://www.suicide referencelibrary.com/148.html.
376. Stack, Simon (2003). A summary of findings from *The Journal of Epidemiology and Community Health* 57: 238–240, accessed on January 24, 2004 at: http://www.psychiatrymatters.md/news/2003/week_12/day_5/p_0000053097.asp.
377. Wingård, C F af. (1846). *Review of the Latest Evils and Present State of the Church of Christ.* Translated from the Swedish. London: Rivington 1846.
378. Souden, cited by Prouvost, Maurice Emile Léon Théodore (1896). *Le Délire Prophétique: étude Historique et Clinique.* Doctoral thesis. Bordeaux: Cassignol, p. 77.
379. Prouvost, op cit., p. 76.
380. Butsch 279: appendix to Letter to C. F. af Wingård, p. 275.
381. Butsch, refer to Wingård, op cit., p. 288.
382. Butsch, refer to Wingård, op cit., 291.
383. Prouvost, op cit., p. 77.
384. Butsch, refer to Wingård, op cit., 275.
385. Butsch, refer to Wingård, op cit., 276.
386. Butsch, refer to Wingård, op cit., 302.
387. Prouvost, op cit., p. 77.
388. "Keyed Up Too Intensely," *The Post-Standard* (Syracuse, New York), January 1, 1951, p. 6.

TAIPING REBELLION

China: 1844-1864

The Taiping Rebellion marked a permanent break with China's traditional past. Though it failed in its object, it embodied ideas and changes in attitude that would in the course of a century transform the country. It also prefigured the way in which that transformation would come about; not by gradual change but by a series of violent revolutions. Such profound changes could be accomplished only by rousing large masses of people to abandon their customary ways and indulge in exceptional collective behavior.[1]

CONTEXT: A combination of circumstances made Chinese society extremely volatile at this time. The existing order, based on principles laid down by K'ung Ch'iu (Confucius) in the 6th century BCE, was a pragmatic and flexible system, capable of maintaining public order even when, as periodically occurred, the state itself was disrupted by dynastic change. Unfortunately these virtues were matched by a tendency to stagnation and rigid resistance to change. Corruption was universal, leading to over-taxation of the general population and widespread banditry. This in turn encouraged the creation of secret societies formed for mutual protection, constituting a kind of underground opposition.

At the period of the Taiping Rebellion, conditions were aggravated by a massive growth in population and by ethnic troubles, as a consequence of which the peasants and lower orders of society, from whom the Taiping rebels would be drawn, felt threatened and unprotected.

Hung Xiu-quan, a young teacher from the Canton delta, inspired the rebellion. In the course of a mental breakdown following an examination failure, he experienced a vision in which he traveled to heaven where he learned that he was in fact the younger brother of Jesus, whose wife was like a mother to him.[2] Although he was reluctant to return to Earth, his father, the Christian God, entrusted him with a mission to go back to China and destroy devils and demons, rid the world of wickedness, and lead humanity to a peaceful and harmonious existence.

Hung's message was of a "Taiping" – a "Heavenly Kingdom of Great Peace" in which all humanity would live as one big mutually supportive family. To bring this about, he would replace the Confucian system with a monolithic state in which all power would devolve directly from the top. Although not hitherto a Christian, he was inspired by Christian teachings and this was reinforced by contact with missionaries, though his understanding of Christian principles was never more than superficial. He traveled the country, started to teach his vision, and attracted followers in

Suppressing the Taiping Outbreak: the French in action.

the Guangxi region where conditions were particularly unstable. He inaugurated the Bai sang-di-hui (The God-worshipping Society), which professed a kind of pseudo-Christian millennarist doctrine. Although the founders considered the teachings important, it is likely that most of those who joined did so for social reasons – the Taiping offered protection in a threatening world. But those who required spiritual authorization received it, as there were reports of miracle healings, speaking in tongues, and ecstasies that favored privileged individuals. "It sometimes happened that while they were kneeling down engaged in prayer, the one or the other of those present was seized by a sudden fit, so that he fell down to the ground, and his whole body was covered with perspiration. In such a state of ecstasy, moved by the spirit, he uttered words of exhortation, reproof, prophecy &c. Often the words were unintelligible, and generally delivered in verse. Loyal followers noted down in a book the more remarkable of these sayings."[3]

Such behavior was evidently in the shaman tradition, to which the Chinese populace were accustomed and which they recognized as either divine or demonic (the distinction between the two was not as polarized as in Christian doctrine). One of those claiming to be inspired in this way was Yang Xiuqing, who in 1848 purported to be possessed by the Holy Ghost of the Christians. Hung was faced with a problem: did these possessions come from the gods or from demons? He decided that three of his followers were indeed receiving divine inspiration, like his own vision, but that the rest were demonic. Since Chinese folk belief recognized such involuntary possession as one of the accidents of everyday life, his decision was accepted, with the result that Hung and Yang were able to impose their authority on the rest.

The way was now open for the sect to move from religious dreaming to political action. By now it was clear that the spiritual beliefs of the society had a more immediate and practical side. The "demons" that must be exterminated included not only the spirits of evil, but their representatives on Earth, the reigning Manchu dynasty and those who supported it. By August 1847, the God Worshippers Society had attracted two thousand followers, mostly peasants and miners. From this nucleus the numbers rapidly grew, thanks to the heady mix of religion, political change, and economic benefits promised by the sect. In three years their numbers swelled to between ten and thirty thousand. Yang, though ruthless and perhaps no more than an opportunist, revealed himself as a dynamic and effective leader, leaving Hung – who showed signs of mental instability – to concern himself with doctrine.

That doctrine was never more than incoherent, and it is questionable whether most of Hung's followers grasped more of it than its earthly promises and a vague notion that there might be even better things to come in the next life. Certainly, despite Hung's principles, it would be absurd to describe the Taiping rebels as Christians, though initially this was what Western observers hoped. Hung promised that those who were killed in battle would ascend to heaven, but also assured those who fought and survived that they would be well rewarded. In the meantime, however, they must put all their strength into the struggle. Not only were the male and female followers separated, but they must abstain from sexual activity until the Taiping cause was achieved. These strictures did not apply to the leaders, though, who were rewarded more immediately by being allowed to possess large harems.

No documents exist that tell of the state of mind of the rank-and-file Taiping rebel. It seems unlikely that so many men and women, from the lowest levels of society, should have come together and achieved so much unless they were inspired by a common dream, and perhaps this in turn inspired them to exceptional courage and sacrifice. But not all were volunteers. When the Taiping took a town or village, the inhabitants were generally conscripted into their ranks, which they were probably glad enough to do, the alternative options being even less attractive. For many there must have been a real fervor and enthusiasm, in addition to the military expertise of their leaders, for initially the rebels swept from success to success, and on March 19, 1853, they took the major city of Nanking, which they made into their headquarters. By now their numbers were over a million; indeed, a government intelligence report estimated more than three million.[4]

But internal strains were appearing within the sect. When a British naval force, maintaining neutrality, sent a cordial message to the Taiping leaders in November 1858, Hung required that he be given the respect due to God's son. Unsurprisingly, Lord Elgin was reluctant to oblige, and a diplomat in his entourage spoke of the "religious eccentricities" of the leaders as damaging the rebels' cause.

Fighting continued as the rebels sought to spread the rebellion further, but by now many of the peasants were disenchanted. Alexander Wylie, the diplomat just mentioned, reported on "the absence of all sympathy with the rebels on the part of the peasantry. Not only do they harry and squeeze these unfortunate people, but press the men into their service by violence, retaining for themselves all the best-looking of their women."[5]

Things were made worse by leadership struggles within the sect. In June 1864, Hung died, possibly by suicide. Although he was now little more than a figurehead, his authority was not disputed and his death led to an open rivalry between the leaders. This in turn led to military defeat, and in July 1864, Nanking was retaken. Government troops killed more than 100,000 men in three days. Those who survived – about the same number – killed themselves rather than be taken, enclosing themselves in buildings that they then set alight. It was the finish of the rebellion.

COMMENT: In November 1864, the *North China Herald* identified imbecility and ignorance as the prime causes of the rebels' failure – a total unawareness of what they were up against. Even if they had achieved the military conquest of the country, they would have been incapable of administering it without the support of those classes they had made their enemies. By alienating the massive administration that worked along Confucian principles, they had deprived themselves of an essential ally. As for popular support, this too they managed to alienate. At the start they inspired thousands, but they soon became just another force imposed on the countryside, filling up their ranks from desperate uprooted groups of the population, at first by voluntary enlistment but more and more through compulsion and terror.[6] Inspired by a visionary prophecy, and believing in the visions and ecstasies of the leaders who manipulated them, they marched in the thousands, eventually the millions, and in the end they died in their millions.

Since the great majority of the rebels were illiterate and uneducated, it is not surprising that we know nothing of the state of mind of the rank-and-file member of the Taiping. It can only be inferred from what they accomplished and what they failed to accomplish. The comment quoted above, that they were unaware of the magnitude of the task they had set themselves, is doubtless justified, but to achieve what they did, including the taking of one of China's major cities, suggests that their leaders succeeded in inspiring their million-plus followers with a remarkable enthusiasm and determination.

TARANTISM

Italy: July and August 1200-1600

The first recorded descriptions of a strange mental "affliction" classified by period physicians as tarantism appeared in Southern Europe in the thirteenth century, in the region that is now Italy. Historian Harold Gloyne described it as a "mass hysterical reaction" to perceived tarantula spider bites.[7] Less common terms used to describe the behavior includes tarantulism, *stellio*, *astaragazza*, and *tarantulismo*. Widespread, seasonal outbreaks persisted on a widespread scale for 400 years, peaking in the seventeenth century after which it rapidly declined to the point where only a handful of twentieth century accounts are recorded. Tarantism was almost exclusively reported during the height of the hot, dry summer months of July and August. According to historian Henry Sigerist:

> People, asleep or awake, would suddenly jump up, feeling an acute pain like the sting of a bee. Some saw the spider, others did not, but they knew that it must be the tarantula. They ran out of the house into the street, to the market place dancing in great excitement. Soon they were joined by others who like them had just been bitten, or by people who had been stung in previous years, for the disease was never quite cured. The poison remained in the body and was reactivated every year by the heat of summer... Music and dancing were the only effective remedies, and people were known to have died within an hour or in a few days because music was not available.[8]

CONTEXT: Tarantism appears to be a local variant of the DANCING MANIA, reflecting the unique social and cultural beliefs in the region known today as Italy.

Tarantism symptoms included breathing difficulties, chest pain, headache, giddiness, fainting, trembling, vomiting, twitching, excessive thirst, appetite loss, general soreness, and delusions. Symptoms resembled typical modern episodes of mass psychogenic illness, and reactions that would be expected from engaging in periods of exhaustive physical activity and/or excessive alcohol consumption. "Victims" occasionally claimed that a sore or swelling was made by a tarantula bite, but such assertions were difficult to verify as the bite appeared similar to that caused by other insects. While the identical species of tarantula is common throughout Southern Europe and is considered relatively harmless, frenzied reactions to perceived bites were almost exclusively reported in the vicinity of the southern Italian state of Apulia. While early medical observers theorized that a single bite from a venomous species of tarantula found only in Apulia could produce tarantism symptoms, more modern investigators testing spiders of the region have not substantiated this theory.[9]

Tarantism was supposedly cured by dancing the tarantella.

While *Latrodectus tarantula* is common in Apulia and can produce psychoactive effects in those it bites, it is not aggressive and moves very slowly. In rare cases its bite could cause symptoms that resemble many characteristic features of tarantism, such as twitching and shaking of limbs, weakness, nausea, and muscle pain. However, its symptoms are temporary and could not account for the range or duration of tarantism symptoms. Further, *Latrodectus tarantula* is found in other regions of the world, including the United States, where tarantism is not recorded.[10] The species most often associated with tarantism, *Lycosa tarantula* – a logical choice because it resides in southern Italy – is aggressive, ferocious in appearance and has a painful bite.[11] However, its bite is not capable of producing symptoms that even remotely resemble tarantism behavior. Also known as the wolf spider, symptoms are typically minor and involve localized pain and itching. Less common reactions included an increased pulse rate, nausea, and light-headedness.[12]

Tarantism is recorded as a history and culture-specific manifestation of mass hysteria due to its psychogenic character and claims that most of those afflicted were female.[13] Further psychogenic indications include the reported necessity of dancing to certain musical scores as the only reliable cure. The most common curative tunes were variations of the tarantella, a dance taking its name in the 18th century from the Italian port city of Taranto. The tarantella is a whirling, fast-paced dance featuring brief, repetitive phrases that increase in intensity.

Other psychogenic features included observations that "victims" were able to exhibit a variety of prohibited acts with impunity, claiming they had been under the influence of tarantism. Other aspects of the behavior were equally conspicuous. For instance, while dancing typically lasted intermittently for days and occasionally weeks, those affected eventually declared themselves "cured," only to relapse in subsequent summers. At other times, "victims" reported being "infected" by simply being in close proximity to those who had been bitten or by simply touching or brushing against a spider. Still others were afflicted summer after summer upon hearing musicians playing certain tunes that were intended to "cure" those who had supposedly been bitten.[14]

Theories Of Tarantism

In 1750, Naples physician Francesco Serao stated that tarantism was prevalent among the poor of Apulia as they were predisposed to depression,[15] while others blamed the condition on the hot, dry climate.[16] Influential Italian medical authority Giorgio Baglivi (1723) theorized that a species of tarantula living in the vicinity of Apulia had a potent venom capable of producing hallucinations, and that dancing to music was the only reliable cure.[17] Medical historian George Rosen discussed tarantism in relation to "psychic epidemics" of the Middle Ages,[18] but remarked on the importance of the historical context. Rosen argued that tarantism (and DANCING MANIAS) were ritualized behaviors that developed from Greek religious ceremonies. However, Rosen assumes that such behaviors were abnormal cathartic reactions to overwhelming stress including floods, famine, and disease.[19] Historian Henry Sigerist, in *Civilization and Disease*, drew similar parallels between ancient Greek rites and tarantism symptoms.[20] He suggested that tarantism may have been a form of covert political activity, providing an outlet for expressing local heathen customs – in this instance a ritual composed mostly of persons suffering from neurosis, insanity, and depression that slowly evolved into the conscious or subconscious guise of being instigated by spider bites, so as to coexist and even thrive, despite the ascendancy of Christianity.[21] Both Rosen and Sigerist assumed that such ceremonies and rituals attracted a disproportionate number of psychologically disturbed individuals. Sigerist even went so far as to suggest that its presence was a function of Apulian-inbreeding, as "there can be no doubt that the great majority of all tarantati were neurotics. Tarantism was a neurosis peculiar to that region."[22]

Historian George Mora concurred with Rosen and Sigerist, underscoring the association between tarantism and collective rituals that the ancient Greek's referred to as telestic or ritual madness. Such rituals acts were intended to produce a catharsis and assure future happiness.[23] The following description involves Corybantoc rites, typically associated with telete rituals. It involves a candidate who "was seated in a chair and the ministrants danced around him and raised a great din. The effect of this was to rouse his excitement and stir his emotions, so that he gradually lost consciousness of all but the whirling rhythm of the dance. This was followed by what was called telete proper, in which, we may suppose, the candidate threw himself into the dance with the rest and yielded to the intoxication of the rhythm. In the end, when all was over, the participants emerged from the tumult to a state of calm and tranquillity, and their minds were at peace."[24]

More recently, sociologist Robert Bartholomew has challenged conventional interpretations of tarantism, contending that episodes were primarily rituals and had little association with mass hysteria.[25] He observes that like contemporary ecstatic religious sects, tarantism adherents worshipped in a discernible pattern, typically commencing their dancing at sunrise, would stop during midday to sleep and sweat, then bathe before resuming the dance until evening, when they would again sleep, sweat, consume a light meal, then sleep until sunrise. This ritual was usually repeated over four or five days, and sometimes for weeks.[26]

COMMENTS: Many of the physical symptoms associated with tarantism likely resulted from sleep deprivation, emotional excitement, and vigorous, prolonged physical activity. Contrary to popular psychiatric portrayals, females were not always overrepresented among participants. For instance, a contemporary study of tarantism in the vicinity of Sardinia, Italy, by C. Gallini found that most "victims" were male, while Ernesto de Martino reported that most participants near Apulia were female.[27] Clearly, episodes were not spontaneous but highly structured, involving strange or unfamiliar customs that were redefined as a psychological abnormality. Bartholomew contends that only by examining the social, cultural, and historical circumstances surrounding the appearance of tarantism is it possible to interpret episodes "as behavioral idioms that have been 'mistranslated' by scholars judging these behaviors per se, removed from their regional context and meaning."[28]

TEACHER HYSTERIA

Pretoria, South Africa: 1987

The teaching staff at a South African primary school was being blamed for triggering a fainting epidemic among students. One day a teacher went into a trance state, had a vision of her classroom smeared with blood and human feces, and then fainted. Other teachers soon reported similar visions before fainting. It wasn't long before several students were collapsing onto the floor and having visions. After sporadic episodes, the situation exploded in 1989 with at least 60 students fainting or falling simultaneously. Many of the students, their parents and teachers believed that witchcraft was responsible. At this point a psychiatric team visited the school, which by now was in chaos with dozens of students screaming, running about, and collapsing. Some were twitching and convulsing; others were hallucinating.

Psychologist Bernadette Wittstock said that some students told of seeing "small, dark people; of women dressed in tattered clothes threatening to hit them with sticks or knives; of frightening animals..."[29] Many students told Wittstock chilling accounts of fearing for their lives: "The figures in the visions called the children to leave the classroom and told them that they would be killed if they discussed their visions with others."[30] Many children were convinced that a witch was casting spells in order to take control of the school. The spells and visions slowly subsided and ceased altogether after several months.

TENNESSEE SCHOOL HYSTERIA

Tennessee: 1998

This reported episode of mass hysteria is well known after a study of the incident appeared in the prestigious *New England Journal of Medicine*. On the morning of November 12, 1998, within 15 minutes of arriving at a McMinnville, Tennessee high school, a teacher detected a "gasoline-like" odor in her classroom. She rapidly developed nausea, headache, dizziness, and breathlessness, and administrators decided to clear the building. During the evacuation more students reported smelling a strange odor and feeling ill, and the fire alarm was activated. Scores of emergency rescue personnel, police, fire trucks, and ambulances from three counties converged on the school. In full view of the evacuees, the initial stricken teacher and several pupils were loaded into ambulances and rushed to hospital as more students reported feeling unwell.

Of the 1,825 pupils and 149 staffers who either attended or worked at the school, 80 pupils, 19 staffers, and one family member were rushed to a local emergency room with a variety of transient symptoms: headache, dizziness, nausea, drowsiness, chest tightness, and breathing difficulty.[31] School was closed until the following Monday. On Tuesday morning, November 17, a similar outbreak occurred at the same school involving 71 persons. An army of personnel from government health agencies descended on the school and conducted a remarkable number and array of tests. Environmental tests of the building were negative, and no medical explanation was evident despite blood and urine tests, 220 air samples, 5 water samples, 8 wipe samples from various surfaces, and soil tests. A questionnaire of students found that symptoms were associated with being female, "seeing another ill person, knowing that a classmate was ill, and reporting an unusual odor at the school."[32] The detection of an odor in the school, and the rapid, prominent reaction to the scene by emergency personnel appear to have further heightened anxiety.

TERRORISM SCARES

Exaggerated public reactions to either real or perceived terrorism threats have prompted a number of episodes of both mass hysteria and social delusion. It is important to note at the onset that, like heretics in religion, terrorism is in the eye of the beholder, and one person's freedom fighter is another's terrorist.

CONTEXT: Every episode involving terrorism attack fears is couched in its unique set of social and cultural circumstances. A major recurring theme is long-standing distrust within a disaffected group, of what is viewed as an oppressive government, which is assumed responsible for an outbreak of illness symptoms. The mass media is influential in both spreading and legitimating the false or exaggerated belief, which engenders great fear. Rumors also play an important role. Chance happenings (precipitating events) such as a flu outbreak further exacerbate the situation.

Jewish Poisoning Scares

In 1321 at Guienne, France, Jews were accused of working in cooperation with criminals to poison drinking water, resulting in an estimated 5,000 Jews being burned at the stake. In 1347, a plague in the form of the Black Death was spread across Europe from rats on ships docking from the Far East. During this period it was widely rumored that the Devil was protecting Jews in return for their poisoning Christian wells. As a result, tens of thousands of Jews were murdered.[33]

In 1630, the Great Poisoning Scare swept across Milan, Italy. According to London journalist CHARLES MACKAY, the episode coincided with pestilence, plague, and a prediction that the Devil and evildoers would poison the city's water supply. On one April morning people awoke and became fearful upon finding "that all the doors in the principal streets of the city were marked with a curious daub, or spot."[34] Soon there was alarm that the sign of the awaited poisoning was at hand. It was believed that corn and fruit had also been poisoned. Many people were executed. One elderly man was spotted wiping a stool before sitting on it and was accused of smearing poison on the seat. He was seized by an angry mob of women and pulled by the hair to a judge, but he died on the way. In another instance, a pharmacist and barber named Mora, who was found with several preparations containing unknown potions, was accused of being in cahoots with the Devil to poison the city. Protesting his innocence, he eventually confessed after prolonged torture on the rack, admitting to cooperating with the Devil and foreigners to poisoning the city and anointing the doors. Under duress he named several accomplices who were eventually arrested and tortured. They were all pronounced guilty and executed. Mackay stated that "The number of persons who confessed that they were employed by the Devil to distribute poison is almost incredible," noting that "day after day persons came voluntarily forward to accuse themselves."[35]

Spy Mania During World War I

During World War I, chemical and bio-terrorism fears grip the United States and Europe as President Wilson warned of German spies being everywhere. There were even rumors that German submarine captains would give themselves influenza, then row ashore and cough in crowded theaters before returning to his vessel. The German scare reached such proportions that foods, streets, schools, businesses, and cities with Germanic names were renamed; communities prohibited German music or theater performances; and suspected traitors were occasionally assaulted, tarred, and feathered, or hanged by vigilantes.[36]

The "Mad Gasser" Of Botetourt

Between December 1933 and February 1934, residents in two rural Virginia counties were terror-stricken after reports that someone was sneaking up to homes at night and spraying a sickish-sweet noxious gas inside. The scare ended in mid-February when police concluded that the affair was a figment of the imagination. The episode began at the Cal Huffman farmhouse in Fincastle, which was reportedly "gassed" three times between Friday evening and Saturday morning December 22-23. At 10 p.m., Mrs. Huffman detected a gas odor, felt nauseated, and assumed that she had been sprayed. Thirty minutes later a gas smell was again detected, and Mr. Huffman phoned police, who found nothing unusual and left at 1 a.m. Minutes later the entire family became ill from fumes, and the Huffman's 20-year-old daughter Alice had fainted. When Dr. S.F. Driver arrived, he mistakenly assessed her condition as grave and administered "artificial respiration." After the third attack, Mr. Huffman and another person thought they may have seen a man running away.

Over the next few weeks the local press published numerous reports of subsequent gassings. At a house in Howell's Mill on January 11, muffled voices were heard outside followed by the smell of gas near a broken window, causing the occupant, a Mrs. Moore, to grab her child and flee. Her only symptom was a vague feeling of numbness. A couple living upstairs were unaffected and unaware of the incident until hearing her screams. By January 23, families in remote sections of the county were sleeping with neighbors, and vigilante farmers were spending their nights patrolling roads and keeping their guns at the ready.

The psychological nature of the scare was soon evident. After several incidents of shooting at, or over, shadowy figures in the night, one police officer warned that the community was so tense that he feared an innocent person would be shot. On January 24, Mamie Brown of Fincastle fled her home, screaming that she had been gassed, but it was quickly determined to have been a prankster. At about this time, Dr. Driver told the Botetourt County Board of Supervisors that not all cases appeared to be genuine and it was disclosed that at one of the homes "attacked," the offending fumes were traced to a coal stove.

In early February, the attacks shifted to Roanoke County. Most of the calls consisted of residents smelling fumes that were traced to mundane sources and few cases people actually becoming sick. In most cases, a common everyday source of the odors was readily detected: coal fumes, burning rubber, exhaust from a passing car. "Gassings" ceased in both counties after the night of the 11th, and Roanoke police concluded that the "gas man" was a product of "the power of suggestion."[37]

The episode must be seen in the context of the times. During the early 1930s, numerous books appeared discussing the perils of gas warfare including J. M. Kenworthy's *New Wars; New Weapons*, and Liddell Hart's *The British Way of Warfare*.[38] In *The Air Menace and the Answer*, Elvira K. Fradkin described America of the early 1930s as living through the "poison gas scare."[39] Numerous documents were published by the League of Nations and as proceedings from the many conferences held on the subject.[40] The year that Botetourt "gassings" began, *The New York Times* published 21 stories under the subject heading of "chemical weapons."[41] Stories described the preparations underway in various countries to defend against possible poison gas attacks in Denmark, England, the Netherlands, Australia, and Germany,[42] as there was a growing sense that chemical weapons were an inevitable part of the post World War I military landscape.[43] Many widely available periodicals of the time published stories on the perils of gas warfare.[44]

The Martian Invasion Panic Of 1938

Many people do not realize that the infamous Martian invasion radio broadcast of October 30, 1938, was actually a chemical weapons scare. In the weeks following the broadcast, Princeton University psychologist Hadley Cantril conducted interviews with a relatively small number of people who reportedly panicked. Twenty percent of his sample stated that during the program, they assumed that the announcer had misperceived what he was looking at and that the so-called Martians were actually Germans taking part in a poison gas raid on the United States. A typical respondent said: "The announcer said a meteor had fallen from Mars and I was sure that he thought that, but in the back of my head I had the idea that the meteor was just a camouflage ... and the Germans were attacking us with gas bombs."[45]

The "Mad Gasser" Of Mattoon

During the first two weeks of September 1944, residents of Mattoon, Illinois, were thrust into the world media spotlight after a series of imaginary gas attacks by a "phantom anesthetist." On Friday night, September 1, Mattoon police received a phone call from a woman and her daughter who said they had felt nauseated and dizzy after being sprayed with a sweet-smelling gas by a mysterious figure lurking near their bedroom window. The woman also said she experienced slight, temporary difficulty in walking. Despite the ambiguous circumstances and police finding nothing, the following evening, on September 2, the incident was afforded sensational coverage in the *Mattoon Daily Journal-Gazette* ("Anesthetic Prowler on Loose"). After seeing the story, two other Mattoon families recounted for police similar "gas attacks" in their homes just prior to the incident.

Before the reports ceased altogether after September 12, police logged over two dozen separate calls involving at least 29 victims, most of whom were females. The University of Illinois' Donald Johnson investigated the episode, concluding that it was a case of mass hysteria.[46] Their symptoms included nausea, vomiting, dry mouth, palpitations, difficulty walking, and in one instance, a burning sensation in the mouth. Given the influential role of the Mattoon news media, it may be that victims were redefining mundane processes as gasser-related such as a panic attack, chemical smell, one's leg "falling asleep," and the consequences of anxiety such as nausea, insomnia, shortness of breath, shakiness, dry mouth, dizziness, etc.

Like its predecessor, the Botetourt gasser, the Mattoon events must be understood within their context. During World War II, both the Allied and Axis powers lived with the fear that poison gas might be used. In *A Higher Form of Killing*, Robert Harris and Jeremy Paxman wrote that "years later it is difficult to appreciate just how great the fear of gas was" for both civilians and military.[47] During the war, rumors abounded in the United States of Axis gas atrocities, prompting numerous journalists to press for retaliation. The year of the Mattoon "attacks," 112 articles appeared in *The New York Times* under the topic of "chemical warfare,"[48] and many other publications at this time discussed the possible use of poison gas and how the Allies should respond.[49] By September 1944, with Germany clearly losing the war, there were fears that this desperate country might use chemical weapons. This threat was viewed as so realistic that the Allies, fearing that the Germans would respond to their June 6, 1944, D-Day invasion of Normandy, devised a plan to counter any German gas attacks with planes loaded with chemical weapons intended to drench select targets.[50] Why Mattoon in September 1944? There was an escaped Nazi on the loose in the area at the time and there had been a wave of robberies and break-ins. Coupled with press reports of possible poison gas use, residents were on edge. The final trigger seemed to be the sensational way in which Mattoon's only daily paper, the *Journal-Gazette*, sensationalized the initial report, resulting in Mattoonites being on the lookout for anything out of the ordinary, including strange odors. As a result residents started redefining mundane events, circumstances, and smells as gasser-related, and the episode was on.[51]

Thai Penis-Shrinking Terrorists Of 1976

During 1976, in northeast Thailand, upwards of 2,000 mostly rural male and female Thai citizens were terror-stricken with the fear that their genitals were shrinking. Men believed their penises were getting smaller while some women were convinced that their breasts or vulva was shrinking. The episode was triggered by rumors that Vietnamese immigrants had deliberately contaminated food and cigarettes with a mysterious powder. Two psychiatrists from the University of British Columbia in Canada were traveling in Thailand at the time and examined admission data from select hospitals, noting that the main complaints "were shrinking of the penis and sexual impotency in men; shrinking and/or itching of the external genitals and frigidity in women, also numbness in the lower abdominal regions."[52]

At the onset of the panic, anti-Vietnamese feelings were strong with claims that some Vietnamese were plotting to overthrow the government. A government analysis of the suspected products found no evidence of any harmful substances that could possibly cause genitals to shrink.[53] The head of the government's Medical Science Department announced that a thorough analysis of various items that were supposedly poisoned, "detected no foreign substance that could possibly cause sexual impotency or contraction of the male sex organ."[54] However, police officers and some journalists undermined attempts by government officials and physicians to calm the situation and reassure citizens that genital shrinking was not occurring. In some Thai newspapers, law enforcement officers were quoted as saying that the offending ingredient was comprised of a "mixture of some vegetable ingredients which could not be detected by medical devices."[55] There were even reports in the *Dao Siam* newspaper on November 15, that police chiefs within the region had been ordered to be on the lookout for any Vietnamese, as it was feared they might try slipping even more poison into certain foods. In northeast Thailand, there is great resentment against

Vietnamese immigrants, as they are economically competitive and clannish. Among Thai residents in the region, it was widely believed that Vietnamese restaurant operators and shopkeepers had sprinkled a "poisonous powder" onto "noodles, rice flour, meat balls, salted pork, iced coffee, soft drinks, and tobacco." Curiously, patients were often able to recall "that foods obtained from Vietnamese establishments had a suspicious taste, or that cigarettes bought there had a funny smell."[56]

Palestinian Poisoning "Plot" Of 1983

For several months in 1983, world media attention was focused on reports that Israelis may have poisoned Palestinian schoolgirls. Between March and April 1983, 947 mostly female residents of the disputed Israeli-occupied Jordan West Bank reported a variety of symptoms that were widely believed in the Arab World at the time to have been the result of chemical weapons. Complaints included headaches, blurred vision, stomach pain, fainting, blindness, and limb weakness. In all, 879 females were affected. Following negative medical tests, it became evident that no gassings had occurred, the hypothesis was discredited, and accordingly, the transient symptoms rapidly ceased.

The episode occurred amid poison gas rumors and a long-standing Palestinian mistrust of Jews. The medical complaints appeared during a fifteen-day period, coinciding with intense media publicity that poison gas was being sporadically targeted at Palestinians. The episode began in, and was predominantly confined to, schools in several adjacent villages. The case became widely known as "the Arjenyattah Epidemic," as they occurred in Arrabah, Jenin and Yattah.[57]

The Soviet Georgia Poisoning Scare Of 1989

A remarkably similar episode occurred at several nearby schools among some 400 adolescent females in Soviet Georgia during political unrest in 1989. The illness outbreak occurred after rumors that students had been exposed to poison gas such as chloropicrin that had been used recently by Russian authorities to disperse a large rally. Intense media publicity surrounding the confirmed use of poison gases, and rumors that the students had been poisoned, precipitated the rapid spread of conversion reactions. The transient complaints mimicked the poison gas symptoms: stomach ache, burning eyes, skin irritation, and dry throat. Media coverage was instrumental in the proliferation of the fears to the wider community.[58]

Fear Overtakes Kosovo

On March 14, 1990, some four thousand residents in the Serbian province of Kosovo, in the former Yugoslavia, were stricken with a mysterious illness that persisted for three weeks. Many of those affected believed they had been poisoned in an attempt at "ethnic cleansing." Symptoms included headache, dizziness, hyperventilation, weakness, burning sensations, cramps, chest pain, nausea, and dry mouth. According to Dr. Zoran Radovanovic, the head of community medicine at Kuwait University, the complaints were psychological in origin prompted by the long-standing ethnic Albanian mistrust of Serbians. The transient symptoms were mostly confined to adolescent ethnic Albanians.[59]

The poisoning scare began when a small group of children at a Podujevo high school reported a flu-like illness, which quickly spread to dozens of schools in the province. Shortly thereafter, "stories began circulating in the Albanian community about a powder, or liquid, alleged to have been put in a classroom by someone of Serbian nationality. An expert from Prishtina was called to investigate the allegation. On March 20, a teacher in another school was called to attend to three children who were said to have collapsed after touching a white powder. The teacher evacuated the classroom and claimed that on re-entry he noticed a strange chemical smell, which convinced him that he too had been poisoned by the Serbs as part of "the war." The teacher left the building immediately, had a severe headache, lost consciousness, and was taken to a hospital in Prishtina.[60]

Dr. Radovanovic concluded that the episode was triggered by respiratory infection in a single classroom. Influential factors included rumors, persons scrutinizing mundane odors and substances, and visits by health officials, which instead of alleviating fears actually seemed to legitimate them. Pre-existing ethnic tension between Serbs and Albanians, and the mass media were also factors. The dramatic proliferation of cases across the province on March 22, coincided with the implementation of an emergency disaster plan whereby ethnic Albanians seized control of public health services.[61]

According to an international team of physicians and human rights specialists who investigated the episode, "mass hysteria, not poisoning, was the reason for the epidemic." Based on an analysis of 86 blood samples, "Tests for liver, lung, renal, and neurological damage revealed nothing untoward except for several instances of raised aspartate aminotransferases, a consequence, possibly, of the fits that many people experienced. Cholinesterase activity – which should be reduced by exposure to organophosphates, one of the poisons suspected – was normal in all the samples. Screening of a random number of samples for organochlorines indicated the presence of some chlorophenols but at concentrations typical for the UK population."[62]

Phantom Iraqi "Gas Attack" At A U.S. School

During February 1991, a pupil fainted at a Rhode Island elementary school three and a half weeks after the onset of the Persian Gulf War. The incident coincided with classmates detecting a strange odor in the building, prompting sudden, extreme anxiety as many students apparently assumed that they were experiencing an Iraqi chemical weapons attack. Eighteen females and three males from four classrooms totaling 86 students and teachers on one end of the third story of a three-story building were stricken with dizziness, headache, and nausea. Four teachers were among those affected. During the Gulf War there was considerable publicity about poison gas attacks on Israel and possibly the United States. The affected seventh- and eighth-graders, and the teachers, were examined at a nearby hospital emergency department where the likelihood of collective hysteria was recognized, the students and the teachers were reassured, and they quickly recovered.[63]

Post-September 11th Terror Scares

The September 11, 2001, terrorist attacks in the United States, and subsequent mailing of anthrax-laced letters, generated widespread media discussion about the likelihood of further chemical or biological attacks. Such media speculation also appears to have been a self-fulfilling prophecy, as the publicity prompted a heightened state of anxiety and alertness and reports of imitative illness directly related to such fears. On September 29, 2001, harmless fumes from oil-based paints set off a bio-terrorism scare at Canyon Creek Middle School in Washington State, sending 16 students to the hospital. An army of rescue personnel rushed to the scene believing a terrorist attack was underway.[64]

Between October 2 and 3, a bio-terror scare swept across Manila in the Philippines when about 1,400 students from several Manila schools flooded local clinics, reporting mild flu-like symptoms: coughing, colds, mild fever. Some of the students were later confirmed as having Type A H1N1 influenza, but health authorities found that many had suffered psychogenic reactions after rumors spread among jittery parents and pupils that it was bio-terrorism. The false story spread rapidly via text messages.[65]

On October 9, a man got into a scuffle with police and sprayed a mysterious substance in a subway station near College Park, Maryland. Suddenly, 35 passengers and transit workers fell ill with nausea, headache, and sore throats. It was later determined that the bottle contained harmless window cleaner.[66] About two weeks earlier in the Los Angeles subway, an unusual odor was detected causing commuters to become anxious, fearing a possible chemical or biological attack. Many reported feeling ill. The subway soon re-opened after tests for the presence of any harmful substances proved negative.[67] The backdrop of these reports was the anthrax scare that gripped the country. Cable News Network reported that no less than 2,300 anthrax false alarms occurred over a two-week span in early October. It seemed as though any powdery substance someone found at work or in school would prompt an evacuation, as emergency personnel, often dressed in bubble suits, would enter the building in dramatic fashion and remove the suspicious powder for testing.[68]

The anthrax scare appears to have given rise to what Princeton University historian Elaine Showalter called "the Bin Laden Itch" (see ITCHING AND RASH FRENZIES) in dozens of schools across the United States. The effects of the anthrax continued to be felt in the form of mass psychogenic illness for years afterwards as hyper-vigilant mailroom workers redefined mundane symptoms as possible biological or chemical weapons. For instance, during May 2003, when two mail sorters at the Naperville, Illinois, City Hall experienced itching of the hands and forearms, police and fire personnel rushed to the scene and locked the building down. As the building was being searched, three more workers who were stationed nearby also reported being itchy. Four were evaluated at a local hospital. Physicians could find no apparent cause and there were no signs of rash or hives. Investigators scoured the building and tested for the presence of anthrax and various chemicals, but all tests were negative. They even tested for traces of the itching powder but without success. [69]

Lastly, in the months following the September 11 terrorist attacks on the United States, there was a big increase in the number of reports of harassment and persecution of persons of Arab or Middle Eastern heritage who were feared to have either been terrorists or in cahoots with them.

COMMENTS: We live in an age preoccupied with environmental concerns that threaten the very existence of life on earth, from depletion of the ozone layer, acid rain, and fear of contaminants in our food, air, and drinking water. In our post-September 11 world, such concerns, in combination with worries over the potential use of nuclear, chemical or biological weapons, is likely to incubate future episodes of pseudo-terror attacks that will be triggered by unfamiliar odors and food poisoning fears.[70]

See also: "MAD GASSER" OF BOTETOURT, "MAD GASSER" OF MATTOON, MARTIAN INVASION "PANIC" OF 1938.

TEXAS EARTHWORM HOAX

Laredo, Texas: 1993

In early March 1993, a newspaper hoax created excitement in Laredo, Texas (population 130,000), after *The Morning Times of Laredo* published a bogus account of a giant 300-pound earthworm measuring 79-feet in length. The creature was reportedly found dead, draped across Interstate 35, tying up traffic.

CONTEXT: The incident highlights the influence of the mass media in the information age, and how susceptible society is to journalistic hoaxes.

According to the story, entomologist Luis Leacky from Laredo State University had located a mucus trail along the Interstate, speculating that the creature had mutated from the nearby Rio Grande. Laredo police and U.S. Border Patrol officers reportedly converged on the scene in rubber gloves, removing the mammoth worm with the help of two cranes and a large truck.[71]

Local police were deluged with hundreds of calls from inquisitive residents as scores of people drove to the scene to glimpse the fictitious worm after the journalist who wrote the story, Carol Huang, wrote: "Because federal environmental guidelines do not outline the proper disposal method for large, earthworm carcasses ... authorities have left the creature in the Target store parking lot until Monday, when zoologists and EPA officials are expected to arrive from Washington."[72] Even before the store opened, a Target worker said that curiosity seekers kept asking if the worm carcass was inside the building.[73]

Huang, who was dismissed from her job the same day, said she wrote the account on her computer as a joke but was flabbergasted to see it appear on page 3A several days later. The news editor who allowed the story to appear, Thomas Sanchez, left his job shortly after the incident, but said the account ran "by accident."[74]

THEORIES OF MASS HYSTERIA

Supernatural Possession

The earliest recorded explanation for episodes of mass hysteria is the supernatural agent hypothesis, which contends that evil or benevolent spirits possesses the victims. This folk theory, popular during the Middle Ages, accounted for incidents of individual and collective demon possession that occurred during reports of DANCING MANIA and TARANTISM. Mass possession attributed to the Devil or his agents was a widely held explanation to account for outbreaks of hysterical fits that swept through European Christian convents between the13th and 16th centuries (see CONVENT HYSTERIA). Symptoms were typified by altered states of consciousness, histrionics, abnormal movements such as twitching, shaking and contractures, and sensations of suffocation and globus (the feeling of a lump in the throat). Similar symptoms and explanations were recorded during the SALEM WITCH TRIALS OF 1692, in addition to historical and modern-day accounts of collective spirit possession in various religious movements of a charismatic or ecstatic nature, i.e., the Dutch and German Anabaptists between 1521 and 1592, French Calvinists between 1686 and 1706, and Janeist convulsionaries of the 1730s. Contemporary reports within a non-Western context continue to be viewed as the work of supernatural forces, such as ancestral bush beings in Papua New Guinea,[75] Islamic *jin* spirits in Malaysia,[76] ancestor spirits in Tanzania,[77] penis-snatching female fox ghosts in China,[78] Christian demons in South Africa,[79] and malevolent spirits of the dead in Thailand.[80]

Feigning Conscious Illness

Another explanation for some episodes is that some or all participants are consciously feigning sickness, or unusual behavior, for monetary or social benefit. This view was supported by Italian Natural History Professor Dominico Cirillo, who suggested in the 1700s that tarantism episodes were the creation of individuals intent on making money for musicians who were needed to perform curative tarantellas.[81] Medical historian Henry Sigerist has suggested that some tarantism "victims" participated out of a desire for companionship.[82] Medieval medical authority Justus Friedrich Hecker commented that "numerous beggars, stimulated by vice and misery, availed themselves of this new complaint to gain a temporary livelihood," while vagabond gangs copied the dance, "roving from place to place seeking maintenance and adventures."[83] A contemporary modification of his theory includes feigning illness for political gain. A classic example occurred in 1983, after 947 mostly Palestinian schoolgirls on the disputed Jordan West Bank were reportedly sickened by "poison gas" attributed to Israeli agents. While several investigations have unambiguously concluded that the episode was psychogenic in nature,[84] several Israeli physicians considered the condition factitious and a deliberate conspiracy among "victims" to promote a negative image of Israeli foreign policy and sympathy for Palestinian supporters.[85]

Some episodes of "mass hysteria" in Malaysia may represent a culturally-conditioned conscious means for the politically weak (mostly Malay females) to critique poor work conditions and effect change. A key issue is differentiating between what is unconscious and what is contrived. It may be difficult to tell the difference between spontaneous outbreaks of mass hysteria in Malaysian factories and deliberate acts of political resistance. (See the kindred section in this entry on "Political Resistance.")

While some medieval demonopath "victims" may have participated unconsciously in the form of conversion symptoms, part of these dramas appear to have included widespread, deliberate deception and fraud. In 1566, l'Hôpital des Enfans Trouves Hospital at Amsterdam, Holland, was the scene of collective convulsions, possession, and delirium. During their exhibitions, the "victims" reportedly vomited quantities of hair, cloth, thimbles, needles, pins, broken pottery, and glass.[86] Miraculous vomiting at a convent of demoniacs in Auxonne, France, during the mid-17th century purportedly included bones, wax, pebbles, and living reptiles. Many "possessed" nuns claimed to have suffered anomalous lacerations from demonic forces or to have been levitated. Similar behaviors were reported among a group of possessed children during a witch accusation panic in Salem, Massachusetts, in 1692, as "nearly all of the children swore repeatedly that they had been pinched, choked and bitten, occasionally exhibiting marks of the bites or pinches on their arms."[87]

Unconscious Feigning Of Illness

The sick role perspective postulates that "victims" are engaged in an unconscious desire to obtain benefits by virtue of their illness status. In their investigation of spasmodic twitching at a Louisiana high school in 1939, Louisiana State University sociologists Edgar Schuler and Vincent Parenton concluded that Helen, the first pupil to exhibit symptoms, received a number of benefits from her illness status, including sympathy, attention, and avoidance of an undesirable situation. Not only did her new status attract considerable interest from friends and school staff, her illness status renewed the waning affection of a boyfriend, and exempted her from mandatory dance classes. The other girls, who soon experienced similar symptoms, were viewed as adopting the sick role to receive secondary gains after observing Helen's success.[88] Some episodes may involve the simultaneous presence of conscious and unconscious efforts by students to achieve specific objectives, though such are often difficult to determine and sometimes prove problematic, as the possibility of unanimous conspiratory deception cannot be excluded. A similar episode of mass hysterical tremor was reported in a Swiss girls' school in Basel in 1893, and then again 11 years later at the same school. In both cases, investigators concluded that the symptoms were an unconscious attempt to avoid school work.[89]

Unconscious Echoing Of Illness Or Behavior (Without Feigning)

Psychologists David Levy and Paul Nail discussed the term "echo contagion" which involves the unconscious spread of illness or acts whereby "an unconflicted recipient imitates or reflects spontaneously the affect or behavior of the imitator."[90] In such episodes, the person being imitated acts in a way that is attractive to the imitator, yet such mimicking of the other other's behavior occurs "at a lower level of cognitive processing," and thus, the responses appear to be relatively involuntary and unconscious.[91] During such echo contagion cases "the responses of the imitator and recipient are relatively exact, and conflict is not necessarily present within the individual."[92]

It is also noteworthy that people do not have to directly observe the "model" as in the case of unconscious imitation of a model of the act. Social Psychologist James Pennebaker has studied social and perceptual factors influencing students who imitate throat irritation and coughing in a college lecture hall.[93] He found that when a student hears another student cough, other students are more likely to begin coughing as a result of the number of coughs heard and their proximity to the coughing. Further, people cough more when there are low external stimulus demands competing for attention. "From a perceptual perspective, hearing another person cough prompts others to monitor quickly their own throat, thus increasing the probability that someone would become aware of throat irritation and emit a cough."[94] Furthermore, this process appears relatively involuntary and unconscious. Of 29 percent of students observed coughing during lectures, when asked by Pennebaker if they recalled hearing any coughing during the lecture, most did not.

Hysterical Identification

Austrian psychoanalyst Sigmund Freud discussed the notion of "hysterical identification" whereby egos engage in psychopathological sympathetic identification. Freud stated: "Identification is a highly important motive in the mechanism of hysterical symptoms... this is the well-known hysterical imitation, the ability of hysterical subjects to imitate all the symptoms which impress them when they occur in others, as though pity were aroused to the point of reproduction." Freud also pointed out that an act of hysterical identification "corresponds to an unconscious end-process." He noted that it is not uncommon for a physician to ward a twitching patient and during a check of the subject the next day observe several others within the same ward twitching."[95]

Freud stated that "psychic infection" occurs in the following way: "As a rule, patients know more about one another than the physician knows about any one of them, and they are concerned about one another when the doctor's visit is over. One of them has an attack today: at once it is known to the rest that a letter from home, a recrudescence of lovesickness, or the like, is the cause. Their sympathy is aroused, and although it does not emerge into consciousness they form the following conclusion: 'If it is possible to suffer such an attack from such a cause, I too may suffer this sort of an attack, for I have the same occasion for it.' If this were a conclusion capable of becoming conscious, it would perhaps express itself in dread of suffering a like attack; but it is formed in another psychic region, and consequently ends in the realization of the dreaded symptoms. Thus identification is not mere imitation, but an assimilation based upon the same aetiological claim; it expresses a just like, and refers to some common condition which has remained in the unconscious."[96]

Low Levels of Chemical Cocktails or Undetected Toxins

Some researchers believe that many cases that are labeled as mass psychogenic illness may actually be the result of combinations of environmental or organic agents. Drs. Halley Faust and Lawrence Brilliant of the School of Public Health at the University of Michigan, contend that the culprit in many "mass hysteria" episodes stems from the interaction of low levels of toxicants, arguing that women and adolescents are vulnerable to their effects due to their relatively lower body weight.

The pair came to their conclusions after investigating an "outbreak" of illness symptoms in Brighton, Michigan, on July 11, 1978. Testing revealed low levels of carbon monoxide, pentane, and ozone in an enclosed room. In addition, there had been heavy cigarette use in the room just prior to the incident and the room's ventilation system was "operating at only 15% of design capacity."[97] While the readings were too low to account for the symptoms, Faust and Brilliant found a correlation between low body weight and psychogenic illness symptoms. While they could not prove it conclusively, they suggest the trigger was either "an undetected toxin or a synergistic combination of low levels of toxins."[98] They note that while mass psychogenic illness is usually declared after investigators have eliminated known biological and chemical substances, eliminating "some of these causes is related to perseverance on the part of the investigator."[99] They also point out that just because testing fails to detect toxic levels, it does not mean they were not originally there. "The fact that clinical laboratory values were normal may imply that the investigators did not ask for certain exotic tests (e.g., pentane in the blood) or that they arrived on the scene too late... and that the toxicant(s) could have cleared before air or blood samples were taken."[100] Symptoms associated with Sick Building Syndrome have also often been labeled as mass hysteria when in fact many or most cases may result from real contaminants resulting from indoor air pollution, inadequate ventilation, and the mixing of various low level substances.[101]

The Misdiagnosis of Physical Illnesses

Some researchers argue that in relatively rare instances, the label of mass psychogenic illness is a misdiagnosis of a disease state such as chorea being mistaken for the hysterical fits reported during the medieval dance manias,[102] or in the case of epidemic malaise, neuromyasthenia, and atypical poliomyclitis, a difficult to detect virus.[103] While the outbreak of epidemic collapse at three British secondary schools during the 1960s was exacerbated by psychogenic elements, a viral infection appears to have played a major role.[104] One team of researchers suggest that involuntary convulsions observed during nocturnal religious revivals in American history may have been triggered by epileptics experiencing seizures induced by flickering torches, which were quickly imitated by emotionally charged, suggestive followers.[105]

Hypnotic Trance

American physician Gary Elkins and colleagues have argued that trance states may play a role in mass hysteria episodes.[106] Elkins compared an incident of mass hysteria to the hypnotic trance state known as "active-alert." They hypothesized that when the first subject becomes ill and receives medical attention, other group members become preoccupied and focused on these disturbing events, fostering a naturalistic trance state. In summarizing this position, they stated: "Alarmed and uncertain of their own feelings, the group members become susceptible to suggestions of illness. These suggestions were received with very little critical or reflexive thought."[107] They also cited other researchers who noted that hypnosis or hypnotic-like states "do not necessarily depend on a formal 'induction' and that people under hypnosis are more responsive to suggestion."[108]

In 1892, Italy's Scipio Sighele viewed crowd behavior as unleashing "primitive" impulses in vulnerable people, a position formulated from Charcot's psychopathological notion of hypnotic suggestibility.[109] Recent works, particularly by psychologists and psychiatrists, draw on similar intellectual roots relative to collective hypnosis in explaining the medieval European fear of witches and mass demon possession. For instance, E.L. Bliss blames much of "the insane idea" surrounding demonophobia on spontaneous "self hypnosis," disregarding more prosaic and plausible explanations: deviance, labeling, conformity dynamics.[110] Casper Schmidt holds a similar "group trance" interpretation of such events.[111]

Political Protest

Some researchers believe that the label of mass hysteria among certain workers in Southeast Asia has been placed on people engaged in either conscious, partially conscious, or wholly unconscious political protest. Depending on the circumstance, the participants in such episodes can be viewed as exhibiting mass illness, while on the other end of the spectrum, they are exclusively feigning. Some cases may involve both. Either way, such "outbreaks" represent a culturally-conditioned means for the politically weak (hence, the over representation of women) to critique unsatisfactory social conditions and affect gradual change. For instance, J. Scott shows how common forms of peasant resistance in rural West Malaysia often involves creative, mundane ways of expressing dissatisfaction with government policies or management rules, including foot dragging, sabotage, desertion, false compliance, and feigned ignorance.[112] Why would Malay females go to such lengths to protest work conditions instead of confronting their repressors? Malay females are enculturated to be obedient and submissive, and hence, they tend to avoid direct confrontation with authority.[113] Malaysian social scientists Raymond Lee and Susan Ackerman have suggested that "mass hysteria" and spirit possession are culturally appropriate ways of indirectly negotiating worker-management problems.[114]

Anthropologist Aihwa Ong has examined the structural and political roots of ideological meanings attached to mass spirit possession "outbreaks" in Malaysian factories, which almost exclusively affect female Malays. She viewed the episodes as mass psychogenic illness-induced ritualized resistance to the imposition of dehumanizing factory conditions that are in stark contrast to traditional Malay conduct codes where people are rarely constrained or preoccupied by Western conceptions of time and material wealth.[115] Ong suggested that collective spirit possession incidents and the common accompanying symptoms such as hyperventilation, nausea, dizziness, fainting, and headache focused public attention on subordinate concerns and amounted to ritualized rebellion. "Spirit possession episodes...are acts of rebellion, symbolizing what cannot be spoken directly, calling for a renegotiation of obligations between the management and workers. However, technocrats have turned a deaf ear to such protests, to this moral indictment of their woeful cultural judgements about the dispossessed...choosing to view possession episodes narrowly as sickness caused by physiological and psychological maladjustment."[116]

However, not all episodes appear to involve unconscious or involuntary symptoms – some may be contrived. Mass hysteria symptoms are typically viewed as spontaneous episodes within familiar social networks while political resistance tactics may seem overly contrived and require detailed collective planning. However, in reality it may not be so easy to distinguish between the two. Ong noted that subversive resistance in many Malaysian factories "were spontaneous, carried out by individual workers independently of each other,"[117] while Scott said they "require little or no coordination or planning," and utilized "implicit understandings and informal networks."[118] Ong even specifically noted that some types of resistance involved an illness feigning strategy in order to leave the shop floor.[119] If several workers leave the shop floor over a short period, it could be "mistranslated" by outsiders unfamiliar with this conduct code of resistance, as "mass psychogenic illness."

Mass Hysteria As Drama

British psychiatrist David Taylor believes episodes of mass hysteria can be viewed as a play or novel, temporarily gaining an external reality in the imagination of the participant. Taylor observed how episodes are typically promoted and maintained by community members such as the relatives of victims. "In these dramas the actors and the audience are equal partners. When the sick are presented to doctors, the doctors are compelled to act from their perspective just as the parents or the crowd acted from theirs. In this way, the medical procedures tend to validate the sickness to the relatives in the same process which invalidates it to the doctors."[120] Taylor emphasizes the importance of understanding the social context of the mass hysteria actors. "Epidemic hysterias arise couched in social settings that enhance emotionality and promote the rapid 'mental acceptance of propositions as true even if beyond observations.' The sorts of events that produce these responses are unavoidable apparent threats that have emerged through some form of ultra-rapid group consensus."[121]

Broad Theories Of Mass Hysteria

Contemporary explanations for the appearance of epidemic hysteria can be divided into five broad theoretical traditions: psychoanalytic, sociological, social psychological, biological, and anthropological. These theories are not mutually exclusive and often share overlapping features. While each perspective emphasizes the influence of different mechanisms and processes in precipitating outbreaks, all converge on the pivotal role of extreme psychosocial stress.

Psychoanalytic Perspectives[122]

Psychoanalytic theories are formulated based upon observations of individual cases of conversion hysteria. It is assumed that the victim is reacting to a state of extreme psychic conflict by subconsciously converting the conflict into physical symptoms. Often the affected body parts are related to the specific conflict. Thus, in singular conversion, a soldier in psychic dissonance over the morality of combat may suffer temporary arm paralysis and be unable to discharge a weapon. Another classic example involves the witness to a traumatic event, who subsequently experiences partial or complete blindness.[123]

Psychoanalytical perspectives have been used to explain the prominence of histrionics and play-acting among mass hysteria victims, which exacerbate outbreaks, especially in enduring episodes involving strict academic discipline. This includes the conscious, subconscious, or partially conscious utilization of the "sick role" to obtain sympathy, attention, and manipulation of cherished or undesirable activities and situations. For example, an outbreak of spasmodic twitching at a Louisiana high school spread after symptoms in the first pupil enabled her to avoid dance classes and rekindle a boyfriend's waning affection. After observing the success of the initial case, six other female students obtained "secondary gains" over the ensuing weeks, as a result of their newly acquired illness status.[124] Dr. Silvio Benaim and his colleagues reported that Louise, the index case in an episode of falling among 16- and 17-year-old schoolgirls near London, admitted to faking "drop attacks" after becoming accustomed to the growing attention that she received from her initial genuine fainting spells.[125] Psychiatrists typically use the term "secondary gains" to refer to symptoms that are only unintentionally produced, while the feigning of symptoms is classified as malingering.[126] Histrionics produced during school outbreaks of epidemic hysteria often do not appear to be intentionally produced with the conscious intent of obtaining secondary benefits, but it appears that considerable feigning may occur in order to convince authority figures to take some immediate action to nullify the perceived threat. This is especially evident in persistent outbreaks where authorities are not perceived as having thoroughly investigated the potential triggering agent. One must remember that even if medical investigators are unable to detect the presence of a toxic gas or biological agent, those experiencing epidemic conversion symptoms and their parents are often convinced that the external agent exists but has not been identified.

Smelser's Value-Added Theory of Social Strains

Prominent California sociologist Neil J. Smelser has outlined a major sociological explanation.[127]

Smelser's theory gained considerable attention following the publication in 1962 of his influential book on collective behavior entitled *Theory of Collective Behavior*. Smelser contends that mass hysteria episodes occur within dysfunctional social orders. Rapid social and cultural changes are believed to produce a disequilibrium within the "normal" state of society. Smelser believes that five factors must be present in order to trigger episodes. First, there must be "structural conduciveness," whereby the structure of society permits the emergence of mass behavior. Hence, a school episode of epidemic hysteria cannot transpire in a "primitive" society that does not have enclosed classrooms and an organized school system. Similarly, a stock market crash cannot occur in communist societies that prohibit private entrepreneurship. The second determinant is "structural strain," which is the existence of stress or conflict, such as an unfamiliar odor or poor student-teacher relations. Third is "growth and spread of a generalized belief," whereby the "strain" – a false, irrational "hysterical belief" – is interpreted by the individual group members in a like manner. The strain must be (a) ambiguous, (b) generate extraordinary anxiety, and (c) result in a redefinition of the situation that is attributed to the stressful agent, and are often exacerbated by (d) "precipitating factors," which are usually specific events that exaggerate the effects of the imaginary threat by "providing 'evidence' that something terrible is at work."[128] For instance, in Seremban, Malaysia, a sudden electrical disruption was believed to confirm the presence of supernatural forces in the school.[129] Prior to the appearance of a mystery "gas" at a Hong Kong school, which affected over 300 students, rumors of a recent toxic gas scare at a nearby school were in circulation and several teachers had discussed the incident with their pupils – some to the point of advising them what action to take if it should occur there.[130]

"Mobilization for action" and "inadequate social control" complete Smelser's determinants. The former category considers how communication and leadership contribute to fostering a mass reaction. This is clearly evident in many episodes where symptoms begin in the older, higher status students and spread to the younger ones. Often the first affected pupil is an influential group member. Finally, "social control" is a counter determinant that is unable to impede or prevent outbreaks. An anxious look, indecision, confusion, or panic by teachers, administrators, medical personnel, or law enforcement officials is counterproductive and fails to contain episodes. Smelser contends that his theory can explain the appearance of such diverse mass behaviors as panics, riots, "crazes," and both norm and value-oriented social movements.

Social Psychological Perspectives: Convergence and Emergent-Norms

There are two prominent social psychological perspectives: convergence and emergent-norm theories. The convergence position holds that students sharing similar predispositions, such as atypical personality traits, are at highest risk of exhibiting psychogenic symptoms following exposure to a stressful stimulus. This view remains unsubstantiated. Several investigators have attempted to differentiate affected versus unaffected pupils within the same group setting by administering standardized personality tests. However, there is no consistent pattern. Some results indicate a tendency for affected pupils to score higher on scales for paranoia,[131] neuroticism,[132] and hysterical traits,[133] while others have found no such correlations.[134] Goldberg noted an association between absenteeism and being affected,[135] while Cole did not.[136] Small et al. identified a relationship between academic performance and being stricken,[137] but Goh found no association.[138] The death of a significant other during early childhood has been correlated with susceptibility to mass psychogenic illness symptoms among elementary school students near Boston,[139] yet this observation was not confirmed in another study by the same investigator.[140] While some researchers have noted that affected pupils possess below average intelligence quotients,[141] others record opposite impressions.[142] Some researchers have correlated mass hysteria episodes with students having disciplinary problems[143] or low socio-economic status.[144]

The emergent-norm perspective rejects the notion that students become "hysterical" per se as a cathartic response to accumulating stress but rather focuses on the influence of sociocultural norms and unique contextual circumstances in structuring episodes.[145] Instead of emphasizing the role of stress per se, or pathological group processes, focus is on the newly emerging definition of the situation from the viewpoint of those affected, creating what William Issac Thomas first described as a self-fulfilling prophesy.[146] In investigating an episode of epidemic hysteria in a Malaysian school, Malaysian anthropologist Raymond Lee and his wife Susan Ackerman emphasized the importance of examining stress "as a matter of definition in a specific sociocultural context rather than as an objective given from which predictions can be made," focusing attention on how victims versus those unaffected retrospectively interpret events.[147] This sociocultural approach examines how victims, observers, and the community at-large explain the episode, and "analyzing the consequences of these interpretations."[148] Whether or not a particular student becomes affected is determined by such factors as physical and visual proximity, social and cultural beliefs, education level, personality traits (not necessarily abnormal), social and spatial distance from the threatening situation, and precipitating events. For instance, students with the strongest social ties with those already affected, or in close physical proximity to the perceived threat, should experience the highest stress levels, as they are most likely to observe the initial index case. The actions of authority figures such as teachers or administrators, either through calm reassurance or expressions of outward anxiety, can validate or defuse situations.

Sociologist Alan Kerckhoff observed that outbreaks are most likely to occur in settings where one or more dramatic illness cases (e.g., fainting, vomiting) or abnormal behavior (e.g., epileptic seizures, drug ingestion) appear.[149] The situation is ambiguous since during the initial incident, students are unaware of the cause. These initial dramatic events must be viewed as a direct threat to the remaining students, thus increasing group stress and associated physiological symptoms (heart palpitations, hyperventilation, etc.). The potential threat must be credible. For instance, if a student were to faint during any given school day, it would not ordinarily precipitate epidemic hysteria syndrome. Yet, if this incident were to occur during the 1991 Middle East War, and coincide with the presence of a strange odor, many of the young, naive schoolchildren might assume that they had been targets in an Iraqi poison gas raid. In fact, a similar scenario was reported at a Rhode Island school during the Persian Gulf War.[150] Similar imaginary threats of poison gas attacks in the Israeli-occupied West Bank[151] and in Soviet Georgia have also occurred.[152] In the two latter instances, political unrest, rumors, and speculative media reports engendered widespread, plausible beliefs that such attacks were a credible possibility. The episode in Soviet Georgia affected about 400 adolescent females who suddenly exhibited symptoms soon after a political rally that was dissipated by Russian troops dispensing toxic gas, including chloropicrin. As is typical in such cases, the transient, benign symptoms reflected the complaints of gas victims: burning eyes, abdominal pain, skin irritation, and dry throat. Instead of representing abnormal responses to stress, it is arguable that pupils are conforming to group norms. Thus, upon seeing a classmate fall ill and soon noting a strange odor, some pupils might assume a connection, triggering immediate and acute conversion reactions.

Of course, what is credible and plausible to one group, culture, or time period, may seem incredible to another. This is especially evident in certain non-Western countries where superstitious beliefs combined with low levels of formal education have contributed to what would appear bizarre by Western standards of normality. An extreme illustration of this point is an episode reported by Legendre.[153] He described an incident that occurred in 1908 affecting twenty males at a school in Szechwan, China, in which the anxious students became convinced that their penises were shrinking. The episode subsided after several days. Before judging the mental stability or gullibility of these students, it is important to examine the sociocultural context. There is a common belief in certain regions of Asia that eating particular foods, or having contact with "ghosts," can cause one's sex organs to rapidly shrink. It is a remarkable example of the power of the self-fulfilling prophesy that Asian men and women continue to experience *koro* epidemics, convinced that they are the victims of a contagious disease that causes their penises and breasts to shrink. Episodes last from a few days to several months and can affect thousands. "Victims" suffer intense anxiety – sweating, palpitations, insomnia – and often take the extreme measure of placing clamps or string onto the organ. Ignorance of human perceptual fallibility, combined with rumors and traditional beliefs, result in frantic citizens intensely scrutinizing their genitalia. Epidemics within the public-at-large have occurred in China as recently as 1987.[154] Similar outbreaks have been reported in Singapore,[155] Thailand,[156] and India.[157] (For a more detailed discussion, see GENITAL SHRINKING SCARES.)

Biological Explanations

Biological theories suggesting innate female susceptibility to epidemic hysteria have been popular until the 1970s. Previously, it was commonly believed that females possessed weaker mental constitutions and were more prone to emotional liability than men, making them prime candidates for episodes. This view has been discredited as sexist, with critics arguing that proponents of a biological basis for cases have not taken into account the influence of gender socialization, as females are typically enculturated to possess emotionally expressive, submissive character traits.[158] Further, there is a transcultural tendency for females to be low in the power hierarchy, which increases their susceptibility to experiencing long-term emotional frustration.

While social factors are undeniable in precipitating school outbreaks, the historical and cross-cultural over representation of females of school age suggests the possibility that biological factors may exacerbate existing social and cultural forces. For instance, classroom social conditions are fairly uniform for both male and female students in many Western countries, yet epidemic hysteria syndrome continues to be reported almost exclusively among females. The same can be argued for worksites. A plausible physiological mechanism for this occurrence is the innate susceptibility of menstruating females to panic disorder and hyperventilation syndrome.[159] Further, the reporting of individual somatic complaints has been associated with the appearance puberty and menstruation, which may help account for the preponderance of schoolgirls being stricken.[160] Hysterical disorders in general may have a biological basis as they are more frequently diagnosed in females, such as somatization disorder, globus hystericus, and psychogenic pain disorder.[161] Further, the incidence of individual conversion disorders appears to be more common in females than males, with reported ratios varying from 2:1 to as high as 10:1. This parallels the range in prevalence ratios of epidemic hysteria episodes in schools.[162]

Anthropological Explanations

Anthropological perspectives focus on the context, social status, and local worldview of pupils, utilizing research by renowned British anthropologist Ioan M. Lewis.[163] This theory was applied to epidemic hysteria episodes in non-Western schools (Malaysia) by Lee and Ackerman.[164] In observing a preponderance of females in spirit possession cults and charismatic religious movements within various cross-cultural settings, Lewis attributed this situation to their low social status and oppression in male-dominated societies where they are low on the power hierarchy. Women in many of these societies often experience, sometimes collectively, trance and possession states, psychomotor agitation (twitching and shaking of the limbs), and anxiety-related transient somatic complaints. Concordantly, females in repressive, intolerable social situations are characteristic features of school life in Malaysia and Central Africa where epidemic hysteria is endemic. While female redress is culturally unacceptable in these societies, males typically believe that spirits possess those affected. Outbreaks of dissociation, histrionics, and psychomotor dysfunction among predominantly female pupils in these countries often include insulting authorities and frank criticism of administration policies. Yet these outbursts are accepted with impunity since their temporary possession status deflects the attribution of blame. As a result, they have developed into idioms of distress and negotiation whereby outbreaks signal to the wider community that something is amiss. The anthropological perspective assumes that females are not susceptible *per se,* but rendered vulnerable through gender socialization.

THEY SAW A GAME STUDY

New England: Fall, 1951

It is an established principle of social psychology that human perception and memory reconstruction are notoriously unreliable and subject to error. This helps to explain why people with folk traditions of extinct or imaginary creatures (e.g., fairies, Bigfoot, the Jersey Devil) report seeing them. However, the extent to which peoples' perceptions are shaped by their beliefs and experiences is remarkable and directly applicable to numerous entries in this Encyclopedia. Human perception is highly selective and reflective of a person's hopes and expectations. For instance, at FATIMA, one person looked to the sky and saw beams of light and became certain it was a miraculous sign of the Virgin Mary; another standing in nearly the same spot, interpreted the display as a natural solar phenomenon.

A classic study on the selective nature of human perception and the tendency to experience what we expect to experience was conducted in 1951 by Princeton University psychologist Hadley Cantril, famous for his study of the 1938 MARTIAN INVASION SCARE. Working with colleague A. Hastorff, the pair examined how two groups of people perceived the same football game based on which side they cheered for. The game was an emotional rivalry between the Princeton Tigers and the Dartmouth Indians. The contest was exceptionally rough and engendered hard feelings on both sidelines.

Both quarterbacks suffered serious injuries and had to leave the game, one with a broken nose and concussion, the other with a broken leg. The game was also riddled with penalties. The following week, students from both schools who were either at the game or saw a film of the event were asked to fill in a questionnaire and write down the number of infractions they saw. It soon became clear that the game was interpreted very differently, depending on whom you rooted for.

When asked to review a game film and count the number of infractions, Princeton supporters "saw" double the number of rule infractions that Dartmouth students reported "seeing," leading Hastorf and Cantril to conclude that group allegiance and membership frames and filters the way in which people experience the world.[165]

THUGGEE

India: 13th century–19th century

The Thugs were a religious sect devoted to the goddess Bhowani, aka Bhagwan, aka Devi, aka Kali, a consort of Shiva and venerated as the goddess of destruction. Whatever their nominal religion or sect, they devoted themselves exclusively to her and worshipped no other deity. The central tenet of their belief was that she wished them to kill people as a sacrifice to her; though a crime in men's eyes, this was meritorious in hers and would bring them posthumous rewards. Figures relating to their clandestine activities are impossible to establish, but an intelligent estimate suggests that between one and three million murders were performed over a 300-year period, until the sect was destroyed by the British administration.[166]

Though the origins of Thuggee are unknown, records show that it was well established by 1290. The name is derived from the sanskrit *sthag,* which has connotations of secrecy. Narratives of highway robbery in the 16th century could well relate to Thuggee, and intermittent events confirm its existence from this time on. The British administration became aware of it at the end of the 18th century, though not until the investigation by Captain William Sleeman in the 1820s did they realize its extent. This was in part due to the fact that foreigners were never attacked for fear of the consequences. Though occasionally Thugs were caught and executed by the Indian authorities, no major effort was made to deal with the problem.

Membership in the sect was hereditary, and necessarily very secret; many Thugs did not even reveal to their wives that they were members. Virtually all were male, though occasionally a wife would assist her husband.

The remarkable feature of Thuggee was its informality. There was no central organization, no priests or hierarchy of any kind, apart from leaders of local groups who had no formal status. There were no rules or teachings, except the oral traditions that governed their activities. Thuggery was a part-time occupation;

when not engaged in it, the Thugs were seemingly normal citizens, often highly respected members of the community for at all other times they were polite, well behaved, and responsible. A captured Thug, Hurree Singh, told Sleeman: "Travellers were frequently reported murdered by robbers, but people thought these must be in the jungle, and never dreamed they were murdered by men they saw every day about them. I was much respected by the people of the town and never suspected until arrested."[167] An English doctor, Dr. Cheek, employed a bearer (senior manservant) who gave perfect service and was a favorite with the children of the household. Once a year he asked to be allowed to return to his family for a month, but it was later found that this was a pretext; in fact he joined his gang and spent his holiday murdering innocent people, subsequently returning to his domestic duties.[168]

Although Bhowani is a Hindu deity, a Thug could be Moslem, Hindu, or Rajput, working together in loyal collaboration. They operated throughout India, in gangs of twenty to fifty, sometimes in even larger numbers – one gang numbered 360. Typically, they would make one expedition a year, lasting four to seven weeks, the members being summoned by secret message. Though altogether they numbered in the thousands, scattered throughout the peninsula, they maintained effective communication between groups, thanks to their own jargon, *ramasi*, and secret signs of recognition.

Ram Luckun Sein, a hereditary thug of Bengal, with his guard.

The murders were invariably carried out on the open road or in stopping-places along the way. Typically, victims were foot or carriage travelers who, because they were far from home, were not known in the locality, and because journeys were long and slow, would not be missed for some time. Investigation, therefore, was likely to be futile. The Thugs, in a party of three or four, would attach themselves to the travelers, ingratiate themselves, and perhaps travel with them in a friendly way for a few days, winning their confidence, before seizing their opportunity and killing their victims. One Thug reported how he and his companions accompanied a party of sixty men, women, and children for 160 miles before a suitable occasion arose.

Each member of the group had his function in the killing, the senior being the one who did the actual strangling. The Thugs rarely killed women, but if they attacked a party of travelers that included women, they too would have to be killed at the risk of offending Bhowani, who liked only male victims. There was a strict rule that the women should not be raped before being killed. Low-caste men were not killed except by error, since they too would not be a suitable sacrifice to Bhowani. If women accompanied the Thug party, their role was to deal with the children, who might either be killed along with the adults or sold to gypsies for the purpose of prostitution or slavery.

The primary motive of the killings was religious, but once dead the victims were robbed. There was never robbery without killing, and the prospect of loot did not influence their decision to kill; they would kill a poor man as readily as a rich man, though they were naturally pleased if they acquired money and valuables as a bonus. This would be divided among the killers, apportioned according to status.

The killings were invariably carried out to a prescribed protocol that had to be strictly observed if they were to provide an acceptable sacrifice to Bhowani. The victims were always strangled, for no blood might be shed. The *ruhmal* – a piece of cloth, about 80 cm long, was used. A typical murder situation was the evening meal, when victims and murders might be sitting in a circle round a fire, talking or singing. At an opportune moment the *ruhmal* was thrown round the victim's neck and pulled tight, while the strangler's companions seized his arms and legs, holding him powerless, and striking him if necessary. Each member of the group had his allotted role, practiced time and time again. Drums and singing would often accompany the murder, to drown the cries of the victims. The bodies were then buried, and this too was a highly skilled matter; the Thugs prided themselves that no one could even detect that the ground had been disturbed where a victim – his skin lacerated to prevent swelling – lay buried. The digging was done with the *kodalee*, a specially designed and consecrated tool.

All this was done in cold blood. A Thug needed no drugs to stimulate him; he was not in an altered state when he performed his deeds. The prescribed *modus operandi* was eminently practical, and a cool head was needed to carry it out. At the same time the killers were inevitably excited, and as they carried out the killing they called upon their deity to witness what they were doing in her name.

Since considerable cunning was required to allay the suspicions of the victim and gain his confidence to the point where he could be attacked, the Thugs regarded it as a battle of wits, much as a con man might congratulate himself on deceiving his victim. They prided themselves on their skills, which were acquired after prolonged training from boyhood on, transmitted from father to son. A young Thug, initiated around the age of 13, would accompany his elders as a spectator until he was hardened enough to be able to participate without weakening. He would practice his movements over and over again. At first he would be simply a *bykureea* (scout), then a *lugha* (burier of the dead), then a *shumseea* (holder of limbs), and finally a *bhurtote* (strangler). A proficient Thug would kill a great many victims in the course of his career. One captive boasted of killing more than a thousand, and others prided themselves on sacrificing five or six hundred to their goddess.

After the killing, the Thugs celebrated with a sacrificial feast of *gur* – unrefined sugar – of which it was said that whoever ate it would desire to become a Thug for the rest of his days. Feringeea, one of the most notorious Thugs, said to Sleeman after his capture, "Let any man once taste of that gur and he will be a Thug although he knows all the trades and has all the wealth in the world...If I were to live a thousand years, I should never be able to follow any other trade."[169]

Thuggee was eventually suppressed during the 1830s by a team of British officers headed by Captain William Sleeman who from 1823 to 1829 had meticulously studied the cult. Since Thuggery was hereditary, he drew extensive family trees that led him from one individual to another, collating the names and the murder-sites identified, or accidentally revealed, by his prisoners. The obstacles were prodigious: "the absence for motive for their murders; the fact that they never murdered near their own homes; the splitting-up of the gang and the return to respectability, after a comparatively short period of absence; their secret language and signs; the support and patronage they obtained from those who benefited by the murders they committed – who asked no questions, providing their palms were well oiled; their respectable appearance and pleasing manners; the reputable, if fictitious reasons given for their absence, had all combined to keep Thuggee secret for centuries."[170] Even when the Thugs were brought into the courts, the problems continued. "The migratory character of the murder-gangs – the difficulty of personal identification – the craft and subtlety of the offenders themselves, the unlimited amount of false swearing and of false impersonation which, at any time, they could bring into our criminal courts..."[171] Many captured Thugs proved willing to save their lives by turning approver (informer), providing Sleeman with information to catch others. He survived three assassination attempts, and in the course of about six years the entire cult had been stamped out and India delivered from a terrible scourge. Altogether, between 1826 and 1835, 1,562 Thugs were tried; 1404 were hanged or transported. The lives of the approvers were spared, but they and their families were detained in a special prison.

COMMENT: "It will have been noticed that the characteristic feature of all these confessions is the total omission of anything approaching remorse or any feeling of sympathy for those who suffered at the hands of the Thugs. This callous disregard for the most elementary principles of civilisation would have been remarkable in savages; in intelligent and often educated Indians, it defies explanation."[172]

This is indeed the almost incomprehensible challenge posed by the Thugs. Time and again, during his interrogations, Sleeman would ask – after an account of killing of children, fathers and husbands, young women – "Do you never feel sympathy for the persons murdered – never pity or compunction?" and invariably he received the answer that Sahib Khan gave him with great emphasis: "Never." The Thugs maintained that the killing was, in effect, done by the goddess; they were simply her servants, and consequently felt no guilt or remorse or compunction. In his remarkable contemporaneous fictional account, *Confessions of a Thug*, based on his own experience of Thuggee, Meadows Taylor has Amir Ali say: "I can never persuade you that I was fully authorized to commit the murders, and only a humble instrument in the hands of Allah. Did I kill one of those persons? No! It was He. Had my *ruhmal* been a thousand times thrown about their necks and the strength of an elephant in my arms, could I have done aught, would they have died, without it was His will? I tell you, Sahib, they would not, they could not."[173]

The operations of the Thugs are extremely well documented, first, thanks to the meticulous work by Sleeman; second, because once apprehended, they were willing to speak freely about their deeds, of which they were proud; and third, because full verbatim records were kept of these confessions. Yet it is hard to enter into the state of mind of the Thugs. Their behavior at their executions is, however, significant. After spending the previous night talking and singing, they were taken to the execution ground. "The indifference these men show on mounting the gallows is truly astonishing. With their own hand, they adjust the halter, pressing the knot close up behind the ear so that it shall not slip, and talking to their companions while doing so with the greatest coolness. Ere the fatal beam can be withdrawn, they jump off and launch themselves into eternity!"[174] Before jumping, they raised their hands and uttered a final invocation to Bhowani. This remarkable imperturbability is confirmed by several eyewitnesses.

This serene self-confidence, even at the moment of death, expresses the Thug's conviction that his deeds, however horrendous to his fellow-men, and even though they were proscribed by his nominal religion, were nonetheless justified because they were performed in honor of the goddess of destruction. The exceptional behavior displayed by the Thugs is not easily accounted for without the religious context of devotion to Bhowanee, whose name was invoked when the killings were done and when the convicted Thugs themselves met death.

Sleeman was not without his critics at the time, and some revisionist assessments of the suppression of Thuggee have suggested that the sect was a monster created in the minds of the British authorities. Noting that most of the evidence was supplied by the approvers, who told their interrogators what they wanted to hear, a different perspective is proposed, whereby the British had their own reasons, associated with the opium trade, for exaggerating the danger and embarking on a campaign of suppression. "While murder was certainly being done on India's roads in the 1820s and thirties, the British reaction was partial, unbalanced and unjust. Thuggee was a social evil but it was not a religious cult; it was a threat to the opium trade. Then, once the demon of an eradication campaign was released, its history ran a similar course to any other witch hunt."[175] This seems an overstatement. Even if it is accepted that the motivation for the suppression of Thuggee contained a measure of self-interest, India was a much safer and healthier place without it. Thuggee was crime on a monstrous scale, and for such criminals to go unpunished was a stain on Indian society, involving an almost unbelievable distortion of social values.

TOLLITIS

New York City: February 1990

Thirty-four tollbooth workers at the New York Triborough Bridge began complaining of headache, nausea, and chest pains. Despite insistence from union members that "toxins" were responsible, investigators could not locate a cause, leading to suspicion that the symptoms were psychogenic in origin.[176]

TOM AND HIS FOLLOWERS

England: 1838

The career of John Nichols Tom and the events leading to the battle of Bossenden Wood involved a relatively small number of people and affected only a limited area in the eastern part of the county of Kent, England, yet they attracted nationwide interest and led to attacks on the Home Secretary in Parliament. John Tom was clearly mad, his aims were confused, and his behavior eccentric, yet he achieved a quite remarkable popularity and a dedicated following that survived his final catastrophe.[177] The small scale of the affair provides an opportunity to see forces and processes in action that in larger incidents are not so easy to discern.

CONTEXT: England at the time of Victoria's accession was a relatively prosperous and progressive nation, but the prosperity was unevenly distributed and progress hampered by an obsolete social structure. Parliamentary reform had been partially initiated, and many institutions were coming under question, but this hardly affected the common people such as those involved in the Tom affair. They were poor and ignorant, uneducated and uncultured, neglected by the church and other authorities, and blest with few social amenities. For someone like Tom to take up their interests and set up as their spokesman was unique and unprecedented. It was no wonder that they should rally round him with hero-worship and adulation.

John Nichols Tom was born in 1799, the son of an innkeeper in Cornwall. Several features of his early life offer clues to his subsequent conduct. The school he attended was notable for the intensity of its religious fervor, elements of which may have been incorporated in his later claims. His family hoped he would better himself by taking up a legal career, and he became a solicitor's clerk. But he left this position and became a wine-merchant's clerk instead. This ability to switch tracks as the occasion arose was characteristic of his later career. He joined the Spenceans, a radical political party considered seditious by the authorities for favoring nationalization of the land; radical politics was always to be part of his program. In 1829, his mother, who had previously showed signs of insanity, had to be committed to a lunatic asylum, where she died. Tom himself received treatment for bouts of mental illness between 1829 and 1832.

His physical characteristics undoubtedly contributed to his appeal. He was tall, strikingly handsome, immensely strong, a fine cricketer, and a champion wrestler. He was very attractive to women and married in 1821. He set up in business as wine-dealer and maltster in Truro, where he seemed to be doing

The last stand of fanatic John Nichols Tom at the battle of Bossenden Wood.

reasonably well. But already his mind was on greater things. In 1832, in a letter to a friend, he wrote: "Some mighty events are germinating in the womb of time, preparatory to the arrival of the millennium," adding that he knew that he was destined to play "a very prominent part" in them.[178]

Later that year he abruptly vanished from view for several months. It is likely he spent some time in London under the name of "Squire Thompson," then he moved to Canterbury, in Kent, where he at first gave his name as "Count Moses Rostopchein Rothschild," of illustrious Jewish ancestry, but later revealed that this was a temporary alias he had assumed, and that in reality he was Sir William Percy Honeywood Courtenay, Knight of Malta, Rightful Heir to the Earldom of Devon, by which name he was known for the rest of his life. A real Sir William Courtenay existed, but he lived unobtrusively on the continent in consequence of "unspeakable offences," and he was not bothered that a stranger was using his name.

At Canterbury, Tom went out of his way to make himself known, partly by his appearance – he dressed in extravagant costume, with long hair making him resemble the popular likeness of Jesus – and partly by his activities. He entered politics in grandiose style, delivering speeches and distributing printed addresses that skillfully blended demagogic bravura with sound and practicable ideas. The mix of sense and nonsense was calculated to appeal to popular mentalities. He offered extravagant tales about his early life, telling of diplomatic missions for the government in the Holy Land (in fact he never once went out of England). He scattered money lavishly, and it was said that every week he had sent from London by coach an oyster-barrel full of fresh sovereigns (£1 coins). He became immensely popular among the common people of the city, who had no fondness either for the authorities or the established church, and were delighted to find someone who promised to "annihilate for ever the TITHES, taxation upon all the shopkeepers and productive classes…slavery, sinecures and placemen, beginning from the very throne to the meanest situation under Government…"[179]

Though so far as actions went he could give them only promises, this – together with his flamboyant style, personal charm, striking appearance, and gift for oratory – made him the lion of the day:

> Courtenay was so pressed by his admirers with invitations to eat, that he was obliged to run or ride from house to house, taking a snack at each, and usually ending the day with a banquet given by a number of his new-found friends. At the local literary society's debates and concerts he was the most honoured of guests, and the audiences listened spellbound to the speeches he made. Women particularly were fascinated by him, and many an ambitious mother laid plans to catch the Knight of Malta for her daughter. The more enthusiastic of his followers would pay him almost divine honours, picking up the hem of his coat and kissing it.[180]

His popularity did him little good when election time came. While the winning candidate received 3,476 votes, the two others two or three thousand, Tom received precisely three, one from his proposer, one from his seconder, the third from a friend. The explanation was simple: those who made up his fanatical following were the lower classes of the town who were not eligible to vote.

Discouraged for a while, he soon resumed his political activities, making an extravagant intervention in a smuggling trial, which led to a charge of perjury and swindling. Though he was clearly either mad or guilty, his popularity was maintained, and he was a hero still. As he was taken to jail, his followers shouted, "We will rescue you! We will have you out!" and crowds thronged the streets outside the jail. Somehow they were made to disperse, and the matter ended peacefully.

When his trial came, the court was a scene of wild enthusiasm. "The tumult was general, and almost beyond description. Shouts of 'Courtenay! Courtenay!' resounded through the court room, mingled with boos, hisses, catcalls, and screams of hysterical laughter."[181] The local newspaper commented: "Never was a scene so completely disgraceful ever witnessed in a court of justice. All order, all decorum, all regard to common decency were alike set at defiance by the deluded followers of this mountebank impostor."

No doubt this was fair comment, but it shows the extraordinary effect Tom had on his followers. Somehow his personality overrode his absurdity and blinded them to his manifest guilt. Furthermore, this was not tied to any particular preaching or teaching; neither now or at any other time did he present a coherent program, platform, policy, or philosophy. The appeal was, quite simply, his own self.

In the matter of the smuggling, he was so blatantly guilty of perjury that nothing his legal advisors could say as to his good intentions could persuade the jury to find him innocent, but it was decided, reasonably enough, that he was of unsound mind. In October 1833, he was committed to the County Lunatic Asylum. The Medical Superintendent gave his personal opinion in a letter: "On the subject of your enquiry, whether I consider him 'harmless,' 'provided his friends are willing to take him', I can only say that though I believe he himself would harm no-one, I cannot answer for the conduct of others, who might be excited by his unsound and extravagant opinions."[182]

He was a model patient and distinguished himself on the cricket field. In 1837 he was released and entrusted to the care of friends in the countryside east of Canterbury. There, he realized that the agricultural unrest among the country folk provided him with the opportunity to reestablish himself as a popular hero. There had been many very violent demonstrations against working conditions, severely suppressed by the authorities, and in the absence of any other leader, the common people in the neighborhood thought that Tom, with his imposing presence and flair for oratory, offered them a hope of seeing their wrongs put right. He claimed, and doubtless sincerely believed, that heaven had entrusted him with a mission, and his followers were as convinced as himself. One of them, a smallholder named Wills, asserted that Tom's mission was divine, and his promises began to become millennarist in tone. His education stood him in good stead as he asserted his divine nature – that he was the reincarnation of Jesus Christ, that his body was the temple of the Holy Ghost. His appearance had always resembled the popular image of Jesus, and now he claimed that Jesus had selected his body for his comeback. In proof of this he showed them the nail marks on his hands – the stigmata from the crucifixion that had terminated his first life on Earth.[183] Though his followers still looked to him for political and economic benefits, now their veneration embodied a spiritual aspect. Dazzled by his assurances that he was about to usher in the Millennium, they became not followers but disciples. One of them subsequently deposed: "He said he was not an earthly man, but could slay ten thousand men by striking his right hand on the muscle of his left arm, and then vanish."[184]

His main activity now was riding about the district on his white horse, attended by some of his disciples, stopping in villages to make speeches, and inviting the people to join him. His arrival was the signal for popular excitement. Children were brought out to be blessed, sick people to be touched. But few – only about twenty – actually left home and employment to join his travelling party.

Nevertheless, the authorities began to be alarmed by this person who went around preaching sedition and what amounted to rebellion. It was reported that Tom was collecting a large mob and inciting them to violence. The magistrates issued a warrant, and early on May 31, 1838, John Mears, a plumber and High Constable of Boughton-under-Blean, was instructed to arrest him. His brother Nicholas offered to accompany him in case of danger, and a third man joined them. At Bossenden Farm they found Tom, who instantly pulled a pistol from his belt and fired at point-blank range. Nicholas Mears dropped dead. Tom then drew his sword and made to attack John Mears who took to his heels, along with Daniel Edwards. Tom turned to his followers, smoking pistol in hand, and cried "I am the Saviour of the World!" Though his followers were appalled and alarmed, they were so captivated by him that they made no attempt to leave him. After delivering an inflammatory address, he administered a kind of sacrament of bread and water from the well, then he went with them to his breakfast of bread and cheese.

Now there could be no doubt that the authorities would act. Soldiers were summoned from Canterbury. In the course of the morning Tom retired into Bossenden Wood with his followers. Addressing his tiny army, he declared. "This is the day of judgment, this is the first day of the Millennium, and the day I will put the crown on my head."[185] He assured them that because he was divine, no bullets or weapon could injure either him or those with him. Amazingly, they believed him, and the party, which now numbered 37, was overtaken by a kind of hysterical frenzy. One shouted adoringly to Tom, "Go on, go on – Till I drop, I'll follow thee!" Another burst into fanatical shouts, sobs, and cries.

The troops came from Canterbury in a coach for the three officers and the magistrates, and wagons for the men who numbered about a hundred. These formed into two parties and approached Tom and his followers through the wood, from opposite directions. It was about three o'clock. The weather was hot and sultry.

Tom was dressed in the smock and broad-rimmed hat which he habitually wore. Only one other of his followers had a firearm; the rest were armed simply with cudgels and staves. Lieutenant Bennett, approaching from the south, without waiting for the other party, advanced impetuously. Tom advanced to meet him and shot him dead. His followers, brandishing their staves and believing themselves invulnerable, rushed fiercely on the soldiers. Chaos ensued. There was a brief but bloody hand-to-hand engagement that lasted for three or four minutes among the bushes and trees. Tom and his men fought bravely enough, but against hopeless odd. They were not only outnumbered three to one but were fighting with sticks against guns. When their staves were lost in the fighting, they fought on with their fists or kicked with their hobnailed boots. Not more than sixty shots were fired, but at the end of the engagement, there were twenty dead or wounded. Eight of the rebels were killed, including Tom himself. Major Armstrong later declared that throughout his career he had never seen such fanatical courage.[186]

As chance would have it, the sultry afternoon erupted in a thunderstorm just as the fighting ended.

One of Tom's followers, wounded Alexander Foad, complained, "Little did I think this morning that this was going to happen to me! Courtenay told us that bullets would not harm him or us!" Another devoted disciple, Sarah Culver, made desperate attempts to reach Tom's body. Tom had told her that if he was injured in the fighting, she should put water on his lips, he would then revive. On hearing of his death the woman filled a vessel with water, walked half a mile with it, and placed it on his lips. Despite her devotion, she failed to restore him to life. Instead she was arrested along with Tom's other supporters.[187]

The death of Tom did not immediately bring the affair to an end. A London newspaper, *The Globe*, reported:

> The excitement throughout the eastern division of Kent continues to increase, and the fanaticism which Courtenay's insanity has given rise to is in no degree abated by the death of the impostor. Many of the agricultural population, as well as several of the trading class, still labour under the grossest delusion with respect to the character of Courtenay and his deceased followers. Several of the labourers expressed their strongest conviction that the whole of them would rise again this day. Such indeed is the infatuation upon this subject that yesterday a female of respectability, who has for some time past been a believer in Courtenay's declaration that he was from heaven and had come down upon earth to judge the people of this world, said the account of "Sir William's" death was a falsehood; that he was still alive, and that the person shot was some rough fellow who had been going about representing him.
>
> For some months after, a board fixed to a tree close to where Tom died, surrounded with hooks to discourage anyone from moving it, spelled out the words: "OUR REAL TRUE MESSIAH, KING OF THE JEWS." Evidently one of his followers, at least, was sufficiently literate to write his epitaph.[188]

COMMENT: The affair made a great sensation and became a political issue. Lord John Russell, the Home Secretary, observed, "If I had not the information upon the best authority, if I had not seen and received the accounts that have been transmitted to me, I could not have believed that such utter and entire ignorance prevailed in Kent."[189]

Rogers, who compiled what is probably the best account of Tom's career, gives his opinion that "if Courtenay were alive today he would be classed as a paranoiac."[190] But it is the conduct of his followers that is the greater puzzle. Tom's personality was clearly a very strong one, and his gradual transition from political matters to messianic divine mission no doubt caught the imagination of some. They had no serious wrongs that needed to be put right; this went deeper than agrarian reform. Mrs. Hadlow, whose son was wounded in the battle, insisted that he was a holy man and had been inspired by God. Mrs. Wright, whose husband had been in the fight and who was in prison for it, confessed, "we was told that he would surely rise again, and me and a neighbour sat up the whole of that blessed night reading the Bible, and believing the world was to be destroyed on the morrow!"[191]

Inquiry into the affair revealed that of the 45 involved in the affair, 14 were completely illiterate, 20 could only read a little, and only 11 could both read and write.[192] Only one had any education; the rest had learned to read and write in Sunday school. Compared with Tom, they were woefully ignorant in all respects. No wonder he dazzled them.

TONSIL AND ADENOID RIOTS

New York City: circa 1920

Dr. Josephine Baker, director of Child Hygiene for the New York City Health Department from 1908 to 1913, recounted a remarkable incident. Dr. Baker said that in about 1920 she got a phone call about a serious commotion at a public school on the city's lower east side. Upon investigating, she came to a schoolyard "clogged with a mob of six or seven hundred Jewish and Italian mothers wailing and screaming in a fine frenzy and apparently just on the point of storming the doors and wreaking the place. Every few minutes their hysteria would be whipped higher by the sight of a child ejected from the premises bleeding from the mouth and nose and screaming with sheer panic. In view of what I saw when I had fought my way inside, I would not have blamed the mothers if they had burned the place down. For the doctors had coolly descended on the school, taken possession, lined the children up, marched them past, taken one look down each child's throat, and then two strong arms seized and held the child while the doctor used his instruments to reach down into the throat and rip out whatever came nearest to hand, leaving the boy or girl frightened…and bleeding savagely." Dr. Baker said there had been no psychological preparation or parental warning. After ordering a halt to proceedings, she pacified the mob of mothers who eventually went home.[193]

CONTEXT: The autonomous actions by the physicians involved, and their disregard for the feelings of the parents and their children, reflect the power and conceit that typified the American medical community during this period.

TOULOUSE POSSESSED VILLAGE

France: 1681

The hysteric outbreak in a parish on the outskirts of Toulouse, in southern France, demonstrates vividly the readiness with which such a malady can spread.[194] Fortunately, two competent doctors were appointed to investigate it, giving us a clear picture of how such an epidemic is diffused in a narrow community.

CONTEXT: The outbreak took place in a small village community, at the height of the summer season when temperatures in this region can be extremely high. It does not seem to have been specifically religious in character, though it should be borne in mind that religion was a central part of peasant life. However, it is hard to say to what extent the Devil was regarded as a religious being, to what extent a folklore figure.

A woman of the village, Marie Clusette, was the first to succumb. She ran through the streets jumping and dancing, committing all kinds of extravagance, crying out that she was Robert and that he was the master of the world. The populace felt sure she had become possessed by a demon named Robert. A crowd formed to observe this interesting spectacle. Marie took refuge in the church, where she stripped off her clothes and continued dancing until she fell to the floor in convulsions. Adults and children crowded into the church to see her.

This spectacle was renewed during the following days, to the astonishment of the populace. Some time later a woman aged about 40, Jeanne Ponchique, behaved in just the same way, dancing in the street and ending up in the church. In August, a young girl named Jeanne, of pale complexion, was also afflicted. She rolled on the ground, sobbing, talking to herself and twisting in convulsive efforts.

During September, a young girl named Françoise followed, with pains in the right arm. In October young Marie-Anne did the same, as did Françoise-Denise who had warm sensations in her left arm and cold sensations in her right.

Towards the end of December, five other women of the village and a boy succumbed to the same malady. At this stage the Parliament of Toulouse ordered two doctors, Bayle and Grangeron, to carry out an investigation and assign a cause for the ailment, which was popularly attributed to the Evil One.

Four young women were examined by the doctors: Marie-Anne, who had been placed in a children's home, and three other young women, who had been placed in a religious house. All complained of headaches and stomach troubles, bouts of hiccups, swellings of the stomach and rumbling, and tightening of the throat. Every so often they would fall to the ground, and their bodies would twist in convulsions. This happened most frequently when they were in church, or after some argument or quarrel.

Between their fits they talked to themselves. They had a small but rapid pulse, and they would swallow all kinds of objects, such as pieces of material and pins. Françoise-Denise vomited a bent pin and a piece of ribbon wrapped round another pin. Questioned, she said she had swallowed them accidentally but begged the doctors to say nothing about it. But Jeanne D. and Marguerite C. and some others also vomited pins, though perhaps all country women hold pins in their mouths while sewing, they do not all swallow them – clearly this was no individual accident. The doctors' report stated:

> These pins could simply be in their mouths, where this sort of person puts them when dressing or undressing, and they could have forgotten they'd put them there by reason of distraction or simple negligence such as are customary with melancholic persons…The pins could then have been swallowed during sleep, or while eating… It is a symptom of melancholia, to swallow whatever comes to hand, without taking note of it, as happens to pale-complexioned girls who swallow earth, coal, chalk and even excrement. And it is often seen that people whose minds are on something else will put into their mouth whatever they have in their hands, and then swallow it without thinking: and someone observed that these people often had pins in their hands. Once in the stomach, the pins could cause hiccups and lead to convulsive movements of the stomach. It is pointless to argue that they vomited the pins during exorcisms, because they vomited them also during feigned or simulated exorcisms.[195]

Some of them claimed that the devil was speaking through their mouths, and so exorcisms were resorted to in the presence of the doctors, a councilor and a big crowd of people, but they had no effect except to exacerbate the trouble. Some of the exorcisms were genuine; others were deliberately simulated by the priests (that is to say, they employed Latin words which had no meaning). It was observed that there was no difference in the effect they had on the girls, whether they were true or false. The effect of the exorcisms on some girls was to send them into convulsions; on others to render them calm, and this happened whether the exorcism was genuine or otherwise.

Although this was a period when diabolic possession was still frequently diagnosed, the doctors concluded otherwise:

> Having found nothing in the various accidents or affections reported of these girls which could not be produced by bad dispositions, such as humours of the brain or other parts of the body, we judge that none of these accidents or affections, either individual or collective, can be construed as evidence of witchcraft, possession or obsession.

Interestingly, too, they felt the need to explain how the malady spread:

> What may seem at first sight extraordinary about this story, is that many people are afflicted in the same way in a small locality; but it is important to remember that a certain Clusette was the first to be affected in this way, and that she drew the attention of the entire community on her by her extravagances; and that all, old or young, followed her everywhere, and that fathers and mothers brought along their children to see her behavior and hear the follies she uttered; that she was the one topic of gossip in the village; that it was the one subject of conversation among families, where everyone had their own opinion on the matter according to their prejudices with regard to witches and their spells, which are common topics among the ignorant, who are by nature timid and superstitious; that Jeanne Pouchique was affected shortly after, and a quantity of others followed. We should remember, too, that the first attack of Clusette was most violent inside the church, where she fell in convulsions, which doubled the general astonishment, especially when it was said that it was in the church that the other subjects had their most severe attacks…Consequently, if we imagine a crowd of people of all ages and sex who run after Clusette to watch her extravagances, we shall have no difficulty in understanding that these follies may have made a strong impression on the minds of people who had never seen anything of the sort in all their lives, especially among the young. If we further remind ourselves that the minds of all these people were filled with notions of witches and magic, we can see how these folk would inevitably attribute to the devil these things which seemed like prodigies, since it was their custom of this kind of people to regard the devil as the author of all that is extraordinary…[196]

COMMENT: Although this was a period when diabolic possession was still often diagnosed – as indeed the victims themselves claimed and their fellow townsfolk accepted as a matter of course – it is to the doctors' credit that they went in the face of public opinion and issued a clear-cut statement, which Calmeil suggests may have been the first unambiguous skeptical statement of its kind.

The women suffered from melancholia crossed with epilepsy, according to the doctors. The noted researcher Saintyves considered this case an example of mythomanie, partly conscious and partly unconscious.

See also: CONVENT HYSTERIA, DEMON POSSESSION.

TOXIC BUS CONTROVERSY

Vancouver, British Columbia, Canada: May 25, 2004

What happened on a public TransLink bus in Western Canada on one spring day in 2004 continues to stir controversy and hard feelings among some public servants in the city of Vancouver and members of the British Columbia health community. Officially it is known as "police file #04-128479." Some residents think that the file contains evidence of a chemical weapons attack, but some of Canada's top medical experts say it has all the hallmarks of mass hysteria.

This much everyone can agree on: On Tuesday May 25, at about 1 p.m., a man walked to the front of a public bus and, before stepping off in downtown Vancouver, made a vague remark to the effect that "his day was about to take a turn." From where the man got off and over the next ten kilometers, the driver began to feel nauseous and vomited; he asked if anyone else felt ill? When another passenger said yes, the driver pulled the bus to the side of the road and called for medics. As the two responding paramedics arrived and began to treat the driver and hear his account of events, they too began to feel unwell. More help was summoned. This time the response was overwhelming. With images of September 11th still fresh, sixty people from government agencies and four detectives were soon on what became known as "the toxic bus case," checking for clues, following leads, and testing the bus for hazardous agents. It looked like a scene from *CSI Miami* on steroids. Fearing a biological attack, nineteen people, including the bus driver, emergency personnel, and journalists, were briefly quarantined.

Joyce Horton, traveling from Richmond to Vancouver to see her daughter, recalled the incident. "He said how's your day going... and the bus driver said good. Then the man said 'it won't be for long.'"[197]

Police launched an urgent search for the man, described as an olive-skinned male in his mid-20s, with an average build and "5 o'clock shadow." He was said to have a pencil-thin mustache and gold neck chain. This description, suggesting the possibility that he may have been Middle Eastern, likely heightened suspicion and fear. He seemingly disappeared into thin air. The incident happened on B-line bus #98 – "the Richmond Express," at the intersection of 49th and Granville Avenue in Vancouver, where the man got off.[198]

Air samples of the bus were negative and everyone soon recovered. Investigators went through every inch of the bus. When they found brown pellets, they thought they might have a vital clue. They scooped them up and waited for the lab results. The finding: thyme, mud, mungo pinecones, and acorns – a dead-end.

Shortly after the incident, University of British Columbia epidemiologist Dr. Richard Mathias said the episode was a textbook example of anxiety. "An unknown substance which turns out to be harmless, somebody getting sick, nausea, vomiting, all of those kinds of things are associated with this." How does it start? Mathias said: "Somebody starts to get sick and then it rapidly spreads to other people... quite a classic presentation for this sort of thing."[199]

In early June, Vancouver's chief medical health officer, Dr. John Blatherwick, concurred with Dr. Mathias' assessment. He too was convinced the episode was "mass anxiety" and closed the case. This clearly irritated the Vancouver police. At a press conference, Constable Sarah Bloor rejected Dr. Blatherwick's statement, noting that "he is not involved in the investigation and that he is misinformed. The investigation remains active, as toxicology results are still not complete."[200] The paramedics union backed the police. At this point it was getting personal. The battle lines were drawn. It was up to science to resolve the issue.

On June 25, Vancouver Police held a press briefing, triumphantly announcing that after painstaking investigation, they had finally identified the chemical agent used in the "attack." Chemist Robert Lockhart was introduced to discuss the findings: "A trace level of Methyl Chloride was found, which in high concentrations is capable of killing someone. While it is impossible to say how much of the gas the victims were exposed to or how it came to be delivered into the air on the bus, it would have taken a fairly high concentration to force the gas into some of the materials on the bus, such as seat fabric and the air filters. No Methyl Chloride was found in any of the samples taken from the back of the bus."[201]

It was also revealed that when the Royal Canadian Mounted Police laboratory had turned up nothing in their tests, a private firm was hired and more in-depth tests were ordered. In a scene reminiscent of the TV drama *Cold Case*, Inspector Chris Beach said: "When nothing was discovered, because of the potential seriousness of the case... our investigators were not satisfied that this file could be concluded and we had more sophisticated tests done by Dr. Lockhart. These tests revealed the presence of this chemical, whose side effects are consistent with what the victims suffered and which should not have been found on the bus."[202] One of the lead investigators, Rodger Shepard, defended the department's interpretation of the methyl chloride findings: "You're talking about two very senior ambulance attendants and they're not going to have psychosomatic symptoms, they've seen everything."[203] Police urged those who felt sick to go back to their doctors for more tests.[204]

On the surface, the announcement seemed straightforward. The press briefing made headlines across Canada and the world: A mysterious chemical attack on a Canadian bus. Was it Al-Qaida? A crazy man, someone with a grudge, or both? Either way, it seemed that the case that had already been closed once by Dr. Blatherwick had been cracked wide open, except for finding the perpetrator. But while Vancouver police were congratulating each other and the paramedics were saying, "we told you so," cracks were beginning to appear and the case would soon unravel.

What was the motivation? How was the chemical released? Why hasn't he attacked again? Why was there an absence of medical findings in the victims? Couldn't the methyl chloride have come from another source, perhaps the air, and built up in small quantities over time? Why hadn't the police at the press briefing acknowledged this possibility and instead announced with certainty that a chemical attack took place? Why hadn't the other bus filters been checked as a control? During the first three media briefings, not a single remark was made about anyone on the bus smelling an odor at the time. During the June 25 briefing, when methyl chloride was "identified" as the cause, police said that after the mystery man left, some passengers detected an odor. It is conspicuous that no mention of an odor is mentioned in any of the earlier briefings. Could the "victim's" memories be playing tricks on them?

A Complete Absence Of Objective Findings

Following the press briefing, Dr. Blatherwick stood firm; he had seen no hard evidence to indicate any diagnosis other than mass hysteria. During the press conference, it was observed that methyl chloride is potentially deadly. True, but so are drinking water and table salt if one consumes too much. Dr. Blatherwick said he suspects that if other bus air filters had been checked, they too would likely have yielded similar concentrations of methyl chloride.[205] The U.S. Environmental Protection Agency says that methyl chloride is "formed in the oceans by natural processes" and "has been detected at low levels in air all over the world." It is also found in cigarette smoke, burning wood, plastics and coal – even aerosol propellants and chlorinated swimming pools.[206] Yet a team of 60 specialists went through the bus and all they could come up with was a minuscule amount of methyl chloride. Dr. Blatherwick also noted that some of the symptoms were not consistent with methyl chloride even if it had been present in higher amounts. What they were consistent with was anxiety.

Dr. Robert Lockhart, of the chemical technology company Vizon SciTec, which did the testing on the filters, said the amount of the chemical found was 27 parts per million. When asked by a reporter for *The Richmond Review* whether "testing other bus filters might serve as a control with which to gauge these findings," he said there had been no request to do so.[207]

Blatherwick's mass hysteria position infuriated paramedics. In a sharply-worded letter to *The Richmond Review* on July 8, Stuart Myers, representing the Ambulance Paramedics of B.C. CUPE Local 873, said "our paramedics were not victims of mass hysteria as the doctor alludes to. These two paramedics have close to 50 years of combined experience, the majority of that experience in one of the busiest ambulance stations in Canada." He also noted: "I know these paramedics personally and they exemplify compassion, commitment, competence, caring and professionalism."[208] This may be true, but these qualities do not inoculate anyone from anxiety. Soldiers see a lot in the line of duty, but cases of "shell shock" Post Traumatic Stress Disorder and other anxiety-related conditions are common. Further, one of the paramedics never got on the bus but still reported feeling sick. How could this be? Some theorized that while treating the bus driver, he had "exhaled the gas" that was breathed in by the paramedic![209]

Myers continued his criticism. "For Dr. Blatherwick to suggest that they are victims of mass hysteria leads me to believe that he has a narrow and limited understanding of the paramedic profession. These paramedics have suffered enough indignity due to this event, from having to defecate and vomit in a bucket while quarantined in the back of an ambulance to being stripped naked and scrubbed with a car brush to decontaminate." He further said that Dr. Blatherwick's statements "only add to these indignities as he belittles and dismisses their exposure and illness as 'hysteria.'"[210]

When interviewed nearly a year after the incident, Dr. Mathias remained confident of the diagnosis. He said that, while the emergency room doctor was convinced there was a problem, "the medical conditions were not confirmed by any objective measurements... He had no objective physical signs or laboratory tests that supported a specific exposure." He continued: "People not on the bus (a journalist) developed similar symptoms that receded spontaneously as she moved away from the site. No responder who was among the ill had any objective confirmation of illness."[211]

About six weeks after the incident, Dr. Reka Gustafson, a Vancouver health officer, gave a structured questionnaire to ten people who reported symptoms in the incident – at least nine of whom were examined at St. Paul's Hospital. The symptoms varied considerably. The most common were eye irritation and headache (4), pressure behind the eye, thirst, vomiting, belching, frequent or excessive urination (3), dizziness, dry mouth, loss of coordination, stomach pain, fear and anxiety (2), lightheadedness, shortness of breath, and tremor (1). The key findings: "although the bus driver and one passenger got ill, the other estimated 20 to 50 passengers did not. In addition...first responders who boarded the bus prior to the paramedics and did so without personal protective equipment did not get ill. Similarly, the bus mechanic who boarded the bus with the paramedic also remained asymptomatic. One symptomatic paramedic boarded the bus, while the other did not. Therefore, symptoms were not limited to those who boarded the bus and most of those who did board the bus were not ill. Thus, results of this investigation are not consistent with a point source of an inhaled substance causing illness on a bus."[212]

Dr. Gustafson noted that symptoms such as nausea and vomiting are seen with many conditions. Further, the more exotic symptoms, such as excessive belching and polyuria (frequent or excessive urination), were experienced "only by the three individuals quarantined together. The passenger who did not have an opportunity to discuss her experience with others at the scene did not experience dry mouth, thirst, polyuria and belching." As a result, Dr. Gustafson said that it was unlikely that all of the symptoms were associated with the same exposure, and that based on the evidence the outbreak epidemiology "is not consistent with an inhaled exposure to a toxic chemical. Alternate hypotheses may be suggested by additional details from chemical analyses."[213]

CONTEXT: The "war on terror" following the September 11, 2001, attacks on the United States resulted in a variety of ordinarily mundane events and circumstances being redefined as terror related. There was considerable media speculation during this period, that mass public transport was a likely target.

In the final analysis, Dr. Mathias thought the way the incident was described – as mass hysteria – was a key factor in the backlash against a psychological cause.[214] Given the absence of objective findings and the symptoms displayed, mass hysteria remains the most likely diagnosis.

TOXIC COURTHOUSE

Toronto, Canada: late 1990s and ongoing

Since at least 1997, controversy has swirled around

the healthiness of the 179,326-square-foot, four-story Newmarket Courthouse on Eagle Street, which is the workplace of 330 full-time employees and sees about 1,100 visitors daily. Despite intense scrutiny of the building by health authorities and an estimated 20 million dollars in renovations aimed at making the building healthier, no significant safety problems were uncovered. In 2003 a judge studied the evidence and ruled that the building was indeed safe.

A timeline of key events involved in the saga is as follows:

Late February/Early March 2000: "Toxic mold" is discovered at the Newmarket Courthouse.

June 29, 2000: a survey of 239 Courthouse workers is released. Forty-one percent said they had experienced symptoms that are consistent with so-called Sick Building Syndrome, such as nose, throat and eye irritation.[215]

June 30, 2000: the courthouse is ordered closed by Attorney General James Flaherty in an effort to remove toxic mold. Journalist Harold Levy reported that prior to the building being close, "many court staff refused to enter it on their doctor's advice, and at least 13 of the 25 judges and justices of the peace who usually work there were refusing to preside over courts."[216]

March 6, 2001: a 50 million dollar class action lawsuit was filed in a Canadian court on behalf of "all persons who, during the period 1979 to the present, were exposed to toxic moulds, harmful gases and substances while on the premises of the courthouse." The suit sought $15 million in damages such as pain, suffering, and failure to enjoy life. Thirty-five million dollars was sought for conduct that was deemed to be "high-handed outrageous and reckless." In failing to protect the building's occupants, the suit claimed that workers in the courthouse have suffered "an unusual number of health complaints, including headaches, nausea, fatigue, dizziness, migraines, asthma, irritability, cancer and respiratory diseases."[217]

Late June, 2001: After being closed for nearly a year to remove toxic mold, the courthouse is reopened after a massive, multi-million dollar renovation project that included the modification or replacement of the following systems: heating, humidifying, plumbing, air conditioning, ventilation and ducts. In addition, carpets were replaced, new drinking fountains were installed, and the windows were sealed. The building's exterior was worked on in order to eliminate potential moisture points. Throughout the renovation process, the building's health was monitored by such groups as a health and safety committee, the owner, Ontario Realty Corporation, and ProFac, its manager.[218] Attorney Morris Manning claimed that between September 2001 and July 2002, there had been at least 65 complaints from people in the courthouse as to feeling stuffy, experiencing temperature extremes, and having impeded airflow in the building.[219] Within days of the building reopening, Val Erwin, of the courthouse government/employee joint health and safety committee, said she began to receive health complaints from workers. Within a few weeks she would express her puzzlement, noting: "I get copies of the test results. They are not telling us lies. It is all so baffling."[220]

July 2002: Judge Bruce Shilton told a television reporter that "something is wrong with the courthouse."[221]

August 2002: it was made public that even after the cleanup, toxic mold had been found on five occasions. Ghous Siddiqui, a manager for ProFac, told a court that these were relatively small amounts of mold and that it was "totally impossible" to eliminate all mold from the building. He also said that it was only after the spring of 2000 did health complaints spike after it was announced that the courthouse was contaminated with toxic mold.[222]

August 7, 2002: Hours before a hearing to determine whether the Newmarket Courthouse is safe or still poses a threat from mold, court reporter Joan Abel, 63, is taken from the building and off to hospital after experiencing breathing problems. As news of the incident spread through the building, a member of the Courthouse health committee, Pauline Tapping, said other workers in the building became anxious. She also revealed that Abel had experienced two previous attacks and that "She is a highly allergic person." At least eight others reported ailments ranging from dizziness to nausea, coughing and plugged ears, though none required hospital treatment. Shortly after the incident, a hearing resumed in which Dr. Om Malik, an occupational health specialist, testified that many of the symptoms being reported at the Courthouse were psychogenic in nature, noting that the "power of suggestion is definitely a factor in this."[223] He also told the court that such incidents are common: "The literature is full of those kinds of incidents, where a large number of people show symptoms (and) investigations show that there is no physical basis for it."[224]

August 28, 2002: Joan Abel returns to the Courthouse to proclaim that it is still a health hazard, and that her illness was just the tip of the iceberg: "They said they fixed the problem, but they haven't." Abel said the only reason she was returning to work was because she was employed on contract, so no work, no pay.[225]

September 2002: The *Toronto Star* reports that about a year earlier, concern over toxic mold resulted in a tax fraud case being moved to another building after several of those involved in the case felt unwell. Attorney Howard Morton who took part in the proceedings, said: "I don't think I'm a hypochondriac. But (one day)...we were all experiencing discomfort. I noticed the judge's eyes were red, I was short of breath, one of the accused was having a really bad day, and hardly 15 seconds went by without the judge, me, the court reporter, or the court clerk, either coughing or clearing the throat."

When asked why the building remained open in the face of claims of unhealthy working conditions at the Courthouse, Government spokesman Brendan Crawley responded that "all recent tests, air quality tests, air pressure tests by independent engineering firms confirm that both air quality and air pressure are at normal levels..."[226]

Based on "incident report forms" returned by 50 courthouse employees, over 300 complaints were recorded at the facility since reopening, including nosebleeds, headaches, sore throats, itchy eyes, ear pain, ear pressure, ringing in the ears, rashes, running noses, and trouble concentrating.[227]

Meanwhile, two court employees were formally refusing to work in the building, saying that the site was a threat to their health. Jocelyn Redgrift and June McRae informed their supervisor of their notice of refusal to work.[228]

September 30, 2002: It is reported that a judge set to preside over a murder trial scheduled to be heard at the Newmarket Courthouse quit the trial fearing that his health problems may be related to the building. According to a transcript obtained by the *Toronto Star*, the Justice said: "On August 28th, I developed what has been diagnosed at this time as an Eustachian tube dysfunction in my right ear." He concluded by stating: "Until further medical investigations have been conducted...it has been recommended that I not sit on this lengthy matter in this courthouse."[229]

October 30, 2002: Citing a serious ear problem, Justice Vibert Lampkin, who was given the task of determining whether the courthouse was safe, withdrew from the case.[230] Meanwhile, defense attorney Morris Manning said that after spending "$20 million to get the building in shape, and people are (still) getting sick,"[231] the situation was an embarrassment to the Ontario Attorney General.

October 31, 2002: A *Toronto Star* editorial called on the attorney general to look into the case of the toxic courthouse more closely. As for suggestions of mass hysteria being the culprit, the editorial argued that this is unlikely as those involved "are rational, respected people raising serious concerns."[232]

On the same date, it was revealed that the traces were minor, despite concerns over the detection of mold after the courthouse was cleaned up and renovated. In fact, mold levels in the air outside the buildings tested higher than inside![233]

March 18, 2003: Federal prosecutor Morris Pistyner stated: "The evidence shows that the Newmarket courthouse has never been healthier, that it is getting healthier all the time and will be the envy of other courthouses." He also observed that relatively minor problems with the building were being overstated, noting: "The courthouse is not a surgical operating room. It is not a perfect place, nor was it ever intended to be."[234]

March 27, 2003: Justice Peter Tetley issued a long-awaited 16-page ruling, declaring that based on an analysis of the evidence presented to him, the Newmarket courthouse was healthy. "There is no evidence that toxic mould is present within this facility."

In rendering his decision, Tetley reviewed 47 exhibits and 1,000 pages of testimony over a 15-day period.[235]

TOXIC MOULD FEARS

Worldwide: 1990s to present

While U.S. lawsuits over the supposed toxic impact of indoor mould has increased dramatically in recent years, two California experts contended that most reports of mold-related breathing problems, memory loss, and difficulty concentrating are in the minds of the beholders. UCLA psychiatrist Mohan Nair said that of the 50 patients referred to him for treatment of mold-related psychosomatic symptoms, many have a history of hypochondriasis, past false claims, and depression. A toxicologist at the University of Southern California Medical Center, Ashok Jain, estimated that 70 to 80% of mold-related "lawsuits have no medical basis." While admitting that mold is a toxic agent, he said: "But it's just not that bad."[236]

CONTEXT: The upsurge in the number of mold-related illnesses in the United States and Canada since the 1990s appear to reflect social factors including alarmist media reports and news of legal proceedings in high profile cases.

TSUNAMI RUMORS

Asia: December 2004 - January 2005

In the wake of the December 26, 2004, tsunami or tidal wave disaster that killed in excess of 220,000 people in coastal areas across Asia, and to a lesser extent, Africa, rumors of further tsunamis reeked havoc. On Friday, December 31, 2004, about 20 Malaysian women fainted after hearing rumors that more tsunamis were on the way, triggering a rush to higher ground. The incident occurred in the northern state of Kedah. A similar panic was reported to the south on the island of Penang. Malaysian police reported receiving several phone calls claiming that meteorological authorities were warning of further tidal waves. Meanwhile, similar rumors were spread across the country via hand-held text messengers.[237]

Journalist Robert Marquand in the vicinity of Galle, Sri Lanka, reported that rumors were rampant in the uncertainty and fear in the wake of the tsunami. In scores of coastal villages, new tsunami rumors were creating social instability. Soon after the disaster, a popular Sri Lankan astrologer appeared on national television to predict with certainty the arrival of a second tidal wave between the 3rd and 8th of January 2005. This presentation was convincing, with the astrologer even betting his own life in guaranteeing that the event would materialize. It did not.[238] Compounding the problem, senior members of the Sri Lankan government were making statements in support of the astrological prediction. One official even claimed that "astrology is a sub-branch of the sciences."[239]

In the aftermath of the Asian tsunami, Snopes.com, an internet site that documents cyber rumors and urban legends, noted a flurry of tidal wave-related accounts that could not be verified and were of dubious origin. These include claims that tsunami orphans were being offered for sale in Malaysia via mobile phone text messages. The Deputy Inspector General of the Malaysian Police, Musa Hassan told the Agence France Presse that "preliminary investigations found that no children are offered for sale."[240]

CONTEXT: In the aftermath of major disasters, rumors are common as residents seek reassurance and certainty during a period that is unsure and uncertain. The process may help to relieve anxiety and may reinforce existing stereotypes or beliefs. For instance, the tsunami disaster occurred during a period of widespread anti-Muslim sentiment and may have added to the plausibility that Islamic Malaysians may have been ruthlessly trafficking in orphaned babies and children.

TULIP MANIA

Holland: 1634-1637

Over a three year period, "Tulip Mania" or "tulipomania" swept across Holland as people paid fantastic prices for certain varieties of tulip bulbs. London journalist CHARLES MACKAY popularized the episode during the mid-nineteenth century, remarking that many citizens lost their senses in the rush to possess tulip bulbs. According to Mackay, many even neglected their jobs, becoming overwhelmed by the herd instinct in the obsessive desire to obtain tulip bulbs. "In 1634, the rage among the Dutch to possess them was so great that the ordinary industry of the country was neglected, and the population, even to its lowest dregs, embarked in the tulip trade. As the mania increased ...[by] 1635, many persons were known to invest a fortune of 100,000 florins in the purchase of forty roots."[241] Mackay records that in February 1637, the price of bulbs crashed and many people went broke.

CONTEXT: A contemporary analysis of the Tulip Mania, examining the event within its socio-historical context, suggests that the episode was an illusion involving relatively poor tavern-goers who wagered huge sums of money in the speculation market, knowing full well that their contracts were not enforceable in the courts.

According to one account, a sailor had been away from Holland for several years, only to return in ignorance of the tulip craze. Spotting what he thought was an onion, he "slipped it into his pocket, as a relish for his herring." The "onion" the man had eaten was actually a rare *Semper Augustus* bulb worth 3,000 florins. "Little did he dream that he had been eating a breakfast whose cost might have regaled a whole ship's crew for a twelvemonth..."[242] By Mackay's estimates, 12 robust sheep were worth 120 florins, eight pigs valued at 240 florins, and four oxen worth 480 florins.[243] When the market for tulip bulbs crashed, "Substantial merchants were reduced almost to beggary, and many a representative of a noble line saw the fortunes of his house ruined beyond redemption."[244] Today, the tulip mania is synonymous with stock market irrationality and "the madness of crowds" to use Mackay's oft used phrase.

More recently, Brown University economist Peter Garber has challenged Mackay's version of events. Garber argues that to label this event as mass irrationality is misguided. He claims that the reports of the mania were greatly exaggerated and constitute a mass delusion in itself. While some varieties reached astronomical heights and suddenly tumbled, he says the economic consequences were not nearly as devastating as Mackay claimed. In terms of supply and demand, bulbs can be propagated and sold at considerable profit, and the eventual drop in prices is virtually inevitable as the greater the number of bulbs produced and sold, the less scarce and valuable they become. Garber's research demonstrated that exorbitant tulip prices were being paid for newly discovered rare bulbs, and based on the laws of supply and demand, the eventual price decline was the inevitable result of their rapid proliferation. The high prices paid for rare bulbs were rational and often made solid business sense as rare bulbs could produce expensive hybrids that often yielded lucrative returns on their initial investment.[245] After the "crash," rare varieties of tulip bulbs continued to fetch high prices – a pattern that continues to the present day.[246]

Garber documented how Dutch tulip futures contracts were illegal and reports of a major economic collapse in Holland as a result of the tulip trade were unfounded. Indeed, the price of Dutch East India Company shares actually rose during the period of the supposed "crash," from 229 in 1636 to 412 by 1639.[247] In February 1637, there *was* a sharp decline in the price of common bulbs that were traded in futures markets housed in taverns. However, Garber viewed this event as a game played by commoners who had accumulated little wealth, but for entertainment purposes, made enormous bets with each other – bets that could not be enforced in court. "These markets consisted of a collection of people without equity making ever-increasing numbers of 'million dollar bets' with one another with some knowledge that the state would not enforce the contracts. This was no more than a meaningless winter drinking game, played by a plague-ridden population that made use of the vibrant tulip market."[248]

Garber documented how an array of scholars through the years have propagated the myth of the Dutch tulip mania, making claims based on inadequate and secondhand research, many citing Mackay's non-scholarly popularization of the myth. These include economist John Kenneth Galbraith and contemporary writers for *The Wall Street Journal* and *The Economist.*[249] Gaber doubted that the tulip mania myth would disappear quickly due to its appealing nature. "The wonderful tales from the tulipmania are catnip irresistible to those with a taste for crying bubble, even when the stories are so obviously untrue. So perfect are they for didactic use that financial moralizers will always find a ready market for them..."[250] Also see: CRAZE.

Sources

1. Michael, Franz (1966). *The Taiping Rebellion.* Seattle: University of Washington Press, pp. 1-20.
2. Michael, op cit., p. 26.
3. Esherick, Joseph W. (1987). *The Origins of the Boxer Uprising.* Berkeley: University of California Press, p. 375, quoting a contemporary commentary.
4. Michael, op cit., p. 70.
5. Michael, op cit., p. 133, citing Alexander Wylie.
6. Michael, op cit., p. 197.
7. Gloyne, Harold F. (1950). "Tarantism: Mass Hysterical Reaction to Spider Bite in the Middle Ages." *American Imago* 7:29-42. See p. 29.
8. Sigerist, Henry E. (1943). *Civilization and Disease.* Ithaca, New York: Cornell University Press, pp. 218-219.
9. Gloyne, op cit., p. 35.
10. Bartholomew, Robert E. (2000). *Exotic Deviance: Medicalizing Cultural Idioms–From Strangeness to Illness.* Boulder, CO: University Press of Colorado, p. 149.
11. Bartholomew, op cit., p. 149.
12. Australian Museum Online, http://www.amonline.net.au/factsheets/wolf_spiders.htm. Accessed March 3, 2003.
13. Sigerist, op cit., p. 218; Rosen, op cit., p. 204.
14. Bartholomew, op cit., pp. 133-134.
15. Serao, F. (1750). *Idem, Della Tarantula Ovvero Falangio di Puglia.* Naples, Italy.
16. Turnbull, A. (1771). Letter from Mr. Turnbull to Archibald Menzies of Kildares, Esq. dated from Delphos, concerning Italy, the Alleged Effects of the bite of the Tarantula, the Grecian antiquities. Pp. 100-115. In *Essays and Observations Physical and Literary.* Edinburgh: Balfour; Katner, W. (1956). *Das Ratsel des Tarentismus. Eine Atiologie der Italienischen Tanzkrankheit* [The Mystery of Tarantism: An Etiology of Italian Dancing Illness]. *Nova Acta Leopoldina* (n.s. 18, number 124), Leipzig, Germany: Barth.
17. Baglivi, Giorgio. (1723). *The Practice of Physick.* London: A. Bell.
18. Rosen, op cit., p. 15.
19. Rosen, op cit., pp. 42-43.
20. Sigerist, op cit., p. 225.
21. Bartholomew, op cit, p. 135.
22. Sigerist, op cit, p. 226.
23. Mora, George (1963). "A Historical and Socio-Psychiatric Appraisal of Tarantism." *Bulletin of the History of Medicine* 37:417-439. See p. 430.
24. Mora, op cit., p. 430.
25. Bartholomew, op cit., pp. 127, 132-139, 142, 146, 149, 151.
26. Russell, op cit., p. 413.
27. de Martino, E. (1966). *La Terre du Remords* [The Land of Self-Affliction] (translated from Italian by Claude Poncet). Paris: Gallimard; Gallini, C. (1988). *La Ballerina Variopinta: Une Festa Guarigione in Sardegna* [The Multi-Colored Dancer: A Healing Festival in Sardinia]. Naples: Liguori.
28. Bartholomew, op cit., p. 146.
29. Wittstock, Bernadette, Rozental, Lydia, and Henn, Charlene (1991). "Mass Phenomena at a Black South African Primary School." *Hospital and Community Psychiatry* 42:851-853. See p. 852.
30. Wittstock, Rozental and Henn (1991).op cit., p. 852.
31. Jones, Timothy F., Craig, Allen S., Hoy, Debbie, Gunter, Elaine W., Ashley, David L., Barr, Dana B., Brock, John W., and Schaffner, William. (2000). "Mass Psychogenic Illness Attributed to Toxic Exposure at a High School." *The New England Journal of Medicine* 342(2):96-100.
32. Jones et al., op cit, p. 96.
33. "A Overview of 2000 Years of Jewish Persecution–Anti-Judaism: 1201 To 1800 CE." http://www.religioustolerance.org/jud_pers3.htm.
34. Mackay, Charles. (1852). *Memoirs of Extraordinary Popular Delusions and the Madness of Crowds Volume 2.* London: Office of the National Illustrated Library, p. 264.
35. Mackay (1852). op cit., p. 264.
36. MacDonnell, F. (1995). *Insidious Foes.* New York: Oxford University Press; Mount, G.S. (1993). *Canada's Enemies: Spies and Spying in the Peaceable Kingdom.* Toronto: Dundurn Press; Kitchen, M. (1985). "The German Invasion of Canada in the First World War." *The International History Review* 7(2):245-260
37. Bartholomew, Robert, and Wessely, Simon. (1999). "Epidemic Hysteria in Virginia: The Case of the Phantom Gasser of 1933-34." *The Southern Medical Journal* 92(8):762-769.
38. Kenworthy, J.M. (1930). *New Wars; New Weapons.* London: E. Matthews & Marrot; Hart, L. (1933). *The British Way of War.* New York: The Macmillan Company; Lefebure, V. (1931). *Scientific Disarmament.* London: Mundamus; Duffield, M. (1931). *King Legion.* New York: Jonathan Cape and Harrison Smith.
39. Fradkin, E.K. (1934). *The Air Menace and the Answer.* New York: The Macmillan Company, p. 1.
40. For a partial bibliography, see Fradkin, op cit., pp. 321-322.
41. Anonymous. (1933). *The New York Times Index.* New York: R.R. Bowker.
42. Ibid.
43. Anonymous. (1933). "Gas in the Next War" [editorial]. *The New York Times,* January 3, 1933, p. 22.
44. See, for example: Gesner, G.D. (1931). "Morning After." *Forum and Century* 86:240-246 (October); Gilchrist, H.L. (1931). "Effects of Chemical Cases; Research Work of Chemical Warfare Service, U.S. Army." *U.S. Bureau of Labor Statistics Bulletin* 536:293-306; McDarment, C. (1931). "Clouds of Death." *Popular Mechanics* 55:177-179 (February); Mills, J.E. (1932). "Chemical Warfare." *Foreign Affairs* 10:444-452 (April); Anonymous. (1932). "False Faces [Gas Masks] for Everyone." *Popular Mechanics* 57:970-971 (June); Anonymous. (1932). "New Shelter from Poison Gas Tested in France." *Popular Science Monthly* 121:38 (October); Anonymous. (1932). "Chemicals in Warfare." *Literary Digest* 114:32 (October 15); Anonymous (1932). "Poison Gas." *Review of Reviews* 86:56 (September). Anonymous. (1933). "First Aid for Ghouls." *World Tomorrow* 14:55 (January); Moore, J.M. (1933). "War We Intend to Avoid." *Forum* 89:218-223 (April); Phillips, T.R. (1933). "Debunking Mars' Newest Toys." *Saturday Review of Literature* 205:23 (March 4); St. John, A. (1934). "Will Gas Destroy Populations in the Next War?" *Literary Digest* 117:17 (March 3).
45. Cantril, H. (1940[1947]). *The Invasion From Mars: A Study in the Psychology of Panic.* Princeton, New Jersey: Princeton University Press, p. 160.
46. Johnson, Donald Max. (1945). "The 'Phantom Anesthetist' of Mattoon: A Field Study of Mass Hysteria." *Journal of Abnormal and Social Psychology* 40:175-186.
47. Harris, R., and Paxman, J. (1991). *A Higher Form of Killing: The*

Secret Story of Chemical and Biological Warfare. New York: The Noonday Press, p. 108.

48. Anonymous. (1934). *The New York Times Index*, op cit.

49. Roosevelt, F.D. (1943). "Statement on Poison Gas." *Current History* 4:405 (August); Lindley, E.K. (1943). "Thoughts on the Use of Gas in Warfare." *Newsweek* 22:24 (December 20); Marshall, J. (1943). "We are Ready with Gas if the Axis Turns on the Gas." *Collier's* 112:21 (August 7); Scott, E.W. (1944). "Role of the Public Health Laboratory in Gas Defense." *American Journal of Public Health* 34:275-278 (March); Wood, J.R. (1944). "Chemical Warfare: A Chemical and Toxicological Review." *American Journal of Public Health* 34:455-460 (May); Sanders, V. (1945). "Our Army's Defense Against Poison Gas." *Popular Science* 146:106-111 (February).

50. Brown, F.J. (1968). op. cit., p. 244.

51. Ladendorf, Robert, and Bartholomew, Robert E. (2002). "The Mad Gasser of Mattoon: How the Press Created an Imaginary Chemical Weapons Attack." *The Skeptical Inquirer* 26(4):50-54, 58 (July-August).

52. Jilek, W. G., and Jilek-Aall, L. (1977a). "A Koro Epidemic in Thailand." *Transcultural Psychiatric Research Review* 14:56-59. See p. 57 for quote.

53. Jilek and Jilek-Aall. (1977a). op cit.; Jilek, W. G., and Jilek-Aall, L. (1977b). "Mass Hysteria with Koro Symptoms in Thailand." *Schweizer Archive Neurologie Neurochirurgie un Psychiatrie* 120(2):257-259.

54. Jilek and Jilek-Aall, 1977a, op cit., p. 58.

55. Jilek and Jilek-Aall, 1977a, op cit., p. 58.

56. Jilek and Jilek-Aall, 1977a, op cit., p. 58.

57. Modan, Baruch, Tirosh, Moshe, Weissenberg, Emil, Acker, Cilla, Swartz, T.A., Coston, Corina, Donagi, Alexander, Revach, Moshe, and Vettorazzi, Gaston (1983). "The Arjenyattah Epidemic." *The Lancet* ii:1472-1474.

58. Goldsmith, M.F. (1989). "Physicians with Georgia on their Minds." *Journal of the American Medical Association* 262:603-604.

59. Radovanovic, Zoran. (1995). "On the origin of mass casualty incidents in Kosovo, Yugoslavia, in 1990." *European Journal of Epidemiology* 11:1-13.

60. Hay, Alastair, and Foran, John (1991). "Yugoslavia: Poisoning or Epidemic Hysteria in Kosovo?" *The Lancet* 338(8776):1196 (November 9).

61. Radovanovic, op cit.

62. Hay and Foran, op cit.

63. Rockney, R.M., and Lemke, T. (1992). "Casualties From a Junior High School During the Persian Gulf War: Toxic Poisoning or Mass Hysteria?" *Journal of Developmental and Behavioral Pediatrics* 13:339-342; Rockney, R.M., and Lemke, T. (1994). "Response." Letter. *Journal of Developmental and Behavioral Pediatrics* 15 (1):64-65.

64. Durbin, K., Vogt, T. (2001). "Fumes ..." *Columbian*, September 29, 2001.

65. Villanueva, R.L., Payumo, M.C., and Lema, K. (2001). "Flu Scare Sweeps Schools." *Business World* (Philippines), October 3, 2001, p. 12.

66. Lellman, L. (2001). "Suspicious Incident Forces Subway's Closing." *Rutland Daily Herald*, October 10, p. A3.

67. Becerra, H, Malnic E. "Complaints of Dizziness Shut Down Subway." *The Los Angeles Times*, September 27, 2001.

68. CNN (2001). "Special report live with Aaron Brown." Atlanta, Georgia, October 16, 10-11pm.

69. Rozek, Daniel (2003). "Unexplained Itching Strikes Naperville Workers." *Chicago Sun-Times*, May 24, 2003.

70. A case involving an imaginary gasser pre-dating the Botetourt and Mattoon episodes occurred in 1910 and involved Halley's Comet. Newspaper reports, bolstered by an irresponsible astronomer, claimed that the comet might veil earth in a mist of poison gas. Some alarmed citizens went so far as to stuff rags in doorways. Davidson, K. (1999). Letter to Robert Bartholomew dated February 11; Sagan, C. (1980). *Cosmos*. New York: Random House, p. 80.

71. Martinez, Yleana (1993). "A Long, Tall Texas Tale." *American Journalism Review* 15(4):11 (May).

72. Matrinez, op cit.

73. Martinez, op cit.

74. Martinez, op cit.

75. Frankel, S. (1976). "Mass Hysteria in the New Guinea Highlands: A Telefomin Outbreak and its Relationship to Other New Guinea Hysterical Reactions." *Oceania* 47:105-133.

76. Teoh, J., Soewondo, S., and Sidharta, M. (1975). "Epidemic Hysteria in Malaysia: An Illustrative Episode." *Psychiatry* 8(3):258-268.

77. Ebrahim, G.J. (1968). "Mass Hysteria in School Children, Notes on Three Outbreaks in East Africa." *Clinical Pediatrics* 7:437-438.

78. Tseng, W. S., Mo, K. M., Hsu, J., Li, L. S., Ou, L. W., Chen, G. Q., and Jiang, D. W. (1988). "A Sociocultural Study of Koro Epidemics in Guangdong, China." *American Journal of Psychiatry* 145 (12):1538-1543; Tseng, W. S., Mo, K. M., Li, L. S., Chen, G. Q., Ou, L. W., and Zheng, H. B. (1992). "Koro Epidemics in Guangdong, China: A Questionnaire Survey." *The Journal of Nervous and Mental Disease* 180 (2):117-123.

79. Carlisle, Adrienne (1999). "Stress may have Caused 'Mass Hysteria." *South African Dispatch*, May 29, 1999, online at http://www.dispatch.co.za/1999/05/29/easterncape/CAUSED.HTM; Bridgraj, Ajith (1999). "A Mysterious 'Madness.'" *The Teacher* at http://www.teacher. co.za/9908/demon.html.

80. Bhatiasevi, Aphaluck. (2001). "Belief in Ghosts Sparks Hysteria: Students Freak Out at School Camp." *Bangkok Post*, February 4, 2001.

81. Cirillo, D. (1770). "A Letter to Dr. William Watson, F.R.S. giving some Account of the Manna Tree and the Tarantula." *Philosophical Transactions of the Royal Society* (London) 60:233-238.

82. Sigerist, H. E. (1943). *Civilization and Disease*. Ithaca, New York: Cornell University Press, p. 221.

83. Hecker, J.F.C. (1970[1837]). *The Dancing Mania of the Middle Ages* (translated by B. Babington). New York: B. Franklin, pp. 3-4.

84. Modan, B., Tirosh, M., Weissenberg, E., Acker, C., Swartz, T., Coston, C., Donagi, A., Revach, M., and Vettorazzi, G. (1983). "The Arjenyattah Epidemic." *The Lancet* ii:1472-1476.

85. Hafez, A. (1985). "The Role of the Press and the Medical Community in an Epidemic of Mysterious Gas Poisoning in the Jordan West Bank." *American Journal of Psychiatry* 142:833-837; Stewart, James R. (1991). "The West Bank Collective Hysteria Episode: the Politics of Illness." *The Skeptical Inquirer* 15: 153-160.

86. Madden, R. R. (1857). *Phantasmata or Illusions and Fanaticisms of Protean Forms Productive of Great Evils*. London: T.C. Newby, p. 253.

87. Caulfield, E. (1943). "Pediatric Aspects of the Salem Witchcraft Tragedy: A Lesson in Mental Health." *American Journal of Diseases of Children* 97:788-802. See p. 793.

88. Schuler, E.A., Parenton, V.J. (1943). "A Recent Epidemic of Hysteria in a Louisiana High School." *Journal of Social Psychology* 17:221-235.

89. Aemmer, F. (1893). *Eine Schulepidemie von Tremor Hystericus* [A School Epidemic of Hysterical Tremor]. Inaugural dissertation, Basel; Truper, J. (1908). "Zur Frage der Schulerselbstmorde." *Zeitschrift fur Kinderforschung* 143:75-86.

90. Levy, D.A., and Nail, P.R. (1993). "Contagion: A Theoretical and Empirical Review and Reconceptualization." *Genetic, Social and General Psychology Monographs* 119 (3):235-283. See p. 270.

91. Levy and Nail, op cit., p. 270.
92. Levy and Nail, op cit., p. 270.
93. Pennebaker, J.W. (1980). "Perceptual and environmental determinants of coughing." *Basic and Applied Social Psychology* 1:83-91.
94. Pennebaker (1980). op cit., p. 87.
95. Freud, Sigmund (1911). *The Interpretation of Dreams.* Translation of 3d edition by A.A. Brill, with introduction by A. A. Brill. New York: Macmillan. The copyright on the 1911 edition has expired and this work is now in the public domain, accessed July 1, 2003, at: http://psychology.about.com/library/classics/blfreud_dream.htm.
96. Freud, Sigmund (1911). op cit.
97. Faust, H. S., and Brilliant, L. B. (1981). "Is the Diagnosis of 'Mass Hysteria' an Excuse for Incomplete Investigation of Low-Level Environmental Contamination?" *Journal of Occupational Medicine* 23:22-26. See p. 23.
98. Faust and Brilliant, op cit., p. 24.
99. Faust and Brilliant, op cit., p. 25.
100. Faust and Brilliant, op cit., p. 25.
101. Bauer, R.M., Greve, K.W., Besch, E.L, Schramke, C.J., Crouch, J., Hicks, A., Ware, M.R., and Lyles, W.B. (1992). "The Role of Psychological Factors in the Report of Building-Related Symptoms in Sick Building Syndrome." *Journal of Consulting and Clinical Psychology* 60(2) 213-19; Ryan, C.M., and Morrow, L.A. (1992). "Dysfunctional Buildings or Dysfunctional people: An Examination of the Sick Building Syndrome and Allied Disorders." *Journal of Consulting and Clinical Psychology* 60(2)220-224.
102. Guthrie, D. (1960). *A History of Medicine.* New York: Thomas Nelson and Sons, p. 100.
103. Stricklin, A., Sewell, M., and Austas, C. (1990). "Objective Measurements of Personality Variables in Epidemic Neuromyasthenia Patients." *South AfricanMedical Journal of Epidemiology* 132:1120-1129.
104. Pollock, G., and Clayton, T.M. (1964). "Epidemic Collapse: A Mysterious Outbreak in 3 Coventry Schools." *British Medical Journal* ii:1625-1627.
105. Massey, E. W., Brannon, W. L. Jr., and Riley, T. L. (1981). "The 'Jerks': Mass Hysteria or Epilepsy?" *Southern Medical Journal* 74(5):607-609.
106. Elkins, G.R., Gamino, L.A., and Rynearson, R.R. (1988). "Mass Psychogenic Illness, Trance States, and Suggestion. *American Journal of Clinical Hypnosis* 30:267-275.
107. Gamino LA, Elkins G.R., Hackney, K.U. (1989). "Emergency Management of Mass Psychogenic Illness." *Psychosomatics* 30:446-449. See p. 448.
108. Gamino et al. (1989). op cit., p. 448.
109. Sighele, S. (1892). *La Foule Criminelle, Essai de Psychologie Collective* (translated from Italian by P. Vigny). Paris: Felix Alcan.
110. Bliss, E.L. (1986). *Multiple Personality, Allied Disorders, and Hypnosis.* New York: Oxford University Press, p. 224.
111. Schmidt, C.G. (1984). "The Group-Fantasy Origin of AIDS." *Journal of Psychohistory* 12 (1):37-78.
112. Scott, J. C. (1985). *Weapons of the Weak.* New Haven, CT: Yale University Press.
113. Ackerman (1980). op cit.
114. Lee, R. L., and Ackerman, S. E. (1980). "The Sociocultural Dynamics of Mass Hysteria: A Case Study of Social Conflict in West Malaysia." *Psychiatry* 43:78-88. See p. 85.
115. Ong, A. (1988). "The Production of Possession: Spirits and the Multinational Corporation in Malaysia." *American Ethnologist* 15(1):28-42; Ong, A. (1987). *Spirits of Resistance and Capitalist Discipline: Factory Women in Malaysia.* Albany, New York: State University of New York Press.
116. Ong (1988). op cit., p. 38.
117. Ong (1987). op cit., pp. 210-211.
118. Scott (1985). op cit., p. xvi.
119. Ong (1987). op cit., p. 203.
120. Taylor, D.C. (1989). "Hysteria, Belief, and Magic." *British Journal of Psychiatry* 155:91-398, cited in Bartholomew, Robert E. (1994). "Tarantism, Dancing Mania and Demonopathy: The Anthro-Political Aspects of 'Mass Psychogenic Illness." *Psychological Medicine* 24:281-306, see p. 300.
121. Taylor (1989). op cit.
122. The follow section on the five broad theories of mass hysteria is excerpted from Bartholomew, R. E., and Sirois, F. (1996). "Epidemic Hysteria in Schools: An International and Historical Overview." *Educational Studies* 22(3):285-311. See pages 287-292.
123. Mohr, P.D., and Bond, M.J. (1982). "Epidemic Blindness." *British Medical Journal* 284:961-962.
124. Schuler, E.A., Parenton, V.J. (1943). "A Recent Epidemic of Hysteria in a Louisiana High School." *Journal of Social Psychology* 17:221-235.
125. Benaim, S.M., Horder, J., Anderson, J. (1973). "Hysterical Epidemic in a Classroom." *Psychological Medicine* 3:66-73.
126. American Psychiatric Association (1994). *Diagnostic and Statistical Manual of Mental Disorders.* Fourth edition. Washington, DC, American Psychiatric Association, p. 457.
127. Smelser, N.J. (1962). *Social Change in the Industrial Revolution.* London: Routledge and Kegan Paul.
128. Smelser, N.J. (1971). "Theoretical Issues of Scope and Problems." Pp. 89-94. in *Readings in Collective Behavior* edited by Robert R. Evans. Chicago: Rands McNally. See. p. 92.
129. "Hysteria at School During Blackout." *The Star* (Malaysia), April 30, 1988.
130. Wong, S.W., Kwong, B., Tam, Y.K., and Tsoi, M.M. (1982). "Psychological Epidemic in Hong Kong." *Acta Psychiatrica Scandinavica* 65:421-436. See p. 430.
131. Goldberg, E.L. (1973). "Crowd Hysteria in a Junior High School." *Journal of School Health* 43:362-366.
132. McEvedy, C.P., Griffith, A., and Hall, T. (1966). "Two School Epidemics." *British Medical Journal* ii:1300-1302; Moss and McEvedy (1966). op cit.
133. Knight, J.A., Friedman, T.I., and Sulianti, J. (1965). "Epidemic Hysteria: A Field Study." *American Journal of Public Health* 55:858-865.
134. Olson, W. C. (1928). "Account of a Fainting Epidemic in a High School." *Psychology Clinic* (Philadelphia) 18:34-38; Olczak, P., Donnerstein, E., Hershberger, T., and Kahn, I. (1971). "Group Hysteria and the MMPI." *Psychological Reports* 28:413-414; Teoh, J., and Yeoh, K. (1973). "Cultural Conflict in Transition: Epidemic Hysteria and Social Sanction." *Australian and New Zealand Journal of Psychiatry* 7:283-295; Tam, Y.K., Tsoi, M.M., Kwong, G.B., and Wong, S.W. (1982). "Psychological Epidemic in Hong Kong, Part 2, Psychological and Physiological Characteristics of Children who were Affected." *Acta Psychiatrica Scandinavica* 65:437-449; Wong et al. 1982, op cit.
135. Goldberg, op cit.
136. Cole, T.B. (1990). "Pattern of Transmission of Epidemic Hysteria in a School." *Epidemiology* 1:212-218.
137. Small, G.W., Propper, M.W., Randolph, E.T., and Eth, S. (1991). "Mass Hysteria Among Student Performers: Social Relationship as a

Symptom Predictor." *American Journal of Psychiatry* 148:1200-1205.

138. Goh, K.T. (1987). "Epidemiological Enquiries into a School Outbreak of an Unusual Illness." *International Journal of Epidemiology* 16(2):265-270.

139. Small et al. 1991, op cit.; Small, G.W., and Nicholi, A.M. (1982). "Mass Hysteria Among Student Performers: Early Loss as a Predisposing Factor." *Archives of General Psychiatry* 39:721-724.

140. Small, G., and Borus, J. (1983). "Outbreak of Illness in a School Chorus. Toxic Poisoning or Mass Hysteria?" *New England Journal of Medicine* 308:632-635.

141. Knight et al. (1965). op cit.; "Epidemic Hysteria: A Field Study." *American Journal of Public Health* 55:858-865; Michaux, L., Lemperiere, T., and Juredieu, C. (1952). "Considerations Psychpathologiques sur une Epidemie d'hysterie Convulsive dans un Internat Professionnel" [Considerations of an Epidemic of Convulsive Hysteria in a Boarding School]. *Archives Francaises Pediatrie* (Paris) 9:987-990.

142. Olson, W.C. (1928). "Account of a Fainting Epidemic in a High School." *Psychology Clinic* (Philadelphia) 18:34-38; Schuler and Parenton (1943). op cit.; Theopold (1955). "Induzierter Amplexus neuralis bei Madchen einer Schulklasse" [Induced Neural Amplexus in Girls in a School Class]. *Monatsschrift fur Kinderheilkunde* 103.

143. McEvedy, C. P., Griffith, A., and Hall, T. (1966). "Two School Epidemics." *British Medical Journal* ii:1300-1302.

144. Johnson, D. M. (1945). "The 'Phantom Anesthetist' of Mattoon: A Field Study of Mass Hysteria." *Journal of Abnormal Psychology* 40:175-186; Parigi, S., and Biagiotti, F. (1956). "Su di una Epidemia di Isterismo" [On an Epidemic of Hysteria]. *Rassegna de Studi Psichiatrici* (Siena) 45:1112-1114.

145. Kerckhoff, A. C. (1982). "A Social Psychological View of Mass Psychogenic Illness." Pp. 199-215. In M. Colligan, J. Pennebaker, and L. Murphy (eds.), *Mass Psychogenic Illness: A Social Psychological Analysis*. Hillsdale, New Jersey: Lawrence Erlbaum; Lee RL (1979). *The Social Meaning of Mass Hysteria in West Malaysia and Singapore*. Ph.D. thesis, University of Massachusetts.

146. Thomas, W.I. (1923). *The Unadjusted Girl.* Boston, Little, Brown.

147. Lee, R.L., and Ackerman, S.E. (1980). "The Socio-Cultural Dynamics of Mass Hysteria: A Case Study of Social Conflict in West Malaysia." *Psychiatry* 43:78-88. See p. 79.

148. Lee and Ackerman (1980). op cit., p. 79.

149. Kerckhoff (1982). op cit.

150. Rockney, R.M., and Lemke, T. (1992). "Casualties from a Junior High School during the Persian Gulf War: Toxic Poisoning or Mass Hysteria?" *Journal of Developmental and Behavioral Pediatrics* 13:339-342.

151. Modan, B., Tirosh, M., Weissenberg, E., Acker, C., Swartz, T., Coston, C., Donagi, A., Revach, M., and Vettorazzi, G. (1983). "The Arjenyattah Epidemic." *The Lancet* ii:1472-1476.

152. Goldsmith, M.F. (1989). "Physicians with Georgia on their Minds." *Journal of the American Medical Association* 262:603-604.

153. Legendre, J. (1936). "A Propos du Koro: Une Curieuse Epidemie" [On Koro: A Curious Epidemic]. *La Presse Medicale* (Paris):1534.

154. Tseng, W.S., Mo, K.M., Li, L.S., Chen, G.Q., Ou, L.W., and Zheng, H. B. (1992). "Koro Epidemics in Guangdong, China: A Questionnaire Survey." *The Journal of Nervous and Mental Disease* 180 (2):117-123.

155. Mun, C.I. (1968). "Epidemic Koro in Singapore." Letter. *British Medical Journal* i:640-641 (March 9).

156. Jilek, W.G. (1986). 'Epidemics of 'Genital Shrinking' (Koro): Historical Review and Report of a Recent Outbreak in Southern China." *Curare* 9:269-282. See p. 273.

157. Dutta, H., Phookan, R., and Das, P.D. (1982). "The Koro Epidemic in Lower Assam." *Indian Journal of Psychiatry* 24:370-374.

158. Parsons T. (1955). "Family Structures and the Socialization of the Child." In T. Parsons and R. Bales (Eds.), *Family, Socialization, and the Interaction Process* (35-131). New York: The Free Press; Colligan and Murphy (1979). op cit.

159. Klein, D.F. (1993). "False Suffocation Alarms, Spontaneous Panics, and Related Conditions: An Integrative Hypothesis." *Archives of General Psychiatry* 50:306-317.

160. Aro, H., and Taipale, V. (1987). "The Impact of Timing of Puberty on Psychosomatic Symptoms Among Fourteen to Sixteen Year-old Finnish Girls." *Child Development* 58:261-268.

161. American Psychiatric Association (1994). op cit.

162. American Psychiatric Association (1994). op cit., p. 455.

163. Lewis, I.M. (1971). *Ecstatic Religion*. Harmondsworth, England: Penguin.

164. Lee and Ackerman (1980). op cit.

165. Hastorff, A. & Cantril, H. (1954). "They Saw a Game." *Journal of Abnormal and Social Psychology* 49:129-134.

166. Sleeman, James Lewis (1933). *Thug*. London: Sampson Low, Marsto, p. 236: unless otherwise indicated, most of the information in this entry is from this source.

167. Sleeman, op cit., p. 127.

168. Sleeman, op cit., p. 27.

169. Sleeman, op cit., p. 16.

170. Sleeman, op cit., pp. 107-8.

171. Sleeman, op cit., p. 123.

172. Sleeman, op cit., p. 56.

173. Taylor, Philip Meadows (1974[1839]). *Confessions of a Thug*. Original publication 1839: reprinted London: Folio Society, p. 215.

174. Anonymous writer in *The Bengal Chronicle*, 17 July 1832, quoted by Sleeman, p. 133.

175. Rushby, Kevin (2002). *Children of Kali*. London: Constable. Rushby, p. 178.

176. "The Toll Workers' Illness: Was it all in their Minds.' *The New York Times*, March 12, 1990, p. A16, cited in Shorter, Edward (1992). *From Paralysis to Fatigue: A History of Psychosomatic Illness in the Modern Era*. New York: The Free Press, p. 270.

177. Unless otherwise noted, all details are taken from Rogers 1962.

178. Matthews, Ronald (1936). *English Messiahs*. London: Methuen, p. 146.

179. Tom's election address December 5, 1832: cited by Rogers, p. 21.

180. Matthews, op cit., p. 136.

181. Rogers, op cit., p. 53.

182. quoted by Rogers, op cit., p. 72.

183. Thurston, Herbert (1934). *Beauraing and Other Apparitions*. London: Burns Oates & Washbourne, p. 201, describes these stigmata as "undoubtedly artifact," but his editor, Father Crehan, inclines towards an unconscious simulation, comparing it with other dubious stigmata: "Neither in Tom's case nor in that of, say, Christina of Stommelm, can one readily assume a conscious self-wounding."

184. Alfred Payne, quoted by Thurston, op cit., p. 198.

185. Thurston, op cit., p. 199.

186. Rogers, P.G. (1961). *Battle in Bossenden Wood*. Oxford: University Press, p. 137.

187. *The Gentleman's Magazine*, July 1838, reported by Thurston, op cit., p. 199.

188. Matthews, op cit., p. 15.

189. Russell, cited by Rogers, op cit., p. 175.

190. Rogers, op cit., p. 208.
191. Rogers, op cit., p. 218.
192. Rogers, op cit., p. 219.
193. T.E.C. Jr. (1978). "Dr. S. Josephine Baker and the Tonsil and Adenoid Riot at a New York City Public School about 1920." *Pediatrics* (New York) 62(4): 559 (October).
194. Calmeil, L.F. (1845). *De la Folie, Consideree Sous le Point de vue Pathologique, Philosophique, Historique et Judiciaire* [On the Crowd, Considerations on the Point of Pathology, Philosophy, History and Justice]. Paris: Baillere, volume 2, p. 171: unless otherwise indicated, all details are from this source.
195. Saintyves 1912: 160.
196. Calmeil, op cit., volume 2, p. 177.
197. (2004) "Passenger said she Heard Man Make Cryptic Remark before B.C. Driver Fell Ill." CNews, May 26, accessed arch 28, 2005 at: http://cnews.canoe.ca/CNEWS/Canada/2004/05/25/472732-cp.html.
198. Highlights From Morning Media Briefing Vancouver Police Department. May 26, 2004, accessed March 27, 2005 at: http://www.City.Vancouver.Bc.Ca/Police/Media/Summaries/2004may26.Htm; Highlights From Morning Media Briefing," May 28, 2004. "Update – Contaminated Bus Incident."
199. Crawford, Tiffany (2004). "Mystery Illness - Or Anxiety - On Vancouver Bus." Canadian Press bureau, May 30, 2004, accessed March 27, 2005 at: http://www.canada.com/search /story.html? id=57ecc518-8b7c-4a8b-97b0-deb5b4c5074d.
200. Vancouver Police Department, "Highlights From Morning Media Briefing," June 11, 2004, "Contaminated Bus Update."
201. "Highlights from Morning Press Conference" by the Vancouver Police Department on June 25, 2004. "Update - Toxic Bus."
202. "Highlights from Morning Press Conference" by the Vancouver Police Department on June 25, 2004. "Update - Toxic Bus."
203. Crawford, Tiffany (2004). "Chemical Probable Cause of Bus Mystery." June 25. C-News Canada, accessed March 27, 2005 at: http://cnews.canoe.ca/CNEWS/Canada/2004/06/25/pf-514533.html.
204. "Dangerous Chemical Detected on 'Toxic Bus.'" CBC News, Canadian Broadcasting Corporation, June 25, 2004, accessed March 28, 2005 at: http://vancouver.cbc.ca/regional/ servlet/PrintStory?filename=bc_bus20040625®ion=Vancouver.
205. van den Hemel, Martin (2004). "Toxic Bus Mystery Continues. Health Officer not Convinced by Finding of Dangerous Chemical." The Richmond Review, July 3-4, 2004, accessed March 27, 2005 at: http://www.yourlibrary.ca/community/richmondreview/archive/RR20040708/ morenews.html.
206. van den Hemel, Martin (2004). op cit.
207. van den Hemel, Martin (2004). op cit.
208. Myers, Stuart (2004). "Paramedics did not Suffer Mass Hysteria." Letter to the Editor, *The Richmond Times*, July 8. Myers is Director of public education for the Ambulance Paramedics of B.C., CUPE Local 873.
209. Personal communication (2004), between John Blatherwick MD, chief medical Health officer, Vancouver Coastal Health Authority, #800-601 West Briadway, Vancouver, British Columbia V5Z 4C2, Canada, and Robert Bartholomew, March 30, 2005.
210. Myers, Stuart (2004). op cit.
211. Personal communication (2004), between Richard Mathias MD, Professor of Epidemiology at the University of British Columbia, Canada, and Robert Bartholomew, March 28, 2005.
212. Gustafson, Reka (2004). "Summary of Findings of Epidemiologic Investigation of Bus Incident." Vancouver, British Columbia: The Author. I am grateful for Dr. Gustafson for providing me with a copy of his report.
213. Gustafson, Reka (2004). "Summary of Findings of Epidemiologic Investigation of Bus Incident." op cit.
214. Personal communication (2004). op cit.
215. Levy, Harold (2002). "Fear Spreads Among Court Workers." *Toronto Star*, August 28, 2002, p. B2.
216. Levy, Harold 2002). "Court Staff Report Health Problems." *Toronto Star*, September 6, p. B2.
217. Levy, Harold (2001). "Lawsuit Launched Over Toxic Mould." *Toronto Star*, March 7, p. 3.
218. Ferenc, Leslie (2001). "Courthouse Reopens After Mould Repairs." *Toronto Star*, June 28, 2001, p. 4.
219. Small, Peter (2002). "Mould Found 5 Times After Cleanup." *Toronto Star*, August 7, 2002, p. 5.
220. Levy, Harold 2002). "Court Staff Report Health Problems." op cit.
221. Levy, Harold (2002). "Mould Prompts Quiet Case Transfer." *Toronto Star*, September 5, p. B4.
222. Small, Peter (2002). "Mould Found 5 Times After Cleanup." op cit.
223. Levy, Harold (2002). "Fear Spreads Among Court Workers." op cit.
224. Levy, Harold (2002). "Fear Spreads Among Court Workers." op cit.
225. Swainson, Gail (2002). "Court Workers Often Sick." *Toronto Star*, August 29, 2002, p. B4.
226. Levy, Harold (2002). "Mould Prompts Quiet Case Transfer." op cit.
227. Levy, Harold (2002). "Court Staff Report Health Problems." op cit.; "Courthouse Too 'Sick,' Lawyer Argues." *Toronto Star*, March 18, 2003, p. B4.
228. Levy, Harold (2002). "2 Court Staff Refuse to Enter Building." *Toronto Star*, September 9, 2002, p. B3.
229. Levy, Harold (2002). "Judge Quits Trial, Cites Toxic Mould." *Toronto Star*, October 25, 2002, p. B5.
230. Levy, Harold (2002). "Judge Fears Building Caused Illness." *Toronto Star*, October 30, p. B1.
231. Levy, Harold (2002). "Judge Fears Building Caused Illness." op cit.
232. Anonymous (2002). "Toxic Testimony." *Toronto Star*, October 31, p. A32.
233. Anonymous (2002). "Courthouse Confounds Occupants." *Toronto Star*, October 31, p. B8.
234. "Courthouse Too 'Sick,' Lawyer Argues." op cit.
235. Pron, Nick (2003). "Courthouse Found Free of Toxic Mould, Judge Rules." *Toronto Star*, March 28, p. B7.
236.(2005). "Worst Effects of Toxic Mould 'are all in the Mind.'" *New Scientist* 185(Number 2490):17 (March 12).
237."Tsunami rumors trigger panic in Malaysian coastal towns." http://asia.news.yahoo. com/050101/ap/d87b29kg1.html, accessed January 10, 2005.
238. Marquand, Robet (2005). "Rumors, False Reports Mar Cleanup." Online edition of The Christian Science Monitor, January 6, 2005. Http://www.csmonitor.com/2005/0106/p06s01-wosc.html, accessed January 10, 2005.
239. Marquand (2005). op cit.
240. "Orphans for Sale." Accessed January 11, 2005 at: http://www.snopes.com/inboxer/hoaxes/ orphans.asp.
241. Mackay, Charles. ([1841]1852). *Memoirs of Extraordinary Popular*

Delusions and the Madness of Crowds Volume 1, second edition. London: Office of the National Illustrated Library, p. 90.
242. Mackay, op cit., p. 92.
243. Mackay, op cit., p. 91.
244. Mackay, op cit., p. 95.
245. Garber, Peter M. (1989). 'Tulipmania.' *Journal of Political Economy* 97:535-560; Garber, Peter M (1990). "Who put the Mania in the Tulip Mania?" Pp. 3-32. In Eugene N. White (editor). *Crashes and Panics: Lessions from History*. Homewood, Illinois: Business One Irwin.
246. Garber, Peter M. (2000). *Famous First Bubbles: The Fundamentals of Early Manias*. Cambridge, Massachusetts: MIT Press.
247. Garber (2000). op cit., p. 77.
248. Garber (2000). op cit., p. 81.
249. Garber (2000). op cit., pp. 128-129.
250. Garber (2000). op cit., p 83.

U

UGANDAN RUNNING SICKNESS

Kayayimba, Uganda: July 2002

An episode of running, demon possession, visions, and various aches and pains was reported in the Ugandan village of Kayayimba during July 2002, affecting about 30 inhabitants, mostly female. At one primary school, 18 students were affected as students removed all of their clothing, began screaming, and perpetrating violent acts. One 24-year-old housewife, Annette Muhairwe, said: "All of a sudden, I felt pain in the chest. My hand was aching and heavy. Sometimes, I could see snakes, then fire, but I could not touch them. Even if I tried to show other people, they could not see these things."[1]

CONTEXT: Mass hysteria episodes with motor dysfunction, such as running, have been widely reported in Uganda and surrounding countries. They appear to reflect long-term exposure to superstitious beliefs that are thought to represent a threat.

According to Dr. M. Kizito, health director for the Kiboga District, the underlying stress that triggered the hysteria was an epidemic of cerebral malaria that was sweeping through the area. Julius Kayiira, a psychologist with the Uganda mental health, said the intense stress triggers mass suggestibility that is incubated in a setting of fear and witchcraft beliefs. "It is a kind of collective consciousness. Something unusual happens and attracts people's attention, then people behave that way because of fear. And that fear develops because of what they believe in."[2]

See also: LAUGHING EPIDEMICS, RUNNING AND CLIMBING.

ULSTER REVIVAL

Northern Ireland: 1859

This remarkable religious revival is interesting in that it was not a planned affair, such as the AMERICAN REVIVALS, nor imposed from above, as in METHODISM, but it seems to have sprung spontaneously from a number of ordinary people meeting over a butcher's shop.[3]

CONTEXT: Ireland was a disturbed and unhappy country at this time, for reasons economic, political, and religious. Economically, the effects of the catastrophic potato famine of the previous decade were still painful, leading to heavy emigration especially to North America. Politically, there was active resistance to the British government and British landowners, and agitation for Home Rule, which frequently involved acts of terrorism. Religiously, there was conflict between the Catholics (mainly in the south) and the Protestants (mainly in the north), which exacerbated the political divisions of the island.

A "fellowship meeting" over a butcher's shop in the county of Antrim, in the spring of 1855, was the occasion that gave the start to a movement in Protestant Northern Ireland. A preacher had suggested to his congregation, "Could you not gather at least six of your careless neighbours... to your own house or some other convenient place... and spend an hour reading and searching the word of God?" From this small beginning, the idea spread to neighboring towns and villages, and then farther afield, until the movement exploded in full force in 1859.

One way that news of the revival spread was by commercial travelers. The Reverend Crockett, in County Tyrone, told of such traveling salesmen who, after doing business in Derry and Antrim, "saw and bore witness to the great change wrought in the hearts of those with whom they were brought in contact."[4]

From small indoor gatherings, the scene changed to massive outdoor meetings at which preachers roused the populace to repentance and conversion and where several thousand people remained all day long in prayer and praise. These occasions were characterized by emotional outbursts:

I saw a young girl in great distress about her soul, weeping bitterly; her mother stood by and said, "Oh, dear, why do you take on so?" The girl threw the shawl from her shoulders, dug her long bony fingers into the flesh of her naked bosom, and cried out, with bated breath, "It's sin, sin, sin, cursed sin, here." The mother: "Oh, no, you were always a good girl." "Mother," said the girl, "don't talk that way to me; I'm tempted sorely enough to think I'm not so bad, but oh, I am bad, very bad; oh, what a great sinner I am."[5]

James Heron, of Rathfriland, was present at a meeting where

...the solemn stillness was soon broken by a faint cry on the opposite side of the platform. I had scarcely time to turn myself, when, sudden as a gunshot, a strong woman sent forth an unearthly scream at my very side. In a moment she was upon her knees, crying, as she clapped and wrung her hands alternately in wild excitement, "Oh! my heart. Oh! my hard heart." The crowd was convulsed, and shook like aspens in the breeze. The voice of the speaker was soon drowned amid the shrieks: the air was filled with groans and screams for mercy... It was not till long after nightfall that a large portion of the helpless mourners were carried to their homes.[6]

At Ballymena, in May 1959,

...careless men were bowed in unaffected earnestness, and sobbed like children. Drunkards and boasting blasphemers were awed into solemnity and silence...A man fell to his knees in the market-place and called on the people around him by loud and desperate cries expressive of the most appalling agony, such as might be expected from a man who felt himself suddenly attacked and sinking under the repeated and deadly blows of an assassin."[7]

At Broughshane, near Ballymena, one morning in the same month a number of young women working in a spinning factory were affected.

Immediately intense excitement spread among the workers, and within an hour twenty or thirty persons of both sexes were laid prostrate. The business of the entire establishment was interrupted, and, as a matter of necessity, it was closed. When re-opened two days after, nearly half the usual hands were absent.[8]

Business of all kinds was affected. "For about six weeks almost all agricultural operations, and indeed every kind of secular employment, were suspended, no man being able to think of or attend to anything but the interests of his soul."[9] Because drink was suddenly perceived as pernicious, the business of public houses fell off, so much so that two in Ballymena were obliged to close. As the revival spread north into Coleraine, so did the excitement; soon the entire community was caught up in the movement. People referred to the effects as if it were a disease – a person "took it" or "caught it" like an infection. On June 9, 1859, nearly a hundred persons suffering from the prostration of religious meetings were carried into the town hall and sheltered till morning. In July, after a meeting at Dromara, which was attended by about a thousand people, seven young people were found on the roadside with their backs against the ditch, their faces toward heaven, supplicating mercy.

By contrast with earlier revivals in America, the Ulster preachers did their best to discourage these emotional responses: but in vain. One of them, Dr. Gibson, recorded:

Anxious to repress any tendency to mere excitement, I endeavoured to set forth in the most didactic and unimpassioned strain the way of salvation, avoiding every allusion that might be calculated to awaken mere emotion in any of the audience. I had not, however, proceeded far, until there arose from a female voice a despairing and yet tender cry... she had to be borne from the place of meeting. This case was soon after succeeded by another and another, until it became necessary to suspend the address... The affected parties were taken to the library until they recovered enough to be taken home. [10]

The movement spread eastwards to Belfast, where about the beginning of September a new feature appeared, as a number of people received "'marks,' being neither less nor more than appearances on the body, resembling printed characters, impressed thereon, as it was represented, by a Divine agency..." A young woman, unbarring her bosom or her arm, "...would exhibit to the admiring onlookers a mystic word or symbol, impressed so legibly that all might read and understand. What if the lettering were somewhat indistinct, or if the sacred name was incorrectly spelled? For this she was in no wise accountable. All unbelief would vanish before the preternatural authentication."[11]

To the populace, the marks were a manifestation of STIGMATA. When the Reverend William Brakey of Lisburn denounced them as imposture, he encountered fierce resentment from those of his parishioners who believed that the marks were a sign from the Holy Spirit.

Another feature was prolonged sleep. An individual would fall asleep voluntarily, waking several days later at a time he had predicted, and telling of the divine revelations he had received while asleep. A medical man, Dr. McCosh, accused the sleepers of being impostors and pointed out that this was a favorite trick of Oriental entertainers. But the entertainers made no claim to the divine revelations, which the Ulster sleepers experienced in their dreams. Observers marveled at "the occasional suspension of the bodily powers, as indicated by the loss of speech, sight, and hearing; the subjects of them affected as if in a trance – deaf, dumb, blind, and motionless – while they would frequently fall into a sleep, in which they continued for hours, and the commencement and termination of which they intimated beforehand to the bystanders."[12]

It seemed as though the revival experience brought out remarkable mental abilities. The Reverend M'Askie of Colgherney reported the case of an

> ...amiable young girl who was stricken at a meeting. When returning to consciousness, or rather, when recovering the use of speech — for she appeared to be totally unconscious of the presence of any one, as she lay with eyes turned up to heaven and fixed — for about four hours she continued repeating sermons and other addresses delivered by myself during the previous month. In many instances she repeated whole passages of them verbatim. Pausing at intervals, she would exclaim, "Oh, what have I not heard!" and then she would resume the repetition of some striking passages with a fluency and an accuracy that were perfectly astonishing... Not less than one hundred Scripture texts were repeated, and sometimes half a chapter at once, with the greatest accuracy, and all bearing upon her own case. I have had frequent opportunities of conversing with her since, and, what is very strange, many of the passages so fluently repeated that night seem to be quite forgotten, and the portions of Scripture she could not repeat with the same accuracy.[13]

Many claimed to see visions. In County Down, Dr. Given was preaching when a woman was strongly affected. "Tears flowed copiously and, mingled with big drops of perspiration, wetted the shawl that lay around her shoulders. She felt extremely weak, but, anxious to escape observation, made an effort to get out of the church... I observed her face become deadly pale, and she sank apparently unconscious in the aisle. It was no fainting fit... she thought she saw the Saviour, clothed in a white garment reaching down to the feet, approach her..."[14] The Reverend Richard Smyth of Armagh reported, "One of the most trying and really distressing cases that came under my observation was that of a girl who imagined herself in hell for three hours, and still out of the depths of hell cried to Jesus for mercy. Her face during this time gave one the idea of a lost soul... At the end of three hours she fell into a kind of trance, for four hours she seemed to be in the regions of the blest. Of the "visions" she had during that time she never wished to speak..."[15]

Children were affected along with the adults. The Reverend M'Alister of Armagh reported how a boy came up to him in the street in breathless haste, exclaiming, "Come, sir, the girls in the school are all crying for mercy." He went in, and found some lying on the floor, some in the arms of the teacher or the monitor, some in the arms of other children. Floods of tears were flowing from these guilt-ridden innocents, who were crying out to God for mercy, to take the stony heart out of them and give them a heart of flesh. On another occasion he was confronted with young persons of both sexes, from 12-to-22 years of age, all "agonising under conviction of sin," one calling himself a hypocrite, another admitting to mocking God, another despairing, "I am lost! I am a child of the devil; for I have told lies, and the devil is the father of lies!"[16]

Compared with the Kentucky camp-meetings or even the Methodist revival in England, the Ulster Revival was a relatively peaceful affair, having more in common with the recent 1857 prayer revival in America (See AMERICAN REVIVALISM). Nonetheless, preachers were outspoken in their denunciations of sin and their depictions of the torments that await the damned, and their congregations were equally eloquent in their response. Time and again the reports include such phrases as "the entire scene was unlike one of earth," or "the whole congregation moved and excited as if the judgment day had come."[17]

COMMENT: *The Edinburgh Medical Journal*, commenting on the revival a few months later, had this to say: "The anti-revivalists are quite in error if they imagine that when they have proved the "cases" to be hysterical, they have disposed of the whole case. It is quite possible that even in these instances salutary impressions may co-exist with the ebullitions of emotional feeling, and the symptoms of actual disease."[18]

This dilemma troubled the churchmen on the spot. Gibson commented, "It is most distressing to hear of young females being fifty, a hundred, and, as in one case of which I am advised, two hundred times 'stricken.'" He detected a streak of exhibitionism in such behavior and recommended isolation.[19] But while the churchmen felt they should discourage such outbursts, whose hysterical character they deplored, they were also compelled to acknowledge the benefits: "Drunkards have been reformed, prostitutes reclaimed, thieves have become honest – Sabbath-breakers, profane swearers, scoffers, neglecters of ordinances, and worthless characters of all descriptions have been awakened or converted."[20]

Even if many of these benefits proved short-lived, the churchmen had little doubt that overall the effects were to be welcomed. "Was it a time to look on with scrutinizing or censorious eye, when the heavens were rending and the earth was shaking at the presence of the Lord? ...Shall we refuse to recognize the presence and the power of the Eternal, even though some strange things should have happened, and here and there a few should have been disordered by unhealthy stimulants and injudicious treatments?"[21] The Ulster Revival was led by churchmen who were concerned to play down, as much as possible, the emotional element involved. But for all their efforts, the populace expressed their feelings in displays of exceptional behavior, raising questions that have yet to be satisfactorily answered.

UMHAYIZO BEWITCHMENT HYSTERIA

South Africa: 19th and 20th centuries

In portions of South Africa, especially the region encompassing Natal, the Eastern Cape, and Zululand, it has long been a common practice for schoolboys who have been rebuffed in their attempts to date or marry a girl to consult a native healer in order to intervene magically and change the girl's mind. Occasionally, girls who have turned away romantic advances by boys begin to fear that they may be the subject of a "love spell" placed on them by a disgruntled suitor conspiring with a native healer. In the wake of concerns that they may be the subject of magical warfare, over the course of weeks or months the tension in the girl and her friends builds to greater and greater levels of intensity. Suddenly, under the prolonged strain, one or more girls experience what can be described as "bewitchment hysteria." In these regions, such reactions are common among schoolgirls. Stories of girls "charming" boys are unheard of. It's always the other way around.

As early as 1900, there have been many accounts of South African students being stricken with episodes of strange behavior known as *umhayizo*. It usually begins with fits of crying, hyperactivity, and the irresistible urge to run. It is commonly believed that they are being pulled like a magnet toward their lover. Most girls eventually pass out from the mental strain. Historian Julie Parle and anthropologist Fiona Scorgie noted a pattern: "Teaching activities are regularly interrupted by the sound of high-pitched wailing, classroom doors being flung open and the sight of at least one girl running out into the courtyard, screaming and cradling her head in her arms. Usually, she is soon followed by others, for the *umhayizo* is apparently 'infectious:' one girl's screaming sets off others."[22]

UNTERZELL OUTBREAK

Germany: 1738

In most cases of convent hysteria, those who are afflicted, or those who are concerned for the welfare of those who are afflicted, look for an external agency that is responsible – either Satan or someone acting under his command. It is rare for the trouble to have its origins with the community itself, but this seems to have been the case at Unterzell.[23]

CONTEXT: Unterzell is "about a league" from Würzburg, on the Main, in Germany. Even at this late date, the witch mania was still persistent in Germany, and this doubtless influenced the course of events, for which there seems no external cause.

The troubles seem to have begun with various poltergeist phenomena. Every night the sisters would hear what seemed to be the sound of carriages and carts crossing their dormitory; or they would be frightened by cries coming from the garden beneath their windows; or, if in bed, they would feel a pressure on them, and battering, pinching, and stifling, so that in the morning they could hardly get up, and sometimes they had marks from the blows they had received. To fight off the evil the cells were closed and holy water sprinkled about. For a while this had a beneficial effect, but soon the phenomena recommenced.

One day one of the sisters, waving her discipline (a scourge used for inflicting penance) round her, succeeded in chasing away the spirit who was tormenting her. The following day, the sisters noticed that one of their number, Sister Renata, had a trace of blood in one of her eyes. This immediately suggested to their minds that she was the spirit responsible for the trouble, though they could not be certain. However, other sisters fell ill, and it was noticed that it was those who were most helpful and useful who were afflicted, and they supposed that magic of some kind was at work. Four sisters were affected, and then the ailment spread outside the convent when the family of the provost was affected.

Soon other symptoms began to be reported by other sisters. When they went to bed, they were ravished out of themselves without really sleeping, and becoming clairvoyant in this state, they saw before them all sorts of persons, among others Sister Renata, who tormented them in all sorts of ways without their being able to defend themselves. The following day they suffered from internal pains that got worse when they went to the church, from which they were chased against their will as if by an irresistible force. If they were singing in the choir, they continually lost and recovered their voice, or else the sound they made was like a savage yell. They trembled, their necks were swollen, and their chests shook with convulsive movements. They were fearful and desperate.

Sister Maria-Renata Saenger was already unpopular in the convent. She was said to have practiced magic in her early life, before she was forced by her parents, who had little money, to enter the religious life. Although she entered it reluctantly, she resolved to make the best of it, did her duty efficiently, and became sub-prioress and might have become prioress except for her coldness with other sisters. Her relations with the other nuns verged on hostility; she kept herself to herself, working with herbs. Then in 1738 the prioress commanded her to get rid of the many cats with which she surrounded herself, saying they made too much noise and caused too much trouble.

Though she had no choice but to obey, this order hurt her deeply and increased the antagonism between her and the others. So it was no surprise when she was suspected of practicing magic.

The nuns who fell ill, the doctors affirmed, were all otherwise in good health. There was no natural cause for their illness, and they were certainly not faking. At this stage, however, no one thought of sorcery or possession.

Among the afflicted sisters was Cecile Pistorini. The demon had begun to speak through her mouth in 1745, but since she was a newcomer of Italian origin and spoke German poorly (though she came from Hamburg), she was generally disregarded and disliked. Sister Renata particularly disliked her, and now that she was ill, Renata said it was imposture on Cecile's part and she deserved to be punished. Yet no one could see why this poor girl should wish to practice imposture. Despite her convulsions and other torments, and despite the blasphemies and ill-speaking she uttered, Cecile could not bring herself to believe that she was really possessed by a demon – she simply saw herself as a poor sinner abandoned by God.

Finally, though, it was decided to exorcise her. This had a temporary beneficial effect, but then the illness came back, and the sisters noted that she got worse when Sister Renata came near her, or breathed on her face, or whispered in her ear. When this happened, it was as though she had been struck by a ball of fire, traversing her body, after which the convulsions began almost at once. All this added to the suspicions against Renata, the more so when one of the most respected of the sisters, who was close to her death, accused Renata of being responsible for the trouble that was afflicting the convent. But the nuns were reluctant to take any firm measures against her, and resorted to prayers that the almighty would come to their rescue.

On the third day of the exorcisms, five of the sisters, who had been silent hitherto, began to speak in the midst of violent convulsions. They, too, cried out that it was Renata who was the author of all the evil. As it was the Church's teaching that, under exorcism, the demons possessing a human are compelled to speak truth, this was strong evidence, and it was confirmed when, about a fortnight later, three more sisters were exorcised, and all affirmed unanimously the same thing.

Now the whole convent fell into the profound despair, and Renata seemed affected as much as any. The demons continued to accuse her, naming the year, the day, and the hour of occasions when she had practiced her criminal magic, some of them as much as 12 years previously.

The provost begged the abbot of Oberzell to start an investigation. He heard all the nuns under oath, and when he found Renata so blamed by all, he resolved to send her away. But before he could do so, she herself confessed voluntarily to all: yes, she was a sorceress; yes, she had made a covenant with the Demon; yes, she attended the sabbats of the witches; yes, she had had carnal intercourse with a Demon and other Satanists; yes, she had retained the Holy Sacrament in her mouth at the mass and later stabbed it with needles; yes, she was attended by a familiar in the form of a rat; and yes, she had by her enchantments caused the possessed nuns to be in the state they were. All this and more she had done, but now she repented sincerely. The sisters who kept watch on her reported that when she was left to herself she was constantly on her knees, praying.

But the nocturnal harassments continued, and it seemed evident that somehow or other Renata was still responsible for them, even though she was now watched night and day and claimed to be penitent about her wrongdoing. When her room was searched, herbs and roots were found that were taken to be magical, indeed poisonous, though she had always been a skilful herbalist. The demons, speaking through the possessed nuns, mocked her seeming conversion and accused her of insincerity. And, whatever the cause, the sisters continued to suffer hideously disturbed nights.

Up until that time, the convent had done its best to keep matters secret, hoping they would not become known outside the community. But the terrible noises of howling were heard not only throughout the cloister, but even in the neighboring homes. Renata was assigned a new confessor in the hope that he would determine how things stood. At first he was inclined to believe her sincere, but the strength of accusation against her, and the continuing phenomena, made him doubt. It was resolved to send her to the castle of Marienberg. But even then the nightly harassment of the nuns continued, and she was handed over to the secular authorities, who found her guilty of practicing magic and condemned her to be burned. This was done on January 21, 1749, eleven years after the trouble started. She must have been about 70 years old by then, but the Church was convinced of her guilt and proscribed the maximum penalty. She died calmly and apparently in repentance.

COMMENT: The happening at Unterzell has been interpreted in very divergent ways. For Montague Summers, for example, Renata was unquestionably a Satanist, an agent of the Evil One, and deserved everything that happened to her.[24]

Johann Görres commented that "many writers have blamed the severity of the sentence, but it is difficult to explain the facts except as an intervention on the part of the demon... Otherwise we would have to suppose that everyone concerned in the affair was involuntarily mistaken. And if that was the case, if the possessed sisters and Renata herself were nothing but maniacs, if the superior and the judges were idiots, then there are no certain signs to distinguish madness from sanity."[25]

However, the fact that the convent continued to be troubled after she had been put to death is certainly suggestive of her innocence. The manifestations did not cease entirely until a long sequence of further exorcisms had been carried out.

By that date, the witch mania had lost almost all of its impetus, and in any other country Renata Saenger would likely have been punished by banishment or sequestration. But she was a victim of the fact that in Germany the mania persisted until the 1770s.

See also: CONVENT HYSTERIA, DEMON POSSESSION.

URBAN LEGENDS

Folklorist Jan Harold Brunvand popularized the term "urban legend" in his study, *The Vanishing Hitchhiker: Urban Legends and Their Meanings* (1981), which describes a broad spectrum of such stories.[26] Folklorists, sociologists, and social psychologists sometimes refer to urban legends as contemporary legends, urban myths, or urban folklore. These narratives, which pass mostly by word of mouth, are usually thought to be of recent origin and are commonly said to have happened in a metropolitan environment – hence the word "urban." Brunvand stated that urban legends involve improbable events that are repeated as truth and embellished with local details. Urban legends are essentially enduring rumors that reappear from time to time in different places in slightly altered form. Typically attributed to a media source or what folklorists sometimes call "FOAF"' (friend of a friend stories), they are usually impossible to verify. The basic themes of many contemporary urban legends can be traced back centuries, and in some cases even millennia. Brunvand believes that urban legends have hidden meanings that function to fulfill psychological needs. He states that for legends to persist in modern society "as living narrative folklore," they must contain three key elements: "a strong basic story-appeal, a foundation in actual belief, and a meaningful message or 'moral.'"[27] In other words, they must tell an interesting story, be believable, and offer a lesson to be learned.

Sociologist Erich Goode identified seven key factors necessary for the propagation of urban legends: a *dramatic story* containing a *moral or message* that reflects *current fears*, with some *element of truth*. These narratives are attributed to a *credible source* (e.g., scientists, journalists), contain *local details*, and are often *repeated in the mass media,* lending a further factual appearance (e.g., "I read it in a book" or "I saw it on TV," so it must be true).[28]

Most experts agree with Brunvand that urban legends function to fulfill psychological needs by containing an underlying moral or message about current fears; they also enhance the status of the storyteller for conveying important news. The spread of urban legends can be reduced by providing education in critical-thinking, heeding advice from experts, identifying key components, and attempting to verify facts by contacting those specifically alleged to be involved. As a general rule of thumb, if you cannot verify it with a first-hand source, it's probably not true. It is beyond the limits of human nature to prevent the appearance and proliferation of urban legends. We can only limit their spread and acceptance through awareness. Urban legends typically function as "cautionary tales."

A classic urban legend is "the snake in the blanket" story, which is one of many urban legends that have circulated across Western countries in recent years. It goes something like this: A woman is shopping for a new coat at a large, well-known department store. She tries one on, and upon placing her hand in the pocket, screams in pain, collapses, and dies by the time ambulance personnel arrive. Later, it is discovered that the coat was made in a foreign country with poor standards of quality control, where one or many eggs had been laid in the pocket, from

UFO reportedly crash lands near Berlin, New York, in 1964. Accounts of crashed flying saucers and government coverups have been common since the latter 19th century.

which a small, venomous snake had hatched on the lengthy trip from some poor overseas country. While details of this story vary from place to place, such as the name of the store or country where the inferior quality import was produced, there is one feature that never varies – the coat (sometimes it's a sweater, blouse, or other cloth item) is always from a foreign country. The lesson is clear. Don't buy imports – Buy American.[29]

Product rumors about contaminated food are a common basis of urban legends. Perhaps the most prominent is the "Kentucky Fried Rat" story, which has circulated across the United States. It usually involves a husband and wife who get a drive-thru order of chicken at KFC (Kentucky Fried Chicken). The wife remarks about the funny taste, only to realize that she has been munching on a rat! Suddenly she goes into shock, is rushed to a hospital, and eventually dies. Folklorist Gary Fine examined 115 different versions of this story and made an interesting finding. In every case the victim is a woman – who has clearly neglected her traditional responsibilities for preparing the family meals as she did not make supper the night they went to KFC. Her reward is the fried rat.[30]

Another popular urban legend holds that a flying saucer crashed in the New Mexico desert during the summer of 1947; the U.S. government supposedly recovered the craft and has kept it hidden from the public. This story is widely believed as true, and acted upon as such, by millions of people around the world. Richard Greenwell studied various versions of this story and observed that the typical informant "must remain anonymous (he is usually retired from the Air Force) [and] relates that a saucer crashed somewhere in the southwest deserts of Arizona, New Mexico, or even...Mexico." Greenwell stated that the informant is usually taken to the site blindfolded, and the craft is sometimes described as protruding from a crater in the sand. "The informant may describe how he glimpsed the dead bodies of small beings, sometimes in a tent, and these were often reportedly shipped in heavily protected trunks to Wright-Patterson Air Force Base."[31] A classic illustration of urban legends being "living folklore," and as such dynamic and ever evolving to fit the times and popular preoccupations and beliefs, is the status of the Roswell saucer "crash." While during the 1980s, Greenwell noted that the typical informat said he must remain anonymous, this element has now changed and isn't true anymore, though it was at one point in the story.

Stories of crashed UFOs are not new. While dozens of crashed UFOs have been reported at sites around the world since 1947, reports of crashed extraterrestrial spacecraft date back to at least the middle nineteenth century. For example, in a letter to the *Houston Post* of May 2, 1897, John Leander wrote that an elderly sailor from El Campo, Texas – identified only as "Mr. Oleson" – claimed to have been shipwrecked on a tiny uncharted Indian Ocean Island in 1862. He said that during his ordeal, an immense airship sporting gigantic wings crashed into a rock cliff. Inside were the bodies of twelve-foot-tall creatures with dark, bronze skin. "Their hair and beard were also long and as soft and silky as the hair of an infant." The surviving sailors lived inside the wrecked airship and eventually "summoned courage to drag the gigantic bodies to the cliff and tumble them over." After building a raft and being rescued by a passing Russian vessel, Oleson retained a ring from the thumb of one of the creatures as the only proof of the events. Two and a quarter inches in diameter, it "[was] made of a compound of metals unknown to any jeweler...and [was] set with two reddish stones." As luck would have it, by the time the vessel reached port, the remaining sailors died, leaving Oleson as the sole survivor.

This story bears an uncanny resemblance to Roswell. The account is a secondhand narrative of alien creatures in a space vessel crashing at a remote location. The craft was destroyed and foreign writing is found inside. The alien bodies were disposed of and the debris lost. A piece of confirming evidence was retained in the form of an immense ring with unknown properties, but the witness failed to allow public scrutiny.

Urban legends often form the foundations of mass delusions, moral panics, and outbreaks of mass hysteria. For example, the Satanic Ritual Abuse Scare of the 1980s and 1990s spread rapidly throughout the United States in the wake of contemporary myths about the existence of a network of Satanic cults kidnapping and sacrificing children. Urban legends typically reinforce popular stereotypes and prevailing public opinions. The Catholic Scare of 1830 to 1860 was incubated amid a flurry of exaggerated stories demonizing Roman Catholics and their ambitions of overthrowing the United States government. Many outbreaks of mass hysteria in Africa and Asia involving trance and possession states were preceded by local urban myths about demonic forces inhabiting a particular school or factory. Hence, urban legends often provide the backdrop for stories that are linked to a specific location, and the resultant pent-up stress.

Sources

1. Wendo, Charles (2002). "Uganda: A Village Possessed by Mass Hysteria." All Africa Global Media, July 6, 2002.
2. Wendo, op cit.
3. Gibson, William ([1860]1909). *The Year of Grace.* [first published 1860, Edinburgh & London]. Oliphant, Anderson & Ferrier 1909, unless otherwise indicated, information is drawn from this source.
4. Gibson, op cit., p. 160.
5. Gibson, op cit., p. 41.
6. Gibson, op cit., p. 132.
7. Davenport 1905 p. 79, citing Gibson 1860 but omitted from 1909 edition.
8. Gibson, op cit., p. 34.
9. Gibson, op cit., p. 36.
10. Gibson, op cit., p. 73.
11. Gibson, op cit., pp. 100-101.
12. Gibson, op cit., pp. 93-94.
13. Gibson, op cit., p. 158.
14. Gibson, op cit., p. 115.
15. Gibson, op cit., p. 142.
16. Gibson, op cit., pp. 168-169.
17. Gibson, op cit., p. 179.
18. Gibson, op cit., p. 230 quoting the *Edinburgh Medical Review* of January 1860.
19. Gibson, op cit., p. 236.
20. Gibson, op cit., p. 116.
21. Gibson, op cit., p. 237.
22. My thanks to Julie Parle for allowing me to cite this brief passage from her unpublished paper with Fiona Scorgie.
23. Görres, Johann Joseph von (1845[1855]). *La Mystique Divine, Naturelle et Diabolique.* Paris: Poussielgue-Rusand, translated from the German Christliche Mystik in 1855, Volume 5, p. 257.
24. Summers, Montague (1927). *The Geography of Witchcraft.* London: Kegan Paul, Trench, Trubner, p. 506.
25. Görres, op cit., Volume 5, p. 265.
26. Brunvand, Jan Harold. (1981). *The Vanishing Hitchhiker: American Urban Legends and Their Meanings.* New York: W.W. Norton.
27. Brunvand (1981). op cit., p. 21.
28. Goode (1992). op cit., pp. 324-330.
29. Brunvand (1981). op cit., pp. 160-171; Fine, Gary Allen. (1989). "Mercantile Legends and the World Economy: Dangerous Imports from the Third World." *Western Folklore* 48:169-177.
30. Robertson, Ian (1987). *Sociology* (third edition). New York: Worth, pp. 545-546.
31. Story, Ronald Dean. (1980). *The Encyclopedia of UFOs.* New York: Doubleday, p. 88.

VACCINATION HYSTERIAS

Iran, Jordan, England, Spain, Congo, Philippines: Late 20th century

Several instances of mass hysteria have been associated with inoculations against disease.

CONTEXT: While there are only a few reports of vaccine-related cases of mass hysteria, this could be expected as "the majority of vaccines are administered to infants and young children, who are not likely to react in this way given their inability to perceive vaccines as a threat and to interact as a group."[1] Elements common to most episodes appear to a small number of children exhibiting illness symptoms, either during or shortly after inoculation, which trigger anxiety among other vaccinated children, their parents, and school officials. Episodes are typically exacerbated by preliminary, inaccurate mass media reports suggesting an association between the illness symptoms and a "bad" batch of vaccine.

Tetanus Vaccine Scare In Iran And Jordan

On October 6, 1992, schoolgirls in the tiny village of Hanza (population 920), in the Islamic Republic of Iran, were inoculated against tetanus. The next three days were uneventful, and no adverse effects were reported. On the fourth day, one girl fainted in class, complaining of blurred vision, headache, tremors, and "burning" hands. Over the next several days, nine of her schoolmates, all of whom had received tetanus shots on October 6, began exhibiting similar "seizures."

An investigation revealed that the initial "victim" had a long history of pseudo-seizures with nearly identical accompanying symptoms as those reported during her classroom "fit." At the time of her "attack," she was under the care of a neurologist and was later diagnosed with conversion disorder and depression. The other girls became anxious after observing the INDEX CASE, fearful that she was suffering from some type of adverse reaction to the inoculation.

The symptoms persisted in the girls for about five weeks amid rumors that a bad batch of vaccine had caused a "brain disease." The episode subsided when one of the visiting investigators, Dr. M.T. Yasamy, invited students, parents and local officials to a public meeting, during which he had himself injected with a dose of vaccine with the same serial number batch from which the 26 girls had received their injections. After this meeting, Dr. Yasamy met with five of the afflicted pupils individually, reassuring them that their symptoms were of psychological origin. Their symptoms quickly subsided. As for the other five students, their symptoms persisted longer but soon subsided as well. Two were treated at home in nearby villages, and three were hospitalized and soon discharged after reassurance.[2]

Between 1992 and September 27, 1998, the tetanus-diphtheria vaccine (commonly referred to as "Td," had been given to all Jordanian students in the first and tenth grades. On the morning of September 29, 1998, at the Eben-Al Abas School, the entire class of tenth grade students, 160 in all, was injected with Td vaccine. During the session, two pupils "felt faint" and were immediately examined by a doctor.[3] The examinations were unremarkable and they were soon returned to class. That evening, several students reported feeling ill at home with lightheadedness and headaches, but none was ill enough to see a physician.

The next day, upon arriving at school at the usual time of 6:45 a.m., a boy who had reported feeling sick the previous night stumbled while entering the school gates and cut his lip. School officials sent the boy to the hospital to be examined, fearing that his fall was the result of fainting. Shortly after the boy was sent to the hospital, another boy who had been ill the night before said he felt faint while going to class. By 7:30 a.m., about 20 students had either fainted or reported feeling sick, alarming the staff. Ambulances and health authorities rushed to the scene. Initially suspecting food or water contamination, they realized after a quick assessment of the situation that those reporting illness symptoms were only those who had been vaccinated the previous day. In all, 55 students from the school, all age 15, were examined at the hospital.

Television and newspaper reporters quickly appeared on the scene and suggested vaccination as the likely cause. At noon the Ministry of Health ordered a halt to all vaccinations nationwide. At 6 p.m. the health minister made a nationwide announcement "that any student with side effects from the Td vaccine...be admitted to the hospital for observation."[4] Over the next several days, more than 800 Jordanians reported side effects from their Td inoculation, of which 122 were hospitalized. The episode occurred during a crisis of confidence in the Jordanian government in the wake of a water pollution scare, as there were many press claims at the time that the water supply was harmful to children's health. The episode also coincided with rumors that the vaccination program could be harmful.[5] In making their diagnosis of mass hysteria for the symptoms in the vast majority of subjects, and ruling out a reaction to the vaccine, the identical batch of Td vaccine was dispensed in two other countries without any incident.

A British Incident

A routine school vaccination turned out to be far from routine at a secondary school in Dumfries, England, in March 2000. Dr. Peter Spafford was at the Wallace Hall Academy in Thornhill as part of a meningitis vaccination program. Several hundred pupils were sitting in their classrooms anxiously awaiting their injections, when word quickly circulated that one of the students, 11-year-old Hannah Henshall had become ill and was transported to hospital. The girl suffered side effects and was hospitalized as a precaution. Dr. Spafford said that it was common for one or two pupils to have a reaction. An eyewitness said that once the ambulance arrived, "It was pretty chaotic. There were children lying on the floor at the school entrance." [6] According to Dr. Spafford: "The episode really was hysterical in nature. The kids got themselves very worked up."[7] Before the vaccination was canceled, several students had fainted.[8]

Scares In Spain And Congo

There have been additional reports of vaccine-associated mass hysteria,[9] including psychosomatic symptoms among students after inoculations in Spain for hepatitis B,[10] and in the Democratic Republic of Congo after administering the polio vaccine.[11] In the latter instance, groundless rumors of a poison vaccine causing many children to die had serious consequences. Many parents refused to have their children inoculated against polio and unnecessarily taxed the medical system as many adults were rushing their newly immunized children to doctors, fearing that they might soon die from the inoculation. According to Dr. Moussa Traore of the World Health Organization (WHO) in Kinshasa: "If there was really a spike in child mortality in Kivu, the WHO would be the first to know about it because we have offices reporting back to us in all the provinces. Furthermore, we would've been on-site in a flash..."[12] He called for anyone caught deliberately spreading the rumors to be prosecuted for threatening the well being of thousands of children in the region who might otherwise be vaccinated. Pierre Kandolo of the region's Expanded Vaccination Program, noted that: "We've given these vaccinations since 1998 to millions of children all across the country and we've never heard of anyone dying as a result."[13]

During 1995, officials from the World Health Organization (WHO) expressed grave concerns over the circulation of widespread rumors in the Philippines that their anti-tetanus vaccine was harmful. Rumors held that small amounts of human chorionic gonadotropin were present in the tetanus toxoid – amounts sufficient to induce abortion. The result was a 45 percent decrease in the number of people getting vaccinated. WHO officials estimated that the scare would result in the deaths of about 350 babies during the year as a result of tetanus. The disease is a serious problem for newborns, as native midwives often deliver babies with unsanitary utensils, including dirty knives that are used to cut the umbilical cord. WHO blamed the church for starting the campaign against tetanus vaccinations, noting that the pro-tetanus campaign had been successful in immunizing millions of Filipino females in order to prevent tetanus in both the mother and newborn.[14]

VAMPIRISM

Vampirism acutely and vividly displays the interplay between popular beliefs and real-life practices. The subject of worldwide belief, and hardly less widespread disbelief, has become the subject of a vast popular mythology from which it is not always easy to extricate the core reality. Yet this very confusion is a testimony to the powerful appeal of this extraordinary social behavior.

Ostensibly, vampirism is not a social behavior. Vampires do not hunt in packs; theirs is a solitary activity. However, because vampires are perceived as behaving according to a pattern, consensus stereotypes have been created to which each individual instance more or less conforms. This is not to say that there is only one way to be a vampire. Around the core definition there are countless derivative behaviors to which the label has been loosely, and often confusingly, attached.

A naked vampire sucks blood from his victim.

There is a further sense in which vampirism is a collective activity, and that is the belief that it is transferable, contagious, and even epidemic by nature: "In Transylvania the belief prevails that every person killed by a nosferatu [vampire] becomes in turn a vampire, and will continue to suck the blood of other innocent people until the evil spirit has been exorcised, either by opening the grave of the suspected person and driving a stake through the corpse, or firing a pistol-shot into the coffin."[15]

Because vampirism has attracted a vast popular interest, manifesting not only in life but in books and films, fan clubs, operas, conventions, and more, it is important to distinguish between vampirism as a psychosocial practice and the popular vampire mythology which, as with witches or ghosts, tends to obscure the subject. While these peripheral manifestations are also of sociological interest, they are secondary to the more strictly defined core behavior.

"A vampire may be defined as (1) the spirit of a dead person, or (2) his corpse, re-animated by his own spirit or by a demon, returning to sap the life of the living, by depriving them of blood or of some essential organ, in order to augment its own vitality."[16] This is essentially the core definition on which this entry focuses. The *Oxford English Dictionary* is substantially in agreement but usefully extends the definition: "Vampire: A preternatural being of a malignant nature (in the original and usual form of the belief, a re-animated corpse), supposed to seek nourishment, or do harm, by sucking the blood of sleeping persons: a man or woman abnormally endowed with similar habits." We are not here concerned, that is to say, with demons who possess the bodies of the dead and use them to haunt the living, nor with living witches, such as the Malayan *penangglan* who in other respects behaves like a vampire.[17] Many writers, notably Montague Summers,[18] for all their valuable research, have muddied the waters by dragging in necrophiliacs, necrophagiacs, necrosadists, and a multitude of ghosts who wouldn't be seen dead sucking blood.

To clarify the confusion, this entry separates the subject into five phases that loosely represent a series of developments, though with a substantial overlap: Folklore vampirism, Epidemic vampirism, Romantic vampirism, Fantasy vampirism, and Clinical vampirism.

Folklore Vampirism

Vampirism is one expression among many of the belief in survival after death, which in turn leads to the belief that the dead can return to visit the living, whether as a physical being or as a spirit. Usually these returns are perceived as malevolent, and alongside the belief that they happen, there exists a vast technology designed to prevent them from returning: corpses are mutilated or subjected to magical practices, amulets and talismans are worn or fixed by the door, and efforts are made to placate the dead and encourage them to stay put.

The belief in survival, in one form or another, goes back to the beginnings of history, and so it can plausibly be claimed that vampirism has co-existed with that belief. Most commentators consider that certain inscriptions and artifacts from Babylonia, Assyria, and Ancient Greece testify to vampire beliefs, in that spirits of the dead are described or depicted rising from the grave to harass the living. Such beliefs vary from one culture to another. Often the malevolent dead are supposed to be a particular category of persons – those who had died abruptly, or who died with a grudge against the living (wives suspected of adultery were especially liable to receive unwelcome posthumous visits), or who have not been buried, or if buried, not according to protocol. Freud has suggested that all the living consider all the dead as being likely to be malevolent, through their own guilty feelings towards the dead, and that this is how the "loved one" came to be transformed into a figure of fear and hate.[19]

Such beliefs span space as well as time. "The Caffres [Kaffirs] believe that men of evil life, after death may return during the night in corporeal form and attack the living, often wounding and killing them. It seems that these revenants are much attracted by blood… even a few drops will help to vitalize their bodies."[20] In virtually every culture there has existed a store of anecdotal reference that can be drawn upon whenever popular fears set people looking to account for a mysterious event. The revenant became a convenient universal scapegoat to whom could be attributed any otherwise inexplicable illness, accident, or catastrophe. Some of these behaviors were sufficiently vampire-like to be used to justify claims that vampirism has always existed.

Yet more often than not the essential features of vampirism were lacking. For example, Vlad Tepes ("The Impaler"), Voivoide (prince) of Walachia in eastern Europe, known as Dracula because he was the son of the notoriously cruel Voivoide Dracul, was the subject of widespread chronicling. "The cruelties of Voivoide Dracula shocked and fascinated Renaissance Europe, and were legendary in his lifetime."[21] Four centuries later, he would be a crucial source for Stoker's novel, discussed herein. Yet there is no evidence whatever that Vlad indulged in vampire-like behavior. Apart from the Stoker connection, the real-life Dracula is irrelevant to the vampire phenomenon.[22]

And so it is with legend after legend, cited by writers such as Montague Summers, as evidence of continuity in the vampire tradition. The 12th century English chronicler William of Newburgh tells of a malevolent revenant at Alnwick, Northumberland, who returned to Earth and walked the streets, frightening the populace and causing the dogs to howl all night long. His corrupting body tainted the air and gave rise to an outbreak of plague. The authorities decided to disinter his corpse, which was found to be uncorrupted. Striking the corpse with a spade, they let forth a flood of fresh blood, from which they concluded that the ghost had sustained itself by taking blood from the living. The body was forthwith burnt.[23] The similarity to vampire stories is clear, yet the evidence, such as it is, is merely circumstantial; the crucial element, the sucking of blood, is absent. And so it is throughout the records; no clear-cut instances of vampirism occur in the early legends. All we have are beliefs, on the one hand, in survival and malicious return, and on the other, legends of non-human creatures such as the lamia, a kind of succubus-like entity that might indeed suck the vitality from a living person. So far as the folklore record goes, there is no prehistory of vampirism; it was born in the 18th century.

Nevertheless, the fact that these stories were told indicates that beliefs in revenants, and their power to do ill, were latent in people's minds, and when circumstances favored, they would be brought out to serve as explanations.

Epidemic Vampirism

The word "vampire" first appeared in English in 1734, and was borrowed from the Hungarian to denote a phenomenon that was currently being discussed throughout Europe. What can be termed the rebirth of vampirism took place in Eastern Europe in the early 18th century. In 1727, from the village of Meduegna, near Belgrade, Serbia, comes the case of Arnod Paole, who died after falling from a hay-cart. Some four weeks after his burial, some villagers began to complain that he was haunting them, and four of them died. The suspicion arose that he was a vampire, for he told his wife that while doing military service in Kosovo he had had to kill a vampire, and feared its revenge. When his grave was opened, his body looked as fresh as though it had not been dead for a day. New skin and new nails had made their appearance and there was fresh blood in the mouth. A stake was forthwith driven through his body, at which the undead man was heard to groan. The body was then burnt to ashes. For good measure, the bodies of the four whom Paole was supposed to have killed were also burned, lest they be infected.

Even this did not halt the deaths. Determined to completely eradicate vampirism in the village, the authorities opened every grave that could possibly be infected. Their report, dated June 7, 1732, tells of twelve more bodies that, on exhumation, were found in good condition. While most were young – one was 8, another 10 – it also included a 60-year-old man. Seven, at least, had died of an illness.[24] One of the victims was "a girl named Stanoska, daughter of the heyduk [nobleman] Jotiutso, who went to bed in perfect health, awoke in the middle of the night trembling violently and uttering terrible shrieks, declaring that the son of the heyduk Milloc, who had been dead nine weeks, had nearly strangled her in her sleep. She fell into a languid state and died at the end of three days. Sixteen-year-old Millo was exhumed and found to be a vampire."[25]

Such cases aroused considerable interest, and the fact that they were immediately diagnosed as vampires shows that the concept was already clearly established. In 1733 a Serbian commentator wrote: "Vampires issue forth from their caves in the night, attack people sleeping quietly in their beds, suck out all their blood from their bodies and destroy them."[26] The term itself seems to have come into general use at this time.

Among the academics of central Europe the initial response to the vampire epidemic was a rationalist one in which there was no question of taking the stories literally. It was left to a respected French scholar, Dom Augustin Calmet, to propose an open-minded approach to the matter. His thoughtful examination of the subject in 1746 was widely discussed and very popular. Indeed, the fact that it was so popular, despite the mockery of Voltaire and the Encyclopedists, is an indication of just how incomplete the rationalism was that the great minds of the Enlightenment believed was replacing popular superstitions and vulgar errors.

Calmet reported a number of cases, including that of Peter Plogojowitz of the village of Kisolova, Hungary, who, ten weeks after his burial, appeared, in the course of eight days, to nine residents of the village, some old, some young, during their sleep, and throttled them so severely that they died in less than 24 hours. His widow confirmed his return, stating that he had asked for his slippers; she was so frightened that she fled from the village. The villagers requested permission to exhume Peter's body. Reluctantly, the authorities did so and found that the body was in a good state, not smelling, and had traces of fresh blood in his mouth, which led them to believe he had sucked the blood of the living. The villagers pierced his body with a pointed stake, causing fresh scarlet blood to gush forth, also by the nose and mouth. He also expelled something from that part of his body which modesty forbids to name. The body was then burnt to ashes.[27]

By telling such stories, Calmet laid the foundation for vampire studies. He identified the vampire as one who, neither living nor dead, remains in some intermediary state where he requires blood to sustain him. His chief difficulty was that he couldn't understand how the dead individual could leave his grave as a physical entity. The solution would be, according to some versions of the legend, is that he didn't: that it was only his spirit that did so. But this created further difficulties, such as how the blood would be passed on to the corpse.

COMMENT: Herbert Mayo, while accepting the facts of the Eastern European cases, was inclined to doubt that "these fresh-looking and well-conditioned corpses had some mysterious source of preternatural nourishment" and suggested instead "a notion not so monstrous, but still startling enough: that the bodies, which were found in the so-called Vampyr state, instead of being in a new or mystical condition, were simply alive in the common way, or had been so for some time subsequent to their interment." In short, Mayo saw them as the bodies of people who had been buried alive, and whose life, where it yet lingered, was finally extinguished through the ignorance and barbarity of those who disinterred them.[28]

Barber shows that there is no need to have recourse to this horrifying theory. Drawing on our present knowledge, he wrote: "How difficult it is, even now, to be sure of what we are seeing when dealing with a corpse. Consider how much harder it would have been for a Serbian peasant in the eighteenth century to know what to expect of a body, which has so many resources at its disposal. It can stiffen and relax, bleed at the mouth and nose, grow, shrivel, change color with dazzling versatility, shed its skin and nails, appear to grow a beard, and even burst open."[29] He also cites precedents for sounds heard at vampire's graves, the disturbed earth about them, and many other features that the 18th century attributed to vampirism.

So far as that century's vampire mania was concerned, Barber suggested: "It is probably not going too far to suggest that a vampire might be defined as a corpse that comes to the attention of the populace at a time of crisis and is taken for the cause of that crisis."[30] But to the popular mind, whatever the authorities might say, vampirism was a fact. Had they not opened the graves and seen the evidence with their own eyes?

The socio-political context played a part. "Vampire attacks were invariably reported from border areas where Catholic Hungarians and Orthodox Serbs and Walachians intermingled."[31] Plogojowitz was a Slav; his religion was Orthodox. It is significant that the authorities of the Imperial government, sent to investigate the outbreak, were unable to speak the language of the community. This was a marginal and insecure population in which recourse to traditional beliefs provided an illusion of security.

To the Roman Catholic Church vampirism was not a problem, since it was a matter of their doctrine that such practices were the work of the Evil One to whom all forms of deceit are possible. When vampires began to appear in Bohemia in the early 18th century, the Church treated them, along with witches, as accomplices of Satan. The Cardinal-bishop of Olmütz reported that graves were opened and the public executioner cut off the suspect's head, opened his chest with a halberd, then struck an iron stake through the body.[32] For the Catholic Church, as for peasants whether Catholic or Orthodox, vampirism was a fact.

Romantic Vampirism

Though Calmet did his best to be neutral in his approach, this was not enough for him to escape the ridicule of the intellectuals of the Enlightenment. The entry in Diderot's Encyclopédie (circa 1760) reads:

> Vampire: this is the name given to supposed demons who during the night draw blood from the bodies of the living, and carry it to corpses from whose mouths, nostrils and ears blood is seen to exude. Father Calmet has written an absurd book on the subject, of which one wouldn't have thought him capable, but which serves to prove how the human spirit is swept along by superstition.[33]

But however the prophets of the Enlightenment might scoff, the popular fascination with vampirism continued to spread, notably among writers of the romantic cast, who can be seen as representing a reaction to the reasoned approach typified by Voltaire and the Encyclopedists. The surge of interest created by the Eastern European epidemic in the early 18th century led to a vast literature which, in the long run, would lead to the confection of a new mythology in which the malevolent revenant was romanticized into a living menace. The "Gothick" novels of Horace Walpole, Mrs. Radcliffe, and their kind – if they did not feature vampirism per se – created an emotional climate in which the vampire was quite at home. Inspired by Byron, John Polidoro, a friend of the Shelleys, wrote a short story featuring a vampire. Keats wrote a poem about the lamia, a folklore entity with vampire-like habits. In France Nodier staged a drama and Baudelaire wrote a celebrated poem, both entitled *Le Vampire*.

In the 19th century, the renewed fascination with the occult, most notably manifested by animal magnetism and spiritualism, embraced all kinds of mysterious phenomena: vampirism came in for its share of attention. The prominent French spiritualist Z. J. Piérart proposed a solution to the question that had bothered Calmet, how the physical vampire left his grave to obtain physical blood.[34] He suggested that the process took place on "the astral plane" – it wasn't the physical body that left the tomb, but the astral body, which could pass through solid matter. Theosophist Franz Hartmann developed this suggestion into a theory of "psychic vampirism" to explain "a certain class of cases in which the usual order of nature seems to be reversed and where the vegetative life of a corpse in the grave is kept active by the exertions made for its sustenance by the animal soul. The cases referred to are those of so-called vampires, which means that corpses which are actually dead, because the true life of the spirit has entirely departed from them, still remain connected with a certain form of animal or 'astral' consciousness which keeps the body from decomposition and procures for it the means of sustaining its existence. These vampires are called 'Pisachas' in India, and are described as the astral bodies of the dead, from which the soul has departed: they are supposed to be a kind of 'shell' or ghost, wandering about or clinging to the living, from whom they extract vitality for the purpose of supplying the corpse in the grave with a kind of artificial life."[35] However, transforming the vampire's excursion into an out-of-body experience merely replaces one difficulty with another, for it does not account for the fact that the blood seen on the lips of the disinterred vampire is no astral substance but real-life gore.

Most vampire writing of the period is characterized by romance rather than realism, where such difficulties can be ignored or skirted. Yet the book which changed vampirism forever achieved its effect by building a sensational story on what seemed to be a solid foundation of authentic detail. Irish author Bram Stoker's 1897 *Dracula* carried conviction by presenting its exotic incidents as though they were the sort of thing one must expect to encounter if one ventures into Transylvania. Immensely popular in its own right, it was followed by spin-offs of every kind, notably on film and television. The result has been to reinforce the original model, to the extent that Count Dracula is today one of the best known of all fictional creations.

Ironically, Stoker's creation bears scarcely any relation to either folklore vampirism or the epidemic vampirism of the previous century. The name of Dracula was purloined from an individual who certainly never practiced vampirism, and in countless other ways – the literary persona of the vampire, the emphasis on drinking blood – he modified, distorted, borrowed, and manipulated his basic materials. He was, after all, creating a fiction with no other purpose than to entertain his readers. He could hardly have guessed that his creation, like Daphne du Maurier's Svengali, Mary Shelley's Frankenstein, Robert Louis Stevenson's Dr. Jekyll, or Oscar Wilde's Dorian Gray, would transcend its fictional embodiments and achieve an archetypal status to which millions would respond.

FANTASY VAMPIRISM

Stoker's book, and the subsequent staging and filming of his story or stories derived from it, led to a further revised perception of the vampire in popular culture. The image of the vampire has been transformed, finding expression in countless media manifestations, and ultimately in the popular mind. The "blood-sucking" element is virtually the only thing it has in common with traditional vampirism; the trappings are largely derived from Stoker or from films inspired by him.

The crucial change from folklore to fantasy vampirism is that the protagonists are not dead. For although they often behave as if they are dead, they do not need blood in order to survive. They may crave it, consciously, for the power they think it will give them, or they may be unaware with what motivation they yield to this urge, which they are apt to describe as irresistible. But the craving for blood is primarily a psychological one, even though it may conceivably become a physiological one as the result of addiction.

The fact that fantasy vampirism largely consists of vicarious game-playing in the form of fantasy literature and cinema, or of participatory role-playing in the form of clubs, conventions, and individual manifestations, seems at first to trivialize the vampire myth, but what it really does is confirm its cultural and psychosocial significance. Though fantasy vampirism is prima facie an artificial construct, this was, after all, equally the case with romantic vampirism and even folklore vampirism; these are all human creations, drawing on the same psychosocial factors as the original. The appeal to young people of the 21st century may be different in kind from the terror it aroused in 18th century Wallachian peasants, but it is no less forceful, and it is just as likely to lead to psychopathological behavior.

The ingredients of the myth explain its enduring appeal. Blood itself is a precious substance that symbolizes life itself, natural vitality and vital force. To see it spilt or shed is shocking. The act of taking someone else's blood, then, ranks with murder and rape as one of the ultimate interpersonal assaults. For most people it is accompanied by fear and horror, for a minority it is strongly appealing, perhaps the more so because it is forbidden and clandestine. Psychologist Richard Noll shares Freud's view that an important element in vampirist behavior is the breaking of a taboo; for the vampirist, the antisocial aspect is part of the appeal.

When a victim loses his/her vitality from unknown causes, loss of blood would be on the short list of possible explanations, and in a culture that accepts magic, it is a short step to the supposition that someone is responsible for causing the loss. Yet blood sucking, which in fantasy vampirism has become the dominant characteristic, was actually extremely rare in folklore or in the alleged 18th century cases. "This supposed habit seems to be merely a folkloric means of accounting for two unrelated phenomena: unexplained deaths and the appearance of blood at the mouth of a corpse."[36] It remained for fantasy vampirism to make this the predominant characteristic of the myth.

In the folklore legends, sexual harassment was an occasional feature, but it does not seem as though the satisfying of sexual lust was ever even a fringe benefit in the 18th century cases. When the body of Plogojowitz was exhumed, *wilde Zeichen* (wild signs) were observed. This is generally taken to mean that it had an erection, but no great importance was attached to this, and victims do not seem to have complained on this score.

In fantasy-vampirism, on the other hand, the erotic element is strongly marked and plays a crucial part in the deeper psychological significance of the vampire. In the cinema, the victim is nearly always an attractive young lady in her nightdress, while the villain, though he inspires horror, may also fascinate and even charm, creating a conflict in the mind of the heroine.

Clinical Vampirism

The emergence of psychology, psychoanalysis, and psychiatry meant that extraordinary behaviors such as vampirism could be catalogued. For Freud, the underlying sexual element was fundamental; for Jung, vampirism was the expression of a timeless component of the collective unconscious. Robert McCully suggested: "It would seem that some long forgotten archetype somehow got dislodged from the murky bottom of the past and emerged to take possession of the modern individual."[37] Noll proposed that "the modern phenomenon called 'clinical vampirism' is perhaps best understood in terms of the primitive theory of a disease caused by the violation of a taboo."[38]

It is this interplay between centuries-old traditional beliefs and present-day behavior that makes vampirism particularly interesting. Although clinical vampirism has only recently been added to the repertoire of pathological behaviors, the activity itself may be presumed to have occurred throughout human history, and real-life cases, such as the Alnwick Castle case cited by William of Newburgh, are likely to have confirmed the folklore even if they did not actually cause it to be created. The population would have known how to fit such an event into their belief-system, even though vampirism per se was not at that time recognized.

Clinical vampirism retains the central feature of traditional vampirism: the craving for blood. Subjects, who it has been suggested should be termed "vampirists" to distinguish them from "true" vampires,[39] differ from the latter by the fact that they are alive. Vampirism is regarded as a chronic element, which may emerge in the personality of an individual. It is possible that the entire history of the vampire, from its folklore beginnings through the 18th century epidemics to the current fascination, reflects a primeval urge that takes various forms of expression according to prevailing cultural conditions. The writings of both Freud and Jung would support this view.

Several gruesome crimes in which blood played a prominent role have been presented as vampire-related: notably those of Fritz Haarmann in Hannover, Germany, in 1924, and Haerm and Algren in Sweden, in 1988. However, Gordon Melton correctly points out that these examples "are only tangential to what traditionally has been thought of as vampirism. They are serial killers with, among other problems, a blood fetish. The blood was not the object of their quest, and the drinking of blood was just one of the more gruesome (and somewhat superficial) practices in which they engaged."[40]

Be that as it may, there is no doubt that clinical vampirism occurs, though extremely rarely and not always in a recognizable form. Fouché, Napoléon's chief of police, had to deal with a man named Rafin, who seems to have shared his attentions between the living and the dead, paying nocturnal visits to the cemetery of Father Lachaise and also frequenting young ladies who, as a result, lost their color and their health.[41] In 1867 a Portuguese seaman naming himself James Brown, aboard a Boston fishing vessel on the Labrador fishing grounds, killed two fellow crewmen, keeping their bodies in a hold where he drank their blood. He was condemned to life imprisonment, but killed two others before dying insane.[42] In 1952, 27-year-old Estrelita Florescio, a maidservant in the Philippines, was jailed for attacking a small boy, biting his face and body and drinking the blood from the wounds. She had done this on many previous occasions; she said she had an irresistible urge to do it, which she claimed to have acquired from a man she formerly lived with. Except for her craving, she behaved quite normally.[43] More recent cases were presented by Noll in 1992. Ironically, all three vampirists whose cases were narrated by Hemphill and Zabow "found cannibalism revolting and films about Dracula 'rubbbish.'"[44]

Apart from the craving for blood, the same authors identify two other behavioral characteristics of the vampirist: a preoccupation with death and an uncertainty as to their own identity. This triad of characteristics recurs in the cases they cite and can be observed in many other cases, including the case history we present below.

These cases present the essential feature – the craving for blood – and reinforce the supposition that clinical vampirism is a chronic pathology of the human mind, and the possibility that the activities of vampirists gave rise to the entire mythology. But perhaps with equal probability it can be argued that it was the existence of a vampire mythology that created the fantasy that vampirists turn into reality.

CONCLUSION: It is reasonable to conclude that the vampire myth is a social construct, whose basis is legendary fears and traditional beliefs which themselves can be seen as springing from an instinctive reverence/fear for blood. The myth took a social form in periodic cases when an individual followed through on this primitive blood lust, and particularly when in 18th century eastern Europe it led to widespread interest when a supposed epidemic was created as inexplicable happenings occurred in a population sensitized by social and political marginalization. This widespread interest gave it a wider acceptance thanks to its strong psychological appeal – the probability of survival, the symbolic significance of blood, and the fascination of entities with superhuman attributes and powers. This appeal is universal but varies from one individual to another, which is why, in the course of this wider diffusion, the stereotype has been modified to satisfy a variety of needs. If, today, the vampire retains a wider fascination than ever, it is because it has become a protean entity that can wear as many disguises as a Barbie doll.

Case History: John George Haigh (1909-1949)[45]

Born into a solid middle-class and deeply religious family of the Plymouth Brethren persuasion, Haigh enjoyed a seemingly normal childhood in Yorkshire. He was an intelligent child, a choirboy at Wakefield cathedral. The first outward signs of trouble came in his 20s, when his diminished sense of right and wrong led to a series of unsuccessful criminal activities. Dismissed from one company for suspected theft, he was later convicted of a hire-purchase fraud involving cars, and served 15 months in prison. After a failed attempt to go straight, he set up as a bogus solicitor for which he served four years in prison. Soon after his release, in 1934, he was in prison again for theft. While in prison, his recently married wife left him and gave up their child for adoption.

In 1944 he was working as an accountant in London. He had respectable and well-to-do friends, and his outward life was quiet and respectable. He was friendly with a teenage girl, the daughter of the family with whom he was lodging, but she was unaware that he was still married.

In February 1949 he was charged with the murder of Mrs. Deacon, a 69-year-old widow who lived in the hotel where he also lived.

Details of his private life now came to light. He told of a childhood of austerity and prohibition. From the age of 6 he enjoyed the taste of blood, licking scratches, and sometimes cutting himself deliberately to suck the cut. He fantasized about blood, accidents, and death, and about Jesus bleeding on the cross. In 1944, blood dripped into his mouth from a scalp wound and an acute craving took hold of him. He realized that he would have to kill to obtain blood. His first victim was a friend, William McSwan, for whom he once worked as a chauffeur. He lured him to a basement in Pimlico, London, where he killed him; he had previously installed apparatus for disposing of the corpses in an acid bath. He told McSwan's parents that their son had run away to Scotland to avoid being called up for the war; he even went to the trouble of traveling to Scotland to send postcards purportedly from his victim. He planned to take over McSwan's business, but realized that to do this he must get rid of the McSwan couple. In July 1945 he killed them in the same way as their son. Forging their signatures, he acquired their property and took a room at the Onslow Court Hotel, Kensington, where he lived for the rest of his life.

A compulsive gambler, he rapidly spent the money he had acquired and in 1947, to obtain more, he targeted a Dr. and Mrs. Henderson, who had advertised a house for sale. By now he had transferred his equipment to a workshop at Crawley, West Sussex. On February 12, he lured Dr. Henderson there on the pretext of seeing an invention and shot him in the head with a stolen revolver. The following day, after luring Mrs. Henderson by telling her that her husband had taken ill, he shot her also. By means of forgery he obtained their property and was again financially stable. He explained to relatives that the Hendersons had gone to South Africa to avoid being charged with performing an illegal abortion.

Once again he was soon out of funds due to gambling, and by the end of 1948 he needed another well-to-do victim. He selected Mrs. Deacon, a resident of the hotel, luring her to his workshop on the same pretext as before. But the police, investigating her disappearance and checking on the other residents of the hotel, learned of his criminal record and became suspicious. The workshop was located and searched, and the remains of Mrs. Deacon were found. Haigh was identified by the jeweler to whom he tried to sell Mrs. Deacon's valuables, and by Mrs. Deacon's clothes, which he had sent to the cleaners.

After first trying to lie his way out of his situation, he switched tack, admitted to the killings, and attributed them to his vampirism. He told how, before the killings, he had cycles of dreams about blood, starting early in the week and culminating on Friday. He claimed that his primary motive was an irresistible craving for blood, not gain nor sexual perversion. He would club or shoot the victim in the head, plug the wound, incise the neck, draw a cupful of blood, and drink it for four or five minutes "after which I felt better." The process of dissolving the body took a few days, after which he would dispose of the remains as rubbish. He confessed to three other killings – a woman from Hammersmith, a young man named Max, and a girl from Eastbourne.

Although the killings were carefully planned, and he showed considerable ingenuity in his cover stories and in his acquisition of his victims' property, he was caught as a result of surprising carelessness. Of his crimes, he said: "I was impelled to kill by wild blood demons, the spirit inside commanded me to kill." He was unconcerned about his trial and did not appeal against sentence. However, he asked a policeman about conditions at Broadmoor (Britain's best-known asylum for the criminally insane), which suggests that he expected to be found insane. Nevertheless, a panel of psychiatrists found that he presented no symptoms of mental illness, and he was hanged in London on August 10, 1949.

We have only Haigh's word for it that blood was his motivation, and his record shows a lifelong propensity to concoct false stories. At his trial the prosecution used the clear indications of malice aforethought to invalidate any defense on grounds of insanity. After his conviction, two other psychiatrists examined him and both took the view that the vampirism claims were a sham, a fantasy designed to conceal his cold-blooded murders for gain.

However, R E. Hemphill and T. Zabow re-evaluated him as a vampirist on the strength of his personal history and his behavior that displayed a fragility of identity approaching multiple personality.[46] The contrast between his respectable everyday life and the ruthlessness of his murders matches the behavior of other vampirists. Additionally, it may be significant that he kept detailed records of his murders, possibly to enable him to re-live the events.

Ultimately, the case of Haigh is equally relevant to the development of vampirism, whether he practiced vampirism or merely fantasized about doing so. Whether his claims are true or false, they are living testimony to the ability of the vampire myth to survive.

VERZEGNIS OUTBREAK

Italy: 1878

This outbreak occurred in the Friuli district of Italy in January 1878, two months after a Jesuit father preached with great pomp at a highly emotional retreat. The first person to be afflicted was Annamaria Valcon, a young woman in her 20s, who for eight years previously had presented symptoms of hysteria together with convulsions, which led to the suspicion that she was possessed by a demon. She was now subjected to public exorcism at the Pardon de Clauzetto, a well-known place of pilgrimage, and this had the effect of giving a definitive form to her malady. Her convulsions now became true "demoniac" seizures with displays of anger, profanity, shouting, and delirium. A seizure could be triggered by the sound of church bells, the visit of a priest, or the sight of a sacred object.

Until her exorcism she was the only person to be afflicted, but after July 1878, several other women were taken with convulsions. The epidemic made rapid progress thanks to a religious ceremony, performed in the parish church, to which all the "possessed" women were brought. Doctors noted, as at the very similar outbreak at MORZINE, a total absence of the erotomania, which so often characterizes this kind of outbreak.

The manifestations continued for about a year, although prompt action by the authorities arranged for those afflicted to be isolated and sequestrated as far as possible, as had recently proved effective at MORZINE. Following a report by Dr. Franzolini, troops were stationed in the area and the sick women were taken to the hospital at Udine. After about a year, thanks to this principle of isolation, all signs of the epidemic had gone.[47]

VIRGIN MARY, APPARITIONS OF

Worldwide: 1830 to present

Religious visions are almost always an individual experience, but though they occur in isolation, they present so many shared features as to create a shared pattern. This is particularly true of apparitions of Mary, mother of the first century prophet Jesus of Nazareth. So many people have claimed to see her that there has grown a kind of consensus regarding the manner of her manifestation and what the apparition should do and say. This in turn governs the actions of the visionary. So though each case is personalized, it occurs within cultural guidelines in which the behavior both of the visionary and of Mary herself are confined within recognized parameters. For some, this is evidence of their authenticity; for others, it is an indication of a culture-shaped behavior-pattern.

Although visions of Mary have been reported periodically since her death, the number escalated during the 19th century and proliferated dramatically in the latter half of the 20th century. Apart from the theological implications, they certainly constitute a remarkable sociological phenomenon.

The Virgin Mary as suposedly seen by the visionaries at Garabandal, northern Spain.

CONTEXT: Roman Catholics experience virtually all encounters with Mary. The rare exceptions are likely to involve individuals who are somehow involved with the Church, the 1842 vision that led to the conversion of the Jew Alphonse Ratisbonne being a notable example.[48] The encounters occur in most Catholic communities, though those of France, Italy, and Spain have attracted the most attention. The visionaries are of either sex, though predominantly female, and of all ages, though adolescents figure disproportionately. Political and economic crises, particularly wars, encourage apparitions, but local affairs may also be reflected.[49] The years 1947-8, which also witnessed the birth of the FLYING SAUCER MANIA, saw a very great many visions of Mary. During this time, the world was troubled by fears of nuclear warfare between Soviet Russia and the West.

The teaching of the Roman Catholic Church is that apparitions of Mary are veridical. Consequent upon Pius XII's 1950 pronouncement, it is an article of Catholic dogma that she was taken bodily to Heaven at the termination of her earthly existence. Consequently it is Mary in person who is performing these visits, and the visionaries are experiencing face-to-face encounters with the mother of a Palestinian religious figure who left our Earth some time after the death of her son two thousand years ago. Theologians offer various explanations as to the process involved, particularly as to whether the events should be seen as wholly miraculous or as partially miraculous but making use of scientifically acceptable processes.

Outside the Catholic Church, it is generally supposed that these incidents are delusions, though it is recognized that the experience may serve a psychological purpose for the individual visionary.

Any assessment of the phenomenon must depend on whether or not the Church's view is accepted. It is not the concern of this Encyclopedia to take sides in this matter, but inevitably the question of authenticity affects any attempt to evaluate the nature of the behavior. If the events are what they are claimed to be, there is no point in looking more deeply for socio-psychological processes. But if they are not, if the Catholic Church is as deluded as skeptics suggest, then the continued popularity of the phenomenon is an important area of behavioral research. There are many problems facing the belief that the apparitions are veridical, and the Church is well aware of them. Even if it is accepted that a certain number are what they claim to be, it is certain that most are not, leaving the Church with the responsibility for deciding which are genuine and which are spurious. Our entry on the LOURDES visions illustrates the difficulties facing the authorities.

Visions of Mary have been reported periodically since her death and many hundreds of specific claims are recorded, some only perfunctorily but others in great detail. However, until modern times – the 19th century – the great majority of the stories were anecdotal, stock items that were almost obligatory in the repertoire of religious professionals such as Teresa of Avila. No attempt was made to verify or investigate them. They were either accepted at face value, or if the circumstances were dubious, supposed to be simulations practiced by the Evil One. Claims of sightings virtually died out in the 18th century – there were only six known cases compared with 34 in the previous century.

What changed matters was a series of high-profile apparitions in 19th century France, where a stronger intellectual approach was encouraged by a lively mutual antagonism between the religious and secular communities. As a result, when Mary was said to appear at the Rue du Bac, Paris (1830), at La Salette (1846), at Lourdes (1858), and at Pontmain (1870), her visits were not only fully covered by the press, whether favorably or skeptically, but also vigorously debated in pamphlets and books. Even the relatively minor affair narrated in our case history in this entry was headline news in the late 20th century. From being private visions within a religious enclave, they became public events taking place in fields and on hillsides.

They have also been more widely commented upon, for in 1970 Pope Paul VI lifted the ban on writing about new apparitions. In recent years, Lourdes and other historic sightings have been meticulously chronicled in retrospect by commentators who, even if predisposed to accept the event as veridical, nevertheless realized that if they were to satisfy the incredulous, they had to address the difficulties. In recent years, the sharpest skeptical writing has come from within the Church; the Medjugorje sightings, in particular, have aroused vigorous controversy from many commentators, including local clergy.[50] One redoubtable Catholic critic of the Medjugorje sightings is Joachim Bouflet, whose *Faussaires de Dieu* is a massive parade of false or deluded claimants.[51] Yet even the most pragmatic Catholic commentators often accept a select few apparitions as genuine.

What distinguishes visions of Mary since 1830 is that virtually all are experienced by lay persons, as opposed to religious professionals. This is not to say that priests and nuns no longer receive them, but their experiences do not attract the interest that is aroused when "ordinary" people have them. This democratization of the visionary experience is without doubt the most significant feature of the current proliferation. To believers, it is a further sign of Mary's virtue that she bestows her favors on simple, obscure individuals. By contrast, behavioral scientists look to a psychosocial interpretation.

The very marked increase in the number of visionary claims since 1940 has, similarly, been explained in quite different ways by believers and unbelievers. Two serious books by Catholic writers – *Why the Virgin Appears Today*[52] and *Multiple Apparitions of the Virgin Today*[53]– address this question and attribute the increase to Mary's concern for humankind at a time of world discord and diminishing piety. "Beyond doubt these events underline the grave turning point at which humankind finds itself, in an age of scientism, rationalism and atheism."[54] Sociologists, on the other hand, tend to see the escalation of apparition experiences as the expression of a yearning for divine certainty at a time of political and social uncertainty.

Though the number of claimed visions is in the several hundreds, only a very small number are fully recognized as authentic by the Roman Catholic Church, which is generally cautious in its acceptance. Opinion is often bitterly divided, and in some cases the authorities will openly state their belief that the vision is false.[55] This may have the effect of stifling interest, but it also may, on the contrary, encourage defiance. The Catholic historian René Laurentin points out that, for theologians, apparitions of Mary, along with other miraculous phenomena such as moving or bleeding images, are "at the foot of the ladder as regards the values of the Church,"[56] but so far as the public is concerned, no other type of religious occasion attracts such intense popular interest. The claimed visions at Necedah (1959) in the United States, at Garabandal (1961) in Spain, at San Damiano (1961) in Italy, and Medjugorje (1981) in Croatia have none of them received the approval of the Church, yet they attract crowds of devoted pilgrims. Those that have been approved – Lourdes, Fatima – draw millions.

There is no such thing as a typical visionary experience, but following the sightings at La Salette (1846) and Lourdes (1858) something like a consensus stereotype has been created:

• Mary generally appears to an individual, or to a small closely bonded group, in a rural context; minding sheep is a typical setting. Most visionaries are young and of limited education. The peasant children of Lourdes, Fatima, and Garabandal are typical.

• Though she usually appears only once, Mary quite frequently pays a series of visits. In such cases she may announce, at the start, how many there will be. (Lourdes, Fatima, Vallensanges).

• The visionaries, during the apparition, go into a trance, ecstasy, or some kind of altered state. Tests may show that they are insensible to normal sensory stimuli – e.g., a candle flame was held against Bernadette's arm and she apparently did not notice, and more sophisticated tests have been carried out on the Medjugorje group.

• Where Mary appears to a group, one of them is likely to play a leading role. (Lucia at Fatima, Conchita at Garabandal, Vicka at Medjugorje.)

• If Mary appears in public, no one other than the chosen visionaries shares the experience.

• Mary delivers messages, usually in the form of a warning, that her son Jesus is angry with humankind and unless people repent she will be unable to persuade him to stay his hand. She may make specific requests, asking for better observance of the Sabbath or a return to old liturgical practices. She may request fasting, or greater use of the rosary. She may speak out against environmental pollution. The messages, which are made public only in the form of what the visionaries report, are simplistic and repetitive. At Heede, Germany, in 1937, she said, "Everything that will happen will be terrible, no one has seen anything like it since the creation of the world. With a few chosen faithful I will build my kingdom…the hour is near," and similar threats have been uttered to many visionaries.[57] The naiveté of the messages has not discouraged commentators from reading profound significance into Mary's words.[58]

• Her messages sometimes include "secrets" which the visionaries must not reveal, or only on particular conditions. But the text of the "third secret" of Fatima, when finally revealed, consisted of the same old threats along with a number of prophecies which turned out to be mistaken, such as that in the latter half of the 20th century there would be a cataclysmic world war in which the seas would evaporate.[59]

• She speaks to the visionary in her own language – if necessary, a patois. (La Salette, Lourdes.)

• She may promise to perform a miracle but later refuse on the grounds that the people do not deserve it. If a possibly miraculous event occurs, it is ambiguous, for example, the dancing sun reported at several locations. (See entry: FATIMA.)

• She may indicate the existence of a healing stream, supposedly hitherto unknown, which possesses miraculous healing properties. (The existence of the "miracle" stream at Lourdes was already known, and geologically predictable.)

• She wishes that a chapel, or even a basilica, be built on the site of her apparition. (La Salette, Lourdes, La Talaudière.) At Kerizinen in 1938, Mary asked for an oratory, while at Dozulé in 1972, she asked Madeleine Aumont to erect a giant crucifix.

• Mary may prescribe a pattern whereby she visits regularly, perhaps on a certain day each month; this enables people to assemble in the expectation of being present at a vision, if only at second hand, and perhaps experiencing something marvelous, even miraculous. This is true of San Damiano (since 1961), La Ladeira (since 1962), Escorial (since 1980), although the Church accepts none of these. At Escorial, Amparo Cuevas, the visionary, dictated the messages into a tape recorder as she received them, and they were then broadcast to the crowd. At Medjugorje (since 1981), Mary has appeared to the visionaries every single evening.

What arises from this consensus is a kind of checklist against which any subsequent visionary experience can be tested. An apparition would be suspect if it was not in general conformity, while the presence of these features serves as confirmation that it is authentic. The miracle of the "dancing sun" has become a folklore item to which pilgrims have testified at La Ladeira in Portugal, San Damiano in Italy, and La Taludière in France.

At the same time, there are considerable variations from one apparition to another. Mary herself, for instance, is perceived very differently, and often does not resemble the conventional image of the Virgin. At Lourdes, Bernadette saw "a young girl" who only at her 16th appearance revealed her identity, and then only in an oblique way, describing herself ungrammatically as "the Immaculate Conception." (Emile Tizané, a former policeman, noted that of 57 well-documented cases, Mary identify herself in only 27.[60]) Physically the Mary of Lourdes did not resemble the conventional images, and when a sculpture was created for the Grotto at Lourdes, Bernadette complained that it did not resemble her vision at all.[61] At Fatima, too, the artist's drawing made on the children's testimony was very different from the images that are sold to pilgrims as "Our Lady of Fatima," or which the children would have seen in their church.[62]

Not only does Mary look different, but her age ranges from that of a young girl to a woman of about 30, though never older, according to Laurentin.[63] Yet Mary is said to have died an old woman.

Collective Visions

Although most apparitions are to one individual only, a considerable number are collective. Tizané, studying 154 sightings, found that 64 were seen by more than one.[64] Some are shared within a large crowd, but the evidence for these is ambiguous at best (Cluj, Romania 1948; Hasmos, Hungary, 1949). More interesting are cases where Mary appears to a small group of three or four, because these collective cases ostensibly support the case for a veridical event occurring outside the mind of any one individual.[65] At Garabandal, Spain, in 1961,[66] and at Medjugorje, Croatia, in 1981,[67] the visionaries gave every appearance of participating simultaneously in a shared experience. However in 1984, one of the Garabandal visionaries, Mari-Cruz Gonzales, revealed that the so-called ecstasies had been "an innocent joke" that became a "monstrous farce,"[68] while a Catholic critic has demonstrated that the "scientific" testing of the Medjugorje visionaries was worthless.[69]

The fact that there is generally one member of the group who plays the leading role has led some critics to propose an explanation along the lines of a *folie à deux*. Nevertheless the synchronicity of the visionaries at Garabandal and Medjugorje is impressive, and those who are reluctant to accept the possibility that all may be simultaneously responding to the presence of Mary have suggested that some such extrasensory means as are employed by flights of birds may be operating. Unfortunately no way has been found to test such hypotheses.

Public Response

Most apparitions are initially met with skepticism, but this does not persist long as far as the populace is concerned, whereas the authorities, ecclesiastical or secular, are likely to be more on their guard. Communities welcome such events in principle, but naturally they do not wish to be deceived. Primitive reality testing is sometimes carried out – Bernadette at Lourdes, when she went to meet Mary for the second time, took some holy water to throw at the vision in case it was a demon.

Where the authorities themselves find it hard to decide whether or not an apparition is authentic, the great mass of people must decide for themselves. Father Thurston, widely respected for his sensible approach to marvelous claims, found grounds for accepting the visions of Bernadette at Lourdes while rejecting those of her fellow townspeople. Frère Michel de la Sainte Trinité has massively documented Fatima, demonstrating it to be authentic, and Medjugorje, demonstrating it to be a fraud.[70] Joachim Bouflet, the most ruthless debunker of false apparitions, was nonetheless a believer that some are authentic. Objective criteria are hard to formulate and even harder to apply. Ultimately the evaluation will be a subjective one.

If the Catholic Church is justified in its belief that the apparitions are authentic, there would seem to be little point in conducting scientific tests on the visionaries to "prove" that they are having a genuine experience. The visitation of Mary is already so far outside scientific acceptance that any lesser aspects are negligible by comparison. For theologians, there is ultimately no question of a "scientific" explanation. Laurentin affirms that "If Christ or Mary wish to manifest, it's a question of a communication sui generis [of its own kind]."[71] Nevertheless the Church goes through the motions of "scientific" testing, the object being to convince unbelievers that it is willing to work as far as possible within the parameters of scientific possibility.

To those standing outside the belief-system, which holds that such visitations can be genuine, the apparent gullibility of the Church is bewildering. Apart from the fact that the reappearance of Mary flies in the face of what is considered physically possible, and therefore constitutes a miracle, the events teem with improbabilities and inconsistencies. To take Lourdes alone, the enormous commercial enterprise which attracts millions of pilgrims a year, its infrastructure of hotels, tourist services, shops and eating-places, medical facilities, etc. rests on the testimony of a 14-year-old girl, unsupported by a scrap of confirmatory evidence of any kind. Such a situation is unlikely to arise in any other field of activity.

The Visionaries

Laurentin has expressed the view that "there would be no apparitions without the receptivity of the subject,"[72] a rather curious admission since one would suppose that Mary has the power to appear to whomsoever she chooses. Although most visionaries are presented as simple, innocent individuals, no obvious characteristic seems to mark them out as appropriate recipients of such a privilege – there were countless young girls ostensibly as fit as Bernadette for the honor. The two visionaries of La Salette lived somewhat unexemplary lives after their great experience, and the subsequent careers of the Medjugorje visionaries, even while some of them are still enjoying the divine visitations, are less than edifying. It is not easy to reconcile their prosperous lives as hotel keepers, etc., with the privilege of an otherworldly experience transcending anything that most people know.

Because visionaries tend to be simple people, unaware of the complex problems incurred by seeing an apparition, it is inevitable that the clergy play a prominent part in counseling and directing them. Their attitude may range from prudent caution to enthusiastic affirmation, from well-meaning guidance to outright manipulation.[73]

Although marginal to the experience itself, it is notable that a cult may grow around a particular sighting or cluster of sightings. This will have a snowball effect, attracting pilgrims. If they continue to come, accommodations are constructed, shops and services are provided, and in the course of time a considerable commerce is created. This is notable at Guadalupe, Mexico, and at Lourdes, France, both of which attract millions of pilgrims each year. Fatima is another favored destination, as are such unauthorized sites as San Damiano and Medjugorje. This touristification, which evidently has a financial aspect, has aroused vigorous criticism from outsiders. While many Catholics deplore this – the devoted Catholic convert and writer Joris-Karl Huysmans, was vehement in his denunciation of Lourdes[74] – the Church authorities, though embarrassed, must also be gratified. Successive popes have made their pilgrimages to Fatima, giving their personal support to a site that, to all but the faithful, is embarrassingly dubious.

COMMENT: The paradox of Mary's otherworldly visits, like that of encounters with aliens, is that, if authentic, they would be of profound significance not only for the individuals concerned but for humankind as a whole. The fact that outside the Roman Catholic Church interest in them is relatively low can only be attributed to a general perception that they are not authentic. Despite the best efforts of the Church, the veridicality of the events rests on the subjective testimony of individuals, or at best a small group of like-minded children. Mary herself, like the aliens, refrains from providing any evidence that would authenticate the claims.

The question, why it is so often Mary who is the apparent, is a complex one, and a vast literature has sought to answer it. The fact that virtually nothing is known about her has not prevented huge structures of meaning from being attributed to her.[75] It is clear that great numbers of people are drawn towards the Mary-figure. If, as Catholics claim and as seems ostensibly to be the case, the initiative is Mary's and it is her decision to make these hundreds of visits, then of course there is nothing more to be said. But if the instigation is coming, albeit unconsciously, from the visionaries, then the whole question of Mary's status becomes relevant.

The vast literature devoted to the cult of Mary offers explanations of many kinds, but the root fact is inescapable: no other entity-sighting experience carries an emotional charge of such intensity, in which the desire of the individual is supported by a vast communal devotion and authorized by doctrinal approval. If, in contrast to the Church's claim, a psychosocial approach is adopted, the visionaries are self-selected, and here again there is a substantial literature offering explanations. Michael Carroll, for example,[76] has offered a persuasive interpretation along Freudian lines: "In the case of female seers, the whole point of the apparition is to provide the young girl with a way of identifying with Mary and thus vicariously enjoying her own Oedipal fantasy, which is to have sexual intercourse with the father."

Jung offers an alternative perspective, in which Mary becomes an archetype, sharing with numerous other female divinities the role of "mothers in a figurative sense" in which fertility is combined with maidenhood, answering a longing for redemption, for maternal solicitude and sympathy, and for the magic authority of the female.[77] Mary has also been perceived as the successor to pre-Christian mother-deities. Robert Graves and Geoffrey Ashe have each presented an intelligent case along these lines.[78]

Hilary Evans has proposed a psychosocial approach, in which the encounter is the expression of a need on the visionary's part, perhaps an identity crisis. It takes the form of a vision of Mary because this is the culturally acceptable form in the visionary's milieu; under a different cultural umbrella she would see extraterrestrial aliens, folklore entities, or a kindly revenant. The two elements – the individual's need and society's myth – combine in a fantasy that, however sincerely experienced, has no reality outside the fantasy-forming mind of the visionary.[79]

Case History

The case of Blandine Piégay is not a "classic" sighting, and the Church does not accept her claims. It is unlikely that Blandine will ever become a saint. On the other hand, it is evident that the encounter was a significant and positive event in her personal life. In September 1981 Blandine Piégay was a 14-year-old schoolgirl, Catholic, living with her parents in the French mining village of La Talaudière, near Saint-Etienne:[80]

> I was in the garden with my father feeding our rabbits, when all of a sudden, by chance, I looked up at the sky and there I saw an angel. Wherever I looked, the angel was there. After a bit I told my father, but of course he didn't believe me too much. So I waited until my mother came back from market. When she arrived I told her what I had seen, but she told me to come into the house or people might hear me and think we were crazy. So we went indoors and I told everything and she didn't know what to say. Then I told it to all my family, none of them believed me and that's how it was till the end of September. Then, about the 15th of October, I left home to go to school. And the angel that I had seen in the garden spoke to me. He announced that I would see the Holy Virgin on 31 October in the kitchen at 16:25 and after that he vanished. I cannot explain how I felt, I can't find the words. All that I can say is that I awaited the day with impatience. I thought I was dreaming, I asked myself if all this could be true. I was sure that for me it was real, that the angel was speaking the truth. But there was still the matter of convincing all the others, but I put my trust in the Holy Virgin.
>
> So the first apparition took place on the 31 October in the kitchen. The Holy Virgin was very beautiful, never on Earth was there a woman like her. So beautiful, so beautiful. During the early days of the apparitions, she stayed from 5 to 10 minutes. Later, she wanted my father to be present at the apparitions, and after that, as she instructed me, I began to tell others about the apparitions. But seeing them all incredulous, I despaired. The Holy Virgin promised that she would make a sign, so that everyone would believe.
>
> The great sign took place on Easter Day (11 April 1982), she asked that a big crowd should gather. On the day, there were 30 coachloads, nearly 10,000 persons in all. To celebrate Easter, she made the sun turn: there was a dance of the sun, it changed colour. Other people saw other signs. It was so beautiful, the people cried out "Alleluia!" There were miracles of healing and all sorts of things. After that, the Holy Virgin appeared every Saturday and on the feasts of the Virgin. Her principal message is to pray and do penance. She has given me also some secrets: she asks many things concerning the Church. Mary wants the mass to be read in Latin, contrary to recent pronouncements by the Vatican. She complains much about the clergy. She recommends the use of the

rosary or the chaplet. She announces also terrible punishments if people do not convert.

Blandine was said by her schoolteacher to be epileptic, though this is unconfirmed: she seems in all other respects a healthy and balanced person. The apparitions were preceded by an outbreak of poltergeist phenomena in the Piégays' home – movements of furniture, unaccountable sounds. A neighbor compared it to being on board a ship during a storm. The angel who appeared is Sainte Nicole of Orly, unlisted in the catalogs of saints, but who, Blandine assures us, died at her own age, 14, and had become an angel. She told Blandine that in three weeks' time her periods would start, and then the domestic disturbances would cease. And indeed, so it happened.

Mary visited Blandine every Saturday, around 5 p.m. Her father, 80 percent blind, stayed in the room, hearing but not seeing the Virgin. Her brother, listening at the door, heard voices but saw nothing. Mary expressed a wish that a basilica, or at least a chapel, be erected in the Piegays' vegetable garden in honor of Notre-Dame de Talaudière. She then uttered threats – if the world continues to offend God, she will no longer be able to stay the hand of her son, there will be punishments. But she also gave good advice: Blandine should not eat so many sweets, and her father should not drink so much. She wished that the Church return to the Latin mass, that priests to go back to wearing the soutane (cassock), and that communion directly to the mouth be reinstituted– three points currently favored by Father Lefevre and his traditionalist followers who disagree with recent Catholic pronouncements. The parish priest was embarrassed by the affair, and though he recognized Blandine as a pious child, he doubted that her visions were authentic, and counseled her parents to prevent her spending too much time contemplating the images of saints.

But to his dismay, news of Blandine's encounters was already spreading, first among neighbors, then a letter from Blandine's mother to a friend, recounting the whole affair, was somehow picked up, copied, and distributed more widely, attracting people from far and wide. Already Blandine had looked for, and found, a "miraculous" spring, though in this mining district, where the ground is subject to subsidence and other effects, water is not hard to find. On April 11, Easter Day, crowds gathered in the thousands, though the newspapers reckoned it was closer to 3,000 than her 10,000. Among the pilgrims was the Abbé Krohn who would subsequently attack the Pope at Fatima.

The left-wing mayor, totally skeptical, moved among the crowds, warning them that they could ruin their eyesight by staring at the sun. Although Blandine claimed that Mary had given a "sign," no unambiguous miracle took place. "Numerous people claim to have seen, about 5 p.m., celestial signs, notably crosses in the sun, which began to rotate: one witness declared that it changed colour from mauve to red to green."[81] During the following days some thirty of the pilgrims received medical treatment for eye ailments. Others, hoping for a miracle cure, touched Blandine's dress or solicited her prayers. There were rumors that some had been healed.

Despite these claims, the lack of support from the Church, and the failure of Mary to present a more dramatic "sign," and perhaps Blandine's lack of charisma caused interest in the event to fade quite quickly. For a few weeks, though, Blandine was headline news. Thereafter, though she maintained the veracity of her experience, and the shrine erected in her orchard was devotedly maintained, the visionary faded from public sight. In Bouflet's *Faussaires de Dieu* she received a three-page mention, appearing not as a liar but as deluded, seeking refuge in a private world.[82]

Although apparitions of Mary vary considerably in detail, the main lines are generally pretty much the same, and there is scarcely a feature of Blandine's apparition experience that cannot be duplicated in other cases. Mary's demand that people repent or convert, for otherwise she will not be able to stay the wrathful arm of her son; the request for a basilica or at least a chapel; the "discovery" of a miraculous spring and the rumors of miraculous healing; the spinning, color-changing sun – all these make her experience stereotypical from start to finish. This is not to say that, for Blandine herself, the experience was nothing but delusion. Unquestionably it was not only real to her but profoundly meaningful. But it is likely that the reality, and the meaning, had relevance only to Blandine herself.

VIRGINIA FAINTING EPIDEMIC

Norfolk, Virginia: April 1967

Some 60 students fainted at the Ocean View Elementary School, in Norfolk. School physician, Dr. George Hand, described the incident as "simple fainting on the part of a few" that triggered "hysteria on the part of many."[83] About 60 children were affected, ranging in age from 9 to 13. A gas leak was initially suspected but was later ruled out. Thirty-eight of the children were examined at hospitals and released. All quickly recovered. The episode lasted four hours.[84]

Dr. Hand said, "I've read about things like this, but you have to see it to believe it." According to a local reporter, Dr. Hand, the school's on-call physician, was joined by "15 police cars, six motorcycles, three fire engine companies and four deputy chiefs' cars which converged on the school..."[85]

VIRTUAL LIFE

Worldwide: Late 20th/Early 21st century

The opening years of the 21st century are witnessing a remarkable transformation of the computer game into a lifestyle behavior, drawing millions of "players" into participation in a community activity that, apart from constituting one of the most massive manifestations of extraordinary group behavior in this Encyclopedia, bears far-reaching implications for the behavioral sciences. In the words of "Isador" on the Second Life website, "Second Life is not a game, it's a virtual world"[86] or as a headline in *New Scientist* expressed it, "A life less ordinary offers far more than just escapism."[87]

CONTEXT: Computer games were a natural exploitation of the personal computer as a game-playing device, enabling players to find entertainment in cleverly constructed situational scenarios in which they were not passive spectators but active participants. Through the last decades of the 20th century, these became more elaborate and sophisticated, requiring players to deploy considerable skill within the situations devised by the manufacturers, developing strategies and role-playing techniques. By the early 21st century, these games had reached a high degree of complexity and were played avidly by millions worldwide. By the end of 2005 the Chinese government estimated 24 million players in China alone. In 2007, a reasonable guess would have more than 50 million players worldwide and growing rapidly. Already by October 2002 it was estimated that 80 percent of South Koreans under 25 were playing games, and Korean psychiatrist Kim Hyun Soo observed that "game players don't have social relationships anymore. Young people are losing the ability to relate to others, except through games." Traditional group activities are being replaced by computer gaming, often with worrying consequences: "People who become addicted are prone to violence even when they are not playing. They clash in the games, and then they meet later and fight face to face." [88]

For the most part, the scenarios are harmless escapism: players compete in sporting events or zap hostile forces in fantastic adventures such as dungeons & dragons, combatting space invaders, monsters and menaces of every kind. The majority is competitive and even aggressive, and there is considerable concern at the climate of violence they engender. Then, around 2003, an astonishing development took place: games were created in which players were invited, not simply to participate in a scenario devised by others, but to enter as individuals. They were encouraged to create secondary personas for themselves (known as avatars) who, rather than act within the constraints of a programmed scenario, were free to "be themselves" – which can of course involve fantasy adventures if they choose, but can also be something as straightforward as purchasing property, wearing new clothes, and adopting new lifestyles. Virtual currency is used to pay for virtual items; on Second Life the currency is Linden Dollars, worth some 170 to the real-world dollar.

Such a development, seeking an outlet for self-expression by transcending the limits of real life, is not in itself astonishing. There have been foreshadowings throughout history, and it could be argued that most of literature and drama are tentative searches for second lives.

Imperfection in the real world has always existed. This is why people kept working hard to change the real world or to create things like literature or movies.

We regard virtual reality as one very powerful tool to enable people to do things that they could never do in real life. For some of us that might mean flying or living in a villa. For IBM it might mean company meetings with people across the planet. For some it might mean leading a social life again, like some of our friends who are ill and cannot leave their bed. Quoting Anshe Chung:[89] "But only with computer technology – the possibilities made available by the worldwide web – did what had hitherto been individual fantasy explode into a communal one: the fantasy that everyone, anyone, could create for themselves a second persona and live an alternative life as that second self."

This new development has been a phenomenal success: the scale of "virtual emigration" is mind-boggling. The most sophisticated of the sites, Second Life, created in 2003, claimed some 9 million "residents" by summer 2007. Other English-language sites include "There," "Active Worlds," and for adult visitors, "Red Light Center," and there are surely others worldwide, especially in Asia. Even though the claimed figures do not necessarily reflect active and continuous participation, the scale of these activities is remarkable: huge numbers of people are spending a significant part of their lives as fantasy beings in a fantasy world largely of their own making.

Because it is user-defined rather than imposed by the manufacturer, participation in sites like Second Life can embrace an almost unlimited range of activities and behavior. At the immediate level, residents can choose their appearance – customize their bodies and their clothing – and select from a menu of gestures, enabling their avatars to mimic real-life movements such as bowing or blowing kisses. Once they have acquired a virtual body, they can interact socially, join virtual communities, purchase virtual property, and attend classes, workshops, and other group activities. Guidance is provided at every stage. Membership is initially free, though as activities become more elaborate, expenses accrue – to purchase virtual property, for example.

Increasingly, schools and universities are coming to appreciate the value of virtual-world simulations as learning tools. Second Life has more than 100 virtual "islands" for educational purposes. Teaching Islands offer a range of educational resources, ranging from workshops on specific topics to a visitable planetarium. Libraries create virtual reference desks staffed by real-life librarians. Because of the global character of virtual facilities, resources that were beyond the reach of individual establishments become available to students. When so much has already been achieved in so brief a period of time, the future potential of virtual-world environments is unlimited. These spaces are no longer just a place for individuals to interact through computer-mediated reality, but instead become significant structures and mechanisms of social order and cooperation within the real world.[90]

Psychosocial Implications

Second Life participation/activity has obvious similarities to many forms of behavior, some of which are featured elsewhere in this Encyclopedia. Dissociation and multiple personality are the most obvious, but many activities on the frontiers of human personality and experience, some of them spontaneous (such as lucid dreaming), others intentional (such as spiritualism and automatic writing), have caused people to behave in ways suggestive of a secondary, alternative personality.

True, the second selves of Second Life are not real, but virtual. But that is equally true of the fantasy lives lived by the alters of multiple personality disorder, or the possessors of imaginary companions, or the victims of diseases such as Capgras or Munchhausen syndromes. The fact that some are voluntary, others involuntary, may not be as significant as at first appears, because *any* form of behavior can be revealing of subconscious hopes, wishes, fears, or anxieties.

"People come to virtual worlds," said Philip Rosedale, the CEO of Second Life, "sometimes because they think they can be more anonymous, and hide behind a pretended identity with greater skill than in the real world. But Second Life is going to pull out of you a little more than you wanted to say. You go into it thinking you're in control. I think what happens is, you're not in control."[91]

As with multiple personalities and other psychological strategies, so the "second life" process can be seen as a life-enhancing strategy with positive therapeutic value. Thus William Wise, dissatisfied with life as a male, was enabled to realize his ambition to live as a female thanks to his female avatar: "I liked myself so much better as Jani – she was fun, happy, even bold and witty, while the real-life me was overwhelmed with fear and self-doubt." [92] As Tim Guest discovered: "A journey into virtual worlds also becomes a journey into the self." [93] At the same time, Second Life offers the opportunity for an infinite diversity of educational, environmental, and social experiences. Thus a simulation of imprisonment in the notorious American prison at Guantanamo Bay enables visitors – in their virtual personas - to experience what it is like to be arrested and imprisoned. As Anil Ananthaswamy observed, "Second Life has morphed from a virtual playground into a force for change in the real world."[94]

A notable instance of Second Life experience is its use by the disabled, enabling them to live virtual lives free from their disabilities. Already there are indications that this can be beneficial, though there could well be a downside if residents feel frustrated because only in their fantasy lives can they enjoy such freedom. Moreover, it is evident that such a resource could be used for evil as well as beneficent purposes. Already there have been episodes of "gang" assaults, such as virtual vandalizing targeting the virtual sites of perceived "enemies."[95] Nevertheless, the potential is infinite, and overwhelmingly positive. The "second life" concept could even be perpetuated to confer a kind of immortality: one Second Life resident offers, for a fee, to continue your virtual self's life after your real death.[96]

Sources

1. Kharabsheh, S., Al-Otoum, H., Clements, J., Abbas, A., Khuri-Bulos, N., Belbesi, A., Gaafar, T., and Dellepiane, N. (2001). "Mass Psychogenic Illness Following Tetanus-Diphtheria Toxoid Vaccination in Jordan." *Bulletin of the World Health Organization* 79(8):764-770. 2001;79(8):764-770. See p. 769.

2. Yasamy, M.T., Bahramnezhad, A., and Ziaaddini, H. (1999). "Post-vaccination Mass Psychogenic Illness on an Iranian Rural School." *East Mediterranean Health Journal* 5(4):710-715.

3. Kharabsheh, op cit., p. 765.

4. Kharabsheh, op cit., p. 765.

5. Kharabsheh, op cit., p. 767.

6. Mackay, Caitlin (2000). "Jab Fears Spark School Hysteria." *The Mirror*, March 21, p. 12.

7. Mackay, op cit.

8. Oakeshott, Isabel (2000). *Scottish Daily Record*, March 21, p. 15.

9. D'Argenio, P., Citarella, A., Intorcia, M., and Aversano, G. (1996). "An Outbreak of Vaccination Panic." *Vaccine* 14(13):1289-1290 (September).

10. Peiro EF, Yanez JL, Carraminana I, Rullan JV, Castell J. (1996). "Study of an outbreak of hysteria after hepatitis B vaccination" (in Spanish). *Med Clin* (Barc) 107(1):1-3 (June 1).

11. Djata, Itcha (2001). "Reports of Poison Vaccine Sow Panic in Congo." *Congo Kinshasa News*, http://www.afrol.com/ News2001/ drc011_polio_ poison.htm, accessed April 18, 2003.

12. Djata, op cit.

13. Djata, op cit.

14. Anonymous (1995). "Tiff Over Anti-Tetanus Vaccine now Erupted into Battle. International (Philippines)." *Vaccine Weekly* (July 24):11-13.

15. Wright, Dudley (1924). *Vampires and Vampirism*. London: Rider, p. 5.

16. MacCullough, J.A., in Hastings 1921, volume 12, p. 591.

17. Skeat, Walter William (1900). *Malay Magic*. London: Macmillan, p. 328.

18. Summers, Montague (1928). *The Vampire, his Kith and Kin*. London: Kegan Paul, Trench, Trubner & Company; Summers, Montague (1929). *The Vampire in Europe*. New York: E.P. Dutton.

19. Freud 1912, p. 59.

20. Summers, 1928, op cit., p. 13.

21. Ronay, Gabriel (1972). *The Dracula Myth*. London: W H Allen, p. 68.

22. McNally and Florescu 1972: passim.

23. Summers, 1929, op cit., p. 88

24. Mayo, Herbert. (1851). *On the Truths Contained in Popular Superstitions*. Edinburgh: Blackwood, p. 24 et seq.

25. Wright, op cit., p. 80.

26. Johann Heinrich Zopfius, in *Dissertatio de Vampiris Serviensibus*, Halle 1733.

27. Calmet, Dom Augustin (1746). *Dissertations sur les Apparitions des Anges, des Demons et des Esprits, et sur les Revenans et Vampires*. Paris: De Bure l'Ainé, p. 399.

28. Mayo, op cit., p. 31.

29. Barber, Paul (1988). *Vampires, Burial and Death*. New Haven: Yale University Press, p. 119.

30. Barber, op cit., p. 125.

31. Ronay, op cit., p. 21.

32. Ronay, op cit., p. 31.

33. Diderot and D'Alembert (circa 1760). *Encyclopédie Universelle*. Paris, entry entitled 'Vampire.'

34. Melton, J. Gordon (1994). *The Vampire Book*. Detroit: Gale research, p. 463.

35. Hartmann, Franz (1895). *Buried Alive*. Boston: Occult Publishing House, p. 101.

36. Barber, op cit., p. 100.

37. Robert S. McCully, "A Case of Auto-vampirism," in Noll, op cit., p. 48. Noll, Richard (1992). *Vampires, Werewolves and Demons*. New York: Brunner/Mazel.

38. Noll, op cit., 17.

39. Hemphill, R.E., and Zabow, T., "Clinical Vampirism," in Noll, op cit., p. 62.

40. Melton, op cit., p. 633.

41. de Lamothe-Langon, E.L. (1988). *Les après-diners de S.A.S. Cambacères*, cited in Mozzani 1988, p. 212.
42. Shay, V.B. (1949). "James Brown, Vampire." *Fate Magazine*, November, p. 59.
43. "Human Vampire." *Fate Magazine* (March, 1953), p. 46.
44. Hemphill & Zabow in Noll, op cit., p. 66.
45. Case history compiled from internet sources: BBC Crime case closed, author Chris Summers, and Serial Killers Casefiles, both 2003.
46. Hemphill & Zabow in Noll, op cit., p. 61 et seq.
47. Richer, Paul (1885). *Etudes Cliniques de la Grande Hystérie*. Paris: Delahaye et Lecrossnier, p. 858; Prouvost, Maurice Emile Léon Théodore (1896). *Le Délire Prophétique: étude Historique et Clinique*. Doctoral thesis. Bordeaux: Cassignol, p. 80.
48. Laurentin, René (1991). *Le 20 Janvier 1842 Marie pparait à Alphonse Ratisbonne, and Preuves et Documents sur L'apparition de Marie à Alphonse Ratisbonne*. Paris: O.E.I.L.
49. Bertin, Georges (Director) (1999). *Apparitions/Disparitions*. Paris: Desclée de Brouwer.
50. Notably Sivric, Ivo (1989). *The Hidden Side of Medjugorje*. Saint-François-du-Lac, Québec: Psilog. Originally published in French, *La Face Cachée de Medjugorje* 1988.
51. Bouflet, Joachim (1999). *Thérèse Neumann*. Paris: Editions du Rocher; Bouflet, Joachim (2000). *Faussaires de Dieu*. Paris: Presses de la Renaissance.
52. Turi, Anna-Maria (1988). *Pourquoi la Vierge Apparaît Aujourd'hui*. Paris: Félin.
53. Laurentin, René (1988). *Multiplication des Apparitions de la Vierge Aujourd'hui*. Paris: Fayard.
54. Bur, Jacques (1994). *Pour Comprendre la Vierge Marie*. New York: Continuum. Translated as *How to Understand the Virgin Mary*,1992, p. 124.
55. Notably Garabandal 1961, San Damiano 1961, Bayside 1970, Medjugorje 1981.
56. Laurentin 1988, op cit., p. 18.
57. Turi, op cit., p. 31.
58. Turi, op cit., passim.
59. Turi, op cit., p. 83.
60. Tizané, E. (1977). *Les Apparitions de la Vierge*. Paris: Tchou.
61. Laurentin, René (1957). *Lourdes, Documents Authentiques*. Paris: Lethielleux, volume 7, p. 52.
62. Fernandes, Joaquim, and D'Armada, Fina (1981). *Intervençåo Extraterrestre em Fatima*. Lisbon: Libraria Bertrand, p. 32.
63. Laurentin 1988, op cit., p. 33.
64. Tizané, op cit., p. 299.
65. For example Pontmain (1870), Fatima (1917), Garabandal (1961), Medjugorje (1981).
66. Sanchez-Ventura y Pascual, Francisco (1966). *La Vierge est-elle Apparue à Garabandal?* [translated from Spanish *Las Apariciones no son un mito by M & G du Pilier*] Paris: Nouvelles Editions Latines.
67. Joyeux, Henri, et Laurentin, René (1985). *Etudes medicales et Scientifiques sur les Apparitions de Medjugorje*. Paris: OEIL.
68. Press report in *La Vanguardia*, 9 June 1984: her recantation is not accepted by believers.
69. Michel de la Sainte Trinité, Frère (1991). *Medjugorje en Toute Vérité*. Saint-Parres-lès-Vaudes: Contre-Reforme Catholique, p. 344.
70. Michel, op cit.; Michel de la Sainte Trinité, Frère (1983). *Toute la Vérité sur Fatima*. Saint-Parres-lès-Vaudes: Renaissance Catholique.
71. Laurentin cited by Turi, op cit., p. 49.
72. Laurentin 1988, op cit., p. 15.
73. Bertin, op cit., p. 270: Sivric, op cit., passim.
74. Huysmans, Joris-Karl (1906). *Les Foules de Lourdes*. Paris: Stock.
75. For a fairly straightforward exposition, see Bur, op cit., 1992.
76. Carroll, Michael P. (1986). *The Cult of the Virgin Mary*. Princeton University Press, p. 144.
77. Jung, Carl Gustav (1954). Psychological Aspects of the Mother Archetype. [translated from German Von den Wurzeln des Bewusstseins.] Zurich: Rascher, in *Collected Works Volume 9*, Part 1, p. 81.
78. Graves, Robert (1948). *The White Goddess*. London: Faber & Faber; Ashe, Geoffrey (1976). *The Virgin*. London: Routledge & Kegan Paul.
79. Evans, Hilary (1984). *Visions, Apparitions, Alien Visitors*. Wellingborough: Aquarian, p. 103; Evans, Hilary (1987). *Gods, Spirits, Cosmic Guardians*. Wellingborough: Aquarian, p. 51, etc.
80. Blandine's account is from a personal communication (Evans), supplemented by items from the periodicals of the time.
81. *France-Soir*, 13 April 1982.
82. Bouflet 2000, op cit., p. 189.
83. "Epidemic of Fainting Spells." *Syracuse Herald-Journal*, April 15, 1967, p. 1.
84. "Epidemic of Fainting Spells." op cit.
85. "60 Pupils Faint in Brief Epidemic." *The Gettysburg Times*, April 17, 1967, p. 6.
86. Second Life website, August 2007.
87. *New Scientist*, 25 August 2007, p. 26.
88. French, Howard W. (2002). "Korea's real rage for Virtual Games." *New York Times*, 9 October.
89. Guest, Timothy (2007). *Second Lives: A Journey Through Virtual Worlds*. New York: Random House, p. 335.
90. Wikipedia: Emerging Virtual Institutions.
91. Guest, op cit., pp. 78-79.
92. *New Scientist*, 25 August 2007.
93. Guest, op cit., p. 80.
94. *New Scientist*, 25 August 2007.
95. *New Scientist*, 1 September 2007.
96. Guest, op cit., p. 342.

WACKY WALLWALKER FAD

The result of a brilliant advertising strategy and willingness to take a risk, Harvard business graduate Kenneth Hakuta was running Tradex, a modest import-export business in 1982 when Japanese relatives sent him some *takos* – a popular octopus-like toy that when hurled against a wall would stick and slowly descend by the pull of gravity, one limb over the other.[1] After obtaining rights to sell the toy in the U.S. under the name "Wacky Wallwalker," Hakuta had to overcome another hurdle – he had no advertising budget. Hakuta made the rounds to different toy stores, tossing his WallWalker against a wall and the toy "sold itself."[2] After an initial wave of interest, sales began to drop, so in a bold effort to rekindle his fad, he refused to sell any more of the toys or to allow anyone to license the name or image. He then made agreements with major companies like Kellogg's and persuaded them to give WallWalkers away as a prize. Kelloggs agreed and sold 75 million boxes with WallWalkers.[3] Described by some as "Dr. Fad," Hakuta wrote and promoted a popular book: *How to Create a Fad and Make a Million Dollars*.[4]

CONTEXT: The success of the Wacky Wallwalker seems to have rested with the boldness, tenacity, and business savvy of Kenneth Hakuta.

Hakuta made $20 million dollars by selling 220 million Wallwalkers over a five-year period before the fad faded.[5] Japanese manufacturers could produce the toy for about 20 cents each. Hakuta would buy them for about 33 cents, ship them by air to the U.S., paying an import duty of 12.3%, then sell them to retailers or wholesalers for about 75 cents, for which they would be typically sold for $1.50 to $2.00.[6]

See also: FADS.

WASHING MANIA

India: 20th century

Psychiatrist Dhirendra Nath Nandi of the Girindra Sekhar Clinic in Calcutta reports encountering an unusual case of psychological contagion sometime prior to 1985 in a small village in West Bengal, India – the same village that a WIFE ABUSE HYSTERIA had taken place. One day an educated housewife began exhibiting what locals refer to as "washing mania." Soon several other village women reported "catching" the mania which involved the exhibition of compulsive rituals. Each morning the woman would recite the Ramayana and the Mahabharata, two of India's classic scriptural tales, during which time women from the neighborhood would gather around and admire her storytelling. Soon, four audience members "developed 'washing' rituals identical to those of the revered storyteller."[7] Nandi states that the woman involved was clearly highly respected by fellow villagers, being wealthy, well educated, and intelligent. "She held a special position among the women because of [an] ability to read and interpret tales, that would otherwise have been inaccessible to the literate women."[8] When the four regular listeners also exhibited the washing rituals, their relatives were agitated and stopped them from attending any more recitals. Three of the women soon stopped engaging in the rituals, while a fourth who was believed suffering from obsessive-compulsive disorder continued to engage in the ritual.[9]

CONTEXT: Within the mass hysteria literature,

it is well established that many episodes are triggered by a socially dominant group member who initially exhibits certain signs or symptoms and who quickly become imitated by other members. Unfortunately, the specific nature of the washing rituals are not discussed.

WATER MONSTER PANIC

Shanghai, China: August 1947

An "amphibious monster" scare claimed its third victim when a cargo boat employee leaped into the Whangpoo River and drowned after hearing screams that he attributed to the creature. Earlier, two people were beaten to death after panic-stricken residents believed they were somehow linked to the monster. Thousands of boat people were keeping a nightly vigil, standing watch to protect the community from the creature.[10]

WEATHER AND HUMAN BEHAVIOR

The effect on human behavior of climate in general, and prevailing weather conditions in particular, has been the subject of substantial speculation, though only limited research. However, there is persuasive scientific evidence to confirm the popular perception that certain climatic conditions affect individual behavior. Little attention has been paid to possible effects on collective behavior, but there are grounds for thinking that they could be a contributing factor.

For example, studies by Israeli scientist Felix Gad Sulman show that "weather-sensitive patients encompass about 30% of any population, no matter of what ethnic origin."[11] He concentrated particularly on the effects of the hot, dry winds that are traditionally associated throughout the Mediterranean region with unpleasant effects on health and behavior. He found that when the Sharav of the eastern Mediterranean is blowing, nearly half of a sample population displayed an irritation syndrome due to serotonin hyperproduction, resulting in tension, irritability etc., and a similar proportion displayed an exhaustion syndrome due to adrenal deficiency, resulting in depression and apathy. Moreover, 13% displayed an intermittent thyroid syndrome due to latent hyperthyreosis, resulting in tension, irritability, confusion, and anxiety.

The Sharav produces these effects because it carries a high proportion of positively charged ions, generated by the friction of sand particles. (Despite their labels, negative ions have a beneficial effect on health, while positive ions are harmful.) Similar conditions are brought about by the Föhn, a wind that blows in Alpine regions, though here the positive ions are produced by whirling snow on the mountain ridges.[12]

Such conditions can also occur in artificial contexts. Indoor environments without sufficient negative ions exert an adverse effect on morale and performance. For example, tests in a Swiss textile mill showed a loss of 22 working days in an area where negative ionizers were installed as against 64 in an identical area without ionizers. Similarly, a Johannesburg bank, where staff had complained of headaches and irritability, reported that when ionizers were installed absenteeism dropped, operator error fell from 2.5% to 0.5%, and staff morale soared.[13]

Though the findings are piecemeal and sometimes ambiguous, it has been shown that changes in the weather correlate with statistics for suicide and aggressive crime. Neurotics, psychopaths, alcoholics, and drug addicts were found to be specially affected by Dutch researcher Solco Tromp who investigated several such effects. He concluded that "there is hardly an organ of the human body which escapes the effects of changes in the meteorological environment, and these effects are reflected either directly or indirectly in the mental processes of man."[14]

Helmut Tributsch, in his study of prediction of earthquakes by animals, affirmed that they sense forthcoming weather changes by sensing changes in air electricity. These may precede pressure changes by 24 to 48 hours, so that animals become "aware" of menacing weather long before any outward signs are observed, and take appropriate action. Deer, for example, congregate in the open rather than in the forest, or near young trees, which are not likely to be felled by high winds.[15]

While animals are apparently more sensitive than humans to such indications, it is clearly possible that humans may also be affected by such changes without being consciously aware of them, and that their behavior could be influenced thereby. Though such subtle influences are probably unlikely to be more than a contributing factor to human behavior, it could well be an enabling, and even a precipitating, factor in some cases of extraordinary behavior. This could take place directly, affecting a crowd *en masse*, but perhaps more probably indirectly, affecting in the first place one of Sulman's "weather-sensitives," triggering behavior that communicates to others by suggestion or imitation.

See also: LUNAR INFLUENCE.

WELSH PEDOPHILE PANIC

North Wales: 1960s to the present

The tragic saga of the hunt for an alleged pedophile ring operating within the social services and police force in North Wales in the late 20th/early 21st century is a classic example of interplay between media rashness and official over-reaction, public concern and private opportunism. The result of this dangerous mix was a sustained investigation that has been compared to a witch-hunt, which led to hundreds of innocent persons being convicted of wrongdoing and thousands more besmirched by association.[16]

Allegations that abuse was taking place in 75% or even 100% of care homes (institutions where homeless or deprived children, mostly adolescent boys, are looked after by the authorities) in Wales coincided with an outbreak of satanic abuse claims in America and to a lesser extent in Britain. (See SATANIC ABUSE.) In Wales, as in the U.S., allegations that under normal circumstances would have been seen to be implausible, and frequently impossible, were accepted with minimal, if any, checking and acted upon regardless of their wider implications. Contrary to normal procedures, where official action is a response to discovered fact or spontaneous accusation, the majority of these allegations were obtained as the result of "trawling" – that is, the authorities, acting on the presumption that criminal acts had indeed taken place, questioned everyone who might have been a victim of such acts, witnessed them, or knew of them. While on the face, this procedure seems an effective way of circumventing the natural reluctance of witnesses to testify, it is potentially dangerous as it is liable to produce fabricated accusations or false memories "recalled" by suggestible people. Such procedures, coupled with the flagrant manipulation of public opinion by the media, which like the authorities were convinced that the allegations were founded on fact, constituted extraordinary behavior of a very sinister kind.

This over-response was not, of course, without some basis in fact. Inevitably, where many hundreds of care workers were involved in caring for many thousands of adolescents, occasional instances of sexual abuse did indeed occur, and a few isolated individuals were correctly convicted. But the great majority of accusations were found to be without substance, and not a scrap of evidence was found to support allegations of an organized pedophile ring.[17]

In 1984, a 42-year-old social worker, Alison Taylor, made statements to the North Wales Police asserting that abuse had taken place at Bryn Estyn, the care home where she had been briefly employed, though previously she had written favorably of her ten-week stay there without any suggestion that she was aware of any wrong-doing. When police investigation revealed no abuse, she made further accusations, and as a result was dismissed from her post in 1987. Maintaining her charges, she became the principal source of allegations of abuse at this and other care homes. When the police failed to find any substance to her allegations, she extended her claims to embody a cover-up by the authorities to conceal the existence of organized pedophilia whereby the authorities conspired to victimize the boys in their care.[18]

"The idea that children in North Wales care homes had fallen prey to an extensive pedophile ring and that senior police officers might be a part of this ring, and were systematically interfering with any investigations designed to expose it, was a compelling one. The proposition that such a conspiracy of evil had been accidentally uncovered by a lone residential social worker, who had been sacked for trying to expose it, was almost as intriguing."[19] Although, when checking Taylor's allegations, a lawyer found at least 32 of them to be without substance, the media saw her as a courageous whistleblower who had dared to disclose a massive and widespread scandal to which authorities at a high level were party.[20] Sensing a story of great public interest, the *Independent on Sunday*, a generally responsible paper much respected for its fearless investigative journalism, sent a reporter to investigate. With Taylor as his principal informant, Dean Nelson submitted an article that the paper, with only perfunctory hesitation and without seeking confirmation, published in December 1991. Given the prevailing social climate, the story snowballed.

The effect of these "disclosures," seemingly well documented, naming names and locations, at a time when the myth of ritual abuse had yet to be debunked and related cases in Britain were fresh in the public memory, was decisive. Other newspapers and television had no choice but to follow where the *Independent* had led. In turn, as the media assailed them with further "revelations," the general public could hardly doubt that a massive and widespread public scandal was indeed being brought to light. This public concern, in its turn, forced the authorities to inquire more deeply into the matter. Thus began what would become the largest police inquiry into organized sexual abuse, or indeed into any form of child abuse, in the whole of the British Isles. Before it had run its course, more than three thousand statements would be taken from more than two thousand witnesses.[21]

The great majority of these statements were accepted at face value. In fact, simple investigation would have shown the implausibility of many of them. Some suspects had incompatible sexual orientations, such as heterosexuals being accused of homosexual abuse.[22] One man, after watching a television documentary in 1997, "recalled" that he had been abused by a particular staff member, yet the latter did not arrive at Bryn Estyn till three years after the youth left and the two never met. Another witness told of watching a staffer performing oral sex with a boy, but it was subsequently shown that the man's flat could not be seen from the dormitory window where the accuser claimed to be.[23] A further witness claimed to have been sexually abused by 49 different people, and physically abused by 26; lawyers who examined his case concluded it was "a transparent fabrication."

Such false accusations were the result of the way the allegations were obtained. Transcripts show that police systematically asked leading questions during the trawling operations. Thus one witness, questioned at the tribunal, told how he had been asked "had I witnessed any sexual abuse from Mr. H, had I been abused, did I know anyone that was being abused, them sort of questions."[24] Another highlighted the attraction of financial compensation as an incentive to fabricate claims: "When the police from North Wales took a statement at my address, they told me, if I was abused, I would get money in compensation. I was just dumbfounded when he came out with it...I feel that most people thought they would get compensation just saying it, that's why most people have come forward, trying to make a quick buck out of the system...the police putting pressure on people to come forward saying you get compensation. I am willing to bet my life on it that when I went there in 1975 to 1977 no person was abused by staff at Bryn Estyn school."[25]

However obtained and however dubious, the mounting heap of testimony persuaded the public, as it had the media, that the abuse had been real, and that Bryn Estyn must be the center of an organized pedophile ring. North Wales Police, accused not only of involvement in the crime but also of seeking to cover it up, felt compelled to take action. As dawn broke on Sunday March 15, 1992, a force of some forty police officers swooped simultaneously on the homes of 17 people, arresting 16 men and one woman, all but one of them former Bryn Estyn staff, searching their homes, seizing videos and photographs. They included people who had been universally admired and liked and against whom – until these allegations – no criticism had been made. "Why the North Wales Police chose to make their arrests in this dramatic manner has never been made clear. The only possible explanation, however, is that they still entertained a real suspicion that Bryn Estyn was at the centre of an organised pedophile ring and it was this that made the simultaneous arrests necessary."[26]

According to police figures, at least 650 adolescents claimed they had been subjected to physical or sexual abuse while in care in Welsh homes over the twenty-year period of the 1970s-1980s. Allegations were made against 365 different people in 30 homes. One consequence was to implicate by association *every* social worker, whether specifically accused or not. At Bryn Estyn, for example, if the allegations were true, it would not have been possible for anyone working there not to be aware of what was going on. Consequently all were considered guilty, if not of participating, then of complicity by keeping quiet. "The publicity was horrendous…we were hammered, absolutely hammered," said one of the victims of this wholesale accusation.[27]

Yet, by the end of 1995, only five people had been prosecuted and only four convicted as a result of the police investigation. It might have been supposed that this was because the others were innocent; instead, as whistleblower Taylor had suggested, the authorities were accused of mounting a cover-up to conceal the fact that police officers were members of the pedophile ring they were supposed to be investigating. One high-ranking officer was actually named in the *Independent's* article as having raped adolescent boys at Bryn Estyn. In November 1994, he successfully sued for libel this newspaper and other media that repeated the accusation. Yet even after this verdict, the authorities failed to realize the necessity of looking more closely at the allegations they received.

To clear up the situation, in 1996 a tribunal was set up under sir Robert Waterhouse. It was the largest Tribunal of Inquiry in British history. It would take two years to hear the evidence and compile its report, *Lost in Care*, at an estimated cost of £15 million. It was clear from the outset that the Tribunal was acting in the belief that there was genuine substance to the accusations. "There seemed to be a presumption that abuse on a massive scale had taken place…given the wording of these terms of reference the Tribunal could be forgiven for concluding that its principal task was to confirm the reality of such abuse and not to investigate whether it had taken place."[28] Its conclusion was that "the evidence before us has disclosed that for many children who were consigned to Bryn Estyn, in the 10 or so years of its existence as a community home, it was a form of purgatory or worse from which they emerged more damaged than when they had entered and for whom the future had become even more bleak." Though this ran counter to abundant testimony from the former inmates of the home, the account rendered by the tribunal was generally accepted by the media, and consequently by the public who had no reason to doubt that the story unearthed by the police and by investigative journalists was based on thorough and meticulous investigation of the allegations.

Alison Taylor, whose claims had triggered the whole matter, was now hailed as a popular heroine who, despite rejection of her claims and sacking from her post, had dared to blow the whistle on the scandal. As a result, she was the recipient of widespread media attention and public admiration. Yet she herself, along with the journalists and officials to whom she had passed her dubious information and helped to fabricate claims, must have been aware that many if not most of their accusations were dubious at best and were often outright invention. Their only justification could have been that they were acting in a good cause.

In their zeal to establish the facts, the authorities, here as in the satanic abuse epidemic in the United States, failed to appreciate the effects of the psychological climate within which the testimony was obtained: "All of this creates a situation ripe for false allegations of abuse—which, it should be stressed, often does not mean stories that are consciously or systematically made up. False allegations are fundamentally untrue. However, in a climate where individuals are continually confronted with the possibility they may have been abused and the awareness that their peers were allegedly abused, and when they are offered rewards for saying they were abused, they become highly suggestible, to the point where it is possible for them to believe that they were abused by a particular person in a particular way, even if it never happened in reality."[29]

Not all the evidence went unquestioned. When in 2000 former football manager David Jones, a well-known and widely respected figure, went on trial for alleged abuse crimes, skepticism was widely voiced and he was cleared of the charges. But this was not enough for people to have second thoughts about other accused people who might have been equally innocent. It was not until 2005, when Richard Webster published the massive result of his investigations, that an alternative narrative of the matter was made available to the public.

COMMENT: Webster estimates that by year's end 2004, the investigating authorities had received allegations from some ten thousand former residents of care homes, in consequence of which some seven to nine thousand care workers had been placed under suspicion, if not faced with outright accusation. Most of these were not formally charged, but in every case lives were blighted and a great many careers wrecked, even apart from the 100 or so people who he claims were wrongfully convicted.[30] "From the day that the *Independent on Sunday* published its sensational story about North Wales, what had come into being was a narrative of immense power. Given the fact that this story was rapidly accepted by politicians, senior police officers and social workers, it was all but inevitable, in view of its ingredients, that a witch-hunt would result."[31] The broader implications of Webster's investigation were widely recognized. Professor Mary de Young, of Grand Valley State University, commented: "From a sociological point of view it is particularly interesting, because it does reveal that moral panics are not always fueled by wild speculation, outrageous emotions or wide-eyed zealots. Instead they can be based on reasonable claims (whether true or false), the requisite emotional response to those claims, and by well-intentioned, although almost always quite self-interested, people."[32]

However, not everyone was convinced by Webster's investigation. The abuse of children is an emotional subject that discourages a cool, rational approach. Despite six hundred pages that documented countless errors and shortcomings, falsification and fabrications, exaggeration and prejudice on the part both of the investigating authorities and of the media, many remained convinced that wholesale abuse had indeed taken place over two decades, concealed by a conspiracy of silence that ensured that only now, when the spotlight of media and public attention was directed to it, was the truth emerging. In May 2005, Wrexham Council refused permission for a public meeting at which Webster was to have been a speaker.[33]

Yet, despite the immense publicity that had been directed to the Welsh care homes and everyone associated with them, despite the far-reaching investigations conducted over many years, not a scrap of evidence was ever found that a pedophile ring, or anything like it, ever existed. The allegations on which this fantasy was erected were shown, in countless instances, to be unfounded or contradicted by the facts. Instead, the media, the authorities, and the general public allowed themselves, in all sincerity, to be deluded into acceptance of a myth that embodied their deep-seated fears.

WELSH REVIVAL

Wales: 1904-1905

The religious revival among the Protestant Christians of Wales, in 1904-1905, resembled other such revivals in its general features – the seemingly spontaneous upsurge of religious feeling in diverse locations, the rapid spread of enthusiasm from one community to another, the intense display of emotion, the influence of charismatic preachers, and the widespread repentance and conversions in which sinners claimed to "find God" and to be "born again."

The feature that distinguished this particular revival was the extraordinary proliferation of ostensibly paranormal happenings, observed so widely as to constitute a collective phenomenon of interest to

Egryn Chapel, North Wales, is a focal point during the well-witnessed luminous manifestations which seemed to accompany the revivalistic preaching of Mary Jones.

students not only of religious behavior but also sociologists, anthropologists, and psychical researchers. Though treated as marginal by historians of the revival,[34] these phenomena attracted considerable attention at the time not only among those participating in the revival but by people who read of them in the national media. A century later these phenomena await a satisfactory explanation. What might have passed, in other circumstances, as one-off individual experiences, became, in this particular context, a collective expression of the emotionality engendered by the climate of the revival.

CONTEXT: A feature of religious life in Wales, among the predominantly Methodist and Baptist communities, was the periodic outbreak of revivals intended to revivify the faith of those already within the church and to recruit new adherents into the fold.[35] In 1904, it was widely felt that the country was due for such a revival. A newspaper correspondent spoke of "low attendance at Sunday services, fellowship and prayer meetings, of a decline in Bible reading and family worship. The remedy proposed was a penitent and humble pleading with God for another divine visitation in revival throughout the land."[36]

We are not here concerned with the history of the revival. What is relevant, however, is the intensity with which it was taken up by the community and the fervor with which religious ideas became matters of everyday debate. It was this ferment that provided the setting for the phenomena, and which presumably caused them to occur. Throughout the country, meetings large and small were marked with displays of emotion, cries of guilt and repentance, and pleas for divine help. At a meeting led by the charismatic preacher Evan Roberts, "the whole congregation fell on their knees and in their fervor beat upon the seats and became almost beside themselves in their frenzy." Roberts also observed: "Order gave place to confusion. Some were shouting 'No more, Lord Jesus, or I die!' others cried for mercy. The noise of weeping, singing and praising, together with the sight of many who had fainted or lay prostrate on the ground in an agony of conviction, was as unbelievable as it was unprecedented."[37] The journalist W. T. Stead said of a meeting he attended: "As a study of the psychology of crowds, I have seen nothing like it. You feel that the thousand or fifteen hundred persons before you have become merged into one myriad-headed, but single-minded personality."[38]

Not everyone approved of such behavior. Referring to this exaggerated behavior, Peter Price, a congregational minister, described, in January 1905, the revival as "bogus...a sham...a mockery, a blasphemous travesty..."[39] But during the several months of its duration, the community was strongly affected. When Mary Jones (a central figure in these events) embarked on her mission, "within a fortnight of registering her oath [a private pledge to do what she could] she had converted every adult, with three exceptions, in the whole district."[40]

"The policemen tell me that the public houses are nearly empty, the streets are quiet, and swearing is rarely heard...The pit-ponies could no longer understand the miners' instructions because of the absence of oaths and curses...At Llanfair in Anglesey all public houses except one were closed...It was claimed that 'three months of the revival had done more to sober the country than the temperance effort of many years.'"[41] Conversions and pledges of 80,000-100,000 were claimed, though there is no saying how many were permanent. Chester hospital reported that ten patients suffering from "religious mania" had been admitted.[42]

This was the social context in which attention was directed to certain specific features that seemed to many of those participating in the revival to be supernatural, and which even to outsiders defied attempts at natural explanation.

Exceptional Eloquence

Many commented on "the wonderful eloquence displayed by unlettered persons in prayer and speaking, and not a few men have claimed that the eloquence is proof of direct Divine inspiration."[43] Thus one priest reported how a group of between 20 and 30 young people aged between 15 and 25 took part in extempore prayer for about six weeks. "I heard dozens of prayers that for piquancy of expression, richness of cadence, and fervency of utterance would have done credit to a Saint Christostom. And this from the mouths of young folk whose knowledge would hardly be level with the requirements of the fourth standard! Their utterances consisted for the most part of Bible and Prayer Book expressions, so arranged and fitted together as to form a coherent and beautifully worded prayer." After the revival they "relapsed into their former state of silence and calmness of mind."[44] Another priest told of a girl of 18 who could scarcely read and had no opportunity for culture, having been brought up in the most squalid surroundings, who "gives expression to the most refined and literary sentiments, couched in admirable phraseology."[45]

These verbal outpourings were "nearly always in the words of the Bible or hymns which they have learned or known from infancy." As with the CEVENNES PROPHETS, it is likely that lifelong familiarity with the Scriptures in households where religious talk was constant would mean that this material was readily retrievable. This does not make the performances any the less remarkable, but it does mean that they can be accounted for in terms of psychology rather than divine inspiration. As Fryer, who conducted an on-the-spot investigation for the Society for Psychical Research, concluded, "it is not surprising that those who are stirred to the depths of their feelings should break out into fervent utterance of the sonorous periods they have taken in with their mother's milk."

Transfiguration

> From two different and widely separated districts I have reports that a distinct change of countenance took place in some of the persons affected... Young people became pale and their eyes wore a faraway listless look. One said that for days after he had prayed he saw people move like ghosts in the street... One girl's appearance, previously coarse, has become quite refined – she has a Madonna-like face.[46]

Those so affected were supposed to have been infused with some heavenly influx. Even if a psychological explanation is preferred, the process whereby such alterations should manifest under the influence of the prevailing mental climate, to such a degree that they impressed observers, is a curious feature of the revival.

Visions and dreams

Many of those participating in the revival reported visionary experiences. Two of the principal preachers, Evan Roberts and Mary Jones, both traced their involvement to visions that convinced them they were entrusted with a mission they were obliged to perform. The mission of Mrs. Jones "was heralded by a mysterious manifestation, threatened by an apparition, and has ever been accompanied by signs in the heavens and portents upon the earth...In December 1904 she had prayed long and earnestly to be allowed to become the accepted medium for spreading the Spirit of Revival throughout Merionethshire, and particularly to be the means of converting her immediate neighbours among whom she had spent her life unnoticed and unnoticing. In the stillness of the night the Saviour appeared to her in bodily form clothed in bright raiment..."[47]

A young man in Glamorgan was converted after being visited by a spirit who held a long dialogue with him, urging him to act, together with a series of visions of "a beautiful light, pure, and brighter than any light I have ever seen, and clusters of something very soft and white falling upon me gently and covering me all over." Another young man, tormented by guilt for his inability to believe in the divinity of Jesus, gained conviction when he "saw a lighted candle emerge from the font of St. Mary's church and the figure of an angel shielding it."

On December 12, 1904, a Mr. J. reported:

> I had this heavenly vision which the tongue of man cannot relate or describe appropriately: I beheld a light approaching the earth...it came downwards and stood before me, about the size of a man's body, and in the bright and glorious light I beheld there the face of a man, and by looking for the body in the light a shining white robe was covering it to its feet and it was not touching the earth and behind its arms there were wings appearing and I was seeing every feather in the wings...the whole was heavenly beyond description. On each hand there were brown spots and they were the marks of the nails, and then I recognised him as Jesus, and I went forward shouting "O my blessed Jesus" and then he ascended on his wing without noise.[48] [49]

A few days later, a housewife who disapproved of her husband's churchgoing prepared to do her weekly laundry while he was at church. But on approaching the washtub, she had a vision of her four children, all of whom had died in infancy. They appeared as in the life but dressed in white. "I could hear the singing of the hymn 'O Paradise' until it died away in the distance." She saw Jesus Christ behind the children "as natural as you see him in a picture."[50]

A woman reported: "I saw a great expanse of beautiful land, with friendly faces peopling it. Between me and the golden country was a shining river, crossed by a plank. I was anxious to cross but feared that that the plank would not support me. But at that moment I gave myself to God and there came over me a great wave of faith and I crossed in safety."[51]

Many other such visions were reported. Though the great majority was benign, there were a few which were taken to be of the Evil One. Mary Jones herself, returning home after a service, walking down the lane to her farm, saw a figure approaching which she took to be her brother come to meet her. But the man turned abruptly and walked ahead of her towards the farm. Realizing it was not her brother, she began singing one of the revival hymns, at which point the man stopped, turned, and was transformed into an enormous black dog, which ran before her for a while before eventually running off.[52] At Abergynolwyn, others saw a figure that turned into a dog, and "an exceptionally intelligent young woman of the peasant class" was visited in her bedroom three nights in succession by a man dressed in black.[53]

Auditory Phenomena

There were many reports of mysterious sounds, ranging from thunder and bangs to the sound of bells, music, and singing. (These phenomena, like the displayed eloquence, were also reported by the CEVENNES PROPHETS.)

Three parishioners of Llangadfan heard bells ringing over their heads during a service on January 29, 1905, though the rest of the congregation heard nothing. Another heard something like a thunderclap followed by "lovely singing in the air." The same month a workman heard strange music like the vibration of telegraph wires only much louder, although there were no wires of the kind anywhere near. Another was frightened by "lovely singing" while on the road near his house. At Christmas 1904, a Cardiganshire vicar reported:

> I was riding to see some parishioners who lived about three miles up the hillside. As I was gradually ascending I fancied I heard voices singing. I took little notice for the moment, believing it was pure fancy. Gradually the voices seemed to increase in volume, until at last they became quite overpowering. I was trying to imagine it could be nothing outside myself, as it were, but the wonderful harmony seemed to be borne on me entirely from the outside, and was as real to my senses as anything I have ever heard. The moment the refrain would come to an end it would be restarted, the volume becoming greater and greater. To me it was an exquisite sensation. When about arriving at my destination the voices suddenly ceased.[54]

A particularly remarkable incident was the conversion of a young Frenchwoman, Mademoiselle Saillens, who was accompanying her father on a tour of Wales. She "was converted through the hearing of a solo in French, which everyone heard in the singer's native Welsh."[55]

While auditory hallucinations are not uncommon, their occurrence within the revival context is a striking instance of the effect of the prevailing cultural climate.

Luminous Phenomena

By far the most striking feature of the revival, and the one which attracted an outside interest in the revival that might not otherwise have occurred, was the proliferation of luminous phenomena of various kinds. Lights appeared when Mary Jones first embarked on her mission, and they were particularly associated with her throughout the Revival, though they were by no means confined to her.

Unexplained lights had been seen in Wales before the revival. Evelyn's memoirs mentions a "fiery exhalation" in 1694 that lasted many months, destroyed many barns and thatched houses and killing cattle. Curiously, it was easily dispelled by any great noise such as sounding a horn or discharging a gun. Other mysterious lights were recorded in 1830, 1875, and 1877:

> We saw twelve at the same time; two were very bright, the one of a red, the other of a blue colour. They were inland, but from what we could observe they did not confine themselves to marshy ground, although at first they seemed to rise from the ground where we knew there were swamps. Others watched them for about an hour and a half...on our way home we saw a bright light which we all thought was a lamp put out to direct us home, the night being so dark and our course across country.

A Welsh folklore tradition concerns the *tarwe*, a slow-moving light considered to have religious significance, often heralding a death. It may travel several miles, but is not seen to originate or terminate.

The lights seen during the revival were of all kinds, and so were the ways in which they were seen. Some were seen by everyone in the vicinity, while others seemed to be subjective in that some could see them while others could not. Most were flashes or stars, but sometimes a whole area would be illuminated; on occasion shapes such as a "luminous arch" were seen. The lights were often seen moving or hovering, especially in relation to Egryn Chapel where Mary Jones was preaching. "Herself and family speak of these lights just as they would of the farm stock. 'We cannot start yet,' she told me on the occasion of my visit, 'the lights have not yet come. I never go without them.' A few minutes later, on going out to see, she returned saying 'Come. It is time to go. The lights have come.' As one would say, 'The cab is ready!'"[56] This account is not easily reconciled with that of a Mr. Bernard Redwood, who was sent to investigate the reported lights. After interviewing Mary Jones he reported:

> It is obvious to me that the woman is a religious maniac, and that no reliance can be placed on her statements, which were vague and indefinite...I saw several lights which might have appeared to be abnormal to the overwrought imagination, but when resolved by a fieldglass turned out to be farm lanterns...in view of the fact that Mrs. Jones solemnly stated that Venus, which was particularly brilliant at that period, was a new star, had only appeared since the Revival, and was situated only a short distance above her house, I think we may dismiss these lights as phantasies of overwrought brains.[57]

By contrast Fryer, who investigated the phenomena on behalf of the Society for Psychical Research, concluded: "Having made all allowance for persons who mistook meteors, brightly-shining planets, farm lanterns, railway signals, and bodies of ignited gases for tokens of heavenly approval of Mrs. Jones and the Revival, there remain sufficient instances of abnormal phenomena to encourage further inquiry."[58]

It was widely believed that the lights accompanied Mary Jones as she traveled on her mission journeys. The lights sometimes manifested indoors; the chapel gallery was flooded with light during a service led by her. But mostly they appeared outdoors: "a group of men, returning from a service, overtook a light and knelt down in the middle of the road and, bathed in its effulgence, held an impromptu open-air prayer-meeting – then proceeded homeward rejoicing."

Many of the accounts are very explicit. Mr. J. of Merionethshire saw a light about five o'clock in the evening.

> The first form in which it appeared to me was that of a pillar of clear fire quite perpendicular. It was about 40 centimetres wide and about 3 metres in height. Suddenly another small fire began by its side some three metres distant from the first. It rapidly increased until it assumed the same measurement and form as the first. Then another small fire arose on the other side of the first pillar until there were three of the same size and form. And as I gazed upon them I saw two arms of fire extending upwards from the top of each of the pillars...[they then diminished and disappeared].[59]

Mr. M. saw "balls of light, deep red, ascending from one side of the chapel where Mary Jones was preaching. The light reappeared after the service, and as Mrs. Jones drove past us going home in her carriage, within a yard of us, there appeared a brilliant light, twice, tinged with blue. Seconds later huge balls of light, so brilliant and powerful that we were dazed for a second or two."

Sometimes the lights were accompanied by music. Mrs. H. saw lights ascending in the sky like a cross, with dozens of small balls of fire dancing back and fro behind the crosses. "And we heard a voice singing." On other occasions she heard singing "like a well-trained choir."[60]

Witnesses insisted on the reality of what they saw. A Mr. P., describing lights he and his brother had seen, declared: "I am not of an excitable nature, therefore do not run away with the idea that what I saw was pure imagination, because if you do, you will be altogether mistaken."[61] Moreover, it was not only participants in the revival who saw the lights. When reports of the phenomena became more widely known, London newspapers sent reporters down to Wales to investigate.

> The whole of the circumstances have been subjected to the closest scrutiny. It has created almost a literature of its own. There is hardly a newspaper in the kingdom but has had something to say of it in its editorial or its correspondence columns. Half a dozen leading daily papers, both London and provincial, have sent their "special correspondents" down to investigate the matter on the spot. In some cases these have been accompanied by scientists, armed with the latest apparatus, who have spent night after night on the bare mountain side just above the little chapel of Egryn, in the vain attempt to determine the real character and source of these "Lights." And the smart London journalists and the accurate scientists have alike been baffled. The "Lights," though showing themselves again and again, have eluded every attempt to "capture" them by snapshot photography, by the most delicate electrical installations, or by any of the other ingenious means devised for accurately determining their character.[62]

Reporters from both the *Daily Mirror* and the *Daily Mail* testified to witnessing the lights. *The Mir-*

ror correspondent wrote: "Suddenly, without the faintest warning, a soft shimmering radiance flooded the road at our feet. Immediately it spread around us, and every stick and stone within twenty metres was visible...it was a little suggestive of the bursting of a firework bomb...Everyone saw this extraordinary light, but while it appeared to me of snowy whiteness, the rest declared it was a brilliant blue."[63]

The Daily Mail reporter was equally sure of what he observed:

> I had decided the whole thing was a local superstition. Half an hour later my views had changed. At 8.15 I was on the hillside. In the distance, about 1.5 kilometres away, I could see the three lighted windows of the tiny Egryn chapel, where service was going on. It was the only touch of light in the miles of countryside. Suddenly I saw what appeared to be a ball of fire above the roof of the chapel. It came from nowhere, and sprang into existence instantaneously. It had a steady, intense yellow brilliance, and did not move. It seemed to be at twice the height of the chapel, say 15 metres, and it stood out with electric vividness against the encircling hills beyond. Suddenly, it disappeared, having lasted about a minute and a half. [About 15 minutes later] two lights flashed out, one on each side of the chapel. They seemed about 30 metres apart, and considerably higher in the air than the first one. They shone out brilliantly and steadily for a space of thirty seconds, then they both began to flicker...they became steady again [then] they disappeared.[64]

The same reporter saw more lights that night and on subsequent occasions. He was just one of a great many witnesses who saw the lights at different times and in different places.

COMMENT: Although extraordinary behavior characterizes many religious revivals, including many described in this Encyclopedia, the 1904-1905 Welsh Revival was unique in being characterized by such a spate of seemingly paranormal incidents. These phenomena undoubtedly played their part in raising the feelings of those who participated in the revival; there were many who believed that the lights observed in the vicinity of Mary Jones were of divine origin, and this was taken as evidence that God favored the Revival. At the same time, they were something of a distraction in that, for many, the question of their nature took precedence over their divine status as signs conveying Heaven's blessing on the work of spiritual regeneration.

The *Cambrian News* in March 1905 didn't at all approve:

> The worse than silly talk about revival, visions and flashes and spirit compellings goes on. The revival is being discredited and the neurotics are monopolising attention...The individuals who begin to see visions, hear voices and rappings cannot be too carefully tended by their friends. Mr. Evan Roberts and Mrs. Mary Jones must take care of their stomachs and nerves, they may be upset. God is not reduced to conjuring tricks of a low order.[65]

The history of luminous phenomena in the area lends strong support to the view that the lights had their origin in the geophysical features of the terrain, but this does little to explain the synchronicity with the revival. The fact that journalists from London, who we may suppose to be hard-headed to the point of skepticism, saw the lights for themselves, likewise suggests that the lights were physically real, rather than products of the heated imaginations of the participants in the revival. Without their testimony, it would be tempting to accept the most obvious explanation: that the sightings were subjective, induced by suggestion. But the sheer number of incidents, and the fact that so many were collective, makes this implausible. Researchers Kevin and Sue McClure, after considering various theories, admitted that no natural or scientific explanation seemed to cover the facts, and they were evidently prepared to accept a paranormal explanation of some kind.[66]

WERTET OUTBREAK

Flanders: 1550-1553

The outbreak in a convent at Wertet, or Uvertet, in Flanders, is a characteristic instance of CONVENT HYSTERIA, though with some significant individual features. The affair drew the attention of Johann Weyer (1515-1588), who provided a detailed account of the nuns' behavior, together with his own comments.[67]

CONTEXT: The outbreak is one of several that disturbed convents throughout Western Europe during the 15th and 16th centuries. While each incident seems to have been independent of the others, the occurrence of so many such outbreaks displaying common features, close in time and often in location, suggests that a shared emotional climate favored such manifestations, and that news spread easily from one location to another.

Weyer opens his report by saying: "The torments that the devils inflicted on several nuns enclosed at

Wertet are marvellous and horrible." They began when a poor woman who during Lent borrowed salt (then a precious commodity) from the convent and repaid it in double shortly before Easter, after which little white balls were found in the dormitories, like sugar sweets but of salty taste. Then the nuns heard a sound like a man in pain, and voices urging them to get up to attend a sick nun, but when they went to her cell they found nothing.

The sisters were harassed in various ways. When they needed to urinate, they were prevented from using the chamber pot, and involuntarily soiled their beds with their urine. They would be pulled from their beds and dragged backwards across the floor as if in a sack, their limbs totally relaxed. They were tickled on the soles of their feet until they feared they would die laughing. Some had their hair pulled out; others had limbs and head twisted into contortions. Some vomited a black bitter liquid, although for the fifty days of Lent they had been fasting, taking in nothing but horseradish without bread. Some were reportedly raised in the air to the height of a man's head, then dropped abruptly onto the ground. Some took to walking on their knees, as if kneeling, while others scrambled up trees, clambering with their feet like cats and coming down again head foremost. When thirteen of their friends entered the monastery to rejoice with those who seemed to be almost cured, the nuns failed to recognize them, lost their powers of speech, and fell backwards from the table where they were seated.

Given the beliefs of the time, it seemed evident that the nuns were under some kind of malevolent spell. A local midwife, though widely respected for her charitable works, came under suspicion after she had visited the nunnery carrying a black cat in a basket, which escaped and could not be found. Accused by the nuns, she was thrown into prison along with seven others suspected of worshipping the devil. Though Weyer was convinced she was innocent, she was tortured to get her to confess, which she refused to do, and she died from her treatment. However, this failed to put an end to the nuns' behavior, which persisted for three years before it eventually faded away.

COMMENT: The claim of the nuns to be possessed by devils was generally accepted by Weyer as well as by the authorities. He said firmly: "There is no doubt that Satan possessed these nuns."[68] But he disagreed with the authorities as regards the role of witchcraft, insisting that none was involved. In his opinion the accused midwife who was tortured to death was completely innocent.

For German author Görres, writing 300 years later, Satan is still perceived as the party responsible: "What was involved was some of these lutins (imps) and farfadets (elves),"[69] which the devil employs to tempt his victims into doubt by their mischievous tricks. A century later, he might have proposed a poltergeist.

French doctor Calmeil, on the other hand, writing in 1845,[70] saw no reason to invoke any outside agency. For him, the nuns were suffering from a psychosocial affliction he labels *hystérie-démonopathie*, born of the stresses of life in an enclosed community, together with the fact that the outbreak occurred towards the end of Lent, when the nuns had been fasting on a very inadequate diet for 50 days. The diagnosis seems plausible. It is easy to guess that under such circumstances the inmates would be rendered suggestible, vulnerable to any untoward happening. Madden suggests that the salty "sweets" may have been nothing more than lumps of crystallized lime falling from damp walls, but to which the excitable nuns gave a more sinister interpretation.[71]

See also: CONVENT HYSTERIA, DEMON POSSESSION.

WHEEZING MALADY

Tampa, Florida: January-October 2003

In January 2003, a girl attending Gaither High School in Tampa, Florida, began to have breathing trouble. There was no obvious cause. Then in late July, a spate of breathing difficulties befell 13 other girls at the school. The final report by Hillsborough County health officials was that psychogenic stridor triggered by anxiety could explain the raspy sound that could be heard when the girls would inhale. The mass hysterical wheezing theory sparked outrage among some of the girls' parents.

Most of the students became ill during a three-week period between mid-September and early October. Eight of those affected were in the school's Starettes dance group, four were members of the marching band, one was a friend of a dance member, and one belonged to neither group. The epidemic occurred shortly after the Starettes and band members attended a music camp between July 21 and 25. During the camp, workers refinished the Gaither gym floor and repainted the school's auditorium, both of which were near where the girls were practicing.

In September when the girls' breathing problems developed, there was speculation that fumes from the polyurethane and paint could have been responsible for the outbreak. School officials hired an environmental firm to test the building's air quality. After tests were conducted over several weeks, scientists at Chastain-Skillman Inc. concluded that there had been no "obvious indications of adverse indoor environmental quality conditions that would indicate a potential health concern."

A Health Department investigation found no relationship between the girls' illnesses and chemical fumes at the school. "While the dance team and band members were exposed to both paint and polyurethane fumes, these exposures cannot explain all of the illness experienced by the ill students. Two of the affected students were not in the school during the week of the band camp. One of the affected students had a bout of stridor six months prior to the band camp (although she did have a recurrence in late August 2003)."

Health Department Epidemiologist David Atrubin said that epidemic stridor was suggested as an explanation after several other possible causes were eliminated. "We waited for the results of the environmental testing and the infectious disease testing. When you put them all together, then you start looking for alternative explanations," he said.[72]

WHITECHAPEL MURDERS SCARE

London: 1888

A series of five murders that took place over a three-month period between August-November 1888 gave rise to the biggest panic of its kind ever experienced by Londoners, rousing an interest that has scarcely died down after more than a century. The horrific nature of the killings, the fact that we have detailed knowledge of the circumstances, combined with the fact that the killer was never caught or even positively identified, not only defied the best efforts of a very competent police force at the time but has been a challenge ever since to countless investigators and armchair theorists.

All five victims were, if not professional prostitutes, at best women of loose repute. The first victim in the series, on August 31, was 43-year-old Mary Ann "Polly" Nichols. A newspaper report the following morning asserted that "no murder was ever more ferociously and more brutally done." The second, on September 8, was "Dark Annie" Chapman, aged 47. On September 30, two more were killed: "Long Liz" Stride, aged 45, and Catherine Eddowes, aged 46. The first four were killed in the street, but the fifth,

The powerless police– a satirical comment after the first three (or four) Whitechapel murders.

Mary Jane Kelly, at 25 the youngest of the victims, was killed indoors. With this killing the spate of murders stopped, a fact that only added to the mystery.

However, popular concern extended the catalogue. Previous to the Nichols murder there had been three killings: "Fairy Fay" in 1887, and Emma Smith and Martha Turner in 1888. After Kelly there were two more: Anne McKenzie in 1889 and Frances Coles in 1891. None of these is now considered to be a victim of the same killer, but at the time it seemed logical to the terrified populace to chalk up their names to the same killer's score.

All the murders took place at night in a geographically limited area, the Whitechapel district of London, which was then a rough and squalid quarter. All were extremely brutal, yet painstakingly carried out with savage yet precise mutilation. Kelly, for instance, was nearly beheaded by a cut to her throat; her abdomen was partially ripped open, across and downwards, the entrails wrenched away and removed, but the liver excised and placed between the feet. One of her hands was placed inside her stomach, both breasts were severed from the body, the left arm was nearly amputated, the nose had been cut off, the forehead skinned, and the thighs and calves stripped of flesh. While such savagery suggested insanity, it also indicated a considerable degree of surgical skill. From the start the investigators were looking for a man with medical experience.

The horrific circumstances produced an intense public reaction. Already, by the second killing, the public – encouraged by the press – was fascinated by the case. The *Penny Illustrated Paper* reported that a large crowd had congregated at the site of Chapman's murder, and neighbors were charging spectators to inspect the scene from their windows. Inevitably, this interest led to a spate of rumors. A huge array of suspects were considered, ranging from the eminent surgeon Sir William Gull to the Duke of Clarence, by way of the painter Walter Sickert and the poet James Kenneth Stephen. The famous philanthropist Dr. Barnardo, who performed good works in the district, came under suspicion, as he had been seen talking with the victim Stride four days before she was killed. Such circumstantial evidence made it possible to draw up a plausible case against each of these people, but none was ultimately convincing and despite a great deal of police activity, none was ever arraigned.

Apart from these celebrity suspects, a string of dubious characters were taken into custody, and some actually charged, but each in turn was released as the evidence proved insufficient. For example, a man named Pizer had been seen speaking with Chapman shortly before her death; moreover he was a leatherworker who used sharp-bladed knives in his profession. But he had a solid alibi for Nichols' murder, and his appearance was quite at variance with the description of Chapman's killer given by possible witnesses.

In September 1888, a letter was delivered at the Central News Agency, addressed to "The Boss." It purported to be from the killer, and went into some detail about the murders. "I am down on whores and shant quit ripping them till I do get buckled" (caught). However, the letter is not generally considered genuine, and is suspected to be the handiwork of a journalist intent on building up a sensational story. If so, it certainly succeeded, for it was signed, "Jack the Ripper" – a name that was immediately seized on by the public and which has stuck to the case ever since.

After the double event of September 30, morbid interest turned to panic. That the killer should strike twice in one night, when the whole district was on the lookout for him, showed that Londoners were challenged by someone who combined an almost reckless fearlessness with his other qualities – including an intimate knowledge of the labyrinthine alleys and courtyards of the district; sufficient familiarity with the local population to select his victims with care; and a horrifying degree of medical expertise, combined with the callousness required first to attack the victims with such savagery and then subject their corpses to such macabre mutilations. Nothing less than a monster, it was thought, could carry out such calculated assaults.

Indeed, some theorists, focusing on the frenzied character of the killings, looked to a real monster – a baboon, such as the one featured in Poe's *Rue* Morgue tale, was proposed. Others concentrated on the question of motivation. There were those – Sir Arthur Conan Doyle among them – who suspected a woman, avenging the death of her sister who had been enticed into prostitution and died. The large Jewish population of the area combined with the meticulous mutilation led others to suspect Judaic ritual slaughter. Then and later there were false confessions that had to be followed up before being rejected. Both at the time, and ever since, a prodigious quantity of surmise and supposition was created, but leading to no satisfactory conclusion.

Public interest and alarm were greater than with any of the previous London "monsters." At the height of the panic, more than a thousand letters every week were addressed to the police, offering advice and suggestions for catching the killer. The careful selection of the victims meant that others living outside the monster's killing ground could feel relatively safe – except that the simple knowledge that such a fiend was at work in the London streets was cause for alarm. In face of the police failure to catch the killer, self-appointed vigilante groups patrolled the streets. Letters to the press targeted police inefficiency – quite unjustifiably, as the police effort was massive: 80,000 leaflets distributed to local residents, house-to-house questioning, and searches by plain clothed policemen and policewomen working undercover. The panic died down only with the fifth killing, and even then was liable to start up again at a fresh incident, even if clearly not by the same hand. For the monster was never caught.

WHITE SLAVERY SCARE

United States and Europe: 1907 to 1917

The "white slavery scare" was a form of MORAL PANIC that occurred across the United States and Europe during the first two decades of the 20th century. It was triggered by an anti-prostitution crusade led by the female Suffragette movement and fundamentalist Protestants. During the episode, widespread public outrage was prompted by the publication of false stories that young women were being kidnapped and forced to work as prostitutes by certain organized crime gangs. As a result, hundreds of people involved in adulterous relationships, or young men living with a lover outside of marriage, were branded as participating in white slavery, with some even imprisoned.[73]

CONTEXT: D. J. Guy believes the white slavery scare was a means for society to quell the growing desire for female independence, with the many purported horror stories serving as "cautionary tales" against venturing out alone.[74]

French sociologist Edgar Morin documented how white slavery rumors gripped the city of Orleans, France in May 1969. His book, *Rumour in Orleans*, documented in painstaking detail, claims that young women were being drugged while trying on clothes in the fitting rooms of Jewish-operated clothing boutiques and then smuggled out of the country through secret tunnels, only to be sold as prostitutes in North Africa. According to the accounts, authorities failed to stop these sinister crimes as the Jews had bribed them. Morin concluded that the rumors functioned as a cautionary tale to the younger generation about the dangers posed by the wearing of mini-skirts and

Cover of an American book.

the frequenting of *avant-garde* boutiques and how it inevitably leads to moral degradation and prostitution.[75]
See also: MORAL PANIC.

WIFE ABUSE HYSTERIA

India: 1973 and ongoing

In October 1983, a team of psychiatrists were researching mental illness in West Bengal, India, when they heard reports that eight women in a small village had been experiencing ongoing fits of hysteria for over ten years. The "outbreak" began when Mr. P. came home intoxicated at midday and beat up his wife. Mrs. P. told investigators: "For some time...[she] crouched quietly in a corner of the room, then suddenly she uttered a strange cry and developed a bizarre convulsive seizure." News of the beating and seizure quickly spread throughout the neighborhood, and in rapid succession six other wives, a divorcee, and Mrs. P.'s daughter.[76] Soon similar occurrences were being reported among the same eight women. Episodes followed a uniform pattern that was usually triggered by stressful situations such as arguments with an alcoholic spouse or cruel mother-in-law. The most common cause was "the husband's beating of one of the wives. As soon as the victim of the assault fell into the fit, the other women, identifying with her, had fits of their own."[77] The victims ranged in age from 20 to 40, were illiterate, smoked and rolled their own tobacco, abstained from alcohol, and were not particularly fond of one another. They were all very poor and felt trapped in unhappy relationships. Each of the abusive men had alcohol abuse problems.

CONTEXT: The abused rural Indian housewives could not address their sad plight through traditional Indian means of redress. Their "fits" seem to represent a form of unconscious or partially conscious creative response to their plight, serving to publicize their situation to the community at-large.

In addition to each of the women exhibiting "hysterical fits," during seizures, two of the women experienced temporary paralysis of an arm or leg. Investigators stated: "When we interviewed the women separately, they all told us that they had felt a strange sensation of fire or heat in their bellies that spread to their chests and heads and was immediately followed by a seizure."[78] During "outbreaks," those affected would receive care and attention from their friends and neighbors. The investigating psychiatrists concluded that "this behavior had served to satisfy deep-seated psychological needs."[79]
See also: WASHING MANIA.

WINDIGO PSYCHOSIS

Canada: 1800s and ongoing

Native Canadians of the Algonquin peoples are subject to periodic outbreaks related to a supernatural naked giant to which they give many names but which is chiefly known as the *windigo* or *wendigo*, or *weetigo*, etc.[80] Seven to ten meters in height, this entity lives in the forest and must be placated with donations of human flesh. Those who have seen it report it as fearsome to see, but few have done so for it is skilled at keeping out of sight. "As you travel, it is always behind your back. No matter how quickly you may turn, it moves faster, as you tramp through bush or forest, hill or desert, with no other company but your thoughts, you become slowly aware that Wendigo follows you. You may struggle against the temptation to swing round, but at last you turn and there is nothing..."[81]

Apart from its huge size, it has two features not always shared by folk monsters. It is widely believed to possess a heart of ice (though the Ojibwa sometimes extend this to its entire body, seeing it as "a giant skeleton of ice"), and it is cannibalistic. If a hunter fails to return from an expedition, it is supposed that he is a victim of the windigo. Though it may be male or female, it is a solitary creature, and should two meet, a fatal combat often follows, the winner eating the loser. To kill a windigo is likely to be beyond the power of an ordinary person, but a shaman may succeed in doing so by using sorcery and invoking the aid of friendly spirits.

Thus described, the windigo sounds like a folklore entity like so many others, however, what is remarkable is that to this day it is firmly believed to be a real creature. It is a source of constant dread. As recently as 1950, some 1,300 Saulteaux living at Island Lake, 500 km northeast of Winnipeg, were thrown into panic throughout an entire summer by the report that a windigo was roaming the district. Natives avoided Packwash Lake, about 160 km northwest of Sioux Lookout in northwestern Ontario, because they believed it to be the home of a windigo who claimed at least one victim a year.

The belief that humans are at risk of being attacked and eaten by the windigo can be classified as folklore, but another aspect of this belief is much more serious: the widespread fear that one may be possessed by it. This medical condition constitutes the so-called "windigo psychosis" of which Morton Teicher, writing in 1962, stated that seventy cases had been identified. Two years previously, Seymour Parker described the malady in these terms:

> The wittiko psychosis, a bizarre form of mental disorder involving obsessive cannibalism, has been reported by many investigators for the area between Lake Winnipeg and Labrador. The illness is associated mainly with the Cree and Ojibwa Indians who inhabit Canada's forested northland. Although this mental disturbance has been reported for both sexes, it usually affects males who have spent varying periods alone in the frozen forest in an unsuccessful hunt for food. The initial symptoms are feelings of morbid depression, nausea, and distaste for most ordinary foods, and sometimes periods of semi-stupor. Gradually, the victim becomes obsessed with paranoid ideas of being bewitched and is subject to homicidal (and occasionally suicidal) thoughts. He feels that he is possessed by the wittigo monster, a fierce cannibalistic being, to whose will he has become subjected. The conviction of the existence of a wittiko monster is not evidence of pathology, since this is a socially shared belief among the Ojibwa. If the illness progresses beyond this stage, the individual begins to see those around him (often close family members) as fat, luscious animals which he desires to devour. Finally, the wittiko sufferer enters a stage of violent homicidal cannibalism. It is commonly thought that once this stage is reached and the person has tasted human flesh, the craving will not leave him and he must be killed.[82]

Today, many anthropologists consider the windigo "psychosis" to be a mythical construction, like many other supposed ailments in this Encyclopedia. In his 1982 study, anthropologist Lou Marano, drawing both on archival research and on years of fieldwork, found no reliable evidence for what was considered at the time to be a classic culture-specific disorder, but which was created when ethnographic data about the subarctic people were taken out of context.

Marano asserted that when windigo psychosis is viewed from the group psychodynamic perspective, rather than as individual psychopathology, "the crucial question becomes, not what causes a person to become a cannibalistic maniac, but under what circumstances a Northern Algonkian is likely to be accused of having become a cannibalistic maniac and run the risk of being executed as such."[83] He contended that tribal members executed for going on a cannibalistic rampage are not experiencing a culture-specific variant of hysteria unique to Northern Algonkians, but are victims of more mundane activities such as witch-hunts or triage homicide – that is, culling individuals who have become a liability to the welfare of the tribe.

However, while accepting that the windigo "psychosis" is shaped by its environmental context, it is clear from instances such as the one presented in our case history – and it is certainly not unique – that as with so many other cases of extraordinary behavior studied in this Encyclopedia, the dynamic exerted by the psychology of the individual plays as much a part in it as the dynamic of the cultural group to which he belongs. Whether or not it is appropriate to label this behavior a psychosis, it seems certain that those who believe themselves, or are believed, to be possessed by the windigo, are – like the 17th century nuns in our CONVENT HYSTERIA entries who were believed to be possessed by demons—individuals who are working out their own personal problems within the framework of their societies beliefs.

Case History

We have chosen the following narrative dating from circa 1800 because it relates to a period when the Native Canadians were relatively uncontaminated by contact with the authorities, so that the events were seen by observers as a clear-cut social puzzle.

> A sad affair took place a few months past on the shores of the Lake of the Woods. About twenty families were together for hunting and fishing. One morning a young man of about twenty-two years of age, on getting up, said he felt a strong inclination to eat his sister. As he was a steady young man and a promising hunter, no notice was taken of this expression. The next morning he said the same and repeated the same several times in the day for a few days. His parents attempted to reason him out of this horrid inclination; he was silent and gave them no answer. His sister and her husband became alarmed, left the place, and went to another camp. He became aware of it; and then said he must have human flesh to eat, and would have it; in other respects, his behavior was cool, calm and quiet. His father and relatives were much grieved; argument had no effect on him, and he made them no answer

to their questions. The camp became alarmed, for it was doubtful who would be his victim. His father called the men to a Council, where the state of the young man was discussed, and their decision was that an Evil Spirit had entered into him, and was in full possession of him to make him become a man eater (a Weetego). The father was found fault with for not having called to his assistance a Medicine Man, who by sweating and his songs to the tambour and rattle might have driven away the evil spirit before it was too late. Sentence of death was passed on him, which was to be done by his father. The young man was called, and informed of the resolution taken, to which he said, I am willing to die. The unhappy father arose, and placing a cord about his neck, strangled him, to which he was quite passive; after about two hours, the body was carried to a large fire, and burned to ashes, not the least bit of bone remaining. This was carefully done to prevent his soul and the evil spirit which possessed him from returning to this world...It may be thought the Council acted a cruel part in ordering the father to put his son to death: this was done to prevent the law of retaliation, which might have been made a pretext of revenge by those who were not his friends.[84]

COMMENT: A. I. Hallowell proposed that the young man was motivated by incestuous desires, which were "solved in almost an ideal fashion by his culture," which provided the opportunity for displacement by disguising it in the form of the windigo belief.[85] While we need not accept this suspiciously Freudian interpretation, we can recognize the interplay between individual psychology and tribal context. It is quite clear from this account that this was a case of an individual overtaken by a mental state peculiar to his culture; that is, the young man would not have behaved in this way unless he had been a member of a community where such conduct, though condemned, was recognized as a real possibility. The narrator points out that this "horrid disposition" to cannibalism was wholly confined to the inhabitants of this particular forest region, for no such disposition was known among the Indians of the Plains, nor among the Chippeway Indians whose hunting grounds were in a different forest region. From this perspective, then, his behavior was social rather than individual. In a sense, neither the killer nor his people believed that he was accountable for his intentions: rather, it was the spirit of the windigo that had possessed him. We can be sure that the father, in killing his son, believed he was safeguarding the tribe from a malignant entity.

In that particular case, the "possession" was checked before the victim could carry out his intentions, but this was only because it took place in the summer camp when several families had come together for communal activities, so that the man's possession came to public knowledge in good time. During the winter months, when owing to the scarcity of game the families separate and live in isolation, each hunter operating in his own stretch of the forest, it may be months before the tribe learns that a man has become possessed and performed acts of cannibalism, generally involving his own family.

In 1879, the government hung a Native Canadian named Swift Runner for murder. A hunter living alone with his family, he had killed his wife, his three children, and his mother-in-law, all of whom he had eaten. (He acknowledged that his mother-in-law was a bit tough.) There was no question of food shortage, as he had plenty of dried meat hanging around his camp. He acknowledged his guilt and, like the young man in our case history, accepted his punishment without demur. In another case from the same period, a man who had eaten his entire family told the judge, "You might as well hang me because I'm going to kill lots more."[86]

It cannot be said that the enigma of the windigo "psychosis" has been satisfactorily resolved. The question remains, why are individuals of this particular tribal group driven to behave in this particular way, which in any other cultural setting would be considered a pathological crime?

WINDSHIELD PITTING SCARE

United States and Canada: 1954

During March 1954, police in the city of Bellingham in northwest Washington State, were baffled by reports that a ghostly sniper was shooting at car windshields. The situation soon reached crisis proportions. During a one-week period in early April more than 1,500 windshields were reported damaged. Despite the massive number of "attacks," Police Chief William Breuer had no suspects and no tangible evidence. Authorities surmised that the most likely weapon "was a BB-gun barrel attached to a compressor in a sparkplug socket, fired from a moving car."[87] At the height of the episode people across the city of 34,000 placed various items over their windshields for protection

– from newspapers to doormats and even plywood. Meanwhile, downtown parking garages were under heavy security. The phantom pellet-shooter seemed to be everywhere – even police cars reported being struck.[88]

CONTEXT: The wave of pitting reports coincided with near saturation media publicity on the atomic bomb tests in the Pacific and its potentially harmful effects, especially in the form of radioactive fallout.

In lieu of a lack of evidence for vandals as being responsible for most of the damage, by mid-April local and national media began emphasizing the mysterious nature of the damage. On April 12, a reporter for *Life* Magazine came to Bellingham and referred to the episode as "ghostly" and the perpetrators as "phantom"-like.[89] In time, as reports of the mysterious windshield "attacks" moved closer to Seattle, 80 miles to the south, there was widespread media speculation that the "pits" were somehow related to highly publicized U.S. military hydrogen bomb tests in the Pacific Marshall Islands on March 1.

Concern over the possible harmful effects of the tests by radioactive fallout dominated world news during March and early April. For instance, on March 18, at least 23 Japanese tuna fishermen were sickened by radiation poisoning after a cloud of atomic ash hit their vessel, *Fukuryu Maru* (*Lucky Dragon*).[90] As news of the incident reached Japan, 36 people in Yokohama became ill after eating what was thought to have been radioactive fish but was later identified as food poisoning.[91] Soon several more Japanese vessels were identified as being "slightly radioactive."[92] The populace was in a state of "near-hysteria."

By March 21, the U.S. military, surprised by the power of the blast, announced that it was tripling the radius of the danger zone for ships to avoid.[93] Two days later it was reported that at least three of the *Lucky Dragon* fishermen might soon die.[94] At the same time, California Democratic representative Chet Hilifield described the tests as having been "out of control."[95] The following day it was reported that 92 crewmen on a U.S. Navy tanker had been mildly contaminated by atomic fallout.[96] Newspaper accounts of fallout contamination concerns continued through mid-April, including a report of radioactive snow in Montana, described as only a trace, posing a threat that was "practically nil."[97]

Reports of strange pit marks on windshields first reached Seattle on the evening of April 14, and by the end of the next day, weary police had answered 242 phone calls from concerned residents reporting tiny pit marks on over 3,000 vehicles.[98] In some cases, whole parking lots were reportedly affected. The reports quickly declined. On April 16 police logged 46 pitting claims, and 10 on the 17th, after which no more reports were received. The sudden presence of the "pits" created widespread anxiety as public consensus quickly shifted from vandals to atomic fallout.

At the height of the incident on the night of April 15, Seattle Mayor Allan Pomeroy sought emergency assistance from Governor Arthur Langlie and U.S. President Dwight Eisenhower. The identical dispatches read in part: "What appeared to be a localized outbreak of vandalism in damaging auto windshields and windows in the northern part of Washington State has now spread throughout the Puget Sound area...Urge appropriate federal (and state) agencies be instructed to cooperate with local authorities on emergency basis."[99] On the 15th, Island County Sheriff Tom Clark stated: "I'll tell you right now that human beings are not doing it...radioactive stuff from some of those hydrogen bomb blasts may be responsible."[100] Two deputy sheriffs reported that five holes actually appeared in a truck windshield as they were inspecting it.[101] Similar stories were common. A Seattle woman said pit "blemishes" appeared before her eyes. "It was like a bubbling action in the glass," she said.[102] Two prominent members of the AFL teamsters union at Portland said that "pinhead-sized pits" suddenly appeared on their vehicles in the parking lot.[103] Meantime, Seattle Police Chief H.J. Lawrence stated his view that "a chemical agent" was responsible.[104] On the 16th, at the urgent request of the Governor, the University of Washington Environmental Research Laboratory (ERL) was assigned to investigate the strange pits. That same day the mayor stated that initial analysis at a police lab indicated that the "ash" found on cars could be "atomic material."[105] Seattle insurance companies, faced with a sudden influx of claims for damaged windshields, undertook an urgent investigation of their own.[106]

In Portland, Oregon, the vandalism theory was widely touted for windshield damage in that city until the 18th,[107] when a sensational front-page story appeared. "A shower of miniature, spherical, featherweight pellets, resembling those linked with Seattle's windshield pox mystery, swept in from the sea Saturday."[108] While the possibility of fallout was discussed, the objects were said to have not been radioactive.[109] In Coos Bay, Oregon, a B.F. Smith told of washing his car and noticing a lone pit mark, but upon returning an hour later, counting 50.[110]

While atomic fallout was the leading explanation, other theories abounded. Many people reported that tiny pit marks grew into dime-sized bubbles embedded within the glass, leading to a folk theory that sand flea eggs had somehow been deposited in the glass and later hatched.[111] Others attributed the pits to electro-magnetic radiation from Seattle's nearby Jim Creek naval base, cosmic rays, resin rains, tiny meteors, and meteoric dust.[112] One woman phoned a newspaper reporter and was emphatic that her neighbor was using thought waves to create the pits. "I can see her now in the window," she stated.[113] Portland, Oregon officials favored "mass hysteria."[114] A chemist suggested volcanic ash,[115] while biologist Paul Parizeau said the particles may be radiolarian skeletons – tiny one-celled sea animals that sink to the ocean floor after death and pile up. "Any tremendous upheaval such as that caused by the H-bomb blast would throw these minute skeletons high into the stratosphere."[116] Other explanations included excrement from seagulls eating radioactive fish to extraterrestrials.[117]

On April 18, reports of windshield pitting spread to other parts of the country: Oregon, California, Ohio, Illinois, and Kentucky.[118] Even a Flying Tiger airliner reportedly had mysterious pockmarks on the windshield to the extent that the shield was replaced.[119] By the 19th the reports had spread to Canada.[120] By the 20th, after several Ohio used car dealerships reported pock marks on nearly 100 vehicles, one auto dealer claimed that "pock marks" appeared on his glasses.[121] By the 21st, some authorities were openly ridiculing the affair. An unnamed scientist at the University of California was quoted as saying: "The Berkeley scientific community is monumentally uninterested..."[122] On the 22nd, pit mania reached the town of Gardiner as tiny "holes or pock marks were found...in virtually all the store windows" along main street.[123] The next day, a team of scientists that was investigating a mysterious yellow substance that covered parts of Clifton, Oregon on the 20th identified the culprit as harmless pollen.[124]

Hydrogen-Bomb Hysteria

On June 10, the ERL of the University of Washington released its findings. In the wake of rumors such as the existence of radioactive fallout, and by a few initial cases amplified in the media, residents began looking *at* instead of *through* their windshields.[125] The report drew four major conclusions. First, it was observed that "virtually all" of the windshield damage was of the "impact" variety, "caused by some hard object striking the glass with sufficient force to chip, pit, or crack it."[126] Second, it identified the mysterious black, sooty grains that dotted many Seattle windshields as cenospheres – tiny particles produced by the incomplete combustion of bituminous coal, and to a minor extent, from other materials. These particles had been a common feature of everyday life in Seattle, and could not pit or penetrate windshields.[127] Third, scientists found that the pits could not be produced under "laboratory or controlled field conditions by any means other than impact," which was entirely consistent with the type of damage reported.[128] Lastly, the report refuted claims by observers who stated that the pits often appeared suddenly over a short period of time. Despite considerable testimony from reputable citizens "to the effect that windshields were pitted by some mysterious cause in the space of a few minutes or hours during the 'epidemic,' it has not been possible to substantiate a single one of these statements by scientific observation. Actually, the observed facts tend to contradict such statements."[129]

As the pitting reports coincided with the H-Bomb tests, media publicity on the windshield damage seems to have reduced tension about the possible consequences of the tests – "something was bound to happen to us as a result of the H-bomb tests –

windshields became pitted – it's happened – now that threat is over."[130] Secondly, the very act of phoning police and appeals by the mayor to the governor and even the president of the United States "served to give people the sense that they were 'doing something' about the danger that threatened."[131 132]

COMMENT: A similar episode occurred near Esher, England, between 1950 and 1953, when police received more than 50 reports of projectiles targeting vehicles on a small stretch of road in the London outskirts. It was commonly believed that a person or persons were targeting vehicles with either bullets or BBs, resulting in broken windscreens (the British term for windshield). In a study of the episode, Paul Chambers and Robert Bartholomew noted that many of the drivers reporting "attacks" were locals who were well aware of the sniper rumors and more likely to contact police "than passing motorists who might attribute an incident to loose stones." Soon the *Esher News* took a major interest in the "shootings," actively campaigning to get authorities to look more closely at the claims. As a result, the *Esher News* promoted the idea of the phantom sniper or snipers by publishing 40 articles on the topic over a three-year period.[133] This heavy press profile, loose stones, and heavy traffic combined to create the local belief in the phantom sniper of Esher.

WITCH MANIA

Western Europe: circa 1350 to 1750

The witch mania in Europe was the most persistent and widespread instance of extraordinary social behavior in human history. Though the myth that sustained it was delusory to the point of absurdity, it seemed to those involved to possess sufficient plausibility to authorize appalling perversions of justice and the infliction of horrific cruelties over a period of three centuries.

Witchcraft, loosely defined as the organized practice of magic, has been and remains prevalent throughout human society. Overtly or covertly, it manifests in every culture, though in widely differing forms, depending on whether the practice is central or marginal to the culture's belief-system.

Inevitably, the practice of magic from time to time leads to extraordinary individual behavior, and collective outbreaks occur periodically. However, by far the biggest and most catastrophic of such outbreaks came about not from witchcraft practices per se, but from a perception of them, which led to the creation of a witchcraft myth. This began in the late Middle Ages, from about 1350, when the Christian Church in Western Europe initiated its witch hunt, and continued till about 1750 when what had been suspected by a few came to be openly recognized by the many – that the mania was founded upon a delusion.

The mania covered the entirety of Western Europe as far east as Poland, though with varying intensity. It was at its most extreme in Germany, where more than 100,000 victims are estimated, and where procedures were harshest – torture was mandatory and execution was by burning alive. France was almost equally

At the sabbat, witches copulate with Satan.

affected. Spain and Portugal were more restrained, though conspicuous by their spectacular auto-da-fés. In Italy and Poland the hunt was less fierce, and still less so in Scandinavia, apart from the notable MORA outbreak. England had a milder share, though with little or no use of torture and with hanging rather than burning; the hunt was fiercer in Scotland.

CONTEXT: A confluence of many social factors contributed in the 14th century to make the population of Western Europe uneasy, and perhaps unusually suggestible. The Black Death of 1347-1400, the worst of many periodic plagues, killed off a third of the population. Wars and popular uprisings, and the widespread banditry, pillage, and disorganization that followed further disrupted a way of life, which for the majority was little more than subsistence, with the ever-present threat of crop failure, floods, and other natural disasters.

However, these conditions were chronic, and cannot of themselves explain how the witch mania came about. Nor can it be attributed to the Reformation and the Counter-Reformation, which tore Western Europe apart with conflicting interpretations of the Christian faith, for on the question of witchcraft the rival churches were of one mind. At most, the religious contest contributed an added dimension of instability to people's lives.

The requisite precipitating factor was imposed by the Church of Rome, which pronounced that witchcraft was a heresy that not only presented an intolerable challenge to its teachings, but threatened to engulf Western Europe in the worship of Satan, God's enemy. To eradicate it was a matter of the utmost urgency if mankind was to be saved. It was soon joined in the pursuit of this aim by the newly formed Protestant churches, and the secular authorities, sometimes reluctantly but more often enthusiastically, supported their efforts.

The European witch mania was all the more extraordinary in that witchcraft, in the organized form in which it was perceived as so great a menace, simply did not exist. Popular magic certainly existed, at all levels of society; and ceremonial magic fascinated a small elite. Certainly too there were sorcerers and magicians who could be categorized as witches, by others if not by themselves, as people who claimed special powers of supernatural origin. But the witch culture against which the Christian Churches took up arms was an artificial construct created by their theologians. It was only remotely associated with the kind of social magic practiced by, say, the Azande tribes of Africa or Native American peoples. In the words of historian George Burr, "the witchcraft our fathers feared and fought was never universal, in place or time. It belonged alone to Christian thought and modern centuries."[134]

The Christian Church's doctrine had its origin in the scriptural tradition that some of God's angels had rebelled against him. Defeated, they were expelled from Heaven and assigned to Hell, where their principal activity is to sabotage God's creation by all possible means. Their aim is to persuade humans to switch allegiance from God to Satan, and this they do by acting on individuals by either fear or inducement. The Church perceived practitioners of magic as the devil's agents, who must be sought out and destroyed.

The literature of witchcraft is vast, and ranges from total belief in the reality of demonic witchcraft to total skepticism. Whether the Evil One exists, and whether witches were his agents, remain open questions for many, and consequently the events constituting the European witch mania can be interpreted in a variety of ways.

What is less open to question, however, are the facts themselves. Since those responsible for putting the Church's intentions into practice were nominally working by legal authority, an enormous quantity of archival material in the form of court records is available, together with the commentaries of some of those involved, such as judges and inquisitors, or the observers and critics on the sidelines.

What follows is a brief and necessarily oversimplified overview of the events of the mania, setting aside the questions, first, whether the victims of the inquisitors were indeed agents of the Devil; second, even if they were, whether they were heretics who represented a real danger to the Church; and third, even if they were heretics, whether a Church professing love, mercy, and forgiveness was justified in torturing and burning them alive.

From Sorcery To Witchcraft[135]

The history of the witch mania can be divided into four approximate phases. First, until circa 1350, witchcraft in the traditional form of sorcery is substantially tolerated. Circa 1350 to 1450, it comes to be re-classified as heresy, and condemned in consequence. Circa 1450 to 1650, the perceived heretics are hunted, identified, and eradicated. Circa 1650, the mania gradually subsides as its sustaining beliefs are increasingly questioned.

Until the 14th century, sorcery was practiced widely, and in a sense this constituted witchcraft though it was almost entirely a practical matter, with no formal theoretical basis; it was folklore, popular wisdom, a commonplace of everyday life. It was punishable only if harm was done; no one was executed simply for practicing it, and indeed Charlemagne in the 10th century prohibited the burning of witches as being itself a pagan custom. From the Church's point of view, guidance was provided by the Canon Episcopi, a 9th century document which was regarded as sufficiently authoritative that in the 12th century it was embodied in the Canon Law of the Catholic Church. In essence, it denied the whole idea of witchcraft. The supposed arts of witches, the sabbat and flight included, were illusions or fantasies originating in dreams. Far from witchcraft being considered a heresy, it was the belief in witchcraft that was heretical.

In the course of the 14th century, however, theologians within the Roman Church brought about a change of attitude, which in effect was tantamount to a 180° reversal of the Canon Episcopi. Now witchcraft was considered not only a fact, but a heretical fact: a witch was a heretic who by definition was perpetrating treason against God by allying him/herself to the Devil. Now it was disbelief in witchcraft that was judged to be heretical and therefore punishable.

How this extraordinary volte-face came about has been the subject of much discussion. Social factors no doubt played a part. Europe had been devastated by plagues and wars, but these were nothing new; they had afflicted the populace oftentimes before without bringing about a witch mania. The Reformation and Counter-Reformation, wherein Catholics and Protestants competed for men's souls, concerned scholars and churchmen but hardly affected the man in the street.

Without the Church to formulate the image of witchcraft, the mania would surely not have come about. There might have been local disturbances, but not an epidemic that rolled across the map of Europe. For that to take place, a wide and powerful authority was needed, and at that time there was only one effective authority that transcended geographical or political boundaries: the Church.

In December 1484, Pope Innocent VIII promulgated the *Bull Summis Desiderantes Affectibus,* which deplored the spread of witchcraft in Germany and bestowed authority to end it on his beloved sons Jakob Sprenger, the dean of Köln University, and Heinrich Kramer, both Dominican fathers. With that mandate, the witch mania can be said to have become official.

Two years later the two Dominicans issued *Malleus Maleficarum* ("The Hammer of Witches").[136] This was an account of witchcraft that amounted to a manual for witch-hunters, describing witches' practices, providing hints for identifying them, questioning them, and punishing them. In so doing, it embodied a wide spectrum of folklore beliefs, rumors, and hearsay, and re-presented them as a formal heresy. Compacts with the Devil, succubi and incubi, the ability to assume animal shapes, and to fly through the air – all was grist for the authors' mill, and became consensus doctrine.

By presenting witchcraft as a new heresy and dissociating it from the old peasant sorcery, they were able to add urgency to their mission, to spread the fear that humankind was threatened by a new menace. This was readily taken up by many secular authorities. In the south of France, Pierre de Delancre, the royally appointed witch-hunter, believed his region was being afflicted by demons who had been driven from Asia by Christian missionaries. He had received reports by wine-traders from Britain who had seen them airborne over the Atlantic and heading in his direction.[137] At the Arras witch-trials in 1459, the Dominican inquisitor insisted that one in three nominal Christians was secretly a witch.[138]

Though it was only one of many treatises on the witch-menace, the *Malleus Maleficarum* was immensely popular, being reprinted some twenty times in the coming two centuries, apart from more than thirty translations. The opening sentence proclaims the authors' position: "The belief that there are such beings as witches is so essential a part of the Catholic faith that obstinately to maintain the opposite opinion manifestly savours of heresy." Since disbelief in witches was heresy, since the ways to recognize a witch were so many and varied, and since the means of extracting a confession – torture of every kind – was a legitimate procedure, the book constituted, in effect, a license to kill.

It is this universal applicability of the witch myth that explains why Protestants, though they jettisoned much of Rome's traditional teaching, retained a belief in the power of the Evil One, in the prevalence of his agents, and consequently in the need to eradicate witchcraft. Had Protestants rejected the *Malleus Maleficarum* as a contemptible production of the Church of Rome, the witch-mania might have been half as devastating. But belief in the Devil was part of the primitive church teaching to which Protestants claimed to be returning, so they accepted the *Malleus* as a laudable return to fundamental Christian principles. The consequence was that the authorities in Scotland and Switzerland were no less ruthless than those in France and Germany.

The man in the street, even if he could read, was unlikely to read the *Malleus*, but its teachings became the model for the witch hunters, and thus became imposed on the populace at large. The model was not entirely an artificial construct. Indeed, one of the reasons it took hold of the popular imagination was that it was built on existing beliefs. Though the "wise woman" living on the edge of the village was a valued member of the community, she was also the object of fear and suspicion, so it was not difficult for the inquisitors to persuade the community to see her as an agent of the devil. Village sorcerers had always been suspected of practicing magic on their neighbors by bringing about cattle sickness and harvest failure, impotence and miscarriages, and fatal accidents of every kind. They were widely believed to be capable of magical flight, and the nocturnal activities of "ladies of the night" under various names were a staple of popular dread.[139] But now these activities were seen as part of a larger plan, executed as part of a collective effort.

Many of the elements were already present in people's minds. What the churchmen did was to weave them into a coherent system, restructuring traditional beliefs into an explicit, logical myth. Because so much of it was what people had always believed, they did not question the new rationale. Now, when they were arrested and questioned, it was not the old crimes of sorcery but the new witchcraft heresy to which they confessed. What the churchmen now had to do was to convince the world that these collective practices were a reality.

The Sabbat

So long as the witches' activities were confined to working magic on neighbors, they provided no evidence of large-scale collective practice. Even though the sorceress might confess that her powers came to her from the Evil One, this did not show that humankind were under a massive demonic threat. Consequently, the concept of the sabbat was crucially important to the elaboration of the witch-myth. Not simply because it was evil in itself, but because it was a group activity. It was in their accounts of the sabbat that the witches' relationship with the Devil was most conspicuously demonstrated, and it was in their acceptance of the sabbat as a reality that the credulity of the inquisitors was most clearly revealed.

Like the other ingredients of the witch-myth, the sabbat possessed a frail basis in fact. Occasional gatherings of sorcerers did indeed take place, for the purpose of working magic or even invoking the Evil One.[140] But it is a far cry from these pathetic reunions in nearby woods to the dramatic sabbats on distant hilltops to which scores, hundreds, sometimes thousands of witches claimed to fly on broomsticks or goat-back. The sheer logistics of these events was evidence of collective effort. Transportation and catering had to be organized; child-minding or child-murder arranged; dancing and the ritual presentation, arse-kissing and copulation, had to be ordered. All this was vital evidence that witchcraft was a collective, not an individual affair. Inquisitor Pierre le Broussard summed up the testimony he elicited from the witches he interrogated at Arras in 1459-60:

> They spread an ointment, given them by the Devil, on a wooden stick, and all over their hands: then they put the stick between their legs and fly off over towns, woods and water, led by the Devil himself to the place of assembly. There they find tables laden with wine and food, and the Devil presents himself to them, sometimes in the form of a goat, sometimes as dog or monkey, but never in human form. They make offerings to the Devil and worship him. Many give him their souls or at least part of their bodies. Then with candles in their hands they kiss the arse of the goat that is the Devil.
>
> The accused told him…When the paying of homage was over, they all walked over a cross spitting on it, scorning Christ and the Trinity. Then they exposed their hinder parts to the sky and the heavens above in sign of their disregard for God. After drinking and eating their fill, they all had intercourse. The Devil appeared either as man or woman, and the men had intercourse with him in the form of a woman and the women in the form of a man. They also committed sodomy and practised homosexuality and other monstrous crimes against God and nature.[141]

Accounts of the sabbat often vary from this. For instance, in our case history that follows, Satan appears in human form. But invariably, proceedings at the sabbats verge on the delirious. If a witch's relative died, the body would be exhumed and taken to the sabbat where it would be served up as food, a husband offering his dead wife or son to his fellow-guests. The witches declared human flesh, even of decaying corpses, to be tastier than mutton or chicken.[142]

It is not always easy to see what the witches themselves would get out of their relationship. They received no earthly rewards – they remained the poor village men and women they had always been. The judges of Lorraine took it for granted that if a witch made a pact with the Evil One, she would prostitute herself to him, "it being the property of the Evil Spirit, as soon as he has seduced women or girls, to have carnal copulation with them."[143] But this was a doubtful pleasure. Satan, though sometimes described as handsome and charming, was more often depicted as a gigantic toad, or a hairy goat; kissing his bare arse (or his lips, if in toad form) cannot have been much fun. An accused woman of Marzelay, admitting that she had lain with the Devil, said she preferred the embraces of her husband.[144] Satan's organ and sperm were unpleasantly cold, and at his banquets the food was tasteless.[145]

Nevertheless, the devoted ladies would fly there, night after night, to dance with the demons, to pledge themselves and their children to his service, to kill and eat babies, and perform acts of black magic. Jeanne Dilusson, who was 29 years old, told the inquisitors that "the sabbat was a real Paradise, one enjoyed oneself more than words can tell: those who went found the time pass so quickly, such was the pleasure and enjoyment, that one could not leave without the greatest regret."[146]

This was just what the inquisitors wanted to hear. It reinforced the image they were anxious to project. As early as 1458, inquisitor Nicolas Jacquier had claimed that the sabbat was a physical reality.[147] To account for this contradiction of the Canon Episcopi, he asserted that the witches of his day were of recent origin – some theologians dated the creation of the new sect to 1404 – and had nothing to do with the victims of hallucination who constituted the former image of the witch.

But to establish the witch-menace as reality, it was necessary to establish the sabbat as reality.

Accusation And Trial

The churchmen, by creating a stereotype, authorized a myth that could be manipulated to serve their purpose. It provided a universal scapegoat that could be blamed for all disasters and afflictions, all accidents and calamities. And the more it was used, the more its efficacy was confirmed. From being used to explain why your cattle were sick or your children born dead, it escalated to explaining bad harvests and floods – whatever the catastrophe, large or small, there were the witches to take the blame. Not every village had Jews or ethnic minorities who could be accused of bringing misfortune, but every village possessed a potential witch, often many of them. For the great achievement of the inquisitors was to show that anyone and everyone could be guilty of witchcraft:

> Even piety and virtue were no shield from suspicion. A careless gesture, look or word, whether one was rich or poor, great or lowly, honest housewife or innocent maid no less than the malevolent or debauched, could pass for malignant spells if that gesture, look or word happened to coincide with one of the thousand and one accidents of human life: none could feel safe from denunciation, arrest, torture and the stake. It was enough simply to be different from one's neighbour: beauty, talent, artistic skills were grounds for suspicion; a fortune rapidly acquired

could be the devil's work. Everything and anything in everyday life could furnish a pretext for an accusation of sorcery; nothing, absolutely nothing, guaranteed anyone's immunity.[148]

Because the crime involved matters outside human experience – demonic forces – the witch-hunters felt justified in suspending the normal rules of law. In almost every instance, the proceedings were a travesty of established procedure. The initial accusations, which came generally from informers or were extracted from prisoners during torture, were never closely investigated, hardly even questioned. The accusation itself was sufficient grounds for arresting the individual and throwing her into prison, from which it was very difficult for her to extricate herself. The widely applied Law of Talion required that an accuser making false accusation, or one that he could not substantiate, himself incurred punishment; this was waived entirely in witchcraft trials, so that a village woman could accuse her neighbor with little risk. Pastor Wilhelm Lutz, at Nordlingen in 1594, noted: "There are people who have informed on their mothers-in-law, their wives or husbands, denouncing them as witches."[149]

Though procedures varied considerably, the basic scenario was that the Church would interrogate the accused until a confession was made, at which point the witch would be handed over to the secular authorities for punishment. He would be shaved over the entire body, in case demons might be lurking in his hair, or magic charms be hidden there, or his hair be concealing devils' marks.

Simply to be detained in prison was a severe punishment in itself. Even in England, where conditions were relatively humane, more then one in ten witches died in captivity from sickness, cold, and malnutrition; in continental Europe, the figure was much higher. If a prisoner died in prison, or in the course of being tortured, this was attributed to the Devil, seeking to protect his own by stopping the mouth of a prisoner who might otherwise reveal further names.

The Confession

Never did the inquisitors obtain a scrap of evidence that the sabbats actually took place. All they had were the confessions of those who claimed to have attended them. Yet such confessions were crucial to the sustaining of the myth, and the eliciting of them was the primary aim of the interrogations. Torture was almost universally used. Particularly in Germany, a voluntary confession was rarely accepted, for it was believed that only a confession obtained by torture was likely to be true. If the first confession seemed inadequate, the torture would be repeated, for "more often than not the extent of the confessions appears to have been directly proportional to the length of torture."[150]

As for the content of the confessions, there was no limit to what the inquisitors were prepared to believe. Not simply changing into animals, flying through the air, and magical practices of every kind, but matters of everyday human experience. In Protestant Pomerania, after torture, a ten-year-old girl admitted that she had already given birth to two children after coupling with demons and was pregnant with a third; no one saw fit to question her statement, and she was burnt at the stake.[151]

No less important than the witch's confession of what she had done was her naming of those who she had done it with. Obviously no witch went alone to the sabbat, so the inquisitors insisted that the accused name her companions. Thereby they were able to arrest others, for it was taken for granted that the names given by a tortured witch would truly be of other witches. The inquisitors do not seem to have considered the possibility that, on the rack, a witch might name names at random, or persons against whom she had a grudge, hoping to be spared further torture.

Even if we accept that the church interrogators felt they were justified in obtaining a confession by whatever means, there are countless instances of gratuitous cruelty that can be explained only by supposing that the judges and executioners were deranged. Thus in 1462, at Chamonix in Savoie, a woman named Pernette, who had confessed (no doubt at the interrogator's suggestion) that she had eaten children at the sabbat, was forced to sit naked on a red-hot iron for three minutes before being burned alive.[152]

An important question is whether the confessions blurted out by accused witches sprang from their own beliefs, or were imposed by inquisitors by suggestion or by leading questions. Historian Richard Kieckhefer has effectively demonstrated that while the populace believed in sorcery, magic, and miracles, and indeed in the powers of the devil, it was not from such traditions that the diabolical association of witchcraft came, but rather it was imposed on the accused by their judges. He cites cases in which the earlier part of the interrogation is concerned only with sorcery, such as was common practice in village life, but the notion of diabolic pacts and acts – the grounds for heresy – comes in at a later stage. He suggested plausibly that the latter part of the confession came only after torture, and that the inquisitor put the words into the victim's mouth.[153] Witch-hunter Pierre De Lancre candidly said of his interrogations, that they were "so many traps to make the accused fall into confession."[154]

A feature of the witch trials that has puzzled historians has been that many "confessions" were made spontaneously and voluntarily. Thus in 1461, at Lausanne, two subjects confessed voluntarily to having venerated the devil. If they hoped by this means to escape torture, they were sadly disappointed, for one of the judges insisted on torture to make sure the accused was telling not only the truth, but the whole truth.[155]

That external suggestion alone does not account for witches' confessions is clear when we descend to detail. Again and again, when we read the case histories, we find witches freely confessing to esoteric details without any evidence of torture, and it was this spontaneity, rather than the confessions themselves, that convinced rational men that the details were true. It was because he had heard confessions given without torture that Paolo Grillandi, a judge of witches in central Italy in the early 16th century, was converted to the belief that witches were transported bodily to the sabbat.[156]

Apart from the fact that "free confession" was often a euphemism applied to the accused's final affirmation that his previous statement was true, and does not mean that that original confession was made voluntarily, the circumstances under which it was obtained were anything but "free." Even if physical torture were not used to obtain it, the stress of arrest, accusation, imprisonment, and interrogation, set in a context of extreme social pressure, would ensure that there was little free will in the matter.

Execution

Once obtained, the confession was sufficient to justify execution. If the victim recanted, protesting he had confessed under torture, he would be tortured again to recant his recantation. It was rare to escape the consequences. Maria Hollin, who kept the Crown Inn in Nordlingen, was tortured 56 times in 11 months and kept in a stinking dungeon between visits to the torture-chamber. Amazingly, she survived, thanks to legal intervention by her hometown of Ulm. She is one of the exceedingly rare instances of escape from the stake. We can only wonder what her physical and psychological state must have been after such an ordeal.[157]

Though technically the secular court was free to override the church's findings, it rarely did so, for a judge to set an accused witch free would be to risk being seen as a friend of the Devil. But in any case, the secular authorities were generally of one mind with the inquisitors. They carried out their share of the proceedings with grisly legal punctiliousness (thanks to which, the court records are available for us to examine). The executions were carried out with pomp and circumstance, often after a parade through the streets. In continental Europe witches were generally burned alive, but this was forbidden in England, where they were hanged.

Estimates as to how many supposed witches in all were executed vary widely. Robbins, drawing on various authorities, proposed a grand overall estimate of 200,000, more than half of these in Germany, about 1000 in England, with the remainder in Scotland or continental Europe.[158] Sociologist Erich Goode, citing more modern sources, places the figure closer to half a million.[159]

The End Of The Mania

Even though few contemporary observers can have been aware of the overall effect of the mania, they were surely aware of its extent, and the intensity of particular instances. The great majority took the view that the Church knew best, and that the widespread purge was necessary if mankind was to be saved, and that it could be achieved only by dispatching the heretics to the next world for their own sakes.

However, from the start there were a few lone voices who questioned the validity of the myth. Many, while accepting the existence of the Devil, questioned whether he was responsible; some shared the view of Jean Weyer that most witches were sick. Some, like the English writer Reginald Scot, went further in their skepticism. Gradually, the voice of reason prevailed, and little by little the mania lost its impetus. This occurred at varying dates in different regions: in Holland, in 1610, and in England in 1684. Scotland took longer, but things were over by 1727; in France in 1745; in Germany in 1775, in Switzerland in 1782, in Poland in 1793, and in Italy in 1791.[160]

COMMENT: The fundamental question posed by the European witch mania is how so many people could participate in so manifest a delusion throughout so long a period. Historians of the subject have looked in many directions for answers – social, political, and economic, as well as psychosocial. Spanish scholar Baroja makes a crucial point: "The nature of witches and the acts they are believed to carry out cannot be determined without taking into account the concept of reality of the times and circles in which they move…This is the essential problem for those who investigate witches and witchcraft. What is the nature of reality in a world where there are witches? Above all, what do those who believe themselves to be the victims of witchcraft believe to be real?"[161]

For the myth to be sustained, the sabbat needed to be acknowledged as a reality, and for this, the confessions – which were the only evidence – must be acknowledged as true. But this testimony was often less than convincing. While a witch at Domjevin, in Lorraine, insisted that her copulation with the Devil was a physical reality, another at Saint-Nicolas averred that hers took place during sleep. Two accused witches stated that the devil took them by force, a third said her will was so paralyzed that she did not even desire to resist. Yet several witches claimed to have resisted the devil successfully. A woman of Amance told the devil that she had not been a whore during her youth and had no intention of becoming one in her maturity.[162]

Few of these women denied or even questioned that they had encountered the devil in physical form; it was only with regards what they did with him that they presented different levels of reality. It is the same with regards the flight to the sabbat. Most witches insisted on the reality of the flight, on broomstick, goat or whatever, but a minority claimed that the journeying took place in sleep, or "in the spirit."[163]

What the inquisitors succeeded in putting across was the reality behind these confessions. Once that reality was established, the rest followed with remorseless inevitability.

No one can read the original accounts of the sabbat without noting their resemblance to present-day satanic ritual abuse. Is it simply a question that the later mania, consciously or unconsciously, lifted details from the old accounts? Or are these characteristic behaviors part of the collective unconscious, liable to resurrect when circumstances favor them?

In both cases, some commentators point to the concurrence of testimony as evidence of reality. How could so many people give similar testimony if it wasn't real? It does not seem to have occurred to them that this convergence can be accounted for by leading questions by interrogators and folklore traditions stored in the collective unconscious.

Case History

The trial of Isabeau Cheyne was not a sensational case, but a typical small-town hearing in southeastern France. The questions and answers show how traditional folklore beliefs were assimilated into the newly formulated myth, so that a simple-minded peasant came to be perceived as an affiliate of an international conspiracy, thus justifying the judges in condemning her as a witch rather than a sorceress.

The year 1656, on the 7th day of April, in the salle de l'auditoire of the baillage of Vivarais, at the seat of Villeneuve-de-Berg, before us, Antoine de Serre, lieutenant of the prévost des maréchaux, assisting Maître Pierre Tardieu, counsellor of the king, judge of the baillage.

Having commanded to come before us Isabeau Cheyne, prisoner detained in the gaol of Villeneuve, and having made known to her our quality as prévost, that our jurisdiction is sovereign, and that there is no appeal from our judgments and sentences; and asked whether she is willing to reply before us to the charges and accusations laid against her;

Asked her name, age, quality, place of residence, and what religion she professes. - Replied that her name is Isabeau Cheyne, from Saint-Martin-l'Inférier en Barris, aged 50 or thereabouts, professes the Roman Catholic faith.

Asked why she was made prisoner? - Said that the woman la Peytière is the cause, she having informed the sieur de Pampellonne that the prisoner had caused harm to la Damoiselle de Pampellonne, his wife;

Asked if it was true that she had done harm to la Damoiselle? what harm? why? how? and in what place? - Replied that it is indeed true: that she, together with Madeleine Lacroze, known as la Peytière, Jeanne, known as Leyriasse, and Louise, known as la Rouge, about ten weeks ago, caused harm to la Damoiselle, in the form of a curse, which caused her to be very angry, so that la Damoiselle had struck her, accusing her of saying she would not be able to bear children. The prisoner, being in a wood of Andance with the evil one and several others, in order to do harm to la Damoiselle, was given a piece of writing by the evil one, which was put in a basket.

Asked who she meant by the evil one? - Replied, the devil.

Asked if she is a witch, and how long she has been one? - Replied that she has been a witch for about 11 years.

Asked how she became a witch? - Replied that 11 years ago, having a leg ailment, she sought out a woman who lived in Montelimar, who cured her with the help of the devil. Two or three weeks later she paid a second visit to this woman, who took her to sabbats in various places, in the woods, on hills. When she was there, the devil spoke to her for the first time, and promised to give her much money, of which she had need, being poor. In fact, he gave her several pieces of money, but when she got home they had turned into leaves.

Asked how this woman of Montelimar travelled to the sabbat? - Replied that the devil gave her an ointment with which she coated a staff, which carried them to the sabbat, leaving the house by the chimney.

Asked what she did with the devil at the sabbat? what was given her or promised? - Replied that she gave her body to the devil, having promised to be always his. In fact the devil laid with her, but she cannot remember if this happened the first time she went to the sabbat or the second.

Asked if the devil laid with her several times? - Replied, three or four times.

Asked if the devil appeared to her as a man or a beast? - Replied that he was always in the form of a big black man, about 30 years of age.

Asked how often she attended the sabbat? - Replied that she doesn't remember well, but thinks it was about thirty times.

Asked if the other women she named were with her? - Replied that she often found herself with la Peytière, thrice with Leyriasse, and once with la Rouge.

Asked if the devil had lain with these others? - Replied that she does not know and doesn't want to tell lies.

Asked if she had practised magic by means of the aiguillette [charm in the form of a knot] on newly-married men, notably Jean Guilhon, [to render them impotent]? - Replied that she had never done so, the only knot she had was the one on her skirt.

Asked if she had cured la Damoiselle of the evil by her magic? - Replied that she was taken, about a fortnight ago, to the chateau of Pampellonne, where the sieur de Pampellonne ordered her to cure his wife, saying that if she did so she would not be punished but set free; which was also promised by the sieur de Cheysserie, brother of la Damoiselle; upon which, the prisoner said prayers in the chapel of the chateau, calling on the Holy Virgin and all the saints in Paradise, and her prayers worked so well that la Damoiselle was partially cured; but because the evil spell can't be cured without passing it on to someone else, she gave it to a sheep which died the next day.

Asked if la Damoiselle was entirely cured? - Replied that she and the other women gathered in a ravine of the chateau, and prayed together for the cure of la Damoiselle, after which each of the four took a small piece of wood, and begged Jesus-Christ to take the evil from la Damoiselle and take it to a desert place where no bread or wine could be cultivated; having struck the ground with the wood, they threw it away, and commanded Satan to quit the body of of the lady, and having thrown their magic charm into the woods, they counselled la Damoiselle to make a pilgrimage to Rochambeau; which she did, and was cured of her affliction.

Asked if the evil was transferred to anyone else? - Replied that it was transferred to a bull which died the same moment that la Damoiselle arrived at Rochambeau.

Asked if it is true that she worked evil on a child named Grausau, of la Bastide, causing its head to swell and be deformed? - Replied that she and Peytière went with the evil one to the house, where they took the form of cats and entered the house by the cattery, took the child from beside his parents, and carried it to the sabbat on a hill named le Charnier. There they drank the blood of the child, sucking it out through its eyes; after which the devil took the child back to its home, where it died a few days later.

Asked why she had done this to the child? - Replied that the child's father had a grudge against her and constantly spoke ill of her.

[The prisoner admitted doing the same to the child of her neighbour Valette, who had killed her chickens; and on another occasion, she and la Peytière stifled a child of one Roumegier, who had spoken ill of her, as it lay beside its parents in bed: on these occasions also, she and la Peytière transformed themselves into cats.]

Asked how and where the witches' sabbat took place, at what time and on what days? - Replied that they took place on Thursdays, from 9 or 10 till midnight, at which time, on the crowing of the cock, the whole assembly disappeared. They were held here or there, on barren hill-tops where nothing will grow.

Asked what was done at the sabbats and who was present? - Replied that the devil was there in human shape, and little devils in the form of cats, with bells on their legs, at the sound of which the devil and the witches would dance round a fire which the devil had prepared.

Asked if the devil spoke to them, and what he said? - Replied that he did speak, telling them he was their comrade and good friend, and he would never let them go short if they gave themselves to him body and soul, which she had never done as regards her soul though she had given him her body.

Asked if she had seen any men at the sabbat? - Replied no.

Asked if she recognised any other women at the sabbat? - Gave the name of five others from nearby villages.

Asked if she was married, and had children? - Replied that she had never been married but had a child by Badovin de Pampellonne, 24 or 25 years ago.

Asked if she had any marks on her body? - Replied that all her life she has had a mark on her left armpit.

Asked if she repented of the harm she had caused? - Replied that she did repent, and asked forgiveness of God and of the present company.

Exhorted to tell the truth - Said she had done so.

Called back to ask if she persisted in her statements - Did so, but was unable to sign her name to them.[164]

It is a measure of the firm hold that the witch myth had taken in the popular mind, that Isabeau's judges were prepared to believe that she and her companions had turned themselves into cats and travelled on broomsticks to distant sabbats, quite apart from the rest of her statement. They therefore condemned her to be burnt alive, which was done in the place of Villeneuve-des-Berg, "to the great edification and satisfaction of the inhabitants who came in crowds to watch her suffer and die."[165]

However, Isabeau's execution is not on record, and if her repentance was considered sincere, it is possible that her punishment was reduced to a flogging, and perhaps banishment, as was done with other convicted sorceresses.[166]

WONDER HORSE MANIAS

United States and Europe: 17th to 20th centuries

In the early years of the 20th century, a German horse named Clever Hans created a global sensation when it was claimed that he could answer complicated mathematical questions by tapping out the correct answers with his foot. For instance, if someone asked Hans, what is 20 minus 10, he would tap his foot 10 times. Soon, calculating "wonder horses" were appearing in circuses and public exhibitions. Hans' owner, Wilhelm von Osten, had been conducting experiments with a variety of animals on the assumption that they had intelligence similar to the level of humans. After failing in his experiments, he came across Hans, who did indeed appear as if he could solve the math questions posed to him. Hans even passed a series of experiments while being observed by a panel of prestigious scientists – answering questions correctly even when his owner was not present. The mystery was solved when it was realized that Hans could not answer the question if he could not see the questioner. As psychologist Dennis Coon remarks: "It seems that questioners always lowered their heads (to look at Hans' foot) after asking a question. That was Hans' cue to start tapping. When Hans had tapped the correct number, a questioner would always look up to see if Hans was going to stop. This was Hans's cue to stop tapping!"[167] Clever Hans had become a channel "through which the information the questioner unwittingly put into the situation was fed back to the questioner."[168]

It was only after prolonged and meticulous investigation that observers were able to establish the imperceptible movements that indicated the correct solutions to the horses. Therefore, it wasn't extraordinary behavior on the part of either the horses or their "trainers" that made this phenomenon so remarkable, as the fact that the explanation was so hard to detect and eluded so many seemingly competent observers—nevertheless, the explanation was there, for all to see, if only they knew what to look for.

While Hans is the most famous "genius horse," he was just one in a long line of calculating horses that were a mainstay in European circus acts for centuries.[169] One of the earliest recorded examples was Morocco, the famous "dancing horse" who performed remarkable feats in Europe during the 16th century. One observer of Morocco, Samuel Rid, wrote about the horse in 1616, sagely noting that Morocco was responding to cues from his master, who "will bid his horse to tell how many (dice) you or he have thrown. Then the horse paws with his foot whiles (sic) the master stands stone still. Then when his master sees he hath pawed so many as the first dice shews (sic), itself, then he lifts up his shoulders and stirs a little." Rid continued: "Then he bids him to tell what is on the second die, and then of the third die, which the horse will do accordingly, still pawing with his foot until his master sees he hath pawed enough, and then stirs. Which, the horse marking, will stay and leave pawing. And note, that the horse will paw an (sic) hundred times together, until he sees his master stir. And note also that nothing can be done but his master must first know, and then his master knowing, the horse is ruled by him by signs."[170] Among Morocco's amazing abilities, he was said to perform complex mathematical calculations. Some thought that Morocco got his powers from consorting with Satan, and as such the horse and his owner were charged with being in cahoots with the devil. Both were saved when Morocco, appearing before church officials, knelt, as if to convey that he was remorseful of his collusion.[171]

Other wonder horses of the early 20th century included Zarif, the math whiz of Elberfeld, England, and Lady Wonder, the so-called talking horse of Richmond, Virginia, who would press keys on a giant typewriter-like contraption and supposedly tap out answers to questions with her nose.[172] The subtle-cuing of Lady Wonder was revealed by magician Milbourne Christopher in a series of clever experiments in 1956. Christopher told the horse's trainer, Claudia Fonda, that his name was actually John Banks. Later he asked Lady Wonder if she knew his name. The horse promptly nudged the levers, spelling: B-A-N-K-S. In another demonstration, a bystander would write down a number and Lady Wonder would then guess what it was by nosing down the appropriate lever on the typewriter device. With pencil and paper, Banks made a motion in the shape of the number 9. But in reality, it was a clever ruse. He didn't touch the paper until the down stroke, producing the number 1. Christopher then concentrated on the number 1. Lady tapped down the lever for 9. Christopher determined that when Lady's head was over the key for the correct number or letter, her trainer would slightly move her training rod. As Joe Nickell observed: "That was enough to cue the swaying mare to stop and nudge that lever. Thus, Lady was revealed to be a well-trained animal, not a telepathic one."[173]

The horse named Clever Hans with his handler and tutor Wilhelm von Osten.

Sources

1. Edmondson, Brad (1987). "Doctor Fad Knows Marketing." *American Demographics* 9(5):23-24. (May).
2. Panati, Charles. (1991). *Panati's Parade of Fads, Follies, and Manias.* New York: HarperCollins, p. 435.
3. Panati, op cit. p. 435.
4. Hakuta, Ken, Williams, Catherine, and Carlson, Margaret B. (1988). *How to Create your Own Fad and make a Million Dollars*. New York: Morrow.
5. Panati, op cit., pp. 434-435.
6. Hakuta, Kenneth (1983). "Sticking to it; Japan's Wall Walker goes far. Ken Hakuta." *Time* 121:92 (April 25); "Creepy; A New Hit Toy." *Fortune* 107, p. 12 (March 7, 1983); Panati, op cit., p. 434.
7. Nandi, Dhirendra Nath, Banerjee, G., Bera, Shibani, Nandi, Sabyasachi, and Nandi, Parthasarathi (1985). "Contagious Hysteria in a West Bengal Village." *American Journal of Psychotherapy* 39(2):247-252. See p. 251.
8. Nandi, et al., op cit., p. 251.
9. Nandi, et al., op cit., p. 251.
10. "Monster Scare Causes Deaths." *Reno Evening Gazette*, August 27, 1947.
11. Sulman, Felix Grad (1980). *The Effect of Air Ionization, Electric Fields, Atmospherics and Other Electric Phenomena on Man and Animal.* Springfield Illinois: Charles C. Thomas, p. 127.
12. Tributsch, Helmut (1982). When the Snakes Awake [translation of German original: *Wenn die Schlangen Erwachen* 1978]. Cambridge, Massachusetts: MIT Press, p. 157.
13. Soyka, Fred, with Edmonds, Alan (1977). *The Ion Effect.* Toronto: Lester and Green, pp. 107-108.
14. Tromp, Solco W., "Effects of Weather and Climate on Mental Processes in Man," cited in Angoff, Allan, and Shapin, Betty (editors) (1974). *Parapsychology and the Sciences.* New York: Parapsychology Foundation, p. 136.
15. Tributsch, op cit., p. 158.
16. The primary source is Webster 2005, together with items published on the internet as a consequence of Webster's investigation. See, Webster, Richard (2005). *The Secret of Bryn Estyn: The Making of a Modern Witch Hunt*. Oxford: Orwell Press.
17. Webster, op cit., p. 92.
18. Webster, op cit., p. 161.
19. Webster, op cit., p. 144.
20. Webster, op cit., p. 156.
21. Webster, op cit., p. 104.
22. Webster, op cit., p. 518.
23. Webster, op cit., p. 209.
24. Webster, op cit., p. 223.
25. Webster, op cit., p. 224.
26. Webster, op cit., p. 238.
27. Webster, op cit., p. 303.
28. Webster, op cit., p. 422.
29. Jennie Bristow, "The Making of a Modern Witch-Hunt" on the Spiked Liberties website, accessed 24 March 2005.
30. Webster, op cit., pp. 529, 550.
31. Webster, op cit., p. 536.
32. Quoted on orwellpress.co.uk.
33. ICNorth Wales/icnetwork.co.uk.
34. For example, Evans 1969 and Orr 1973 make little or no mention of the phenomena. Refer to: Evans, Eifion (1904). *The Welsh Revival of 1904.* Bridgend, Wales: Bryntirion Press, reprinted in 1969/1987; Orr, J. Edwin (1973). *The Flaming Tongue: Evangeli-*

cal Awakenings 1900. Chicago: Moody press.
35. Orr, J. Edwin (1965). *The Light of the Nations.* Exeter: Paternoster, p. 140; Orr, 1973, op cit., p. 1.
36. Evans, 1969, op cit., p. 45.
37. Evans, 1969, op cit., p. 90.
38. Stead quoted by Evans, 1969, op cit., p. 127.
39. Evans, 1969, op cit., pp. 131-132.
40. Evans, Beriah G. (1905). "Merionethshire Mysteries." *Occult Review* 1(3):114 (March).
41. Evans, 1969, op cit., pp. 110, 161.
42. Quoted in Kevin and Sue McClure (1970). *Stars and Rumours of Stars.* Privately published, circa 1970, p. 3.
43. Fryer, A.T. (1905-1907). "Psychological Aspects of the Welsh Revival." *Proceedings of the Society for Psychical Research* XIX, p. 91.
44. Fryer, op cit., p. 123.
45. Fryer, op cit., p. 135.
46. Fryer, op cit., p. 92.
47. Evans, 1969, op cit., p. 114.
48. Fryer, op cit., p. 95.
49. Fryer, op cit., pp. 124, 139.
50. Fryer, op cit, pp. 131-132.
51. *The Western Mail,* quoted in Lowe, Lowe, Karen (2004). *Carriers of the Fire.* Llanelli, Wales: Shedhead Productions, p. 110.
52. Evans, 1969, op cit., p. 117.
53. Evans, 1969, op cit., p. 118.
54. Fryer, op cit., p. 136.
55. Quoted from Winifred Pearce Knight in royal service, in Orr, op cit., p. 19.
56. Evans, 1969, op cit., p. 119.
57. Fryer, op cit., p. 147.
58. Fryer, op cit., p. 98.
59. Fryer, op cit., pp. 148-149.
60. Fryer, op cit., p. 150.
61. Fryer, op cit., p. 157.
62. Evans, 1969, op cit., p. 179.
63. McClure, op cit., p. 12.
64. McClure, op cit., pp. 13-14.
65. *Cambrian News,* March 1905 quoted by Lowe, p. 115.
66. Kevin and Sue McClure, *Stars and Rumours of Stars.* Privately published, circa 1970.
67. Wier, Jean. [Weyer, Johann] (1885). *Histoires, Disputes Et Discours Des Illusions Et Impostures Des Diables, Des Magiciens Infames, Sorcières Et Empoisonneurs.* Translated from the Latin original, published 1563. Paris: Bureaux du Progrès Médical.
68. Wier, op cit., Volume 1, p. 529.
69. Görres, Johann Joseph von (1845). *La Mystique Divine, Naturelle et Diabolique.* Paris: Poussielgue-Rusand, 1855, translated from the German Christliche Mystik, Volume 5, p. 269.
70. Calmeil, L.F. (1845). *De la Folie, Consideree Sous le Point de vue Pathologique, Philosophique, Historique et Judiciaire* [On the Crowd, Considerations on the Point of Pathology, Philosophy, History and Justice]. Paris: Baillere, Volume 1, p. 255.
71. Madden, R. R. (1857). *Phantasmata or Illusions and Fanaticisms of Protean Forms Productive of Great Evils.* London: T.C. Newby, volume 2, p. 239.
72. Mabe, Logan (2003). "School Finds No Cause for Illness. Officials are Left to Wonder: Is the Malady that Struck 14 Gaither High School Students all in their Heads?" St. *Petersburg Times* (Florida).
73. Victor, Jeffery S. (1998). "Moral Panics and the Social Construction of Deviant Behavior: A Theory and Application to the Case of Ritual Child Abuse." *Sociological Perspectives* 41(3):541-565. See p. 548.
74. Guy, D.J. (1991). *Sex and Danger in Buenos Aires: Prostitution, Family and Nation in Argentina.* Lincoln, Nebraska and London: University of Nebraska Press.
75. Morin, Edgar (1971). *Rumours in Orleans.* New York: Pantheon Books.
76. Nandi, Dhirendra Nath, Banerjee, G., Bera, Shibani, Nandi, Sabyasachi, and Nandi, Parthasarathi (1985). "Contagious Hysteria in a West Bengal Village." *American Journal of Psychotherapy* 39(2):247-252.
77. Nandi et al., op cit., p. 248.
78. Nandi et al., op cit., p. 248.
79. Nandi et al., op cit., p. 251.
80. Teicher, Morton I. '"Windigo" Psychosis Among Algonkian-Speaking Indians.' *International Journal of Parapsychology* pp. 5-33 (reprint, no date).
81. Page, Michael, and Ingpen, Robert (1985). *Encyclopedia of Things that Never Were.* London: Landsdowne/Dragon's World, p. 83.
82. Seymour Parker (1982). "The Wittiko Psychosis in the Context of Ojibwa Personality and Culture." *American Anthropologist* 62:602 (1960) reprinted in Corliss, William R. [compiler] (1982). *The Unfathomed Mind.* Glen Arm MD: Sourcebook Project, p. 76.
83. Marano, L. (1982). "Windigo Psychosis: The Anatomy of an Emic-Etic Confusion." *Current Anthropology* 23(4):385-412.
84. Tyrrel, J.B.. "David Thompson's narrative of his explorations in Western America 1784-1812," quoted in Teicher, op cit.
85. Halowell. A.I. "Psychic Stresses and Culture Patterns" in *American Journal of Psychiatry* 1936, cited by Teicher.
86. Teicher, op cit.
87. "A New Look for Windshields. In Bellingham, Wash. 1,500 Cars are Damaged by Ghostly Little Pellets." *Life* (12 April, 1954):34-35. See p. 34.
88. "Bellingham Vandals Break Windows." *Seattle Post-Intelligencer,* March 23, 1954, p. 8; "'Buckshot Gang' Resumes Reign of Vandalism." *Seattle Post-Intelligencer,* March 30, 1954, p. 1.
89. "A New Look for Windshields," op cit.
90. "Boat Hit by Atomic Ash OK'd." *Seattle Post-Intelligencer,* March 18, 1954, pp. 1, 8.
91. "Boat Hit by Atomic Ash OK'd." op cit., p. 1.
92. "Eight More Nippon Craft Radioactive." *Seattle Post-Intelligencer,* March 19, 1954, p. 3.
93. "Danger Area Tripled: H-Blast Zone Radius Set at 450 Miles." *Seattle Post-Intelligencer,* March 21, 1954, p. 1.
94. "3 H-Bomb Victims Face Death. Doctor Reports on Fishermen." *Seattle Post-Intelligencer,* March 23, 1954, p. 1, 2.
95. "Witness Says: Hydrogen Test 'Out of Control." *Seattle Post-Intelligencer,* March 23, 1954, p. 2.
96. "H-Bomb Test: US Vessel Showered by Ashes." *Seattle Post-Intelligencer,* March 24, 1954, p. 3.
97. "H-Tainted Snow Falls in Montana." *Seattle Post-Intelligencer,* April 1, 1954, p. 7.
98. Medalia, Nahum Z., and Larsen, Otto. (1958). "Diffusion and Belief in a Collective Delusion." *American Sociological Review* 23:180-186. See p. 180.
99. "Mayor Wires Ike and Langli: President's Aid Askled in Windshield Mystery. NW Police Summoned." *Seattle Post-Intelligencer,* April 16, 1954, pp. 1, 6. Also see: "Windshield Dilemma: Mayor's Call for U.S. Aid Answered. Reports Vary on Cooperation." *Seattle Post-Intelligencer,* April 18, 1954, pp. 1, 6.

100. "Sheriff Believes Clue in H-Bomb Fallout." *Portland Oregonian*, April 15, 1954, p. 1.
101. "Mayor Wires Ike and Langli," op cit., p. 6.
102. "Windshields Shattered at Beaverton." *Portland Oregonian*, April 16, 1954, p. 6.
103. Scientists Discount 'Glass Pox.'" *Portland Oregonian*, April 17, 1954, p. 1.
104. "Mayor Wires Ike and Langli," op cit., p. 1.
105. "Mayor Wires Ike and Langli," op cit., p. 1; "Scientists Discount 'Glass Pox.'" op cit.
106. "Broken Windshield Epidemic Spreads; Damage Here Slight." *Portland Oregonian*, April 16, 1954, p. 1, 14.
107. "Washington Spreads Mesh for Windshield Crackers." *Portland Oregonian*, April 15, 1954, p. 1; "Broken Windshield Epidemic Spreads." op cit.; "Mystery Lacking in City's Glass Loss, Portland Police Favor Vandalism Idea." *Portland Oregonian*, April 17, 1954, p. 5.
108. "Mystery Pox on Car Glass Invades State." *Portland Oregonian*, April 18, 1954, p. 1.
109. Mystery Pox on Car Glass Invades State." op cit.
110. Mystery Pox on Car Glass Invades State." op cit.
111. "Hatching of Sand Fleas in Glass Suggested in Windshield Pocking; Even FBI Called into Case." *Portland Oregonian*, April 25, 1954, p. 17; Medalia and Larsen, op cit.
112. "Windshield Pox: Theories Range from Gremlins to Supersonics." *Seattle Post-Intelligencer*, April 16, 1954, p. 6; "U Scientists Skeptical in Glass Puzzle. Meteoric Bits Found in Laurelhurst District." *Seattle Post-Intelligencer*, April 17, 1954, pp. 1, 4; "Meteor Pellets may be Answer to Car Damage." Seattle Post-Intelligencer, April 17, 1954, p. 4; "Meteor 'Dust' Theory Eyed." *Portland Oregonian*, April 20, 1954, p. 14.
113. "Seattle 'Theorized' by Dots Before Eyes." *Seattle Post-Intelligencer*, April 20, 1954, p. 9.
114. "Windshields Shattered at Beaverton." op cit.
115. "Glass Seen Unaffected by Pellets." *Portland Oregonian*, April 19, 1954, p. 1.
116. "Windshield Pits Theorized as Shells of Sea Animal Disturbed by H-Blast." *Portland Oregonian*, April 20, 1954, p. 14.
117. "Seattle 'Theorized' by Dots Before Eyes." op cit.
118. "Windshield Pellets Show Tails Similar to Comets." *Portland Oregonian*, April 20, 1954, p. 1; "Windshield Blemish Spreads South; Ohio Cars also Marred by Pox." *Seattle Post-Intelligencer*, April 18, 1954, p. 6.
119. "Windshield Blemish Spreads South..." op cit.
120. "Windshield 'Pit' Puzzle Grows." *Seattle Post-Intelligencer*, April 19, 1954, p. 1.
121. "Pocks Mark Appear on Spectacles." *Portland Oregonian*, April 20, 1954, p. 14.
122. "His Windshield Still Unscathed." Portland Oregonian, April 21, 1954, p. 1.
123. "Maine Windows Develop Holes." *Portland Oregonian*, April 22, 1954, p. 1.
124. "Dust Declared to be Pollen." *Portland Oregonian*, April 23, 1954, p. 1
125. Bovee, Harley H. (1954). "Report on the 1954 Windshield Pitting Phenomenon in the State of Washington" (mimeographed). Environmental Research Laboratory, University of Washington, June 10, summarized by Bovee in the *Occupational Health Newsletter* 3(5) (May 1954), p. 3. Published by the University of Washington, Environmental Health Division, presently known as Department of Environmental Health, School of Public Health and Community Medicine, Box 357234, Seattle, Washington 98195-7234.
126. Bovee, op cit.
127. Bovee, op cit.
128. Bovee, op cit.
129. Bovee, op cit.
130. Medalia and Larsen, op cit., p. 186.
131. Medalia and Larsen, op cit., p. 186.
132. We are grateful to Chuck Flood for gathering the press reports used in this entry.
133. Chambers, Paul, and Bartholomew, Robert E. (2001). "The Phantom Sniper of Esher England: How a Community Created an Imaginary Assailant." Pp. 169-182. In Bartholomew, Robert E. (2001). *Little Green Men, Meowing Nuns and Headhunting Panics: A Study of Mass Psychogenic Illness and Social Delusion*. Jefferson, North Carolina: McFarland, p. 182.
134. Quoted by Robbins, Rossell Hope (1959). *The Encyclopedia of Witchcraft and Demonology*. London: Spring Books, p. 550.
135. This section has been compiled by drawing on Baissac, Jules (1890). *Les Grands Jours de la Sorcellerie*. Paris: Klincksieck; Cohn, Norman (1975). *Europe's Inner Demons*. London: Chatto-Heinemann for Sussex University Press; Delcambre, Etienne (1948). *Le Concept de la Sorcellerie dans le Duché de Lorraine*. Nancy: Société d'Archéologie Lorraine; Robbins, op cit.; Russell, Jeffrey B. (1989). *A History of Witchcraft*. London: Thames and Hudson; Trevor-Roper, Hugh (1967). *The European Witch-Craze of the 16th and 17th Centuries*. London: Penguin, and numerous other sources.
136. Sprenger, Jakob and Kramer, Heinrich (1928[1486]). *Malleus Maleficarum*. Translated into English by Montague Summers. London: Rodker, p. 1.
137. De Lancre, Pierre (1613). *Tableau de l'inconstance des Mauvais Anges et des Demons*. Paris: Buon, p. 37.
138. Cohn, op cit., p. 231.
139. Cohn, op cit., pp. 211, 217.
140. Delcambre, op cit., volume 1, p. 129.
141. Baroja, Julio Caro (1964). *The World of the Witches*. Original: Madrid 1961: translated by Nigel Glendinning. London: Weidenfeld and Nicolson, pp. 90-91.
142. Baissac, op cit., pp. 118-119.
143. *Archives Départementales de Meurthe-et-Moselle*, cited in Delcambre, op cit., volume 1, p. 67.
144. Delcambre, op cit., p. p. 79.
145. Baissac, op cit., p. 33.
146. Baissac, op cit., p. 121.
147. Delcambre, op cit., volume 1, p. 132.
148. Baissac, op cit., p. 132.
149. Robbins, op cit., p. 305.
150. Kieckhefer, Richard (1976). *European Witch Trials*. London: Routledge & Kegan Paul, p. 89.
151. Baissac, op cit., p. 723.
152. Robbins, op cit., p. 517.
153. Kieckhefer, op cit., pp. 73-74.
154. Delancre, op cit., 410.
155. Kieckhefer, op cit., p. 89.
156. Trevor-Roper, op cit., p. 49.
157. Robbins, op cit., p. 304.
158. Robbins, op cit., p. p. 180.
159. Goode, Erich. (2001). *Deviant Behavior* (sixth edition). Upper Saddle River, New Jersey: Prentice-Hall, pp. 344-345.
160. Robbins, op cit., p. 551.
161. Baroja, op cit., p. xiii.

162. Delcambre, op cit., volume 1, p. 68, citing departmental archives.
163. Delcambre op cit., volume 1, p. 161.
164. Reprinted in Dalmas, J-B. (1865). *Les Sorcières du Vivarais Devant les Inquisiteurs de la Foi.* Privas, p. 171.
165. Dalmas, op cit., p. 1865.
166. Régné, Jean (1913). *La Sorcellerie en Vivarais.* Paris: Alcan, p. 27.
167. Coon, Dennis. (2000). *Introduction to Psychology: Exploration and Application* (eighth edition). Pacific Grove, California: Brooks/Cole Publishing, p. 29.
168. Hyman, Ray. (1981). "The Psychic Reading." Pp. 168-181. In Thomas A. Sebeok and Robert Rosenthal (editors). *The Clever Hans Phenomenon: Communication with Horses, Whales, Apes, and People.* New York: New York Academy of Sciences, p. 170.
169. Sebeok, Thomas A., and Umiker-Sebeok, Jean. (1979). "Performing Animals: Secrets of the Trade." *Psychology Today* 13(6):78-91. See p. 78.
170. Rid, Samuel (1612). *The Art of Juggling or Legerdemain*, cited in Kinney, Arthur, F. (1973). *Rogues, Vagabonds, and Sturdy Beggars.* Barre. MA: The Imprint Society, p. 290.
171. Nickell, Joe (1992). "Investigative Files: Psychic Pets and Pet Psychics." *The Skeptical Inquirer* (November-December), accessed April 15, 2006 at http://www.csicop.org/si/2002-11/pet-psychic.html.
172. Rickard, Robert, and Michell, John. (2001). "Calculating Horses." In *Unexplained Phenomena: A Rough Guide Special.* London: Rough Guides Limited, pp. 328-333.
173. Nickell, op cit.

XENOGLOSSOSSY

Xenoglossy refers to the rarely reported ability of a person to speak or write in a language to which they had never been consciously exposed. At fist glance, it may appear that this entry is inappropriate for this Encyclopedia, in that only individuals display the phenomenon and there is no apparent group behavior involved. However, xenoglossy has played an undeniable role in promoting major religious movements such as Hinduism as it offers "proof" of reincarnation. Indeed, Dr. Ian Stevenson, arguably the foremost expert on the subject, observed that cases of xenoglossy were found "particularly in the Buddhist and Hindu countries of South Asia…"[1] Also known as "xenoglossia" (from *xeno* meaning strange or foreign, and *glossa* meaning tongue), most cases involve people who communicate words and phrases for which they profess to have no understanding of their meaning. According to *Webster's Dictionary*, xenoglossy is the "purported use (as by a medium) while in a trance state of a language unknown to the individual under normal circumstances."[2] Persons exhibiting xenoglossy typically do so under certain conditions: altered states of consciousness, mediumship, and hypnosis. Some cases are voluntarily induced, as with mediums summoning spirits or gods in an effort to communicate; others involve claims of involuntary possession by demons. We provide two case histories.

Xenoglossy In The Séance Room

On October 15, 1926, in a private home in New York City, the American direct-voice medium George Valiantine gave a sitting to a small group. Because the medium had previously channeled an entity who spoke in some indecipherable foreign tongue, a distinguished linguist, Neville Whymant, was invited to be present, although he had no particular interest in psychical research. In the course of the sitting, Valiantine began to speak in what Whymant recognized as Chinese, though it was a style of Chinese he was not used to: he realized it was the Chinese of Confucius's day, the 6th century BCE. "The Chinese to which we were now listening was as dead colloquially as Sanskrit or Latin… If this was a hoax, it was a particularly clever one, far beyond the scope of any of the sinologues [scholars of Chinese] now living." The speaker gave the name K'ung-fu-tzu (Confucius), though it was not clear whether he purported to be the philosopher in person or was merely giving the name as a reference.

Since ancient Chinese was Whymant's special field of expertise, he was able to verify not only that the speaker was perfectly versed in the language, but that he was exceedingly knowledgeable about its literature – far more knowledgeable than himself. Whymant asked several questions and received unhesitating answers that were correct not only as to language but also as to scholarship. He then inquired about some poems that were the subject of some doubts among scholars. In one instance, the entity explained that the poem had been incorrectly copied and provided the correct readings, whereupon the sense of the poem became apparent. Later, when Whymant gave the first words of an obscure poem, the speaker not only continued reciting it but interpreted its meaning. There were only half a dozen Chinese scholars in the world possessing the kind of knowledge required to understand the questions, let alone answer them, and speaking, moreover, with the correct intonation and fluency. Altogether, over the course of 12 sessions, Valiantine spoke in 14 foreign languages, some recognized by Whymant, others by other specialists.[3]

Xenoglossy Under Hypnosis

Carroll Jay, an American Methodist minister in Ohio, has often used hypnosis for healing purposes. On May 10, 1970, he was treating his wife Dolores for back pains, when to his surprise she answered his question in German. A few days later he tried to evoke the personality that had spoken, and she announced: "Ich bin Gretchen." Questioning brought out further speech, which neither Jay nor his wife (in her waking state) could understand. Ian Stevenson, who spoke German, investigated the case, and in the course of nineteen conversations, he found that "Gretchen" responded intelligently to his questions in fluent, if not always correct, German. She gave details of her life, from which Stevenson concluded that she was most likely a small-town Catholic girl who had died at age 16, most likely around 1876. She was intelligent but uncultured and could provide no verifiable information about her existence. Indeed, some of the details she supplied appeared to be incorrect, but this could have been because the investigation was wrongly directed. Dolores herself knew no German and could not recall ever having been exposed to German speech, let alone having the facility to conduct an intelligent conversation.[4]

COMMENT: Many cases of apparent xenoglossy have been reasonably explained as cryptomnesia, in which the subject is unwittingly repeating words that they had heard earlier in their life and stored in their memory, perhaps not even aware of hearing them. The writer Samuel Coleridge told of a young woman of about 25 who in a delirium spoke Latin, Greek, and Hebrew. The languages had apparently been stored in her mind since she was a child of 9-to-13; when her foster-father had been accustomed to declaim aloud in those languages. Such recall is in itself a remarkable phenomenon, but it does not seem adequate to account for either of these two case histories.[5]

XHOSA CATTLE KILLING PROPHECY

South Africa: 1856

In 1856, the Xhosa people[6] of South Africa, in obedience to instructions from their spirit ancestors, commenced a massive slaughter of the cattle on which most of them depended for their livelihood. At the same time they destroyed their stored grain and ceased cultivating their fields. They did these things in the belief that their cattle – many of which were wasted with lung-disease – would be more than replaced by new and superior cattle provided by their spirit ancestors, who would themselves rise from the dead, bringing with them foods and other goods in such abundance that the Xhosa would never again have to toil on their farmlands. The white colonial administrators and settlers would be driven into the sea, and the Xhosa would once again rule their ancestral lands.

Not all the Xhosa subscribed to these prophecies, but the great majority did, including many of the most influential chiefs. The consequence, when the promised benefits failed to materialize, was catastrophic. Without animals or crops, some 40,000 Xhosa – more than a third of the population – died of starvation, and many more were compelled to abandon their derelict farms and migrate either to neighboring territories or to find work in the towns. The original population of 105,000 was reduced to some 26,000. The Xhosa people, as a nation, virtually ceased to exist.

CONTEXT: Jeff Peires, author of the only in-depth study of the episode, concluded: "I believe that the Cattle-Killing was a logical and rational response, perhaps even an inevitable response, by a nation driven to desperation by pressures that people today can barely imagine."[7] But the response can be seen as logical and rational only in the light of the situation in which the Xhosa people found themselves at this time. Their exceptional behavior was the response to exceptional circumstances.

Chief among these circumstances was the political situation. South Africa was under the administration, direct or indirect, of the British colonial government. The "Kaffir Wars" left most of the region demoralized and subordinate to British control, and though the

Xhosa chiefs still ruled their tribes, they did so within constraints imposed by the British governors. The consequent resentment and frustration created the mental climate in which the fatal prophecies were uttered. Even when the process of cattle killing had begun, the administrators could have taken measures to check its spread. Instead, their policies not only failed to check it but even facilitated its spread to such a degree that they were suspected, though mistakenly, of having deliberately fomented it. The administration's policies were directed almost wholly by self-interest, and though many individuals displayed genuine concern for the well-being of the native population, the overall view was that the Xhosa were an inferior people who did not know what was good for them, and that the sooner they adopted the values of Christian Britain, the better for them. The cynical cast of mind of the governor, Sir George Grey, was well expressed in this comment: "Instead of nothing but dangers resulting from the Xhosa having during the excitement killed their cattle and made away with their food, we can draw very great permanent advantages from the circumstance, which may be made a stepping-stone for the future settlement of the country."[8]

The Xhosa themselves were by no means blameless. Inter-tribal rivalries and jockeying for power were part of their way of life, and notions of witchcraft and sorcery underlay their every activity.

A millennarist view of life was built in to native attitudes. During the 1840s a witch-finder named Mlanjeni, urging his people to discard witchcraft and sorcery, taught that he had power to make his followers invulnerable, to fill the white man's guns with water, and to drive them out of the country – provided sacrifices were made to the spirits, including the killing of all dun- and cream-colored cattle. Such notions were prevalent throughout the Xhosa region, predisposing the people to give a respectful hearing to any prophet who might arise in their midst, should the occasion arise.

That occasion arose in 1853, when an epidemic of lung-sickness began to spread among the cattle of the Xhosa. Though it was prevalent also in other parts of Africa, the effects were felt particularly here where the people were demoralized by the "Kaffir" wars. It came naturally to them to suppose that the sickness was the result of magic, and the implication was that the magic originated with the whites, who were intent on devastating the natives even further. The lung-sickness epidemic, combined with the notion of sacrifice – almost any major transaction was sealed by the slaughter of an animal – led to the movement taking the form that it did. The coming of new healthy herds to replace those that had been contaminated by magic was the central feature of the prophecy.

A further contributing factor was Britain's involvement in the Crimea, where the British and French were currently at war with Russia. Since in the African mind the British were associated with colonialist oppression, it was supposed that the Russians were a black-skinned people like themselves. When they had defeated the British, they would surely come to liberate the subjugated Africans and join with the New People – the resurrected ancestors – in driving the whites into the sea.

Nongqawuse's Vision And Prophecies

Onto minds conditioned by such ideas, the news that a young girl was receiving messages from the spirits had an immediate and forceful impact. Nongqawuse was an orphan, raised by her uncle Mhlakaza who lived near the mouth of the Gxara River in independent Xhosaland in today's Eastern Cape. She was aged 14 or 15 when, one day in April 1856, she and her young cousin Nombanda went to keep birds off her uncle's crops. She heard her name called by two strangers standing in a small bush adjoining the field, who gave her a dramatic message: "Tell that the whole community will rise from the dead, and that all cattle now living must be slaughtered, for they have been reared by contaminated hands, because there are people about who deal in witchcraft. There should be no cultivation, but great new grain pits must be dug, new houses must be built, and great strong cattle enclosures must be erected. The people must leave their witchcraft."[9]

By all accounts Nongqawuse was not a particularly intelligent girl; one witness described her as "having a silly look… she appeared to me as if she was not right in her mind."[10] Her cousin stated, "I frequently accompanied Nongqawuse to a certain bush where she spoke with people… I neither saw them nor did I hear them speak till after I had constantly visited the bush with her."

On the following day, the strangers appeared again and asked how their message had been received. She told them it was thought to be either a joke or a fairy-tale. They asked that her uncle should, after making a sacrifice, come to them. Though he did not see the strangers, he received a message from voices that only Nongqawuse could hear. From her description, Mhlakaza recognized that one of them was his dead brother, the girl's father. This convinced him that the messages must be authentic, and as a religious visionary, he was able to interpret the messages, which he lost no time in communicating to the chiefs.

Nongqawuse was neither the first nor the last young Xhosa girl to emerge as a prophet, but her messages came at a crucial time and became the definitive expression of the nation's hopes. The attitude of the Xhosa to girls who claimed to see visions was similar to that of the Roman Catholic Church to visionaries such as Bernadette of Lourdes who two years later would claim to receive divine messages from the mother of Jesus. In both cases, the messages were received with serious attention but also with some reserve. Just as a Christian visionary was taken under the wing of the Church, a Xhosa visionary would customarily be "managed" by an acknowledged diviner, such as Mhlakaza, who now interpreted his niece's prophecies and clarified the instructions brought to Nongqawuse by the messengers of the gods.

As vision succeeded vision, the prophecies took firmer shape. New People were coming to rescue the Xhosa: they were ancestors, the heroes of old, restored to life. They would bring with them wonderful new cattle – Nongqawuse had seen their horns peeping below the rushes (the spirits were believed to reside under water, rivers or the sea). Wagons and clothes, guns and ammunition would miraculously appear, and food in abundance, even "such food as the English eat." At the same time, the living would be made young again; cripples would have their limbs restored, the blind would see. On the appointed day, a blood red sun – or in some versions two suns, for the prophecies were not always consistent – would appear in the sky at sunrise. There would be a great storm, and a tremendous wind would sweep the white folk into the sea, and then the Xhosa would rule once again in their own lands.

But there was a price to be paid. First, the people must kill the cattle they presently owned, which had been contaminated by witchcraft – the lung-sickness. They must destroy their stores of corn, which were similarly impure. They should cease cultivation but build large enclosures for the new cattle, and dig deep grain-pits for the corn that would miraculously appear. They should build new houses for themselves. Furthermore, they should abandon the practice of witchcraft.

Nongqawusa's messages were quickly recounted to the chiefs and the Xhosa people generally. The prevailing epidemic of lung-sickness among the cattle predisposed them to accept the prophecies. It was logical to ascribe the lung-sickness to sorcery, to accept that witchcraft was at work, that they were contaminated, and that they must purify themselves.

But not everyone believed. From the start, the prophecies polarized the Xhosa into two parties, believers and skeptics, with a great many who wavered, uncertain whether to believe or disbelieve. The prospect was certainly an attractive one – but could one really believe the utterances of a young girl? Many came to visit the Gzarha River site of the visions, but most saw nothing, so uncertainty prevailed despite the wish to believe. In July 1856, Sarhili, the senior chief, came to see for himself. He too, was initially uncertain, but eventually he became a reluctant believer. He himself commenced the slaughter by killing his favorite ox, an animal known to all. His decision carried great weight, and many who had hesitated hitherto began to slaughter their livestock.

When word reached the colonial authorities, the accounts were not taken seriously. A few who had the interests of the African people at heart recognized the potential danger and did what they could to discourage belief in the prophecies. But even when the Xhosa began to slaughter their cattle in great numbers, the authorities prevaricated and no official action was taken.

Initially, a great many households killed some of their animals, but when there was no immediate sign, the slaughter halted to await developments. Streams of visitors came to consult Nongqawusa, who was still frequently seeing the strangers. No one else had seen anything more tangible than vague shapes in the bushes or out at sea – shapes that Nongqawusa assured them were the New People, preparing to emerge when the sacrifices had been performed. Those who wished to believe, believed; others returned to their tribes as uncertain as ever. Nongqawusa became ill and her cousin Nombanda, who had been with her on the first occasion, took her place. Though she was only about nine years old, many visitors preferred her. But still no one else saw anything.

In August came the First Disappointment. Nongqawusa had specified a certain date, but the appointed day came – and dawned as usual. There was widespread disillusion, but Nongqawusa pointed out that the instructions had not been carried out – many unbelievers had killed none of their cattle, and even the believers had killed or sold only part of their herds. Not all the grain had been destroyed, and many were still cultivating their fields. The effect of the disappointment, consequently, was to encourage the believers to be more active in killing their cattle and destroying their food stores. Within two weeks the killing had recommenced on a bigger scale than ever.

Now the killing was fueled by further rumors, directed against the skeptics. Those who continued to cultivate their lands would be punished. It was said that a woman who tried to work her fields had been fixed to the ground, unable to move. Hostility increased between the believers and the skeptics, and the believers avoided the company of unbelievers, fearing the contamination of witchcraft. Often families were divided, fathers accepting the prophecies, their sons skeptical. Women were almost unanimous in believing the prophecies, and reproached their men folk when they were reluctant to slaughter their animals.

In such a mental climate, every circumstance took on significance. Encouragement was given to the believers when the governor Sir George Grey, sensing the restless state of the province, decided to make a demonstration of authority, and directed a warship to the mouth of the river close to Nongqawuse's home. The captain, drunk, neglected to take on board a pilot; he took the wrong course at the river mouth, overturned a boat, and then just steamed away. The incident was promptly transformed by rumor into a foretaste of the fate destined for the white men; the spirits, as a sign of things to come, had effected the "destruction" of the ship.

Cattle were now being slaughtered in great quantities. Since the spirits ordained that only cattle killed that day should be eaten, the countryside was soon littered with putrefying carcasses, which predators subsequently picked to skeletons.

In October a new date was announced: the cattle must be killed within eight days, and then the dead would arise. Many cattle were duly killed, but when the day came, nothing happened. As always in such cases, an explanation was found for the failed prophecy. This time blame was attributed to the skeptics who refused to kill their animals, and the antagonism between believers and unbelievers led to growing acts of violence.

The total number of cattle deliberately slaughtered by the Xhosa can only be estimated, especially as many would have died of the lung-sickness anyway. Estimates range between 150,000 and 200,000. Along with the quantities of grain-stores destroyed, this represented virtually the entire wealth of the people. When the New People arrived, of course, they would be repaid a hundred-fold. But in the meantime, the country was starving. In September the first deaths from starvation were recorded. By December 1856 the Xhosa were in a serious situation: "There can be no recovery now," commented Commissioner Brownlee, one of the few white administrators to show real concern for the Xhosa.[11] The euphoria that had characterized the early stages of destruction, when people feasted on their slaughtered cattle and enjoyed the leisure of doing no work, gave way to frustrated waiting, resentment of the unbelievers, and serious concern for the future. Many farms were deserted as thousands of families moved into Cape Colony to take employment in the towns, while others scattered among their neighbors to east and north.

By January the Xhosa were in a desperate situation. The time was long past when crops could be planted, and the great majority of the cattle and other animals had been slaughtered. Now there was nothing for the Xhosa to do but wait for the promises to be fulfilled. A hope that the full moon of January 10 would see that fulfillment proved deceptive. Stormy meetings took place. Sandile, the great chief, though filled with misgivings, committed himself publicly, slaughtering his remaining cattle. The prophecies crystallized, and Nongqawuse declared that "on the eighth day – certainly before the end of the ninth day – the resurrection would take place. The sun would rise late, blood-red, and set again, upon which it would be as black as night. A terrible storm would follow, with thunder and lightning; and then the dead would rise."[12] But February 16, 1857, dawned like any other day. All that day, and all the following day, the people sat, watching the skies in anticipation of a sign. None came. Stunned by "the Great Disappointment," the Xhosa chiefs and their people had to recognize that the promises would not be fulfilled and that all their sacrifices had been futile.

Aftermath

Although the "exceptional behavior" treated of in this entry is that of the Xhosa people only, the story would be incomplete without a brief account of the consequences, particularly because it was widely believed, among the Xhosa, that those consequences were the cause of the cattle killing. There had to be some explanation for such a catastrophe, and they came to believe that it had been nothing less than a conspiracy on the part of the colonial government to destroy the tribal system of the Xhosa people and subjugate them entirely to British rule.

This theory was balanced by another, widely held among the white administration and settlers, to the effect that it was a conspiracy deliberately created by the Chiefs to rouse the people against the whites, to start a new Kaffir War, and drive them into the sea. In fact, it is quite clear that neither of these conspiracy theories had any substance whatsoever. Each was an instance of self-deception, both parties seeking to exculpate themselves from responsibility for the catastrophe.

In *A History of South Africa*, the Hon. A. Wilmot, a South African legislator, wrote: "A great statesman grasped the helm of the State when Sir George Grey became Governor and High Commissioner in 1854...A strong police force and a system of espionage were established. By means of the latter every detail of the plot to kill all the cattle and then drive the hated white man into the sea was fully discovered. The necessary precautions were taken with the result that rebellion was made impossible and 70,000 Kafirs died of starvation."[13]

Since Wilmot's time, more has been disclosed about the conduct of the British Colonial administration in South Africa. In regard to the Xhosa cattle-killing, Peires, with access to Grey's private records, has been able to demonstrate a considerable divergence between what Grey chose to report to London and what was in fact happening in the region he governed. The "great statesman" is revealed as guilty of duplicity, deceit, and outright lying. Continually overriding the warnings and suggestions of his subordinates on the ground, he emerges as an arrogant and ruthless autocrat who saw the cattle massacre as a heaven-sent opportunity to further British interests at the expense of native Africans – an opportunity that he seized and exploited to a degree that permanently changed the course of African history, while leaving an indelible stain on the history of British colonialism.

COMMENT: Though unique in many respects, the Xhosa cattle-massacre has interesting parallels with other events narrated in this Encyclopedia.

The readiness of the native Africans to accept the unsubstantiated word of the adolescent Nongqawuma is paralleled by the readiness of the Roman Catholic Church to accept the equally unsubstantiated declaration by Bernadette Soubirous of her encounters with the Virgin Mary, which by coincidence occurred just two years later. See LOURDES.

The belief in spirits and their continued involvement in mundane affairs is paralleled by the growth of the spiritualist movement, first in America and then in Europe, which by coincidence had escalated a few years earlier with the claims of the Fox sisters. See

SPIRITUALISM.

The belief in gifts being miraculously brought from elsewhere is paralleled by the cargo cults that proliferated in the 20th century in many under-privileged parts of the world, particularly those which had been subjected to colonial infringement. See CARGO CULTS.

A movement that in some respects paralleled the Xhosa cattle-killing arose in the Transkei seventy years later. In 1926-27, following the teachings of Marcus Garvey, a West Indian promoter of black rights who claimed that black people would win freedom only when Afro-Americans returned to their ancestral homes in Africa, Wellington Buthelezi initiated what became known as "the Wellington movement." He predicted that "American blacks would arrive in aeroplanes from which they would bomb all whites and African non-believers with burning lumps of charcoal."[14] By way of sacrifice to help bring this about, men were ordered to slaughter all their pigs and white fowls.[15] However, after a brief flurry of popularity, the movement faded and no mass killing of animals took place.

Sources

1. Stevenson, Ian (1997). *Where Reincarnation and Biology Intersect.* Praeger: Westport, CT. Quote from back cover.

2. Babcock Gove, Philip (editor-in-chief) (1986). *Webster's Third New International Dictionary of the English Language Unabridged.* Springfield, Massachusetts: Merriam-Webster, Incorporated, p. 2644.

3. Whymant, Neville (1931). *Psychic Adventures in New York.* London: Morley & Mitchell.

4. Stevenson, Ian (1984). *Unlearned Language.* Charlottesville: University Press of Virginia; Jay, Carroll E. (1977). *Gretchen I Am.* New York: Wyden Books.

5. Coleridge, Samuel Taylor (1974). *Biographia literaria.* Cited in Stevenson, Ian. "Xenoglossy: A Review and Report of a Case." *Proceedings of the American Society for Psychical Research*, volume 31 (February), p. 2.

6. 'Xhosa' is approximately equivalent to the popular though derogatory term 'Kaffir.'

7. Peires, J B. (1989). *The Dead Will Arise.* Johannesburg: Ravan Press, p. x.

8. Quoted by Peires, op cit., p. 247.

9. Quoted by Peires, op cit., p. 79.

10. Peires, op cit., p. 311.

11. Peires, op cit., p. 150.

12. Peires, op cit., p. 155.

13. Wilmot, Hon. A. (1901). *The History of South Africa.* Kegan, Paul, Trench and Trübner, p. 124.

14. Account published on www.sahistory.org.za'specialprojects/garveyism.

15. Wilson, Monica, and Thompson, Leonard [editors] *The Oxford History of South Africa.* Oxford: University Press 1969, p. 259.

ZEITOUN LUMINOUS PHENOMENA

Zeitoun, Egypt: 1968-1971

From April 1968 to May 1971, in excess of 100,000 people reported observing Virgin Mary apparitions above a Coptic Orthodox Church in the Cairo suburb of Zeitoun, Egypt. Witnesses descriptions varied between two main types: small bright, short-lived lights nicknamed "doves," and more enduring, less intense, diffuse patches of glowing light. The observations began several months after the brief 1968 Egyptian-Israeli war, when on the night of April 2, an Islamic mechanic claimed to see a young lady atop the Church of the Virgin Mary. Fearful she was about to commit suicide, he sought help and soon a crowd gathered around the church. A priest eventually concluded that the figure was, in fact, the Virgin Mary. Over the next several years the "Virgin" was observed on various occasions lasting anywhere from a few minutes to several hours.[1]

CONTEXT: When Canadian neuropsychologist Michael Persinger and his American colleague John Derr analyzed seismic activity in the region from 1958 to 1979, they found an unprecedented peak in earthquakes during 1969. They concluded that some people were predisposed by their religious background and social expectation to interpret a natural phenomenon – a display of earthquake lights emanating from a nearby fault line – as related to the Virgin Mary.

Psychiatrist Ramzy Yassa believed the episode was a reflection of the massive loss of self-esteem in the wake of the demoralizing Egyptian defeat at the hands of Israel, an event that seriously eroded Egyptian confidence. Yassa remarked: "In a general way, we can see the phenomenon as an attempt to recoup on this loss [of the Israeli war]. The purported appearance of a celestial being is gratifying to the community."[2] As for why a Christian symbol might become the focus of interest in a predominately Muslim country, Yassa speculated that "It may be in the light of a recent Egyptian experience under British rule, that the Coptic divinities are felt to be more powerful since their community was more affluent and successful than the Islamic portion of the community...Or it may be that the Coptic church has a richer tradition of heavenly visitations than Islam."[3]

ZIMBABWE ZOMBIE SCHOOL

Msengezi, Zimbabwe: September 2002

During September 2002, a "mysterious hysteria" was reported to be sweeping through a co-educational school operated by the Methodist Church in rural Zimbabwe in Southeastern Africa. Symptoms included shaking of the hands, legs, and shoulders, and what was described as a state of "sleepwalking" as if they were zombies. Some victims appeared to be possessed by spirits and seemed to be hallucinating. The outbreak began on Saturday September 7, when the first three pupils were affected. The next day there were five more cases. By Monday the 9th, 21 students were afflicted. Eventually the total reached 24. The episode occurred at Moleli High School in Msengezi about 80 kilometers west of Harare and only involved female students, mostly from Form One and Two.[4] According to school officials, concerned parents had withdrawn 14 girls who had been exhibiting symptoms.

One of the students had to be admitted to the

Kutama Mission Hospital in Zvimba after becoming violent. Doctors gave her a sedative to calm her. She has since been withdrawn from the school by her parents. Some worried parents were said to be consulting with both physicians and prophets. As for the other affected girls, doctors were prescribing phenobarbitone and painkillers. This practice upset some psychiatrists who complained that it was inappropriate without first conducting a thorough history of the students. A surprising aspect of the case was the absence of symptoms once the students returned to their homes, and its reappearance once they returned to the premises. At the time of the outbreak, there were rumors that ghosts were haunting the girls' hostel – the spirits of 22 students who drowned on Lake Chivero when their boat overturned in 1995. It was believed that their spirits were afflicting those affected. Amid the ghost stories, at night the girls claimed to hear voices in their hostel and the sounds of footsteps and a screaming child.

The chief education psychologist from The Ministry of Education, Sport and Culture, Kwadzanai Nyanungo, said the episode was triggered by "rumours and fear." She said that every year her department learns of one or two cases somewhere in the country. She says that part of the blame lies with the failure of the teaching staff to address the rumors in a timely manner. According to Nyanungo, "Schools should take care of the kids and parents must watch their kids and assist them to get confidence."

The Secretary-General of the Zimbabwe National Traditional Healers' Association, Dr. Peter Sibanda, disagreed with the government's approach. He noted that a similar outbreak of hysteria had broken out at the school about a decade earlier and it was successfully handled using native healers. Dr. Sibanda said that an exorcist was sent to the school and it was learned that a disgruntled former employee, who was not being paid his pension, had apparently cast a spell. He said the hysteria stopped after locals were summoned "to discipline the man." Dr. Sibanda said he believes that some small-scale farmers in the vicinity of Msengezi had supernatural creatures known as *tokoloshis* that may have been responsible for the school hysteria. "If these [beings] lack socialisation, they go out to prey on females in the vicinity, in this case girls at Moleli High School," said Dr. Sibanda, who thought that the outbreak could be quelled if, with the community's consent, a native healer was sent to the school to capture the *tokoloshis*.

ZOOT SUIT RIOTS

California: 1942-1943

Anxiety was rife across southern California in the Summer of 1942, after nine members of a Mexican-American youth gang in Los Angeles were convicted of murdering Jose Diaz in a quarry pit in what would become known as the Sleepy Lagoon episode. The trial was characterized by sensational press coverage by the *Los Angeles Times* of the perceived mounting threat by Mexican-American youths or "Pachuo gangs." At the same time, journalists and police officers began to describe young Mexican-Americans in the region as "hoodlums" and "baby gangsters."[5] Those involved in the murder received lengthy prison terms. After the trial, and fueled by press exaggeration of the threat to society posed by Mexican-American youth gangs, a series of confrontations erupted between American servicemen and "zoot suiters" in several California cities including Oakland, San Jose, and Delano.[6] These suits were popular in the 1940s and consisted of a long sport jacket, shoulder pads, and high pants. Many L.A. Mexican-Americans commonly wore them. The biggest confrontation occurred in the streets of downtown and East Los Angeles during the first two weeks of June of 1943.

CONTEXT: The zoot suit riots were a reflection of the longstanding status of Mexican Americans and other minority citizens, intensified during a period of xenophobia coinciding with the onset of World War II.

On June 3, a group of Mexican-American boys beat up some U.S. sailors while they were walking through Los Angeles. While no one was seriously hurt, the next night hundreds of sailors crisscrossed the streets of L.A. in cabs, stopping whenever they spotted "zoot suiters," then jumped out and assaulted them. By June 5, scores of sailors, accompanied by soldiers and civilians roamed the Mexican quarter, seeking out more zoot suiters, and later, anyone with dark skin. Police made 27 arrests that night – all zoot suiters, and not a single serviceman.[7] In his acclaimed book *North From Mexico*, attorney Carey McWilliams related his own eyewitness account from downtown Los Angeles, noting that he watched as "a mob of several thousand soldiers, sailors, and civilians, proceeded to beat up every zoot suiter they could find. Pushing its way into the important motion picture theaters, the mob ordered the management to turn on the house lights and then ran up and down the aisles dragging Mexicans out of their seats. Streetcars were halted while Mexicans, and some Filipinos and Negroes, were jerked out of their seats, pushed into the streets and beaten with a sadistic frenzy."[8]

The mass media applauded the military personnel for "cleaning up the city" of Hispanic gang members. "The use of the stereotyped image of the zoot suit appeared in all the publicity, and what was simply a teenage fad was linked in the minds of readers with such characterizations as 'gang,' 'roughneck,' 'subversive,' and so forth. The press and radio leaped on the bandwagon."[9] The rioting finally stopped on or about June 13, soon after the L.A. City Council passed a resolution making it illegal to wear a zoot suit, and military authorities ordered the city to be off limits to all servicemen.[10] The riots were a reflection of the long-standing, widespread discrimination and racism in America against persons of Mexican heritage at the time, which was fueled by the mass media, despite estimates that 98 percent of those victimized were United States citizens.[11]

Sources

1. Johnston, F. (1980). *When Millions Saw Mary*. Chulmleigh, England: Augustine Publishing; Persinger, Michael, and Derr, John. (1989). "Geophysical Variables and Behavior: LIV. Zeitoun (Egypt) Apparitions of the Virgin Mary as Tectonic Strain-Induced Luminosities." *Perceptual and Motor Skills* 68:123-12.
2. Yassa, R. (1980). "A Sociopsychiatric Study of an Egyptian Phenomenon." *American Journal of Psychotherapy* 34:246-251. See p. 250.
3. Yassa, op cit., p. 250.
4. Tsiko, Sifelani (2002). "Mysterious Hysteria Hits Moleli High School." *The Zimbabwe Herald* Online (Zimbabwe) Friday, 13 September 2002.
5. Griswold del Castillo, Richard, "The Los Angeles 'Zoot Suit Riots' Revisited: Mexican and Latin American Perspectives," *Mexican Studies* 16(2) (Summer 2000): 367–392. See p. 370.
6. Griswold, op cit., p. 370.
7. Marden, Charles, Meyer, Gladys, and Engel, Madeline H. (1992). *Minorities in American Society* (sixth edition). New York: HarperCollins, p. 272.
8. McWilliams, Carey. (1968). *North from Mexico: The Spanish-Speaking People of the United States*. New York: Greenwood Press, p. 249, cited in Griswold, p. 370.
9. Marden, op cit., p. 273.
10. Marden, op cit., p. 273.
11. Griswold, op cit., p. 391; McWilliams, Carey. (1943). *The New Republic*, June 21, p. 819.

Index

A

Abdullah, Jariah, 283
Abu Ghraib Prison (abuse), 275-77
Ackerman, Susan, 173, 652, 655-656
altered states of consciousness, 7-8
  Amsterdam outbreak of 1566, 17
  Anabaptists, 21
  animal noises, 26
  Auxonne possession outbreak, 33
  Botswana school outbreak, 310
  Boxer Rising movement, 56
  Cargo "cults," 70
  convent hysteria, 322
  copycat behaviour, 100
  cross-cultural female oppression, 172-74
  cross-cultural presentation, 6
  dance frenzies (Japan), 116
  dancing mania, 118
  fantasy-prone people, 162
  female susceptibility (social vs. biological), 172-74, 656
  German school in 1892, 362
  ghost dance, 208
  glossolalia, 212
  goblin attacks in Zimbabwe, 212
  headings for, 7-8
  hypnotic trance and mass hysteria, 651-52
  hysteria, 255, 621
  Islamic ecstatic sects, 282
  Landes outbreak, 308
  Lille convent outbreak, 313
  lycanthropy, 337
  Malaysia, 369, 382
  mass hysteria, 361
  mass motor hysteria, 364-65, 376
  Methodist revival, 404
  Morzine, 424
  motor hysteria, 430
  Multiple Personality Disorder, 437
  Papua New Guinea, xvi
  paranormal phenomena, 474

altered states of consciousness, *cont.*
  phantom pregnancy attacks, 501-02
  possession, 515-16
  profanity and blasphemy, 519
  running, jumping and climbing, 544-45
  Salem witchhunts, 565
  school outbreaks of mass hysteria, 375, 578, 381
  Singapore factory hysteria, 588
  small group scares, 593
  snake handler sect, 597
  South Africa, 383
  spirit possession in India, 603-05
  spititualism, 609
  St. Medard Convulsionnaries, 559
  Swedish preaching epidemic, 627-29
  teacher hysteria in South Africa, 642
  theories of mass hysteria, 649
  Ulster revival, 682
  Urban myths, 688
  Virgin Mary apparitions, 702
  work settings, 368-70
  Xenoglossy, 745
Andree, Salmon August, 23-25, 145, 211, 224, 499, 546
Animal noises, epidemics of, 25-26, 100, 535
  barking, 13, 16-17, 25-26, 53-54, 57, 105, 248, 300, 307-08, 310, 341, 357, 361, 427, 530, 557
  bellowing (like bulls), 26, 311
  bleating, 341, 361
  braying, 341
  cackling, 25-26, 310-11
  chattering (like monkeys), 25, 310
  hee-hawing (like donkeys), 26
  hooting, 25, 310
  howling, 68, 307, 310, 530
  meowing, 25, 71-73, 105, 261, 310, 361, 557
  parrots, horses and hounds in Hungary, xiii
  roaring, 25-6, 310-11, 530
  whinnying (like horses), 341, 357

anthrax scare, 277, 286, 363, 647, 648
Arnold, Kenneth, 48, 177-180
Audubon, John, 40-41

B

Back, Kurt, 366
Backman, E. Louis, 119-20
Baglivi, Giorgio, 641
Bainbridge, William Sims, 468
Baring-Gould, Sabine, 334
Barkun, Michael, xi,
Baroja, Julio Caro, 738
Barr, John, 70
Barthélemy, Toussaint, 620
Bartholomew, Robert Emerson, 4, 98-99, 120, 161, 173, 200, 203-05, 351-52, 369, 373-75, 380, 488, 509, 518, 592-93, 641, 731
Bass, Ellen, 156
Bavent, Madeleine, 106, 329-30
Bechterew, Vladimir Mikhailovich [now spelled Bekhterev], v, 47-48, 300-02, 356, 358, 546, 601
Bekker, Balthasar, 17-18, 248, 419
Ben-Yehuda, Nachman, 421-23
Bequette, Bill, 48, 177-179
Bennett, James Gordon, 15
Bennett, Sir Courtney, 9, 490, 542
Bergen, Edgar, 467
Billings, Dorothy K., 517-18
Bin Laden Itch, 286, 648
Blatherwick, John, 667
Bloecher, Ted, 179
Bodin, Jean, 290, 304
Boekelsen, Jan, 20-23
Bogardus, Emory Stephen, 152
Bondeson, Jan, 314, 316
Boone, Daniel, 40
Bouflet, Joachim, 266, 701, 703, 706
Bourgignon, Antoinette, 376
Bourguignon, Erika, 7, 174
Boyer, Paul, 407, 561, 565
Burton-Bradley, Sir Bruton G., 70
Braithwaite, William C., xvi
Bromley, David G., 573
Brunvand, Jan Harold, 685-86
Bulgatz, Joseph, 345
Bullard, Thomas E., 3, 6, 527, 546
Burnham, William H., 170
Businessmen's Revival, 9, 14-15, 185

C

Calmeil, Louis Florentin, xi, 16, 18, 35, 108, 308, 321, 463, 560, 666, 722
Calmet, Dom Augustin, 693-95
Campbell, Terence W., 157
Cantril, Hadley, 465, 468, 644, 657
Capron, Eliah Wilkinson, 606, 608, 611
cargo "cults," ix, 69-70, 103, 361, 409, 751
  Filo, 175-76
  Mangzo, 359
  Naked, 459-60
  President Johnson, 517-18
Carnes, Mark C., 185
Carré de Montgeron, Louis-Basile, 556-60
Carroll, Michael P., 705
Cartwright, Edmund, 362, 368
Cavendish, Richard, 571
Chambers, Paul, 731
choral and concert collapses
  California concert, 67
  Massachusetts, 390
  Milwaukee, Wisconsin, 182
  Ohio fainting fits, 464
  Oklahoma stadium collapse, 464-65
  Rolling Stones Mania, 540
  Starpoint High School, 616-17
Chronic Fatigue Syndrome, 175, 258, 520, 585-86
Code of Handsome Lake, 246
Cohen, Stanley, 420, 422
Cohn, Norman, 23, 582-83
Coleman, Loren, 100-103, 625-26
Colligan, Michael J., 172, 364, 374
Collin de Plancy, J., 89
Collins, Tony, 126
Convent hysteria, xvi, 8, 13, 99, 104-109, 128, 290, 361, 402, 423, 427, 435, 474, 507, 516, 565, 584, 619, 621, 628, 649, 727
  Aix, 106-07, 311
  Auxonne, France, 32-36

Convent Hysteria, *cont.*
Cambrai, France, 68-69
Chinon, France, 91-92
Kentorff, Germany, 298-99
Koln, Germany, 302-04
Lille, France, 311-13
Loudun, France, 317-22
Louviers, France, 328-32
Madrid, Spain, 355-56
Meowing nuns, 73
Milan, Italy, 404-05
Nijmegen, Netherlands, 461-62
Nimes, France, 462-63
profanity and blasphemy, 518-519
Santen, Germany, 566-67
Unterzell, Germany, 683-685
Wertet, Flanders, 721-22
Coon, Dennis, 386-87, 740
Cornelisz, Jeronimus, 42-45
Cornwell, John, 374
Courtenay, Sir William, ix, 662, 664
Crazes, 109-11
facilitated communication, 151
Florida Land Boom, 110, 176
Klondike Gold Rush, 109
mass hystera, 256
Mississippi Bubble, 109-10
moral panic, 422
oat bran, 464
Smelser, Neil J., 654
south sea bubble, 110
stock market crash of 1929, 110-11, 176
tulip mania, 672-74
Cros, Léonard, 326-27

D
Day, Benjamin, 416
Darnton, Robert, 72
Davidson, Keay, 180, 468
Davis, Laura, 156
De Lancre, Pierre, 16, 336, 733, 737
De Martino, Ernesto, 121, 641
Drake, Richard, 247
Dwight, Theodore, 74

E
Edamaruku, Sanal, 247, 413-14
Edwards, Jonathan, 9-10, 15, 536
Eliade, Mircea, 70
Elliott, Diana, 158
Ellis, Havelock, 391, 396
End-of-the-world-scares
Anabaptists, 19-20
aurora borealis, 32
Bezpopovtzy sect, 49-51
Bird Flu, 53
Cevennes Prophets, 78, 81
Fatima, Portugal, 169
Halifax disaster, 237, 239
Halley's Comet, 242-44
Lille, France, 312
London, 313-314
Maliovanny sect, 356-59
Mars earthquake panic, 360
Millerite, 406-07
Miracle Hen of Leeds, 413
New Zealand, 480
Perm, Russia, 388
Pittsburgh furnace scare, 506
Scotland, 581
Siberia, Russia, 388
South America, 408
Spouse Dropping Revival, 614
Sweden, 628
Tom and his followers, 663-64
Uganda, 389
Virgin Mary, 702
see also, Martian invasion scares
Estrade, Jean-Baptiste, 327
Evans, Bergen, 540
Evans, Hilary, 437, 460, 705
Evans, Robert R., 624
exaggerated illness threats
Mad Cow, 346-47
SARS,567-68
Bird Flu, 51-53
extreme social conditions
Batavia shipwreak, 41-45
Halifax disaster, 235-39
Iraq prison abuse affair, 275-77

extreme social conditions, *cont.*
  Iraq mutiny, 274

F

fads, 103, 151-54
  barking-off squirrels, 40-41
  defined, 151
  feather tickling, 170
  goldfish swallowing, 213-14
  and hysteria, 256
  hula-hoop, 249-50
  and medicine, 255
  Melin, Arthur Spud, 399
  miniature golf, 412
  streaking, 624-25
  versus crazes, 109, 111
  versus fashions, 163-65
  wacky wallwalker, 711
Fantasy-prone people, 160-163
  and alien abductions, 161
  hypnotic susceptibility, 162
  out-of-body experiences, 162
  physiological effects, 162-63
  psychic phenomena, 162
  spiritual themes, 163
fashion, defined, 163
Figuier, Louis, 322
Filo movement, 175-76
Finch, Jack, 504
Fine, Gary, 687
Finot, Jean, 133-34, 548
Flammarion, Camille, 242
flappermania, 164-65
Fox, George, 529
Frankel, Stephen, 181-82
Freedman, Lawrence, 225-26
Freeman, Derek, 518
Frere, Jean-Claude, 31
Freud, Sigmund, 26, 45, 195, 212, 364, 376, 396, 435, 598, 650, 692, 696-97, 705, 728
Fuller, Ronald, 575
Fumento, Michael, 51-52, 225, 239, 568

G

Garber, Peter M., 257, 673
Gasparin, Comte Agénor de, 613
Geertz, Clifford, xii
Genital Shrinking Scares, 194-203
  China, 196-97
  India, 198-99, 201
  Singapore, 198-200
  Thailand, 197-98
Genital Vanishing Scares, 203-06
  Benin, 204
  European witch scare, 206
  Nigeria, 203-04
  Sudan, 205-06
Gibbs-Smith, Charles H., 214, 483-84,
Ginu movement, 359
Gnu'u, Keama, 175-76
Goode, Erich, 109, 421-23, 468, 686, 737
Görres, Johann Joseph von, 685, 722
Goss, Michael, 239
Granfield, Robert, 251
Graves, Robert, 705
Great Awakening in Massachusetts, 9-10
Grégoire, M., 14
Gridley, Josiah A., 611
Griffiths, Arthur, 194
Gustafson, Reka, 669
Gutman, Jeremiah, 387

H

Hafez, Albert, 472, 474
Haining, Peter, 615
Hakuta, Ken, 711
Hall, Lesley A., 393
Hammond, Charles, 609
Hare, Robert, 610
Harris, Robert, 645
Hayes, Wiebbe (and Hayes' Island), 42-45
Hecker, Justus Friedrich, 117-19, 649
Heim, Roger, 440
Hell-Fire Club, 582
Hempenstall, P., 70
Herschel, Sir John, 416-17
Higgins, Julia, 247

Hoaxes,
airship mania (USA, 1897), 214-224
BBC *Ghostwatch* Scare, 45-46
BBC radio hoax, 46-47
cyber ghost scare, 111
earthworm (Texas), 648
Hook, The, 504-05
Moon Hoax, The Great, 416-18
New England Airship, 483-86
New York Zoo Scare, 460-61
New Zealand Zeppelin scare, 482
nuclear disaster, 463
see also, *War of the Worlds* scares
Howard, George S., 161, 592-93
Howard, Leland, 299-300
Huang, Carol, 648
Huggins, Sir William, 242
Hulbert, Harold, 354-55
Huxley, Aldous, 322

I

Ilechukwu, Sunny, 203-05
imaginary and contentious conditions,
Battered Wife Syndrome, 45
Chronic Fatigue Syndrome, 175, 258, 520, 585-86
Fibromyalgia, 174-75
Genital shrinking scares, 194-203
Genital vanishing scares, 203-206
Gulf War Syndrome, 224-226
Jumping Frenchmen of Maine, 294-96
Masturbation delusion, 391-397
Multiple Personality Disorder, 430-439
Railway Spine, 532
Repetition Strain Injury, 371-73
Riveter's Ovaries, 540
Royal Free Disease, 371
Sick Building Syndrone, 364, 373-74, 651, 670
Telegraphist's Cramp, 371-73
Tollitis, 661
Windigo psychosis, 726-28
Imbert-Goubeyre, A., 618
Irving, Edward, 278-80
Israeli, Raphael, 473

J

Janet, Pierre, 129, 432,
Jeanne des Anges, Soeur, 8, 318
Jones, Candy, 411
Jones, Francis, 145
Jones, Jim, x, 386-87
Jones, Margaret, 561
Jones, Mary, 716-21
Jones, Sally, 402
Jonestown, 49, 386-87
Jordan, Furneaux, 45

K

Kapferer, Bruce, 173-74
Kapferer, Jean-Noel, 542
Karlsen, Carol F., 566
Kastein, Joseph, 555
Kaye, Jefferson, 62-64
Kentucky space creatures scare, 593-94
Kentucky Revival, 9-14
Kerckhoff, Alan C., 172
Kieckhefer, Richard, 366, 655
Kinsey, Alfred C., 395-96
Klass, Phillip J., 5
Kleinman, Arthur, 256, 363
Knightley, Phillip, 504-05
Knox, Ronald A., 46-47
Kottak, Conrad P., 69, 246
Kramer, Heinrich, 206, 733

L

Lanternari, Vittorio, 70
LaPiere, Richard T., 110
Lasserre, Henri, 325-26
Laughing Epidemics, ix, 25, 203, 309-11
Anabaptists, 20
Africa and stress, 475
Botswana, 310
copycat behavior, 100
European schools, 362
Franz Mesmer, 311
Holy Laugh, 13-14
Irvingites, 279

Laughing Epidemics, *cont.*
 Jaca possession festival, 290
 Klikuschestvo shouting mania, 300
 Methodist revival, 403
 Miliovanny affair, 357
 Morzine, 425
 motor hysteria, 310
 Sardine factory, 567
 Singapore, 369, 588
 Tanganyika, 309
 Tanzania, 309
 Toronto Blessing, 25-26, 310-11
 Uganda, ix, 309, 680
 Welsh jumpers, 292, 309
 Zambia, 382
Laurentin, René, 326, 703-04
LaVey, Anton Szandor, 573-75
Lavington, George, 11, 401-04
Leaming, Barbara, 467
Lebon, Gustave, x
Lee, Raymond, 173, 373, 652, 655
Lefebvre, Georges, 58-59, 61
Levine, Justin, 468
Levine, Richard, 360
Levy, David, 384
Lewis, Ioan M., 173-74, 656
Lippmann, Walter, 339
Locke, Richard Adams, 416-17
Loftus, Elizabeth, 159-59
Lucas-Dubreton, J., 95
Luhman, Reid, 538

M

MacDonnell, Francis, 496
Mackay, Charles, xii, xv, 153, 254, 257, 345, 406, 481, 643, 672-73
Macionis, John, 164
Madden, Richard Robert, 312-13, 321-22, 356, 462, 567, 722
Mahan, Asa, 611
Maliovanny, Kondrath, 356-59
malingering, defined, 255
Malleus Maleficarium (The Hammer of Witches), 129, 733-34
Marchetti, D. Jean [Giovanni], 267-68, 271
marching band collapses, 359-360
 Pigsty hysteria (1972), 505-06
 Mississippi football pep squad (1952), 154
Martindale, C. C., 168
mass hysteria, defined, 360-61, 376, 501
mass hysteria by proxy, 477
mass hysteria, theories of, 648-656
 anthropological explanations, 656
 biological explanations, 656
 conscious feigning, 649
 dramatic theory, 653
 hypnotic trance, 651-52
 hysterical identification, 650-51
 physical ('real') illness, 651
 political protest, 652
 psychoanalytic perspectives, 653
 Smelser's value-added theory, 653-54
 social psychological perspectives, 654-56
 supernatural explanations, 648-49
 unconscious echoing, 650
 undetected toxins, 651
Mathias, Richard, 667, 669
Matthisson, Jan, 20-22
Maude, Aylmer, 137, 140
McCarthy, Joseph , 533-34
Mead, Margaret, 518
Mecklin, John Moffatt, 9
Melton, J. Gordon, 389, 697
Mikkelson, Barbara, 252
Milgram, Stanley, 276-77
Miller, Bess, 473
Miller, David L., 153, 164, 208, 468, 516, 539
Miller, Jerry, 624
Miller, Norman, 366
Miller, Perry, 14
Miller, William, 406-07
Millerites, 406-07
Modan, Barauch, 473
Monestier, Martin
Monster Scares,
 Bear Man, 415
 London Monster, 194, 314, 475
 London Monster social panics, 314-15
 Chupacabra, 96
 Face Scratcher, 273

Monster Scares, *cont.*
fantasy-prone people, 161
goblin attacks, 212-13
Indian Ocean space creatures, 687
Indian Wolf Man, 416
Kentucky space creatures, 593-94
lycanthropy, 333-39
Martian invasion scares (see individual cases)
Monkey Man, 413-415
nuns, 108, 329
Philippine devil hysteria, 503-04
school vampire scare, 577
small group scares, 592-95
Springheel Jack, 614-16
Texas earthworm hoax, 648
vampirism, 691-699
water monster, 712
Windigo psychosis, 726-28
Zimbabwe zombie school, 752
moral panics, xvi, 420-23
Catholic Scare, 73-74
child abduction panic of 1750, 83-86
Cholera Panic, 92-95
defined, 420-21
False Memory Syndrome, 155-59
garrotting scares, 193-94
London Monster scare, 315-17
London Monster social panics, 314-15
masturbation delusion, 391-397
Popish Plot, 103, 314-15, 421, 509-515
Red Scares, 532-34
Salem witchhunts, 561-566
Satanic cult and ritual abuse scare, 568-70
Scowerers and Mohocks, 581-82
suicide epidemics, 101
urban legends, 687
Welsh pedophile ring, 713-16
Whitechapel murders scare, 723-25
white slavery scare, 725-26
witch mania, 731-740
Multiple Personality Disorder, defined, 431-32

N
Nagin, C. Ray, 251
Nail, Paul, 384
Naylor, James, 529
Nevius, John L., 128
Nickell, Joseph, 247, 741
Nissenbaum, Stephen, 561, 565
Nitzkin, Joel, 499-501
Noll, Richard, 696-97
Norton, Mary Beth, 566
Nynauld, Jean de, 339

O
obedience to authority study, 276-77
Oesterreich, T.K., 130, 301, 516, 603
Ofshe, Richard, 437
Ong, Aihwa, 652
Owen, Nancy H., 75-76

P
Parker, Arthur C., 246
Paxman, Jeremy, 645
Pazder, Lawrence, 568
Peires, J.B., 746, 750
Pendergrast, Mark, 155-56, 568
Pfister, Oskar, 212
phantom attackers, 592-95
Halifax slasher, 239-42
Hammersmith ghost, 194, 244-45
Montreal slasher, 416
Kelly, Kentucky space creatures, 593-94
London Monster, 315-317
mad gasser of Mattoon, Illinois, 350-355
mad gasser of Botetourt, Virginia, 347-350
Mundrabilla, Australia, 595
phantom drug siege in Michigan, 594-95
phantom hatpin stabber, 501
phantom slasher of Taipei, 502-503
phantom sniper of Esher, 731
small group scares, 592-595
Springheel Jack, 475, 614-616
see also, Phantom Aircraft Scares, 477-99
Phoon, W.H., 369-70, 588

photosensitive epilepsy, 508-09
Picart, Bernard, 1-2
Pokémon hysteria (Japan), 508-09
Poray Madeyski, Boleslas de, 623
post-September 11th terror scares, 647-48
  anthrax, 277, 286, 363, 399, 647, 648
  Arab Americans targeted, 534, 648
  Canyon Creek School, Washington, 647
  College Park, Maryland, 647
  irradiated mail scare, 277-78
  Manila, Philippines, 647
  Melbourne Airport Mystery Illness, 399
  Naperville, Illinois, 648
  Toxic Bus Controversy, 667-69
Prince, Morton, 432-33
Prince, Samuel Henry, 235, 237
Proctor, Richard, 243

Q

Queen Filo (cargo "cult"), 176
Queen Mary, 47
Quito, Ecuador (riot), 143-144

R

Radford, Benjamin, 509
Reay, Marie, 440-41
Richardson, Miles, xii
Richer, Paul, 296, 430, 508
Rid, Samuel, 740
Riots,
  celebration riots, 540
  Civil War draft riots, 540
  commodity riots, 539
  coordinated versus uncoordinated, 538
  protest riots, 539-40
  race riots, 538-39
  stages of, 538-39
Robbins, Rossell Hope, 333, 737
Rommel, Kenneth M., 76
Rottmann, Bernhard, 18-19
Rumors, 541-44
  American Airship wave, 214, 216, 224
  American invasion of Canada, 9, 490-94, 542

Rumors, *cont.*
  anxiety hysteria, 27
  Australian airship mania, 482
  death of V. Bekhterev, 48
  Bird Flu, 53
  Brigand Fear of 1789, 58-61
  British Zeppelin scare, 486
  Catholic scare, 73-74. 387, 688
  cattle mutilations, 76
  child abduction panic of 1750, 83-85
  German child-eating scare, 86
  children's crusades, 87
  Chinese needle scare, 90
  cholera panic of 1832, 92, 94-95
  Coca-Cola, 543
  collective anxiety attacks, 98
  conspiracy theories, 103
  cyber ghost scare, 111
  dance frenzies (Japan), 116
  defined, 541
  extraordinary social behaviour, xvi
  Edison Star sightings, 144-145
  Fatima, Portugal,167
  fumigation hysteria, 187
  genital shrinking scares, 196-200
  genital vanishing scares, 205-206
  ghost rockets (Scandinavia), 191, 209-210
  ghost school in Kenya, 208
  German invasion of New Hampshire, 496-97
  Great Smurf Scare, 543
  Gulf War Syndrome, 225
  Halifax disaster of 1917, 236-37, 239
  Hammersmith Ghost scare, 244-45
  headhunting scares, 246-47, 543
  Hurricane Katrina, 251-52
  hysteria and, 256
  hysterical schoolgirls in Fiji, 262
  imaginary London riot, 47
  Indian 'evil spirit' school, 72
  Indian Monkey Man scare, 413-14
  Indian witch of 2005, 273
  Italian mummy curse fits, 440
  JFK assassination, 543
  Kentucky Fried Rat, 687
  London Monster Scare, 316

Rumors, *cont.*
- Louisiana twitching epidemic, 323
- lycanthropy, 334-35
- mad gasser of Mattoon, 354
- mass hysteria, 361-63, 754-56
- mass suicide, 389
- Milan poisoning scare of 1630, 405-06
- moral panics, 421
- Morzine 'possessed' town, 423, 426
- Multiple Personality Disorder, 434
- New England airship hoax, 486
- New York Zoo scare, 461
- New Zealand Zeppelin scare, 479-80
- Osama bin Laden, 542
- Palestinian poisoning panic, 471, 473
- Paul McCartney is dead, 543
- Pearl Harbor attack, 541
- phantom sniper of Esher, England, 731
- phantom slasher of Taipei, 502-03
- Popish Plot, 509, 511-15
- Riveter's Ovaries, 540
- Roswell crashed saucer, 543, 686-87
- Russian-Poland balloon scare of 1892, 546
- Sabbatai Zevi (the Messiah), 551-54
- Salem witch-hunts, 563
- Satanic cult scare, 568-69, 687-88
- Satanism, ix, 573
- Scandinavian ghost flier, 498
- schools, 377, 380-81, 385
- school vampire scare, 577
- school writing tremors, 578
- snake in the blanket legend, 686
- South African monoplane scare, 488
- Springheel Jack scare, 615
- Starpoint High School, 616-17
- terrorism scares, 643, 645-47
- tsunami, 672
- urban legends, 686-87
- vaccination scares, 689-90
- Virgin Mary appariations, 706
- Whitechapel murders scare, 724
- white slavery scare, 725
- windshield-pitting episode, 730
- witch mania, 731, 733
- work settings, 374-75

Rumors, *cont.*
- Xhosa cattle killing, 749
- zombie school, 753

S

Saintyves, Pierre, 268, 333, 666
Sanchez, Thomas, 648
Santos, Lucia, 166-68
Marto, Francisco and Jacinta, 166
Sherif, Muzafer, 478
Shibutani, Tamotsu, 541
Shorter, Edward, 107-08, 519-20, 568
Showalter, Elaine, 258, 284, 585-86, 648
Shweder, Richard A., xiv, 205
Sick Building Syndrome, 364, 373-74, 651, 670
Simon, Benjamin, 4-5, 7
Sirois, Francois, 171, 369, 380
Sjahrir, Soetan, 246
Skiff, Nolan, 177
Sleeman, James Lewis, 657-60
Smelser, Neil J., 205, 368, 653-54
Smith, Michelle, 568
Spanos, Nicholas P., 212, 437
Sprenger, Jakob, 206, 733
Stevenson, Ian, 745-46
Stevenson, Robert Louis, 626, 695
Stewart, James R., 75
Strieber, Whitley, 5
Suicide, mass
- Austria (1889), 626
- Bavaria (1886), 626
- Bezpopovtsy, 625
- Copycat Effect, 99-103, 627
- cultural relativity, 387, 389
- cults, 387, 475
- *Deer Hunter, The*, 626
- Defense Industry Suicide Clusters, 121-127
- Egypt (1967), 625
- France (1793), 626
- Gothe's novel as trigger, 101, 626
- Guyana, 386-87
- Heaven's Gate, 386
- Hungary (1936), 626
- Japan (1933), 626

Suicide, mass, *cont.*
- Lord Castleragh as trigger, 626
- Masada (74 BCE), 625
- mass hysteria, 256, 361
- Micronesia, 101-03
- Perm Providence (Russia, 1868), 388
- Peru (2000), 389-90
- share market crash (1929), 625
- Siberia (1896), 388(1887), 625
- Sicily (1887), 625
- Solar Temple (Canada, 1997), 389
- Solar Temple (Switzerland, 1994), 389
- suicide clubs, 626
- suicide clusters, 627
- Uganda (2000), xv
- Vietnam (1975), 625

Summers, Montague, 331, 333, 339, 685, 691
Sybil, 433, 435-36
Szasz, Thomas S., 201, 225, 396

T

Taguba, Antonio, 276
Terrorism Scares, 642-648
- Halifax disaster, 237
- Jewish poisoning scares, 643
- Kosovo poisoning scare (1990), 646-47
- Mad Gasser of Mattoon, 644-45
- Mad Gasser of Botetourt, 643-44
- Martian invasion panic (1938), 644
- Palestinian poisoning plot (1983), 646
- phantom Iraqo gas attack, 647
- post-September 11th terror scares, 647-48
- spy mania during World War I, 643

Tesk, 459-60
Tillinghast, Wallace E., 484-86
Thoreau, Henry David, xiv
Thurston, Herbert, 269, 326, 619-21, 703
Tizané, E., 703
Toibin, Colm, 270
Tributsch, Helmut, 712
Tseng, Shing Tseng, 196, 200

U

Umhayizo bewitchment, 683
Underwood, Alfred Clair, 536

V

Valentino, Rudolph, 182, 540-41
vampire defined, 691-92, 694
Veblen, Thorstein, 164
Victor, Jeffrey S., 98-99, 420-21, 569-70
Volk, Stephen, 46

W

Walsh, Le comte Théobald, 612
War of the Worlds scares, xvi, 475, 478
- Buffalo, New York (1968, 1971), 62-64
- Chile (1944), 90
- Ecuador (1949), 143-44
- Orson Welles broadcast (1938), 465-69
- Portugal (1988, 1998), 515
- Rhode Island (1974), 536-37
- South Carolina Martian panic (1939), 601-02

Warfield, Benjamin B., 146, 280
Wasson, R. Gordon, 440
Welles, Orson, 47, 62, 64, 90, 144, 465, 467, 469, 478, 515, 536-37, 602, 630
Wells, H.G. (Herbert George), 63, 90, 143, 465-67, 479, 486
Wesley, John, xvi, 13, 57-58, 81, 291, 294, 400-04, 535-36
Wessely, Simon, 225-26, 310, 361, 365, 373
Westrum, Ron, 594
wish-fulfillment, collective
- Alien Abduction Belifs, 3-7
- American airship wave, great, 214-224
- Andree balloon mania, 23-25
- Australian airship mania (1909), 482-83
- children's crusades, 88-89
- Edison Star sightings, 144-45
- facillitated communication, 150-51
- Fatima solar phenomenon, 165-70, 325, 657
- Florida Land Boom, 176

wish-fulfillment, collective, *cont.*
Flying saucers (origin of), 25, 48, 130, 145, 162, 177-80, 211, 257, 361, 478, 593, 686-87, 700
Hindu milk miracle, 247-48
images that move, weep and bleed, 266-273
Klang, Malaysia, 282-84
Lourdes 324-28, 750
Louviers, 328-332
Medjugorje, 701-04
Miraculous hen of Leeds, 413
Morzine, 424
pipe dream rumors, 542
stigmata, ix, xiii, 476, 618-623, 663, 697
Virgin Mary, appearances of, 699-706
Xhosa cattle killing prophesy, 746-751
Zeitoun luminous phenomena, 752
see also, "cargo cults"
Wier, Jean [Weyer, Johann], 17, 105, 107, 129, 291, 298-99, 303-04, 322, 461, 566-67, 721-22, 738
Wild Man behavior (New Guinea), 518

X

Xante, Spain (bleating nuns), 361
Xenoglossy defined, 745
X-Files, 225
Xhosa (of South Africa), 746-751
Xhosaland, 747

Y

Yap, Pow Meng, 195
Yassa, Ramzy, 752
yin versus *yang* forces, 196

Z

Zeehan, Tasmania, mystery lights, 483
Zeitoun, Egypt, Virgin Mary appearance at, 752
Zimbardo, Philip, 275-77, 624
Zion-on-Earth, 19, 20-21, 23
Zond 4 moon probe (Russian), 478
zoot suit defined, 753
Zoroastrianism, 28, 570

CPSIA information can be obtained
at www.ICGtesting.com
Printed in the USA
LVHW100048090820
662713LV00025B/583